PRIVATE INTERNATIONAL LAW OF
REINSURANCE AND INSURANCE

LLOYD'S INSURANCE LAW LIBRARY

Editor-in-Chief
Malcolm A Clarke

The Law of Insurance Contracts
by Malcolm A Clarke
Looseleaf

The Law of Insurance Contracts
5th edition
by Malcolm A Clarke
(2006)

Good Faith and Insurance Contracts
second edition
by Peter MacDonald Eggers, Patrick Foss
and Simon Picken
(2004)

Product Liability: Law and Insurance
edited by Mark Mildred
(2001)

Reinsurance Practice and Law
Barlow Lyde & Gilbert
Looseleaf

Private International Law of Reinsurance and Insurance
by Raymond Cox, Louise Merrett and Marcus Smith
(2006)

PRIVATE INTERNATIONAL LAW OF REINSURANCE AND INSURANCE

BY

RAYMOND COX, Q.C.
B.A. (Oxon)

LOUISE MERRETT
M.A. (Cantab)

AND

MARCUS SMITH
B.C.L., M.A. (Oxon)

FOREWORD BY
SIR FRANCIS JACOBS, Q.C.
Advocate General, Court of the European Communities 1988–2006

INSURANCE LAW LIBRARY

EDITOR-IN-CHIEF
MALCOLM A. CLARKE

informa law
from Routledge

First published 2006 by Informa Law

Published 2014
by Informa Law from Routledge
2 Park Square, Milton Park, Abingdon, Oxon OX14 4RN

and by Informa Law from Routledge
711 Third Avenue, New York, NY, 10017, USA

Informa Law is an imprint of the Taylor & Francis Group, an informa business

British Library Cataloguing in Publication Data
A catalogue record for this book is available from the British Library

ISBN-13: 978-1-84311-532-8 (hbk)

Typeset in 10/12pt Postscript Times
by Tony Lansbury, Tonbridge, Kent

MIX
Paper from responsible sources
FSC™ C013985
www.fsc.org

Printed in the United Kingdom
by Henry Ling Limited

FOREWORD

The rules of private international law play a very important role in insurance and reinsurance cases. The fundamental issues – namely, which courts have jurisdiction, and which is the applicable law – are of special importance in this field, if only because of the international character of the insurance market. This book therefore has a key role in the understanding of the subject.

In recent years, the traditional approaches of both the common law and the civil law to these fundamental issues of private international law have been largely replaced by common European rules. The consequences have been far-reaching.

Rules on jurisdiction were laid down by the Brussels Convention, now superseded, for most but not all purposes, by the (directly applicable) Brussels Regulation. The Brussels Regulation applies as between the Member States of the European Union, with the exception of Denmark, to which the Convention continues to apply. The Convention and the Regulation may also, in certain circumstances, apply in relation to third countries. In cases involving certain other European countries, on the other hand, the similar, but not identical, regime of the Lugano Convention will apply. All of these regimes differ radically from the common law.

As for choice of law, the rules are laid down for some purposes by the Rome Convention, for some purposes by European legislation in the form of the Insurance Directives. Here too, therefore, there are important demarcation issues. The Convention rules do not apply to contracts of insurance which cover risks situated in the territories of the Member States of the European Union. Thus it is only where the risk is situated outside the European Union that the Convention rules will apply. Where the risk is situated within the Union, the Insurance Directives will apply. But the exclusion of the Rome Convention does not apply to contracts of reinsurance; here therefore the Convention rules do apply. In this field again, the European schemes are novel, especially perhaps from the vantage point of the common lawyer.

The role of the common law in this field is now somewhat residual. However, it is still necessary to consider the scope and evolving content of the common law, and the contrast between the common law and the various European regimes is illuminating in itself.

All of these regimes are helpfully and systematically expounded and discussed in this book.

The book's valuable comparison of the European regimes and the common law may dispel some widely held assumptions. It is often assumed that the common law prefers detailed rules, while European law favours principles. In this field, at least, the reverse is the case. The common law has developed principles of great generality, and has preferred a flexible approach, epitomised by the doctrine of *forum non conveniens*. The European regimes, in contrast, are designed to furnish specific solutions in specific areas, with the aim of promoting the essential goals of uniformity and legal certainty.

Those values are necessary to the effort to ensure that it will be clear at the outset which State's courts have jurisdiction, and that a judgment once given by a competent court will be recognised and enforced, without further ado, in other States.

With the same aims, the European system has the advantage of providing a mechanism for uniform interpretation of the rules, by preliminary rulings of the European Court of Justice, which has developed a substantial body of case-law in this field.

Common lawyers have, however, strongly criticised some aspects of this case law, where the traditionally more flexible approach of the English courts has fallen foul of the perceived scheme of the European system, relying as it seems necessary to do on unqualified acceptance of the jurisdiction of other Member States' courts. Thus the ECJ's rejection of, for example, anti-suit injunctions as practised by English courts has been the subject of much concern. Indeed it is difficult to find any other area of ECJ case law which has given rise to as much controversy.

Fortunately perhaps, such debates have not loomed large overall in the subject of this book. It will be widely welcomed for the clarity of the guidance which it provides to practitioners in Europe and beyond.

Francis Jacobs
Fountain Court Chambers
November 2006

PREFACE

The initial idea for this book arose from the observation that there was a torrent of judgments handed down each year which concern conflicts of law issues in the context of reinsurance and insurance. It was not hard to see why that should be. Reinsurance and insurance business is of course frequently international in nature, and cases may be large, so disputes are to be expected. But reinsurance contracts are also very different from many other types of contracts in their terms and the manner in which they are agreed, and it is obvious that the peculiarities of reinsurance were very far from the minds of the drafters of the Brussels Regulation and Rome Convention. Applying the provisions of those European rules, and much of the case law on them, to (re)insurance business is often extraordinarily difficult, as will be seen. Good examples of this would include such bread and butter issues as the incorporation of jurisdiction clauses, or the effect of assignment, subrogation and contribution. Some insurance business is, by contrast, governed by very specific, idiosyncratic codes within the Brussels Regulation and Insurance Directives which have tended to give rise to their own peculiar problems. Some recent themes in the development of the common law have also been of particular significance in relation to (re)insurance business, such as the availability of negative declarations and anti-suit injunctions.

We were also struck by the absence of any previous book dedicated to this area. Research has had to be directed to books on conflicts generally, or on reinsurance and insurance generally. In either case the relevant subject was necessarily only a small part of a much broader canvas. In this book we have accordingly sought to focus on the relatively unchartered waters of the application of the European rules and common law as they apply to (re)insurance business. We have sought to avoid attempting any treatment of the conflict of laws generally, or (re)insurance business generally.

We deal with the decisions we had to make about the approach and structure of the book in Chapter 1, Part E. Our material dictated that we dealt with reinsurance before insurance. We also found that the weightiest issues tended to arise in relation to reinsurance rather than insurance, because of the existence of the special codes for conflicts in relation to some insurance. Accordingly, although it may seem unnatural from a domestic law point of view, we have placed reinsurance before insurance in the title to this book.

Looking to the future we have in mind the possibility of incorporating into a future edition a treatment of jurisdiction and choice of law in relation to disputes with brokers who play such an important role in (re)insurance business, and aspects of enforcement.

There are many we are happy to thank. We are most grateful to Professor Sir Francis Jacobs QC for contributing his Foreword. Sir Francis was good enough to give us some corrections to the proofs of Part 1. We also thank Professor Malcolm Clarke and David Railton QC for most helpful comments on drafts of parts of the book. Sushma Ananda did a great deal of checking and correcting of the proofs and Simon Atrill researched some of the European case law. Needless to say all errors and omissions are our own. Christine Child, chambers' librarian, went way beyond the call of duty in responding quickly, precisely and cheerfully to endless requests for materials. We are deeply indebted to our publishers who have been a model of encouragement, assistance and patience, and above all to our families who have put up with so much intrusion into their time during the preparation of this book.

We have endeavoured to state the law as at 1 September 2006.

RC, MS
Fountain Court Chambers, London
LM
Trinity College, Cambridge
19 November 2006

BIBLIOGRAPHY AND ABBREVIATIONS

Briggs/Rees: A. Briggs and P. Rees, *Civil Jurisdiction and Judgments* (4th ed., 2005).
Cheshire/North: P. M. North and J. J. Fawcett, *Cheshire & North's Private International Law* (13th ed., 1999).
Chitty: H. Beale, *Chitty on Contracts* (29th ed., 2004).
Clarke: M. Clarke, *The Law of Insurance Contracts* (5th ed., 2006).
Clarkson/Hill: C. M. V. Clarkson and J. Hill, *The Conflict of Laws* (3rd ed., 2006).
Collier: J. G. Collier, *Conflict of Laws* (3rd ed., 2001).
Craig/De Burca, P. Craig and G. De Burca, *European Law* (3rd ed., 2003).
Cruz, Desantes, Real and Jenard: *Cruz, Desantes, Real and Jenard report on the Brussels Convention*, 1990 OJ C.189/35.
Dicey/Morris/Collins: L. Collins, *Dicey, Morris & Collins The Conflict of Laws* (14th ed., 2006).
Evrigenis and Kerameus: *Evrigenis and Kerameus Report on the Brussels Convention*, 1986 OJ C.298/1.
Fentiman: R. Fentiman, *Foreign Law in English Courts* (1998).
Giuliano-Lagarde: *Giuliano-Lagarde Report on the Rome Convention*, 1980 OJ C.282/1.
Hartley: T. C. Hartley, *The Foundations of European Community Law* (5th ed., 2003).
Jenard: *Jenard Report on the Brussels Convention*, 1979 OJ C.59/1.
Jenard and Moller: *Jenard and Moller Report on the Brussels Convention*, 1990 OJ C.189/57.
Kahn-Freund: O. Kahn-Freund, *General Problems of Private International Law* (1st ed., 1980).
Kaye, Civil Jurisdiction: Kaye, *Civil Jurisdiction and Enforcement of Foreign Judgments* (1987).
Kaye, European Case Law: Kaye, *European Case Law in the Judgment Convention* (Chichester, 1998).
Lando/Beale: O. Lando and H. Beale, *Principles of European Contract Law* (1st ed., 2000).
Layton/Mercer: A. Layton Q.C. and H. Mercer, *European Civil Practice* (2nd ed., 2004).
Merkin (Insurance): R. Merkin, *Colinvaux & Merkin's Insurance Contract Law* (1st ed., 2002).
Merkin (Arbitration): R. Merkin, *Arbitration Law* (2004).
Mustill: M. Mustill, *The Law and Practice of Commercial Arbitration in England* (2nd ed., 1999).
North (1982) and North (1993): P. M. North (ed), *Contract Conflicts* (1st ed., 1982)
P. M. North, *Essays in Private International Law* (1st ed., 1993).
Nygh: P. Nygh, *Autonomy in International Contracts* (1999).
Plender/Wilderstein: R. Plender and M. Wilderstein, *The European Contracts Convention* (2nd ed., 2001).
Redfern/Hunter: A. Redfern and M. Hunter, *Law and Practice of International Commercial Arbitration* (4th ed., 2004).
Schlosser: *Schlosser report on the Brussels Convention*, 1979 OJ C.59/71.

Seatzu: F. Seatzu, *Insurance in Private International Law* (2003).
Worthington: S. Worthington, *Commercial Law and Commercial Practice* (2003).
Yeo: T. M. Yeo, *Choice of Law for Equitable Doctrines* (2004).
Zamir/Woolf: I. Zamir and I. Woolf, *The Declaratory Judgment* (3rd ed., 2002).

TABLE OF CONTENTS

PART II: JURISDICTION

TABLE OF CASES

TABLE OF LEGISLATION

EUROPEAN UNION AND CONVENTIONS

PART I

OVERVIEW

CHAPTER 1

INTRODUCTION

A. THE IMPORTANCE OF PRIVATE INTERNATIONAL LAW QUESTIONS IN (RE)INSURANCE DISPUTES

1.1 Questions of private international law loom large in reinsurance and insurance disputes, as witnessed by the sheer volume of reported cases concerning conflicts of law and (re)insurance. In the first place, this is because many (re)insurance risks – particularly those involving the London market and London (re)insurers – are complex, high value and, above all, international in nature. Secondly, it is often the case that the contracts setting out the terms on which such risks are (re)insured are not as clear as they might be on such questions. Thirdly, in large value disputes, one or more of the parties involved will be inclined, because of actual or perceived advantages in the litigation they are involved in, to seek to take private international law questions in the course of such proceedings. The prevalence of arbitration clauses may go some way to diminish but does not prevent this tendency.

1.2 These questions of private international law can broadly be characterised under two heads: jurisdictional questions – dealt with in Part II of this book – and choice of law questions – dealt with in Part III. Generally speaking, jurisdictional questions will arise and be determined before the hearing of any substantive dispute, whereas choice of law questions tend to form a part of such disputes, and indeed play a significant role in determining the substantive issues which arise for decision. Of course, this is not to deny that choice of law can be very relevant to jurisdiction issues, but the order of discussion flows from these considerations.

B. THE COMMON LAW APPROACH

1.3 The essential characteristics of the common law approach to jurisdictional disputes may be said to be, firstly, that jurisdiction was available on the ground of the presence of the defendant within the jurisdiction and other broad or exorbitant grounds which might be expected to give some sort of connection between the dispute and the jurisdiction; but, secondly, that potential excesses of jurisdiction were tempered by the principle of *forum non conveniens* under which the court would decline jurisdiction in favour of another clearly more appropriate forum. Choice of law was based on the express, implied or imputed choice of the parties.

1.4 Although (re)insurance disputes involved their own particular "spin" on such questions, the fundamental private international law tests were the same, whether the dispute was a (re)insurance dispute or some other civil or commercial piece of litigation. In other words, private international law questions in (re)insurance disputes tended to involve the application of common and widely understood principles, albeit that the application of such principles involved factors specific to (re)insurance, for instance, the mode of contracting and administering which is often different from that in other areas, and the *situs* of the risk (re)insured.

C. THE EVOLUTION OF EUROPEAN PRIVATE INTERNATIONAL LAW

1.5 Time was when these jurisdiction and choice of law questions were the more-or-less exclusive province of the common law. This is certainly now no longer the case. The past two decades have seen a progressive displacement of these common law principles in favour of European laws (either incorporated into English law by Act of Parliament or delegated legislation, or else "directly applicable" rules requiring no incorporating Act). Thus, as regards jurisdictional questions, the process began with the Brussels Convention of 1968, incorporated into English law (in a form amended in the light of the UK's accession to the EEC as it was then known) by the Civil Jurisdiction and Judgments Act 1982. This 1982 Act is, itself, now a dead letter, and the Brussels Convention has for most purposes been re-born as an EU Regulation, comprehensively entitled "Council Regulation (EC) No 44/2001 of 22 December 2000 on jurisdiction and the recognition and enforcement of judgments in civil and commercial matters" and referred to herein as "the Brussels Regulation".

1.6 The common law test for choice of law questions has similarly been displaced, chiefly by the Rome Convention of 1980, incorporated into English law by the Contracts (Applicable Law) Act 1990. Before this decade is out, it is likely that the Rome Convention (and implementing legislation such as the Contracts (Applicable Law) Act 1990), will have gone the way of the Brussels Convention, and have been incorporated into a directly applicable and directly effective Regulation.

1.7 As will be seen, the Rome Convention does not apply to most contracts of insurance, whereas it is applicable to contracts of reinsurance. Insurance questions tend to be dealt with by the so-called insurance directives.

1.8 Even this brief overview shows that the history of European law involvement in private international law questions is a long one. It is also complicated and the final chapter of this history has by no means yet been written. The evolution of this corpus of European law is important not just in historical, but also in legal terms. Thus, for instance, it is this historical evolution which explains which countries are party to what convention (the Brussels Regulation has variants on its theme). This, in turn, affects not merely the specific provisions applicable to private international law questions, but also the extent of the involvement of the European Court of Justice in the determination of such questions. For this reason, the historical development of European law in this area is described in Chapter 2.

D. CHARACTERISTICS OF EUROPEAN RULES OF PRIVATE INTERNATIONAL LAW

1.9 European rules of private international law have a number of characteristics which it is important to note at the outset. These relate to:

(1) *The essential nature of the rules*. As will be seen, the fundamental nature of the European rules is in marked contrast to the common law principles that European law has displaced.

(2) *An overlay of social engineering in the rules*. Certain contracts – generally those perceived to involve individuals requiring protection under the law – tend to be singled out for special treatment under European law. Thus, it is no longer the case that one regime fits all, with special factors forming, if anything, a subsidiary matter to be considered under the umbrella of generally formulated principles. Rather, the rules applicable to a given contract tend to vary according to the nature of the contract.

(3) *The need for a common interpretative approach*. The fundamental *raison d'etre* of the European private international law rules is to provide consistent jurisdictional and choice of law rules across the EU. That implies an application of a common European approach to such rules, as opposed to a narrow national approach.

These characteristics are considered in turn below.

1. The essential nature of the rules

1.10 In distinct contrast to the rules of common law that they have largely displaced, the European rules seek to minimise the exercise of judicial discretion or judgment and maximise certainty of outcome by creating a whole raft of very specific rules, designed to cater for and to provide an ostensibly clear answer to the wide range of different jurisdictional and choice of law questions which may arise in the course of civil litigation. Such a rule-based approach is, of course, in large part a question of legal policy and/or a reflection of the different legal traditions represented in the European Union. What can be said is that the European rules will seem very alien to anyone brought up on the common law approach to jurisdiction and choice of law. The common law tended to evolve principles capable of extremely brief articulation, but which were deceptive in their brevity and simplicity, because of their broad brush and (particularly as regards jurisdiction) discretionary nature. By discretionary, we do not, of course, seek to suggest that the rules are in any way arbitrary. It was simply that the common law approach involved the weighing of a number of potentially countervailing factors, often requiring evidence, and certainly involving a fundamental exercise of judgement as regards such factors.

1.11 The European rules are by contrast tightly formulated to deal with specific issues or questions. Of critical importance is the characterisation of the relevant question or issue, as this will determine which rules will resolve that issue. Thus, for instance, the determination whether a contract is one of reinsurance or insurance (and, if the latter, whether the insurance relates to risks situated within the EU) is critical as to whether the Rome Convention or the insurance directives apply. Of course, no set of rules is ever likely to be completely comprehensive or completely certain, and it may fairly be said of many European law provisions that the difficult questions that are overtly discussed as "judgemental" questions under the common law regime arise in hidden form when seeking to delimit the scope of application of one or other rule of European law.

2. An overlay of social engineering in the rules: consumer protection, etc

1.12 The Brussels Regulation contains a series of provisions dealing specifically with certain types of contract. Examples are consumer contracts and employment contracts and – important for present purposes – contracts of insurance. Similarly, the Rome Convention tends to apply only to reinsurance contracts, with insurance contracts (at least those involving risks situated in the EU) being regulated by the insurance directives.

1.13 This differentiation between different types of contract reflects a public policy agenda on the part of the European law-makers. The respective positions of the participants – or perceived participants – to specific contracts are deemed to require special treatment. This special treatment is not a reflection of the different legal approaches of the Member States of the EU. Its source is very different – public policy – which, of course, also finds expression in UK national legislation. For present purposes, the importance of this public policy overlay is that the rule-based nature of European law is accentuated. It becomes necessary – more-or-less at the outset of any legal inquiry – to distinguish between different types of contract: as a direct result, contracts of insurance are (to an extent) separated from other forms of contract; and contracts of insurance and reinsurance need to be distinguished. Although, of course, it is wrong to say that insurance and reinsurance contracts are governed by wholly different and separate regimes – they are not – it is necessary to bear in mind that some of the rules applicable to such contracts are unique to them.

3. The need for a common interpretative approach

1.14 The fundamental *raison d'etre* of the European private international law rules is to provide consistent jurisdictional and choice of law rules across the EU. Thus, the aim of the jurisdictional rules is that whichever national court is confronted with a piece of international litigation, that court will apply the same principles in order to determine whether or not it has jurisdiction. Equally, where a national court is seised of dispute, the approach of that court to the choice of law questions before it should be common to the EU.

1.15 Obviously, this implies a common approach to the difficult questions of construction that arise out of the European private international law rules, and to the application of those rules. This is dealt with in two related ways. In the first place, national courts are injuncted to eschew narrow, national approaches to construction; a broad, "Community" approach needs to be adopted. Secondly, and reinforcing this, questions of construction can (to varying degrees) be referred to the European Court of Justice for an authoritative, EU-wide, determination. Questions of interpretation are considered in Chapter 3.

E. APPROACH AND STRUCTURE OF THIS BOOK

1.16 The nature of the European private international law rules largely determines the structure of this book. Part I deals with matters of common interest to both the rules on jurisdiction and the rules on choice of law – namely, the history of the development of these rules (Chapter 2) and the manner in which these rules are to be interpreted in order to facilitate a common, EU-wide, approach (Chapter 3).

1.17 The division of the rest of the book into two parts – jurisdiction (Part II) and choice of law (Part III) – reflects the essential division (both in European law, and in the common law) between these two areas. Within each Part, the approach is similar. First, and critically given the regimented European approach, the various different potentially applicable regimes are described and the tests for determining which regime is applicable in any given case stated. This involves differentiating between:

(1) The various different applicable European regimes. In particular, it has been necessary to distinguish between the regimes applicable to contracts of reinsurance and contracts of insurance;
(2) The extent to which the common law still has a role; and
(3) Arbitration proceedings.

The different jurisdictional regimes are described in Chapter 4. The different choice of law regimes are described in Chapter 9.

1.18 In the following chapters – Chapters 5–8 and 10–13 respectively – the different regimes are themselves described. The relationship between the European rules, the rules of common law and the rules applicable in arbitration proceedings are dealt with in this order. Clearly, given the priority of the European rules over the rules of common law (which have a limited application, whether by virtue of the terms of the European rules or outside them), the European rules need to be dealt with first. So far as the rules applicable in arbitration proceedings are concerned, these are expressly not derived from the Brussels Regulation nor the Rome Convention, but are self-standing. Their treatment last is simply a reflection of the fact that they are coloured by the European and common law rules, whose analysis precedes them.

1.19 Within the analysis of the European rules, contracts of reinsurance have been considered before contracts of insurance. Within the choice of law context, this approach was informed by the need to consider the Rome Convention first, and the insurance directives second – this because the insurance directives in many cases refer implicitly, or sometimes explicitly, back to provisions in the Rome Convention. The Rome Convention, as has been described, excludes from its scope the insurance of risks situated within the EU.

1.20 So far as the European jurisdictional rules are concerned, the same approach was taken: reinsurance first, insurance thereafter. The analytical need to do so was not so compelling as with the choice of law rules; but in terms of consistency, this approach was preferred. It also enabled the "pure" diet of Brussels to be considered first, without the specific provisions applicable to insurance (but not reinsurance) contracts.

F. TERMINOLOGY

1.21 It is apparent that there are a number of relevant treaties, conventions and instruments. In this book, we refer to:

(1) The Brussels Regulation 44/2001. This is headed "Council Regulation (EC) No 44/2001 of 22 December 2000 on jurisdiction and the recognition and enforcement of judgments in civil and commercial matters", and this is how it is referred to in subsequent Commission regulations.[1] It is simply called "the Regulation" in the Civil Jurisdiction Judgments Order 2001, SI No. 3929. There are other regulations to which reference will be made so we will use the shorthand "the Brussels Regulation".[2]

(2) Those states which are bound by the Brussels Regulation are referred to in the Regulation as "Member States" (Article 1(3)) and we adopt this usage although it has the disadvantage that it always has to be remembered that the Member States do not include Denmark which is a Member State of the EU.[3]

(3) The Brussels Convention refers to whichever version of the convention is relevant to the discussion. The Lugano Convention has never been substantially amended (although Poland became a party to it) so that the problem does not arise. Parties to the Brussels and Lugano Conventions are referred to as "Contracting States" in accordance with the terms of those treaties.

(4) The Rome Convention is referred to as such.

(5) The Financial Services and Markets Act 2000 (Law Applicable to Contracts of Insurance) Regulations 2001[4] bring into force under English law the choice of law rules in various insurance directives which apply to insurance contracts and are referred to as "the Insurance Regulations".

1. E.g. Commission Regulation (EC) No 1937/2004 of 9 November 2004 amending annexes I to IV of the Brussels Regulation.

2. Reference is also often made to the "Brussels I Regulation" to distinguish it from the Brussels II Regulation which deals with jurisdiction in matrimonial matters and which is not relevant for our purposes.

3. Sometimes the Member States, i.e. not including Denmark, are referred to as "the Regulation States". As we will see, in accordance with Article 1 and 2 of the Protocol on the position of Denmark annexed to the Treaty on European Union, Denmark is not bound by the provisions of the Brussels Regulation. However, the Commission has negotiated an agreement between the European Community and Denmark extending the provisions of the Regulation to Denmark and this decision was approved by the Council on 27 April 2006 (2006/325/EC OJ L 120/22). See para. 2.72 below.

4. SI 2001/2635 as amended by SI 2001/3542.

HISTORICAL OVERVIEW OF THE EUROPEAN PRIVATE INTERNATIONAL LAW RULES

A. THE HARMONISATION OF EU JURISDICTION RULES

2.1 A description of the context of the Brussels Regulation could perhaps be confined to the powers under which the regulation itself was made, and the objectives of those powers. However, the Brussels Regulation replaces the Brussels Convention for the Member States and differences between the regulation and the Brussels Convention shed light on the regulation. It is clear that in many if not most ways the Brussels Regulation will be interpreted consistently with the Brussels Convention. It is therefore important to know the context of the Brussels Convention. It is also convenient to deal with the history of the Brussels Convention and the Lugano Convention in one go.

2.2 This chapter therefore considers, in chronological terms:

(1) the original Brussels Convention made between the six original Member States;
(2) the amended Brussels Convention to which Denmark, Ireland and the UK became parties;
(3) the re-amended Brussels Convention to which Greece became a party;
(4) the Lugano Convention made between the states of the EEC and members of EFTA;
(5) the re-re-amended Brussels Convention to which Spain and Portugal became parties;
(6) the re-re-re-amended Brussels Convention to which Austria, Sweden and Finland became parties; and
(7) the Brussels Regulation.

2.3 Having considered the development of the Brussels Regulation we will then outline the historical background to other parallel European developments; namely the Rome Convention and the insurance directives.

1. 1957 EEC treaty

2.4 The predecessor of the Brussels Regulation was the Brussels Convention, the origins of which are to be found in the Treaty establishing the European Economic Community (the EEC Treaty).[1] There were originally six parties to the EEC Treaty: Belgium, France, Germany, Italy, Luxembourg and the Netherlands. The EEC Treaty was signed on 25 March 1957 and came into force on 1 January 1958.

2.5 The focus of the EEC treaty was on the economic integration of the Member States. Essentially it established a common market, a customs union and certain common policies. Article 2 of the EEC Treaty stated that the task of the Community was "by establishing a common market and progressively approximating the economic policies of member states, to promote economic activities ... and closer relations".[2] Article 3 described in very general terms some of the anticipated activities of the Community for the purposes in Article 2. The treaty specifically provided for the creation of certain institutions including a Court of Justice

1. Rather confusingly the EEC Treaty was re-named by the Treaty of Maastricht, and its provisions were to some extent re-numbered.
2. As referred to below the provisions of the EEC Treaty have been extensively amended and extended.

to serve the Community, for the Community to have legal personality, for the creation of a custom union, for a common market for agriculture, free movement of workers, services and capital, for common policies on transport, competition, and tax in order to promote the common market, the economy and social policy.

2.6 Towards the end of the original EEC Treaty was Part Six, headed "General and Final Provisions", which contained miscellaneous provisions, including a provision at Article 220 that the Member States shall, so far as is necessary, enter into negotiations with each other with a view to securing for the benefit of their nationals amongst other things "the simplification of formalities governing the reciprocal recognition and enforcement of judgments of courts or tribunals and of arbitration awards".

2.7 It is this apparently obscure provision in Article 220 relating to judgments and awards which was destined to become the basis of the development of the wide regime of co-operation in matters of civil jurisdiction which existed until the Brussels Regulation was made.

2.8 The EEC Treaty has been heavily amended by the Single European Act, and the treaties of Maastricht, Amsterdam and Nice. These are noted below. Other amendments have been made but are not relevant.

2. 1968 Brussels Convention

2.9 At the time the EEC Treaty was agreed, there were a series of widely differing bilateral conventions between the Member States relating to enforcement of judgments.[3] As mentioned, Article 220 of the EEC Treaty had provided that Member States would negotiate simpler formalities concerning the recognition and enforcement of judgments.

2.10 In 1960, pursuant to Article 220 of the EEC Treaty, the Commission invited the Member States to set up a committee of experts to consider proposals for negotiations.[4] The Commission's view which has often been cited in the interpretation of the Convention was that "a true internal market between the six States will be achieved only if adequate legal protection can be secured. The economic life of the Community may be subject to disturbances and difficulties unless it is possible, where necessary by judicial means, to ensure the recognition and enforcement of the various rights arising from the existence of a multiplicity of legal relationships. As jurisdiction in both civil and commercial matters is derived from the sovereignty of member states, and since the effect of judicial acts is confined to each national territory, legal protection and, hence, legal certainty in the common market are essentially dependent on the adoption by the member states of a satisfactory solution to the problem of recognition and enforcement of judgments."[5]

2.11 The committee of experts produced a draft report and draft Convention which led to the Brussels Convention which was signed on 27 September 1968 and came into force on 1 February 1973 for an unlimited period.[6] The text of that report formed the Jenard report on

3. *Jenard*, 1979 OJ C.59/1, Chap. II.

4. The Commission was one of the institutions of the Community created by the EEC Treaty consisting of a number of individual Commissioners originally appointed by the governments of Member States but since the Nice Treaty (see below) now appointed by the Council (see below) whose main functions have been described as formulating proposals for policies, steering those policies towards adoption, co-ordinating national policies and overseeing execution: Hartley, p. 11.

5. *Jenard,* 1979 OJ C.59/1, Chap. 1.

6. "Convention" like "protocol" is simply another word for a Treaty, as to which see further Halsbury, 4th ed., vol. 18, para. 655 and, e.g., s.1(4) of the European Communities Act 1972. "Convention" is frequently employed for an agreement to which a large number of countries are parties whereas "protocol" is now used principally for an instrument subsidiary to a treaty. Ratification of the treaty will normally *ipso facto* ratify the protocol: *R* v. *Foreign Secretary, ex p. Rees-Mogg* [1994] QB 552, 564 (CA). For the significance of the use of protocols in the founding treaties of the EU see Beaumont, *Current Law Statutes Annotated*, 1993, vol. 2, para. 32-10. Protocols relating to

the Brussels Convention which is an official commentary on the Brussels Convention describing its genesis and effect.[7]

2.12 Two purposes of the Contracting States in agreeing the Treaty were recorded in the recitals.[8] They desired to implement Article 220 of the EEC Treaty in which they undertook to simplify formalities governing recognition and enforcement of judgments. They were also anxious to strengthen the "legal protection" of persons in the Community. This seems to be a reference to the approach of the Commission (para. 2.10 above) which had linked legal protection and legal certainty.

2.13 Perhaps the major and enduring feature of the Brussels Convention, followed in the Lugano Convention and the Brussels Regulation, was that it set out rules for the international jurisdiction of the courts of the Member States which were part of the national law of Member States governing whether or not those courts had jurisdiction in respect of original proceedings (sometimes called a "double" system).[9] The alternative would have been a much less ambitious system of rules (sometimes called a "single" system) which would not alter the international jurisdiction of the courts in respect of proceedings but would only apply in relation to the recognition and enforcement of judgments obtained in another country. However, the experts favoured the former system over the latter because they considered it "would allow increased harmonisation of laws, provide greater legal certainty, avoid discrimination and facilitate the 'free movement' of judgments".[10]

2.14 This feature of directly applicable rules under the Brussels Convention was crucial because it led to "an autonomous system of international jurisdiction in relations between the member states".[11] In essence what this meant was that the rules created their own code which was to be applied by all Member States and which did not depend on national laws of jurisdiction or the methods of interpretation of such national laws. This process of establishing an autonomous system was aided by the agreement of Member States in a declaration to the Convention that the European Court of Justice had jurisdiction to give rulings on the interpretation of the Brussels Convention (see paras 2.18 *et seq.*).

2.15 Furthermore, it is now clear that the uniform rules of jurisdiction contained in the Brussels Convention apply whenever there is an international element; it is not necessary that there is a connection with two or more Convention States.[12] Thus despite the fact that the origins of the Convention lie in Article 220 and accordingly the working of the internal market, the European Court of Justice has made clear its view that achieving an internal market can also require removing disparities between national legislations on jurisdiction.[13] It is very unlikely that the European Court of Justice would reach a different conclusion as to the scope of the Brussels Regulation.

---

interpretation by the European Court of Justice were entered into under the Brussels Convention and the Rome Convention: see paras 2.19 and 3.19 below.

7. Preamble to the Jenard report on the Brussels Convention, 1979 OJ C.59/1, 7. See further para. 3.10 below.
8. See paras 3.5–3.6 below for the interpretation of treaties by reference to their objectives.
9. Such treaties are said to be of "double treaty" type: Jenard and Moller, para.13.
10. *Jenard,* 1979 OJ C.59/1.
11. *Jenard,* 1979 OJ C.59/1.
12. C-281/02; *Owusu* v. *Jackson* [2005] ECR I-1383, [2005] QB 801.
13. It is sufficient to observe in that regard that the consolidation as such of the rules on conflict of jurisdiction and on the recognition and enforcement of judgments, effected by the Brussels Convention in respect of cases with an international element, is without doubt intended to eliminate obstacles to the functioning of the internal market which may derive from disparities between national legal systems on the subject: see, by analogy, as regards harmonisation Directives based on Article 95 EC intended to improve the conditions for the establishment and working of the internal market, (Joined Cases C-465/00 and 138 and 139/01) *Rechnungshof* v. *Österreichischer Rundfunk* [2003] ECR I-4989, 5034-5035 [41] and [42].

"If this hardens into law, it will mean that it will never be admissible to argue that an absence of actual connection to the internal market means that the Convention is inapplicable. This marking out of territory by the court was deadly serious. It was intended to warn off those who might advance similar arguments about lack of connection to the internal market to trim or undermine the scope of the Judgments Regulation. It will also serve to prevent those who may advance similar arguments to cast doubt on the treaty basis of Regulations, present and to come, governing choice of law in contract, tort and unjust enrichment, family law, etc. Disparities in any of these areas of national law may, just as speciously, be said to obstruct the internal market. Careful and precise legal arguments about the legal basis for such legislation will be impotent against a boilerplate paragraph, bolted into every judgment, which will say that any disparities between national legislation will impede the functioning of the internal market, and that legislation to eradicate such disparities is therefore within the competence of the organs of the European Union. Left unchallenged, this appalling claim removes every limitation on the extent to which English private international law may be dismantled."[14]

2.16 However, the code of rules established by the Brussels Convention was not completely autonomous. It was autonomous in the sense that interpretation is independent of the national law of Member States, but interpretation of the Convention is not independent from the body of law relating to the Community. The European Court of Justice has established that Community law is to be interpreted as a whole, which means that the Brussels Convention may be interpreted in accordance with other provisions of the EEC treaty, laws made under the treaty, and the ensuing plethora of law which may be called Community law (see further para. 2.21 below). This also means that the Brussels Convention will not necessarily be interpreted in accordance with the normal rules of international law applicable to treaties.[15]

2.17 The Brussels Convention also differed fundamentally from previous conventions in that amongst other things it primarily allocated jurisdiction according to the *domicile* of the defendant rather than nationality: it applied to anyone domiciled in a Member State regardless of nationality, it defined rules of exclusive jurisdiction, outlawed certain exorbitant bases of jurisdiction, and relied on rules which did not include judicial discretion in allocating jurisdiction.[16]

3. 1971 Protocol on the European Court of Justice

2.18 At the same date as they signed the Brussels Convention in 1968 the parties had made a Joint Declaration that they would examine the possibility of conferring jurisdiction on the European Court of Justice because they wanted "to ensure that the Convention is applied as effectively as possible" and were "anxious to prevent differences on the interpretation of the Convention from impairing its unifying effect".

2.19 The result was an agreement between the states to confer jurisdiction to interpret the Brussels Convention on the European Court of Justice after a request for a ruling in carefully defined circumstances. In essence, the Court is empowered to provide definitive preliminary interpretations of the Convention as a matter of law which the national court then has to apply. The agreement was made by a Protocol signed on 3 June 1971 which came into force on 1 September 1975, and was the subject of an official report describing its genesis and effect.[17]

2.20 The recitals to the Protocol stated that it was agreed having regard to the declaration annexed to the Brussels Convention (para. 2.14 above). The objective of the Protocol was

14. A. Briggs, "The Death of Harrods: Forum Non Conveniens and the European Court" (2005) LQR 535, 539. See also C. Hare, "Forum Non Conveniens in Europe: Game Over or Time for Reflexion" (2006) JBL 157, 165.

15. Hartley, p. 89; Layton/Mercer, p. 308.

16. *Jenard,* 1979 OJ C.59/1, 8.

17. Jenard report on the Protocols: C59/66.

therefore plainly to ensure that the Brussels Convention was given a uniform interpretation in all Contracting States and so promote its unifying effect on the Community.

2.21 There was another reason why this was an important step: it gave the power to make definitive rulings on the autonomous interpretation of the Convention to the same body as had the power to interpret the EEC Treaty and laws made under it, and so enabled the Convention to be interpreted in accordance with Community law as a whole.[18]

4. 1972 UK joined the Community

2.22 The UK, together with Denmark and Ireland, agreed to become a member of the Community by an Accession Convention signed on 22 January 1972 which came into force on 1 January 1973.[19] The Six became Nine. At the same time the UK and Denmark left EFTA. The construction of an "ever closer union" in the spirit of the EEC Treaty was recorded as an objective of the Accession Convention in the recitals.

2.23 The 1972 Accession Convention provided that the new members became a party to the EEC Treaty but that they undertook to accede to the Conventions provided for in Article 220 of the EEC Treaty which included the Brussels Convention, and to enter into negotiations to make the necessary adjustments.[20]

2.24 The EEC Treaty and 1972 Accession Convention were given effect under English law by the European Communities Act 1972 which was given Royal Assent on 17 October 1972 but did not have practical effect until 1 January 1973 when the Convention came into force by Article 2. Legislation was required to give effect to the Treaty under the laws within the UK because "treaties are not self-executing. They create rights and obligations on the international plane, not on the domestic plane."[21]

5. 1978 UK signed the Brussels Convention

2.25 As with the preparation of the Brussels Convention in 1972 a committee of experts was convened to work on a draft of what became the 1978 Accession Convention and produced a report for the governments which is known as the Schlosser report, after the rapporteur for that committee.[22]

2.26 The negotiations for the Accession Convention must have been lengthy. It was not until six years after acceding to the EEC Treaty that the UK, Denmark and Ireland agreed to

18. See para. 2.16 above and Chapter 3 below. Article 177 of the EEC Treaty conferred jurisdiction on the European Court of Justice in relation to the interpretation of the EEC Treaty.

19. Norway signed the Accession Convention but did not ratify following a referendum. The opportunity was taken to agree various amendments to the EEC Treaty. The six founder members became nine: Belgium, France, Germany, Italy, Luxembourg, the Netherlands, Denmark, Ireland and the UK.

20. Article 1 of the Accession Convention incorporated the terms of the Act of Accession. Articles 2 and 3 of the Act of Accession set out terms on which the UK joined the EEC. Article 3(2) contained the undertaking to negotiate the Brussels Convention.

21. *R* v. *Foreign Secretary, ex p. Rees-Mogg* [1994] QB 552, 567 (CA) *per* Lloyd LJ; Halsbury's Laws, 4th ed. (1996), vol 8(2), para. 802. Hence the Brussels Convention was later brought into effect under the laws within the UK by the Civil Jurisdiction and Judgments Act 1982. Section 2(1) of the European Communities Act 1972 provided in essence that provisions intended to be directly applicable of the EEC Treaty, the 1972 UK Accession Convention and other specified treaties were to be given legal effect under the laws within the UK. The list of treaties covered by this subsection has been expanded to include later treaties, including the Single European Act, Maastricht, Amsterdam and Nice. Section 2(2) of the European Communities Act 1972 empowered the Crown by Order in Council and any Minister or department by regulation to make provision for the purpose of implementing any Community obligation of the UK or related matters to be carried into effect.

22. 1979 OJ C.59/71. Chapter 1 of the report refers to the work done on the draft Accession Convention before the committee of experts was set up.

become parties to the Brussels Convention and 1971 Protocol. The Accession Convention was signed on 9 October 1978.

2.27 The 1978 Accession Convention made some significant changes to the Brussels Convention for the original six members, although not many of these are relevant for our purposes. The objectives were not altered (see paras 2.12–2.14 above). The main relevant changes were to the special jurisdiction under section 3 in relation to insurance.[23] The accession of the UK was described as introducing a "totally new dimension" to the insurance business within the EEC, primarily because of the size of the Lloyd's market for international insurance of large risks.[24] However, the modifications to the existing Convention were modest.[25]

2.28 Other than that, the only relevant change of any significance was that Article 17(1) of the Brussels Convention was amplified to give effect to exclusive jurisdiction agreements in international trade which were in accordance with the ordinary course of trade or commerce even if not in or evidenced in writing.[26]

2.29 One significant clash highlighted by the Schlosser report on the 1978 Accession Convention was in relation to *forum non conveniens*. Schlosser pointed out that the idea that a national court has discretion in the exercise of jurisdiction "does not generally exist in Continental legal systems" (para. 76). The majority of the committee of experts came down in favour of rejecting the introduction of such discretionary powers into the Brussels Convention and in the end the UK and Ireland did not press for them. The implications of this are still being worked out in the decisions of the European Court of Justice (see Chapter 5, Section I below).

2.30 Another clash which remains unresolved was in relation to the scope of the arbitration exclusion in Article 1(4) of the Brussels Convention (see para. 8.21 below).

2.31 The 1978 Accession Convention did not itself come into force for over eight years until 1 November 1986 as between Contracting States other than the UK, and until 1 January 1987 as between the UK and other Contracting States.[27] By the time the 1978 Brussels Convention came into force in the UK it had already been revised in 1982 on the accession of Greece but no substantial amendments had been made on that occasion.

2.32 The Civil Jurisdiction and Judgments Act 1982 made some other changes to English law apart from implementing the treaties:

(1) The Brussels Convention did not define "domicile" which was broadly similar in the original six parties to the Brussels Convention.[28] However, the concept of domicile was very different under English law and the Civil Jurisdiction and Judgments Act 1982 therefore introduced a new definition for the purpose of the Brussels Convention.[29]
(2) The Brussels Convention treated the UK as one country for the purpose of allocating jurisdiction and the Civil Jurisdiction and Judgments Act 1982 introduced a new uni-

23. See further Chapter 6 below.
24. *Schlosser*, para. 136.
25. *Schlosser*, paras 136–152a.
26. See further para. 5.41 below; *Schlosser*, para. 179. At common law a choice of English law is a ground of jurisdiction. To cater for parties who had agreed such a clause intending it to operate as a choice of jurisdiction the Accession Convention included a transitional provision in Article 35 in respect of contracts agreed in writing before the Convention came into force.
27. The 1978 Brussels Convention, the amended 1971 Protocol and the 1978 Accession Convention were given the force of law within the UK by the Civil Jurisdiction and Judgments Act 1982 which came into force on 1 January 1987: Civil Jurisdiction and Judgments Act 1982 (Commencement No 1) Order 1984 SI 1553.
28. *Schlosser*, para. 71.
29. See para. 5.115 below.

form code based on the Brussels Convention for allocating jurisdiction within the UK.[30]

(3) Section 25 of the Civil Jurisdiction and Judgments Act 1982 gave the English courts power to grant interim relief in support of substantive proceedings in a Contracting State.[31]

(4) Section 49 of the Civil Jurisdiction and Judgments Act 1982 provided that nothing in the Act would prevent a court from staying proceedings on the ground of *forum non conveniens* insofar as that was not inconsistent with the Brussels Convention (as to which see para. 5.296 below).

6. 1982 Greece signed the Brussels Convention

2.33 Greece became a party to the EEC Treaty by an Accession Convention signed on 28 May 1979 which came into force on 1 January 1981. The Nine became Ten.[32]

2.34 In preparation for the accession of Greece to the Brussels Convention a committee of experts was again set up and prepared a report commenting on the 1982 Brussels Convention and amended 1971 Protocol known as the Evrigenis and Kerameus report. Although no substantial amendments were made to the Brussels Convention on the accession of Greece the report nevertheless to some extent analysed what was described as the "autonomous law of the Contracting parties" (para. 4) under the Brussels Convention. It also summarised Greek law relating to jurisdiction and judgments (section II).

7. 1986 The Single European Act

2.35 On 17 February 1986 the first major reform of the EEC Treaty was agreed in the form of a new treaty called the Single European Act (SEA).[33]

2.36 The SEA stated that the objective of the Community and European Political Co-operation (a new structure formalising co-operation in foreign policy) was "to contribute together to making concrete progress towards European unity" (Article 1).

2.37 Changes were made by the SEA to introduce co-operation in relation to economic and monetary union, social cohesion (reducing disparities between regions), and in the development of European Political Co-operation in relation to "any foreign policy matters of general interest" (Article 30). The objectives of the Community were no longer confined to economic integration as they had been stated to be in 1957 (para. 2.5 above) but now embraced "European unity" which now included at least an element of political co-operation, mainly in relation to foreign policy, but also the environment and new technologies.

2.38 One of the specific aims of the SEA was the completion of the internal market by removing trade barriers between Contracting States. The SEA accordingly introduced a new Article 8a into Part 1 of the EEC Treaty which set out the principles of the EEC. This

30. See Chapter 5, Section K below.

31. See, generally, para. 5.249 below.

32. The Accession Convention was given legal effect in the UK by an amendment to the European Communities Act 1972: European Communities (Greek Accession) Act 1979 given Royal Assent on 20 December 1979. Greece signed the Brussels Convention and the 1971 Protocol both as amended in 1978 by an Accession Convention signed on 25 October 1982. The 1982 Brussels Convention came into force as between Greece and the Contracting States other than the UK on 1 April 1989, over six years after having been signed. In the case of the UK the 1982 Brussels Convention came into force on 1 October 1989.

33. See para. 2.24 above for the enactment of treaties by legislation. The SEA was brought into law in the UK by the European Communities (Amendment) Act 1986 (in force 7 November 1986) and under Article 33 came into force on 1 July 1987.

provided that the Community would adopt by the end of 1992 measures with the aim of progressing the internal market, i.e. an area without internal frontiers in which the free movement of goods, persons, services and capital was ensured. To this end it made a number of significant amendments to the procedures for enacting Community rules with the aim of making reforms to the internal market easier to enact.

2.39 As has been seen (para. 2.10 above) one of the specific objectives of the Brussels Convention as originally drafted was to strengthen legal protection of persons within the Community, and this apparently was linked to the objective of the EEC Treaty of achieving a "true internal market". That remained the objective in later revisions of the Brussels Convention. The agreement of Member States in the SEA to complete the internal market enhanced the importance of this objective.

8. 1988 Lugano Convention signed by EFTA countries and the Community

2.40 The European Free Trade Association (EFTA) is essentially an association of countries outside the European Union formed for the purpose of promoting free trade.[34] It must be distinguished from European Economic Area (EEA) – (see para. 2.59 below). Because of the large amount of trade between the Community and EFTA countries there was an obvious interest in establishing a treaty like the Brussels Convention to regulate jurisdiction and enforcement of judgments to replace the web of bilateral treaties (listed in Article 55 of the Lugano Convention) which existed.

2.41 Accordingly in 1985 a working party of experts was set up to draft a Convention between the Community and EFTA member countries. They rejected the notion of the EFTA members simply becoming parties to the Brussels Convention, because the Brussels Convention was based on Article 220 of the EEC Treaty, and subject to interpretation by the European Court of Justice and is a "Community instrument" and it was considered difficult to ask non-Member States to sign it for reasons set out in the Jenard and Moller report.[35] Instead the committee of experts drafted a parallel Convention to the Brussels Convention and a report commenting on it known as the Jenard and Moller report.[36]

2.42 The Lugano Convention set out a code with some differences from the 1982 Brussels Convention, but most of these were incorporated into the 1989 Brussels Convention on the accession of Spain and Portugal.[37]

2.43 The Lugano Convention was opened for signature on 16 September 1988 following an international conference and came into force on 1 January 1992 as between Contracting States which had ratified other than the UK, and on 1 May 1992 as between the UK and other Contracting States.[38]

2.44 The EFTA countries with which the Lugano Convention was made were Austria, Finland, Iceland, Norway, Sweden, and Switzerland. Subsequently Austria, Finland and Sweden joined the Community and they are now parties to the Brussels Regulation. The Lugano Convention continues to apply in relation to Iceland, Norway and Switzerland.

34. See, generally, *Jenard and Moller*, paras 8–9, for the background.

35. *Jenard and Moller*, para. 9.

36. 1990 OJ C.189, 7.

37. The particular changes made by the Lugano Convention but not made by the 1989 Brussels Convention are identified in chapter 4 of the official report on the 1989 Brussels Convention.

38. In the case of the UK the Lugano Convention was given effect within the UK by the Civil Jurisdiction and Judgments Act 1991 from 1 May 1992. The Act amended the Civil Jurisdiction and Judgments Act 1982 so that section referred to the Lugano Convention. A copy of the Lugano Convention is at Schedule 3C to the Civil Jurisdiction and Judgments Act 1991. It also included the Jenard and Moller report as an official report which was an aid to interpretation: SI 1992 No. 745.

2.45 Liechtenstein is a special case. It became a full member of EFTA in 1991 but has not acceded to the Lugano Convention.

2.46 The Lugano Convention applied to Poland briefly between 1 August 2000 and the accession of Poland to the European Union on 1 May 2004 when Poland too became a party to the Brussels Regulation (para. 2.75 below).[39]

2.47 Work on the revision of the Lugano Convention has been frozen pending work on revision of the Brussels Convention to bring it into line with the Brussels Regulation.[40] The European Court of Justice has recently confirmed that the European Community has exclusive competence to conclude any new convention to replace the existing Lugano Convention (Lugano Opinion, 7 February 2006). Thus any new convention will be concluded between the EFTA states on the one hand and the EU itself on the other.

9. 1989 Spain and Portugal join the Brussels Convention

2.48 Spain and Portugal had become members of the Community by an Accession Convention signed on 12 June 1985 which came into force on 1 January 1986. The Ten became the Twelve Member States.[41]

2.49 In 1989 a working party of experts was as usual set up to draft an Accession Convention to the Brussels Convention. A draft explanatory report on the Convention was prepared. After agreement of the Accession Convention this report was amended and is known as the Cruz, Desantes Real and Jenard report.[42]

2.50 The 1989 Brussels Convention (sometimes known as the San Sebastian Convention) was signed on 26 May 1989 and came into force as between Contracting States which had ratified it not including the UK on 1 February 1991. The 1989 Brussels Convention came into force in the UK on 1 December 1991.[43]

2.51 The only substantive amendments made to the Brussels Convention in 1989 were to incorporate some but not all of the innovations which had been included in the Lugano Convention (as referred to in para. 2.42 above).

10. 1992 European Union (EU) created, and European Community christened, by the Treaty on European Union (the Maastricht Treaty)

2.52 This major treaty was signed by the Member States of the Community on 7 February 1992. Its title is the Treaty on European Union, but it is also commonly known as the Maastricht Treaty. The Maastricht Treaty came into force between those countries which had ratified it on 1 November 1993. It came into legal effect within the UK on 20 July 1993 by amendment to the European Communities Act 1972.[44]

39. Under Article 62 the Lugano Convention was open to accession by other States. Poland acceded to the Lugano Convention on 1 February 2000. That accession was brought into effect under English law by an amendment to the Civil Jurisdiction and Judgments Act 1982 by an order in council SI 2000 No. 1824 under s.14 of the Civil Jurisdiction and Judgments Act 1982 (see para. 2.33 above for the same procedure in relation to the accession of Greece to the Brussels Convention).

40. 39th Annual Report of EFTA, p. 36.

41. The Accession Convention was given legal effect in the UK by an amendment to the European Communities Act 1972: The European Communities (Spanish and Portuguese Accession) Act 1985 was given Royal Assent on 19 December 1985.

42. 90/C 189/06.

43. Civil Jurisdiction and Judgments Act 1982 (Amendment Order) 1990 SI 1990 No. 2591 which amended the Civil Jurisdiction and Judgments Act 1982 in a similar way as the amendment on the Accession of Greece (para. 2.33 above). The 1989 Brussels Convention is scheduled to that statutory instrument in its amended form. The Act was amended to include the Cruz, Desantes, Real and Jenard report as an official aid to interpretation within the UK.

44. European Communities (Amendment) Act 1993, in force on 20 July 1993 under section 7. This enacted into domestic law within the UK Titles II to IV of the Maastricht Treaty. Although the UK also agreed in the Maastricht

2.53 In short, the Maastricht Treaty was a substantial push forward by Contracting States towards greater economic and political integration, in particular by agreement to eventual monetary union, and to greater co-operation in foreign policy, security and defence policy, asylum and immigration policy, criminal and civil judicial matters.[45]

2.54 Since some Member States did not agree to the Community dealing with all these matters the Contracting States agreed to establish among themselves a new entity called the European Union (EU) consisting of the Community established by the amended EEC Treaty, as well as separate structures for inter-governmental co-operation in relation to foreign and security policy and for co-operation in asylum and immigration policy, criminal and civil judicial matters.

2.55 These three constituents of the EU are very commonly referred to as the "three pillars" of the EU, although not so defined in the Treaty itself: the Community pillar, the Common Foreign and Security Policy pillar, and the Justice and Home Affairs pillar (respectively pillars one, two and three). Matters within pillars two and three were not to be handled by the Community but by the governments of the Contracting States themselves, i.e. by means of inter-governmental agreement alone upon the recommendation of the Council.

2.56 In relation to pillar one, the Maastricht Treaty made many changes to the EEC Treaty, not least by re-naming it the Treaty establishing the European Community (EC), and renaming the EEC the European Community.[46] The UK did not agree to all the extensions to the tasks of co-operation within the Union and famously opted out of an agreement on social policy.[47]

2.57 In relation to pillar three, the Maastricht Treaty included a set of apparently comprehensive provisions relating to co-operation in civil judicial matters (although they were expressly subject to Article 220 of the treaty establishing the EU which it will be recalled was the original basis of the Brussels Convention (see para. 2.10 above)). These included Title VI "Provisions on co-operation in the fields of justice and home affairs". The governments of the Member States retained control of the formulation and implementation of policy under pillar three since it was up to them to agree, or not, to Conventions recommended by the Council alone in relation to co-operation in civil matters, albeit the Commission could suggest initiatives to the Council (Article K.3). The Council, or Council of the European Union to give it its full title, is a body formed from ministers drawn from the government of each Member State and takes most of the important decisions within the EU.[48]

2.58 The result of the Maastricht Treaty was that it remained the position that co-operation in civil matters between Member States would be handled by governments under pillar three and accordingly that any development in judicial co-operation would be strictly controlled

Treaty to Titles I, V and VI setting up the EU, and the second and third pillars of the EU referred to below those Titles were not enacted into domestic law by the European Communities (Amendment) Act 1993. Apparently the view of the government was that they did not need to since they were concerned with inter-governmental policy rather than rights, although there is some room for doubt about this: see generally Beaumont, *Current Law Statutes Annotated*, 1993, vol. 2, 32–6 to 32–7, 32–20. However, the terms of Titles I and VI are relevant to the interpretation of Titles II to IV of the Maastricht Treaty and have been taken into account in interpreting the Brussels Convention: see Beaumont, *Current Law Statutes Annotated*, 1993, vol. 2, 32–20. In *R* v. *Foreign Secretary, ex p. Rees-Mogg* [1994] QB 552 the Court of Appeal rejected an argument that parts of the Maastricht Treaty (the Social Policy protocol and Title V relating to foreign policy) could not be ratified by the UK.

45. For the background see *Craig/De Burca*, p. 22; Beaumont, *Current Law Statutes Annotated*, 1993, vol. 2, 32–1.

46. The provisions of the Treaty Establishing the EC as amended by the Maastricht Treaty are helpfully reproduced at Beaumont, *Current Law Statutes Annotated*, 1993, vol. 2, 32–27.

47. Protocols on certain provisions relating to the UK, and Protocol on social policy, both annexed to the Maastricht Treaty.

48. Not to be confused with the unhelpfully named European Council which is a body formed of Heads of Government and Foreign Ministers. See, generally, *Hartley*, pp. 19, 25.

by the governments and not by the Community. However, as we will see, the picture changed again when the Treaty of Amsterdam was agreed.

11. 1992 European Economic Area (EEA) formed

2.59 The EEA is, in essence, a treaty between the EU and, currently, Iceland, Liechtenstein and Norway under which some of the free trade policies of the EU are as between the EU and Iceland, Liechtenstein and Norway. Switzerland, which is a member of EFTA, decided after a referendum not to become a part of the EEA. The treaty, called the Agreement on the EEA was given legal effect in the UK by an amendment to the European Communities Act 1972 and came into force on 1 January 1994.[49]

2.60 The EEA agreement did not include agreement in relation to the field of judicial co-operation in civil matters in pillar three of the Maastricht Treaty, and did not supersede the Lugano Convention. It is not relevant to the jurisdiction rules relating to reinsurance and insurance, but it is referred to in relation to the insurance choice of law regulation (Chapter 11).

12. 1994 Austria, Finland and Sweden joined the Brussels Convention

2.61 Austria, Finland and Sweden became members of the Community by a Treaty of Accession signed on 24 June 1994 which came into force on 1 January 1995. Norway signed the Treaty of Accession but following its rejection in a referendum never ratified it. The Twelve became Fifteen Member States. The Treaty of Accession was given legal effect in the UK by an amendment to the European Communities Act 1972.[50] The Treaty of Accession made no significant changes to the Treaty Establishing the EC or Maastricht Treaty.

2.62 The new States undertook in Article 3 of the Act of Accession annexed to the Treaty of Accession to accede to the Brussels Convention. This time no committee of experts was established. On 29 November 1996 the Accession Convention to the 1996 Brussels Convention was signed and came into force as between Contracting States which had ratified it (not including the UK) on 1 December 1998. The 1996 Brussels Convention came into force in the UK on 1 January 2001.[51]

13. 1997 Treaty of Amsterdam amended the treaties of EC and EU

2.63 The third major reform of the EU was made by the Treaty of Amsterdam which was signed on 2 October 1997 and came into force as between those countries which had ratified it on 1 May 1999. It was brought into effect within the UK by amendment to the European Communities Act 1972.[52]

2.64 In short, for our purposes the main importance of the Treaty of Amsterdam was that it enabled the Brussels Regulation to be issued by the Council rather than the Member States having to agree a new treaty (see para. 2.57 above). The newly created area of judicial

49. European Economic Area Act 1993, in force 5 November 1993.

50. European Union (Accessions) Act 1994 given Royal Assent on 3 November 1994.

51. Civil Jurisdiction and Judgments Act 1982 (Amendment Order) 2000 SI 2000 No. 1824 which amended the Civil Jurisdiction and Judgments Act 1982 in a similar way as the amendment on the Accession of Greece (para. 2.33 above). The 1996 Brussels Convention is scheduled to that statutory instrument in its amended form.

52. European Communities (Amendment) Act 1998, s.1, enacting Articles 2–9 and 12 of and the Protocols to the Treaty of Amsterdam. The UK agreed to Article 1 of the Treaty of Amsterdam which in particular amended the recitals to the Maastricht Treaty, and pillars 2 and 3 but these were not enacted into law within the UK by the European Communities (Amendment) Act 1998 although they have influenced the interpretation of the Brussels Convention. See generally Chapter 3.

co-operation in civil matters under the Maastricht Treaty was taken away from the powers of Member States and handed back to the Community.

2.65 These changes were achieved by removing Title VI (judicial co-operation in civil matters from the Maastricht Treaty) and placing it within an amended Title IV of the Treaty Establishing the EC concerned with the free movement of persons, called "Visas, Asylum, Immigration and other policies related to free movement of persons".[53] In effect, this removed the area from pillar three to pillar one of the EU.

2.66 The new Title IV of the Treaty Establishing the EC required the Council "in order to establish progressively an area of freedom security and justice" to "adopt measures in the field of judicial co-operation in civil matters as provided for in Article 73m" (now re-numbered Article 65) which provided:

"Measures in the field of judicial cooperation in civil matters having cross-border implications, ... insofar as necessary for the proper functioning of the internal market, shall include:

(a) improving and simplifying:
   - the system for cross-border service of judicial and extrajudicial documents;
   - cooperation in the taking of evidence;
   - the recognition and enforcement of decisions in civil and commercial cases, including decisions in extrajudicial cases;

(b) promoting the compatibility of the rules applicable in the member states concerning the conflict of laws and of jurisdiction;

(c) eliminating obstacles to the good functioning of civil proceedings, if necessary by promoting the compatibility of the rules on civil procedure applicable in the member states."[54]

2.67 It will be seen that the objectives in relation to Title VI and judicial co-operation are stated by the Treaty Establishing the EC in very broad terms, and specified inclusively, i.e. without specification of limits.

2.68 The position is complicated because the UK is not bound by measures in this area unless it opts in. By a Protocol to the Treaty of Amsterdam the UK along with Ireland opted out of the new Title VI to the Treaty Establishing the EC. Article 2 of the Protocol provided that:

"none of the provisions of Title [IV] of the Treaty establishing the European Community, no measure adopted pursuant to that Title, no provision of any international agreement concluded by the Community pursuant to that Title, and no decision of the Court of Justice interpreting any such provision or measure shall be binding upon or applicable in the United Kingdom or Ireland; and no such provision, measure or decision shall in any way affect the competences, rights and obligations of those States; and no such provision, measure or decision shall in any way affect the acquis communautaire nor form part of Community law as they apply to the United Kingdom or Ireland."

2.69 However, the UK or Ireland can notify the Council within 3 months of any proposal being made that it wishes to take part in the adoption and application of such a proposal.[55]

14. Brussels Regulation

2.70 On 14 July 1999 the Commission made a proposal for a Council regulation on jurisdiction and enforcement of judgments in civil and commercial matters.[56] The Regulation was adopted on 22 December 2002 and came into force on 1 March 2002.[57]

53. Article 2 Treaty of Amsterdam.

54. Article 2.15 Treaty of Amsterdam.

55. Article 3 of the Protocol. Denmark also opted out of the provisions but, unlike the UK and Ireland, did not retain a power to opt in.

56. COM [1999] 348 final, 1999 OJ C.376.

57. The Brussels Regulation applies to legal proceedings instituted after 1 March 2002 (Article 66(1)) and contains transitional provisions dealing, *inter alia*, with judgments in proceedings commenced before that date.

2.71 The Brussels Regulation was thus a community measure adopted under the new Treaty of Amsterdam mechanism. Unlike a Treaty, as a directly applicable community measure it did not need to be implemented into national law.[58] The position of the UK and Ireland was potentially problematic, but, in March 1999, the UK and Ireland had indicated their intention to adopt Community instruments in relation to judicial co-operation in civil matters, that is, they elected to opt in to the Regulation.

2.72 Denmark, which did not retain any power to opt in, was not bound by the Brussels Regulation. By an agreement made between the EC and Denmark in 2005 Denmark agreed to apply the Brussels Regulation as between it and other Member States with some minor changes of no relevance for our purposes.[59] The aim was that there should be a uniform application and interpretation of the Brussels Regulation (Article 1). The agreement has been adopted by the Council and will come into effect on the first day of the sixth month following notification by Denmark of its adoption of the agreement.[60] Until that agreement is in force, the Brussels Regulation does not apply as between Denmark and other Member States; the Brussels Convention and the Lugano Convention will apply within their scope. EFTA countries (Iceland, Norway and Switzerland) continue to be bound by the Lugano Convention.

2.73 The Brussels Regulation has accordingly now superseded the Brussels Convention. Although it was modelled on the Convention it made a number of substantive changes, and, rather confusingly, the numbering of many of the Articles has changed which needs to be borne in mind when reading the cases.[61] Some changes codified the effect of European Court of Justice decisions on the Convention, others were new. The changes which are particularly relevant for our purposes will be discussed in detail below. In summary:

(1) modifications are made to the special jurisdiction rules for contract under Article 5(1);
(2) the Regulation makes it clear that the provisions relating to tort in Article 5(3) apply when the harmful event has yet to occur;
(3) by Article 60 a new autonomous community meaning for the domicile of companies is introduced;
(4) changes are made to the special rules relating to jurisdiction in insurance and consumer contracts;
(5) non-exclusive jurisdiction clauses are expressly recognised in Article 23; and
(6) by Article 30 a new definition of when a court is "seised" of proceedings is introduced.

15. 2001 Nice Treaty amended the treaties of EC and EU

2.74 The fourth and most recent important reform of the EU was the agreement of the Nice Treaty on 26 February 2001. This Treaty came into force on 1 February 2003.[62] The Nice Treaty made important changes to the Maastricht Treaty and the Treaty Establishing the EC, mainly concerned with institutional arrangements in preparation for expansion of the EU, but none of significance for our purposes.[63]

58. Section 2(1) of the European Communities Act 1972. The merits of a Regulation over a Convention were also discussed by the Commission in relation to the Rome Convention, see fn. 87 below.

59. 16 November 2005, L.299/62.

60. Notice of Council Decision 27 April 2006, L. 120/22; Article 12 of the agreement.

61. The Regulation is based on the recommendations of a working party that was originally set up to consider reform of the Brussels and Lugano Conventions.

62. It was given legal effect under the laws within the UK by an amendment to the European Communities Act 1972. European Communities (Amendment) Act 2002 given Royal Assent on 26 February 2002 enacting Articles 2–10 of the Nice Treaty. Article 1 of the Nice Treaty made amendments to the Maastricht Treaty but has not been enacted into the laws of the UK because of the view of the government that the other parts of the Nice Treaty concern the inter-governmental pillars two and three of the EU (para. 2.52 above).

63. See, generally, *Craig/De Burca*, p. 44.

16. 2003 Accession of ten new members to the EU and Brussels Regulation

2.75 On 16 April 2003 the Member States signed an Accession Treaty with 10 new Member States of the EU. The new Member States were: Czech Republic, Estonia, Cyprus, Latvia, Lithuania, Hungary, Malta, Poland, Slovenia, and the Slovak Republic. The Accession Treaty came into force on 1 May 2004 (Article 3 of the Accession Treaty). The Accession Treaty was given legal effect in the UK by an amendment to the European Communities Act 1972.[64] The Accession Treaty made no significant changes to the Treaty Establishing the EC or Maastricht Treaty.

2.76 Under the terms of the Treaty the effect of accession was that the new Member States became bound by the acts already adopted by the institutions of the EU including the Brussels Regulation.[65] As for the UK, the effect of section 2(1) of the European Communities Act 1972 was that from 1 May 2004 the Brussels Regulation applied, under the laws within the UK, as between all the Member States including the new Member States. Bulgaria and Romania are currently scheduled to become members of the EU in 2007 and therefore subject to the Brussels Regulation.

B. THE HARMONISATION OF EU CHOICE OF LAW RULES

2.77 As we have seen, Article 220 of the original EEC Treaty, relating to judgments and awards, became the basis of the development of the wide regime of co-operation in matters of civil jurisdiction which existed until the Brussels Regulation was made.

2.78 The major feature of the Brussels Convention, followed in the Lugano Convention and the Brussels Regulation, was that it set out rules for the international jurisdiction of the courts of the Member States as well as providing rules guaranteeing the recognition and enforcement of judgments from other Member States. Thus it adopted a "double" system rather than simply providing for the reciprocal enforcement of judgments within the Community (see para. 2.13 above).

2.79 However, whilst the Brussels Convention made huge inroads towards harmonisation in the fields of jurisdiction and enforcement, the Community was not content to leave it at that. Each of the Member States had a separate and in many cases very different legal system. Thus each state, for example, has its own contract law, its own rules relating to insurance contracts and its own regulations concerning the offering of insurance business. Thus, whilst litigants could now in theory predict very accurately which state they could sue or be sued in, and would know that a judgment obtained in a Member State would almost certainly be enforceable throughout the Community, it remained the case that the claimant by exercising any choice of jurisdiction allowed to him under the jurisdictional rules could still exercise an enormous impact on the result of the case. Thus "forum shopping" remained a very real prospect despite the implementation of the jurisdictional rules. The prospect of forum shopping meant that there remained uncertainty and a lack of uniformity in the system and accordingly the guarantee of legal rights to all those in the community remained fundamentally flawed.

2.80 The most radical and far reaching solution to forum shopping and indeed all conflict of law issues would be the adoption of a community legal code. If each Member State had the same law of contract, tort, regulation of insurance business, etc, it would make no difference what court heard any matter since there would no longer be any "choice of law". However,

64. European Union (Accessions) Act 2003 given Royal Assent on 13 November 2003.
65. Article 2 of the Act attached to the Accession Treaty.

whilst work continues towards harmonisation of substantive laws (particularly, as we will see, in insurance) it is unlikely to be achieved in anything but relatively defined areas.[66]

2.81 At the same time, therefore, work has continued on an alternative approach namely the harmonisation of choice of law rules. Thus, if it were the case that whatever court heard a matter would apply the same choice of law rule the same substantive law would then be applied to the dispute (whether that be the law of England, France or Germany) wherever the case was heard. Applicable law would thus be predictable and certain and also there would no advantage in starting the proceedings in any particular state since all courts would end up deciding the dispute by applying the substantive law of the same state.[67]

1. Development of the Rome Convention

2.82 The first proposal on the harmonisation of conflict of law rules (8 September 1967) was extended to the Commission by the Permanent Representative of Belgium, in the name of his own Government and those of the Netherlands and Luxembourg, and was an invitation to collaborate with the experts of the Member States in the unification of private international law and the codification of the rules of conflict of laws within the Community. In his opening address to the subsequent meeting of experts the then Director General for the Internal Market and Approximation of Legislation at the Commission noted that compared with the unification of substantive law, unification of the rules of conflict of laws is more practicable and that:

"This proposal should bring about a complete unification of the rules of conflict. Thus in each of our six countries, instead of the existing rules of conflict and apart from cases of application of international Agreements binding on any member state, identical rules of conflict would enter into force both in member states' relations *inter se* and in relations with non-Community States.... The great advantage of this proposal is undoubtedly that the level of legal certainty would be raised, confidence in the stability of legal relationships fortified, agreements on jurisdiction according to the applicable law facilitated, and the protection of rights acquired over the whole field of private law augmented."[68]

2.83 He also commented specifically on the subject of forum shopping. Having referred to the Brussels Convention and the fact that the outcome of the rules introduced may be to enable the parties to give preference to the court of a state whose law seems to offer a better solution to the proceedings he continued:

"To prevent this 'forum shopping', increase legal certainty, and anticipate more easily the law which will be applied, it would be advisable for the rules of conflict to be unified in fields of particular economic importance so that the same law is applied irrespective of the State in which the decision is given."[69]

2.84 At the next meeting on 20 to 22 October 1969, the government experts agreed that a start should be made on matters most closely involved in the proper functioning of the common market, more specifically:

(1) the law applicable to corporeal and incorporeal property;
(2) the law applicable to contractual and non-contractual obligations;
(3) the law applicable to the form of legal transactions and evidence; and

66. Harmonisation of substantive law has been achieved in some limited areas, but even the "European contract law" project does not aim at either the uniformisation of contract law nor at the adoption of a European civil law code. Even if one day there is closer harmonisation of contract law in the Community, it is quite possible that this will concern only certain particularly important aspects and that the applicable law will still have to be determined for non-harmonised aspects (see the comments of Commission in its Green Paper on the Rome Convention at para.1.6. (COM (2002) 654 final)).

67. On the desirability of each court applying the same choice of law rules see Staughton LJ in *MacMillan Inc.* v. *Bishopsgate Investment Trust plc (No. 3)* [1996] 1 WLR 387, 391–392.

68. This passage is set out in *Giuliano-Lagarde*, 1980 OJ C.282/1, 4.

69. *Giuliano-Lagarde*, 1980 OJ C.282/1, 5.

(4) general matters under the foregoing heads (*renvoi*, classification, application of foreign law acquired rights, public policy, capacity and representation).

2.85 As for the legal basis for the work, it was the unanimous view that the proposed harmonisation, without being specifically connected with the provisions of Article 220 of the EEC Treaty, would be a natural sequel to the Convention on jurisdiction and enforcement of judgments.

2.86 Eventually, at a meeting in June 1972, the group completed a preliminary draft convention but it was limited to the law applicable to contractual and non-contractual obligations.[70]

2.87 Following the accession of the UK, Denmark and Ireland to the Community in 1973 the Commission extended the Group to include experts from the new Member States. The accession of the new States and the need for them to consult on the work lead to a delay of some three years. Work started again in 1975. At its meeting in March 1978 the Group decided to limit the convention to contracts alone and begin negotiations for a second Convention on non-contractual obligations (often referred to as Rome II) after the first had been worked out.[71]

2.88 At the meeting in February 1979 the group finished the draft Convention and instructed Professors Giuliano and Lagarde to draw up the report. The report was duly finalised at a meeting from 18 to 20 June 1979 and was transmitted to the Council and Governments.

2.89 An ad hoc working party then met twice early in 1980 to finalise the Convention text and consider whether the Court of Justice should be given jurisdiction to interpret the Convention. This work resulted eventually in the Rome Convention, which opened for signature in Rome on 19 June 1980.[72] Like the original Brussels Convention, and unlike Council Regulation (EC) 44/2001 which replaced it, the Rome Convention (as a "mere" treaty) had no direct effect in the United Kingdom and needed to be specifically implemented. The Convention was ratified by the UK on 29 January 1991 and was implemented in the United Kingdom by the Contracts (Applicable Law) Act 1990, which provides that the Convention shall have force of law in the United Kingdom.[73] The majority of the Act's provisions came into force on 1 April 1991.[74] The Convention, according to its own terms, has no retrospec-

70. This draft also covered some of the general issues identified in heads 3 and 4 above (it dealt with, for example, public policy, the exclusion of *renvoi* and formalities). It had been agreed that the report on the law applicable to property would be discussed later as a comparative study of the principal laws on security rights was needed first.

71. Political support for Community legislation covering non-contractual obligations was provided by the Vienna Action Plan (1999 OJ C.19/1) on how best to implement the provisions of the Treaty of Amsterdam which stipulated that a certain number of measures in the field of judicial co-operation in civil matters would be taken within two years of the Amsterdam Treaty coming into force. One of the measures identified by the Vienna Action Plan was "drawing up a legal instrument on the law applicable to non-contractual obligations". The Commission came forward with a preliminary draft in May 2002. Following consultation, a formal proposal was adopted in July 2003 which was followed by a revised proposal published in February 2006 for a regulation on the law applicable to non-contractual obligations (COM (2006) 83 final, 21 February 2006). Political agreement was reached in the Council of Ministers in April 2006 and a common position adopted on 1 June 2006. A second reading of the Regulation is anticipated at the end of 2006 and the Regulation will enter into force 18 months after adoption (see T. Petch, "The Rome II Regulation: An Update" [2006] JIBLR 21(8) 449). Denmark has an "opt out" as Title IV of the Treaty Establishing the European Community as we have seen does not apply to Denmark, but the UK and Ireland have "opted in".

72. It was signed on that day by plenipotentiaries of the following Member States: Belgium, Germany, France, Ireland, Italy, Luxembourg and the Netherlands. The United Kingdom signed on 7 December 1981.

73. Section 2(1) of the Act.

74. Section 7 of the Act provides that the Act shall come into force on such day as the Lord Chancellor and the Lord Advocate may by order made by statutory instrument provide; and different days may be appointed for different provisions or different purposes. Sections 1, 2(1) (insofar as it relates to the Rome Convention and the Luxembourg Convention as defined in s.1), 2(2) to (4), 3(3)(a), 4 to 9 and Schedules 1 to 4 came into force on 1 April 1991: Contracts (Applicable Law) Act 1990 (Commencement No. 1) Order, SI 1991/707. Sections 2(1) (insofar as it relates to the Brussels Convention as defined in s.1), 3(1), (2) and (3)(b) came into force on 1 March 2005: Contracts (Applicable Law) Act 1990 (Commencement No. 2) Order, SI 2004/3448.

tive effect and will only apply "to contracts made after the date on which this Convention has entered into force with respect to that State".[75] Thus, the Convention has no effect as regards contracts concluded before 1 April 1991 and the common law will continue to apply to such contracts.

2. The Insurance Directives

2.90 As we have seen, the need for free movement of judgments as well as the need for greater legal certainty and the need to discourage forum shopping are all aims which are clearly apparent in the development of comprehensive rules on jurisdiction in the Brussels Convention, and choice of law in the Rome Convention. But the achievement of the internal market is also defined by the implementation of some more specific basic freedoms including the free movement of goods and services (see Article 14(2) of the EC Treaty inserted by the Single European Act of 1986). In the field of insurance this specific aim is more clearly apparent than in the areas already discussed.

2.91 Two of the substantive rights which the European Union seeks to uphold and which are essential to achieving a single market, are the right of establishment and the right to provide services. Freedom of establishment concerns the pursuit of an economic activity through a fixed establishment in another Member State for an indefinite period. In the case of companies, two forms of establishment are envisaged: primary (that is, setting up a company in another Member State); or secondary (which means setting up a branch or agency in another Member State). Once a company has established itself or a branch in the host state, it must enjoy the same benefits and advantages available to national companies. The right to provide services relates to the freedom to provide services on a temporary basis by a person established in one Member State to a recipient established in another.

2.92 Thus, insurance companies established in one Member State are guaranteed the right to set up a branch in another Member State or to provide services on a temporary basis in another Member State. National laws subjecting insurance undertakings to mandatory rules as regards their financial position, the conditions of insurance which they provide and providing for registration and/or supervision to check that such rules are complied with, will have the effect of restricting both of these freedoms. But such national laws are common, and the insurance sector has been identified as a particularly sensitive area from the point of view of the protection of the consumer, both as a policy-holder and as an insured person. Thus, in *Commission* v. *Germany* (the insurance cases),[76] the European Court of Justice found that German rules requiring insurance companies wishing to provide insurance in Germany to be authorised in Germany could be justified on the grounds of consumer protection.

2.93 In order to further the aim of a single market in insurance products, it was therefore decided that steps should be taken towards harmonising the substantive laws of the Member States under which insurance is provided. This is what the insurance directives primarily seek to achieve.

2.94 The first directive (Directive 73/239 of 24 July 1973)[77] is aimed at freedom of establishment and required each Member State to make the taking up of the business of direct insur-

75. Article 17.

76. C-205/84 *Commission v. Germany* [1986] ECR 3755.

77. EC law draws a distinction between contracts of "general insurance" (or "non-life insurance") and "long-term insurance" (or "life-insurance").The EU rules as regards general or non-life insurance are stated in three directives: Directive 73/239 of 24 July 1973; Directive 88/357 of 22 June 1988; and Directive 92/49 of 18 June 1992. The EU rules regarding long term or life insurance are again stated in three directives: Directive 79/267 of 5 March 1979; Directive 90/619 of 8 November 1990; and Directive 92/96 of 10 November 1992.

ance subject to official authorisation (Article 6) and also to impose requirements relating to sufficient reserves and an adequate solvency margin (Articles 15 and 16). The directive then lays down rules governing the relationship between the legislation and supervising authority of the state in which the head office is situated on the one hand, and the legislation and authorities in the state where the company wishes to set up branches or agencies on the other.

2.95 The second directive (Directive 88/357 of 22 June 1988) continues the process by turning to the provision of services. Article 13 requires Member States to allow undertakings established in one Member State to cover various risks in another Member State subject to the provision of certain information. The third directive (Directive 92/49 of 18 June 1992) seeks to complete the single insurance market, in particular by introducing a single authorisation applicable to both establishment and services. That single authorisation is issued by the authorities of the Member State in which an insurance undertaking has its head office and allows the undertaking to carry on business throughout the community under the right of establishment or freedom to provide services.

2.96 The role of insurance contract law in this development is more complicated. The ability of insurers to offer products throughout the EU is hampered if each individual state is entitled to apply its own (different) insurance laws to the product. The Commission's original approach to this problem was twofold. For insurance involving transportation or large risks it focused on a conflict of laws solution: parties would be free to specify a law, usually the law of the insurer, thereby ensuring that products were subject to the same insurance law. As to other risks, the harmonisation of European insurance contract law would guarantee that policies were subjected to the same law and at the same time would guarantee the protection of the basic rights of the insured. However, the harmonisation of insurance contract law has proved to be extremely difficult to achieve. Eventually, the second insurance directive therefore adopted a solution based entirely on the conflict of laws. As we will see, it allows choice in relation to transportation and large risks, but in other cases choice is more limited and usually the law of the policy holder will apply.[78]

2.97 This is how it comes about that different conflict of law rules apply to insurance, in addition to those in the Rome Convention, to provide split codes for choice of law in contract in the fields of insurance and reinsurance.[79]

2.98 The choice of law rules contained in the various insurance directives are implemented into English law by the Insurance Regulations. Part II of the Regulations governs contracts of general insurance. Part III of the Regulations governs contracts of long term insurance. These Regulations came into force on 1 December 2001.[80]

2.99 Prior to the 2001 Insurance Regulations, the general or non-life directives were implemented by the Insurance Companies (Amendment) Regulations 1990[81] and the Insurance Companies (Third Insurance Directives) Regulations 1994.[82] These Regulations caused the EU rules to be implemented in section 94B of the Insurance Companies Act 1982 and Schedule 3A, Part I to that Act.[83] The long-term or life directives were implemented by

78. This hardly constitutes a harmonised approach to private international law and for that reason work continues on a European insurance contract code. See para. 2.107 below.

79. We come back to the genesis of the insurance directives in paras 11.1–11.5 below as a question arises as to whether the code is indeed comprehensive or whether it excludes contracts of insurance where the risk is within the EU but the insurer is established outside the EU.

80. See Regulation 1, which provides that the Regulation shall come into force on the day on which s.19 of the 2000 Act shall come into force. Section 19 came into force on 1 December 2001: SI 2001/3538.

81. SI 1990/1333, as amended by SI 1993/174.

82. SI 1994/1696.

83. See describing the previous regime L. Collins, *Dicey & Morris, The Conflict of Laws* (13th ed., 2000), para. 33-139.

the Insurance Companies (Amendment) Regulations 1993,[84] which inserted into the Insurance Companies Act 1982 a new section 94B(1A) and a new Part II of Schedule 3A.[85]

3. The future of the Rome Convention and insurance directives

2.100 As we have seen, the Treaty of Amsterdam amending the Treaty on European Union and the Treaty establishing the European Community entered into force on 1 May 1999 (para. 2.63 above). It included Article 65 on "measures in the field of judicial co-operation in civil matters". Thus under the Treaty the Community was given the power to make community legislation in the spheres covered by both the Brussels Convention and the Rome Convention.

2.101 As we have also seen the Treaty's application is subject to:

(1) the Protocol on the position of the UK and Ireland; and
(2) the protocol on the position of Denmark.

2.102 The effect of (1) is that UK and Ireland are not bound by measures under Title IV but that they may "opt in" to negotiations on proposed measures, and may accept measures in the adoption of which they have not participated. By contrast, under (2) not only is Denmark not bound by such measures it does not contain any provision allowing Denmark to opt in to particular measures.

2.103 Thus, when the Brussels Convention was turned into a Regulation the position of the UK, Ireland and Denmark was complex. As we have seen the UK opted in to the Brussels Regulation and so is bound. The position of Denmark is more complex (see para. 2.72 above).

2.104 In January 2003, the Commission published a "Green Paper" on the conversion of the Rome Convention into a Community instrument and its modernisation.[86] Paragraph 2 of the Green Paper noted that the Rome Convention is the only private international law instrument still in the form of an international treaty.[87]

2.105 On 15 December 2005 a proposal for a Regulation on the law applicable to contractual obligations ("Rome I") was proposed by the Commission.[88] Under the protocol the UK had three months to opt in to the proposal – it has chosen not to do so. If the Regulation is subsequently adopted, the UK will have a purely national decision whether it would nevertheless wish to be a party. If the decision is taken not to become a party to a Rome I Regulation, the UK will remain a party to the Rome Convention.

2.106 Article 22(1) of the proposed Regulation provides that it shall not prejudice the application or adoption of Acts of the institutions of the European Communities which in relation to particular matters lay down choice-of-law rules relating the contractual obligations – a list of such Acts currently in force is provided in Annex 1 and includes the insurance

84. SI 1993/174.

85. See *Dicey & Morris*, 13th ed., *op. cit.*, para. 33-178.

86. COM (2002) 654 final.

87. The Commission referred to a number of advantages that would result from changing the Rome Convention into a Regulation. Two of the main advantages are that referrals to the ECJ would then be under the same terms as the Brussels Regulation, and, being a Community Instrument, new members of the Community would be automatically bound by its provisions. The position in relation to the Rome Convention is that, because it takes the form of a Treaty rather than a Community instrument proper, it does not automatically apply to new Member States. In relation to the 10 Member States who joined the EU in 2004, as a result of the signatures of all the Member States to an accession convention on 14 April, 2005, the Rome Convention should have entered into force in the new Member States by the end of 2005 (see S. Dutson, "A Dangerous Proposal – the European Commission's Attempt to Amend the Law Applicable to Contractual Obligations" (2006) JBL 608).

88. COM (2005) 650 final.

directives. Thus, even if a Regulation comes into force, it seems that for the time being at least the insurance directives will also remain.[89]

2.107 In the meantime, work continues on the harmonisation of substantive law, including insurance contract law.[90] Indeed, there are those who think that this is the only solution in the insurance field.[91] Advocates of a European insurance law code argue that the only way of achieving the often conflicting aims of a single market in insurance (which requires products to be transparent and also capable of being transported throughout the community) and adequate protection of the consumer is through the harmonisation of substantive insurance law. As we have seen the current system provides for a far-from-harmonised conflict of laws solution. The relationship between the various regimes as well as the application of the regimes themselves causes considerable difficulties in the insurance and reinsurance context as we will see in Part III of this book.

89. Including a special conflicts rule on insurance contracts in the Rome I Regulation would do much to improve the current situation. This is the solution proposed by the Max Planck Institute in its Comments on the European Commission's Green Paper on the Conversion of the Rome Convention into a Community Instrument.

90. Recent developments in this area are helpfully summarised in M. Clarke and H. Heiss, "Towards a European Insurance Contract Law? Recent Developments in Brussels" in (2006) JBL 600. They refer to an initiative opinion by the European Economic and Social Committee, 15 December 2004, and two EC Commission communications commenting on the harmonisation of contract law in general and insurance contract law in particular (2003 and 2004). See also *Lando/Beale*.

91. See J. Basedow, "The case for a European Insurance Contract Code" (2001) JBL 569–586; J. Basedow, "Insurance Contract Law as Part of an Optional European Contract Act" (2003) LMCLQ 498 and M. Clarke and H. Heiss, "Towards a European Contract Law? Recent Developments in Brussels" in (2006) JBL 600.

CHAPTER 3

INTERPRETATION

A. INTRODUCTION

3.1 As we have seen, the result of the developments discussed in Chapter 2 is that private international law issues in insurance and reinsurance, both in the context of jurisdiction and choice of law, are now governed by a complex patchwork of statutory schemes enacting into law various European Conventions and Directives, European Regulations as well as residual areas which remain governed by the common law. The existence of European rules, whether implemented by statute or applying directly, raises issues of interpretation which are discussed in this chapter. Some of the issues are common to all European legislation and will therefore apply to both jurisdiction and choice of law, in other areas more specific considerations will need to be addressed. But the underlying principle is one of uniformity. The aim of achieving a single European market, with consistency and uniformity throughout, would be undermined if the courts of each Member State interpreted community provisions in a different way.

3.2 This need for a uniform interpretation and application of community rules is met in a number of ways, each of which will be outlined in this chapter. First and foremost has been the development of an autonomous approach to interpretation. One of the key features of European Court of Justice case law, reflected in the approach taken by the courts of the Member States themselves, is the adoption of a "purposive" or "teleological" approach to construction which in turn leads to autonomous or independent community meanings for the terms used in community instruments. Other means by which the aim of uniformity is achieved are (a) the power and duty of national courts to make references to the European Court of Justice and to take into account decisions of the European Court of Justice and other national courts on questions of interpretation; and (b) the use of other sources, particularly the official reports.

3.3 As a preliminary matter it is also important to note that the text of European legislation is written in all official languages of the European Union and all of them are "equally authentic". Thus, although the English versions of both the Brussels Convention and Rome Convention are appended for convenience to the enacting legislation, all versions are equally authentic.[1] Thus, English courts will have to be prepared to consider the texts of the Brussels Regulation and the Rome Convention in other languages, where there are material differences between the texts.

B. AUTONOMOUS INTERPRETATION

3.4 It is a general principle of English law that treaties that have been incorporated into the law of the UK (such as the Brussels Convention or the Rome Convention, but not the Brussels Regulation) are to be construed on broad principles, rather than in the strict manner accord-

1. See Article 68 of the Brussels Convention and Article 33 of the Rome Convention which provide that, in each case, the Convention was "drawn up in a single original", the various languages texts being "equally authentic". See, e.g., *Caledonia Subsea* v. *Microperi,* 2002 SLT 1022 at [25] where the court considered the French version of the text of the Rome Convention considered at para. 10.88 below; and Schlosser, para. 152, on the meaning of "*preneur d'assurance*" in the various authentic versions of the Brussels Convention (para. 6.10 below).

ing to which statutes are generally construed.[2] Article 18 of the Rome Convention reinforces this, providing that in the interpretation and application of the Convention rules, "regard shall be had to their international character and to the desirability of achieving uniformity in their interpretation and application".[3]

3.5 But in the European context, these general principles have been refined and developed into a new approach to the interpretation of community instruments; that is a "purposive" or "theological" approach.[4] The approach the courts will take (for example to the interpretation of the insurance directives) is described by Hobhouse LJ in *Credit Lyonnais* v. *New Hampshire Insurance Co Ltd*.[5]

> "It is clear from the recitals to the [insurance] directive that one of its purposes is to protect the interests of policyholders. It therefore has a similar character to those articles of the Rome and Brussels Conventions which make special provision for classes of contract where it is considered that the parties are not or may not be in an equal bargaining position and considerations of policy are to be applied.... such concerns underlie and inform the understanding of the drafting of provisions such as these. Similarly it is always important to have in mind that they are intended to have a uniform international application. Their provisions and the Acts by which they are incorporated into English law should not be given a construction deriving from specifically English concepts which are not within the scheme of the relevant international convention."

3.6 The "purposes" by reference to which legislation is to be interpreted are to be identified from the preamble or recitals, the text of the instrument itself and from its context.[6] Some purposes are common to all the European legislation under consideration. Thus, courts very often refer to the fact that the interpretation adopted should be one which contributes to legal certainty.[7] Certainty is required in order to "eliminate obstacles to legal relations and to strengthen in the Community the legal protection of persons therein established" which is the ultimate object of the Brussels Regulation and the Rome Convention.[8]

3.7 Another overriding aim which is apparent in the jurisdiction rules is the need to avoid inconsistent decisions and, linked to this, the need to trust the courts of the other Member States.[9] Other considerations are relevant in specific contexts: thus the court has stressed that those provisions which allow a defendant to be sued in a Member State other than that of his domicile (principally those in Article 5 of the Brussels Regulation) should be construed narrowly (since the fundamental purpose behind the jurisdictional rules is to allow a defendant to defend himself in his own state). Other provisions may have been guided by different aims – such as the protection of a particularly vulnerable party as in the context of the insur-

2. *Stag Line Ltd* v. *Foscolo, Mango & Co Ltd* [1932] AC 328, 350 (*per* Lord MacMillan). Lord MacMillan was considering the rules in the Schedule to the Carriage of Goods by Sea Act 1924. The Act was the outcome of an International Conference.

3. Although as Morrison J. noted at para. 14 in *Definitely Maybe (Touring) Ltd* v. *Marek Lieberberg* [2001] 1 WLR 1745 "although Article 18 of the Rome Convention encourages a uniform interpretation of the Convention, that is less easy to achieve than to say".

4. This technique has been applied by the European Court of Justice fairly consistently in relation to the Brussels Convention and other community treaties and measures – see Plender/Wilderstein, para. 2.01.

5. [1997] 2 Lloyd's Rep. 1, 5.

6. The European Court of Justice has established that Community law is to be interpreted as a whole, which means that the provisions under consideration must be interpreted in accordance with other provisions of the EEC Treaty, laws made under the Treaty and all other Community law.

7. See Briggs/Rees, para. 2.04.

8. See, in relation to the Brussels Convention, C-33/78 *Etablissements Somafer SA* v. *Saar-Ferngas AG* [1978] ECR 2183, 2190. The preamble to the Rome Convention confirms that it aspires to advance the process of unification of which the Brussels Convention forms part.

9. See for the importance of these considerations Gasser, Grovit and Owusu, discussed in Chapter 5, Section I, below.

ance directives as seen above and the special rules which apply to consumers in both the Brussels Regulation and Rome Convention. The approach to construction in a case where European legislation is in issue is thus to ascertain the purposes behind the provision and then to seek to give the provision an independent community meaning which is consistent with those purposes.[10]

3.8 As we will see in the following chapters, autonomous meanings have been given to a number of the basic features of the community legislation which will be discussed. Thus, whether a case involves a "civil or commercial matter" will depend on an autonomous meaning of that phrase developed in the case law of the European Court of Justice and the national courts, not any English law definition which would apply in a purely domestic case (see paras 5.3 below). Similarly, as we will see, "matters relating to contract", "matters relating to tort", the meaning of a "branch or agency" and many other concepts have been given an independent community meaning.

3.9 This purposive approach to construction and the search for an independent community meaning are clearly vital. But there are other special considerations which may apply in situations involving European legislation and which must also be borne in mind when a question of construction arises.

1. Official Commentaries

3.10 As we have seen, the Conventions are each supplemented by a report written by members of the working group who were responsible for drafting the Convention, giving background and an explanation of the text. The most important for our purposes are the Jenard report[11] which accompanied the Brussels Convention, the Schlosser report[12] which accompanied the amended Brussels Convention on the accession of the UK, and the Giuliano-Lagarde[13] report which accompanied the Rome Convention. In each case, the enacting legislation expressly permits the English courts to consider the relevant Report in ascertaining the meaning and effect of any provision in the Convention.[14] National courts as well as the European Court of Justice make reference to the various reports as a matter of course and numerous references will be found to them in the following chapters. In any case where there is a doubt about the construction of a particular provision the relevant official report may well be the best place to start.[15]

3.11 Reference to other *travaux préparatoires* or preparatory work is more difficult. The general approach of English courts to *travaux préparatoires* has been cautious. Such references should be "rare" and should only be made where the material involved is "public and accessible" and "clearly and indisputably points to a definite legislative intention".[16] This is likely to be particularly so in the case of the Conventions for two reasons. In the first place, the existence of the reports referred to above. Given that the purpose of these reports was clearly to provide an authoritative opinion as to the purpose and meaning of the relevant

10. See Briggs/Rees, para 2.07.
11. 1979 OJ C.59/1.
12. 1979 OJ C.59/71.
13. 1980 OJ C.282/1.
14. See s.3 of the 1982 Act in relation to the Brussels Convention and s.3(3) of the 1990 Act in relation to the Rome Convention.
15. Indeed the reports are also sometimes used interchangeably. For example, Giuliano-Lagarde was used as an aid to the construction of the insurance directives in *AMICC* [2003] EWCA Civ 206 at para. 18.
16. *Fothergill* v. *Monarch Airlines Ltd* [1981] AC 251, 278A-E (*per* Lord Wilberforce), 283A-D (*per* Lord Diplock) and 287E-G (*per* Lord Fraser).

Conventions – they are each published in the *Official Journal*[17] and were written by persons who played a role in the drafting of the Convention – it may be questioned whether reference to the *travaux préparatoires* could provide any real help in establishing a definite legislative intention.

3.12 Secondly, although English law permits recourse to the *travaux préparatoires* of an international treaty, this is not the case as regards all states party to the Rome Convention. Reference to such materials may, therefore, result in inconsistencies in interpretation being introduced.[18]

3.13 There is no official report accompanying the Brussels Regulation. It is likely that in practice the courts will continue to have recourse to the reports already referred to.[19]

2. References to the European Court of Justice

3.14 The position is complex and differs depending on the instrument involved.

3.15 The European Court of Justice was given jurisdiction in relation to the Brussels Convention by a Protocol originally agreed in 1971 (see paras 2.13–2.21 above).[20] In general, it *allowed* but did not require references to be made by appellate courts, but provided that a reference *shall* be made by the House of Lords together with all other final courts of appeal, wherever a decision on interpretation is necessary to enable it to give judgment.

3.16 In relation to the Brussels Regulation the position is different. The procedure is set out in Article 68 of the EC Treaty which provides: "Where a question of the interpretation of [the Brussels Regulation] is raised in a case pending before a court or tribunal of a Member State against whose decision there is no judicial remedy under national law, that court or tribunal shall, if it considers that a decision on the question is necessary to enable it to give judgment, request the Court of Justice to give a ruling thereon." Thus the only court which can now make a reference is the House of Lords.[21]

3.17 As it is not a European Treaty, the Lugano Convention is not within the jurisdiction of the European Court of Justice.[22]

17. Significantly, no *travaux préparatoires* have been published in this way. Although the written submission put forward by the commission for the adoption of the draft form of the Brussels Regulation can be found at 1999 OJ C/376.

18. As regards the EC Treaty, objections to the use of *travaux préparatoires* have been expressed: C–2/74 *Reyners* v. *Belgium* [1974] ECR 631, 666 (*per* Advocate General Mayras). *Cf.* the suggestion that the Brussels Convention is to be interpreted by reference to the principles set out in Articles 31–33 of the Vienna Convention on the Law of Treaties (May 23, 1969, Cmnd 7964), which includes by Article 32 that recourse may be had to *travaux préparatoires* when the application of ordinary canons of construction would lead to an absurd or unreasonable result or would leave the meaning ambiguous or obscure. For a summary of this debate on this issue see Plender/Wilderstein, paras 2.08–2.09.

19. A practice which has been said to be "justifiable in practice if not technically well-founded as a matter of law": Briggs/Rees, para 1.14.

20. Attached as Schedule 2 to the CJJA 1982.

21. See *Through Transport Mutual Insurance Association (Eurasia) Ltd* v. *New India Assurance Association Co Ltd* [2004] EWCA Civ 1598; [2005] 1 Lloyd's Rep. 67 at [29].

22. Although the Lugano Convention is not subject to definitive interpretation by the European Court of Justice efforts were made in the 2nd protocol to secure consistency of interpretation between the Lugano Convention and the Brussels Convention through judicial consultation (see *Jenard and Moller*, para. 110). In particular, it was recognised in the recitals to the Lugano Convention and in a Declaration by EFTA Member States annexed to the Convention that the Lugano Convention had been negotiated on the basis of European Court of Justice decisions on the interpretation of provisions in the Brussels Convention which were largely reproduced in the Lugano Convention and that their courts should pay due account to those rulings. Conversely, in a second declaration by Community members appended to the Lugano Convention it was agreed that in the future the European Court of Justice had to pay due account to case law on the Lugano Convention (1988 OJ C.319/37, 40). In practice, national courts have tended to treat the question of whether a decision arises under the Brussels or Lugano Convention as irrelevant: see Briggs/Rees, para. 3.02.

3.18 The position in relation to the Rome Convention is more complicated. At the time the Rome Convention was concluded, there was considerable controversy over the question of referrals to the European Court of Justice. Clearly, without such a mechanism there is a danger that the courts in each Member State will interpret the Convention differently, jeopardising the harmonisation of conflict rules that the Convention seeks to achieve. But some countries have internal problems relating to allowing such a reference. Furthermore, some Member States, including the United Kingdom, argued that provision for the European Court of Justice to have jurisdiction at all was undesirable as it was feared that foreign businessmen would opt for trial outside England, and indeed the Community, rather than face the prospect of a referral to the European Court of Justice on choice of law.

3.19 Eventually, on 19 December 1988, two Protocols on the interpretation of the Rome Convention were signed in Brussels, namely "the first Protocol on the interpretation by the Court of Justice of the European Communities of the Convention" and "the second Protocol conferring on the Court of Justice of the European Communities certain powers to interpret the Convention".[23] The reference in section 3(1) of the 1990 Act to the "Brussels Protocol" is a reference to the first Protocol.[24]

3.20 The first Protocol defines the scope of the jurisdiction of the European Court of Justice and the conditions under which that jurisdiction is to be exercised. States accept the jurisdiction of the European Court of Justice under this Protocol. The concerns over compulsory references were dealt with by providing that the courts *may* rather than *must* request a ruling, unlike the position under the Brussels Regulation.[25] In exercising its discretion, the referring court is entitled to take into account any appropriate factor, including the wishes of the party not to refer.

3.21 The second Protocol confers powers on the European Court of Justice to interpret the Rome Convention, i.e. it gives the European Court of Justice the power to deal with references made under the first Protocol.

3.22 The coming into force of the two Protocols was inter-related. The first Protocol had to be ratified by seven States in respect of whom the Rome Convention was in force.[26] It would then enter into force three months later, unless the second Protocol was itself not in force. If the second Protocol enters into force on a later date, then the first Protocol would enter into force on the same date.[27]

3.23 The second Protocol needed to be ratified by all the States party to the treaty establishing the European Economic Community. That only occurred with the ratification of Belgium on 5 May 2004.

3.24 As has been described,[28] the Rome Convention may eventually be turned into a Community instrument. References to the European Court of Justice would then also be under Article 234 of the EU Treaty. From a Community standpoint, this would have the advantage that the European Court of Justice would have identical jurisdiction over all Community private international law instruments. In particular, such references would no longer be optional.

3.25 In relation to the Insurance Directives, as Community "acts", Directives are susceptible to preliminary reference under Article 234 of the Treaty.[29] The position is thus the same as for the Brussels Regulation.

23. [1989] OJ L48.
24. Section 1(c).
25. See para. 3.16 above.
26. Article 6 of the first Protocol. All EC Member States, except Belgium and Ireland, have ratified the first Protocol.
27. Article 6 of the first Protocol.
28. See para. 2.104 above.
29. See Hartley, pp. 272–273.

3.26 The English courts must determine cases in accordance with the principles laid down by any relevant decision of the European Court of Justice.[30] Thus, if there is a European Court of Justice decision on the meaning of "relating to contract" in the context of the Brussels Convention, the English court must take notice of such decision if the same issue arose before it, arguably whether in the context of the Rome Convention, the insurance directives, or the Lugano Convention, and regardless of whether or not that court would have had the power to make a reference itself on the particular point.[31]

3. Other sources

3.27 In addition to having regard to the different languages in which the Convention has been expressed (see para. 3.3 above), English Courts may properly have regard to foreign case law[32] (although the level of the court deciding the case in question and the process of law reportingmust be borne in mind[33]) and relevant text books and articles[34] when considering the construction of community legislation.

30. Section 3 of the 1982 Act in relation to the Brussels Convention; s.3 of the 1990 Act in relation to the Rome Convention and s.3 of the European Communities Act 1972 in relation to the Brussels Regulation.

31. The European Court of Justice itself has referred to the Rome Convention when construing the Brussels Convention (C-133/81 *Ivenel* v. *Schwab* [1982] ECR 1891) and its Advocates General have done the same on several occasions (see Plender/Wilderstein, p. 6). However, the solutions to jurisdictional problems addressed by the Brussels Convention cannot always be transported to the field of choice of law. See the decision of the European Court of Justice in *Six Constructions Ltd* v. *Humbert* [1989] ECR 341 discussed in Plender/Wilderstein, para. 2.04.

32. *James Buchanan & Co Ltd* v. *Babco Forwarding and Shipping (UK) Ltd* [1978] AC 141, 161E-H (*per* Lord Salmon). Indeed the courts have done so in Rome Convention cases, e.g. *Samcrete Egypt Engineers and Contractors* v. *Land Rover Exports Ltd* [2001] EWCA Civ 2019 at para. 42.

33. *Fothergill* v. *Monarch Airlines Ltd* [1981] AC 251, 275G-276B (*per* Lord Wilberforce) and 284C-E (*per* Lord Diplock).

34. *Fothergill* v. *Monarch Airlines Ltd* [1981] AC 251, 274G-H (*per* Lord Wilberforce), 283H-284B (*per* Lord Diplock) and 287D-E (*per* Lord Fraser). See, in relation to foreign articles, *Samcrete, op. cit.*, and in relation to text books, *Marconi Communications International Ltd* v. *PT Pan Indonesian Bank Ltd TBK* [2005] EWCA Civ 422 at [49].

PART II

JURISDICTION

CHAPTER 4

LEGAL REGIMES DETERMINING JURISDICTION

A. INTRODUCTION

4.1 There are three main regimes governing the *in personam* jurisdiction of the English court[1]:

(1) the first is the Brussels regime (which is derived from the Brussels Convention);
(2) the second is the Lugano Convention; and
(3) thirdly there are traditional rules which apply in all other cases, referred to as the common law (although in fact many of the rules are enshrined in statute).

4.2 Special rules apply to allocate jurisdiction within the UK. Special rules also apply to arbitration (considered in Chapter 8 below).

4.3 Together these regimes make up a complex patchwork of regulation which will apply to determine all questions of jurisdiction arising out of contracts of insurance and reinsurance. The process of considering whether or not the English court has jurisdiction in relation to a particular dispute must begin by identifying the applicable regime. Working out which regime applies can be tedious but is important.

4.4 Generally speaking only one set of rules will apply to a particular dispute. If the Brussels Regulation applies, the Brussels Convention will not. However, the picture is slightly more complicated. The European rules sometimes apply national law, including English common law, as a form of delegated legislation in which case the European rules may modify the operation of the common law (see para. 4.10 below).

B. IDENTIFYING THE REGIME TO APPLY

1. Do the European rules apply?

4.5 The first question is to decide if the European rules apply (that is whether the matter is governed by the Brussels regime or the Lugano Convention). Some issues are relevant equally to the Brussels Convention, the Brussels Regulation and the Lugano Convention: thus in relation to all European regimes this depends on

(1) whether or not the matter is a "civil and commercial matter". Reinsurance and insurance disputes are invariably civil or commercial matters.[2]
(2) whether or not the matter is excluded or another Convention applies. The relevant exclusion in relation to reinsurance and insurance is arbitration (see Chapter 8). As to other conventions, see para. 5.4 below.
(3) whether or not the matter is international. The Brussels Convention only applied where there was an international element involved:

1. Admiralty proceedings "*in rem*" are directed against property rather than an individual defendant, usually a ship.
2. Public law claims are not included in civil and commercial matters; see, generally, Briggs/Rees, p. 46.

It alters the rules of jurisdiction in force in each Contracting State only where an international element is involved. It does not define this concept, since the international element in a legal relationship may depend on the particular facts of the proceedings of which the court is seised. Proceedings instituted in the courts of a Contracting State which involves only persons domiciled in that State will not normally be affected by the Convention; Article 2 simply refers matters back to the rules of jurisdiction in force in that State. It is possible, however, that an international element may be involved in proceedings of this type. This would be the case, for example, where the defendant was a foreign national, a situation in which the principle of equality of treatment laid down in the second paragraph of Article 2 would apply, or where the proceedings related to a matter over which the courts of another State had exclusive jurisdiction (Article 16), or where identical or related proceedings had been brought in the courts of another State (Article 21 to 23).[3]

In *Owusu* v. *Jackson*[4] the European Court of Justice held that the element of internationality could be supplied even where the dispute was as between the courts of a Member State and those of a non-Member State, with the result that since the Brussels Convention conferred jurisdiction on the UK the court had no power to stay proceedings under the common law. There is no reason to think that this element is not equally applicable to the Lugano Convention and Brussels Regulation.

4.6 The next question is which of the various European rules applies. Once the European rules have allocated jurisdiction to the UK, the allocation of jurisdiction within the UK is governed by the Civil Jurisdiction and Judgments Act 1982 (see paras 4.25–4.26 below).

(i) Brussels Regulation

4.7 As we have seen, the Brussels Regulation applies to all proceedings commenced after 1 March 2002.[5] It superseded the Brussels Convention as from that date (Article 68). The Member States as at that date were: Austria, Belgium, Finland, France, Germany, Greece, Ireland, Italy, Luxembourg, the Netherlands, Portugal, Spain, Sweden, UK and Denmark.[6]

4.8 On 1 May 2004 the following countries acceded to the EU and thereby became bound by Brussels Regulation from that date: Cyprus, the Czech Republic, Estonia, Hungary, Latvia, Lithuania, Malta, Poland, Slovakia and Slovenia.[7]

4.9 The geographical scope of the Brussels Regulation is governed by Article 229 of the Treaty Establishing the EC (see para. 2.71 above). Gibraltar is a part of the UK for the purpose of the Brussels Regulation, but not the Channel Islands[8] or the Isle of Man (Article 229).

4.10 The Brussels Regulation applies to all proceedings falling within its scope, regardless of the domicile or nationality of the parties. Having said that, *in general*, the Brussels Regulation only seeks to set out rules which apply where the defendant is domiciled in a Member State. Where the defendant is not domiciled in a Member State the Brussels Regulation expressly states that the national law applicable under the choice of law rules of the forum (in England, the common law) applies. This is the effect of Article 4 of the Brussels Regulation which provides:

3. *Jenard*, p. 8.
4. C-281/02; [2005] ECR I-1383; [2005] QB 801.
5. As to commencement of proceedings see Article 30 and para. 5.274 below.
6. The position of Denmark has been considered at para. 2.72 above.
7. Some other minor amendments were made to the Brussels Regulation: Regulation 1496/2002; 1937/2004; 2245/2004. The text of the Brussels Regulation in the Appendix is the amended version.
8. *Groupama* v. *Channel Islands* [2002] Lloyd's Rep. IR 843.

"If the defendant is not domiciled in a Member State, the jurisdiction of the courts of each Member State shall, subject to Articles 22 and 23, be determined by the law of that Member State."

4.11 However, even where the defendant is not domiciled in a Member State the field is not entirely left to the national law: in special cases the Brussels Regulation lays down rules conferring jurisdiction regardless of domicile:

(1) where the court has mandatory jurisdiction under Article 22;
(2) where there is a jurisdiction agreement in favour of the courts of a Member State under Article 23.
(3) (possibly) where the defendant has entered an appearance under Article 24.

4.12 In all other cases, national conflict rules (i.e. the common law) apply under Article 4, subject to the rules about *lis pendens* in Articles 27–30.

(ii) Brussels Convention

4.13 If the Brussels Regulation does not apply because proceedings were commenced before 1 March 2002 the Brussels Convention may apply. The scope of the Brussels Convention is not materially different from that of the Brussels Regulation.

4.14 Because the Brussels Convention is a treaty it took effect as between the Contracting States from the dates when they acceded to the treaty. The Contracting States were Belgium, France, Germany, Italy, Luxembourg and the Netherlands from 1973, the UK, Denmark and Ireland from 1978, Greece from 1981, Spain and Portugal from 1986, and Austria, Finland and Sweden from 1994. The term "Contracting State" is used in the Brussels Convention to refer to parties to it, and is useful to distinguish parties to the Brussels Convention from Member States which are parties to the Brussels Regulation. The Brussels Convention came into force in the UK on 1 January 1987 (see, generally, para. 2.31 above).[9]

4.15 The treaty was also altered from time to time, sometimes significantly. This fact means that it is important to know precisely which version of the Brussels Convention applies. We have recorded the major changes in the development of the Brussels Convention in Chapter 2. Changes to particular provisions are also outlined in Chapter 5.

(iii) Lugano Convention

4.16 If neither the Brussels Regulation nor the Brussels Convention applies the Lugano Convention may. Again the scope of the Lugano Convention is not materially different from that of the Brussels Regulation. There are few differences between the Lugano Convention and the Brussels Regulation or the Brussels Convention (see, generally, para. 2.42 above).

4.17 The Lugano Convention essentially extended the Brussels Convention so as to apply as between countries party to the Brussels Convention and countries party to the European Free Trade Association (see generally para 2.40 above). It remains in force as between Member States within the Brussels Regulation and Denmark on the one hand and the EFTA states (except Liechtenstein) on the other.

4.18 The Lugano Convention came into force on 1 January 1992 as between Contracting States which had ratified other than the UK, and on 1 May 1992 as between the UK and other Contracting States.

9. The Foreign and Commonwealth Office maintains a list of signature and ratification details at *www.fco.gov.uk*.

4.19 The EFTA countries with which the Lugano Convention was made were Austria, Finland, Iceland, Norway, Sweden, and Switzerland. In 1994 Austria, Finland and Sweden joined the Community and they are now parties to the Brussels Regulation. The Lugano Convention continues to apply in relation to Iceland, Norway and Switzerland.

2. European rules summary

4.20 In summary, the Brussels Regulation will apply to proceedings in relation to matters within its scope commenced after 1 March 2002. The Brussels Convention will continue to apply to proceedings within its scope commenced before 1 March 2002, and as between Denmark and Contracting States under the Brussels Convention until the agreement with Denmark to apply the Brussels Regulation takes effect (see para. 2.72 above). The Lugano Convention continues to apply as between Iceland, Norway, Switzerland, Denmark and Member States under the Brussels Regulation.

4.21 As regards matters within the material scope of these regimes (as is likely in the case of (re)insurance) the allocation of jurisdiction hinges on the defendant's domicile:

(1) if the defendant is domiciled in a Member State or in Norway, Switzerland or Iceland, he must be sued in the courts of his domicile and can be sued in the courts of another Member State only in accordance with the terms of the Regulation (Article 3). As we will see he may be sued in the courts of another Member State in certain circumstances in matters relating to contract (Article 5(1)) or tort (Article 5(3)), where there is a relevant branch or agency in another state (Article 5(5)) or where he is a necessary party to proceedings in another state (Article 5(6)). Special rules apply to insurance contracts (Articles 8–15).

(2) However, if the proceedings come with Article 22 (for example, the proceedings have as their object rights *in rem* in immoveable property) the courts of that state will have exclusive jurisdiction.

(3) If there is a jurisdiction agreement in favour of another Member State:
   (i) and one of the parties is domiciled in a Member State, that court shall have exclusive jurisdiction (Article 23(1));
   (ii) and none of the parties is domiciled in a Member State, the courts of the other Member States shall not have jurisdiction unless the courts of the chosen jurisdiction has declined jurisdiction (Article 23(3)).

(4) Where the defendant has entered an appearance under Article 24 the court will have jurisdiction if the defendant is domiciled in a Member State, and possibly will do so even if he is not so domiciled.

(5) In all other cases the English court applies common law rules of jurisdiction (Article 4). Proceedings can be served as of right if the defendant is present in the jurisdiction. Otherwise permission to serve out of the jurisdiction will be required under CPR 6.20.

(6) However, other than in the situation referred to in paragraph (2) above (i.e. exclusive jurisdiction under Article 22), in all of the cases discussed above, if proceedings concerning the same cause of action and between the same parties have already been brought in the courts of another Member State, any court other than that first seised must stay its proceedings (Article 27); if those proceedings are related any court other than the court first seised may stay proceedings before it (Article 28).

3. Reinsurance and insurance under the European rules

4.22 If the European rules apply, they will determine jurisdiction in relation to most reinsurance and insurance disputes, other than in relation to arbitration (see Chapter 8). Reinsurance is governed by the ordinary jurisdiction rules under the Brussels Regulation, and Brussels and Lugano Conventions, dealt with in Chapter 5. Insurance has its own code within the European rules: it is contained in section 3. These rules are dealt with in Chapter 6.

4. Does the common law apply?

4.23 The common law will apply if none of the European rules apply. It will also apply where proceedings are commenced which are within the scope of the Brussels Regulation against a defendant who is not domiciled in a Member State and none of the other bases of jurisdiction under the Brussels or Lugano regimes apply.

4.24 The system of common law is very different from that of the European rules. Proceedings may be served outside the jurisdiction without permission if the defendant is present in the jurisdiction when served, or submits to the jurisdiction. Otherwise the court may grant permission to serve a defendant out of the jurisdiction on specified grounds, essentially where there is a connection between the dispute and England and Wales. The court always has a discretion to stay proceedings on grounds of *forum non conveniens*, or to order an anti-suit injunction to prevent proceedings in foreign jurisdictions. The court has strictly limited powers in relation to arbitrations, dealt with in Chapter 8. The common law jurisdiction rules applicable to reinsurance and insurance do not differ and we deal with them together in Chapter 7.

5. Jurisdiction within the UK

4.25 Sometimes the European rules allocate jurisdiction to a particular court within the UK, such as, in matters relating to contract, the courts for the place of performance of the obligation in question (para. 5.129 below). There is then no need for any further rules to allocate jurisdiction within the UK.

4.26 In other cases jurisdiction is allocated by the European rules to the UK without specifying which part of the UK. Section 16 of the Civil Jurisdiction and Judgments Act 1982 then allocates jurisdiction within the UK according to rules set out in Schedule 4. Those rules were amended with effect from 1 March 2002 when the Brussels Regulation came into force, and apply to all proceedings commenced after that date.[10] The rules contained in Schedule 4 are similar to those contained in the European rules, except that there are no special rules for insurance which is therefore covered by the same rules as reinsurance.

10. The Civil Jurisdiction and Judgments Order 2001, SI 2001 No. 3929, paragraph 6.

CHAPTER 5

REINSURANCE JURISDICTION – BRUSSELS REGULATION

A. INTRODUCTION

5.1 We consider the relevant rules in this order[1]:

B. Preliminary matters: is the subject-matter of the dispute within the Brussels Regulation? Does another convention apply? Does Article 22 give mandatory jurisdiction? Has the defendant entered an appearance within Article 24?
C. Is there a choice of jurisdiction agreement under Article 23?
D. Is there jurisdiction based on the defendant's domicile under Article 2 or the operations of a branch under Article 5(5)?
E. Is there jurisdiction based on matters relating to a contract under Article 5(1)?
F. Is there jurisdiction based on matters relating to tort under Article 5(3)?
G. Is there jurisdiction in respect of a claim against a co-defendant, third party or counterclaim under Article 6?
H. Is there jurisdiction to grant provisional or protective measures under Article 31?
I. Preventing conflicting decisions: declining jurisdiction, stay and anti-suit injunctions under Articles 27–30.
J. Jurisdiction within the UK under Schedule 4 of the Civil Jurisdiction and Judgments Act 1982 (under which stay for *forum non conveniens* is still available).

B. PRELIMINARY MATTERS

5.2 A number of questions need to be addressed in any reinsurance dispute before getting to what is usually the heart of the matter: jurisdiction under an exclusive jurisdiction agreement or founded on matters relating to a contract or tort. Of these preliminary matters the most important is whether or not the arbitration exclusion applies. We consider the following main headings:

(1) Is the subject-matter within the Brussels Regulation?
(2) Does another convention apply?
(3) Does Article 22 give mandatory jurisdiction?
(4) Has the defendant entered an appearance under Article 24?

1. Is the subject-matter within the Brussels Regulation?

5.3 The Brussels Regulation applies in "civil and commercial matters" (Article 1). It is set out in Appendix 1.1. Although this concept has an autonomous meaning, reinsurance and insurance disputes are invariably civil or commercial matters.[2] The question then is whether or not the Brussels Regulation excludes the dispute from the purview of the regulation, in particular because it is concerned with arbitration. Reinsurance disputes often involve the possibility of arbitration, and this exclusion is potentially very important. Arbitration is considered in Chapter 8.

1. See, generally, Briggs/Rees on the hierarchy of rules under the Brussels Regulation at pp. 30 and 700, to which we are indebted.
2. Public law claims are not included in civil and commercial matters; see, generally, Briggs/Rees, p. 46.

2. Does another convention apply?

5.4 Article 71(1) prevents the Brussels Regulation from applying where other specialised conventions on jurisdiction apply:

> "This Regulation shall not affect any conventions to which the member states are parties and which in relation to particular matters, govern jurisdiction or the recognition or enforcement of judgments."

5.5 The Jenard report listed the specialised conventions to which the parties to the Brussels Convention were a party.[3] The Schlosser report at Annex II listed the specialised conventions to which the UK was a party, including various Conventions relating to carriage by rail and air, and the arrest of ships.[4] It does not appear that there are any specialised conventions which would apply to disputes involving reinsurance and insurance.

5.6 A novel question which has been asked is whether Article 71 could be applied to the right to a trial within a "reasonable time" under Article 6 of the European Convention for the safeguard of Human Rights and political Freedoms (ECHR) so as to enable the court to disapply the Brussels Regulation where delays in the judicial system are extreme.[5] In *Gasser* v. *MISAT*[6] the Austrian court asked whether the fact that court proceedings in a Member State take an unjustifiably long time (for reasons largely unconnected with the conduct of the parties) so that material detriment may be caused to one party could mean that Article 21 (*lis alibi pendens*) should not apply to proceedings in the court. It was suggested that this was the position in for example Italy, Greece and France.[7] In its judgment the European Court of Justice was very clear that any such interpretation of the Brussels Convention would be manifestly contrary to the letter, spirit and aim of the Brussels Convention, that there was no provision in the Brussels Convention which would allow Article 21 (now Article 27) not to be applied, and would be inconsistent with the mutual trust between Member States in respect of each other's legal systems on which the Brussels Convention was based. Although no specific reference was made to Brussels Convention Article 57 (which was the same as Brussels Regulation Article 71) it is clear that Article 6 of the ECHR is not considered a relevant provision under Article 71 of the Brussels Regulation.

5.7 The purpose of Article 71 was to ensure that in areas where the Brussels Regulation and the specialised conventions could apply the latter would prevail.[8] Broadly, if a specialised convention does not apply the Brussels Regulation will apply, but numerous further questions arise in that event which we do not consider here since they do not arise in relation to reinsurance and insurance disputes.

5.8 Mention should also be made of Article 67 which provides that the Brussels Regulation does not prejudice the application of provisions governing jurisdiction and judgments in specific matters contained in community instruments or national legislation harmonised pursuant to such instruments.[9]

3. Does Article 22 give mandatory jurisdiction?

5.9 Article 22 of the Brussels Regulation confers exclusive jurisdiction on particular courts in respect of specific international[10] proceedings. Unlike most of the Brussels Regulation

3. Page 59.
4. See further details at Kaye, Civil Jurisdiction, p. 199.
5. Briggs/Rees, p. 68.
6. C-116/02 *Erich Gasser GmbH v. MISAT Srl* [2003] ECR I-14693; [2005] 1 QB 1.
7. Opinion of Advocate General Leger in C-116/02 *Erich Gasser v. MISAT* [2003] ECR I-14693 at [25], [85].
8. *Jenard*, 1979 OJ C.59/1, 60.
9. For instance, the Unfair Terms in Consumer Contracts Regulation SI 1999/2083 may deprive a jurisdiction agreement of effect in spite of Article 23 of the Brussels Regulation: see Briggs/Rees, p. 70.
10. The Brussels Regulation only applies where proceedings have an international element: see para. 2.15 above.

Article 22 applies "regardless of domicile". Where it applies Article 22 is very important since the jurisdiction it confers is exclusive which means that no other provision of the Brussels Regulation may be relied on to ground jurisdiction.

5.10 The proceedings singled out in Article 22 for exclusive jurisdiction are a mixed bag of proceedings relating to the validity of decisions of companies or associations including partnerships, and the enforcement of judgments, as well as other proceedings relating to rights *in rem* in land and tenancies, entries in public registers, and the registration of patents and similar rights. Of these, proceedings relating to companies are considered below. The other specified proceedings are not relevant to the reinsurance and insurance proceedings with which we are concerned.[11]

5.11 Article 22(2) of the Brussels Regulation provides that:

"The following courts shall have exclusive jurisdiction, regardless of domicile: ...

2. in proceedings which have as their object the validity of the constitution, the nullity or the dissolution of companies or other legal persons or associations of natural or legal persons, or of the validity of the decisions of their organs, the courts of the member state in which the company, legal person or association has its seat. In order to determine that seat, the court shall apply its rules of private international law."

5.12 The wording of potential concern here in relation to reinsurance and insurance proceedings is "the validity of the decisions of their organs". This Article was in substantially the same form when Jenard identified the purpose of the mandatory provision as being to avoid conflicting judgments as regards the validity of the decisions of a company's organs, and made the point that it was in the country of the seat that information about the company will have been made public.[12]

5.13 The authorities have clarified that the slightly strange wording "have as their object" means no more than that the subject-matter of the proceedings must be the decisions of the organs,[13] and that only proceedings which are principally concerned with the validity of the decisions of the organs will fall within Article 22.[14]

5.14 On its face this wording is potentially extremely wide in its application. As has been pointed out, since a company can only operate through the decisions of its human organs and agents, or of those of its controlling company, every set of proceedings in which a company takes part is to some extent capable of involving a decision of one of its organs.[15] Could Article 22(2) apply, for instance, to a dispute with a reinsured as to whether or not an underwriting agent for reinsurers had authority, actual or ostensible, to bind business? Could it apply to whether or not the knowledge of the reinsured's broker was to be imputed to the reinsured so as to enable the reinsurers to avoid for non-disclosure?

5.15 The problem is that the reported decisions on Article 22(2) (referred to below) have been largely concerned with the validity as between the company and its directors or agents of the decisions of the organs of the company, and not, so far, with the validity as against third parties of the decisions of organs, so the questions raised above have not been specifically considered.

5.16 Article 22(1) calls for proceedings to be characterised as concerning the validity of the decisions of the company's organs for the purpose of allocating jurisdiction. The European Court of Justice has made it clear in relation to Article 22(1) that the question whether or not

11. Proceedings concerning insurance of land clearly would not have as their object rights *in rem* within Article 22(1).

12. Page 35. Article 22(2) differed from its predecessor Article 16(2) of the Brussels Convention in that Article 22(2) refers to the "validity of the decisions of their organs" rather than simply "the decisions of their organs", although in any event Article 16(2) had been interpreted in England as referring to validity of the decisions and not simply all decisions: *Newtherapeutics* v. *Katz* [1991] Ch. 226.

13. *Grupo Torras* v. *Al-Sabah* [1996] 1 Lloyd's Rep. 7, 15 (CA).

14. See Article 25; *Jenard*, 1979 OJ C.59/1, 34.

15. Kaye, Civil Jurisdiction, p. 945.

proceedings can be characterised as having as their object rights *in rem* in property depends on an autonomous definition under community law.[16] As usual, the reason is the need for consistency at the jurisdictional level in characterising claims or proceedings under numerous divergent systems of national law. For the same reason it is likely that the same approach applies to the characterisation of proceedings under Article 22(1).

5.17 In arriving at such an autonomous definition of relevant proceedings the law will not give the Article a greater width than is required for its objective.[17] The objective of Article 22(2) is plainly that, by way of exception to the general rule that defendants should be sued in the country in which they are domiciled (Article 2), proceedings which concern questions which are better determined in the country of the seat of the company (because of local knowledge) should be determined there.[18] As Mance J has said: "The exercise envisaged by Article 16 (now Article 22) only really works if the court bears in mind the underlying rationale of the Article and (viewing the litigation overall) attempts to assess whether it is likely to be so closely connected with matters of local company law and internal corporate decision-making in respect of one particular company that it should not be tried anywhere but in the courts of the state of that company's seat."[19]

5.18 Where the proceedings have as their subject-matter the constitution or dissolution of companies it is easy to see why the country of the seat is likely to be best placed to determine the action. The law governing constitution or dissolution will often be that of country of the seat,[20] and the overall factual and legal picture of the workings of a company necessary (especially in relation to dissolution) is probably going to be best viewed by the courts of the country where it has its seat.

5.19 On the other hand, where the proceedings have as their subject-matter the validity of the decisions of organs of the company, the proceedings may relate to:

(1) the internal management of the company (e.g. whether or not the company authorised a decision), or
(2) the external effect of decisions of organs of the company on relations with outside parties (e.g. whether or not a decision made by an organ bound the company as against the third party).

5.20 As to internal management, Article 22(2) does not apply to all proceedings. In *Grupo Torras* v. *Al-Sabah*[21] the Court of Appeal held that Article 22(2) did not apply to all proceedings concerning internal management and did not apply to proceedings against the directors essentially for having misappropriated the monies of the companies since, if the allegations were true, there was never any question as to the validity of the decisions of the directors.

5.21 As for the external effect of, for instance, underwriting decisions made by an agent of a reinsurer, this will depend on the law governing the reinsurance between the reinsurer and reinsured, and the facts giving rise to the dispute (see the provisions of the Rome Convention on agency at para. 9.60). These may well have nothing to do with the law of the country of the seat of the reinsurer. Nor is there any reason to think that the courts of the country of the seat would be better placed than other courts to determine the external effect of decisions.

16. C-261/90 *Reichert* v. *Dresdner Bank* [1990] ECR I-2149.
17. *Grupo Torras* v. *Al-Sabah* [1995] 1 Lloyd's Rep. 374, 402, Mance J.; affirmed [1996] 1 Lloyd's Rep. 7 (CA).
18. *Jenard*, 1979 OJ C.59/1, 35.
19. *Ibid*.
20. That may often be the case, but is not always so. In England the definition of the seat is governed by s.43(2) of the CJJA 1982 which provides that a company may have its seat in the UK if its central management and control is exercised in the UK, or it is incorporated under English law.
21. *Ibid*. See also *Speed Investments Ltd and another* v. *Formula One Holdings Ltd and others* [2004] EWCA Civ 1512, [2005] 1 BCLC 455.

Indeed in many cases the result of applying Article 22(2) would be ludicrous. Although he was not specifically concerned with the external effect of decisions of the company's organs, Stuart Smith LJ was surely correct in *Grupo Torras* v. *Al-Sabah*[22] when he said at 15:

"The objective of Art. 16(2) [now 22(2)] is to confer exclusive jurisdiction to decide questions concerning the constitution and internal management of a company on the courts of the member state in which the company has its seat. It is generally accepted as a matter of private international law that the law of the place of incorporation determines the capacity of the company, the composition and powers of the various organs of the company, the formalities and procedures laid down for them, the extent of an individual member's liability for the debts and liabilities of the company, and other matters of that kind. The objective of Art. 16(2) is to confer exclusive jurisdiction to determine all such questions on the courts of the state where the company has its seat. The other paragraphs of the Article follow a similar logic."

4. Has the defendant entered an appearance under Article 24?

5.22 Article 24 confers jurisdiction on a court of a Member State where a defendant enters an appearance in that court:

"Apart from jurisdiction derived from other provisions of this Regulation, a court of a member state before which a defendant enters an appearance shall have jurisdiction. This rule shall not apply where appearance was entered to contest the jurisdiction, or where another court has exclusive jurisdiction by virtue of Article 22."

5.23 The significance of Article 24 is that it confers jurisdiction on a court in circumstances where the court would otherwise not have jurisdiction under the Brussels Regulation. Thus, if an English domiciled reinsured commenced proceedings in London against a French domiciled reinsurer relying on the ground that the contract was made in London (CPR 6.20(5)(a)) but in breach of an exclusive jurisdiction agreement in favour of the courts of Paris, the English courts would not have jurisdiction: Article 23(1). However, the defendant reinsurers could choose not to contest the English proceedings and enter an appearance by serving a defence or acknowledging service and the English court would have jurisdiction because of Article 24.[23]

5.24 Why in such a case would the defendant reinsurers choose not to contest the jurisdiction? Usually reinsurers prefer home advantage. However, there may, for instance, be related proceedings in London, and the defendant reinsurers may perceive an advantage in having the claim against it heard in the same court as the related proceedings. The other possible situation in which Article 24 will be called into play is, of course, where although the defendant reinsurers did not intend to enter an appearance it is said that they inadvertently did so.

5.25 The European Court of Justice has made clear that the objective of Article 24 is to give effect to a choice by a defendant:

"Article 18 [now Article 24] in particular is based on the idea that, by entering an appearance before the court seised of the proceedings by the plaintiff, without contesting that court's jurisdiction, the defendant is by implication signifying his consent to the hearing of the case by a court other than that designated by the other provisions of the convention."[24]

As Jenard said "Article 18 governs jurisdiction implied from submission".[25]

22. [1996] 1 Lloyd's Rep. 7 (CA).

23. See the example at *Jenard*, 1979 OJ C.59/1, 38; *Gasser* v. *MISAT* [2004] 1 Lloyd's Rep. 222, 229. If the defendant reinsurers did not enter an appearance the court would have to declare that it had no jurisdiction since the defendant was domiciled in a Member State unless the claimant could show that the court had jurisdiction under the Brussels Regulation: Article 26(1).

24. C-48/84 *Spitzley* v. *Sommer* [1985] ECR I-787 at [15].

25. Page 38.

5.26 Article 24 expressly states that it does not apply if another court has exclusive jurisdiction under Article 22. But it is not stated to be subject to any other provision of the Brussels Regulation. Jenard concluded that: "the only cases in which a court must declare that it has no jurisdiction and where jurisdiction by submission will not be allowed are those in which the courts of another State have exclusive jurisdiction."[26] The European Court of Justice has repeatedly confirmed that Article 24 confers jurisdiction in relation to international proceedings[27] even if there is a binding exclusive jurisdiction agreement under Article 23.[28] The parties are in effect taken to have consented to jurisdiction *also* being available under Article 24. However, Article 24 jurisdiction is not exclusive and jurisdiction under either Article 23 or 24 would be available.[29] In other words, the choice to submit to the jurisdiction only prevails over the *exclusivity* of the jurisdiction agreement. It also follows that although in matters relating to insurance Articles 8–14 set out special provisions for jurisdiction, Article 24 confers an additional ground of jurisdiction.[30] However, although Article 24 provides a ground of jurisdiction such proceedings may be stayed or declined under the *lis alibi* Articles 27 to 30 (see para. 5.250).[31]

5.27 Although in his report Jenard gave an example of how Article 24 extended jurisdiction in a case where a defendant *domiciled* in a Member State was sued in another country (at page 38), the wording of Article 24 is wide enough to apply to proceedings in a Member State whatever the domicile of the parties. For instance, if, in the example considered above, the reinsurers were domiciled in the USA, would Article 24 apply? There are differing views as to whether or not Article 24 should apply[32] but the wording seems wide enough, and, if it did apply, the beneficial effect would be to enable the uniform controls on multiplicity of proceedings in Articles 27 to 30 to be applied to relevant proceedings throughout the Member States.[33]

5.28 As to what amounts to entering an appearance within Article 24, Jenard commented that "Unlike the case of conventions based on indirect jurisdiction, the defendant may, by virtue of the Convention, rely on its provisions in the court seised of the proceedings and plead lack of jurisdiction. It will be necessary to refer to the rules of procedure in force in the State of the court seised of the proceedings in order to determine the point in time up to which the defendant will be allowed to raise this plea, and to determine the legal meaning of the term 'appearance'."[34] However, the characterisation of the steps for an entry of appearance under Article 24 must depend on an autonomous definition for the purpose of the Brussels

26. *Ibid.*

27. The Brussels Regulation only applies to proceedings with an international element: see para. 2.15 above.

28. C-150/80 *Elefanten Schuh GmbH* v. *Jacqmain* [1981] ECR I-1671 at [17]; C-48/84 *Spitzley* v. *Sommer* [1985] ECR I-787 at [26]; C-201/82 *Gerling Konzern Speziale Kreditversicherung AG* v. *Amministrazione del Tesoro dello Stato* [1983] ECR I-2503.

29. As was argued in C-201/82 *Gerling* v. *Amministrazione del Tesoro* [1983] ECR I-2503 at [21].

30. By Article 8 the insurance provisions apply without prejudice to Articles 4 and 5(5). Article 8 makes no reference to Article 24 and Article 24 is expressed to be subject only to Article 22. The insurance rules are also subject to an express agreement (Article 13). In effect, the jurisdiction under Article 24 is a special form of jurisdiction by the consent of the parties.

31. In *Rank Film Distributors* v. *Lanterna Editrice SRL* [1992] IL Pr 58 an argument was raised but not decided that because an entry of appearance overrode an exclusive jurisdiction agreement, and an exclusive jurisdiction agreement overrode the *lis alibi pendens* provisions, an entry of appearance created a jurisdiction not subject to the *lis alibi pendens* provisions. However, the jurisdiction created by entry of appearance is not exclusive, so there does not appear to be any reason to exclude the *lis alibi pendens* provisions, as there does if there is an effective exclusive jurisdiction agreement. In any event the basic premise that Article 23 trumps Article 21 has been shown to be false in *Gasser* v. *MISAT* [2004] 1 Lloyd's Rep. 222, see para. 5.280.

32. There are some views that Article 24 can be interpreted more narrowly, but the wording of Article 24 appears to be clear: see Layton and Mercer, p. 746.

33. Compare, however, Article 23(3) which expressly applies where neither party is domiciled in a Member State (para. 5.110 below). The effect is that the provisions of Articles 27 to 30 apply to such proceedings.

34. *Jenard*, 1979 OJ C.59/1, 38.

Regulation. A uniform approach is required at the jurisdiction level. Hence, in *Elefanten Schuh GmbH* v. *Jacqmain,*[35] where the European Court of Justice had to consider whether or not there had been an entry of appearance under Article 18 of the Brussels Convention (now Brussels Regulation Article 24) if the defendant put in a defence on the merits at the same time as contesting jurisdiction, it said this (para. 16):

"… the [court below] asks in this regard whether jurisdiction must be contested *in limine litis*. For the purposes of interpreting the convention that concept is difficult to apply in view of the appreciable differences existing between the legislation of the contracting states with regard to bringing actions before courts of law, the appearance of defendants and the way in which the parties to an action must formulate their submissions. However, it follows from the aim of Article 18 that if the challenge to jurisdiction is not preliminary to any defence as to the substance it may not in any event occur after the making of the submissions which under national procedural law are considered to be the first defence addressed to the court seised."

In other words, Article 24 would not apply provided that the challenge to jurisdiction is not made after the defence on the merits is put forward.

5.29 In fact, the European Court of Justice has not sought to give any autonomous meaning to entry of appearance for the purposes of Article 24 other than in two respects. Firstly, a defendant can defend on the merits at the same time as contesting jurisdiction, as in *Elefanten*. Secondly, Article 24 has been held to apply to a *claimant* who does not contest the jurisdiction of the court to hear a counterclaim, just as it does to a defendant who does not contest jurisdiction for a claim.[36] Subject to those two qualifications, what is an entry of appearance is determined by the national law of the court seised.[37] The differences between the law and procedures of Member States do not make this a problem because there is only ever one court which can be seised of the proceedings to which the defendant has submitted.

5.30 As far as English law is concerned, the defendant is treated as having accepted the court's jurisdiction if he files an acknowledgment of service and does not apply to challenge jurisdiction within 14 days after filing the acknowledgment: CPR 11. If the defendant does not serve an acknowledgement of service but simply serves a defence without at the same time challenging jurisdiction he would thereby accept the jurisdiction.[38] Pending an application to challenge the jurisdiction the defendant will only lose the right to challenge the jurisdiction if there are acts which amount to: "a representation that the defendant is abandoning the option … to challenge the jurisdiction at any time until … the expiry of the appropriate period under the rules."[39] The cases show that the defendant may make interlocutory applications to the court or take steps such as seeking disclosure of documents referred to in the particulars of claim, agreeing an extension of time for the defence, requesting security for costs,[40] and (after an express reservation) requesting time for disclosure of assets without being treated as having accepted the jurisdiction.[41] But arguing that injunctions should be discharged on the merits without expressly reserving the right to challenge the jurisdiction did amount to an acceptance of the jurisdiction.[42] The safest course for a defendant is always to make any step without prejudice to a challenge to the jurisdiction.

35. C-150/80 *Elefanten Schuh GmbH* v. *Jacqmain* [1981] ECR I-1671.
36. C-48/84 *Spitzley* v. *Sommer* [1985] ECR I-787. Where the counterclaim arose from the same contract or facts as the claim the court would in any event have jurisdiction under Article 6(3).
37. *Jenard*, 1979 OJ C.59/1, 38.
38. CPR 10.1(3)(b); 10.2(b). *Cf. SSQ* v. *Backes* [2002] 1 Lloyd's Rep. 465 where service of a counterclaim at the same time as challenging the jurisdiction did not amount to entry of an appearance.
39. *Caltex* v. *Taurus,* 22.2.2000 (CA, unrep.); *SSQ* v. *Johann* [2002] 1 Lloyd's Rep. 465, 474.
40. *Kurz* v. *Stella* [1992] Ch 196; *Hewden Stuart Heavy Cranes* v. *Gottwald*, 13.5.92 (CA, unrep.).
41. *The Xing Su Hai* [1995] 2 Lloyd's Rep. 15.
42. *Caltex* v. *Taurus* 22.2.2000 (CA, unrep.).

5.31 We consider entering an appearance and procedure generally in relation to challenging the jurisdiction later (para. 7.19).

C. IS THERE A CHOICE OF JURISDICTION AGREEMENT UNDER ARTICLE 23?

1. Introduction

5.32 The most relevant parts of Article 23 are[43]:

"1. If the parties, one or more of whom is domiciled in a member state, have agreed that a court or the courts of a member state are to have jurisdiction to settle any disputes which have arisen or which may arise in connection with a particular legal relationship, that court or those courts shall have jurisdiction. Such jurisdiction shall be exclusive unless the parties have agreed otherwise. Such an agreement conferring jurisdiction shall be either:

(a) in writing or evidenced in writing; or
(b) in a form which accords with practices which the parties have established between themselves; or
(c) in international trade or commerce, in a form which accords with a usage of which the parties are or ought to have been aware and which in such trade or commerce is widely known to, and regularly observed by, parties to contracts of the type involved in the particular trade or commerce concerned...

3. Where such an agreement is concluded by parties, none of whom is domiciled in a member state, the courts of other member states shall have no jurisdiction over their disputes unless the court or courts chosen have declined jurisdiction."

5.33 Since reinsurance contracts often contain an agreement as to jurisdiction Article 23 is of great importance. It should come as no surprise therefore that many of the English cases and some of the European Court of Justice consequently arise from reinsurance disputes. Insurance contracts relating essentially to large risks also need to be considered because jurisdiction agreements in such contracts are given effect by Article 14, and so fall outside the insurance code in section 3 of the Brussels Regulation. In practice, the main (but not exclusive) preoccupation of such cases has proved to be whether or not references in the reinsurance or insurance contracts amount to jurisdiction agreements within Article 23, in other words, whether or not there is a jurisdiction agreement in writing within Article 23(1)(a). This reflects the fact that if (re)insurance contracts include a jurisdiction agreement it is usually made express in some form or another. Only rarely is it sought to incorporate a jurisdiction agreement through a practice of the parties, or a usage in the industry.

5.34 Although, as we shall see, the policy of the Brussels Regulation has been in broad terms to give effect to agreements for jurisdiction over other rules in the Brussels Regulation, questions have arisen in two particular areas. Firstly, the Achilles heel of jurisdiction agreements is that even if proceedings are started in one Member State in blatant breach of the jurisdiction agreement in favour of another Member State it is the court first seised which must decide the effect of the jurisdiction agreement. As we shall see there is, as yet, no effective appeal to the court provided for in the jurisdiction agreement, although the cases have considered anti-suit injunctions and damages for breach of contract. Secondly, there have been a number of cases on what the correct approach should be in cases not specifically identified by Article 23, e.g. where one or more of the parties is domiciled in a Member State but the jurisdiction agreement is in favour of a non-Member State.

43. Note that under Article 67 certain legislation may deprive Article 23 of effect, for example the Unfair Terms in Consumer Contracts Regulation SI 1999/2083: see para. 5.8.

5.35 We start by considering the general effect of Article 23, its development, its place in the hierarchy of the Brussels Regulation, and its objectives. For the purposes of exposition we then consider the main questions which arise from the point of view of a party seeking to rely on the clause under these main headings:

(1) What approach should be adopted to decide if a jurisdiction agreement is within Article 23(1)?
(2) What is the burden and standard of proof?
(3) Is the jurisdiction agreement within Article 23(1)?
(4) Does the jurisdiction agreement apply to the dispute?
(5) What can you do if proceedings have been commenced in breach of an exclusive jurisdiction agreement?

To distinguish the agreement relating to jurisdiction from the rest of the contract between the parties we refer to the "jurisdiction agreement" (or sometimes "jurisdiction clause" if in writing) as distinct from the "underlying contract".

(i) General effect of Article 23

5.36 Article 23 may apply where the jurisdiction agreement is exclusive or non-exclusive. Where the jurisdiction agreement is exclusive, no court of a Member State will have jurisdiction under any other rule in the Brussels Regulation *except* under the special codes relating to insurance, consumer and employment contracts; under the mandatory jurisdiction rules in Article 22; where a party has entered an appearance under Article 24 (see para. 5.26, *supra*); and where there is another jurisdiction convention under Article 71.[44]

5.37 The other main circumstances in which Article 23(1) does not apply are as follows:

(1) If the proceedings do not have an international element (see para. 2 15).[45]
(2) Neither party is domiciled in a Member State.
(3) The jurisdiction agreement is not in favour of the courts of a Member State.
(4) The claimant denies that the underlying contract containing the jurisdiction agreement was made.[46]

5.38 If proceedings are commenced in the courts of another Member State contrary to a jurisdiction agreement within Article 23, the court first seised must decide the issue of jurisdiction; and any other court must stay its proceedings in the meantime. Article 23 does not enable a court other than the court first seised to avoid a stay under Articles 27 or 28 (para. 5.280).

(ii) Development of Article 23

5.39 Article 23 has developed significantly from its beginnings in Article 17 of the Brussels Convention, mainly in the direction of relaxing the formal requirements for there to be an effective jurisdiction agreement whilst maintaining the objective of requiring there to be a real consensus. It can be important to an understanding of the cases to know the state of the relevant Article at the time.[47]

44. See Article 23(5).

45. For an example of a case where both parties were domiciled in Germany and had agreed a jurisdiction agreement in favour of Austria but the court declined to apply Article 23 for lack of an international element see *The European Legal Forum 2004*, judgment 10, p. 1.

46. *Andromeda* v. *O W Bunker* [2006] EWHC 777 (Comm.); but it does apply where the claimant claims a declaration the contract is void: C-269/95 *Benincasa* v. *Dentalkit* [1997] ECR I-3767 at [25]. See para. 5.97 below.

47. See, e.g., *SSQ* v. *Backes* [2002] 1 Lloyd's Rep. 465, 481 (Judge Havelock-Allan QC).

5.40 Article 17 of the Brussels Convention (the predecessor of Article 23) stated that:

"If the Parties, one or more of whom is domiciled in a Contracting State, have, by agreement in writing or by an oral agreement evidenced in writing, agreed that a court or the courts of a Contracting State are to have jurisdiction to settle any disputes which have arisen or which may arise in connection with a particular legal relationship, that court or those courts shall have exclusive jurisdiction...

If the agreement conferring jurisdiction was concluded for the benefit of only one of the parties, that party shall retain the right to bring proceedings in any other court which has jurisdiction by virtue of this Convention."

5.41 In 1978 the United Kingdom became a party to the Brussels Convention and the first sentence of Article 17 was amended to read:

"If the parties, one or more of whom is domiciled in a Contracting State, have agreed that a court or the courts of a Contracting State are to have jurisdiction to settle any disputes which have arisen or which may arise in connection with a particular legal relationship, that court or those courts shall have exclusive jurisdiction. Such an agreement conferring jurisdiction shall be either in writing or evidenced in writing or, in international trade or commerce, in a form which accords with practices in that trade or commerce of which the parties are or ought to have been aware. Where such an agreement is concluded by parties, none of whom is domiciled in a Contracting State, the courts of other Contracting States shall have no jurisdiction over their disputes unless the court or courts chosen have declined jurisdiction."

The second sentence of the 1978 version apparently relaxed the formalities required in international trade. This seems to have been a reaction to the decision of the European Court of Justice in *Segoura* v. *Bonadakarian*.[48] There, goods had been subject to an oral sale contract, and on delivery the seller delivered his standard terms incorporating a jurisdiction agreement. This situation has featured in many of the cases in the European Court of Justice although it is not common in (re)insurance disputes. The European Court of Justice took the view that the protection of the buyer from having imposed a jurisdiction agreement which had not been specifically agreed required that the jurisdiction agreement had to be specifically agreed in writing, unless the oral agreement was made in the framework of a "continuing trading relationship" based on standard terms including a jurisdiction agreement when the jurisdiction agreement would be incorporated. This would in fact have been allowed by the original wording of Article 17 under which the jurisdiction agreement had to be in writing or evidenced in writing as interpreted in *Segoura* v. *Bonadakarian*.[49] However, the change in 1978 went further, so that in international trading an underlying contract could incorporate a jurisdiction agreement, even if there was not an already established relationship, if the terms to be included (including the jurisdiction agreement) were well known to both parties or the industry.[50]

5.42 The third sentence of the 1978 version made clear that if, for instance, a US reinsured and reinsurer chose the courts of England even though the place of performance was in France, Article 5 would only confer jurisdiction if the courts of England declined jurisdiction. Schlosser said of this change (at para. 177):

"proceedings can be brought before a court within the Community by parties who, although both domiciled outside the Community, have agreed that that court should have jurisdiction. There is no reason for the Convention to include rules on the conditions under which the court stipulated by such parties must accept jurisdiction. It is however important for the Community to ensure, by means of more detailed conditions, that the effect of such an agreement on jurisdiction is recognised throughout the EEC. The new third sentence of the first paragraph of Article 17 is designed to cater for this. It covers the situa-

48. C-25/76; [1976] ECR I-1851.
49. C-25/76; [1976] ECR I-1851.
50. *Schlosser*, para. 179; *SSQ* v. *Backes* [2002] 1 Lloyd's Rep. 465, 481 (Judge Havelock-Allan QC).

tion where despite the fact that both parties are domiciled outside the Community, a court in a Community State ("X") would, were it not for a jurisdiction agreement, have jurisdiction, e.g. on the ground that the place of performance lies within that State. If in such a case the parties agree that the courts of another Community State are to have exclusive jurisdiction, that agreement must be observed by the courts of State X, provided the agreement meets the formal requirements of Article 17. Strictly speaking, it is true, this is not necessary adjustment. Such situations were possible before, in relations between the original member states of the Community. However, owing to the frequency with which jurisdiction is conferred upon United Kingdom courts in international trade, the problem takes on considerably greater importance with the United Kingdom accession to the Convention than hitherto."

5.43 An amended form of Article 17(1) was agreed as part of the Lugano Convention in 1988 (although it came into force later), and, in this altered form, found its way into the version of the Brussels Convention amended on the accession of Spain and Portugal in 1989. The first paragraph was replaced with this:

"If the parties, one or more of whom is domiciled in a Contracting State, have agreed that a court or the courts of a Contracting State are to have jurisdiction to settle any disputes which have arisen or which may arise in connection with a particular legal relationship, that court or those courts shall have exclusive jurisdiction. Such an agreement conferring jurisdiction shall be either:

(a) in writing or evidenced in writing, or
(b) in a form which accords with practices which the parties have established between themselves, or
(c) in international trade or commerce, in a form which accords with a usage of which the parties are or ought to have been aware and which in such trade or commerce is widely known to, and regularly observed by, parties to contracts of the type involved in the particular trade or commerce concerned.

Where such an agreement is concluded by parties, none of whom is domiciled in a Contracting State, the courts of other Contracting States shall have no jurisdiction over their disputes unless the court or courts chosen have declined jurisdiction."

5.44 Article 17(1)(b) in the 1989 version seems to have been directed at covering what was already covered by the decision in *Segoura* v. *Bonadakarian*,[51] that is, the incorporation of a jurisdiction agreement in terms which governed an existing relationship. According to the Jenard and Moller report (para. 58) it was thought that this statement of the meaning of Article 17 in the 1968 Brussels Convention should be explicitly reflected in the Lugano Convention. Oddly, this was done by simply adding Article 17(1)(b), apparently as a subset of Article 17(1)(a). Article 17(1)(c) encapsulated the change which had been made in 1978.[52]

5.45 Finally, in 2001, when the Brussels Regulation was issued, the opportunity was taken to delete the provision which had become Article 17(4) that if the jurisdiction agreement was concluded for the benefit of only one of the parties, that party shall retain the right to bring proceedings in any other court which has jurisdiction by virtue of this Convention,[53] and to introduce a sentence stating that the jurisdiction conferred by Article 23 "would be exclusive unless the parties have agreed otherwise".[54]

(iii) Objectives of Article 23

5.46 A number of different themes are frequently referred to by the European Court of Justice in construing Article 23 which are discussed further below:

51. C-25/76; [1976] ECR I-1851.
52. Cruz report, para. 26; *SSQ* v. *Backes* [2002] 1 Lloyd's Rep. 465, 481 (Judge Havelock-Allan QC). The word "practice" was changed to "usage" which apparently reflects the word used in the majority of versions of the Brussels Convention: C-159/97 *Trasporti* v. *Hugo Trumpy* [1999] ECR I-1597, note 1.
53. C-22/85 *Anterist* v. *Credit Lyonnais* [1986] ECR I-1951.
54. *Evialis* v. *SIAT* [2004] Lloyd's Rep. IR 187, 203.

(1) Article 23 is based upon the policy of recognising the freedom of the parties to decide on jurisdiction.[55]
(2) The objective of the formal requirements in Article 23 is to ensure that the consensus between the parties is in fact established.[56]
(3) The requirements of Article 23 must be "strictly construed" because Article 23 derogates from the standard jurisdiction elsewhere in the Brussels Regulation,[57] and so as to promote legal certainty.[58]

2. What approach should be adopted to decide if a jurisdiction agreement is within Article 23(1)?

5.47 Article 23(1) refers to the parties having agreed that a court is to have jurisdiction. By what law is it to be decided whether or not such an agreement was validly made? In summary, the position appears to be as follows.

5.48 First, the applicable law of the underlying contract clearly applies to the terms of the contract other than the jurisdiction agreement. The Brussels Regulation is not intended to alter the substantive law of the contract generally. Article 23(1) is concerned with the jurisdiction agreement not the contract as whole.[59]

5.49 Second, it is also clear, at least in the English cases, that the meaning of the jurisdiction agreement must be interpreted in accordance with applicable law of the underlying contract in order that the court can then consider whether or not the jurisdiction agreement is within the definition of Article 23(1).[60] In other words, what is the jurisdiction agreement trying to do?[61] In practice, it is often perfectly clear that the jurisdiction agreement allocates jurisdiction to the courts of one country when the parties are domiciled in different countries, and the court progresses straight to the next question as to whether or not that jurisdiction agreement is within the Article 23 definition. In some cases, however, there may be doubt as to whether or not the so-called jurisdiction agreement is in fact to be interpreted as allocating jurisdiction. The court then has to decide what the jurisdiction agreement means before it can consider whether or not the jurisdiction agreement falls within the Article 23 definition.[62] It decides the meaning of the jurisdiction agreement according to the applicable law of the underlying contract.

5.50 One such example is *Evialis* v. *SIAT*[63] referred to above in which a French company Evialis bought goods from Italian sellers. The sellers were insured by an Italian company

55. C-23/78 *Meeth* v. *Glacetal* [1978] ECR I-2133 at [5], also stressing in the context of Article 23 the overall objective of the Brussels Regulation of avoiding "superfluous proceedings".

56. C-24/76 *Estasis Salotti* v. *RUWA* [1976] ECR I-1831 at [7]. C-784/79 *Porta-Leasing* v. *Prestige* [1980] ECR I-1517 at [5]; C-221/84 *Berghoefer* v. *ASA* [1985] ECR I-2699 at [15]; C-313/85 *Iveco* v. *van Hool* [1986] ECR I-3337 at [5]; C-106/95 *MSG* v. *Le Gravieres* [1997] ECR I-911 at [15]; C-116/02 *Gasser* v. *MISAT* [2004] 1 Lloyd's Rep. 222, 229.

57. C-25/76 *Galeries Segoura Sprl* v. *Firma Rahim Bonadakarian* [1976] ECR I-1851 at [6]; C-221/84 *Berghoefer* v. *ASA* [1985] ECR I-2699 at [13]; C-106/95 *MSG* v. *Le Gravieres* [1997] ECR I-911 at [14].

58. C-150/80 *Elefanten Schuh GmbH* v. *Jacqmain* [1981] ECR I-1671 at [25]; C-269/95 *Benincasa* v. *Dentalkit* [1997] ECR I-3767 at [27], [29]; C-159/97 *Trasporti* v. *Hugo Trumpy* [1999] ECR I–1597 at [34]; C-116/02 *Gasser* v. *MISAT* [2004] 1 Lloyd's Rep. 222, 229.

59. C-269/95 *Benincasa* v. *Dentalkit* [1997] ECR I-3767 at [24].

60. The Rome Convention does not apply to choice of law clauses: Article 1(2)(d). At common law the law governing the contract would usually be held to govern the jurisdiction clause and hence would govern questions such as initial validity, interpretation, etc. Compare the position in relation to the law applicable to an arbitration clause.

61. See, e.g., *Evialis* v. *SIAT* [2004] Lloyd's Rep. IR 187, 204; *British Sugar* v. *Babbini* [2005] 1 Lloyd's Rep. 332 (HH Judge Seymour QC) where the agreement stated "for any dispute, the court of exclusive jurisdiction is that of Forli", being a place in Italy. One issue was whether this was to be read as purely domestic in effect (Forli as opposed to any other place in Italy) or as regulating international jurisdiction also. The judge considered the distinction between "*competenza*" and "*giurisdizione*" in Italian law.

62. This distinction is not always made clear; e.g. *AIG* v. *Ethniki* [2000] Lloyd's Rep. IR 343, 351, CA.

63. [2004] Lloyd's Rep. IR 187; *Insured Financial Structures* v. *Elecktrocieplownia* [2003] QEG BVI 1260, 1264 (CA) on the Lugano Convention; *cf.* the approach in *British Sugar* v. *Babbini* [2005] 1 Lloyd's Rep. 332, 343 (HH Judge Seymour QC).

SIAT. The insurance was agreed by declaration to an open cover, and the certificate included a service clause which stated "Address for legal proceedings in UK: WK Webster and Co 6 Lloyd's Avenue London EC3N 3AX (United Kingdom)". However, another clause of the general conditions contained in the open cover stated: "The competent court, at the choice of the plaintiff, is exclusively that of the court office of the place in which is located the head office of the insurer or the agency which is in charge of the policy or in whose offices the contract was located [i.e. Italy]". The insured relied on Article 23 to found jurisdiction for the English proceedings, and relied on the service clause in the certificate which was to be construed under Italian law as the applicable law. It was not disputed that the service clause only applied to service of proceedings on the insurers. Smith J. made clear at p. 204 that "while the court will apply autonomous community law in order to decide whether Article 23 of the Regulation is satisfied, in so far as the court needs to interpret the contract between the parties in order to do so, the court will, I take it, interpret it in accordance with its applicable law" (see also p. 202). He found that it was highly likely that the insurance contract conferred on the English courts non-exclusive jurisdiction. Clause 16 of the general conditions had to be read as having been modified so as to confer "a further option about where to proceed to insurers"[64] rather than as stipulating the only available jurisdiction as it appeared to do. In *Standard Steamship* v. *GIE*[65] the question was whether or not a joint entrant of a P&I club was bound by the club rules which contained a jurisdiction agreement. The rules were governed by English law, and Cooke J. construed the jurisdiction agreement in the rules under English law to see whether or not the requirements of Article 23(1) were met.[66] It has also been held that in construing jurisdiction agreements under English law where the Brussels Regulation applies the court should lean towards a construction which gives effect to jurisdiction under Article 2, i.e. against the jurisdiction agreement providing for a jurisdiction other than the domicile of the defendant. In *Ocarina Marine* v. *Marcard*[67] Rix J. considered jurisdiction agreements in various loan agreements:

"I approach the construction of these clauses applying English canons of construction, as I am required to do. The loan agreements, the assignments and the charges are all governed by English law. In applying canons of English construction to the relevant clauses, I think I am entitled to bear in mind, and I do, that the formal requirements of Art. 17 of the Convention have been interpreted to mean that consent has to be clearly and precisely shown, and that any jurisdiction agreed for the purpose of Art. 17 may be a derogation from the general rule contained in Art. 2. In the case of genuine ambiguity or uncertainty as to the correct construction of such a jurisdiction agreement I therefore consider that the English court should resolve such ambiguity or uncertainty in favour of a construction which leaves the underlying jurisdiction required by Art. 2 untouched."

5.51 The law applicable to the underlying contract also applies to the determination of which documents and communications comprise that contract (including the jurisdiction agreement); but this is subject to community law which may not give effect to any constraints in the applicable law on a party establishing a jurisdiction agreement for the purposes of Article 23(1).

5.52 Thirdly, once the meaning of the jurisdiction agreement is ascertained in accordance with the applicable law you still need to know whether or not that comes within the formal requirements of Article 23(1). For many purposes the Article 23 definition of what is a jurisdiction agreement is autonomous. It does not depend on the applicable law or the national law. What is not clear is whether the validity of the underlying contract or jurisdiction agreement

64. At p. 205.
65. [2005] Lloyd's Rep. IR 407.
66. See p. 413.
67. [1994] 2 Lloyd's Rep. 524, followed in *Standard Steamship* v. *GIE* [2005] Lloyd's Rep. IR 407, 413.

under the applicable law or national law is ever relevant to whether or not the jurisdiction agreement falls within the Article 23(1) definition, and, if so, to what extent (see para. 5.97).

5.53 Lastly, if it is concluded that the jurisdiction agreement is within the definition of Article 23 the court then has to decide whether or not the jurisdiction agreement covers the dispute between the parties. This depends on the meaning of the jurisdiction agreement under the applicable law of the underlying contract. The European Court of Justice has on many occasions reminded referring courts of this fact.[68] In *Standard Steamship* v. *GIE*[69] (referred to above) the jurisdiction agreement in the rules of the P&I club stated that "The Member hereby submits to the jurisdiction of the High Court of Justice of England in respect of any action brought by the Club to recover any sums which the Club may consider to be due to it from a Member" and the question was whether or not this was wide enough to apply to a claim brought by the club against an insured joint entrant which was not a member of the club. That was determined under the applicable law of the club rules which was English law. In cases where it is possible under community law to rely on a jurisdiction agreement against a third party, or where a third party seeks to rely on a jurisdiction agreement, perhaps after an assignment or on subrogation (para. 5.71 below) it will be necessary to scrutinise the wording of the jurisdiction agreement under the applicable law to see whether or not the wording is wide enough to cover the dispute.

3. Burden and standard of proof

5.54 In a case where a party relies on Article 23(1) to establish jurisdiction within England on whom is the burden of proof? If the English court would not have jurisdiction apart from Article 23 the burden must of course be on the party relying on Article 23(1) to bring a claim within the English court.[70] But, if the English court would otherwise have jurisdiction under Article 2 or some other provision of the Brussels Regulation, and a party applies for a stay under Article 23(1) in favour of some other jurisdiction, who has the burden of establishing that Article 23(1) applies? Is the burden on the party relying on Article 23(1), or on the other party to establish that it does not apply? There is no guidance from the European Court of Justice as yet. The English cases at first instance go each way.[71] In *Konkola* v. *Coromin*[72] Rix LJ reviewed the authorities and without deciding the point preferred the view that the burden was on the party relying on Article 23(1) (at para. 95): "It seems to me to be counter-intuitive to think that, where a statutory jurisdiction has been established but an exceptional jurisdiction elsewhere is put forward based on a contract which must be clearly shown to have the assent of both parties, it remains the burden of the claimant to prove a negative rather than that of the applicant who challenges the established jurisdiction to prove that he is entitled to rely on the clause in question. After all, Article 23 comes in a section of the Regulation (section 7) called 'Prorogation of Jurisdiction'."

5.55 To what standard must a party prove its side of the argument on factual disputes? If factual disputes arise during a hearing relating to whether or not a jurisdiction agreement is

68. C-23/78 *Meeth* v. *Glacetal* [1978] ECR I-2133; C-214/89 *Powell Duffryn* v. *Petereit* [1992] ECR I-1745 at [36].

69. [2002] 1 Lloyd's Rep. 407, 413–414; *Provimi* v. *Roche* [2003] 2 All ER 683.

70. See, e.g., *Standard Steamship* v. *GIE* [2005] Lloyd's Rep. IR 407, 416.

71. Burden on the party seeking to establish English jurisdiction: *Carnoustie Universal* v. *International Transport Workers Federation* [2002] 2 All ER 657 para. 45; *Provimi* v. *Roche* [2003] 2 All ER 683 (Comm), para. 55. Burden on the party relying on Article 23: *Knauf* v. *British Gypsum* [2002] 1 WLR 907, the point was left open on appeal: [2002] 1 Lloyd's Rep. 199 (CA); *Bank of Tokyo-Mitsubishi* v. *Baskan* [2004] 2 Lloyd's Rep. 395 para. 194.

72. [2006] 1 Lloyd's Rep. 410; *Royal and Sun* v. *Exel* [2006] EWCA Civ 629, para. 62; *WPP* v. *Benatti* [2006] EWHC 1641 (Comm), para. 54.

binding, the court will usually have to deal with the dispute summarily and not after full disclosure and cross examination. At the interlocutory stage the process is necessarily summary. Under the common law the corresponding test is that there must be a "good arguable case" for the ground of jurisdiction relied on (see para. 7.23) and the same test is applied in relation to disputes relating to the application of for instance Article 5 (see para. 5.137).

5.56 What is clear is that on any basis the test to be applied where a party relies on Article 23(1) is that the case for the jurisdiction of the English courts is at least a "good arguable case".[73] What is not yet clear is when, and in what circumstances, if any, the test should be higher than this, or at any rate should be at the tougher end of a flexible scale of what is a good arguable case. As well as the point that the issues have to be decided summarily, the courts have taken into account the following points[74]:

(1) In some cases the factual issue in dispute is the dispute which will be the subject of the trial, or at least is likely to form a significant part of the evidence in relation to the subject of the trial, and the court will therefore not wish to be seen to be closing its mind on that issue. In other cases the factual dispute on the Article 23 application will be as to an issue such as domicile which will not arise at trial and which therefore the court will be less reluctant to appear to take a view on, albeit on imperfect evidence.

(2) Where it is clear that a court of a Member State has jurisdiction under another Article of the Brussels Regulation, especially the default jurisdiction under Article 2, the court will be reluctant to make a finding which departs from that established jurisdiction on the basis of the existence of a jurisdiction agreement unless the consent of the parties is clearly and precisely demonstrated.

5.57 In *IP Metal* v. *Ruote*[75] Waller J. preferred a test that it must be highly likely that the party relying on the jurisdiction agreement would have succeeded at trial rather than that there was merely a good arguable case under Article 23(1). In that case the jurisdiction agreement in a sale of goods contract was in favour of London, but the defendant Italian buyers started proceedings in respect of one consignment in Italy, and sought a stay of later English proceedings. Other related proceedings were taking place in England. Waller J. explained why he preferred a test that the case be "highly likely" (at p. 63):

> "I believe that where the argument in relation to Art. 17 (now Article 23) is whether a consensus has been reached, that is likely to distinguish the Art. 17 situation from an Art. 5 situation. It is likely in such a situation that the court will wish to be more certain that the party alleging the consensus is right, because it is likely that the argument is only of relevance when jurisdiction is being decided ... where there is a risk that there could be irreconcilable judgments on jurisdiction or proper law and thus ultimately even on the merits (as in this case), the English court will, as I see it, want to be as clear as possible, and at least form the view that it is highly likely, that if the matter were tried out the plaintiff would succeed in his argument on the jurisdiction agreement."

5.58 In *Canada Trust* v. *Stolzenberg (No 2)*[76] the Court of Appeal confirmed that the "good arguable" test applied to a claim that the court had jurisdiction under Article 6 of the Lugano Convention. Waller LJ took the opportunity to say that following the decision by the House of Lords in *Seaconsar*[77] he was "probably wrong" to reject the good arguable test in *IP Metal*, even though the court might be in a different position under Article 23(1) from that under

73. *Canada Trust* v. *Stolzenberg (No. 2)* [1998] 1 WLR 547, CA; [2002] 1 AC 1, HL.
74. See the useful *obiter* discussion by Rix LJ in *Konkola* v. *Coromin* [2006] EWCA 5, at paras 74–98.
75. [1993] 2 Lloyd's Rep. 60, affirmed [1994] 2 Lloyd's Rep. 560, CA.
76. [1998] 1 WLR 547, CA, affirmed [2002] 1 AC, HL.
77. [1994] 1 AC 438.

Articles 5 or 6,[78] apparently because after *Seaconsar* the flexibility of the good arguable test had become evident. He explained this at p. 555:

"It is I believe important to recognise, as the language of their Lordships in *Korner*'s case [1951] AC 869 demonstrated, that what the court is endeavouring to do is to find a concept not capable of very precise definition which reflects that the plaintiff must properly satisfy the court that it is right for the court to take jurisdiction. That may involve in some cases considering matters which go both to jurisdiction and to the very matter to be argued at the trial, e.g. the existence of a contract, but in other cases a matter which goes purely to jurisdiction, e.g. the domicile of a defendant. The concept also reflects that the question before the court is one which should be decided on affidavits from both sides and without full discovery and/or cross-examination, and in relation to which therefore to apply the language of the civil burden of proof applicable to issues after full trial is inapposite ... It is also important to remember that the phrase which reflects the concept 'good arguable case' as the other phrases in *Korner*'s case 'a strong argument' and 'a case for strong argument' were originally employed in relation to points which related to jurisdiction but which might also be argued about at the trial. The court in such cases must be concerned not even to appear to express some concluded view as to the merits, e.g. as to whether the contract existed or not. It is also right to remember that the 'good arguable case' test, although obviously applicable to the *ex parte* stage, becomes of most significance at the *inter partes* stage where two arguments are being weighed in the interlocutory context which, as I have stressed, must not become a 'trial'. 'Good arguable case' reflects in that context that one side has a much better argument on the material available. It is the concept which the phrase reflects on which it is important to concentrate, i.e. of the court being satisfied or as satisfied as it can be having regard to the limitations which an interlocutory process imposes that factors exist which allow the court to take jurisdiction.

The civil standard of proof has itself a flexibility depending on the issue being considered and the concept 'good arguable case' has a similar flexibility. It is natural, for example, in a case concerned with a contract where the jurisdiction depends on whether the breach took place within the jurisdiction, but where the issue to be tried will be whether there was a contract at all, not to wish to give even the appearance of pre-trying the central issue, even though the concept of being satisfied must apply both to the existence of the contract and the place of the breach. It is equally natural for the court in the process of being satisfied to scrutinise most jealously that factor which actually provides jurisdiction. It is equally natural that where the foundation of jurisdiction is domicile, i.e. an issue that will not arise at the trial, that particular scrutiny of the material available takes place in the context of the limitations applied to an interlocutory process."

5.59 Later cases have seen the courts at first instance not speaking with one voice on the relevant test. Reference has been made simply to a good arguable case,[79] to one side having "much the better of the argument",[80] or simply "the better of the argument",[81] and to a good arguable case in the sense of "highly likely" to succeed if the questions were tried.[82] It appears that where a party relies on Article 23(1) to justify setting aside English proceedings over which the English court would otherwise have jurisdiction the courts are not generally content simply to adopt the same good arguable case as would be applied for instance if there were a dispute about whether or not the defendant was domiciled in England. Rather the court will, within the confines of the summary procedure, and having regard to the need not to appear to close its mind on issues which will be central at trial, require that the good arguable case be better than the opposing argument. The same would apply where the English court is first seised of proceedings commenced in reliance on an English jurisdiction agreement but it

78. Nourse LJ agreed with Waller LJ; Pill LJ said nothing about this point. The point was not argued in the House of Lords [2002] 1 AC 1, 13.

79. *Glencore* v. *Metro* [1999] 2 Lloyd's Rep. 632, 642.

80. *Provimi* v. *Roche* [2003] EWHC 961; *Knauf* v. *Peters* [2002] 1 Lloyd's Rep. 199, 205 (David Steel J.), left open on appeal at 216; and in relation to reliance on Article 5(1) *Deutsch Ruckversicherung AG* v. *La Fondaria* [2002] Lloyd's Rep. IR 475, 478–479; *Konkola* v. *Coromin* [2006] EWCA 94, CA; *WPP* v. *Benatti* [2006] EWHC 1641 (Comm), para. 61.

81. *Bank of Tokyo-Mitsubishi* v. *Baskan* [2004] 1 Lloyd's Rep. 395.

82. *Prifti* v. *Mussini* [2004] 1 Lloyd's Rep. 528, 534; *Evialis* v. *SIAT* [2004] Lloyd's Rep. IR 187, 204; *Standard Steamship* v. *GIE* [2002] Lloyd's Rep. 407, 415–416.

is clear that subject to the Article 23(1) argument another Member State would have jurisdiction under the Brussels Regulation.[83] A similar tendency can be seen where the issue on which the jurisdiction of the English court depends is not one which will be litigated at trial.

4. Is the jurisdiction agreement within Article 23?

5.60 Having considered how to approach the question whether or not a jurisdiction agreement is within Article 23(1), we now consider the limits of what is an agreement for jurisdiction within Article 23(1). This predominantly depends on community law, although it must be remembered that the applicable law will apply to the interpretation of the underlying contract and clause; which documents and communications comprise the underlying contract, and the creation of rights and liabilities by an agent for a principal or the transfer of rights and liabilities to a third party. Community law has developed incrementally so that the cases have built upon each other over time by small steps. Most of the attention in the cases has been focused on the questions of what the formalities require, and (a question of particular significance to reinsurance) when a jurisdiction agreement in one contract can be incorporated into another contract.

5.61 Article 23(1) will *only* apply if –

(i) the courts of a Member State are selected;
(ii) one or more of the parties are domiciled in a Member State (compare Article 23(3));
(iii) the jurisdiction agreement was made in connection with the legal relationship which is the subject of the dispute;
(iv) a third party is involved, in limited circumstances; and
(v) the requisite formalities have been met.

5.62 However, it is no bar to Article 23(1) applying that –

(1) the defendant disputes the existence of the contract, or that it remains binding;
(2) the contract is not valid under the applicable law.

(i) Are the courts of a Member State selected?

5.63 Article 23(1) only confers jurisdiction if the jurisdiction agreement chooses the courts of a Member State.[84] If it does (and one or more parties is domiciled in a Member State) the jurisdiction agreement will allocate jurisdiction; if not, Article 23(1) will not confer jurisdiction at all. In this discussion we are only concerned with jurisdiction agreements which choose the courts of Member States.[85]

5.64 An exclusive jurisdiction agreement is one which specifies that the courts of only one state have jurisdiction. A non-exclusive jurisdiction agreement is one which specifies that the courts of more than one states have jurisdiction in addition to any others which have jurisdiction under other rules.

5.65 Article 23 applies whether the jurisdiction agreement is exclusive or non-exclusive. There have been attempts to argue that Article 23(1) should not apply to non-exclusive jurisdiction agreements which have been rejected. In *Meeth* v. *Glacetal*[86] it was argued that a clause

83. If the English court were not first seised the court for the Member State which was first seised would decide the issue.
84. C-387/98 *Coreck Maritime* v. *Handelsveem* [2000] ECR I-9337 at [17]–[19].
85. See para. 5.108 for cases where the courts of a non-Member State are chosen.
86. C-23/78 *Meeth* v. *Glacetal* [1978] ECR I-2133.

providing that each party to a contract could only commence proceedings in the country of the domicile of the other was not within Article 17 of the Brussels Convention (now Article 23(1) of the Brussels Regulation) as it only referred to an agreement that the courts of "a Contracting State" in the *singular* have jurisdiction. The European Court of Justice rejected this argument. A choice of two or more courts would fall within the Article. This approach would give effect to the primacy of the parties' intentions and the objective of avoiding multiple proceedings. In *Kurz* v. *Stella*[87] it was argued that a non-exclusive jurisdiction agreement in favour of England could not be within Article 17 of the Brussels Convention. The basis for this was that Article 17 provided that the courts selected "shall have jurisdiction"; that must mean the courts of the selected state alone would have jurisdiction; if Article 17 applied to a non-exclusive jurisdiction agreement its effect would therefore be to convert the agreement into an exclusive jurisdiction agreement; since that cannot have been intended non-exclusive jurisdiction agreements simply fell outside Article 17. Hoffmann J rejected the argument (at p. 203):

> "This argument in my judgment misinterprets what Article 17 means when it says that the chosen or 'prorogated' jurisdiction is to be exclusive. It does not mean 'unique', that the parties are limited to choosing a single jurisdiction. It means only that their choice, whatever it is, shall (subject to the exceptions made in the fifth sentence) have effect to the exclusion of the jurisdictions which would otherwise be imposed on the parties by the earlier Articles of the Convention. Once the parties have availed themselves of Article 17 by the prescribed method, jurisdiction becomes a question of the intention of the parties. But (subject always to the fifth sentence) the Article does not limit their choice or the language in which it can be expressed. Nor does it prevent them from including in their choice, expressly or by implication, courts which would otherwise have had jurisdiction under the Convention. Jurisdiction thus conferred is still based exclusively on the intention of the parties rather than imposed by the general law and is therefore within the terms of Article 17."

The wording of Article 23(1) has now been altered so as to state that "such jurisdiction shall be exclusive unless the parties have agreed otherwise" which makes express the way in which it was interpreted in *Kurz*.

5.66 How precise does the jurisdiction agreement need to be? It need not name the country with jurisdiction provided that it can be identified from the description with precision. In *Société Peloux* v. *AXA*,[88] for example, the jurisdiction agreement in the insurance policy referred to the court of the domicile of the policy-holder and was given effect.

5.67 Can the parties by-pass Article 23(1) by agreeing the place for performance orally and relying on Article 5 to give jurisdiction to the courts of the place of performance? A genuine agreement as to the place of performance will be given effect under Article 5, regardless of the formalities in Article 23 (see para. 5.189 below).

(ii) Is one or more of the parties domiciled in a Member State?

5.68 Article 23(1) only confers jurisdiction if one or more of the parties was domiciled in a Member State. We consider the position if neither party was so domiciled at para. 5.108 below. Domicile is considered at para. 5.111 below. The relevant parties are the parties to the original contract. As will be seen in some circumstances the jurisdiction agreement may be enforced by or against a third party provided that the requirements of Article 23(1) were met by the agreement between the original parties (para. 5.71). It would seem to follow that in such a case one or more of the parties to the original contract must be domiciled in a Member State, and the domicile of the third party would not be relevant for this purpose.[89] It is

87. [1992] Ch 197; *Insured Financial Services* v. *Tychy* [2003] QB 1261.
88. C-112/03, [2005] ECR I-3707; C-387/98 *Coreck Maritime* v. *Handelsveem* [2000] ECR I-9337.
89. C-387/98 *Coreck Maritime* v. *Handelsveem* [2000] ECR I-9337 at [20].

clear that Article 23(1) applies if a party was domiciled in a Member State both at the date of the jurisdiction agreement and when proceedings were initiated.[90]

(iii) Was the jurisdiction agreement made in connection with the legal relationship which is the subject of the dispute?

5.69 Article 23(1) is expressed only to apply to jurisdiction agreements which arise "in connection with a particular legal relationship" between the parties. In *Powell Duffryn* v. *Petereit*[91] the European Court of Justice said that the purpose of that wording is (at para. 31):

"to limit the scope of an agreement conferring jurisdiction solely to disputes which arise from the legal relationship in connection with which the agreement was entered into. Its purpose is to avoid a party being taken by surprise by the assignment of jurisdiction to a given forum as regards all disputes which may arise out of its relationship with the other party to the contract and stem from a relationship other than that in connection with which the agreement conferring jurisdiction was made."

5.70 It therefore appears that the autonomous definition of a jurisdiction agreement would exclude from Article 23(1) an agreement which on its proper construction under its applicable law would apply to a legal relationship other than the one in connection with which the agreement was made. *Powell Duffryn* was not such a case, and, in practice, it is difficult to conceive of a jurisdiction agreement which is broad enough to cover a dispute, but in respect of which it could also be said that the jurisdiction agreement affected a legal relationship other than the one in connection with which the jurisdiction agreement was made. If, for example, a reinsurer wrote a reinsurance for years 1 and 2, but only included a jurisdiction agreement for year 2, it might be said that the reinsurer could not rely on the jurisdiction agreement in respect of a dispute concerning year 1 since that was "a legal relationship other than that in connection with which the agreement conferring jurisdiction had been made". But this would not always be the right result. If, for instance, the parties intended that the jurisdiction agreement should govern both years 1 and 2, and made this clear in the jurisdiction agreement inserted into the contract for year 2, the relationship in connection with which the jurisdiction agreement was agreed could be said to be the relationship created by the contracts for both years. If that is right Article 23(1) should apply.

(iv) Is a third party involved?

5.71 If a jurisdiction agreement was originally agreed between two parties, may it be relied upon either *by* a third party to found jurisdiction under Article 23(1), or *against* a third party by one of the original parties? The answer differs according to whether the subject-matter is reinsurance or insurance. As will be seen, claims governed by section 3 of the Brussels Regulation are subject to special rules, the effect of which is that a third party claiming through the policy-holder insured or beneficiary may enforce a jurisdiction agreement made between other parties, but the insurer may not (see para. 6.30). In relation to matters outside section 3 of the Brussels Regulation, this differential approach does not apply. In *Tilly Russ* v. *Goeminne Hout*[92] a bill of lading issued by the carrier to the shipper and containing a juris-

90. However, it is not clear if the Article applies if (a) a party ceases to be so domiciled after the jurisdiction agreement but before the proceedings were initiated, or (b) if a party only became domiciled in a Member State after the jurisdiction agreement was made but before proceedings were initiated. Briggs/Rees, p. 112, and Dicey/Morris/Collins, para. 12-101, suggest that Article 23 should apply in case (b) as well as (a); *cf.* Layton/Mercer, p. 696, which accepts case (a) but not (b).

91. C-214/89, [1992] ECR I-1745.

92. C-71/83, [1984] EC 2417; C-387/98 *Coreck Maritime* v. *Handelsveem* [2000] ECR I-9337; *Andromeda* v. *O W Bunker* [2006] EWHC 777 (Comm).

diction agreement was apparently indorsed by the shipper to the cargo owner who was the notify party. Could the jurisdiction agreement be enforced against the third party although the third party had made no separate contract with the carrier? The court's approach was essentially that the purpose of Article 23(1) was met if there had been a consensus between the original parties, and that if the applicable law allowed assignment of the rights of a party (about which Article 23(1) said nothing) it would be "alien" to the purposes of Article 23(1) not to apply Article 23(1), i.e. if a jurisdiction agreement has been agreed it should be enforced. The court held that in agreeing to transfer the bill the shipper could confer no more rights than he had, and the third party therefore took the rights subject to the obligations including the jurisdiction agreement. Article 23(1) should therefore apply to the jurisdiction agreement even though it had not been separately agreed between carrier and third party. This approach must surely depend upon the terms of the jurisdiction agreement. If the clause excepted claims by the third party presumably it would not be enforced against the third party.

5.72 This approach has been applied to enforcement of a jurisdiction agreement in a contract of sale against an assignee of the seller's rights. In *Glencore* v. *Metro*[93] Moore-Bick J. rejected an argument based on *dicta* in *Firswood* v. *Petra Bank*[94] that the assignee had to be aware of the existence of the jurisdiction agreement at the time of the assignment. *Tilly Russ* implied no such requirement.

5.73 Accordingly, if a reinsurance contract is validly assigned under the applicable law, a jurisdiction agreement in the reinsurance would in principle be enforceable by the assignee if the original jurisdiction agreement met the Article 23(1) requirements. Such a clause would also be enforceable against the assignee since it does not relate to insurance. The same approach would presumably apply where a third party is subrogated to the rights of a party to the reinsurance contract.[95]

5.74 What is the position if the jurisdiction agreement is made between agents? In *Standard Steamship* v. *GIE*[96] brokers for the insured obtained insurance cover through an agent for the insurers, including a jurisdiction agreement. It was argued that for Article 23 consensus had to be shown as between the principal and any other contracting party, and not between the agent for the principal and that other party. If the jurisdiction agreement made by the agent bound the principal as a matter of the applicable law it is difficult to see why that jurisdiction agreement should not be the one tested by Article 23(1). This is the result Cooke J. arrived at (at p. 420):

> "In *The Tilly Russ*, the *Main Schiffahrts* decision and some of the insurance authorities cited to me, the business was plainly transacted between one or more agent for the parties. At no point, however, does this seem to have given rise to argument, although on the facts it may not have made any difference. Insurance and reinsurance and shipping almost invariably involve the use of agents in agreeing to contracts in standard form which regularly include jurisdiction agreements. If the agent has appropriate authority to bind the principal, the principal has put the agent in the position where the agent's consensus is that of the principal and no further enquiry beyond the agent's consensus is therefore required. Provided therefore that there is actual authority or ostensible authority on the part of the agent, the issue is whether or not the requirements of Article 23 are satisfied, as between the agent and the third party."

(v) Have the formalities under Article 23(1) been met?

5.75 As has been said the formalities required by Article 23(1) have undergone a good deal of change over the years, with the result that care needs to be exercised in looking at the older

93. [1999] 2 Lloyd's Rep. 631, 644–646.
94. 13.12.95 (unrep., CA).
95. Compare the very different position under Article 5(1) considered at para. 5.146 below; and the incorporation of choice of law clauses considered at para. 5.80.
96. [2005] 1 Lloyd's Rep. 407.

authorities (para. 5.39). Whether or not the formalities have been met is a matter of community law (para. 5.60 above), although it is noticeable that, on occasion, the English court considers the English law as to incorporation as a kind of cross check.[97]

5.76 It is sometimes suggested that on top of the requirements as to formalities there is an overarching requirement that there be evidence of a real consensus between the parties. It is quite easy to find statements in the European Court of Justice which appear to indicate this, such as: "Article 17 [now Article 23] imposes upon the court before which the matter is brought the duty of examining, first, whether the clause conferring jurisdiction upon it was in fact the subject of a consensus between the parties, which must be clearly and precisely demonstrated."[98] It is suggested, however, that it would be more accurate to say that whilst the *purpose* of the formalities in Article 23(1) is to ensure that a consensus exists, if the formalities have been met jurisdiction will exist without any further enquiry into consensus. It is the formalities which matter. More recent decisions of the European Court of Justice have made clear that if the formalities under Article 23(1)(c) are met the contract is "presumed to exist".[99] The presumption is probably irrebutable for the purposes of Article 23: the requirement of legal certainty would no doubt not allow a continuing debate as to the application of Article 23(1) if the formalities had been met.

WAS THE JURISDICTION AGREEMENT MADE IN WRITING?

5.77 Article 23(1)(a) applies to jurisdiction agreements in writing or evidenced in writing which by Article 23(2) includes communications by electronic means. In many, if not most, reinsurance cases this is the relevant provision; in other words the parties to such business tend to rely on some wording of the contract as incorporating a jurisdiction agreement rather than a practice between the parties or a trade usage, although there are exceptions referred to below. The leading case on jurisdiction agreements in writing (not evidenced in writing) is early and took a strict line. In *Estasis Salotti* v. *RUWA*[100] the European Court of Justice considered a case where a signed contract for the sale of goods included on the back general conditions of sale including a jurisdiction agreement. The face of the contract did not refer to the general conditions, but it did refer to previous offers by the seller which themselves referred to the general conditions. The incorporation of the jurisdiction agreement was therefore in two stages. The court identified the purpose of the requirements as ensuring there was a real consensus (at para. 7): "by making such validity subject to the existence of an 'agreement' between the parties, Article 17 [now 23] imposes on the court before which the matter is brought the duty of examining, first, whether the clause conferring jurisdiction upon it was in fact the subject of a consensus between the parties, which must be clearly and precisely demonstrated. The purpose of the formal requirements imposed by Article 17 is to ensure that the consensus between the parties is in fact established." The mere fact that the jurisdiction agreement was on the back of a signed contract did not mean that there had been a real consent. However, an express reference on the face of the contract to the general conditions would suffice: it did not have to refer to the jurisdiction agreement. A reference on the face of the contract to *previous* offers which referred to the general conditions would also suffice but (para. 12): "only in the case of an express reference, which can be checked by a party exercising reasonable care, and only if it is established that the general conditions including the

97. See, e.g., *Siboti* v. *BP France* [2003] 2 Lloyd's Rep. 364, 367.
98. C-25/76 *Segoura* v. *Bonadakarian* [1976] ECR I-1851 at[6]; see further para. 5.41 above.
99. C-106/95 *MSG* v *Le Gravieres* [1997] ECR I-911; C-159/97 *Trasporti* v. *Hugo Trumpy* [1999] ECR I-1597.
100. C-24/76, [1976] ECR I-1831.

clause conferring jurisdiction have in fact been communicated to the other contracting party with the offer to which reference is made."

5.78 The rather mechanistic effect of *Estasis* can be summarised as being: it is not enough that the jurisdiction agreement is contained in terms on the back of the contract if the terms are not referred to on the face of the contract. A reference on the face of a contract to a document or terms which include a jurisdiction agreement may suffice; alternatively a reference on the face of the contract to a document which itself refers to terms including the jurisdiction agreement may suffice. More recently *Estasis* has been mitigated by the introduction of looser requirements in Article 23(1)(b) and (c), but despite its somewhat rigid approach it remains the main authority on agreements made in writing.[101]

5.79 However, is it necessary that the document referred to in the contract have been *received* by the person to be bound? In *Estasis* the contract was two stages removed from the jurisdiction agreement: it referred to a previous offer which itself referred to the conditions which included the jurisdiction agreement. The court seemed to say that in such a case the conditions must have been communicated to the recipient with the offer. But what about the common case where the contract is only one stage removed from the jurisdiction agreement, i.e. the contract refers to a document which includes the jurisdiction agreement? In *Credit Suisse Financial* v. *Société General*[102] the claimant made a written contract for a bond put option. The contract expressly referred to the ISDA Master Agreement which was a set of standard terms including a jurisdiction agreement in favour of England. In other words the contract was one stage removed from the jurisdiction agreement. It was argued that *Estasis* required that the ISDA Master Agreement be communicated to the defendant before the contract was made in order for Article 23 to apply. The Court of Appeal held that provided the reference was sufficiently clear possession of the document referred to was *not* required:

"To my mind the question is simply whether the express reference in the written contract in the present case amounts to a clear and precise demonstration that the clause conferring jurisdiction was the subject of a consensus between the parties ... It seems to me to be clear from the judgment in [*Estasis*] *Salotti* that the court considered that a guarantee of real consent does exist where there is an express reference in the written contract itself by way of incorporation of other written terms which include a clause conferring jurisdiction. Indeed, given such an express reference, it seems to me self-evident that the profferee of the written contract, by signing without reservation, has agreed in writing the incorporated terms (and thus the clause conferring jurisdiction) for the simple reason that the very words of the signed written contract itself are to that effect. To my mind the fact (if such it be) that Mr Mossler in the present case did not have a copy of the Master Agreement in his possession and readily available to him, or, as he said in his Affidavit, that he thought the reference to the Master Agreement was a standing clause (whatever that may mean) is neither here nor there; for in truth Mr Mossler, by signing the confirmation, did agree in writing that the terms of the Master Agreement formed part of the contract he was making."[103]

5.80 Incorporation by reference often occurs in (re)insurance contracts. In *Denby* v. *Hellenic*[104] insurance against cancellation of ferries was placed in London by brokers on a slip prepared by them and signed by underwriters which referred to the contract form being

101. Followed in *Tilly Russ* (*supra*), para. 16; *Credit Suisse* v. *Société General* [1997] CLC 168, CA; *Lafarge* v. *Fritz* [2000] 2 LLR 689, 697 (HHJ Peter Bowsher).

102. [1996] 5 Bank LR 220; [1997] CLC 168; [1997] IL Pr 165, CA.

103. *Per* Saville LJ with whom the rest of the court agreed. See also *AIG* v. *QBE* [2002] Lloyd's Rep. IR 22: "It follows from the decisions in *Estasis Salotti* v. *RÜWA* and *Crédit Suisse Financial Products* v. *Société Générale d'Enterprises* that a provision which purports to incorporate into the contract by express reference a body of terms which is clearly identified will normally satisfy the requirements of Article 17, whether or not those terms were available to the contracting parties at the time the contract was made", *per* Moore Bick J. at p. 27; *Siboti* v. *BP France* [2003] 2 Lloyd's Rep. 364.

104. [1994] 1 Lloyd's Rep. 320.

the MAR form. The MAR form included a term providing for the jurisdiction of English courts. Rix J. concluded that there was clearly a jurisdiction agreement "in writing or evidenced in writing" since the insured's own brokers had put forward the slip incorporating the well known MAR form, and it had been signed by underwriters. In *Evialis* v. *SIAT*[105] goods were insured pursuant to an open cover. The open cover was signed by the brokers for the underwriters and comprised a front page, signature page specific to the cover, general conditions and certain special agreements, Institute clauses, and a number of appendices. The cover seems to have been operated by the brokers who signed a separate certificate of cover and issued it to the insured. The general conditions included a jurisdiction agreement in favour of Italy. The certificate stated that it was issued under the open cover (calling it a policy), but also referred to various clauses including a clause providing for service of proceedings in London. The court found that the service clause referred to in the certificate had been incorporated for the purposes of Article 23(1) by the express reference in the certificate, and that it operated as a non-exclusive jurisdiction agreement. The jurisdiction agreement in the general conditions in the open cover itself was also incorporated by the reference in the certificate to the open cover, but had to read as modified so as to provide a further option as to where proceedings could be commenced. No mention is made of whether or not the insured had received a copy of the open cover before the contract was made although it appears the contract was two stages removed from the jurisdiction agreement.

5.81 In *Standard Steamship* v. *GIE*[106] the relevant insurance contract was made in emails between agents for the underwriters and the brokers for the insured. The emails referred to existing certificates of entry to the club which expressly referred to the bye-laws and rules of the club (see pp. 417–418). The contract in the emails was therefore two stages removed from the rules containing the jurisdiction agreement. Cooke J. held that by: "referring to the Certificates of Entry which themselves refer to the Club Rules in circumstances where there were existing Certificates and the contents of the Club Rules were well-known to [the brokers], including the jurisdiction agreement, the agreement to the jurisdiction agreement was made in writing or at least was evidenced in writing for the purposes of Article 23" (p. 417). The fact that the brokers knew of the content of the rules may have provided extra comfort in *Standard Steamship* but was not essential, as appeared from *Credit Suisse*.

5.82 What if, for example, the reinsurance contract is in slip form and expressly states "wording as original" or some such? Often what has happened is that the underlying insurance contract in respect of a foreign company incorporates a jurisdiction agreement in favour of the foreign insured where the risk is situated. The reinsurance may have been placed in London. In this situation the question is one of incorporation of one contract into another. It is therefore different from the situation discussed above where the contract in question refers to a document at one or two stages removed. The English courts have uniformly held that the jurisdiction agreement in the underlying insurance is not incorporated into the reinsurance contract by *general* words. In *AIG* v. *Ethniki*[107] a Greek property was insured in respect of earthquake risks by Greek insurers under a policy incorporating a jurisdiction agreement in

105. [2004] 1 Lloyd's Rep. 187, the terms are at p. 193; see also *Crédit Suisse Financial Products* v. *Société Générale d'Enterprises* [1997] CLC 168.

106. [2002] Lloyd's Rep. 407.

107. [1999] Lloyd's Rep. IR 221, 227 quoting from Colman J's judgment in *OK* v. *Vitol* [1995] 1 Lloyd's Rep. 160; affirmed [2000] Lloyd's Rep. IR 343 (CA); followed in *Assicurazione* v. *Sigorta* [2002] Lloyd's Rep. IR 480, 484; *Arig Insurance* v. *Sasa* (10.2.98 unrep.) where "policy wording as original" in the reinsurance did not incorporate the jurisdiction agreement in the underlying contract of insurance; *cf. Gan* v. *Tai Ping* [1999] Lloyd's Rep. IR 472, CA, "as original" in the reinsurance slip did not incorporate a provision for Taiwanese law in the insurance into the reinsurance.

favour of Athens. The insurers were reinsured facultatively under a slip placed in London which stated "Conditions: wording as original". Colman J. considered cases on incorporation of charterparty terms into sale contracts, and arbitration clauses and concluded that:

> "general words of incorporation will not normally be construed as wide enough to incorporate any provision from the other contract unless that provision is part of the subject-matter of that contract and not merely ancillary to it, such, for example, as an arbitration clause or a jurisdiction agreement. Such ancillary provisions will not generally be treated as relevant or germane to the rights and obligations of the parties under the incorporating contract. I do not suggest that this is an invariable rule of construction and that there can never be a case where general words will be construed as incorporating such ancillary provisions. That would depend upon the surrounding circumstances and the relationship between the parties to the incorporating contract ... such cases are likely to be extremely uncommon ..."

The Court of Appeal upheld this result and Evans LJ said that the question was: "did the parties to the contract in which the general words of incorporation appear intend that their contract should include the particular term from the other contract referred to?"[108] In *Dornoch* v. *Mauritius*[109] a reinsurance of an excess premises and transit policy stated "Conditions: to follow all terms and conditions of the primary policy together with riders and amendments applicable thereto covering the identical subject-matter and risk". The Court of Appeal held that the general words did not incorporate into the reinsurance a jurisdiction agreement in the underlying policy but merely specified the subject-matter and risk reinsured.

5.83 Even if the commercial background suggests that the parties might have been content for the jurisdiction agreement to apply it will be difficult for general words to suffice to incorporate the jurisdiction agreement from the underlying contract. In *AIG* v. *QBE,*[110] the claimant AIG had issued a policy of material damage insurance which included a jurisdiction agreement in favour of France. The reinsurance was placed by Luxembourg brokers with an English company QBE through its Paris office on terms which stated: "Conditions: all terms, clauses and conditions as original." Neither the fact the reinsurance referred to *all* terms being incorporated, nor that the centre of gravity of the reinsurance was largely located in France persuaded the judge that the jurisdiction agreement had been incorporated. The judge made the distinction between incorporating from a separate contract and from a separate document: (at p. 28):

> "The incorporation of the terms of one contract into another related contract between different parties raises rather different questions from those which arise when one party to a contract seeks to incorporate by reference a set of standard trading terms. In the former case most, but not all, of the terms of the original contract are likely to be directly relevant to the substance of the contract into which they are to be incorporated. In these circumstances it becomes necessary to decide which terms the parties intended to incorporate and which they did not. In many cases the answer will be that in the absence of specific language the court will not be able to infer with confidence that the parties did intend to incorporate any terms other than those which are germane to their own contract ... in the context of contracts of reinsurance jurisdiction agreements, being ancillary in nature and having no bearing on the definition of the risk, are not germane to the substance either of the underlying policy or of the reinsurance contract. In those circumstances general words of incorporation will not suffice to demonstrate with sufficient certainty to satisfy the requirements of Article 17 the existence of the necessary consensus."

5.84 Again, in *Prifti* v. *Musini*[111] Spanish insurers agreed a personal accident insurance which included a Spanish jurisdiction agreement, and then obtained 98% facultative reinsurance on the London market on a slip which stated (for 1999): "Full reinsurance clause: being

108. [2000] Lloyd's Rep. IR 343, 351 (CA).
109. [2006] EWCA Civ 389, CA.
110. [2002] Lloyd's Rep. IR 22.
111. [2004] Lloyd's Rep. IR 528.

a reinsurance of and warranted subject to the same terms and conditions (excluding limits and rates) as and to follow the settlements of the reassured." The fact that the insurance was in essence a "front" so that reinsurers bore the real risk and yet had agreed a Spanish jurisdiction agreement in the underlying contract did not mean that when it came to disputes relating to the reinsurance it was intended that the jurisdiction agreement should apply. The exclusion of rates and limits from the words of incorporation did not mean that everything else was meant to be incorporated: there were terms other than the jurisdiction agreement which plainly could not have been incorporated into the reinsurance and were not rates and limits.

5.85 The approach of the English courts to incorporation was summarised by Gross J. in *Siboti* v. *BP France*[112] (at p. 372):

"(i) The construction and effect of Art. 17 [now Article 23] was to be determined by reference to Community law rather than the proper law of the contract. (ii) In Community law, there was a need to be confident that the jurisdiction clause had been effectively drawn to the attention of the other contracting party so as to satisfy the requirement of genuine consensus. (iii) Community law recognised the validity of incorporation by reference, provided that the body of terms to be incorporated was clearly identified and whether or not it was available to the contracting parties at the time of entry into the contract. (iv) For the purposes of Art. 17, Community law, like English law, regarded jurisdiction clauses as ancillary to the substantive provisions of the contract. In many cases, general words of incorporation would only suffice to incorporate terms germane to the subject-matter of the contract and not terms ancillary thereto; the reason is that in the absence of specific language, the Court may not be able to conclude that the parties have demonstrated clearly and precisely the existence of a consensus to incorporate clauses which are ancillary to the subject-matter of their contract. (v) While, in Community law, the language of the contract was emphasised, rather than extrinsic factors, this did not entail ignoring the commercial background; to the contrary, in each case the court must construe the language of the contract in context and inquire whether a consensus on the subject-matter of the jurisdiction clause had been clearly and precisely demonstrated. It was, however, to be kept in mind that the commercial background could not always be relied upon to make good deficiencies in the language which the parties had chosen to use."

5.86 The result is that in reinsurance cases jurisdiction agreements in the underlying insurance will not usually be incorporated by general words of incorporation in the reinsurance. If there is no other express jurisdiction agreement in the reinsurance, actions against the reinsurer will have to be founded on some other provision of the Brussels Regulation, often that relating to the domicile of the reinsurer.

WAS THE JURISDICTION AGREEMENT EVIDENCED IN WRITING?

5.87 When is a jurisdiction agreement evidenced in writing within Article 23(1)(a)? If there was an earlier oral agreement to jurisdiction that may form the basis of a jurisdiction agreement evidenced in writing. In *Segoura* v. *Bonadakarian*[113] the German seller of goods orally agreed the sale, and on delivery handed over standard terms including the jurisdiction agreement. The jurisdiction agreement was not incorporated. The European Court of Justice seems to have proceeded on the basis that the oral contract did not refer to the standard terms or jurisdiction agreement. On that basis the mere existence of the oral contract did not help, and a later unilateral presentation of the standard terms by the seller would not suffice for Article 23, unless that was agreed in writing by the buyer. However, if there had been a trading rela-

112. [2003] 1 Lloyd's Rep. 364. Although this case concerns incorporation of a jurisdiction agreement from a charterparty into a bill of lading which has been distinguished as a "special and possibly unique" situation by the Court of Appeal in *AIG* v. *Ethniki* [2000] Lloyd's Rep. IR 343, 351, the general statement quoted was based on the judgment of Colman J. in *AIG* v. *Ethniki* and is equally applicable to reinsurance and insurance cases.
113. C-25/76, [1976] ECR I-1851.

tionship on the basis of written standard terms (including a jurisdiction agreement), and an oral contract for sale on the basis of those terms, that could have sufficed for Article 23(1)(a):

"it would be otherwise where an oral agreement forms part of a continuing trading relationship between the parties, provided also that it is established that the dealings taken as a whole are governed by the general conditions of the party giving the confirmation, and these conditions contain a clause conferring jurisdiction. Indeed, in such a context, it would be contrary to good faith for the recipient of the confirmation to deny the existence of a jurisdiction conferred by consent, even if he had given no acceptance in writing" (para. 11).

5.88 It follows that if, in *Segoura*[114] the oral contract had expressly referred to the jurisdiction agreement, and then had been followed by delivery of the standard terms, that would have sufficed for Article 23. Thus in *Tilly Russ* (*supra*) where a bill of lading was signed by the carrier, and included a jurisdiction agreement on the back, the European Court of Justice confirmed that Article 23(1)(a) would have been satisfied if there had been a prior oral agreement "expressly relating to the jurisdiction agreement" (para. 17). Given that an express reference in writing to standard terms will incorporate a jurisdiction agreement contained in the standard terms (para. 5.77 above) it should follow (although not mentioned in *Tilly Russ*) that a reference in the oral contract to the standard terms alone, if confirmed in writing, and not objected to, would suffice. The written confirmation can emanate from either party.[115]

5.89 The requirement that the written confirmation not be objected to is part of a concept of good faith which is sometimes referred to by the European Court of Justice. The idea seems to be that the jurisdiction agreement will be binding if it would be contrary to good faith for a party to deny it, and that would be the case if he had not objected to a written confirmation of a contract which included the jurisdiction agreement.[116] In *IP Metal* v. *Ruote*[117] Waller J. summarised the cases:

"there are threads running through the decisions of the European Court, to which I have been referred, to the following effect. (i) There is an expectation that a party will exercise reasonable care (see [*Estasis Salotti* v. *RUWA*] p. 1842 para. 13). (ii) It is, or can be, contrary to good faith to deny the existence of a term where for example an oral agreement forms part of a continuing trading relationship during which a term has been brought expressly to the attention of one of the parties (see *Segoura*, p. 1862, para. 11). (iii) There is an expectation that if a document is sent purporting to confirm an oral agreement, the terms should be objected to within a reasonable time if those terms are not to apply (see Sir Gordon Slynn AG (as he then was) in his advice in *Berghofer*, p. 17)."

This suggests that, if a party does object to the written confirmation of the oral contract, he will not be bound by the jurisdiction agreement for the purposes of Article 23. The effect of such an objection is still unresolved. In *Berghofer ASA*[118] the European Court of Justice simply said (at para. 15) that: "it would ... be a breach of good faith for a party who did not raise any objection subsequently to contest the application of the oral agreement. It is not necessary in this case to decide the question of whether and to what extent objections raised by the other party to the written confirmation of an oral agreement could, in an appropriate case, be taken into consideration."

5.90 However, it is not necessary that the contract which is confirmed in writing should be oral. In *Powell Duffryn* v. *Petereit*[119] the European Court of Justice held that a person who

114. *Ibid.*
115. C-221/84 *Berghoefer* v. *ASA* [1985] ECR I-2699.
116. C-221/84 *Berghoefer* v. *ASA* [1985] ECR I-2699 at [15]; *IP Metal* v. *Ruote* [1993] 2 Lloyd's Rep. 60, 66 (Waller J.), affirmed [1994] 2 Lloyd's Rep. 560, CA.; *SSQ* v. *Backes* [2002] 1 Lloyd's Rep. 465, 481 (HHJ Havelock-Allan).
117. [1993] 2 Lloyd's Rep. 60, 66; affirmed [1994] 2 Lloyd's Rep. 560, CA.
118. C-221/84, [1985] ECR I-2699.
119. C-214/89, [1992] ECR I-1745.

became a shareholder of a company could be bound by a jurisdiction agreement contained in its Articles even if he had not made an oral contract to become a shareholder beforehand. By becoming a shareholder the shareholder agreed to its Articles. Thus, in *Middle East Tankers* v. *Abu Dhabi Container Lines* it was held that a contract made by conduct to buy goods on standard terms including a jurisdiction agreement fell within Article 23(1)(a):

> "It seems to me that if a party who is willing to supply goods presents a document which contains either on the face of the document or by reference to documents which the other party already has, offering to supply goods on particular terms, including a jurisdiction agreement, and the party to whom that document is proffered orders the goods and takes delivery of the goods upon that basis, that is the clearest evidence that he is agreeing to the written terms, and in my judgment that is sufficient to satisfy Art. 17(a) [now Art. 23(1)(a)] as constituting evidence in writing".[120]

WAS THE JURISDICTION AGREEMENT IN ACCORDANCE WITH THE PRACTICES BETWEEN THE PARTIES?

5.91 As has been said the background to Article 23(1)(b) was the *Segoura* v. *Bonadakarian*[121] decision (see paras 5.44, 5.87 above). There does not appear to have been a European Court of Justice decision on this part of Article 23. It has however been applied in a few English cases. Article 23(1)(b) requires that there be practices between the parties which clearly means that there should be some evidence of an *existing* contractual relationship on terms which include a jurisdiction agreement.[122] Nor is it necessary that there was a prior oral agreement to the jurisdiction agreement: "it is immaterial whether the jurisdiction agreement was the subject of a prior oral agreement. It is enough, in order to establish consensus, that the claimant can show that by virtue of the practices adopted between the parties during their continuing trading relationship, the terms of business of one of them govern the relevant transactions and that those terms of business include an agreement conferring jurisdiction."[123]

5.92 The main question is often what evidence is required to show a practice between the parties? This can be difficult to establish. In *Standard Steamship* v. *GIE*[124] (referred to above, para. 5.81) there was little direct evidence of the previous dealings of the parties. But the underlying contract was negotiated between experienced brokers and agents for underwriters, and the judge inferred that the email exchanges between them relating to the relevant entry into the club would have been typical, and that such dealings would have been commonplace, and therefore that Article 23(1)(b) applied in the alternative to other grounds.[125]

WAS THE JURISDICTION AGREEMENT IN ACCORDANCE WITH A USAGE IN INTERNATIONAL TRADE?

5.93 Article 23(1)(c) was also introduced in 1978 it seems as a reaction to the *Segoura* v. *Bonadakarian*[126] decision, although it deals with a different problem from that identified in

120. [2002] 2 Lloyd's Rep. 643, 652, *per* HHJ Dean QC.
121. C-25/76, [1976] ECR I-1851.
122. *Middle East Tankers* v. *Abu Dhabi Container Lines* [2002] 2 Lloyd's Rep. 643, 652, HHJ Dean QC.
123. *SSQ* v. *Backes* [2002] 1 Lloyd's Rep. 465, 481 (HHJ Havelock-Allan).
124. [2002] 1 Lloyd's Rep. 407; *Consumenten/TDK*, Court D'appel de Luxembourg, 16 February 2000, ECJ database Case 2001/48 at *http://www.jura.uni-sb.de/convention-bruxelles/en/2001/48-2001* where it was held that a jurisdiction clause contained in the general conditions on the back of all the invoices which, over the years preceding the dispute, were accepted and paid without any protest, was valid under Article 21 if the parties were in an established commercial relationship, and the invoices of which payment was sought formed part of ongoing business relations between the parties.
125. At p. 418.
126. C-25/76, [1976] ECR I-1851.

that case (see para. 5.44 above). A number of questions arise. First, was the jurisdiction agreement agreed "in international trade"? In *Standard Steamship* v. *GIE*[127] Cooke J. considered that *marine* insurance fell within this requirement. That case concerned a company which had obtained employers' liability cover as a joint entrant to a P&I club. Cooke J. held that (at p. 418):

"insurance, including liability insurance in respect of maritime matters is a matter of international trade or commerce. It is so closely allied to the trading and shipping of goods that it is part and parcel of international trade and the price of goods is regularly expressed by reference to it – in terms such as 'C & F' or 'CIF'. P&I insurance is so intimately connected with the carriage of goods and commerce that it forms part of it for the purposes of Article 23, whether or not there is urgency in concluding contracts, which LDFS [the joint entrant] suggested was the rationale for the sub-paragraph. Since the cover here is akin to crew cover and involved the joint entry of LDFS on a much wider form of cover for Festival [the Member], the usage in question is one which relates to Club covers as a whole and, in my judgment is undoubtedly one which is well recognised in international trade or commerce and is certainly one of which, on the evidence, Ferrari [the broker] was well aware."

This judgment was clearly closely tied to the facts of that case, and referred to the link between the insurance and international trade in goods. But what if for example the insurance covered banking liabilities, or personal accident liabilities? Or there was a reinsurance of for example property risks in a foreign country? There does not seem to be any reason why the service of providing insurance cover in return for premium should not itself be regarded as trade or commerce, and, if it is provided internationally, why it should not be regarded as international trade or commerce.

5.94 Second, as to the "form which accords with a usage", the only relevant requirements are those of Article 23(1)(c), and any particular requirements of governing or national law relating to evidence of a binding usage are not relevant for Article 23.[128]

5.95 Third, there must be a usage.[129] Whether or not a usage exists is not determined by the governing or national law, or international trade in general, but the evidence in relation to the branch of trade or commerce in question.[130] Further:

"it is not necessary for such a course of conduct to be established in specific countries or, in particular, in all the Contracting States. The fact that a practice is generally and regularly observed by operators in the countries which play a prominent role in the branch of international trade or commerce in question can be evidence which helps to prove that a usage exists. The determining factor remains, however, whether the course of conduct in question is generally and regularly followed by operators in the branch of international trade in which the parties to the contract operate."[131]

5.96 Fourth, as to the parties' knowledge of the usage, it is enough if the parties ought to have been aware of the usage. Further, "actual or presumed awareness of a usage on the part of the parties to a contract can be made out, in particular, by showing either that the parties had previously had commercial or trade relations between themselves or with other parties operating in the sector in question, or that, in that sector, a particular course of conduct is sufficiently well known because it is generally and regularly followed when a particular type of contract is concluded, so that it may be regarded as being an established usage".[132] The

127. [2002] 1 Lloyd's Rep. 407.

128. C-159/97 *Trasporti* v. *Hugo Trumpy* [1999] ECR I-1597 at [39].

129. In the English version of the Brussels Convention the word was changed from practice to usage in 1989 (para. 5.44 above).

130. C-106/95 *MSG* v. *Le Gravieres* [1997] ECR I-911; para. 5.52 above.

131. C-159/97 *Trasporti* v. *Hugo Trumpy* [1999] ECR I-1597 at [27].

132. C-159/97 *Trasporti* v. *Hugo Trumpy* [1999] ECR I-1597 at [43].

parties who must be aware of the usage are the original parties to the contract, even if the jurisdiction agreement in the contract may be enforced by or against a third party (para. 5.71 above).[133]

(vi) Article 23 may apply even if the contract is disputed

5.97 If the defendant disputes that the contract was *ever made* Article 23 may still apply to the claim by the claimant. An example is *Benincasa* v. *Dentalkit*[134] in which Dentalkit had made a franchise contract with Benincasa relating to a shop in Germany. The contract included a jurisdiction agreement in favour of Italy. Benincasa later claimed the contract was void and started proceedings in Germany for a declaration that the contract was void. Certainty required that Article 23 applied, even though the clause might eventually be held void. A mere dispute as to whether or not the underlying contract was void would not affect Article 23 jurisdiction. This would depend on whether or not the person invoking Article 23 jurisdiction had proved the claim to a sufficient standard: see para. 5.54. (Of course it was always possible that when the court applied the applicable law to determine the true interpretation of the jurisdiction agreement the court would conclude that it was not meant to apply if the underlying contract was void. But that did not mean that Article 23 did not apply.)

5.98 On the other hand, if a claimant asserts that it never became a party to a jurisdiction agreement, and there is no evidence that it had accepted the jurisdiction agreement, Article 23 would not apply.[135]

5.99 In *Benincasa* the dispute was about the existence of the contract. What if the applicable law was English law and the evidence was that the underlying contract lacked contractual intention, or consideration, or was made as a result of duress, misrepresentation, non-disclosure or fraud? Under the applicable law the jurisdiction agreement may be void or unenforceable. The European Court of Justice has not so far had to consider such attacks on the underlying contract. In applying Article 23 should the court simply rely on the applicable law to determine whether or not the contract is enforceable in some (and, if so, which) circumstances? Or should community law be developed so that the available attacks on a jurisdiction agreement are the same across all Member States? There has been much debate among writers on this point. Some have argued that questions of validity of the jurisdiction agreement such as questions of capacity, the need for consideration, or the possibility of post-contract incorporation of terms should be determined by the applicable law.[136] Others argue that "agreement" within Article 23 is an entirely independent concept and that the European Court of Justice will have to develop in time rules relating to for instance contracts induced by duress.[137] As will be seen below, the European Court of Justice has shown itself ready to find a jurisdiction agreement exists contrary to the applicable law in some cases because of the need under Article 23 for consistency and certainty. It seems likely the court would wish to apply the same approach to all issues which could affect the validity of the jurisdiction agreement.

133. *Ibid.*, para. 42.

134. C-269/95, [1997] ECR I-3767.

135. *Andromeda* v. *O W Bunker* [2006] EWHC 777 (Comm).

136. Layton/Mercer, p. 693; Kaye, Civil Jurisdiction, p. 1073. In *Knauf* v. *Peters* [2002] 1 Lloyd's Rep. 199, 216, the Court of Appeal left open the question whether or not a jurisdiction agreement cannot be established under Article 23 unless valid under its applicable law.

137. Briggs/Rees, p. 133. See also the debate as to whether or not a dispute is a "matter relating to a contract" within Article 5(1) if the claim is that the contract is void for duress, undue influence or mistake at para. 5.159 below.

5.100 In other cases, Article 23 may be satisfied even if under the law applicable in the forum there would be no contract. For instance, in *Iveco* v. *van Hool*[138] there was an exclusive sales concession agreement between the Italian vehicle supplier and Belgian sales agent containing a jurisdiction agreement in favour of Italy. The sales concession had expired and nothing had been put in its place, although the parties continued to deal with each other. The European Court of Justice's approach was that (a) if under the applicable law the sales concession contract continued after expiry, the court then simply had to ask itself whether or not the formal requirements of Article 23 were satisfied by the expired sales concession agreement; but (b) if under the applicable law the sales concession was not renewed after expiry "it is necessary to consider whether the jurisdiction agreement, in so far as it forms part of a set of terms which were tacitly taken over from a previous written agreement that has expired and which continued to serve as the legal basis for the contractual relations between the parties, satisfies the conditions laid down by Article 17 [now Article 23]" (para. 7). It is case (b) which is interesting because the court made no reference to the applicable law. It was clearly envisaged that, even though under the applicable law the sales concession contract would not be binding any more, nevertheless the jurisdiction agreement could be binding for the purpose of Article 23. In other words, community law alone would decide whether or not there was a binding jurisdiction agreement. The court then said that the formalities could have been satisfied if after the expiry of the sales concession contract the agreement "continued to serve as the legal basis for the contractual relations" (para. 9) and one party had confirmed in writing the jurisdiction agreement or the contract containing the jurisdiction agreement and the other had not objected. This did not make it clear whether or not the confirmation had to be before the expiry of the sales concession or after, but presumably it was before since the question of expiry would not have arisen if after. However, the key point was that the court was saying that under community law there could be a binding jurisdiction agreement if there was conduct demonstrating an intention to deal on the basis of an expired contract.

5.101 Again, in *Powell Duffryn* v. *Petereit*[139] the European Court of Justice had to consider whether or not a term of the statutes of a company providing for jurisdiction amounted to a jurisdiction agreement within Article 23. The relationship between shareholders was viewed as contractual in some Member States, but as institutional, normative or *sui generis* in others. The court held that (para. 13):

> "The concept of 'agreement conferring jurisdiction' is decisive for the assignment, in derogation from the general rules on jurisdiction, of exclusive jurisdiction to the court of the Contracting State designated by the parties. Having regard to the objectives and general scheme of the Brussels Convention, and in order to ensure as far as possible the equality and uniformity of the rights and obligations arising out of the Convention for the Contracting States and persons concerned, therefore, it is important that the concept of 'agreement conferring jurisdiction' should not be interpreted simply as referring to the national law of one or other of the States concerned."

The court took the view that the links between shareholders were such that for the purposes of Article 23 "a clause conferring jurisdiction in the statutes of a company limited by shares is an agreement, within the meaning of Article 17 of the Brussels Convention, which is binding on all the shareholders" (para. 18). The result is that in Member States where the relationship between shareholders is not contractual under the national law, under community law a jurisdiction agreement in the company's statutes will be contractual for the purposes of Article 23. In this case the court then quite separately considered whether or not the juris-

138. C-313/85, [1986] ECR I-3337.
139. C-214/89, [1992] ECR I-1745

diction agreement satisfied the formalities, and held that they were met if the jurisdiction agreement was in the statutes of the company and made available publicly.

5.102 Further, as will be seen, requirements of the applicable law which put further restrictions on the existence of a jurisdiction agreement beyond those in Article 23 will not prevent there being a jurisdiction agreement within Article 23. In *Elefanten Schuh GmbH* v. *Jacqmain*[140] the European Court of Justice ruled that Article 23 lays down formal requirements for jurisdiction agreements for the purpose of ensuring legal certainty, and that Member States were therefore not free to lay down formal requirements other than those laid down by Article 23. This meant a provision of Belgian law that a contract of employment was void if not written in Dutch for the Netherlands cultural community did not prevent the jurisdiction agreement (in favour of Germany) from being effective under Article 23. Again, in *Trasporti Castelleti* v. *Trumpy*[141] the European Court of Justice confirmed that a provision of Italian law that in order for a usage to be valid the other party must be or ought to have been aware of it, and that jurisdiction agreements must be specifically agreed in writing could not affect the validity of the jurisdiction agreement under Article 23.

5.103 Accordingly, even if it is *accepted* that the underlying contract or jurisdiction agreement is not binding under the applicable law, that is by no means necessarily the end of the jurisdiction agreement for the purposes of Article 23. If the underlying contract (which includes the jurisdiction agreement) is not even a contract under national law, or has not been renewed under the applicable law, or does not comply with a requirement as to form under the applicable law, there may nevertheless be a jurisdiction agreement within Article 23 applying community law.

5. What can be done if proceedings have been commenced in breach of an exclusive jurisdiction agreement?

5.104 This depends on whether or not Article 23(1) applies to the exclusive jurisdiction agreement.

(i) If Article 23(1) applies to the exclusive jurisdiction agreement

5.105 We are here concerned with a case where the jurisdiction agreement is effective under Article 23(1). This means it is assumed that the jurisdiction agreement meets the formalities requirements of Article 23; that is, was made between parties at least one of whom is domiciled in a Member State and the courts chosen are those of a Member State (see para. 5.61 above). Cases where Article 23(1) does not confer jurisdiction are considered in para. 5.108 below). It is also assumed that the jurisdiction agreement confers jurisdiction on one court only, rather than conferring jurisdiction on a court in addition to any other court which has jurisdiction under the Brussels Regulation.

5.106 In such cases, if the jurisdiction agreement is, say, between X and Y and in favour of England, but Y commenced proceedings in France, has the English court jurisdiction to hear the English proceedings? We consider the options in detail in the section on priority of jurisdiction generally (para. 5.250). At this stage it may be helpful if we briefly summarise the options which have become much clearer since the landmark decisions of the European Court of Justice in *Gasser* v. *MISAT*[142] and *Turner* v. *Grovit*.[143] The English court would not have

140. C-150/80, [1981] EC I-1671.
141. C-159/97, [1999] ECR I-1597.
142. [2004] 1 Lloyd's Rep. 222.
143. [2004] 2 Lloyd's Rep. 169.

jurisdiction: the French court as the court first seised would have to decide whether or not it had jurisdiction, and the English court would have to stay any proceedings before it which involved the same cause of action or was related under Articles 27 or 28. Neither would the English court have power to issue an anti-suit injunction against the party bringing the proceedings in the other Member State. The French court would have to decide the issue about jurisdiction, however clearly X and Y had agreed that jurisdiction was to be given to courts of England. There is no way under the Brussels Regulation of ensuring by agreement that questions of jurisdiction are only given to the courts of one Member State or only effectively decided by that court. However, provided that the French court did determine that the jurisdiction agreement should be enforced, and dismissed the French proceedings, it is possible for X to include a claim for damages for breach of the jurisdiction agreement.[144] Clearly, if there is a danger that Y will commence proceedings in France or another Member State contrary to the jurisdiction agreement (and usually it is not possible to rule that out) X must commence English proceedings as soon as practicable (*pace* the Civil Procedure Rules) unless X is prepared for the effect of the jurisdiction agreement to be decided by a foreign court.

5.107 If the position is reversed, and the jurisdiction agreement is in favour of the courts of France, but Y has commenced proceedings in England, the English court as the court first seised would be bound to determine the issue of jurisdiction. X would apply to the English court for dismissal of the English proceedings, and in due course to the French court for damages for breach of the jurisdiction agreement.

(ii) If Article 23(1) does not apply to the jurisdiction agreement

5.108 Article 23(1) may not confer jurisdiction either because the jurisdiction agreement is in favour of the courts of a non-Member State, or because parties not domiciled in a member state have chosen the courts of a Member State.

5.109 If a jurisdiction agreement between X and Y is in favour of, say, the courts of New York, and Y starts proceedings in England, Article 23 simply does not apply.[145] It seems that the English court would have to apply its national conflicts rules: "If a court within the Community is applied to despite such an agreement, its decision on the validity of the agreement depriving it of jurisdiction must be taken in accordance with its own *lex fori*. In so far as the local rules of conflict of laws support the authority of provisions of foreign law, the latter will apply. If, when these tests are applied, the agreement is found to be invalid, then the jurisdictional provisions of the 1968 Convention become applicable."[146] In other words, if X is domiciled in England, and the jurisdiction agreement is valid under English conflicts rules, it is likely that Y will not be able to rely on Article 2 to ground a claim for jurisdiction despite the jurisdiction agreement. Even though not mentioned in Article 23, a jurisdiction agreement in favour of a non-Member State will take precedence over jurisdiction granted by, for example, Article 2. It also appears that the court may also stay proceedings in order to give effect to an exclusive jurisdiction favour of a non-Member State (para. 7.67 below).

144. *Union Discount* v. *Zoller* [2002] 1 WLR 1517, CA. It is a much more difficult question whether damages could have been claimed if the French court heard the case on the basis that the jurisdiction agreement did not apply whereas the English court would have held that it did: see Merrett, "The Enforcement of Jurisdiction Agreements Within the Brussels Regime" [2006] 55 ICLQ 315.

145. C-387/98 *Coreck Maritime* v. *Handelsveem* [2000] ECR I-9337 at [16]–[19].

146. *Schlosser*, para. 176; C-387/98 *Coreck Maritime* v. *Handelsveem* [2000] ECR I-9337 at [16]–[19]; *Konkola* v. *Coromin* [2005] 2 All ER (Comm) 637, 660, Colman J, affirmed on other points [2006] EWCA 5, CA.

5.110 If a jurisdiction agreement between X and Y who are both domiciled in New York is in favour of the courts of England, Article 23(1) does not apply.[147] Article 23(3) makes clear in this situation that no courts of any Member States other than England would have jurisdiction unless the English court declined jurisdiction.[148] The English court would apply its national conflict rules (considered in Chapter 7 below). If the English court declined jurisdiction the jurisdiction of other Member States would be governed by the Brussels Regulation.

D. IS THERE JURISDICTION BASED ON THE DEFENDANT'S DOMICILE UNDER ARTICLE 2 OR THE OPERATIONS OF A BRANCH UNDER ARTICLE 5(5)?

5.111 Article 2 of the Brussels Regulation provides:

"Article 2

1. Subject to this Regulation, persons domiciled in a member state shall, whatever their nationality, be sued in the courts of that member state.

2. Persons who are not nationals of the member state in which they are domiciled shall be governed by the rules of jurisdiction applicable to nationals of that State."

5.112 This is the fundamental rule of the Brussels Regulation. There are rules which for good reason take precedence (Articles 22, 23 and 24) and which derogate from it (Articles 5, 6 and section 3 considered below), but the default position, often referred to in the consideration of other rules, is that the defendant should be sued in the courts of his domicile.

5.113 When is a defendant "sued"? It seems likely that the concept will be autonomous in view of the need for a uniform approach across Member States. In *The Ikarian Reefer (No. 2)*[149] it was held that a claim for costs against a non party under section 51 of the Supreme Court Act 1981 following proceedings on a claim on an insurance did not amount to "suing" the defendant since it did not involve "pursuing a substantive cause of action" (p. 137).

5.114 What is the domicile of the defendant? In the case of a company Article 60 provides a single general definition for the purposes of the Brussels Regulation[150]:

"Article 60

1. For the purposes of this Regulation, a company or other legal person or association of natural or legal persons is domiciled at the place where it has its: (a) statutory seat, or (b) central administration, or (c) principal place of business.

2. For the purposes of the United Kingdom and Ireland "statutory seat" means the registered office or, where there is no such office anywhere, the place of incorporation or, where there is no such place anywhere, the place under the law of which the formation took place."[151]

147. C-387/98 *Coreck Maritime* v. *Handelsveem* [2000] ECR I-9337 at [16]–[19].

148. *Schlosser*, para. 177.

149. [2000] 1 Lloyd's Rep. 129.

150. The corresponding requirements for the domicile of a company for the Brussels and Lugano Conventions are similar and appear from the Civil Jurisdiction and Judgments Act 1982, s.42.

151. Article 22(2) confers mandatory jurisdiction in relation to proceedings relating to the constitution of a company and other bodies, or the validity of decisions (as to which see para. 5.12 above), and, to avoid the problem of there being more than one domicile which is possible under Article 60, special provision for domicile is made by Article 22(2) and in England SI 2001/3929, para. 10: "(1) The following provisions of this paragraph determine where a company, legal person or association has its seat for the purposes of Article 22(2) (which confers exclusive jurisdiction over proceedings relating to the formation or dissolution of such bodies, or to the decisions of their organs). (2) A company, legal person or association has its seat in the United Kingdom if and only if – (a) it was incorporated or formed under the law of a part of the United Kingdom; or (b) its central management and control is exercised in the United Kingdom. (3) Subject to sub-paragraph (4), a company, legal person or association has its seat in a Regulation State other than the United Kingdom if and only if – (a) it was incorporated or formed under the law of that state; or (b) its central management and control is exercised in that state. (4) A company, legal person or association shall not be regarded as having its seat in a Regulation State other than the United Kingdom if – (a) it has

5.115 In the case of an individual, partnership or other party the court seised of the matter must apply its "internal law" under Article 59. In other words, unlike the position in relation to companies, there has been no harmonisation of the laws of Member States in relation to domicile. The requirements of English law for the purposes of the Brussels Regulation[152] appear from the Civil Jurisdiction and Judgments Order 2001[153]:

"Domicile of individuals (section 41)
… (2) An individual is domiciled in the United Kingdom if and only if –
(a) he is resident in the United Kingdom; and
(b) the nature and circumstances of his residence indicate that he has a substantial connection with the United Kingdom.
(3) Subject to sub-paragraph (5), an individual is domiciled in a particular part of the United Kingdom if and only if –
(a) he is resident in that part; and
(b) the nature and circumstances of his residence indicate that he has a substantial connection with that part.
(4) An individual is domiciled in a particular place in the United Kingdom if and only if he –
(a) is domiciled in the part of the United Kingdom in which that place is situated; and
(b) is resident in that place.
(5) An individual who is domiciled in the United Kingdom but in whose case the requirements of sub-paragraph (3)(b) are not satisfied in relation to any particular part of the United Kingdom shall be treated as domiciled in the part of the United Kingdom in which he is resident.
(6) In the case of an individual who –
(a) is resident in the United Kingdom, or in a particular part of the United Kingdom; and
(b) has been so resident for the last three months or more,
the requirements of sub-paragraph (2)(b) or, as the case may be, sub-paragraph (3)(b) shall be presumed to be fulfilled unless the contrary is proved.
(7) An individual is domiciled in a state other than a Regulation State if and only if –
(a) he is resident in that state; and
(b) the nature and circumstances of his residence indicate that he has a substantial connection with that state."

1. Does the dispute arise out of the operations of branch, agency or other establishment: Article 5(5)?

5.116 Under Article 5(5) a person domiciled in a Member State may in another Member State, be sued "as regards a dispute arising out of the operations of a branch, agency or other establishment, in the courts for the place in which the branch, agency or other establishment is situated". In selecting the activity of the branch rather than a specific cause of action as the link between the dispute and the jurisdiction Article 5(5) differs from the other grounds of special jurisdiction under Article 5.[154] The purpose of Article 5(5) is to treat the place where a branch, agency or other establishment carries on business with third parties in a similar way to the treatment of the domicile of the defendant under Article 2.[155] The justification for this is the likelihood of a particularly close link between the dispute and the State in which the branch, agency or other establishment is established rather than that where the defendant is domiciled,[156] although the Article will apply even if that is not the case. As will be seen, in

its seat in the United Kingdom by virtue of sub-paragraph (2)(a); or (b) it is shown that the courts of that other state would not regard it for the purposes of Article 22(2) as having its seat there." Under Article 9(2) an insurer may be deemed domiciled in the Member State where it has a branch, agency or other establishment (see para. 6.16).

152. The requirements for the Brussels and Lugano Conventions are similar and appear from Brussels Convention Article 53 and the Civil Jurisdiction and Judgments Act 1982, Part V.

153. SI 2001/3929.

154. *Durbeck* v. *Den Norske Bank* [2003] QB 1160, CA, at [42].

155. *Ibid.*, at [43].

156. C-33/78 *Somafer* v. *Saar-Ferngass* [1978] ECR I-2183 at [7].

essence Article 5(5) requires that the defendant has set up or appeared to set up a branch office or something very like it, in that the defendant can control the business of the branch, agency or other establishment, and the branch, agency or other establishment appears to the claimant to be able to deal with business on behalf of the defendant.

5.117 There are two key requirements for Article 5(5) to apply: there must be a branch, agency or other establishment, and the dispute must arise out of the operations of the branch. The concepts of branch, etc, and operations have an autonomous meaning under community law because of the need for there to be a uniform definition across the Member States.[157] It is for the national court seised of the matter to decide as a matter of fact whether or not the requirements of Article 5(5) have been met in fact.

5.118 The wording of Article 5(5) makes it clear that where it applies it serves to allocate jurisdiction to the courts of the place where the branch is located, so that if, for example, that place is London there is no room to apply the provisions allocating jurisdiction within the UK. It is also clear that the branch must be that of the defendant, and the position of the claimants is irrelevant in this respect.[158]

5.119 Article 5(5) only applies where the defendant is domiciled in a Member State: where the defendant is for example domiciled in the USA jurisdiction will be determined under Article 4 by the conflicts rules in the court seised even if it has a branch in a Member State. However, in the case of an insurer section 3 of the Regulation in effect applies Article 5(5) regardless of where the defendant is domiciled: Article 9(2).[159]

(i) What is a branch?

5.120 The cases in the European Court of Justice have concerned sales agencies. In *de Bloos* v. *Bouyer* the grantor of an exclusive sales agency was not liable to proceedings in the courts of the location of the sales agent because the business of the agent was not subject to the "direction and control of the parent body".[160] Even though the grantor would presumably have had some rights of direction in relation to the business the subject of the exclusive sales agency these could not be sufficient in the view of the European Court of Justice. The same essential characteristics applied to an "other establishment" as to a branch or agency.[161] It was also emphasised in *Somafer* v. *Saar-Ferngas*[162] that it was not enough for the branch to have a local contact address, there needed to be a place of business with an appearance of permanency and a local management. In *Blanckaert* v. *Willems*[163] the court held that Article 5(5) did not apply in a case of an independent commercial agent "who merely negotiates business, inasmuch as his legal status leaves him basically free to arrange his own work and decide what proportion of his time to devote to the interests of the undertaking which he agrees to represent and whom that undertaking may not prevent from representing at the same time several firms competing in the same manufacturing or marketing sector, and who, moreover, merely transmits orders to the parent undertaking without being involved in either their terms or their execution". On the other hand, the appearance of being a branch or agency will suffice even

157. *Ibid.*, at [8].
158. *Jenard*, 1979 OJ C.59/1, 26; *New Hampshire* v. *Strabag* [1990] 2 Lloyd's Rep. 61, 68 (Potter J.); approved *New Hampshire* v. *Strabag* [1992] 1 Lloyd's Rep. 361 (CA) where the reinsurance had been written by an underwriter in the London branch office of the US claimant reinsurer.
159. *Jenard*, 1979 OJ C.59/1, 26.
160. C-14/76 *De Bloos* v. *Bouyer* [1976] ECR I-1497 at [20].
161. *Ibid.*, at [21].
162. C-33/78, [1978] ECR I-2183 at [12].
163. C-139/80, [1981] ECR I-137, at [13].

if the parent concern and branch are independent. In *Schotte* v. *Parfums Rothschild*[164] the claimant had entered into contracts with a French company for goods but all its negotiations and post contract dealings were with the German company. The German company bore a similar name to the defendant. This was presumably no accident since the two companies had common management although it was apparently accepted that technically the German company was not a branch or agent. The European Court of Justice found that nevertheless the German company was an "establishment" of the French company. This was on the basis that even if the entity in question was independent it sufficed if the entity in question acted like a branch or agent in its dealings with third parties. In this case the German company had negotiated contracts in the name of the French company and was described as being used by the latter as "an extension of itself" (para. 7). In *Lloyd's Register of Shipping* v. *Société Campenon Bernard*[165] the court concluded that a branch is "an entity capable of being the principal, or even exclusive, interlocutor for third parties in the negotiation of contracts".

5.121 It is therefore apparent that the requirements for Article 5(5) to apply are exacting: the branch must have been established with a degree of permanency and local management, and where contracts are concerned the branch must be, or appear to be capable of itself negotiating contracts with the third party rather than acting as a letterbox. But the branch must also still be subject to the overriding direction and control of the defendant.[166] It seems clear from this that Article 5(5) cannot apply to the ordinary situation in which, for example, a reinsured in Germany instructs a London broker to place business with London reinsurers. The brokers are clearly agents of the reinsured, but that agency alone does not make them subject to the overall direction and control of the reinsured in the conduct of their business; usually the reinsured will be one of many independent clients of the brokers and the comments in *Blanckaert* will apply.[167] Thus in *New Hampshire* v. *Strabag*[168] Potter J had no difficulty in deciding that Article 5(5) did not apply to a claim against a German reinsured which had employed London brokers to place business in London with the branch office of the claimant.

5.122 In the (re)insurance context these cases would have bearing on a possible claim by an assured in the courts at the location of, for example, a branch office for the insurer or perhaps an underwriting agent for the reinsurer.

164. C-218/86, [1987] ECR I-4905.

165. C-439/83, [1995] ECR I-961 at [19].

166. See also the summary of the main European Court of Justice cases at *Jenard/Moller*, pp. 99–100 including this summary of *Somafer*: "The Court has given an autonomous interpretation to the concepts of 'operations of a branch, agency or other establishment' – (a) the concept of branch, agency or other establishment implies a place of business which has the appearance of permanency, such as the extension of a parent body, has a management and is materially equipped to negotiate business with third parties so that the latter, although knowing that there will if necessary be a legal link with the parent body, the head office of which is abroad, do not have to deal directly with such parent body but may transact business at the place of business constituting the extension; (b) the concept of 'operations' comprises – (1) actions relating to rights and contractual or non-contractual obligations concerning the management properly so-called of the agency, branch or other establishment itself such as those concerning the situation of the building where such entity is established or the local engagement of staff to work there, (2) actions relating to undertakings which have been entered into at the above mentioned place of business in the name of the parent body and which must be performed in the Contracting State where the place of business is established, (3) actions concerning non-contractual obligations in which the branch, agency or other establishment has engaged at the place in which it is established on behalf of the parent body."

167. It is plain from *Schlosser*, para. 150, that it was intended that neither Article 5(5) nor Article 9(2) should apply to "an independent insurance broker of the type common in the United Kingdom".

168. [1990] 2 Lloyd's Rep. 61, 68 (Potter J.); approved *New Hampshire* v. *Strabag* [1992] 1 Lloyd's Rep. 361 (CA). In *Cerbi SA/MBJ International,* 17 November 1999, Case 2001/42 on ECJ database at *http://www.jura.uni-sb.de/convention-bruxelles/en/2001/42-2001* the Corte di Cassazione in Italy held that Article 5(5) did not apply where an Italian insured had placed business via an Italian producing broker, and Lloyd's brokers, with Lloyd's insurers.

(ii) What are the operations?

5.123 Article 5(5) refers to a dispute arising "out of the operations" of the branch. This requirement establishes the nexus between the dispute and the activities carried on by the branch.[169] In other words, not all disputes involving a branch will fall within Article 5(5). However, the operations need not take place in the country in which the branch is established, whether the claim is in contract or tort.[170] Where the claim is in contract the nexus can be derived from the negotiations between the claimant and the branch.[171] Where the claim is in tort the court will consider all the circumstances giving rise to the dispute.[172]

E. IS THERE JURISDICTION BASED ON MATTERS RELATING TO A CONTRACT UNDER ARTICLE 5(1)?

1. Introduction

5.124 Article 5(1) provides:

"A person domiciled in a member state may, in another member state, be sued:

1. (a) in matters relating to a contract, in the courts for the place of performance of the obligation in question;

(b) for the purpose of this provision and unless otherwise agreed, the place of performance of the obligation in question shall be:

– in the case of the sale of goods, the place in a member state where, under the contract, the goods were delivered or should have been delivered,

– in the case of the provision of services, the place in a member state where, under the contract, the services were provided or should have been provided;

(c) if subparagraph (b) does not apply then subparagraph (a) applies."

5.125 Article 5(1) confers jurisdiction in matters relating to contract and is thus potentially one of the main sources of jurisdiction in reinsurance cases (along with jurisdiction agreements under Article 23, and the default jurisdiction under Article 2). Many reinsurance cases concern claims under Article 5(1) for negative declarations by reinsurers concerned to establish jurisdiction in courts other than those of the domicile of the reinsured.

5.126 The need for uniformity in relation to concepts used in the Brussels Regulation is seen again in the autonomous definition given to matters relating to a contract. The result is no less than the construction from scratch of the fundamentals of a law of contract within community law. In the reinsurance context the difficulties are compounded because reinsurance is not well represented in EU case law. Particular areas of debate include the following:

(1) The application of Article 5(1) to claims involving subrogation, contribution and assignment has barely been scratched.

(2) One of the main questions, yet to be resolved, is whether Article 5(1)(b) applies to reinsurance. Article 5(1)(b) in essence provides an autonomous definition of the place for performance in relation to contracts for services. If it applied it would confer jurisdiction on the place where the claims were payable. If Article 5(1)(b) does apply

169. C-33/78 *Somafer* v. *Saar-Ferngass* [1978] ECR I-2183 at [11]; *Durbeck* v. *Den Norske Bank* [2003] QB 1160, CA, at [40].

170. C-439/93 *Lloyd's Register of Shipping* v. *Société Campenon Bernard* [1995] ECR I-961 at [20] (departing from C-33/78 *Somafer* v. *Saar-Ferngass* [1978] ECR I-2183 at [13]); *Durbeck* v. *Den Norske Bank* [2003] QB 1160, CA, at [40]–[46].

171. *Durbeck* v. *Den Norske Bank* [2003] QB 1160, CA, at [40].

172. *Ibid.*, at [46].

to reinsurance many of the questions referred to below would disappear and the usage of the Article could be expected to diminish. However, it is suggested that it does not apply to reinsurance (para. 5.179) and that the general provisions of Article 5(1) therefore apply.

(3) A major question is whether or not a claim by reinsurers to avoid based on non-disclosure or misrepresentation is a matter relating to a contract within Article 5(1). Here, at least, we have the authority of the House of Lords that such a claim is a matter relating to a contract, but the issue has not been the subject of a decision of the European Court of Justice and must be regarded as debateable, although it is suggested that the decision of the Lords should be followed.

5.127 It is noticeable that the European Court of Justice has to a large extent sought to make the rules mechanistic and therefore easy to apply even if the results are not in accordance with the object of Article 5(1). The court has sought to avoid fragmentation of disputes, and to interpret the rules in a way that means that where possible only one court will have jurisdiction, even if that means having to identify the principal obligation or the principal place for performance from among a number of candidates. On the other hand, the court has determinedly resisted attempts to incorporate *forum non conveniens* type judgments into the application of Article 5(1), and has also shown itself unafraid to say that if a particular claim does not comfortably fit Article 5(1) without stretching, the Article simply does not apply, and the claimant must resort to the general jurisdiction under Article 2.

5.128 We start by considering the general effect of Article 5(1), its development, its place in the hierarchy of the Brussels Regulation, and its objectives. We then consider how Article 5(1) is to be applied. The main questions are:

(1) Is this a matter relating to a contract?
(2) What is the obligation in question?
(3) What is the place for performance?

Although it is necessary to consider each question in turn it will be found that the answers are often inter-dependent; for example, whether or not the matter relates to a contract may well depend on what is the obligation in question.[173]

(i) General effect of Article 5(1)

5.129 Article 5(1) operates where the place for performance is within a Member State.[174] If the place for performance is not a Member State the Article cannot apply since it only confers jurisdiction on the courts of Member States. Where it operates Article 5(1) confers jurisdiction not just on a jurisdiction but on the courts for the place where the contract was to be performed. The effect is that if the contract was to be performed in London, Article 5(1) confers jurisdiction on the courts for England without having to have recourse to the Civil Jurisdiction and Judgments Act 1982 to allocate jurisdiction within the UK.[175]

5.130 Article 5(1) allocates jurisdiction for the obligation in question, not to all obligations arising from a contract. Consequently, unless the court is able to identify a principal and accessory obligation which are lumped together for Article 5(1), the result will be that the Article may allocate jurisdiction to different jurisdictions.[176]

5.131 As has been said, the jurisdiction conferred by Article 5(1) is additional to any other jurisdiction conferred by the Brussels Regulation. The claimant need not use it.

173. See, e.g., *Kleinwort Benson* v. *Glasgow* [1999] 1 AC 153, and para. 5.160 below.
174. C-32/88 *Six Constructions* v. *Humbert* [1989] ECR I-341 at [19].
175. *Jenard*, 1979 OJ C.59/1, 22.
176. See C-420/97 *Leathertex* v. *Bodetex* [1999] ECR I-6747, and para. 5.183 below.

(ii) Development of Article 5(1)

5.132 Article 5(1) originally provided that "a person domiciled in a Contracting State may, in another Contracting State, be sued: 1. in matters relating to a contract, in the courts for the place of performance of the obligation in question". The Jenard report made clear that the obligation in question was intended to be the obligation on which the claim was based, and emphasised that the intention was to avoid a situation in which a number of courts had jurisdiction over a matter relating to a contract.[177] In 1978 upon the accession of the UK to the Brussels Convention, versions of Article 5(1) in other languages were amended so as to make clear that the obligation in question was the obligation on which the claim was based.[178] In 1988 when the Lugano Convention was agreed Article 5(1) was, on the request of the EFTA states, amended to make specific provision for contracts of employment (a course which had been considered and rejected in 1968).[179] When the Brussels Regulation came into force in 2002 Article 5(1) was amended so as to add sub-paragraphs (b) and (c) and to provide an autonomous definition of the place for performance of the obligation in question in the case of contracts for sale of goods and the provision of services. The result is that the terms of Article 5(1) of the Brussels Regulation are very different from those of the Brussels and Lugano Conventions.

(iii) Objectives of Article 5(1)

5.133 A number of different themes are frequently referred to by the European Court of Justice in construing Article 5(1) (in its different forms) which are discussed further below:

(1) The freedom of choice in Article 5(1) was introduced "in view of the existence in certain well-defined cases of a particularly close relationship between the dispute and the court" which is the court for the place for performance of the obligation in question.[180]
(2) A major purpose of Article 5(1) is to promote certainty as to the applicable jurisdiction,[181] or as it has been put Article 5(1) "should be interpreted in such a way as to enable a normally well-informed defendant reasonably to foresee before which courts, other than those of the State in which he is domiciled, he may be sued'.[182]
(3) The regulation should be construed so as to avoid as far as possible the multiplication of the bases of jurisdiction in relation to one and the same legal relationship.[183]
(4) Because the special jurisdiction under Article 5 derogates from the general jurisdiction based on domicile that jurisdiction must be "interpreted restrictively"[184] or, as it has been put, "must not lead to an interpretation going beyond the situations envisaged by the [Brussels Regulation]".[185]

177. *Jenard*, p. 23.
178. For example, in French Article 5(1) became "*en matière contractuelle, devant le tribunal du lieu où l'obligation qui sert de base à la demande a été ou droit être exécutée*". The reason was to bring the texts into line with other language texts which were more specific: *Jenard*, 1979 OJ C.59/1, 111; *Schlosser*, para. 133; C-420/97 *Leathertex* v. *Bodetex* [1999] ECR I-6747 at [32]; see Layton and Mercer, p. 424 for other language versions.
179. *Jenard*, 1979 OJ C.59/1, 24; *Jenard and Moller*, para. 36.
180. C-12/76 *Tessili* v. *Dunlop* [1976] ECR I-1473 at [13]; C-34/82 *Martin Peters* v. *Zuid* [1983] ECR I-987 at [11]; C-266/85 *Shenevai* v. *Kresicher* [1987] ECR I-239 at [18].
181. C-266/85 *Shenevai* v. *Kresicher* [1987] ECR I-239 at [17]; C-26/91 *Handte* v. *TMCS* [1992] ECR I-3967 at [12]; C-288/92 *Custom Made* v. *Stawa* [1994] ECR I-2913 at [15]; *Kleinwort Benson* v. *Glasgow* [1999] 1 AC 153, 164, 171.
182. C-440/97 *GIE Groupe Concorde* v. *Panjan* [1999] ECR I-6307, para. 24; C-256/00 *Besix* v. *WABAG* [2002] ECR I-1699 at [26], [54].
183. C-125/92 *Mulox* v. *Geels* [1993] ECR I-4075 at [11], [21]; C-256/00 *Besix* v. *WABAG* [2002] ECR I-1699 at [27]; and *Jenard*, 1979 OJ C.59/1, 22.
184. C-189/87 *Kalfelis* v. *Schroder* [1988] ECR I-5565 at [19].
185. C-26/91 *Handte* v. *TMCS* [1992] ECR I-3967 at [14].

(iv) What approach should be adopted to decide if a claim is within Article 5(1)?

5.134 Whether or not a dispute is a matter relating to a contract depends on an independent concept of community law "which for the purposes of the [Brussels Regulation] must be interpreted by reference chiefly to the system and objectives of the [Brussels Regulation] in order to ensure that it is fully effective".[186]

5.135 The obligation in question has to be determined according to community law. But as the European Court of Justice has pointed out this does not mean that the applicable law is irrelevant. "Some of the questions which might arise in this context, such as identification of the contractual obligation forming the basis of proceedings, as well as the principal obligation where there are several obligations, could hardly be resolved without reference to the applicable law."[187] The place which is the principal place for performance is a matter of the applicable law, as well as the obligation which is the principal obligation and therefore the obligation in question. The choice of applicable law falls to be determined under the Rome Convention and therefore ought to yield the same result in whichever Member State it arises (Chapter 9 below).

5.136 The place for performance has to be determined by the national law of the court seised in accordance with its conflicts rules; i.e. according to the applicable law as determined by the court seised.[188]

5.137 The burden is on the claimant to show that there is a good arguable case in relation to the obligation alleged by him.[188a]

2. Is this a matter relating to contract?

(i) Introduction

5.138 Is a claim in respect of a reinsurance contract a matter relating to contract for the purposes of Article 5(1)? In an ordinary case of a claim on a reinsurance contract which is denied by reinsurers on grounds say that the loss has not occurred, the question will be whether or not reinsurers are bound by the contract to pay the claim. The dispute is clearly a matter relating to a contract. In this example no-one disputes the contract. In other cases reinsurers may bring the claim, seeking a negative declaration on the ground that the loss did not occur. The result is the same: the dispute is clearly a matter relating to a contract. As will be seen, where a negative declaration is sought the obligation in question is that upon which the reinsurers rely to establish that they are not liable under the contract. The reinsurers rely on the obligation only to pay where a loss occurred, and the dispute is a matter relating to a contract. The same would apply if reinsurers denied liability for example on grounds that the reinsurance excluded the claim.

5.139 More difficulty arises, however, where the existence and validity of the contract are disputed. In particular we consider below questions which have arisen as to whether or not Article 5(1) applies where:

(1) both parties accept that a contract apparently made was not made or is void;
(2) the claimant asserts that a contract apparently made was not made or is void, for example for illegality, duress or undue influence;

186. C-34/82 *Martin Peters* v. *Zuid* [1983] ECR I-987 at [10]; C-9/87 *Arcado* v. *Haviland* [1988] ECR I-1539 at [10]; C-26/91 *Handte* v. *TMCS* [1992] ECR I-3967 at [10].

187. C-440/97 *GIE Groupe Concorde* v. *Panjan* [1999] ECR I-6307 at [26].

188. *Ibid.*, at [27].

188a. *Canada Trust* v. *Stolzenberg (No. 2)* [1998] 1 WLR 547, CA; [2002] 1 AC 1, HL; para. 5.56 above.

(3) the claimant asserts that a contract apparently made was voidable; for example reinsurers seek a negative declaration on the ground a reinsurance was avoided for non-disclosure or misrepresentation.

Apart from these questions the other major questions in relation to what is a matter relating to a contract concern third parties.

(ii) What is a contract?

5.140 On the basic question of what is a contract where that is in dispute for the purposes of Article 5(1) there is comparatively little guidance from the European Court of Justice.[189] First, it has to be remembered that this question is a question of characterisation which depends ultimately on community law rather than any national law (para. 5.134). That said, in order to undertake the characterisation of the matter at the level of community law, it is still necessary to analyse the legal relationship between the parties under the law governing that relationship applying the conflicts rules of the court seised. In other words, any characterisation of the relationship under, say, English law, would not determine the characterisation under community law, but the incidents of the relationship under English law would be relevant to the characterisation under community law.[190]

5.141 Probably the leading case on what is a matter relating to a contract is *Handte* v. *TMCS*[191] where a sub-buyer claimed against the manufacturer with whom the sub-buyer had no direct contract. Such a direct action was apparently classified as contractual under French law.[192] The European Court of Justice held that the notion of what is a matter relating to a contract within Article 5(1) is an autonomous one, and that it could not apply if there is no "obligation freely assumed by one party towards another".[193] The court's approach was in essence to give Article 5(1) a narrow interpretation since it is a derogation from the general principle that a defendant should be sued in his country of domicile, and because of the need for certainty. The court would not stretch Article 5(1) beyond what was clearly envisaged by the Article. That meant there had to be in some sense a genuine assumption of an obligation in contract.

5.142 The court also stated that (para. 19):

"the application of the special jurisdictional rule laid down by Article 5(1) of the Convention to an action brought by a sub-buyer of goods against the manufacturer is not *foreseeable* by the latter and is therefore incompatible with the principle of legal certainty. Apart from the fact that the manufacturer has no contractual relationship with the sub-buyer and undertakes no contractual obligation towards that buyer, whose *identity and domicile* may, quite reasonably, be unknown to him, it appears that in the great majority of Contracting States the liability of a manufacturer towards a sub-buyer for defects in the goods sold is not regarded as being of a contractual nature" [emphasis added].

The references to the claim by the sub-buyer not being foreseeable, and his identity and domicile being unknown, seem merely to be put forward by the court as additional reasons

189. See further Plender, *The European Contracts Convention* (2nd ed., 2001) p. 52, who concludes that the comparative law of contract in Member States indicates certain commonly accepted elements in the definition of a contract: contract implies a voluntary agreement giving rise to obligations enforceable by law, and consideration is not essential to regard an obligation as contractual although the lack of it may go to validity.

190. See further para. 9.13 as to what is a contract under the Rome Convention.

191. C-26/91, [1992] ECR I-3967.

192. Para. 6 of the judgment; and see further para. 20 of the opinion of Advocate General Jacob who described the claim under French law as based on an assignment from the direct buyer to the sub-buyer, alternatively as based on subrogation. Since the decision in *Frahuil* it would apparently be necessary to ask whether or not the manufacturer authorised the direct buyer to enter into an agreement with the sub-buyer which led to the claim in subrogation: see para. 5.147 below.

193. C-26/91 *Handte* v. *TMCS* [1992] ECR I-3967 at [15].

why the obligation was not freely assumed on the facts of that case. However, in theory there does not seem to be any reason why a party may (a) decide not freely to assume an obligation towards a third party even if he knows the identity and domicile of the third party, or, conversely, (b) freely to assume an obligation towards a third party even though he does not know his identity and domicile.

5.143 The effect of *Handte* was to exclude from Article 5(1) cases where an obligation was imposed by the applicable law towards a third party unless in some sense the party to be bound had intended to assume the obligation.[194]

5.144 In *Handte* the European Court of Justice did not treat a dispute as a matter relating to a contract although the claim was classified by the applicable law as contractual. In *Reunion* v. *Spliethoff*[195] it was not clear that national law classified the claim as contractual. Underwriters were subrogated to the claims of the insured who was the consignee of damaged goods, and sought to bring claims against the physical carrier and master as representative of the owners and charterers of the vessel, neither of whom had signed the bill of lading and with whom there was therefore no direct contractual relationship. The European Court of Justice held that there was no "obligation freely assumed" by the defendants to the consignee. Since the action was not a matter relating to a contract it was therefore a claim in tort under Article 5(3).[196] This claim to jurisdiction therefore failed on the ground that the liability of the defendants to the insured was not an obligation freely assumed (however, it also appears that the insurer's claim would have failed even if the defendants had freely assumed an obligation to the insured because a claim based on a right of subrogation is not a matter relating to a contract (see para. 5.146 below)). On the other hand there are examples of cases where there has under community law been a matter relating to a contract even if there would be no contract under the applicable law.[197]

(iii) Claims involving third parties

5.145 A third party may become entitled to enforce a reinsurance contract under English law by reason for instance of novation, subrogation, or assignment, or become entitled to payment by way of contribution. Does Article 5(1) give jurisdiction in such cases? Novation seems straightforward. Under English law, in the case of a novation of a reinsurance to a new party,[198] the new party enters into a fresh contract with the original parties to the contract. The parties to the new contract would have freely assumed obligations to each other, and Article 5(1) would apply to the new contract.

SUBROGATION

5.146 In *Reunion* referred to above (para. 5.144) the European Court of Justice denied a subrogation claim made by the third party to the original contract on the basis that an obligation to the party had not been freely assumed. However, it should not be assumed a claim made by way of subrogation may never fall within Article 5(1). In 1995 in *Atlas Shipping* v. *Suisse*

194. Compare the enforcement by third parties of jurisdiction agreements (see para. 5.71).

195. C-51/97, [1999] ECR I-6511; see also C-167/00 *VKI* v. *Henkel* [2002] ECR I-8111.

196. At para. 24.

197. C-34/82 *Martin Peters* v. *Zuid* [1983] ECR I-987 at [13] (obligations owed by association to one member were contractual for Article 5(1) even if not under the applicable law): C-27/02 *Engler* v. *Janus* [2005] ECR I-481 (unilateral offer letter could create an obligation freely assumed within Article 5(1) if accepted by recipient).

198. As to novation generally, see *Chitty on Contracts* (29th Ed., 2004) para. 19-085, and in relation to insurance contracts, see Clarke, para. 6-1.

Atlantique[199] Rix J. resisted the notion that *Handte* insisted on privity of contract for Article 5(1) to apply. That was an unusual claim by brokers or sub-brokers acting for the sellers on the sale of a ship against buyers who had deducted from the sale price commission payable to the claimants but not paid it over. The claim was that the buyers were trustees of the commission because of the terms of the sale contract between seller and buyer. Rix J. held that the claim was a matter relating to a contract, essentially because (p. 193) "the obligation being enforced, albeit with the aid of equitable principles, is the contractual obligation owed by the buyers to the sellers to pay the brokers". The judge distinguished *Handte* principally on the ground that the buyers freely assumed the obligation towards the claimants, even if they did not know that English law would give the claimants a direct claim (p. 194):

"It seems to me that it is too narrow a reading of [*Handte*] to say that it insists upon privity of contract between the parties to the litigation. If it did, then not even the legal assignee of a contract could bring a claim to enforce the contract and maintain jurisdiction within Art. 5(1). It has to be borne in mind that the decision in *Handte* is about the problems which arise out of a chain of contracts. In such a case, because the sub-buyer and the manufacturer are not in direct contractual relations, there is no obligation freely entered into between the parties; on the contrary, each may have entered into contracts with their direct contractual partners on different terms. Moreover, the identity and domicile of the ultimate sub-buyer may be entirely unknown to the manufacturer, so that he cannot predict the court in which he may be sued. In these circumstances the jurisdictional connecting factor of the place of performance may become an arbitrary touchstone. None of this reasoning applies to the case before me of a contract between A and B to pay C. There is only one contractual obligation in question; there is privity between the parties to it; the obligation was freely entered into by those parties; although neither of them may have realised that English law would give to the plaintiffs an independent right to enforce the buyers' promise to the sellers to pay the brokers, they both knew the identity and domicile of the plaintiffs and, *ex hypothesi*, both intended to benefit them by means of the contracted payment. Moreover, both parties to the contract will also be parties to the litigation, in the promissee sellers' case either as plaintiffs or as co-defendants. In these circumstances the fact that performance of the obligation is to take place in the brokers' domicile is exactly what the buyers must have anticipated, and the appropriateness of there being jurisdiction in the courts of the country of that domicile is consistent with the rationale behind Art. 5(1)...."

5.147 The European Court of Justice confirmed that *Handte* did not mean that no claim made by or against a third party could come within Article 5(1) in *Frahuil* v. *Assitalia*[200] decided in 2004. A French company, Frahuil, imported goods into Italy and engaged Vegetoil as forwarding agent to carry out customs clearance. Assitali gave a guarantee to the Italian authorities in respect of the payment by Vegetoil of customs duties, and, when Vegetoil failed to pay those sums Assitalia paid the authorities and made a claim in the Italian courts by way of subrogation against Frahuil for reimbursement under two specific provisions of the Italian Civil Code. The European Court of Justice held that since Frahuil was not a party to the guarantee, the subrogation claim could not be a matter relating to a contract within Article 5(1). Frahuil was apparently not to be treated as having freely assumed the obligation which was imposed by Italian law.

5.148 However, the court did say the result might have been different if Frahuil had *authorised* Vegetoil to enter the guarantee with Assitalia:

"it appears that Frahuil instructed Vegetoil to carry out the formalities of customs clearance. It is therefore a matter for the referring court to examine the legal relationship between Frahuil and Vegetoil in order to establish whether that relationship permitted Vegetoil, on behalf of Frahuil, *to enter into a contract such as the contract of guarantee* in question in the main proceedings.... Article 5(1) of the Convention must be interpreted as meaning that 'matters relating to a contract' do not cover the obligation which a guarantor who paid customs duties under a guarantee obtained by the forwarding agent seeks to enforce in legal proceedings by way of subrogation to the rights of the customs authorities and

199. [1995] 2 Lloyd's Rep. 188.
200. C-265/02, [2004] ECR 1-1543.

by way of recourse against the owner of the goods, if the latter, who was not a party to the contract of guarantee, did not authorise the conclusion of that contract" [emphasis added].[201]

5.149 This tantalising passage has opened up important possible claims by and against third parties, and is potentially of much wider application than *Atlas* which in itself was quite a narrow decision because the third party was an express beneficiary of the original contract. What are the requirements if a claim by third party is to be treated as a matter relating to a contract? It does not appear that the court considered that it was necessary that Frahuil had authorised *the subrogation claim* – merely that it had authorised Vegetoil to enter into the guarantee which formed the basis for the subrogation claim under Italian law. Nor does it appear that the court required that Assitalia had made an *agreement* with Frahuil, or even that Frahuil's authority to enter the guarantee should be part of a contract between Frahuil and Vegetoil. The key facts seem to have been that Italian law treated Assitalia as entitled to pursue contractual rights against Frahuil, and that Frahuil in fact authorised the guarantee agreement. In other words, the court's approach was simply to look to see whether or not the party to be bound, Frahuil, had freely assumed *the obligation, which Italian law treated as contractual*, towards Assitalia by permitting Vegetoil to make a guarantee. If so, the claim by the party seeking to enforce the contract, Assitalia, would be a matter relating to a contract. The decision in *Atlas* was plainly correct in light of *Frahuil* even if the facts were different: the buyers agreed to pay the claimants even if they did not know English law would give the claimants a direct claim. The same result as in *Atlas* would now follow in the case of a claim by a third party under the Contracts (Rights of Third Parties) Act 1999, section 1(1), which confers a direct right of action on a third party if the contract states that he may enforce a contract term or purports to confer a benefit on him.

5.150 How would this approach apply to insurance?[202] Suppose, for example, that the insured had a claim for breach of contract against its accountants which its insurers, having paid the loss in full, are entitled to enforce by way of subrogation. Will the accountants be treated as having *authorised* the insured to enter into the insurance? Presumably, rarely, if ever. The accountants may not even know of the insurance, but even if they do, it does not appear that knowledge alone will suffice: a party may *know* that the other may do something without *authorising* it.

5.151 *Frahuil* concerned a claim by the third party. But suppose the claim had been by an original party to the contract against the third party, possibly for a negative declaration? The European Court of Justice cases have not so far considered this situation. It is suggested, however, that, consistently with the comments above, the correct approach here should be to look at whether or not the defendant, the third party, could be said to have freely assumed any obligation it owed to the original party. If, in *Frahuil*, the importer Frahuil had made a claim against the third party, Assitalia, the question would have been whether or not Assitalia had freely assumed an obligation towards Frahuil by giving the guarantee to Vegetoil.

CONTRIBUTION

5.152 What if a reinsurer X pays a claim in full and has a claim in contribution against another reinsurer Y?[203] Under English law the right to contribution arises in equity.[204] If Y

201. At [25]–[26].

202. Other than insurance governed by Section 3 of the Brussels Regulation. As to reinsurance, a claim between reinsurers liable for the same loss will be dealt with by claim for contribution, which is considered below.

203. If X has not paid in full, and is sued by the reinsurer, X might seek to join Y to the proceedings relying on Article 6.

204. *Halsbury's Laws*, Vol. 25 (4th ed., 2003), para. 210.

has not authorised the reinsured to enter into the reinsurance with X the same result should follow as in *Frahuil*, and the claim by X against Y for contribution would not be a matter relating to a contract.

5.153 When might Y be treated as having authorised the reinsured to enter another reinsurance? One possibility is if the reinsurance contract between Y and the reinsured contained, as is common, a clause stipulating that Y is only to pay his rateable proportion of the loss,[205] does it follow that Y has authorised the other reinsurance? Much will depend on the wording of the particular clause. However, such a clause could only operate if the reinsured has other reinsurance in respect of the same loss as that for which Y was liable, and in such a case the other reinsurer would necessarily have a claim to contribution from Y if it had paid the loss. Y could always have excluded a claim under its reinsurance if the reinsured obtained other reinsurance. By inserting the rateable contribution clause Y can be taken to have permitted the reinsured to obtain other reinsurance. It therefore seems likely that Y will be treated as having freely assumed the potential obligation to pay contribution to any other reinsurers, and that X's claim for contribution against Y will be a matter relating to a contract. Authorisation of insurance by an insured may also arise if, as commonly happens, the reinsured is a captive insurer, and the insured intends that the reinsured will be fully reinsured.

ASSIGNMENT

5.154 Assignment is here used to refer to the transfer from A to B of rights A has against C under a reinsurance contract, as distinct from a novation contract between all three parties (see para. 5.145). Under English law rights under a reinsurance contract are generally assignable without the consent of the reinsurer, subject to the provisions of the contract.[206] We are here generally concerned with a voluntary assignment by agreement between assignor and assignee.[207]

5.155 There have not as yet been any reported decisions on the treatment of assignment under Article 5(1). In *Atlas* (para. 5.146 above) Rix J. plainly thought that a claim based on assignment should be a matter relating to a contract.[208] However, such a view risks falling foul of the approach in *Handte* because an original party to the contract may not know of or anticipate that the other will assign the contract or a claim under it to a third party. On the basis of *Frahuil* if the original reinsured A assigns to B a reinsurance contract or the monies payable under a reinsurance contract, a claim by B against the reinsurers would only be a matter relating to a contract if the assignment was authorised by the reinsurers. If the original contract permitted A to assign the contract it may be taken that C has authorised the assignment (see para. 5.150 above).

5.156 On the other hand would a claim, for example, by the reinsurers *against* the assignee for a negative declaration be a matter relating to a contract? It is suggested that in accordance with the approach in *Frahuil* the question is whether or not the assignee had freely assumed the obligation which the applicable law treated as contractual to reinsurers by entering into the assignment. If so, the claim against the assignee would be a matter relating to a contract, regardless of whether or not reinsurers authorised the assignment.

205. As to which see Clarke, *The Law of Insurance Contracts* (4th ed.), para. 28-9A.

206. In the case of an assignment of the entire contract of (re)insurance the assignee must have an insurable interest in the subject-matter of the insurance whereas in the case of an assignment of the right to recover claim monies no such interest is necessary. See, generally, *Clarke*, para 6-3D in relation to insurance contracts: the position in relation to reinsurance contracts is the same.

207. An example of an assignment by operation of law would be that on the insolvency of the reinsured under the Third Party (Rights Against Insurers) Act 1930.

208. Page 194.

(iv) Implied terms

5.157 The European Court of Justice has not so far had to consider whether or not a dispute relating to terms implied by the applicable law would be a matter relating to a contract. Many important terms of a contract will be implied under the applicable law, for example an obligation on a reinsured to take all proper steps to have the amount of a claim fully and carefully ascertained.[209] Under English law the basis for the implication may for instance be that both parties would have agreed to them, or business efficacy. It would obviously be wrong to exclude claims based on such terms from Article 5(1) on the basis that they were not freely assumed. Such implied terms may be described as freely assumed because a party has voluntarily entered into a contract which included them. English cases have so far treated a claim based on an implied term as a matter relating to a contract.[210] Lord Millett was surely correct in *Agnew* v. *Länsförsäkringsbolagens*[211] (considered below, para. 5.170) when he said:

"Nor am I impressed by the argument that 'the obligation in question' must be an obligation voluntarily undertaken and contained in the contract as distinct from one imposed as extra by law. All contractual obligations are voluntary, whether they are contained expressly in the contract or imposed on the contracting parties by law. No one is compelled to undertake contractual obligations. If the parties voluntarily enter into a contract, they seldom express all the contractual terms in the contract. It is often necessary for the law to imply terms into the contract. Many terms, for example, are implied by statute into a contract for the sale of goods. Sometimes such terms are subject to express provision to the contrary; sometimes they cannot be excluded by the contract. While it is customary to describe them as implied terms of the contract, it is equally and often more correct to describe them as legal incidents of the contract. It is not necessary to incorporate them expressly into the contract in order to make them contractual obligations within the meaning of Article 5(1)."[212]

Implied terms are different from the obligations towards third parties imposed by law and the subject of the claims in *Handte* and *Reunion*. The correct approach would seem to be to determine which terms should be implied under the applicable law and then to decide whether or not a dispute relating to that contract with that content, express or implied, should be characterised under community law as a matter relating to a contract.

(v) Tort

5.158 The concept of contract does not however overlap with the liability of a defendant in tort (see para. 5.208). Further, if a court has jurisdiction under Article 5(1) because the dispute is a matter relating to a contract, it will not thereby have jurisdiction in matters relating to tort.[213] The European Court of Justice pointed out that there are other ways under the Brussels Regulation to ensure all claims are heard in one court:

"Whilst it is true that disadvantages arise from different aspects of the same dispute being adjudicated upon by different courts, it must be pointed out, on the one hand, that a plaintiff is always entitled to bring his action in its entirety before the courts for the domicile of the defendant and, on the other, that Article 22 of the Convention allows the first court seised, in certain circumstances, to hear the case in its entirety provided that there is a connection between the actions brought before the different courts."[214]

209. This was the implied term relied on in *AIG* v. *Ethniki* [2000] Lloyd's Rep. IR 343 where the Court of Appeal applied Article 5(1) (see para. 5.186 below).

210. *AIG* v. *Ethniki* (above); *Raffeisen* v. *National Bank of Greece* [1999] 1 Lloyd's Rep. 408 where Tuckey J. held that a claim on an implied term of a security agreement fell within Article 5(1).

211. [2001] 1 AC 223.

212. At p. 264. Lord Millett dissented, but on this point the rest of the Lords agreed: pp. 242, 253, 234 and 247.

213. C-189/87 *Kalfelis* v. *Schroder* [1988] ECR I-5565 at [18]–[21]; C-32/88 *Six Constructions* v. *Humbert* [1989] ECR I-341 at [20]; C-167/00 *VKI* v. *Henkel* [2002] ECR I-8111 at [36]; C-96/00 *Gabriel* v. *Schlank* [2002] ECR I-6367 at [33]–[34].

214. C-189/87 *Kalfelis* v. *Schroder* [1988] ECR I-5565 at [20]; C-420/97 *Leathertex* v. *Bodetex* [1999] ECR I-6747 at [41]. This approach is also apparent from the decision in C-256/00 *Besix* v. *WABAG* [2002] ECR I-1699 at [50] in relation to the place for performance.

(vi) What if a party claims that the contract was not made or is not binding?

5.159 Some of the most difficult questions in relation to Article 5(1) concern the application of the Article to cases where claims are made in relation to contracts which are alleged not to have been made or to be binding (see generally para. 5.138 above). A reinsurer may claim that a reinsurance contract was never made, or claim to avoid a contract for non-disclosure or misrepresentation. Is a dispute as to any of these a matter relating to a contract? The issues have to a large extent not yet been considered by the European Court of Justice. It seems useful to start by considering the three main relevant European Court of Justice cases on the application of the Brussels Regulation where a party denies a contract was made. We then consider the main issues not covered by those decisions, such English cases as there have been on them, and their application to reinsurance.

CONTRACT NOT BINDING: THE EUROPEAN CASES

5.160 What if a defendant denies a contract was made which is relied on by the claimant? In *Effer* v. *Kantner*[215] the claimant claimed fees from the defendant but the defendant denied that it had any contract with the claimant. Was the claim a matter relating to a contract? The European Court of Justice made clear at para. 7 that:

> "in the cases provided for in Article 5(1) of the convention, the national court's jurisdiction to determine questions relating to a contract includes the power to consider the existence of the constituent parts of the contract itself, since that is indispensable in order to enable the national court in which proceedings are brought to examine whether it has jurisdiction under the convention. If that were not the case, Article 5(1) of the convention would be in danger of being deprived of its legal effect, since it would be accepted that, in order to defeat the rule contained in that provision it is sufficient for one of the parties to claim that the contract does not exist. On the contrary, respect for the aims and spirit of the convention demands that that provision should be construed as meaning that the court called upon to decide a dispute arising out of a contract may examine, of its own motion even, the essential preconditions for its jurisdiction, having regard to conclusive and relevant evidence adduced by the party concerned, establishing the existence or the inexistence of the contract."

As will be seen the obligation in question under Article 5(1) is that on which the claimant bases his claim (para. 5.174). The effect of *Effer* is that even if that obligation is denied by the defendant because he denies the contract exists the claim is still treated as a matter relating to a contract within Article 5(1). The court seems to have been concerned not to make it too easy for defendants to avoid Article 5(1) jurisdiction or to overcomplicate the area. Of course, at trial it may turn out that the defendant is correct although that will not retrospectively affect the jurisdiction of the court.

5.161 What if the claimant alleges that he is entitled to set aside a contract because of breach of contract by the defendant? The decision in *Effer* would indicate that this ought to be a matter relating to a contract. This was confirmed in *de Bloos* v. *Bouyer*[216] where a Belgian distributor made a claim against the French grantor of the distributorship contract supplier based on "unilateral breach" of contract for "dissolution" of the contract and for damages. The European Court of Justice was asked whether or not the obligation in question was exclusively the obligation forming the basis of the contract (which it was), but in answering that question assumed that a claim to dissolve a contract based on a breach of the contract by the other party could be a matter relating to contract (at para. 14): "In a case where the plaintiff asserts the right to be paid damages or seeks a dissolution of the contract on the

215. C-38/81 [1982] ECR I-825; *Kleinwort Benson* v. *Glasgow* [1999] 1 AC 153, 165; C-27/02 *Engler* v. *Janus* [2005] ECR I-481, para. 46.

216. C-14/76, [1976] ECR I-1497.

ground of the wrongful conduct of the other party, the obligation referred to in Article 5(1) is still that which arises under the contract and the non-performance of which is relied upon to support such claims."

5.162 Finally, what if the claim is for compensation for breaching a duty of good faith imposed by law in the conduct of negotiations for a contract never made? In *Tacconi* v. *HWS*[217] an Italian company sued a German company in Italy for compensation because the German company had broken off negotiations for a contract, in breach of its duty of good faith and contrary to Article 1337 of the Civil Code under Italian law.[218] In a remarkably brief judgment the European Court of Justice concluded (at para. 22) that "while Article 5(1) of the Brussels Convention does not require a contract to have been concluded, it is nevertheless essential, for that provision to apply, to identify an obligation, since the jurisdiction of the national court is determined, in matters relating to a contract, by the place of performance of the obligation in question", and that there was no obligation freely assumed by one party to the other in that case. The liability of the German company stemmed from Article 1337 of the Italian code rather than from contract, and was therefore governed by Article 5(3) in relation to tort.

5.163 *Tacconi* was the first occasion in which the question of the application of Article 5(1) to a pre-contractual dispute had arisen.[219] In most legal systems of the Member States there is apparently some form of liability for breaking off negotiations without cause, having created an expectation that a contract will be entered into.[220] So far as English law is concerned the Advocate General pointed out that liability arising from breaking off negotiations was not part of English law, but that there could be some forms of liability in such a case:

> "liability can be based of the doctrine of misrepresentation. However, I consider that the legal concept of estoppel by representation is more important. In accordance with this legal concept, a party may not withdraw a previous statement if the other party has suffered harm as a result of that statement. Thus, this legal concept is – albeit not identical – comparable with notions in continental law such as the protection of good faith and legitimate expectations. Finally, it should be noted that in so far as liability arises as a result of negotiations which have been broken off, this is based on actions which constitute a tort. A clear distinction must be drawn between such liability and liability in connection with failure to fulfil contractual obligations."[221]

The reference to a possible claim under English law for misrepresentation seems to have been to a possible claim for damages for negligent or even fraudulent misrepresentation. Under English law such a claim may obviously be made in tort based on *Hedley Byrne* v. *Heller*[222] or if a contract has been concluded, under the Misrepresentation Act 1967. The reasoning of the Advocate General would suggest that such claims would not be a matter relating to a contract although it remains an open question. It would depend on whether or not the obligations are to be regarded as freely assumed by the person bound.

217. C-334/00, [2002] ECR I-7357.

218. See the opinion of Advocate General Geelhoed in C-334/00 *Tacconi* v. *HWS* at [2002] EC I-7357 at [13]. The law is summarised at para. 59 of the opinion: "In Italian law Article 1337 of the Codice Civile contains a specific provision governing pre-contractual liability. Parties must act in good faith during negotiations over and the formation of a contract. A party who breaks off negotiations without just cause, having created an expectation that a contract will be entered into, is liable for the negative contractual interest. Such negative interest specifically includes lost opportunities in addition to expenses. The positive interest is not compensated for, that is to say the other party need not be placed in the situation in which it would have been had the contract actually been concluded. The legal requirement which is not observed when negotiations are broken off abruptly is intended to prevent the other party suffering harm as a result of the fact that it is involved in negotiations and not because the negotiations did not ultimately result in a contract. Fault is not required."

219. Opinion of Advocate General Geelhoed in C-334/00 *Tacconi* v. *HWS* at [2002] EC I-7357 at [57].

220. *Ibid.*, at [58].

221. *Ibid.*, at [63].

222. [1964] AC 465.

5.164 In summary, these decisions of the European Court of Justice establish that:

(1) If a defendant denies that a contract has been made, a claim based on terms of the contract will still be a matter relating to a contract: *Effer*.
(2) Even if the claim is that the claimant is entitled to dissolve a contract for breach of a term by the defendant, the dispute is still a matter relating to a contract: *de Bloos*.
(3) A claim based on statute for compensation for breach of a duty to negotiate a contract in good faith is not a matter relating to a contract: *Tacconi*.

BOTH PARTIES ACCEPT CONTRACT NOT BINDING

5.165 What if both parties accept that the contract is not binding? In such a case there will be no issue for the court at trial even as to the making of the contract. So why should the court for the place for performance of some obligation which is part of the non binding contract be the most appropriate to hear the dispute? In *Kleinwort Benson* v. *Glasgow*[223] the claimant sought to recover sums paid to the defendant under swap transactions later held *ultra vires* and void. A majority of the House of Lords held that where there was no issue that the contract was void the dispute could not be a matter relating to a contract within Article 5(1). The essential reason was that in such a case the obligation in question could never be a contractual obligation under a contract which did not exist:

"I have to confess that I find it very difficult to see how such a claim can fall within Article 5(1). It can only do so if it can properly be said to be based upon a particular contractual obligation, the place of performance of which is within the jurisdiction of the court. Where however, as here, the claim is for the recovery of money paid under a supposed contract which in law never existed, it seems impossible to say that the claim for the recovery of the money is based upon a particular contractual obligation. In truth, the claim in the present case is simply a claim to restitution, which in English law is based upon the principle of unjust enrichment; and claims of this kind do not *per se* fall within Article 5(1)"[224]

The decision demonstrates the importance of the obligation in question to the question whether or not the dispute is a matter relating to a contract.

CLAIMANT ALLEGES NO CONTRACT WAS MADE

5.166 What if the claimant alleges that no contract was ever concluded but the defendant contends that there was a contract? One view is that it may simply be said Article 5(1) cannot not apply because the claimant cannot base his claim on an obligation which is part of the contract so how would the obligation in question be identified. Another view is that there is no reason not to apply the same approach as in *Effer* (para. 5.160 above) the trial court will presumably have to decide the issue of whether or not the contract was made in any event, and will be the court for place for performance of some obligation relied on by the defendant, so why is not that court likely to be best placed to have jurisdiction for the trial. The courts have wavered between these views but it is submitted that the former is the better view. In *Boss Group* v. *Boss France*[225] the claimant manufacturer claimed in English proceedings a decla-

223. [1999] 1 AC 153.
224. Lord Goff at p. 167.
225. [1997] 1 WLR 351; cited with approval by Lord Clyde in *Kleinwort Benson* v. *Glasgow* [1999] 1 AC 153, 182, but *cf. Agnew* below; in *USF* v. *Aqua Technology* [2001] 1 All ER (Comm) 856 (Aikens J.) the claimant claimed a negative declaration that there was no distributorship contract, alternatively that if there was a contract it was not for exclusive distribution via the defendant. It was accepted without argument following *Boss* that Article 5(1) applied where a claimant claimed there was no contract, and held that the obligation in question was the obligation to deal exclusively with the defendant.

ration that it had not made a distributorship contract which the French defendant company contended had been made. The Court of Appeal held that Article 5(1) applied:

> "To my mind there are 'matters relating to a contract' in the present case. There is a lively dispute between the parties as to whether there is a contract between them under which the defendants are the exclusive distributors for the plaintiffs in France. It is true that the plaintiffs, who seek to sue here, are asserting that no such contract exists, but equally the defendants are asserting the contrary. In my judgment, the fact that it is this way round does not make the Article inapplicable. Article 5(1) is not confined to actions to enforce a contract or to obtain recompense for its breach, but refers generally to 'matters relating to a contract'." [226]

The court in *Boss* thus looked at the claim by the *defendant* that there was a contract, and concluded that he could not at the same time maintain there was a contract and that the matter did not relate to a contract. The problem with this is that the approach of the European Court of Justice is that the obligation in question must be the obligation in the contract on which the claimant bases his claim (see below). If the claim is to dissolve a contract because of breach of a term by the other party the obligation in question is that obligation the non-performance of which is claimed to entitle the claimant to dissolution (*de Bloos*). But if the claimant denies the contract *his* claim can never be based on an obligation in the contract whatever the defendant claims. It can be argued that the substance of the issue the court would have to decide in a case like *Boss* is similar to a case where the claimant asserts the contract, but that does not answer the difficulty of identifying the obligation in question: there may be obligations in the contract to be performed in more than one country which is one reason why there has to be a rule that the obligation in question is the one relied on by the claimant.[227]

5.167 The decision in *Boss* has been followed in at first instance in England. In *USF* v. *Aqua Technology*[228] the claimant sought a negative declaration that there was no distributorship contract, alternatively that if there was a contract it was not for exclusive distribution via the defendant. It was accepted without argument following *Boss* that Article 5(1) applied where a claimant claimed there was no contract, and held that the obligation in question was the obligation to deal exclusively with the defendant. Further, in *Equitas* v. *Wave*[229] reinsurers claimed a negative declaration that there was no foundation to an apparent claim by the insured that the reinsurance terms for profit commission were tortious in that they induced the reinsured to refuse to pay valid claims. The application was undefended. The court relied on *Boss* and *USF* in deciding that a dispute could be a matter relating to tort even if the claimant denied that there had been a tort committed (para 11):

> "The purpose of Arts. 5(3) and 5(1) is to prescribe the courts in which matters relating to torts and contracts may be determined. Such matters include whether or not a contract has been made or a tort committed as well as the consequences, if it has. It would seem to me inconsistent with that underlying purpose if it were otherwise – with the result that X who claims that he is the victim of a breach of a contract or a tort committed by Y may sue in the court prescribed, but Y, who claims that there was no contract to be breached and no tort committed, may not avail himself of the same facility."

However, it is doubtful that Article 5(1) may be equated with Article 5(3) in this way; Article 5(1) requires an obligation in question to be identified and the European Court of Justice has made clear that this has to be the obligation on which the claim is based which is why it is difficult to see that Article 5(1) may apply where the claimant denies there ever was any

226. Saville LJ at p. 405, giving the judgment of the court.

227. The concern expressed in *Effer* that defendants could negate the effect of Article 5(1) by simply denying the contract was binding is not applicable here.

228. [2001] 1 All ER (Comm) 856, Aikens J.

229. [2005] EWHC 923 (Comm), Clarke J.

contract and therefore does not base his claim on any part of it; but no such reasoning applies in the case of Article 5(3). *Equitas* is therefore of little help in relation to Article 5(1).

5.168 In *Kleinwort Benson* v. *Glasgow*[230] (*supra*) Lord Clyde (who was part of the majority) referred to *Boss* with apparent approval (p. 182). On the other hand in *Agnew* v. *Länsförsäkringsbolagens*[231] Lord Millett described the approach in *Boss* as "doubtful" (at p. 264) and Lord Cooke (with whom Lord Nicholls agreed) seemed to consider that Article 5(1) applied where the claimant sought to set aside a contract for breach of the duty of good faith, but might not apply where the claim was that a contract was void *ab initio* (e.g. for failure to comply with a requirement as to form, lack of contractual power or uncertainty), presumably because the claimant could not base his claim on an obligation in the contract. Lord Hope was alone in approving the approach in *Boss* (at p. 258). In summary, whatever its merits the approach in *Boss* is not consistent with the approach of the European Court of Justice in insisting that the obligation in question is the obligation on which the claim is based and is therefore doubtful.

CLAIM TO AVOID FOR NON-DISCLOSURE OR MISREPRESENTATION

5.169 If a reinsurer seeks to *avoid* a reinsurance for non-disclosure or misrepresentation in the placing, and claims a negative declaration to that effect, is the dispute a matter relating to a contract? There are a couple of important features to note about such a claim under English law. First, the claim is for a declaration that the claimant is not liable under the reinsurance. However, unlike the case where the claimant claims that there never was a contract (considered above), here the claimant asserts that the contract was made but seeks to avoid an existing contract. Unless and until avoided the contract is on foot. Second, the claim to avoid is based breach of the duty of good faith in the negotiations for the reinsurance. The duty is imposed by the general law if the contract is classified as *uberimmae fidei*. The obligation to perform the duty which is relied on by the claimant is not a part of the terms of the reinsurance contract. The remedy is not damages, but avoidance of the concluded reinsurance contract.[232] The decision in *Tacconi* (above) does not directly apply to the question of avoidance of a reinsurance contract under English law for breach of the duty of good faith. No contract was made in *Tacconi*. The liability under Italian law did not affect an existing contract.

5.170 The English courts have held that the claim to avoid for non-disclosure or misrepresentation is a matter relating to a contract. In *Trade Indemnity* v. *Forsakringsaktiebolaget Njord*[233] reinsurers sought a declaration in the English court that they were entitled to avoid two surplus treaty reinsurances of the Swedish reinsured in respect of the insurance of financial guarantees, performance bonds, advance payments bonds and other forms of bonds and borrowing liabilities for non-disclosure and misrepresentation. The reinsurers claimed a negative declaration of no liability and restitution of the net amounts paid out under the reinsurances. The issue of whether or not the matter related to a contract was not much argued, and Rix J. readily accepted that it was, albeit that he went on to find that the obligation in question could not be the obligation to make a fair presentation (as to which see para. 5.181

230. [1999] 1 AC 153.

231. [2001] 1 AC 223, 246; see also *Andromeda* v. *O W Bunker* [2006] EWHC 777 (Comm), para. 25, where it was held that if a claimant denies that a contract was made there is no jurisdiction under Article 23, para. 5.37 above.

232. See generally *Agnew* v. *Länsförsäkringsbolagens* [2001] 1 AC 223.

233. [1995] 1 Lloyd's Rep. 367.

234. At p. 380.

below).[234] In *Agnew* v. *Länsförsäkringsbolagens*[235] the claimant reinsurers sought to avoid primary and excess layer facultative reinsurance placed with them via London brokers of the defendant Swedish reinsured in respect of suppliers and manufacturers guarantee insurance business. The ground relied on was misrepresentation by the reinsured and non-disclosure through its brokers. The majority view was that a claim that a contract was voidable and could be set aside for non-disclosure was a matter relating to a contract. They plainly viewed this approach as consistent with the purpose of Article 5(1) because it would allow jurisdiction to be founded where the disclosure and correct representation had to be made. The vital question was whether or not the obligation to comply with the duty of good faith could be the obligation in question even though it was not part of the reinsurance contract. The majority emphasised that without the making of the contract the matter would not come before the court at all.[236] The remedy of avoidance for lack of good faith could only affect a concluded contract. It was a quirk of English law that the duty of good faith arose under the general law rather than an implied term. *Kleinwort Benson* was to be distinguished because it was accepted that there was never any contract in that case at all.[237] By contrast it was suggested that a claim to avoid for duress, undue influence or misrepresentation could not fall within Article 5(1) since there could be no place for performance of such a negative obligation, unlike the positive obligation to disclose material facts and make correct representations.[238]

5.171 It is suggested that if and when the issue comes before the European Court of Justice the court should uphold the decision in *Agnew*. Under Article 5(1) the classification of the obligation as contractual or not depends on community law not the applicable law (para. 5.134 above). It is open to the court at the community law level to classify the obligation to comply with the duty of good faith as contractual if it has been freely assumed and is sufficiently linked to the contract. This is clearly demonstrated by the view of the European Court of Justice in *Frahuil* that a dispute as to obligations *imposed by Italian law* in favour of a third party could be a matter relating to a contract for Article 5(1) (see the discussion at para. 5.147). The fact that the source of the duty was the general law did not prevent a free assumption of that obligation. In that case the applicable law imposed the right of Assitalia to enforce against Frahuil the contractual rights of Vegetoil. English law imposes on the parties a right of the reinsurers to avoid the reinsurance contract. The link between the right to avoid and the contract is sufficient to classify the obligation as contractual under community law. The question is whether or not the reinsured freely assumes it, but that he does in entering into the reinsurance contract, just as he assumes the duties imposed by implied terms. The decision in *Tacconi* (para. 5.162 above) is clearly distinguishable because there the obligation imposed did not affect the concluded contract but was to pay compensation for breaking off the negotiations. The result of *Agnew* can also be said to be in accordance with the purpose of locating jurisdiction in the place with the closest connections to the substance of a dispute.

235. [2001] 1 AC 223. The decision was on the Lugano Convention and it was therefore not possible to refer the case to the European Court of Justice. Pester, "Reinsurance, Good Faith and Article 5(1) of the Brussels Convention" (2000) LMCLQ 289.

236. Lord Woolf at pp. 240–241, Lord Cooke at pp. 246–247. Lord Nicholls agreed with them. Lords Hope and Millett dissented. Lord Hope did not consider the obligation to act in good faith could be characterised as contractual and therefore could not be the obligation in question. Lord Millett considered that the obligation to act in good faith was in the nature of a condition precedent to the formation of a fully binding contract rather than a contractual obligation. *Cf. Trade Indemnity* at p. 382 where Rix J. posed the question why, if avoidance for non-disclosure or misrepresentation would be a matter relating to a contract, would not avoidance for negligent or fraudulent misrepresentation also (as to which see para. 5.210). Ultimately he considered that obligations which arise before the contract are not apposite to be the subject-matter of Article 5(1) which is concerned with where contracts are to be performed.

237. At pp. 239, 247.

238. At p. 241, Lord Woolf; see also p. 266, *per* Lord Millett, dissenting.

CLAIM OF BREACH OF WARRANTY

5.172 In *Fisher* v. *Unione Italiana*[239] the claimants were retrocessionaires and the defendants reinsurers in respect of facultative personal accident risk in respect of the banker, Roberto Calvi who died in notorious circumstances. The retrocession agreement included a warranty as to the size of the retention by the reinsurers. The retrocessionaires claimed a negative declaration that they were under no liability on the retrocession because of a breach of that warranty by the reinsurers. Colman J's approach was that:

"The 'obligation in question' has the following essential characteristics: (i) it is a promissory term of or at least a duty closely connected with the contract, such as the duty to disclose all material facts in a reinsurance contract; (ii) there is a dispute relating to its performance; (iii) the plaintiff has formulated his claim for relief in the proceedings on the grounds of the performance or non-performance of that obligation. The place of performance of that obligation must be shown to be the country in which the proceedings sought to be sustained have been started. It follows that, where one party claims a negative declaration that he is not bound to perform a contract on a basis which he formulates by reference to a particular obligation in the contract and that obligation is in dispute, that will be the obligation in question and it will be to the courts of the country where that obligation falls to be performed that Article 5(1) jurisdiction will be accorded. The process of identification of the obligation in question thus depends crucially on the way in which the plaintiff has formulated his claim for relief. Where he advances a claim for a negative declaration which he formulates on the basis of non-performance of a term of the contract by the other party, it can safely be said that it is that term which is the obligation in question for the purposes of Article 5(1)."

In the result the judge found that the claim was based on breach of the warranty as to retention which was to be performed in Italy and jurisdiction was therefore denied. The approach to negative declarations in *Fisher* is in keeping with the decision in *de Bloos* (*supra*).

CLAIM FOR RESTITUTION

5.173 One consequence of a contract being held not binding may be that one party has a claim to restitution of monies paid under the contract. If, for example, claims have been paid under a reinsurance contract later avoided, reinsurers may seek to recover the claim monies wrongly paid out, possibly on the ground that the consideration for the payment has totally failed or on the ground of payment by mistake.[240] Will a dispute as to such a claim for restitution be a matter relating to a contract? In *Kleinwort Benson* v. *Glasgow* (above) a majority of the House of Lords denied that a claim in restitution for monies paid out under illegal swap transactions was capable of being a matter relating to a contract. The majority plainly viewed a claim to restitution as based on unjust enrichment even if a contract was in some sense in the background and therefore not a matter relating to a contract, although Lord Goff did allow that (p. 167) "very exceptionally" it may be said that for the purposes of the Brussels Regulation the claim is based on a contractual obligation and is therefore within Article 5(1), citing as an example a claim for money had and received on a total failure of consideration (p. 171). Unless the claim can be said for the purposes of community law to be based upon an obligation freely assumed by the defendant it is difficult to see the rationale for considering that Article 5(1) may apply. Essentially, the liability to the claim for money had and received would have to be seen as being part of the package of obligations assumed in entering into the contract, like an implied term. In the case of total failure of consideration, this view seems justifiable because the claim only arises where there has been a contract, and the consideration has failed. Where a reinsurance contract is avoided for non-disclosure or misrepresentation it similarly seems justifiable, following *Agnew* (para. 5.170 above), to say

239 [1998] CLC 682.

240. See, generally, *Halsbury's Laws*, Vol. 40(2) (4th ed., 2000), para. 1305.

that the obligation of good faith was freely assumed as a part of the package of liabilities when the contract was agreed.

3. What is the obligation in question?

5.174 If the matter is one relating to a contract the next question is what is the obligation in question. The obligation in question "refers to the contractual obligation forming the basis of the legal proceedings… The obligation to be taken into account is that which corresponds to the contractual right on which the plaintiff's action is based."[241] This has been said to be based on the need to avoid multiple courts having jurisdiction where the contract contains multiple obligations (though it of course does not deal with the cases where the claimant pleads more than one obligation – see para. 5.183). It has also been said that: "the place in which that obligation is to be performed usually constitutes the closest connecting factor between the dispute and the court having jurisdiction over it, and it is this connecting factor which explains why, in contractual matters, it is the court of the place of performance of the obligation which has jurisdiction".[242]

5.175 Under Article 5(1)(a) a defendant may be sued in the place for performance of the obligation in question. Once the obligation in question has been identified the applicable law under the conflicts rules of the forum will determine where that obligation was to be performed. However, under Article 5(1)(b) it is now provided that in the case of sale of goods and in the case of provision of services the place for performance is always where the goods were or were to be delivered or the services were or were to be provided (subject to a different agreement by the parties[243]). Article 5(1)(b) was introduced at the time of the Brussels Regulation. Its genesis appears from the Commission's comments in the proposal for the Brussels Regulation:

> "to remedy the shortcomings of applying the rules of private international law of the State whose courts are seised, the second subparagraph of Article 5(1) gives an autonomous definition of the place for performance of 'the obligation in question' in two specific situations … In the case of the provision of services, it will be the place where, still under the contract, the services were or should have been provided. This pragmatic determination of the place of performance applies regardless of the obligation in question, even where this obligation is the payment of the financial consideration for the contract. It also applies where the claim relates to several obligations. The rule may, however, be 'displaced' by an explicit agreement on the place of performance."[244]

Article 5(1)(b) therefore adopts the "characteristic obligation" approach, that is, jurisdiction is to be determined by reference to the place for performance of the obligation which determines the nature of the contract which is intended to make it more likely that the place identified

241. C-14/76 *De Bloos* v. *Bouyer* [1976] ECR I-1497 at [10], [13]; C-266/85 *Shenevai* v. *Kresicher* [1987] ECR I-239 at [18]; C-420/97 *Leathertex* v. *Bodetex* [1999] ECR I-6747 at [32], which pointed out that the 1978 version of the Brussels Convention was amended in certain language versions to specify that the obligation in question is the obligation which forms the basis of the claim; see also C-256/00 *Besix* v. *WABAG* [2002] ECR I-1699 at [44]. In employment cases only, a different approach was adopted to the interpretation of Article 5(1) but this has now been overtaken by Section 6 of the Brussels Regulation: C-133/81 *Ivenel* v. *Schwab* [1982] ECR I-1891; *Mercury* v. *Loerke*, *The Times*, 21 October 1991, CA; C-256/00 *Besix* v. *WABAG* [2002] ECR I-1699. For more notes on the history of this part of Article 5(1) see Layton/Mercer, p. 434. Where the obligation relied on is to pay liquidated damages in the event of a breach of contract it appears that the obligation in question is the obligation the non performance of which led to the liability to pay damages: C-14/76 *De Bloos* v. *Bouyer* [1976] ECR I-1497 at [14]–[17].

242. C-266/85 *Shenevai* v. *Kresicher* [1987] ECR I-239 at [18].

243. *Continuity Promotions Ltd* v. *O'Connor's Nenagh Shopping Centre Ltd* [2006] All ER (D) 39 (Feb), HHJ Langan, where an agreement in a sale of goods as to place of payment was not enough to found an implied agreement at to place of delivery so as to displace Article 5(1)(b).

244. Proposal for a council regulation on jurisdiction and the recognition and enforcement of judgment in civil and commercial matters, 99/0154 (CNS), p. 14.

will be the factual centre of the dispute. As we shall see, however, the new rule appears to be particularly ill-suited to reinsurance business.

5.176 In the case of many disputes relating to contracts for services, for example the provision of advice or designs, the dispute is likely to be about the services which were provided. The place for the provision of those services may therefore be best suited to deal with the dispute. In such cases the effect of Article 5(1)(b) is always to locate jurisdiction in the place where the services were to be performed, and to prevent Article 5(1) locating jurisdiction in, for example, the jurisdiction where payment was to be made because that is the obligation on which the claimant relies. It is not obvious what sort of residual contracts were intended to fall outside Article 5(1)(b) and therefore to fall within 5(1)(a), but examples might be a joint venture agreement or an undertaking not to do something in a certain country.

5.177 The main question is does Article 5(1)(b) apply to the provision of reinsurance or insurance (so far as not covered by section 3 of the Brussels Regulation)? Is the provision of (re)insurance the provision of a service for this purpose? As a matter of language it is certainly possible: the EU Action Plan for Financial Services has identified reinsurance as a sector which requires action at Community level in order to complete the internal market for financial services.[245] Insurance is within the definition of "services" in Article 5 of the Rome Convention on the applicable law (although not within "services" in Article 13 of the Brussels Convention on which Article 5 of the Rome Convention was modelled).[246]

5.178 If reinsurance and insurance were within Article 5(1)(b) the place for performance of the obligation in question would be the place where the services should have been provided. The result would be that whatever the obligation in question the place for performance would always be that where the services should have been provided. In other words, everything would depend on identification of the place where the services should have been provided and nothing would turn on identification of the obligation in question which hitherto has been a major question under Article 5(1).[247] On one view if Article 5(1)(b) did apply the services would presumably be the payment of claims by reinsurers and insurers.[248] The question would therefore be where such claims had to be paid. Under English law in the absence of specific agreement it is likely that claims are payable at the place of the reinsured. However, currently reinsurers often seek a negative declaration on the basis of a failure to disclose or make a correct representation at the place of the reinsurers, frequently by a broker who is situated in the same place as the reinsurers, and jurisdiction is established at the place of the reinsurers. The effect of applying Article 5(1)(b) to reinsurance would therefore be profound.[249]

5.179 It is, unfortunately, not clear whether or not reinsurance and insurance do fall within Article 5(1)(b). It has been accepted without argument in the authorities that Article 5(1)(a) applies and not Article 5(1)(b).[250] The primary problem with applying Article 5(1)(b) is that in reinsurance and insurance cases there is no reason to think that the jurisdiction where claims are to be paid would be likely to be to the jurisdiction with which the dispute has its closest connection. The position is very different from many ordinary contracts for services where the dispute is likely to be closely connected to the place for performance of the service. This consideration suggests that where, as in contracts of reinsurance and insurance, the

245. See recitals to Directive 2005/68/EC on Reinsurance

246. *Giuliano-Lagarde*, para. 2 on Article 5, and see para. 10.99 below.

247. The drafting method chosen to render obsolete in this way the inquiry as to the obligation in question in cases of goods and services is inept to say the least, but the wording seems clear.

248. See further the discussion at para. 10.67 below. Another view there discussed is that the service is the provision of cover which is provided by the reinsurer (or insurer) at his place of business.

249. See para. 10.67 and the views of Clarke there referred to.

250. *Prifti* v. *Musini* [2004] Lloyd's Rep. IR 528, para. 12; *Mora* v. *AXA* [2005] 2 Lloyd's Rep. 769, 773, CA.

contract is for the payment of money the contract should not fall within Article 5(1)(b). If, as is suggested, Article 5(1)(b) does not apply to reinsurance and insurance, the next question is what is the obligation in question. We consider the issues which arise below on the basis that Article 5(1)(b) does not apply to reinsurance and insurance.

(i) Claim by reinsured

5.180 In a claim by the reinsured the obligation in question will usually be the obligation on the reinsurers to pay claims whatever the ground on which reinsurers may deny the claim. In *Deutsche Ruck* v. *La Fondaria*[251] the claimant was a German company and front reinsurer within a pool of foreign reinsurers managed by a Dutch agency Inter Community Reinsurance Agency BV (ICRA) but in reality administered by London agents. The claimant claimed that it was reinsured by other pool members under implied retrocession agreements in respect of inwards reinsurance business for a pool of retrocessionaires. The obligation in question was the obligation of the retrocessionaires to make payment under the implied retrocessions. The general rule of English law that the debtor must seek out the creditor (see para. 5.190 below) was argued in *Deutsche Ruck* so as to place jurisdiction in the countries where the reinsurers carried on business, but the judge found that there was sufficient evidence that the implied agreement was that payment had to be made in London where the pool was effectively administered.

(ii) Claim by reinsurers

5.181 There are of course many grounds on which the reinsurers may deny liability and seek a negative declaration. If the claim is for a negative declaration that the reinsurers are entitled to avoid for breach of the duty of good faith, it is now clear from *Agnew* that the obligation in question is the obligation to disclose or to represent the risk fairly (see para. 5.170 above).[252] In other cases where the claim is for a negative declaration the obligation in question will be the obligation on the non-performance of which the claimant relies.[253] The obligation in question is not an inconsistent obligation which is asserted by the defendant.[254]

5.182 A distinction may be drawn in this context between obligations which are promissory and non-promissory. An obligation is promissory in nature if the reinsured promises or warrants something. Where the reinsurers rely on a breach of warranty to deny liability the obligation in question will be the obligation which was warranted: see *Fisher* v. *Unione Italiana*[255] referred to above. Other examples where reinsurers have sought negative declarations on the basis of failure to perform an obligation which appears to be promissory in nature are: a failure to mitigate,[256] allowing an underlying insurance to lapse,[257] failure to co-operate in relation to claims,[258] and failure to pay premiums.[259] However, in many cases reinsurers

251. [2002] Lloyd's Rep. IR 475; see also *Citadel* v. *Atlantic* [1982] 2 Lloyd's Rep. 543, 548, CA; *OUI* v. *IGI* [1992] 1 Lloyd's Rep. 439.

252. *Agnew* v. *Länsförsäkringsbolagens* [2001] 1 AC 223, 239, 246.

253. *Fisher* v. *Unione Italiana* [1998] CLC 682.

254. *Royal and Sun* v. *MK Digital* [2006] EWCA Civ 629 at [104]: "In effect, [the claimant's] submission is that a claim form which asserts non-liability can be expanded, *sub silentio*, to embrace a repudiation of any liability of any kind which could possibly be asserted against the claimant and to insist that the obligation in question can be found accordingly. In my judgment, if that was so, it would entirely undermine the logic and purpose of Article 5(1). It would enable any party to rush to court to make a claim for a declaration of non-liability in the widest possible form and then seek to find in such a claim form support for first seisure by means of an *ex post facto* rationalisation of the obligation in question."

255. [1998] CLC 682.

256. *Evialis* v. *SIAT* [2004] Lloyd's Rep. IR 187.

257. *New Hampshire* v. *Strabag* [1992] 1 Lloyd's Rep. 361.

258. *ACE* v. *Zurich* [2001] 1 Lloyd's Rep. 618.

259. *Gatoil* v. *Arkwright* [1985] 1 AC 255.

deny liability on the basis of obligations which are *non promissory* in nature. For example the reinsurer may claim that he simply did not contract with the reinsured, the loss did not fall within the scope of the reinsurance, the reinsurance excluded the loss, the claim is time-barred, or the loss did not occur. In such cases the reinsured has not failed to perform an obligation; the reinsurer is simply not under an obligation. If the reinsurer seeks a negative declaration it is difficult to see how his claim can be said to rely on non-performance of a particular obligation. There is no authority on the place of performance in relation to such non promissory obligations. However, if it is not possible to identify a place for performance of the obligation in question the European Court of Justice has held that Article 5(1) simply does not apply (see paras 5.184, 5.194). Similarly, if the claimant reinsurer cannot demonstrate a place for performance of an obligation on the reinsured on which the reinsurer relies because the claim is not based on a promissory obligation the reinsurer simply cannot rely on Article 5(1).[260] The reinsurer would have to fall back on Article 2 jurisdiction based on domicile.

(iii) What if there is more than one obligation in question?

5.183 Where the claim is in respect of more than one obligation the aim of the courts has been to try to avoid forcing different claims in relation to the same contract to be brought in different courts. The European Court of Justice has therefore adopted the test of finding where possible which is the principal obligation in question.[261] This approach was first aired in *Shenevai* v *Kreischer* (although the question did not in fact arise in that case): "the court before which the matter is brought will, when determining whether it has jurisdiction, be guided by the *maxim accessorium sequitur* principle; in other words, where various obligations are at issue, it will be the principal obligation which will determine its jurisdiction".[262] Obligations other than the principal obligation are therefore to be regarded as "accessory". Jurisdiction in respect of both principal and accessory obligations is available in the place for performance of the principal obligation.

5.184 It is for the national court to decide on the relative importance of the obligations relied on by the claimant. This emerges from the European Court of Justice decision in *Leathertex* v. *Bodetex*[263] which considered what happens if obligations are held to be of *equal* importance. A Belgian company, Bodetex, had been appointed the commercial agent for Belgium and the Netherlands by an Italian company, Leathertex. Bodetex claimed compensation in lieu of notice on the termination of the contract which was due to be paid in Belgium, and arrears of commission which was due to be paid in Italy. The Belgian Court of Appeal held that the two obligations were "equal in rank" preliminary to holding that Article 5(1) meant that jurisdiction in Belgium in respect of both claims could be founded on the place for performance of one of them. The European Court of Justice rejected an argument that the priority of the obligations should be decided at community law level (at para. 21): "it is for the national court to assess the relative importance of the contractual obligations at issue in the main proceedings and for the Court of Justice to interpret the Convention in the light of the findings made by the national court."[264] However, the court also held that if there was

260. See the comments of Lord Millett in *Agnew* v. *Länsförsäkringsbolagens* [2001] 1 AC 223, 266.

261. See, e.g., C-133/81 *Ivenel* v. *Schwab* [1982] ECR I-1891 at [18].

262. C-266/85, [1987] ECR I-239 at [19].

263. C-420/97, [1999] ECR I-6747; George Panagopoulos, "Jurisdiction in relation to a contract split between two states" (2000) LMCLQ 150–153.

264. The basis of the claim for compensation for termination without due notice was apparently the failure product pay commission, and it was argued that at community law level it should be open to the court to decide that the payment of commission was the principal obligation.

no principal obligation then the doctrine in *Shenevai* could not apply with the result that Article 5(1) had to be applied to each of the separate obligation in questions, and the two claims would have to be brought in different jurisdictions (or the claimant could sue the defendant in his country of domicile in respect of all claims). The court rejected an argument that Article 28 (which applies to related actions) could confer jurisdiction: it only applied where jurisdiction was established under other provisions of the Brussels Regulation.[265] This approach reflects the consistent view of the European Court of Justice that since Article 5(1) is a derogation from the general jurisdiction under Article 2, it should not strain to fit cases within Article 5(1), and this in effect outweighs the counter-argument against fragmentation in some cases.[266]

5.185 However, there is no other guidance as yet from the European Court of Justice as to when an obligation should be regarded by a national court as principal under the national law. The English cases have provided some clarification. The leading case is *Union Transport* v. *Continental Lines*[267] in which the English claimant company entered into a contract with brokers for the Belgian defendant shipowners for the charter of a vessel to be nominated by the defendants. The claimants began proceedings claiming that the defendants had failed to nominate a vessel (which had to be done in England) or to provide a vessel (which did not). The House of Lords decided that nomination of the vessel was the principal obligation. That obligation was characterised as "the more fundamental obligation" and "the real ground of complaint".[268] The main reasons for this were that a charter which called for a vessel to be nominated was quite different from a charter of a named vessel; nomination triggered other obligations under the contract; and until there had been a nomination there could be no duty to cause a vessel to proceed to the loading port.

5.186 The court considered how to apply this approach to reinsurance in *AIG* v. *Ethniki*[269] where a Greek property was insured in respect of earthquake risks by Greek insurers who were reinsured facultatively under a slip placed in London. The reinsurers claimed negative declarations on the basis of breach of the claims control clause in failing to give notice of the claim in 72 hours (to be done in England), as well as damages for failing to ascertain the claim properly on being notified of it (which was to be done in Greece or outside the UK), in breach of the full reinsurance clause and an implied term. Colman J. distinguished cases where the claimant relied on "inter-dependent" obligations where breach of one could affect performance of another from cases where the claim was based on *alternative* and independent claims. The question of what was the principal obligation depended on the connection between the court and the place for performance of the obligation relied on. There was no room for appeal to *forum non conveniens* type arguments in the debate about the principal obligation.[270] Colman J. considered the claims control clause was the principal obligation. The Court of Appeal confirmed that view. The correct inquiry was to "ask whether AIG's claim for a declaration of non-liability *depends or is based principally (or 'substantially')* on the alleged breaches of the claims control clause or on the accompanying allegations of breaches of the insurance company's obligation to investigate the claim fully and timeously in Greece" (emphasis added).[271] The claims control clause was the principal obligation because (p. 349): "If notice had been given, then a London adjuster could and allegedly would have been

265. C-420/97 *Leathertex* v. *Bodetex* [1999] ECR I-6747 at [38]; C-150/80 *Elefanten* v. *Schuh Mode* [1981] ECR I-1671 at [19].
266. See, e.g., C-256/00 *Besix* v. *WABAG* [2002] ECR I-1699.
267. [1999] 1 WLR 15.
268. By Lord Goff at pp. 22–23.
269. [1999] Lloyd's Rep. IR 221, Colman J.; [2000] Lloyd's Rep. IR 343, CA.
270. Following C-288/92 *Custom Made* v. *Stawa* [1994] ECR I-2913.
271. Page 359, *per* Evans LJ.

appointed forthwith, and AIG's reliance on [the reinsured] for information and for investigating and responding to the claim would have been greatly reduced, probably extinguished altogether." The two claims were therefore in practice to some extent inter-dependent. The principal obligation did not depend on which arose first in time, or on the way that the obligations were pleaded by the claimant. It is clear from AIG that the court should weigh up the competing obligations to see which is the principal without reference to where they are to be performed. This approach seems consistent with *Union Transport* where the court sought "the real ground of complaint", i.e. that obligation the non performance of which was the most important part of what the claimant claimed It seems unlikely that a dead heat of the sort the Belgian court found in *Leathertex* will occur frequently, bearing in mind that the relative importance of obligations is a matter for the court seised, and the inconvenience of fragmenting disputes about one contract that *Leathertex* would cause.

4. What is the place for performance?

5.187 The place for performance must be decided under the national law which is applicable according to the conflicts rules in the court seised, and is the place stipulated by the contract as the place for performance which must be within a Member State (see para. 5.129) [272] The application of the Rome Convention on applicable law should ensure that the applicable law is the same within the Member States.[273] The purpose of the rule is that the dispute should be heard in the court best placed to hear the dispute. However, in *Custom Made* v. *Stawa*[274] the European Court of Justice made it clear that the place for performance of the obligation relied on by the claimant should be applied even if the result is that the court with jurisdiction is not that with the closest connection to the dispute (para. 15):

"The place of performance of the obligation was chosen as the criterion of jurisdiction because, being precise and clear, it fits into the general aim of the Convention, which is to establish rules guaranteeing certainty as to the allocation of jurisdiction among the various national courts before which proceedings in matters relating to a contract may be brought: It has been submitted, certainly, that the criterion of the place of performance of the obligation which specifically forms the basis of the applicant's action, a criterion expressly laid down in Article 5(1) of the Convention, may in certain cases have the effect of conferring jurisdiction on a court which has no connection with the dispute, and that, in such a case, the criterion explicitly laid down should be departed from on the ground that the result it yields would be contrary to the aim of Article 5(1) of the Convention. That last argument cannot be accepted, however. The use of criteria other than that of the place of performance, where that confers jurisdiction on a court which has no connection with the case, might jeopardise the possibility of foreseeing which court will have jurisdiction and for that reason be incompatible with the aim of the Convention. The effect of accepting as the sole criterion of jurisdiction the existence of a connecting factor between the facts at issue in a dispute and a particular court would be to oblige the court before which the dispute is brought to consider other factors, in particular the pleas relied on by the defendant, in order to determine whether such a connection exists and would thus render Article 5(1) nugatory. Such an examination would also be contrary to the purposes and spirit of the Convention, which requires an interpretation of Article 5 enabling the national court to rule on its own jurisdiction without being compelled to consider the substance of the case (see Case 34/82, *Peters* v. *ZNAV* [1983] ECR 987, paragraph 17). It follows that under Article 5(1), in matters relating to a contract, a defendant may be sued in the courts for the place of performance of the obligation in question, even where the court thus designated is not that which has the closest connection with the dispute."

5.188 Article 5(1)(b) stipulates the place for performance in the case of contracts for the provision of services. It is assumed in this discussion that Article 5(1)(b) does not apply to reinsurance (see para. 5.179).

272. C-12/76 *Tessili* v. *Dunlop* [1976] ECR I-1473, para. 13; *Mora* v. *AXA* [2005] 2 Lloyd's Rep. 769.
273. C-440/97 *Groupe Concorde* v. *Panjan* [1999] ECR 6307 at [30], and see Chapter 10.
274. C-288/92, [1994] ECR I-2913.

5.189 Where the parties specifically agree the place for performance the effect of Article 5(1) is that the agreement is capable of having the effect of a jurisdiction agreement without complying with the formalities in Article 23. However, such an agreement will be effective under Article 5(1) provided that the place specified is genuinely the place for performance (para. 5.67 above). The reason for Article 5 jurisdiction is that there is an objective link between the legal relationship and the court designated by Article 5. Under Article 23 the link is supplied by the parties' intentions, provided they have been manifested in a way which meets the formalities required.[275] However, in *MSG* v. *Les Gravieres*[276] the parties agreed that the place for performance was Germany although in fact performance (chartering a barge for service in French waterways) had little or nothing to do with Germany. The European Court of Justice had no trouble holding that (para. 33): "to specify a place of performance which has no actual connection with the real subject-matter of the real contract becomes fictitious and has as its sole purpose the determination of the place of the courts having jurisdiction. Such agreements conferring jurisdiction are governed by Article 17 of the Convention [now Article 23] and are therefore subject to specific requirements as to form."

(i) Claim by the reinsured

5.190 Usually the claim by the reinsured will be for the sums payable under the reinsurance, i.e. the claim payments. Where no place for performance has been specified in the contract the general position under English law is that: "the promissory must seek out the promissee and perform the contract wherever he may happen to be. This rule applies not only to contracts for the payment of money, but to all promises for the performance of which the concurrence of the promissee is necessary. If, however, a debtor gives notice to his creditor of his intention to pay at a certain time at a convenient place, and the creditor makes no objection to the notice, he will be deemed to waive the necessity of a personal tender unless he attends at the place specified."[277] This rule will often mean that under English law jurisdiction in respect of a claim for payment of sums due under a reinsurance will be located in the place of the reinsured who is the creditor. Can it be said that payment of claims had to be made to the broker? A mere provision that claims were to be collected through the broker constituted no more than a notice to insurers that the insured authorised the brokers to collect claims, and without more did not mean that claims must be paid through the broker.[278] However, in other cases it has been possible to find an implied agreement that claims be paid to the broker. In *Deutsche Ruck* v. *La Fondaria*[279] (considered at para. 5.180 above) Steel J. found that there was a good arguable case that the sums claimed under a reinsurance of pool members were payable not at the place of the reinsurers, but in London where the pool was administered. In a "transparent and (probably ineffectual)"[280] attempt to avoid regulation

275. C-129/83 *Zelger* v. *Salinitri* [1980] ECR I-89; *Gerling* (*supra*).

276. C-106/95, [1997] ECR I-911; C-129/83 *Zelger* v. *Salinitri* [1980] ECR I-89; *Lohmann/Societa Esercizio Cantieri*, Corte di Cassazione, 22 January 2002, ECJ database 2003/39 at *http://www.jura.uni-sb.de/convention-bruxelles/en/2003/39-2003* where a clause fixing the place for performance included in standard terms annexed to a draft contract and signed only by the proposer were regarded as binding following performance of the contract.

277. *Halsbury's Laws*, Vol. 9(1) (4th ed., 1998), para. 490; the general rule does not apply where the promissee was in England when the promise was made and subsequently went abroad before breach, *op. cit.*, para. 491; *Chitty*, para. 21-054.

278. *The Stolt Marmaro* [1985] 2 Lloyd's Rep. 428.

279. [2002] Lloyd's Rep. IR 475; *Citadel* v. *Atlantic* [1982] 2 Lloyd's Rep. 543; compare *Domicrest* v. *SBC* [1999] 1 Lloyd's Rep. 80 where Rix J. rejected a submission that there was an implied agreement to pay a creditor at the place of the debtor.

280. At p. 479.

under the Insurance Companies Act 1974 the reinsurers signed the reinsurances proposed outside the UK, but recommendations were made by London agents; the London pool managers dealt with all accounting, and payments by and to pool members passed through London bank accounts.

(ii) Claim by the reinsurer

5.191 Where the claim is for a negative declaration because of non-disclosure or misrepresentation the place for performance is the place where the correct disclosure or representation should have been made.[281] In London disclosure and representations will often be required to be made via the placing broker for the reinsured at the place where the reinsurer or his agent is (whether or not there is a producing broker), and the courts in England will therefore have jurisdiction under Article 5(1).

5.192 Obviously care must be taken to establish the correct obligation in question.[282] Where reinsurers rely on a breach of warranty to deny liability, the place for performance is the place where the warranty should have been performed; for example, a warranty as to retention,[283] a claims co-operation clause,[284] and a clause requiring the loss to be asserted.[285] If premium is payable through the accounts of the broker the place for payment will be where those accounts are to be paid; and similar questions may arise as in relation to payment of claims through the broker (para. 5.180 above).

(iii) What if there could be more than one place for performance?

5.193 The problem of what to do where there is more than one place for performance is in some ways similar to the problem where there is more than one obligation in question. As has been seen the approach of the European Court of Justice in the cases is that the national court should identify where possible the principal obligation relied upon (para. 5.183). That approach avoids so far as possible fragmenting parts of a dispute between different jurisdictions. It seems obvious that the same approach should be applied where there is more than one possible place for performance. In relation to employment cases the European Court of Justice has indeed held that where there was more than one place for performance it is the principal place for performance (if there is one) which is relevant.[286] It is true that employment disputes were treated differently under Article 5(1) from disputes relating to other contracts and the obligation in question was deemed to be the obligation on the employee to work (para. 5.132 above), but that should not affect the approach where there is more than one place for performance.

5.194 However, there may be cases where it is not possible to identify the principal place for performance. One of these is where a party gives a negative undertaking e.g. not to

281. *Agnew* v. *Länsförsäkringsbolagens* [2001] 1 AC 223; *Fisher* v. *Unione Italiana* [1998] CLC 682; *cf. Trade Indemnity* v. *Forsakringsaktiebolaget Njord* [1995] 1 Lloyd's Rep. 367, and *supra*, para. 5.170.

282. Fine distinctions may be made: e.g. *Chailease* v. *CAI* [2000] 1 Lloyd's Rep. 348, CA, where the obligation in question was to pay sums due under a letter of credit not to examine and take up documents presented, and *Viskase* v. *Kiefel* [1999] 3 All ER 362, CA, where the obligation to supply a machine which was reasonably fit for purpose was to be performed at the place for delivery since it was a once and for all obligation which could only be performed on delivery, rather than an obligation to do whatever is necessary from time to time to ensure the machine fulfilled its purpose.

283. *Fisher* v. *Unione Italiana* [1998] CLC 682.

284. *AIG* v. *Ethniki* [2000] Lloyd's Rep. IR 343.

285. *Ibid.*

286. C-125/92 *Mulox* v. *Geels* [1993] ECR I-4075 at [24].

supply anyone else, or to compete anywhere. Based on the objective of promoting legal certainty the European Court of Justice has interpreted Article 5(1) as requiring that the obligation in question must have only one place for performance. If there can be no principal place for performance the consequence is that Article 5(1) does not apply. In *Besix* v. *WABAG*[287] where the relevant obligation in a joint venture was not to enter into a competing contract with another party anywhere in the world, the European Court of Justice held that the place for performance could not be identified:

"Where parties have agreed a contractual obligation not to do something, applicable without any geographical limit, that approach does not avoid a multiplicity of competent courts, since it leads to the result that the places of performance of the obligation in question are in all the Contracting States. It also involves the risk that the claimant will be able to choose the place of performance which he judges to be most favourable to his interests. Consequently, that interpretation does not make it possible to identify the court most qualified territorially to determine the case. Furthermore, it is likely to reduce the predictability of the competent court, so that it is incompatible with the principle of legal certainty ... By its very nature, an obligation not to do something, which, like that in question in the main proceedings, consists in an undertaking to act exclusively with a contracting partner and a prohibition restraining those parties from committing themselves to another partner for the purpose of submitting a joint tender for a public contract and which, according to the parties' intention, is applicable without any geographical limit and must therefore be honoured throughout the world – and, in particular, in each of the Contracting States – is not capable of being identified with a specific place or linked to a court which would be particularly suited to hear and determine the dispute relating to that obligation. By definition, such an undertaking to refrain from doing something in any place whatsoever is not linked to any particular court rather than to any other. In those circumstances jurisdiction can, in such a case, be determined solely in accordance with Article 2 of the Brussels Convention, which provides a certain and reliable criterion."[288]

The court rejected the suggestion that the place for performance should be that jurisdiction in which the breach actually took place, partly because that would not resolve the problem where the breach occurred in more than one jurisdiction. The insistence in *Besix* on the place for performance being in one country overturns the approach previously adopted in English cases of permitting English jurisdiction where the obligation in question was capable of being performed in the UK and other countries.[289] Where, however, the negative undertaking is not to communicate with customers within one country there is no reason why that country should not be the place for performance.[290]

5.195 The effect of *Besix* is to focus attention on the precise terms of the contract. Where a clause relating to payment under a reinsurance stipulates that payment may be made for instance to the broker in London or to the reinsured in another jurisdiction can Article 5(1) apply? In *Mora* v. *AXA*[291] shipowners claimed against insurers the sums due under an average guarantee which provided that insurers "undertake to pay to the shipowners or to the Average Adjusters". The shipowners and adjusters were in different jurisdictions. The Court of Appeal accepted that where a contract specifies two or more alternative places for payment or performance the question whether or not the promisor has the right to select depends on the intention of the parties to be ascertained from the contract and the surrounding circumstances, but also held that the natural meaning of the words was that it was for the promisor to choose. The argument centred on whether or not that approach was over-literal and did not

287. C-256/00, [2002] ECR I-1699 at [24].

288. At [34]–[35], [49]–[50].

289. *Medway* v. *Meurer* [1990] 2 Lloyd's Rep. 112; *Boss Group* v. *Boss France* [1997] 1 WLR 351; *USF* v. *Aqua Technology* [2001] 1 All ER (Comm) 856.

290. *Kenburn* v. *Bergmann* [2002] EWCA 98, CA.

291. [2005] 2 Lloyd's Rep. 769, CA.

give effect to business common sense.[292] Accordingly the term in the reinsurance referred to above is liable to be interpreted so as to allow payment in more than one jurisdiction with the result that Article 5(1) cannot apply, unless there are compelling business reasons why that should not be so.[293]

F. IS THERE JURISDICTION BASED ON MATTERS RELATING TO TORT UNDER ARTICLE 5(3)?

1. Introduction

5.196 Under Article 5(3) a person domiciled in a Member State may, in another Member State, be sued "in matters relating to tort, delict or quasi-delict, in the courts for the place where the harmful event occurred or may occur". The application of Article 5(3) involves characterising the dispute as a matter relating to tort, etc, and characterising the place where the harmful event occurred or may occur which involves two questions: what was the place of the harmful event; what was the place of the event giving rise to the harmful event.

5.197 Many of the same general comments made in relation to Article 5(1) apply to Article 5(3) (para. 5.124). Article 5(3) only applies where the defendant is domiciled in another Member State. This is apparent from the opening words of the Article.[294] Nor can Article 5(3) apply where the harmful event occurs outside any Member State. Other questions arise as to how Article 5(3) applies where the harmful event occurred in more than one Member State, or partly in one Member State and partly in a non-Member State which are considered below.

5.198 The wording of Article 5(3) also makes it clear that where it applies it serves to allocate jurisdiction to the courts of the place where the harmful event occurred, so that if, for example, that place is London there is no room to apply the provisions allocating jurisdiction within the UK.

5.199 Article 5(3) does not confer accessory jurisdiction: "a court which has jurisdiction under Article 5 (3) over an action in so far as it is based on tort or delict does not have jurisdiction over that action in so far as it is not so based".[295]

(i) Development of Article 5(3)

5.200 When the Brussels Regulation was introduced three words were added to Article 5(3) so as to read: "in the courts for the place where the harmful event occurred or may occur". The aim was to make it clear that claims for preventive injunctions relating to tort were covered by Article 5(3).[296]

(ii) Objectives of Article 5(3)

5.201 There is a substantial overlap in the objectives of Article 5(1) and Article 5(3):

(1) Like Article 5(1), Article 5(3) is a derogation from the default jurisdiction of domicile under Article 2 and to be interpreted restrictively, in the sense of not going beyond

292. See, e.g., the approach in *Sirius* v. *FAI* [2004] 1 WLR 3251 (HL).

293. Compare the position if no place for performance is specified when English law will imply a place for performance – see para. 5.190 above.

294. Compare Article 5(4) which permits a civil claim for damages or restitution based on an act giving rise to criminal proceedings to be brought whatever the domicile of the defendant; *Jenard*, 1979 OJ C.59/1, 26.

295. C-189/87 *Kalfelis* v. *Schroder* [1988] ECR I-5565 at [19]. This was based on the need to interpret restrictively derogations from the general jurisdiction under Article 2. It was pointed out that it is always open to a claimant to bring all possible claims against a defendant in the courts for the domicile of the defendant. C-68/93 *Shevill* v. *Presse Alliance* [1995] ECR I-415.

296. *Schlosser*, para. 134; *Explanatory Memorandum to Brussels Regulation*, p. 14. Article 5(3) of the Brussels Convention was interpreted as wide enough to cover anticipated torts: C-167/00 *VKI* v. *Henkel* [2002] ECR I-8111 at [49].

cases expressly envisaged by the Brussels Regulation.[297] Another way in which this has been put is to say the scope of the derogation should be such as to enable a reasonably well-informed defendant reasonably to predict in which courts other than that of his domicile he may be sued.[298]

(2) The additional jurisdiction under Article 5(3) is justified by: "reasons relating to the sound administration of justice and the efficacious conduct of proceedings ... The courts for the place where the harmful event occurred are usually the most appropriate for deciding the case, in particular on the grounds of proximity and ease of taking evidence."[299]

(3) Efforts to interpret Article 5(3) so as to confer jurisdiction on the claimant's domicile will be looked on warily: the need to avoid multiplication of available jurisdictions "militates against any interpretation of the Convention which, otherwise than in the cases expressly provided for, might lead to recognition of the jurisdiction of the courts of the plaintiff's domicile and would enable a plaintiff to determine the competent court by his choice of domicile".[300]

(iii) Approach to Article 5(3)

5.202 Key elements of Article 5(3) are subject to an autonomous definition because of the need for uniformity of approach across Member States. Thus, the question what are matters relating to tort, delict or quasi-delict, what is the place where the harmful event occurred, what is damage, and what is the event giving rise to damage are all to be decided according to community law. However, the role of Article 5(3) is not to unify national laws in relation to what is a tort or how it may be proved, so the applicable law as determined by the conflicts rules in the forum will determine whether or not there is a tort, and the evidence required of the existence and extent of harm.[301] Accordingly, the fact that under English law damage is presumed in libel actions does not mean that Article 5(3) cannot apply.[302] The correct approach is to apply the conflicts rules of the court seised to decide the law applicable to the tort, etc, and under that law to identify the elements necessary to establish the claim relied on, and then to apply the autonomous definition under community law to, for instance, whether or not the dispute is a matter relating to tort within Article 5(3).[303]

5.203 We consider the issues which arise under following main headings:

(1) Is this a matter relating to tort, delict or quasi-delict?
(2) What is the place where the harmful event occurred?

2. Is this a matter relating to tort, delict or quasi-delict?

5.204 It has been said in this context that "Like the proverbial elephant, tort is easier to recognise than to define".[304] For the purposes of (re)insurance disputes there may not be

297. C-189/87 *Kalfelis* v. *Schroder* [1988] ECR I-5565 at [19]; C-168/02 *Kronhofer* v. *Maier* [2004] ECR I-6009 at [14].

298. C-26/91 *Handte* v. *TMCS* [1992] ECR I-3967 at [14], [18]; C-364/93 *Marinari* v. *Lloyds Bank* [1996] QB 217, [1995] ECR I-2719 at [13]; C-168/02 *Kronhofer* v. *Maier* [2004] ECR I-6009 at [20]; C-18/02 *Danmarks* v. *LO Landsorganisationen* [2004] ECR I-1417 at [36]; *London Helicopters* v. *Heliportugal* [2006] EWHC 108 at [16].

299. C-167/00 *VKI* v. *Henkel* [2002] ECR I-8111 at [46]; C-21/76 *Bier* v. *Mines de potasse d'Alsace* [1976] ECR I-1735 at [11].

300. C-220/88 *Dumez* v. *Hessiche Landesbank* [1990] ECR I-49 at [19].

301. C-68/93 *Shevill* v. *Presse Alliance* [1995] ECR I-415; C-18/02 *Danmarks* v. *LO Landsorganisationen* [2004] ECR I-1417 at [43].

302. C-68/93 *Shevill* v. *Presse Alliance* [1995] I-415.

303. *Ibid.*, at [38]–[39].

304. Opinion of the Advocate General Jacobs in C-167/00 *VKI* v. *Henkel* [2002] ECR I-8111 at [31], citing Advocate General Warner; it covers "a wide diversity of kinds of liability": C-21/76 *Bier* v. *Mines de potasse d'Alsace* [1976] ECR I-1735 at [18].

many cases where the matter is in doubt. The "liability" of the defendant will usually be the subject of a claim to compensate the claimant for wrongdoing. However, a claim to compensation is not always necessary. In *Equitas* v. *Wave*[305] the court held that a claim for a negative declaration in relation to an alleged tort of procuring a breach of contract was within Article 5(3). In *VKI* v. *Henkel*[306] a consumer association sought an injunction but not damages against an individual to prevent the use of unfair terms in contracts with members of the public. The European Court of Justice said of Article 5(3) that "with regard to consumer protection, it covers not only situations where an individual has personally sustained damage but also, in particular, the undermining of legal stability by the use of unfair terms which it is the task of associations such as the VKI to prevent".[307] It follows from this case that a claim for an injunction alone in respect of an undoubted tort, for example libel, would come within Article 5(3). The approach of the European Court of Justice in *VKI* seemed to be to equate damage to an individual with damage to the public by the use of unfair terms. And in *Danmarks* v. *LO Landsorganisationen*[308] the European Court of Justice held that a dispute as to the legality of industrial action which under Danish law had to be heard in a court which had no jurisdiction to award damages was still within Article 5(3), and that it did not matter that the unlawful action was suspended pending a ruling as to its legality.

5.205 The conduct of the defendant must, it would seem, be in some sense wrongful. In *VKI* the conduct of the defendant was undoubtedly alleged to be wrongful. By contrast, in *Reichert* v. *Dresdner Bank (No. 2)*[309] a creditor objected to a transfer of property which the claimant was entitled to do even if the transferee had acted in good faith. The claim did not fall within Article 5(3). It has been said that "an action which may be directed against a third party who has not committed any wrongful act cannot be regarded as an action which seeks to establish the liability of a defendant".[310] If the liability of the defendant is caused by his wrongful conduct it is very likely that the claim will fall within Article 5(3). If the liability of the defendant is caused by non performance of an obligation which was freely assumed, or the claim is for performance of such an obligation, the claim will fall within Article 5(1).

5.206 In summary, it therefore seems likely that for Article 5(3) to apply the "liability" of the defendant must be founded on some wrongdoing of the defendant, but not on breach of an obligation freely assumed. The liability will often but not always result in a claim for damages. The result is that most claims for damages which are classified under English law as claims in tort fall within Article 5(3).

5.207 The scope of Articles 5(1) and 5(3) have been held to be exclusive, so that if a claim is a matter relating to a contract it cannot be a matter relating to a tort, as will be seen below. Some claims fall neither within Article 5(1) nor 5(3). We consider these three categories with reference to reinsurance below.

(i) Matters which relate to a contract

5.208 If a claim is a matter relating to a contract, it cannot be within Article 5(3): "matters relating to tort, delict and quasi-delict" covers all actions which seek to establish the liability

305. [2005] EWHC 923 (Comm), Simon J.
306. C-167/00, [2002] ECR I-8111.
307. C-167/00 *VKI* v. *Henkel* [2002] ECR I-8111 at [42]; see also the discussion in the opinion of the Advocate General in that case at [40].
308. [2004] 2 Lloyd's Rep. 162.
309. C-261/90 *Reichert* v. *Dresdner Bank (No. 2)* [1992] ECR I-2149.
310. Opinion of the Advocate General Jacobs in C-167/00 *VKI* v. *Henkel* [2002] ECR I-8111 at [40].

of a defendant and which are not related to a "contract" within the meaning of Article 5(1).[311] A matter remains one relating to a contract even if on the same facts the claim can be put as a claim in tort (for instance breach of a contractual and tortious duty of care): such a claim can only be brought within Article 5(1), not 5(3).[312] This is often a crucial point because of the difference in the rules for jurisdiction. If the matter relates to contract jurisdiction may be more likely to be found to be at the place of the reinsurer (which is often the place for performance of the obligation in question) than if the matter relates to tort.

5.209 The English courts have held that a claim to avoid a reinsurance contract for non-disclosure or misrepresentation is a matter relating to contract within Article 5(1) (para. 5.170). If that is right, a claim to rescind a contract for innocent misrepresentation should also fall within Article 5(1) in view of its similarities with a claim to avoid for breach of the duty of good faith, and the fact that it is not based on wrongdoing, at any rate in the sense that connotes fault. This conclusion should not alter if the court awards damages in lieu of innocent misrepresentation under the Misrepresentation Act 1967. It has been suggested that a claim to avoid for duress and undue influence could not fall within Article 5(1) since there could be no place for performance of such a negative obligation[313]; such a claim is therefore likely to fall within Article 5(3).

(ii) Matters which relate to a tort, delict or quasi delict

5.210 Where a claim for misrepresentation is based on negligence or fraud it has been assumed without questioning in several cases in the European Court of Justice that claims for compensation fall within Article 5(3).[314] The English courts have uniformly treated a claim for damages and/or rescission for negligent or fraudulent misrepresentation as falling within Article 5(3).[315]

5.211 A claim for damages in negligence is an archetypal matter within Article 5(3).[316] So also is a claim for damages for conspiracy,[317] and for inducing breach of contract.[318]

5.212 The fate of claims based on constructive trust depends on the basis of the claim made. There are claims based on the implication of the defendant in a breach of trust, and claims based on the defendant having become the owner of property through a transaction which is not challenged but where the claimant asserts that it would now be unconscionable for the defendant to assert a beneficial interest in the property.[319] In the first case of a claim based on the implication of the defendant in a breach of trust, liability may be based on knowing assistance in a breach of trust or unconscionable receipt of trust property. A claim based on dishonest assistance is "a liability in equity to pay damages based on fault"[320] since it

311. C-189/87 *Kalfelis* v. *Schroder* [1988] ECR I-5565 at [17].

312. *Source* v. *TUV Rheinland* [1998] QB 54, 63 (CA).

313. *Agnew* v. *Länsförsäkringsbolagens* [2001] 1 AC 223, 241, Lord Woolf; see also p. 266, *per* Lord Millett, dissenting.

314. C-189/87 *Kalfelis* v. *Schroder* [1988] ECR I-5565; C-168/02 *Kronhofer* v. *Maier* [2004] ECR I-6009.

315. *Minster* v. *Hyundai* [1988] 2 Lloyd's Rep. 621 (negligent misstatement at common law within *Hedley Byrne* v. *Heller* [1964] AC 465); *Domicrest* v. *SBC* [1999] 1 Lloyd's Rep. 80 (negligent misstatement at common law); *Alfred Dunhill* v. *Diffusion* [2002] 1 All ER (Comm) 950 (negligent misrepresentation under the Misrepresentation Act 1967 and at common law); *Bank of Tokyo-Mitsubishi* v. *Baskan* [2004] 2 Lloyd's Rep. 395 (fraudulent and negligent misrepresentation); *London Helicopters* v. *Heliportugal* [2006] EWHC 108, para. 16 (negligent misstatement).

316. *Source* v. *TUV Rheinland* [1998] QB 54, 63 (CA).

317. *Bank of Tokyo-Mitsubishi* v. *Baskan* [2004] 2 Lloyd's Rep. 395, para. 219.

318. C-18/02 *Danmarks* v. *LO Landsorganisationen* [2004] ECR I-1417; *Equitas* v. *Wave* [2005] EWHC 923.

319. *Paragon* v. *Thakerer* [1999] 1 All ER 400, 408–409, Millett LJ; *Halsbury's Laws* (4th ed., 2002), Vol. [16(2)], para. 852.

320. *Casio* v. *Sayo* [2001] EWCA Civ 661, quoting from Chadwick J. in *Arab Monetary Fund* v. *Hashim*, 29.7.94 unrep.; *Dexter* v. *Harley*, *The Times*, 2 April 2001.

depends on the dishonesty of the defendant and is within Article 5(3). A claim of the second type based on unconscionable receipt does not necessarily depend on a claim of dishonesty by the recipient although it may well do so on the facts: the test is whether or not it would be unconscionable for the defendant to retain the benefit received.[321] If, in such a case, dishonesty is alleged the claim will be based on wrongdoing and within Article 5(3).[322] If dishonesty is not alleged, the claim is similar to a claim to title to property, and does not depend on the defendant having been guilty of any wrongdoing: it is therefore treated as not within Article 5(3).[323] Similarly, the fate of claims based on breach of fiduciary duty will also depend on the basis on which the claim is made; if the claim is based on an undertaking freely undertaken it is likely to be treated as falling within Article 5(1), otherwise it will often be based on wrongdoing of the defendant and within Article 5(3).

5.213 If a claim based on subrogation or assignment does not fall within Article 5(1) because, for instance, the defendant did not authorise the making of the contract on which the claim is based (para. 5.146 above) it would not be based on wrongdoing and would not fall within Article 5(3): jurisdiction would usually have to be founded on Article 2. Similarly, claims in contribution against a co-reinsurer which do not fall within Article 5(1) (para. 5.152) cannot be said to be based on wrongdoing and do not fall within Article 5(3), although there is no reason why a claim to contribution under the Civil Liability (Contribution) Act 1978 or its equivalent based on the liability of the defendant for the same damage as the claimant could not fall within Article 5(3) if the basis of the liability was wrongdoing.

(iii) Matters which do not relate to a contract or tort

5.214 The English courts have held that a claim in restitution to recover monies paid under a contract which was *ultra vires* one party and void as unjust enrichment is not founded on an obligation freely assumed or wrongdoing of the defendant and does not fall within Articles 5(1) or 5(3).[324] A claim to account for property held as constructive trustee but not apparently based on any wrongdoing of the defendant was held to be outside Article 5(3).[325] It is otherwise, however, if the constructive trust claim is based on wrongdoing of the defendant, as referred to above. A claim under French law that a transfer of property should not be recognised because it was in fraud of creditors was not within Article 5(3) or Article 5(1).[326] The European Court of Justice emphasised (at para. 19) that such an action is capable of being directed at innocent third parties not guilty of wrongdoing, and did not seek compensation:

> "the action … may be instituted both against dispositions made for consideration by the debtor when the beneficiary acts in bad faith and against transactions entered into without consideration by the debtor even if the beneficiary acts in good faith. The purpose of such an action is not to have the debtor ordered to make good the damage he has caused his creditor by his fraudulent conduct, but to render ineffective, as against his creditor, the disposition which the debtor has made. It is directed not only against the debtor but also against the person who benefits from the act, who is not a party to the obligation binding the creditor to his debtor, even, in cases where there is no consideration for the transaction, where that third party has not committed any wrongful act."

321. *BCCI* v. *Akindele* [2001] Ch 437 (CA); disapproved on a different point *Criterion* v. *Stratford* [2004] 1 WLR 1846 (HL).
322. As it was in *Bank of Tokyo-Mitsubishi* v. *Baskan* [2004] 2 Lloyd's Rep. 395, para. 218; *Dexter* v. *Harley*, *The Times*, 2 April 2001.
323. *Compagnie Andre* v. *Artibell* [2001] SC 653; compare C-261/90 *Reichert* v. *Dresdner (No. 2)* [1992] ECR I-2149.
324. *Kleinwort Benson* v. *Glasgow* [1999] 1 AC 153, 172, 185, 196.
325. *Compagnie Andre* v. *Artibell* [2001] SC 653.
326. C-261/90 *Reichert* v. *Dresdner (No. 2)* [1992] ECR I-2149.

3. What is the "place where the harmful event occurred"?

5.215 The law applicable to the tort under the conflicts laws of the forum will decide whether or not there is a tort, including the circumstances in which the event giving rise to the harm complained of, or the evidence which must be adduced.[327] But, for the purposes of deciding jurisdiction under Article 5(3), the court will for many purposes apply autonomous concepts used in Article 5(3) to the tort alleged under the applicable law. First, the definition of the place where the harmful event occurred is autonomous in order that a uniform approach may be adopted across Member States. In *Bier* v. *Mines de potasse d'Alsace*[328] the European Court of Justice referred to two possible meanings: the place where the damage occurred or the place of the event giving rise to the damage, and decided that it could mean either at the option of the claimant.[329] In the case of each option community law also decides for the purposes of jurisdiction which is the place where the damage occurred, or the place of the event giving rise to the damage. The essential reason for the double test under Article 5(3) seems to be that the "harmful event" within Article 5(3) (i.e. damage) will necessarily have been caused by an event, and there is no reason to exclude from Article 5(3) the event causing the damage.[330]

(i) What is the relevant damage?

5.216 Before dealing with identification of the two places referred to above it is necessary to ask what is the damage which is relevant under the test referred to in *Bier*. The European Court of Justice has given damage an autonomous meaning, and drawn a fairly small radius around the relevant damage by holding that it must be direct not indirect.[331] This distinction has been of most importance in denying claims to establish jurisdiction based on financial loss suffered by a claimant in a place other than that where the harmful event occurred.[332] It is necessary to see where the event giving rise to the damage produced its *initial or direct* effect. The autonomous meaning of damage relevant also means that Article 5(3) may apply even though under the applicable law the tort may not require proof of any damage[333] or may presume that damage has occurred.[334]

(ii) What is the place where the damage occurred?

5.217 The place where the damage occurred must be decided by the court seised.[335] In cases of claims in tort for negligent or fraudulent misrepresentation this will often be the place

327. C-68/93 *Shevill* v. *Presse Alliance* [1995] ECR I-415 at [38].

328. C-21/76 *Bier* v. *Mines de potasse d'Alsace* [1976] ECR I-1735 at [11].

329. C-21/76 *Bier* v. *Mines de potasse d'Alsace* [1976] ECR I-1735 at [19]. If the place where the damage occurred was not available, Article 5(3) would be of little practical use since the place of the event giving rise to the damage is often the same as the domicile of the defendant: C-68/93 *Shevill* v. *Presse Alliance* [1995] ECR I-415 at [27].

330. C-21/76 *Bier* v. *Mines de potasse d'Alsace* [1976] ECR I-1735, para. 16; *Dexter* v. *Harley*, *The Times*, 2 April 2001, para. 17; C-18/02 *Danmarks* v. *LO Landsorganisationen* [2004] ECR I-1417 at [32].

331. C-220/88 *Dumez* v. *Hessiche Landesbank* [1990] ECR I-49 at [20]–[21].

332. C-220/88 *Dumez* v. *Hessiche Landesbank* [1990] ECR I-49 (claim by French parent company in respect of losses suffered in France owing to insolvency of German subsidiaries caused by withdrawal of funds by German bank); *Marinari* v. *Lloyds Bank* [1996] QB 217, [1995] ECR I-2719 (claim for financial consequences suffered in Italy of alleged wrongful imprisonment in England); C-168/02 *Kronhofer* v. *Maier* [2004] ECR I-6009 (claim by Austrian claimant for damages for negligent advice given by telephone from Germany to invest money in Germany which led to losses suffered in Austria); see also Opinion of Advocate General Darmon in C-220/88 *Dumez* v. *Hessiche Landesbank* [1990] ECR I-49, para. 124, for a distinction between where the damage occurred and where it was suffered.

333. C-364/93 *Marinari* v. *Lloyds Bank* [1996] QB 217, [1995] ECR I-2719 at [18].

334. C-68/93 *Shevill* v. *Presse Alliance* [1995] ECR I-415 at [40].

335. C-18/02 *Danmarks* v. *LO Landsorganisationen* [2004] ECR I-1417 at [43].

where a claimant relies upon the representation and sustains loss.[336] In many cases this test may locate jurisdiction in the place where the claimant is domiciled, and is especially significant because the alternative test of the place of the event giving rise to the damage will locate jurisdiction in the place where the representation was made (see below). However, it is always necessary to examine the place where the damage was sustained with care. The key question is what is the relevant damage, and where did that take place, not simply where did reliance begin.[337] Where damage has occurred in more than one Member State the court will have jurisdiction in respect of that damage which occurred in that jurisdiction alone.[338]

(iii) What is the place of the event giving rise to the damage?

5.218 The first question is what is the relevant event. This has been given an autonomous meaning in order that there may be uniformity across Member States.[339] Presumably the place to be regarded as the place of that event is to be decided by the court seised, like the place where the relevant damage occurred (see above). In relation to claims in tort for negligent or fraudulent misrepresentation the relevant event is the issue of the representation, and the place of that is therefore where the representation was issued. This was the conclusion of the European Court of Justice in a claim in defamation: the place where the "libel was issued and put into circulation" was the place of the event giving rise to the damage.[340] It was also assumed by the European Court of Justice in a case of a claim based on a telephone conversation between one country and another.[341] It has since been followed in the English cases in relation to claims in tort for misrepresentation.[342] This approach will often lead to jurisdiction in the Member State in which the defendant is domiciled – hence the importance of the alternative ground of jurisdiction in relation to misrepresentation.

5.219 In the case of a claim of constructive trust based on knowing assistance the English court has held that the event is the act of assistance by the accessory not merely the breach of trust by the principal.[343] As to the place of that event, the English courts have taken a broad view and looked to the substance of the conduct said to be wrongful. Thus in *Casio* v. *Sayo*[344] the relevant event was the assistance by the accessory in using an account in England, and the place where that occurred was where the account was operated, not where knowledge was acquired, or the operation of the account was procured, since without the actual act of

336. *Domicrest* v. *SBC* [1999] 1 Lloyd's Rep. 90, 92; *Alfred Dunhill* v. *Diffusion* [2002] 1 All ER (Comm) 950; *London Helicopters* v. *Heliportugal* [2006] EWHC 108, para. 25. Compare avoidance for non-disclosure or misrepresentation which is a matter relating to a contract within Article 5(1) (para. 5.170 above).

337. Thus, for example, in *Domicrest* the damage occurred where goods were released in reliance on a misrepresentation; in *Raffeisen* v. *Tranos* [2001] IL Pr 85 the damage occurred where a credit facility was agreed and signed, and not where the "chain of reliance", leading to that facility, began.

338. C-68/93 *Shevill* v. *Presse Alliance* [1995] ECR I-415 at [30].

339. C-68/93 *Shevill* v. *Presse Alliance* [1995] ECR I-415 at [24], where the European Court of Justice decided that the place of the event giving rise to the damage in the case of libel was where the publisher of the newspaper was established; C-364/93 *Marinari* v. *Lloyds Bank* [1996] QB 217, [1995] ECR I-2719 where the event giving rise to the damage was the place where the claimant was arrested and securities confiscated.

340. C-68/93 *Shevill* v. *Presse Alliance* [1995] ECR I-415 at [24].

341. C-168/02 *Kronhofer* v. *Maier* [2004] ECR I-6009 at [17].

342. *Domicrest* v. *SBC* [1999] 1 Lloyd's Rep. 80, 92 (negligent misstatement at common law) *Alfred Dunhill* v. *Diffusion* [2002] 1 All ER (Comm) 950 (negligent misrepresentation under the Misrepresentation Act 1967 and at common law); *ABCI* v. *Banque Franco-Tunisienne* [2003] 2 Lloyd's Rep. 146, 160 (CA): *Bank of Tokyo-Mitsubishi* v. *Baskan* [2004] 2 Lloyd's Rep. 395 (fraudulent and negligent misrepresentation); *London Helicopters* v. *Heliportugal* [2006] EWHC 108, para. 29 (negligent misstatement); *Newsat* v. *Zani* [2006] 1 Lloyd's Rep. 707; compare *Minster* v. *Hyundai* [1988] 2 Lloyd's Rep. 621 (negligent misstatement at common law within *Hedley Byrne* v. *Heller* [1964] AC 465).

343. *Casio* v. *Sayo* [2001] EWCA Civ 661, para. 14.

344. [2001] EWCA Civ 661, CA, paras 17–22; *Cronos* v. *Palatin* [2003] 2 Lloyd's Rep. 489, 495.

operating the account to accept and disburse monies the other acts would have been of no use. However, there has to be some act by the accessory within the jurisdiction.[345]

5.220 What if it is not possible to locate the relevant event in one Member State only? A claim of negligence, particularly if it involved an omission to act, may have taken place in more than one Member State, or it may not be possible to identify the place at which the event took place. It may be that the European Court of Justice will adopt a similar approach to that likely to apply where there is more than one place for performance of the obligation in question under Article 5(1) and select the principal place at which the event took place (para. 5.193). If that is not possible it is likely that Article 5(3) will not apply.

G. IS THERE JURISDICTION IN RESPECT OF A CLAIM AGAINST A CO-DEFENDANT, THIRD PARTY OR COUNTERCLAIM UNDER ARTICLE 6?

1. Introduction

5.221 Broadly Article 6 confers an option to bring proceedings against a defendant domiciled in another Member State in jurisdictions in which certain other proceedings are taking place. The relevant parts provide:

"A person domiciled in a member state may also be sued:

1. where he is one of a number of defendants, in the courts for the place where any one of them is domiciled, provided the claims are so closely connected that it is expedient to hear and determine them together to avoid the risk of irreconcilable judgments resulting from separate proceedings;
2. as a third party in an action on a warranty or guarantee or in any other third party proceedings, in the court seised of the original proceedings, unless these were instituted solely with the object of removing him from the jurisdiction of the court which would be competent in his case;
3. on a counter-claim arising from the same contract or facts on which the original claim was based, in the court in which the original claim is pending."

5.222 The common theme running through Article 6 is that a defendant may be sued outside his domicile under Article 6 because of the connection between the claim against that defendant and other proceedings; whether a claim against a co-defendant, other original proceedings in which a third party claim has been made, or proceedings in which a counterclaim has been made. Article 6 only applies where the defendant to be sued is domiciled in a Member State.

5.223 Article 6 is a significant provision in reinsurance disputes because of the prevalence of multi party disputes. There is, for example, scope for a reinsured to bring proceedings against any one of a market of reinsurers in the place where one is domiciled, and for third party proceedings by reinsurers against the reinsured, or a counterclaim against the claimant. Jurisdiction in relation to such claims in insurance is in many respects different (see Chapter 6).

5.224 Article 6(1) does not include any accessory jurisdiction: it only confers jurisdiction in respect of the claim which is within Article 6(1).[346] This seems likely to be the case with the other Article 6 grounds.

5.225 Article 6(2) does not apply if there is an exclusive jurisdiction agreement as between the third party and the party seeking to have him joined.[347] The same would apply to the other grounds under Article 6.

345. *Dexter* v. *Harley*, *The Times*, 2 April 2001, para. 19.

346. C-189/87 *Kalfelis* v. *Schroder* [1988] ECR I-5565 at [19]; *BST Pro Mark/SARL Ergeca*, Court d'Appel Versalles, 30 November 2000, Case 2001/36 at ECJ database *http://www.jura.uni-sb.de/convention-bruxelles/en/2001/36-2001* in relation to Article 6(3).

347. *Jenard*, 1979 OJ C.59/1, 27.

(i) Development of Article 6

5.226 Article 6(1) was amended when the Brussels Regulation was introduced specifically to add a proviso that the claims were sufficiently connected to justify the joinder of the defendant.[348] The other parts of Article 6 have not been amended since the Brussels Convention was introduced.

(ii) Objectives of Article 6 generally

5.227 The reason for Article 6(1) jurisdiction was to "obviate the handing down of irreconcilable judgments".[349] Article 6(2) jurisdiction is justified as being in the "interests of justice", since it enables a necessary party to an existing dispute to be joined.[350] The need to promote predictability and certainty at all stages has also been emphasised.[351] Article 6 is to be construed restrictively since it is a derogation from Article 2.[352]

(iii) Approach to Article 6 generally

5.228 A number of concepts have autonomous meanings because of the need for uniformity in the application of Article 6 across Member States as referred to below. However, the European Court of Justice has emphasised that the Brussels Regulation is not intended to supersede the procedural law of the Member States which must be applied to decide whether or not claims may be joined, provided that the effectiveness of the Brussels Regulation is not impaired.[353] Under Article 6(2) the national court may apply its own procedural requirements for the joinder of a third party to an existing action, as long as the effectiveness of the Brussels Regulation is not impaired, for example by requiring that the third party be domiciled in the Member State of the court seised.[354]

5.229 If the anchor defendant is domiciled in England Article 6(1) will confer jurisdiction on "the courts for the place where [he] … is domiciled", i.e. England, so that there is no need to apply the provisions for the allocation of jurisdiction within the courts of the UK. The same would apply to Articles 6(2) and 6(3).

5.230 We consider the issues which arise under the following main headings:

(1) Article 6(1): one of a number of defendants
(2) Article 6(2): third party proceedings
(3) Article 6(3): counterclaim.

2. Article 6(1): one of a number of defendants

5.231 If X has brought proceedings against Y and Z in Y's domicile, Article 6(1) may confer jurisdiction on the court seised against Z even though Z is not domiciled there. Sometimes Y is referred to as the anchor defendant.[355] The effect is that if any one of a market of reinsurers is domiciled in for example England then all other reinsurers domiciled in any Member State may be sued in the same proceedings in England.[356] Or the reinsured may commence

348. *Explanatory Memorandum to Brussels Regulation*, p. 14
349. *Jenard*, 1979 OJ C.59/1, 26.
350. *Jenard*, 1979 OJ C.59/1, 27.
351. *Canada Trust* v. *Stolzenberg (No. 2)* [2002] 1 AC 1, 11, an Article 6(1) case.
352. C-189/87 *Kalfelis* v. *Schroder* [1988] ECR I-5565, paras 8, 19; *Jordan* v. *Baltic* [1999] 2 AC 128, 134.
353. C-365/88 *Kongress* v. *Zeehage* [1990] ECR I-1845 at [18]–[19]; C-77/04 *GIE* v. *Zurich* [2005] ECR I-4509 at [34].
354. C-365/88 *Kongress* v. *Zeehage* [1990] ECR I-1845 at [22].
355. E.g., *Canada Trust* v. *Stolzenberg (No. 2)* [2002] 1 AC 1, 6.
356. Compare the position in relation to insurance where co-insurers may only be sued in the courts of a Member State in which proceedings are brought against the leader: Article 9(1)(c) and para. 6.17 below.

proceedings against the reinsurer and join the broker (if domiciled in a Member State) as a defendant in the event that the reinsurer is not held liable.

5.232 The concept of an irreconcilable judgment under Article 6(1) has an autonomous meaning. In *Reunion* v. *Splieterhoff*[357] in French proceedings French insurers claimed to be subrogated to the claim by the owners of cargo for damage against an Australian carrier in contract, and a Dutch carrier in tort. The court pointed out *obiter* that if such claims had been made against the same defendant it was clear that Article 5(3) would not confer jurisdiction except for the tort claim,[358] and drew the conclusion from this that the claim in contract and in tort therefore "cannot be regarded as connected" for the purposes of Article 6(1).[359] This seems debateable. The rule that there is no jurisdiction under Article 5(3) in respect of claims not covered by the Article is concerned with not derogating from Article 2 jurisdiction any further than expressly required by the special jurisdiction under Article 5. It is not concerned with preventing irreconcilable judgments, as is Article 6(1). It is therefore difficult to understand the relevance of Article 5(3) to the ambit of Article 6(1). Nor is it clear why the approach to irreconcilable judgments under Article 6(1) should be different from that under Article 28(3), in relation to which it would not matter that claims were in tort and contract if there was a risk that the judgments would be conflicting (see para. 5.290).[360] Further, the European Court of Justice has often stressed in the context of Articles 5(1) and (3) that a claimant can always fall back on Article 2 jurisdiction and avoid fragmentation of claims in contract and tort against the same defendant by bringing them all in the courts of the defendant's domicile. Article 6, however, is the only way of mitigating the effect of fragmentation where various disputes arise out of a single set of facts involving different parties.

5.233 In *Watson* v. *First Choice*[361] the Court of Appeal plainly regarded the apparently rigid rule laid down in *Reunion* as liable to give rise to arbitrary and unjustified distinctions and too strict. In principle, it would have preferred to adopt the wider approach taken under Article 28(3). The Court of Appeal referred the matter to the European Court of Justice but the matter was settled. However, the weight of English authority is that a broad approach should be adopted in deciding whether or not there is a risk that judgments will be irreconcilable. This was encapsulated by Hirst LJ in *Gascoine* v. *Pyrah*: "In many cases it will be only the legal consequence of the separate judgments that will give rise to a real risk of irreconcilability, but the courts must look at the substance of the claims against the different defendants and assess the risk giving due weight to the possibility of conflicting determinations of factual and other issues common to each of the claims".[362] In *Andrew Weir* v. *Wartsila*[363] the English court held *Reunion* did not apply where the claimant had claims in contract and tort against the anchor party and against the other defendant. Although the relevant contracts were different there was a risk of irreconcilable judgments on causation and fact which was enough for Article 6(1). There was also such a risk in relation to the separate tort claims.

357. C-51/97, [1998] ECR I-6511.

358. The result of C-189/87 *Kalfelis* v. *Schroder* [1988] ECR I-5565 (see para. 5.208 above).

359. Para. 50; and see further the explanation of Advocate General Cosmas at paras 70–72.

360. Briggs/Rees, p. 207, takes the view that the decision in *Reunion* results from a misreading of Article 6(1) and is simply wrong and should not be followed.

361. [2001] 2 Lloyd's Rep. 339; Case 2003/23 in Oberlandsgericht Düsseldorf on European Court of Justice database at *http://www.jura.uni-sb.de/convention-bruxelles/en/2003/23-2003* the summary of which states "It is sufficient that there is a possibility of reaching different conclusions on preliminary issues, such as the validity of a declaration".

362. 25 May 1993, CA; *Casio* v. *Sayo* [2001] EWCA Civ 661, CA; *Latchin t/a Dinkha Latchin Associates* v. *General Mediterranean Holidays SA and another* [2003] EWCA Civ 1786; *ET Plus* v. *Welter* [2006] 1 Lloyd's Rep. 251, Gross J., para. 59.

5.234 There is also a question as to whether or not Article 6(1) requires that the anchor defendant be a party to the same proceedings as those against the defendant to be sued. In *Masri* v. *Consolidated Contractors*[364] the claimant had commenced the first proceedings in England against an English defendant claiming damages for breach of contract. When the English defendant denied that it was a party to the contract, the claimant commenced a second set of proceedings against Greek defendants making the same claim in the alternative against parties associated with the English defendant in the first proceedings. The Court of Appeal took the view that the purpose of Article 6(1) was to prevent irreconcilable judgments which it would not do if Article 6(1) could only apply if the anchor English defendant was a party to the second set of proceedings.

5.235 Subject to these points, the approach to Article 6(1) is that it is up to the procedural law of the court seised to decide whether or not joinder of the claims is permissible,[365] and whether or not there is a risk of irreconcilable judgments.[366]

5.236 If it is not expedient to hear the claims together, perhaps because there is no arguable claim against the new defendant, Article 6(1) will not apply.[367] In other cases there may be no real or serious issue to be tried against the anchor defendant in which case Article 6(1) will not apply.[368] As to timing, the claims must be related when the proceedings are instituted.[369] In England this is when the claim form is issued.[370]

5.237 Article 6(1) only confers jurisdiction on "the courts for the place where any one of them [the defendants] is domiciled". It therefore is of no avail if jurisdiction for the original proceedings was not based on the domicile of a defendant under Article 2, but on some other special ground of jurisdiction such as those in relation to exclusive jurisdiction agreements, submission, contract or tort.[371] This could be very inconvenient, although it might be pointed out that if the claimant sued the original defendant in the court of his domicile under Article 2, fragmentation could be avoided as all relevant parties could be brought before that court. Whilst this argument may have general application, it would not help in an Article 23 case (jurisdiction agreement) where Article 2 jurisdiction is not available.

3. Article 6(2): third party proceedings

5.238 If there are original proceedings between X and Y in England, Article 6(2) would confer jurisdiction on the English court in respect of a claim by X against a third party, Z. It seems likely that what are "third party proceedings" within Article 6(2) should be treated as an autonomous concept under community law because of the need for uniformity across Member States.[372] It has been suggested that the third party proceedings would therefore include a case where a third party voluntarily joined in proceedings.[373] An English court has

363. [2004] 2 Lloyd's Rep. 377.
364. [2006] 1 Lloyd's Rep. 391, CA; *cf. Barclays* v. *Glasgow* [1994] QB 404, CA.
365. E.g., CPR 7.3, all claims may be joined in one action which can "conveniently" be dealt with.
366. C-189/87 *Kalfelis* v. *Schroder* [1988] ECR I-5565 at [12].
367. *The Rewia* [1991] 2 Lloyd's Rep. 325; *Molnlycke* v. *Proctor* [1992] 1 WLR 112 where Dillon J. suggested that it would be "improper" to join a party under Article 6(1) for the purpose of obtaining disclosure since there were other channels for such applications; *Qingdao* v. *Grace (The Xing Sui)* [1995] 2 Lloyd's Rep. 15.
368. *Qingdao* v. *Grace (The Xing Sui)* [1995] 2 Lloyd's Rep. 15. It is probably not necessary to go any further and show in English proceedings that there is a good arguable case in the merits against the anchor defendant: *ET Plus* v. *Welter* [2006] 1 Lloyd's Rep. 251, Gross J., para. 59.
369. C-189/87 *Kalfelis* v. *Schroder* [1988] ECR I-5565 at [12]; *Canada Trust* v. *Stolzenberg (No. 2)* [2002] 1 AC 1; *Messier-Dowty* v. *Sabena* [2000] 1 WLR 2040, CA; *Petrotrade* v. *Smith* [1998] 2 All ER 346.
370. *Canada Trust* v. *Stolzenberg (No. 2)* [2002] 1 AC 1.
371. C-51/97 *Reunion* v. *Spliethoff's* [1998] ECR I-6511 at [44].
372. *Kinnear* v. *Falconfilms* [1996] 1 WLR 920, 926; *The Ikarian Reefer (No. 2)* [2000] 1 WLR 603.
373. Briggs/Rees, p. 210.

held that the original proceedings would generally have to be active for the third party proceedings to be within Article 6(2) except for example "where it is necessary that the same tribunal which has already tried the issue in the main action should determine similar or related issues in the third party claim".[374] Where a third party brings further third party proceedings the further third party proceedings may come within Article 6(2).[375]

5.239 In reinsurance cases it often occurs that a defendant wishes to join another party to the proceedings; possibly because he wishes to claim an indemnity or contribution (possibly from his own reinsurer),[376] or because the defendant claims a breach of duty by the third party (such as a broker) in the event that the defendant is held liable.

5.240 Article 6(2) is subject to a proviso that the claim by X against Y has not been instituted solely with the object of removing Z from the jurisdiction which would be competent against him. The proviso is, however, narrowly targeted:

> "It is important in my view to have regard to two features of the proviso: the first is that the word 'these' in the phrase 'unless these were instituted' refers, both as a matter of syntax and good sense, to the 'original proceedings' and not to the third party proceedings. The second is that the word 'solely' emphasises that the motive for the institution of the original proceedings, presumably the motive for their institution in the forum where they have been brought, has to be directed exclusively to the attempt to draw the third party away from his proper Convention forum. The test, in other words, is a narrow one designed to meet a situation where the plaintiff and the defendant are effectively in collusion to bring a claim against a third party in the plaintiff's or defendant's domicile, or otherwise where, even without collusion, the plaintiff has no good reason to sue the defendant, but is hoping that by doing so the defendant will, with the aid of Article 6(2), bring the third party within the plaintiff's domicile. If there was good reason to sue the defendant in the domicile where he was sued, then it could hardly be said that the original proceedings were instituted 'solely' with the object of affecting the forum where the third party is sued."[377]

In *GIE* v. *Zurich*[378] the insured commenced proceedings in France against its French insurers in respect of a sum paid to a car park owner in respect of its liability to the owners of cars damaged in the car park. The French insurers sought to make a third party claim for contribution against a Spanish insurer, Zurich, which covered the owners of the cars. The European Court of Justice confirmed that if French law allowed the third party proceedings against Zurich there was no other requirement under Article 6(2) for any connection between the third party proceedings and the original proceedings. But the court seised had to be satisfied the proviso did not apply (paras 32, 36):

> "It is for the national court seised of the original claim to verify the existence of such a connection, in the sense that it must satisfy itself that the third-party proceedings do not seek to remove the defendant from the jurisdiction of the court which would be competent in the case. Article 6(2) of the Convention is applicable to third-party proceedings between insurers based on multiple insurance, in so far as there is a sufficient connection between the original proceedings and the third-party proceedings to support the conclusion that the choice of forum does not amount to an abuse."

5.241 In *Kongress Agentur* v. *Zeehage*[379] the original defendant to Dutch proceedings was domiciled in Germany and the European Court of Justice held that Article 6(2) applied where a defendant domiciled in a Member State is sued in another. The court did not consider the case where the original defendant was not domiciled in a Member States, and jurisdiction was

374. *Waterford* v. *Nagli*, 8.4.1988, Aldous QC; see also *British Sugar* v. *Babbini* [2005] 1 Lloyd's Rep. 332, 345 (HH Judge Seymour QC).

375. C-77/04 *GIE* v. *Zurich* [2005] ECR I-4509 at [34].

376. *Kinnear* v. *Falconfilms* [1996] 1 WLR 920.

377. *Hough* v. *P&O* [1999] QB 834, 841, Rix J.

378. C-77/04, [2005] ECR I-4509 at [36].

379. C-365/88, [1990] ECR I-1845 at [12]; *British Sugar* v. *Babbini* [2005] 1 Lloyd's Rep. 332, 345 (HH Judge Seymour QC).

established under the conflicts laws of the court seised (under Article 4), but there does not appear to be any reason why it should not confer jurisdiction in such a case. In other words, unlike Article 6(1), it does not appear to be necessary to find an anchor defendant under Article 6(2).

5.242 If there is an exclusive jurisdiction between the original defendant and the third party Article 6(2) would not apply. Article 6(2) is permissive, and allows a party to rely upon it where it applies, as distinct from Article 23 which is mandatory (see para 5.36 above).[380]

4. Article 6(3): counterclaim

5.243 If there are original proceedings between X and Y in England Article 6(3) confers jurisdiction on the court seised in respect of a counterclaim by Y against X arising from the same contract or facts as the claim.

5.244 The connecting factor between the counterclaim and the original proceedings is the fact that the counterclaim arises from the same contract or facts. As to what is a "counterclaim" an autonomous definition almost certainly applies, and has been narrowly drawn.[381] A number of features have been discussed:

(1) The concept does not include a case where the matters relied on by the defendant would not operate as a defence to the claimant's claim so as to extinguish the claim, although it would include a claim which would support a "separate judgment or decree".[382] In English law this distinction appears to correspond to that between a set off and a counterclaim.[383] Thus Article 6(3) applies to counterclaims leading to a separate judgment. Article 6(3) has no application to set-off; if the defendant has a claim which amounts to a defence, it is an integral part of the proceedings and does not involve the claimant being sued, so Article 6(3) is not necessary.

(2) Further, "counterclaim" probably does not include a claim against someone other than the claimant to the original proceedings. In *Jordan* v. *Baltic*[384] the English company claimant issued proceedings in England against a Lithuanian insurer claiming sums due under a policy to reimburse it for expenses incurred because of a top six placing in the constructors' racing championship. The insurer claimed to have avoided the policy for conspiracy. The House of Lords denied that the insurer could add other parties domiciled in the Republic of Ireland to the English proceedings because "counterclaim" in Article 12(2) (which concerns claims by insurers) only included a claim between existing parties. It is not clear if the same result would apply to Article 6(3). The reasoning deployed by the House of Lords in reaching its conclusion would not apply outside the area of insurance covered by section 3 of the Brussels Regulation. However, it has been suggested that the European Court of Justice may take a similar

380. *Hough* v. *P&O* [1999] QB 834, 843.

381. *Jordan* v. *Baltic* [1999] 2 AC 128, 134.

382. C-341/93 *Danvaern* v. *Schufabriken Otterbeck* [1995] ECR I-2053 at [18].

383. *Halsbury's Laws* (4th ed., 1999), vol. 42, para. 409: "Set-off is distinguishable from counterclaim both in its application and in its effect. In its application set-off is limited to money claims, whereas counterclaim is not so limited. Any claim in respect of which the defendant could bring an independent claim against the plaintiff may be enforced by counterclaim subject only to the limitation that it must be such as can conveniently be tried with the plaintiff's claim. Thus not only claims for money, but also other claims such as a claim for an injunction or for specific performance or for a declaration may be the subject of a counterclaim. In its effect set-off is essentially different from counterclaim in that set-off is a ground of defence, a shield and not a sword, which, if established, affords an answer to the plaintiff's claim wholly or *pro tanto*, whereas counterclaim as such affords no defence to the plaintiff's claim, but is a weapon of offence which enables a defendant to enforce a claim against the plaintiff as effectually as in an independent action. Where facts pleaded by way of counterclaim constitute a set-off they may be additionally pleaded as such."

384. *Jordan* v. *Baltic* [1999] 2 AC 128, 134–135 in relation to Article 12(2).

view to the scope of Article 6(3), and treat a counterclaim against a new party as a third party proceedings within Article 6(2).[385] The effect would be that if the reinsured commenced proceedings against the reinsurer who counterclaimed against both the reinsured and broker, Article 6(3) would not apply to the claim against the broker; however, Article 6(2) would apply provided that there was a risk of irreconcilable judgments.

(3) A "counterclaim" does not include a claim *by* a party other than the defendant to the original proceedings. The English court has held that where a claimant brought proceedings against a defendant, and that defendant together with another party issued CPR Part 20 proceedings for declarations against the claimant, Article 6(3) does not apply.[386]

5.245 Like Article 6(2), Article 6(3) does not require that there be an anchor defendant domiciled in the Member State of the court seised, and would apply to original proceedings against a defendant domiciled within another Member State, or indeed in a non-Member State.

H. IS THERE JURISDICTION TO GRANT PROVISIONAL OR PROTECTIVE MEASURES UNDER ARTICLE 31?

5.246 If there are substantive proceedings being carried on in another Member State when will the English court have jurisdiction to make an order on the application of one of the parties for example for the preservation or production of documents, or a freezing injunction? Or if proceedings are going on in England when will the courts of another Member State have jurisdiction to make such orders?

5.247 Under Article 31: "Application may be made to the courts of a Member State for such provisional, including protective, measures as may be available under the law of that State, even if, under this Regulation, the courts of another Member State have jurisdiction as to the substance of the matter." This provision has not been changed since the Brussels Convention was agreed.

5.248 The leading case on such applications is the European Court of Justice decision in *Van Uden* v. *Deco-Line*.[387] Dutch carriers commenced arbitration proceedings in Holland against a German charterer for unpaid charter hire, and then applied to the Dutch courts for an order for interim payment on the grounds that the charterers were not getting on with the arbitration and the non payment of sums due was affecting its cash flow. A number of important points were made in the judgment:

(1) If the court hearing an application for provisional or protective measures is also the court seised of the substantive proceedings under Articles 2 and 5 to 23 of the Brussels Regulation the jurisdiction conferred by Articles 2 and 5 to 23 of the Brussels Regulation will carry with it the jurisdiction necessary for the provisional or protective measures (para. 19).

(2) The role of Article 31 is to permit additional jurisdiction "falling outside the system set out in" Articles 2 and 5 to 23 of the Brussels Regulation "whereby a court may order provisional or protective measures even if it does not have jurisdiction as to the substance of the case. Under that provision, the measures available are those provided for by the law of the State of the court to which application is made" (para. 20).

385. Briggs/Rees, p. 214.

386. *Dolfus Mieg* v. *LBJ Regents Limited*, *The Times*, 19 April 2003, Havelock-Allan QC; *cf. Canada* v. *Oerlikon*, 23 May 1997, Tuckey J.; Petrochilos, "Arbitration and interim measures: in the twilight of the Brussels Convention" (2000) LMCLQ 99.

387. C-391/95, [1998] ECR I-7091. Petrochilos, "Arbitration and Interim Measures: In the Twilight of the Brussels Convention" (2000) LMCLQ 99.

(3) Arbitration is excluded from the scope of the Brussels Regulation by Article 1(4), and so are "proceedings ancillary to arbitration proceedings, such as the appointment of arbitrators, the fixing of the place of the arbitration or the extension of the time-limit for making awards" (para. 32). Article 31 could not confer jurisdiction in relation to those matters since they were excluded from the Regulation.

(4) However, "provisional measures" are "not in principle ancillary to arbitration proceedings but are ordered in parallel to such proceedings and are intended as measures of support. They concern not arbitration as such but the protection of a wide variety of rights. Their place in the scope of the Convention is thus determined not by their own nature but by the nature of the rights which they serve to protect" (para. 33). The result was that Article 31 could "confer jurisdiction on the court" in relation to provisional or protective measures even if the substantive proceedings had been referred to arbitration (para. 34).

(5) The classification of an application as for "provisional, including protective, measures" under Article 31 depended on 2 particular matters: (a) "the expression provisional, including protective, measures within the meaning of Article 24 of the Convention [Article 31 of the Brussels Regulation] is to be understood as referring to measures which, in matters within the scope of the Convention, are intended to preserve a factual or legal situation so as to safeguard rights the recognition of which is otherwise sought from the court having jurisdiction as to the substance of the case" (para. 37) and (b) there had to be a "real connecting link between the subject-matter of the measures sought and the territorial jurisdiction" of the Member State before which the measures were sought (para. 40).

(6) An application for an interim payment might pre-empt the decision on the substance of the case and therefore not be a provisional or protective measure. However, that was not necessarily so: "interim payment of a contractual consideration does not constitute a provisional measure within the meaning of Article 24 unless, first, repayment to the defendant of the sum awarded is guaranteed if the plaintiff is unsuccessful as regards the substance of his claim and, second, the measure sought relates only to specific assets of the defendant located or to be located within the confines of the territorial jurisdiction of the court to which application is made" (para. 47).[388]

5.249 Reference therefore must be made to the national laws of each Member State to see what provisional or protective measures are available under that law. As to English law, section 25 of the Civil Jurisdiction and Judgments Act 1982 confers on the High Court the power to grant "interim relief" where proceedings within the scope of the Brussels Regulation are or are to be commenced in another Member State, provided that the court may refuse to do so if it is "inexpedient".[389] The interim relief the High Court can grant is listed in CPR 25.1,[390] and includes a freezing injunction (*Mareva*), a search order (*Anton Piller*), interim injunction, interim declaration, an order for the detention or inspection of property, an order for disclosure or inspection against a non-party, and an order for payment into court. As to whether a claim for security for costs would be within Article 24 or not: Petrochilos, "Arbitration and Interim Measures: In the Twilight of the Brussels Convention", LMCLQ (2000) 99, 105.

388. Applied *Cogenius/Apothek Schothorst*, Hoge Rad, 8 February 2001, Case 2001/54 ECJ database at *http://www.jura.uni-sb.de/convention-bruxelles/en/2001/54-2001*.

389. Such power extends to the case where jurisdiction is doubtful because the issue to be tried relates to the jurisdiction of the court: s.24(1). Until s.25(1) came into force in 1987 the effect of the decision of the House of Lords in *The Siskina* [1979] AC 210 was that protective injunctions, such as a freezing injunction, could only be granted in support of a cause of action in England. Since 1987 the section applies to proceedings in countries which are party to the Brussels or Lugano Conventions or a state subject to the Brussels Regulation.

390. Section 25(7).

On an application under Article 31 for interim relief in support of proceedings in another Member State the claimant must apply for permission under CPR 6.21(4).[391]

I. PREVENTING CONFLICTING DECISIONS: DECLINING JURISDICTION, STAY AND ANTI-SUIT INJUNCTIONS

1. Introduction

5.250 It often happens that there is a risk of conflicting decisions of courts in different jurisdictions. How are the courts seised of proceedings in different jurisdictions to decide which proceedings should be allowed to continue? How can a court seised of such proceedings manage either the proceedings before it, or the proceedings in the other state so as to avoid conflicting decisions? Should it decline jurisdiction in respect of the proceedings before it, or stay the proceedings? Should it even prevent one party from pursuing proceedings in another jurisdiction? Does it make a difference if one set of proceedings is in a non-Member State?

5.251 Section 9 of the Brussels Regulation is concerned with some of these questions:

"Section 9

Lis pendens – related actions

Article 27

1. Where proceedings involving the same cause of action and between the same parties are brought in the courts of different member states, any court other than the court first seised shall of its own motion stay its proceedings until such time as the jurisdiction of the court first seised is established.
2. Where the jurisdiction of the court first seised is established, any court other than the court first seised shall decline jurisdiction in favour of that court.

Article 28

1. Where related actions are pending in the courts of different member states, any court other than the court first seised may stay its proceedings.
2. Where these actions are pending at first instance, any court other than the court first seised may also, on the application of one of the parties, decline jurisdiction if the court first seised has jurisdiction over the actions in question and its law permits the consolidation thereof.
3. For the purposes of this Article, actions are deemed to be related where they are so closely connected that it is expedient to hear and determine them together to avoid the risk of irreconcilable judgments resulting from separate proceedings.

Article 29

Where actions come within the exclusive jurisdiction of several courts, any court other than the court first seised shall decline jurisdiction in favour of that court.

Article 30

For the purposes of this Section, a court shall be deemed to be seised:

1. at the time when the document instituting the proceedings or an equivalent document is lodged with the court, provided that the plaintiff has not subsequently failed to take the steps he was required to take to have service effected on the defendant, or
2. if the document has to be served before being lodged with the court, at the time when it is received by the authority responsible for service, provided that the plaintiff has not subsequently failed to take the steps he was required to take to have the document lodged with the court."

5.252 The general effect of the regime expressly provided for in the Brussels Regulation is as follows:

391. Article 31 permits the courts of Member States to exercise any jurisdiction they may have under the national law to grant protective measures, but does not of itself confer jurisdiction: *The Siskina* [1979] 1 AC 210, 259–260, *per* Lord Diplock. Since the Brussels Regulation does not of itself confer any jurisdiction in respect of a claim for protective measures the claimant must seek permission to serve out of the jurisdiction even if the defendant is domiciled in a Member State.

(1) It only applies where the relevant proceedings are in Member States; it does not expressly deal with the situation where one of the relevant proceedings is before the courts of a non-Member State. However, Articles 27 and 28 apply whatever the *domicile* of the parties.

(2) The approach is meant to be as simple and automatic as possible, leaving as little as possible to the discretion of the courts The European Court of Justice has referred to the "objective and automatic character of the *lis pendens* mechanism".[392] There is no principle of *forum non conveniens* at all in this context.

(3) Timing and trust are all. The court first seised must alone be trusted by all other courts to decide whether or not it has jurisdiction under the Brussels Regulation. If it decides that it does, any other proceedings involving *the same cause of action* must be stayed or declined.

(4) The only tools available to a court are to stay or decline its own proceedings; in particular, it may *never* issue an anti-suit injunction in respect of proceedings in a court of another Member State.

(5) It has therefore become crucial to be the first to commence proceedings and thereby force any battle to be decided in the desired jurisdiction. This has encouraged forum shopping and pre-emptive strikes by well-advised parties.

(6) A court seised of subsequent related proceedings is permitted to stay those proceedings on case management grounds, or even to decline jurisdiction, provided the issues can be decided by the court first seised. To this limited extent the court second seised may in effect decide the court first seised is the better forum.

5.253 A key question not specifically addressed by the Brussels Regulation is whether or not proceedings in a Member State may be stayed or declined in favour of proceedings in a non-Member State on *forum non conveniens* grounds. Before dealing with the latter question it is convenient to deal with the situations which are specifically covered by section 9 of the Brussels Regulation.

5.254 In the discussion which follows it will for convenience be assumed that proceedings are to be or have been commenced in England and in another Member State, and the question is what, if anything, should be done by the court about the English action. The two actions will be referred to as competing actions or proceedings. Similar questions would arise in relation to proceedings begun in any two Member States.

5.255 Neither Article 27 nor Article 28 apply to matters excluded from the Brussels Regulation, such as arbitration. This was the decision of the Court of Appeal in *Through Transport* v. *New India*.[393] The court second seised in that case could therefore proceed to consider whether or not the arbitration exception applied in spite of Article 27 without having to wait for the court first seised to determine the question of the arbitration exception (see further para. 8.34 below).

(i) Development of section 9

5.256 Article 27 was amended when the Lugano Convention was agreed so that it was no longer required that the second court seised "decline" jurisdiction, but instead the second court was permitted to stay the proceedings until the jurisdiction of the first court had been established. The initial wording was thought too radical because an action often had to be brought to stop time running and opinions differed as to the effect on the running of time of

392. C-111/01 *Gantner* v. *Basch* [2003] ECR I-4207 at [30].
393. [2005] 1 Lloyd's Rep. 67.

an action which had been declined.[394] The court second seised must decline jurisdiction once the jurisdiction of the court first seised is established.

5.257 Article 28(1) was amended when the Brussels Regulation was introduced so that a stay could be sought if both related actions were pending *at any stage* in another jurisdiction, rather than as previously stated only if the actions were pending *at first instance*. This means a stay may be ordered even if one or both actions are under appeal. Conversely, Article 28(2) was amended so that the court second seised could decline jurisdiction only while both actions were pending at first instance, rather than as before at any stage in the proceedings, otherwise the parties would lose the benefit of the two stage procedure.[395] The amendment to Article 28(2) also made clear that the law of the court first seised (rather than the court second seised) must permit the consolidation of proceedings in the event that the court second seised declines jurisdiction.

5.258 Article 30 was also introduced into the Brussels Regulation to define for the first time the time when a court became seised.[396]

(ii) Objectives of section 9

5.259 The main object of Articles 27 and 28 is to avoid conflicting judgments and thereby facilitate the proper administration of justice in the EU.[397] Section 9 "is intended, in the interests of the proper administration of justice within the community, to prevent parallel proceedings before the courts of different Contracting States and to avoid conflicts between decisions which might result therefrom".[398] In particular, Article 27 is important because if irreconcilable judgments are given they may not be recognised under Article 34(3). The European Court of Justice has also said that it follows from that main object that they must be interpreted broadly.[399]

5.260 Two principles which have hit the forefront in this context relate to trust and certainty. The European Court of Justice has emphasised that courts of other Member States are to be trusted to make decisions on jurisdiction which impinge on other courts: "the Brussels Convention is necessarily based on the trust which the Contracting States accord to each other's legal systems and judicial institutions".[400] The court has also reiterated in this context the principle that the operation of the Brussels Regulation should be as certain as possible: "the principle of legal certainty requires, in particular, that the jurisdictional rules which derogate from the general rule laid down in Article 2 of the Brussels Convention should be interpreted in such a way as to enable a normally well-informed defendant reasonably to foresee before which courts, other than those of the State in which he is domiciled, he may be sued".[401]

5.261 We consider the questions which arise under these main headings:

(1) Is there exclusive jurisdiction within Article 29?
(2) Are there proceedings involving the same cause of action under Article 27?
(3) Are there related actions under Article 28?
(4) *Owusu*: can proceedings in a Member State be stayed in favour of a non-Member State?

394. *Jenard and Moller*, para. 64.
395. *Explanatory Memorandum to Brussels Regulation*, p. 19.
396. *Explanatory Memorandum to Brussels Regulation*, pp. 19–20.
397. *Jenard*, 1979 OJ C.59/1, 41; C-220/88 *Dumez* v. *Hessiche Landesbank* [1990] ECR I-49; C-351/89 *OUI* v. *New Hampshire* [1991] ECR I-3317 at [15]–[16]; C-406/92 *The Tatry* [1994] ECR I-5439 at [51].
398. C-144/86 *Gubisch* v. *Palumbo* [1987] ECR I-4861 at [8].
399. C-351/89 *OUI* v. *New Hampshire* [1991] ECR I-3317 at [16].

2. Is there exclusive jurisdiction under Article 29?

5.262 If the English court has mandatory jurisdiction in respect of proceedings (under Article 22, see para. 5.9) then under Article 29 it must exercise that jurisdiction unless another court also has exclusive jurisdiction and was first seised. The time when each court becomes seised of an action is now defined by Article 30. In forming the view that it has exclusive jurisdiction the English court would necessarily have to decide that no other Member State had jurisdiction, even if there were proceedings pending in another Member State. No judgment given by the court first seised would be entitled to recognition under the Brussels Regulation because of Article 35(1). Rather, the court first seised must declare of its own motion that it has no jurisdiction: Article 25. The English Court of Appeal has therefore concluded that the court second seised should not stay the proceedings under Article 27 which is inapplicable but should proceed to hear them.[402]

5.263 Mandatory jurisdiction under Article 22 will prevail over an exclusive jurisdiction agreement under Article 23: Article 23(5). An exclusive jurisdiction agreement which selected one of two or more countries would only confer jurisdiction on one court.[403] Article 29 will not apply if a court has jurisdiction under a non-exclusive jurisdiction agreement

3. Are there proceedings involving the same cause of action under Article 27?

(i) Effect of Article 27

5.264 The aim of Article 27 is to make the decisions of the courts before which competing proceedings are brought as clear cut as possible and to eliminate the possibility of one court examining the jurisdiction of another court. In *OUI* v. *New Hampshire*[404] US insurers provided cover to a French retailer in respect of the costs of extended warranties and reinsured their liability with English reinsurers in London who later sought to avoid for non-disclosure and misrepresentation. The US insurers brought proceedings in France claiming the sums due under the reinsurances and reinsurers commenced subsequent proceedings in London for a negative declaration. The European Court of Justice held that Article 27 applied in respect of the English proceedings even though the US insurers were not domiciled in a Member State, and even though the jurisdiction had been asserted against the US insurers on the basis of the English conflicts rules which apply in accordance with Article 4. The English court had stayed the English proceedings pending the decision of the French court on jurisdiction, and was not permitted itself to examine whether or not the French Court had jurisdiction under the Brussels Regulation but had to await the decision of the French court.

5.265 The effect is therefore that a court only has two choices under Article 27: either to decline jurisdiction or stay the proceedings. Normally it will decline jurisdiction. It may only stay where the jurisdiction of the court first seised is contested, but in no case may the court second seised review the jurisdiction of the court first seised.[405]

5.266 Article 27 applies where the competing proceedings are both in courts of Member States. However, the Article makes no reference to the domicile of the parties and applies

400. *Gasser* v. *MISAT* [2004] 1 Lloyd's Rep. 222, 231.

401. C-281/02 *Owusu* v. *Jackson* [2005] ECR I-1383, [2005] QB 801, para. 40; see also *Konkola* v. *Coromin* [2005] 2 All ER (Comm) 637, 659, Colman J.; affirmed on other points [2006] EWCA 5, CA.

402. *Speed Investments* v. *Formula One* [2005] 1 WLR 1936, 1947.

403. C-23/78 As in *Meeth* v. *Glacetal* [1978] ECR I-2133 (para. 5.65 above).

404. [1991] ECR I-3317.

405. C-351/89 *OUI* v. *New Hampshire* [1991] ECR I-3317 at [25].

wherever the parties are domiciled, whether in Member States or not.[406] Article 27 ceases to apply if the court first seised gives judgment.[407]

(ii) Same cause of action?

5.267 Article 27 requires the court to classify a proceeding as one which involves "the same cause of action and ... the same parties", that is, that there is a *lis pendens*. Sometimes such proceedings are referred to as parallel proceedings, as opposed to related proceedings under Article 28. It is clear that the meaning of these concepts is autonomous because of the need for uniformity across Member States.[408] Although the English text of Article 27 only refers to "cause of action" the European Court cases have interpreted this to mean:

(1) the proceedings have the same "*cause*", from French, meaning the same facts and rule of law as their basis, and
(2) the proceedings have the same "*objet*", again from French, meaning the same end in view.[409]

5.268 In *Gubisch* v. *Palumbo* it was held that a claim (a) for sums due under a sale of goods involved the same cause as alternative claims that (b) the contract had never been made, or could be set aside for lack of consent, or discharged for delay in delivery. Both types of claims were concerned with the contractual relationship. They shared the same *objet* since they were both essentially concerned with the binding effect of the contract:

"it is apparent that the action to enforce the contract is aimed at giving effect to it, and that the action for its rescission or discharge is aimed precisely at depriving it of any effect. The question whether the contract is binding therefore lies at the heart of the two actions. If it is the action for rescission or discharge of the contract that is brought subsequently, it may even be regarded as simply a defence against the first action, brought in the form of independent proceedings before a court in another contracting state."[410]

5.269 Similarly, a claim for sums due under a reinsurance involves the same cause of action as one to avoid the contract for non-disclosure and misrepresentation.[411] In *Evialis* v. *SIAT*[412] Italian underwriters commenced proceedings in Italy against the French insured claiming that they were not liable for a loss on various grounds, and the insured later commenced proceedings in England relying on a non-exclusive jurisdiction clause and claiming the sums due under the insurance. The court looked to the "central or essential issue" in both proceedings and concluded that it was whether or not the insurers were liable in respect of the loss, and therefore Article 27 applied.

5.270 In England it has also been held at first instance that proceedings in which the sole claim is to give effect to a jurisdiction agreement, and not for substantive relief in the underlying dispute, do not have the same cause of action as other proceedings which seek relief in

406. *Ibid.*, at [18].

407. *Tavoulareas* v. *Alexander G Tsavliris and Sons Maritime Co. (No. 2)* [2005] EWHC 2140.

408. C-144/86 *Gubisch* v. *Palumbo* [1987] ECR I-4861 at [11]; C-406/92 *The Tatry* [1994] ECR I-5439 at [46].

409. C-406/92 *The Tatry* [1994] ECR I-5439 at [38]–[40]. The matter is best explained by Bingham LJ in *Haji-Ioannou* v. *Frangos* [1999] 2 Lloyd's Rep. 337, 349–351, referring to C-144/86 *Gubisch* v. *Palumbo* [1987] ECR I-4861 and C-351/89 *OUI* v. *New Hampshire* [1991] ECR I-3317. Although the English version of Article 27 has been drafted with the phrase "cause of action" it is not to be interpreted as it would be in English law: *Sarrio* v. *Kuwait* [1999] 1 AC 32, 40; *Glencore* v. *Shell* [1999] 2 Lloyd's Rep. 692, 697; *JP Morgan* v. *Primacom* [2005] 2 Lloyd's Rep. 665, 672.

410. C-144/86 *Gubisch* v. *Palumbo* [1987] ECR I-4861 at [16]; *The Tatry* [1994] ECR I-5439 at [33].

411. Hirst J. held that the cause of action was the same in *OUI* v. *New Hampshire* [1992] 1 Lloyd's Rep. 218, 225. The case was referred to the European Court of Justice where the point was conceded: C-351/89 [1991] ECR I-3317 at [9], following *Gubisch*.

412. [2004] Lloyd's Rep. IR 187.

the underlying dispute, so that Article 27 cannot apply in such cases.[413] However, this approach seems unlikely to be followed since the Court of Appeal has doubted that "a dispute as to jurisdiction can properly be characterised as a 'cause of action' at all".[414]

5.271 In determining whether or not actions involve the same cause of action only the claims must be taken into account. A claim of set-off made in a defence is not relevant:

"Article 21 of the Convention [Article 27 of the Brussels Regulation] adopts a simple method to determine, at the outset of proceedings, which of the courts seised will ultimately hear and determine the dispute. The court second seised is required, of its own motion, to stay its proceedings until the jurisdiction of the court first seised is established. Once that has been established, it must decline jurisdiction in favour of the court first seised. The purpose of Article 21 of the Convention would be frustrated if the content and nature of the claims could be modified by arguments necessarily submitted at a later date by the defendant. Apart from delays and expense, such a solution could have the result that a court initially designated as having jurisdiction under that Article would subsequently have to decline to hear the case."[415]

(iii) Same parties?

5.272 The concept of "between the same parties" has an autonomous meaning because of the need for uniformity in the application of Article 27.[416] It applies to the extent that there is an overlap in parties, even if not complete:

"Consequently, where some of the parties are the same as the parties to an action which has already been started, Article 21 [Article 27 of the Brussels Regulation] requires the second court seised to decline jurisdiction only to the extent to which the parties to the proceedings pending before it are also parties to the action previously started before the court of another Contracting State; it does not prevent the proceedings from continuing between the other parties. Admittedly, that interpretation of Article 21 involves fragmenting the proceedings. However, Article 22 [Article 28 of the Brussels Regulation] mitigates that disadvantage. That Article allows the second court seised to stay proceedings or to decline jurisdiction on the ground that the actions are related, if the conditions there set out are satisfied."[417]

The court second seised is not required to stay proceedings or decline jurisdiction in respect of parties to which Article 27 does not apply. Where parties are sham the English court may look behind sham companies to see who are the real parties to proceedings.[418]

5.273 Insurers or reinsurers who claim by way of subrogation may find that Article 27 applies if there are existing proceedings involving the insured or reinsured. In *Drouot Assurances* v. *Consolidated*[419] cargo owners and cargo insurers had commenced proceedings in the Netherlands against the vessel owner for a declaration of non liability to contribute to the general average in respect of the costs of refloating the vessel. Subsequently the hull insurers claimed from the cargo owners and cargo insurers in French proceedings a contribu-

413. *Continental Bank* v. *Aekos* [1994] 1 WLR 588, 595; *Toepfer* v. *Molino* [1996] 1 Lloyd's Rep. 510, 513; *Toepfer* v. *Cargill* [1997] 2 Lloyd's Rep. 98, Colman J, referred to European Court of Justice by the CA [1998] 1 WLR 379.

414. *Toepfer* v. *Cargill* [1998] 1 WLR 379, 387, CA; *Eviclis* v. *SIAT* [2004] Lloyd's Rep. IR 187, 206.

415. C-111/01 *Gantner* v. *Basch* [2003] ECR I-4207 at [30].

416. C-406/92 *The Tatry* [1994] ECR I-5439 at [46].

417. C-406/92 *The Tatry* [1994] ECR I-5439 at [33]–[34]; for an example involving reinsurance see *AGF* v. *Chiyoda* [1992] 1 Lloyd's Rep. 325, 339.

418. *Turner* v. *Grovit* [2000] 1 QB 345, 363, CA: "the deployment of CSA, a Spanish company, as claimant in Madrid is nothing but a device to confer putative jurisdiction on the Spanish court. That is not only in the circumstances of the case abusive upon ordinary principles of our domestic law. In addition, for this court to treat it as reality rather than the sham and pretence which it plainly is, and accordingly to deny what is otherwise the clearly established jurisdiction of the tribunal under Article 21, would in my judgment tend to undermine what Lord Goff of Chieveley has called in *Airbus Industrie GIE* v. *Patel* [1999] 1 AC 119, 132B, 'the primary purpose of the Convention [*viz.*] to ensure that there shall be no clash between the jurisdictions of member states of the Community'."

419. C-351/96, [1998] ECR I-3075.

tion to the general average costs. The question was whether or not under Article 27 the hull insurers could be treated as the same person as their insured which was the defendant in the Netherlands proceedings. The European Court of Justice accepted that this was a question for the national court, but did not hold back from expressing the view that the hull insurers did not bring their claim by way of subrogation, but in their own right as a party entitled to a contribution to general average, having paid towards the costs of refloating (para. 23). If, however, the insurers had brought a claim by way of subrogation, and other proceedings had involved the insured, Article 27 might have applied:

> "It is certainly true that, as regards the subject-matter of two disputes, there may be such a degree of identity between the interests of an insurer and those of its insured that a judgment delivered against one of them would have the force of *res judicata* as against the other. That would be the case, *inter alia*, where an insurer, by virtue of its right of subrogation, brings or defends an action in the name of its insured without the latter being in a position to influence the proceedings. In such a situation, insurer and insured must be considered to be one and the same party for the purposes of the application of Article 21 of the Convention" (para. 19).[420]

(iv) When does the court become seised?

5.274 The time when a court becomes seised will determine priority of proceedings. In the light of *Gasser* priority is more important than ever. The question when a court was seised of a matter used to be left to the national law of the court seised.[421] However, differences in the laws of different Member States led to uncertainty and arbitrary difficulties[422] and Article 30 was accordingly introduced at the time of the Brussels Regulation.

5.275 If, as in England, national law requires proceedings to be issued first, then served on the defendant, the court will be deemed to be seised when the claim form was issued.[423] However, this is provided the claimant can show he has "taken the steps he was required to take to have service effected". If so, the proceedings will have priority even if other proceedings were commenced after issue but before the time for service. If the claimant does not take the steps he was required to take Article 30 would not deem his proceedings to have priority. Presumably if the court extended time for the claimant to serve proceedings, and the claimant served within the extended period, the claimant would still have taken "the steps he was required to take" and Article 30 would apply. If, however, the national law requires service first, before proceedings are lodged with the court, the court will be deemed seised when the documents comprising the proceedings are received by the authority responsible for service.

5.276 What if there are defects in the procedure followed to institute proceedings? In *WPP* v. *Benatti*[424] it was held that the effect of any such defects depends on the national law of the court where it is said proceedings have begun. In that case the original claim form issued in England did not identify every claim, and was incorrectly endorsed with a reference to the Brussels Convention and not the Brussels Regulation. The amended claim form was not served with a copy of an order joining a party, and the Particulars of Claim did not include any jurisdiction endorsement. None of these failures was so serious that the court would

420. It seems the French proceedings could have been stayed under Article 28, but the question was not raised: Opinion of the Advocate General at [1998] ECR I-3075 at [30].

421. *Jenard*, 1979 OJ C.59/1, 42.

422. As in *Knauf* v. *Peters* [2002] 1 Lloyd's Rep. 199; see further *Explanatory Memorandum to Brussels Regulation*, p. 20.

423. An English court only became seised of proceedings for the purpose of Article 21 of the Brussels Convention once the proceedings had been both issued and served which was the moment when they were definitively pending: *The Sargasso* [1994] 3 All ER 180, CA.

424. [2006] EWHC 1641 (Comm).

make an order invalidating the steps under CPR 3.10, and, unless it did so, the steps were effective, and the proceedings instituted when the claim forms were issued. On the other hand under Italian law the Italian court had not become seised of related proceedings in Italy because the defendant had declined service as it was entitled to do, and because no translation accompanied the Italian writ. Article 30(2) therefore did not apply.

5.277 Where there are multiple defendants it has been held in England that as soon as the court was seised of the proceedings in relation to one defendant it was seised of the proceedings in relation to all.[425]

5.278 If a party is added to existing proceedings by amendment when are those proceedings "brought" against him for the purposes of Article 27? Under English law, if the claim form has been served, the permission of the court will be required: CPR 19.2. The new party does not become a party until the amended claim form is served on him: Practice Direction to CPR 19, para. 13.3. Presumably on the date when the court gives permission for the amendment (CPR 17.1) Article 30 will apply because the document instituting proceedings has been lodged with the court, and, provided that the amended proceedings are duly served, the court will therefore be seised of the proceedings against the new defendant on the date of the permission for the amendment.[426] In *AGF* v. *Chiyoda*[427] there was a programme of reinsurance over two years which involved various reinsured, reinsurers and retrocessionaires. Reinsurers commenced English proceedings claiming avoidance of the year one programme for misrepresentation and non-disclosure against the reinsured. Subsequently the reinsured commenced Italian proceedings to enforce the reinsurance for both years. In the English action reinsurers then sought leave to amend the proceedings by adding claims in respect of the year two programme. There was something of a catch 22. If the Italian proceedings were the same cause of action or related to the English proceedings, the Italian proceedings should not continue and the English court would have jurisdiction to make the amendments. But if the Italian proceedings continued the amended claims would undoubtedly have been related proceedings to the Italian proceedings and the English proceedings could not continue in relation to the amendments. The court held that the key point was that following *OUI* only the Italian court could decide if the Italian proceedings were related to the English proceedings and therefore whether or not Italian jurisdiction should be declined or the action stayed. The English court could not therefore proceed to deal with the amendment application until the Italian court had decided on jurisdiction.

5.279 If there is no longer a *lis* pending in the court first seised when the question of jurisdiction arises in the court second seised there is no possibility of conflicting judgments and Article 27 does not apply.[428]

425. *Grupo Torras* v. *Al-Sabah* [1995] 1 Lloyd's Rep. 374, 415–421, Mance J. The subsequent decision of the European Court of Justice in *The Tatry* (*supra*) that Article 27 applies between multiple parties on a defendant-by-defendant basis suggests that the court might adopt a similar approach in relation to the time of service. But, as Mance J. demonstrated, there are real practical difficulties with that approach which have not been addressed by *The Tatry*. The Court of Appeal in *Grupo Torras* left the point open [1996] 1 Lloyd's Rep. 7, 19. However, following the introduction of Article 30 the point is likely to be of much less significance. Provided the proceedings are issued against all defendants at the same time, the fact that they are served at different times no longer makes any difference; the court will be deemed seised in relation to all defendants when the claim form was issued.

426. It is a question of fact when the document is lodged and unaffected by the doctrine of relation back of an amendment: *Grupo Torras* v. *Al-Sabah* [1996] 1 Lloyd's Rep. 7, 24; *cf. AGF* v. *Chiyoda* [1992] 1 Lloyd's Rep 325, 341.

427. [1992] 1 Lloyd's Rep. 325, 341.

428. *Prudential Assurance* v. *Prudential Insurance* [2003] 1 WLR 2295, 2307 (CA); *International Nederladen* v. *CAA* [1997] 1 Lloyd's Rep. 80, 93. If a court has stayed proceedings it does not cease to be seised of them: *ROFA Sport* v. *DHL* [1989] 1 WLR 902.

(v) Gasser: *The court second seised must always stay or decline jurisdiction in favour of court first seised (except if there is mandatory jurisdiction)*

5.280 It is now clear that even if there is an exclusive jurisdiction agreement in favour of the court second seised, the latter court must stay the proceedings or decline jurisdiction. In *Gasser* v. *MISAT*[429] Italian buyers of goods brought proceedings in Italy for a declaration a sale contract had been terminated. There was an exclusive jurisdiction agreement in the contract in favour of Austria, and the Austrian buyers commenced later proceedings in Austria for sums due. The European Court of Justice held that the court second seised had to stay or decline jurisdiction. There could be no exception even where proceedings were apparently in breach of an exclusive jurisdiction agreement.[430] It took the view that the court second seised (para. 48) "is never in a better position than the court first seised to determine whether the latter has jurisdiction". The principal justification for this approach was that there could be disputes about the existence or binding nature of the exclusive jurisdiction agreement. A party may have entered an appearance, or the formal requirements of Article 23 may not have been met. The Brussels Regulation was based on the "mutual trust" (para. 72) of Member States in the courts of each state. The only exception to the rule that the court second seised must always wait for the court first seised to decide on its own jurisdiction is where there is mandatory jurisdiction under Article 22 in favour of the court second seised (para. 5.262 above). As has been said, the Brussels Regulation: "creates a closed system in which it is assumed that every contracting state will come to a similar decision about jurisdiction".[431]

5.281 The effect of the decision in *Gasser* is of course to encourage forum shopping; that is, the commencement of proceedings at the first possible moment in the jurisdiction of choice regardless of an exclusive jurisdiction agreement: "Freedom to forum shop by seeking negative declaratory relief is inherent in the European Court of Justice's decisions".[432]

5.282 A party may choose a particular court because, for example, he believes that he stands a better chance of denying that the exclusive jurisdiction was effective under Article 23 in that jurisdiction, or he may simply know that proceedings will be very protracted in that jurisdiction which will put pressure on the defendant to concede or settle. In *Gasser* it was argued that proceedings were notoriously long in countries such as Italy, France and Greece. The tactic of starting proceedings in such jurisdictions to force excessive delays is sometimes called "the Italian torpedo" because of its devastating effect on the efficacy of the exclusive jurisdiction agreement. The phrase has its origins in an article by an Italian lawyer indicating how litigants facing patent infringement actions in other EU states could turn the delays in the Italian judicial system to their advantage.[433] It is highly questionable that the court second seised is never in a better position to decide the issue as to jurisdiction than that first seised: this seems to ignore the advantage of having issues as to jurisdiction decided by the court chosen by the parties.[434]

5.283 The effect of *Gasser* is to undermine the effect of the agreement, cause uncertainty and hand unscrupulous parties an unfair commercial advantage. Even if there are disputes

429. C-116/02; [2003] ECR I-14693; [2005] 1 QB 1.

430. *OUI* v. *New Hampshire* [1991] ECR I-3317, para. 26, seemed to indicate that a different approach should apply where the court second seised had exclusive jurisdiction, as it would do under Article 23 where there was an exclusive jurisdiction clause, but the court in *Gasser* rejected this approach.

431. *OT Africa* v. *Magic* [2005] 2 Lloyd's Rep. 170, 180, Rix LJ.

432. *Tavoulareas* v. *Alexander G Tsavliris and Sons Maritime Co.* [2004] 1 Lloyd's Rep. 445, 446, Mance LJ.

433. M. Franzosi, "World-wide Patent Litigation and the Italian Torpedo", [1997] EIP Rev 382, cited in Hartley, "The European Union and the Systematic Dismantling of the Common Law of Conflict of Laws", [2005] 54 ICLQ 813.

434. It is possible to avoid the effect of *Gasser* by commencing a claim for provisional or protective measures under Article 31 since Articles 27 and 28 do not prevent the court seised of the claim for provisional or protective measures from having jurisdiction.

about whether or not there is an exclusive jurisdiction agreement it is surely better that those issues are decided by the court designated in the exclusive jurisdiction agreement in case it is effective than by a court which was clearly not designated by the exclusive jurisdiction agreement but may have been chosen because of its protracted delays.

5.284 The court must stay or decline jurisdiction of its own motion, but as a matter of practicalities a "court will not always have to examine of its own motion whether the same proceedings are pending in the courts of another country, but only when the circumstances are such as to lead the court to believe that this may be the case".[435] Once the jurisdiction of the court first seised is established the court second seised must decline jurisdiction.[436]

(vi) Turner: *No anti-suit injunction in respect of proceedings in another Member State*

5.285 The English court has powers to grant anti-suit injunctions to prohibit proceedings in other jurisdictions. These are examined in relation to proceedings not involving the Brussels Regulation at para 7.95 below. The only methods of control mentioned in section 9 are that a court seised of proceedings may either stay them or decline jurisdiction. Can a court of a Member State grant anti-suit injunctions in respect of proceedings in another Member State?

5.286 The English courts took the view that there was nothing in the Brussels Regulation or Convention which was inconsistent with the exercise of the power to grant an anti-suit injunction.[437] In *Turner* v. *Grovit*[438] an employee brought English proceedings against an English company, Harada, claiming unfair dismissal. An associated Spanish company, CSA, subsequently commenced Spanish proceedings against the employee claiming damages for breach of contract. The Court of Appeal took the view that CSA had no claim; the Spanish proceedings had been commenced in order to pressure the employee into giving up his claim and were an abuse; the Spanish proceedings involved the same cause of action between the same parties (CSA was a sham) as the English action; the English tribunal was the court first seised, and therefore Article 27 applied. It made an order that the individual behind CSA and Harada discontinue the Spanish proceedings, in other words, an anti-suit injunction.

5.287 The European Court of Justice overturned this decision. It emphasised, as in *Gasser*, that the Brussels Regulation "is necessarily based on the trust which the Contracting States accord to one another's legal systems and judicial institutions" (para. 24) and that:

> "a prohibition imposed by a court, backed by a penalty, restraining a party from commencing or continuing proceedings before a foreign court undermines the latter court's jurisdiction to determine the dispute. Any injunction prohibiting a claimant from bringing such an action must be seen as constituting interference with the jurisdiction of the foreign court which, as such, is incompatible with the system of the Convention" (para. 27),

and even though indirect and intended to prevent abuse was "counter to the principle of mutual trust" (para. 28).[439] Further,

435. *Jenard*, 1979 OJ C.59/1, 41.

436. *OUI* v. *New Hampshire* [1992] 1 Lloyd's Rep. 218, 225. This case was later referred to the European Court of Justice by the Court of Appeal which gave judgment on different points (Article 27 applies irrespective of domicile; if the court second seised cannot examine the jurisdiction of the court first seised).

437. E.g., *Continental Bank* v. *Aekos* [1994] 1 WLR 588, 597, CA.

438. C-159/02, [2004] ECR I-3656, [2005] 1 AC 101. Hartley, "The European Union and the Systematic Dismantling of the Common Law of Conflict of Laws", [2005] 54 ICLQ 813; Dickinson, "A Charter for Tactical Litigation in Europe?", (2004) LNCLQR 273.

439. This insistence on mutual trust is despite the difficulties of delay in some legal systems and lack of public confidence in the judiciary and judicial corruption in others: see the EU Commission report in 2003 on the accession of the ten new Member States at *http://ec.europa.eu/comm/development/body/organisation/eu_enlargement_en htm* and quoted in Dickinson, "A Charter for Tactical Litigation in Europe?", (2004) LNCLQR 273.

"the argument that the grant of injunctions may contribute to attainment of the objective of the Convention, which is to minimise the risk of conflicting decisions and to avoid a multiplicity of proceedings, cannot be accepted. First, recourse to such measures renders ineffective the specific mechanisms provided for by the Convention for cases of *lis alibi pendens* and of related actions. Second, it is liable to give rise to situations involving conflicts for which the Convention contains no rules. The possibility cannot be excluded that, even if an injunction had been issued in one Contracting State, a decision might nevertheless be given by a court of another Contracting State. Similarly, the possibility cannot be excluded that the courts of two Contracting States that allowed such measures might issue contradictory injunctions" (para. 30).

5.288 The effect of *Turner* is that it is now clear that an anti-suit injunction is not available in respect of proceedings in another Member State. Even if proceedings are commenced which are an abuse the court seised of the (abusive) proceedings must deal with them. Although *Turner* was decided in the context of Article 27 it would appear to be intended by the European Court of Justice that an anti-suit injunction would be incompatible with the Brussels Regulation in any context, including cases where proceedings are commenced in breach of an exclusive jurisdiction agreement (see para. 5.106).[440] There is a question as to whether or not an anti-suit injunction can be granted where proceedings have been commenced in a Member State in breach of an arbitration clause (see para. 8.34). *Turner* does not apply to anti-suit injunctions in respect of proceedings in a non-Member State (para. 7.103 below).

5.289 The effect of *Gasser* and *Turner* is to put paid to the idea that the English court could decline to order a stay where a defendant to English proceedings had, by an abuse of proceedings, led a claimant to delay proceedings in England in order to create the opportunity to commence proceedings in another jurisdiction.[441] Claimants may be expected to seek to strike early and to strike broadly in terms of parties and claims so as to prevent proceedings from taking place in a jurisdiction which is not preferred.[442] By including in a jurisdiction agreement a term requiring that claims by related parties arising out of the same relationship be brought in a particular court it may be possible at least to reduce the scope for side-stepping the jurisdiction agreement.[443]

4. Are there related actions under Article 28?

(i) Related actions?

5.290 It is first necessary under Article 28 to characterise actions pending in different Member States as "related". This concept is defined in Article 28(3).[444] Actions are deemed related where they are so closely connected that it is expedient to hear and determine them together to avoid the risk of irreconcilable judgments resulting from separate proceedings. When is there a risk of irreconcilable judgments? If Article 28 was confined to cases where the same cause of action was involved it would merely cover the same cases as Article 27, at least where the same parties were involved.[445] It follows that Article 28 must have been intended to cover cases where, although the causes of action are not the same, it is expedient they should be heard in one jurisdiction. This is the view the European Court of Justice has adopted. In *The Tatry*[446] that court held that proceedings by one group of cargo owners

440. For an argument that *Turner* may be avoided where the foreign court has violated ss.3, 4 or 6 of the Brussels Regulation see Briggs/Rees, p. 437.

441. See, e.g., *The Filiatra Legacy* [1994] 1 Lloyd's Rep. 513, 515; *Turner* v. *Grovit* [2000] 1 QEG BVI 345, CA.

442. Dickinson, "A Charter for Tactical Litigation in Europe?", (2004) LNCLQR 273, 279.

443. *Ibid.*

444. C-406/92 *The Tatry* [1994] ECR I-5439 at [51].

445. Compare *Sarrio* v. *Kuwait* [1999] 1 AC 32, 40.

446. C-406/92; [1994] ECR I-5439.

against shipowners for damage to cargo were related to proceedings by another group of cargo owners in a different Member State in respect of damage to cargo on board the same vessel where the contracts with cargo owners were separate but in the same terms. Separate trials would involve the risk of conflicting decisions even though there was no risk of mutually exclusive legal consequences since the contracts were separate. In reaching that decision the European Court of Justice took a broad view of "related actions" in Article 28 (para. 52): "In order to achieve proper administration of justice, that interpretation must be broad and cover all cases where there is a risk of conflicting decisions, even if the judgments can be separately enforced and their legal consequences are not mutually exclusive". Consequently the term "irreconcilable" in Article 27(3) was wider than the same term in Article 34(3) which is concerned with non-recognition of judgments (para. 54): "The objectives of the two provisions are different. Article 27(3) of the Convention [Article 34(3) of the Brussels Regulation] enables a court, by way of derogation from the principles and objectives of the Convention, to refuse to recognise a foreign judgment. Consequently the term "irreconcilable … judgment" there referred to must be interpreted by reference to that objective. The objective of the third paragraph of Article 22 of the Convention [Article 28(3) of the Brussels Regulation], however, is, as the Advocate General noted in his Opinion (paragraph 28), to improve coordination of the exercise of judicial functions within the Community and to avoid conflicting and contradictory decisions, even where the separate enforcement of each of them is not precluded". The effect is that there may be a risk of irreconcilable judgments even though the causes of action and the parties are not the same. There was an obvious risk in *The Tatry* that factual issues relating to the cause of the damage to the cargo on the same vessel would be resolved in conflicting ways.

5.291 In *Sarrio* v. *Kuwait* [447] the claimant commenced proceedings in Spain alleging that the defendant was liable for sums due from a company in which it was interested (Grupo Torras). The claimant later brought proceedings in England for damages for misrepresentations made by the defendant in relation to a transaction with Grupo Torras. The Lords rejected the argument that only "primary" issues of fact or law necessary for a court to reach its judgment on a particular case were relevant. That view would only increase delay, complexity and costs. The reference to actions being so closely connected that it is expedient to hear and determine them together was important (p. 40):

"To my mind these wide words are designed to cover a range of circumstances, from cases where the matters before the courts are virtually identical (though not falling within the provisions of Article [27]) to cases where although this is not the position, the connection is close enough to make it expedient for them to be heard and determined together to avoid the risk in question. These words are required if 'irreconcilable judgments' extends beyond 'primary' or 'essential' issues, so as to exclude actions which, though theoretically capable of giving rise to conflict, are not sufficiently closely connected to make it expedient for them to be heard and determined together. The words would hardly be necessary at all if the Article was to be confined as suggested. Indeed, in that event, it seems to me that quite different words would have been used."

5.292 In *Prifti* v. *Musini* [448] Spanish insurers, Musini, insured a football club, Real Sociedad, in respect of personal accident and sickness of its players, and reinsured all but 2% of this liability in London with the claimant. Real Sociedad commenced proceedings in Spain for payment under the insurance in respect of injury to a player which Musini denied on grounds that the injury was related to an earlier injury, and the player's condition had not been disclosed. Reinsurers subsequently commenced proceedings in England seeking a negative

447. [1999] 1 AC 32.
448. [2004] Lloyd's Rep. IR 528.

declaration of no liability on two grounds (a) avoidance and (b) the claim was excluded by a pre-existing condition clause. Andrew Smith J. found the actions were related within Article 28 because the reinsurers' second case was based on the pre-existing condition of the player, and there was a risk that the Spanish and English courts would reach irreconcilable judgments on that factual issue. However, to meet this objection, reinsurers gave an undertaking not to rely on the case that the claim was excluded by the pre-existing condition of the player. That left avoidance as the only issue which would depend on whether or not Musini should have disclosed the report they had received on the player, rather than his true condition, so that Article 28 no longer applied.

(ii) Stay or decline jurisdiction?

5.293 Even if there is a risk of irreconcilable judgments there is still a question as to whether or not it is "expedient" that actions be heard together. Thus in *JP Morgan* v. *Primacom*[449] Cooke J. would not have stayed the English proceedings under Article 28 which were related to German proceedings on the ground that it was not expedient that they be heard together: the English proceedings depended on the effect of contracts under English law while the German proceedings would seek to apply German public policy considerations to those contracts. If it is expedient the proceedings are deemed related.

5.294 However, even if proceedings are related, it still appears that the court has to decide whether or not it should order a stay. Under Article 28 the court "may" stay proceedings if actions are related (rather than "shall" stay or decline jurisdiction under Article 27).[450] No doubt the court would decline to order a stay if there was evidence that defendants had indulged in sharp practice to mislead claimants into delaying the issue of proceedings so as to create the opportunity to commence proceedings in another jurisdiction.[451] In the sequel to *Prifti* (referred to above) the court had to decide whether or not it should order a stay. After the decision of Andrew Smith J. Musini commenced Part 20 proceedings in the English proceedings against Willis which had broked the reinsurance and an associated broker which had broked the insurance claiming that the brokers were liable if the reinsurance did not respond. The brokers and reinsurers then joined together in seeking a stay of the English proceedings pending the determination of the Spanish proceedings (in spite of the fact that reinsurers had successfully resisted a stay before Andrew Smith J.). Clarke J. approached the matter on the basis that he essentially had to exercise a "discretion" on "case management grounds" (para. 19). Clarke J. ordered a stay because a lengthy and expensive trial in England could be rendered unnecessary if in whole or in part Musini were not held liable to the insured or it were held that the pre-existing condition clause had been incorporated.

5.295 Another example of the exercise of this discretion occurred in *Sarrio* referred to above. At first instance, having lost on the point that the actions were related, the claimants sought to limit the stay of the English proceedings until they had added the misrepresentation case to the Spanish proceedings, content that when that was done the English proceedings should be dismissed. By the time the English proceedings reached the House of Lords the claimants still had not added the misrepresentation case to the Spanish proceedings (apparently taking the view it would delay those proceedings) and the Lords decided that instead of a stay there should be an order declining jurisdiction in favour of the Spanish proceedings, in effect forcing the claimants to make the misrepresentation case in those proceedings or not at all.

449. [2005] 2 Lloyd's Rep. 665, 674.

450. There is some debate as to whether what the court is doing is exercising a discretion or making a judgment: compare *AGF* v. *Chiyoda* [1992] 1 Lloyd's Rep. 325, 339, *Prifti* v. *Musini (No. 2)* [2006] Lloyd's Rep. IR 221, 226.

451. See, e.g., *The Filiatra Legacy* [1994] 1 Lloyd's Rep. 513, 515; *Turner* v. *Grovit* [2000] 1 QB 345, CA.

(iii) Owusu: *Can proceedings in a Member State be stayed in favour of a non-Member State?*

5.296 Section 9 specifically empowers a court seised to stay proceedings in favour of the courts of another Member State in certain circumstances. It says nothing about a stay in favour of proceedings in a *non*-Member State. Suppose a reinsurer brings proceedings against a reinsured in England but the reinsured argues that the proceedings should be stayed pending the determination of related proceedings in New York. The reinsured may for example, be domiciled in England in which case Article 2 would confer jurisdiction; he may be domiciled in New York but there may be an exclusive jurisdiction agreement conferring jurisdiction on the English courts within Article 23; or he may have entered an appearance under Article 24. The issue is whether the provisions of the Brussels Regulation which confer jurisdiction on the English courts are inconsistent with the English court exercising a power to stay on any grounds.

5.297 In *Owusu* v. *Jackson*[452] a British claimant commenced proceedings in England for breach of contract and damages for personal injury suffered in Jamaica against an English defendant, Jackson, who let his accommodation in Jamaica, and various Jamaican companies which owned the beach where he was injured. The defendants sought a stay of the English proceedings on the grounds of *forum non conveniens* in favour of Jamaica where the accident took place, and most of the defendants were. The Court of Appeal referred the case to the European Court of Justice[453] which emphatically held that Article 2 conferred international jurisdiction *solely* on the basis of the domicile of Jackson. An "international element" (para. 25) was required, but was met by the fact that the injury took place in Jamaica, the question being whether proceedings could take place in England or Jamaica. The Brussels Regulation was intended to facilitate the working of the internal market. But that did not mean it could only apply to disputes relating to jurisdiction between *two or more* Member States. It could fulfil that purpose by in effect harmonising to some extent rules for jurisdiction involving a single member state and possible proceedings in a non-Member State.[454] That being so, the question was whether there could be a derogation from Article 2 based on a principle of *forum non conveniens*. The court's view was that *forum non conveniens* was inconsistent with Brussels Regulation. The Brussels Regulation made no provision for a stay for *forum non conveniens* as such.[455] Legal certainty required that a normally well informed defendant be able reasonably to foresee before which court he may be sued, and the principle of *forum non conveniens* would not do that. Moreover, the principle was only recognised in a limited number of Member States.

5.298 The effect of *Owusu* is therefore that in the case of proceedings in a Member State which are based on Article 2 jurisdiction no stay may be ordered in favour of any court, whether in a Member State or not, except under the rules in section 9, and not on the ground of *forum*

452. C-281/02, [2005] ECR I-1383, [2005] QB 801. Hartley, "The European Union and the Systematic Dismantling of the Common Law of Conflict of Laws", [2005] 54 ICLQ 813; Hill, "Stays and Proceedings and the Brussels Convention", [2005] 54 ICLQ 933; Briggs, "The Death of Harrods: Forum Non Conveniens and The European Court", (2005) 121 LQR 535; Hare, "Forum Non Conveniens in Europe: Game Over or Time for Reflexion?", (2006) JBL 157.

453. [2002] EWCA Civ. 87, [2003] PIQR 186. The question had been left open in *Lubbe* v. *Cape* [2000] 2 Lloyd's Rep. 383, 394, HL.

454. Compare the decision that Article 2 applies provided only that the defendant is domiciled in a Member State. It does not matter if the claimant is domiciled in a non-Member State. Article 2 therefore harmonises the conflicts rules of the Member States in relation to cases where the debate is between the courts of a member state and a non-Member State. See, generally, para. 5.111 above.

455. Though Article 28 allows a court to stay proceedings on case management grounds in certain circumstances. The decision in *Owusu* was contrary to the Court of Appeal decision in *Re Harrods* [1992] Ch 72 which had been followed in many English decisions, e.g. *Travelers Casualty and Surety Company of Europe Ltd and others v. Sun Life Assurance Company of Canada (UK) Ltd and another* [2004] Lloyd's Rep. IR 846.

non conveniens as such.[456] It is suggested that where the English court has jurisdiction under Article 4, it may stay the proceedings in favour of another Member State. Article 4(2) provides that the claimant may avail himself of the "rules of jurisdiction there in force" which under English law includes the power to stay proceedings.[457] Would the decision apply to prevent a stay on the basis of an exclusive jurisdiction agreement in favour of courts of a non-Member State? Article 23 does not refer as such to the case where a defendant domiciled in a Member State agreed to a jurisdiction agreement in favour of a non-Member State. But, since the policy of the Brussels Regulation is to give effect to jurisdiction agreements in favour of courts of Member States, it would be strange and inconsistent for it to prevent courts from giving effect to jurisdiction agreements in favour of non-Member States. This is in effect what Colman J. held at first instance in *Konkola* v. *Coromin*.[458] A Zambian insured commenced proceedings in England against Bermudan insurers for the sums due under various insurances. In Part 20 proceedings insurers claimed to be indemnified by reinsurers all domiciled in Brussels Regulation or Lugano states. Reinsurers claimed that the reinsurance was subject to an exclusive jurisdiction agreement in favour of Zambia, and sought a stay of the English proceedings. Colman J. held at para. 101 that *Owusu* did not mean that the court could not stay proceedings against a party domiciled in a Member State where there was an exclusive jurisdiction agreement in favour of the courts of a non-Member State. There was already the authority of *Schlosser* that although the Brussels Regulation makes no specific provision for exclusive jurisdiction agreements in favour of a non-Member State, the court should in such cases give effect to the jurisdiction agreement if valid under the conflicts rules in the court seised, and, only if invalid, apply the jurisdictional provisions in the Brussels Regulation. The application of the discretionary approach of the common law where there was a jurisdiction agreement to which the Brussels Regulation did not apply was not inconsistent with *Owusu*.[459] The court could, therefore, under its own conflict rules give effect to the jurisdiction agreement. Others suggest that the lacuna can be filled by giving the Brussels Regulation a reflexive effect. Thus, where a non-Member State asserts jurisdiction on a basis which is accepted under the Brussels Regulation as conferring exclusive jurisdiction on that court, the principles inherent in the Brussels Regulation to deal with such situations will be applied. If the formalities under Article 23 are complied with a stay may be granted.[460]

5.299 However, where the jurisdiction agreement is in terms non-exclusive (see para. 5.36 above) the effect of Article 23 is to confer additional jurisdiction on the court of a Member State, and it would seem to follow from the reasoning in *Owusu* that the court chosen could not decline jurisdiction.

456. It remains to be seen whether the same principle applies if the proceedings in a Member State are based on another Brussels Regulation ground, such as Articles 5(1), (3) or (5). There is little in the reasoning of the European Court of Justice to suggest that it will not.

457. Hartley, "The European Union and the Systematic Dismantling of the Common Law of Conflict of Laws", [2005] 54 ICLQ 813; *cf.* Briggs, "The Death of Harrods: Forum Non Conveniens and The European Court" (2005) 121 LQR 535.

458. [2005] 2 All ER 637, affirmed on other points on other points [2006] EWCA 5, CA; see generally Dicey/Morris/Collins, para. 12-103.

459. Para. 176, and see further para. 5.108 above.

460. See W. Kennet, "Forum Non Conveniens In Europe" [1995] CLJ 553; Peel, "Forum Non Conveniens And European Ideals" (2005) LMCLQ 363–377; Briggs, "Allocation Of Jurisdiction: EC Law: Forum Non Conveniens: Stay Of Proceedings" (2005) LMCLQ 378–382; Briggs/Rees, p. 261. Hartley, "The European Union and the Systematic Dismantling of the Common Law of Conflict of Laws" [2005] 54 ICLQ 813; Hare, "Forum Non Conveniens in Europe: Game Over or Time for Reflexion?" (2006) JBL 157, 161.

J. JURISDICTION WITHIN THE UK UNDER SCHEDULE 4 OF THE CIVIL JURISDICTION AND JUDGMENTS ACT 1982

5.300 As has been seen, in some cases the Brussels Regulation allocates jurisdiction to the courts of a particular place, for example uner Article 5(1) which allocates jurisdiction to the courts for the place for performance of the obligation in question (see para. 5.129).

5.301 In other cases the Brussels Regulation merely allocates jurisdiction to the UK without specifying which jurisdiction within the UK is to have jurisdiction. For example, Article 23 will simply allocate international jurisdiction to the courts of the UK if a jurisdiction agreement refers to the courts of the UK. In the latter cases, the allocation of jurisdiction as between the different domestic jurisdictions of the UK will be determined according to a code for domestic jurisdiction which is similar to that for international jurisdiction contained in the Brussels Regulation. This domestic jurisdiction code is provided for by section 16 of the Civil Jurisdiction and Judgments Act 1982, and set out in Schedule 4 to that Act.[461] Schedule 4 applies where the subject-matter of the dispute would fall within the Brussels Regulation and the defendant is domiciled in the UK (or would fall within the mandatory provisions of Article 22 of the Brussels Regulation).[462] The focus of this book is on the international jurisdiction; however, it is of interest to note two differences between the Brussels Regulation and Schedule 4.[463] First, under Schedule 4 the courts of the UK are free to apply the doctrine of *forum non conveniens*: section 49 of the Civil Jurisdiction and Judgments Act 1982.[464] Second, there is not within Schedule 4 a special regime for insurance contracts as there is in section 3 of the Brussels Regulation; insurance contracts are dealt with like any other contract under Schedule 4.

461. Section 16 and Schedule 4 were amended by the Civil Jurisdiction and Judgments Order 2001 (SI 2001 No. 3929) so as to bring their provisions into line with the Brussels Regulation, and apply to all proceedings commenced after 1 March 2002 (when the Brussels Regulation came into force): Article 1. The unamended versions of section 16 and Schedule 4 previously applied a code for domestic jurisdiction similar to the Brussels Regulation.

462. Section 16(1) of the Civil Jurisdiction and Judgments Act 1982. However, section 16 and Schedule 4 do not *only* apply where international jurisdiction has been conferred on the UK courts by the Brussels Regulation: they apply where there is any question as to which domestic jurisdiction within the UK is to have jurisdiction.

463. See, generally, Briggs/Rees, p. 272.

464. Compare the position under the Brussels Regulation at para. 5.285.

CHAPTER 6

INSURANCE JURISDICTION UNDER THE BRUSSELS REGULATION

A. INTRODUCTION

6.1 In this chapter we deal with the regime applicable to insurance under section 3 of the Brussels Regulation which provides:

"Section 3 Jurisdiction in matters relating to insurance

Article 8

In matters relating to insurance, jurisdiction shall be determined by this Section, without prejudice to Article 4 and point 5 of Article 5.

Article 9

1. An insurer domiciled in a Member State may be sued:
   (a) in the courts of the Member State where he is domiciled, or
   (b) in another Member State, in the case of actions brought by the policyholder, the insured or a beneficiary, in the courts for the place where the plaintiff is domiciled,
   (c) if he is a co-insurer, in the courts of a Member State in which proceedings are brought against the leading insurer.
2. An insurer who is not domiciled in a Member State but has a branch, agency or other establishment in one of the Member States shall, in disputes arising out of the operations of the branch, agency or establishment, be deemed to be domiciled in that Member State.

Article 10

In respect of liability insurance or insurance of immovable property, the insurer may in addition be sued in the courts for the place where the harmful event occurred. The same applies if movable and immovable property are covered by the same insurance policy and both are adversely affected by the same contingency.

Article 11

1. In respect of liability insurance, the insurer may also, if the law of the court permits it, be joined in proceedings which the injured party has brought against the insured.
2. Articles 8, 9 and 10 shall apply to actions brought by the injured party directly against the insurer, where such direct actions are permitted.
3. If the law governing such direct actions provides that the policyholder or the insured may be joined as a party to the action, the same court shall have jurisdiction over them.

Article 12

1. Without prejudice to Article 11(3), an insurer may bring proceedings only in the courts of the Member State in which the defendant is domiciled, irrespective of whether he is the policyholder, the insured or a beneficiary.
2. The provisions of this Section shall not affect the right to bring a counter-claim in the court in which, in accordance with this Section, the original claim is pending.

Article 13

The provisions of this Section may be departed from only by an agreement:
1. which is entered into after the dispute has arisen, or
2. which allows the policyholder, the insured or a beneficiary to bring proceedings in courts other than those indicated in this Section, or
3. which is concluded between a policyholder and an insurer, both of whom are at the time of conclusion of the contract domiciled or habitually resident in the same Member State, and which has the effect of conferring jurisdiction on the courts of that State even if the harmful event were to occur abroad, provided that such an agreement is not contrary to the law of that State, or

4. which is concluded with a policyholder who is not domiciled in a Member State, except in so far as the insurance is compulsory or relates to immovable property in a Member State, or
5. which relates to a contract of insurance in so far as it covers one or more of the risks set out in Article 14.

Article 14

The following are the risks referred to in Article 13(5):

1. any loss of or damage to:
   (a) seagoing ships, installations situated offshore or on the high seas, or aircraft, arising from perils which relate to their use for commercial purposes;
   (b) goods in transit other than passengers' baggage where the transit consists of or includes carriage by such ships or aircraft;
2. any liability, other than for bodily injury to passengers or loss of or damage to their baggage:
   (a) arising out of the use or operation of ships, installations or aircraft as referred to in point 1(a) in so far as, in respect of the latter, the law of the Member State in which such aircraft are registered does not prohibit agreements on jurisdiction regarding insurance of such risks;
   (b) for loss or damage caused by goods in transit as described in point 1(b);
3. any financial loss connected with the use or operation of ships, installations or aircraft as referred to in point 1(a), in particular loss of freight or charter-hire;
4. any risk or interest connected with any of those referred to in points 1 to 3;
5. notwithstanding points 1 to 4, all 'large risks' as defined in Council Directive 73/239/EEC(7), as amended by Council Directives 88/357/EEC(8) and 90/618/EEC(9), as they may be amended."

6.2 The basic reason for the special rules in section 3 is that it was felt when the Brussels Convention was agreed that public policy or social considerations required enhanced protection for the weaker party in certain types of contracts, including insurance.[1] The main aim of section 3 is that the claimant in proceedings against an insurer should be entitled to commence proceedings in his own domicile among other places, and any actions by an insurer should generally be commenced in the courts in which the other party is domiciled, except in very limited cases. The power of either party to contract out of the ordinary rules should also be very restricted.

6.3 The scheme of section 3 is that in matters relating to insurance it alone applies. It has thus been described as "a self contained and exclusive code governing insurance".[2] Some of the rules in section 3 therefore duplicate those in the rest of the Brussels Regulation.[3] Where section 3 confers a ground of jurisdiction, and that ground is utilised by a party, the court is required to accept jurisdiction[4] unless some other court has mandatory jurisdiction or is first seised when section 9 will apply (para. 5.250). Where section 3 does not apply the conflicts laws in the court seised will apply which may include the Brussels Regulation.[5]

6.4 Generally section 3 only applies where the defendant (whether insurer or policy-holder) is domiciled in a Member State (or has a branch, etc, in a Member State),[6] and only applies where there is an international element (see para. 2.15).[7] Where it applies section 3 may allocate jurisdiction to a particular part of the UK,[8] or even to a particular court[9]; if not, it may allocate jurisdiction to the UK and jurisdiction within the UK will be allocated by the Civil Jurisdiction and Judgments Act 1982.[10]

1. *Jenard*, p. 28.
2. *Jordan* v. *Baltic* [1999] AC 127, 133 (HL).
3. E.g. Article 9(1) and Article 2.
4. *S&W Berisford* v. *New Hampshire* [1990] 1 Lloyd's Rep. 454, 461.
5. *Jenard*, p. 31.
6. *Jenard*, pp. 30, 33.
7. *Jenard*, p. 33.
8. E.g. Article 10, which refers to the courts for the place where the harmful event occurred.
9. E.g. Article 11(1) permits joinder to existing proceedings.
10. There is no equivalent under the CJJA 1982 to Section 3, and jurisdiction is allocated within the UK according to the ordinary rules applicable to contracts.

1. Development of Section 3

6.5 The 1978 version of the Brussels Convention on the accession of the UK made a number of changes. It deleted a provision in Article 8 of the 1968 version (Article 9 of the Brussels Regulation) which had provided that an insurer could also be sued in the place of the domicile of his agent for insurance if that place was mentioned in the policy or proposal.[11] The provision now in Article 13(3) of the Brussels Regulation that the parties were at the time of the conclusion of the contract domiciled in the same Member States was introduced in 1978, as were the provisions now in Articles 13(4), (5), and Article 14(1)–(4) which extended the circumstances in which effective jurisdiction agreements could be made because it was recognised that in the types of commercial business identified there was not the need for social protection.[12]

6.6 In 2001 the Brussels Regulation made some further changes. Article 9(1)(b) of the Brussels Regulation logically extended the available jurisdiction from that in which the policy-holder claimant was domiciled to those in which insured or beneficiary were domiciled,[13] and made clear that the Article was only to apply to a claimant policy-holder, insured or beneficiary. The provision now in Article 14(5) relating to large risks was also introduced.

2. Objectives in interpreting Section 3

6.7 The purpose of section 3 is to protect the party deemed to be weaker than the other party to the contract.[14] "In relation to insurance, consumer contracts and employment, the weaker party should be protected by rules of jurisdiction more favourable to his interests than the general rules provide for".[15] Reference has also been made to the objective of avoiding conflicting judgments.[16]

6.8 We consider the issues which arise under these heads:

(1) Who are the policyholder, insured and beneficiary?
(2) What are matters relating to insurance?
(3) Proceedings against insurer.
(4) Proceedings by insurer.
(5) Jurisdiction agreements.

B. WHO ARE THE POLICY-HOLDER, INSURED AND BENEFICIARY?

6.9 The concepts of the policy-holder, insured and beneficiary used in the original Brussels Convention, and ever since, are undefined and appear likely to be autonomous because of the need for uniformity across the Member States. Although section 3 confers protection on all three parties it can be important to distinguish between them: Article 11(3) only allows joinder of the policyholder and insured; and Articles 13(3) and (4) only apply to jurisdiction agreements with a policy-holder.

11. The background to this provision is at *Jenard*, p. 31.
12. *Schlosser*, para. 140.
13. *Explanatory Memorandum to Brussels Regulation*, p. 15.
14. C-201/82 *Gerling* v. *Amministrazione del Tesoro* [1983] ECR I-2503, para. 17; C-412/98 *Group Josi* v. *UGIC* [2000] ECR I-5925 at [39]; *Jordan* v. *Baltic* [1999] AC 127, 134 (HL).
15. Recitals to the Brussels Regulation, para. (13).
16. *S&W Berisford* v. *New Hampshire* [1990] 1 Lloyd's Rep. 454, 460, Hobhouse J.

6.10 In essence, it appears likely that the policy-holder is the original contracting party.[17] The beneficiary is a party who is not the policy-holder but who has become entitled to payment of the claim, for example because of an assignment of the right to the claim or he is a loss payee.[18] The insured is the party whose loss is insured, for example a named driver under a motor insurance policy. Some light is thrown on these distinctions by Schlosser, para. 152:

"The previous authentic texts to the 1968 Convention use the term '*preneur d'assurance*' and the equivalent in German, Italian and Dutch; the nearest English equivalent of the term proved to be 'the policy-holder'. However, this should not give rise to the misunderstanding that the problems arising from a transfer of legal rights are now any different from those existing before the accession of the new member states to the Convention. The rightful possessor of the policy document is not always the '*preneur d'assurance*'. It is of course conceivable that the whole legal status of the other party to the contract with the insurer might pass to another person by inheritance or some other means, in which case the new party to the contract would become the *preneur d'assurance*. However, this case must be clearly distinguished from the transfer of individual rights arising out of the contract of insurance, especially in the form of assignment of the sum assured to a beneficiary. Such an assignment may be made in advance and may be contingent, for instance, upon the occurrence of a claim. In this event it is conceivable that the insurance policy might be passed on to the beneficiary at the same time as the assignment of the right to the sum assured so that he can claim his entitlement from the insurer, if the case arises. The beneficiary would not thereby become the *preneur d'assurance*. Hence, where a court jurisdiction is dependent on individual characteristics of the '*preneur d'assurance*', the situation remains unchanged as a result of prior assignment of any claim to the sum assured which might arise, even if the policy document is transferred at the same time." [19]

C. WHAT MATTERS RELATE TO INSURANCE?

6.11 Section 3 only applies in "matters relating to insurance" (Article 8). It is now clear that it does not apply to reinsurance; that is, it does not apply as between the reinsured and reinsurer, or to relations between reinsurers.[20] However, section 3 will apply to any direct action by the insured against the reinsurer. In the *Explanatory Memorandum to the Brussels Regulation* it is simply said that Article 8 and therefore section 3 would apply to "actions brought by policy-holders against reinsurers" (p. 15). In *Group Josi* v. *UGIC*[21] the European Court of Justice confirmed (para. 75) section 3 applies:

"where, under the law of a Contracting State, the policy-holder, the insured or the beneficiary of an insurance contract has the option to approach directly any reinsurer of the insurer in order to assert his rights under that contract as against that reinsurer, for example in the case of the bankruptcy or liquidation of the insurer. In such a situation, the plaintiff is in a weak position compared with the professional reinsurer, so that the objective of special protection inherent in Article 7 *et seq.* of the Convention justifies the application of the special rules which it lays down."

Any such action would relate to the rights of the policy-holder against the insured and therefore can be said to be a matter relating to insurance, even though a direct claim were made against the reinsurer.

17. See *Bonello/Credit Commercial*, 22 February 2000, Cour de Cassation, Case 2000/34 ECJ database at *http://www.jura.uni-sb.de/convention-bruxelles/en/2000/34-2000* where it was held that Article 9(2) did not apply to an action by the beneficiaries of the estate of the policyholder.

18. C-112/03 *Societe Peloux* v. *Axa* [2005] ECR I-3707 at [34]. The policy-holder was a parent company, and the policy covered a subsidiary which was not a party to the policy but described by the European Court of Justice as a "beneficiary".

19. See also *Banque Bruxelles Lambert (Suisse)/République du Paraguay et Sezione speciale per l'assicurazione del credito all'esportazione*, 20 August 1998, Swiss Tribunal Federal, Case 1999/35, ECJ database at *http://www.jura.uni-sb.de/convention-bruxelles/en/1999/35-1999*.

20. C-412/98 *Group Josi* v. *UGIC* [2000] ECR I-5925; *Schlosser*, para. 151.

21. C-412/98, [2000] ECR I-5925.

6.12 Would a claim by an insurer based on subrogation against a third party to the insurance fall within section 3? It is difficult to see why it should since the relationship of insurer and insured is not likely to be relevant to the issues between the insurer and third party. In *The Ikarian Reefer (No. 2)*[22] it was held that a claim for costs against a non party under section 51 of the Supreme Court Act 1981 following proceedings on a claim on an insurance was not a "matter relating to insurance".

D. PROCEEDINGS AGAINST INSURER

1. Domicile of the policy-holder, etc

6.13 The basic rule is that the claimant policy-holder, beneficiary, insured, or a relevant injured party[23] may commence proceedings in the Member State in which the *claimant* is domiciled (Article 9(1)(b)). This rule reverses the usual rule.[24] It establishes what may be called "general jurisdiction"[25] for proceedings against the insurer. The general jurisdiction or rule only applies where the claimant and insurer are domiciled in a Member State. If the insurer is not domiciled (or does not have a branch, etc) in a Member State section 3 will not apply and the claimant will need to establish jurisdiction under the conflicts law of the court seised, including the rest of the Brussels Regulation.[26] Formerly, Article 8(2) of the Brussels Convention provided that proceedings could be commenced in the place where the policy-holder was domiciled, but Article 9(2) of the Brussels Regulation now provides that proceedings can be commenced in the domicile of the claimant whether policy-holder, insured or beneficiary.[27] The domicile which is relevant is that at the time when the proceedings were instituted.[28]

6.14 In addition to the general rule there are five rules conferring additional options for jurisdiction against the insurer which are examined in turn below.

2. Domicile of insurer

6.15 The first additional ground of jurisdiction is that an insurer domiciled in a Member State may be sued by any party in the Member State in which the insurer is domiciled (Article 9(1)(a)). This is the equivalent of the usual domicile jurisdiction under Article 2. Again, if the insurer is not domiciled in a Member State this rule will not apply unless the insurer has a branch, etc, in a Member State (see below) and the conflicts laws in the court seised will determine jurisdiction in respect of proceedings against an insurer not domiciled in a Member State under Article 4.

6.16 The second additional ground of jurisdiction is that an insurer not domiciled in a Member State but which has a branch agency or other establishment which is in a Member State, may be sued there by the insured, policy-holder, beneficiary or a relevant injured party,[29] in respect of disputes arising out of that entity (Article 9(2) which is the equivalent

22. [2000] 1 Lloyd's Rep. 129, 138.

23. A relevant injured person is, in respect of liability insurance, one who is entitled under the law of the court seised to make a claim directly against the insurer: Article 11(1), (2).

24. This is one of the few areas in which the Brussels Regulation accords decisive importance to the claimant's domicile being in a Member State: C-412/98 *Group Josi* v. *UGIC* [2000] ECR I-5925, para. 47.

25. *Jenard*, p. 31.

26. *Jenard*, p. 31; *Lassin* v. *Payne* [1995] ILPr 17 (Paris, Court of Appeal).

27. *Jenard*, p. 31.

28. *Ibid.*

29. See above.

of Article 5(5)). The discussion of Article 5(5) applies equally here (para. 5.116). In *S&W Berisford* v. *New Hampshire*[30] this provision was applied where the insurers, New Hampshire, had made the insurance contract through its London office.

3. Proceedings against leading insurer

6.17 The third additional ground of jurisdiction is that an insurer domiciled in a Member State may be sued by any party in another Member State where proceedings have been commenced against a leading insurer: Article 9(1)(c). The lead will not necessarily have the biggest line on a risk, but will usually have set the rate and terms. Again, this rule only applies if the follower is domiciled in a Member State. It is also very limited; not allowing a lead to be joined in the place where proceedings have been commenced against a follower, or a follower to be joined in proceedings against another follower. There is no requirement that the proceedings have been commenced against the lead where he is domiciled,[31] or indeed that the proceedings be based on jurisdiction conferred by the Brussels Regulation. If the proceedings against the lead have been settled the claimant cannot rely on Article 9(1)(c).[32]

4. Liability and immoveable property insurance

6.18 The fourth additional ground of jurisdiction is that an insurer of liability insurance or immovable property[33] may be sued by any party in the courts for the place where the harmful event occurred (Article 10). The harmful event will be what triggers the claim under the policy: see further the discussion of this concept in relation to Article 5(3).[34] Article 10 does not specify in terms that the insurer must be domiciled in a Member State, but that must be the intention. This provision is of particular importance in relation to road accident liability insurance.

6.19 An insurer of liability insurance may also be joined to an action by an injured party against the insured, if the law of the court permits (Article 11(1)).[35] This Article is concerned with third party jurisdiction. English law permits such joinder in appropriate circumstances under the Road Traffic Act 1988 and the Third Parties (Rights Against Insurers) Act 1930. An insurance policy may also include a cut-through clause designed to allow a direct claim.[36] If the injured party is entitled to bring a direct action against the insurer,[37] the injured party is permitted to bring proceedings against the insurer in the circumstances set out in Articles 8–10: Article 11(2). In other words, the injured party has the same options as to jurisdiction as the policyholder, insured or beneficiary. Whether or not the direct action is permitted must be decided according to the conflicts of law rules in the court seised.[38] Further, the policy-holder or the insured may be joined as a party to a direct action by the person injured

30. [1990] 1 Lloyd's Rep. 454, 461.
31. *Schlosser*, para. 149.
32. *Schlosser*, para. 149.
33. Including a policy covering immoveable and moveable property: Article 10. For example a buildings and contents policy would fall within Article 10: *Jenard*, p. 32.
34. Para. 5.215. Article 10 does not include "or may occur" which was added to Article 5(3), as to which see para. 5.200.
35. *Jenard*, pp. 31–32. For example, German law does not so permit (*ibid.*).
36. Clarke, pp. 5-2; e.g. as in *General Star* v. *Stirling Cooke Brown* [2003] Lloyd's Rep. IR 719.
37. Such actions were said by Jenard, p. 32, to be permitted by Belgian, French and Luxembourg law. See *Cigna Insurance Company of Europe/Société The West of England Ship Owners Mutual Insurance Association*, 2 February 1999, Cour de Cassation, France, Case 1999/52, on the ECJ database at *http://www.jura.uni-sb.de/convention-bruxelles/en/1999/52-1999* where it was held that the injured party and not his insurers had to bring the proceedings for Article 11 to apply.
38. *Jenard*, p. 32.

against the insurer if the law governing the direct action permits (Article 11(3)). Presumably the relevant law is the law of the court seised. The purpose of this provision is clearly to prevent different courts from reaching irreconcilable judgments.[39]

5. Jurisdiction agreements

6.20 The fifth ground of additional jurisdiction is if any parties have entered into an effective jurisdiction agreement the insured may commence proceedings in the jurisdiction agreed (Article 13). We consider the limited circumstances in which jurisdiction agreements are effective below.

E. PROCEEDINGS BY INSURER

6.21 The basic rule is that the insurer may *only* bring proceedings in the courts of the Member State in which the defendant, whether insured, policy-holder or beneficiary, is domiciled (Article 12(1)). The rule simply depends on the defendant's domicile in a Member State; it does not matter where the insurer is domiciled. This is apparent from the wording of Article 12(1).[40] Accordingly, a counterclaim by Lithuanian insurers against parties domiciled in Member States was subject to Article 11.[41] The domicile which is relevant is that at the time when the proceedings were instituted.[42] However, there are a number of exceptions to the basic rule which are examined below.

6.22 First, if the defendant is not domiciled in a Member State the general rule does not apply. This is the effect of Articles 4 and 8. The insurer may then commence proceedings against the defendant in any jurisdiction permitted by the law of the court seised. However, if the insured had a branch, agency or other establishment within a Member State (as to which see para. 5.116) jurisdiction may be established there in respect of disputes arising out of the operations of that entity under Articles 5(5) and 8.

6.23 Secondly, if any defendant has entered an appearance under Article 24 the court seised will have jurisdiction (see para. 5.22).[43]

6.24 Thirdly, if the insurer is already a defendant to proceedings brought in accordance with section 3, in which he has counterclaimed, the court will have jurisdiction even against an insured, policy-holder, beneficiary or relevant injured party (Article 12(2)).[44]

6.25 Fourthly, if any parties have entered into an effective jurisdiction agreement the insurer may commence proceedings in the jurisdiction agreed (Article 13). We consider the limited circumstances in which jurisdiction agreements are effective below.

F. IS THERE AN EFFECTIVE JURISDICTION AGREEMENT?

6.26 Article 13 permits agreements conferring jurisdiction in matters relating to insurance in certain specified cases, including a jurisdiction agreement:

39. *Jenard*, p. 32.
40. C-412/98 *Group Josi* v. *UGIC* [2000] ECR I-5925 at [61].
41. *Jordan* v. *Baltic* [1999] AC 127, 133 (HL). As to counterclaims generally, see below.
42. *Jenard*, p. 31.
43. Following C-150/80 *Elefanten Schuh GmbH* v. *Jacqmain* [1981] ECR I-1671 in which the European Court of Justice held that if a party entered an appearance Article 24 applied even if there was a jurisdiction agreement in favour of a different jurisdiction under Article 23. Article 24 does not apply where another court has exclusive jurisdiction by virtue of Article 22, but it appears to override all other provisions, including therefore the specialist insurance rules in section 3.
44. Probably only a counterclaim which is against the original claimant is within Article 11: see generally para. 5.244.

"1. which is entered into after the dispute has arisen, or
2. which allows the policyholder, the insured or a beneficiary to bring proceedings in courts other than those indicated in this Section, or
3. which is concluded between a policyholder and an insurer, both of whom are at the time of conclusion of the contract domiciled or habitually resident in the same member state, and which has the effect of conferring jurisdiction on the courts of that State even if the harmful event were to occur abroad, provided that such an agreement is not contrary to the law of that State
4. which is concluded with a policyholder who is not domiciled in a member state, except in so far as the insurance is compulsory or relates to immovable property in a member state, or
5. which relates to a contract of insurance in so far as it covers one or more of the risks set out in Article 14."

A jurisdiction agreement is of no legal force if it is contrary to Article 13: Article 23(4).

6.27 The purpose of Article 13: "is to prevent the parties from limiting the choice offered by this Convention to the policy-holder, and to prevent the insurer from avoiding the restrictions imposed under [Article 12]".[45] The conditions for there to be a valid jurisdiction agreement are referred to by Jenard as "strictly defined".[46] If an agreement does not comply with Article 13 or purports to exclude a mandatory jurisdiction under Article 22 it has no legal force under the Brussels Regulation: Article 23(5). However, it does not follow that if a jurisdiction agreement complies with Articles 13 and 14 that it will be effective. Article 23 sets out requirements for the form and nature of an effective jurisdiction agreement which are not replicated in Articles 13 and 14 which impose *further* limitations on what is permitted in relation to insurance matters. In other words, the requirements of Article 23 must be met as well as those in section 3.[47]

6.28 With the exception of Article 13(3) Article 13 does not specify that the court chosen should be a court of a Member State. By contrast, Article 23 only applies where the court chosen is in a Member State (para. 5.37). It would be odd to say the least if the more restrictive and protective Article 13 were to give effect to jurisdiction agreements which Article 23 did not. This suggests that Article 13 is restricted to a choice of the courts of a Member State. If so, the choice of the courts of a non-Member State would render the jurisdiction agreement of no legal force under Article 23(5).

6.29 Even if the court has jurisdiction under Article 13 by virtue of a jurisdiction agreement, the court may yet have to decline jurisdiction or stay the action because of *lis alibi pendens* or related proceedings. In *Evialis* v. *SIAT*,[48] Italian underwriters commenced proceedings in Italy against the French insured claiming that they were not liable for a loss on various grounds, and the insured later commenced proceedings in England relying on a non-exclusive jurisdiction clause and claiming the sums due under the insurance. The judge accepted the insured had a sufficient case that the non-exclusive jurisdiction agreement applied, which was effective under Article 13 of section 3 containing the insurance code,

45. *Jenard*, p. 33.

46. *Jenard*, p. 33; C-112/03 *Societe Peloux* v. *Axa* [2005] ECR I-3707 at [31]; compare *Charman* v. *WOC* [1993] 2 Lloyd's Rep. 551, 557, Staughton LJ, suggesting a "liberal or generous" approach to Article 14(4) of the Brussels Regulation on the basis that if someone has sufficient economic power to fall within Article 14(1), (2) or (3), but chooses to insure other risks and property connected in some way, he does not suddenly become a person in need of consumer protection.

47. The matter has not been specifically discussed in the cases but the courts have in practice applied the requirements of Article 23 as well as Articles 13–14; for example: C-201/82 *Gerling* v. *Amministrazione del Tesoro* [1983] ECR I-2503; *Tradigrain* v. *SIAT* [2002] 2 Lloyd's Rep. 553, 558; *Standard Steamship* v. *GIE* [2002] 2 Lloyd's Rep. 407, 415. See also *Société d'études d'investissement pour les affaires (SEIA) SA v. Société nationale de sauvetage en mer (SNSM), Banque nationale de Paris (BNP) et les Souscripteurs des Lloyd's de Londres (Navire "Jet Ruban bleu")*, Case 1998/19 on ECJ database at *http://www.jura.uni-sb.de/convention-bruxelles/en/1998/19-1998.*

48. [2004] 1 Lloyd's Rep. 187, Andrew Smith J.

but held that there was no justification for treating Article 27 as inapplicable to the "quasi-exclusive" regime relating to insurance in section 3, and stayed the English proceedings.

1. Third parties

6.30 If the insured or beneficiary is not a party to the insurance contract can he enforce the jurisdiction agreement to which he is not a party as against the insurer? The effect of recent European Court of Justice decisions is that a non party insured or beneficiary may rely on Article 13 to enforce a jurisdiction agreement in a contract of insurance where he has succeeded to the rights under it, but that the insurer cannot rely on Article 13 to enforce a jurisdiction agreement against a beneficiary who was not a party to the jurisdiction agreement. The asymmetry is said to be justified by the purpose of Article 13 being to protect the weaker party to the contract although that is questionable. In *Gerling* v. *Amminstrazione del Tresoro*[49] the European Court of Justice considered a claim by a third party to enforce a jurisdiction agreement in an insurance policy. The policy was granted by a pool of underwriters and covered an international group of national road transport associations in respect of liability to pay certain sums, and included a jurisdiction agreement in favour of the country of each national association. When the Italian association was wound up its rights under the policy vested in the Italian Treasury by operation of law. Could the Treasury rely on the jurisdiction agreement under Article 23? The Treasury had succeeded to the rights of the insured under the policy by operation of law not by agreement. It therefore had not made any agreement with the insurers. The court pointed to Article 13(2) which contemplated that a jurisdiction agreement could allow proceedings to be brought not just by the original parties to the policy but by persons intended to benefit (it refers to "policyholder, the insured or a beneficiary"). The purpose of the Article 23 requirements was to ensure that consent to the jurisdiction agreement was clearly established, but, if such consensus was established as between the original parties, there was no need to prevent a third party from benefiting from the jurisdiction agreement. The court found nothing in the wording to require a third party to meet the formal requirements (not surprising since Article 23 does not mention third parties at all). The Treasury was therefore able to rely on the jurisdiction agreement although not a party to the original policy.

6.31 The effect of this approach is that community law does not apply to the question whether or not a third party has title to enforce a jurisdiction agreement. That depends on the law applicable under the conflicts rules of the national law of the court seised. Different national laws could of course yield different answers as to whether or not a third party may enforce a jurisdiction agreement; but this potential lack of uniformity has been held, in effect, to be tolerable as part of the system under Article 23. It is interesting to compare this more relaxed approach to that applied to whether or not a claim by a third party under a contract is within Article 5(1) (para. 5.147 above).

6.32 But what if it is the insurer which wishes to enforce a jurisdiction agreement as against a third party? In *Societe Peloux* v. *AXA*[50] a French manufacturer was a subsidiary of a Belgian parent company, and insured by a group policy issued to the Belgian parent by a number of Belgian and other insurers which included a jurisdiction agreement in favour of Belgium. The French subsidiary wished to join the insurers to an action against it in France. Could the insurers rely on the jurisdiction agreement in the policy which had been agreed by the parent company to prevent jurisdiction in France at the suit of the subsidiary? The court

49. C-201/82; [1983] ECR I-2503.

50. C-112/03, [2005] ECR I-3707; *Societe Lutz* v. *Societe Frasgo*, 12 November 1991, Paris Court of Appeal in Kaye, European Case Law, p. 434.

underlined that the policy behind section 3 was to protect the economically weaker party, and that even the rules in Article 13 giving effect to party autonomy do not enable the policy holder to be deprived of the right to sue in the country of his domicile (para. 32). But, if the jurisdiction agreement bound the French subsidiary it would mean the French subsidiary would not be entitled to sue in France but was bound to sue in Belgium. The European Court of Justice was not prepared to allow even this detraction from the protection under section 3. Protection should be extended to a beneficiary under a policy, just as much as to a policy-holder, and therefore Article 13(3) did not apply to a claim by a beneficiary of a policy who was not a party. This approach seems questionable. Why was it to be supposed that the subsidiary company needed the protection of not having to commence proceedings in a place agreed by the parent? Suppose that a loss payee who is not a policyholder of a large contract wishes to avoid having to commence proceedings in the place agreed by the policyholder with the insurer. The justification behind the restrictions in section 3 and in particular Articles 13–14 simply do not apply to a claim by the insurer against the loss payee.

2. Jurisdiction agreement post dispute

6.33 Article 13(1) generally permits jurisdiction agreements made after the dispute has arisen to have effect, but limits the scope for agreements made pre-dispute. The dispute is said by Jenard to arise "as soon as the parties disagree on a specific point and legal proceedings are imminent or contemplated" (p. 33).

3. Jurisdiction agreement conferring additional jurisdiction

6.34 A jurisdiction agreement is effective if it is to the advantage of the policy-holder, insured or beneficiary by conferring jurisdiction on a place additional to those provided for by section 3 (Article 13(2)). Unlike Article 13(1) there is no condition as to the time when the jurisdiction agreement is made.

4. Jurisdiction agreement by insurer and policy-holder in favour of their own Member State

6.35 In effect, an insurer may, if the insurer and policy-holder are domiciled or habitually resident in the same Member State, procure agreement that the courts of that Member State will have jurisdiction even if the harmful event occurred abroad: Article 13(3).[51] This permits the policy-holder to give up by agreement the right to commence proceedings in the place where the harmful event occurred, so long as he may commence them in his domicile or where he is habitually resident. Article 13(3) only refers to a jurisdiction agreement between a policy-holder and insurer; such a clause cannot be enforced by an insurer against a non party insured or beneficiary who is not domiciled in that Member State.[52] Again, unlike Article 13(1) there is no condition as to the time when the jurisdiction agreement is made.

5. Jurisdiction agreement with policy-holder not domiciled in a Member State

6.36 A jurisdiction agreement with a policy-holder not domiciled in a Member State is effective, "except in so far as the insurance is compulsory or relates to immoveable property in a Member State". This provision was originally introduced to the Brussels Convention in 1978 when the UK joined the Convention because of the number of policy-holders not domiciled in the UK who do business in the UK.[53] It allows non-Member State policyholders to choose

51. See *Jenard*, p. 32, for the background to this provision.
52. C-112/03 *Societe Peloux* v. *AXA* [2005] ECR I-3707.
53. *Schlosser*, para. 137.

English jurisdiction and for that choice to be binding. A list of compulsory insurance provisions in different Member States appears in Schlosser, para. 138.

6. Jurisdiction agreement in respect of ships, aircraft, goods in transit and connected risks

6.37 A jurisdiction agreement is effective insofar as it covers one or more of the risks in Article 14: Article 13(5). The specified risks are not thought to be ones in which the parties have inequality of bargaining power. The definitions of the classes of business are complicated, and are the subject of detailed commentary in Schlosser, paras 140–147. In essence they are risks relating to cover for ships, aircraft, goods in transit and connected risks: Articles 14(1) to (4). Large risks under Article 14(5) are considered below.

6.38 Note that Article 13(5) permits a jurisdiction agreement "insofar as it covers" one or more of the risks set out in Article 14. If the jurisdiction agreement covers risks which are not within Article 14 is the jurisdiction agreement valid to any extent? A literal interpretation of "in so far as" might suggest that the jurisdiction agreement would be valid in relation to risks which are within Article 14, and not in relation to those risks which were not. But such an approach hardly seems practical. It could easily lead to disputes being litigated in two jurisdictions which is contrary to one of the purposes of the Brussels Regulation. On the other hand, if the jurisdiction agreement was valid for all risks, even if not within Article 14 it is difficult to see why para. 14(4) was included. Largely for these reasons Staughton LJ interpreted Article 13(5) as meaning that the jurisdiction agreement was *only* permitted if it covered one or more of the risks in Article 14, and *not* permitted if it covered any risks not within Article 14.[54]

6.39 In addition, "any risk or interest connected with any of those" is specified: Article 14(4). This is intended to allow a jurisdiction agreement covering a risk which is sufficiently connected to a risk covering ships and aircraft or the liabilities referred to. The meaning of risk is obvious; as to interest, this probably refers to the subject matter of the risk in Articles 13(1) to (3), i.e. ships, aircraft and goods.[55] What is a sufficient connection? According to Schlosser (para. 147):

> "Insurance against ancillary risks is a familiar practice, especially in United Kingdom insurance contracts. An example would be shipowner disbursements consisting of exceptional operational costs, e.g. harbour dues accruing whilst a ship remains disabled. Another example is insurance against increased value, providing protection against loss arising from the fact that a destroyed or damaged cargo had increased in value during transit. The provision does not require an ancillary risk to be insured under the same policy as the main risk to which it relates."

6.40 In *Charman* v. *WOC*[56] the insurance covered the risk that at the end of a contract to construct a breakwater the policy-holder would not be able to repatriate from Algeria certain equipment which included both sea-going and land-based equipment. The Court of Appeal took a wide view of the connection required under Article 14(4) (at p. 557):

> "For my part I do not accept that there must be a very close connection between the risk or interest in par. (4) and that within pars. (1) to (3). If that is what is meant by saying that the former must be accessory or ancillary to the latter, I do not agree with that interpretation. It seems to me inconsistent with the purpose of art. 12(5) and art. 12A [now Article 13(5) and 14 of the Brussels Regulation]. As

54. *Charman* v. *WOC* [1993] 2 Lloyd's Rep. 551, 558; *Minister for Agriculture, Food and Forestry* v. *Alte Leipziger* [2001] 2 IR 82, para. 43.

55. *Charman* v. *WOC* [1993] 2 Lloyd's Rep. 551, 556, Staughton LJ: "In broad terms it is used to describe property in connection with which a risk can give rise to loss."

56. [1993] 2 Lloyd's Rep. 551.

explained by Professor Schlosser, I take that purpose to be the creation of an exception to the mandatory rules for jurisdiction in insurance cases. The reason for the exception is that some people who take out insurance do not need the special advantage which is accorded to those with less economic power. It was not considered possible to define the class of people who did not need such protection, except by reference to the type of contracts which they entered into. Hence art. 12A. If somebody has sufficient economic power to be in that class and to make a contract of that type, but chooses to insure also for other risks or property connected in some way with the subject matter of marine insurance, it does not seem to me that he suddenly becomes a person in need of consumer protection. There are of course other reasons given by Professor Schlosser for the special treatment of marine insurance. But in my opinion the reason summarised above was its main purpose. It is best served by adopting a liberal or generous interpretation of art. 12A(4), and not the narrow meaning which the owners contend for in this case. I would however say that the extra risks or interests covered by par. (4) must not be disproportionately large compared with those covered by pars. (1) to (3). They must not be the main or almost the main subject-matter of the contract, but a lesser part of it. The tail must not be allowed to wag the dog, or an insurance on land-based property to be converted into an insurance within art. 12A by the inclusion of some trivial marine risk."

In that case there was a sufficient connection between the risk to the seagoing vessels and the land-based equipment because they were all insured against the same risk. There was a sufficient connection between the interests because the equipment was being used for the same venture, and belonged to the same insured. The interest in the maritime risks were primary risks because some 80% by value of the equipment was seagoing.

6.41 In *Tradigrain* v. *SIAT*[57] there were separate insurances for marine carriage of oil, and for the risks of storage of the oil (para. 29). The question was whether or not a jurisdiction agreement in the policy covering the storage risks came within Article 14(4). Colman J. found that the storage risk was connected to the carriage risk "in the sense that it covered the goods after they had ceased to be covered by the marine cover but prior to their availability to the buyer" (p. 560). The connection here seems to have been in the interest (oil), rather than the risk.

6.42 In *Standard Steamship* v. *GIE*[58] the insured company held the duty free and shop concessions on five cruise ships operated by a cruise ship company. The insured basically needed employers' liability cover for its retail employees in its concessions on board ships. It obtained the cover by way of becoming a joint entrant to the P&I club cover which covered the cruise ship company. The insurance treated the retail employees as seamen, and the risks covered included liability for death injury or illness to employees, and liability for such matters arising out of collision or carriage of cargo, repatriation, crew substitute expenses and shipwreck unemployment benefit. The court found that the risks covered were liability arising from the use or operation of ships within Article 13(2), or financial loss connected with the use or operation of ships within Article 14(3), or connected with those risks within Article 14(5). Another ground for the decision was that the relevant risks were the totality of those covered by the P&I cover in respect of the cruise ship company and the insured joint entrant, and the vast majority of those risks were clearly within Article 14.

7. Jurisdiction agreement in respect of large risks

6.43 Under Articles 13 and 14(5) insofar as[59] a jurisdiction agreement covers "large risks" it is permitted. Large risks are as defined in the First Non-Life Insurance Directive, as later amended.[60] In essence large risks are:

57. [2002] 2 Lloyd's Rep. 553. Compare *Minister for Agriculture, Food and Forestry* v. *Alte Leipziger* [2001] 2 IR 82 where the relevant risk was mostly storage with some road transport and not within Article 14.

58. [2005] Lloyd's Rep. IR 407, see para. 5.93 above.

59. As to which see above.

(1) all risks relating to railway rolling stock, aircraft, ships, goods in transit, aircraft liability, and liability for ships;
(2) credit and insolvency risks and suretyship liability where the policy-holder is engaged professionally;
(3) risks covering motor vehicles, fire and natural forces, motor vehicle liability, general liability and miscellaneous financial loss and employment risks, if and insofar as the policy-holder has any two of a balance sheet of €6.2m, a net turnover of €12.8m or an average number of employees during the financial year of 250.[61]

These provisions were first introduced in 1978 on the accession of the UK to the Brussels Convention because it was recognised that commercial risks of the type identified did not warrant the special protection provided in Section 3. The approach in 1978 was to identify the business by class: loss or damage to ships, goods in transit, etc. Schlosser referred to the impossibility of taking as criteria abstract general factors like company turnover or capital or cross-referring to the classes in the Annex to the first non-life insurance directive 73/239/EEC (para. 140). But, in the event, in 2001 when the Brussels Regulation was introduced this was the approach taken to identify additional large risks.

60. Including future amendments: Article 14(5); *Explanatory Memorandum to Brussels Regulation*, p. 15. The concept of "large risks" was originally introduced into the First Non-Life Insurance Directive 73/239/EEC by the Second Non-Life Insurance Directive 88/357/EEC, and is still used for some purposes, e.g. Insurance Intermediaries Directive 2002/92/EC Article 8; and Financial Services and Markets Act 2000 (Regulated Activities) Order 2001, SI 2001/544, para. 72D.

61. The limits were higher before 1 January 2003.

CHAPTER 7

REINSURANCE AND INSURANCE JURISDICTION AT COMMON LAW

A. INTRODUCTION

7.1 Common law jurisdiction rules remain important in relation to reinsurance and insurance because of the prevalence of business in non-EU countries such as the USA, Japan, China, Korea, Russia and Commonwealth countries. In this chapter we deal with the jurisdiction rules applicable under English law where the Brussels Regulation does not apply. By way of a convenient and commonly used shorthand we refer to this law as the common law, as distinct from the law contained in the European legislation, although all the court's exorbitant jurisdiction derives from statute and there may be other particular English legislation which is relevant. The usage is justified because the principles in this area have been and continue to be very largely developed by the courts.

7.2 The approach of the common law to clashes of jurisdiction is very different from the civil law:

"This part of the law is concerned with the resolution of clashes between jurisdictions. Two different approaches to the problem have emerged in the world today, one associated with the civil law jurisdictions of continental Europe, and the other with the common law world. Each is the fruit of a distinctive legal history, and also reflects to some extent cultural differences which are beyond the scope of an opinion such as this. On the continent of Europe, in the early days of the European Community, the essential need was seen to be to avoid any such clash between member states of the same community. A system, developed by distinguished scholars, was embodied in the Brussels Convention on Jurisdiction and the Enforcement of Judgments in Civil and Commercial Matters (1968) (Schedule 1 to the Civil Jurisdiction and Judgments Act 1982), under which jurisdiction is allocated on the basis of well-defined rules. This system achieves its purpose, but at a price. The price is rigidity, and rigidity can be productive of injustice. The judges of this country, who loyally enforce this system, not only between United Kingdom jurisdictions and the jurisdictions of other member states, but also as between the three jurisdictions within the United Kingdom itself, have to accept the fact that the practical results are from time to time unwelcome. This is essentially because the primary purpose of the Convention is to ensure that there shall be no clash between the jurisdictions of member states of the Community. In the common law world, the situation is precisely the opposite. There is, so to speak, a jungle of separate, broadly based, jurisdictions all over the world. In England, for example, jurisdiction is founded on the presence of the defendant within the jurisdiction, and in certain specified (but widely drawn) circumstances on a power to serve the defendant with process outside the jurisdiction. But the potential excesses of common law jurisdictions are generally curtailed by the adoption of the principle of *forum non conveniens* – a self-denying ordinance under which the court will stay (or dismiss) proceedings in favour of another clearly more appropriate forum." [1]

The Brussels Regulation regime has been described as a "closed system", that is, it is one within which the rules are the same for all members, and which is designed to avoid clashes of jurisdiction by laying down precise rules which can lead to rigidity and injustice (see, for example, para. 5.282 above – for the Italian Torpedo). The common law system deals with a "jungle of different, broadly based, jurisdictions all over the world",[2] and is characterised by widely drawn power to serve proceedings outside the jurisdiction but curtailed by the principle

1. *Airbus* v. *Patel* [1998] 1 Lloyd's Rep. 631, 636.
2. *Ibid.*

of *forum non conveniens*.[3] Accordingly, the purpose of the common law of *forum non conveniens* is to avoid cases being heard in inappropriate jurisdictions, not necessarily to avoid all parallel proceedings: "indeed parallel proceedings in different jurisdictions are not of themselves regarded as unacceptable."[4]

7.3 If the court has jurisdiction under the Brussels Regulation it will not have jurisdiction under the common law. The precise line between the application of the Brussels Regulation and the common law is therefore crucial, as to which see chapter 4.

7.4 As to the common law rules themselves, there is a primary distinction to be made between cases where jurisdiction may be established as of right, that is, without permission (presence within the jurisdiction and submission), and cases where the claimant must obtain permission from the court. Where the claimant must obtain permission it is usually because the defendant is situated abroad and it is necessary to rely on an exorbitant ground of jurisdiction or not proceed in England at all. The court has a discretion not to permit such exorbitant service. Wherever the English court has jurisdiction (whether with or without permission) the defendant may challenge the jurisdiction. Where permission to serve out was required the defendant may apply to set aside the permission. The defendant may also apply in any case (whether or not service out was as of right or required permission) for a stay of the English proceedings on *forum non conveniens* grounds. This is a fruitful area of reported cases. Where it is the claimant who wishes in effect to challenge foreign proceedings he may apply to the English court in certain circumstances for an order against a defendant to restrain foreign proceedings (an anti-suit injunction).

7.5 It is convenient to consider the issues which arise under the following headings:

(1) Establishing (re)insurance jurisdiction without permission.
(2) Establishing (re)insurance jurisdiction with permission of the court.
(3) Challenging (re)insurance jurisdiction: setting aside, stay and anti-suit injunction.
(4) Conclusions.

B. ESTABLISHING (RE)INSURANCE JURISDICTION WITHOUT PERMISSION

1. Introduction

7.6 There are a number of principal cases at common law where the claimant may serve proceedings on a foreign defendant without having to obtain permission of the court under CPR 6.20 to service out of the jurisdiction. These cases are:

(1) the defendant is present in England and duly served there;
(2) it is possible to serve the claim form at a place in England specified under Part 23 of the Companies Act 1985 or under CPR 6.5; or
(3) proceedings can be served on an agent under CPR 6.16;
(4) the defendant submits to the jurisdiction of the English court;
(5) the court may have jurisdiction under certain particular statutes (see below).

In cases (1) to (3) service may be made within the jurisdiction even though the defendant is foreign. In case (4) it does not matter where service is made. In case (5) service depends on the statute but in some cases may be made outside the jurisdiction without permission.

3. *Airbus* v. *Patel* [1998] 1 Lloyd's Rep. 631, 636.
4. *Ibid.* See also Hartley, "The European Union and the Systematic Dismantling of the Common Law of Conflict of Laws" [2005] 54 ICLQ 813.

7.7 In all other cases, at common law, it will be necessary to obtain the permission of the court to serve proceedings out of the jurisdiction. In cases where jurisdiction is established as of right the court may still stay the proceedings for *forum non conveniens* but will not do so lightly (see para. 7.102 below).[5]

2. Service within the jurisdiction on a foreign defendant

7.8 There is jurisdiction in respect of proceedings against an individual if he is duly served in England, however short the period for which he is England. The claim must be one *in personam*. Accordingly, in *Colt* v. *Sarlie*[6] the defendant was visiting London for "a few days" and service on him was good.[7] The court retains jurisdiction even if the defendant later leaves the jurisdiction. However, if the claimant later adds a new claim he will have to obtain permission in relation to the new claim if the defendant cannot be served within the jurisdiction at that time.

7.9 Where the claimant does not need the permission of the court he may proceed directly to service. For personal service generally see CPR 6.4; for service by post see CPR 6.5; for service by an alternative method see CPR 6.8; and for service by a contractually agreed method see CPR 6.15.[8] Difficult questions may arise as to whether or not there is jurisdiction, or service was good, if the individual left the jurisdiction at a time when service is deemed to be made.[9] Proceedings may be commenced against a partnership in the name of the firm by leaving the claim form with a partner or a person who at the time of service has the control and management of the partnership business at its principal place of business in England.[10] By this means proceedings may be commenced against partners even if none are present in the jurisdiction. Alternatively, an individual partner may be personally served if present in England.

7.10 There is jurisdiction to commence proceedings against a company if, like an individual, it is present in England when service is made.[11] But it is also possible to serve on foreign companies with a branch or other establishment in England (see sections 725, 694A–695 of the Companies Act 1985). Furthermore, under CPR 6.5 it is possible to serve on a foreign company (that is, companies incorporated abroad) wherever the company carries on business, or has a place of business within the jurisdiction.[12]

7.11 Under CPR 6.19 a claimant can apply to proceed against an overseas defendant by serving on an agent within the jurisdiction provided the contract was entered into within the jurisdiction or through that agent.

5. *Spiliada* v. *Cansulex* [1987] 1 AC 460, 476.

6. [1966] 1 WLR 440.

7. It may be otherwise if there is "fraud inducing the defendant to come into the country", p. 444. Also in such a case the connection with England may be fragile, even though service is as of right, which will bear on any *forum non conveniens* application: *Spiliada* v. *Cansulex* [1987] 1 AC 460, 477.

8. *The Society of Lloyd's* v. *Tropp* [2004] EWHC 33 (Comm), where Lloyd's was entitled to serve proceedings for payment of Equitas premium on a US domiciled defendant by service on Underwriting Agencies (No. 9) in the UK pursuant to a term in a reinsurance and run-off contract made by Underwriting Agencies (No. 9) for the defendant with Equitas.

9. See, e.g., *Barclays Bank* v. *Swaziland* [1989] 1 WLR 506 where service was made through the letterbox at 15.30 and the defendant came into England at 17.30 that day but did not visit the address where service had been made and left the next day; *Chellaram* v. *Chellaram (No. 2)* [2002] 3 All ER 17.

10. CPR 6.4(5).

11. See, generally, *Adams* v. *Cape* [1990] Ch 433 (CA).

12. See, further, Dicey/Morris/Collins, para. 11-082.

3. Submission to the jurisdiction

7.12 A party may by his own conduct act in a way inconsistent with his objecting to the jurisdiction of the court, for example by accepting service, making a counterclaim, or taking a step in the action. If the defendant does not file an acknowledgement of service and apply to the court for an order declaring that the court has no jurisdiction, or should not exercise its jurisdiction, within 14 days of filing acknowledgement of service, he will be treated as having accepted that the court has jurisdiction.[13] The defendant may also submit to the jurisdiction by a term of the contract agreeing to nominate an agent for service within the jurisdiction.[14] By submitting to the jurisdiction a defendant cannot confer on the court jurisdiction which it could not otherwise have.[15]

4. Jurisdiction under particular conventions

7.13 The UK is party to a number of international conventions which provide for international jurisdiction in certain areas, quite apart from the Brussels Regulation (formerly a convention, but now in the form of direct EU legislation). The conventions are implemented by statutes. They concern carriage by air, sea, rail and road, collisions at sea, disputes at Liner Conferences, the employment of crew on aircraft and ships, and pollution by ships.[16] In such cases no permission to serve out is required although the claim form should contain a statement of the grounds on which the claimant is entitled to serve out: CPR 6.19. The Brussels Regulation "shall not affect" any conventions to which Member States are parties which in relation to particular matters govern jurisdiction or judgments: Article 71. This means that the specialised convention will apply to the cases governed by it but otherwise the Brussels Regulation will apply. In *The Tatry*[17] the European Court of Justice held that Article 71: "introduces an exception to the general rule that the Convention [now Regulation] takes precedence over other conventions signed by the Contracting States on jurisdiction and the recognition and enforcement of judgments. The purpose of that exception is to ensure compliance with the rules on jurisdiction laid down by specialised conventions, since in enacting those rules account was taken of the specific features of the matters to which they relate. That being its purpose, Article 57 [now Article 71 of the Brussels Regulation] must be understood as precluding the application of the provisions of the Brussels Convention solely in relation to questions governed by a specialised convention. A contrary interpretation would be incompatible with the objective of the Convention which, according to its preamble, is to strengthen in the Community the legal protection of persons therein established and to facilitate recognition of judgments in order to secure their enforcement. In those circumstances, when a specialised convention contains certain rules of jurisdiction but no provision as to *lis pendens* or related actions, Articles 21 and 22 of the Brussels Convention apply [now Article 27 and 28 of the Brussels Regulation]" (para. 23-4). In relation to the allocation of jurisdiction within the UK, the corresponding provision to Article 71 of the Brussels Regulation is made by the Civil Jurisdiction and Judgments Act, section 17, and Schedule 5, para. 6.

13. CPR 11. The defendant must file evidence in support of the application but not serve the Defence before the hearing of the application.

14. *Montgomery* v. *Liebenthal* [1898] 1 QB 487, 488 CA: "The service of proceedings ... upon a party residing or carrying on business in Scotland or Ireland, by leaving the same at the office of the London Corn Trade Association, together with the posting of a copy of such proceedings to the address in Scotland or Ireland, shall be deemed good service"; *Allison* v. *Limehouse* [1992] 2 AC 105, HL.

15. For example, because courts of another Member State have mandatory jurisdiction under Article 22 of the Brussels Regulation.

16. See, generally, Dicey/Morris/Collins, chapter 15.

17. C-406/92, [1994] ECR I-5439.

C. ESTABLISHING (RE)INSURANCE JURISDICTION WITH PERMISSION

1. Introduction

7.14 In summary, the key questions on an application for permission to serve out of the jurisdiction are:

(1) Whether or not there is a good arguable case that the claim falls within one or more of the heads of jurisdiction under CPR 6.20. The CPR expressly state that the court will not permit service out unless satisfied that this jurisdiction is the proper place in which to bring the claim.[18]
(2) Whether or not there is a serious question to be tried on the merits of the claim.
(3) Whether or not England is the *forum conveniens*.

7.15 If these three matters are established by the claimant the court will, in principle, grant permission to serve out of the jurisdiction.

7.16 In addition to the framework of the three questions above, it may be useful to highlight here some of the general principles applied by the courts in considering applications for permission to serve out. At bottom many of these derive from the serious nature of the application, which is to bring before the English courts a defendant not situate in the jurisdiction.

(1) First and foremost the court will exercise its power to give permission to serve proceedings out of the jurisdiction with caution: "it is a serious question whether the jurisdiction under Order 11 [now CPR 6.20] ought to be invoked, to put a person outside the jurisdiction to the 'inconvenience and annoyance of being brought to contest his rights in this country:'... It is, of course, true to say that any inconvenience involved has been much reduced by modern methods of communication; but the point of principle remains".[19] Respect for the foreign defendant is matched by respect for the foreign jurisdiction which has jurisdiction over the defendant: "the jurisdiction exercised by an English court over a foreign corporation which has no place of business in this country, as a result of granting leave under RSC, Ord. 11, r. 1(1)(f) for service out of the jurisdiction of a writ on that corporation, is an exorbitant jurisdiction, i.e. it is one which, under general English conflict rules, an English court would not recognise as possessed by any foreign court in the absence of some treaty providing for such recognition. Comity thus dictates that the judicial discretion to grant leave under this paragraph of RSC, Ord. 11, r. 1(1) should be exercised with circumspection in cases where there exists an alternative forum, *viz*. the courts of the foreign country where the proposed defendant does carry on business, and whose jurisdiction would be recognised under English conflict rules."[20]
(2) For these reasons, as well as an overarching caution, the court has adopted a restrictive approach to the construction of the jurisdictional rules: any ambiguities in the rules are

18. CPR 6.21(2A). Waller LJ held that the predecessor of this rule was "directed to whether the plaintiff has established that the case falls within one of the heads of jurisdiction" and there is no reason to think that CPR 6.21(2A) is any different: *Canada Trust* v. *Stolzenberg (No. 2)* [1998] 1 WLR 547, 553 CA; affirmed [2002] 1 AC 1, 13 HL; *cf. Marubeni* v. *Mongolian Government* [2002] 2 All ER 873, 890.

19. *Seaconsar* v. *Bank Markazi* [1994] 1 AC 438, 455, *per* Lord Goff; *Societe Generale de Paris* v. *Dreyfus* (1885) 29 Ch. D 239, 242, Pearson J.; *Mackender* v. *Feldia* [1967] 2 QB 590, 599.

20. *Amin Rasheed* v. *Kuwait* [1984] 1 AC 50, 65, HL, *per* Lord Diplock. In *Spiliada* v. *Cansulex* [1987] 1 AC 460, at p. 481 Lord Goff noted that "the word 'exorbitant' is, as used in the present context, an old-fashioned word which perhaps carries unfortunate overtones: it means no more than that the exercise of the jurisdiction is extraordinary in the sense explained by Lord Diplock".

to be resolved in favour of not giving permission[21]; and a claimant must show that the claim falls within the spirit as well as the letter of the rule conferring jurisdiction.[22]

(3) Because the initial application for permission is made by the claimant only, usually without the knowledge or participation of the defendant, and because of its serious nature, the court requires that there be full and frank disclosure by the claimant in relation to the initial application (see further below).

7.17 The feature of the common law which stands out by comparison with the approach under the Brussels Regulation, is the discretion which the court has to decide whether or not to permit service out. The considerations which must be weighed make this approach almost infinitely flexible and responsive to the particular facts of the case. A consequence of this is that it may well not be possible to predict at the time when a dispute arises (and even less possible at an earlier stage) whether or not the English court will assume jurisdiction in relation to a particular dispute. Relevant facts may not be known until the opposing evidence is served. On the other hand, the approach under the Brussels Regulation is diametrically opposite: the constant aim of the European Court of Justice is to ensure that the application of the jurisdiction provisions in the Regulation is as "automatic" as possible[23]; accordingly *forum non conveniens* is outlawed, as is almost any review by one Member State court of the jurisdiction of another Member State court (para. 5.280). It follows that where the common law is relied upon, many jurisdiction disputes in practice centre around the arguments about *forum conveniens*, whether on an application to set aside service out or on a stay application. Such arguments are decisive of jurisdiction but are generally matters of weight and judgment rather than black and white rules. The factors which outweigh all others in arguments about *forum conveniens* are the existence of an arbitration clause or an exclusive jurisdiction agreement; consequently much attention has been paid to them in the cases. It is undeniable that the selection of jurisdictions, the timing of applications in different jurisdictions, the content of proceedings and framing of concessions which may be offered by one party can have a decisive effect on the outcome of a jurisdiction application: in other words there is inevitably scope for careful strategy by the parties.

7.18 We consider the issues under the following heads:

(1) Procedure.
(2) Does the claim fall within CPR 6.20?
(3) Are the merits of the claim sufficiently strong?
(4) Should the court exercise its discretion to give permission – is England the *forum conveniens*?

We deal with arbitration separately in chapter 8.

2. Procedure

7.19 Where permission to serve out is required the application is made in writing under Part 23: see generally CPR 6.21 and Commercial Court Guide B7 and appendix 15. The application is necessarily one-sided and the court requires that the claimant's evidence must be full and frank; if it is not any permission may be set aside.[24] For instance, the applicant should

21. *The Hagen* [1908] P 189, 201; *Finnish Marine* v. *Protective* [1990] 1 QB 1078, 1082.
22. *Atlantic* v. *Milano* [1979] 2 Lloyd's Rep. 240, 245.
23. *Gantner* v. *Basch* [2003] ECR I-4207 at [30].
24. See, generally, *MRG* v. *Engelhard* [2004] 1 Lloyd's Rep. 731; *Ophthalmic Innovations* v. *Ophthalmic Innovations* [2004] EWHC 2948, Lawrence Collins J., para. 44.

draw attention to the fact that it has started or intends to start proceedings in a foreign jurisdiction,[25] or that reinsurance or insurance cover for years previous to the relevant year included a jurisdiction agreement in favour of a different jurisdiction which might ground an argument that such a clause applied to the relevant cover.[26] It is not necessary to argue the case about *forum conveniens* in the supporting evidence though the claimant may obviously do so, provided the court is given the relevant facts about the *forum conveniens*.[27]

7.20 Once permission has been given, and the proceedings served, the claimant may not amend the claim form or Statement of Case unless there is power to serve out of the jurisdiction in relation to it.[28] Because service out of the jurisdiction is an assertion of extra-territorial jurisdiction which could have international repercussions, it is carefully controlled by rules of civil procedure. Irregularities should be cured only in exceptional cases.[29]

7.21 Any application to set aside service of the claim form, or to stay the proceedings must be made in accordance with CPR Part 11. Defects in following the CPR in relation to service out of the jurisdiction will not invalidate the step taken unless the court so orders under paragraph 3.10.[30] The defendant does not submit to the jurisdiction by acknowledging service as required within 14 days of service on him but must exercise care not to take a step in the action thereafter. On an application to set aside permission on the ground of *forum conveniens* it is incumbent on the defendant to identify the issues concerned and state how they may arise in the proceedings.[31]

3. Does the claim fall within CPR 6.20?

7.22 CPR 6.20 states that "a claim form may be served out of the jurisdiction with the permission of the court if –", and then lists 18 categories of claim. These grounds, the "jurisdictional grounds", define the necessary connecting factors between the claim and the English court which under English law justify the English court having jurisdiction.

(i) A good arguable case

7.23 To what standard must a claimant prove the claim is within a ground of jurisdiction? The leading case is *Seaconsar* v. *Bank Markazi*.[32] The claim was for failure to pay sums due under

25. *Tiernan* v. *Magen Insurance* [2000] IL Pr 517, 525–526.
26. *Cf. Burrows* v. *Jamaica* [2002] Lloyd's Rep. IR 466.
27. *Tiernan* v. *Magen Insurance* [2000] IL Pr 517, 526.
28. *Mettall* v. *Rohstoff* [1990] 1 QEG BVI 391, 436 CA: "if the draftsman of a pleading intended to be served out of the jurisdiction under Ord. 11, r. 1(1)(f) (or indeed under any other sub-paragraph) can be reasonably understood as presenting a particular head of claim on one specific legal basis only, the plaintiff cannot thereafter, for the purpose of justifying his application under Ord. 11, r. 1(1)(f), be permitted to contend that that head of claim can also be justified on another legal basis (unless, perhaps, the alternative basis has been specifically referred to in his affidavit evidence, which it was not in the present case). With this possible exception, if he specifically states in his pleading the legal result of what he has pleaded, he is in our judgment limited to what he has pleaded, for the purpose of an Order 11 application"; *A&B* v. *C&D* [1982] 1 Lloyd's Rep. 166, affirmed *sub nom*. *Qatar* v. *Shell* [1983] 2 Lloyd's Rep. 35, CA.
29. *Camera Care Ltd* v. *Hasselblad AB* [1986] 1 FTLR 348; *Ophthalmic Innovations* v. *Ophthalmic Innovations* [2004] EWHC 2948, Lawrence Collins J., para. 43; *cf. WPP* v. *Benatti* [2006] EWHC 1641 (Comm) in relation to defects in service.
30. *WPP* v. *Benatti* [2006] EWHC 1641 (Comm).
31. *Limit (No. 3)* v. *PDV Insurance* [2005] 2 All ER (Comm) 347, 366, CA, where the claim was by a London retrocedent for a declaration of non-liability in respect of clean up costs of damage in Venezuela in circumstances where the issues which would arise along the line from insured to retrocessionaire were far from clear.
32. [1994] 1 AC 439, HL. The differences between RSC Ord. 11 considered in *Seaconsar* and CPR 6.20 are immaterial: *MRG* v. *Engelhard* [2004] 1 Lloyd's Rep. 731, 732, Toulson J.

a letter of credit and jurisdiction was put on the basis (a) that the contract was made in the jurisdiction, or by or through an agent in the jurisdiction, or (b) of a breach of contract within the jurisdiction. The leading speech was that of Lord Goff with which the rest of the Lords agreed, from which a number of points emerge.

7.24 The standard of proof on the jurisdictional ground under CPR 6.20 is that of a "good arguable case".[33] Another equivalent formula is "strong argument".[34] This test is more strict than "serious issue to be tried" which applies in relation to the merits (see para. 7.56 below), but less strict than the ordinary civil burden of the balance of probabilities which applies at trial.[35] On the one hand, applications for permission to serve proceedings out of the jurisdiction are necessarily made at the outset of proceedings, and preliminary in nature so that it is not usually practicable to determine disputed factual matters after cross-examination. On the other, if the court accepts that it has jurisdiction under for instance CPR 6.20(5) it may never have to re-visit the question where the contract was made, and, even if it does, will not set aside jurisdiction because it is determined at trial that the factual basis on which jurisdiction was assumed was erroneous. Such considerations shaped the good arguable case test:

> "It is the concept which the phrase reflects on which it is important to concentrate, i.e. of the court being satisfied or as satisfied as it can be having regard to the limitations which an interlocutory process imposes that factors exist which allow the court to take jurisdiction. The civil standard of proof has itself a flexibility depending on the issue being considered and the concept 'good arguable case' has a similar flexibility. It is natural, for example, in a case concerned with a contract where the jurisdiction depends on whether the breach took place within the jurisdiction, but where the issue to be tried will be whether there was a contract at all, not to wish to give even the appearance of pre-trying the central issue, even though the concept of being satisfied must apply both to the existence of the contract and the place of the breach. It is equally natural for the court in the process of being satisfied to scrutinise most jealously that factor which actually provides jurisdiction. It is equally natural that where the foundation of jurisdiction is domicile, i.e. an issue that will not arise at the trial, that particular scrutiny of the material available takes place in the context of the limitations applied to an interlocutory process."[36]

The test is therefore flexible according to the jurisdictional ground relied on and the issues in the case. However, although the court has power to order a preliminary issue on a jurisdiction dispute, it is seldom that the power is used because trials on jurisdiction issues are "strongly to be discouraged".[37]

7.25 Which elements of the jurisdictional ground must be shown to this standard? It might be thought that it ought merely to be, for instance, the requirement as to the place where the contract was made under CPR 6.20(5)(a); and, if so, the lower test of serious issue to be tried should be applied to whether or not there was a contract, since the place is the only element identified in CPR 6.20(5). However, Lord Goff confirmed in *Seaconsar* that all matters assumed by the jurisdiction ground had to be established to the good arguable case standard. Under CPR 6.20(5)(a), therefore, these are that the contract was made, and made within the jurisdiction. Under CPR 6.20(6) the requirements to be shown to the standard of a good arguable case are that the contract was made, there was a breach, and that the breach was in the jurisdiction.[38]

33. *Seaconsar*, p. 457.
34. *Ibid*., p. 453.
35. *Canada Trust* v. *Stolzenberg (No. 2)* [1998] 1 WLR 547, 558, CA; [2002] 1 AC 1, 13, HL; *MRG* v. *Engelhard* [2004] 1 Lloyd's Rep. 731, 732, Toulson J.; *Carvill* v. *Camperdown* [2005] 2 Lloyd's Rep. 457, 468, CA.
36. *Canada Trust* v. *Stolzenberg (No. 2)* [1998] 1 WLR 547, 555, CA; [2002] 1 AC 1, 13, HL; see also *CGU* v. *Szabo* [2002] 1 Lloyd's Rep. 196, 201.
37. *Attock Cement* v. *Romanian* [1989] 1 WLR 1147, 1156, Staughton LJ; *CGU* v. *Szabo* [2002] 1 Lloyd's Rep. 196, 201.
38. *Seaconsar*, p. 454.

7.26 Sometimes the jurisdictional ground may equate to the cause of action, for example, where the claim is that there was a breach of contract within the jurisdiction. In such a case there is clearly no need to establish the strength of the merits on the cause of action to the different and lower standard which is required. However, some jurisdictional grounds under CPR 6.20 do not overlap or overlap completely with the merits, and a separate question as to the strength of the case on the merits does arise. For instance, if the claim is based on CPR 6.20(1), once the claimant has established a good arguable case that the defendant is domiciled in the jurisdiction, it will still be necessary to go on to establish that the merits of whatever the claim might be are sufficiently strong (see para. 7.56).

(ii) Jurisdictional grounds

7.27 The grounds on which jurisdiction may be assumed by the English court appear from CPR 6.20.[39] Of the 18 grounds of jurisdiction listed in CPR 6.20 the grounds which are mostly relevant to (re)insurance cases are as follows:

(iii) injunction against a defendant from doing something in England;
(iv) third party claims;
(v) contract made in England, governed by English law or with a jurisdiction agreement in favour of England or breached in England;
(vi) tort.

7.28 A claimant may rely on more than one ground, and in practice frequently does so, partly to buttress the argument in relation to *forum conveniens*. Often an important ground of dispute is whether or not the contract is subject to English law, for, if it is, this may provide strong support for the claim that England is the most appropriate forum. For example, it may be said there is evidence the foreign court will not under its choice of law rules apply English law. This is a particularly important potential argument because of the effect under English law of misrepresentation and non-disclosure on a reinsurance or insurance contract,[40] but other differences between English law and the law a foreign court would apply may be significant (para. 7.63).

(iii) Injunction and interim remedy – CPR 6.20(2) and (4)

7.29 The court may give permission to serve out where the claim is for an injunction to do, or refrain from doing, an act in England – CPR 6.20(2). It might be an injunction to prevent a party from issuing proceedings in England contrary to a jurisdiction agreement in favour of a foreign court, or an arbitration clause. It is not possible to use CPR 6.20(2) to confer jurisdiction for an injunction in relation to an act outside the jurisdiction, such as commencing proceedings in a foreign country contrary to a jurisdiction agreement. Such would be the "antithesis" of the rule, or at any rate contrary to the spirit of the rule.[41]

7.30 However, CPR 6.20(4) also now includes the power to grant an injunction in aid of foreign proceedings. Where there are proceedings in another Member State, CPR 6.20(4) specifically confers jurisdiction in relation to a claim for an interim remedy under section

39. For the source and history of the rule making powers of the court, see *Halsbury's Laws* Vol. 37 (4th ed., 2001), para. 8.

40. *Dornoch* v. *Mauritius* [2006] EWCA Civ 389 at [53].

41. *Amoco* v. *British American* [1999] 2 Lloyd's Rep. 772, 778; *Donohue* v. *Armco* [2000] 1 Lloyd's Rep. 579, 599, Sedley LJ, CA; [2002] 1 Lloyd's Rep. 425, HL. See para. 7.103 below for jurisdiction in relation to an anti-suit injunction.

25(1) of the Civil Jurisdiction and Judgments Act 1982.[42] At common law, the English court only had jurisdiction to grant an interim injunction such as a freezing order in aid of substantive proceedings in the English court, but this restriction has been removed by section 25(3) of the Civil Jurisdiction and Judgments Act 1982.[43]

(iv) Third party claims – CPR 6.20(3)

7.31 The court may give permission to serve out where

> "(3) a claim is made against someone on whom the claim form has been or will be served (otherwise than in reliance on this paragraph) and – (a) there is between the claimant and that person a real issue which it is reasonable for the court to try; and (b) the claimant wishes to serve the claim form on another person who is a necessary or proper party to that claim.
>
> (3A) a claim is a Part 20 claim and the person to be served is a necessary or proper party to the claim against the Part 20 claimant."

7.32 In effect the court may assume jurisdiction over a claim against a third party,[44] even though the court would otherwise not have jurisdiction over that claim. The connecting factor and justification is the relationship between the third party claim and the main or anchor proceedings over which the court has jurisdiction.

7.33 It is clear from the wording that it is now not necessary that the anchor proceedings have *already* been served (which sometimes caused procedural problems) and this means that the application under CPR 6.20(3) can be made at the same time as any application for permission in relation to the anchor proceedings. Provided that the third party could have been joined to the proceedings against the anchor defendant if both had been in England the third party will be a proper party.[45] Under CPR 19.2 a party may be joined if it is desirable to add the new party so that the court can resolve all matters in dispute, or there is an issue involving a new party and an existing party which is "connected" to the matters in dispute. A claim in this context is a Part 20 claim (CPR 6.20(3A)) which is any claim other than a claim by a claimant against a defendant, and includes a counterclaim against some person other than the claimant, a claim against any person for a contribution or indemnity or some other remedy, and a claim by a Part 20 defendant (CPR Part 20.2). The definition also includes a counterclaim by a defendant against a claimant, but there is no need for permission in such a case.[46] Accordingly, even if the third party is not a necessary party, he may be a *proper* party: for example, a claim against the broker in the event that the reinsurers' defence succeeds. The claim need not even be alternative as long as there is sufficient overlap between the two claims to make it proper to join the third party.[47]

7.34 It has been said many times that the court will exercise caution or special care in granting permission to bring a third party before it in circumstances where no direct claim could be made: "It must never become the practice to bring foreign defendants here as a

42. That section confers powers on the court to grant interim relief where proceedings have been commenced in a Brussels Regulation state other than the UK (or in another part of the UK) and there are proceedings within Article 1 of the Brussels Regulation in any Member State. It gives effect to Article 31 of the Brussels Regulation and reverses the previous position under the common law. The court need not make an order if it is inexpedient because the court has no jurisdiction over the substantive proceedings: s.25(2).

43. Section 25(3) and Civil Jurisdiction and Judgments Act 1982 (Interim Relief) Order 1997, SI 1997/302 (made under subs (3)).

44. See below.

45. *Goldean Ocean* v. *Martin* [1989] 2 Lloyd's Rep. 390, 395, appeal allowed on other issues [1990] 2 Lloyd's Rep. 215, CA; *Carvill* v. *Camperdown* [2005] 2 Lloyd's Rep. 457, 468, CA.

46. *Derby* v. *Larsson* [1976] 1 WLR 202, HL.

47. *Carvill* v. *Camperdown* [2005] 2 Lloyd's Rep. 457, 468, CA.

matter of course, on the ground that the only alternative requires more than one suit in more than one different jurisdiction."[48] However, it

> "is of course the position that, because of the very nature and wording of the rule, the argument of litigation convenience is able to be advanced by the claimant in every case where leave is sought in relation to Part 20 proceedings. While that will not necessarily be sufficient in itself to persuade the court into a favourable exercise of its discretion, it is, in my view, a factor which may properly encourage a judge to lean in favour of allowing service out of the jurisdiction in the absence of positive counter-indications. As it seems to me, the very existence of the rule and its underlying rationale bring into play the factor of litigation convenience as a matter to be weighed against any reluctance (as opposed to 'caution' in the sense referred to above), on the part of the court when considering whether to exercise its discretion under Ord. 11, r. 4(2)."[49]

The claimant must state in his written evidence the grounds for believing there is a real issue between the claimant and the anchor defendant: CPR 6.21(2). Permission will not be given under CPR 6.20(3) if the claim in the anchor proceedings is bound to fail,[50] or if the purpose is solely to obtain disclosure and there is no substantive claim shown.[51] However, provided the claim in the anchor proceedings is bona fide CPR 6.20(3) may still apply even if the claim against the anchor defendant may or will not be met for lack of funds, and the predominant aim of the claimant in suing him is to anchor the third party claim.[52] Permission was granted to serve contribution proceedings on a third party which had the effect of "out-flanking" an arbitration agreement between the third party and the claimant where contribution would not have been available under the law of the foreign jurisdiction in question.[53]

7.35 This jurisdiction is of particular importance in (re)insurance cases, with many examples of its use. An insured brought proceedings against insurers in England, and insurers wished to join reinsurers so that they were bound by findings in the main action.[54] An insured brought a claim against one broker for negligence in relation to the making of declarations under an open cover and had further or alternative claims against a foreign broker in relation to the same failure.[55] A broker brought proceedings against reinsurers for brokerage and sought to join the foreign reinsured in case it failed against reinsurers.[56] The London placing broker for a reinsurance contract commenced proceedings against the reinsured for premium and sought to join the foreign producing broker in the alternative.[57]

(v) Claims relating to contract – CPR 6.20(5), CPR 6.20(7)

7.36 The court may give permission to serve out where:

> "(5) a claim is made in respect of a contract where the contract – (a) was made within the jurisdiction; (b) was made by or through an agent trading or residing within the jurisdiction; (c) is governed by English law; or (d) contains a term to the effect that the court shall have jurisdiction to determine any claim in respect of the contract …

48. *Goldean Ocean* v. *Martin* [1990] 2 Lloyd's Rep. 215, 222, CA; *Petroleo* v. *Mellitus* [2001] 2 Lloyd's Rep. 203, 209.
49. *Petroleo* v. *Mellitus* [2001] 2 Lloyd's Rep. 203, 210, Potter LJ.
50. *The Brabo* [1949] AC 326, HL.
51. *Unilever* v. *Chefaro* [1994] FSR 135, CA.
52. *Multinational* v. *Multinational* [1983] Ch 258, 279, 287; *Credit Agricole Indosuez* v. *Unicof Ltd* [2004] 1 Lloyd's Rep. 196, 200.
53. *Petroleo* v. *Mellitus* [2001] 2 Lloyd's Rep. 203, CA.
54. *Konkola* v. *Coromin* [2005] 2 All ER (Comm) 637, 660, Colman J., affirmed [2006] EWCA 5, CA.
55. *BP* v. *Aon* [2006] 1 Lloyd's Rep. 549.
56. *Carvill* v. *Camperdown* [2005] 2 Lloyd's Rep. 457, CA.
57. *Heath Lambert Ltd* v. *Sociedad De Corretaje De Seguros* [2005] 1 Lloyd's Rep. 597. Further examples are: *Goldean Ocean* v. *Martin* [1990] 2 Lloyd's Rep. 215, CA (claim by defendant insurers against foreign co-insurers); *SCOR* v. *ERAS EIL* [1992] 1 Lloyd's Rep. 570, CA (claim by defendant brokers/pool managers against their foreign agents).

(7) a claim is made for a declaration that no contract exists where, if the contract was found to exist, it would comply with the conditions set out in paragraph (5)."

7.37 The rule applies where the claim is made "in connection with" a contract. Under the previous version of the rule, RSC Ord. 11, r. 1(1)(d) the rule applied to a claim to "enforce, rescind, annul or otherwise affect" which was interpreted widely to include claims for a declaration that a contract was valid, or had been avoided,[58] or that a party was not in breach of contract, or that a party has suffered no loss resulting from a breach of contract,[59] but not that a contract was never made since such a claim did not "affect" a contract: *Finnish Marine* v. *Protective National Insurance*.[60] The changes to CPR 6.20(5)(a) appear to be intended to minimise argument about the nature of the link required between the claim and the contract; and, just in case, CPR 6.20(7) specifically applies where the claimant seeks a declaration that no contract exists where if it existed it would be within one of the grounds in CPR 6.20(5).

7.38 It is accordingly difficult to foresee many (re)insurance cases where the link between the claim and the contract will not be made out. The rule makes no reference to the parties to the contract. However, the court is unlikely to grant a declaration in relation to a contract between the defendant and a third party without being persuaded that the claim is made to enforce a substantive right of the claimant against the defendant.[61] A claim for interpleader relief is in essence a claim to be released from proceedings not for substantive relief, and therefore not within CPR 6.20(5).[62]

WAS THE CONTRACT MADE IN THE JURISDICTION – CPR 6.20(5)(A)?

7.39 A contract is made when and where it is accepted. In general an acceptance does not take place until it is communicated.[63] Communication of course may take place in many ways. A distinction is drawn between instantaneous communications where the acceptor knows immediately whether or not the acceptance has been properly received, and non-instantaneous communications such as posting where the acceptor is at a distance and will not know straightaway whether or not his acceptance has been successful.[64] In the former case the usual rule that the communication is effective when and where *received* prevails. In the latter case a special rule prevails that the acceptance takes place where and when *sent*, based on the disadvantages of not being able to hold the acceptor to the contract until the communication is received. The archetypal example is that acceptance takes place where posted. Categorising modern methods of communication such as email and faxes can give rise to difficulty.[65] In

58. *Insurance Corporation of Ireland* v. *Strombus International Insurance Co.* [1985] 2 Lloyd's Rep. 138, 142; *BP Exploration Co (Libya) Ltd* v. *Hunt* [1976] 1 WLR 788, in which Kerr J. said, at p. 795: "The words 'or otherwise affect' are very wide; indeed, almost as wide as they can be. A claim for a declaration that a contract has become discharged, whether as the result of frustration, repudiation, or otherwise, is in my view a claim which affects the contract in question. The contrary construction would have serious and highly inconvenient consequences"; *DR Insurance* v. *Central National Insurance* [1996] 1 Lloyd's Rep. 74, 78.

59. E.g., *HIB* v. *Guardian* [1997] 1 Lloyd's Rep. 412, 415–416.

60. [1990] 1 QB 1078, 1083, where the court refused permission to a reinsurer to serve proceedings out of the jurisdiction on the reinsured under a pool scheme run by the Accolade agency for a declaration that the agency had no authority to make contracts on the reinsurers' behalf; *DR Insurance* v. *Central National Insurance* [1996] 1 Lloyd's Rep. 74, 78; *Cool Carriers* v. *HSBC* [2001] 2 Lloyd's Rep. 22, 29.

61. *Cf. Finnish Marine* v. *Protective National Insurance* [1990] 1 QB 1078, 1083, decided under the wording of RSC Ord. 11, although it is not clear why it was not thought that the reinsurers' claim did not directly affect the reinsurance contract; *Cool Carriers* v. *HSBC* [2001] 2 Lloyd's Rep. 22, 29.

62. *Cool Carriers* v. *HSBC* [2001] 2 Lloyd's Rep. 22.

63. See, generally, *Chitty on Contracts* (29th ed., 2004), para. 2-046.

64. *Brinkibon Ltd* v. *Stahag Stahl und Stahlwarenhandelsgesellschaft MbH* [1983] 2 AC 34, 41, 43, 48; *Chitty, op. cit.*, para. 2-048.

65. *Chitty, op. cit.*, para. 2-049.

any event, although the place where the contract was made remains a ground on which the court will assume jurisdiction, it is often a matter of chance in an era of instant international communication where the contract is made, and alone will not count for much when it comes to discretion.[66]

7.40 A (re)insurance contract placed with underwriters in the jurisdiction by an English broker will usually come within the ground of having been made within the jurisdiction.[67] In *Islamic Arab Insurance* v. *Saudi Egyptian American Reinsurance*[68] the claimant reinsured had for years placed reinsurance of its risks in Saudi Arabia through London brokers, Willis, with companies in the London market and international market. In 1984 Willis told the claimant it was unable to complete the reinsurance in the London and international markets, and the claimants began direct negotiations with the defendant company in Saudi Arabia. There was some doubt that reinsurance contracts would be recognised by the Saudi Arabian courts and the court found that despite the direct negotiations there was a good arguable case that it was only intended that matters of principle should be agreed in Saudi Arabia and that the contract was made in London.

WAS THE CONTRACT MADE BY OR THROUGH AN AGENT TRADING OR RESIDING IN ENGLAND – CPR 6.20(5)(B)?

7.41 It was held under the old RSC Ord. 11 that this rule did not apply to a contract made with a defendant by or through the agent of the *claimant*, only a contract by or through an agent of the *defendant*.[69] In other words, the court would only assume jurisdiction over a defendant where *he* employs an agent in the jurisdiction. There is no reason to think the same approach would not apply to the new rule. In the usual case of business placed in London through a London broker the contract will be made through an agent in the jurisdiction even if stamped and initialled elsewhere.[70] A contract can be made *through* an agent even if not by him, for example where the agent has no authority to make the contract as agent but simply transmits offers to his principal for his authorisation. In *Citadel* v. *Atlantic*[71] the Greek reinsurer agreed to an open cover by which it reinsured risks declared to a broker in London. When each risk was declared by submitting the declaration to the broker, a contract came into being between the reinsured and reinsurer which was made through the broker in London. There can occasionally be an issue as to whether or not a London placing broker was in fact acting for the reinsurers rather than the reinsured.[72] It should be remembered that under CPR 6.16 the court may also give permission for service on a principal who is abroad by service on an agent within the jurisdiction of proceedings (see para. 7.6 above). Where it applies this rule enables a claimant to serve proceedings on a defendant principal outside the jurisdiction without having to obtain permission under CPR 6.20.

IS THE CONTRACT GOVERNED BY ENGLISH LAW – CPR 6.20(5)(C)?

7.42 In practice, this can be one of the most important questions in (re)insurance jurisdiction disputes, although it is far from determinative of *forum conveniens* (see para 7.57).[73] The

66. *Cf. Amin Rasheed* v. *Kuwait* [1984] 1 AC 50, 62, HL.
67. E.g. *Burrows* v. *Jamaica* [2002] Lloyd's Rep. IR 466.
68. [1987] 1 Lloyd's Rep. 315, CA.
69. *Union Insurance* v. *Jubilee Insurance* [1991] 1 WLR 415, 417.
70. See, e.g., *Lincoln Life* v. *Employers Re* [2002] EWHC 28 at [11], Moore-Bick J.
71. [1982] 2 Lloyd's Rep. 543, 545, 548, 549; *National Mortgage* v. *Gosselin* (1922) 38 TLR 832, CA.
72. See, e.g., *Tryg Baltica* v. *Boston* [2005] Lloyd's Rep. IR 40, 45.
73. See, e.g., *CGU* v. *Szabo* [2002] 1 Lloyd's Rep. 196, 201–202; *Dornoch* v. *Mauritius* [2006] EWCA Civ 389 at [19].

choice of law rules which determine whether or not a (re)insurance contract is governed by English law are discussed in Part III of this book.

IS THERE AN ENGLISH JURISDICTION AGREEMENT – CPR 6.20(5)(D)?

7.43 The question whether or not there is an English jurisdiction agreement may often involve other questions: for example whether or not a contract was made at all, if it was avoided, whether or not a jurisdiction agreement was incorporated and whether or not the claim falls within the jurisdiction agreement. What is the approach if there is a dispute as to whether or not a jurisdiction agreement was ever made? If there is only one possible law which would apply if the contract was made the court will apply that law (the putative law) to determine whether or not the contract was validly formed.[74] However, in *Dornoch* v. *Mauritius*[75] the question was as to the effect of a condition on a reinsurance slip that simply stated "Jurisdiction clause" where the underlying insurance included a Mauritius jurisdiction clause. It was argued that the question whether or not the jurisdiction clause was incorporated had to be decided according to the law which would apply if it had been incorporated which was said to be Mauritius law. The court rejected this approach, and applied the law of the forum, English law (para. 17): "Our case is not concerned with the existence of an agreement but with one of its terms. Where there is more than one possible putative law (as here) it makes no sense to decide which one to choose by any putative law. At this stage the court has no choice but to apply the law of the forum."

7.44 The applicable law determines whether or not the jurisdiction agreement was incorporated into the relevant contract. In reinsurance cases there is often a question whether a jurisdiction agreement in an underlying insurance was incorporated into a reinsurance slip by words in the reinsurance such as "wording as original". The English law is considered in detail at para. 5.80 above, but here it may be noted that general words of incorporation will not usually suffice to incorporate the jurisdiction agreement into a separate contract.

7.45 The law applicable to the wider contract of which the jurisdiction agreement is said to form a part will usually govern the interpretation of the jurisdiction agreement. That law will therefore determine the legal effect of the jurisdiction agreement. For instance, there may be a question as to the effect of a service of suit clause. In *Burrows* v. *Jamaica*[76] the court found that there were two types of law and jurisdiction clauses in the non-marine Lloyd's market, NMA 1483 the Overseas Jurisdiction Clause, and NMA 1486 the English Jurisdiction clause, and that the agreement to use the Overseas Jurisdiction clause, albeit without actually entering the name of the overseas jurisdiction intended, was a basis for finding that the clause was a jurisdiction agreement in favour of the only possible foreign jurisdiction, Jamaica.

7.46 The applicable law determines whether or not the claim made falls within the jurisdiction agreement. It is a question of construction whether or not an exclusive jurisdiction agreement in favour of England applies to claims which can only be made in a foreign jurisdiction, or under foreign law.[77]

7.47 The usual claim based on a jurisdiction agreement is a claim for an injunction, in effect an order that the jurisdiction agreement should be performed. Can a claimant make a

74. *The Parouth* [1982] 2 Lloyd's Rep. 351, CA; *The Atlantic Emperor* [1989] 1 Lloyd's Rep. 548; Dicey/Morris/Collins, para. 32R-154.

75. [2006] Lloyd's Rep. IR 127, Aikens J.; affirmed [2006] EWCA Civ 389, CA.

76. [2002] Lloyd's Rep. IR 466, 472, see further para. 7.68 below.

77. *Youell* v. *Kara Mara* [2000] 1 Lloyd's Rep. 102, 117 (direct claim of third party against insurer under Louisiana law); *Donohue* v. *Armco* [2002] 1 Lloyd's Rep. 425, 442 HL (RICO claim in the USA).

claim for damages caused by a breach of the jurisdiction agreement as well as or instead of a claim for an injunction? CPR 6.20(5)(d) is wide enough to encompass any such claim. It has been held that damages are available in some circumstances for *legal costs* which are incurred in defending a claim which was brought in breach of a jurisdiction agreement.[78] The possibility of a claim for damages in respect of any award made by a court before which proceedings were commenced in breach of a jurisdiction agreement has been the subject of recent discussion but must be regarded as doubtful where the award was made by the court of a Member State.[79]

IS THE CLAIM IN RESPECT OF A BREACH OF CONTRACT COMMITTED IN ENGLAND – CPR 6.20(6)?

7.48 The court may give permission to serve proceedings out of the jurisdiction where:

"(6) a claim is made in respect of a breach of contract committed within the jurisdiction."

7.49 All three elements – contract, breach and the place of breach must be proved to the requisite good arguable case standard to bring a claim within CPR 6.20(6) (see para. 7.23 above).[80] It follows that under this ground there is no separate requirement to show that there is a serious issue to be tried on the merits, since all the elements of the claim must be shown to the higher standard for the purposes of establishing the jurisdictional ground.[81] Although not stated in the rule, the contract must be between the claimant and the defendant.[82]

7.50 Where the breach consists of a failure to perform the contract, the question is where the terms of the contract required performance. If a defendant was entitled to perform a contract in England *or* abroad, a breach does not fall within the rule.[83] In the case of payment of sums due from the reinsurer or insurer, in the absence of express provision in the contract, English law is that the debtor must seek out his creditor (see generally para. 5.190 above). However, where the agreement is that payments will all be made via the broker, the breach by the reinsurer is in failing to put the broker in funds in the place where the broker is.[84]

7.51 In *Atlantic* v. *Milano*[85] the claimant underwriting agent commenced proceedings in England for damages for breach of an underwriting agreement based on a telex from the insurer in Italy to the agent in the jurisdiction terminating the agency. Lloyd J. held that the repudiation was not accepted and therefore did not terminate the contract. In theory, the claimant might have a claim for breach based on the unaccepted repudiation, but it would not sound in damages, and therefore could not be the claim for which the claimants needed permission to serve out of the jurisdiction.

(vi) Is the claim made in tort?

7.52 The court may permit service out of the jurisdiction where:

"(8) a claim is made in tort where – (a) damage was sustained within the jurisdiction; or (b) the damage sustained resulted from an act committed within the jurisdiction": CPR 6.20(8).

78. *Union Discount* v. *Zoller* [2002] 1 WLR 1517, CA.

79. Tan and Yeo, "Damages and Breach of Exclusive Jurisdiction Clauses", chapter 14 in *Commercial Law and Commercial Practice*, Worthington (ed.), 2003; Tan and Yeo, "Breaking Promises to Litigate in a Particular Forum: Are Damages an Appropriate Remedy?" in [2004] LMCLQ 435; Merrett, "The Enforcement of Jurisdiction Agreements Within the Brussels Regime" in [2006] 55 ICLQ 315.

80. *Seaconsar*, p. 454, Lord Goff.

81. *Ibid.*

82. *Finnish Marine* v. *Protective* [1990] 1 QB 1078, 1083; *cf.* *Union Insurance* v. *Jubilee Insurance* [1991] 1 WLR 415, 417.

83. *Cuban Atlantic Sugar Sales Corporation* v. *Compania de Vapores San Elefterio Limitada* [1960] 1 QB 187, CA.

84. *Citadel* v. *Atlantic* [1982] 2 Lloyd's Rep. 543, 548, CA; *OUI* v. *IGI* [1992] 1 Lloyd's Rep. 439.

85. [1979] 2 Lloyd's Rep. 240, 247.

7.53 This definition is similar to the approach adopted to Article 5(3) of the Brussels Regulation.[86] However, it is probably not helpful to refer to the cases under the Brussels Regulation: even if the wording of the tests is similar. The context of the Brussels Regulation and the common law is different[87]; the question whether or not a claim is made in tort is to be decided under English law even if acts relied on were committed abroad[88]; and the jurisdiction of the English court is discretionary.

7.54 Damage is sustained within the jurisdiction only if it is recoverable damage: "[i]t is enough if some significant damage has been sustained in England".[89] Where the damage consists of being exposed to actions by others in England the damage will have been sustained in England.[90]

7.55 The damage results from an act committed within the jurisdiction where the tort is in substance committed within the jurisdiction, even if not all the acts were committed within the jurisdiction.[91] Where the claim is in respect of misrepresentation the relevant act is the making of the representation and the place where that is done is the place where the representation is issued.[92]

4. Are the merits of the claim sufficiently strong?

7.56 What is the appropriate test of the strength of the case on the cause of action relied on? The court is faced with a number of conflicting considerations. On the one hand, the court is cautious about requiring a foreign defendant to defend proceedings in England. On the other, it can hardly try disputed facts on affidavits, and it would be premature to make definitive findings on disputed facts before trial. The test applied is therefore simply whether there is a serious issue to be tried on the claim.[93] A number of points may be made about this apparently simple test:

(1) There may be a serious issue to be tried even if the issue cannot be resolved by affidavit evidence: "if, at the end of the day, there remains a substantial question of fact or law or both, arising on the facts disclosed by the affidavits, which the plaintiff *bona fide* desires to try, the court should, as a rule, allow the service of the writ. If this approach is correct, the standard of proof in respect of the cause of action can broadly be stated to be whether, on the affidavit evidence before the court, there is a serious question to be tried."[94]

(2) This test is not different from the test under CPR 24.2 in relation to summary judgment. Under that rule summary judgment may be given if a claimant "has no real

86. New wording was adopted in 1987 to bring the jurisdictional ground into line with the decision in *Bier* v. *Mines de potasse d'Alsace* [1976] ECR I-1735 consequent on the Civil Jurisdiction and Judgments Act 1982: *Metall* v. *Rohstoff* [1990] 1 QB 391, 437, CA.

87. *Cf. Morin* v. *Bonham* [2004] 1 Lloyd's Rep. 702, 708.

88. *Metall* v. *Rohstoff* [1990] 1 QB 391, 436, CA, overruled in *Lonhro* v. *Fayed* [1992] 1 AC 448 on other points.

89. *Ibid.*

90. *SCOR* v. *ERAS EIL* [1992] 1 Lloyd's Rep. 570, CA (claim by defendant brokers/pool managers against their foreign agents).

91. *Metall* v. *Rohstoff* [1990] 1 QB 391, 437, CA: the question whether or not damage resulted from an act committed within the jurisdiction "requires the court to look at the tort alleged in a commonsense way and ask whether damage has resulted from substantial and efficacious acts committed within the jurisdiction (whether or not other substantial and efficacious acts have been committed elsewhere)"; overruled in *Lonhro* v. *Fayed* [1992] 1 AC 448 on other points.

92. *Newsat* v. *Zani* [2000] 1 Lloyd's Rep. 707 and the cases there referred to. See also para. 5.218 above in relation to the Brussels Regulation.

93. *Seaconsar*, p. 457.

94. *Seaconsar*, p. 455, Lord Goff.

prospect of success on the claim". The rationale is that the court should not subject a foreign litigant to proceedings which the defendant would be entitled to have summarily dismissed.[95]

(3) If there is no serious issue as to fact but the law is in issue, or the construction of a document, the court may be more ready finally to decide the issue of law.[96] That does not apply if there is, for instance, a dispute as to the custom and practice of the London and European reinsurance markets as to the reinsurers' liability to pay premium to the placing broker.[97]

(4) The fact that the claim form is to be served abroad does not increase the standard of proof required since that fact is accommodated by the separate *forum conveniens* requirement.[98]

(5) "It seems to me to be wholly inappropriate once the question[s] of jurisdiction and *forum* [*conveniens*] are established for there to be prolonged debate and consideration of the merits of the plaintiffs' claim at the interlocutory stage."[99]

(6) The fact that related proceedings are continuing in the jurisdiction cannot make up for the weakness of the merits of the proceedings in question, albeit it will be relevant at the *forum conveniens* stage.[100]

(7) The standard of proof required in relation to the merits does not vary depending on the strength of the *forum conveniens* arguments:

> "Suppose that, for example, the plaintiff's case is very strong on the merits. If so, I cannot see that a case particularly strong on the merits can compensate for a weak case on *forum conveniens*. Likewise, in my opinion, a very strong connection with the English forum cannot justify a weak case on the merits, if a stronger case on the merits would otherwise be required. In truth, as I see it, the two elements are separate and distinct. The invocation of the principle of *forum conveniens* springs from the often expressed anxiety that great care should be taken in bringing before the English court a foreigner who owes no allegiance here. But if jurisdiction is established under r. 1(1), and it is also established that England is the *forum conveniens*, I can see no good reason why any particular degree of cogency should be required in relation to the merits of the plaintiff's case."[101]

(8) The evidence in support of the application for permission to serve out must state that the claimant believes that his claim has a reasonable prospect of success: CPR 6.21(1)(b).

95. *MRG* v. *Engelhard* [2004] 1 Lloyd's Rep. 731, 733, Toulson J.; *Carvill* v. *Camperdown* [2005] 2 Lloyd's Rep. 457, 465, CA, Clarke LJ: "It is, however, important in my opinion to have in mind that the test is not a high one. A claimant has a real prospect of success if its chances of success are not fanciful."

96. *De Molestina* v. *Ponton* [2002] 1 Lloyd's Rep. 271, 281, Colman J.: "if the law is in issue but there is no serious issue to be tried in relation to any conceivably relevant fact, there may in some cases be good reason to determine the question of law at the application stage and decline permission to serve out rather than imposing upon a foreign defendant the inconvenience and expense of subsequently applying to strike out the claim under CPR 3.4.2 or 24.2. There can be no unfairness in declining to postpone argument on the law. A requirement that in all such cases legal argument must automatically be postponed until after permission to serve out has been given would be to perpetuate that procedural formalism against which CPR was directed"; *Chellaram* v. *Chellaram (No. 2)* [2002] 3 All ER 17 at para. 136; *Marubeni* v. *Mongolian Government* [2002] 2 All ER 873, 882 (if the issue of law requires significant facts to be found, the good arguable case test applies); *Nima* v. *The Deves* [2003] 2 Lloyd's Rep. 327, 341, 348, CA.

97. *Carvill* v. *Camperdown* [2005] 2 Lloyd's Rep. 457, 465, CA.

98. *Seaconsar*, p. 455.

99. *Seaconsar*, in the CA at [1993] 1 Lloyd's Rep. 236, 242 *per* Stuart-Smith LJ, approved by Lord Goff at p. 455. Compare the invocation to keep matters short in relation to disputes about *forum conveniens* at para. 7.59 below.

100. *Seaconsar*, p. 456.

101. *Seaconsar*, p. 456.

5. Should the court exercise its discretion to give permission – is England the *forum conveniens*?

7.57 Even if the court is satisfied the claim falls within CPR 6.20, and of the merits of the claim, it still has to decide whether or not to exercise its discretion to permit the service out of the jurisdiction. The court will not give permission unless satisfied that this jurisdiction is the proper place in which to bring the claim.[102] But what does this mean? The leading case on *forum conveniens* is *Spiliada* v. *Cansulex*.[103] Shipowners commenced proceedings in England against Canadian shippers claiming damages for breach of contract arising from loading wet sulphur on board which had damaged their vessel. Another trial had already begun in England of a similar action involving the same shippers and damage to another ship, the *Cambridgeshire*. Should the English court exercise its discretion to permit service on the Canadian shippers? The Lords summarised the law relating to the exercise of the discretion on an application to *stay* for *forum non conveniens* (pp. 476–478) and expressed the view that this approach bore a "marked resemblance" to the approach of the court when exercising its discretion to permit service out (p. 480). It is not surprising that the considerations on an application to serve out are essentially the obverse of those on a submission of *forum non conveniens*. Indeed, where the claimant obtained permission to serve out the defendant will usually seek to set aside that permission on the ground that the claimant has not established that England is clearly the appropriate forum, and will usually only have to seek a stay (and assume the burden of proof that goes with it) where the claimant did not need the permission of the court to serve out.[104] The Lords held that England was the *forum conveniens*, one of the main connecting factors being the efficiency, expedition and economy of the same lawyers dealing with the dispute as with the ongoing related proceedings, the so-called "*Cambridgeshire*" factor, on account of the name of the vessel in relation to which much work had been done by lawyers and experts in England on the question of what the effect of wet sulphur on the holds of ships was, a question of industry-wide importance.[105] We deal with:

(i) the basic approach to *forum conveniens*.
(ii) connecting factors and juridical advantages.
(iii) is there a *lis alibi pendens*?
(iv) is there a jurisdiction agreement?
(v) is there a claim for a negative declaration?
(vi) illustrations of *forum conveniens* in reinsurance and insurance cases.

We deal with arbitration separately in Chapter 8.

(i) The basic approach to forum conveniens

7.58 Adapting the summary given in *Spiliada* in relation to stay for *forum non conveniens*,[106] the approach to *forum conveniens* on an application for permission to serve out is as follows:

(1) The basic principle is that permission will only be granted if the claimant establishes that England is the most appropriate forum, i.e. in which the claimant's claim may be

102. CPR 6.21(2).

103. [1987] 1 AC 460.

104. For example *Limit (No. 3)* v. *PDV* [2005] 2 All ER (Comm) 347, 359; *Trade Indemnity* v. *Forasakrings* [1995] 1 All ER 796, 805.

105. Compare *Societe Nationale Industrielle Aerospatiale* v. *Lee Kui Jak* [1987] AC 871, 898, HL, where the Lords rejected the *Cambridgeshire* factor argument on the facts.

106. For instance, the point that a stay may be less readily granted where the claimant did not require permission to serve out of the jurisdiction at *Spiliada* 476F has no application to the discretion to permit service out.

tried suitably in the interests of the parties and the ends of justice.[107] The test is different from that which applies on an anti-suit injunction (see para. 7.102 below).

(2) The burden of proof is on the claimant to persuade the court to permit service out. Because the jurisdiction is exorbitant the effect is "not merely that the burden of proof rests on the plaintiff to persuade the court that England is the appropriate forum for the trial of the action, but that he has to show that this is clearly so".[108]

(3) Which forum is more appropriate? The court looks first to the "connecting factors" between the dispute and a forum to find the "natural forum" for the dispute, being "that with which the action had the most real and substantial connection".[109] These "will include not only factors affecting convenience or expense (such as availability of witnesses), but also other factors such as the law governing the relevant transaction …, and the places where the parties respectively reside or carry on business".[110] We consider the connecting factors in more detail below. The jurisdiction in which a tort is committed is thus *prima facie* the natural forum for proceedings in relation to it.[111] It must be remembered, however, that in some cases it may not be possible to identify a natural forum – the connecting factors may be inconclusive.[112] However, the court will not give permission unless the claimant can demonstrate that England is clearly the appropriate forum.[113]

(4) If the court concludes that England is clearly the appropriate forum it will ordinarily give permission to serve out. However, there may be circumstances by reason of which justice requires that permission should nevertheless be granted even if England is not on the face of it the most convenient forum.[114] The court will consider all the circumstances going beyond the connecting factors between the dispute and the rival forums.[115] One example would be where the claimant established objectively by cogent evidence that it will not obtain justice in the foreign jurisdiction.

(5) Delay in making the application for permission to serve out may be a ground for refusing permission.[116]

7.59 The issues raised on *forum conveniens* arguments can be many and complex. Nevertheless the aim is that "submissions will be measured in hours and not days. An appeal should be rare and the appellate court should be slow to interfere."[117] In practice this hope is not always fulfilled.[118]

107. *Spiliada*, 476C, 480G, 464H; see Merrett, "Uncertainties in the First Limb of the Spiliada Test", [2004] 54 ICLQ 211 which highlights difficulties in deciding whether or not another forum is "available".

108. *Spiliada*, 481, 476D; *Limit (No. 3)* v. *PDV Insurance* [2005] 2 All ER (Comm) 347, 359, CA.

109. *Spiliada*, 478.

110. *Spiliada*, 478.

111. *Bezerovsky* v. *Michaels* [2000] 1 WLR 1004, HL.

112. *Spiliada*, 477C.

113. *Spiliada*, 481E.

114. This is an oddity of the *Spiliada* test: where permission is sought to serve out, the claimant effectively gets two bites of the cherry: first he can show that England is clearly the more appropriate forum according to the ordinary *Spiliada* considerations. But, secondly, even if he fails at that stage, permission may still be granted if he can show that he will not obtain justice in the appropriate forum.

115. *Spiliada*, 478D.

116. *Schothorst and Schuitema* v. *Franz Dauter GmbH (The Nimrod)* [1973] 2 Lloyd's Rep. 91, 96, *per* Kerr J.: "Inordinate delay for no good reason is a strong factor to be taken into consideration in exercising the court's discretion"; disapproved on a different point: *Castle* v. *Hong Kong* [1984] AC 226, PC.

117. *Spiliada* v. *Cansulex* [1987] 1 AC 460, 465, *per* Lord Templeman. On the restricted approach to appeals on *forum conveniens* see *The Abidan Daver* [1984] AC 398, 420, HL; *SCOR* v. *ERAS EIL* [1992] 1 Lloyd's Rep. 570, 614, CA.

118. E.g. *Dornoch* v. *Mauritius* [2006] EWCA Civ 389 at [11].

(ii) Connecting factors and juridical advantages

7.60 The process of weighing the connecting factors is very sensitive to the facts of different cases, making citation of authority unlikely to help much. Further, the

"factors which the court is entitled to take into account in considering whether one forum is more appropriate are legion. The authorities do not, perhaps cannot, give any clear guidance as to how these factors are to be weighed in any particular case. Any dispute over the appropriate forum is complicated by the fact that each party is seeking an advantage and may be influenced by considerations which are not apparent to the judge or considerations which are not relevant for his purpose." [119]

One particular difficulty which often arises is that the issues have not yet been crystallised. The judge may be called upon to consider issues which may arise in the future as between the parties, or other parties, and on that basis to form a view about the likely consequences of that for the *forum conveniens* argument.[120]

7.61 The weight to be given to the same connecting factor may also vary from case to case. The fact that the Commercial Court has particular experience of dealing with disputes in relation to the London insurance market may be important if the issue is central, but not otherwise.[121] The residence of a party may be important in one case, or insignificant, e.g. if residence is in a tax haven.

7.62 One party or the other may point to a legitimate juridical advantage, that is, an advantage available in one forum and not in another. The mere existence of such an advantage is by no means decisive. The root question remains where the proceedings may be tried suitably for the interests of the parties and the ends of justice.[122] Injustice is not caused by differences between well-recognised systems of law, in matters such as disclosure, or the scale of damages.[123] In the case of a plaintiff seeking to resist a stay of proceedings it was said:

"The plaintiff will not ordinarily discharge the burden lying upon him by showing that he will enjoy procedural advantages, or a higher scale of damages or more generous rules of limitation if he sues in England; generally speaking, the plaintiff must take a foreign forum as he finds it, even if it is in some respects less advantageous to him than the English forum ... It is only if the plaintiff can establish that substantial justice will not be done in the appropriate forum that a stay will be refused."[124]

119. *Spiliada*, 465, *per* Lord Templeman; *Amin Rasheed* v. *Kuwait Insurance* [1984] AC 50, 72, HL: "the court must take into account the nature of the dispute, the legal and practical issues involved, such questions as local knowledge, availability of witnesses and their evidence and expense", *per* Lord Wilberforce.

120. *Limit (No. 3)* v. *PDV Insurance* [2005] 2 All ER (Comm) 347, 366, CA: "The exercise for the judge, as I have said, is one of discretion, not the application of a rigid or mathematical analysis as to probabilities or likelihood, in the individual weighing of relevant factors. Factors to be taken into account include: the nature of the dispute; the legal and practical issues likely to arise, or that could cause significant difficulties in one jurisdiction rather than another if they did arise; questions as to local knowledge; availability of evidence; and efficiency, expedition and economy, not only in the trial of the instant proceedings, but also in related proceedings that, in the interests of justice should be tried in the same jurisdiction and/or with it. Whilst, at the early stage of proceedings at which the issue of *forum conveniens* normally arises for decision, an English court should look beyond theoretical difficulties for trial in one jurisdiction rather than another, it does not follow that it should only take into account such difficulties if it is satisfied that they are likely in the sense of already being evidentially supported, though such evidence where it is available is, of course, helpful. It is permissible, as the judge did here, to form his own view of what is likely and what is not likely though possible, and, in the latter case, to take account of serious problems that would flow from choice of one jurisdiction rather than another if it were to arise." Auld LJ, para. 67; *ACE* v. *Zurich* [2001] 1 Lloyd's Rep. 618, 629, CA.

121. *Burrows* v. *Jamaica* [2002] Lloyd's Rep. IR 466, 474; *Assicurazione* v. *Sigorta* [2002] Lloyd's Rep. IR 480, 484; *cf. Trade Indemnity* v. *Forsakringsaktiebolget Njord* [1995] 1 Lloyd's Rep. 367.

122. *Spiliada*, 482D.

123. *Spiliada*, 482–483; *cf. HIB* v. *Guardian* [1997] 1 Lloyd's Rep. 412, 417 (claim for punitive damages against reinsurance broker not appropriate where relationship governed by English law), and *Travelers Casualty and Surety Company of Europe Ltd and others* v. *Sun Life Assurance Company of Canada (UK) Ltd and another* [2004] Lloyd's Rep. IR 846, 865 (where a claim for punitive damages in the foreign jurisdiction was discounted on the facts).

124. *Lubbe* v. *Cape* [2000] 2 Lloyd's Rep. 383, 390, HL.

Further, it is not appropriate to embark on a comparison of the procedures, methods, reputation or standing of the courts of one country compared to another.[125] The fact that proceedings will take longer in a foreign jurisdiction is not likely to be determinative.[126]

7.63 If English law governs the contract and there are significant issues as to the law, the English court is likely to take the view that this is a weighty factor to take into account in (re)insurance cases. These cases are considered in detail below but in summary:

(1) the differences between English law and the law which would be applied in a foreign jurisdiction may highlight a disadvantage to the claimant if he is not permitted to continue the English proceedings[127];

(2) where a dispute depends on questions of public policy arising *under a foreign law* the court is unlikely to conclude that England would be the *forum conveniens* for the determination of that dispute.[128] On the other hand where *English* law applied and the question relates to English public policy this is a powerful factor in favour of England being the *forum conveniens*.[129] In *OUI* v. *IGI*[130] the reinsureds commenced proceedings in England for payment of sums due under reinsurances arranged through the Accolade underwriting pool. The defence was that the business was written without authorisation and was void for illegality under the Insurance Companies Act 1974. The fact that the main issue would be illegality under English law supported the conclusion that England was the *forum conveniens*.

(3) In some cases the court may view it is as important that an English court *construes* a contract subject to English law "[where] the decision depends upon the construction of a document or documents in one language and the rival courts are, on the one hand, courts whose native language is that of the document and, on the other, courts whose native language is not that of the document, it is in my view clear that the matter may most suitably be tried in the former courts".[131] But if the issues of construction are straightforward the court may not view this as an important point.[132]

7.64 In other cases the fact that English law is the applicable law of the transaction may be of very little importance because the choice of law makes no real difference. In *Amin Rasheed* v. *Kuwait*[133] the insured under a marine policy claimed in respect of the detention of the

125. *Amin Rasheed* v. *Kuwait Insurance* [1984] AC 50, 67, 72, HL; *The Abidan Daver* [1984] AC 398, 410, HL; *The Bergen* [1997] 2 Lloyd's Rep. 710, 715.

126. *Radhakrishna* v. *EIH* [1999] 2 Lloyd's Rep. 249, 253, where there was evidence that disputes in India could take up to 15 years to be resolved.

127. *Spiliada*, 481, 486. See, for example, *Britannia SS Insurance* v. *Ausonia* [1984] 2 Lloyd's Rep. 98, 100; *Standard Steamship* v. *Gann* [1992] 2 Lloyd's Rep. 528 (where serious questions of English law arose as to the relationship of principal and agent and sub-agent and trial in California was therefore described as a "serious disadvantage"); *Gan* v. *Tai Ping* [1999] Lloyd's Rep. IR 229, 241, Cresswell J., affirmed on this point [1999] Lloyd's Rep. IR 472, CA (where the reinsurance was governed by English law and there were substantial issues as to construction of the reinsurance and the effect of a claims co-operation requirement); *Tiernan* v. *Magen Insurance* [2000] IL Pr 517, 525; *Akai* v. *People's Insurance* [1998] 1 Lloyd's Rep. 90, 107 (where the foreign law would have rendered ineffective a jurisdiction agreement which would have been effective under English law); *Tryg Baltica* v. *Boston* [2005] Lloyd's Rep. IR 40, 52; *Dornoch* v. *Mauritius* [2006] EWCA Civ 389 at [53].

128. *CGU* v. *Szabo* [2002] 1 Lloyd's Rep. 196, 201–202.

129. *Dupont* v. *Agnew* [1987] 2 Lloyd's Rep. 585, 594.

130. [1992] 1 Lloyd's Rep. 439, CA; *cf. DR Insurance* v. *Central National Insurance* [1996] 1 Lloyd's Rep. 74.

131. *Seashell* v. *Mutualidad de Seguros* [1989] 1 Lloyd's Rep. 47, 51, Parker LJ. *Assicurazione* v. *Sigorta* [2002] 1 Lloyd's Rep. 1 IR 480, 486, where Colman J. expressed a preference for an English court to deal with a complex English law contract in the technical field of reinsurance.

132. *Lincoln Life* v. *Employers Re* [2002] EWHC 28 at [25]; *Navigators* v. *Atlantic* [2004] Lloyd's Rep. IR 418, 424.

133. [1984] 1 AC 50, HL; *Chase* v. *Ram* [2000] 2 Lloyd's Rep. 418, 421, where the essential dispute was about the facts as to what occurred in Canada, and Timothy Walker J. attached no weight to certain possible points of difference between Alberta law and English law which could increase the liability of underwriters; *Lincoln Life* v.

vessel and crew in Saudi Arabia. Although the policy was subject to English law the central issue was the factual question whether or not the vessel was engaged in smuggling when detained; if so the loss was excluded. The local court in Kuwait was far better suited to deciding that than the English court. Although there were questions of English law, the evidence was that the Kuwaiti court would apply English law, and there was no reason to think the court could not deal with them. Accordingly permission to serve out was set aside.

7.65 If a party would be time-barred in a foreign jurisdiction that may swing the balance away from an otherwise appropriate foreign jurisdiction in favour of granting permission to pursue proceedings in England which would not be time-barred, providing that the claimant acted reasonably in commencing proceedings in England and not unreasonably in allowing the foreign limitation period to pass.[134]

(iii) Is there a lis alibi pendens*?*

7.66 Although there are obvious cases where it would not be appropriate for there to be concurrent proceedings between the parties in different jurisdiction the English court does not assume that concurrent proceedings are to be avoided: everything depends on the particular facts of each case. Foreign proceedings

> "may be of no relevance at all, for example, if one party has commenced the proceedings for the purpose of demonstrating the existence of a competing jurisdiction, or the proceedings have not passed beyond the stage of the initiating process. But if, for example, genuine proceedings have been started and have not merely been started but have developed to the stage where they have had some impact upon the dispute between the parties, especially if such impact is likely to have a continuing effect, then this may be a relevant factor to be taken into account when considering whether the foreign jurisdiction provides the appropriate forum for the resolution of the dispute between the parties."[135]

In practice, the existence of other proceedings is often an important factor to consider. If the foreign proceedings also involve third parties it may be a significant factor in favour of the foreign proceedings.[136]

(iv) Is there a jurisdiction agreement?

7.67 It should be remembered at the outset that the Brussels Regulation will apply if the jurisdiction agreement chooses the courts of a Member State, whether or not any party is domiciled

---

Employers Re [2002] EWHC 28 (Comm) at [25], Moore-Bick J. (where the issues turned only on construction of the slips rather than the application of particular principles of English law); *Nima* v. *The Deves* [2003] 2 Lloyd's Rep. 327, 354, CA (where the dispute in relation to a marine insurance claim was essentially factual and the only concrete example of the application of Thai law at the expense of English law was in relation to a two-year limitation period which the defendant successfully neutralised by waiving the defence); *Navigators* v. *Atlantic* [2004] Lloyd's Rep. IR 418, 424 (where the issues of English law of straightforward points of linguistic analysis of the policy, and the primary disputes were as to the facts); *Munchener* v. *Commonwealth* [2005] Lloyd's Rep. IR 99, 107–108.

134. *Spiliada*, 483–484.

135. *De Dampierre* v. *De Dampierre* [1988] AC 92, 108, *per* Lord Goff (where there were English proceedings and pending proceedings in France which was clearly the more appropriate forum); *Insurance Corporation of Ireland* v. *Strombus* [1985] 2 Lloyd's Rep. 138, 146, CA (where the English proceedings were commenced just before the foreign proceedings, and the English proceedings were stayed); *Du Pont* v. *Agnew* [1987] 2 Lloyd's Rep. 585, 593: "I do not regard this as a case in which the dates of beginning proceedings are significant. As it happens, the English proceedings began first and the Illinois action a month later. It might have been the other way round. I do not think the outcome of these appeals should be affected by what is little more than an accident of timing"; *Meadows* v. *ICI* [1989] 1 Lloyd's Rep. 181, 189, Hirst J., affirmed on *forum conveniens* [1989] 2 Lloyd's Rep. 198, CA; *DR Insurance* v. *Central National Insurance* [1996] 1 Lloyd's Rep. 74, 84; *Sabah* v. *Islamic* [2003] 2 Lloyd's Rep. 571, 582 (an anti-suit injunction case); *Travelers Casualty and Surety Company of Europe Ltd and others* v. *Sun Life Assurance Company of Canada (UK) Ltd and another* [2004] Lloyd's Rep. IR 846, 864; *Navigators* v. *Atlantic* [2004] Lloyd's Rep. IR 418, 424.

136. *Standard Steamship* v. *Gann* [1992] 2 Lloyd's Rep. 528, 536; *Gan* v. *Tai Ping* [1999] Lloyd's Rep. IR 229, 241, Cresswell J., affirmed on this point [1999] Lloyd's Rep. IR 472, CA.

in a Member State. We deal with such jurisdiction agreements in detail at para. 5.32 above, but in summary:

(1) if the jurisdiction agreement is in favour of a Member State and one or more parties is domiciled in a Member State Article 23(1) will apply and there will be no question of *forum conveniens*, stay or anti-suit injunction;
(2) if the jurisdiction agreement is in favour of a Member State and *neither* party is domiciled in a Member State Article 23(3) will apply which means that no court of a Member State other than the court chosen will have jurisdiction unless the court chosen has declined jurisdiction. If the jurisdiction agreement was in favour of the English courts the court would apply English conflicts rules, including *forum conveniens*, stay and anti-suit injunction (although not in respect of proceedings in a Member State);
(3) further, if the jurisdiction agreement is in favour of a non-Member State, the court can probably decline jurisdiction even if it would otherwise have jurisdiction under the Brussels Regulation, e.g. because the defendant is domiciled in a Member State: see *Konkola* v. *Coromin*[137] and para. 5.109 above.

7.68 Where the common law applies, what is the effect of a jurisdiction agreement in favour of England on the *forum conveniens* arguments? The existence of an exclusive jurisdiction agreement in favour of England will create a "strong *prima facie* case" that England is the appropriate forum, but does not oust the jurisdiction of the court to stay the action: "An agreement to submit disputes to the courts of a particular country is a powerful factor when the court comes to exercising its discretion in matters of this kind. It is rare that the court will permit a party to maintain an action in England in breach of an exclusive jurisdiction clause or refuse to exercise its jurisdiction over a defendant if there is an exclusive jurisdiction agreement in favour of the courts of this country."[138]

7.69 The court will give effect to an exclusive jurisdiction agreement in favour of England even if a foreign law decrees otherwise. In *Akai* v. *People's Insurance*[139] an insured commenced English proceedings on an insurance policy containing an exclusive jurisdiction agreement in favour of England. There were proceedings in Australia in respect of the claim under the policy which the Australian court refused to stay on the basis that provisions of the Insurance Contracts Act 1984 had the effect of rendering the choice of jurisdiction ineffective. Thomas J. declined to stay the English proceedings, preferring to give effect to the jurisdiction agreement unless it would be contrary to English public policy (which included international public policy) to give effect to it.[140] In a similar case, had permission been sought to serve out, it is likely that it would be given.

7.70 What if the agreement is for *non* exclusive jurisdiction? In *British Aerospace* v. *Dee Howard*[141] Waller J. considered such a clause in favour of England and suggested the right approach ought to be "that [the applicants] are not entitled to resist the English jurisdiction if an action is commenced in England … Surely they must point to some factor which they could not have foreseen on which they can rely for displacing the bargain which they made, i.e. that they would not object to the jurisdiction of the English Court." Further there is a

137. [2005] 2 Lloyd's Rep. 555 Colman J.; affirmed [2006] 1 Lloyd's Rep. 410, CA.

138. *Burrows* v. *Jamaica* [2002] Lloyd's Rep. IR 465, 470, Moore-Bick J.; *Marubeni* v. *Mongolian Government* [2002] 2 All ER 873, 890–891 and the cases there cited; *Donohue* v. *Armco* [2002] 1 Lloyd's Rep. 425, 433, HL, in the context of a stay application.

139. [1998] 1 Lloyd's Rep. 90.

140. At p. 100.

141. [1993] 1 Lloyd's Rep. 368, 376, followed in many cases since which are summarised in *BP* v. *Aon* [2006] 1 Lloyd's Rep. 549, 553–555, Colman J.

strong *prima facie* case that the jurisdiction referred to in the non-exclusive jurisdiction agreement is an appropriate one.[142] The usual *Spiliada* factors such as connection with a jurisdiction, the whereabouts of parties and documents are less powerful because of the agreement of the parties. Indeed, in a case which has little connection with England it may be that the parties are taken to have agreed on a neutral forum for the resolution of disputes.[143]

7.71 An example of a case where the existence of a non-exclusive jurisdiction agreement was not determinative is *BP* v. *Aon*[144] where the question was whether or not the claimants could have obtained permission to commence proceedings in England on the defendants even though there was a non-exclusive jurisdiction agreement in favour of Illinois. Colman J. held that the non-exclusive jurisdiction agreement:

> "does not go as far as saying that it is agreed that in all circumstances that may in future arise the designated court will necessarily be the court where the case may most suitably be tried for the interests of all parties and the ends of justice. If that were so, the effect of such a clause would be indistinguishable from that of an exclusive jurisdiction clause. The *forum non conveniens* test would be deployed not as a flexible comparative exercise but so as to impose an inflexible constraint analogous to that imposed by a contract.... It is sufficient for it to be shown that although Illinois is an appropriate forum, there is a clear balance of justice and fairness as between the parties in favour of London. By a clear balance I mean one which substantially relies on considerations which would not have been obvious to the parties at the time when they entered into the [contract] and a balance which while not overwhelming, is substantially more than a fine balance" (at pp. 553–555).

7.72 An exclusive jurisdiction clause may only oblige one party to commence proceedings in the assigned jurisdiction, and not the other. This was the situation in *Groupama* v. *Channel Islands*[145] where the clause in a property insurance provided that the "insured will submit any such dispute or difference to the exclusive jurisdiction of the English Courts". The insurance covered the defendant for property damage. The property was occupied by various companies and destroyed by fire. Insurers denied cover on the ground of breach a warranty that waste would be regularly removed from the property. When the insured threatened to commence proceedings in Jersey for payment under the insurance the insurers commenced proceedings for a negative declaration in England. Any foreign proceedings by the defendant would have been in breach of the jurisdiction agreement. There was therefore no basis for treating the clause any differently from an exclusive jurisdiction agreement which obliged both parties to commence proceedings in one jurisdiction (or to arbitrate).[146]

7.73 A voluntary submission to the jurisdiction of the foreign court is capable of being a good reason not to enforce an English jurisdiction agreement.[147]

7.74 Where the jurisdiction agreement is in favour of a foreign jurisdiction the English court will require strong reasons as to why permission should nevertheless be granted (or a stay declined).[148] In *Chase* v. *Ram*[149] insurers commenced proceedings in England seeking a negative declaration in relation to a construction, installation and transit policy in respect of

142. *S&W Berisford* v. *New Hampshire* [1990] 1 Lloyd's Rep. 454, 463.

143. *Akai* v. *People's Insurance* [1998] 1 Lloyd's Rep. 90, 105; *Marubeni* v. *Mongolian Government* [2002] 2 All ER 873, 892; *Sabah* v. *Islamic* [2003] 2 Lloyd's Rep. 571.

144. [2006] 1 Lloyd's Rep. 549.

145. [2002] Lloyd's Rep. IR 843.

146. Although the court does not seem to have taken this strict view of the clause but to have treated it as similar in effect to a non-exclusive jurisdiction agreement. In *Standard Steamship* v. *Gann* [1992] 2 Lloyd's Rep. 528, 531, Hirst J. described such a non mutual jurisdiction clause as being "drafted in standard form typical of the rules of P&I clubs generally, where the member is, of course, both insurer and insured".

147. *Svendborg* v. *Wansa* [1997] 2 Lloyd's Rep. 183.

148. *Akai* v. *People's Insurance* [1998] 1 Lloyd's Rep. 90, 104; *ACE* v. *Zurich* [2001] 1 Lloyd's Rep. 618 (Texas exclusive jurisdiction agreement).

149. [2000] 2 Lloyd's Rep. 418.

a boiler bound for Ghana which was damaged while being transhipped by road in Belgium on the ground that the risk was not as described and/or exclusions in the Institute Cargo Clauses to which the insurance was subject. The insurers were licensed by the Superintendent of Insurance for Alberta which entitled the insured to bring proceedings against the insurers in Alberta. In effect insurers had agreed to confer jurisdiction on the courts of Alberta. It was argued that Canada was not an appropriate forum because the Alberta court would or might not apply the exclusions in the Institute Cargo Clauses and the insured was claiming in Alberta proceedings costs and expenses which would not be recoverable under English law. The judge rejected this argument at p. 421: "Even on the assumption that all this was correct, I can see no injustice to underwriters. They took their own commercial decision to obtain a licence to sell insurance in Alberta, which necessarily involved appointing an attorney for service. Otherwise they could not have got the business in the first place. They take the risk that the local law may be disadvantageous to them. That is part of the price they pay for their licence."

7.75 One important situation in which the court may give permission to serve out even though there is a jurisdiction agreement in favour of another jurisdiction is where there are related proceedings involving a number of parties, only some of whom are bound by jurisdiction agreements.[150] The ends of justice in such a case may require that proceedings all be heard in one jurisdiction even if not that agreed on. In *Donohue* the claim was in conspiracy and there was an overwhelming case that the claim against all defendants should be heard in one foreign jurisdiction even though one of the defendants had the benefit of an exclusive jurisdiction agreement in favour of England.

7.76 However, the mere fact that there is a contingent claim against a third party will not be significant. One typical situation which arises is where reinsurers deny liability and the reinsured makes an alternative claim against a broker, including possibly a foreign producing broker. In practice, the mere existence of such a contingent claim is unlikely to have a significant effect on *forum conveniens*.[151]

(v) Is there a claim for a negative declaration?[152]

7.77 A negative declaration is a claim for a declaration by the court that the claimant is not under a liability to the defendant. It is commonly sought by reinsurers and insurers as a way of establishing that they are not liable on a reinsurance or insurance contract. Usually the (re)insurance is governed by English law which is why the claimant seeks a declaration of no liability from the English court. It may either put a stop to any claim by the reinsured or insured where the facts are not in issue; or, if the facts are in issue, may assist the claimant to prevail in another jurisdiction.[153]

7.78 The courts have become more willing to grant negative declarations than hitherto, and will now assume jurisdiction in respect of such claims provided always that the court is

150. *Donohue* v. *Armco* [2002] 1 Lloyd's Rep. 425, 433–434, HL.

151. *Goshawk* v. *QBD* [2006] EWHC (Comm) 1730; and for a similar approach in the context of an application for an anti-suit injunction see *General Star* v. *Stirling Cooke Brown* [2003] Lloyd's Rep. IR 719, *Tonicstar* v. *American Home* [2005] Lloyd's Rep. IR 32. *Cf. Insurance Corporation of Ireland* v. *Strombus* [1985] 2 Lloyd's Rep. 138, 144, CA (where the court set aside service out partly because of the existence of third party proceedings in the foreign jurisdiction against the placing brokers which could not easily be made in England; however, that was a case where there was a service of suit agreement in favour of a court of competent jurisdiction in the USA, and the claimant claimed a negative declaration at a time when the courts were more hostile to such claims).

152. Bell, "The Negative Declaration in Transnational Litigation" (1995) 111 LQR 674; Zamir/Woolf, pp. 116, 189.

153. Bell, "The Negative Declaration in Transnational Litigation" (1995) 111 LQR 674, 675, on the efficacy of the negative declaration.

the *forum conveniens* and the declaration would be useful.[154] CPR 6.20(7) has been introduced specifically to allow claim for a negative declaration, i.e. that no contract exists where if the contract did exist it would be within CPR 6.20(5). There are, in essence, two questions for the court: "the court will have to consider both the question whether there is justification for seeking that relief and the separate question of whether England is the appropriate forum in which to seek it".[155] In *New Hampshire* v. *Philips*[156] insurers sought a negative declaration against the insured. The insurance policy was governed by English law and a number of questions of law arose on the policy which insurers sought to have decided by the English court (p. 63). There were also numerous significant disputes on the facts which were centred on Illinois. Rix J. summarised the approach to negative declarations in terms approved by the Court of Appeal at p. 61:

"1. There is power to grant a negative declaration in an appropriate case, the fundamental test being whether it would be useful. 2. However, careful scrutiny will be exercised not only to test the utility, or on the other hand the futility of seeking to determine the claim by means of a negative declaration in England, but also to ensure that inappropriate forum shopping is not allowed let alone encouraged. 3. A negative declaration will not be appropriate where it is premature or hypothetical, *viz.* where no claim has been made or threatened against the plaintiffs. 4. The existence of imminent or *a fortiori* current foreign proceedings is always a highly relevant consideration, not only for the purpose of testing the utility of the English claim, but also having in mind the need to avoid the twin dangers of forum shopping and of the vices of concurrent proceedings."

7.79 In that case the policy was governed by English law and the declaration would establish points which significantly curtailed the factual investigation. Unusually, the court accepted that Illinois was the appropriate forum for the trial of the factual issues, but that England remained the appropriate forum for the legal issues:

"It is normally undesirable that one jurisdiction should be seised of issues of law in a dispute while another is seised of issues of fact, let alone that the same issues should be tried in different jurisdictions ... Should then the English court in such a case decline to entertain the application for the negative declaration on the ground that it should be sought, if at all, in the jurisdiction that is appropriate for determination of the facts? I do not believe that it is possible to answer this question as a matter of principle. It must depend on the facts of the particular case and, in particular, on the complexity of the issues of construction and on the likelihood that they will resolve the dispute. There is an obvious anomaly in requiring a plaintiff to resolve a point of law designed to obviate an enquiry into fact, not in the country whose law is applicable, but in the country where the issues of fact should be resolved if the plaintiff fails on the law."

7.80 The danger of forum shopping is a point which is often raised in the context of negative declarations. Parties may seek to commence proceedings for a negative declaration merely in order to establish jurisdiction in one forum and prevent it in another, and not because the proceedings for a negative declaration will actually serve a useful purpose. This is described as forum shopping. If, however, the negative declaration proceedings do serve a useful purpose it is no objection that the claimant's motives include preventing proceedings being continued in another jurisdiction. Forum shopping is not a danger peculiar to claims for negative declarations; it is a danger even if the claimant makes a claim for substantive relief. Equally, there are clearly cases where proceedings are in the appropriate forum even

154. *Meadows* v. *ICI* [1989] 1 Lloyd's Rep. 181, Hirst J., affirmed on *forum conveniens* [1989] 2 Lloyd's Rep. 198, CA, see Bell, *op. cit.*, p. 679, on the history of the courts' approach to negative declarations.

155. *Gan* v. *Tai Ping* [1999] Lloyd's Rep. IR 229, 237, Cresswell J., affirmed on this point [1999] Lloyd's Rep. IR 472, CA.

156. [1999] Lloyd's Rep. IR 58, CA; see also *Insurance Corporation of Ireland* v. *Strombus* [1985] 2 Lloyd's Rep. 138, 144, CA; *HIB* v. *Guardian* [1997] 1 Lloyd's Rep. 412, 416.

though the claim is for a negative declaration. The nature of the relief sought is obviously therefore no test of whether or not the forum will be appropriate, which is why the principle of *forum conveniens* applies whatever the relief sought. In *Boss Group* v. *Boss France*[157] Saville LJ held that seeking a negative declaration was not "a substantive ground for declining jurisdiction" (at p. 358), nor could a charge of forum shopping be made out, because, (at p. 357): "the charge of forum shopping can only be made good by assuming that a party which takes advantage of the Convention exceptions to the general rule of domicile is doing something illegitimate; but that assumption cannot be maintained if in truth one of the exceptions is applicable." This is consistent with the European jurisprudence: see the opinion of Advocate General Tesauro in *"The Tatry"*[158]: "... the bringing of proceedings to obtain a negative finding ... is entirely legitimate in every respect, is an appropriate way of dealing with genuine needs on the part of the person who brings them. For example, he may have an interest, where the other party is temporising, in securing a prompt judicial determination if doubts exist ... deriving from a given contractual relationship...."[159] In *Messier-Dowty* v. *Sabena*[160] the claimant issued English proceedings for a declaration that it was not liable to the defendant. The Court of Appeal resisted attempts to persuade it to follow older authority which had restricted declarations to cases where proceedings had been threatened (at 2050–2051):

> "The approach is pragmatic. It is not a matter of jurisdiction. It is a matter of discretion. The deployment of negative declarations should be scrutinised and their use rejected where it would serve no useful purpose. However, where a negative declaration would help to ensure that the aims of justice are achieved the courts should not be reluctant to grant such declarations. They can and do assist in achieving justice... While negative declarations can perform a positive role, they are an unusual remedy in so far as they reverse the more usual roles of the parties. The natural defendant becomes the claimant and vice versa. This can result in procedural complications and possible injustice to an unwilling 'defendant'. This in itself justifies caution in extending the circumstances where negative declarations are granted, but, subject to the exercise of appropriate circumspection, there should be no reluctance to their being granted when it is useful to do so."

7.81 The key question is therefore whether or not the declaration proceedings may be expected to achieve anything of use in relation to the dispute between the parties. If, as often happens, the reinsurance is governed by English law and the court is being asked to declare that reinsurers are not liable under English law, and this may be expected to give reinsurers a defence in any proceedings in any foreign jurisdiction by the reinsured, the court will usually give permission to serve out.[161] In *Tiernan* v. *Magen*[162] Longmore J. put it this way: "It would be difficult to describe English reinsurers as forum shopping if they ask an English court to decide questions of construction on a reinsurance policy which in English eyes was made in England and governed by English law". If the reinsured contends that the proper law of the reinsurance is that of the foreign jurisdiction, as in *Tiernan*, there is an obvious danger that if the English court does not assume jurisdiction there will be no decision at all according to the law which the English courts would regard as being the proper law (at least on a good arguable case basis).

157. [1997] 1 WLR 351, 357.
158. [1994] ECR I-5439, [1995] All ER (EC) 229.
159. See further Dicey/Morris/Collins, para. 12-042.
160. [2000] 1 WLR 2040, 2050 (CA).
161. See, e.g., *Lincoln Life* v. *Employers Re* [2002] EWHC 28; *Travelers Casualty and Surety Company of Europe Ltd and others* v. *Sun Life Assurance Company of Canada (UK) Ltd and another* [2004] Lloyd's Rep. IR 846, 863; *Tryg Baltica* v. *Boston* [2005] Lloyd's Rep. IR 40, 46.
162. [2000] IL Pr 517, 523.

(vi) Illustrations of forum conveniens *in reinsurance and insurance cases*

7.82 Although generally speaking decisions on the facts of *forum conveniens* cases are unlikely to provide much general assistance, it is worth highlighting some features which have arisen in the particular context of (re)insurance.

NEGATIVE DECLARATIONS

7.83 As has been seen, where reinsurers or insurers seek only a negative declaration the court will be astute to guard against forum-shopping but if the claim may be of value, and the ordinary requirements for service out of the jurisdiction are met, will give permission. In *Lincoln Life* v. *Employers Re*[163] reinsurers commenced proceedings in England for negative declarations in respect of a reinsurance of the defendant's participation in excess of loss reinsurance of aviation insurers in respect of North American light aircraft risks. The issue was whether or not, and to what extent, five claims made on reinsurers which had been settled by the aviation insurers, and passed to the reinsured, were in respect of bodily injury, or covered matters outside the scope of the reinsurance. On an application by the reinsured to set aside permission to serve out, Moore-Bick J. considered that England was the appropriate forum (para. 25):

> "This does not appear to be a case which turns on the application of particular principles of the English law of insurance any more than it turns on the manner in which the law of Kansas or any other American state characterises the nature of the underlying losses. As far as one can see at the moment it will turn on the proper construction of the words used in the slips. These, of course, have to be given their natural and ordinary meaning, but their interpretation is not without its difficulties and it may be that some evidence of market background will be required in order to enable the court to understand them correctly. Such evidence will be available in this country rather than elsewhere. It is not clear at this stage whether it will be necessary to produce much of the documentation relating to the underlying claims since it may be possible to determine the real point in issue without the need for a detailed examination of the underlying claims. However, even if it is necessary to produce copies of the underlying documents, it appears that only five claims are involved. The parties to this dispute carry on business in different places and viewing the matter objectively I do not think that it is likely to prove significantly more inconvenient or expensive overall for them to litigate in this country than elsewhere."

Although there was a danger of forum shopping, the action might serve a useful purpose in resolving the issue by determining their rights and liabilities as a matter of English law and therefore should be allowed to continue (para. 27).

7.84 In other cases negative declaration proceedings by reinsurers in England may involve disputes as to the facts of the inwards claim to the reinsured, or may involve uncertainty and speculation as to the issues, or a possible likelihood of multiple proceedings involving the ultimate insured which will prevent England being the *forum conveniens*. In *Limit (No. 3)* v. *PDV Insurance*[164] retrocessionaires claimed a declaration of non-liability in England in respect of original claims by RDV, the Venezuelan national oil company, in respect of environmental impairment liability. The negative declaration proceedings were commenced before PDV had itself commenced any proceedings, and before the issues as between the various parties in the chain between PDV and retrocessionaires were known. There was therefore "an air of unreality and considerable uncertainty"[165] in the negative declaration proceedings. It was desirable that the issues between all parties be determined in one place, and the centre of gravity of the dispute was in Venezuela, which was therefore the *forum conveniens*.[166]

163. [2002] EWHC 28, para. 11, Moore-Bick J.
164. [2005] 2 All ER (Comm) 347, CA.
165. p. 364.
166. p. 364.

7.85 Another example of a case where permission to serve out was denied because negative declaration proceedings primarily turned on disputed facts was *Trade Indemnity* v. *Forsakrings*[167] where reinsurers commenced English proceedings against the Swedish reinsured seeking a negative declaration based on misrepresentation and non-disclosure relating to gross mismanagement and dubious underwriting practices of the reinsured in Sweden. Although the proper law of the reinsurance placed in London was English, Rix J. held that the focus of the dispute was not so much on the materiality of what was presented to reinsurers but the conduct of the reinsured's business in Sweden. This outweighed the inconvenience of a Swedish court having to decide English law (see further para. 7.90 below).

7.86 Again, in *Navigators* v. *Atlantic*[168] where insurers commenced proceedings in England claiming a declaration that they were not liable under a project insurance policy covering insureds in respect of the building and maintenance of a methanol plant in Texas, USA. The insurance was governed by English law, and the contract for the construction of the plant between the insured and the employers was subject to New York law. Although the claimants relied on the fact that the policy was subject to English law that counted for little because the major disputes were of fact, or would turn on New York law to which the construction contract was subject, and was easily outweighed by other *forum conveniens* factors which pointed to not permitting the English proceedings to continue at the same time as other proceedings already underway in Texas.

ISSUES OF PUBLIC POLICY AND CASES WHERE THE FOREIGN COURT WILL NOT APPLY ENGLISH LAW

7.87 The undesirability of multiple proceedings was also a reason for setting aside service out in *DR Insurance* v. *Central National Insurance*[169] where reinsurers commenced proceedings in England seeking a negative declaration on the basis that business written by the reinsurers through the agency of Stetzel Thomson in London was written contrary to the Insurance Companies Act 1974, illegal and void, so that the reinsurances could not be enforced. The reinsured subsequently commenced New York proceedings to enforce the reinsurances. The evidence was that it was not clear if the New York court would stay the New York proceedings. The English court set aside the permission to serve out largely because of the danger of there being multiple proceedings with the risk of inconsistent judgments, the fact that the reinsurers' claim was only for a negative declaration, and the fact that the claim was based on the illegality of the very business written by the reinsurers.[170] By contrast, in *Dornoch* v. *Mauritius*[171] reinsurers commenced negative declaration proceedings in England against the reinsured Mauritian insurance company in respect of bankers' blanket bond cover granted to a Mauritian bank claiming that they had avoided for non-disclosure and misrepresentation, and also against the bank in tort for damages for deceit and misstatement. The bank had previously commenced proceedings in Mauritius against the reinsured for recovery under the bankers' blanket bond, and after the English proceedings were commenced obtained permission to join reinsurers to the Mauritian proceedings. On the question whether or not the permission to serve the English proceedings on the reinsured should be set aside, the court held that there was a good arguable case that English law applied to the reinsurance, but

167. [1995] 1 All ER 796; and see the insurance case of *Amin Rasheed* v. *Kuwait Insurance* [1984] AC 50, HL.
168. [2004] Lloyd's Rep. IR 418.
169. [1996] 1 Lloyd's Rep. 74; compare *OUI* v. *IGI* [1992] 1 Lloyd's Rep. 439 where a different result was reached in relation to the Accolade underwriting pool and *forum conveniens*.
170. p. 84.
171. [2006] Lloyd's Rep. IR 127, Aikens J.; affirmed [2006] EWCA Civ 389, CA.

that it was likely that the Mauritian court would apply Mauritian law which would deprive reinsurers of defences open to them under English law. This outweighed the danger of inconsistent decisions if the English proceedings continued as well as the Mauritian, indeed, the danger was a point in favour of permitting the English proceedings to continue.

7.88 Even if, unlike in *Dornoch*, the foreign court would apply English law, issues relating to public policy may be particularly important: if the court will be called on to decide English public policy, or if English law applies to the contract but foreign public policy would conflict with the outcome under English law, the court is liable to prefer the English jurisdiction. In *Dupont* v. *Agnew*[172] the insured company was held liable in the USA to punitive damages of US$13m arising from the use of a drug it manufactured and claimed this and other sums under various product liability insurances governed by English law. Proceedings had been commenced in Illinois and England. One of the issues was whether public policy would preclude recovery of the punitive damages. The Court of Appeal considered that this weighed heavily in favour of the proceedings in England:

"This court is necessarily better placed than any other to rule on that question. Du Pont and Endo have been convicted of no crime, and charged with none. There is no decided authority in English law which denies them an indemnity. If English public policy is to be held to deny the right to indemnity in these circumstances, then this court and no other must so hold. I do not regard this as a question capable of fair resolution in any foreign court, however distinguished and well instructed... In the Illinois action attention would, I think, necessarily be directed to ascertaining not what cover the policies according to their proper law afford, but what cover the law of Illinois permits. In the interests of justice to all parties, this should not in my judgment be so. It may not be as relevant, but it is at best a subsidiary, question. The primary question, as I regard it, is the effect of this contract as a matter of English public policy, and that is a question which I do not think any foreign judge could conscientiously resolve with any confidence that he was reaching a correct answer."[173]

7.89 Again, in *Seashell Shipping* v. *Mutualidad*[174] there was a good arguable case that a marine insurance policy of a vessel owned by a Spanish company was governed by English law. The court declined to set aside the permission to serve out on the insurers, one of the prime reasons being that if, as insurers contended, the issue was determined in Spain, the Spanish court would reject the insured's claim on public policy grounds, whereas the English court would not. In *Britannia SS Insurance* v. *Ausonia*[175] the claimant P&I club commenced English proceedings for sums due on reinsurances issued by the defendant Italian insurance company and governed by English law. The main question was whether or not the reinsurances were signed on behalf of the defendant by employees with ostensible authority, or had been ratified. The court declined to set aside permission to serve out, the most important point in favour of England being that the claim was governed by English law, and would be likely to succeed if brought in England, but would fail if brought in Italy because the Italian court would not apply all aspects of English law. In *Tiernan* v. *Magen Insurance*[176] reinsurers commenced proceedings in England for a negative declaration, and the defendant Israeli insurance company sought a stay in favour of proceedings in Israel. What underlay the defendants' contentions was the hope that the Israeli court would apply Israeli law to the reinsurance rather than English law and that this would be to their advantage. Longmore J. regarded English law as applying to the reinsurance, and in principle regarded the fact that the foreign jurisdiction might not apply that law as a factor in favour of English jurisdiction. In *Tryg*

172. [1987] 2 Lloyd's Rep. 585.
173. p. 594, Bingham LJ.
174. [1989] 1 Lloyd's Rep. 47, CA.
175. [1984] 2 Lloyd's Rep. 98, 100, CA.
176. [2000] IL Pr 517, 525.

Baltica v. *Boston*[177] reinsurers commenced proceedings in England for various declarations, including a declaration that the currency of the reinsurances which covered the Argentine railways remained expressed in US dollars and had not been altered by charges in the law of Argentina which converted the currency of the underlying insurance contracts into pesos (a process called pessification). The danger that the Argentine courts would apply pessification to the reinsurance was a factor in favour of English jurisdiction (at p. 52):

"there is a real risk the courts of Argentina might apply the law of Argentina to the reinsurance contracts because of the nature of the pessification decrees, should they be found to be of an international public order nature which prevails over any other principle, or any choice of foreign law. With contracts that are governed by English law, it is right that disputes as to their meaning should be resolved by reference to that law and that law alone, whilst of course taking into account the effect of pessification, if any on the insurances and the character of the cover given to the reinsureds in respect of their liability to their insureds under the law of those insurance contracts."

THE IMPORTANCE OF ENGLISH COURTS RATHER THAN FOREIGN COURTS DETERMINING ISSUES OF ENGLISH LAW

7.90 The court will not compare the courts of one country with another. But in reinsurance cases may give weight to the difficulty which may be faced by a foreign court having to deal with a dispute on documents in English, in a technical field like reinsurance, with English law and experts. The starting point is the statement in *Amin Rasheed* v. *Kuwait*[178] which concerned an insurance claim primarily dependent on factual issues where Lord Diplock said (at p. 67):

"Nor, with respect, can I accept the suggestion of Sir John Donaldson MR that, for the purposes of the application by national courts of the doctrine of comity between one national court and another, the Commercial Court in London is far more than a national or domestic court; it is an 'international commercial court' and that Bingham J. erred in regarding it otherwise. True it is that either directly through a choice of forum clause in commercial contracts or indirectly through an English arbitration clause, the Commercial Court in London is much resorted to by foreign nationals for resolution of disputes; and true it is that its judges have acquired unrivalled expertise in such matters, including marine insurance where that insurance is governed by English law. The latter fact no doubt accounts for the popularity of the court with foreign litigants, but their submission to its jurisdiction in the case of contracts which contain such clauses is voluntary and not, as in the instant case, sought to be forced upon an unwilling defendant in the exercise by an English court of what can be classified only as an exorbitant jurisdiction which it does not recognise as possessed by foreign courts."

and Lord Wilberforce at p. 72:

"It is not appropriate, in my opinion, to embark upon a comparison of the procedures, or methods, or reputation or standing of the courts of one country as compared with those of another."

However, the court will also keep in mind what Lord Goff said in *Spiliada Maritime Corporation* v. *Cansulex*[179]:

"But if the legal issues are complex, or the legal systems very different, the general principle that a court applies its own law more reliably than does a foreign court will point to the more appropriate forum, whether English or foreign."

7.91 The approach of the courts in a reinsurance context can be seen from two contrasting cases. First, in *Trade Indemnity* v. *Forsakringsaktiebolget Njord*[180] a number of reinsurers sought a declaration in the English court that they were entitled to avoid two surplus treaty

177. [2005] Lloyd's Rep. IR 40.
178. [1984] 1 AC 50, HL; *Munchener* v. *Commonwealth* [2005] Lloyd's Rep. IR 99, 107–108.
179. [1987] AC 460 at p. 486, Lord Goff.
180. [1995] 1 Lloyd's Rep. 367 (see para. 5.170 above).

reinsurances of the Swedish reinsured in respect of the insurance of financial guarantees, performance bonds, advance payments bonds and other forms of bonds and borrowing liabilities for non-disclosure and misrepresentation based on what was described as "gross mismanagement" and dubious underwriting practices in the conduct of the business of the reinsured. Rix J. took the view that (at p. 375):

"the real focus of the dispute raised by the plaintiffs' writ is not so much as to the materiality of what was or was not said in Njord's [the reinsured's] placement information, but as to the conduct of Njord's business affairs in Sweden. The proper law of the contracts is, in my view, English law, and there will be English legal issues to be decided; but the main burden of the dispute is a factual one with its centre in Sweden, in connection with which Swedish factual and expert witnesses will have to be called. Here too the submission that the Swedish courts are unfamiliar or less familiar than the Commercial Court in London with respect to the hearing of reinsurance disputes in general or reinsurance disputes under English law in particular is not an appropriate submission. I am in any event confident both that the Swedish Court is far better placed than this Court to hear and determine issues as to the business practices of a Swedish insurance company, and also that it is not unused to applying foreign law."

By contrast in *Assicurazione* v. *Sigorta*[181] the claimant reinsurers commenced proceedings in England for a negative declaration that they had validly avoided English law reinsurances of a Turkish insurance company reinsured in respect of bankers blanket bond policies issued to a Turkish bank, alternatively that they were not liable because of breach of warranty and breach of duty after the claim. Although concurring with the approach in *Amin Rasheed* and *Trade Indemnity* Colman J. emphasised that where there are significant issues in the context of a reinsurance governed by English law this is a factor in favour of English jurisdiction (at p. 486):

"I have no doubt at all that in a case where the meaning of a complex English law contract is in issue, particularly in a technical field such as reinsurance in the London market, it is appropriate to place weight on this factor in determining whether the English courts are clearly the appropriate forum. Indeed, I would go so far as to say that, in determining where the fair trial component of the overriding objective and of the interests of justice component of the *Spiliada* test is most likely to be satisfied, it would be completely unrealistic to leave out of account the fact that a trial before a Turkish court will involve the slips and wordings being translated into Turkish and then construed in translation by the court with the assistance of expert opinions also translated into Turkish as to what the meaning and effect of the English words should be. To the extent that there are issues of non-disclosure in respect of the reinsurance similar problems will arise. They too will have to be determined by reference to English law and expert market evidence."

In that case it was unlikely there would be significant disputes on the facts; the major issues were as to materiality and construction of the primary policies and the reinsurance contracts, and the application of English law to the primary insurances and reinsurances and the *forum conveniens* was England. The key difference between *Trade Indemnity* and *Assicurazione* seems to have been in the extent to which it was expected that each case would involve factual disputes centred on the foreign jurisdiction. But in the former case the court also appears to have been confident that such legal issues as there were in relation to the reinsurance claim could be dealt with satisfactorily, whereas in the latter case the court had no such confidence, apparently primarily because of the language differences.

THE RELEVANCE OF MULTIPLE PROCEEDINGS

7.92 The possibility of multiple proceedings is not determinative. In *Meadows* v. *ICI*[182] an insured commenced proceedings in the Republic of Ireland against the insurer for sums due

181. [2002] 1 Lloyd's Rep. 1 IR 480.

182. [1989] 1 Lloyd's Rep. 181, Hirst J., affirmed on *forum conveniens* [1989] 2 Lloyd's Rep. 198, CA; see also *S&W Berisford* v. *New Hampshire* [1990] 1 Lloyd's Rep. 454; *Irish Shipping* v. *Commercial Union* [1991] 2 QB 206 (CA).

under a financial guarantee insurance, and shortly thereafter the reinsurers commenced English proceedings against the insurer seeking a negative declaration on the basis of misrepresentations made to the brokers who had placed both the insurance and the reinsurance, and the insurers joined the insured as third parties.[183] Hirst J. refused to stay the English proceedings for *forum non conveniens*. The Irish proceedings could not be said to be simply a ploy because the insurer was incorporated there. They had developed to some extent. But the key point was that reinsurers were not a party to the Irish proceedings whereas all three parties were before the English court. This latter fact therefore strongly favoured not staying the English proceedings.

7.93 The position of third parties, in particular a broker, may be significant. In *Konkola* v. *Coromin*[184] the Zambian insured had commenced proceedings in England against its Bermudan insurers for recovery under an all risks policy arising out of a mine collapse in Zambia. Insurers did not need the permission of the court to join the reinsurers as third parties and issued Part 20 proceedings against them. They had also joined the brokers Aon who had placed the reinsurance alleging that if the reinsurance did not cover it Aon were liable. The reinsurers failed to persuade the court that the reinsurance was subject to a jurisdiction agreement in favour of Zambia, and therefore ought to be stayed, but even if such a clause had been incorporated, Colman J. would not have stayed the English proceedings; one of the main reasons being that: "There are clearly cases where the party autonomy principle must yield to the wider interests of justice. Thus, a party to a jurisdiction agreement who will be exposed to the risk of inconsistent decisions, if the agreement is enforced by the granting of a stay, is entitled to invoke the wider interests of justice by inviting the court to exercise its discretion in a manner which removes or substantially reduces that risk" (at p. 575). Largely because it was not clear if there could be proceedings in Zambia which would bind the insurers, reinsurers and brokers Colman J. would have declined to stay the English proceedings in spite of a jurisdiction agreement in favour of Zambia as between the reinsurers and insurers.

7.94 By contrast, in *Munchener* v. *Commonwealth Insurance*[185] the claimant retrocessionaire commenced proceedings in England for a negative declaration that they were not liable on a retrocession since the claim did not fall within the cover, and repayment of sums already paid. Subsequently the retrocedent commenced proceedings in California against the retrocessionaire for the sums due under the retrocession, and contingently against the producing broker based in California. There was no relevant jurisdiction agreement. Did the existence of the claim in the Californian proceedings against the third party producing broker mean that the English proceedings should not be pursued? The court viewed England as clearly the appropriate forum for the dispute apart from the question of the third party claim, and that to allow the third party claim to dictate the jurisdiction would be wrong: "the tail should not be allowed to wag the dog" (at p. 108). It is evident that not much was known about that claim but there was no reason why such a claim against the producing broker could not be made by the retrocedent in the English proceedings if, as seemed sensible, the retrocedent wanted to ensure that the producing broker was bound by any decision in the main proceedings. Alternatively, it would be open to the retrocedent not to make the producing

183. Reinsurers also sought a declaration directly against the insured that insurers were not liable to the insured because of the misrepresentations on which reinsurers relied; but the Court of Appeal held that contrary to the decision of Hirst J. the court had no power to issue a declaration where there was no *lis* between the parties: [1989] 2 Lloyd's Rep. 298.

184. [2005] 2 Lloyd's Rep. 555, Colman J.; affirmed [2006] 1 Lloyd's Rep. 410, CA.

185. [2005] Lloyd's Rep. IR 99, Morison J.

broker a party to the English proceedings and proceed if necessary against the producing broker after the conclusion of the main proceedings.

D. CHALLENGING (RE)INSURANCE JURISDICTION: SETTING ASIDE, STAY AND ANTI-SUIT INJUNCTION

1. Introduction

7.95 We now turn from the initial question of whether or not the court will grant permission to serve proceedings out of the jurisdiction to three other areas:

(1) When can the defendant apply to set aside the permission to serve proceedings out of the jurisdiction?
(2) When can a stay be ordered of proceedings which have been commenced in England?
(3) When can a party be ordered not to pursue proceedings in a different jurisdiction (an anti-suit injunction)?

7.96 The power to set aside permission is in effect a review of the grant of permission. The power to stay proceedings or grant an anti-suit injunction is different: these are two of the weapons of the common law for dealing with the problems of concurrent proceedings in a world of independent jurisdictions:

"as between common law jurisdictions, there is no system as such, comparable to that enshrined in the Brussels Convention. The basic principle is that each jurisdiction is independent. There is therefore, as I have said, no embargo on concurrent proceedings in the same matter in more than one jurisdiction. There are simply these two weapons, a stay (or dismissal) of proceedings and an anti-suit injunction. Moreover, each of these has its limitations. The former depends on its voluntary adoption by the state in question, and the latter is inhibited by respect for comity. It follows that, although the availability of these two weapons should ensure that practical justice is achieved in most cases, this may not always be possible."[186]

2. Will the permission to serve out of the jurisdiction be set aside?

7.97 The application for permission is dealt with on paper and without notice. If the defendant wishes to challenge the service of proceedings on him he must make an application under CPR Part 11 within 14 days of filing acknowledgement of service.

7.98 On the application by the defendant to set aside the burden of showing that England is clearly the appropriate forum remains on the claimant.[187] The relevant time at which the evidence must be considered is at the date when permission was given.[188] Evidence may be given at the hearing as to what has subsequently happened which may throw light on what were relevant factors at the time of the permission, but the permission will not be set aside simply because circumstances have changed. By contrast, where the application is to *stay* for *forum non conveniens* the burden is on the defendant and the evidence must, as a practical matter be considered as at the date of the stay hearing; if circumstances later change in relation to the *forum non conveniens* arguments the defendant may make a fresh application based on the new circumstances.[189]

186. *Airbus Industrie* v. *Patel* [1998] 1 Lloyd's Rep. 631, 637, HL.
187. *Dornoch* v. *Mauritius* [2006] EWCA Civ 389, para. 18; *Islamic Arab Insurance* v. *Saudi Egyptian American Reinsurance* [1987] 1 Lloyd's Rep. 315, 317, CA.
188. *ISC* v. *Guerin* [1992] 2 Lloyd's Rep. 430, 434; *Andromeda* v. *O W Bunker* [2006] EWHC 777 (Comm) para. 25.
189. *Mohammed* v. *Bank of Kuwait* [1996] 1 WLR 1483, 1492, CA.

3. Will a stay be ordered of English proceedings?

(i) Introduction

7.99 The power to order a stay of proceedings, or to strike them out, derives from the inherent jurisdiction of the court. Although the court has jurisdiction to stay proceedings on *forum non conveniens* grounds it clearly may exercise the power in cases outside this narrow context.[190] In particular, the court may stay proceedings on case management grounds even if it would not do so on conflicts grounds.[191]

7.100 This discretionary power is now[192] one of the hallmarks of the common law, distinguishing it from the civil law systems (see para. 7.2). It will be remembered that if proceedings are commenced in another Member State under the Brussels Regulation no stay may be granted (see generally para. 5.285). As to the procedure in relation to a stay application see para. 7.21 above. In some cases it may be possible to overcome obstacles in the way of the grant of a stay of proceedings by appropriate undertakings given by the defendant to the English proceedings in relation to the foreign proceedings.[193]

(ii) When should the court stay English proceedings for forum non conveniens?[194]

7.101 As we have seen, the principles applied by the court in relation to an application to stay proceedings for *forum non conveniens*, and when considering the *forum conveniens* on an application for permission to serve out were set out in the leading case *Spiliada* v. *Cansulex*.[195] The question of what is the *forum conveniens* on a stay application is, in essence, the mirror of the same question on a permission application. We have considered the factors relevant to the *forum conveniens* in detail in relation to the application for permission at para. 7.57 above and these are equally relevant to the *forum conveniens* on a stay application.

7.102 The approach of the court is, however, necessarily different on a stay application from a permission application because in the former the proceedings have already been commenced (with or without permission). The court therefore has established jurisdiction, and the application is by the defendant to persuade the court to exercise its discretion to cause the proceedings not to continue until the stay is lifted. Essentially the burden is on the defendant to justify bringing proceedings over which the court has jurisdiction to a halt. The main differences between a stay and permission application therefore relate to the burden of proof, and the approach is as follows:

190. See, generally, *Halsbury's Laws*, Vol. 37 (4th ed., 2001) paras 926 *et seq.* for the jurisdiction of the court to order a stay of proceedings. The power is referred to by statute: SCA 1981, s.49(3): "(3) Nothing in this Act shall affect the power of the Court of Appeal or the High Court to stay any proceedings before it where it thinks fit to do so, either of its own motion or on the application of any person, whether or not a party to the proceedings"; and CJ&JA 1982, s.49: "Nothing in this Act shall prevent any court in the United Kingdom from staying, sisting, striking out or dismissing any proceedings before it, on the ground of *forum non conveniens* or otherwise, where to do so is not inconsistent with the 1968 Convention or, as the case may be, the Lugano Convention."

191. *Reichhold Norway ASA* v. *Goldman Sachs International* [1999] 2 Lloyd's Rep. 567; *National Westminster* v. *Utrecht* [2001] 3 All ER 733, para. 24-5, CA.

192. It was recognised as a part of English law in *Spiliada* v. *Cansulex* [1987] 1 AC 460.

193. *Societe Nationale Industrielle Aerospatiale* v. *Lee Kui Jak* [1987] 1 AC 871 (HL). For example, an undertaking may be given not to rely on a foreign limitation period: see para. 7.108 below.

194. "I doubt whether the Latin tag *forum non conveniens* is apt to describe this principle. For the question is not one of convenience, but of the suitability or appropriateness of the relevant jurisdiction. However, the Latin tag (sometimes expressed as *forum non conveniens* and sometimes as *forum conveniens*) is so widely used to describe the principle, not only in England and Scotland, but in other Commonwealth jurisdictions and in the United States, that it is probably sensible to retain it": *Spiliada* v. *Cansulex* [1987] 1 AC 460, 474, *per* Lord Goff.

195. [1987] 1 AC 460.

(1) "The basic principle is that a stay will only be granted on the ground of *forum non conveniens* where the court is satisfied that there is some other available forum, having competent jurisdiction, which is the appropriate forum for the trial of the action, i.e. in which the case may be tried more suitably for the interests of all the parties and the ends of justice."[196]
(2) In general, the burden of proof rests on the defendant to persuade the court to grant a stay. The evidential burden in relation to a particular matter advanced by one party will be on that party.
(3) Where jurisdiction was established as of right, that is without permission, the burden on the defendant is to show that there is "another available forum which is clearly or distinctly more appropriate than the English forum".[197] Where jurisdiction was established with permission the defendant will usually apply to set aside the permission.
(4) The court will look first for any reasons why another forum is more appropriate: if the court is not satisfied that there is another available forum which is more appropriate that is usually the end of the matter.[198]
(5) Once the court is satisfied that there is another available forum which is *prima facie* the appropriate forum for trial the burden shifts to the claimant to show that there are special circumstances which mean trial should take place in England.[199]
(6) Where there is no *one* forum which is clearly more appropriate the English forum will win by default, provided it is an appropriate forum.[200]
(7) Which forum is more appropriate? The factors taken into account are considered in detail at para. 7.57 above, including consideration of *lis alibi pendens*, applications for negative declarations and examples of the application of the principles to (re)insurance cases. The interests of all parties are relevant.[201]

4. When can an anti-suit injunction be ordered?

(i) Introduction

7.103 The anti-suit injunction is a draconian remedy, and is accordingly governed by stricter principles than the grant of permission to serve out of the jurisdiction, or a stay of proceedings. An injunction will only be granted where the defendant's conduct is vexatious or oppressive (usually because he has commenced foreign proceedings in breach of an agreement not to do so) and the English forum has an interest in the dispute.

7.104 The source of the power to grant the injunction is the same as any injunction, section 37 of the Supreme Court Act 1981: "the High Court may by order (whether interlocutory or final) grant an injunction in all cases in which it appears to the court to be just and convenient to do so". The discretion so conferred is exercised in accordance with the principles referred to below.

7.105 The anti-suit injunction is not in form directed at the foreign court but at a person who is amenable to the jurisdiction of the English court, against whom an injunction will be

196. *Spiliada*, p. 476.
197. *Spiliada*, p. 477.
198. *Lubbe* v. *Cape* [2000] 2 Lloyd's Rep. 383, 390, HL. See Merrett, "Uncertainties in the First Limb of the Spiliada Test" in [2004] 54 ICLQ 211 which highlights difficulties in deciding whether or not another forum is "available".
199. For example, the inability of a claimant to obtain funds with which to conduct proceedings which would be available by way of legal aid in England could be special circumstances, *Lubbe* v. *Cape* [2000] 2 Lloyd's Rep. 383, 390, HL; as could the inability of the foreign court to deal with a complex group action, *Connelley* v. *RTZ* [1998] AC 854.
200. *Cf. Airbus Industrie* v. *Patel* [1998] 1 Lloyd's Rep. 631, 640, HL.
201. *Lubbe* v. *Cape* [2000] 2 Lloyd's Rep. 383, 389, HL.

an effective remedy.[202] But in substance the anti-suit injunction can be seen as interfering in the process of a foreign court,[203] and in any event may be seen by the foreign court as an infringement of its jurisdiction.[204] In an appropriate case the English court may grant an injunction against seeking an anti-suit injunction in a foreign jurisdiction (anti-anti-suit injunction),[205] or even against a defendant from seeking an injunction in a foreign jurisdiction to stop a claimant from applying in England for an anti-suit injunction (anti-anti-anti-suit injunction). The injunction will be granted on an interim basis if it depends on matters which have not been finally determined as between the parties, such as the existence of a disputed arbitration agreement.[206] It will be remembered that if proceedings are commenced in another Member State under the Brussels Regulation no anti-suit injunction may be granted (see generally para. 5.285). We deal with arbitration separately in Chapter 8.

(ii) Is there jurisdiction to grant an anti-suit injunction?

7.106 If there are proceedings between the parties in England apart from the claim for the anti-suit injunction the court will have jurisdiction over those proceedings and therefore over an anti-suit injunction claimed in respect of them. If the anti-suit injunction is the only relief sought it will be necessary to establish that the English court has jurisdiction. It may be necessary for the claimant to seek permission to serve the defendant out of the jurisdiction. Commonly there will be a claim for breach of a jurisdiction agreement in favour of England, in which case the claimant can rely on CPR 6.20(5)(d) or Article 23 of the Brussels Regulation.

(iii) Should the court exercise its discretion to grant an anti-suit injunction?

7.107 An anti-suit injunction will only be granted if the ends of justice require it, and then only if comity permits.[207] Where the defendant agreed not to bring foreign proceedings either because of a jurisdiction agreement or arbitration agreement the court will be much less averse to granting an anti-suit injunction on comity grounds than where no such grounds exist.

7.108 When considering whether or not to grant an anti-suit injunction the court will need to have "the fullest possible knowledge and understanding of all circumstances relevant to the litigation and the parties before it", and, in particular, as to the likely effect of an injunction on proceedings in the foreign and domestic jurisdictions, as well as on parties not bound by the injunction.[208] In some cases it may be possible to neutralise objections to the grant of, or refusal to grant, an anti-suit injunction by appropriate undertakings given by the claimant or defendant.[209] The court will take into account whether or not the application for the anti-suit

202. *Societe Nationale Industrielle Aerospatiale* v. *Lee Kui Jak* [1987] AC 871, HL. The terminology of "anti-suit injunction" has been described as misleading because it is liable to foster the impression that the order is directed to the foreign court: *Turner* v. *Grovit* [2002] 1 WLR 107 at [23], [26].

203. *Royal Bank of Canada* v. *Centrale Raffeisen-Boerenleenbank* [2004] 1 Lloyd's Rep. 471, 475.

204. As in *Re: the enforcement of an English anti-suit injunction* [1996] IL Pr 320; *OT Africa Line* v. *Hijazy* [2001] 1 Lloyd's Rep. 76, 92; *cf. Navigation* v. *Rustal, The Ivan Zagubanski* [2002] 1 Lloyd's Rep. 106, 126; *West Tankers* v. *RAS, The Front Comor* [2005] 2 Lloyd's Rep. 257, para. 43. The House of Lords has given leave for a leapfrog appeal in this case.

205. As in *General Star* v. *Stirling Cooke Brown* [2003] Lloyd's Rep. IR 719, see below; *Tonicstar* v. *American Home* [2005] Lloyd's Rep. IR 32; *Goshawk* v. *QBD* [2006] EWHC 1730 (Comm), an anti-anti arbitration injunction case.

206. *Navigation* v. *Rustal, The Ivan Zagubanski* [2002] 1 Lloyd's Rep. 106, 127.

207. The principles have been summarised recently by Cooke J. in *Trafigura* v. *Kookmin* [2005] EWHC 2350, para. 42.

208. *Donohue* v. *Armco* [2002] 1 Lloyd's Rep. 425, 430, HL.

209. *Societe Nationale Industrielle Aerospatiale* v. *Lee Kui Jak* [1987] AC 871, HL; *Society of Lloyd's* v. *White, The Times*, 14 April 2000 (undertaking as to limitation).

injunction was launched promptly and before any foreign proceedings were too far advanced; the longer the delay the more likely a court is to refuse the application.[210]

THE ENDS OF JUSTICE

7.109 At bottom an anti-suit injunction will be granted if the ends of justice require it.[211] But in this context this is only in limited circumstances: "Generally speaking, this may occur when the foreign proceedings are vexatious or oppressive."[212] In other cases it has been said that the test is what is "unconscionable",[213] or where there has been "wrongful conduct" by the party to be restrained.[214] The test is not the same as for a stay: proceedings may be stayed for *forum non conveniens* where another forum is the appropriate forum for the trial, but a court may decline to order an anti-suit injunction even if England is the appropriate forum for trial in the ends of justice: "the [power to stay] depends on its voluntary adoption by the state in question and the [power to make a restraining order] is inhibited by respect for comity".[215] The reason is that comity dictates that the English court not interfere indirectly with foreign proceedings simply because it may take a different view about which is the appropriate forum. Further, the mere fact that there are concurrent proceedings is not enough of itself to make foreign proceedings vexatious or oppressive.[216] The court may conclude that foreign proceedings are vexatious or oppressive if England is the natural forum and the ends of justice require that the foreign proceedings not continue, taking account of the injustice to the party seeking the injunction if the foreign proceedings continue, and the injustice to the other party if the foreign proceedings do not continue.[217] In *Societe Nationale Industrielle Aerospatiale* v. *Lee Kui Jak*[218] the widow and administratrix of the estate of a person killed in a helicopter crash in Brunei commenced proceedings in Texas against the helicopter manufacturer for damages. The manufacturer commenced proceedings in Brunei for an anti-suit injunction which ended up before the Privy Council on appeal. The court took the view that Texas was by no means the most appropriate forum for the trial – jurisdiction was founded there only because the manufacturer carried on business there. But that was not ground enough to justify

210. *Akai* v. *People's Insurance* [1998] 1 Lloyd's Rep. 90, 105 (where the court granted an anti-suit injunction on terms that the applicant indemnify the defendant against the costs of further foreign proceedings commenced by the claimant during the period of delay); *Society of Lloyd's* v. *White*, *The Times*, 14 April 2000; *Royal Bank of Canada* v. *Centrale Raffeisen-Boerenleenbank* [2004] 1 Lloyd's Rep. 471, 483.

211. *Societe Nationale Industrielle Aerospatiale* v. *Lee Kui Jak* [1987] AC 871, HL.

212. *Airbus Industrie* v. *Patel* [1998] 1 Lloyd's Rep. 631, 637, HL; although this should not be regarded as the only ground: *Societe Nationale Industrielle Aerospatiale* v. *Lee Kui Jak* [1987] AC 871, HL; *Turner* v. *Grovit* [2002] 1 WLR 107 at [24]; and see *Royal Bank of Canada* v. *Centrale Raffeisen-Boerenleenbank* [2004] 1 Lloyd's Rep. 471 for a case where it was unsuccessfully argued that foreign proceedings were a disclosure exercise and unconscionable or an abuse.

213. "... the threatened conduct must be 'unconscionable'. It is only such conduct which founds the right, legal or equitable ... for the protection of which an injunction can be granted. What is unconscionable cannot and should not be defined exhaustively, but it includes conduct which is 'oppressive or vexatious or which interferes with the due process of the court'. The underlying principle is one of justice in support of the 'ends of justice'. It is analogous to 'abuse of process' it is related to matters which should affect a person's conscience": *Glencore* v. *Exter* [2002] 2 All ER (Comm) 1, Rix LJ, para. 52; *Tonicstar* v. *American Home* [2005] Lloyd's Rep. IR 32, 36; *Trafigura* v. *Kookmin* [2005] EWHC 2350, para. 42. Compare *Airbus* where the Lords seemed to view the test of what was "unconscionable" as more demanding than "vexatious or oppressive", and applicable to a single forum case (as to which see below).

214. *Turner* v. *Grovit* [2002] 1 WLR 107 at [24], Lord Hobhouse.

215. *Airbus Industrie* v. *Patel* [1998] 1 Lloyd's Rep. 631, 637, HL; *Royal Bank of Canada* v. *Centrale Raffeisen-Boerenleenbank* [2004] 1 Lloyd's Rep. 471, 475, CA.

216. *Societe Nationale Industrielle Aerospatiale* v. *Lee Kui Jak* [1987] AC 871, 894, HL.

217. *Societe Nationale Industrielle Aerospatiale* v. *Lee Kui Jak* [1987] AC 871, 895–896, HL.

218. [1987] AC 871, HL.

an anti-suit injunction. The widow and administratrix of the estate offered undertakings in relation to the Texan proceedings which meant trial would be before a judge alone, and there would be no punitive damages. However, it was not clear that the manufacturer would be entitled to bring contribution proceedings in the Texan proceedings against the Malaysian company which owned and operated the helicopter whereas that company was prepared to accept service of proceedings in Malaysia. Thus it would be unjust to deprive the manufacturer of this benefit by allowing proceedings to continue in Texas and an anti-suit injunction was granted.

IS THERE AN ALTERNATIVE FORUM?

7.110 A distinction is drawn between an alternative forum case and a single forum case. In the more common alternative forum cases, there is an alternative forum in which the claim of the foreign claimant may be heard if the anti-suit injunction is granted. In a single forum case there is no other forum in which that claim may be heard if the anti-suit injunction is granted: "In alternative forum cases, it has been stated that the jurisdiction will be exercised as the ends of justice require, and in particular where the pursuit of the relevant proceedings is vexatious or oppressive; in single forum cases, it is said that an injunction may be granted to restrain the pursuit of proceedings overseas which is unconscionable."[219] The grant of an anti-suit injunction in a single forum case is, however, a matter of some doubt.[220]

JURISDICTION AGREEMENT

7.111 If there is an exclusive jurisdiction agreement in favour of England the courts will generally grant an anti-suit injunction unless the foreign proceedings are too far advanced or there is some other very good reason not to do so. The existence of a exclusive jurisdiction agreement is "near-conclusive" as to whether or not an anti-suit injunction should be granted.[221] In *Donohue* v. *Armco*[222] the Armco group of companies commenced New York proceedings against four defendants for damages for fraud; one of the defendants Donohue was a party to an exclusive jurisdiction agreement in favour of England and commenced later English proceedings for an anti-suit injunction to which the other three New York defendants applied to become parties in order themselves to seek anti-suit injunctions. Lord Bingham, with whom the majority agreed, stated at para. 24 that:

"If contracting parties agree to give a particular court exclusive jurisdiction to rule on claims between those parties, and a claim falling within the scope of the agreement is made in proceedings in a forum other than that which the parties have agreed, the English court will ordinarily exercise its discretion (whether by granting a stay of proceedings in England, or by restraining the prosecution of proceedings in the non-contractual forum abroad, or by such other procedural order as is appropriate in the circumstances) to secure compliance with the contractual bargain, unless the party suing in the non-contractual forum (the burden being on him) can show strong reasons for suing in that forum,"

219. *Airbus Industrie* v. *Patel* [1998] 1 Lloyd's Rep. 631, 637, HL.

220. Such an injunction was granted in *Midland Bank* v. *Laker* [1986] QB 689 to restrain an English claimant from pursuing proceedings against an English defendant in the USA claiming damages under US anti-trust legislation. Such a claim could not be brought in England, but it was still unconscionable and unjust for the claimant to invoke the US extra-territorial jurisdiction against a defendant whose dealings with the claimant were entirely in England. An argument was raised in *The Kribi* [2001] 1 Lloyd's Rep. 76 that the anti-suit injunction sought would have the effect of denying the claimant right of access to a court in an ECHR state. Aikens J. rejected the argument on the basis that Article 6 does not provide that a person is to have an unfettered right to choose an ECHR court, but this seems to assume that at least one such court would be available.

221. *Bouygues* v. *Caspian* [1998] 2 Lloyd's Rep. 461, 467, Evans LJ; *Trafigura* v. *Kookmin* [2005] EWHC 2350 at [42], the court will "readily" grant an anti-suit injunction.

222. [2002] 1 Lloyd's Rep. 425.

and later at para. 25 that in such circumstances the court will "in all probability" give effect to the jurisdiction agreement.[223] However, on the facts of *Donohue* the court refused to grant an anti-suit injunction to Donohue, mainly because the proceedings against the other defendants (who were not bound by the arbitration clause) would continue in New York and there was overwhelming sense in having the claims in fraud against all parties decided by one court in one forum. This was enough to outweigh the exclusive jurisdiction agreement. Nor does the fact that the foreign proceedings have already been commenced in breach of the exclusive jurisdiction agreement mean that it is necessary that the claimant first have applied to the foreign court to stay the foreign proceedings, or that the English court should refrain from pronouncing before the foreign court.[224]

7.112 Where the jurisdiction agreement is not exclusive the reasons for not exercising restraint on the grounds of comity diminish considerably. The parties have not agreed that the foreign jurisdiction in question will not have jurisdiction. However, it is clear that to some extent the existence of a non exclusive jurisdiction agreement lightens the burden on the applicant for an anti-suit injunction in showing that foreign proceedings are vexatious or oppressive. In *Amoco* v. *TGTL*[225] Waller J. explained why:

> "First, to agree non-exclusive jurisdiction in my view means ... that the parties agreed to submit to that jurisdiction and cannot object to that court accepting jurisdiction, and that the parties are implicitly agreeing that jurisdiction as appropriate. They are not so agreeing in relation to any other jurisdiction by the term non-exclusive. All the term non-exclusive means is that there is no contractual bargain not to start proceedings elsewhere; any other relevant point for contesting jurisdiction (other than in the place expressly chosen non-exclusively) will be open to the parties. Second, in addition to there being no question of the English court taking on itself a decision as to the natural forum when there is a non-exclusive jurisdiction clause, it seems to me much less likely that a foreign court will be offended if the court, to whose jurisdiction the parties have agreed to submit, grants an injunction, particularly where that court's resources are being used and where proceedings in the foreign court might affect English proceedings, e.g. by the risk of witnesses having to be in two places or by the English process being lengthened by the examination of witnesses who have already given depositions under a foreign procedure. Third, I am doubtful whether a party can rely on a procedural advantage in some country other than the one to whose jurisdiction he has on any view submitted, as a juridical advantage. Putting this point another way, can it seriously have been contemplated that when these parties agreed a non-exclusive jurisdiction clause in favour of England that they were agreeing that if the English courts and its procedures were adopted for the purpose of any action, that, in addition, the same issues could be litigated elsewhere if there was some procedural advantage in the sense of discovery to be gained by so doing."

The effect of the last point is that the court is unlikely to treat a non exclusive jurisdiction agreement as sanctioning concurrent proceedings unless that is spelt out in terms.[226] In *Ace*

223. Following the approach of Millett LJ in *Aggeliki Charis Cia Maritima SA* v. *Pagnan SpA, The Angelic Grace* [1995] 1 Lloyd's Rep 87, 96: "the time has come to lay aside the ritual incantation that this is a jurisdiction which should only be exercised sparingly and with great caution. There have been many statements of great authority warning of the danger of giving an appearance of undue interference with the proceedings of a foreign court. Such sensitivity to the feelings of a foreign court has much to commend it where the injunction is sought on the ground of *forum non conveniens* or on the general ground that the foreign proceedings are vexatious or oppressive but where no breach or contract is involved. In the former case, great care may be needed to avoid casting doubt on the fairness or adequacy of the procedures of the foreign court. In the latter case, the question whether proceedings are vexatious or oppressive is primarily a matter for the court before which they are pending. But in my judgment there is no good reason for diffidence in granting an injunction to restrain foreign proceedings on the clear and simple ground that the defendant has promised not to bring them."

224. *Aggeliki Charis Cia Maritima SA* v. *Pagnan SpA, The Angelic Grace* [1995] 1 Lloyd's Rep 87; *Akai* v. *People's Insurance* [1998] 1 Lloyd's Rep. 90, 107.

225. Unreported, 26 June 2006; *Sabah* v. *Islamic* [2003] 2 Lloyd's Rep. 571, 581; *Royal Bank of Canada* v. *Centrale Raffeisen-Boerenleenbank* [2004] 1 Lloyd's Rep. 471, 478, 480.

226. As it was in *Royal Bank of Canada* v. *Centrale Raffeisen-Boerenleenbank* [2004] 1 Lloyd's Rep. 471.

v. *Zurich*[227] there was in a retrocession agreement a clause on the Service of Suit Form NMA 1998 which provided in part: "It is agreed that in the event of the failure of the Underwriters hereon to pay any amount claimed to be due hereunder, the Underwriters hereon, at the request of the Insured (or Reinsured), will submit to the Jurisdiction of a Court of competent jurisdiction within the United States". The reinsurers sought anti-suit injunction in respect of proceedings in Texas but were unable to point to (at p. 630) "anything unforeseen, no suggestion of any strong or special cause, no identification of some matter which lies beyond considerations of convenience and goes to a matter of justice" and consequently failed to persuade the court to grant an anti-suit injunction.

7.113 It is a question of construction whether or not a jurisdiction agreement in favour of England covers causes of action even though they could not be litigated in this jurisdiction.[228] An agreement not to bring proceedings at all in respect of a specific matter may have the effect of an exclusive jurisdiction agreement for the purpose of an anti-suit injunction.[229]

OTHER *FORUM NON CONVENIENS* CASES

7.114 In cases where the foreign proceedings are not in breach of a jurisdiction agreement the claim for an anti-suit injunction must be based on *forum non conveniens* grounds alone. Such grounds are weak compared with the disadvantages of granting an anti-suit injunction and the court will be reluctant to grant an anti-suit injunction.[230] However, there are cases where an anti-suit injunction will be granted even though there was no agreement not to commence proceedings in another jurisdiction. In *General Star* v. *Stirling Cooke Brown*[231] reinsurers of film finance business had commenced proceedings in England against the placing brokers and their solicitors alleging breaches of duty in relation to their acceptance of the reinsurance. Subsequently, the brokers commenced proceedings in New York for an anti-suit injunction. England was overwhelmingly the appropriate forum for the trial of the issues between the parties (the connections relating to parties, the policies, the acts and omissions relied on, the law and the witnesses were all English). It would also be vexatious and oppressive to allow the New York proceedings to continue when the brokers were in substance seeking a stay of the English proceedings and the correct course would have been to have applied for a stay in the English proceedings; hence an anti-anti-suit injunction was granted against the brokers (i.e. against the brokers pursuing an anti-suit injunction in New York).

COMITY

7.115 Because the anti-suit injunction in this context is concerned with the clash of jurisdictions comity requires that the jurisdiction must be exercised with caution.[232] Comity is behind the basic requirement that an anti-suit injunction will only be granted where the foreign

227. [2001] 1 Lloyd's Rep. 618; *Insurance Corporation of Ireland* v. *Strombus* [1985] 2 Lloyd's Rep. 138, CA; *Excess Insurance* v. *Allendale*, unreported, 8 March 1995, CA; *American International* v. *Abbott* [2004] Lloyd's Rep. IR 815, 824.

228. *Youell* v. *Kara Mara* [2000] 1 Lloyd's Rep. 102, 117 (direct claim of third party against insurer under Louisiana law); *Donohue* v. *Armco* [2002] 1 Lloyd's Rep. 425, 442, HL (RICO claim in the USA).

229. *National Westminster* v. *Utrecht* [2001] 3 All ER 733, para. 32, where the court found that there had been breach of such an agreement and on the strength of that finding made a permanent anti-suit injunction.

230. *Turner* v. *Grovit* [2002] 1 WLR 107 at [25]; *Trafigura* v. *Kookmin* [2005] EWHC 2350, para. 42, a "special factor" is required.

231. [2003] Lloyd's Rep. IR 719. See also *Societe Nationale* at para. 7.109 above.

232. *Airbus Industrie* v. *Patel* [1998] 1 Lloyd's Rep. 631, 637, HL.

proceedings would be vexatious or oppressive (para. 7.109 above). But it also requires that no anti-suit injunction will be granted by the English court unless the English forum has a sufficient interest in the proceedings. In *Airbus* v. *Patel*[233] the English claimants commenced proceedings in Texas against aircraft manufacturers, Airbus, for damages which could include triple damages in relation to the crash of an aircraft in India. Texas did not recognise the principle of *forum non conveniens* and therefore could not decline proceedings on that basis. The Indian courts could not issue an effective anti-suit injunction against the English claimants since none were within that jurisdiction. Airbus therefore sought an anti-suit injunction in England against the claimants domiciled in England. Lord Goff, with whom all of the Lords agreed, stated the principle as being (p. 640): "As a general rule, before an anti-suit injunction can properly be granted by an English court to restrain a person from pursuing proceedings in a foreign jurisdiction in cases of the kind under consideration in the present case, comity requires that the English forum should have a sufficient interest in, or connection with, the matter in question to justify the indirect interference with the foreign court which an anti-suit injunction entails." Accordingly, the English court will not normally[234] intervene even if foreign proceedings are vexatious or oppressive if the English forum has no sufficient interest in the matter in dispute. The fact that Texas had not at that time (although it later did) recognised the principle of *forum non conveniens* and would therefore not decline jurisdiction on that basis was not enough to cause the English court to intervene where there was no link between the English forum bearing in mind that *forum conveniens* is not recognised in many civil law countries. Nor was the fact the courts of India were powerless to prevent the English claimants enough:

> "I am driven to say that [an anti-suit injunction] is not open to the English courts because, for the reasons I have given, it would be inconsistent with comity. In a world which consists of independent jurisdictions, interference, even indirect interference, by the courts of one jurisdiction with the exercise of the jurisdiction of a foreign court cannot in my opinion be justified by the fact that a third jurisdiction is affected but is powerless to intervene. The basic principle is that only the courts of an interested jurisdiction can act in the matter; and if they are powerless to do so, that will not of itself be enough to justify the courts of another jurisdiction to act in their place. Such are the limits of a system which is dependent on the remedy of an anti-suit injunction to curtail the excesses of a jurisdiction which does not adopt the principle, widely accepted throughout the common law world, of *forum non conveniens*."[235]

E. CONCLUSIONS

1. Pursuing litigation in a foreign jurisdiction

7.116 Assume a dispute relating to a reinsurance between a reinsurer incorporated in England and a reinsured incorporated in the USA. If the reinsured wishes to take steps to have any litigation heard in, for example, New York what can he do? It must be assumed throughout this discussion that the reinsured is acting *bona fide*, and that any steps he takes in New York or England are justified; the English court will not give credence or weight to steps which are not *bona fide* and justified. The options for the reinsured are strictly limited if he is a party to an exclusive jurisdiction agreement in favour of England. The reinsured should expect that the reinsurer will readily be able to persuade the English court to enforce the exclusive jurisdiction agreement by anti-suit injunction if necessary (quite apart from any

233. [1998] 1 Lloyd's Rep. 631, HL.

234. The example given by Lord Goff at p. 641 of a case where the court might intervene even without a sufficient interest was if a foreign state exercised jurisdiction such as to deprive it of the respect normally required by comity.

235. *Airbus Industrie* v. *Patel* [1998] 1 Lloyd's Rep. 631, 641; *Turner* v. *Grovit* [2002] 1 WLR 107 at [27]; *Trafigura* v. *Kookmin* [2005] EWHC 2350 at [42], there must be a "clear need for protection".

remedies open to the reinsurer in New York), and will give the reinsurer permission to commence his own proceedings in England against the reinsured. However, even in such a case, if the reinsured is for instance embroiled in litigation in New York involving third parties the English court may exceptionally choose not to enforce the exclusive jurisdiction agreement or permit English proceedings despite the exclusive jurisdiction agreement. The further advanced those foreign proceedings are the less likely the English court is to wish to interfere in them. It is therefore important to consider very carefully whether or not it is possible to challenge the jurisdiction agreement, on the basis that it was not incorporated, was not exclusive, or does not apply to the dispute. Even if the jurisdiction agreement is not exclusive but assigns jurisdiction to the courts of England it is likely to be a significant factor in the eyes of the English court.

7.117 If there is no exclusive jurisdiction agreement there is more scope for the reinsured to persuade the English court not to interfere in any New York proceedings he commences. Again, it will usually be advantageous to the reinsured to start proceedings early and progress them quickly. If the New York proceedings involve third parties, the English court may take this into account, especially if those parties cannot be parties to litigation in England, perhaps because of jurisdiction agreements or arbitration clauses.

7.118 In such a case an important consideration will be whether or not the English court will view the reinsurance as governed by English law; if so the reinsured will need to consider whether or not he should accept that English law would be applied in the New York proceedings, and in any event whether or not he should offer any undertakings so as to neutralise differences between proceedings in England and New York (for example as to limitation). It will be important, if possible, to define the issues between the parties so that they do not involve significant disputes of English law or English public policy. If the reinsured can avoid relying on grounds of public policy under the foreign law that will assist his cause. In any jurisdiction proceedings in England the reinsured will need to have ready evidence from New York lawyers which supports his case as to the issues, the applicable law and the significant juridical differences.

7.119 Where there is no exclusive jurisdiction agreement, if there is no good arguable case that the reinsurance is governed by English law the position of the reinsured may be slightly easier. If the English court would apply New York law to the reinsurance the reinsured will need to consider whether or not the issues and law are such that they would be better dealt with in a New York court rather than an English court. Issues as to public policy in New York would point to the New York jurisdiction.

7.120 The reinsured may consider seeking an anti-suit injunction in New York, but, if the question of English jurisdiction is already before the English court, it is not advisable to do so from the point of view of the English forum.

2. Pursuing litigation in England

7.121 Assume in the above example that the reinsurer wishes any litigation to take place in England. The obverse of much of the above applies. The reinsurer clearly should not submit to any New York proceedings. The reinsurer may confine his claim to a negative declaration provided he can show that the declaration will be of use which will certainly be the case if there is a good arguable case the reinsurance is governed by English law. It would usually be to the advantage of the reinsurer to commence English proceedings as early as possible, and before the reinsured, and to progress them without delay.

7.122 If the reinsurance contains an exclusive jurisdiction agreement the reinsurer will almost certainly obtain and retain permission to serve out of the jurisdiction, unless there are special factors, such as well advanced litigation in New York involving third parties who cannot be made parties in England. The reinsurer is also likely to be able to obtain an anti-suit injunction in respect of any threatened New York proceedings, and, if the need arises, should act without delay. If there is a non-exclusive jurisdiction agreement it is still likely to be a significant aid to the English court retaining jurisdiction.

7.123 If the reinsurance contain no jurisdiction agreement the applicable law will be the next most important factor in relation to jurisdiction. If the reinsurance is governed by English law the reinsurer may well need to consider whether the New York court would apply English law, and, if not, what the consequences of that would be.

CHAPTER 8

REINSURANCE AND INSURANCE JURISDICTION IN ARBITRATION DISPUTES

A. INTRODUCTION

8.1 Reinsurance and insurance agreements will often contain a clause agreeing to arbitration. The aim of an arbitration agreement is, plainly, to remove a dispute from the primary jurisdiction of the state-court system, for adjudication according to a process determined or selected by the parties.[1] This does not, of course, mean that the courts' role is excluded. Rather, the courts' role changes to that of supporting the arbitration agreement, e.g. by deciding whether or not court proceedings should be stayed because of the existence of the arbitration agreement, or to enforce the attendance of witnesses at an arbitration, or to enforce an award. The relationship between arbitration proceedings and court proceedings has aptly been described as a "relay race" in which from time to time the baton passes to the courts from the arbitral tribunal for specific reasons.[2]

8.2 The conflict of laws issues which arise in the context or arbitration are different, and altogether more complex from those which arise generally. This is because, in addition to the jurisdiction rules so far considered, there are specific rules determining the courts' role and powers in relation to arbitration disputes. For the English courts, these rules are contained in the Arbitration Act 1996.

8.3 How these arbitration specific rules interact with the general jurisdiction rules hitherto described is the subject of this chapter. More specifically:

(1) Section 2 considers the substantive juridiction of the English courts over arbitration proceedings.
(2) Section 3 then considers how these provisions interact with the Brussels Regulation. For example, what happens if an EU court is already seised of the matter, or where the defendant is domiciled abroad? What rules determine priority as between the Brussels Regulation and the Arbitration Act 1996? As will be seen, the answer is contained in the Brussels Regulation itself, which (by its own provisions) expressly limits its own application to arbitration disputes. Although it can be said that many disputes as to arbitration will not involve the application of the Brussels Regulation it would be wrong to say that the Regulation will never have effect.
(3) Finally, there is a further complication which ought to be borne in mind from the outset. In a case *not* involving arbitration, if the English court has jurisdiction in relation to a particular matter there will obviously be a further question as to which law is applicable to that dispute. There is often only one choice of law to contend with. Where arbitration is concerned, however, three (or more) choices of law may well need to be considered. In addition to the choice of law governing the substance of the dispute between the parties, the law governing the arbitration agreement, and the procedural law of the arbitration need to be considered separately (see Chapter 13 below).[3]

1. The main reference books in this area include Mustill, *The Law and Practice of Commercial Arbitration in England* (2nd ed., 1999); Redfern and Hunter, *Law and Practice of International Commercial Arbitration* (4th ed., 2004); Merkin (Arbitration), 1991.
2. Redfern/Hunter, p. 330.
3. *Halsbury's Laws* (4th ed., 2003), Vol. 2(3), para. 5.

B. THE JURISDICTION OF THE ENGLISH COURTS IN RELATION TO ARBITRATION PROCEEDINGS

1. The Arbitration Act 1996

8.4 The substantive jurisdiction of the English courts is primarily governed by the Arbitration Act 1996.[4] In general, the English courts have a number of powers enumerated in the Act provided the seat of the arbitration is in England, Wales or Northern Ireland, and a few specific powers even if the seat is not.[5]

8.5 Where the seat is in England, Wales or Northern Ireland the main powers include the power to stay legal proceedings, extend agreed time limits, remove an arbitrator, determine a preliminary point of jurisdiction, secure the attendance of witnesses and determine a challenge to the award for lack of substantive jurisdiction or irregularity.[6] These powers are mandatory which means they have effect even if the parties agree otherwise.[7] The court has other non-mandatory powers, that is, powers subject to the parties' agreement,[8] including the power to appoint an arbitrator, to enforce orders of the arbitral panel, and determine a challenge to the award on a point of law.

8.6 Where the seat of the arbitration is not in England, Wales or Northern Ireland the court has more restricted powers. These powers include the power to stay legal proceedings, enforce an award, make orders for securing the attendance of witnesses and make other orders in support of arbitral proceedings.[9]

8.7 The seat of the arbitration is determined "(a) by the parties to the arbitration agreement, or (b) by any arbitral or other institution or person vested by the parties with powers in that regard, or (c) by the arbitral tribunal if so authorised by the parties, or determined, in the absence of any such designation, having regard to the parties' agreement and all the relevant circumstances".[10] In some cases there may be a dispute about which is the appropriate court to decide the seat.[11]

8.8 An arbitration agreement is an agreement in writing to submit to arbitration present or future disputes (whether they are contractual or not).[12] References in the Arbitration Act 1996 to a party to an arbitration agreement include any person claiming under or through him.[13]

8.9 The procedure for applications to the English court in relation to arbitration is governed by CPR Part 62 which applies to any application affecting arbitration proceedings.[14] An arbitration claim is begun by an arbitration claim form, except where the application is to stay existing English court proceedings in which case the application is made in those proceedings.[15]

4. Arbitration Act 1996, s.1(c). It applies to arbitration commenced on or after 31 January 1997. As to the residual discretion of the court to intervene to support the basic process of arbitration see *Hiscox* v. *Dickson* [2004] 2 Lloyd's Rep. 438, 444. The court retains for instance its inherent jurisdiction to stay proceedings in favour of arbitration where the requirements of the Arbitration Act 1996 are not complied with: *Mackley* v. *Gosport* [2002] EWHC 1315, TCC.

5. Arbitration Act 1996, s.2.

6. See, generally, Schedule 1 to the Arbitration Act 1996; *Hiscox* v. *Dickson* [2004] 2 Lloyd's Rep. 438 (order for access to documents evidencing insurance bound under binding authority).

7. Arbitration Act 1996, s.4(1).

8. Arbitration Act 1996, s.4(2). A choice of a foreign law as the applicable law in respect of a matter provided for a non-mandatory provision is equivalent to an agreement not to apply the non-mandatory provision: s.4(5).

9. Arbitration Act 1996, s.2(2). The court may exercise other powers set out in the Arbitration Act 1996 in support of arbitral proceedings where no seat has been determined and it is appropriate to do so by reason of a connection with England, Wales or Northern Ireland: s.2(4).

10. Arbitration Act 1996, s.3.

11. *Dubai* v. *Paymentech* [2001] 1 Lloyd's Rep. 65; *Arab National Bank* v. *Abdali* [2005] 1 Lloyd's Rep 541.

12. Arbitration Act 1996, ss.5, 6; see s.81 for oral arbitration agreements.

13. Section 82(2). An insurer or reinsurer may become bound by an arbitration agreement by subrogation, or because he is enforcing under statute the rights of a party who was party to the arbitration agreement, see para. 5.145.

14. CPR 62.2(1).

15. CPR 62.3.

8.10 Permission is required to serve the arbitration claim form out of the jurisdiction.[16] It may be given under CPR 62.5 if:

(a) the claimant seeks to – (i) challenge; or (ii) appeal on a question of law arising out of, an arbitration award made within the jurisdiction;
(b) the claim is for an order under section 44 of the 1996 Act[17]; or
(c) the claimant – (i) seeks some other remedy or requires a question to be decided by the court affecting an arbitration (whether started or not), an arbitration agreement or an arbitration award; and (ii) the seat of the arbitration is or will be within the jurisdiction or the conditions in section 2(4) of the 1996 Act are satisfied.

8.11 The applicant must show a good arguable case that there is a substantive dispute falling within the arbitration agreement.[18] The ground at (c) does not enable the court to give power to serve proceedings out of the jurisdiction on a non-party to the arbitration agreement.[19]

2. Proceedings brought in breach of an arbitration agreement

(i) Proceedings before an English court

8.12 Where legal proceedings are brought before an English court, the court is obliged to grant a stay of those proceedings unless satisfied that the arbitration agreement is null and void, inoperative or incapable of being performed.[20] The court has no discretion. This is an important distinction between the law relating to exclusive jurisdiction agreements (where the court may still choose not to stay proceedings in breach of a jurisdiction agreement where there are special reasons) and arbitration agreements.

(ii) Anti-suit injunction in respect of foreign proceedings

8.13 The Arbitration Act 1996 does not make provision for anti-suit injunctions which are therefore governed by the ordinary principles considered at para. 7.95 above.

8.14 Plainly, this is an area where the interaction between English municipal law and the Brussels Regulation is critical. The following paragraphs consider the general approach of the English courts *absent* the Regulation. The effect of the Regulation on arbitration jurisdiction is considered at para. 8.21 below.

8.15 The application for a stay is not made under the Arbitration Act 1996.[21] The court has a discretion to order an anti-suit injunction, but will do so readily where foreign proceedings are in breach of an arbitration agreement, provided that the other requirements for the exercise of the power are met.[22] In *Toepfer* v. *Societe Cargill*[23] Phillips LJ in holding that

16. Unless service can be made on the respondent's solicitors within the jurisdiction under CPR Practice Direction 62.3.1.
17. Power to order the taking of evidence from witnesses and similar orders in support of arbitration.
18. *Mayer Newman* v. *Arbitral Ferro* [1990] 2 Lloyd's Rep. 290, 293, CA.
19. *Vale do Rio* v. *Bao Steel* [2000] 2 Lloyd's Rep. 3.
20. Arbitration Act 1996, s.9(4).
21. *Welex* v. *Rosa* [2003] 2 Lloyd's Rep. 509, 516, CA.
22. The approach is the same as that in relation to exclusive jurisdiction agreements, see para. 7.111 above and *Aggeliki Charis Cia Maritima SA* v. *Pagnan SpA, The Angelic Grace* [1995] 1 Lloyd's Rep. 87; *Society of Lloyd's* v. *White, The Times*, 14 April 2000; *XL Insurance* v. *Owens Corning* [2000] 2 Lloyd's Rep. 500, 509 *Turner* v. *Grovit* [2002] 1 WLR 107 at [25]; *National Westminster* v. *Utrecht* [2001] 3 All ER 733, para. 32; *Navigation* v. *Rustal, The Ivan Zagubanski* [2002] 1 Lloyd's Rep. 106, 124; *Welex* v. *Rosa* [2003] 2 Lloyd's Rep. 509, 517, CA; *Goshawk* v. *QBD* [2006] EWHC 1730 (Comm).
23. [1998] 1 Lloyd's Rep 379, 386 CA; see also *West Tankers* v. *RAS, The Front Comor* [2005] 2 Lloyd's Rep. 257, para. 56, where Colman J. noted that "article II.3 of the New York Convention provides: 'The court of a Contracting State, when seized of an action in a matter in respect of which the parties have made an agreement within the mean-

the judge did not err in principle in granting an anti-suit injunction in protection of an agreement to arbitrate observed:

"The 1958 New York Convention on the Recognition and Enforcement of Foreign Arbitral Awards article II.3 requires the court of a Contracting State to refer the parties to arbitration when an action is commenced in disregard of a binding arbitration clause. It might be thought that there would be much to be said, both as a matter of comity and in the interests of procedural simplicity, if a defendant who was improperly sued in disregard of an arbitration agreement in the court of a country subject to the New York Convention were left to seek a stay of the proceedings in the court in question. It seems, however, that litigants in cases governed by English arbitration clauses are not prepared to trust foreign courts to stay proceedings in accordance with the New York Convention, for it has become the habit to seek anti-suit injunctions such as that sought in the present case. In *The Angelic Grace* [1995] 1 Lloyd's Rep. 87 the Court of Appeal gave its approval to this practice."

8.16 In *XL Insurance* v. *Owens Corning*[24] an insurance policy included an arbitration clause which provided for arbitration in England. The insured began proceedings in Delaware USA for recovery of sums due under the insurance and one of the insurers applied in England for an anti-suit injunction. On the question of discretion the court was mainly influenced to grant the anti-suit injunction by the breach of the arbitration agreement by the insured in commencing proceedings. The insured would not be able to join all insurers in one proceeding in one jurisdiction but that was a consequence of the agreement to arbitrate. As to comity, Toulson J. said at p. 509, the "grant of an anti-suit injunction involves by definition a degree of interference with foreign court procedures, because that is its object. But if the English Court is satisfied that litigation in another country would be a breach of contract to arbitrate the dispute in London, the grant of an injunction involves no disrespect or unfriendliness towards the foreign court, but merely an insistence on parties respecting their own contractual obligations." The fact that the foreign court would not apply an arbitration agreement was a ground for finding the foreign proceedings vexatious or oppressive.[25]

8.17 In *Goshawk* v. *QBD*[26] the claimant reinsurers commenced an arbitration in England under an arbitration clause against the reinsured based in the USA and another company, R, to which the reinsurance had been novated, on the grounds that the reinsurance had been avoided for non-disclosure and misrepresentation. At the same time reinsurers commenced proceedings in the USA against the reinsured in the USA seeking to force the reinsured to arbitrate its claims under the reinsurance, and against the reinsured's parent in tort, presumably for procuring breach of contract. R applied to intervene in the US proceedings and for an anti-arbitration injunction. Reinsurers applied in England for permission to serve out of the jurisdiction on R a claim for an injunction against pursuing the claim to intervene in the US proceedings and to pursue the anti-arbitration proceedings. The English court regarded England as the appropriate forum for the dispute and was not persuaded that R's application to intervene in the US proceedings was anything other than an opportunistic attempt to hijack the US proceedings to avoid the arbitration.

ing of this article, shall, at the request of one of the parties, refer the parties to arbitration, unless it finds that the said agreement is null and void, inoperative or incapable of being performed.' Whereas this provision identifies the duty which rests on the court seised of court proceedings to stay those proceedings and to refer the parties to arbitration, it contains nothing which vests in that court exclusive jurisdiction to enforce that arbitration agreement. In this respect the Convention crucially has no provision equivalent to Article 27 of The Brussels Regulation which vests exclusive jurisdiction in the court first seised of the issue." There was therefore no provision in the Convention equivalent to that which influenced the European Court of Justice in *Turner* v. *Grovit* to deny the ability to issue an anti-suit injunction in the context of the Brussels Regulation.

24. [2000] 2 Lloyd's Rep. 500.
25. At p. 509.
26. [2006] EWHC 1730 (Comm).

8.18 An anti-suit injunction may be granted in respect of foreign proceedings if a party has become bound by an arbitration clause because of an assignment or subrogation. In *Schiffahrtsgesellschaft Detlev von Appen GmbH* v. *Voest Alpine Intertrading GmbH (The Jay Bola)*[27] one of the issues was whether or not the owners of the vessel should be granted an anti-suit injunction against the sub-charterers and their insurers restraining them from pursuing proceedings in Brazil. Insurers argued they were not subject to an arbitration clause in the sub-charter. The court held that the subrogated insurers could only enforce their claim subject to the equities which included the arbitration agreement. By seeking to do so the insurers were acting contrary to equity and were subject to an injunction to restrain them. The availability of the anti-suit injunction did not depend on the burden of the contract being transferred to the insurers, nor on there being a claim for breach of contract against the insurers.[28] This approach has also been applied in the case of a transfer of rights under the Third Parties (Rights against Insurers) Act 1930.[29]

C. APPLICATION OF THE BRUSSELS REGULATION TO ARBITRATION DISPUTES

1. The general approach

8.19 The Brussels Regulation and its predecessors were not intended to apply to jurisdiction in relation to disputes referred to arbitration. This is because arbitration was regarded by the framers of the Brussels Convention as sufficiently regulated by other rules. Thus, the Jenard Report stated:

"There are already many international agreements on arbitration. Arbitration is, of course, referred to in Article 220 of the Treaty of Rome. Moreover, the Council of Europe has prepared a European Convention providing a uniform law on arbitration, and this will probably be accompanied by a Protocol which will facilitate the recognition and enforcement of arbitral awards to an even greater extent than the New York Convention. This is why it seemed preferable to exclude arbitration. The Brussels Convention does not apply to the recognition and enforcement of arbitral awards (see the definition in Article 25); *it does not apply for the purpose of determining the jurisdiction of courts and tribunals in respect of litigation relating to arbitration for example*, proceedings to set aside an arbitral award; and, finally, it does not apply to the recognition of judgments given in such proceedings"[30] (emphasis added).

8.20 When it came to the Schlosser report on the Brussels Convention on the accession of the UK, the experts were divided as to the answer to the related question whether or not enforcement of an award could be refused on the ground that the judgment was obtained in breach of an arbitration agreement. The report merely rehearsed the arguments on both sides:

"In support of the view that this [i.e. refusal of enforcement] would be the correct course, it is argued that since a court in the State addressed is free, contrary to the view of the court in the State of origin, to regard a dispute as affecting the status of an individual, or the law of succession, or as falling outside the scope of civil law, and therefore as being outside the scope of the 1968 Convention, it must in the same way be free to take the opposite view to that taken by the court of origin and to reject the applicability of the 1968 Convention because arbitration is involved. Against this, it is contended that the literal meaning of the word 'arbitration' itself implies that it cannot extend to every dispute affected by an arbitration agreement; that 'arbitration' refers only to arbitration proceedings. Proceedings before national courts would therefore be affected by Article 1, second paragraph, point (4) of the 1968

27. [1997] 2 Lloyd's Rep 279, CA.

28. At p. 285; see also *West Tankers* v. *RAS, The Front Comor* [2005] 2 Lloyd's Rep. 257, 269.

29. *The Padre Island (No. 1)* [1984] 2 Lloyd's Rep. 408, 414; *The Padre Island (No. 2)* [1990] 2 Lloyd's Rep. 191, 200; *cf. Through Transport Mutual* v. *New India Assurance Co.* [2005] 1 Lloyd's Rep. 67, para. 94; *West Tankers* v. *RAS, The Front Comor* [2005] 2 Lloyd's Rep. 257, 269.

30. 1979 OJ C.59/1, 13.

Convention only if they dealt with arbitration as a main issue and did not have to consider the validity of an arbitration agreement merely as a matter incidental to an examination of the competence of the court of origin to assume jurisdiction. It has been contended that the court in the State addressed can no longer re-open the issue of classification; if the court of the State of origin, in assuming jurisdiction, has taken a certain view as to the applicability of the 1968 Convention, this becomes binding on the court in the State addressed."[31]

2. The provisions of the Brussels Regulation

8.21 Article 1 of the Brussels Regulation states that the regulation applies to "civil and commercial matters whatever the nature of the court or tribunal". However, under Article 2:

"2. The Regulation shall not apply to:
...(d) arbitration."

8.22 Thus, the exclusion of the Regulation in the case of arbitration is clearly – even tersely – expressed. It is also clear that the exclusion is a fundamental one, albeit one with limits, as shall be seen.[32] Given the considerations described above, the legal protection granted to those domiciled in the EU in relation to civil and commercial matters is not to be extended to them in relation to arbitration, such matters being regulated elsewhere.

8.23 The Brussels Regulation does not apply to the enforcement of arbitral awards (Article 32).

8.24 Where the Brussels Regulation does not apply, by reason of the foregoing provisions, English municipal law (specifically, the 1996 Act and the common law) will apply.

8.25 Unfortunately, despite the apparent clarity of Article 2(d), a number of difficult questions arise as to the scope of this exclusion. In particular, the following questions fall for consideration:

(1) Does the Brussels Regulation apply where there is a dispute about whether or not an arbitration agreement was made in the first place or whether that agreement is binding?
(2) Is the Brussels Regulation excluded even where the arbitration question at issue is incidental only?
(3) Does the Brussels Regulation apply to determine priority in arbitration matters where more than one court is seised?

As will be seen, the exclusion is wide in the sense that it applies even where there is a dispute about whether or not an arbitration agreement was made or is binding. However, the exclusion only applies where a matter is principally concerned with arbitration (including applications ancillary to arbitration) and not where the matter only incidentally concerns arbitration. There also remains some doubt as to whether or not a court second seised may decide the issue, and as to whether or not it may issue an anti-suit injunction against proceedings in a Contracting State. Where the Brussels Regulation is not excluded, it applies to contracts made and proceedings commenced after 1 March 2002. These questions are considered in turn below.

3. What if the dispute is whether or not an arbitration agreement was made or is binding?

8.26 The exclusion extends to proceedings in which there is a dispute about whether or not an arbitration agreement had been made at all. As has been described,[33] the Jenard Report clearly took the view that disputes as to the arbitration agreement itself fell within the scope of the Article 2(d) exclusion.

31. 1979 OJ C.59/71, 92.
32. See para. 8.30 below.
33. Para. 8.20 above.

8.27 In one of the first cases on the ambit of the identically worded arbitration exclusion in Article 1.2 of the Brussels Convention, *Marc Rich & Co AG* v. *Societa Italiana Impianti PA (The Atlantic Emperor)*,[34] Swiss buyers of oil claimed damages from the Italian sellers for contamination. There was a dispute about whether or not a London arbitration clause had been incorporated into the contract. The sellers began court proceedings in Italy for a declaration of no liability. The buyers then started arbitration proceedings in London and applied to the London court for an order appointing an arbitrator. The European Court of Justice first rejected the claim that the arbitration exclusion was confined to the proceedings before an arbitral tribunal. The exclusion must be interpreted as excluding "arbitration in its entirety, including proceedings before national courts" (para. 18).

8.28 In other words, the code for jurisdiction set out in the Brussels Regulation does not apply to court proceedings covered by the exclusion of "arbitration". The primary reason was that, as the Jenard report explained, the reason why the Contracting States excluded arbitration from the Brussels Convention was because there were already international agreements which applied to arbitration which had to be respected by national courts (including in particular the New York Convention – para. 8.19 above). The court gave effect to that intention by interpreting the exclusion as applying to court proceedings relating to arbitration.[35] The court also rejected an argument that there was a preliminary issue in relation to the buyer's application for the appointment of an arbitrator which was whether or not the contract included an arbitration agreement at all, and that this preliminary issue was within the Convention and not within the arbitration exclusion. The court held that the arbitration exclusion applied if the subject-matter of the dispute was arbitration, even if resolving that dispute would involve deciding a preliminary issue whatever that issue might be (para. 26). It would be contrary to legal certainty if the application of the exclusion varied according to the existence of preliminary issues which might be raised at any time.

8.29 The result was that the buyers were not prevented by the Brussels Convention (in particular the requirement that the court second seised decline jurisdiction) from going on to establish jurisdiction against the sellers under the common law.[36]

4. Incidental questions

8.30 The *Atlantic Emperor* concerned an application for a court order for the appointment of an arbitrator which was within the exclusion. But is any matter relating to an arbitration within the exclusion? The answer is that a distinction is to be drawn between matters which are principally concerned with arbitration and those where arbitration is a subsidiary matter. The origins of the point are in *Jenard* (p. 10): "However, matters falling outside the scope of the Convention do so only if they constitute the principal subject-matter of the proceedings. They are thus not excluded when they come before the court as a subsidiary matter either in the main proceedings or in preliminary proceedings." The Evrigenis/Kerameus report on the

34. C-190/89, [1991] ECR I-3855; [1991] 1 Lloyd's Rep. 342; C-391/95 *Van Uden* v. *Deco-Line* [1998] ECR I-7091 at [31].

35. See *Jenard*, 1979 OJ C.59/1, 13, and p. 1 and para. 18 of the judgment. M. Jenard had in fact given a contrary view in an expert report served for the buyers in the *Atlantic Emperor* case but this was rejected by the Advocate General and not followed by the European Court of Justice: see *Through Transport Mutual* v. *New India Assurance Co.* [2005] 1 Lloyd's Rep. 67 at [27].

36. In fact, the Italian court later held that the arbitration clause was void, but the English Court of Appeal rejected the buyer's claim to an anti-suit injunction because the buyers had submitted to the jurisdiction in Italy by presenting a defence: *Marc Rich & Co. AG* v. *Societa Italiana Impianti PA (The Atlantic Emperor) (No. 2)* [1992] 1 Lloyd's Rep. 624; *Navigacion Maritime Bulgare* v. *Rustlan Trading Limited and others (The "Ivan Zagubanski")* [2002] 1 Lloyd's Rep. 106; *cf. Partenreederei* v. *Grosvenor* [1994] 2 Lloyd's Rep. 287.

accession of Greece to the Brussels Convention also expressed the view that proceedings which are directly concerned with arbitration as their principal issue were excluded from the Convention, such as cases where the court is instrumental in setting up the arbitration body, however, "verification, as an incidental question, of the validity of an arbitration agreement which is cited by a litigant in order to contest the jurisdiction of the court before which he is being sued pursuant to the Convention, must be considered as falling within its scope".[37]

8.31 The European Court of Justice has therefore distinguished between types of claims involving arbitration which fall within the exclusion and those which do not. Claims will only be excluded if "the relief sought in the action can fairly be said to be ancillary to, or perhaps an integral part of, the arbitration process".[38] For this purpose: "the essential subject-matter of a dispute has to be categorised and ... for the purpose of such categorisation a dispute is not to be casually categorised as relating to arbitration merely because what is really a question of construction relates to an arbitration clause."[39]

8.32 It has also been said that the exclusion applies if the "principal focus" of the claim is arbitration.[40] The exclusion therefore applies to proceedings concerning the validity or existence of an arbitration agreement; the appointment of arbitrators; ancillary assistance to arbitration proceedings and the recognition and enforcement of awards.[41] The English courts have held that a claim for an anti-suit injunction is within the exclusion (see below). If the claim relates to a contract which contains an arbitration clause but makes no mention of it or seeks any relief related to an arbitration the claim will not be within the exclusion. A claim against a third party broker is not an integral part of the arbitration process and not within the exception.[42]

5. Priority in arbitration matters where more than one court is seised[43]

8.33 If the party intending to pursue foreign court proceedings has not yet commenced those proceedings, the party seeking arbitration in England may simply proceed to establish jurisdiction under English municipal law. However, if foreign proceedings have already been commenced in a Contracting State, must the English court stay or decline jurisdiction in favour of the court first seised where the cause of action is the same or the actions are related (Articles 27 and 28), or can it make its own decision about the application of the arbitration exclusion? If the English court does decide that the arbitration exclusion applies can it grant an anti-suit injunction against a party domiciled in a Member State?

37. *Evrigenis/Kerameus*, p. 10.

38. *Union de Remorquage et de Sauvetage SA* v. *Lake Avery, The Lake Avery* [1997] 1 Lloyd's Rep. 540, 548, Clarke J.

39. *The Xing Su Hai* [1995] 2 Lloyd's Rep. 15, 21, Rix J.; *Lexmar Corporation and The Steamship Mutual* [1997] 1 Lloyd's Rep. 289, where an application to enforce a compromise agreement on costs relating to arbitration was not within the exclusion.

40. *Navigacion Maritime Bulgare* v. *Rustlan Trading Limited and others (The "Ivan Zagubanski")* [2002] 1 Lloyd's Rep. 106, 118, Aikens J.

41. *Navigacion Maritime Bulgare* v. *Rustlan Trading Limited and others (The "Ivan Zagubanski")* [2002] 1 Lloyd's Rep. 106, 118, Aikens J.; *Union de Remorquage et de Sauvetage SA* v. *Lake Avery, The Lake Avery* [1997] 1 Lloyd's Rep. 540; *Toepfer* v. *Cargill* [1997] 2 Lloyd's Rep. 98, Colman J., referred to European Court of Justice by the CA [1998] 1 WLR 379, where a claim relating to whether or not a dispute had to go to arbitration was within the exclusion.

42. *The Xing Su Hai* [1995] 2 Lloyd's Rep. 15; *Vale do Rio* v. *Bao Steel* [2000] 2 Lloyd's Rep. 3, 5.

43. Beraudo, "The Arbitration Exception of the Brussels and Lugano Conventions; Jurisdiction Recognition and Enforcement of Judgments" in *Journal of International Arbitration* 2001, 13; Haersolte-van Hof, "The Arbitration Exception In The Brussels Convention" in *Journal of International Arbitration* 2001, 27; Ambrose, "Arbitration and the Free Movement of Judgments" in *Arbitration International* (2003) Vol. 19, 3.

8.34 In the *Atlantic Emperor* (para. 8.27 above) the European Court of Justice appears to have assumed that it was open to the English court to decide whether or not the arbitration exception applied, and, if it did, to decide jurisdiction under national conflicts rules, even though proceedings for a declaration of no liability had already been commenced in Italy by the sellers.[44] The outcome of a number of English cases has depended on this decision.[45] However, it will be remembered that in *Erich Gasser GmbH* v. *Misat Srl*[46] (para. 5.280 above) the European Court of Justice has recently held that the *lis pendens* provision in Article 27 overrode an exclusive jurisdiction clause under Article 23. In summary, the European Court of Justice based its interpretation on the need for legal certainty (avoiding inconsistent decisions of different courts) and trust in the courts of other Contracting States. Even if the existence of the exclusive jurisdiction agreement was in dispute the court second seised must await the decision of the court first seised. And in *Turner* v. *Grovit*[47] the European Court of Justice also held that an anti-suit injunction is inconsistent with the Brussels Regulation, and, in particular, the necessity for mutual trust between the courts of Member States (para. 5.285 above). However, in *Through Transport Mutual* v. *New India Assurance Co.*[48] the Court of Appeal held the *lis pendens* provision did not apply to the exclusion for arbitration even though it applied to an exclusive jurisdiction agreement. In essence, insurers ("the Club") of insolvent carriers claimed in London court proceedings a declaration of non-liability and an anti-suit injunction against the defendant insurers ("New India") of shippers in respect of a claim for lost goods. New India had already started Finnish proceedings against the Club relying on a Finnish statute which gave it the right to proceed directly against the insurers where the defendant was insolvent (not unlike the Third Party (Rights against Insurers) Act 1930). Although the insurance policy issued by the Club contained a London arbitration clause the Finnish court held that it had jurisdiction because neither the Club nor New India was a party to the arbitration agreement.

8.35 The Court of Appeal did not uphold the grant of an anti-suit injunction on the facts but was of the view that an anti-suit injunction could be granted where proceedings were commenced in a Member State in breach of an arbitration clause. It held that there was a crucial distinction between an arbitration clause and an exclusive jurisdiction clause: in *Gasser* it had been common ground that the claims in both courts were within the Brussels Convention and governed by Articles 21 and 22 (Articles 27 and 28 of the Brussels Regulation); whereas in *Through Transport* the issue was whether the court proceedings in England for a declaration and anti-suit injunction were within the Convention or not. The Court of Appeal also drew support from arguments of the Advocate General and the reasons of the court in the *Atlantic Emperor*.

8.36 The decision by the Court of Appeal has the merit of deterring parties from deliberately delaying arbitration by quickly seeking a declaration of no liability in a favourable forum (para. 5.282 above), and is in line with the result in the *Atlantic Emperor*. It is, however, doubtful that the European Court of Justice will agree with the decision when called upon to decide

44. Although the question of stay under Article 22 of the Brussels Convention was one of the questions before the European Court of Justice (para. 9 of the judgment) the European Court of Justice decided that the question did not arise once it had decided that the arbitration exclusion applied (para. 30). See articles at Merkin (Arbitration), pp. 1–30, n. 4.

45. See the detailed analysis by Aikens J. in *Navigacion Maritime Bulgare* v. *Rustlan Trading Limited and others (The "Ivan Zagubanski")* [2002] 1 Lloyd's Rep. 106. See also *Partenreederei* v. *Grosvenor* [1994] 2 Lloyd's Rep. 287; *Union de Remorquage et de Sauvetage SA* v. *Lake Avery Inc. (The "Lake Avery")* [1997] 1 Lloyd's Rep 540, 550.

46. Case C-116/02; [2004] 1 Lloyd's Rep. 222.

47. C-159/02, [2004] ECR I-3656, [2005] 1 AC 101.

48. [2005] 1 Lloyd's Rep. 67; followed in *West Tankers* v *RAS, The Front Comor* [2005] 2 Lloyd's Rep. 257, Colman J.; Hill, "Anti-suit injunction and arbitration" in LMCLQ (2006) 166–171.

the issue.[49] The point was apparently not the subject of debate in the European Court of Justice in the *Atlantic Emperor*. More recently, the approach of the European Court of Justice in *Gasser* and *Turner* v. *Grovit* has been that where the Brussels Regulation applies the court first seised is in the best position to decide its own jurisdiction and, moreover, should be trusted to do so by the courts of other Contracting States, regardless of the dangers of forum shopping. The approach in *Gasser* also avoids the problems of inconsistent decisions. There is also a possibility following *Van Uden* v. *Deco-Line*[50] that an anti-suit injunction is not ancillary to arbitration proceedings and not within the arbitration exception (see, generally, para. 8.30 above). In the meantime, Colman J. followed the decision of the Court of Appeal in *West Tankers* v. *RAS, The Front Comor*,[51] but a direct appeal is pending to the House of Lords.

49. Merkin (Arbitration), para. 8.85.
50. C-391/95, [1998] ECR I-7091.
51. [2005] 2 Lloyd's Rep. 257.

PART 3

CHOICE OF LAW

CHAPTER 9

LEGAL REGIMES DETERMINING CHOICE OF LAW

A. INTRODUCTION

9.1 In contracts, the will of the parties is unsurprisingly accorded substantial pre-eminence, and the choice of law rules applicable to contractual questions are no exception. As will be seen, the various treaties and directives applicable to contracts of insurance and reinsurance accord primacy to the contractual will of the parties, as does the common law, when applicable.

9.2 An important anterior question is the source of the parties' autonomy. Is the source of the parties' ability to choose the law governing their contract simply based upon their will or is the parties' autonomy confined to selecting from amongst the options offered by a particular system of municipal law? If the latter is the case, then a further question arises: *which* system of municipal law is applicable?

9.3 In an article lamenting the coming into force of the Contracts (Applicable Law) Act 1990,[1] the late Dr F. A. Mann debated whether the unfortunate consequences of the 1990 Act could be avoided by contracting parties agreeing that the applicable law should be "English law excluding the Act of 1990". Clearly, if choice of law is simply based upon the parties' will, such a choice ought to be given effect to. If, however, the choice of the parties must be based upon the conflicts rules of a particular legal system, then the parties' freedom of choice may be restricted by that system. It may very well be that English law would not give effect to the sort of choice of law contemplated by Dr Mann.

9.4 The prevailing view is that the parties' choice is subject to municipal law, and that the parties' choice can therefore be fettered. This is the prevailing view, not only in England but generally.[2] Indeed, this is the only way of explaining why it is not possible to specify a "floating" applicable law (i.e. a proper law chosen at a time later than the commencement of the contract).[3]

9.5 The relevant municipal law is the law of the forum.[4]

9.6 In English law, the process of determining which law is the proper law involves three stages.[5] First, it is necessary to characterise the issue that is before the court, e.g. is the question regarding the interpretation of a contract. Secondly, the court must identify the "connecting factor" for the issue in question. The connecting factor is the rule of (English) conflict laws that ties the issue before the court to a particular legal system. Thirdly, having identified the connecting factor, the court must apply it so as to identify the applicable legal system.

1. F. Mann, "The Proper Law of the Contract – An Obituary" (1991) 107 LQR 353.

2. As to England, see: *Amin Rasheed Shipping Corporation* v. *Kuwait Insurance Corporation* [1984] AC 50, 61, 65 (*per* Lord Diplock); *El du Pont de Nemours* v. *Agnew* [1987] 2 Lloyd's Rep. 585 (*per* Bingham LJ); North (1993), pp. 185–186; Dicey/Morris/Collins, paras 32-062–32-065. Generally, see Kahn-Freund, pp. 195–196; Nygh, pp. 31–32.

3. As to this, see the authorities cited at para. 10.60 below.

4. As to England, see: *El du Pont de Nemours* v. *Agnew* [1987] 2 Lloyd's Rep. 585 (*per* Bingham LJ). Generally, see Kahn-Freund, p. 197.

5. *MacMillan Inc.* v. *Bishopsgate Investment Trust plc (No. 3)* [1996] 1 WLR 387, 391–392 (*per* Staughton LJ).

9.7 In an ideal world, the answers obtained in these three stages would be the same, in whatever country they were determined.[6] These days, as we have seen (paras 2.77–2.99 above) choice of law questions relating to contracts of insurance and reinsurance are largely governed by treaty and directive in order to achieve a harmonisation of the conflict of law rules applied across the nations of the European Union. Short of harmonising the substantive laws themselves, this is the best way of ensuring that the same outcome occurs whatever the jurisdiction: if each state adopts the same choice of law rules, then the same substantive law should be applied to the case, whatever that substantive law may be.

9.8 The Rome Convention on the Law Applicable to Contractual Obligations ("the Rome Convention") and various EC Directives on Insurance ("the insurance directives") are the instruments whereby such harmony is sought to be introduced. As is the case in relation to the various regimes applicable to jurisdiction, together they make up a complicated patchwork of regulation, which – with some exceptions – will apply to determine all choice of law questions arising out of contracts of insurance and reinsurance, thus leaving the common law with a residual, and peripheral, role. The process of answering a choice of law question in the context of insurance and reinsurance must begin by identifying the applicable legal regime. This question is considered in the next section.

B. IDENTIFYING THE APPLICABLE REGIME

1. Overview

9.9 The various regimes draw a fundamental distinction between contracts of insurance and contracts of reinsurance. Provided the contract of reinsurance was concluded on or after 1 April 1991, the Rome Convention will apply. Contracts of reinsurance concluded before that date will be governed by the common law.

9.10 So far as contracts of insurance are concerned, the Rome Convention will only apply to contracts of insurance covering risks situated outside the territories of the Member States of the European Union. Again, where such contracts were concluded before 1 April 1991, the common law will apply.

9.11 As regards contracts of insurance covering risks situated in the territories of the Member States of the European Union, the Insurance Directives will apply. These distinguish between contracts of "general insurance" (or "non-life insurance") and contracts of "long-term insurance" (or "life insurance"). The Directives will apply to non-life insurance entered into after 1 July 1990[7] and life insurance entered into after 20 May 1993.[8] Contracts concluded before those dates will be governed by the common law.

9.12 A flow diagram, identifying which regime applies when, is shown in Appendix 2.1. In the following sections, the Rome Convention will first be considered, and then the Insurance Directives.

2. Scope of the Rome Convention

9.13 The Rome Convention applies to "contractual obligations" in any situation involving a choice between the laws of different countries. The basic question of what is a contract has already been considered in the context of Article 5(1) of the Brussels Regulation (which

6. See Staughton LJ in *MacMillan Inc.* v. *Bishopsgate Investment Trust plc (No. 3)* [1996] 1 WLR 387, 391–392.

7. The choice of law rules in the Second Non-Life Directive 1988 were initially implemented into English law by the Insurance Companies (Amendment) Regulations 1990 (SI 1990/1333) which entered into force on 1 July 1990.

8. The choice of law rules in the Second Life Directive 1990 were initially implemented into English law by the Insurance Companies (Amendment) Regulations 1993 (SI 1993/174) which entered into force on 20 May 1993.

confers jurisdiction in matters relating to contract – see paras 5.140–5.173 below). As we have already seen in a number of areas in the context of jurisdiction this is a question of characterisation which depends ultimately on community law rather than any individual national law. The key feature of a "contract" is a voluntary agreement giving rise to obligations capable of being enforced by law.[9] It is unlikely that an issue will often arise in reinsurances cases as to whether the reinsurance agreement itself is contractual – it almost certainly will be – although as we will see issues can arise in relation to third parties. Much more difficult is the question of whether the law applicable to that contract will govern issues such as misrepresentation, breach of warranty, subrogation and assignment (these issues will be considered further in para. 9.36 below).

9.14 The rules of the Rome Convention apply "in any situation involving a choice between the laws of different countries": their application is *not* limited to international contracts. Thus the rules apply to a contract of reinsurance concluded between a New York insurer and a New York reinsurers but containing an English choice of law clause. Indeed, if the proceedings arose before the English courts, the Rome Convention would apply to the same contract even if it had a New York choice of law.[10] "Countries" includes for these purposes each territorial unit of a state where each unit has its own rules of law in respect of contractual obligations (Article 19). Thus, and by virtue of section 2(3) of the 1990 Act, the Convention applies where an English court is determining whether Scots law is applicable and vice versa. An English court will similarly apply the Convention in determining whether Jersey law is applicable, although in this case the converse is not the case.

9.15 As we have seen, the Rome Convention applies to *some* contracts of insurance and all contracts of reinsurance, provided of course these contracts were concluded on or after 1 April 1991.[11] Article 1(3) provides:

> "The rules of this Convention do not apply to contracts of insurance which cover risks situated in the territories of the member states of the European Economic Community. In order to determine whether a risk is situated in those territories the court shall apply its internal law."

Thus, the Rome Convention applies to contracts of insurance which cover risks situated outside the territories of the Member States.[12]

9.16 The Rome Convention applies to contracts of reinsurance (Article 1(4)). It does so in a curiously negative way. Article 1(3) provides that "the rules of this Convention do not apply to contracts of insurance which cover risks situated in the territories of the Member States of the European Economic Community". Article 1(4) then goes on to provide that "the preceding paragraph does not apply to contracts of reinsurance".

9.17 What, for purposes of the Convention, is a contract of insurance and a contract of reinsurance? By reference to what rules are such issues is determined? The Convention contains no definition, either of "insurance" or "reinsurance". Although, in many cases, it will be very clear whether a contract is one of insurance or reinsurance, this is by no means always the case. Thus, for instance, it may be difficult to distinguish a contract of insurance from a performance bond, guarantee contract or other contracts of indemnity.[13] Equally, it may be debatable whether a policy is one of insurance or reinsurance.[14]

9. See paras 5.140–5.144 above and Plender/Wilderstein, paras 3-09–3-14.
10. See further, Plender/Wilderstein, paras 3-01–3-104 and 3-15–3-18.
11. See para. 2.89 above.
12. As to the position of EEA States, see para. 11.1 below
13. As to this, see *Clarke*, paras 1-1 and 1-2A.
14. One example of potential difficulty, is the question of stop-loss policies, which Hobhouse LJ considered in *Toomey* v. *Eagle Star Insurance Ltd* [1994] 1 Lloyd's Rep. 516.

9.18 The answer, in this case, lies in the Insurance Directives. As will be seen, the implementation of these Directives into English law involves detailed definitions of what constitutes a "contract of insurance"[15] and, within that definition, what is a contract of general insurance[16] and what is a contract of long-term insurance.[17] As a matter of construction, it will not only be permissible, but obligatory, to refer to these definitions (which are considered below).

9.19 It is clear that when determining whether a risk is situated within the territory of a Member State, the court applies its own internal law,[18] without *renvoi*.[19]

3. The Insurance Directives

(i) The meaning of "general" and "long-term" insurance

9.20 The definitions of general and long-term insurance applicable in English law are to be found, not in the Financial Services and Markets Act 2000 (Law Applicable to Contracts of Insurance) Regulations 2001,[20] but in another order made under the Financial Services and Markets Act 2000, the Financial Services and Markets Act 2000 (Regulated Activities) Order 2001.[21]

9.21 The Regulated Activities Order 2001 defines a "contract of insurance" as[22]:

"... any contract of insurance which is a contract of long-term insurance or a contract of general insurance, and includes –

(a) fidelity bonds, performance bonds, administration bonds, bail bonds, customs bonds or similar contracts of guarantee, where these are:
  (i) effected or carried out by a person not carrying on a banking business;
  (ii) effected not merely incidentally to some other business carried on by the person effecting them; and
  (iii) effected in return for the payment of one or more premiums;

(b) tontines;

(c) capital redemption contracts or pension fund management contracts, where these are effected or carried out by a person who –
  (i) does not carry on a banking business; and
  (ii) otherwise carries on a regulated activity of the kind specified by Article 10(1) or (2);

(d) contracts to pay annuities on human life;

(e) contracts of a kind referred to in Article 1(2) (e)of the first life insurance directive (collective insurance etc); and

(f) contracts of a kind referred to in Article 1(3) of the first life insurance directive (social insurance); ..."

but does not include a funeral plan contract (or a contract which would be a funeral plan contract but for the exclusion in Article 60).

9.22 Contracts of general insurance and contracts of long-term insurance are comprehensively defined in Parts I and II of Schedule 1 to the Regulated Activities Order 2001.[23] Thus, Part I lists the following as contracts of general insurance:

15. See para. 9.21 below.
16. See para. 9.22 below.
17. See para. 9.23 below.
18. Article 1(3).
19. Article 15 provides that if the application of a certain law is specified by the Convention, the court applies the rules of law in force in that country other than its rules of private international law. Thus the English court ignores the question of what substantive law the courts of that country would apply to the dispute.
20. See the definitions of "contract of general insurance" and "contract of long-term insurance" in Regulation 2, which refer on to the Financial Services and Markets Act 2000 (Regulated Activities) Order 2001, SI 2001/544.
21. SI 2001/544.
22. Regulation 3(1).
23. Regulation 3(1) contains definitions referring on to these Parts of Schedule 1.

- accident and sickness insurance;
- insurance against loss of or damage to vehicles used on land and to railway rolling stock;
- insurance upon aircraft and ships;
- insurance against loss of or damage to goods in transit;
- insurance against loss of or damage to property due to fire, natural forces and other events;
- liability insurance;
- credit insurance, suretyship and other forms of financial loss insurance;
- legal expenses insurance and travel assistance insurance.

These categories are specifically defined; and reference should be made to the precise terms of the Regulation, which is set out at Appendix 2.6.

9.23 Part II lists the following as contracts of long-term insurance:

- life insurance and annuities;
- insurance providing for payment on marriage or birth;
- linked long-term insurance;
- permanent health insurance;
- tontines;
- capital redemption contracts;
- pension fund management contracts;
- collective insurance;
- social insurance.

Again, these categories are specifically defined in the Regulations, set out at Appendix 2.6.

(ii) Contracts of general insurance

9.24 These are governed by Part II of the Regulations. This Part applies only to a contract of general insurance which covers risks situated in an EEA State.[24]

9.25 The reference to an EEA State means a state which is a contracting party to the agreement dated 2 May 1992 (adjusted by a protocol dated 17 March 1993) extending the EU internal market to Norway, Ireland and Liechtenstein. The agreement was implemented into English law by the European Economic Area Act 1993 (see para. 2.59 above).[25]

9.26 Where a risk is situated is described by Regulation 2(2), which provides:

"References to the EEA State where the risk covered by a contract of insurance is situated are to –

(a) if the contract relates to buildings and their contents (in so far as the contents are covered by the same contract of insurance), the EEA State in which the property is situated;

(b) if the contract relates to vehicles of any type, the EEA State of registration;

(c) if the contract covers travel or holiday risks and has a duration of four months or less, the EEA State in which the policyholder entered into the contract;

(d) in any other case –

(i) if the policyholder is an individual, the EEA State in which he resides on the date the contract is entered into;

(ii) otherwise, the EEA State in which the establishment of the policyholder to which the contract relates is situated on that date."

(iii) Contracts of long-term insurance

9.27 These are governed by Part III of the Regulations. This Part applies only to a contract of long-term insurance if:

24. Regulation 4(1).

25. Financial Services and Markets Act 2000, Schedule 3, para. 8.

(i) where the policyholder is an individual, he resides in an EEA State;
(ii) otherwise, the establishment of the policyholder to which the contract relates is situated in an EEA State.

C. LIMITS TO THE APPLICABLE REGIME

9.28 Having identified the applicable regime, the next step is to identify which provision in the Rome Convention or, as the case may be, the Insurance Directives, applies. This provision will then serve to identify the applicable law or laws. However, it must not be assumed that the Rome Convention or, as the case may be, the Insurance Directives, will govern every contractual question arising out of a contract of insurance or reinsurance.

1. The Rome Convention

9.29 The Rome Convention provides that it shall apply "to contractual obligations in any situation involving a choice between the laws of different countries" (Article 1(1)). Clearly, in a dispute relating to or arising out of a contract of insurance, it is very likely that this will involve "contractual obligations" and that the Rome Convention will therefore apply (see paras 5.140–5.144 above). But how far does this go? Does it, for instance, extend to the right to avoid for misrepresentation or non-disclosure?

9.30 We will consider these issues in the rational order in which they arise when considering issues arising out of a contract, namely:

- capacity;
- material validity;
- formal validity;
- interpretation;
- performance;
- damages;
- extinction of obligations;
- limitation;
- procedure.

(i) Capacity

9.31 Capacity is generally excluded from the scope of the Rome Convention.[26] The exception is the rule contained in Article 11 of the Convention, which provides:

"In a contract concluded between persons who are in the same country, a natural person who would have had capacity under the law of that country may invoke his incapacity resulting from another law only if the other party to the contract was aware of this incapacity at the time of the conclusion of the contract or was not aware thereof as a result of negligence."

9.32 The rule in Article 11 applies only to natural persons and so is not going to be relevant to contracts of reinsurance. However, it is of relevance to contracts of insurance, insofar as these fall within the scope of the Rome Convention.

(ii) Material validity

9.33 Article 8(1) provides:

"The existence and validity of a contract, or of any term of a contract, shall be determined by the law which would govern it under this Convention if the contract or term were valid."

26. Article 1(2)(a).

9.34 This provision is similar to the approach of the common law.[27] But the position may be complicated when it is alleged that the contract contains an express choice of law. For example, an English company offers to enter a reinsurance with a German reinsurance company on terms which include an express English choice of law clause. Although the purchaser purports to withdraw the offer before the reinsurer replies, the reinsurer accepts the offer. Under English law the revocation is effective, but what would be the position if under German law it was not? There appear to be two possible approaches:

(1) look at the contract as a single entity, including the alleged choice of law clause. The contract, if it exists would be governed by English law, therefore there is no contract; alternatively

(2) consider first the alleged choice of law. Under English law there is no effective agreement as to choice. Thus the putative proper law as regards the remainder of the contract is then decided according to Article 4 (that is the rules which apply in the absence of an express choice) which is likely to be German law. Under German law there is a valid contract.

The first approach appears to be the simpler solution. Although it may allow the parties to pull themselves up by their own bootstraps, any potential unfairness, particularly in relation to consent, is dealt with by Article 8(2) which is considered further below.[28]

9.35 Article 8(1) will govern questions of offer and acceptance, i.e. whether the parties have reached an agreement at all. This goes to the existence of a contract. Questions going to the validity of a contract will include: whether consideration is required, and whether there was an intention to create legal relations.

9.36 More difficult is the question whether invalidating factors – for instance, whether a contract is void for mistake or voidable for misrepresentation or non-disclosure – fall within the scope of Article 8(1). The problem is that such questions arise independently of the contract[29] and (particularly in the context of misrepresentation) can generate rights and remedies which clearly are not contract, e.g. the right to claim damages for negligent misrepresentation.[30] As we have seen, under the Brussels Regulation, such issues (provided they are in issue) are clearly regarded as "matters relating to a contract" under Article 5(1)(a).[31] The issue of whether a contract is void or voidable for whatever reason is, however, intuitively contractual in character and at common law there is authority for application of the proper law.[32] The better view is that such matters fall within the scope of Article 8(1).

9.37 There is a proviso to Article 8(1), contained in Article 8(2) that:

27. *Amin Rasheed Shipping Corp.* v. *Kuwait Insurance Co.* [1984] AC 50.

28. Cheshire/North, p. 588. *Cf.* Clarkson/Hill, p. 208 advocating the second of the alternative solutions.

29. See Chitty, chaps 5 and 6, and in particular, para. 6-001 in relation to misrepresentation.

30. Under s.2(1) of the Misrepresentation Act 1967. Similarly in the context of mistake, mistake may also entitle a party who has paid money under the mistake to recover it back in an action for money had and received (see Chitty, para. 5-004).

31. See, for instance, *Agnew* v. *Länsförsäkringsbolagens AB* [2001] 1 AC 223; *Kleinwort Benson Ltd* v. *Glasgow City Council* [1999] 1 AC 153 and the discussion at paras 5.165–5.173 above. Although different considerations may apply where it is alleged that the contract is void *ab initio*.

32. Yeo, para. 7.88, and *Mackender* v. *Feldia AG* [1967] 2 QB 590, where the claimant was seeking a declaration that an insurance contract was voidable for non-disclosure because of a failure to disclose alleged smuggling activities. It was held that the question of whether the insurer was entitled to repudiate must be determined by the proper law of the policy. See also *Halpern* v. *Halpern* [2006] EWHC 603 (Com), where it was assumed that the proper law of the compromise agreement governed questions of duress and mutual mistake. The reasoning in *Gan Insurance Co. Ltd* v. *Tai Ping Insurance Co. Ltd* [1999] I L Pr 729, is also consistent with the duty of disclose being governed by the proper law of the contract.

"... a party may rely upon the law of the country in which he has his habitual residence to establish that he did not consent if it appears from the circumstances that it would not be reasonable to determine the effect of his conduct in accordance with the law specified in the preceding paragraph."

An example of the situation Article 8(2) is intended to deal with is where a natural person[33] does not respond to an offer made by an insurance company.[34] If, under the law that governs the contract according to Article 8(1), silence is sufficient, then the offeree – apart from the operation of Article 8(2) – will be bound even where the law of the place of his residence interprets his silence as a rejection of the offer. Article 8(2) gives judges a discretion to apply the law of the party's country of residence, although the judge is not bound to do so.[35]

(iii) Formal validity

9.38 Article 9 provides:

"1. A contract concluded between persons who are in the same country is formally valid if it satisfies the formal requirements of the law which governs it under this Convention or of the law of the country where it is concluded.

2. A contract concluded between persons who are in different countries is formally valid if it satisfies the formal requirements of the law which governs it under this Convention or of the law of one of those countries.

3. Where a contract is concluded by an agent, the country in which the agent acts is the relevant country for the purposes of paragraphs 1 and 2."

9.39 Formal validity, according to the Giuliano-Lagarde Report includes "every external manifestation required on the part of a person expressing the will to be legally bound, and in the absence of which such expression of will would not be regarded as fully effective".[36]

9.40 Like Article 8, this Article applies the law which governs the contract under the Rome Convention. But Articles 9(1) and 9(2) also contain references to other laws. Unlike the proviso in Article 8(2), however, these other laws do not serve to render a contract that would otherwise be valid, invalid, but vice versa. Even if a contract is not formally valid under the law governing it, it will nevertheless be formally valid if valid according to the applicable law or the law of the country where the contract was concluded or, if different, the law of the country where either of the parties was when the contract was concluded. Article 9 is very liberal with the result that formal validity will rarely cause a contract to be invalidated.[37]

9.41 Where a contract is concluded by an agent, the country in which the agent acts is the relevant country for the purposes of Article 9.

(iv) Interpretation

9.42 Article 10(1)(a) makes clear that the Convention extends to questions of interpretation.

33. The use of the words "habitual residence" make it clear that the proviso is not intended to apply to corporations. *Cf.* Clarkson/Hill, p. 208.

34. Contracts of reinsurance are unlikely to involve natural persons.

35. See, for example, *Egon Oldendorff* v. *Liberia Corporation* [1995] 2 Lloyd's Rep. 64.

36. *Giuliano-Lagarde*, 1980 OJ C.282/1, 29.

37. The Green Paper considers whether a provision is needed to deal with cases where it is not possible to determine the place where the contractual intention was expressed. This might be a problem with email contracts in particular (para. 3.2.12.3). To facilitate the formal validity of contracts further, the proposed Rome I Regulation provides that a contract is also valid if it satisfies the law of the country in which one or other of the parties has his habitual residence at the time the contract is concluded (Article 10).

(v) Performance

9.43 Article 10(1)(b) makes clear that the Convention extends to questions of performance. Questions such as where payments are to be made,[38] and any time limit within which a claim must be made will all be determined by the applicable law.[39] Other matters covered are the diligence with which the obligation must be performed, the extent to which the obligation can be performed by another person, conditions of performance of the obligation in the case of joint and several or alternative obligations.[40]

9.44 Once again, there is a gloss to this rule. Article 10(2) provides:

"In relation to the manner of performance and the steps to be taken in the event of defective performance regard shall be had to the laws of the country in which performance takes place."

9.45 This provision was intended to cover minor details of performance such as the currency of payment and the date at which lay days (in charterparties re loading, etc) begin to run.[41] The provision does not compel the application of any law other than the applicable law. It simply provides that regard shall be had to the laws of the place of performance; it does not say that those laws must be applied. The purpose of the provision is to allow the court to assess the relevance of the law of the place of performance so as to do justice between the parties. But, inevitably, the provision generates uncertainty.

(vi) Damages

9.46 Article 10(1)(c) makes clear that the Convention extends to the consequences of breach, including the assessment of damages insofar as it is governed by rules of law "within the limits of the powers conferred on the court by its procedural law". The extent to which the assessment of damages is substantive (and therefore governed by the applicable law) rather than procedural (governed by the law of the forum) will be considered in paras 9.56–9.58 below.

(vii) Extinction of obligations

9.47 Article 10(1)(d) makes clear that the Convention extends to the various ways of extinguishing obligations. The applicable law therefore governs frustration, termination for breach and termination for any other reason, e.g. insolvency.

(viii) Limitation

9.48 Article 10(1)(d) makes clear that the Convention extends to prescription and limitation of actions.[42]

38. At common law it had been held that discharge of a contract includes the determination of the place where the policy monies are to be paid (and accordingly that this issue is governed by the applicable law). See *Pick* v. *Manufacturers Life Insurance Co.* [1958] 2 Lloyd's Rep. 93.

39. The Giuliano-Lagarde Report gives as examples of performance, conditions relating to the place and time of performance (1980 OJ C.282/1, 32).

40. *Giuliano-Lagarde*, 1980 OJ C.282/1, 32.

41. Seatzu, p. 116. Examples given in the Giuliano-Lagarde Report are the rules governing public holidays, the manner in which goods are to be examined and the steps to be taken if they are refused (commentary to Article 10, 1980 OJ C.282/1, 33.)

42. Article 10(1)(d). At common law limitation periods had been seen as procedural and thus applied to all claims brought in English courts but the Foreign Limitation Periods Act 1984 adopts a general rule that the limitation rules of the governing law are to be applied subject to a public policy-based exception. The same result is achieved in contractual cases by Article 10(1)(d).

(ix) Consequences of nullity

9.49 Article 10(1)(e) provides that the applicable law will govern the consequences of nullity of a contract. The UK exercised its right of reservation in relation to this provision, the choice of law rules regarding restitution being a matter of some controversy in English common law. The same provision appears in the proposed Rome I Regulation (now Article 11(1)(2)).

(x) Assignment

9.50 Article 12 provides:

> "1. The mutual obligations of assignor and assignee under a voluntary assignment of a right against another person ('the debtor') shall be governed by the law which under this Convention applies to the contract between the assignor and assignee.
>
> 2. The law governing the right to which the assignment relates shall determine its assignability, the relationship between the assignee and the debtor, the condition under which the assignment can be invoked against the debtor and any question whether the debtor's obligations have been discharged."

9.51 Thus, where a contract is entered into between A and B for the assignment of the benefit of an insurance policy between A and C, the mutual obligations between A and B will be governed by the law of the contract between them (Article 12(1)).

9.52 Other questions, such as whether the right is assignable, the relationship between the assignee and the debtor (i.e. between B and C) and the conditions under which it is assignable, including as to notice, are governed by the law applicable to the insurance contract itself (Article 12(2) as interpreted in *Raiffeisen Zentralbank Östereich AG* v. *Five Star General Trading LLC*).[43]

(xi) Subrogation

9.53 Article 13 provides:

> "1. Where a person ('the creditor') has a contractual claim upon another ('the debtor') and a third person has a duty to satisfy the creditor, or has in fact satisfied the creditor in discharge of that duty, the law which governs the third person's duty to satisfy the creditor shall determine whether the third person is entitled to exercise as against the debtor the rights which the creditor had against the debtor under the law governing their relationship, and, if so, whether he may do so in full or only to a limited extent.
>
> 2. The same rule applies where several persons are subject to the same contractual claim and one of them has satisfied the creditor."

9.54 As explained in the Giuliano-Lagarde report, having regard to the fact that the Convention only applies to contractual obligations, it was thought proper to limit the application of the rule adopted in Article 13 to assignment of rights which are contractual in nature. This rule does not apply to subrogation by operation of law when the debt to be paid has its origin in tort (for example, where the insurer succeeds to the rights of the insured against the person causing damage). If the article applies, the law governing the insurance contract will determine whether the insurer is entitled to exercise against the debtor the right which the insured had.

9.55 The proposed Rome I Regulation deals with voluntary subrogation together with assignment. Article 14 applies to statutory subrogation but again only applies to the satisfaction of contractual claims.

43. [2001] EWCA Civ 68; [2001] QB 825.

(xii) Procedure

9.56 Article 1(2)(h) provides that the Convention does not apply to evidence and procedure.[44] This confirms the common law rule that questions of procedure are governed by the *lex fori*. The difficult question is where to draw the line. Under the English common law, a distinction was often drawn between heads of damages (which were substantive) and the assessment or quantification of damages (which was characterised as procedural and accordingly governed by the *lex fori*).[45] Clearly, it will not always be possible to divide issues so neatly. For example, there has always been considerable controversy as to whether a ceiling or cap on damages is more akin to a head of damage than quantification of damages and is thus substantive rather than procedural.[46] However, under Article 10(1)(c) the consequences of breach, including the assessment of damages in so far as it is governed by rules of law and within the limits of the powers conferred on the court by its procedural law are to be governed by the applicable law. This provision clearly envisages that some legal rules concerning the assessment of damages will be governed by the applicable law within the limits of the court's procedural rules. The distinction between substance and procedure has been considered in the recent House of Lords decision in *Harding* v. *Wealands*.[47]

9.57 The Lords had to consider (in the context of a claim in tort) whether various New South Wales statutory provisions concerning damages were procedural and therefore could be ignored since questions of procedure were for the *lex fori* (in this case English law), or were substantive and applied as the law applicable to the tort was the law of New South Wales. The provisions included a cap on recovery, limits on recovery for gratuitous care, a prescribed discount rate, provisions for payment of interest and rules concerning credit for insurance recoveries. The claimant alleged that under these rules he would receive 30% less than he would under English law. At common law, the provisions, with the possible exception of the cap on damages, are likely to have been classified as procedural. But the majority of the Court of Appeal had adopted a much narrower view of procedure, that is, that it was concerned with the mode and conduct of the trial, and on that basis had held that all of the provisions were substantive. This decision was reversed by the House of Lords which unanimously reasserted the distinction between the kind of damage which constitutes an actionable injury (substance) and the assessment of compensation (procedure).[48] Their Lordships held that the rule that quantification of damages must be determined by the *lex fori* was left untouched by the Private International Law (Miscellaneous Provisions) Act 1995.[49] On that basis the rules were all held to be procedural.

9.58 Whether the same approach will be taken under the Rome Convention remains to be seen, but there are at least two reasons why a different view may be taken:

(1) unlike the 1995 Act, the Rome Convention is a community instrument and therefore the courts are not bound by any distinction which was drawn as a matter of English common law[50];

44. But without prejudice to Article 14 which provides that: the law governing the contract under this Convention applies to the extent that it contains, in the law of contract, rules which raise presumptions of law or determine the burden of proof.

45. See, for example, Cheshire/North, pp. 86–88; Clarkson/Hill, pp. 216–217.

46. See Clarkson/Hill, p. 237, preferring the view that the question is one of substance (at least in the context of claims in tort).

47. [2006] 3 WLR 83.

48. *Per* Lord Hoffmann, para. 24, and Lord Roger, paras 66–67.

49. *Per* Lord Hoffmann, paras 34 and 67.

50. Lord Hoffmann stressed that the question was not what the law should be but what Parliament thought the law was in 1995 (para. 51) and Lord Roger also noted that while the policy may be criticised as liable to encourage forum shopping or on some other ground it was the policy of the legislature (para. 64).

(2) Article 10(1)(c) appears to acknowledge that some questions relation to the assessment of damages will be governed by the applicable law.

9.59 Article 14 provides that:

"The law governing the contract under this Convention applies to the extent that it contains, in the law of contract, rules which raise presumptions of law or determine the burden of proof."

(xiii) Agency

9.60 It is important to identify the different contractual issues which can arise in an agency situation. There may be questions relating to:

(1) the relationship between the principal and the agent;
(2) the relationship between the agent and the third party; and
(3) the relationship between the principal and the third party.

Where there are issues relating to a contract in the case of (1) or (2) the law applicable to that contract will be determined by the Rome Convention and the scope of the applicable law will be as discussed in the previous paragraphs. But the question of whether an agent can bind the principal (i.e. issue (3)) is excluded from the Convention. Thus, Article 1(f) provides that the Rome Convention does not apply to the question whether an agent is able to bind a principal to a third party.[51]

Under English conflict of law rules if the question relates to the actual authority of the agent the scope of the agent's authority will be determined according to the law with reference to which the agency is constituted. On the other hand, if the question is whether the agent had ostensible authority to bind the principal the position is less clear. On one view ostensible authority should be governed by the law of the country in which the agent has acted. On another view the question should be determined by the law applicable to the contract created between the agent and the third party (although possibly without reference to any express choice of law made by those parties).[52]

Under the proposed Rome I Regulation, Article 1(f) is deleted and there is a new specific rule on Agency, Article 7, which provides:

"1. In the absence of choice under Article 3, a contract between principal and agent shall be governed by the law of the country in which the agent has his habitual residence, unless the agent exercises or is to exercise his main activity in the country in which the principal has his habitual residence, in which case the law of that country shall apply.

2. The relationship between the principal and third parties arising out of the fact that the agent has acted in the exercise of his powers, in excess of his powers or without power, shall be governed by the law of the country in which the agent had his habitual residence when he acted. However, the applicable law shall be the law of the country in which the agent acted if either the principal on whose behalf he acted or the third party has his habitual residence in that country or the agent acted at an exchange or auction.

3. Notwithstanding paragraph 2, where the law applicable to a relationship covered by that paragraph has been designated in writing by the principal or the agent and expressly accepted by the other party, the law thus designated shall be applicable to these matters.

51. The reasons for this exclusion are unclear. The Giuliano-Lagarde Report states that the exclusion is justified by the fact that it is difficult to accept the principle of freedom of contract on this point, 1980 OJ C.282/1, 13. Whereas the Proposal for the Rome I Regulation states that the reasons for the exclusion were the diversity of the national conflicts rules when the Convention was negotiated and the existence of the Hague Convention of 14 March 1987 on the law applicable to agency (5 December 2005, COM (2005) 650 final).

52. Plender/Wilderstein, paras 4-36–4-39.

4. The law designated by paragraph 2 shall also govern the relationship between the agent and the third party arising from the fact that the agent has acted in the exercise of his powers, in excess of his powers or without power."

These proposals would change the current position in a number of respects:

(1) Contractual issues between the principal and the agent and the agent and the third party (issues (1) and (2) above) would be subject to a special rule as to applicable law. Previously these issues would have been determined by the general rules applicable to all contracts under Articles 3 and 4.

(2) Questions relating to the scope of the agent's authority (i.e. issue (3) above) are no longer excluded from the scope of the regime. Instead a new community-wide rule is introduced applying the law of the country where the agent had his habitual residence – with a limited recognition of express choice of law where that is agreed by all the parties.

2. The Insurance Directives

9.61 The scope of the Insurance Directives should be the same as that of the Rome Convention. This is because, in the case of both contracts of general insurance and contracts of long-term insurance, the Regulation incorporates the Rome Convention subject to the provisions of Parts I and II.[53] Thus, where not expressly dealt with the insurance directives adopt the provisions of the Rome Convention.

53. See Regulation 7(1) and Regulation 10(1).

CHAPTER 10

REINSURANCE AND INSURANCE OF RISKS OUTSIDE THE EEA – CHOICE OF LAW AND THE ROME CONVENTION

A. OVERVIEW

10.1 As has been described, the Rome Convention applies:

(1) to contracts of reinsurance, provided such contracts were concluded on or after 1 April 1991[1]; and
(2) to contracts of insurance, provided (a) that the contract does not cover a risk situated in the territories of the Member States of the European Economic Community[2] and (b) that the contract was concluded on or after 1 April 1991.

10.2 A flow diagram summarising the choice of law regime under the Rome Convention is shown in Appendix 2.2. The choice of law regime operated by the Rome Convention may be summarised as follows:

(1) As regards contracts of reinsurance, the Rome Convention in the first place respects the parties' choice of law where it is expressed or demonstrated with reasonable certainty by the terms of the contract or the circumstances of the case: Article 3. Absent a choice by the parties, the contract is governed by the law of the country with which it is most closely connected: Article 4. The law selected by these Articles will apply to questions of material validity, formal validity, interpretation, performance, damages, extinction of obligations and limitation (see para. paras 9.28–9.59 above).
(2) As regards contracts of insurance falling within the scope of the Rome Convention, the regime is the same as for contracts of reinsurance, except where the contract is a "consumer contract" within Article 5, in which case special rules apply. A contract of reinsurance is inherently not going to be a consumer contract. The law selected by these Articles will apply to the matters referred to above in relation to reinsurance contracts.
(3) The regimes described in (1) and (2) above are both subject to certain limits and exceptions. In particular, the applicable law may be displaced by mandatory rules or on the grounds of public policy (see paras 10.104–10.130 below).

B. PARTIES' CHOICE OF LAW (ARTICLE 3)

10.3 Article 3 gives effect to any choice made by the parties to the contract as to what law should govern. In other words, the will of the parties is accorded a substantial pre-eminence. Thus, the first sentence of Article 3 provides: "A contract shall be governed by the law chosen by the parties." Article 3 goes on to provide[3]:

> "The choice must be expressed or demonstrated with reasonable certainty by the terms of the contract or the circumstances of the case."

1. See paras 2.89 and 9.15 above.
2. As we will see below, now the EEA – see para. 11.1 below.
3. See the second sentence of the Article.

10.4 Article 3 thus applies to much *more* than express choice of law clauses. Provided the terms of the contract "demonstrate" a choice "with reasonable certainty", Article 3 will apply. Moreover, in determining whether a choice of law has been made, Article 3 permits reference not only to "the terms of the contract", but also "the circumstances of the case".

10.5 In short, Article 3 embraces not only *express* choice of law clauses, but many of the situations where the English common law would hold that a choice of law was *implied*. The equivalence (or otherwise) of the concepts of an *implied choice* as opposed to a *choice of law demonstrated with reasonable certainty* is considered at paras 10.38–10.40 below.[4]

10.6 This section first considers express choice of law clauses. It then goes on to consider how choices of law are demonstrated with reasonable certainty.

1. Express choice of law

10.7 The clearest case is where the parties have included an express choice of law provision: for example, the parties might provide that "This contract shall be governed by English law"; or that "Any dispute arising out of this contract shall be decided according to English law". Parties to any international insurance or reinsurance contract would be well-advised to include such a clause in their agreement. This would avoid any uncertainty in determining the applicable law.

10.8 Because of the principle of party autonomy respected by Article 3, few problems arise with express choice of law clauses. But there are pitfalls which are considered in the following paragraphs.

(i) Incorporation of the choice of law clause

10.9 Questions can arise as to whether a clause has or has not been incorporated into the contract. The law governing this issue is, as we have seen,[5] prescribed by Article 8(1): the applicable law is the law which would govern if the contract or term were valid. Thus, if there is a dispute as to the existence or validity of a choice of law clause, an English court will be obliged to determine that question by reference to the putatively chosen law.

10.10 Where English law is the putative law, normal contractual principles of offer and counter-offer will apply. For example, in *The Lincoln National Life Insurance Co.* v. *Employers Reinsurance Corp.*,[6] the wording for the first layer of a reinsurance contract was drawn up by a broker with an express choice of Kansas law. The broker's evidence was that, in his experience, contracts of this kind were always written on the basis that they would be subject to the law and jurisdiction of the country in which the reinsurer had its seat, unless the parties agreed otherwise. The wording was approved by the insurer and copies were then sent to the leading underwriters for their signature, but no response was ever received. It was alleged by the other side that they had prepared a wording naming England. The claim that the parties had expressly chosen Kansas law to govern the contract was rejected by the court. The court held that the evidence could not support a case of custom; and it was accepted that silence in response to an offer of terms could not amount to acceptance.[7]

4. The Green paper comments at 3.4.2 that Article 3 is construed too widely by the English and German courts. One area where there does appear to be a divergence of approach is in the weight to be given to choice of jurisdiction. See further paras 10.35–10.42 below.

5. See paras 9.33–9.34 above.

6. [2002] Lloyd's Rep. IR 853.

7. It was not alleged that Kansas law differed in this respect from English law. The court, accordingly, did not need to deal with the potentially difficult question of whether to apply English law or Kansas law where one party contended for an express choice of Kansas law and the other an express choice of English law.

10.11 Similarly, in *Iran Continental Shelf Oil Company* v. *IRI International Corp.*,[8] each party had provided contractual documentation including an express choice of law provision. The defendant had provided for the law of Texas and the claimant for the law of Iran. In the circumstances, it could not be said that the parties had made an express choice in favour of either Iranian or Texan law: at no point did either party unequivocally accept the other party's terms.

(ii) Slips and subsequent policy wordings

10.12 In *Burrows* v. *Jamaica*,[9] it was common ground that a slip had been scratched and a contract of insurance therefore came into being. The policy wording remained to be agreed. Moore-Bick J. acknowledged that no doubt the parties contemplated that in the course of fleshing out the abbreviated wording of the slip, in order to produce the full policy wording, that contract might be amended and supplemented in some respects. But the court held that this did not detract from the fact that a contract had come into existence on the terms contained in, or evidenced by, the slip itself. Furthermore, the court stressed that it was essential to the manner in which the market operated that the slip should contain or identify all the terms of any real significance that were intended to form part of the contract. The slip included clause NMA 1483.[10] The court noted that this was one of the two established forms of law and jurisdiction clause which were then available to the market: NMA 1483 was the overseas jurisdiction clause and NMA 1486 the English jurisdiction clause. Whilst the wording of NMA 1483 was capable of being completed so as to provide for English law and jurisdiction, that is clearly not what it was intended for and there was no evidence that it had ever been used for that purpose. If it were completed in that way, it would probably be queried by the Lloyd's Policy Signing Office,[11] which is responsible for checking policy wordings before they are issued. If the parties intended to agree English law and jurisdiction, there were other, more appropriate, ways of doing so. Therefore, the court held that the inclusion of NMA 1483 in the slip conditions indicated agreement that the contract was to be subject to foreign law and jurisdiction (which on the facts of the case could only have meant Jamaica). It was all a matter of construing the slip. The court acknowledged that when construing the slip, the court must take into account any relevant evidence of general market background as well as evidence of the circumstances surrounding the particular contract before it, but on the facts there was no such evidence.

10.13 Difficulties can also arise where the wording in the slip is alleged to differ from that contained in the subsequently concluded policy. This is what happened in *Assicurazioni Generali SpA* v. *Ege Sigorta AS*.[12] Colman J. held that the contract of reinsurance as evidenced by the slip included such terms of the policy document as were compatible with the other express provisions of the slip. Although two earlier reinsurance contracts were governed by Turkish law, the clause was not incorporated into the reinsurance as the tendering by the brokers of a form including a Turkish jurisdiction clause was a negligent error which was not picked up when the document was signed; the tendering of wording by a London broker to an underwriter is intended to reflect exactly what has already been agreed in the slip a purely ministerial exercise hence could not constitute a variation of the contract.

8. [2002] EWCA Civ 1024.
9. [2002] 1 All ER Comm 374.
10. This was one of the standard form non-marine market clauses headed overseas jurisdiction clause.
11. Now Ins-sure.
12. [2002] Lloyd's Rep. IR 480.

(iii) Temporary cover

10.14 The difficulties caused by the provision of temporary cover were considered by the court in *Konkola Copper Mines plc* v. *Coromin*.[13] The question was whether a reinsurance contract was subject to the same terms as temporary cover provided on a specific basis, or rather was on the same terms as a global all risks policy entered into at the end of that period. Colman J. held that the evidence supported the latter analysis. The judge held that on the face of the documents the brokers were proceeding on the basis that as far as the reinsurers were concerned their cover was in respect of the global all-risks policy (and therefore subject to the terms of that policy including English law and jurisdiction) rather than the specific temporary cover (which included a Zambian choice of law).

(iv) Express choice by reference

10.15 An express choice can also be made by reference to some external factor, for instance the place of business of the insurer. Whether the choice is effective, turns on the construction of the clause in question.

10.16 In *Compagnie Tunisienne de Navigation SA* v. *Compagnie d'Armement Maritime SA*,[14] a contract was made for the carriage of a number of consignments of oil over a period of some months. The parties adapted a single-voyage charter party form providing that the charterparty was governed by the law of the flag of the vessel carrying the goods. For the first six voyages the defendant had employed ships flying five different flags (only one of which was French). But it was found that at the time of the conclusion of the contract, the parties had assumed that the defendant would be using its own ships, which flew the French flag. The majority of the House of Lords held that the clause was an effective choice of French law since it was reasonable to conclude on the evidence that the parties had chosen French law as the governing law.

10.17 Incorporation of provisions from a different contract may well raise further issues. General words of incorporation may well not be enough to incorporate a choice of law clause.[15] See paras 10.51–10.57 below on whether clauses from an underlying insurance contract will be incorporated into the reinsurance contract.

10.18 When discussing jurisdiction we considered the effect of a jurisdiction agreement in relation to third parties and agents (see paras 5.71–5.74 and 6.30–6.32 above). Similar issues may arise in respect of choice of law clauses. The question is again whether a choice of law originally agreed between two parties may be relied upon either by a third party or against a third party in a dispute with one of the original parties. As we have seen, in *Gerling* v. *Amminstrazione del Tresoro*[16] the European Court of Justice was happy to allow a third party, the Italian Treasury, to rely on a jurisdiction clause in an insurance policy, the rights under which had invested in the Treasury by operation of law. Similarly, one would expect a third

13. [2005] All ER (D) 180. Approved by the Court of Appeal at [2006] EWCA Civ 5.

14. [1971] AC 572.

15. In *Chase* v. *Ram Technical Services Ltd* [2000] 2 Lloyd's Rep. 418, it was submitted that the contract was governed by English law, on the basis that the policy incorporated the Institute Cargo Clauses, the relevant standard form of which (identified by number and date in the policy) provided: "This insurance is subject to English law and practice." The Judge, Mr Justice Timothy Walker, noted that this submission was strong enough to establish the necessary good arguable case. However, he also noted that an eventual finding that the proper law of the contract was English law was far from a foregone conclusion. The words of incorporation were not "Subject to Institute Cargo Clauses" but "Subject to wording based Institute Cargo Clauses". Further, the incorporation was confined to section 2 of the cover, which is odd if the intention was to apply English law to the whole contract. Thus, arguably, what was incorporated were the cargo clauses themselves, but not the choice of law.

16. C-201/82; [1983] ECR I-2503.

party to be able to rely on a choice of law agreement in an insurance or reinsurance contract the rights under which the third party has acquired by operation of law. Similarly, absent the special rules which apply to jurisdiction in insurance contracts, the original party ought also to be able to rely on a choice of law against a third party who will take any rights subject to the choice of law clause.

2. Choice demonstrated with reasonable certainty

(i) The nature of the test

10.19 Article 3 does not apply only to express choices of law. It is sufficient that a choice can be "demonstrated with reasonable certainty by the terms of the contract or the circumstances of the case". The court is not thereby imputing a choice to the parties (which, as we will see, is the function of Article 4). Rather, it is acknowledging that the parties themselves did in fact chose the governing law, albeit that that agreement was not expressly recorded or set out in the contract. As the Giuliano-Lagarde Report describes it, the parties "have made a real choice of law, although this is not expressly stated in the contract".[17]

10.20 This distinction between a choice demonstrated with reasonable certainty (Article 3) and a law imputed or imposed on the parties absent their choice (Article 4) mirrors the similar distinction that exists at common law between a real, but implied, chosen law, and an objectively determined applicable law imposed in the absence of such a choice. The common law rule was set out in the 11th edition of *Dicey & Morris*.[18] The proper law meant the system of law by which the parties intended the contract to be governed, or, where their intention was neither expressed (sub-rule 1) nor to be inferred from the circumstances (sub-rule 2), the system of law with which the transaction has its closest and most real connection (sub-rule 3).

10.21 This analysis was confirmed by the Court of Appeal in *Hellenic Steel Co.* v. *Svolamar Shipping Co Ltd (The Komninos S)*[19]:

> "Mr Collins submitted that no inference could be drawn as to the parties' intended choice of law and that accordingly the case was one to which *Dicey and Morris'* sub-r.3 to r.180 applies (*ibid.* at p. 1190):
>
> When the intention of the parties to a contract with regard to the law governing it is not expressed and cannot be inferred from the circumstances, the contract is governed by the system of law with which the transaction has its closest and most real connection.
>
> Mr Collins pointed out that there is some overlap between the processes envisaged by sub-rr.2 and 3, since the process of construction involved in the application of sub-r.2 necessarily involves (like any other process of construction) consideration of all the surrounding circumstances, which is the essential basis of a decision under sub-r.3. This is true, and has the formidable support of Lord Wilberforce (*Amin Rasheed Shipping Corporation* v. *Kuwait Insurance Co.* [1983] 2 Lloyd's Rep. 365 at p 373; [1984] AC 50 at p. 69). There is nonetheless a clear difference in the purpose for which the surrounding circumstances are considered under the two sub-rules. Under sub-r.2 it is to ascertain the parties' contractual intention (meaning their actual, not their imputed, intention: what they would have said if asked at the time). Under sub-r.3 it is to determine, objectively and irrespective of the parties' intention, with which system of law the transaction has its closest and most real connection. This involves the application of a rule of law, not a process of contractual construction. It is doubtless no accident that this same dichotomy is reproduced in the Rome Convention, scheduled to the Contracts (Applicable Law) Act 1990 but not yet in force."

10.22 There is thus a degree of similarity in the approach of the common law and the approach of the Rome Convention. But, at the end of the day, it is the words of the Convention

17. Commentary to Article 3(3) 1980 OJ C.282/1, 17.
18. Volume 2, p. 1161.
19. [1991] 1 Lloyd's Rep. 370, 373–374 (*per* Bingham LJ).

that apply; and the approach of the common law – however similar – can only provide assistance to the extent that European law as construed by English courts allows.

10.23 When approaching this part of Article 3, the first point to note is that despite use of the word "or", the courts must take into account *both* the terms of the contract and the circumstances of the case.[20]

10.24 English courts have differed as to the width of the Article 3 approach. The question is whether the Article 3 test is essentially similar to the English law test for the implication of a contractual term[21] or whether the Convention takes a different approach. In *ISS Machinery Services Ltd* v. *Aeolian Shipping SA*,[22] Potter LJ inclined to the view that the test was wider than the English law approach to implied terms:

> "... the circumstances which may be taken into account when deciding whether or not the parties have made an implied choice of law under Article 3 of the Rome Convention range more widely in certain respects than the considerations ordinarily applicable to the implications of a term into a written agreement, in particular, by reason of the reference in Article 3 to the circumstances of the case."

10.25 However, in *American Motorists Insurance Co. (AMICO)* v. *Cellstar Corp.*,[23] Mance LJ, having referred to these comments, said that he reserved his view on this point because it seemed to him that even when construing a written agreement at common law, the surrounding circumstances might well be of considerable relevance. In his view, there was considerable similarity between the test for the implication of a term and the approach of Article 3(1)[24]:

> "... Article 3(1) does ... bring to mind the test governing the implication of an implied term at common law, on the grounds that it must have been intended or was so obvious that it went without saying and was one to which the parties would have said 'of course' if anyone had suggested it. The mere fact that it would be 'reasonable' would not suffice."

10.26 At the end of the day, what is directly relevant is that the test of "real choice" contained in the Article is satisfied. The nature of the test is best illustrated by example than by a possibly barren debate as to whether the Article 3 test is similar or not similar to the English law test for implied terms.

3. Instances where the "reasonable certainty" test may be satisfied

(i) Examples in the Giuliano-Lagarde Report

10.27 The Giuliano-Lagarde Report gives three examples of the sort of factual situations in which a choice of law will be demonstrated with reasonable certainty by the terms of the contract or the circumstances of the case[25]:

- standard form contracts;
- jurisdiction and arbitration clauses;
- course of dealing between the parties.

20. This is clear from the examples of implied choice given in the Giuliano-Lagarde Report and the decision of Aikens J. confirming this construction in *Marubeni Hong Kong and South China Ltd* v. *Mongolian Government* [2002] All ER (Comm) 873.

21. I.e. a term will be implied on grounds of business efficacy or on the basis that both parties, if asked, would have readily agreed that such a term should be implied. These tests were summarised by Lord Simm in *BP Refinery (Westernport) Pty Ltd* v. *Shire of Hastings* (1978) ALJR 20. The House of Lords in *Liverpool CC* v. *Irwin* [1977] AC 239 confirmed that it was not enough that the proposed implied term was reasonable, it must be necessary. A full explanation of the position in English law can be found in Chitty, paras 13-004–13-009.

22. [2001] 2 Lloyd's Rep. 641 at p. 645.

23. [2003] IL Pr 370.

24. [2003] IL Pr 370, 393.

25. Commentary to Article 3(1) 1980 OJ C.282/1, 17.

However, the list in the Giuliano-Lagarde Report is not, and is not intended to be, exhaustive.[26] There are other situations which are likely to give rise to a choice of law that can be demonstrated with reasonable certainty. These are considered after the three examples in the Giuliano-Lagarde Report.

(ii) Standard form contracts

10.28 The first example given in the Giuliano-Lagarde Report is where the contract is in a standard form which is known to be governed by a particular system of law, even though there is no express statement to this effect. The report gives as an example a Lloyd's policy of marine insurance.[27] This ground for inferring a choice of law is likely to be particularly important in an insurance and reinsurance context.

10.29 The example given of the use of Lloyd's insurance policies resonates with a number of common law cases where the use of a standard English form of insurance has been held to be grounds for inferring intention that English law should govern the contract. For example, in *Amin Rasheed Shipping Corp.* v. *Kuwait Insurance Co.*,[28] a marine insurance policy was issued by a Kuwait insurance company to a Liberian company carrying on business in the Gulf. The policy was based on the Lloyd's standard form of marine policy. It was held that the policy's provisions pointed to the conclusion that the intention of the parties was that it should be determined in accordance with the English law of marine insurance.[29]

10.30 Similarly, where a contract of reinsurance was made on the London market, the courts at common law were prepared to infer an intention that English law should govern.[30]

10.31 Under the Rome Convention, similar considerations have lead to the implication of a choice of law under Article 3 in insurance and reinsurance cases. In *Gan Insurance Co. Ltd* v. *Tai Ping Insurance Co. Ltd*,[31] the Court of Appeal upheld Cresswell J.'s decision that[32]:

"... there was an implied choice of English law demonstrated with reasonable certainty by the terms of the contract or circumstances of the case as required by Article 3. The judge pointed to the reference to slip policy NMA 1779, full reinsurance clause NMA 416, claims co-operation clause NMA 464, NMA 1685 and the claims co-operation clause itself as demonstrating a choice of clauses commonly found in

26. The Report expressly states that these are "examples" (1980 OJ C.282/1, 17).

27. A related situation, referred to later on in the report, is where references in a contract to specific articles of the French Civil Code leave the court in no doubt that the parties have deliberately chosen French law. But note, the parties may simply have intended to incorporate that particular legal provision into the contract, rather than apply French law to the contract as a whole. See, for example, *DR Insurance Co.* v. *Central National Insurance Co. of Omaha* [1996] 1 Lloyd's Rep 74, 81, a clause referring to s.315 of the New York insurance law was said to be "indicative of an intention to incorporate the provisions of that section into the contract rather than to render the contract as a whole subject to New York law". The crucial difference between these situations is that if all the parties have done is incorporate a particular provision of law into the contract, that provision becomes a term of the contract and will not change even if the law itself does.

28. [1984] AC 50.

29. However, it should be noted that a crucial surrounding circumstance was that it was common ground that there was no indigenous law of marine insurance in Kuwait. Plus the terms of the policy itself (i.e. the adoption of the obsolete language of the Lloyd's SG policy) made it impossible to determine without recourse to English law. Also it should be noted that Lord Wilberforce, although agreeing that English law governed, did not think there was sufficient evidence to imply an actual choice of English law, but in any event objectively determined the contract had its closest and most real connection with England.

30. In *Royal Exchange Assurance Corp.* v. *Sjoforsakrings AB Vega* [1902] 2 KB 384, a policy of reinsurance was executed in Sweden, and place of payment was in England. However, these factors were not conclusive. The Court of Appeal held that it had to gather the intention of the parties from the terms and circumstances The policy was in the form of a Lloyd's policy. The reinsurance policy contained a term adopting with the necessary modifications, the terms of the original policy which was an English policy. Note, however, the reinsurance policy also contained a clause stating that the defendant was bound by the jurisdiction and decision of the English law courts.

31. [1999] IL Pr 729.

32. [1999] IL Pr 729, 741.

contracts of reinsurance placed on the London market. Moreover the procedure adopted was to place the business in London using London brokers who presented the risk to reinsurers in the conventional way in concluding a contract of reinsurance governed by English law."

10.32 In *Tiernan* v. *The Magen Insurance Co. Ltd*,[33] Longmore J. held:

"In my view the contract is governed by English law. I say that by reason either of Article 3 or Article 4 of the Rome Convention … Mr Butcher submits in relation to Article 3 that the contract was placed by London brokers on the Lloyd's market in the conventional way, further that the contract contains London market clauses, not only the claims control clause but the 'so deemed' clauses that have all the hallmarks of clauses framed in London according to English law. I accept those submissions and it follows to my mind that there is in that sense an implied choice of law. I am particularly influenced by the Giuliano-Lagarde Report, where it is stated in terms that a contract may be in a standard form known to be governed by a particular system of law even though there is no express statement to that effect and a Lloyd's policy of marine insurance is instanced. Mr Locket states that may well refer to the old SG form but it seems to me the same considerations apply to the Lloyd's form on which the contract of reinsurance is written in this case."

10.33 In *Tryg Baltica International (UK) Ltd* v. *Boston Compania de Seguros SA*,[34] the claimant maintained that reinsurances were governed by English law. Cooke J. commented:

"Although the defendants do not formally concede this, they do not put forward any positive case or any process of reasoning to justify the application of any other law. The only possible rival contender for applicable law is Argentina, because of the connection with the underlying policies but it appears to me that the most obvious inference from all the circumstances in which the Reinsurances were written is that the parties must have intended English law to apply. The reinsurance contracts were, as already indicated, made in England, in the London market. The presentations were made to Tryg in London, the slips were scratched in London and the wordings were agreed in London on London market forms. The certificates of reinsurance were issued in London by HSBC, operating under the facility agreement and superseded the off-slips which had been scratched by Tryg. All the contractual and relevant pre-contractual documentation is expressed in English. In my judgment Tryg are correct in saying that the reinsurance contracts are governed by English law under the terms of Article 3(1) of the Rome Convention (implied choice of English law) or under Article 4(2) of the same Convention on the basis of Tryg's central administration being in this country."

10.34 In *Assicurazioni Generali SpA* v. *Ege Sigorta*,[35] Colman J. held:

"The contracts of reinsurance were by implication governed by English law. They were made between London brokers and insurers and they referred to various London market provisions such as KFA 81 which is expressly governed by English law. They were also performable in London in as much as claims were to be paid in London through the companies or Lloyd's payout system. They were facultative reinsurances of risks insured under an original primary policy governed by English law."

(iii) Jurisdiction and arbitration clauses

10.35 A choice of jurisdiction is not the same as a choice of law. It is perfectly possible for the parties to provide that the English courts shall have exclusive jurisdiction to hear disputes under a contract, which they also expressly provide is to be governed by French law. The English court would simply apply French law proved as a fact through expert evidence.[36] Similarly, the parties can provide for arbitration in London but intend that the contract be governed by a different law, the arbitrator applying that law to determine the merits of the dispute.[37]

33. [2000] IL Pr 517, paras 11–12.
34. [2005] Lloyd's Rep. IR 40, para. 8.
35. [2002] 2 Lloyd's Rep. 480, 484.
36. On proof of foreign law in English courts see Fentiman, *Foreign Law in English Courts* (1998).
37. For example, in the *Compagnie Tunisienne* case referred to above, the House of Lords held that the contract was expressly chosen to be governed by French law, despite the presence of an arbitration clause providing for

10.36 However, at common law, one of the strongest indications of an implied choice of law is a choice of forum clause. Assuming that the parties have not provided otherwise, the courts at common law readily assume that the parties must have had in mind that the chosen court would apply its own law. Indeed, it is inferred that the parties intend their contract to be governed by the law of the forum chosen as the place where the dispute is to be tried, unless there are strong indications that they did not so intend or may not have intended that result.[38]

10.37 The presumption has often been applied at common law in insurance and reinsurance cases. For example, in *Spurrier* v. *La Cloche*,[39] the Privy Council held that a fire policy issued in Jersey with money payable in Jersey, but which required arbitration in England in accordance with the English Arbitration Acts, was clearly intended to be governed by English law. Similarly in *Norske Atlas Insurance Co. Ltd* v. *London General Insurance Co. Ltd*,[40] a contract of reinsurance subject to arbitration in Norway with arbitrators chosen from Norway, Sweden or Denmark with the Norwegian court choosing in default was held to be intended to be governed by Norwegian law.

10.38 Although the wording of Article 3 differs from common law test, the Giuliano-Lagarde Report confirms that in some cases the choice of a particular forum may show, in no uncertain manner, that the parties intend the contract to be governed by the law of that forum, albeit that this must always be subject to the other terms of the contract and circumstances of the case. This seems to reflect the common law position. The Giuliano-Lagarde Report also refers to the possibility that the choice of a place where disputes are to be settled by arbitration may also indicate that the arbitrator should apply the law of that place.[41]

10.39 The similarity of the Convention test to the common law approach was confirmed in *Egon Oldendorff* v. *Liberia Corp.*[42] The plaintiff claimed that there was a choice of English law on the following grounds:

(i) There was a London arbitration clause by a person conversant with shipping matters;

London arbitration. See also *XL Insurance Ltd* v. *Owens Corning* [2000] 2 Lloyd's Rep. 500. Having held that there was a London arbitration clause in the contract, Toulson J. pointed out that it was possible at least for a different law to govern (a) the underlying contract, (b) the arbitration agreement, and (c) the terms under which the arbitration took place, i.e. the curial law. However, the judge went on to hold on the facts that by stipulating for arbitration in London under the provisions of the Act (other than ss.45 and 69) the parties chose English law to govern the matters which fall within those provisions, including the formal validity of the arbitration clause and the jurisdiction of the arbitral tribunal, and by implication chose English law as the proper law of the arbitration clause.

38. See, for example, *The Komninos S* [1991] 1 Lloyd's Rep. 370. The Court of Appeal held that a clause referring all disputes to the "British Courts" (which the court was happy to assume was a reference to the English courts, any other argument being described as a "lawyer's point") was a strong indication that the parties also intended their agreement to be governed by English law there being no strong indication otherwise (albeit that the Court accepted that other features of the case may have led to the application of Greek law as the law with the closest connection to the case). In the *Compagnie Tunisienne* case referred to above (para. 10.16 above) the court also acknowledged such a presumption. Lord Wilberforce said "that the selection of a certain place for arbitration is an indication that the parties intended the law of that place to govern is a sound general rule" ([1971] AC 572, 596) Lord Diplock also stated that an arbitration clause is generally intended by the parties to operate as a choice of governing law and should be construed unless there are compelling indications to the contrary in the other terms of the contract or the surrounding circumstances of the transaction ([1971] AC 572, 609).

39. [1902] AC 446.

40. (1927) 28 Ll L Rep. 104. A Norwegian company centered into a contract of reinsurance with a London reinsurer. The treaty included an arbitration clause providing for three arbitrators from Norway, Sweden or Denmark, with the Norwegian court to appoint in default and that the arbitration was to be in Norway. MacKinnon J. held that the contract was governed by Norwegian law. The question it was said always depended on intention, if nothing else the inference was the place where the contract was executed. But here the arbitration clause showed a clear intention in favour of Norway. Conversely, in *Maritime Insurance Company Ltd* v. *Assecuranz-Union von 1865* (1935) 52 Ll L Rep. 16 the policy contained a clause providing for arbitration in London which Goddard J. held to be decisive despite the fact that the contract was arguably made in Germany and that the contract was invalid according to English law.

41. Commentary to Article 3 (1980 OJ C.282/1, 17).

42. [1996] 1 Lloyd's Rep. 380.

(ii) The dealings between the parties showed that they conducted negotiations by reference to English law; and
(iii) There was a related contract which was expressly governed by English law.

Clarke J. confirmed that the test under the Convention was very similar to that applied at common law. Any change of emphasis was a small one. On the facts, although it was not a case where the arbitration was to be in London and by London arbitrators or brokers, given it was a well-known English language form of charterparty, containing standard clauses with well-known meanings in English law, and they had chosen a neutral forum, there was enough to imply a choice of English law.

10.40 Thus, as was the case at common law, a choice of England as the exclusive jurisdiction to hear the dispute or place of arbitration under a reinsurance contract leads to a strong inference that English law governs the contract. However, it is important to note that the strength of that inference is affected by a number of other factors:

(i) In the cases discussed so far, England had been chosen as a "neutral" forum and it was in that context that it was assumed that the parties would also have intended the application of a "neutral" applicable law. The inference may be less strong where the forum chosen is the jurisdiction of one of the parties, or where England is chosen as the place to hear the dispute for a different reason, e.g. availability of witnesses.
(ii) In arbitration cases, the inference will be stronger where, not just the place of arbitration is chosen, but where there is also provision for an English arbitrator or someone familiar with English law or practice, or where the parties also provide for arbitration in accordance with the English Arbitration Acts.[43]

10.41 An interesting example of how the two presumptions so far discussed interact is *King* v. *Brandywine Reinsurance Co.*[44] The case was one of many which resulted from the *Exxon Valdez* disaster. In this instance; it concerned claims made by Exxon, the owner of the cargo on board at the time, against its insurers, in relation to various expenses it had incurred in the clean up process, as well as claims made against it by the Government and local parties affected by the disaster. Exxon's insurers settled some of the claims and judgments were made in respect of others by the court in Texas. The case concerned claims subsequently made by the claimant reinsurers against the defendants who were the retrocessionaires of the claimants. It was common ground that under the terms of the retrocessions the claimants had to prove that the losses were covered by the primary policy as well as being within the terms of the outward retrocessions. Various issues arose, but, in particular, there was a dispute as to whether the clean up expenses came within the provisions of the main insurance policy (GCE policy), Section I, in relation to "removal of debris". In order to consider that issue, the court considered the proper law of the GCE policy. At first instance, Colman J. found that the GCE policy was governed by English law. The Court of Appeal disagreed. Although it was accepted that the common law had always paid great attention to the market in which the insurance was placed and the location of the lead underwriters (both England in this case), in this case the crucial factor was the presence of an arbitration clause in the GCE policy. That clause provided for arbitration in New York at the request of either party. It could therefore be implied that the law they would apply would be New York law. The inference in favour of New York law was consistent with the service of suit clause in favour of New York and the non-

43. The presumption will be weaker if the clause applies only to a narrow category of disputes: see Jonathan Hirst QC (sitting as a judge of the High Court) in *Travelers Casualty and Surety Company of Europe Ltd* v. *Sun Life Assurance Company of Canada (UK) Ltd* [2004] Lloyd's Rep. IR 846.
44. [2005] EWCA Civ 235; [2005] 1 Lloyd's Rep. 655.

mandatory arbitration clause in favour of New York. Viewed as a whole, these factors pointed to an inferred choice in favour of New York law.[45]

10.42 The German courts, like the English courts, have held that a jurisdiction clause is a "significant indicator" ("*gewichtiges Indie*") of a choice of law.[46] The French courts have taken a much stricter view of Article 3. The French view is that a jurisdiction clause does not create a presumption that there has been a choice of law in favour of that jurisdiction.[47]

(iv) Course of dealing between the parties

10.43 The Giuliano-Lagarde Report refers to two situations where the course of dealing between the parties might be relevant. First, it is said that a previous course of dealing between the parties under contracts containing an express choice of law may leave the court in no doubt that the contract in question is to be governed by the law previously chosen, where the choice of law clause has been omitted in circumstances which do not indicate a deliberate change of policy by the parties. This is relatively straightforward. For instance, if previous reinsurance contracts between the parties have expressly been governed by English law and there is no evidence that there has been a deliberate change of policy, this may be sufficient to infer an express choice of English law in a later contract. For example, in *Marubeni Hong Kong and South China Ltd*,[48] an express choice appeared in an earlier draft of the contract. Aikens J. held the parties were anxious to get a neutral jurisdiction, there was no evidence that they had decided specifically to reject the clause and that they were worried about the ability of the Mongolian courts to deal with the issue. On that basis there was a choice of law in favour of England.

10.44 Secondly, the Report notes that other matters that may impel the court to the conclusion that a real choice of law has been made might include an express choice of law in related actions between the same parties. This raises an interesting question in reinsurance cases, namely, what is the relevance, if any, of an express choice of law in the insurance contract itself? Although contracts of insurance and reinsurance can be intimately related (e.g. where there is a facultative reinsurance of a risk or a fronting arrangement), the contracts are not between the *same* parties: there is, instead, one common party to each contract – the insurer/reinsured. It cannot, therefore, be said that the Report is stating that the relationship between insurance and reinsurance contracts is a factor to be taken into account. Then again, the Report does not purport to set out a comprehensive list of factors. This point is specifically considered in paras 10.51–10.57 below.

(v) Other factors not expressly considered in the Giuliano-Lagarde Report

10.45 English courts have sometimes drawn an inference as to choice of law from factors such as the currency and place of payment and from the supposed intention of the parties to

45. The key provision was the mandatory arbitration clause. It appears that the service of suit clause and/or non-compulsory arbitration clauses would not by themselves have rebutted the presumption in favour of English law. *EI Du Pont de Nemours* v. *Agnew* [1989] 2 Lloyd's Rep. 585 was distinguished on that basis (paras 43–49). This seems to be a classic example of a series of conflicting indications and it is hard to believe that it was possible to demonstrate with "reasonable certainty" what the parties could have intended. The contrast with the French view (see para. 10.42 above) is stark.

46. See the judgment of the Bundesgerichtshof of 13 June 1996 [1998] IP Rax 108.

47. See Lagarde in Rev crit dip (2006) 95 (1) 94, 96, referring to V. Larrsbau Terneyre Droit de la famille, Oct. 2005, comm. 203; ME Ancel, Droit et patrimoine, Nov. 2005, p. 113. See also the decision of the tribunal d'arrondisement de Luxembourg in *Winters Arnhem BV* v. *SA Coedeux Rivista di dritto internazionale private e processuale,* 1991, p. 1092, in which the court refused to find a choice of law in favour of Luxembourg from a Luxembourg jurisdiction agreement.

48. [2002] 2 All ER (Comm) 873.

create or include a valid contract or term therefore (*inference in favorem negotii*[49]). The status of such factors under the Convention is not discussed in the Giuliano-Lagarde Report.

10.46 For a factor to be relevant the critical test is whether it demonstrates a real choice by the parties. Article 3 does not permit the court to *infer* a choice of law that the parties *might* have made in circumstances where they had no clear intention of making a choice, this case being governed by Article 4. Many factors – such as the factors considered above – may justify an inferred choice, but be insufficient (at least on their own) to show a real choice. The following factors are considered below:

- follow London clauses;
- lead policies;
- the effect of insurance contracts on contracts of reinsurance.

In each of these cases, the English courts have held – applying common law principles – that English law applies. They are helpful as examples, but are no more than that. In particular, the key Article 3 test of whether there was sufficient evidence to infer an *actual* choice of law was not, for obvious reasons, considered.

(vi) Follow London clauses

10.47 In *Armadora Occidental SA* v. *Horace Mann Insurance Co.*,[50] a fleet of 29 vessels was insured through policies effected in the US by US brokers. 30% of the risk was placed on the London market, 39% on the US market and the remainder in various other jurisdictions. Service outside the jurisdiction was allowed against one of the US insurers on the basis that the contract was governed by English law. That decision was upheld by the Court of Appeal. The case was decided at common law and Lord Denning answered the question which country had the closest and most real connection on that basis. In many respects, that country would appear to be the US, but Lord Denning held that the existence of a "follow London" clause was crucial to a different outcome. The object of the clause was that any negotiations regarding any claims should be undertaken in the first instance by a London underwriter. So far as the London policies were concerned, they were clearly governed by English law and therefore the negotiations would be dealt with according to English law. The underlying inference therefore was that the insurance with respect to the American policies was also governed by English law. The existence of a New York suable clause made no difference as even if a claim had been brought in NY and the NY court had held that NY law applied, that law would recognise the follow London clause and would therefore apply English law.

(vii) Lead policies

10.48 In *Cantieri Navali Riuniti Spa* v. *Omne Justitia NV*,[51] a vessel was owned by a Liberian corporation and hull insurance was underwritten by a large number of insurers. The policies included a clause stating that any suit may be brought against the insurers in the US. The benefit of the policies was assigned to the claimant. Goff LJ considered the lead policy which was a contract made in London with an English insurance company through brokers working in London under a policy incorporating clauses introduced by the London brokers who were

49. For example, in the case of contracts of insurance connected with states in which such contracts might be invalid by Muslim law the courts will be ready to infer that the parties would not have intended the contract to have been governed by that system of law: see *Islamic Arab Ins. Co.* v. *Saudi Egyptian American Reinsurance Co.* [1987] 1 Lloyd's Rep 315, 320.

50. [1978] 1 All ER 407.

51. [1985] 2 Lloyd's Rep. 428.

accustomed to working in accordance with English law and practice. Given that contract was governed by English law, the court held that it was reasonable to assume that so were all the other policies given the existence of the following clause: "All terms, clauses, wording and conditions as is or may be added to Policy issued by Fenton [the first named underwriter] for the identical subject matter and period."

10.49 In *EI Du Pont de Nemours & Co.* v *Agnew*,[52] the defendant insurers insured the claimant against product liability claims. The insurers claimed that they were not required to indemnify for that part of a judgment relating to punitive damages. The lead policy was issued in London on the familiar Lloyd's form. It must, it was held, be a *prima facie* inference that a following policy is governed by the same law as the policy it follows.[53] The Court of Appeal considered it plain that the proper law of the policy was English law. It was a Lloyd's policy negotiated by London brokers.

10.50 For similar reasons an excess policy on same risk as a primary policy is likely to be governed by the law of the latter.[54]

(viii) The effect of insurance contracts on contracts of reinsurance

10.51 The extent to which a contract reinsuring a contract of insurance is so connected with the contract that a real choice of law as regards the reinsurance can be inferred out of the relationship will depend on essentially two different factors: first, the extent to which the insurance itself demonstrates a clear choice of law, which the parties to the reinsurance can have taken into account; and, secondly, the closeness of the relationship between the insurance and the reinsurance.[55] Thus, as to the first factor, clearly if the insurance does not itself evince a real (or, at least, a clear) choice, it is unlikely that the insurance can have much effect on the choice of law for the reinsurance. As to the second factor, there is much more likelihood of a close connection between an insurance and a reinsurance where the reinsurance is facultative rather than treaty.

10.52 The question is, how far such connections result in a demonstrable choice of law. The question is of some significance because – with the limited exception of contracts of insurance covering risks that are not situate within the EU – different regimes will govern the contracts.

10.53 Particularly where there is a facultative reinsurance of a risk, it is very often the clear commercial purpose of the reinsurance contract to provide cover corresponding to that contained in the original cover. If the laws governing the two contracts are different, that might be difficult to achieve. For example, in *Vesta* v. *Butcher*,[56] the original insurance policy was governed by Norwegian law. According to Norwegian law, the particular misrepresentation at issue did not render the contract of insurance null and void as it did not contribute to the loss, hence the insurer was liable to pay. The reinsurance contract was governed by English law. According to English law the misrepresentation did render the contract null and void, accordingly the reinsurer argued that he did not have to pay.

10.54 There are two possible approaches. First, the courts could rely on the fact that the insurance contract is either chosen or found to be governed by law X as a reason for finding

52. [1987] 2 Lloyd's Rep. 585.

53. See also *Travelers Casualty and Surety Company* [2004] Lloyd's Rep. IR 846 where the judge, Jonathan Hirst QC, took into account the proper law (where it was possible to determine) of policies which the policy in issue was to follow. However, because only two of the three policies referred to were governed by the law contended for the indication was less powerful (para. 57).

54. See *Clarke*, 2-4B1.

55. See paras 5.80–5.86 above.

56. [1989] AC 852.

that the reinsurance contract is also governed by law X under Article 3 (because the parties must have intended that result). If the reinsurance contract contains an express provision in favour of law Y, the court could rely on *dépeçage*[57] and hold that common provisions were governed by law X with the rest of the contract being governed by law Y.[58] This was the approach of judge at first instance in *Vesta* v. *Butcher*.[59] It is supported by cases in other areas where the courts have taken into account the governing law of another related contract. For example, in *Bank of Baroda* v. *Vysya Bank Ltd*[60] great weight was given to the commercial convenience of the same law governing all the contracts in the letter of credit relationship (that approach being confirmed by the Court of Appeal in *Marconi Communications International Ltd* v *PT Pan Indonesian Bank TBK*).[61] Similarly, there is often a strong presumption that a guarantee or performance bond is governed by the same law as that which governs the underlying transaction.[62]

10.55 Alternatively the court could see the contracts (which after all are between different parties) as independent. The potential problem could then be solved, as a matter of English law, assuming English law governs the reinsurance contract, by construing the reinsurance contract in accordance with law X which governs the insurance contract. This was the approach adopted by the Court of Appeal and House of Lords in *Vesta* v. *Butcher* both of which held that the reinsurance contract was in its entirety governed by English law. As a matter of English law as the law governing the contract, it was possible when interpreting the contract to resort to the Norwegian governing law so that the same meaning could be given to terms common to both policies. It was a contract in which the parties "are deemed to have used the same dictionary", in this case a Norwegian legal dictionary, to ascertain the meaning of the terms and conditions. This decision was followed in *Groupama Navigation et Transports* v. *Catatumb CA Seguros*[63] where a very similar problem arose. It was accepted that the insurance contract was governed by Venezuelan law according to which, like Norwegian law, there had to be a causal connection between the breach of warranty and the loss. The reinsurance contract was governed by English law. The Court of Appeal held that the incorporated warranties from the insurance policy had to have the same meaning in both

57. See para. 10.61 below.

58. This is referred to as the "hybrid solution" in Clarke, para. 2.1C.

59. See also Collins/Dicey/Morris, para. 33-215, where the learned editors, having referred to Articles 3 and 4 of the Rome Convention, state that it could be concluded that, if the clear contractual intent was that the legal effect of the clauses which define the scope of the cover should be the same in the re-insurance contract and the original insurance contract, the parties may have demonstrated with reasonable certainty that part of the re-insurance contract should be governed by the same law as governs the original insurance contract. Although they also accept that the difficulty is to establish when there would be such certainty.

60. [1994] 2 Lloyd's Rep. 87.

61. [2005] 2 All ER (Comm) 325. The same is not necessarily true in relation to the letter of credit arrangements and the underlying transaction which are separate and independent commercial transactions: see *Attock Cement Co. Ltd* v. *Romanian Bank for Foreign Trade* [1989] 1 Lloyd's Rep. 572.

62. See, e.g., *Wahda Bank* v. *Arab Bank* [1996] 1 Lloyd's Rep. 470, 472. The court in *Samcrete Egyptian Engineer & Contractors SAE* v. *Land Rover Exports Ltd* [2002] CLC 533 left open the question of whether choice of law in a related contract could be relevant under Article 4 as well as under Article 3. See also *Royal Exchange Assurance Corporation* v. *Vega* [1902] 2 KB 384. A policy of reinsurance was executed in Sweden, and place of payment was in England. However, these factors were not conclusive. The Court of Appeal held that it had to gather the intention of the parties from the terms and circumstances. The policy was in the form of a Lloyd's policy. The reinsurance policy contained a term adopting with the necessary modifications, the terms of the original policy which was an English policy. The reinsurance policy also contained a clause stating that the defendant was bound by the jurisdiction and decision of the English law courts. Lagarde, writing in the *Virginia Journal of International Law* (1981) 22 Virginia J. of Int. Law 91 at pp. 97–98, has also stated that rebuttal might be appropriate where a subcontract might be governed by the same law governing the principal contract between the contractor and the employer rather than by the law of the country in which the subcontractor has his place of business.

63. [2000] 2 Lloyd's Rep. 350.

contracts and that similar warranties expressly included in the slip should not be construed so as to have a different effect.[64] This seems to be the solution currently favoured by the English courts. It means that – at least when the reinsurance is governed by English law – a mismatch in the applicable law need not lead to different outcomes. It is difficult to conceive of a different solution where one reinsurance contract covers liability under a number of insurance contracts which are or may be governed by different laws, as may occur under a reinsurance treaty.

10.56 The first approach – allowing a choice of law in the insurance to affect the reinsurance choice – appears to be an approach that is not especially favoured. The courts are not quick to find that an express choice of law in an original insurance policy is expressly incorporated into the reinsurance contract. For example, in *Gan Insurance Co. Ltd* v. *Tai Ping Insurance*, the underlying insurance contract was expressly governed by Taiwanese law. However, the court rejected the argument that the reference in the reinsurance contract to "as original" incorporated that choice into the reinsurance contract.[65] Similarly, in *Assicurazioni Generali*, the judge held that even if the original policy did contain a Turkish jurisdiction clause, the clause was not incorporated into the reinsurance as general words of incorporation in a reinsurance contract will not generally incorporate jurisdiction clauses from the primary policy, not being germane to the risk insured but being merely ancillary provisions which the parties to the reinsurance would not normally intend to incorporate (a similar argument would no doubt have been made in relation to choice of law).

10.57 Similar issues were raised in *CGU International Insurance plc* v. *Astrazeneca Insurance Co. Ltd.*[66] The case concerned an excess liability policy and reinsurance policy which it was conceded were both governed by English law. The insured settled a number of claims and sought an indemnity from his insurer which was paid in full. The insurer sought to be indemnified by reinsurers who declined to pay the full amount. Arbitration proceedings were commenced. Preliminary issues arose as to (i) which system of law would determine the reinsured's liability to the original insured, and (ii) which law would determine the reinsurer's liability to the reinsured under the reinsurance policy. By a majority the arbitral tribunal decided that the law of Iowa applied to the underlying insurance and for the purposes of establishing consequent liability on the part of the reinsurer reasoning that if the original insured had been forced to bring a claim, that claim would have been brought in Iowa under a US service of suit clause in the original insurance. The Iowa court would have applied Iowa law. The reinsurers appealed and the appeal was allowed. English law would determine both liabilities where no claim had been brought and there was no follow settlements clause.

4. Restrictions on the parties' choice: impossible choices

10.58 Although Article 3 confers considerable freedom on the parties, that freedom is not absolute.

64. The insurance policy contained warranties as to the vessels being classed at all times. The vessels were not but it was assumed that that was not causative of loss and that the insurers would therefore have to pay under Venezuelan law. These warranties were incorporated into the reinsurance contract which also contained an express provision providing that "warranted existing class maintained". The Court of Appeal held that this express term had to be construed as having the same effect as the same provision in the insurance contract.

65. *Cf.* Seatzu, p. 95, who says that an implied choice of law is present in a reinsurance contract which embodies some terms of an underlying insurance and states that these terms should be interpreted "back to back" or "as original" or "as more fully described" in the original policy wording.

66. [2005] EWHC 2755 (Comm); [2005] All ER (D) 92.

(i) Choice confined to the choice of the law of a given municipal system

10.59 The choice of law must be a choice of law of a municipal legal system, rather than, for example, a code, a religious law, or the *lex mercatoria*.[67]

(ii) "Floating" choice of law clauses

10.60 At common law, the applicable law must exist and be identifiable at the time when the contract is made. This is because a contract cannot exist in a vacuum without reference to a proper law. It is said to follow that it is not possible to specify a "floating" applicable law (that is, a proper law chosen at a time later than the commencement of the contract), for example, by providing that one party has the option to determine the applicable law in the future by selecting the applicable law from a list of alternatives.[68] It seems that this is also the case under Article 3 of the Convention.[69]

(iii) Dépeçage

10.61 The concept of *dépeçage* refers to the fact that the parties may choose different laws to apply to different parts of a contract. There seems to be no problem in principle to different parts of a contract being governed by different laws except in relation to "the general obligation" of a contract. It would be unworkable, for example, for issues such as whether the contract is discharged by frustration or whether the innocent party can withhold performance, not to be governed by a single law. Article 3 expressly provides that by their choice the parties can select the law applicable to the whole or a part only of the contract. But the choice must be logically consistent, i.e. it must relate to elements in the contract which can be governed by different laws without giving rise to contradictions.[70] Application of *dépeçage* has sometimes been advocated as a possible solution where a contract of insurance is

67. The Green Paper (para. 3.2.3) notes that it is common practice in international trade for the parties to refer not to the law of one or other state but directly to the rules of an international convention, to customs of international trade, to the *lex mercatoria* or private codifications such as the UNIDROIT principles. Such a choice would not be allowed under Article 3 of the Convention. See also *Seatzu*, pp. 97–98. In *Shamil Bank of Bahrain EC* v. *Beximco Pharmaceuticals* [2004] 1 WLR 1784 the Court of Appeal held that a contract could not be governed by Shari'a religious law which is not simply "principles of law" but principles which apply to other aspects of life and behaviour (paras 35–37). See also *Halpern* v. *Halpern* [2006] EWHC 603 (Comm) where Clark J. confirmed that similarly it was not possible under the Rome Convention to agree to apply "Jewish law". Nor could a general reference to Jewish law amount to an incorporation as terms of the contract of the relevant provisions of Jewish law. The position may change under the proposed Rome I Regulation (see para. 10.62 below) and different principles apply in relation to arbitration (see paras 13.25–13.26 below).

68. See, confirming this principle, *Star Shipping AS* v. *China National Foreign Trade Transportation Corp., "The Star Texas"* [1993] 2 Lloyd's Rep. 445. A charter contained an unusual arbitration clause which provided "any dispute arising under the charter to be referred to arbitration in Beijing or London in Defendant's option". It was argued that this incorporated into the contract a floating proper law clause, which English law will not countenance and that therefore the arbitration clause was invalid. Although the Court of Appeal confirmed that such clauses are not possible, it rejected the argument that that was the effect of the contract. There was no intention to create a floating applicable law. If no place was given for the arbitration there could be no argument that the parties intended as the proper law wherever the arbitration eventually took place. The Supreme Court of Canada in *Imperial Life Assurance Co. of Canada* v. *Colmenares* (1967) 62 DLR (2d) 138 also took the view that a contract cannot have a proper law that shifts from time to time. See also *EI Du Pont de Nemours* v. *Agnew* [1987] 2 Lloyd's Rep. 585.

69. Article 3(2) provides that the parties can at any time decide to subject the contract to a law *other than that which previously governed it* (emphasis added). This appears to confirm that although the parties can expressly agree to change the governing law they must start with a fixed law. *Cf.* Seatzu, p. 96. Steyn LJ in *The Star of Texas, op. cit.*, commented that because it was common ground that Article 3(2) of the Convention was not applicable (arbitration agreements being excluded from the scope of the Convention) even if Article 3(2) permits a floating applicable law that could not affect the present dispute.

70. See Giuliano-Lagarde Report Commentary to Article 3(1) 1980 OJ C.282/1, 17 giving the example of an "index-linking clause", which may be made subject to a different law, to repudiation of the contract for non-performance which could not be subject to two different laws (one for the vendor and one for the purchaser) and

potentially governed by a different law from the reinsurance contract but, as we saw in paras 10.51–10.57, this is not a solution currently favoured by the courts.[71]

5. Proposals in the Rome I Regulation

10.62 In the proposed Rome I Regulation, Article 3 is amended in three ways:

(1) to include a reference to the behaviour of the parties rather than a purely hypothetical will[72];
(2) expressly to refer to the fact that "if the parties have agreed to confer jurisdiction on one or more courts or tribunals of a Member State to hear and determine disputes that have arisen or may arise out of the contract, they shall also be presumed to have chosen the law of that Member State"[73]; and
(3) to provide in order "further to boost the impact of the parties will" that parties may choose as the applicable law a non-state body of law, including UNIDROIT principles or the Principles of European Contract Law, but not the *lex mercatoria*.[74]

C. APPLICABLE LAW IN THE ABSENCE OF CHOICE (ARTICLE 4)

1. Introduction

10.63 To the extent that the law applicable to the contract has not been chosen in accordance with Article 3, the court must look to Article 4 of the Convention. This provides that "the contract shall be governed by the law of the country with which it is most closely connected". Again, dépeçage is possible but only by way of exception (Article 4(1)).

10.64 This is a very different process from that carried out under Article 3. The court is not interested in the intentions of these particular parties; rather the court determines *objectively* the law of the country with which the contract is most closely connected. At common law, the test to be applied is straightforward to state, if not apply. The contract is governed by the system of law with which the transaction has its closest and most real connection (see Chapter 12 below and particularly paras 12.2–12.4) Although, at first sight, the Convention appears to share many of the features of the common law test, appearances are deceptive.

10.65 Article 4 contains a series of presumptions, intended to identify the law with which the contract is most closely connected.[75] These presumptions are, however, not conclusive, but can be displaced or disregarded if "it appears from the circumstances as a whole that the contract is more closely connected with another country".[76] The Convention gives no indication as to the circumstances when the presumption that a law of a particular country should

generally, Collins/Dicey/Morris, paras 32-047–32-053. Furthermore, a contract cannot in its entirety be governed by two laws: *Shamil Bank of Bahrain* v. *Beximco Pharmaceuticals Ltd* [2003] 2 All ER (Comm.) 849 where it was held that a contract could not be governed both by English law and Shari'a law.

71. Composite policies like that considered by the Court of Appeal in *AMICO* will be regarded as a single, probably multipartite contract subject to one governing law ([2003] IL Pr 370 at [20]).

72. It is difficult to know what is meant by this.

73. Compare the view of the French courts referred to at para. 10.42 above. The presumption seems to be limited to jurisdiction clauses, not arbitration clauses. It also refers only to a jurisdiction agreement in favour of a Member State. It would seem very odd if a jurisdiction agreement in favour of a non-Member State did not benefit from the same presumption.

74. It is unclear whether this change would allow reference to Shari'a law or Jewish law: *cf. Shamil Bank and Halpern* v. *Halpern*, *op. cit.*, referred to at para. 10.59 above.

75. The presumptions are contained in Articles 4(2)–(4) of the Convention. For contracts of insurance and reinsurance the relevant presumption is Article 4(2) which, as will be seen, is itself not without difficulty.

76. Article 4(5).

govern can be "disregarded" and – not surprisingly – this has become an area of considerable judicial controversy. In the following sections, the presumption applicable in contracts of insurance and reinsurance will first be considered; and then the manner in which the presumed law can be displaced by another law.

2. The presumed law in insurance and reinsurance cases

10.66 There are specific presumptions that apply to rights in immovable property (Article 4(3)) and contracts for the carriage of goods (Article 4(4)). These are not relevant for present purposes. In the context of reinsurance contracts, it is the general presumption set out in Article 4(2) that will apply. Article 4(2) provides:

> "Subject to the provisions of paragraph 5 of this article, it shall be presumed that the contract is most closely connected with the country where the party who is to effect the performance which is characteristic of the contract has, at the time of conclusion of the contract, his habitual residence, or in the case of a body corporate or unincorporated, its central administration. However, if the contract is entered into in the course of that party's trade or profession, that country shall be the country in which the principal place of business is situated or, where under the terms of the contract performance is to be effected through a place of business other than the principal place of business, the country in which that other place of business is situated."

This is a complicated, multi-layered, provision. Essentially, it is necessary to:

(1) identify the performance which is characteristic of the contract;
(2) identify the party who is to effect that performance (i.e. the characteristic performer);
(3) find the relevant territorial connection for that party.

These stages are considered in turn.

(i) Stages (i) and (ii): Performance characteristic of the contract and the party effecting that performance

10.67 The idea explained by the Giuliano-Lagarde Report is to identify the function which the legal relationship involved fulfils in the economic and social life of any country.[77] Identifying the characteristic performance should be no problem in a unilateral contract. In a bilateral contract, where the counter-performance takes the form of money, the identity of characteristic performer is also clear. The characteristic performance is that for which the payment is due. That performance can be of a service, as well as say a sale of goods. It thus includes the provision of insurance services.[78] Although it might crudely be said that in contracts of insurance and reinsurance both sides pay money (one side the premium; the other side the indemnity), the characteristic performance is the provision of the indemnity, that is the payment of the loss. That is the service for which the (re)insured is paying. The (re)insurer is also the party who assumes the greater risk.[79]

77. Commentary on Article 4(2); 1980 OJ C.282/1, 20.

78. *Ibid.*

79. The notion of characteristic performance is one which the drafters of the Convention adopted from Swiss law. Where there are two performances involving the payment of money, the characteristic performer is the party carrying the greater risk – see D'Oliveira, "Characteristic Obligation in the Draft EEC Obligation Convention" (1977) 25 Am J Comp L as discussed in Clarkson/Hill, pp. 186–187. On reinsurance services *cf.* Merkin (Insurance), para. 4.2.24. See Clarke, para. 2-8. The author notes that there is some question as to whether the relevant service provided is the insurance money or the cover. Faced with this debate the author believes there must be some temptation to avoid it and fall back on Article 4(5). But whilst there may well be such a debate in either case the insurer is identified as the provider of the characteristic service and accordingly it is his territorial connection which is indicated. See also *Vögeli* v. *Müller,* 2 May 1973, 99 (11) BGZ 315 referred to in Plender/Wilderstein, para. 6.14: in a contract of insurance, the characteristic performance is that of the insurer.

10.68 Identifying characteristic performance is particularly difficult where the agreement involves multiple obligations. For example, in *Print Concept GmbH* v. *GEW (EC) Ltd*[80] the German claimant undertook to distribute in Germany, Austria and Switzerland air-cooled drying systems supplied by the defendant English company under an exclusive distribution agreement. The question arose whether the characteristic performance was the supply of the machines by the defendant, or the marketing and selling of the machines by the claimant. The English court of appeal decided that the "real meat" of the contract and therefore the characteristic performance was the supply of the products by the defendant. But to identify the "real meat" on a case by case basis misses the point. The *characteristic performance* is that which distinguishes this type of contract generically from others. The essential characteristic of an exclusive distribution agreement, that which distinguishes it from a normal contract of sale, is the penetration of the market by the distributor.

(ii) Stage (iii): Relevant territorial connection

10.69 Here there are a number of alternatives: "habitual residence"; "central administration"; "principal place of business"; "other place of business". Because the (re)insurer is effecting the performance which is characteristic of the contract, it is necessary to apply the relevant territorial connection to the (re)insurer.

10.70 Given that the (re)insurer will be entering into the contract "in the course of that party's trade or profession", the relevant territorial connection is "the country in which the principal place of business is situated or, where under the terms of the contract the performance is to be effected through a place of business other than the principal place of business, the country in which that other place of business is situated".

10.71 It is usually a relatively straightforward matter to identify the principal place of business of the reinsurance company. The problem is the qualification: what is meant by performance being "under the terms of the contract to be effected through another place of business"?[81]

10.72 A relatively clear example is *Sierra Leone Telecommunications Co. Ltd* v. *Barclays Bank Plc.*[82] It was noted that at common law, as a general rule, the contract between a bank and its customer was governed by the law of the place where the account was kept, that this is a rule of the greatest commercial importance and that there is a risk of grave difficulty and confusion if some other law was held to be the governing law. Cresswell J. held that the same result could be reached under the Rome Convention: repayment is to be effected through the branch where the account is kept for the purposes of the Article 4(2) presumptions. These principles were applied in *Bank of Baroda* v. *Vysya Bank Ltd*,[83] where Mance J. held that the obligations of an Indian confirming bank under a letter of credit were to be effected through its London branch.

10.73 However, outside the context of the particular branch of a bank the position is less clear. Two decisions have to be contrasted. First, in the *Iran Continental Shelf* case, the parties entered into an agreement for the refurbishment of one of the claimant's oil rigs in Iran. The defendant undertook to provide parts as well as some services in Iran. The defendant was a

80. [2002] CLC 352.

81. The Giuliano-Lagarde Report simply states that "According to the last part of paragraph 2, if the contract prescribes performance by an establishment other than the principal place of business it is presumed that the contract has the closest connection with the country of that other establishment" (Commentary to Article 4(2); 1980 OJ C.282/1, 21).

82. [1998] 2 All ER 820.

83. [1994] 2 Lloyd's Rep. 87.

Delaware corporation with its principal place of business in Texas, but it also had an office in England. The question was whether the contract "was to be effected" through that English office. The judge, McCombe J., held it was not. The English office was no more than a conduit of communication between Iran and Texas. The Court of Appeal disagreed. In both the contract itself and the bill of lading under which the parts were shipped, the address of the seller was given as the English office. The reason for this was that the parties had used the English office to get round a decree in Iran preventing purchases from being made directly from the USA. The court held that the obligations under the CFR contract were, under the terms of the contract, effected through the Defendant's English office. Clarke LJ, *obiter*, doubted whether "to be effected through" should be construed so narrowly as to require the contractual obligation to be performed through that place of business (although on the facts it was in this case).

10.74 Secondly, in *Ennstone Building Products Ltd* v. *Stanger Ltd*,[84] the claimant was a supplier of stone. The defendant provided testing and consultancy services. The defendant's principal place of business was in England but it also had an office in Scotland. The Court of Appeal held that even though both parties had clearly envisaged that the defendant would undertake the characteristic performance through its Scottish office, that was not enough. It must be a term of the contract, whether express or implied, that the defendant is bound to perform through that place of business such that a failure to do so would be a breach. Furthermore, the court would not imply a term that performance *must* be through that office simply on the basis that both parties anticipated performance through the Scottish office; one would not normally imply a term requiring an individual employee to be engaged even if both parties envisaged the work being carried out by him. The judgment in *Iran Continental Shelf* was handed down on the same day as that in *Ennstone* and that case was not cited.

10.75 The *Ennstone* interpretation is a very strict interpretation. It is not enough that all the parties intended performance to be from a particular place of business: it must be a breach of contract for it not to be so performed.[85]

10.76 How might these principles be applied in the context of insurance and reinsurance contracts? The question might arise in the following way. A (re)insurance company's principal place of business is in New York. But the contract was entered into by its London office with brokers based in London, the premium was paid to that office, there was a requirement that claims be submitted to that office. However, payment of any claims had to be made through the New York principal office. It is very tempting to argue that a contract placed on the London market by London brokers is a contract the performance of which is to be effected through a place of business in London. But this is not what Article 4(2) refers to: even if the contract was arranged in London, it is the performance and not the entering into the contract which is determinative.

10.77 According to Article 4(2), what is relevant is where the *performance* of the contract is to take place. If the relevant performance is where the obligation to indemnify exists, then questions of where the contract was placed or the risk evaluated (central to a (re)insurer's acceptance of a risk, but not on this test central to his characteristic performance) are all irrelevant. What will be relevant is whether the contract specifies the place of business which must make the payment. Since it will be rare for a contract of insurance to do this (much more

84. [2002] EWCA Civ 916; [2002] WLR 3059.

85. Hill, "Choice of law in contracts under the Rome Convention: the approach of the UK courts" [2004] ICLQ 325, prefers this stricter view on the basis of certainty. But the downside is that the presumption may end up pointing to a place far removed from the actual performance of the contract in practice. As we will see, this may well lead to great reliance on rebutting the presumption under Article 4(5).

common is an obligation as to where payment must be received), it would appear that derogation from the law of the principal place of business is likely to be rare.[86]

3. Disregarding the Article 4(2) presumption: the effect of Article 4(5)

(i) Article 4(5)

10.78 It will usually be relatively straightforward to apply the Article 4(2) presumption and come up with an applicable law. Indeed, the whole point of having presumptions is that they are easy to apply and result in a clear and predictable answer. But Article 4(2) is expressly said to be subject to Article 4(5). It is in applying the Article 4(5) "exception" that real difficulties arise.

10.79 It is because it is recognised that the Article 4(2) presumption will not always produce a satisfactory result, that Article 4(5) exists. It provides[87]:

> "… the presumptions in paragraphs 2, 3 and 4 shall be disregarded if it appears from the circumstances as a whole that the contract is more closely connected with another country."

10.80 So, the country identified by application of the presumption in Article 4(2) need not be applied in every case and "shall" be disregarded if the contract is more closely connected with another country. The problem, to which the Convention provides no explicit answer, is what is the test as to when the Article 4(2) presumption can be disregarded in favour of another country with which the contract is more closely connected. There have been a number of recent cases both here and elsewhere in Europe on this point and it is a question which has caused some disagreement as to correct approach both in the UK and abroad.

(ii) Alternative tests for displacing the presumption

10.81 Essentially, there are three alternative tests. First, and at one extreme, the Article 4(2) presumption could be given the greatest possible weight, so that it can only be disregarded if the law identified has no real connection with the dispute. This was the approach adopted by the Dutch court in *Societe Nouvelle des Papeteries de l'Aa SA* v. *BV Machinefabriek BOA*.[88]

86. In *AMICO*, Mance LJ, having held that there was a choice of law in favour of Texas under Article 3, went on to consider Article 4(2). He noted that the policy stipulated that in the event of total loss, the insured should contact what was clearly a centralised main claims department in New Jersey. He then stated, having regard to all the circumstances, that the policy still provided by implication for performance by Amico through its Houston office. But even if the second sentence of Article 4(2) did not itself apply to point towards Texas law, the presumption that would result in favour of Illinois (where the insurance company was incorporated and had its principal place of business) under the first sentence was obviously displaced by the circumstances connecting the policy with Texas ([2003] IL Pr 370, para. 47). The circumstances relied on concerning the entering into of the policy were: that it was a global transportation policy entered into through an underwriting office in Houston, the named insured was also a Texas corporation, the policy was negotiated during meetings in Texas, the insured's principal office was in Houston, a Texas mailing address was given and the broker was based in Texas.

87. The first part of Article 4(5) says that the presumption shall not apply if the characteristic performance cannot be determined. It is not clear why it is necessary to say so: surely it is impossible to apply Article 4(2) if one of the fundamental premises on which that section operates cannot be ascertained. The classic example referred to in the Giuliano-Lagarde report is a contract of barter. This is unlikely to prove problematic in a (re)insurance context, where it is clear that the characteristic performance is that of the (re)insurer (para. 10.67 above).

88. 1992 Nederlands Jurisprudentie 750, noted and discussed by Struychen, "Some Dutch Reflections on the Rome Convention, Article 4(5)" in [1996] LMCLQ 18; and Hill, "Choice of law in contracts under the Rome Convention", *op. cit.*, p. 339. The case was concerned with a contract for the purchase by the French plaintiffs of a paper press from the Dutch defendants. The negotiations for the sale took place in France. The offer and the contract were in the French language. The buyers ordered the press from the seller's agent in France. The sellers confirmed the order in French, exchanged further technical details with the buyers, delivered the machine in France and

Alternatively, and at the other extreme, the court could look at all the factors connecting the contract to various systems of law, and if more point to another country than the country selected under Article 4(2), then Article 4(5) can be applied. The presumption thus operates only as a tie-breaker when the laws of two countries are otherwise equally connected. Finally, some course in between these two extremes could be adopted.

10.82 There are problems with both of the extreme positions. The first test – which gives the presumption the greatest possible weight – serves to deprive the exception to the presumption of a great deal of its effect. It will only apply in the most extreme of cases and does not appear consistent with the language used in Article 4(5). The first option renders the exception one that will almost never pertain. However, some limited support for this approach might be taken from the Giuliano-Lagarde Report, which states that Article 4(5) provides for the possibility of disregarding the presumptions in Articles 4(2), (3) and (4) when "*all* the circumstances show the contract to have closer connections with another country. In this case, the law of that other country is applied" (emphasis added).[89]

10.83 By contrast, the second option – which elevates the Article 4(5) test to one of almost equal standing with the Article 4(2) presumption –deprives the presumption of almost all effect, so that in every case it will be necessary to consider the Article 4(5) test and balance the law it selects against the law selected by the Article 4(2) presumption. Some English judges have taken the view that this accords with the wording of the Article, which does not refer to Article 4(5) being an "exception" to a more general rule. In *Crédit Lyonnais* v. *New Hampshire Insurance Co. Ltd*,[90] the issue was whether two insurance contracts were governed by English or French law. The Rome Convention did not apply directly, but Hobhouse LJ referred to the relationship between Articles 4(2) and 4(5) in the following way:

> "The word used in Article 4 of the Rome Convention is 'presumption'. The commentators refer to it as a 'rebuttable' presumption. But para. 5 of the Article goes further: it provides that where the 'characteristic performance' cannot be determined the presumption in para. 2 is not to be made and, in any case, the presumptions in paras 2 to 4 ...
>
> ... shall be disregarded if it appears from the circumstances as a whole that the contract is more closely connected with another country.
>
> The presumption is therefore displaced if the court concludes that it is not appropriate in the circumstances of any given case. This, formally, makes the presumption very weak but it does not detract from the guidance that para. 2 gives as to what is meant by 'the country with which it is most closely connected' and does not detract from the need to look for a geographical connection. This reading of Article 4 is also supported by the commentators."

However, Hobhouse LJ did seem to acknowledge that the factor identified in Article 4(2) must be given due weight, seeming to accept that it (at the very least) must act as a weighting factor in the Article 4(5) analysis.

---

assembled it there. The price was paid in French francs. The presumption under Article 4(2) clearly pointed to Dutch law as the applicable law. However, this was the only connection with relevance to the place of business of the sellers. According to Struycken, the Supreme Court stated a general rule of thumb, as follows: "The Court of Appeal apparently and rightly proceeded from the view that it follows from the wording and the structure of Article 4, as well as from the uniformity in the application of the law which has been intended with the Convention, that this exception to the main rule of s.2 has to be applied restrictively, to the effect that the main rule should be disregarded only if, in the special circumstances of the case, the place of business of the party who is to effect the characteristic performance has no real significance as a connecting factor" (emphasis added). This approach received some support from Lord Marnoch in the Inner House of Court of Session in Scotland in *Caledonia Subsea Ltd* v. *Microperi Srl* 2001 SC 716 (OH) 2003 SC 70, but the majority adopted a different approach – see, further, para. 10.88 below.

89. Commentary to Article 4(5); 1980 OJ C.282/1, 22.

90. [1997] 2 Lloyd's Rep. 1, 5.

10.84 Although, as we have seen, there is authority to support both of the extreme positions,[91] it is unlikely that the English courts will adopt either extreme. The better approach is one that accepts that Article 4(2) will provide the usual rule (thereby giving the presumption some clear role), but that the exception has a greater role to play then merely when the Article 4(2) selected law has no real connection with the dispute. The approach is that the Article 4(2) presumption will be applied unless the evidence clearly demonstrates[92] either a preponderance[93] or (more likely) a *clear* preponderance[94] of factors in favour of another country. The difference between a preponderance and a clear preponderance is obviously one of degree; and, of course, other tests could be formulated – some commentators have formulated a test based on an *overwhelming* preponderance of factors in favour of another country,[95] which brings this middle test much closer to extreme first test.

(iii) The case-law

10.85 It is worth reviewing the decisions that form the basis for this middle way. In *Samcrete Egyptian Engineer & Contractors SAE* v. *Land Rover Exports Ltd*,[96] the defendant acted as guarantor in relation to the distribution obligations of another group company which had been appointed by the claimant English manufacturer, Land Rover, as its exclusive distributor in Egypt. The distribution agreement itself was expressly governed by English law. Applying the Article 4(2) presumption, the characteristic performance was that of the guarantor whose principal place of business was in Egypt. But should Egyptian law be disregarded under Article 4(5)? Potter LJ noted that while a straight reading rendered the Article 4(2) presumption formally very weak,[97] unless there was at least a rule of thumb requiring a preponderance of factors, the other way the intention of the convention was likely to be subverted. Thus:

"[Article 4(2) should] only be disregarded in circumstances which clearly demonstrate the existence of connecting factors justifying the disregarding of it."

On the facts, he allowed the presumption to be displaced in favour of English law, on the basis that England was the place of payment under the guarantee (i.e. was the place where the characteristic performance was to take place) and where the goods were to be delivered.[98] The tendency of English judges to give special significance to the place where the characteristic performance is to be effected is apparent in a number of these cases and will be referred to further below (see para. 10.88 below).

91. A "weak" view of the presumption is also supported by the Italian Corte di Cassazione in its decision of 10 March 2000 No. 58, Riv.dir.int.priv.proc. 2000, p. 773. The court ignored the presumption in a case relating to a dispute concerning the execution of a sale involving the delivery and mortgage of machines. The view that Article 4(2) is only guidance is also supported by the French Court of Appeal at Versaille in *Bloch* v. *Lima*, 6 Feb 1991 (noted and criticised by Lagarde in Rev.crit.dip. 1991, p. 745).

92. See *Samcrete Egyptian Engineer & Contractor SAE* v. *Land Rover Exports Ltd* [2002] CLC 533, para. 10.85 below; *Ennstone Building Products Ltd* v. *Stanger Ltd* [2002] EWCA Civ 916, [2002] WLR 3059, para 10.88 below and *Waldwiese Stiftung* v. *Lewis* [2004] EWHC 2589, para. 10.89 below.

93. See *Samcrete* and *PT Pan Indonesian Bank Ltd TBK* v. *Marconi Communications International Ltd* [2005] EWCA Civ 422, para. 10.96 below.

94. See *Definitely Maybe (Touring) Ltd* v. *Marek Lieberberg Konzertagentur GmbH (No. 2)* [2001] 1 WLR 1745 at para. 10.86 below and *Caledonia Subsea Ltd* v. *Microperi SRL* 2001 SC 716 (OH) 2003 SC 70 at para. 10.88 below.

95. Hill, "Choice of law in contracts under the Rome Convention", *op. cit.*, p. 350.

96. [2002] CLC 533, 545.

97. See the comments of Hobhouse LJ in *Crédit Lyonnais*, para. 10.83 above.

98. A similar conclusion was reached by the French court in a case where a French company was a distributor in France of an Italian company's products. The distribution agreement was governed by Italian law. The presumption pointed to French law governing the guarantee but the court held that Article 4(5) applied in favour of Italian law (see O. Lando, "Some issues relating to the law applicable to contractual obligations" (1996/97) *Kings College Law Journal*, p. 55.

10.86 In *Definitely Maybe (Touring) Ltd* v. *Marek Lieberberg Konzertagentur GmbH (No. 2)*,[99] the claimant, a company based in England, provided the services of pop groups, including the group Oasis, to concert organisers. The defendant, a German-based company, engaged the services of the group for a concert in Germany at which eventually only one of the two members of Oasis played. They declined to pay the full price and the question arose as to the law applicable to the contract. It was common ground that it was the claimants who were to effect the characteristic performance, that they were located in England and therefore that the Article 4(2) presumption pointed to England. The dispute centred on whether Article 4(5) could be applied. On the one hand it was recognised that if the presumption was to be displaced whenever there was a divergence that the presumption would be of little weight or value. Article 4(2) must have been inserted to provide a "normal rule". The judge, Morison J., then went on to consider the factors said to show a closer connection to Germany than England. He held that the centre of gravity was Germany and that if Article 4(5) applied alone, that would be the governing law. He then referred to the two schools of thought about the relationship between the two sections. He rejected the view of the Dutch court that the presumption becomes a rule of law to which Article 4(5) must be treated as an exception is not (yet) the language of the Convention. Instead he held (at para. 15) that:

"it seems to me that the presumption in Article 4(2) shall be disregarded according to the words but that in carrying out that comparative exercise due weight must be given to the factor identified in Article 4(2).

But on the facts, Article 4(5) was again applied. Performance by both parties was to be in Germany. Thus, there was a 'clear preponderance' of factors in favour of Germany."

10.87 In *Ennstone* (the facts of this case have already been referred to in para. 10.74 above), the court refused to apply Article 4(5), stating that if the presumption was to be of any real significance, it must be taken to apply except where evidence clearly shows that the contract is more closely connected with another country.

10.88 The fullest consideration of the issues comes in a Scottish case, *Caledonia Subsea Ltd* v. *Microperi Srl*.[100] The jurisdiction of the Scottish court depended on whether a contract was governed by Egyptian or Scottish law. A Scottish company had agreed to provide diving services on an Egyptian pipeline. There was no doubt that the relevant place of business was in Scotland. As to whether that presumption should be disregarded, Lord President Cullen reviewed both the strong and weak models referred to above and stated:

"As has been observed in a number of decisions and by commentators, each of the two schools of thought in their extreme forms are open to significant objection. If the only real significance of para 2 is that of providing a 'tie-breaker', it is difficult to understand why the paragraph was given the prominence which it occupies in the arrangement of Article 4 … On the other hand, to treat the presumption in para. 2 as so powerful that it must be applied unless there is no connecting factor with the country which has been identified, appears to run contrary to the language of Article 4 which makes para. 2 'Subject to' (in the French text '*Sous réserve du*') para. 5 and to deprive the latter of much of its significance.

It appears that thus far the English courts have not reached a definitive view as to the interrelationship of paras 2 and 5 but have preferred to deal with each case on its circumstances. As we have noted earlier, there is as yet no guidance from the European Court of Justice …

In my view Article 4 intended to accord a special significance to the place of business of the principal performer as the indicator of the country with which the contract had the closest connection. I am not disposed to agree with the view that this was because in most cases the contract was likely to be performed in that country; or with the view suggested by *Dicey and Morris* at para. 32-124 that the presumption may most easily be rebutted in those cases where the place of performance differs from the place of business of the party whose performance is characteristic of the contract, a statement approved by Mance J. at p. 93 in *Bank of Baroda* v. *Vysya Bank Ltd*. If the framers of Article 4 had intended to

99. [2001] 1 WLR 1745.

100. SRL 2001 SC 716 (OH), 2003 SC 70.

attach such significance to the place of performance they could have readily indicated that, but they did not do so. Indeed when the place of performance is such an obvious candidate as the test, the fact that it is not mentioned suggests a movement away from it. Furthermore, it is important to bear in mind the significance of the social and economic factors which are mentioned in the report. No doubt the place where the contract is performed is of relevance, either directly or indirectly, but it may be only one of a number of factors to be assessed in the exercise under para. 5. In the result I consider that the presumption under para. 2 should not be 'disregarded' unless the outcome of the comparative exercise referred to in para. 5 – which, unlike para. 2, may involve difficulty and uncertainty – demonstrates a clear preponderance of factors in favour of another country."

10.89 In *Waldwiese Stiftung* v. *Lewis*,[101] Mann J. held:

"I shall not treat the presumption as being weak and I shall investigate whether the circumstances in this case 'clearly demonstrate the existence of connecting factors justifying the disregarding of the presumption' or '[whether] the evidence clearly shows that the contract is more closely connected with another country'; in each case the emphasis being on the word 'clearly'. Otherwise, the presumption would be too easily robbed of the effect which it is obviously intended to have.[102]

10.90 The Court of Appeal in *PT Pan Indonesia Bank Ltd TBK* v. *Marconi Communications International Limited*[103] agreed that the presumption should only be disregarded in circumstances which demonstrate a "preponderance of contrary connecting factors".[104]

(iv) The application of Article 4(5) in reinsurance cases

10.91 As we have seen, the application of the Article 4(2) presumption to reinsurance cases is likely to lead to the application of the law of the reinsurer's principal place of business or possibly (but much less likely, for the reasons given in paras 10.76–10.77 above) the branch or office where the reinsurance was entered into. This will often lead to a different result than that which was reached at common law. At common law the courts tended to focus on the market by reference to which the contract was made, and also on the role of brokers in the process. This focus tended to lead to the application of English law to contracts of reinsurance entered into on the London market by London brokers *regardless* of the place of business of the (re)insurer. Indeed the courts often stressed the importance of English law governing in this situation.[105] The problems of applying the Article 4(2) presumption to reinsurance contracts are that

101. [2004] EWHC 2589 *per* Mann J., at [28].

102. See also *Ophthalmic Innovations International (UK) Ltd* v. *Ophthalmic Innovations International Incorporated* [2004] EWHC 2948. The claimant was an importer and distributor of the defendant's optical equipment into the UK. The defendant, a US co with its principal place of business in California agreed to indemnify the claimant against any claims brought as a result of the sale of its products. The judge, Lawrence Collins J., refused to allow service out of the jurisdiction holding that the indemnification agreement was not governed by English law. There was no evidence justifying disregarding the presumption in favour of Californian law. The fact that payments might be due in England and third party claims might be in England was not sufficient. On the contrary the form and language of the document showed they were US documents and the distribution agreement was expressly governed by Californian law.

103. [2005] EWCA Civ 422.

104. At para. 44. The Court of Appeal rejected any stricter approach, specifically that suggested by Lord Marnoch in *Caledonia* at paras 46–48. See, further, para. 10.81 above.

105. For example, in *Maritime Insurance Company* v. *Assekuranz Union von 1865* (1935) 52 Ll L Rep 16 the policy contained a clause providing for arbitration in London which was held to be decisive despite the fact that the contract was arguably made in Germany and that the contract was invalid according to English law. Goddard J. commented that otherwise every reinsurance contact made by an English company in a foreign country would be intended to governed by that foreign law which would not be welcomed by English companies. That of course is the effect of the Article 4(2) presumption. See also the Court of Appeal in *Citadel Insurance Co.* v. *Atlantic Union Insurance Co. SA* [1952] 2 Lloyd's Rep. 543, where all members of the court stressed the importance of the finding that a reinsurance contract entered into on the London market through London brokers was governed by English law to the London reinsurance market. See also *Trade Indemnity Plc* v. *Forsakringsatiebolaget Njord* [1995] 1 All ER 796 where Rix J. stressed the very strong imputation seen in cases like *Forsikringsakjeselskapet Vesta* v. *Butcher* [1989] AC 852 that London reinsurance is governed by English law.

"In re-insurance the re-insurer is the party who assumes the risk, and he is therefore to effect the performance which is characteristic of the contract. Nevertheless, it is the re-insurer party who organises his coverage. In many cases he has the same risk covered by server re-insurers in different countries who each take a part. If the law of the re-insurer governed each of these contracts the re-insured party would be subject to different laws in respect of the same risk. He would have to meet different requirements as regards the information to be given when the contracts are being made, and to make sure that his claims handling meets the demands of the law of each of the re-insurers. In practice this would mean that the re-insurer party would have to comply with the law which in each case puts the strictest requirements on the re-insured party."[106]

10.92 It may be that the Convention effected a dramatic change in the choice of law in (re)insurance cases, but that is unlikely for a number of reasons. In the first place, the significance of Article 3 must not be forgotten, in particular the circumstances where a choice may be "demonstrated" by the terms of the contract or the circumstances of the case, without there having been an express choice of law.[107] That said, the extent to which Article 3 can apply where the common law would have *imputed* a choice of law must be questioned. The distinction between implied actual choice and imputed choice was often blurred at common law.[108] But that sort of shading is not possible under the Convention. Whilst some cases of imputed choice may fall within Article 3, the European Court of Justice is unlikely to support too wide an interpretation of Article 3 when it eventually hears Rome Convention cases, since a wide interpretation of Article 3 undermines the "certainty" sought to be achieved by the presumptions in Article 4, whilst departing too far from the parties' real choice.

10.93 As we have seen, the presumed choice of law imposed by Article 4(2) uses as a connecting factor the principal place of business of the (re)insurer.[109] Since this is – given the nature of contracts of insurance – an inappropriate connecting factor,[110] its application is likely to result in displacement by the Article 4(5) exception.

10.94 The next question is what law will Article 4(5) point to in (re)insurance cases? Two preliminary points to note are first that Article 4 refers to the *country* with which the contract is most closely connected, rather than the *system of law*.[111] However, arguably, country includes the legal system so the debate may well be somewhat sterile.[112]

106. O. Lando, "Some Issues Relating to the Law Applicable to Contractual Obligations" in (1996/97) *Kings College Law Journal* 55, p. 71.

107. See paras 10.19–10.57 above.

108. See para. 12.4 below. Good examples are *Tiernan* v. *Magen*, and *Tryg Baltica* (paras 10.32–10.33 above). See also *DR Insurance Co.* v. *Central National Insurance Co. of Omaha* [1996] 1 Lloyd's Rep. 74, 81–82: "... when parties enter a particular market in order to transact business they can usually be taken to intend that their relationship will be governed by the system of law in place in that market. Whether it be viewed as an implied choice of law or simply the application of the system of law which has the closest connection with the transaction, the result will be the same", in that case that English law governed (*per* Moore-Bick Q.C. sitting as a deputy judge of the High Court), at 81–82.

109. See para. 10.67 above.

110. To illustrate the problem, the following are cases at common law where the courts found that English law governed, but which would *prima facie* be decidedly differently under the Rome Convention unless Article 4(5) applies: (i) Lord Wilberforce in *Amin Rasheed Shipping Corp.* v. *Kuwait Insurance Co.* [1984] AC 50; and in the Court of Appeal, *Armadora Occidental SA* v. *Horace Mann Insurance Co.* [1977] 1 WLR 1098, CA (as will be seen in Chapter 12 below in both cases it was held that the closest and most real connection was with English law); and the following cases discussed in para. 12.13 below; (ii) *Citadel Insurance Co.* v. *Atlantic Union Insurance Co. SA* [1982] 2 Lloyd's Rep. 543; (iii) *Afia Worldwide Insurance Co.* v. *Deutsche Ruck Versicherings AG* (1983) 133 NLJ 621; (iv) *Britannia Steamship Insurance Association* v. *Ausonia Assicurazioni* [1984] 2 Lloyd's Rep. 98; (v) *Overseas Union Insurance* v. *Incorporated General Insurance* [1992] 1 Lloyd's Rep. 63.

111. See Collier, p. 204.

112. *Cf. Rossano* v. *Manufacturers' Life Insurance Company* [1963] 2 QB 352. An Egyptian national resident in Egypt purchased endowment policies from the Egyptian branch of a company incorporated in Ontario. McNair J. concluded that the proper law of the contract was the law of Ontario because that was the legal system with which they were most closely connected, albeit that the country with which they were most closely connected was arguably Egypt (p. 369).

10.95 A potentially more significant problem is that factors relating to the particular parties' intentions are relevant *only* to Article 3. As we have seen, London market factors are often treated as relevant to an express choice of law, but it is questionable how far they should also be relevant to the objective assessment undertaken under Article 4(5). Some support for the application of Article 4(5) in such cases is found in *The Lincoln National Life Insurance Co.* v. *Employers Reinsurance Corp.*[113] The court confirmed that the party who is to effect characteristic performance for the purposes of Article 4(2) is the reinsurer. In the present case, however, each of the parties had their principal place of business in various jurisdictions, and it would make little sense to hold that each claimant's obligations was governed by the law of a different country. Clearly, it was held, it was necessary to consider whether the contracts had a close connection with one country whose law would then apply to govern all the obligations arising under them. Although the contracts were not made by reference to a standard English form, nor were they all made in the London market (in the sense of being placed by London brokers direct with London underwriters) all the contracts were negotiated through brokers in London and were made in the usual manner of the London market, that is, by the scratching of a slip. Two other factors which pointed strongly towards England were the nature of the cover itself which was specialist cover developed in the London market and that the slips incorporated by reference a number of standard London market clauses.

10.96 In *Groupama Navigation et Transports* v. *Catatumbo CA Seguros*[114] it was common ground that the reinsurance contract was governed by English law, but Mance LJ commented[115]:

"Neither the insurance nor the reinsurance expressly states its governing law … But in this case, to legal ears, it speaks for itself. The insurance was issued in Venezuela in Spanish covering a Venezuelan risk and provided for the jurisdiction of the Maracaibo Court if arbitration was not agreed. The reinsurance was placed by London brokers with the appellant reinsurers through their French underwriting agents for their 50% share and the MAR 91 slip policy form which is incorporated provides for the English Courts to have exclusive jurisdiction."

The extent to which the Article 4(2) presumption can be displaced is clearly critical here.[116] A different approach to Article 4(5) can be seen in *Marconi Communications Int'l* v. *PT Pan Indonesian Bank Ltd*.[117] Under the terms of a contract of sale, the price was payable by letter of credit to be established and authorised by a bank in London. The buyers established various letters of credit, including one issued by an Indonesian bank who directed the defendant bank in London. The claimant drew on the defendant bank and the court was asked to determine the proper law of the contract between the claimant and the defendant bank. The court noted that Article 4(2) assumed an ability to identify a single party charged with a single characteristic performance; which was not the case with a letter of credit. The overall purpose was to achieve payment for the goods. The most important factual element was therefore the place where the documents were to be presented and where payment was to be made. Therefore there was a "valid reason and commercial logic" why Article 4(5) should be applied.[118]

113. [2002] Lloyd's Rep. IR 853.
114. [2000] 2 Lloyd's Rep. 350.
115. At para. 25.
116. A different approach, perhaps more in keeping with the aim of achieving predictable outcomes in different jurisdictions, would be to have a different presumption in the case of (re)insurance contracts; for example that the law of the re-insured party govern the contract of reinsurance. See O. Lando, "Some Issues Relating to the Law Applicable to Contractual Obligations", *op. cit.*, p. 71. This is not an approach which has found favour even under the proposed Rome I Regulation which as discussed below removes the Article 4(5) case by case solution to the problem (see para. 10.98 below).
117. [2005] EWCA Civ 422.
118. Para. 66. See also the judgment of the Cour d'appel de Versailles in *Bloch* v. *Lima*, 1991, referred to in Plender/Wilderstein, para. 6-17. Mr Bloch, resident in France, was the manager of a French company which distributed Italian products. Mr Bloch had signed a document in Italy guaranteeing the debts of the French company. The

(v) No characteristic performance in a (re)insurance contract

10.97 Some writers[119] maintain that it is impossible to identify the characteristic performance in insurance and reinsurance contracts. If that is right, then Article 4(2) does not apply and a court would proceed directly to an application of Article 4(5). It is difficult to see how this can be right. However, they reflect the profoundly unsatisfactory choice of law rules in the absence of express choice (as regards (re)insurance) contained in the Rome Convention.

4. The proposed Rome I Regulation

10.98 The most important change proposed in the Rome I Regulation is that the presumption set out in Article 4(2) will become a fixed rule, and the exception in Article 4(5) is therefore abolished. Thus, by Article 4(1) to the extent that the law has not been chosen, the contract shall be governed by, in the case of a contract for the provision of services, the law of the country in which the service provider has his habitual residence.[120] By Article 18, for companies the principal establishment shall be considered to be the habitual residence save that where the contract is concluded in the course of operation of a subsidiary, branch or other establishment, or if under the contract, performance is the responsibility of such an establishment, this establishment shall be considered the habitual residence. The justification for this change is that "since the cornerstone of the instrument is freedom of choice, the rules applicable in the absence of choice should be as precise and foreseeable as possible so that the parties can decide whether or not to exercise their choice". This change, if adopted, could have considerable significance in the (re)insurance context. As we have seen, in many cases (unless it is possible to rely on Article 3) the only way to avoid the conclusion that the contract is governed by the law of the country of the (re)insurer is to rely on the Article 4(5) exception. Under the proposed Rome I Regulation such a solution would no longer be possible. This change clearly has the potential of imposing on the parties to international (re)insurance contracts a law which they had no expectation would govern the contract between them. If the Regulation comes into force in this form, this change is one which all parties to such transactions must be aware of.[121]

D. CONSUMER CONTRACTS (ARTICLE 5)

1. The definition of a consumer contract

10.99 Under the Rome Convention, special rules apply to consumer contracts.[122] These are defined in Article 5(1) as:

---

guarantee was valid under Italian law but not under French law. The Article 4(2) presumption pointed to France. The court held that Italian law applied, placing weight on the language used, the place where the contract was signed and the residence of the creditor. But it also seems that the court was influenced by what was just and reasonable, seeking to apply the conflict rule that the contract of guarantee should be governed by the same law as that governing the underlying debt.

119. See, for example, Merkin (Insurance), para. 4.2.24.

120. It also sets out certain contracts and identifies the characteristic performer. In the context of some of these cases, e.g. in relation to distribution contracts, this seems like a fairly blunt tool: compare the analysis of the Court of Appeal in *Print Concept* referred to in para. 10.68 above.

121. See further S. Dutson, "A Dangerous Proposal – the European Commission's Attempt to Amend the Law Applicable to Contractual Obligations" in (2006) JBL 608.

122. These provisions reflect the fact that the consumer is presumed to be in a weaker bargaining position which requires special protection to be afforded to that party (see the Giuliano-Lagarde Report commentary to Article 5 1980 OJ C.282/1, 23). Although no special rules existed at common law in a choice of law context, this policy is apparent in statutes such as the Unfair Contract Terms Act 1977.

"... a contract the object of which is the supply of goods or services[123] to a person (the consumer) for a purpose which can be regarded as being outside his trade and profession."

Article 5 will not apply to reinsurance, but contracts of insurance entered into by an individual in his private capacity,[124] for example car insurance, holiday insurance, house contents insurance or life insurance will be subject to the rules set out in Article 5.[125]

A difficult question arises as to whether these provisions apply to contracts covered by the insurance directives (see further para. 11.39 below).

2. Effect of Article 5

10.100 Where there is a consumer contract as defined in Article 5(1), Article 5 has two effects, described in Articles 5(2) and 5(3).

(i) Article 5(2): continued application of mandatory rules

10.101 Article 5(2) provides that even if a law has been chosen according to the provisions of Article 3, this shall not have the effect of depriving the consumer of the protection afforded to him by the mandatory rules of the law of the country in which he has his habitual residence:

(i) if in that country the conclusion of the contract was preceded by a specific invitation addressed to him[126] or by advertising,[127] and he had taken all the steps necessary on his part for the conclusion of the contract[128]; or

(ii) if the other party or his agent received the consumer's order in that country.[129]

The effect of this provision as regards "mandatory rules" is considered in para. 10.115 below.

(ii) Article 5(3): non-application of Article 4

10.102 In the absence of an express choice of law pursuant to Article 3, Article 5 modifies Article 4. If one of the two conditions described in para. 10.101 above are met, the contract will be governed by the law of the country in which the consumer has his habitual residence. This is an absolute rule. It does away with the Article 4 presumptions (which would tend to reach the opposite conclusion) and is not subject to Article 4(5) (thus this law cannot be displaced in favour of any other).

10.103 The Rome I Regulation proposes a new rule applying only the law of the place of the consumer's residence. It also replaces the conditions with a "targeted" activity criterion (new Article 5).

123. Including insurance (see Giuliano-Lagarde Report commentary to Article 5, 1980 OJ C.282/1, 23).

124. Or "primarily" outside his trade or profession (see Giuliano-Lagarde Report commentary to Article 5, 1980 OJ C.282/1, 23).

125. In the proposed Rome I Regulation, the definition of a consumer contract is changed to make it clear that the non-consumer party has to be acting in the course of his or her business. There is some debate about whether this is the case under the Rome Convention, but in any case it will always be the case in an insurance contract.

126. E.g. by mailshot or email.

127. The advertisement must have been directed to the consumer in that country. See the Giuliano-Lagarde Report commentary on Article 5, 1980 OJ C.282/1, 24 and the comments in Dicey/Morris/Collins, para. 33-09–33-010, and Seatzu, p. 107.

128. By this is meant the factual rather than legal steps necessary so avoiding difficulties such as the post rule, etc (see Giuliano-Lagarde Report commentary on Article 5, 1980 OJ C.282/1, 24).

129. There is considerable overlap between this and the first condition. An example of when this provision might apply is where a consumer has addressed himself to the stand of a foreign firm at a fair or exhibition taking place in the consumer's country or to a branch or agency of the firm in that country even though the firm has not advertised in that country in a relevant way. It would also apply to "cross-border excursion selling" (Giuliano-Lagarde Report commentary to Article 5, 1980 OJ C.282/1, 24).

E. DISPLACEMENT OF THE APPLICABLE LAW: MANDATORY RULES AND PUBLIC POLICY

1. Introduction

10.104 The applicable law selected by Articles 3 or 4 may be displaced or supplemented by mandatory rules and/or rules of public policy. The application of mandatory rules is essentially positive in effect. If there is a rule which is "mandatory" in effect (the meaning of this will be considered further below) it will be applied regardless of the law applicable to the contract. By contrast, the use of the doctrine of public policy is essentially negative: the application of the applicable law may be refused if it is incompatible with public policy.

(i) Mandatory rules

10.105 Article 3 of the Rome Convention allows the parties to choose the law they wish to govern the contract. Under Article 3, there are no limits on that choice. The parties are free to chose any law they please regardless of whether it is connected in any way to them or the contract. However, that does not mean that such a choice of law can effectively serve to displace certain laws of a country having a specific connection with the parties or the dispute. For example, a reinsurance contract is entered into between two English companies in relation to an English insurance policy covering risks in England. Article 3 allows the parties to select, e.g., French or New York law to govern the contract. But, notwithstanding that choice, certain rules of English law will nevertheless apply. Such rules are known as "mandatory" rules. A number of provisions in the Rome Convention provide for the application of the mandatory rules of countries whose law is not the applicable law.[130]

(ii) Rules of public policy

10.106 The applicable law may be limited, i.e. not applied, by reason of the public policy of the *lex fori*: Article 16. As stated, this is essentially a negative doctrine: the applicable law is simply not applied because it is inconsistent with public policy.

2. Mandatory rules

(i) Two different types of mandatory rule

10.107 Rules can be mandatory in two different ways, although the distinction is referred to differently and is not always consistently drawn.[131] As we have seen, the Rome Convention in Article 4 provides for an applicable law where the parties to the contract have not made an effective choice of law pursuant to Article 3. Because Article 3 provides an unfettered choice of law, the parties to a contract may use that freedom to escape provisions in the law that would otherwise apply. Generally speaking, they will be permitted to do so. Thus, if English

130. E.g. Articles 3(3) and 7.

131. The distinction is referred to in contrasting ways in the different language versions of the Convention. In the French text they are *dispositions impératives* (Article 3(3)) and *lois de police* (Article 7). The two different types of mandatory rules are referred to in the Green Paper. It explains the difference by pointing out that what is special about mandatory rules within the meaning of Article 7 (which it notes are designated by the term "overriding rules" by English writers) is that the court does not even apply its conflict rules to see what law would be applicable and assess whether its context might be repugnant to the values of the forum but automatically applies its own law. The definition of rules within Article 7 proposed:

> "national provisions compliance with which has been deemed to be so crucial for the protection of the political, social or economic order in the member state concerned as to require compliance therewith by all persons present on the national territory of that member state and all legal relationships within that State."

law was the applicable law *but for* an effective (Article 3) choice of some other law, the parties could (by choosing another law) avoid its effect. Mandatory rules of the first type prevent the parties from excluding their operation in this way. Where English law is the "default", in the sense that but for the parties' choice, it would apply, the parties are not permitted (whether by an express choice of law, or otherwise), to derogate from that rule. For example, under the Landlord and Tenant Act 1985 in a lease of residential premises for a term of less than seven years there is an implied statutory covenant to keep the structure and exterior in repair. The Act provides that an agreement which purports to exclude or limit this obligation is void. A choice of law provision is one such exclusion or limitation. In effect, the provisions of the Landlord and Tenant Act will apply if the contract would otherwise be governed by English law, but for an express choice of another law.[132]

10.108 The intervention of English law in this way is regarded as legitimate[133] because the contract has a connection with England – but for the Article 3 choice, English law would apply. However, this need not be the only reason why a mandatory rule might bite on a contract. The second type of mandatory rule applies to a contract irrespective of the applicable law. In other words, even if the parties have chosen a law other than English law pursuant to Article 3 *and* English law would *not* be the "default" law pursuant to Article 4, the mandatory rule still applies. Clearly, rules of comity and public international law will restrict the extent to which mandatory rules of this sort can apply.[134] The intervention of English law in this way is clearly not legitimised by the fact that English law is the law applicable in default, and there will – in the case of this type of mandatory rule – be some other factor connecting English law with the contract. An example of such a provision is the Employment Rights Act 1996, which provides in section 204(1) that "for the purposes of this Act it is immaterial whether the law which (apart from this Act) governs any person's employment is the law of the United Kingdom, or if a part of the United Kingdom, or not". Thus section 204 secures the benefits of the Act to employees who work here for foreign employers and whose contracts of employment may well be governed by foreign law. It is the employee's presence in the jurisdiction that constitutes the connecting factor. Another example of such a rule, according to the European Court of Justice, is to be found in the Commercial Agents Regulations. In *Ingmar GB Ltd v. Eaton Leonard Technologies Inc.*,[135] the European Court of Justice, disagreeing with the English High Court, held that the Commercial Agents (Council Directive) Regulations applied to an agency contract entered into between a Canadian company and an English agent despite the fact that there was an express choice of Californian law. The European Court of Justice held that the regulations, the purpose of which is to guarantee certain rights to commercial agents, apply regardless of the law applicable to the contract, where the commercial agent carries on his activity in a Member State even though the principal is established in a non-member country. The fact that the agent carries on activities within the EU is thus the relevant connecting factor.

132. *The Hollandia* [1983] AC 565 concerned the Carriage of Goods by Sea Act 1971, the Schedule to which contains certain of the Hague-Visby rules and provides by s.1(2) that the provisions of these rules "shall have the force of law". Included are rules providing that exclusion clauses other than those provided in the rules shall be null and void. A dispute arose under a bill of lading which specified that it was governed by the law of the Netherlands. It purported to include a limitation clause which was valid under Dutch law as well as an exclusive jurisdiction clause in favour of the Netherlands. The House of Lords held that since the Hague-Visby rules were to be treated as if they were part of directly enacted statute law of the UK, Article III rendered null and void the provision, as well as the choice of law and exclusive jurisdiction clauses which would subject the dispute to a jurisdiction whose substantive laws provided for a lower maximum limit.

133. Within limits, of course. The extent to which the parties' choice of law can be overridden in this way is considered in paras 10.112–10.114 below.

134. Dicey/Morris/Collins, para. 32-077.

135. C-381/98, [2000] ECR I-9305.

10.109 We shall refer to mandatory rules of the first type as "non-excludable mandatory rules" and rules of the second type as "overriding mandatory rules". However, it should be noted that labels, although convenient, can be dangerous, and may be inconsistently applied. An interesting statute in this context is the Unfair Contract Terms Act 1977. Section 27(2) provides:

"... the Act has effect notwithstanding any contract term which applies or purports to apply the law of some other country outside the UK where (a) the term is for the purpose of evading the Act and/or (b) the contract was made by a consumer resident in the UK."

Thus, this appears to be a provision which cannot be derogated from by contract in certain situations, i.e. it appears more like a non-excludable mandatory rule because it will only apply if the contract would, absent the choice of foreign law, be governed by English law.[136] But UCTA is very often referred to as an overriding statute in this context.[137] The Unfair Terms in Consumer Contracts Regulations 1999 which implement rules which mean that certain types of contractual terms are not binding on consumers operates in a way similar to UCTA. It is expressly provided that the regulations apply notwithstanding any contract term that applies or purports to apply the law of a non-Member State if the contract has a close connection with the territory of the Member State.

10.110 Of course, even overriding mandatory rules are not overriding in all circumstances. They only apply in specific circumstances, albeit that those circumstances are not defined by reference to what is the "default" law. In all cases of overriding mandatory rules, it is of particular importance to determine the scope of application of the rule, i.e. the defined *situation* or *circumstance* where the rules are mandatory.

10.111 The two types of mandatory rule are dealt with in different parts of the Convention. Article 3(3) deals with non-excludable mandatory rules; and Article 7 deals with overriding mandatory rules.

(ii) Article 3(3): non-excludable mandatory rules

10.112 Article 3(3) provides:

"The fact that the parties have chosen a foreign law, whether or not accompanied by the choice of a foreign tribunal, shall not, where all the other elements relevant to the situation at the time of the choice are connected with one country only, prejudice the application of rules of the law of that country which cannot be derogated from by contract, hereinafter called 'mandatory rules'."

Thus, where the contract in question is connected to a given country, the parties cannot through their Article 3 choice affect the application of those laws of that country which would have been applied but for the choice of law clause. Party autonomy is fundamentally respected, but within the limits set out in Article 3(3). The choice of law is not invalidated; it is superseded only to the extent to which it conflicts with those mandatory rules.

10.113 Article 3(3) only applies where *all* the elements relevant to the situation at the time of the choice (apart from party choice of law and party choice of jurisdiction) are connected with *one* country only. This is quite a stringent test, because the presence of a single element pointing to another country (apart from choice of law and choice of jurisdiction) will render Article 3(3) inapplicable. The test is also an uncertain one, since neither the text of the Convention nor the Giuliano-Lagarde Report give any guidance as to which elements are

136. See Collier, p. 197, which refers to UCTA in the context of Article 3(3) and says that Article 7(2) deals with a slightly different type of mandatory rule.

137. See, e.g., Dicey/Morris/Collins, para. 1-058, and Clarkson/Hill, p. 199.

relevant to the situations. It is to be noted, however, that the relevant "elements" are defined by reference to the *situation at the time of the choice*, which is clearly wider than simple elements relevant to the *contract*.

10.114 Under the proposed Rome I Regulation the rule in Article 3(3) is retained (now in Article 3(4)). Article 5(4) would extend the rule to mandatory community law: thus where the parties choose the law of a non-Member State, that choice shall be without prejudice to the application of such mandatory rules of Community law as were applicable to the case.

(iii) Consumer contracts

10.115 As we have seen (para. 10.101 above) where there is a consumer contract as defined in Article 5(1), a law chosen in accordance with Article 3 shall not, in certain circumstances, deprive the consumer of protection afforded to him by the mandatory rules of the state of his habitual residence. Thus, similarly to Article 3(3), this rule applies to allow the application of non-excludable rules despite an express choice of a different law. But in this case, the exception applies only to the benefit of the consumer, and wherever the law chosen is not the law of his habitual residence. The effect is that in certain circumstances a consumer cannot be deprived of the protection of the law of his habitual residence.

(iv) Article 7: Overriding mandatory rules

10.116 Article 7 of the Convention provides:

> "1. When applying under this Convention the law of a country, effect may be given to the mandatory rules of the law of another country with which the situation has a close connection, if and in so far as, under the law of the latter country, those rules must be applied whatever the law applicable to the contract. In considering whether to give effect to these mandatory rules, regard shall be had to their nature and purpose and to the consequences of their application or non-application.
> 2. Nothing in this Convention shall restrict the application of the rules of the law of the forum in a situation where they are mandatory irrespective of the law otherwise applicable to the contract."

10.117 Article 7(1) was opposed by the UK delegation because it was a recipe "for confusion,... for uncertainty ... for expense ... and for delay ...".[138] Because of this opposition, Contracting States were given a right of reservation in relation to Article 7(1), which was made use of by the UK, Germany, Ireland and Luxembourg.[139] Article 7(1) does, therefore, not form part of English law. The right of Member States to enter reservations relating to Articles 7(1) and 10(1)(e) may need to be examined in the context of the aim of establishing a genuine area of justice and if the Rome Convention becomes a Regulation.[140]

10.118 By Article 7(2), the English courts can continue to apply overriding rules of English law (provided of course that the situation falls within the scope of that rule) regardless of the law that would otherwise be applicable.

(v) Mandatory and overriding statutes in (re)insurance cases

10.119 The scope for mandatory or overriding rules in reinsurance cases is likely to be quite limited. Most of the examples discussed so far reflect a social policy of protecting the

138. North, *Contract Conflicts* (1982) at pp. 19–20.

139. Dicey/Morris/Collins, para. 32-143. Subsequently, Portugal, Latvia and Slovenia have derogated from Article 7(1) on their accession to the 1980 Rome Convention.

140. See the Green Paper, para. 2.2. There is no right of reservation in the proposed Rome I Regulation itself. However, since the proposed Article 8(3) gives the court a discretion to take into account foreign mandatory rules, it may well be that in practice English courts would very rarely and only in very exceptional circumstances chose to do so (see S. Dutson, "A Dangerous Proposal – the European Commission's Attempt to Amend the Law Applicable to Contractual Obligations" in (1996) JBL 608, 616).

individual who is a weaker party in a transaction. Reinsurance contracts are commercial transactions where such considerations will rarely be relevant.[141]

10.120 By contrast, insurance contract law within the EU is to a high degree mandatory and regulates aspects of the product itself.[142] However, that is not the case in English insurance law.[143] Mandatory rules are most likely to be relevant to life insurance and motor insurance.[144]

10.121 However, an example of a potentially mandatory provision in the context of reinsurance and insurance is seen in *DR Insurance Co.* v. *Central National Insurance Company of Omaha*.[145] Moore-Bick QC (sitting as a Deputy Judge of the High Court), indicated, *obiter*, that his view was that the provisions of section 132 of the Financial Services Act 1986 and the Insurance Companies Acts 1974–1982 were overriding. According to these provisions, contravention of section 2 of the 1982 Insurance Companies Act, which prohibits the making of contracts of insurance by an unlicensed insurer, make the contract unenforceable by the insurer (although not by the insured).[146] The claimant (the successor in title to certain reinsurance business) sought a declaration that each of three contracts of reinsurance was void and unenforceable as having been effected or carried out in contravention of the 1982 Act. As we have already seen in para. 10.92 above, the judge (Moore-Bick Q.C.) held that the contract was governed by English law. It was accepted that on that basis there was an arguable case that section 132 applied. However, the judge went on to say that in his view the relevant provisions of the Act were overriding statutes accordingly they would have applied even if he was wrong and the contract was governed by New York law. He indicated that there were two factors which supported that view: first that the statutory provisions were designed for the protection of insureds. If they could be circumvented simply by the choice of a foreign law to govern the contract much of their efficacy would be lost; secondly, the statutes were worded so as to regulate conduct of a specified kind. Although this case was decided at common law, it would be decided the same way under Article 7(2).[147]

10.122 Another example is the cancellation rules introduced pursuant to the Financial Services Act 1986.[148] A choice of law other than English law will not prevent the application of these rules.[149]

10.123 The Rome I Regulation proposes a definition of international mandatory provisions which is inspired by the recent European Court of Justice decision in *Arblade* (C-369/96).

141. See, for example, the cases on the English stamp duties Acts. It is clear from the cases of *Norske Atlas Insurance Co. Ltd* v. *London General Insurance Co. Ltd* (1927) 43 TLR 541 and *Maritime Insurance Company* v. *Assekuranz Union von 1865* (1935) 52 Ll L Rep. 16 that the provisions of those Acts rendering unenforceable a policy which had not been stamped only applied when the proper law of the contract was English law.

142. See M. Clarke and H. Heiss, "Towards a European Insurance Contract Law? Recent Developments in Brussels" (2006) JBL 600. Indeed this is often said to be one of the reasons why hardly any cross border services are being provided by insurers. Because under the Brussels Regulation the policyholder is likely to be able to bring proceedings in his home state insurers will have to comply with the particular mandatory rules of that state. As a result the insurer is essentially barred from selling one and the same insurance product everywhere in the EU.

143. The concept of mandatory rules is not one that is well developed in the UK – see I. MacNeil, "The Legal Framework in the UK for Insurance Policies sold by EC Insurers under Freedom of Services" in [1995] 44 ICLQ 19, 30. Insurance is excluded from the scope of the UCTA 1977 (s.15(3)(i)).

144. Seatzu, p. 110.

145. [1996] 1 Lloyd's Rep. 74.

146. These provisions have now been replaced by provisions in the Financial Services and Markets Act 2000 making it an offence for any person to effect a contract of insurance in the UK unless authorised and rendering contracts entered into by such persons unenforceable against the other party (s.26(1)).

147. Dicey/Morris/Collins, fn 38, para. 33-214. However, the law relating to authorisation and supervision of insurance companies is now to a large extent harmonised by Community law in any event under the Insurance Directives discussed in the next chapter.

148. Financial Services (Cancellation) Rules 1989 and associated rules, described in detail in I. MacNeil, *op. cit.*, p. 34.

149. See I. MacNeil, *op. cit.*, p. 34.

Under that definition, considerations underlying the legislation can be taken into account only in terms of the exceptions to Community freedoms expressly provided for by the Treaty. Thus, the rules must be crucial for safeguarding a state's political, social or economic organisation.

3. Public policy

10.124 Article 16 of the Rome Convention provides:

> "The application of a rule of the law of any country specified by this Convention may be refused only if such application is manifestly incompatible with the public policy ('ordre public') of the forum."

This Article allows the English court to disregard a rule of foreign law that would otherwise be applicable, by virtue of Articles 3 or 4, where to apply it would be manifestly incompatible with English public policy. Thus, whereas Article 7(2) is essentially positive in effect – it allows a mandatory rule of English law to be overlaid on the contract otherwise governed by a different law – Article 16 is negative, it simply provides for the blanking out of a rule of another law.

10.125 The use of the word "manifestly" stresses that the use of the exception must be restrictively applied.

This condition, which is to be found in all the Hague Conventions since 1956, requires the court to find special grounds for upholding an objection.[150]

10.126 A good example of the operation of public policy and the interaction with the applicable law is *Royal Boskalis Westminster NV* v. *Mountain*.[151] The claimants, five Dutch companies, owned and operated a dredging fleet which was insured against war risks by the defendant insurers. The insurance policy was expressly governed by English law. Two of the plaintiffs formed a joint venture with the Iraqi authorities, that agreement being governed by Iraqi law and providing for arbitration in France. When war broke out the claimants were forced (*inter alia*, by threats to use their personnel as part of a "human shield") to enter into a finalisation agreement in order to secure release of the fleet and its personnel, and as part of that agreement waived all claims under the joint venture contract. The claimants then claimed to be indemnified against those losses under a sue and labour clause in the insurance policy. The Court of Appeal, applying English law as the proper law of the insurance contract, held that a loss which could form the basis of an indemnity under the policy had only been suffered if the claimants had indeed lost the payments they would otherwise have been entitled to under the joint venture agreement. That question in turn depended on whether if those amounts had been claimed in an arbitration in France, the arbitrators would have held that the waiver contained in the finalisation agreement was binding or not. The fact that it was valid according to Iraqi law was one thing. But it would still be open to the arbitrators as a matter of French public policy to refuse to give effect to the agreement. In the absence of evidence to the contrary it was assumed that English public policy was the same as French public policy in this regard, and it was not seriously disputed that the English court would not as a matter of public policy give effect to the agreement; indeed in the opinion of the Court of Appeal any civilised tribunal would do the same. Although the case was decided at common law, the result would be likely to be the same under the Rome Convention. Thus, even though the contract was valid according to its governing Iraqi law, it would be contrary to English public policy to enforce a contract entered into in those circumstances. A similar example might be insurance on the property of an alien enemy national in time of armed conflict.[152]

150. Giuliano-Lagarde Report commentary on Article 16, 1980 OJ C.282/1, 38.
151. [1999] QB 674.
152. See Seatzu, p. 112.

10.127 Another area where considerations of public policy often arise is in the area of exchange control. In this context, for example, such controls may render payment under a policy illegal in a particular jurisdiction. It is important to identify two different factual situations. First, a reinsurance or insurance contract requires payment to be made, say in New York, in a situation where it is illegal from the outset for such a payment to be made. This is often referred to as "initial illegality". Alternatively, in the same situation, the payment might have been legal when the contract was entered into but rendered illegal some time later either when new regulations were made or due to a change in factual circumstances, e.g. a change in the exchange rate. This is often referred to as "supervening illegality". In the first situation, initial illegality, if the contract is governed by New York law, it will not be enforced. But if the contract is governed by English law or French law, where no such restrictions exist, will the contract be enforced by the English courts where payment is illegal by the law of the place of performance? The answer at common law seemed to be no. For example, in *Foster* v. *Driscoll*,[153] a contract for the supply and sale of whisky which it was intended should be smuggled into the US in violation of the Prohibition laws was not enforced, and in *Regazzoni* v. *KC Sethia (1944) Ltd*,[154] a seller in India agreed to sell jute bags to a Swiss buyer knowing that the buyer intended to redeliver them to South Africa which would have been an offence under Indian law, the contract was not enforced. The courts appear to have refused to apply the applicable law of the contract, under which performance was allowed, on the grounds of public policy based on comity and respect for the laws of the place of performance.

10.128 Some have questioned whether this is legitimately a matter of public policy, which, as we have seen, is essentially negative in effect, when the result appears to be the application of the laws of another country, specifically the law of US and India respectively, rather than disapply an otherwise applicable law. Some doubt whether this should or should any longer be a rule of English law,[155] regardless of whether it can be fitted into the Rome Convention. But even if it was a legitimate common law rule, the separate question arises as to whether this result can be achieved under the Rome Convention. This result would clearly be possible under Article 7(1)[156] of the Rome Convention but given that provision is not in force there is an argument that should not be forced into Article 16.[157]

10.129 A limited role for public policy in this area seems to have been envisaged in *Akai Pty Ltd* v. *People's Insurance Co. Ltd*.[158] The defendant had insured the claimant, a New South Wales company, by a comprehensive credit insurance policy. The contract was expressly governed by English law and was subject to an exclusive jurisdiction clause in favour of the

153. [1929] 1 KB 470.

154. [1958] AC 301.

155. See, for example, F. Reynolds, "Contracts illegal by the *lex loci solutionis*" in (1992) 108 LQR 553 noting that "almost all the leading common law academic writers are against the exception".

156. Note in this regard that the Green Paper cites *Regazzoni* as being precisely the kind of situation to which Article 7(1) applies.

157. *Cf.* Collier, pp. 217–218, who states that public policy is being used to exclude the rule of law which would make the contract valid. This is also the view expressed by the UK government in its response to the Green Paper where it is stated (para. 25) that in fact *Regazzoni* is not relevant to Article 7(1), it was held contrary to English public policy to give effect to the contract: the court did not and could not have enforced the Indian legislation. Another suggestion is that these cases could come under Article 7(2), but, as Cheshire/North, p. 586, note, to regard a common law rule of public policy based on the comity of nations and which therefore only applies in international cases, as an overriding domestic law rule under Article 7(2) would appear to be a fiction (at p. 586). See also Seatzu, p. 112: "the rule that a contract, whether lawful by its governing law or not, is invalid if performance of it is illegal according to the law of the place where the insurance or reinsurance contract is to be performed is a third and final example of a situation in which public policy can be invoked in insurance and reinsurance cases". The first two cases cited were insurance on the property of an enemy alien (see para. 10.126 above) and insurance for unlawful acts.

158. [1998] 1 Lloyd's Rep. 90.

English courts. By section 8 of the Insurance Contracts Act 1984 applicable in New South Wales which contained restrictions on the ability of an insurer to limit its liability, if the proper law of a contract of insurance would be the law of an Australian state but for an express provision to the contrary, the provisions applied. The Australian court held that section 8 of the 1984 Act applied, that the contract was governed by Australian law under which a time limit was likely to be void. Thomas J. noted that it was accepted that the contract was governed by English law and that the question was whether as a matter of English public policy the choice of law clause should be disregarded. The public policy relied on was comity or respect for the Australian public policy set out in the Act. He noted that if this had been a Rome Convention case[159] Article 7(1) has not been enacted (the inference being that if it had been a Rome Convention that would have been the appropriate provision). But he also noted that the court in an appropriate case can take account of the public policy with which there is a close connection[160] but he said the provisions here were not of that nature. This decision accordingly seems to confirm that there will be situations where English public policy requires giving respect to the laws of another state but that the situations when this principle applies will be limited.

10.130 Supervening illegality raises rather different questions. Again if the contract is governed by New York law the situation is clear (because questions of performance and discharge are governed by the applicable law – see paras 9.43–9.45 and 9.47 above). But if the contract is governed by English or French law the answer may well depend on the law of the particular country. In English law, the contract may well have been frustrated. The case often cited in this context is *Ralli Bros* v. *Compania Naviera Sota y Aznar*.[161] An English firm chartered a Spanish steamship from the Spanish owners to carry jute from Calcutta to Barcelona. The charterparty was held to be governed by English law. By a Spanish decree the freight on jute was not to exceed a certain sum. Owing to alterations in the rate of exchange that limit was exceeded by the time the cargo arrived in Barcelona. The Court of Appeal held that the charterparty was an English contract but that as that part of the contract dealing with the obligation to pay freight had to be performed in Spain, and as by the law of Spain the payment was illegal, that part of the contract was invalid and could not be enforced against the charterers. Warrington LJ expressly decided on the basis of an implied condition that the obligation of the charterers contemplated that payment by Spaniards to Spaniards in Spain should not be illegal by the laws of that country.[162] Viewed in this way the case was simply decided on the basis of the English law of frustration and causes little difficulty in this context.[163] However, the case is sometimes referred to as a further example of the rule of public policy that the court will not enforce a contract illegal by its place of performance, i.e. as being analogous to the comity cases discussed in paras 10.127–10.129 above. However, the former view is to be preferred as otherwise the same difficulties as discussed above arise.

159. It was not because choice of court is excluded from the scope of the Convention.

160. He gave the example of *E I Du Pont de Nemours & Co., op. cit.*, where Bingham LJ observed that it was an open question whether the English court would give effect to Illinois law on the irrecoverability of punitive damages under a contract of insurance.

161. [1920] 2 KB 287.

162. p. 296. See also Scrutton LJ, p. 304: "where a contract requires an act to be done in a foreign country, it is, in the absence of very special circumstances, an implied term of the continuing validity of such a provision that the act to be done in the foreign country shall not be illegal by the law of that country. This country should not in my opinion assist or sanction the breach of the laws of other independent States."

163. See Collier, p. 219, whose view is that this is clearly simply an application of English rule on frustration.

CHAPTER 11

INSURANCE OF RISKS IN THE EEA: CHOICE OF LAW AND THE INSURANCE DIRECTIVES

A. THE SCOPE OF THE INSURANCE DIRECTIVES

11.1 The Insurance Directives apply to contracts of insurance covering risks situated in an EEA State.[1] But unfortunately, in several significant respects, the precise scope of the Insurance Directives and the overlap between the various regimes is unclear. In particular, it is unclear which regime applies where the risk is situated in an EEA State but the insurer is established outside the EEA. Article 1(3) of the Rome Convention, as we have seen, provides that the rules of the Convention do not apply to contracts of insurance which cover risks situated in the territories of the Member States of the EEC. This exclusion is not drafted by reference to the place of business of the insurer. One would assume that the Rome Convention and the directives would be back and, thus, one would then turn to the specialist insurance directives, expecting that they would apply instead. At first sight it appears they do, applying whenever the risk is situated in an EEC state.[2] Thus the Insurance Directives appear to plug the gap left by Article 1(3). Unfortunately the position may not be as simple as at first appears.

11.2 It has been suggested[3] that an examination of the history of the Directives shows that their scope is actually narrower than it appears. The history of the Directives was considered in detail in Chapter 2. As we have seen, the Insurance Directives were implemented against the background of two of the substantive rights which the EU seeks to uphold, i.e. the right of establishment and the right to provide services. Thus, it is argued that the subject of the Insurance Directives are those to whom the two fundamental community rights are given; that is, insurers established in the EU.

11.3 However, the scope of the first Directive merits further consideration. One of the ways of promoting freedom of establishment is to harmonise rules on authorisation amongst the Member States. But there is no reason why those rules should not then apply to any insurance provider in fact providing services in that state regardless of whether they were guaranteed the right to do so under the Treaty. Thus, it is acknowledged in the preamble to the first Directive that "the coordinated rules concerning the taking-up and pursuit of the business of direct insurance within the Community should, in principle, apply to all undertakings entering the market, consequently also to agencies and branches where the head office of the undertaking is situated outside the Community". The rules in the first Directive are in two parts: Title II contains the rules applicable to undertakings whose head offices are situated within the Community, including the requirement of authorisation under Article 6; Title III contains rules applicable to agencies and branches established within the Community and belonging to undertakings whose head offices are outside the Community including, under Article 23(1),

1. See para. 9.24 above (as regards contracts of general insurance) and para. 9.27 above (as regards contracts of long-term insurance).

2. The Insurance Regulations apply more widely than the insurance directives themselves as they apply to risks in EEA states not just EU states (in other words including Liechtenstein, Norway and Iceland). Thus the scope of the Rome Convention, which is superseded by the Regulations, (Article 20) is actually narrower than Article 1(3) suggests. Although Article 20 gives precedence to national law implementing the EU directives which of course themselves only cover EU states.

3. See the Court of Appeal in *AMICO*, *op. cit.*, para. 26.

an obligation to make access to the relevant insurance business subject to official authorisation. Thus, the first Directive applies to any insurer setting up a branch or agency within the EU although those with a head office outside the EU will have no right to do so.

11.4 Thus, the basic premise on which the above argument was built, that is, that the first directive applies only to insurers established within the EU, is questionable. Accordingly, even if the fact that the choice of law rules are inserted in Title I of the second Directive is enough to demonstrate the intention that they are to have the same scope as the *first* Directive, it is not only undertakings established in the Community which fall within the scope of the first Directive. The second Directive provides that for the purposes of Title I and II, undertaking means any undertaking which has received official authorisation under Articles 6 *or 23* of the first Directive (including therefore branches or agencies established in a Member State where the head office is outside the Community) whereas for the purposes of Titles III and V (which contains the provisions peculiar to the freedom to provide services) undertaking means only those authorised under Article 6. Article 7, which contains the conflict of laws provisions, is in Title II. Accordingly, on any view, the provisions seem to apply to the situation where the insurer has a branch or agency in the EU which has been authorised under Article 23 of the first Directive, even if its head office is outside the EU. But given that the first Directive potentially applies to all insurers who may wish to open a branch in the EU, there seems to be no reason, based on the directives themselves, why the conflicts provisions should be limited in any way, provided of course that the risk is situated in the EU.

11.5 This debate may in any event be academic. Regardless of any debate which might be had about the scope of the directives, the English Insurance Regulations, which implement the directives, appear to apply to contracts of insurance which cover risks situated in an EEA state (without reference to the place of establishment of the insurer).[4]

B. OVERVIEW

11.6 As we have seen, the insurance directives draw a fundamental distinction between contracts of general insurance and contracts of long-term insurance.[5] The choice of law rules as regards both types of contract are contained in the Financial Services and Markets Act 2000 (Law Applicable to Contracts of Insurance) Regulations 2001, general insurance being dealt with in Part II and long term insurance in Part III.[6]

11.7 As regards non-life business, although the parties are given some freedom of choice over the applicable law, there are – in contrast to the Rome Convention – substantial limits to that freedom. The extent of that freedom depends on the type of non-life insurance in question, and the Regulations draw a series of distinctions as to this. In the absence of choice, or where the parties' choice is invalid because of the limits imposed by the insurance directives, there are provisions which identify the relevant law. These are very different to those in the Rome Convention. This is, of course, a matter of great significance given that it is the Rome Convention that applies to reinsurance.

11.8 As regards life business, the position is similar. Although there is an element of freedom of choice, that choice is more fettered than in the case of the Rome Convention. In

4. Although ultimately leaving the question open, this was a solution referred to by the Court of Appeal in *AMICO* (at para. 27) and is also supported in Dicey/Morris/Collins, *The Conflict of Laws*, para. 33-136.

5. The meanings of these concepts are considered at paras 9.20–9.27 above.

6. See paras 9.24–9.27 above.

the absence of choice, or where there has been an ineffective choice, an applicable law is selected.

11.9 Although the primary aim of the choice of law provisions in the Insurance Directives was to achieve a uniform regime across the EEA, there is a clear secondary aim of protecting the weaker party to the transaction. This is reflected in the restrictions on the parties' freedom of choice.

11.10 The following sections consider the choice of law rules applicable first to contracts of general insurance and then to contracts of long-term insurance.

C. NON-LIFE BUSINESS

1. Expression of choice

11.11 Regulation 6(1) provides that:

"Any choice made by the parties under regulation 4 must be expressed or demonstrated with reasonable certainty by the terms of the contract or the circumstances of the case."

These words echo the wording of Article 3(1) of the Rome Convention, and it is most likely that the words will be construed in similar fashion.[7]

2. Extent to which the parties are permitted a choice

11.12 However, the extent to which Regulation 4 actually permits the parties to the contract to exercise free choice in the applicable law is circumscribed, in marked contrast to the Rome Convention regime, where, as we have seen, party autonomy is paramount: the parties may generally choose whatever law they want to govern the contract (Article 3 of the Rome Convention) subject only to the possibility of the court applying particular mandatory rules or disregarding the law chosen on the grounds of public policy.

11.13 The position under the Regulations is, on the face of it, very different. There are various provisions which appear to limit substantially the freedom of parties to choose what law to apply to their non-life policy of insurance. The provisions are also extremely complex. Essentially, if the risk is a large risk, parties are permitted to choose any law to govern the contract. If not, depending on the precise circumstances, that choice must be either an identified law (such as the law of the EEA state where the risk is situated or the state where the policyholder resides) or any law which the law of those countries allows. As we will see, if one of the countries identified through this process is England, the parties are accorded a wide freedom of choice because the wide freedom under Article 3 of the Rome Convention is applied.

(i) Large risks

11.14 If the risk is a "large risk", the parties may choose any law as the applicable law (Regulation 4(7)).[8] Large risks are defined in Article 5(d) of the first non-life insurance Directive as[9]: railway rolling stock, aircraft; ships; goods in transit; liability for ships; credit

7. As to which, see paras 10.3–10.62 above. See further the Court of Appeal in *AMICO*, *op. cit.*, who decided that there was no reason to distinguish between the two regimes on this question (para. 18). However the two regimes will diverge if the new Article 3 Rome I Regulation is accepted – see para. 10.62 above.

8. This is achieved in a nicely convoluted way, by disapplying the significant restrictions on choice contained in Regulations 4(2), 4(3) and 4(4).

9. Regulation 2(1) defines "large risk" by reference to Article 5(d) of the first non-life insurance directive, Directive 73/239.

and suretyship insurance which relates to a business carried on by the policyholder; and in relation to policyholders who carry on a business insurance of land vehicles, insurance against fire and natural forces, insurance against damage to property, motor vehicle liability insurance, general liability insurance and insurance against miscellaneous financial loss.[10]

(ii) Non-large risks

11.15 Where the risk is not a large risk, then the first step is to identify the EEA State in which the risk is situated, a question considered at paras 9.26–9.27 above. Once this has been ascertained, it must be asked whether or not the policyholder resides in the EEA State in which the risk is situated. Where the policyholder resides in the EEA State in which the risk is situated, Regulation 4(2) applies. Where the policyholder does not, Regulation 4(3) applies.

11.16 The test for where the policyholder resides is stated in Regulation 2(3). Where the policyholder is an individual, he resides in the country in which he has his habitual residence.[11] Otherwise, the policyholder resides in the country in which he has his central administration.[12]

(iii) Policy-holder resident in the EEA State in which the risk is situated: Regulation 4(2)

11.17 Where the policyholder resides in the EEA State in which the risk is situated, the applicable law is the law of that EEA State, *unless*, if such a choice is permitted under the law of that EEA State, the parties to the contract choose the law of another country.

11.18 If the policyholder and risk are situated in England, then English law will either be the applicable law or – if the parties have chosen an applicable law – English law will be the arbiter of whether that choice is a permitted one. The relevant English rules are those contained in the Rome Convention. This is not because the Rome Convention applies to such contracts – it obviously does not – but because it is deemed so to apply for these purposes by the provisions of the Regulation.[13] It follows that in this case the parties will have a wide freedom of election.

11.19 Where the risk is situated in another EEA state, the English court will have to inquire as to the regime in that EEA state. This is likely to be diverse, because the Rome Convention (as we have seen) does not of itself apply. Some states may have done as the UK has done, and provided that the Rome Convention should apply. But insurance law is elsewhere quite highly regulated, and many countries will not have a choice of law regime as liberal as the UK.[14] The inquiry into whether a choice of law provision is valid or not is thus likely to be a lengthy one.[15]

(iv) Policy-holder not resident in the EEA State in which the risk is situated: Regulation 4(3)

11.20 If the policyholder does not reside in the EEA state in which the risk is situated, then the parties may choose as the applicable law either:

10. They were chosen on the basis of the economic relevance of the risk and the bargaining power of the policy holder: see Seatzu, p. 133.

11. Regulation 2(3)(a).

12. Regulation 2(3)(b).

13. See Regulation 7(3), which provides that in determining what freedom of choice the parties have under the law of a part of the United Kingdom, the 1990 Act is to be treated as applying to the contract.

14. According to the Max Planck Institute's response to the Green Paper, Austria and Italy also allow a choice wider than that under the directives, while Belgium, Germany, France and Spain have been much more restrictive.

15. It may be questioned whether this is in accordance with the consumer-orientated approach of the insurance directives. Hopefully, the problem will be more academic than real, because most insurers will be sued in the jurisdiction of the policyholder: see Article 9(1)(b) of the Brussels Regulation.

(i) the law of the EEA state in which the risk is situated (Regulation 4(3)(a)); or
(ii) the law of the country in which the policyholder resides (Regulation 4(3)(b)).[16]

If any of those states – provided they are an EEA State – grant a greater freedom of choice, the parties may take advantage of that freedom (Regulation 4(5)).

11.21 Thus, if England is *either* the state in which the risk is situated *or* the country where the policyholder resides, the parties' choice of law will generally be unfettered.[17] If England is *neither* the state in which the risk is situated *nor* the country where the policyholder resides, then the inquiry as to whether the parties' choice of law is a valid one will require examination of the choice of law provisions of *two* states.[18] Even if neither of these states allows a freedom of choice, the parties will still be entitled to choose the law of one of those two countries.

(v) Policy-holder carrying on a business: Regulation 4(4)

11.22 If the policyholder carries on a business and the contract covers two or more risks relating to that business which are situated in different EEA States, the parties may choose as the governing law:

(i) the law of any of those EEA States (Regulation 4(4)); or
(ii) the law of the country in which the policyholder resides (Regulation 4(4)).[19]

If any of those states – provided they are an EEA State – grant a greater freedom of choice, the parties may take advantage of that freedom (Regulation 4(5)). As before, if one of these states is the UK, the parties' freedom of choice will largely be respected; if the UK is not one of these states, then the process of inquiry may be a long one.[20]

(vi) Insured risks limited to events occurring in one EEA State: Regulation 4(6)

11.23 Regulation 4(6) provides:

"… if the risks covered by the contract are limited to events occurring in one EEA State other than the EEA State in which the risk is situated, the parties may choose the law of the former EEA State as the applicable law."

Thus, if, for example, a motor insurance is confined to accidents in a country other than the EEA State of registration, the parties to the contract may select the law of that country. Note that this provision does *not* allow for a choice which would be allowed by the law of that EEA State and thus is narrower than those previously discussed.

(vii) Other restrictions on the parties' choice: impossible choices

11.24 Although these are not matters expressly considered in the Insurance Directives or the Regulation, the parties' choice of law is likely to be confined to the choice of the law of a given municipal system[21]; "floating" law clauses are unlikely to be permitted[22]; and *dépeçage*

16. Note that this does not have to be an EEA State.
17. For the reason given in para. 11.18 above.
18. For the reason given in para. 11.19 above.
19. Note that this does not have to be an EEA State.
20. See paras 11.18–11.19 above.
21. See para. 10.59 above.
22. See para. 10.60 above.

by express choice of different laws to govern different parts of the contract is likely to be permitted.[23] In other words, the position will be as it is for the Rome Convention.

3. Applicable law in the absence of choice or valid choice

11.25 If the parties have either not made an express choice or have made a choice which is not valid according to the provisions discussed above the position is as follows.

(i) Where the policy-holder resides in the EEA State in which the risk is situated

11.26 If the policyholder resides in the EEA State in which the risk is situated the applicable law will be the law of that EEA State (Regulation 4(2)). This appears to be an absolute rule.[24]

(ii) All other cases

11.27 In all other cases, the applicable law is the law of the country, from amongst those considered in the relevant paragraph, which is most closely connected with the contract (Regulation 4(8)). However, where a severable part of the contract has a closer connection with another relevant country, the law applicable to that part, is, by way of exception, the law of that relevant country. This provision in Regulation 4(8) mirrors a similar provision in Article 4(1) of the Rome Convention and expressly envisages *dépeçage* in exceptional circumstances.[25]

11.28 For the purposes of this provision, the contract is rebuttably presumed to be most closely connected with the EEA state in which the risk is situated (Regulation 4(9)).

(iii) Identifying potentially applicable laws

11.29 The regulation requires the court first to identify the potentially applicable laws. In other words, the court must review the "relevant" sub-paragraphs in Regulation 4 and list the potentially applicable laws. The material wording of the regulation is as follows:

"... the applicable law is the law of the country, from amongst those considered in the relevant paragraph ('the relevant countries'), which is most closely connected with the contract."

This must be a reference to Regulations 4(3), 4(4), 4(6) and 4(7). Regulation 4(2), as we have noted, lays down a single applicable law for cases where the risk and the policyholder are situated in the same state,[26] and is therefore not relevant to this exercise. The better view is that Regulation 4(5), also, cannot be relevant, because (on any sensible reading) it presumes an actual choice of law by the parties. It would be a strange situation if the correct approach were to consider *first* the law of which country was most closely connected with the contract and *then* go on to debate whether the law of that country permitted reference to the law of yet another country, the parties having made no actual choice.[27]

23. See para. 10.61 above. *Dépeçage* is clearly envisaged in Regulation 4(8).
24. *Cf.* the possibilities explored by the Court of Appeal in *AMICO, op. cit.*, at para. 31.
25. See para. 10.63 above
26. See para. 11.26 above
27. This is the view of Dicey/Morris/Collins, para. 33-180. *Cf.* the view of the Court of Appeal in *AMICO, op. cit.*, at para. 30 that Regulation 4(8), in referring to "the relevant paragraph" without limitation, was wide enough to embrace *any* law which it was open to the parties to choose under whichever is or are the relevant sub-paragraph(s) in the particular case.

11.30 Applying this approach, and by way of example, where the policyholder does not reside in the EEA State in which the risk is situated, there are two potentially applicable laws to choose from by virtue of Regulation 4(3): the law of the EEA State in which the risk is situated; and the law of the country in which the policyholder resides. If the policyholder carries on a business, then Regulation 4(4) will add other candidates. So too will Regulation 4(6) if the risk is limited to events occurring in one EEA State other than the EEA State in which the risk is situated.

(iv) Identifying the country most closely connected with the contract

11.31 The next step is to determine which of these countries is most closely connected with the contract. This gives rise to two questions:

(i) What factors can be taken into account when making this comparison?
(ii) If, having identified which country is most closely connected with the contract, and this is not the EEA State in which the risk is situated, what is the strength of the presumption in Regulation 4(9).

These two questions are considered in turn below.

11.32 It is to be noted that the test appears to be which *country* is most closely connected with the contract, rather than which *legal system*. If anything, this allows for a reference to a wider range of factors than would be the case if the test were connection with a legal system (see para. 10.94 above). In *Crédit Lyonnais* v. *New Hampshire Insurance Co. Ltd*,[28] the Court of Appeal stated that it considered links with the subject-matter and performance of the contract and their connection with a particular country to be relevant to determining with which country a contract was most closely connected. Hobhouse LJ went on[29]:

"In the present case such factors are exclusively English. The subject-matter of the contract is risks which relate to property and activity in the UK. This is clearly stated in the 'territoriality clause'. The performance of the contract by the payment of premiums and payment of claims is again either expressly or by the contemplation of the parties to take place in England. Both parties are ... established in England ... There is no element of performance that is geographically connected with France ... The factors relied on by the defendants in argument ... are largely irrelevant to the statutory criteria. Thus references to French francs and provisions of the French penal code do not themselves relate to the location of the performance of the contract nor to the location of either of the performing parties. Similarly the genesis of the contract and its emanation from a world-wide programme negotiated in France is not relevant."

The Court of Appeal criticised the reasoning of the judge below (Miss B Dohmann QC sitting as a deputy judge), in so far as she appeared to have been asking herself whether there was material from which an intention to contract by reference to the French legal system could be inferred. Once it was seen that there was no choice, the question of choice or absence of choice becomes irrelevant to the question of ascertaining with what state the contract is most closely connected. Thus, the factors which can be considered are limited but in the same way as under Article 4 of the Rome Convention.[30]

28. [1997] 2 Lloyd's Rep. 1, 6.
29. At p. 7.
30. See paras 10.95–10.96 above. The same distinction between factors relevant to intention and those relevant to object assessment of closest connection should be apparent in the context of Articles 3 and 4 of the Rome Convention. *Cf.* Dicey/Morris/Collins, para. 33-180, which states that the formulation of Regulation 4 limits the factors by reference to which the most closely connected country may be determined. Regard may not be had to the law of the place of incorporation, central administration, currency in which premiums are paid, etc.

(v) Rebutting the presumption

11.33 As we have seen, there has been a considerable debate in the context of Article 4 of the Rome Convention as to the strength which should be given to presumptive applicable law. In theory, the same debate could arise under the regulations. But in many cases, the exercise will be much more limited, as only a very limited number of laws will be "candidates" for selection.[31] In *Crédit Lyonnais*, Hobhouse LJ, as we have seen,[32] noted that the wording of Article 4(5) of the Rome Convention could be said to make the presumption formally very weak, but went on to stress the difference in the wording under the Insurance Directives:

"The only qualification is the word 'rebuttable'. There are no words such as those included in Article 4(5) of the Rome Convention which displace the presumption if it appears from the circumstances as a whole that there is a closer connection with another country. It is understandable why the directive should have been more tightly drafted since a more general qualification of the presumption would effectively displace the policy of the directive that the location of the insured should be the primary consideration." [33]

11.34 As we have seen, the Article 4(5) exception may be particularly important in (re)insurance cases where, at common law, the courts often stressed the importance of the contract being governed by English law where it was entered into on the London market and this will not always be the result under Articles 3 and 4(2) of the Convention. A similar problem may arise in cases governed by the insurance directives. At common law, indemnity contracts were sometimes held to be governed by the law of the insurer's head office, but more recently the courts recognised the importance of contracts drawn up by reference to a particular market (see paras 12.11–12.12 below). By comparison under the insurance regulations, the presumption is that the contract is governed by the law of the state where the risk is situated (and indeed this is conclusive if the policyholder also resides there). Thus, again the result may well be different from at common law unless such factors can be relied on as founding an actual choice of law or the court is prepared to rebut the presumption. However, given that the place where the risk is situated has been chosen specifically in the insurance context as the law which presumptively applies, there will clearly be less sympathy for displacing that law in favour of English law even if the insurance contract was placed on the London market in a form consistent with English law.

4. Displacement of the applicable law: mandatory rules and public policy

(i) Non-excludable mandatory rules

11.35 Regulation 5(2) provides:

"If the parties to the contract choose the applicable law under regulation 4 and if all the other elements relevant to the situation at the time when the parties make their choice are connected with one EEA state only, the application of the mandatory rules of that EEA state is not prejudiced."

Although this provision is similar to Article 3(3) of the Rome Convention discussed in paras 10.112–10.114 above, there are some potentially significant differences. In the first place, it

31. The number will, of course, depend on the applicable provision(s) of the Regulation.

32. See para. 10.83 above.

33. [1997] 2 Lloyd's Rep. 1, 6. One situation suggested in Dicey/Morris/Collins as to when the presumption might be rebutted is where the contract covers two or more risks situated in different EEA states if, for example, the policyholder entered into the contract at his place of habitual residence or central administration or where the policyholder insures the buildings and contents of his holiday home in Italy by entering into a contract at the place where he habitually resides, say England (para. 33-182). In *AMICO, op. cit.*, the Court of Appeal indicated *obiter* that the presumption in favour of the Member State where the risk was situated would if necessary have been rebutted given that it was a group policy to cover risks situated all over the world (para. 46).

only allows the application of the mandatory rules of another EEA State. Even if all the elements of a contract are connected with a non-EEA State, that state's mandatory rules cannot be had regard to. Secondly, Article 3(3) of the Rome Convention refers to choice of a "foreign law", but as referred to above, this is likely to include a choice of English law when all other elements point to another state. Article 3(3) refers to choice of a foreign law *whether or not accompanied by the choice of a foreign tribunal*. This could make a difference in a situation where there is an express choice of English law, and an English jurisdiction clause but all other elements point to France. Such a case could clearly come within Article 3(3) and the mandatory rules of France would be applied. But under Regulation 5(2), it may be argued that another element points to England other than the choice of law.[34]

11.36 Where a contract is otherwise connected with another EEA state in determining whether the laws of that state are mandatory the question is whether that state regards them as mandatory.[35]

(ii) Overriding mandatory rules

11.37 Regulation 5(1) provides:

"Nothing in regulation 4 restricts the application of the mandatory rules of any part of the UK, irrespective of the applicable law of the contract."

This provision is very similar to Article 7(2) of the Rome Convention discussed in paras 10.107–10.122 above.[36]

11.38 See paras 10.119–10.122 above for examples of mandatory rules in an insurance and reinsurance context. Mandatory rules are of potentially greater relevance to direct insurance than to reinsurance because of the absence in a reinsurance context of a party in a weaker bargaining position. For example, the Financial Services Act 1986 gives the Securities and Investments Board the power to make rules to enable a person who has entered into an investment agreement to rescind the contract. The rules adopted by the Board generally allow cancellation within a period of 14 days. A choice of applicable law other than English or Scots law will not prevent the application of these rules which are likely to be mandatory within the meaning of the insurance directives.[37]

11.39 As noted above, it is unclear whether Article 5 of the Rome Convention applies to insurance contracts expressly referred to by the second non-life Directive. In the context of non-life insurance the directives draw a distinction between large risks and mass risks. It seems that this is the relevant distinction rather than between consumer and non consumer contracts. However no such distinction is drawn in the context of life insurance.[38]

34. Dicey/Morris/Collins, para. 33-166, conclude that it is unlikely that this substantial effect was intended (p. 261). *Cf.* Seatzu, p. 148.

35. Rather oddly Regulation 7(2) provides "in determining whether the mandatory rules of another EEA state should be applied in accordance with regulation 5(2) where the parties have chosen the law of a part of the UK as the applicable law, the 1990 Act is to be treated as applying to the contract. See Dicey/Morris/Collins, para. 33-167.

36. This provision implements the first paragraph of Article 7(2) of the Insurance Directives. The second paragraph of Article 7(2) is modelled on Article 7(1) of the Rome Convention and provides a discretion to the court to apply overriding rules where they form part of the law of the Member State where the risk is situated or the Member State imposing any obligation to take out insurance. This provision, like Article 7(1) of the Rome Convention, is not implemented in the Insurance Regulations.

37. See I. MacNeil, "The legal framework in the United Kingdom for insurance policies sold by EC insurers under freedom of services" (1995) 44 ICLQ 19.

38. See Seatzu, pp. 147–148, 172.

(iii) Public policy

11.40 Although there is no express provision dealing with public policy, a similar power to ignore otherwise applicable law probably exists at common law (see para. 12.17 below) and, in any event, Regulation 7 provides that subject to the preceding provisions the Contracts Applicable law Act 1990 (including, therefore, Article 16 discussed in paras 10.124–10.130 above) is to be treated as applying to the contract.

D. LIFE BUSINESS

11.41 Part III of the Regulation applies to contracts of long-term insurance where the risk is situated in an EEA State.[39]

1. Express choice of the parties

11.42 Oddly, unlike the provision relating to general insurance, Part III contains no statement as to how the parties should make their choice of law clear.[40] It is likely, however, that the same approach as informs the Rome Convention[41] and general insurance[42] will apply, and that a choice will either have to be made expressly or demonstrated with reasonable certainty.

2. Restrictions on express choice

11.43 Just as is the case with general insurance, the parties are given a rather circumscribed right to choose the applicable law. A choice will only be allowed if such a choice is permitted under the law of the EEA state of the commitment (Regulation 8(2)), which means, if the policyholder is an individual the EEA state in which he resides on that date or otherwise the EEA state in which the establishment of the policyholder to which the contract relates is situated on that date (Regulation 2(1)). Because, as we have seen, England has chosen to adopt the Rome Convention in this regard, if the commitment is in England the parties will be free to chose any governing law (para. 11.18 above).

11.44 Furthermore, if the policyholder is an individual and he resides in one EEA state but is a national or citizen of another EEA state, the parties to the contract may choose the law of the EEA state of which he is a national or citizen as the applicable law. In practice, this provision will only be important where the law of his place of residence does not allow free choice of law (so will not be needed if he is resident in England). The meaning of this regulation seems relatively clear but the application may be difficult particularly in cases where a country has units to which different laws apply or where someone has dual nationality.[43]

3. Applicable law in the absence of choice

11.45 If the parties have not chosen any other law, the contract will be governed by the law of the EEA state of the commitment (Regulation 8(2)). There are no exceptions to this rule. At common law, contracts of life insurance were very often governed by the law of the country

39. See para. 9.27 as to the test for this.

40. Regulation 6, which deals with choice of law, is part of Part II and only applies to general insurance – as is also clear from the reference to Regulation 4.

41. See paras 10.3–10.61 above.

42. See para. 11.11 above.

43. For example the UK. What law does this allow a British citizen to chose? Dicey/Morris/Collins conclude that such a citizen could choose the law of any part of the UK, e.g. the law of Scotland or of England. In cases of dual nationality or citizenship again the learned editor favours broad interpretation allowing choice of either (at paras 33-202–33-204). Another possibility is to limit the choice to the country with which he is most closely connected (see Seatzu, p. 169).

where the insurer or the insurers head office was situated.[44] Under the Regulation, in the absence of express choice the law, the residence or place of establishment of the policyholder will apply. There is no prospect of rebutting this result. Thus the "opposite" result is reached.[45]

4. Limits to the applicable law

11.46 Again the question arises as to whether the consumer provisions in Article 5 of the Rome Convention applies (as to which see para. 11.39 above). Regulation 9 provides that nothing in Regulation 8 affects the application of the mandatory rules of any part of the UK, irrespective of the applicable law of the contract. This provision is identical to Regulation 5(1) in the context of non long-term insurance and as already discussed is almost identical to Article 7(2) of the Rome Convention.[46] It is likely that the court will also ignore any otherwise applicable law if it contravenes English public policy (see para. 11.40 above).

E. SCOPE OF THE APPLICABLE LAW

11.47 The directives themselves do not contain provisions like Articles 8 and 10 of the Rome Convention dealing with the scope of the applicable law (see paras 9.28–9.60 above). But in the absence of any rules to the contrary these provisions of the Rome Convention will apply.[47]

44. See paras 12.8–12.10 below.

45. Clarke, para. 2-4B2, submits that in any event the common law cases like *Rossano* are the exception rather than the rule and that the location of the insured always carries more weight than that of the insurer's head office. This is also the trend in the US.

46. Again the UK used its right to make a reservation in relation to Article 4(4)(2) of the insurance directives (the equivalent of Article 7(1) of the Rome Convention). There is no equivalent to Regulation 5(2) (Rome Convention Article 3(3)) in relation to life insurance.

47. Regulations 7(1) and 10(1) provide that subject to the preceding provisions of the regulation, the 1990 Act is to be treated as applying to the contract for the purposes of determining the applicable law. See also Seatzu, p. 175.

CHAPTER 12

REINSURANCE AND INSURANCE: CHOICE OF LAW UNDER THE COMMON LAW

A. THE SCOPE OF THE COMMON LAW

12.1 The common law will continue to apply to:

(1) contracts of reinsurance entered into before 1 April 1991;
(2) contracts of insurance where the risk is situated outside the Member States entered into before 1 April 1991;
(3) contracts of insurance where the risk is situated inside a Member State entered into:
  (a) in the case of non-life insurance, before 1 July 1990; and
  (b) in the case of life insurance before 20 May 1993;
(4) contracts of insurance entered into by Friendly Societies before 1 February 1993[1];
(5) contracts of insurance where the risk is situated within a Member State but the contract falls outside the scope of the insurance directives.[2]

B. THE APPROACH AT COMMON LAW

1. Introduction

12.2 As was stated in Chapter 1, although at common law (re)insurance disputes involve their own particular "spin", the fundamental private international law tests for choice of law are the same whether the dispute relates to (re)insurance or some other contractual dispute. Thus, at common law, the starting point is that every contract is governed by its "proper law". When the parties have expressed their intention as to what law should govern, that intention, in general, determines the proper law. When there is no express selection, an intention can be inferred from the terms and nature of the contract and from the general circumstances of the case. Otherwise the contract is governed by the system of law with which the transaction has its closest and most real connection, in other words through the application of an "objective test".[3]

12.3 This has been referred to as a tripartite hierarchy of express, inferred and objective choice.[4] However, there is some overlap between the final "objective" stage and the earlier two steps. In theory, in any given case, the court first looks to whether it can determine the actual intention of the parties as to which law should govern. If no such intention is expressed and cannot be inferred from the terms of the contract or circumstances of the case, then the court carries out an objective assessment. However, the factors which the court will consider

1. When the Friendly Societies Act 1991 entered into force. Contracts entered into by friendly societies are now governed by rules very similar to those in the insurance regulations.

2. See, generally, I. MacNeil, "The legal framework in the United Kingdom for insurance policies sold by EC insurers under freedom of services" [1995] ICLQ 19, 22–23. The question of whether this includes cases where the insurance is provided by an insurer with no establishment in the EEA is discussed in paras 11.1–11.5 above.

3. The objective test of "closest and most real connection" was adopted by the Privy Council in *John Lavington Bonython* v. *Commonwealth of Australia* [1951] AC 201: "the system of law by reference to which the contract was made or that with which the transaction has its closest and most real connection."

4. See High Court of Australia in *Akai Pty Ltd* v. *People's Insurance Co. Ltd* (1997) 188 CLR 418.

at the first and second stages are very similar and often could lead to a conclusion under either test.[5] Moreover, even at the third stage there was often a suggestion that the reason why the contract is governed by the system of law with the closest and most real connection is because that is what the parties would have intended.[6] However, whilst it is possible to see "imputed" intention as reflecting what the parties would have agreed to had they thought about it, there is an important distinction between this and the actual intention (whether express or implied) of these particular parties.

12.4 A good example of the blurring of the distinction in a (re)insurance context is *DR Insurance Co.* v. *Central National Insurance Co. of Omaha*.[7] Moore-Bick QC (sitting as a Deputy Judge of the High Court) held:

> "... when parties enter a particular market in order to transact business they can usually be taken to intend that their relationship will be governed by the system of law in force in that market unless they provide some clear indication to the contrary. Whether it be viewed as an implied choice of law or simply the application of the system of law which has the closest connection with the transaction, the result will be the same."

The fact that the reinsurance business was written in the London market through a London broker in accordance with the normal practices of that market was a strong indication that it was governed by English law. At common law, this overlap does not matter. But for the reasons already explored above, the distinction is much more significant under the Rome Convention and insurance directives.

2. Application of the common law in (re)insurance cases

(i) Express choice

12.5 The simplest cases are where the contract is expressly governed by a particular law. For example, in *Anderson* v. *Equitable Assurance Society of the United States*,[8] a life insurance contract was expressly governed by English law. Therefore, English law governed the performance of the contract, including payment. Thus, the sums due under the policy were to be paid in the sterling equivalent to the sum in DM referred to in the contract at the current rate of exchange (which was virtually zero). Similarly, in *Perry* v. *Equitable Life Assurance Society of the United States of America*,[9] the life insurance contract contained an express provision that it was governed by Russian law. Thus payment was to be made in accordance with Russian law.

(ii) Implied choice

12.6 We have already seen a number of examples in (re)insurance cases where the court has implied a choice of law.[10]

5. For example, in *Armadora Occidental SA* v. *Horace Mann Insurance Co.* [1977] 1 WLR 520, Kerr J. applied the second test (that is, of implied actual choice) and his decision as to the proper law was upheld by the Court of Appeal but on the basis of the third test (that is, closest connection) aff'd at [1977] 1 WLR 1098. Similarly, in *Amin Rasheed Shipping Corp.* v. *Kuwait Insurance Co.* [1984] AC 50 Lord Wilberforce reached the same result on the basis of the third head that the rest of their Lordships had reached on the basis of the second head.

6. See, for example, *Spurrier* v. *La Cloche* [1902] AC 446 where the PC held that the intention of the parties is the true criteria. See also *Pick* v. *Manufacturers Life Insurance Co.* [1958] 2 Lloyd's Rep. 93 where the court did not clearly distinguish between implied intention and the objective test of closest connection, saying it was all a matter of construing the implied terms of the contract.

7. [1996] 1 Lloyd's Rep. 74, 81–82. See also *Trade Indemnity plc* v. *Forsakringsaktiebolaget Njord* [1995] 1 All ER 796, where the judge held that there was a presumption that reinsurance written on the London market is written on the basis of an "implied or imputed" English proper law.

8. (1926) 134 LT 554.

9. (1929) 45 TLR 468.

10. See paras 10.29–10.30 and 10.27 above.

(iii) Imputed choice

12.7 In the absence of actual choice (whether express or implied), the courts at common law have to identify the system of law with which the contract has its closest and most real connection. The court weighs the connecting factors and chooses the law with the closest connection, or where the contract has its "centre of gravity". It is helpful to draw a broad distinction between life insurance, indemnity insurance and reinsurance.

(iv) Life insurance

12.8 At common law, in the absence of an express choice of law, life insurance contracts are usually held to be governed by the law of the country in which the insurer carries on business. Where the insurer is present in more than one country, the contract is usually held to be governed by the law where the insurer's head office was situated.[11] For example, in *Pick* v. *Manufacturers Life*,[12] a life insurance policy was issued by a Canadian company whose head office was in Ontario. The insured was a German national resident at the time in Palestine. Although the insurance company had a branch in Tel Aviv and technically the contract may be said to have been entered into in Palestine, on the facts of the case that was of little relevance. There was no evidence to suggest that the contract was connected with that office and there was no one authorised to enter policies from that office, the policies being issued by the head office in Canada. Furthermore, the policies were on a common form issued by the head office, and the court decided that Ontarian law was the proper law of the contract.

12.9 Similarly in *Rossano* v. *Manufacturers Life Insurance Co.*,[13] a life insurance policy issued by the same Canadian company to an Egyptian assured was also held to be governed by the law of Ontario. Even though some contact was made with a branch in Egypt, and that branch may have had some authority with regard to interim policies, the policy itself needed head office approval and the foreign form policy used was based upon the terms of an Ontario statute.[14]

12.10 From these cases, it can be seen that the reason why the law of the place where the insurer's head office is found is usually preferred as the proper law is that the insurance was usually issued on a standard form which it would be intended should receive a uniform interpretation. If that form was based on the local law of the head office, the inference will obviously be even stronger (as was the case in *Rossano*). Furthermore, in practice, the head office would usually reserve to itself the ultimate decision (*cf.* the position of a bank where each branch manager usually has more discretion).[15]

(v) Indemnity insurance

12.11 Again, there was some focus on the head office of the insurer. For example, in *Greer* v. *Poole*,[16] a policy of marine insurance effected with English underwriters by an English

11. *Cf. Rowlett, Leakey and Company* v. *Scottish Provident Institution* [1927] 1 Ch 55. The plaintiff English company insured the life of their MD, who owed money to the company, through three policies entered into through the defendant insurer's London office, the Head Office being in Scotland. A question arose as to the interpretation of a provision in the policy excluding cover in the event of suicide. The Court of Appeal held that the proper law of the contract was English law and the fact that the insurers happened to be a Scottish institution was immaterial, the contract having to be performed in London and effected in London.

12. [1958] 2 Lloyd's Rep. 93.

13. [1963] QB 352.

14. The Supreme Court of Canada took a very similar view in *Imperial Life Assurance Co. of Canada* v. *Colmenares* (1967) 62 DLR (2d) 138.

15. *Cf.* the view of Clarke referred to in fn. 45, para. 11.45 above that these cases should be the exception rather than the rule.

16. (1880) 5 QBD 272.

merchant relating to goods shipped in France was governed by English law except so far as the parties had expressly stipulated that it should be construed according to French law. Similarly, *Atlantic Underwriting Agencies Ltd* v. *Compagnia Assicurazione di Milano SPA*,[17] actually concerned the proper law of an underwriting agency agreement, but Lloyd J., in holding that the contract was governed by Italian law relied on the fact that the insurance contracts, which it was the object of the contract to procure for the Italian insurance company would, in all probability, be governed by Italian law in the absence of an express provision to the contrary.

12.12 In more recent cases, however, increasing weight has been paid to the market in which the (re)insurance contract was made. In particular the use of standard forms in marine insurance sometimes even led the court to find an actual implied intention at the second stage. See the cases referred to in paras 10.29–10.30 above.

(vi) Reinsurance

12.13 As referred to above, in reinsurance cases emphasis is usually placed on the fact that contracts are entered into on the London market by London brokers. For example, in *Citadel Insurance Co.* v. *Atlantic Union Insurance Co. SA*,[18] marine insurance brokers in New York arranged open cover through London reinsurance brokers with Greek reinsurers (who in turn reinsured themselves all round the world). The head underwriters were a US company and the insurance was also eventually taken up by the Canadian claimants. The claimants applied for leave to serve out of the jurisdiction and one of the grounds relied on was that the contract of reinsurance was governed by English law. All the members of the Court of Appeal focused on the importance of the case to the London reinsurance market; all agreed that the contract was governed by English law. Kerr LJ (with whom Oliver LJ agreed) held that England was the system of law with the closest connection. The centre of gravity of the business was the brokers in London. In *Afia Worldwide Insurance Co.* v. *Deutsche Ruck Versicherings AG*,[19] the jurisdiction of the court depended on the proper law of various reinsurance contracts. It was held that as regards the claims brought under contracts containing an arbitration clause there could be no doubt it being accepted that the presence of the clause was a sufficient indication of an intention to have the contracts governed by English law. But in relation to the other contracts, the fact that one party made a contract with an implied choice cannot lead to the conclusion that a different party, albeit the contract was brokered through the same medium, had the same intention. Hence they had to determine objectively the centre of gravity of the transaction. It was held to be London, and English law was the law with which the transaction had the closest connection on the following grounds: the contracts were negotiated in London; the approval of the reinsurer's agent was communicated by a document sent to the London brokers in London; the documents were in English; and where there were documents other than slips, they were either on the English broker's standard form or in forms commonly used in the London market and finally claims and accounts were handled in London. In *Overseas Union Insurance* v. *Incorporated General Insurance*,[20] the defendant reinsurer was a South African reinsurance company. The reinsurance contract was made through a London underwriter. The court of appeal upheld the judge's decision that the contract was governed by English law. The only possible alternative was South African law,

17. [1979] 2 Lloyd's Rep. 240.
18. [1982] 2 Lloyd's Rep. 543.
19. (1983) 133 NLJ 621.
20. [1992] 1 Lloyd's Rep. 439.

but both parties had intended to comply with English law and registration (by showing that the business was accepted elsewhere so not subject to the authority required under the Insurance Companies Act 1974).[21]

3. Scope of the proper law

(i) Contractual issues determined by reference to the proper law

12.14 At common law, proper law "is the law which governs the contract and the parties' obligations under it; it is the law which determines (normally) its validity and legality, its construction and effect and the conditions of its discharge."[22] Thus, it was well established that the proper law determined a contract's material or essential validity, its interpretation and effect and its discharge.[23] Most authorities supported the view that the formation of the contract was governed by the putative proper law.[24] A contract was formally valid if in accordance with governing law or the law of the place where it was made.

12.15 At one time, limitation was seen as procedural, hence courts would always apply English limitation periods, but the Foreign Limitation Periods Act 1984 made it clear that limitation was a matter of substance and therefore subject to the proper law.

12.16 To a large extent, this mirrors the scope of the applicable law under the Rome Convention (see paras 9.29–9.60 above).

(ii) Limits on choice of law

12.17 At common law, effect was given to the parties' choice of law only if their choice was *bona fide*, legal and a choice which there was no reason for avoiding on grounds of public policy.[25] It was also well established that the courts would refuse a choice of law clause if that law was designated for the objective of evading mandatory rules of English law.[26]

21. In *Britannia Steamship Insurance Association* v. *Ausonia Assicuraziono* [1984] 2 Lloyd's Rep. 98 it was not disputed that the proper law of the reinsurance contract was English law because the contract had its closest and real connection with English law.

22. *Amin Rasheed*, *op. cit.*, p. 69.

23. Proper law of the contract also governed the question of how policy monies were to be paid – i.e. how contractual obligations are discharged – see *Pick* v. *Manufacturers Life Insurance Co.* [1958] 2 Lloyd's Rep. 93.

24. See, generally, Dicey/Morris/Collins, para. 32-007.

25. See Lord Wright in *Vita Food Products Inc.* v. *Unus Shipping Co.* [1939] AC 277, 290.

26. See Dicey/Morris/Collins, para. 32-140, and Seatzu, p. 109. *Cf.* the view expressed in the Giuliano-Lagarde Report when discussing Article 7 (at para. 1) that "despite the opinion of some jurists, it must be frankly recognised that no clear indication in favour of the principle in question seems discernible in English cases"; 1980 OJ C.282/1, 27. See also Clarke, para. 2-28.

CHAPTER 13

REINSURANCE AND INSURANCE: CHOICE OF LAW IN ARBITRATION DISPUTES

A. INTRODUCTION

13.1 If the insurance or reinsurance contract contains an arbitration clause, the picture in relation to choice of law changes completely. In this chapter we consider the choice of law rules which will apply in such cases. In particular, we consider the extent to which the various regimes already discussed will apply to arbitrators.

B. THE DIFFERENT CHOICE OF LAW ISSUES WHICH ARISE IN ARBITRATIONS

13.2 As we have already seen (see para. 8.3 above), a number of different choice of law issues arise in the context of arbitration. The arbitrators must determine:

(1) the law governing the agreement to submit the dispute to arbitration;
(2) the law governing the reference to arbitration;
(3) the law which regulates the conduct of the arbitration; and
(4) the law which regulates the substantive rights of the parties.[1]

13.3 It is only the last of these issues, the law which regulates the contract or other matter from which the dispute has arisen, that also arises in court proceedings. The various regimes which apply to determine choice of law in insurance and reinsurance contracts have been discussed in detail in Chapters 9 to 12. The extent to which arbitrators are bound by these same regimes is a difficult question. But first we will consider briefly the arbitration-specific choice of law questions referred to at (1) to (3) above.[2]

C. THE LAW GOVERNING THE AGREEMENT TO SUBMIT THE DISPUTE TO ARBITRATION

13.4 An arbitration clause in a contract constitutes a self-contained contract collateral to the main contract of which it forms part.[3] The law governing this self-contained agreement need not be the same as that which governs the rest of the contract and must be determined separately.[4]

13.5 The law which governs the arbitration agreement will govern a number of issues, notably: whether the agreement to arbitrate is valid; the interpretation of the arbitration agreement, and in particular whether the arbitrator has jurisdiction over a specific issue; and

1. See the recent decision of Clark J. in *Halpern* v. *Halpern* [2006] EWHC 603 at [44]. In that case a further question arose, namely the law applicable to a compromise of the dispute.

2. A more detailed picture can be obtained from any of the main reference books listed in fn 1, para. 8.1 above.

3. The principle of separability was recognised by English law prior to the passing of the 1996 Arbitration Act but was given statutory force by s.7 of that Act. See, further, Merkin (Arbitration), para. 3-2.

4. See, for example, *Sumitomo Heavy Industries Ltd* v. *Oil and Natural Gas Commission* [1994] 1 Lloyd's Rep. 45.

whether an agreement to arbitrate has been frustrated. It will also be relevant to the other choice of law questions. Thus, the law governing the arbitration agreement will be applied to decide whether there has been an agreement as to curial law (i.e. issue (3) above).[5]

13.6 The Rome Convention does not apply to agreements to arbitrate (Article 1(2)(d)). Nonetheless, an arbitration clause is usually governed by the same law as that which governs the contract of which it forms part. It will only be in exceptional cases that the laws differ.[6] For example, in *Deutsche Schachtbau-und-Tiefbohrgellschaft mbH* v. *Ras Al Khaimah National Oil*,[7] an arbitration agreement providing for arbitration in Geneva was governed by Swiss law, notwithstanding that the contract, which was to be performed in R'As Al Khaimah, had been held by the arbitral tribunal to be governed by general principles of law. Thus, usually an arbitration agreement in an insurance or reinsurance contract will be governed by the law applicable to the contract it is contained in, determined in accordance with the relevant choice of law regime as has been described in detail in the preceding chapters. The main situation where this will not be the case is where the underlying contract is governed by law A, but provides for arbitration in state B, which may be chosen as neutral territory. In such a case it is likely that the presumption that the agreement to arbitrate will be governed by the same law as the law of the arbitration will outweigh any other presumption.[8]

13.7 All questions relating to the formulation of an arbitration agreement are governed by the law which would govern if it were validly concluded, i.e. by its putative proper law.[9]

D. THE LAW GOVERNING THE REFERENCE TO ARBITRATION

13.8 There is in theory a distinction between the agreement to arbitrate and the actual reference to arbitration which constitutes a contract in its own right. In theory, at least, that contract is capable of having its own proper law. But the overwhelming likelihood is that they will be governed by the same law. Indeed, there is no case where the courts have held that the law applicable is different to that which governs the agreement to arbitrate.[10] Thus, the laws at (1) and (2) above are nearly always the same.

E. THE LAW GOVERNING THE ARBITRAL PROCEEDINGS

13.9 The law governing the arbitral proceedings, often referred to as the curial law, will govern procedural aspects of the arbitration, such as appointment of arbitrators, the conduct of the proceedings, and challenge to the award. The law of the arbitration will also be applied, as we will see, to decide what law the arbitrators are to apply to decide the substantive issues (i.e. issue (4) above).[11]

5. See *Sumitomo Heavy Industries Ltd* v. *Oil and Natural Gas Commission* [1994] 1 Lloyd's Rep. 45.

6. Indeed, it is often an arbitration agreement itself which leads to a finding that the underlying contract is governed by the law of the place chosen for arbitration (see paras 10.35–10.41 above).

7. [1990] 1 AC 295.

8. As was the case in *Deutsche Schachtbau-und-Tiefbohrgesellschaft mbH* v. *Ras Al Khaimah National Oil Co.* [1987] 2 All ER 769. See, further, Merkin (Arbitration), para. 7-8.

9. See *XL Insurance Ltd* v. *Owens Corning* [2000] 2 Lloyd's Rep. 500.

10. See Merkin (Arbitration), para. 7.60. See also *Sumitomo*, *op. cit.*, where Potter LJ made it clear that although the contract which regulates the individual reference to arbitration is an agreement subsidiary to but separate from the arbitration agreement itself, the governing law will very rarely differ from that which governs the arbitration agreement itself.

11. See paras 13.17–13.18 below.

13.10 The 1996 Arbitration Act tells us when English procedural law applies.[12] The application of the Act, and thus the curial law, depends on a number of factual questions. Most significant is whether the seat of the arbitration is in England.

13.11 The juridical seat of an arbitration is not necessarily the place where the hearings physically take place. The seat may be designated by the parties themselves or they may agree to delegate the decision to the arbitrators (see para. 8.7 above). In the absence of any express designation, the court will have to determine the seat. The seat has to be determined at the outset of the arbitration. The court will consider the parties agreement and all the relevant circumstances at the time when the arbitration was commenced. These circumstancesinclude any connections with one or more particular countries that can be identified in relation to:

(1) the parties;
(2) the dispute;
(3) the proposed procedures in the arbitration, including the place of any interlocutory or final hearings; and
(4) the issue of the award.[13]

13.12 Although the place where any hearings take place is clearly significant, it can be outweighed by other factors, particularly if that place is purely fortuitous or the hearings were held there to meet to convenience of the arbitrators or particular witnesses.[14]

13.13 If the seat of the arbitration is in England, the 1996 Act will apply in its entirety. Thus various procedural rules set out in that Act will apply. However, some of those provisions are mandatory (for example, the provisions relating to the court's powers of supervision such as the power to set aside or remit an award for lack of jurisdiction or serious irregularity and certain of the provisions relating to the court's support of the process such as the duty to stay court proceedings, the power to extend time limits and the power to secure the attendance of witnesses, as well as the duty of the tribunal to act fairly and impartially), while the others are non-mandatory (for example, the power to appeal on questions of law). It is possible for the parties to contract out of the non-mandatory provisions and chose their own rules in that regard. This can be done in a number of ways:

(1) the parties may have agreed to arbitration in England in accordance with English law but have specifically excluded certain of the non-mandatory provisions. This is what happened in *XL Insurance Ltd* v. *Owens Corning*[15] where the parties had agreed to hold their arbitration in London but had excluded section 45 (application to the court for a ruling on a preliminary point of law) and section 69 (appeal on a point of law);
(2) the parties may have agreed to arbitrate in accordance with the rules of one of the institutional arbitration organisations, for example they may have incorporated the Rules of the London Court of International Arbitration or the UNCITRAL Arbitration Rules. To the extent that those rules are inconsistent with non-mandatory provisions in the 1996 Act the rules will apply;

12. It does not address the more general question of what is the curial law of the arbitration but in practice this separate question will rarely arise. Issues relating to the procedural aspects of arbitration arise in English courts only if (1) there is a dispute as to how an English arbitration has been conducted, or (2) the English court is asked to intervene in an arbitration. Both of these situations are comprehensively dealt with by the 1996 Act. The question of whether a foreign award can be refused recognition or enforcement on the basis that the procedure was defective is governed by the New York Convention 1958 which is implemented in Part III of the 1996 Act.

13. Section 3 of the 1996 Act as interpreted by Aikens J in *Dubai Islamic Bank PJSC* v. *Paymentech Merchant Services Inc.* [2001] 1 Lloyd's Rep. 65.

14. See Merkin (Arbitration), para. 1.30.

15. [2000] 2 Lloyd's Rep. 500.

(3) the parties may have chosen a different curial law. Where the procedural rules imposed by that law differ to the non-mandatory provisions in the 1996 Act the curial law will apply.

13.14 A little more needs to be said about (3) above. Section 5(5) of the 1996 Act provides:

"The choice of a law other than the law of England and Wales or Northern Ireland as the applicable law in respect of a matter provided for by a non-mandatory provision of this Part is equivalent to an agreement making provision about that matter.

For this purpose an applicable law determined in accordance with the parties' agreement, or which is objectively determined in the absence of any express or implied choice, shall be treated as chosen by the parties."

13.15 Thus, a choice of curial law other than English law, whether expressly or impliedly chosen by the parties or imposed by the court, will incorporate any rules of that law which are inconsistent with the non-mandatory provisions of the 1996 Act. This situation will in practice usually only arise in a case where England is the seat of the arbitration but the parties have expressly chosen a different curial law. In the absence of an express agreement or strong implication to this effect, the inference that the parties when contracting to arbitrate in a particular place consented to having the arbitral process governed by the law of that place is irresistible.[16] This will usually be the case, even if the law governing the arbitration agreement differs.[17]

13.16 If the seat of the arbitration is not England, the 1996 Act has only limited application, whether or not the parties have chosen English law as the curial law. Certain provisions apply regardless of the seat of the arbitration namely those relating to the stay of proceedings and the enforcement of arbitral awards (sections 9–11 and section 66). There are also certain procedures exercisable by the English court in relation to foreign arbitrations (for example, the power to secure the attendance of witnesses and the power to grant interim injunctions (section 44)) but the English courts can refuse to act if there is no necessary link with the domestic jurisdiction (section 2(3)). These powers are likely to be used particularly sparingly where the seat is abroad and the arbitration is governed by a foreign curial law.[18] Finally, the provisions relating to the separability of the arbitration agreement and the death of a party (sections 7 and 8) apply where English law is the law applicable to the arbitration agreement, regardless of the seat of the arbitration.

F. THE LAW GOVERNING THE SUBSTANCE OF THE DISPUTE

13.17 Section 46 of the 1996 Act provides:

"(1) The arbitral tribunal shall decide the dispute –
   (a) in accordance with the law chosen by the parties as applicable to the substance of the dispute, or
   (b) if the parties so agree, in accordance with such other considerations as are agreed by them or determined by the tribunal.

(2) …

(3) If or to the extent that there is no such choice or agreement, the tribunal shall apply the law determined by the conflict of law rules which it considers applicable."

16. See *Channel Tunnel Group Ltd* v. *Balfour Beatty* [1991] 1 All ER 127 and *Sumitomo Heavy Industries Ltd* v. *Oil and Natural Gas Commission* [1994] 1 Lloyd's Rep. 45.

17. See *James Miller & Partners Ltd* v. *Whitworth Street Estates (Manchester) Ltd* [1970] AC 583.

18. *Commerce and Industry Insurance Co. of Canada* v. *Lloyd's Underwriters* [2002] 1 Lloyd's Rep. 219.

13.18 Thus, where the seat of the arbitration is England, and unless the parties have agreed otherwise, section 46 sets out the approach which the arbitrators should take to determine the standards by which the merits of the dispute are to be judged.

1. Express choice of law

13.19 The first point to note is that the parties are free to agree the law applicable to the dispute. As we have seen, in contracts, the will of the parties is accorded substantial pre-eminence. Unsurprisingly, the same respect for party autonomy is accorded in the context of arbitration, itself a process founded on the consent and agreement of the parties.

13.20 However, even this apparently simple first step may be more complex than appears. First, are the parties free to choose any law? This is a question of considerable significance in an insurance and reinsurance context. As we have seen, whereas under the Rome Convention party autonomy is given primary importance under Article 3, if the contract is an insurance contract to which the insurance directives, as implemented into English law by the insurance regulations, applies the parties' freedom to choose the applicable law may well be much curtailed. A similar question would arise in a consumer contract which in a domestic context would be governed by Article 5 of the Rome Convention. By choosing to arbitrate have the parties effectively contracted out of these provisions, or is their freedom to choose within the limits otherwise allowed by English law (assuming English law is the law which governs the arbitration)? This question may well depend on the fundamental question of principle raised at the beginning of Chapter 9, i.e. what is the source of the parties' autonomy (see paras 9.2–9.4 above). Is the source of the parties' ability to choose the law governing their contract simply based upon their will or is the parties' autonomy confined to selecting from amongst the options offered by a particular system of municipal law? If the latter is the case, then a further question arises: *which* system of municipal law is applicable? In this context is it the 1996 Act without more, or the 1996 Act incorporating the relevant provisions of English law – if so is that the rule which would apply in domestic court proceedings or do different rules apply to arbitrations?

13.21 For a number of reasons, the respect given to party autonomy should prevail:

(1) The special conflict rule for arbitration set out in section 46(1) of the 1996 Act appears to make the obligation absolute.

(2) Traditionally national law was the only basis for party autonomy and determined the conditions and limits within which it could be exercised. But due to the universal acceptance of party autonomy in most developed legal systems some argue that party autonomy operates as a right in itself. Thus the rule has a special transnational or universal character and has binding effect because it has been agreed and adopted by the parties. Thus party autonomy is the most prominent and widely accepted (and possibly only) international conflict of law rule.[19]

(3) There is no reason why provisions such as the Rome Convention, binding on English courts, should apply to arbitrators. This point is developed further in paras 13.30–13.31 below.

13.22 There may well be, however, an exception for the application of mandatory rules that are contrary to international public policy. Although the arbitrator is not an organ of the state and so is not obliged to apply mandatory rules, his duty to enable awards to be enforceable as

19. Much has been written about party autonomy and conflict of law issues in international arbitration: see for example, Blessing, (1997) 14(4) J Int'l Arb 23; Voser (1996) 7 Am Rev. Int'l Arb 319; Hochstrasser (1994) 11(1) J Int'l Arb 57; Wortmann, (1998) 14 Arb Int 97.

well as to support the whole system of arbitration ought to require him, at the very least, not to apply any rules which are contrary to international public policy.[20]

13.23 The second problem that arises is whether section 46(1) (a) allows for an implied choice of law? It refers to the law "chosen by the parties" but it would be strange if the arbitrators could not give effect to such an implied intention. But again the question arises as to how such an intention should be ascertained. The following appear to be options:

(1) Apply the relevant regime which would apply if the case were a domestic case before the domestic courts, i.e. either the Rome Convention, insurance regulations or the common law.
(2) Apply special rules developed specifically in the context of arbitration cases. In practice this debate may well end up being somewhat academic. The basis on which an implied choice will be found seem relatively clear and well accepted. For example, there are a number of cases at common law which establish that the nominated seat of the arbitration is to be regarded as the best evidence of an implied choice of law. The case law was reviewed by the House of Lords in *Compagnie d'Armement Maritime SA* v. *Compagnie Tunisienne de Navigation,*[21] their Lordships confirming that the presumption the proper law follows the forum is strong but not conclusive. This presumption also operates to found a choice of law expressed with reasonable certainty for the purposes of Article 3 of the Rome Convention.[22] An arbitrator considering the same contract may well also feel that the fact that the parties have chosen to arbitrate under a particular law is because they assumed the tribunal would be applying that law to the substantive dispute before it and may well therefore imply a choice of law on the same basis.

13.24 The next important point to note is that under section 46(1)(b) the parties are free to choose to apply "such other considerations as are agreed by them or determined by the tribunal". This provision confirms that the parties can incorporate equity clauses into their agreement to arbitrate.[23]

13.25 There are two different types of such agreement. First are equity clauses, otherwise known as "honourable engagement" or "*amiable compositeur*" provisions, which purport to allow arbitrators to decide the dispute without applying the strict principles of the governing law. The only class of contracts in English law which commonly use such clauses are reinsurance treaties.[24] There is no clear English common law authority on their meaning. The weight of authority favours an interpretation which upholds the agreement and the arbitration clause but holds that the clause does not relieve the arbitrators from their usual duty to apply the governing law of the contract. Thus they have limited effect. They do not turn the contract into a "gentleman's agreement"; they merely oust technicalities and strict construction[25] and possibly allow the arbitrators to draw upon their own practical experience without the need for formal proof.[26]

20. See, further, the articles cited in fn 19 above.
21. [1971] AC 572.
22. See *Giuliano-Lagarde*, 1980 OJ C.282/1, 17, and *Egon Oldendorff* v. *Liberia Corporation* [1995] 1 Lloyd's Rep. 64 and paras 10.35–10.41 above.
23. This confirms the position at common law. See *Home and Overseas Insurance Co. Ltd* v. *Mentor Insurance Co. (UK) Ltd* [1990] 1 WLR 153. It also allows the parties to chose a religious law such as Shari'a law or Jewish law: *cf.* the position under the Rome Convention discussed in para. 10.59 above.
24. See Merkin (Arbitration), para. 7.47.
25. See Lord Denning in *Eagle Star Insurance Co* v. *Yuval Insurance Co. Ltd* [1962] 1 Lloyd's Rep. 357.
26. See Evans J. in *Overseas Union Ins.* v. *AA Mutual International Ltd* [1988] 1 FTLR 421.

13.26 Secondly, the parties may chose to adopt a version of the so-called *lex mercatoria*. In 1994 the Governing Council of the International Institute for the Unification of Private Law (UNIDROIT) published the Principles of International Commercial Contracts (the UNIDROIT principles). The UNIDROIT principles are drafted as articles supported by comments and cover areas such as formation, validity, interpretation, performance and breach of contract. Since 1982 the Commission on European Contract Law has been working to establish principles of European Contract Law (PECL). In both cases they set forth general rules for international contracts and shall be applied when the parties have agreed that their contract is to be governed by them or where the parties have agreed that their contract shall be governed by "general principles of law, the *lex mercatoria* or the like". Thus, the following has been put forward as a description of the *lex mercatoria*:

"a non-national law to be applied to international commercial contracts. Its main elements are the international customs and usages of international trade, the international conventions, the rules which have been established for this purpose such as the UNIDROIT Principles and the PECL, and the rules which are common to most of the states engaged in international trade or to the states connected with the contract. When the judge or arbitrator cannot find guidance in these rules he will apply the rule which appeared to him to be the most appropriate and equitable. In so doing he may consider national laws, the works of legal writers and the published arbitral awards. This judicial process is partly an application of the existing rules and partly a selective and creative process. In applying the *lex mercatoria* the arbitrator does not decide the case *ex aequo et bono*, he does not act as an *amiable compositeur*. He bases his decision on rules."[27]

Other rules which may now be regarded as part of the *lex mercatoria* include the Convention on Contracts for the International Sale of Goods 1989.

13.27 In this respect at least, the choice of law regime applicable to arbitrators expressly differs from that in the Rome Convention which allows a choice of the law of a municipal legal system only.[28]

2. No express or implied choice of law

13.28 The question becomes even more complex where there is no express choice of law.[29] The 1996 Act provides that the tribunal shall apply "the law determined by the conflict of laws rules which it considers applicable". The following points should be noted:

(1) The section does not allow the arbitrators to apply directly whatever law they think appropriate (although the parties may include such an express provision[30]), they can choose what conflict of law rule to apply and then apply that rule to determine the applicable law. A delegated choice of law allows the arbitrators to choose what law is

27. O. Lando, "Dicey & Morris, The Conflict of Laws: A Review" (1998) 47 ICLQ 394, 401.

28. See, for example, *Shamil Bank of Bahrain* v. *Beximco Pharmaceuticals Ltd* [2004] EWCA Civ 19 and *Halpern* v. *Halpern* [2006] EWHC 603. Although this may change under the proposed Rome I Regulation (see para. 10.62 above).

29. The DAC in its report on the 1996 Act recognised that the wording of the Model law, which is identical to s.46(3), was problematic and that the proper interpretation of the provision raised complex questions. The DAC felt it best to adopt the wording of the Model law in the hope that the problems would not be insurmountable.

30. Many arbitration rules, including the rules of UNCITRAL and ICC delegate to the arbitrators the power to choose the system of law to be applied. See, for example, the ICC rules which provide that "the parties shall be free to agree upon the rules of law to be applied by the Arbitral Tribunal to the merits of the dispute. In the absence of any such agreement the Arbitral Tribunal shall apply the rules of law which it determines to be appropriate" (Article 17.1). The common law recognised the validity of such clauses and the inviolability of the arbitrator's choice. See Merkin (Arbitration), para. 7.43.

to be applied. This must take precedence over any other conflict rules including those in the Rome Convention.[31]

(2) The section refers to the arbitrators applying the conflict of law rules which it considers applicable, note not appropriate.

13.29 Thus the question arises again as to whether the arbitrators will be required to determine the regime which would apply were these domestic court proceedings or whether their discretion is wider.

13.30 Again, there are good reasons why arbitrators sitting in England should not be bound to apply English conflict of law rules.

13.31 Traditionally the choice of law process constitutes an attempt to localise a legal issue in a national legal system. National conflict of laws rules codify states' policies with regard to choice of law. These principles are particularly apparent in the European context. The aim of the Rome Convention is to facilitate the free market by providing free movement of judgements (which in turn necessitates common rules on jurisdiction and choice of law). Also apparent is the secondary aim of protection of consumers. These are aims which the sovereign has signed up to as part of its accession to a common European market and the conflict of law rules are part of this broader picture.

13.32 By contrast, the power of the arbitral tribunal to determine the rules to apply to the merits of the dispute can be considered an extension to the principle of party autonomy. International arbitrators are under a duty to the parties rather than the sovereign thus they need not implement or follow state policies. Consequently, their analysis of the applicable law can be based on an analysis of the substantive rules themselves rather than the source of the rules through the application of conflict of law rules.

13.33 But assuming the arbitrators are not bound to apply English conflict of law principles, how do they determine the applicable law? Section 46(3) requires the arbitrators to select an applicable conflict of law system. But need that be a national system at all?

13.34 The better view seems to be that section 46(3) gives a general discretion to apply any conflict of law rule, not necessarily the rules of a particular country (the tribunal could pick from an international convention, academic writing or indeed any other rule it wished), still less the rules of a particular country that a judge would apply on the facts of the case.[32]

13.35 Thus, it is possible that a contract will have a different applicable law depending on whether or not there is an arbitration clause. Some might think this result surprising: often arbitration clauses are inserted at the last minute and seen as peripheral or at least purely procedural (more recently an arbitration clause may have been inserted to avoid the consequences of the *Gasser* decision (see paras 5.280–5.284 above). It is important to remember that through the impact on the choice of law issues discussed above, an agreement to arbitrate may also affect the parties' substantive rights and liabilities.

31. *Cf.* Merkin (Arbitration), para. 7.45. He suggests that there may be a reconciliation possible between s.46 and the Rome Convention if the choice made by the arbitrators is an express choice under Article 3. But that solution would not help if the arbitrators choose a rule or law which is not permitted under the insurance regulations which do not, of course, give the parties full freedom of choice.

32. See Dicey/Morris/Collins, para. 16-038. The learned editor notes that an arbitrator should be wary of assuming that solutions adopted within the EU are necessarily a safe guide to the determination of applicable conflict rules for a dispute where the parties and subject-matter are outside the EU. Merkin agrees to some extent in that he agrees that s.46(3) gives the arbitrators a discretion to choose whichever conflict of laws rules they think appropriate – a discretion which could not be challenged in court, but he also says that if they select English conflict of law rules those rules would be the Rome Convention (or presumably the relevant regime such as the insurance regulations) (Merkin (Arbitration), para. 7.42). Indeed, he states that if the arbitrators having decided to apply English conflict rules have failed to apply the Rome Convention that is an error of English law which could be challenged in court.

APPENDIX 1

JURISDICTION MATERIALS

APPENDIX 1.1

COMPARATIVE TABLE OF BRUSSELS REGULATION (EC) 44/2001 AND BRUSSELS CONVENTION (1998)

Council Regulation (EC) No. 44/2001 of 22 December 2000 on jurisdiction and the recognition and enforcement of judgments in civil and commercial matters

THE COUNCIL OF THE EUROPEAN UNION,

HAVING REGARD to the Treaty establishing the European Community, and in particular Article 61 (c) and Article 67(1) thereof,

HAVING REGARD to the proposal from the Commission,

HAVING REGARD to the opinion of the European Parliament,

HAVING REGARD to the opinion of the Economic and Social Committee,

WHEREAS:

(1) The Community has set itself the objective of maintaining and developing an area of freedom, security and justice, in which the free movement of persons is ensured. In order to establish progressively such an area, the Community should adopt, amongst other things, the measures relating to judicial cooperation in civil matters which are necessary for the sound operation of the internal market.

(2) Certain differences between national rules governing jurisdiction and recognition of judgments hamper the sound operation of the internal market. Provisions to unify the rules of conflict of jurisdiction in civil and commercial matters and to simplify the formalities with a view to rapid and simple recognition and enforcement of judgments from Member States bound by this Regulation are essential.

(3) This area is within the field of judicial cooperation in civil matters within the meaning of Article 65 of the Treaty.

(4) In accordance with the principles of subsidiarity and proportionality as set out in Article 5 of the Treaty, the objectives of this Regulation cannot be sufficiently achieved by the Member States and can therefore be better achieved by the

1968 Brussels Convention on jurisdiction and the enforcement of judgments in civil and commercial matters (consolidated version) (1998)

Official Journal C 027, 26/01/1998

PREAMBLE

THE HIGH CONTRACTING PARTIES TO THE TREATY ESTABLISHING THE EUROPEAN ECONOMIC COMMUNITY,

DESIRING to implement the provisions of Article 220 of that Treaty by virtue of which they undertook to secure the simplification of formalities governing the reciprocal recognition and enforcement of judgments of courts or tribunals,

ANXIOUS to strengthen in the Community the legal protection of persons therein established,

CONSIDERING that it is necessary for this purpose to determine the international jurisdiction of their courts, to facilitate recognition and to introduce an expeditious procedure for securing the enforcement of judgments, authentic instruments and court settlements,

HAVE DECIDED to conclude this Convention and to this end have designated as their plenipotentiaries ...

Brussels Regulation 44/2001	Brussels Convention (1998)
Community. This Regulation confines itself to the minimum required in order to achieve those objectives and does not go beyond what is necessary for that purpose. (5) On 27 September 1968 the Member States, acting under Article 293, fourth indent, of the Treaty, concluded the Brussels Convention on Jurisdiction and the Enforcement of Judgments in Civil and Commercial Matters, as amended by Conventions on the Accession of the New Member States to that Convention (hereinafter referred to as the "Brussels Convention"). On 16 September 1988 Member States and EFTA States concluded the Lugano Convention on Jurisdiction and the Enforcement of Judgments in Civil and Commercial Matters, which is a parallel Convention to the 1968 Brussels Convention. Work has been undertaken for the revision of those Conventions, and the Council has approved the content of the revised texts. Continuity in the results achieved in that revision should be ensured. (6) In order to attain the objective of free movement of judgments in civil and commercial matters, it is necessary and appropriate that the rules governing jurisdiction and the recognition and enforcement of judgments be governed by a Community legal instrument which is binding and directly applicable. (7) The scope of this Regulation must cover all the main civil and commercial matters apart from certain well-defmed matters. (8) There must be a link between proceedings to which this Regulation applies and the territory of the Member States bound by this Regulation. Accordingly common rules on jurisdiction should, in principle, apply when the defendant is domiciled in one of those Member States. (9) A defendant not domiciled in a Member State is in general subject to national rules of jurisdiction applicable in the territory of the Member State of the court seised, and a defendant domiciled in a Member State not bound by this Regulation must remain subject to the Brussels Convention. (10) For the purposes of the free movement of judgments, judgments given in a Member State bound by this Regulation should be recognised and enforced in another Member State bound by this Regulation, even if the judgment debtor is domiciled in a third State. (11) The rules of jurisdiction must be highly predictable and founded on the principle that jurisdiction is generally based on the defendant's domicile and jurisdiction must always be available on this ground save in a few well-defined situa-	

Brussels Regulation 44/2001	Brussels Convention (1998)
tions in which the subject-matter of the litigation or the autonomy of the parties warrants a different linking factor. The domicile of a legal person must be defmed autonomously so as to make the common rules more transparent and avoid conflicts of jurisdiction.	
(12) In addition to the defendant's domicile, there should be alternative grounds of jurisdiction based on a close link between the court or the action or in order to facilitate the sound administration of justice.	
(13) In relation to insurance, consumer contracts and employment, the weaker party should be protected by rules of jurisdiction more favourable to his interests than the general rules provide for.	
(14) The autonomy of the parties to a contract, other than an insurance, consumer or employment contract, where only limited autonomy to determine the courts having jurisdiction is allowed, must be respected subject to the exclusive grounds of jurisdiction laid down in this Regulation.	
(15) In the interests of the harmonious administration of justice it is necessary to minimise the possibility of concurrent proceedings and to ensure that irreconcilable judgments will not be given in two Member States. There must be a clear and effective mechanism for resolving cases of lis pendens and related actions and for obviating problems flowing from national differences as to the determination of the time when a case is regarded as pending. For the purposes of this Regulation that time should be defined autonomously.	
(16) Mutual trust in the administration of justice in the Community justifies judgments given in a Member State being recognised automatically without the need for any procedure except in cases of dispute.	
(17) By virtue of the same principle of mutual trust, the procedure for making enforceable in one Member State a judgment given in another must be efficient and rapid. To that end, the declaration that a judgment is enforceable should be issued virtually automatically after purely formal checks of the documents supplied, without there being any possibility for the court to raise of its own motion any of the grounds for non-enforcement provided for by this Regulation.	
(18) However, respect for the rights of the defence means that the defendant should be able to appeal in an adversarial procedure, against the declaration of enforceability, if he considers one of the grounds for non-enforcement to be present. Redress procedures should also be available to the claimant where his application for a declaration of enforceability has been rejected.	

Brussels Regulation 44/2001	Brussels Convention (1998)
(19) Continuity between the Brussels Convention and this Regulation should be ensured, and transitional provisions should be laid down to that end. The same need for continuity applies as regards the interpretation of the Brussels Convention by the Court of Justice of the European Communities and the 1971 Protocol should remain applicable also to cases already pending when this Regulation enters into force.	
(20) The United Kingdom and Ireland, in accordance with Article 3 of the Protocol on the position of the United Kingdom and Ireland annexed to the Treaty on European Union and to the Treaty establishing the European Community, have given notice of their wish to take part in the adoption and application of this Regulation.	
(21) Denmark, in accordance with Articles 1 and 2 of the Protocol on the position of Denmark annexed to the Treaty on European Union and to the Treaty establishing the European Community, is not participating in the adoption of this Regulation, and is therefore not bound by it nor subject to its application.	
(22) Since the Brussels Convention remains in force in relations between Denmark and the Member States that are bound by this Regulation, both the Convention and the 1971 Protocol continue to apply between Denmark and the Member States bound by this Regulation.	
(23) The Brussels Convention also continues to apply to the territories of the Member States which fall within the territorial scope of that Convention and which are excluded from this Regulation pursuant to Article 299 of the Treaty.	
(24) Likewise for the sake of consistency, this Regulation should not affect rules governing jurisdiction and the recognition of judgments contained in specific Community instruments.	
(25) Respect for international commitments entered into by the Member States means that this Regulation should not affect conventions relating to specific matters to which the Member States are parties.	
(26) The necessary flexibility should be provided for in the basic rules of this Regulation in order to take account of the specific procedural rules of certain Member States. Certain provisions of the Protocol annexed to the Brussels Convention should accordingly be incorporated in this Regulation.	
(27) In order to allow a harmonious transition in certain areas which were the subject of special provisions in the Protocol annexed to the Brussels Convention, this Regulation lays down, for a transitional period, provisions taking into consideration the specific situation in certain Member States.	

Brussels Regulation 44/2001	Brussels Convention (1998)
(28) No later than five years after entry into force of this Regulation the Commission will present a report on its application and, if need be, submit proposals for adaptations. (29) The Commission will have to adjust Annexes I to IV on the rules of national jurisdiction, the courts or competent authorities and redress procedures available on the basis of the amendments forwarded by the Member State concerned; amendments made to Annexes V and VI should be adopted in accordance with Council Decision 1999/468/EC of 28 June 1999 laying down the procedures for the exercise of implementing powers conferred on the Commission,	
HAS ADOPTED THIS REGULATION:	WHO … HAVE AGREED AS FOLLOWS:
CHAPTER I: SCOPE	TITLE I: SCOPE
Article 1 1. This Regulation shall apply in civil and commercial matters whatever the nature of the court or tribunal. It shall not extend, in particular, to revenue, customs or administrative matters.	*Article 1* This Convention shall apply in civil and commercial matters whatever the nature of the court or tribunal. It shall not extend, in particular, to revenue, customs or administrative matters.
2. The Regulation shall not apply to:	The Convention shall not apply to:
(a) the status or legal capacity of natural persons, rights in property arising out of a matrimonial relationship, wills and succession; (b) bankruptcy, proceedings relating to the winding-up of insolvent companies or other legal persons, judicial arrangements, compositions and analogous proceedings; (c) social security; (d) arbitration.	1. the status or legal capacity of natural persons, rights in property arising out of a matrimonial relationship, wills and succession; 2. bankruptcy, proceedings relating to the windingup of insolvent companies or other legal persons, judicial arrangements, compositions and analogous proceedings; 3. social security; 4. arbitration.
3. In this Regulation, the term "Member State" shall mean Member States with the exception of Denmark.	
CHAPTER II: JURISDICTION **Section 1: General provisions**	TITLE II: JURISDICTION **Section 1: General provisions**
Article 2 1. Subject to this Regulation, persons domiciled in a Member State shall, whatever their nationality, be sued in the courts of that Member State.	*Article 2* Subject to the provisions of this Convention, persons domiciled in a Contracting State shall, whatever their nationality, be sued in the courts of that State.
2. Persons who are not nationals of the Member State in which they are domiciled shall be governed by the rules of jurisdiction applicable to nationals of that State.	Persons who are not nationals of the State in which they are domiciled shall be governed by the rules of jurisdiction applicable to nationals of that State.

Brussels Regulation 44/2001	Brussels Convention (1998)
Article 3	*Article 3*
1. Persons domiciled in a Member State may be sued in the courts of another Member State only by virtue of the rules set out in Sections 2 to 7 of this Chapter.	Persons domiciled in a Contracting State may be sued in the courts of another Contracting State only by virtue of the rules set out in Sections 2 to 6 of this Title.
2. In particular the rules of national jurisdiction set out in Annex I shall not be applicable as against them.	In particular the following provisions shall not be applicable as against them: …
Article 4	*Article 4*
1. If the defendant is not domiciled in a Member State, the jurisdiction of the courts of each Member State shall, subject to Articles 22 and 23, be determined by the law of that Member State.	If the defendant is not domiciled in a Contracting State, the jurisdiction of the courts of each Contracting State shall, subject to the provisions of Article 16, be determined by the law of that State.
2. As against such a defendant, any person domiciled in a Member State may, whatever his nationality, avail himself in that State of the rules of jurisdiction there in force, and in particular those specified in Annex I, in the same way as the nationals of that State.	As against such a defendant, any person domiciled in a Contracting State may, whatever his nationality, avail himself in that State of the rules of jurisdiction there in force, and in particular those specified in the second paragraph of Article 3, in the same way as the nationals of that State.
Section 2: Special jurisdiction	**Section 2: Special jurisdiction**
Article 5	*Article 5*
A person domiciled in a Member State may, in another Member State, be sued:	A person domiciled in a Contracting State may, in another Contracting State, be sued:
1. (a) in matters relating to a contract, in the courts for the place of performance of the obligation in question; (b) for the purpose of this provision and unless otherwise agreed, the place of performance of the obligation in question shall be: – in the case of the sale of goods, the place in a Member State where, under the contract, the goods were delivered or should have been delivered, – in the case of the provision of services, the place in a Member State where, under the contract, the services were provided or should have been provided, (c) if subparagraph (b) does not apply then subparagraph (a) applies;	1. in matters relating to a contract, in the courts for the place of performance of the obligation in question; in matters relating to individual contracts of employment, this place is that where the employee habitually carries out his work, or if the employee does not habitually carry out his work in any one country, the employer may also be sued in the courts for the place where the business which engaged the employee was or is now situated;
2. in matters relating to maintenance, in the courts for the place where the maintenance creditor is domiciled or habitually resident or, if the matter is ancillary to proceedings concerning the status of a person, in the court which, according to its own law, has jurisdiction to entertain those proceedings, unless that jurisdiction is based solely on the nationality of one of the parties;	2. in matters relating to maintenance, in the courts for the place where the maintenance creditor is domiciled or habitually resident or, if the matter is ancillary to proceedings concerning the status of a person, in the court which, according to its own law, has jurisdiction to entertain those proceedings, unless that jurisdiction is based solely on the nationality of one of the parties;
3. in matters relating to tort, delict or quasi-delict, in the courts for the place where the harmful event occurred or may occur;	3. in matters relating to tort, delict or quasi-delict, in the courts for the place where the harmful event occurred;

Brussels Regulation 44/2001	**Brussels Convention (1998)**
4. as regards a civil claim for damages or restitution which is based on an act giving rise to criminal proceedings, in the court seised of those proceedings, to the extent that that court has jurisdiction under its own law to entertain civil proceedings;	4. as regards a civil claim for damages or restitution which is based on an act giving rise to criminal proceedings, in the court seised of those proceedings, to the extent that that court has jurisdiction under its own law to entertain civil proceedings;
5. as regards a dispute arising out of the operations of a branch, agency or other establishment, in the courts for the place in which the branch, agency or other establishment is situated;	5. as regards a dispute arising out of the operations of a branch, agency or other establishment, in the courts for the place in which the branch, agency or other establishment is situated;
6. as settlor, trustee or beneficiary of a trust created by the operation of a statute, or by a written instrument, or created orally and evidenced in writing, in the courts of the Member State in which the trust is domiciled;	6. as settlor, trustee or beneficiary of a trust created by the operation of a statute, or by a written instrument, or created orally and evidenced in writing, in the courts of the Contracting State in which the trust is domiciled;
7. as regards a dispute concerning the payment of remuneration claimed in respect of the salvage of a cargo or freight, in the court under the authority of which the cargo or freight in question: (a) has been arrested to secure such payment, or (b) could have been so arrested, but bail or other security has been given; provided that this provision shall apply only if it is claimed that the defendant has an interest in the cargo or freight or had such an interest at the time of salvage.	7. as regards a dispute concerning the payment of remuneration claimed in respect of the salvage of a cargo or freight, in the court under the authority of which the cargo or freight in question: (a) has been arrested to secure such payment, or (b) could have been so arrested, but bail or other security has been given; provided that this provision shall apply only if it is claimed that the defendant has an interest in the cargo or freight or had such an interest at the time of salvage.
Article 6 A person domiciled in a Member State may also be sued:	*Article 6* A person domiciled in a Contracting State may also be sued:
1. where he is one of a number of defendants, in the courts for the place where anyone of them is domiciled, provided the claims are so closely connected that it is expedient to hear and detennine them together to avoid the risk of irreconcilable judgments resulting from separate proceedings;	1. where he is one of a number of defendants, in the courts for the place where anyone of them is domiciled;
2. as a third party in an action on a warranty or guarantee or in any other third party proceedings, in the court seised of the original proceedings, unless these were instituted solely with the object of removing him from the jurisdiction of the court which would be competent in his case;	2. as a third party in an action on a warranty or guarantee or in any other third party proceedings, in the court seised of the original proceedings, unless these were instituted solely with the object of removing him from the jurisdiction of the court which would be competent in his case;
3. on a counter-claim arising from the same contract or facts on which the original claim was based, in the court in which the original claim is pending;	3. on a counter-claim arising from the same contract or facts on which the original claim was based, in the court in which the original claim is pending;
4. in matters relating to a contract, if the action may be combined with an action against the same defendant in matters relating to rights *in rem* in immovable property, in the court of the Member State in which the property is situated.	4. in matters relating to a contract, if the action may be combined with an action against the same defendant in matters relating to rights in rem in immovable property, in the court of the Contracting State in which the property is situated.
Article 7 Where by virtue of this Regulation a court of a Member State has jurisdiction in actions relating	*Article 6a* Where by virtue of this Convention a court of a Contracting State has jurisdiction in actions relat-

Brussels Regulation 44/2001

to liability from the use or operation of a ship, that court, or any other court substituted for this purpose by the internal law of that Member State, shall also have jurisdiction over claims for limitation of such liability.

Section 3: Jurisdiction in matters relating to insurance

Article 8

In matters relating to insurance, jurisdiction shall be detennined by this Section, without prejudice to Article 4 and point 5 of Article 5.

Article 9

1. An insurer domiciled in a Member State may be sued:

(a) in the courts of the Member State where he is domiciled, or

(b) in another Member State, in the case of actions brought by the policyholder, the insured or a beneficiary, in the courts for the place where the plaintiff is domiciled,

(c) if he is a co-insurer, in the courts of a Member State in which proceedings are brought against the leading insurer.

2. An insurer who is not domiciled in a Member State but has a branch, agency or other establishment in one of the Member States shall, in disputes arising out of the operations of the branch, agency or establishment, be deemed to be domiciled in that Member State.

Article 10

In respect of liability insurance or insurance of immovable property, the insurer may in addition be sued in the courts for the place where the harmful event occurred. The same applies if movable and immovable property are covered by the same insurance policy and both are adversely affected by the same contingency.

Article 11

1. In respect of liability insurance, the insurer may also, if the law of the court permits it, be joined in proceedings which the injured party has brought against the insured.

2. Articles 8, 9 and 10 shall apply to actions brought by the injured party directly against the insurer, where such direct actions are permitted.

3. If the law governing such direct actions provides that the policyholder or the insured may be joined as a party to the action, the same court shall have jurisdiction over them.

Brussels Convention (1998)

ing to liability from the use or operation of a ship, that court, or any other court substituted for this purpose by the internal law of that State, shall also have jurisdiction over claims for limitation of such liability.

Section 3: Jurisdiction in matters relating to insurance

Article 7

In matters relating to insurance, jurisdiction shall be determined by this Section, without prejudice to the provisions of Articles 4 and 5 point 5.

Article 8

An insurer domiciled in a Contracting State may be sued:

1. in the courts of the State where he is domiciled, or

2. in another Contracting State, in the courts for the place where the policy-holder is domiciled, or

3. if he is a co-insurer, in the courts of a Contracting State in which proceedings are brought against the leading insurer.

An insurer who is not domiciled in a Contracting State but has a branch, agency or other establishment in one of the Contracting States shall, in disputes arising out of the operations of the branch, agency or establishment, be deemed to be domiciled in that State.

Article 9

In respect of liability insurance or insurance of immovable property, the insurer may in addition be sued in the courts for the place where the harmful event occurred. The same applies if movable and immovable property are covered by the same insurance policy and both are adversely affected by the same contingency.

Article 10

In respect of liability insurance, the insurer may also, if the law of the court permits it, be joined in proceedings which the injured party had brought against the insured.

The provisions of Articles 7, 8 and 9 shall apply to actions brought by the injured party directly against the insurer, where such direct actions are permitted.

If the law governing such direct actions provides that the policy-holder or the insured may be joined as a party to the action, the same court shall have jurisdiction over them.

Brussels Regulation 44/2001	Brussels Convention (1998)
Article 12 1. Without prejudice to Article 11 (3), an insurer may bring proceedings only in the courts of the Member State in which the defendant is domiciled, irrespective of whether he is the policyholder, the insured or a beneficiary.	*Article 11* Without prejudice to the provisions of the third paragraph of Article 10, an insurer may bring proceedings only in the courts of the Contracting State in which the defendant is domiciled, irrespective of whether he is the policy-holder, the insured or a beneficiary.
2. The provisions of this Section shall not affect the right to bring a counter-claim in the court in which, in accordance with this Section, the original claim is pending.	The provisions of this Section shall not affect the right to bring a counterclaim in the court in which, in accordance with this Section, the original claim is pending.
Article 13 The provisions of this Section may be departed from only by an agreement: 1. which is entered into after the dispute has arisen, or 2. which allows the policyholder, the insured or a beneficiary to bring proceedings in courts other than those indicated in this Section, or 3. which is concluded between a policyholder and an insurer, both of whom are at the time of conclusion of the contract domiciled or habitually resident in the same Member State, and which has the effect of conferring jurisdiction on the courts of that State even if the harmful event were to occur abroad, provided that such an agreement is not contrary to the law of that State, or	*Article 12* The provisions of this Section may be departed from only by an agreement on jurisdiction: 1. which is entered into after the dispute has arisen, or 2. which allows the policy-holder, the insured or a beneficiary to bring proceedings in courts other than those indicated in this Section, or 3. which is concluded between a policy-holder and an insurer, both of whom are domiciled in the same Contracting State, and which has the effect of conferring jurisdiction on the courts of that State even if the harmful event were to occur abroad, provided that such an agreement is not contrary to the law of that State, or
4. which is concluded with a policyholder who is not domiciled in a Member State, except in so far as the insurance is compulsory or relates to immovable property in a Member State, or 5. which relates to a contract of insurance in so far as it covers one or more of the risks set out in Article 14.	4. which is concluded with a policy-holder who is not domiciled in a Contracting State, except in so far as the insurance is compulsory or relates to immovable property in a Contracting State, or 5. which relates to a contract of insurance in so far as it covers one or more of the risks set out in Article 12a.
Article 14 The following are the risks referred to in Article 13(5): 1. any loss of or damage to: (a) seagoing ships, installations situated off-shore or on the high seas, or aircraft, arising from perils which relate to their use for commercial purposes; (b) goods in transit other than passengers' baggage where the transit consists of or includes carriage by such ships or aircraft; 2. any liability, other than for bodily injury to passengers or loss of or damage to their baggage: (a) arising out of the use or operation of ships, installations or aircraft as referred to in point l(a) in so far as, in respect of the latter, the law of the Member State in which such aircraft are registered does not prohibit agreements on jurisdiction regarding insurance of such risks;	*Article 12a* The following are the risks referred to in point 5 of Article 12: 1. any loss of or damage to: (a) sea-going ships, installations situated off-shore or on the high seas, or aircraft, arising from perils which relate to their use for commercial purposes; (b) goods in transit other than passengers' baggage where the transit consists of or includes carriage by such ships or aircraft; 2. any liability, other than for bodily injury to passengers or loss of or damage to their baggage: (a) arising out of the use or operation of ships, installations or aircraft as referred to in point I (a) above in so far as the law of the Contracting State in which such aircraft are registered does not prohibit agreements on jurisdiction regarding insurance of such risks;

Brussels Regulation 44/2001

(b) for loss or damage caused by goods in transit as described in point l(b);

3. any financial loss connected with the use or operation of ships, installations or aircraft as referred to in point l(a), in particular loss of freight or charterhire;

4. any risk or interest connected with any of those referred to in points 1 to 3;

5. notwithstanding points 1 to 4, all "large risks" as defined in Council Directive 73/239/EEC, as amended by Council Directives 88/357/EEC and 90/618/EEC, as they may be amended.

Section 4: Jurisdiction over consumer contracts

Article 15

1. In matters relating to a contract concluded by a person, the consumer, for a purpose which can be regarded as being outside his trade or profession, jurisdiction shall be determined by this Section, without prejudice to Article 4 and point 5 of Article 5, if:

(a) it is a contract for,the sale of goods on instalment credit terms; or

(b) it is a contract for a loan repayable by instalments, or for any other fonn of credit, made to finance the sale of goods; or

(c) in all other cases, the contract has been concluded with a person who pursues commercial or professional activities in the Member State of the consumer's domicile or, by any means, directs such activities to that Member State or to several States including that Member State, and the contract falls within the scope of such activities.

2. Where a consumer enters into a contract with a party who is not domiciled in the Member State but has a branch, agency or other establishment in one of the Member States, that party shall, in disputes arising out of the operations of the branch, agency or establishment, be deemed to be domiciled in that State.

3. This Section shall not apply to a contract of transport other than a contract which, for an inclusive price, provides for a combination of travel and accommodation.

Article 16

1. A consumer may bring proceedings against the other party to a contract either in the courts of the Member State in which that party is domiciled or in the courts for the place where the consumer is domiciled.

2. Proceedings may be brought against a consumer by the other party to the contract only in the

Brussels Convention (1998)

(b) for loss or damage caused by goods in transit as described in point 1 (b) above;

3. any financial loss connected with the use or operation of ships, installations or aircraft as referred to in point 1 (a) above, in particular loss of freight or charter-hire;

4. any risk or interest connected with any of those referred to in points I to 3 above.

Section 4: Jurisdiction over consumer contracts

Article 13

In proceedings concerning a contract concluded by a person for a purpose which can be regarded as being outside his trade or profession, hereinafter called "the consumer", jurisdiction shall be determined by this Section, without prejudice to the provisions of point 5 of Articles 4 and 5, if it is:

1. a contract for the sale of goods on instalment credit terms; or

2. a contract for a loan repayable by instalments, or for any other form of credit, made to finance the sale of goods; or

3. any other contract for the supply of goods or a contract for the supply of services, and

(a) in the State of the consumer's domicile the conclusion of the contract was preceded by a specific invitation addressed to him or by advertising and

(b) the consumer took in that State the steps necessary for the conclusion of the contract.

Where a consumer enters into a contract with a party who is not domiciled in a Contracting State but has a branch, agency or other establishment in one of the Contracting States, that party shall, in disputes arising out of the operations of the branch, agency or establishment, be deemed to be domiciled in that State.

This Section shall not apply to contracts of transport.

Article 14

A consumer may bring proceedings against the other party to a contract either in the courts of the Contracting State in which that party is domiciled or in the courts of the Contracting State in which he is himself domiciled.

Proceedings may be brought against a consumer by the other party to the contract only in the

Brussels Regulation 44/2001	**Brussels Convention (1998)**
courts of the Member State in which the consumer is domiciled. 3. This Article shall not affect the right to bring a counter-claim in the court in which, in accordance with this Section, the original claim is pending.	courts of the Contracting State in which the consumer is domiciled. These provisions shall not affect the right to bring a counter-claim in the court in which, in accordance with this Section, the original claim is pending.
Article 17 The provisions of this Section may be departed from only by an agreement: 1. which is entered into after the dispute has arisen; or 2. which allows the consumer to bring proceedings in courts other than those indicated in this Section; or 3. which is entered into by the consumer and the other party to the contract, both of whom are at the time of conclusion of the contract domiciled or habitually resident in the same Member State, and which confers jurisdiction on the courts of that Member State, provided that such an agreement is not contrary to the law of that Member State.	*Article 15* The provisions of this Section may be departed from only by an agreement: 1. which is entered into after the dispute has arisen; or 2. which allows the consumer to bring proceedings in courts other than those indicated in this Section; or 3. which is entered into by the consumer and the other party to the contract, both of whom are at the time of conclusion of the contract domiciled or habitually resident in the same Contracting State, and which confers jurisdiction on the courts of that State, provided that such an agreement is not contrary to the law of that State.
Section 5: Jurisdiction over individual contracts of employment	
Article 18 1. In matters relating to individual contracts of employment, jurisdiction shall be determined by this Section, without prejudice to Article 4 and point 5 of Article 5. 2. Where an employee enters into an individual contract of employment with an employer who is not domiciled in a Member State but has a branch, agency or other establishment in one of the Member States, the employer shall, in disputes arising out of the operations of the branch, agency or establishment, be deemed to be domiciled in that Member State.	
Article 19 An employer domiciled in a Member State may be sued: 1. in the courts of the Member State where he is domiciled; or 2. in another Member State: (a) in the courts for the place where the employee habitually carries out his work or in the courts for the last place where he did so, or (b) if the employee does not or did not habitually carry out his work in any one country, in the courts for the place where the business which engaged the employee is or was situated.	

Brussels Regulation 44/2001

Article 20

1. An employer may bring proceedings only in the courts of the Member State in which the employee is domiciled.

2. The provisions of this Section shall not affect the right to bring a counter-claim in the court in which, in accordance with this Section, the original claim is pending.

Article 21

The provisions of this Section may be departed from only by an agreement on jurisdiction:

1. which is entered into after the dispute has arisen; or

2. which allows the employee to bring proceedings in courts other than those indicated in this Section.

Section 6: Exclusive jurisdiction

Article 22

The following courts shall have exclusive jurisdiction, regardless of domicile:

1. in proceedings which have as their object rights *in rem* in immovable property or tenancies of immovable property, the courts of the Member State in which the property is situated.

However, in proceedings which have as their object tenancies of immovable property concluded for temporary private use for a maximum period of six consecutive months, the courts of the Member State in which the defendant is domiciled shall also have jurisdiction, provided that the tenant is a natural person and that the landlord and the tenant are domiciled in the same Member State;

2. in proceedings which have as their object the validity of the constitution, the nullity or the dissolution of companies or other legal persons or associations of natural or legal persons, or of the validity of the decisions of their organs, the courts of the Member State in which the company, legal person or association has its seat. In order to determine that seat, the court shall apply its rules of private international law;

3. in proceedings which have as their object the validity of entries in public registers, the courts of the Member State in which the register is kept;

4. in proceedings concerned with the registration or validity of patents, trade marks, designs, or other similar rights required to be deposited or registered, the courts of the Member State in which the deposit or registration has been applied for, has taken place or is under the terms of a Community instrument or an international convention deemed to have taken place.

Brussels Convention (1998)

Section 5: Exclusive jurisdiction

Article 16

The following courts shall have exclusive jurisdiction, regardless of domicile:

1 (a) in proceedings which have as their object rights in rem in immovable property or tenancies of immovable property, the courts of the Contracting State in which the property is situated;

(b) however, in proceedings which have as their object tenancies of immovable property concluded for temporary private use for a maximum period of six consecutive months, the courts of the Contracting State in which the defendant is domiciled shall also have jurisdiction, provided that the landlord and the tenant are natural persons and are domiciled in the same Contracting State;

2. in proceedings which have as their object the validity of the constitution, the nullity or the dissolution of companies or other legal persons or associations of natural or legal persons, or the decisions of their organs, the courts of the Contracting State in which the company, legal person or association has its seat;

3. in proceedings which have as their object the validity of entries in public registers, the courts of the Contracting State in which the register is kept;

4. in proceedings concerned with the registration or validity of patents, trade marks, designs, or other similar rights required to be deposited or registered, the courts of the Contracting State in which the deposit or registration has been applied for, has taken place or is under the terms of an international convention deemed to have taken place;

Brussels Regulation 44/2001	Brussels Convention (1998)
Without prejudice to the jurisdiction of the European Patent Office under the Convention on the Grant of European Patents, signed at Munich on 5 October 1973, the courts of each Member State shall have exclusive jurisdiction, regardless of domicile, in proceedings concerned with the registration or validity of any European patent granted for that State;	
5. in proceedings concerned with the enforcement of judgments, the courts of the Member State in which the judgment has been or is to be enforced.	5. in proceedings concerned with the enforcement of judgments, the courts of the Contracting State in which the judgment has been or is to be enforced.
Section 7: Prorogation of jurisdiction	**Section 6: Prorogation of jurisdiction**
Article 23	*Article 17*
1. If the parties, one or more of whom is domiciled in a Member State, have agreed that a court or the courts of a Member State are to have jurisdiction to settle any disputes which have arisen or which may arise in connection with a particular legal relationship, that court or those courts shall have jurisdiction. Such jurisdiction shall be exclusive unless the parties have agreed otherwise. Such an agreement conferring jurisdiction shall be either:	If the parties, one or more of whom is domiciled in a Contracting State, have agreed that a court or the courts of a Contracting State are to have jurisdiction to settle any disputes which have arisen or which may arise in connection with a particular legal relationship, that court or those courts shall have exclusive jurisdiction. Such an agreement conferring jurisdiction shall be either:
(a) in writing or evidenced in writing; or	(a) in writing or evidenced in writing; or
(b) in a form which accords with practices which the parties have established between themselves; or	(b) in a form which accords with practices which the parties have established between themselves; or
(c) in international trade or commerce, in a form which accords with a usage of which the parties are or ought to have been aware and which in such trade or commerce is widely known to, and regularly observed by, parties to contracts of the type involved in the particular trade or commerce concerned.	(c) in international trade or commerce, in a form which accords with a usage of which the parties are or ought to have been aware and which in such trade or commerce is widely known to, and regularly observed by, parties to contracts of the type involved in the particular trade or commerce concerned.
2. Any communication by electronic means which provides a durable record of the agreement shall be equivalent to "writing".	
3. Where such an agreement is concluded by parties, none of whom is domiciled in a Member State, the courts of other Member States shall have no jurisdiction over their disputes unless the court or courts chosen have declined jurisdiction.	Where such an agreement is concluded by parties, none of whom is domiciled in a Contracting State, the courts of other Contracting States shall have no jurisdiction over their disputes unless the court or courts chosen have declined jurisdiction.
4. The court or courts of a Member State on which a trust instrument has conferred jurisdiction shall have exclusive jurisdiction in any proceedings brought against a settlor, trustee or beneficiary, if relations between these persons or their rights or obligations under the trust are involved.	The court or courts of a Contracting State on which a trust instrument has conferred jurisdiction shall have exclusive jurisdiction in any proceedings brought against a settler, trustee or beneficiary, if relations between these persons or their rights or obligations under the trust are involved.
5. Agreements or provisions of a trust instrument conferring jurisdiction shall have no legal force if they are contrary to Articles 13, 17 or 21, or if the courts whose jurisdiction they purport to	Agreements or provisions of a trust instrument conferring jurisdiction shall have no legal force if they are contrary to the provisions of Articles 12 or 15, or if the courts whose jurisdiction they

Brussels Regulation 44/2001	Brussels Convention (1998)
exclude have exclusive jurisdiction by virtue of Article 22.	purport to exclude have exclusive jurisdiction by virtue of Article 16. If an agreement conferring jurisdiction was concluded for the benefit of only one of the parties, that party shall retain the right to bring proceedings in any other court which has jurisdiction by virtue of this Convention. In matters relating to individual contracts of employment an agreement conferring jurisdiction shall have legal force only if it is entered into after the dispute has arisen or if the employee invokes it to seise courts other than those for the defendant's domicile or those specified in Article 5 (1).
Article 24 Apart from jurisdiction derived from other provisions of this Regulation, a court of a Member State before which a defendant enters an appearance shall have jurisdiction. This rule shall not apply where appearance was entered to contest the jurisdiction, or where another court has exclusive jurisdiction by virtue of Article 22.	*Article 18* Apart from jurisdiction derived from other provisions of this Convention, a court of a Contracting State before whom a defendant enters an appearance shall have jurisdiction. This rule shall not apply where appearance was entered solely to contest the jurisdiction, or where another court has exclusive jurisdiction by virtue of Article 16.
Section 8: Examination as to jurisdiction and admissibility	**Section 7: Examination as to jurisdiction and admissibility**
Article 25 Where a court of a Member State is seised of a claim which is principally concerned with a matter over which the courts of another Member State have exclusive jurisdiction by virtue of Article 22, it shall declare of its own motion that it has no jurisdiction.	*Article 19* Where a court of a Contracting State is seised of a claim which is principally concerned with a matter over which the courts of another Contracting State have exclusive jurisdiction by virtue of Article 16, it shall declare of its own motion that it has no jurisdiction.
Article 26 1. Where a defendant domiciled in one Member State is sued in a court of another Member State and does not enter an appearance, the court shall declare of its own motion that it has no jurisdiction unless its jurisdiction is derived from the provisions of this Regulation. 2. The court shall stay the proceedings so long as it is not shown that the defendant has been able to receive the document instituting the proceedings or an equivalent document in sufficient time to enable him to arrange for his defence, or that all necessary steps have been taken to this end. 3. Article 19 of Council Regulation (EC) No 1348/ 2000 of 29 May 2000 on the service in the Member States of judicial and extrajudicial documents in civil or commercial matters shall apply instead of the provisions of paragraph 2 if the document instituting the proceedings or an equivalent document had to be transmitted from one Member State to another pursuant to this Regulation.	*Article 20* Where a defendant domiciled in one Contracting State is sued in a court of another Contracting State and does not enter an appearance, the court shall declare of its own motion that it has no jurisdiction unless its jurisdiction is derived from the provisions of the Convention. The court shall stay the proceedings so long as it is not shown that the defendant has been able to receive the document instituting the proceedings or an equivalent document in sufficient time to enable him to arrange for his defence, or that all necessary steps have been taken to this end.

Brussels Regulation 44/2001	Brussels Convention (1998)
4. Where the provisions of Regulation (EC) No 1348/2000 are not applicable, Article 15 of the Hague Convention of 15 November 1965 on the Service Abroad of Judicial and Extrajudicial Documents in Civil or Commercial Matters shall apply if the document instituting the proceedings or an equivalent document had to be transmitted pursuant to that Convention.	The provisions of the foregoing paragraph shall be replaced by those of Article 15 of the Hague Convention of 15 November 1965 on the service abroad of judicial and extrajudicial documents in civil or commercial matters, if the document instituting the proceedings or notice thereof had to be transmitted abroad in accordance with that Convention.
Section 9: Lis pendens – related actions	**Section 8: Lis pendens – related actions**
Article 27 1. Where proceedings involving the same cause of action and between the same parties are brought in the courts of different Member States, any court other than the court first seised shall of its own motion stay its proceedings until such time as the jurisdiction of the court first seised is established. 2. Where the jurisdiction of the court first seised is established, any court other than the court first seised shall decline jurisdiction in favour of that court.	*Article 21* Where proceedings involving the same cause of action and between the same parties are brought in the courts of different Contracting States, any court other than the court first seised shall of its own motion stay its proceedings until such time as the jurisdiction of the court first seised is established. Where the jurisdiction of the court first seised is established, any court other than the court fust seised shall decline jurisdiction in favour of that court.
Article 28 1. Where related actions are pending in the courts of different Member States, any court other than the court first seised may stay its proceedings. 2. Where these actions are pending at first instance, any court other than the court first seised may also, on the application of one of the parties, decline jurisdiction if the court first seised has jurisdiction over the actions in question and its law permits the consolidation thereof. 3. For the purposes of this Article, actions are deemed to be related where they are so closely connected that it is expedient to hear and determine them together to avoid the risk of irreconcilable judgments resulting from separate proceedings.	*Article 22* Where related actions are brought in the courts of different Contracting States, any court other than the court first seised may, while the actions are pending at first instance, stay its proceedings. A court other than the court first seised may also, on the application of one of the parties, decline jurisdiction if the law of that court permits the consolidation of related actions and the court first seised has jurisdiction over both actions. For the purposes of this Article, actions are deemed to be related where they are so closely connected that it is expedient to hear and determine them together to avoid the risk of irreconcilable judgments resulting from separate proceedings.
Article 29 Where actions come within the exclusive jurisdiction of several courts, any court other than the court first seised shall decline jurisdiction in favour of that court.	*Article 23* Where actions come within the exclusive jurisdiction of several courts, any court other than the court first seised shall decline jurisdiction in favour of that court.
Article 30 For the purposes of this Section, a court shall be deemed to be seised: 1. at the time when the document instituting the proceedings or an equivalent document is lodged with the court, provided that the plaintiff has not subsequently failed to take the steps he was required to take to have service effected on the defendant, or	

Brussels Regulation 44/2001	**Brussels Convention (1998)**
2. if the document has to be served before being lodged with the court, at the time when it is received by the authority responsible for service, provided that the plaintiff has not subsequently failed to take the steps he was required to take to have the document lodged with the court.	
Section 10: Provisional, including protective, measures	**Section 9: Provisional, including protective, measures**
Article 31 Application may be made to the courts of a Member State for such provisional, including protective, measures as may be available under the law of that State, even if, under this Regulation, the courts of another Member State have jurisdiction as to the substance of the matter.	*Article 24* Application may be made to the courts of a Contracting State for such provisional, including protective, measures as may be available under the law of that State, even if, under this Convention, the courts of another Contracting State have jurisdiction as to the substance of the matter.
CHAPTER III: RECOGNITION AND ENFORCEMENT	TITLE III: RECOGNITION AND ENFORCEMENT
Article 32 For the purposes of this Regulation, "judgment" means any judgment given by a court or tribunal of a Member State, whatever the judgment may be called, including a decree, order, decision or writ of execution, as well as the determination of costs or expenses by an officer of the court.	*Article 25* For the purposes of this Convention, "judgment" means any judgment given by a court or tribunal of a Contracting State, whatever the judgment may be called, including a decree, order, decision or writ of execution, as well as the determination of costs or expenses by an officer of the court.
Section 1: Recognition	**Section 1: Recognition**
Article 33 1. A judgment giveng in a Member State shall be recognised in the other Member States without any special procedure being required.	*Article 26* A judgment given in a Contracting State shall be recognized in the other Contracting States without any special procedure being required.
2. Any interested party who raises the recognition of a judgment as the principal issue in a dispute may, in accordance with the procedures provided for in Sections 2 and 3 of this Chapter, apply for a decision that the judgment be recognised.	Any interested party who raises the recognition of a judgment as the principal issue in a dispute may, in accordance with the procedures provided for in Sections 2 and 3 of this Title, apply for a decision that the judgment be recognized.
3. If the outcome of proceedings in a court of a Member State depends on the determination of an incidental question of recognition that court shall have jurisdiction over that question.	If the outcome of proceedings in a court of a Contracting State depends on the determination of an incidental question of recognition that court shall have jurisdiction over that question.
Article 34 A judgment shall not be recognised:	*Article 27* A judgment shall not be recognized:
1. if such recognition is manifestly contrary to public policy in the Member State in which recognition is sought;	1. if such recognition is contrary to public policy in the State in which recognition is sought;
2. where it was given in default of appearance, if the defendant was not served with the document which instituted the proceedings or with an equivalent document in sufficient time and in such a way as to enable him to arrange for his defence,	2. where it was given in default of appearance, if the defendant was not duly served with the document which instituted the proceedings or with an equivalent document in sufficient time to enable him to arrange for his defence;

Brussels Regulation 44/2001	Brussels Convention (1998)
unless the defendant failed to commence proceedings to challenge the judgment when it was possible for him to do so;	
3. if it is irreconcilable with a judgment given in a dispute between the same parties in the Member State in which recognition is sought;	3. if the judgment is irreconcilable with a judgment given in a dispute between the same parties in the State in which recognition is sought;
	4. if the court of the State of origin, in order to arrive at its judgment, has decided a preliminary question concerning the status or legal capacity of natural persons, rights in property arising out of a matrimonial relationship, wills or succession in a way that conflicts with a rule of the private international law of the State in which the recognition is sought, unless the same result would have been reached by the application of the rules of private international law of that State;
4. if it is irreconcilable with an earlier judgment given in another Member State or in a third State involving the same cause of action and between the same parties, provided that the earlier judgment fulfils the conditions necessary for its recognition in the Member State addressed.	5. if the judgment is irreconcilable with an earlier judgment given in a non-contracting State involving the same cause of action and between the same parties, provided that this latter judgment fulfils the conditions necessary for its recognition in the State addressed.
Article 35	*Article 28*
1. Moreover, a judgment shall not be recognised if it conflicts with Sections 3, 4 or 6 of Chapter II, or in a case provided for in Article 72.	Moreover, a judgment shall not be recognized if it conflicts with the provisions of Sections 3, 4 or 5 of Title II, or in a case provided for in Article 59.
2. In its examination of the grounds of jurisdiction referred to in the foregoing paragraph, the court or authority applied to shall be bound by the findings of fact on which the court of the Member State of origin based its jurisdiction.	In its examination of the grounds of jurisdiction referred to in the foregoing paragraph, the court or authority applied to shall be bound by the findings of fact on which the court of the State of origin based its jurisdiction.
3. Subject to the paragraph I, the jurisdiction of the court of the Member State of origin may not be reviewed. The test of public policy referred to in point 1 of Article 34 may not be applied to the rules relating to jurisdiction.	Subject to the provisions of the fust paragraph, the jurisdiction of the court of the State of origin may not be reviewed; the test of public policy referred to in point I of Article 27 may not be applied to the rules relating to jurisdiction.
Article 36	*Article 29*
Under no circumstances may a foreign judgment be reviewed as to its substance.	Under no circumstances may a foreign judgment be reviewed as to its substance.
Article 37	*Article 30*
1. A court of a Member State in which recognition is sought of a judgment given in another Member State may stay the proceedings if an ordinary appeal against the judgment has been lodged.	A court of a Contracting State in which recognition is sought of a judgment given in another Contracting State may stay the proceedings if an ordinary appeal against the judgment has been lodged.
2. A court of a Member State in which recognition is sought of a judgment given in Ireland or the United Kingdom may stay the proceedings if enforcement is suspended in the State of origin, by reason of an appeal.	A court of a Contracting State in which recognition is sought of a judgment given in Ireland or the United Kingdom may stay the proceedings if enforcement is suspended in the State of origin, by reason of an appeal.

Brussels Regulation 44/2001	Brussels Convention (1998)
Section 2: Enforcement	**Section 2: Enforcement**
Article 38 1. A judgment given in a Member State and enforceable in that State shall be enforced in another Member State when, on the application of any interested party, it has been declared enforceable there. 2. However, in the United Kingdom, such a judgment shall be enforced in England and Wales, in Scotland, or in Northern Ireland when, on the application of any interested party, it has been registered for enforcement in that part of the United Kingdom.	*Article 31* A judgrnent given in a Contracting State and enforceable in that State shall be enforced in another Contracting State when, on the application of any interested party, it has been declared enforceable there. However, in the United Kingdom, such a judgment shall be enforced in England and Wales, in Scotland, or in Northern Ireland when, on the application of any interested party, it has been registered for enforcement in that part of the United Kingdom.
Article 39 1. The application shall be submitted to the court or competent authority indicated in the list in Annex II. 2. The local jurisdiction shall be determined by reference to the place of domicile of the party against whom enforcement is sought, or to the place of enforcement.	*Article 32* 1. The application shall be submitted: (...) 2. The jurisdiction of local courts shall be determined by reference to the place of dornicile of the party against whom enforcement is sought. If he is not domiciled in the State in which enforcement is sought, it shall be determined by reference to the place of enforcement.
Article 40 1. The procedure for making the application shall be governed by the law of the Member State in which enforcement is sought. 2. The applicant must give an address for service of process within the area of jurisdiction of the court applied to. However, if the law of the Member State in which enforcement is sought does not provide for the furnishing of such an address, the applicant shall appoint a representative *ad litem*. 3. The documents referred to in Article 53 shall be attached to the application.	*Article 33* The procedure for making the application shall be governed by the law of the State in which enforcement is sought. The applicant must give an address for service of process within the area of jurisdiction of the court applied to. However, if the law of the State in which enforcement is sought does not provide for the furnishing of such an address, the applicant shall appoint a representative *ad litem*. The documents referred to in Articles 46 and 47 shall be attached to the application.
Article 41 The judgment shall be declared enforceable immediately on completion of the formalities in Article 53 without any review under Articles 34 and 35. The party against whom enforcement is sought shall not at this stage of the proceedings be entitled to make any submissions on the application.	*Article 34* The court applied to shall give its decision without delay; the party against whom enforcement is sought shall not at this stage of the proceedings be entitled to make any submissions on the application. The application may be refused only for one of the reasons specified in Articles 27 and 28. Under no circumstances may the foreign judgment be reviewed as to its substance.
Article 42 1. The decision on the application for a declaration of enforceability shall forthwith be brought to the notice of the applicant in accordance with	*Article 35* The appropriate officer of the court shall without delay bring the decision given on the application to the notice of the applicant in accordance with

Brussels Regulation 44/2001	**Brussels Convention (1998)**
the procedure laid down by the law of the Member State in which enforcement is sought. 2. The declaration of enforceability shall be served on the party against whom enforcement is sought, accompanied by the judgment, if not already served on that party.	the procedure laid down by the law of the State in which enforcement is sought.
Article 43 1. The decision on the application for a declaration of enforceability may be appealed against by either party. 2. The appeal is to be lodged with the court indicated in the list in Annex III. 3. The appeal shall be dealt with in accordance with the rules governing procedure in contradictory matters. 4. If the party against whom enforcement is sought fails to appear before the appellate court in proceedings concerning an appeal brought by the applicant, Article 26(2) to (4) shall apply even where the party against whom enforcement is sought is not domiciled in any of the Member States.	
5. An appeal against the declaration of enforceability is to be lodged within one month of service thereof. If the party against whom enforcement is sought is domiciled in a Member State other than that in which the declaration of enforceability was given, the time for appealing shall be two months and shall run from the date of service, either on him in person or at his residence. No extension of time may be granted on account of distance.	*Article 36* If enforcement is authorized, the party against whom enforcement is sought may appeal against the decision within one month of service thereof. If that party is domiciled in a Contracting State other than that in which the decision authorizing enforcement was given, the time for appealing shall be two months and shall run from the date of service, either on him in person or at his residence. No extension of time may be granted on account of distance.
	Article 37 1. An appeal against the decision authorizing enforcement shall be lodged in accordance with the rules governing procedure in contentious matters: (…)
Article 44 The judgment given on the appeal may be contested only by the appeal referred to in Annex IV.	2. The judgment given on the appeal may be contested only: (…)
Article 45 1. The court with which an appeal is lodged under Article 43 or Article 44 shall refuse or revoke a declaration of enforceability only on one of the grounds specified in Articles 34 and 35. It shall give its decision without delay. 2. Under no circumstances may the foreign judgment be reviewed as to its substance.	
Article 46 1. The court with which an appeal is lodged under Article 43 or Article 44 may, on the appli-	*Article 38* The court with which the appeal under Article 37(1) is lodged may, on the application of the

Brussels Regulation 44/2001	**Brussels Convention (1998)**
cation of the party against whom enforcement is sought, stay the proceedings if an ordinary appeal has been lodged against the judgment in the Member State of origin or if the time for such an appeal has not yet expired; in the latter case, the court may specify the time within which such an appeal is to be lodged.	appellant, stay the proceedings if an ordinary appeal has been lodged against the judgment in the State of origin or if the time for such an appeal has not yet expired; in the latter case, the court may specify the time within which such an appeal is to be lodged.
2. Where the judgment was given in Ireland or the United Kingdom, any form of appeal available in the Member State of origin shall be treated as an ordinary appeal for the purposes of paragraph 1.	Where the judgment was given in Ireland or the United Kingdom, any form of appeal available in the State of origin shall be treated as an ordinary appeal for the purposes of the first paragraph.
3. The court may also make enforcement conditional on the provision of such security as it shall determine.	The court may also make enforcement conditional on the provision of such security as it shall determine.
Article 47 1. When a judgment must be recognised in accordance with this Regulation, nothing shall prevent the applicant from availing himself of provisional, including protective, measures in accordance with the law of the Member State requested without a declaration of enforceability under Article 41 being required.	*Article 39* During the time specified for an appeal pursuant to Article 36 and until any such appeal has been determined, no measures of enforcement may be taken other than protective measures taken against the property of the party against whom enforcement is sought.
2. The declaration of enforceability shall carry with it the power to proceed to any protective measures.	The decision authorizing enforcement shall carry with it the power to proceed to any such protective measures.
3. During the time specified for an appeal pursuant to Article 43(5) against the declaration of enforceability and until any such appeal has been determined, no measures of enforcement may be taken other than protective measures against the property of the party against whom enforcement is sought.	
	Article 40 If the application for enforcement is refused, the applicant may appeal: (...) 2. The party against whom enforcement is sought shall be summoned to appear before the appellate court. If he fails to appear, the provisions of the second and third paragraphs of Article 20 shall apply even where he is not domiciled in any of the Contracting States.
	Article 41 A judgment given on an appeal provided for in Article 40 may be contested only: (...)
Article 48 1. Where a foreign judgment has been given in respect of several matters and the declaration of enforceability cannot be given for all of them, the court or competent authority shall give it for one or more of them.	*Article 42* Where a foreign judgment has been given in respect of several matters and enforcement cannot be authorized for all of them, the court shall authorize enforcement for one or more of them.

Brussels Regulation 44/2001	**Brussels Convention (1998)**
2. An applicant may request a declaration of enforceability limited to parts of a judgment.	An applicant may request partial enforcement of a judgment.
Article 49 A foreign judgment which orders a periodic payment by way of a penalty shall be enforceable in the Member State in which enforcement is sought only if the amount of the payment has been finally determined by the courts of the Member State of origin.	*Article 43* A foreign judgment which orders a periodic payment by way of a penalty shall be enforceable in the State in which enforcement is sought only if the amount of the payment has been finally determined by the courts of the State of origin.
Article 50 An applicant who, in the Member State of origin has benefited from complete or partial legal aid or exemption from costs or expenses, shall be entitled, in the procedure provided for in this Section, to benefit from the most favourable legal aid or the most extensive exemption from costs or expenses provided for by the law of the Member State addressed.	*Article 44* An applicant who, in the State of origin has benefited from complete or partial legal aid or exemption from costs or expenses, shall be entitled, in the procedures provided for in Articles 32 to 35, to benefit from the most favourable legal aid or the most extensive exemption from costs or expenses provided for by the law of the State addressed. However, an applicant who requests the enforcement of a decision given by an administrative authority in Denmark in respect of a maintenance order may, in the State addressed, claim the benefits referred to in the first paragraph if he presents a statement from the Danish Ministry of Justice to the effect that he fulfils the economic requirements to qualify for the grant of complete or partial legal aid or exemption from costs or expenses.
Article 51 No security, bond or deposit, however described, shall be required of a party who in one Member State applies for enforcement of a judgment given in another Member State on the ground that he is a foreign national or that he is not domiciled or resident in the State in which enforcement is sought.	*Article 45* No security, bond or deposit, however described, shall be required of a party who in one Contracting State applies for enforcement of a judgment given in another Contracting State on the ground that he is a foreign national or that he is not domiciled or resident in the State in which enforcement is sought.
Article 52 In proceedings for the issue of a declaration of enforceability, no charge, duty or fee calculated by reference to the value of the matter at issue may be levied in the Member State in which enforcement is sought.	
Section 3: Common provisions	**Section 3: Common provisions**
Article 53 1. A party seeking recognition or applying for a declaration of enforceability shall produce a copy of the judgment which satisfies the conditions necessary to establish its authenticity.	*Article 46* A party seeking recognition or applying for enforcement of a judgment shall produce: 1. a copy of the judgment which satisfies the conditions necessary to establish its authenticity; 2. in the case of a judgment given in default, the original or a certified true copy of the document which establishes that the party in default was

Brussels Regulation 44/2001	Brussels Convention (1998)
	served with the document instituting the proceedings or with an equivalent document.
2. A party applying for a declaration of enforceability shall also produce the certificate referred to in Article 54, without prejudice to Article 55.	*Article 47* A party applying for enforcement shall also produce: 1. documents which establish that, according to the law of the State of origin the judgment is enforceable and has been served; 2. where appropriate, a document showing that the applicant is in receipt of legal aid in the State of origin.
Article 54 The court or competent authority of a Member State where a judgment was given shall issue, at the request of any interested party, a certificate using the standard form in Annex V to this Regulation.	
Article 55 1. If the certificate referred to in Article 54 is not produced, the court or competent authority may specify a time for its production or accept an equivalent document or, if it considers that it has sufficient information before it, dispense with its production. 2. If the court or competent authority so requires, a translation of the documents shall be produced. The translation shall be certified by a person qualified to do so in one of the Member States.	*Article 48* If the documents specified in point 2 of Articles 46 and 47 are not produced, the court may specify a time for their production, accept equivalent documents or, if it considers that it has sufficient information before it, dispense with their production. If the court so requires, a translation of the documents shall be produced; the translation shall be certified by a person qualified to do so in one of the Contracting States.
Article 56 No legalisation or other similar formality shall be required in respect of the documents referred to in Article 53 or Article 55(2), or in respect of a document appointing a representative *ad litem*.	*Article 49* No legalization or other similar formality shall be required in respect of the documents referred to in Articles 46 or 47 or the second paragraph of Article 48, or in respect of a document appointing a representative *ad litem*.
CHAPTER IV: AUTHENTIC INSTRUMENTS AND COURT SETTLEMENTS	TITLE IV: AUTHENTIC INSTRUMENTS AND COURT SETTLEMENTS
Article 57 1. A document which has been formally drawn up or registered as an authentic instrument and is enforceable in one Member State shall, in another Member State, be declared enforceable there, on application made in accordance with the procedures provided for in Articles 38, *et seq*. The court with which an appeal is lodged under Article 43 or Article 44 shall refuse or revoke a declaration of enforceability only if enforcement of the instrument is manifestly contrary to public policy in the Member State addressed. 2. Arrangements relating to maintenance obligations concluded with administrative authorities	*Article 50* A document which has been formally drawn up or registered as an authentic instrument and is enforceable in one Contracting State shall, in another Contracting State, be declared enforceable there, on application made in accordance with the procedures provided for in Article 31 *et seq*. The application may be refused only if enforcement of the instrument is contrary to public policy in the State addressed.

Brussels Regulation 44/2001	Brussels Convention (1998)
or authenticated by them shall also be regarded as authentic instruments within the meaning of paragraph 1.	
3. The instrument produced must satisfy the conditions necessary to establish its authenticity in the Member State of origin.	The instrument produced must satisfy the conditions necessary to establish its authenticity in the State of origin.
4. Section 3 of Chapter III shall apply as appropriate. The competent authority of a Member State where an authentic instrument was drawn up or registered shall issue, at the request of any interested party, a certificate using the standard form in Annex VI to this Regulation.	The provisions of Section 3 of Title III shall apply as appropriate.
Article 58 A settlement which has been approved by a court in the course of proceedings and is enforceable in the Member State in which it was concluded shall be enforceable in the State addressed under the same conditions as authentic instruments. The court or competent authority of a Member State where a court settlement was approved shall issue, at the request of any interested party, a certificate using the standard form in Annex V to this Regulation.	*Article 51* A settlement which has been approved by a court in the course of proceedings and is enforceable in the State in which it was concluded shall be enforceable in the State addressed under the same conditions as authentic instruments.
CHAPTER V: GENERAL PROVISIONS	TITLE V: GENERAL PROVISIONS
Article 59 1. In order to determine whether a party is domiciled in the Member State whose courts are seised of a matter, the court shall apply its internal law.	*Article 52* In order to determine whether a party is domiciled in the Contracting State whose courts are seised of a matter, the Court shall apply its internal law.
2. If a party is not domiciled in the Member State whose courts are seised of the matter, then, in order to determine whether the party is domiciled in another Member State, the court shall apply the law of that Member State.	If a party is not domiciled in the State whose courts are seised of the matter, then, in order to determine whether the party is domiciled in another Contracting State, the court shall apply the law of that State.
Article 60 1. For the purposes of this Regulation, a company or other legal person or association of natural or legal persons is domiciled at the place where it has its: (a) statutory seat, or (b) central administration, or (c) principal place of business. 2. For the purposes of the United Kingdom and Ireland "statutory seat" means the registered office or, where there is no such office anywhere, the place of incorporation or, where there is no such place anywhere, the place under the law of which the formation took place.	*Article 53* For the purposes of this Convention, the seat of a company or other legal person or association of natural or legal persons shall be treated as its domicile. However, in order to determine that seat, the court shall apply its rules of private international law.
3. In order to determine whether a trust is domiciled in the Member State whose courts are seised of the matter, the court shall apply its rules of private international law.	In order to determine whether a trust is domiciled in the Contracting State whose courts are seised of the matter, the court shall apply its rules of private international law.

Brussels Regulation 44/2001	Brussels Convention (1998)

Article 61
Without prejudice to any more favourable provisions of national laws, persons domiciled in a Member State who are being prosecuted in the criminal courts of another Member State of which they are not nationals for an offence which was not intentionally committed may be defended by persons qualified to do so, even if they do not appear in person. However, the court seised of the matter may order appearance in person; in the case of failure to appear, a judgment given in the civil action without the person concerned having had the opportunity to arrange for his defence need not be recognised or enforced in the other Member States.

Article 62
In Sweden, in summary proceedings concerning orders to pay (betalningsföreläggande) and assistance (handräckning), the expression "court" includes the "Swedish enforcement service" (kronofogdemyndighet).

Article 63
1. A person domiciled in the territory of the Grand Duchy of Luxembourg and sued in the court of another Member State pursuant to Article 5(1) may refuse to submit to the jurisdiction of that court if the final place of delivery of the goods or provision of the services is in Luxembourg.
2. Where, under paragraph 1, the final place of delivery of the goods or provision of the services is in Luxembourg, any agreement conferring jurisdiction must, in order to be valid, be accepted in writing or evidenced in writing within the meaning of Article 23(1)(a).
3. The provisions of this Article shall not apply to contracts for the provision of financial services.
4. The provisions of this Article shall apply for a period of six years from entry into force of this Regulation.

Article 64
1. In proceedings involving a dispute between the master and a member of the crew of a seagoing ship registered in Greece or in Portugal, concerning remuneration or other conditions of service, a court in a Member State shall establish whether the diplomatic or consular officer responsible for the ship has been notified of the dispute. It may act as soon as that officer has been notified.
2. The provisions of this Article shall apply for a period of six years from entry into force of this Regulation.

Brussels Regulation 44/2001	Brussels Convention (1998)
Article 65 1. The jurisdiction specified in Article 6(2), and Article 11 in actions on a warranty of guarantee or in any other third party proceedings may not be resorted to in Germany and Austria. Any person domiciled in another Member State may be sued in the courts: (a) of Germany, pursuant to Articles 68 and 72 to 74 of the Code of Civil Procedure (Zivilprozessordnung) concerning third-party notices, (b) of Austria, pursuant to Article 21 of the Code of Civil Procedure (Zivilprozessordnung) concerning third-party notices. 2. Judgments given in other Member States by virtue of Article 6(2), or Article 11 shall be recognised and enforced in Germany and Austria in accordance with Chapter III. Any effects which judgments given in these States may have on third parties by application of the provisions in paragraph 1 shall also be recognised in the other Member States.	
CHAPTER VI: TRANSITIONAL PROVISIONS	TITLE VI: TRANSITIONAL PROVISIONS
(...)	(...)
CHAPTER VII: RELATIONS WITH OTHER INSTRUMENTS	TITLE VII: RELATIONSHIP TO OTHER CONVENTIONS
Article 67 This Regulation shall not prejudice the application of provisions governing jurisdiction and the recognition and enforcement of judgments in specific matters which are contained in Community instruments or in national legislation harmonised pursuant to such instruments.	(...)
(...)	
Article 71 1. This Regulation shall not affect any conventions to which Member States are parties and which in relation to particular matters, govern jurisdiction or the recognition or enforcement of judgments.	*Article 57* 1. This Convention shall not affect any conventions to which the Contracting States are or will be parties and which in relation to particular matters, govern jurisdiction or the recognition or enforcement of judgments.
(...)	(...) 3. This Convention shall not affect the application of provisions which, in relation to particular matters, govern jurisdiction or the recognition or enforcement of judgments and which are or will be contained in acts of the institutions of the European Communities or in national laws harmonized in implementation of such acts.

THE JENARD REPORT

Council: Report on the Convention on jurisdiction and the enforcement of judgments in civil and commercial matters

(Signed at Brussels, 27 September 1968)

BY MR P. JENARD

Director in the Belgian Ministry of Foreign Affairs and External Trade

A committee of experts set up in 1960 by decision of the Committee of Permanent Representatives of the Member States, following a proposal by the Commission, prepared a draft Convention, in pursuance of Article 220 of the EEC Treaty, on jurisdiction and the enforcement of judgments in civil and commercial matters. The committee was composed of governmental experts from the six Member States, representatives of the Commission, and observers. Its rapporteur, Mr P. Jenard, Directeur d' Administration in the Belgian Ministry for Foreign Affairs and External Trade, wrote the explanatory report, which was submitted to the governments at the same time as the draft prepared by the committee of experts. The following is the text of that report. It takes the form of a commentary on the Convention which was signed in Brussels on 27 September 1968.

[2] CONTENTS

Note: Page numbers of the original report are given in square brackets. In this Appendix footnotes in the original Jenard Report are for convenience numbered consecutively throughout the report; in the original report footnote numbers started afresh on each page.

[3] CHAPTER I: PRELIMINARY REMARKS

By Article 220 of the Treaty establishing the European Economic Community, the Member States agreed to enter into negotiations with each other, so far as necessary, with a view to securing for the benefit of their nationals the simplification of formalities governing the reciprocal recognition and enforcement of judgments of courts or tribunals and of arbitration awards.

The fact that the Treaty of Rome requires the Member States to resolve this problem shows that it is important. In a note sent to the Member States on 22 October 1959 inviting them to commence negotiations, the Commission of the European Economic Community pointed out that

> "a true internal market between the six States will be achieved only if adequate legal protection can be secured. The economic life of the Community may be subject to disturbances and difficulties unless it is possible, where necessary by judicial means, to ensure the recognition and enforcement of the various rights arising from the existence of a multiplicity of legal relationships. As jurisdiction in both civil and commercial matters is derived from the sovereignty of Member States, and since the effect of judicial acts is confined to each national territory, legal protection and, hence, legal certainty in the common market are essentially dependent on the adoption by the Member States of a satisfactory solution to the problem of recognition and enforcement of judgments."

On receiving this note the Committee of Permanent Representatives decided on 18 February 1960 to set up a committee of experts. The committee, consisting of delegates from the six Member countries, observers from the Benelux Committee on the unification of law and from the Hague Conference on private international law, and representatives from the EEC Commission departments concerned, met for the first time from 11 to 13 July 1960 and appointed as its chairman Professor Billow then Ministerialdirigent and later Staatssekretar in the Federal Ministry of Justice in Bonn, and as its rapporteur Mr Jenard, directeur in the Belgian Ministry for Foreign Affairs.

At its 15th meeting, held in Brussels from 7 to 11 December 1964, the committee adopted a Preliminary Draft Convention on jurisdiction and the recognition and enforcement of judgments in civil and commercial matters, and the enforcement of authentic instruments (document 14371IV/64). This preliminary draft, with an explanatory report (document 2449/IV/65), was submitted to the Governments for comment.

The comments of the Governments, and those submitted by the Union of the Industries of the European Community, the Permanent Conference of Chambers of Commerce and Industry of the EEC, the Banking Federation of the EEC, the Consultative Committee of the Barristers' and Lawyers' Associations of the six EEC countries (a committee of the International Association of Lawyers), were studied by the Committee at its meeting of 5 to 15 July 1966. The draft Convention was finally adopted by the experts at that meeting.

The names of the governmental experts who took part in the work of the committee are set out in the annex to this report.

CHAPTER II: BACKGROUND TO THE CONVENTION

It is helpful to consider, first, the rules in each of the six countries governing the recognition and enforcement of foreign judgments.

A. THE LAW IN FORCE IN THE SIX STATES

In Belgium, until the entry into force of the Judicial Code (Code Judiciaire), the relevant provisions as **[4]** regards enforcement are to be found in Article 10 of the Law of 25 March 1876, which contains Title I of the Introductory Book of the Code of Civil Procedure.[1]

1. Article 10 of the Law of 1876 provides that: They (courts of first instance) shall also have jurisdiction in relation to judgments given by foreign courts in civil and commercial matters. Where there exists a treaty concluded on a basis of reciprocity between Belgium and the country in which the judgment was given, they shall review only the following five points:
    1. whether the judgment contains anything contrary to public policy or to the principles of Belgian public law;
    2. whether, under the law of the country in which the judgment was given, it has become *res judicata*;
    3. whether, under that law, the certified copy of the judgment satisfies the conditions necessary to establish its authenticity;
    4. whether the rights of the defendant have been observed;

Where there is no reciprocal convention, a court seised of an application for an order for enforcement ' has jurisdiction over a foreign judgment as to both form and substance, and can re-examine both the facts and the law. In other words, it has power to review the matter fully.[2, 3]

As regards recognition, text-book authorities and case-law draw a distinction between foreign judgments relating to status and legal capacity and those relating to other matters. The position at present is that foreign judgments not relating to the status and legal capacity of persons are not regarded by the courts as having the force of *res judicata*.

However, foreign judgments relating to a person status or legal capacity may be taken as evidence of the status acquired by that person.[4] Such foreign judgment thus acts as a bar to any new proceedings for divorce or separation filed before a Belgian court if the five conditions listed in Article 10 of the Law of 1876 are fulfilled, as they "constitute no more than the application to foreign judgments of rules which the legislature considers essential for any judgment to be valid".

In the *Federal Republic of Germany*, foreign judgments are recognized and enforced on the basis of reciprocity.[5] The conditions for recognition of foreign judgments are laid down in paragraph 328 of the Code of Civil Procedure (Zivilprozeßordnung):

"I. A judgment given by a foreign court may not be recognized:

1. where the courts of the State to which the foreign court belongs have no jurisdiction under German law;
2. where the unsuccessful defendant is German and has not entered an appearance, if the document instituting the proceedings was not served on him in person either in the State to which the court belongs, or by a German authority under the system of mutual assistance in judicial matters;
3. where, to the detriment of the German party, the judgment has not complied with the provisions of Article 13(1) and (3) or Articles 17, 18, and 22 of the Introductory Law to the Civil Code. (Einführungsgesetz zum Bürgerlichen Gesetzbuch), or with the provisions of Article 27 of that Law which refer to Article 13(1), nor where, in matters falling within the scope of Article 12(3) of the Law of 4 July 1939 on disappearances certifications of death, and establishment of the date of decease (RGBI. I, p. 1186), there has been a failure to comply with the provisions of Article 13 (2) of the Introductory Law to the Civil Code, to the **[5]** detriment of the wife of a foreigner who has been declared dead by judgment of the court[6];
4. where recognition of the judgment would be contrary to 'good morals' (gegen die guten Sitten) or the objectives of a German law;
5. where there is no guarantee of reciprocity.

II. The provision in (5) above shall not prevent recognition of a judgment given in a matter not relating to property rights where no court in Germany has jurisdiction under German law."

The procedure for recognizing judgments delivered in actions relating to matrimonial matters is governed by a special Law (Familienrechtsänderungsgesetz) of August 1961 (BGBI. I, p. 1221, Article 7).

---

5. whether the jurisdiction of the foreign court is based solely on the nationality of the plaintiff.

Article 570 of the Judicial Code contained in the Law of 10 October 1967 (supplement to the Moniteur belge of 31 October 1967) reads as follows:

"Courts of first instance shall adjudicate on applications for orders for the enforcement of judgments given by foreign courts in civil matters, regardless of the amount involved. Except where the provisions of a treaty between Belgium and the country in which judgment was given are to be applied, the court shall examine, in addition to the substance of the matter:

1. whether the judgment contains anything contrary to public policy or to the principles of Belgian public law;
2. whether the rights of the defendant have been observed;
3. whether the jurisdiction of the foreign court is based solely on the nationality of the plaintiff;
4. whether, under the law of the country in which the judgment was given, it has become *res judicata*;
5. whether, under that law, the certified copy of the judgment satisfies the conditions necessary to establish its authenticity." These provisions will enter into force on 31 October 1970 at the latest. Before that date an *arrêtè royal* (Royal Decree) will determine the date on which the provisions of the Judicial Code enter into force.

2. Graulich, Principes de droit international privé, No 248 *et seq.*
3. Rigaux, L' efficacite des jugements etrangers en Belgique, Journal des tribunaux, 10.4.1960, p. 287.
4. Cass. 16. 1. 1953 Pas. I. 335.
5. Riezler, Internationales Zivilprozeßrecht, 1949, p. 509 *et seq.*
6. These Articles of the Introductory Law to the Civil Code provide for the application of German law in many cases: condition of validity of marriage, form of marriage divorce, legitimate and illegitimate paternity, adoption, certification of death.

Enforcement is governed by Articles 722 and 723 of the Code of Civil Procedure, which read as follows:

Article 722

"I. A foreign judgment may be enforced only where this is authorized by virtue of an order for enforcement.

II. An application for an order for enforcement shall be heard either by the Amtsgericht or the Landgericht having general jurisdiction in relation to the defendant, or otherwise by the Amtsgericht or the Landgericht before which the defendant may be summoned under Article 23."

Article 723

"I. An order for enforcement shall be granted without re-examination of the substance of the judgment.

II. An order for enforcement shall be granted only if the foreign judgment has become *res judicata* under the law of the court in which it was given. No order for enforcement shall be granted where recognition of the judgment is excluded by Article 328."

In France, Article 546 of the Code of Civil Procedure (Code de procedure civile) provides that judgments given by foreign courts and instruments recorded by foreign officials can be enforced only after being declared enforceable by a French court (Articles 2123 and 2128 of the Civil Code).

The courts have held that four conditions must be satisfied for an order for enforcement to be granted: the foreign court must have had jurisdiction; the procedure followed must have been in order; the law applied must have been that which is applicable under the French system of conflict of laws; and due regard must have been paid to public policy.[7]

The Cour de cassation recently held (Cass. civ. 1er Section, 7 January 1964 – Munzer case) that the substance of the original action could not be reviewed by the court hearing the application for an order for enforcement. This judgment has since been followed.

In Italy, on the other hand, the Code of Civil Procedure (Codice di procedura civile) in principle allows foreign judgments to be recognized and enforced.

Under Article 796 of the Code of Civil Procedure, any foreign judgment may be declared enforceable in Italy by the Court of Appeal (Corte d'appello) for the place in which enforcement is to take place (Dichiarazione di efficacia) .

Under Article 797 of the Code of Civil Procedure, the Court of Appeal examines whether the foreign judgment was given by a judicial authority having jurisdiction under the rules in force in Italy; whether in the proceedings abroad the document instituting the proceedings was properly served and whether sufficient notice was given; whether the parties properly entered an appearance in the proceedings or whether their default was duly recognized; whether the judgment has become res judicata; whether the judgment conflicts with a judgment given by an Italian judicial authority; whether proceedings between the same parties and concerning the same claim are pending before an Italian judicial authority; and whether the judgment contains anything contrary to Italian public policy.

However, if the defendant failed to appear in the foreign proceedings, he may request the Italian court to review the substance of the case (Article 798). In such a case, the Court may either order enforcement, or hear the substance of the case and give judgment.

[6] There is also in Italian law the "delibazione incidentale" (Article 799 of the Code of Civil Procedure) which, however, applies only to proceedings in which it sought to invoke a foreign judgment.

Luxembourg. Under Article 546 of the Luxembourg Code of Civil Procedure (Code de procedure civile), judgments given by foreign courts and instruments recorded by foreign officials can be enforced in the Grand Duchy only after being declared enforceable by a Luxembourg court (see Articles 2123 and 2128 of the Civil Code).

Luxembourg law requires seven conditions to be satisfied before an order for enforcement can be granted: the judgment must be enforceable in the country in which it was given; the foreign court must have had jurisdiction; the law applied must have been that applicable under the Luxembourg rules of conflict of laws; the rules of procedure of the foreign law must have been observed; the rights of the defendant must have been observed; due regard must have been paid to public policy; the law must not have been contravened (Luxembourg, 5.2.64, Pasicrisie luxembourgeoise XIX, 285).

7. Batiffol, Traité élémentaire de droit international privé, No 741 *et seq.*

Luxembourg law no longer permits any review of a foreign judgment as to the merits.

In the *Netherlands*, the Code of Civil Procedure (Wetboek van Burgerlijke Rechtsvordering) lays down the principle that judgments of foreign courts are not enforceable in the Kingdom. Matters settled by foreign courts may be reconsidered by Netherlands courts (see Article 431 of the Code of Civil Procedure).

The national laws of the Member States thus vary considerably.

B. EXISTING CONVENTIONS

Apart from conventions dealing with particular matters (see p. 10), various conventions on enforcement exist between the Six; they are listed in Article 55 of the Convention. However, relations between France and the Federal Republic of Germany, France and the Netherlands, France and Luxembourg, Germany and Luxembourg, and Luxembourg and Italy are hampered by the absence of such conventions.[8]

There are also striking differences between the various conventions. Some, like those between France and Belgium, and between Belgium and the Netherlands and the Benelux;, Treaty, are based on "direct" jurisdiction; but all the others are based on "indirect" jurisdiction. The Convention between France and Italy is based on indirect jurisdiction, but nevertheless contains some rules of direct jurisdiction. Some conventions allow only those judgments which have becom *res judicata* to be recognized and enforced whilst others such as the Benelux Treaty and the Conventions between Belgium and the Netherlands Germany and Belgium, Italy and Belgium and Germany and the Netherlands apply to judgments which are capable of enforcement.[9] Some cover judgments given in civil matters by criminal courts, whilst others are silent on this point or expressly exclude such judgments from their scope (Conventions between Italy and the Netherlands, Article 10, and between Germany and Italy, Article 12).

There are various other differences between these treaties and conventions which need not be discussed in detail; they relate in particular to the determination of competent courts and to the conditions governing recognition and enforcement. It should moreover be stressed that these conventions either do not lay down the enforcement procedure or give only a summary outline of it.

The present unsatisfactory state of affairs as regards the recognition and enforcement of judgments could have been improved by the conclusion of new bilateral conventions between Member States not yet bound by such conventions.

[7] However, the Committee has decided in favour of the conclusion of a multilateral convention between the countries of the European Economic Community, in accordance with the views expressed in the Commission letter of 22 October 1959. The Committee felt that the differences between the bilateral conventions would hinder the "free movement" of judgments and lead to unequal treatment of the various nationals of the Member States, such inequality being contrary to the fundamental EEC principle of non-discrimination, set out, in particular, in Article 7 of the Treaty of Rome.

In addition, the European Economic Community provided the conditions necessary for a modern, liberal law on the recognition and enforcement of judgments which would satisfy both legal and commercial interests.

C. THE NATURE OF THE CONVENTION

Some of the bilateral conventions concluded between the Member States, such as the Convention between France and Belgium of 8 July 1899, the Convention between Belgium and the Netherlands of 28 March 1925 , and the Benelux Treaty of 24 November 1961 are based on rules of direct jurisdiction, whilst in the others the rules of jurisdiction are indirect. Under conventions of the first type known also as "double treaties", the rules of jurisdiction laid down are applicable in the State of origin, i.e. the State in which the proceedings originally took place; they therefore apply independently of any proceedings for recognition and enforcement, and permit a defendant who is summoned before a court which under the convention in question would not have jurisdiction to refuse to accept its jurisdiction.

Rules of jurisdiction in a convention are said to be "indirect" when they do not affect the courts of the State in which the judgment was originally given, and are to be considered only in relation to recognition and enforcement. They apply only in determining cases in which the court of the State in which

8. It should be noted that at the time of writing this report the Benelux Treaty has not yet entered into force and there is no agreement existing between Luxembourg on the one hand and Belgium and the Netherlands on the other.

9. The Franco-Belgian convention, in spite of the provisions of Article 11 (2) which impose the condition of *res judicata* nevertheless applies to enforceable judgments even if there is still a right of appeal (see Niboyet, Droit international privé français, T. VII 2022).

recognition or enforcement of a judgment is sought (the State addressed) is obliged to recognize the jurisdiction of the court of the State of origin. They can therefore be taken as conditions governing the recognition and enforcement of foreign judgments and more specifically, governing supervision of the jurisdiction foreign courts.

The Committee spent a long time considering which of these types of convention the EEC should have. It eventually decided in favour of a new system based on direct jurisdiction but differing in several respects from existing bilateral conventions of that type.

Although the Committee of experts did not underestimate the value and importance of "single" conventions, (i.e. conventions based on rules of indirect jurisdiction) it felt that within the EEC a convention based on rules of direct jurisdiction as a result of the adoption of common rules of jurisdiction would allow increased harmonization of laws, provide greater legal certainty, avoid discrimination and facilitate the "free movement" of judgments, which is after all the ultimate objective.

Conventions based on direct jurisdiction lay down common rules of jursidiction, thus bringing about the harmonization of laws, whereas under those based on indirect jurisdiction, national provisions apply, without restriction, in determining international jurisdiction in each State.

Legal certainty is most effectively secured by conventions based on direct jurisdiction since, under them, judgments are given by courts deriving their jurisdiction from the conventions themselves; however in the case of conventions based on indirect jurisdiction certain judgments cannot be recognized and enforced abroad unless national rules of jurisdiction coincide with the rules of the convention.[10]

Moreover, since it establishes, on the basis of mutual agreement, an autonomous system of international jurisdiction in relations between the Member States, the Convention makes it easier to abandon certain rules of jurisdiction which are generally regarded as exorbitant.

Finally, by setting out rules of jurisdiction which may be relied upon as soon as proceedings are begun in the State of origin, the Convention regulates the problem of *lis pendens* and also helps to minimize the conditions governing recognition and enforcement.

[8] As already stated, the Convention is based on direct jurisdiction, but differs fundamentally from treaties and conventions of the same type previously concluded. This is not the place to undertake a detailed study of the differences, or to justify them; it will suffice merely to list them:

1. the criterion of domicile replaces that of nationality;
2. the principle of equality of treatment is extended to any person domiciled in the Community, whatever his nationality;
3. rules of exclusive jurisdiction are precisely defined;
4. the right of the defendant to defend himself in the original proceedings is safeguarded;
5. the number of grounds for refusal of recognition and enforcement is reduced.

In addition, the Convention is original in that:

1. the procedure for enforcement obtaining is standardized;
2. rules of procedure are laid down for cases in which recognition is at issue;
3. provision is made for cases of conflict with other conventions.

CHAPTER III: SCOPE OF THE CONVENTION

The scope of the Convention is determined by the preamble and Article 1.

It governs international legal relationships, applies automatically, and covers all civil and commercial matters, apart from certain exceptions which are exhaustively listed.

I. INTERNATIONAL LEGAL RELATIONSHIPS

As is stressed in the fourth paragraph of the preamble, the Convention determines the international jurisdiction of the courts of the Contracting States.

It alters the rules of jurisdiction in force in each Contracting State only where an international element is involved. It does not define this concept, since the international element in a legal relationship may depend on the particular facts of the proceedings of which the court is seised. Proceedings instituted in the courts of a Contracting State which involves only persons domiciled in that State will not normally be affected by the Convention; Article 2 simply refers matters back to the rules of jurisdiction

10. Weser, Les conflits de juridictions dans le cadre du Marché Commun, *Revue Critique de droit international privé 1960*, pp. 161–172.

in force in that State. It is possible, however, that an international element may be involved in proceedings of this type. This would be the case, for example, where the defendant was a foreign national, a situation in which the principle of equality of treatment laid down in the second paragraph of Article 2 would apply, or where the proceedings related to a matter over which the courts of another State had exclusive jurisdiction (Article 16), or where identical or related proceedings had been brought in the courts of another State (Article 21 to 23).

It is clear that at the recognition and enforcement stage the Convention governs only international legal relationships since *ex hypothesi* it concerns the recognition and enforcement in one Contracting State of judgments given in another Contracting State.[11]

II. THE BINDING NATURE OF THE CONVENTION

It was decided by the committee of experts that the Convention should apply automatically. This principle is formally laid down in Articles 19 and 20 which deal with the matter of examination by the courts of the Contracting States of their international jurisdiction. The courts must apply the rules of the Convention whether or not they are pleaded by the parties. It follows from this, for example, that if a person domiciled in Belgium is sued in a French court on the basis of Article 14 of the French Civil Code, and contests the jurisdiction of that court but without pleading the provisions of the Convention, the court **[9]** must nevertheless apply Article 3 and declare that it has no jurisdiction.[12]

III. CIVIL AND COMMERCIAL MATTERS

The Committee did not specify what is meant by "civil and commercial matters", nor did it point to a solution of the problem of classification by determining the law according to which that expression should be interpreted.

In this respect it followed the practice of existing conventions.[13]

However, it follows from the text of the Convention that civil and commercial matters are to be classified as such according to their nature, and irrespective of the character of the court or tribunal which is seised of the proceedings or which has given judgment. This emerges from Article 1, which provides that the Convention shall apply in civil and commercial matters "whatever the nature of the court or tribunal". The Convention also applies irrespective of whether the proceedings are contentious or non-contentious. It likewise applies to labour law in so far as this is regarded as a civil or commercial matter (see also under contracts of employment, page 24).

The Convention covers civil proceedings brought before criminal courts, both as regards decisions relating to jurisdiction, and also as regards the recognition and enforcement of judgments given by criminal courts in such proceedings. It thereby takes into account certain laws in force in the majority of the Contracting States,[14] tends to rule out any differences of interpretation such as have arisen in applying the Convention between Belgium and the Netherlands[15] and, finally, meets current requirements arising from the increased number of road accidents.

The relevant provisions of the treaty and conventions already concluded between the Member States vary widely, as has already been pointed out in Chapter I (A).

11. A. Bülow, Vereinheitlichtes internationales Zivilprozeßrecht in der Europäischen Wirtschaftsgemeinschaft – Rabels Zeitschrift für auslandisches und internationales Privatrecht, 1965, p. 473 *et seq*.

12. Tribunal civil de Lille, 9. 11. 1953 , Revue critique de droit international privé, 1954, p. 832.

13. This problem is not dealt with in any treaty on enforcement. See also the report by Professor Fragistas on the Preliminary Draft Convention adopted by the Special Commission of the Hague Conference on private international law, preliminary document No 4 for the tenth session, p. 11.

14. In *Belgium*, see Article 4 of the Law of 17 April 1878 containing the Introductory Title of the Code of Criminal Procedure.

In the *Federal Republic of Germany*, see Article 403 *et seq*. of the Code of Criminal Procedure.

In *France*, see Article 4 of the Code of Criminal Procedure.

In *Luxembourg*, any person who claims to have suffered loss or injury as a result of a crime or other wrongful act may, under Article 63 of the Code of Criminal Procedure, be joined as a civil party.

In the *Netherlands*, see Articles 332 to 337 of the Code Criminal Procedure, and Articles 44 and 56 of the Law Judicial Procedure, which gives jurisdiction to the justices of the peace or to the courts up to F 200 and 500 respectively.

15. In interpreting the 1925 Convention between Belgium and the Netherlands, the Netherlands Court of Cassation held in its judgment of 16.3.1931 (NJ 1931, p. 689) that Articles 11 and 12 did not affect orders by criminal courts to pay compensation for injury or loss suffered by a party.

The formula adopted by the Committee reflects the current trend in favour of inserting in conventions clauses specifying that they apply to judgments given in civil or commercial matters by criminal courts. This can in particular be seen in the Benelux Treaty of 24 November 1961 and in the work of the Hague Conference on private international law.

It should be noted that the provisions of Article 5 (4) of the Convention in no way alter the penal jurisdiction of criminal courts and tribunals as laid down in the various codes of criminal procedure.

As regards both jurisdiction and recognition and enforcement the Convention affects only civil proceedings of which those courts are seised, and judgments given in such proceedings.

However, in order to counter the objection that a party against whom civil proceedings have been brought might be obstructed in conducting his defence criminal sanctions could be imposed on him in the same proceedings, the Committee decided on a solution identical to that adopted in the Benelux Treaty. Article II of the Protocol provides that such persons may be defended or represented in criminal courts. Thus they will not be obliged to appear in person to defend their civil interests.

The Convention also applies to civil or commercial matters brought before administrative tribunals.

The formula adopted by the Committee is identical to that envisaged by the Commission which was given the task at the fourth session of the Hague Conference on private international law of examining the Convention of 14 November 1896 in order to draw up common rules on a number of aspects of private international law relating to civil procedure. It reported as follows:

> "The expression 'civil or commercial matters' is very wide and does not include only those matters which fall within the jurisdiction of civil tribunals and commercial tribunals in countries where administrative tribunals also exist. Otherwise there would be a wholly unjustifiable inequality between the Contracting States: service abroad of judicial **[10]** instruments could take place on a wider scale for countries which do not have administrative tribunals than for countries which have them. In brief, the Convention is applicable from the moment when private interests become involved…"[16]

Thus, for example, decisions of the French Conseil Etat given on such matters may be recognized and enforced.[17]

IV. MATTERS EXCLUDED FROM THE SCOPE OF THE CONVENTION

The ideal solution would certainly have been to apply the Convention to all civil and commercial matters. However, the Committee did not feel able to adopt this approach, and limited the scope of the Convention to matters relating to property rights for reasons similar to those which prevailed when the Hague Convention on the recognition and enforcement of foreign judgments in civil and commercial matters was drafted, the main reason being the difficulties resulting from the absence of any overall solution to the problem of conflict of laws.

The disparity between rules of conflict of laws is particularly apparent in respect of matters not relating to property rights, since in general the intention of the parties cannot regulate matters independently of considerations of public policy.

The Committee, like the Hague Conference on private international law, preferred a formula which excluded certain matters to one which would have involved giving a positive definition of the scope of the Convention. The solution adopted implies that all litigation and all judgments relating to contractual or non-contractual obligations which do not involve the status or legal capacity of natural persons, wills or succession rights in property arising out of matrimonial relationship, bankruptcy or social security must fall within the scope of the Convention, and that in this respect the Convention should be interpreted as widely as possible.

However, matters falling outside the scope of the Convention do so only if they constitute the principal subject-matter of the proceedings. They are thus not excluded when they come before the court as a subsidiary matter either in the main proceedings or in preliminary proceedings.[18]

16. See The Hague Conference on private international law – documents of the fourth session (May to June 1904), p. 84.

17. Weser, Traité franco-belge du 8.7.1899, No. 235.

18. Bellet, "L'elaboration d'une convention sur reconnaissance des jugements dans le cadre du Marché commun", Clunet, 1965.

A. Status , legal capacity, rights in property arising out of a matrimonial relationship, wills , succession

Apart from the desirability of bringing the Convention into force as soon as possible, the Committee was influenced by the following considerations. Even assuming that the Committee managed to unify the rules of jurisdiction in this field, and whatever the nature of the rules selected, there was such disparity on these matters between the various systems of law, in particular regarding the rules of conflict of laws, that it would have been difficult not to re-examine the rules of jurisdiction at the enforcement stage. This in turn would have meant changing the nature of the Convention and making it much less effective. In addition, if the Committee had agreed to withdraw from the court enforcement all powers of examination, even in matters not relating to property rights, that court would surely have been encouraged to abuse the notion of public policy, using it to refuse recognition to foreign judgments referred to it. The members of the Committee chose the lesser of the two evils, retaining the unity and effectiveness of their draft while restricting its scope. The most serious difficulty with regard to status and legal capacity is obviously that divorce, a problem which is complicated by the extreme divergences between the various systems of law: Italian law prohibits divorce, while Belgian law not only provides for divorce by consent (Articles 223 , 275 *et seq*. of the Civil Code), which is unknown under the other legal systems apart from that of Luxembourg, but also, by the Law of 27 June 1960 on the admissibility of divorce when at least one of the spouses is a foreign national, incorporates provisions governing divorces by foreign nationals who ordinarily reside in Belgium.

The wording used, "status or legal capacity of natural persons", differs slightly from that adopted in the Hague Convention, which excludes from its scope judgments concerning "the status or capacity of persons or questions of family law, including personal or financial rights and obligations between parents and children or between spouses" (Article 1 (1)). The reason for this is twofold. Firstly, family law in the six Member States of the Community is not a concept distinct from questions of status or capacity; secondly, the EEC Convention unlike the Hague Convention, (Article 5 (2)) even where the obligation stems from the status of the persons and irrespective of whether rights **[11]** and duties between spouses or between parents and children are involved.

Moreover, in order to avoid differences of interpretation, Article 1 specificies that the Convention does not apply to the status or legal capacity of natural persons, thereby constituting a further distinction between this Convention and the Hague Convention which specifies that it does not apply to judgments dealing principally with "the existence or constitution of legal persons or the powers of their organs" (Article 1 (2) third indent).

With regard to matters relating to succession, the Committee concurred in the opinion of the International Union of Latin Notaries.

This body, when consulted by the Committee considered that it was necessary, and would become increasingly so as the EEC developed in the future, to facilitate the recognition and enforcement of judgments given in matters relating to succession, and that it was therefore desirable for the six Member States to conclude a convention on the subject. However, the Union considered that it was essential first to unify the rules of conflict of laws.

As is pointed out in the Memorandum of the Permanent Bureau of the Hague Conference on private international law,[19] from which this commentary has been taken, there are fairly marked differences between the various States on matters of succession and of rights in property arising out of a matrimonial relationship.

1. As regards succession, some systems of law make provision for a portion of the estate to devolve compulsorily upon the heirs, whereas others do not. The share allocated to the surviving spouse (a question which gives rise to the greatest number of proceedings in matters of succession because of the clash of interests involved) differs enormously from country to country. Some countries place the spouse on the same footing as a surviving child, or grant him or her a certain reserved portion (Italy), while others grant the spouse only a limited life interest (for example, Belgium).

   The disparities as regards rules of conflict of laws are equally marked. Some States (Germany, Italy and the Netherlands) apply to succession the national law of the *de cujus*; others (Belgium and France) refer succession to the law of the domicile as regards movable property and, as regards

19. The Hague Conference on private international law, recognition and enforcement of foreign judgments in matters relating to property rights. Memorandum, with Annexes, by the Permanent Bureau. Preliminary document No. 1 of January 1962 for the Special Committee, p. 10

immovable property, to the law of the place where the property is situated; or (as in Luxembourg) refer to the law of the place where the property is situated in the case of immovable property, but subject movable property to national law.

2. As regards rights in property arising out of matrimonial relationship, the divergences between the legal – systems are even greater, ranging from joint ownership of all property (Netherlands) through joint ownership of movable property and all property acquired during wedlock (France, Belgium and Luxembourg) or joint ownership of the increase in capital value of assets (Federal Republic of Germany) to the complete separation of property (Italy).

There are also very marked divergences between the rules of conflict of laws, and this provokes positive conflicts between the systems. In some States the rules governing matrimonial property, whether laid down by law or agreed between the parties, are subject to the national law of the husband (Germany, Italy and the Netherlands); in the other States (Belgium, France, and Luxembourg) matrimonial property is subject to the rules impliedly chosen by the spouses at the time of their marriage.

Unlike the preliminary draft the Convention does not expressly exclude gifts from its scope. In this respect follows the Hague Convention, though gifts will of course be excluded in so far as they relate to succession.

However, the Committee was of the opinion that there might possibly be grounds for resuming discussion of these problems after the Judgments Convention had entered into force, depending on the results of the work currently being done by the Hague Conference and by the International Commission on Civil Status.

It should be stressed that these matters will still be governed, temporarily at least, by existing bilateral conventions, in so far as these conventions apply (see Article 56).

B. Bankruptcy

Bankruptcy is also excluded from the scope of this Convention.

A separate Convention is currently being drafted, since the peculiarities of this branch of law require special rules.

Article 1 (2) excludes bankruptcy, proceedings relating to the winding-up of insolvent companies or other legal persons judicial arrangements compositions and analogous proceedings, i.e. those proceedings which, **[12]** depending on the system of law involved, are based on the suspension of payments, the insolvency of the debtor or his inability to raise credit, and which involve the judicial authorities for the purpose either compulsory and collective liquidation of the assets or simply of supervision.

Thus the Convention will cover proceedings arising from schemes of arrangement out of court, since the latter depend on the intention of the parties and are of purely contractual nature. The insolvency of non-trader (*déconfiture civile*) under French law, which does not involve organized and collective proceedings cannot be regarded as falling within the category "analogous proceedings" within the meaning of Article 1 (2).

Proceedings relating to a bankruptcy are not necessarily excluded from the Convention. Only proceedings arising directly from the bankruptcy[20] and hence falling within the scope of the Bankruptcy Convention of the European Economic Community are excluded from the scope of the Convention.[21]

Pending the conclusion of the separate Convention covering bankruptcy, proceedings arising directly from bankruptcy will be governed by the legal rules currently in force, or by the conventions which already exist between certain Contracting States, as provided in Article 56.[22]

C. Social Security

The Committee decided, like the Hague Conference,[23] to exclude social security from the scope of the Convention. The reasons were as follows.

20. Benelux Treaty, Article 22 (4), and the report annexed thereto. The Convention between France and Belgium is interpreted in the same way. See Weser, Convention franco-belge 1899, in the *Jurisclasseur de droit international*, Vol. 591 , Nos 146 to 148.

21. A complete list of the proceedings involved will be given in the Bankruptcy Convention of the European Economic Community.

22. These are the Conventions between Belgium and France, between France and Italy, and between Belgium and the Netherlands, unless the latter convention has been abrogated by the Benelux Treaty on its entry into force.

23. The Hague Conference on private international law, extraordinary session. Final Act, see Article 1 of the Convention.

In some countries, such as the Federal Republic of Germany, social security is a matter of public law, and in others it falls in the borderline area between private law and public law.

In some States, litigation on social security matters falls within the jurisdiction of the ordinary courts, but in others it falls within the jurisdiction of administrative tribunals; sometimes it lies within the jurisdiction both.[24]

The Committee was moreover anxious to allow current work within the EEC pursuant to Articles 51, 117 and 118 of the Treaty of Rome to develop independently, and to prevent any overlapping on matters of social security between the Convention and agreements already concluded, whether bilaterally or under the auspices of other international organizations such as the International Labour Organization or the Council Europe.

Social security has not in fact hitherto given rise conflicts of jurisdiction, since judicial jurisdiction has been taken as coinciding with legislative jurisdiction which is determined by Community regulations adopted pursuant to Article 51 of the Treaty of Rome; however the recovery of contributions due to social security bodies still raises problems of enforcement. This matter should therefore be the subject of a special agreement between the Six.

What is meant by social security?

Since this is a field which is in a state of constant development, it did not seem desirable to define it expressly in the Convention, nor even to indicate in an annex what this concept covers, especially as Article 117 of the Treaty of Rome states that one of the Community s objectives is the harmonization of social security systems.

Nevertheless, it should be pointed out that in the six countries benefits are paid in the circumstances listed in Convention No 102 of the International Labour Organization on minimum standards of social security, namely: medical care, sickness benefits, maternity allowances, invalidity benefits, old age and survivors pensions benefits for accidents at work and occupational diseases family allowances and unemployment benefits.[25] It may also be useful to refer **[13]** to the definition given in Articles 1 (c) and 2 of Council Regulation No 3 on social security for migrant workers which, moreover, corresponds to that laid down in Convention No 102 of the ILO.

However, the litigation on social security which is excluded from the scope of the Convention is confined to disputes arising from relationships between the administrative authorities concerned and employers or employees. On the other hand, the Convention applicable when the authority concerned relies on a right of direct recourse against a third party responsible for injury or damage, or is subrogated as against a third party to the rights of an injured party insured by it since, in doing so, it is acting in accordance with the ordinary legal rules.[26]

D. Arbitration

There are already many international agreements on arbitration. Arbitration is, of course, referred to in Article 220 of the Treaty of Rome. Moreover, the Council of Europe has prepared a European Convention providing a uniform law on arbitration, and this will probably be accompanied by a Protocol which will facilitate the recognition and enforcement of arbitral awards to an even greater extent than the New York Convention. This is why it seemed preferable to exclude arbitration. The Brussels Convention does not apply to the recognition and enforcement of arbitral awards (see the definition in Article 25); it does not apply for the purpose of determining the jurisdiction of courts and tribunals in respect of litigation relating to arbitration for example, proceedings to set aside an arbitral award; and, finally, it does not apply to the recognition of judgments given in such proceedings.

CHAPTER IV: JURISDICTION

A. GENERAL CONSIDERATIONS

1. Preliminary remarks

Underlying the Convention is the idea that the Member States of the European Economic Community wanted to set up a common market with characteristics similar to those of a vast internal market.

24. Étude de la physionomie actuelle de la sécurité sociale dans les pays de la CEE. Série politique sociale 3 – 1962, Services des publications des Communautés européennes. 8058/1/IX/1962/5.

25. Tableaux comparatifs des régimes de sécurité sociale applicables dans les États membres des Communautés européennes. Third edition, Services des publications des Communautés européennes 8122/1/VII.1964/5.

26. See Michel Voirin, note under Cass. 16. 2. 1965, Recueil Dalloz 1965, p. 723.

Everything possible must therefore be done not only to eliminate any obstacles to the functioning of this market, but also to promote its development. From this point of view, the territory of the Contracting States may be regarded as forming a single entity: it follows, for the purpose of laying down rules on jurisdiction, that a very clear distinction can be drawn between litigants who are domiciled within the Community and those who are not.

Starting from this basic concept, Title II of the Convention makes a fundamental distinction particular in Section 1, between defendants who are domiciled in a Contracting State and those who are domiciled elsewhere.

1. If a person is domiciled in a Contracting State, he must in general be sued in the courts of that State in accordance with the rules of jurisdiction in force in that State (Article 2).
2. If a person is domiciled in a Contracting State, he may be sued in the courts of another Contracting State only if the courts of that State are competent by virtue of the Convention (Article 3).
3. If a person is not domiciled in a Contracting State that is, if he is domiciled outside the Community, the rules of jurisdiction in force in each Contracting State, including those regarded as exorbitant, are applicable (Article 4).

The instances in which a person domiciled in a Contracting State may be sued in the courts of another Contracting State or must be so sued, in cases of exclusive jurisdiction or prorogation of jurisdiction are set out in Sections 2 to 6. Section 7, entitled "Examination as to jurisdiction ... and admissibility", is mainly concerned with safeguarding the rights of the defendant.

Section 8 concerns *lis pendens* and related actions. The very precise rules of this Section are intended to prevent as far as possible conflicting judgments being given in relation to the same dispute in different States.

[14] Section 9 relates to provisional and protective measures and provides that application for these may be made to any competent court of a Contracting State, even if under the Convention, that court does not have jurisdiction over the substance of the matter.

2. Rationale of the basic principles of Title II

The far-reaching nature of the Convention may at first seem surprising. The rules of jurisdiction which it lays down differ fundamentally from those of bilateral conventions which are based on direct jurisdiction (the Conventions between France and Belgium, and between Belgium and the Netherlands, the Benelux Treaty, the Convention between France and Switzerland) and apply not only to nationals of the Contracting States but also to any person, whatever his nationality, who domiciled in one of those States.

The radical nature of the Convention may not only evoke surprise but also give rise to the objection that the Committee has gone beyond its terms of reference, since Article 220 of the Treaty of Rome provides that States should enter into negotiations with a view to securing "for the benefit of their nationals" the simplification of formalities governing the recognition and enforcement of judgments. The obvious answer to this is that the extension of the scope of the Convention certainly does not represent a departure from the Treaty of Rome provided the Convention ensures, for the benefit of nationals, the simplification of formalities governing the recognition and enforcement of judgments. Too strict an interpretation of the Treaty of Rome would moreover, have led to the Convention providing for the recognition and enforcement only of those judgments given in favour of nationals of the Contracting States. Such a limitation would have considerably reduced the scope of the Convention, which would in this regard have been less effective than existing bilateral conventions.

There are several reasons for widening the scope of the Convention by extending in particular the rules of jurisdiction under Title II to all persons, whatever their nationality, who are domiciled in a Contracting State.

First, it would be a retrograde step if common rules of jurisdiction were to be dependent on the nationality of the parties; the connecting factor in international procedure is usually the domicile or residence of the parties (see, for example, Article 3 (1) and (2) of the Hague Convention of 15 April 1958 concerning the recognition and enforcement of decisions relating to maintenance obligations towards children; the Hague Convention of 15 April 1958 on the jurisdiction of the contractual forum in matters relating to the international sale of goods; Article 11 of the Benelux Treaty; and Article 10 (1) of the Hague Convention on the recognition and enforcement of foreign judgments in civil and commercial matters).

Next, the adoption of common rules based on nationality would have caused numerous difficulties in applying the Convention. This method would have necessitated the introduction of different rules of jurisdiction depending on whether the litigation involved nationals of Contracting States, a national of a Contracting State and a foreign national, or two foreign nationals.

In some situations the rules of jurisdiction of the Convention would have had to be applied; in others national rules of jurisdiction. Under this system the court would, at the commencement of proceedings, automatically have had to carry out an examination of the nationality of the parties, and it is not difficult to imagine the practical problems involved in, for example, establishing the nationality of a defendant who has failed to enter an appearance.

If the Convention had adopted the nationality of the parties as a connecting factor, it might well have been necessary to introduce a special provision to deal with the relatively frequent cases of dual nationality.

The Convention would thus have had to solve many problems which do not strictly speaking fall within its scope. Using nationality as a criterion would inevitably have led to a considerable increase in the effect of those rules of jurisdiction which may be termed exorbitant. Thus, for example, a judgment given in France or Luxembourg on the basis of Article 14 of the Civil Code in an action between a national of France or Luxembourg and a national of a non-Member State of the Community would have had to be recognized and enforced in Germany even if the foreign national was domiciled in Germany and a generally recognized jurisdiction, that of the defendant's domicile, thus existed.

By ruling out the criterion of nationality, the Committee is anxious not only to simplify the application of the Convention by giving it a unity which allows a uniform interpretation, but also, in fairness, to allow foreign nationals domiciled in the Community, who are established there and who thereby contribute to its **[15]** economic activity and prosperity, to benefit from the provisions of the Convention.

Moreover, the purpose of the Convention is also, by establishing common rules of jurisdiction, to achieve, in relations between the Six and in the field which it was required to cover, a genuine legal systematization which will ensure the greatest possible degree of legal certainty. To this end, the rules of jurisdiction codified in Title II determine which State's courts are most appropriate to assume jurisdiction, taking into account all relevant matters; the approach here adopted means that the nationality of the parties is no longer of importance.

3. Determination of domicile

As already shown, the rules of jurisdiction are based on the defendant's domicile. Determining that domicile is therefore a matter of the greatest importance.

The Committee was faced with numerous questions which proved difficult to resolve. Should the Convention include a common definition of domicile? Should domicile possibly be replaced by the concept of habitual residence? Should both domicile and habitual residence be used? Should the term "domicile" be qualified?

1. Should the Convention include a common definition of domicile?

   The first point to note is that the concept of domicile is not defined in the Conventions between France and Belgium, Belgium and the Netherlands Germany and Belgium, and Italy and Belgium, nor in the Benelux Treaty.

   It is, however, defined in the Conventions between France and Italy (Article 28), between Italy and the Netherlands (Article 11), and between Germany and Italy (Article 13); but these Conventions are all based on indirect jurisdiction.

   At first, the Committee thought of defining domicile in the Convention itself, but it finally rejected this course of action. Such a definition would have fallen outside the scope of the Convention, and properly belongs in a uniform law.[27] To define the concept of domicile in international conventions might even be dangerous, as this could lead to a multiplicity of definitions and so to inconsistency.

   Moreover, such definitions run the risk of being superseded by developments in national law.

2. Should domicile be replaced by habitual residence?

   This course was similarly rejected. It was pointed out that the term "habitual" was open to conflicting interpretations, since the laws of some of the Member States provide that an entry in the population registers is conclusive proof of habitual residence.

27. The concept of domicile has been specified by the European Committee for Legal Cooperation, set up by the Council of Europe, as one of the basic legal concepts which should be defined.

The adoption of this course would, moreover represent a divergence from that followed under the laws of the Contracting States, the majority of which use domicile as a basis of jurisdiction.[28]

Adopting habitual residence as the sole criterion would have raised new problems as regards jurisdiction over persons whose domicile depends or may depend on that of another person or on the location of an authority (e.g. minors or married women).

Finally, in a treaty based on direct jurisdiction, it is particularly important that jurisdiction should have secure legal basis for the court seised of the matter. The concept of domicile, while not without drawbacks, does however introduce the idea of a more fixed and stable place of establishment on the part of the defendant than does the concept of habitual residence.

3. Should both domicile and habitual residence be adopted?

   In a treaty based on direct jurisdiction , the inclusion of both criteria would result in the major disadvantage that the number of competent courts would be increased. If the domicile and the place of habitual residence happened to be in different States, national rules of jurisdiction of both the States concerned would be applicable by virtue of Article 2 of the Convention, thus defeating the object of the Convention. Moreover, the inclusion of both criteria could increase the number of cases of *lis pendens* and related actions. For these reasons the Committee preferred finally to adopt only the concept of domicile.

4. Should the concept of domicile be qualified?

   In view of the varied interpretations of the concept of domicile, the Committee considered that the implementation of the Convention would be facilitated by the inclusion of a provision specifying the law to be applied in determining domicile. The absence of such a provision might give rise to claims and disclaimers of jurisdiction; the purpose of Article 52 is to avoid this.
   Article 52 deals with three different situations:

   (i) where the court of a Contracting State must determine whether a person is domiciled in that State;
   (ii) where the court must determine whether a person is domiciled in another Contracting State; and finally,
   (iii) where the court must determine whether a person's domicile depends on that of another person or on the seat of an authority.

28. *Belgium*
Law of 25 March 1876 containing Title I of the Introductory Book of the Code of Civil Procedure.
Article 39: Except in the case of amendments and exceptions provided for under the law, the court of the defendant's domicile shall be the only court having jurisdiction.

Judicial Code:
Article 624: Except in cases where the law expressly determines the court having jurisdiction a plaintiff may, institute proceedings:

1. in the court of the domicile of the defendant or of one of the defendants.

Federal Republic of Germany
Code of Civil Procedure, Article 13: A person shall in general be subject to the jurisdiction of the courts of his domicile.

France
Code of Civil Procedure, Article 59 (1): In actions personam the defendant shall be sued in the court of his domicile or, where he has no domicile or, in the court of his place of residence.

Italy
Code of Civil Procedure, Article 18: Except where the law otherwise provides, the competent court shall be the court for the place where the defendant has his habitual residence or his domicile or, where these are not known the court for the place where the defendant is resident.

Luxembourg
Article 59 of the Code of Civil Procedure corresponds to Article 59 of the French Code of Civil Procedure.

Netherlands
Code of Civil Procedure, Article 126:
1. In actions in personam or actions relating to movable property, the defendant shall be sued in the court of his domicile.

[16] Article 52 does not deal with the case of a person domiciled outside the Community. In this case the court seised of the matter must apply its rules of private international law.

Nor does Article 52 attempt to resolve the conflicts which might arise if a court seised of a matter ruled that a defendant were to be considered as having his domicile in two other Contracting States, or in one Contracting State and a third country. According to the basic principles of Title II the court, having found that a person is domiciled in some other Contracting State, must, in order to determine its own jurisdiction, apply the rules set out in Article 3 and in Sections 2 to 6 of the Convention.

In most disputed cases it will be necessary to determine where the defendant is domiciled.

However, when applying certain provisions of the Convention, in particular Article 5 (2) and the first paragraph of Article 8 , the rules set out will be used to determine the plaintiff 's domicile. For this reason Article 52 does not specify either the defendant or the plaintiff since, in the opinion of the Committee, the same provisions for determining domicile must apply to both parties.

Under the first paragraph of Article 52, only the internal law of the court seised of the matter can determine whether a domicile exists in that State. It follows that, if there is a conflict between the *lex fori* and the law of another Contracting State when determining the domicile of a party, the *lex fori* prevails. For example, if a defendant sued in a French court is domiciled both in France, because he has his principal place of business there, and in Belgium, because his name is entered there in the official population registers, where the laws conflict the French court must apply only French law. If it is established under that law that the defendant is in fact domiciled in France, the court need take other law into consideration. This is justified on various grounds. First, to take the example given, a defendant, by establishing his domicile in a given country, subjects himself to the law of that country. Next, only if the *lex fori* prevails can the court examine whether it has jurisdiction; as the Convention requires it to do, in cases where the defendant fails to enter an appearance (Article 20).

Where the courts of different Contracting States are properly seised of a matter – for example, the Belgian court because it is the court for the place where the defendant's name is entered in the population registers, and the French court because it **[17]** is the court for the place where he has his principal place of business – the conflict may be resolved by applying the rules governing *lis pendens* or related actions.

The second paragraph covers the case of a defendant who is not domiciled in the State whose courts are seised of the matter. The court must then determine whether he is domiciled in another Contracting State, and to do this the internal law of that other State must be applied

This rule will be applied in particular where a defendant is sued in the courts of a Contracting State in which he is not domiciled. If the jurisdiction of the court is contested, then, following the basic principles of Title II, whether or not the court has jurisdiction will vary according to whether the defendant is domiciled in another Contracting State or outside the Community. Thus, for example, a person domiciled outside the Community may properly be sued in Belgium in the court for the place where the contract was concluded[29] while a person domiciled in another Contracting State and sued in the same court may refuse to accept its jurisdiction, since Article 5(1) of the Convention provides that only the courts for the place of performance of the obligation in question have jurisdiction. Thus if a defendant wishes to contest the jurisdiction of the Belgian court, he must establish that he is domiciled in a Contracting State.

Under the second paragraph of Article 52 the Belgian court must, in order to determine whether the defendant is domiciled in another Contracting State, apply the internal law of that State.

The Committee considered it both more equitable and more logical to apply the law of the State of the purported domicile rather than the *lex fori*.

If a court, seised of a matter in which the defendant was domiciled in another Contracting State, applied its own law to determine the defendant s domicile the defendant might under that law not be regarded as being domiciled in the other Contracting State even though under the law of that other State he was in fact domiciled there. This solution becomes all the more untenable when one

29. See Article 634 of the Judicial Code and Article 4 of the Convention.

realises that a person establishing his domicile in a Contracting State can obviously not be expected to consider whether this domicile is regarded as such under a foreign law.[30]

On the other hand, where the law of the State of the purported domicile has two definitions of domicile,[31] that of the Civil Code and that of the Code of Civil Procedure, the latter should obviously be used since the problem is one of jurisdiction.

The third principle laid down by Article 52 concerns persons such as minors or married women whose domicile depends on that of another person or on the seat of an authority.

Under this provision national law is applied twice. For example, the national law of a minor first determines whether his domicile is dependent on that of another person. If it is, the national law of the minor similarly determines where that domicile is situated (e.g. where his guardian is domiciled). If, however, the domicile of the dependent person is under his national law not dependent on that another person or on the seat of an authority, the first or second paragraph of Article 52 may be applied to determine the domicile of the dependent person. These two paragraphs also apply for the purpose of determining the domicile from which that of the dependent person derives.

The members of the Committee were alive to the difficulties which may arise in the event of dual nationality, and more especially in determining the domicile of a married woman. For example, where a German woman marries a Frenchman an acquires French nationality while retaining her German **[18]** nationality, her domicile under French law[32] is that of her husband, whereas under German law she can have a separate domicile, since German law no longer provides that a married woman has the domicile of her husband.[33] In cases of this kind the Committee considered that the usual rules relating to dual nationality should be applied. Thus even if she has a separate domicile in Germany, that person may be sued in France in the court for the husband's domicile, since the French court must apply French law. If, however, she is sued Germany in the court for the place of her own domicile, the German court will apply German law and declare that it has jurisdiction.

Finally, it should be made clear that the concept of domicile within the meaning of the Convention does not extend to the legal fiction of an address fur service of process.

B. COMMENTARY ON THE SECTIONS OF TITLE II

Section 1

General provisions

Section 1 sets out the main principles on which the rules of jurisdicition laid down by the Convention are founded:

1. the rule that a defendant domiciled in a Contracting State is in general to be sued in the courts of that State (Article 2);
2. the rule that a person domiciled in a Contracting State may in certain circumstances be sued in the courts of another Contracting State (Article 3);
3. the rule that a person domiciled outside the Community is subject to all applicable national rules of jurisdiction (Article 4).

This Section also embodies the widely applied principle of equality of treatment,[34] which is already enshrined in Article 1 of the Convention between France and Belgium of 8 July 1899, Article 1 of the

30. Niboyet, Traité de droit international prive fransçais Vol. VI, No. 1723: "It is submitted that domicile is not systematically determined according to the *lex fori* but according to the law of the country where the domicile is alleged to be. French law alone can therefore determine whether a person is domiciled in France; but whether a person is domiciled in any particular foreign country is a matter, not for French law, but for the law of the country concerned."

31. Such might for example be the case in Belgium, where Article 102 of the Civil Code provides that the domicile of a Belgian in so far as the exercise of his civil rights is concerned is where he has his principal establishment while Article 36 of the Judicial Code provides that, for the purpose of that Code, a person is deemed to be domiciled in the place where his name is entered in the official population registers.

32. French Civil Code, Article 108: "A married woman has no domicile other than that of her husband."

33. BGB, Article 10, repealed by the Gleichberechtigungsgesetz. (Law on equal rights of men and women in the field of civil law) of 18 June 1957.

34. Weser, Revue critique de droit international privé, 1960, pp. 29–35.

Convention between Belgium and the Netherlands of 28 March 1925 and Article 1 of the Benelux Treaty of 24 November 1961. Whilst this principle thus forms an integral part of treaties based on direct jurisdiction, in this Convention it also ensures implementation of the mandatory rules of the Treaty of Rome. Article 7 of that Treaty lays down the principle of non-discrimination between nationals of Member States of the Community.

Specific provisions applying the general principle set out in Article 7 of the Treaty of Rome to the right of establishment are laid down in Article 52 *et seq.* of that Treaty.

During the preparation of the General Programme on establishment, the Economic and Social Committee of the European Communities drew particular attention to this aspect of the problem by requesting that equality of treatment as regards legal protection be achieved in full as quickly as possible.

Article 2

The maxim "*actor sequitur forum rei*" which expresses the fact that law leans in favour of the defendant, is even more relevant in the international sphere than it is in national law.[35] It is more difficult, generally speaking, to defend oneself in the courts of a foreign country than in those of another town in the country where one is domiciled.

A defendant domiciled in a Contracting State need not necessarily be sued in the court for the place where he is domiciled or has his seat. He may be sued in any court of the State where he is domiciled which has jurisdiction under the law of that State.

As a result, if a defendant is sued in one of the courts of the State in which he is domiciled, the internal rules of jurisdiction of that State are fully applicable. Here the Convention requires the application of the national law of the court seised of the matter; the Convention determines whether the courts of the State in question have jurisdiction, and the law of that State in turn determines whether a particular court in that State has jurisdiction. This solution seems equitable since it is usual for a defendant domiciled in a State to be subject to the internal law of that State without it being **[19]** necessary for the Convention to provide special rules for his protection. It is, moreover, an extremely practical solution because it means that in most cases the court will not have to take the Convention any further into consideration.

Defendants are usually sued in the courts of the State in which they are domiciled. This is true of proceedings in which there is no international element. It is also true of proceedings with an international element in which, by application of the traditionally accepted maxim "*actor sequitur forum rei*" the defendant is sued in the courts of the State of his domicile. The Convention does not therefore involve a general reversal of national rules of jurisdiction nor of the practice of judges and lawyers. In fact, judges and lawyers will need to take account of the changes effected by the Convention only in cases where a defendant is sued in a court of a State where he is not domiciled, or in one of the few cases in which the Convention has laid down common rules of exclusive jurisdiction.

The second paragraph of Article 2 embodies the principle of equality of treatment where a foreigner is domiciled in the State of the forum. Such foreigner whether he is defendant or plaintiff, is governed in that State by the same rules of jurisdiction as its nationals, or more precisely, as its nationals who are domiciled in that State, where, as in Italy, the law of that State determines the jurisdiction of its courts according to whether the national concerned is domiciled in its territory.

As a result, Article 52 of the Belgian Law of 25 March 1876 will no longer be applicable as such to foreigners domiciled in Belgium.[36]

The positive aspect of equality of treatment is set out in the second paragraph of Article 4.

Article 3

Article 3 deals with those cases in which a defendant domiciled in a Contracting State may be sued in another Contracting State. This Article lays down the principle that a defendant may be sued otherwise than in the courts of the State where he is domiciled only in the cases expressly provided for in the Convention. The rule sets aside the rules of exorbitant jurisdiction in force in each of the Contracting States. However, these rules of jurisdiction are not totally excluded; they are excluded only in respect of persons who are domiciled in another Contracting State. Thus they remain in force with respect to persons who are not domiciled within the Community.

35. See report by Professor Fragistas – Hague Conference on private international law – preliminary doc No. 4, May 1964, for the tenth session.

36. This Article provides, in particular, that foreigners who are domiciled or resident in Belgium may be sued before a court of the Kingdom either by a Belgian or by a foreigner.

The second paragraph of Article 3 prohibits the application of the most important and best known of the rules of exorbitant jurisdiction. While this paragraph is not absolutely essential it will nevertheless facilitate the application of certain provisions of the Convention (see, in particular, Article 59).

The following are the rules of exorbitant jurisdiction in question in each of the States concerned.

In Belgium

Articles 52, *52bis* and 53 of the Law of 25 March 1876 which govern territorial jurisdiction in actions brought by Belgians[37] or by foreigners against foreigners before Belgian courts, and Article 15 of the Civil Code which corresponds to Article 15 of the French Civil Code.

In Germany

The nationality of the parties does not in general affect the rules of jurisdiction. Article 23 of the Code of Civil Procedure lays down that, where no other German court has jurisdiction, actions relating to property instituted against a person who is not domiciled in the national territory come under the jurisdiction of the court for the place where the property or subject of the dispute is situated.

German courts have in a number of cases given a very liberal interpretation to this provision, thereby leading some authors to state that Article 23 "can be likened to Article 14 of the French Civil Code".[38]

In France

1. Article 14 of the Civil Code provides that any French plaintiff may sue a foreigner or another Frenchman in the French courts, even if there is no **[20]** connection between the cause of action and those courts.
2. Article 15 of the Civil Code provides that a Frenchman may always be sued in the French courts by a Frenchman or by a foreigner, and can even insist on this.

Despite the fact that Articles 14 and 15 in terms refer only to contractual obligations, case law has extended their scope beyond contractual obligations to all actions whether or not relating to property rights. There are thus only two limitations to the general application of Articles 14 and 15: French courts are never competent to hear either actions in rem concerning immovable property situated abroad or actions concerning proceedings for enforcement which is to take place abroad.[39]

In Italy

1. Article 2 of the Code of Civil Procedure provides that an agreement to substitute for the jurisdiction of Italian courts the jurisdiction of a foreign court or arbitral tribunal will be valid only in the case of litigation between foreigners, or between a foreigner and an Italian citizen who is neither resident nor domiciled in Italy, and only if the agreement evidenced in writing.
2. (a) Under Article 4 (1) of the Code of Civil Procedure, a foreigner may be sued in an Italian court if he is resident or domiciled in Italy, or if he has an address for service there or has a representative who is authorized to bring legal proceedings in his name, or if he has accepted Italian jurisdiction unless the proceedings concern immovable property situated abroad.
2. (b) Under Article 4 (2) of the Code of Civil Procedure, a foreigner may be sued in the courts of the Italian Republic if the proceedings concern property situated in Italy, or succession to the estate of an Italian national, or an application for probate made in Italy, or obligations which arose in Italy or which must be performed there.
3. The interpretation given to Article 4 by Italian case law means that an Italian defendant may always be sued in the Italian courts.[40]

In Luxembourg

Articles 14 and 15 of the Civil Code correspond to Articles 14 and 15 of the French Civil Code.

Luxembourg case law applies the same principles of interpretation as French case law.

37. Répertoire pratique du droit beige, under "competence" – No. 17518 *et seq.* – (see Judicial Code, Articles 635, 637 and 638).

38. Weser, Revue critique de droit international privé, 1959, p. 636; Rosenberg, Lehrbuch des deutschen Zivilprozeßrechts, ninth edition, paragraph 35 I 3.

39. Batiffol, *op. cit.*, No. 684 *et seq.*

40. Morelli, Diritto processuale civile internazionale, pp. 108–112.

In the Netherlands

Article 126 (3) of the Code of Civil Procedure provides that, in personal matters or matters concerning movable property, a defendant who has no known domicile or residence in the Kingdom shall be sued in the court for the domicile of the plaintiff. This provision applies whether or not the plaintiff is a Netherlands national.[41]

Article 127 provides that a foreigner, even if he does not reside in the Netherlands, may be sued in a Netherlands court for the performance of obligations contracted towards a Netherlander either in the Netherlands or abroad.

Article 4

Article 4 applies to all proceedings in which the defendant is not domiciled in a Contracting State, and provides that the rules of internal law remain in force.

This is justified on two grounds:

First, in order to ensure the free movement of judgments, this Article prevents refusal of recognition or enforcement of a judgment given on the basis of rules of internal law relating to jurisdiction. In the absence of such a provision, a judgment debtor would be able to prevent execution being levied on his property simply by transferring it to a Community country other than that in which judgment was given.

Secondly, this Article may perform a function in the case of lis pendens. Thus, for example, if a French court is seised of an action between a Frenchman and a defendant domiciled in America, and a German court is **[21]** seised of the same matter on the basis of Article 23 of the Code of Civil Procedure, one of the two courts must in the interests of the proper administration of justice decline jurisdiction in favour of the other. This issue cannot be settled unless the jurisdiction of these courts derives from the Convention.

In the absence of an article such as Article 4, there would be no rule in the Convention expressly recognizing the jurisdiction of the French and German courts in a case of this kind.

The only exception to the application of the rules of jurisdiction of internal law is the field of exclusive jurisdiction (Article 16).[42] The rules which grant exclusive jurisdiction to the courts of a State are applicable whatever the domicile of the defendant.

However, the question arises why the Committee did not extend the scope of the provision limiting the application of rules of exorbitant jurisdiction to include in particular nationals of Member States regardless of their place of domicile.

In other words, and to take another example based on Article 14 of the French Civil Code, why will it still be possible for a French plaintiff to sue in the French courts a foreigner, or even a national of a Member State of the Community, who is domiciled outside the Community?

The Committee thought that it would have been unreasonable to prevent the rules of exorbitant jurisdiction from applying to persons including Community nationals domiciled outside the Community. Thus, for example, a Belgian national domiciled outside the Community might own assets in the Netherlands. The Netherlands courts have jurisdiction in the matter since the Convention does not recognize jurisdiction based on the presence of assets within a State. If Article 14 of the French Civil Code could not be applied, a French plaintiff would have to sue the Belgian defendant in a court outside the Community, and the judgment could not be enforced in the Netherlands if there were no enforcement treaty between the Netherlands and the non-member State in which judgment was given.

This, moreover, was the solution adopted in the Conventions between France and Belgium, and between Belgium and the Netherlands, and in the Benelux Treaty, which, however, take nationality as their criterion.[43]

The second paragraph of Article 4 of the Convention constitutes a positive statement of the principle of equality of treatment already laid down in the second paragraph of Article 2. An express provision was considered necessary in order to avoid any uncertainty.[44] Under this provision, any person domi-

41. Weser, Revue critique de droit international privé, 1959, p. 632.

42. The third paragraph of Article 8, which concerns jurisdiction in respect of insurers who are not domiciled in the Community but have a branch or agency there, may also be regarded as an exception.

43. The Convention between France and Belgium is interpreted to mean that a Frenchman may not rely on Article 14 of the Civil Code to sue in France a Belgian domiciled in Belgium, but may do so to sue a Belgian domiciled abroad. Batiffol, Traité élémentaire de droit international privé No. 714.

44. According to French case law on the Treaty of 9 February 1842 between France and Denmark, a Danish national may not rely on Article 14 of the French Civil Code.

ciled in a Contracting State has the right, as plaintiff, to avail himself in that State of the same rules of jurisdiction as a national of that State.

This principle had already been expressly laid down in the Convention between France and Belgium of 8 July 1899 (Article 1 (2)).

This positive aspect of the principle of equality of treatment was regarded as complementing the right of establishment (Article 52 *et seq.* of the Treaty of Rome), the existence of which implies, as was stated in the General Programme for the abolition of restrictions on freedom of establishment of 18 December 1961,[45] that any natural or legal person established in a Member State should enjoy the same legal protection as a national of that State.

The provision is also justified on economic grounds. Since rules of exorbitant jurisdiction can still be invoked against foreigners domiciled outside the European Economic Community, persons who are domiciled in the Member State concerned and who thus contribute to the economic life of the Community should be able to invoke such rules in the same way as the nationals of that State.

It may be thought surprisIng that the Convention extends the "privileges of jurisdiction" in this way, since equality of treatment is granted in each of the States to all persons, whatever their nationality, who are domiciled in that State.

[22] It should first be noted that such treatment is already granted to foreigners in Belgium, the Federal Republic of Germany, Italy and the Netherlands, where the rules of exorbitant jurisdiction may be invoked by foreigners as well as by nationals. The second paragraph of Article 4 therefore merely brings into line with these laws the French and Luxembourg concepts, according to which Article 14 of the Civil Code constitutes a privilege of nationality.

Secondly, the solution adopted in the Convention follows quite naturally from the fact that, for the reasons already given, the Convention uses domicile as the criterion for determining jurisdiction. In this context it must not be forgotten that it will no longer possible to invoke the privileges of jurisdiction against persons domiciled in the Community, although it will be possible to invoke them against nationals of the Community countries who have established their domicile outside the territory of the Six.

Section 2

Special jurisdiction

Articles 5 and 6

Articles 5 and 6 list the situations in which a defendant may be sued in a Contracting State other than that of his domicile. The forums provided for in these Articles supplement those which apply under Article 2. In the case of proceedings for which a court is specifically recognized as having jurisdiction under these Articles the plaintiff may, at his option, bring the proceedings either in that court or in the competent courts of the State in which the defendant is domiciled.

One problem which arose here was whether it should always be possible to sue the defendant in one of the courts provided for in these Articles, or whether this should be allowed only if the jurisdiction of that court was also recognized by the internal law of the State concerned.

In other words, in the first case, jurisdiction would derive directly from the Convention and in the second there would need to be dual jurisdiction: that of the Convention and that of the internal law on local jurisdiction. Thus, for example, where Netherlands law on jurisdiction does not recognize the court for the place of performance of the obligation, can the plaintiff nevertheless sue the defendant before that court in the Netherlands? In addition, would there be any obligation on the Netherlands to adapt its national laws in order to give that court jurisdiction?

By adopting "special" rules of jurisdiction, that is by directly designating the competent court without referring to the rules of jurisdiction in force in the State where such a court might be situated, the Committee decided that a plaintiff should always be able to sue a defendant in one of the forums provided for without having to take the internal law of the State concerned into consideration. Further, in laying down these rules the Committee intended to facilitate implementation of the Convention. By ratifying the Convention, the Contracting States will avoid having to take any other measures to adapt their internal legislation to the criteria laid down in Articles 5 and 6. The Convention itself determines which court has jurisdiction.

Adoption of the "special" rules of jurisdiction is also justified by the fact that there must be a close connecting factor between the dispute and the court with jurisdiction to resolve it. Thus, to take the

45. *Official Journal of the European Communities* 15.1.1962 , p. 36 *et seq.*

example of the *forum delicti commissi*, a person domiciled in a Contracting State other than the Netherlands who has caused an accident in The Hague may, under the Convention, be sued in a court in The Hague. This accident cannot give other Netherlands courts jurisdiction over the defendant. On this point there is thus a distinct difference between Article 2 and Articles 5 and 6, due to the fact that in Article 2 domicile is the connecting factor.

Forum contractus (Article 5 (1)) including contracts of employment

There are great differences between the laws of the Six in their attitude to the jurisdiction of the *forum contractus*; in some countries this jurisdiction is not recognized (the Netherlands, Luxembourg), while in others it exists in varying degrees. Belgian law recognizes the jurisdiction of the courts for the place where the obligation arose, and also that of the courts for the place where the obligation has been or is to be performed[46]; Italian law recognizes only the jurisdiction of the courts for the place where the obligation arose and where it has been performed[47]; German law in general recognizes only the jurisdiction of the courts for the place where the obligation has been **[23]** performed[48]; and, finally, French law recognizes the jurisdiction of the forum contractus only to a limited extent and subject to certain conditions.[49]

Some of the conventions concluded between the Six reject this forum, while others accept it in varying degrees. Article 2 (1) of the Convention between France and Belgium provides that, where a defendant is neither domiciled nor resident in France or Belgium, a Belgian or French plaintiff may institute proceedings in the courts for the place where the obligation arose or where it has been or is to be performed. [50]

Article 4 of the Convention between *Belgium and the Netherlands* provides that in civil or commercial matters a plaintiff may bring a personal action concerning movable property in the courts for the place where the obligation arose or where it has been or is to be performed.

In Article 3 (5) of the Convention between *Belgium and Germany*, jurisdiction is recognized where, in matters relating to a contract, proceedings are instituted in a court of the State where the obligation has been or is to be performed.

Article 14 of the Convention between *France and Italy* provides that if the action concerns a contract which is considered as a commercial matter by the law of the country in which the action is brought, a French or Italian plaintiff may seise the courts of either of the two countries in which the contract was concluded or is to be performed.

The Convention between *Belgium and Italy* (Article 2 (5)) recognizes jurisdiction where, in matters relating to a contract, an action is brought before the courts of the State where the obligation arose, or where it has been or should have been performed.

There are no provisions on this subject in the Conventions between *Italy and the Netherlands*, *Germany and Italy*, and *Germany and the Netherlands*.

Finally, the Benelux Treaty adopts Article 4 of the Convention between Belgium and the Netherlands, but includes a Protocol which in Article 1 lays down that Article 4 shall not apply where Luxembourg concerned if the defendant is domiciled or resident in the country of which he is a national.[51]

Article 5 (1) provides a compromise between the various national laws.

The jurisdiction of the forum is, as in German law limited to matters relating to contract. It could have been restricted to commercial matters, but account must be taken of the fact that European integration will mean an increase in the number of contractual relationships entered into. To have confined it to commercial matters would moreover have raised the problem of classification.

Only the jurisdiction of the *forum solutionis* has been retained, that is to say the jurisdiction of the courts for the place of performance of the obligation on which the claim is based. The reasons for this are as follows.

The Committee considered that it would be unwise to give jurisdiction to a number of courts, and thus possibly create conflicts of jurisdiction. A plaintiff already has a choice, in matters relating to a contract between the competent courts of the State where the defendant is domiciled, or, where there is more than

46. Articles 41 and 52 of the Law of 25 March 1876, Article 624 of the Judicial Code.
47. Articles 4 and 20 of the Code of Civil Procedure.
48. Article 29 of the Code of Civil Procedure.
49. Articles 59 (3) and 420 of the Code of Civil Procedure.
50. On the serious controversy to which this Article has given rise, see Weser, Traité franco-belge du 8 juillet 1899. Étude critique, p. 63 *et seq.*; also *Jurisclasseur de droit international*, vol. 591 , Nos 42 and 45.
51. For the reasons for this limitation, see the report on the negotiations.

one defendant, the courts for the place where anyone of them is domiciled, or finally, the courts for the place of performance of the obligation in question.

If the Committee had adopted as wide-ranging a provision as that of the Benelux Treaty, which recognizes also the jurisdiction of the courts for the place where the obligation arose, this would have involved very considerable changes for those States whose laws do not recognize that forum, or do so only with certain restrictions.

There was also concern that acceptance of the jurisdiction of the courts for the place where the obligation arose might sanction, by indirect means, the jurisdiction of the forum of the plaintiff. To have accepted this forum would have created tremendous problems of classification, in particular in the case of contracts concluded by parties who are absent.

The court for the place of performance of the obligation will be useful in proceedings for the recovery of fees: the creditor will have a choice between the courts of the State where the defendant is domiciled and the courts of another State within whose jurisdiction the services **[24]** were provided, particularly where, according to the appropriate law, the obligation to pay must be performed where the services were provided. This forum can also be used where expert evidence or inquiries are required. The special position of Luxembourg justified, as in the Benelux Treaty, the inclusion of a special provision in the Protocol (Article I).

Contracts of employment

In matters relating to contracts of employment in the broadest sense of the term, the preliminary draft of the Convention contained a provision attributing exclusive jurisdiction to the courts of the Contracting State either in which the undertaking concerned was situated, or in which the work was to have been or had been performed. After prolonged consideration the Committee decided not to insert in the Convention any special provisions on jurisdiction in this field. Its reasoning was as follows.

First, work is at present in progress within the Commission of the EEC to harmonize the provisions of labour law in the Member States. It is desirable that disputes over contracts of employment should as far as possible be brought before the courts of the State whose law governs the contract. The Committee therefore did not think that rules of jurisdiction should be laid down which might not coincide with those which may later be adopted for determining the applicable law.

In order to lay down such rules of jurisdiction, the Committee would have had to take into account not only the different ways in which work can be carried out abroad, but also the various categories of worker: wage-earning or salaried workers recruited abroad to work permanently for an undertaking, or those temporarily transferred abroad by an undertaking to work for it there; commercial agents, management, etc. Any attempt by the Committee to draw such distinctions might have provided a further hindrance to the Commission's work.

Next, in most Member States of the Community the principle of freedom of contract still plays an important part; a rule of exclusive jurisdiction such as that previously provided for in Article 16 would have nullified any agreements conferring jurisdiction.

The general rules of the Convention will therefore apply to contracts of employment. Thus, in litigation between employers and employees, the following courts have jurisdiction: the courts of the State where the defendant is domiciled (Article 2); the courts for the place of performance of the obligation, if that place is in a State other than that of the domicile of the defendant (Article (1)); and any court on which the parties have expressly or impliedly agreed (Articles 17 and 18). In the case of proceedings based on a tort committed at work (Article 2 Nos and of the Arbeitsgerichtsgesetz), Article 5 (3), which provides for the jurisdiction of the courts for the place where the harmful event occurred, could also apply. It seems that these rules will, for the time being, prove of greater value to the persons concerned than a provision similar to that of the former Article 16 (2), which could not be derogated from because it prohibited any agreement conferring jurisdiction.

The rules on the recognition and enforcement of judgments will probably ensure additional protection for employees. If the law of the State addressed had to be applied to a contract of employment, the courts of that State, upon being seised of an application for recognition or enforcement of a foreign judgment would, on the basis of Article 27 (1), which permits refusal of recognition (or enforcement) on grounds of public policy in the State addressed, be able to refuse the application if the court of the State of origin had failed to apply, or had misapplied, an essential provision of the law of the State addressed.

Once the work of the Commission in this field has been completed, it will always be possible to amend the provisions of the Convention, either by means of an additional Protocol, or by the drafting of a convention governing the whole range of problems relating to contracts of employment, which would, under Article 57, prevail over the Convention.

Maintenance obligations (Article 5 (2))

Matters relating to maintenance are governed by the Convention.

The Convention is in a sense an extension of the Hague Convention of 15 April 1958 concerning the recognition and enforcement of decisions relating to maintenance obligations in respect of children,[52] since **[25]** it ensures the recognition and enforcement of judgments granting maintenance to creditors other than children and also of the New York Convention of 20 June 1956 on the recovery abroad of maintenance.[53]

The Committee decided that jurisdiction should be conferred on the forum of the creditior, for the same reasons as the draftsmen of the Hague Convention.[54] For one thing, a convention which did not recognize the forum of the maintenance creditor would be of only limited value, since the creditor would be obliged to bring the claim before the court having jurisdiction over the defendant.

If the Convention did not confer jurisdiction on the forum of the maintenance creditor, it would apply only in those situations where the defendant against whom an order had been made subsequently changed residence, or where the defendant possessed property in a country other than that in which the order was made.

Moreover the court for the place of domicile of the maintenance creditor is in the best position to know whether the creditor is in need and to determine the extent of such need.

However, in order to align the Convention with the Hague Convention Article 5 (2) also confers jurisdiction on the courts for the place of habitual residence of the maintenance creditor. This alternative is justified in relation to maintenance obligations since it enables in particular a wife deserted by her husband to sue him for payment of maintenance in the courts for the place where she herself is habitually resident, rather than the place of her legal domicile.

The Convention also supplements the New York Convention of 20 June 1956 on the recovery abroad of maintenance. The latter is limited to providing that a forwarding authority will transmit to an intermediate body any judgment already given in favour of a maintenance creditor, and that body will then have to begin proceedings for enforcement or registration of the judgment, or institute new proceedings altogether.

This Convention, by simplifying the formalities governing enforcement will thus facilitate implementation of the New York Convention.

As regards maintenance payments, the Committee did not overlook the problems which might be raised by preliminary issues (for example, the question of affiliation). However, it considered that these were not properly problems of jurisdiction, and that any difficulties should be considered in the chapter on recognition and enforcement of judgments.

It was suggested that, in order to avoid conflicting judgments, it might be desirable to provide that the court which had fixed the amount of a maintenance payment should be the only court to have jurisdiction to vary it. The Committee did not think it necessary to adopt such a solution. This would have obliged parties neither of whom had any further connection with the original court, to bring proceedings before courts which could be very far away. Moreover, any judgment by a second court, in order to vary that of the first court would have to be based on changed facts, and in those circumstances it could not be maintained that the judgments were in conflict.[55]

Forum delicti commissi (Article 5 (3) and (4))

This jurisdiction is recognized by the national laws of the Member States with the exception of Luxembourg and the Netherlands, where it exists only in respect of collisions of ships and of road accidents.

The following are applicable in Belgium, Articles 41 and 52 (3) of the Law of 1876[56]; in Germany, Article 32 of the Code of Civil Procedure; in France, Article 59 (12) of the Code of Civil Procedure and

52. In force on 1.9.1966 between Belgium, France, Germany, Italy and the Netherlands.

53. In force on 1.9.1966 between Belgium, France, Germany, Italy and the Netherlands.

54. Hague Conference on private international law, documents for the eighth session, p. 315.

55. For a similar view, see the Hague Conference on private international law, documents for the ninth session. Report on the draft Convention concerning the recognition and enforcement of decisions relating to maintenance obligations in respect of children, p. 321.

56. Article 626 of the Judicial Code.

This jurisdiction is incorporated in the bilateral conventions by the following provisions: Article 4 of the Convention between Belgium and the Netherlands and Article 4 of the Benelux Treaty, which cover all obligations concerning movable property, whether statutory, contractual or non-contractual[57]; Article 2 (b) of the Convention between Belgium and Italy; Article 3 (1) (6) of the Convention between Germany **[26]** and Belgium; Article 15 of the Convention between France and Italy; Article 2 (4) of the Convention between Germany and Italy; and Article 4 (1)(e) of the Convention between Germany and the Netherlands.

The fact that this jurisdiction is recognized under most of the legal systems, and incorporated in the majority of the bilateral conventions, was a ground for including it in the Convention, especially in view of the high number of road accidents.

Article 5 (3) uses the expression "the place where the harmful event occurred". The Committee did not think it should specify whether that place is the place where the event which resulted in damage or injury occurred or whether it is the place where the damage or injury was sustained. The Committee preferred to keep to a formula which has already been adopted by number of legal systems (Germany, France).

Article 5 (4) provides that a civil claim may be brought before a court seised of criminal proceedings; this is in order to take into account the rules of jurisdiction laid down by the various codes of criminal procedure. A civil claim can thus always be brought, whatever the domicile of the defendant, in the criminal court having jurisdiction to entertain the criminal proceedings even if the place where the court sits (place of arrest, for example) is not the same as that where the harmful event occurred.

Jurisdiction based on a dispute arising out of the operations of a branch agency or other establishment (Article 5 (5))

This jurisdiction exists in the bilateral conventions already concluded between the Contracting States: the Conventions between Italy and Belgium (Article 2 (3)), between Belgium and Germany (Article 2 (1)(4)), between France and Belgium (Article 3 (2)), between France and Italy (Article 13), between Italy and the Netherlands (Article 2 (3)), and between Belgium and the Netherlands (Article 5 (3)); the Benelux Treaty (Article 5 (4)); and the Conventions between Germany and the Netherlands (Article 4 (1)(d)), and between Germany and Italy (Article 2 (3)).

This provision concerns only defendants domiciled in a Contracting State (Article 5), that is, companies or firms having their seat in one Contracting State and having a branch, agency or other establishment in another Contracting State. Companies or firms which have their seat outside the Community but have a branch, etc, in a Contracting State are governed by Article 4, even as regards disputes relating to the activities of their branches, but without prejudice to the provisions of Article 8 relating to insurance.

More than one defendant (Article 6 (1))

Where there is more than one defendant, the courts for the place where anyone of the defendants is domiciled are recognized as having jurisdiction. This jurisdiction is provided for in the internal law of Belgium,[58] France,[59] Italy,[60] Luxembourg[61] and the Netherlands.[62]

It is not in general provided for in German law. Where an action must be brought in Germany against a number of defendants and there is no jurisdiction to which they are all subject, the court having jurisdiction may, subject to certain conditions, be designated by the superior court which is next above it (Article 36 (3) of the German Code of Civil Procedure).

This jurisdiction is also provided for in the Conventions between Italy and the Netherlands (Article 2 (1)), between Italy and Belgium (Article 2 (1)), between France and Italy (Article 11 (2)), and between Germany and Italy (Article 2 (1)). However, under the latter Convention, jurisdiction depends on the existence of a procedural requirement that the various defendants be joined.

It follows from the text of the Convention that, where there are several defendants domiciled in different Contracting States, the plaintiff can at his option sue them all in the courts for the place where anyone of them is domiciled.

57. Report on the negotiations, p. 17.
58. Articles 39 and 52 (10) of the Law of 25 March 1876, and Article 624 of the Judicial Code.
59. Article 59 (4) of the Code of Civil Procedure.
60. Article 33 of the Code of Civil Procedure.
61. Article 59 (2) of the Code of Civil Procedure.
62. Article 126 (7) of the Code of Civil Procedure.

In order for this rule to be applicable there must be a connection between the claims made against each of the defendants, as for example in the case of joint debtors.[63] It follows that action cannot be brought solely with the object of ousting the jurisdiction of the courts of the State in which the defendant is domiciled.[64]

[27] Jurisdiction derived from the domicile of one of the defendants was adopted by the Committee because it makes it possible to obviate the handing down in the Contracting States of judgments which are irreconcilable with one another.

Actions on a warranty or guarantee, third party proceedings, counterclaims

(a) Actions on a warranty or guarantee (Article 6 (2))

An action on a warranty or guarantee brought against a third party by the defendant in an action for the purpose of being indemnified against the consequences of that action, is available in Belgian,[65] French,[66] Italian,[67] Luxembourg[68] and Netherlands[69] law.

The proceeding which corresponds to an action on a warranty or guarantee in Germany is governed by Articles 72, 73 and 74 and Article 68 of the Code of Civil Procedure.

A party who in any proceedings considers that, if he is unsuccessful, he has a right of recourse on a warranty or guarantee against a third party, may join that third party in the proceedings (Article 72) (Streitverkündung – *litis denunciatio*).

The notice joining the third party must be served on that party and a copy must be sent to the other party (Article 73). No judgment can be given as regards the third party, but the judgment given in the original proceedings is binding in the sense that the substance of the judgment cannot be contested in the subsequent action which the defendant may bring against the third party (Article 68). Under the German Code of Civil Procedure the defendant can exercise his right of recourse against the third party only in separate proceedings.

Actions on a warranty or guarantee are governed by the bilateral Conventions between Belgium and Germany (Article 3 (10)), between France and Belgium (Article 4 (2)), between Belgium and the Netherlands (Article 6 (2)), between Italy and the Netherlands (Article 2 (4)), between Belgium and Italy (Article 2 (10)), and between Germany and the Netherlands (Article 4 (1)(c)), and also by the Benelux Treaty (Article 6 (3)).

This jurisdiction is, in the opinion of the Committee, of considerable importance in commercial dealings, as can be seen from the following example: A German exporter delivers goods to Belgium and the Belgian importer resells them. The purchaser sues the importer for damages in the court for the place of his domicile for example in Brussels. The Belgian importer has a right of recourse against the German exporter and consequently brings an action for breach of warranty against that exporter in the court in Brussels, since it has jurisdiction over the original action. The jurisdiction over the action on the warranty is allowed by the Convention although the warrantor is domiciled in Germany, since this is in the interests of the proper administration of justice.

However, under Article 17, the court seised of the original action will not have jurisdiction over the action on the warranty where the warrantor and the beneficiary of the warranty have agreed to confer jurisdiction on another court provided that the agreement covers actions on the warranty.

Moreover, the court seised of the original action will not have jurisdiction over an action on the warranty if the original proceedings were instituted solely with the object of ousting the jurisdiction of the courts of the State in which the warrantor is domiciled.[70]

The special position of German law is covered by Article V of the Protocol.

Under this provision, the jurisdiction specified in Article 6 (2) in actions on a warranty or guarantee may not be resorted to in the Federal Republic of Germany, but any person domiciled in another Contracting State may be summoned before the German courts on the basis of Articles 72 to 74 of the Code of Civil Procedure.

63. Morel, Traité élémentaire de procedure civile, No. 264.
64. Cass. française 1924, D.P. 1925, Vol. 13.
65. Articles 50 and 52 of the Law of 25 March 1876, Article 181 of the Code of Civil Procedure.
66. Articles 59 (10) and 181 to 185 of the Code of Civil Procedure.
67. Articles 32 and 36 of the Code of Civil Procedure.
68. Articles 59 (8) and 181 to 185 of the Code of Civil Procedure.
69. Article 126 (14) of the Code of Civil Procedure.
70. See Article 181 of the Belgian, French and Luxembourg Code of Civil Procedure, and Article 74 of the Netherlands Code of Civil Procedure.

Judgments given against a guarantor or warrantor in the other Contracting States will be recognized and enforced in Germany.

Judgments given in Germany pursuant to Articles 72 to 74 will have the same effect in the other Contracting States as in Germany.

Thus, for example, a guarantor or warrantor domiciled in France can be sued in the German court having jurisdiction over the original action. The German law **[28]** judgment given in Germany affects only the parties to the action, but it can be invoked against the guarantor or warrantor. Where the beneficiary of the guarantee or warranty proceeds agaist the guarantor or warrantor in the competent French courts, he will be able to apply for recognition of the German judgment, and it will no longer be possible to re-examine that judgment as to the merits.

It is clear that, following the principles which apply to enforcement, a judgment given in an action on a guarantee or warranty will have no effects in the State in which enforcement is sought other than those which it had in the country of origin.

This principle, which already applied under the Conventions between Germany and Belgium (Article 3 (10)) and between Germany and the Netherlands (Article 4 (1)(i)), is thus incorporated in the provision governing relations between the Federal Republic of Germany and the other Member States of the Community.

(b) Third party proceedings

While a third party warranty or guarantee necessarily involves the intervention of an outsider, it seemed preferable to make separate provision for guarantors or warrantors and for other third parties. The simplest definition of third party proceedings is to be found in Articles 15 and 16 of the Belgian Judicial Code, which provides that:

> "Third party proceedings are those in which a third party is joined as a party to the action.
> They are intended either to safeguard the interests of the third party or of one of the parties to the action, or to enable judgment to be entered against a party, or to allow an order to be made for the purpose of giving effect to a guarantee or warranty (Article 15).
> The third party's intervention is voluntary where he appears in order to defend his interests.
> It is not voluntary where the third party is sued in the course of the proceedings by one or more of the parties (Article 16)."

(c) Counterclaims (Article 6 (3))

The bilateral conventions on enforcement all recognize jurisdiction over counterclaims: see the Convention between Belgium and Germany (Article 3 (1) (10)) (counterclaims); the Convention between Italy and Belgium (Article 2 (1) (10)) (dependent counterclaims); the Convention between France and Belgiul1l (Article 4 (2)) (counterclaims); the Convention between Belgium and the Netherlands (Article 6) (counterclaims, third party proceedings and interlocutory proceedings); the Convention between France and Italy (Article 18) (claims for compensation, interlocutory or dependent proceedings, counterclaims); the Convention between Italy and the Netherlands (Article 2 (4)) dependent proceedings, counterclaims); the Convention between Germany and Italy (Article 2 (5)) (counterclaims); the Benelux Treaty (Article 6) (counterclaims, third party proceedings and interlocutory proceedings); and the Convention between Germany and the Netherlands (Article 4 (1)(i)) (counterclaims and actions on a warranty or guarantee).

It has been made clear that in order to establish this jurisdiction the counterclaim must be related to the original claim. Since the concept of related actions is not recognized in all the legal systems, the provision in question, following the draft Belgian Judicial Code states that the counterclaim must arise from the contract or from the facts on which the original claim was based.

Sections 3 to 5

Insurance, instalment sales, exclusive jurisdiction

General remarks

In each of the six Contracting States, the rules of territorial jurisdiction are not as a rule part of public policy and it is therefore permissible for the parties to agree on a different jurisdiction.

There are, however, exceptions to this principle: certain rules of jurisdiction are mandatory or form part of public policy, either in order to further the efficient administration of justice by reducing the number of jurisdictions and concentrating certain forms of litigation in a single forum, or else out of social considerations for the protection of certain categories of persons, such as insured persons or buyers of goods on instalment credit terms.

In view of the Convention's structure and objectives, it was necessary to deal with this matter under the Convention. Failure to take account of the problem raised by these rules of jurisdiction might not only have caused recognition and enforcement to be refused in certain cases on grounds of public policy, which would be contrary to the principle of free movement of judgments, but also result, indirectly, in general re-examination of the jurisdiction of the court of the State of origin.**[29]**

Several solutions were open to the Committee.

The first is found in many bilateral Conventions, and enables the court of the State in which recognition or enforcement is sought to refuse to recognize the jurisdiction of the court of the State of origin where, in the former State, there are "rules attributing exclusive jurisdiction to the courts of that State in the proceedings which led to the judgment".[71]

This system would have been unsatisfactory not only because it gives rise to the objections already set out above, but because it would have introduced into the Convention an element of insecurity incompatible with its basic principles. It is no solution to the problem, and only postpones the difficulties, deferring them until the recognition and enforcement stage.

Another possible solution would have been a general clause like that contained in the Convention between Belgium and the Netherlands or the Bendux Treaty (Article 5 (1)), which takes into consideration the internal law of the Contracting States.[72] Such a clause could however, lead to difficulties of interpretation since the court of the State of origin must, where its jurisdiction is contested, apply the internal law of the State which claims to have exclusive jurisdiction.

Moreover, while such a solution might be acceptable in a Treaty between three States, it would be much more difficult to incorporate it in a Convention between six States where it is not always possible to determine in advance the State or States in which recognition or enforcement may be sought

A third solution would have been to draw up a list the individual jurisdictions which would be exclusive and which would thus be binding on all the Contracting States. Such a list would answer the need of the parties for information regarding the legal position, allow the court to give judgment on the basis of a definite common rule, remove any element of uncertainty and ensure a balance between the parties to contractual arrangements.

The considerations underlying the various provisions of the Convention are complex. Sections 3 and 4, for example, concerning insurance and instalment sales and loans, are dictated by social considerations and are aimed in particular at preventing abuses which could result from the terms of contracts in standard form.

Section 5 (Article 16) contains a list of situations in which the courts of a Contracting State are acknowledged as having exclusive jurisdiction, since the proper administration of justice requires that actions should be brought before the courts of a single State.

The Convention deals with the two categories differently. The first category has been placed in an intermediate position between the general rules of jurisdiction and the rules which are wholly exclusive.

The following system adopted:

1. For matters falling within Section 3 and 4 there is no single jurisdiction. A choice, albeit a limited one, exists between the courts of different Contracting States where the plaintiff is a protected person, that is, a policy-holder, a buyer or a borrower. In matters falling under exclusive jurisdictions pursuant to Section 5, the parties have no choice between the courts of serveral Contracting States.
2. The parties may, in certain circumstances, derogate from the provisions of Sections 3 and 4 (Articles 12 , and 18). The provisions of Section 5 may not however, be derogated from, either by an agreement conferring jurisdiction (second paragraph of Article 17) or by an implied submission to the jurisdiction (Article 18).

71. Convention between Germany and Belgium, Article 3 (2); Convention between Italy and the Netherlands (end of Article 2); Convention between Italy and Belgium (end of Article 2).

72. Article 5 (1) of the Convention between Belgium and the Netherlands reads as follows: "Where a domicile conferring jurisdiction has been chosen in one of the two countries for the enforcement of an instrument, the courts for the place of domicile chosen shall have exclusive jurisdiction over litigation relating to that instrument, save for exceptions and modifications enacted or to be enacted under the national law of one of the two States or by international agreement."

3. The rules in Section 3 and 4 are applicable only where the defendant is domiciled in a Contracting State, whereas those in Section 5 apply regardless of domicile.

[30] However, contravention of the provisions of Sections 3 and 4, as well as of those of Section 5 , constitutes a ground for refusing recognition and enforcement (Articles 28 and 34).

Section 3

Jurisdiction in matters relating to insurance

Rules of exclusive or special jurisdiction relating to insurance exist in France (Article 3 of the Law of July 1930 concerning contracts of insurance), in Belgium (Law of 20 May 1920, added as Article 43 bis to the Law of 25 March 1876 on jurisdiction), in Germany (§48 of the Gesetz über den Versicherungsvertrag (Law on contracts of insurance)), and in Italy (Article 1903 (2) of the Civil Code, Article 124 of the Consolidated Law on private insurance). In Luxembourg, the Law of 16 May 1891 on contracts of insurance does not include any provision on jurisdiction. This is due to the small size of the Grand Duchy, which comprises only two judicial arrondissements. However, the Law of 16 May 1891 concerning the supervision of insurance matters governs jurisdiction in regard to foreign insurance companies. This Law requires an insurer resident abroad who is transacting insurance business in the Grand Duchy to appoint a general representative domiciled Luxembourg who will represent him there judicially and extrajudicially. This representative must give an address for service of process in the judicial arrondissement in which he is not domiciled. Either the domicile of the general representative or his address for service founds jurisdiction in respect of actions arising from contracts of insurance. In the Netherlands, there are no special provisions concerning the jurisdiction of the courts insurance matters. As regards foreign life-assurance companies, the Netherlands Law of 22 December 1922 recognizes rules analogous to those of the Luxembourg Law of 16 May 1891. The rules are approximately the same in Germany.

Section 3 was drawn up in cooperation with the European Insurance Committee.

The provisions of this Section may be summarized as follows: in matters relating to insurance, actions against an insurer domiciled in a Contracting State may be brought in the following courts, i. e. either:

(i) In the courts of the State where he is domiciled (Article 8), or, subject to certain conditions, in the courts for the place where he has a branch (Articles 7 and 8); or

(ii) (a) in the courts for the place where the policy-holder is domiciled (Article 8);

(b) in the courts of the State where one of the insurers is domiciled, if two or more insurers are the defendants (Article 8);

(c) in the courts for the place where the agent who acted as intermediary in the making of the contract of insurance has his domicile , if there is provision for such jurisdiction under the law of the court seised of the matter (Article 8);

(d) 1. in respect of liability insurance, the insurer may in addition be sued:

(1) in the courts for the place where the harmful event occurred (Articles 9 and 10),

(2) as a third party, in the court seised of the action brought by the injured party against the insured if, under its own law, that court has jurisdiction in the third party proceedings (Article 10);

2. in respect of insurance of immovable property, the insurer may in addition be sued in the courts for the place where the harmful event occurred. The same applies if movable and immovable property are covered by the same insurance policy and both are adversely affected by the same contingency (Article 9).

Where an insurer is the plaintiff, he may in general bring an action only in the courts of the State in which the defendant is domiciled, irrespective of whether the latter is the policy-holder, the insured or a beneficiary.

Agreements conferring jurisdiction which depart from these rules have no legal force if they were entered into before the dispute arose (Article 12).

Article 7

Article 7 specifies that jurisdiction in matters relating to insurance is governed solely by Section 3 of Title II.

Specific exceptions are made by the references to Articles 4 and 5 (5), which concern respectively defendants domiciled outside the Community and disputes arising out of the operations of a branch agency or other establishment.

It follows from the first of these exceptions that jurisdiction is determined by the law of the court seised of the matter including the rules of exorbitant jurisdiction, where the defendant, whether he is the insurer or the policy-holder, is domiciled outside the Community. However, as an exception to the general rules of the Convention, an insurer domiciled outside the Community who has a branch or an agency in a **[31]** Contracting State is, in disputes relating to the operations of the branch or agency, deemed to be domiciled in that State. This exception, which contained in the last paragraph of Article 8 , was adopted because foreign insurance companies can establish branches or agencies in other States only by putting up guarantees which in practice place them in the same position as national companies. However, the exception applies only to branches or agencies, i.e. when the foreign company is represented by a person able to conclude contracts with third parties on behalf of the company.

The second exception again relates to branches or agencies, and also to other establishments, which, as appears from the reference back to Article 5(5), depend from a company whose seat is in a Contracting State. The result is that such a company may be sued in the courts for the place in which the branch, agency or establishment is situated, in all disputes arising out of their operations.

Article 8

Article 8 lays down general rules of jurisdiction in proceedings instituted against an insurer in matters relating to insurance.

First, the courts of the State where the insurer is domiciled have jurisdiction. This provision determines only general jurisdiction, namely the jurisdiction of the courts of the State where the insurer is domiciled. Each State must then apply its internal law to determine which court has jurisdiction. However, if the insurer is sued outside the State in which he is domiciled, the proceedings must be instituted in specifically determined court, in accordance with the principles already adopted in Article 5.

Secondly, an action may be brought in a State other than that in which the insurer is domiciled, in the courts for the place where the policy-holder is domiciled. "Policy-holder" is to be taken to mean the other party to the contract of insurance. Where the insured or the beneficiary is not the same person as the policy-holder their place of domicile is not taken into consideration. As was noted in particular by the European Insurance Committee, the insurer, as a supplier of services , enters into a business relationship with the other contracting party (the policy-holder). Because of their direct contact it is right and proper that the insurer can be sued in the courts for the place where the policy-holder domiciled. But it would be unreasonable to expect the insurer to appear in the court of the insured or of a beneficiary, since he will not necessarily know their exact domicile at lhe time when the cause of action arises.

The domicile of the policy-holder which is relevant here is the domicile existing at the time when the proceedings are instituted.

Thirdly, if two or more insurers are defendants in the same action, they may be sued in the courts of the State where anyone of them is domiciled. This provision is identical to that in Article 6 (1), which does not apply here since the Section relating to insurance applies independently of the rest of the Convention.

Furthermore, an insurer may be sued in a State other than that in which he is domiciled, in the courts for the place where the agent who acted as intermediary in the making of the contract of insurance is domiciled, but subject to two conditions: first, that the domicile of the agent who acted as intermediary is mentioned in the insurance policy or proposal, and, secondly, that the law of the court seised of the matter recognizes this jurisdiction. It is not recognized in Belgium or in France although it is in Germany[73] and in Italy (Article 1903 of the Civil Code). The reference to the insurance proposal takes account of the usual practice in Germany. Insurance companies there in general use data-processing systems, so that the place of the agency often appears in the policy only in the form of a number referring back to the insurance proposal. The insurance proposal, within the meaning of the Convention, means of course, the final proposal which forms the basis of the contract.

The expression "the agent, who acted as intermediary in the making of the contract of insurance" includes both an agent through whom the contract was directly concluded between the company and the policy-holder and also an agent who negotiated the contract to conclusion on behalf of the company. The significance **[32]** of the last paragraph of Article 8 is made clear in the commentary on Article 7.

73. §48 of the Gesetz über den Versicherungsvertrag:
"1. If an insurance agent has acted as intermediary in the making of the contract, or has concluded the contract, then in actions against the insurer arising out of the insurance contract the court for the place where, at the time when the contract was negotiated through the agent or concluded the agent had his agency or, in the absence of an agency, has domicile, shall have jurisdiction.
2. The jurisdiction defined in paragraph 1 may not be excluded by agreement."

Article 9

Article 9 allows an insurer to be sued in a State other than that in which he is domiciled in the courts for the place where the harmful event occurred, but without prejudice to the application of Article 12(3). This jurisdiction applies only in respect of liability insurance and insurance of immovable property. It extends to movable property in cases where a building and the movable property it contains are covered by the same insurance policy. This also applies if the movables are covered by an endorsement to the policy covering the immovable property.

Article 10

Article 10 contains rules of special jurisdiction for liability insurance cases. This provision is of particular importance in relation to road accidents.

Under the first paragraph of Article 10, in an action brought by the injured party against the insured, the latter may join the insurer as a third party if the court seised of the matter has jurisdiction in such a case under its own law. This is not possible in the Federal Republic of Germany.[74]

The problem arose whether consolidation of the two actions should be allowed even where the insurer and the insured are both domiciled in the same State, which it must be assumed for the purposes of this argument, is different from the State of the court seised of the matter. For example, where an accident is caused in France by a German domiciled in Germany who is insured with a German company, should third party proceedings, which are recognized under French law, be possible even though the litigation concerns a contract of insurance between a German insured person and a German insurer? As it is subject to German law, should this contract not be litigated in a German court? The contractual relationship between the insurer and the policy-holder would then fall outside the scope of the proceedings relating to personal liability.

While acknowledging the relevance of this question, the Committee was of the opinion that it would be unwise to introduce rules of jurisdiction which would depart from national laws and which could also jeopardize the system in force following the introduction of the green card.[75]

The compromise solution adopted by the Committee is to reduce the scope of the first paragraph of Article 10 by inserting, under Article 12 (3), a provision that, if the policy-holder and the insurer are both domiciled in the same Contracting State, when the contract is concluded they may agree to confer jurisdiction on the courts of that State. Such an agreement must not, however, be contrary to the law of that State.

Under the second paragraph of Article 10 the insurer may also, in respect of liability insurance, be sued directly by the injured party[76] outside the State in which he is domiciled in any court which, under Articles 7 to 9, has jurisdiction over actions brought by the policy-holder against the insurer.

Where, however, under the first paragraph of Article 8 the court for the place where the policy-holder is domiciled has jurisdiction, there is no provision giving jurisdiction to the court for the place where the injured party is domiciled. The phrase "where such direct actions are permitted" has been used specifically to include the conflict of laws rules of the court seised of the matter.[77]

Under the last paragraph of Article 10 , the insurer may join the policy-holder or the insured as parties to the action brought against him by the injured party. In the interests of the proper administration of justice, it must be possible for the actions to be brought in the same court in order to prevent different courts from giving judgments which are irreconcilable. This procedure will in addition protect the insurer against fraud.[78]

74. See Article V of the Protocol.

75. Insurance against civil liability in respect of motor vehicles is compulsory in all Community countries except Italy.

Belgium: Law of 1 July 1956.

France: Law of 27 February 1958, Decree of 7 January 1959.

Germany: Law of 7 November 1939.

Luxembourg: Law of 10 June 1932, Implementing Regulations of 28 October 1932 and 24 December 1932.

Netherlands: Law of 30 May 1963, Decree of 23 June 1964.

76. Direct actions are recognized under Belgian, French and Luxembourg law. Under German and Netherlands law they are recognized only with regard to compulsory insurance against civil liability in respect of motor vehicles.

77. The rules of conflict must be used to decide whether the law to be applied is the law of the place where the harmful event occurred, the law governing the contract of insurance or the *lex fori*.

78. J. Wautier, L' assurance automobile obligatoire, Brussels 1947.

[33] *Article 11*

Article 11 relates to actions brought by the insurer against the policy-holder, the insured or a beneficiary.

The courts of the State in which the defendant is domiciled when the proceedings are instituted have exclusive jurisdiction. Again, this is a provision dealing with international jurisdiction; local jurisdiction within each State will be determined by the internal law of that State.

Article 11 does not apply where the defendant is domiciled outside a Contracting State, that is to say, outside the Community. In such cases Article 4 applies.

The second paragraph corresponds to the provisions of Article 6 (3).

Article 12

Article 12 relates to agreements conferring jurisdiction. Agreements concluded before a dispute arises will have no legal force if they are contrary to the rules of jurisdiction laid down in the Convention.

The purpose of this Article is to prevent the parties from limiting the choice offered by this Convention to the policy-holder, and to prevent the insurer from avoiding the restrictions imposed under Article 11.

A number of exceptions are, however, permitted. After a dispute has arisen , that is to say "as soon as the parties disagree on a specific point and legal proceedings are imminent or contemplated",[79] the parties completely regain their freedom.

Certain agreements conferring jurisdiction which were concluded before the dispute arose are also permissible. First, there are those made to the advantage of the policy-holder, the insured or a beneficiary, which allow them to bring proceedings in courts other than those specified in the preceding Articles.

Certain other agreements conferring jurisdiction are allowed under Article 12 (3), but only in the strictly defined circumstances therein specified which have been explained in the commentary on Article 10.

Section 4

Jurisdiction in matters relating to instalment sales and loans

This Section relates to the sale of goods where the price is payable in a series of instalments, and to the sale of goods where the sale is contractually linked to a loan (Abzahlungsgeschäfte). The rules here adopted are similar to those applicable in the national law of several of the Member States and, like them, stem from a desire to protect certain categories of persons. Article 13 provides that this Section applies independently of the rest of the Convention and, like Article 7, without prejudice to the provisions of Articles 4 and 5(5).

Article 14 determines the rules of jurisdiction.

In actions against a seller or a lender, proceedings may be instituted by the buyer or borrower either in the courts of the State in which the defendant is domiciled or in the courts of the State in which the buyer or borrower is domiciled.

Actions by a seller or a lender may in general be brought only in the courts for the place where the buyer or borrower is domiciled when the proceedings are instituted.

The third paragraph, relating to counterclaims, corresponds to Article 6 (3).

Article 15, which relates to agreements conferring jurisdiction, contains under (3) a provision analogous to that of Article 12(3), but for different reasons. In actions brought by a seller of a lender, it is rather difficult to determine jurisdiction where the buyer borrower establishes himself abroad after the contract has been concluded. To protect these persons, they should ideally be sued only in the courts of the State where they have established their new domicile. For reasons of equity the Committee has however provided that where a seller and a buyer, or a lender and a borrower, are both domiciled or at least habitually resident in the same State when the contract is concluded, they may confer on the courts of that State jurisdiction over all disputes arising out of the contract on condition that such agreements are not contrary to the law of that State.

The criterion of habitual residence allows agreements conferring jurisdiction to be concluded even where a buyer or borrower remains domiciled in a Contracting State **[34]** other than that in which he is resident. It follows, for example, that a seller or lender need not sue the defendant abroad in the courts of

79. Braas, Précis de procedure civile, Vol. I, No. 795.

the State in which the defendant is domiciled, if when the proceedings are instituted, the defendant is still resident in the State in which the contract was concluded.

Section 5

Exclusive jurisdiction

Article 16

Article 16 lists the circumstances in which the six States recognize that the courts of one of them have exclusive jurisdiction. The matters referred to in this Article will normally be the subject of exclusive jurisdiction only if they constitute the principal subject-matter of the proceedings of which the court is to be seised.

The provisions of Article 16 on jurisdiction may not be departed from either by an agreement purporting to confer jurisdiction on the courts of another Contracting State, or by an implied submission to the jurisdiction (Articles 17 and 18). Any court of a State other than the State whose courts have exclusive jurisdiction must declare of its own motion that it has no jurisdiction (Article 19). Failure to observe these rules constitutes a ground for refusal of recognition or enforcement (Articles 28 and 34).

These rules, which take as their criterion the subject-matter of the action, are applicable regardless of the domicile or nationality of the parties. In view of the reasons for laying down rules of exclusive jurisdiction it was necessary to provide for their general application even in respect of defendants domiciled outside the Community. Thus, for example, a Belgian court will not, on the basis of Article 53 of the Law of 1876 or of Article 637 of the draft Judicial Code, which in actions against foreigners recognize the jurisdiction of the courts of the plaintiff, have jurisdiction in proceedings between a Belgian and a person domiciled, for example in Argentina, if the proceedings concern immovable property situated in Germany. Only the German courts will have jurisdiction.

Immovable property

Under Article 16 (1), only the courts of the Contracting State in which the immovable property is situated have jurisdiction in proceedings concerning rights *in rem* or tenancies of, immovable property.

The importance of matters relating to immovable property had already been taken into consideration by the authors of the Treaty of Rome since, under Article 54 (3)(c) of that Treaty, the Commission and the Council must enable "a national of one Member State to acquire and use land and buildings situated in the territory of another Member State", in so far as this does not conflict with the principles laid down in Article 39 (2) relating to agricultural policy.

The problems which the Committee faced in this connection did not in fact relate to the recognition and enforcement of judgments, since these questions are governed by the provisions of the conventions already concluded between Member States, all of which apply in civil and commercial matters, including immovable property, but rather to the choice of rules of jurisdiction.

The laws of all the Member States include in this respect special rules of jurisdiction[80] which generally speaking, have been incorporated in the bilateral conventions, whether they are based on direct[81] or indirect[82] jurisdiction.

However, the rules laid down in the Convention differ from those in the bilateral agreements in that the Convention lays down rules of exclusive jurisdiction. The Convention follows in this respect the Treaty between France and Germany settling the question of the Saar, Article 49 of which provides that the courts "the country in which the immovable property is situated shall have exclusive jurisdiction in all disputes regarding the possession or ownership of such property and in all disputes regarding rights in rem in such property".

As in that Treaty, the exclusive jurisdiction established by Article 16 (1) applies only in international relations; the internal rules of jurisdiction in force in each of the States are thus not affected.

In other words, the Convention prohibits the courts of one Contracting State from assuming jurisdiction in **[35]** disputes relating to immovable property situated in another Contracting State; it does not,

80. Belgium: Article 8 of the Law of 25 March 1876, amended by the Arrêté royal of 3 January 1935; Article 52 of the Law of 1876; Federal Republic of Germany, Article 24 of the Code of Civil Procedure; France, Article 59 (5) of the Code of Civil Procedure; Italy, Articles 4 and 21 of the Code of Civil Procedure; Luxembourg, Article 59 (3) and (4) of the Code of Civil Procedure; Netherlands, Article 126 (8) of the Code of Civil Procedure.

81. Convention between Belgium and the Netherlands (Article 10).

82. Conventions between Germany and Belgium (Article 10); between France and Italy (Article 16); between Italy and the Netherlands (Article 2 (6)); between Germany and Italy (Article 2 (7)); between Belgium and Italy (Article 2 (8)); and between Germany and the Netherlands (Article 4 (1)(f)).

in the State in which the immovable property is situated, prevent courts other than that for the place where the property is situated from having jurisdiction in such disputes if the jurisdiction of those other courts is recognized the law of that State.

A number of considerations led the Committee to provide a rule of exclusive jurisdiction in this matter. In the Federal Republic of Germany and in Italy, the court for the place where the immovable property is situated has exclusive jurisdiction, this being considered a matter of public policy. It follows that, in the absence of a rule of exclusive jurisdiction, judgments given in other States by courts whose jurisdiction might have been derived from other provisions of the Convention (the court of the defendant's domicile, or an agreed forum) could have been neither recognized nor enforced in Germany or Italy.

Such a system would have been contrary to the principle of "free movement of judgments".

The Committee was all the more inclined to extend to international relations the rules of jurisdiction in force in the Federal Republic of Germany and in Italy, since it considered that to do so was in the interests of the proper administration of justice. This type of dispute often entails checks, enquiries and expert examinations which have to be made on the spot. Moreover, the matter is often governed in part by customary practices which are not generally known except in the courts of the place, or possibly of the country, where the immovable property is situated. Finally, the system adopted also takes into account the need to make entries in land registers located where the property is situated.

The wording adopted covers not only all disputes concerning rights in rem in immovable property, but also those relating to tenancies of such property. This will include tenancies of dwellings and of premises for professional or commercial use, and agricultural holdings. In providing for the courts of the State in which the property is situated to have jurisdiction regards tenancies in immovable property, the Committee intended to cover disputes between landlord and tenant over the existence or interpretation of tenancy agreements, compensation for damage caused by the tenant, eviction, etc. The rule was not intended by the Committee to apply to proceedings concerned only with the recovery of rent, since such proceedings can be considered to relate to a subject-matter which is quite distinct from the rented property itself.

The adoption of this provision was dictated by the fact that tenancies of immovable property are usually governed by special legislation which, in view of its complexity, should preferably be applied only by the courts of the country in which it is in force. Moreover several States provide for exclusive jurisdiction in such proceedings, which is usually conferred on special tribunals.

Companies and associations of natural or legal persons

Article 16 (2) provides that the courts of the State in which a company or other legal person, or an association of natural or legal persons, has its seat, have exclusive jurisdiction in proceedings which are substance concerned either with the validity of the constitution, the nullity or the dissolution of the company, legal person or association, or with the decisions of its organs.

It is important, in the interests of legal certainty, to avoid conflicting judgments being given as regards the existence of a company or association or as regards the validity of the decisions of its organs. For this reason, it is obviously preferable that all proceedings should take place in the courts of the State in which the company or association has its seat. It is in that State that information about the company or association will have been notified and made public. Moreover, the rule adopted will more often than not result in the application of the traditional maxim "*actor sequitur forum rei*". Such jurisdiction is recognized in particular in German law and, as regards non-profit making organizations, in Luxembourg law.

Public registers

Article 16 (3) lays down that the courts of the State in which a public register is kept have exclusive jurisdiction in proceedings relating to the validity or effects of entries in that register. This provision does not require a lengthy commentary. It correspond to the provisions which appear in the internal laws of most of the Contracting States; it covers in particular entries in land registers, land charges registers and commercial registers.

[36] *Patents*

Article 16 (4) applies to proceedings concerned with the registration or validity of patents, trade marks, designs or other similar rights, such as those which protect fruit and vegetable varieties, and which are required to be deposited or registered.

A draft convention has been drawn up by the EEC countries relating to patent law. The draft includes rules of jurisdiction for the Community patent, but it will not apply to national patents, which thus fall within the scope of the Judgments Convention.

Since the grant of a national patent is an exercise of national sovereignty, Article 16 (4) of the Judgments Convention provides for exclusive jurisdiction in proceedings concerned with the validity of patents.

Other actions, including those for infringement of patents, are governed by the general rules of the Convention.

The expression "the deposit or registration has been applied for" takes into account internal laws which, like German law, make the grant of a patent subject to the results of an examination. Thus, for example, German courts will have exclusive jurisdiction in the case of an application to the competent authorities for a patent to be granted where, during the examination of the application, a dispute arises over the rights relating to the grant of that patent.

The phrase "is under the terms of an international convention deemed to have taken place" refers to the system introduced by the Madrid Agreement of 14 April 1891 concerning international registration of trade marks, revised at Brussels on 14 December 1900, at Washington on 2 June 1911, at The Hague on 6 November 1925 and at London on 2 June 1934, and also to the Hague Arrangement of 6 November 1925 for the international registration of industrial designs revised at London on 2 June 1934. Under this system the deposit of a trade mark, design or model at the International Office in Berne through the registry of the country of origin has the same effect in the other Contracting States as if that trade mark, design or model had been directly registered there. Thus where a trade mark is deposited at the International Office at the request of the German authorities, the French courts will have exclusive jurisdiction in disputes relating, for example, to whether the mark should be deemed to have been registered in France.

Enforcement of judgments

Article 16 (5) provides that the courts of the State in which a judgment has been or is to be enforced have exclusive jurisdiction in proceedings concerned with the enforcement of that judgment.

What meaning is to be given to the expression "proceedings concerned with the enforcement of judgments"?

It means those proceedings which can arise from "recourse to force, constraint or distraint on movable or immovable property in order to ensure the effective implementation of judgments and authentic instruments".[83]

Problems arising out of such proceedings come within the exclusive jurisdiction of the courts for the place of enforcement.

Provisions of this kind appear in the internal law of many Member States.[84]

Section 6

Prorogation of jurisdiction

This section includes Article 17, on jurisdiction by consent, and Article 18 , which concerns jurisdiction implied from submission.

Article 17

Jurisdiction deriving from agreements conferring jurisdiction is already a feature of all the Conventions concluded between Member States of the Community, whether the rules of jurisdiction are direct or indirect: see the Convention between France and Belgium (Article 3), and between Belgium and the Netherlands (Article 5); the Benelux Treaty (Article 5); the **[37]** Convention between France and Italy (Article 12), between Germany and Italy (Article 2 (2)), between Italy and the Netherlands (Article 2 (2)), between Italy and Belgium (Article 2 (1) (2)), between Germany and Belgium (Article 3 (2)), and between Germany and the Netherlands (Article 4 (1)(b)).

83. Braas, Précis de procedure civile, Vol. I, No. 808.

84. See Lerebours-Pigeonnière, Droit international privé, seventh edition, p. 9; Loussouarn, No. 411: French courts have exclusive jurisdiction over measures for enforcement which is to take place in France (preventive measures, distress levied on a tenant's chattels, writs of attachment and applications for enforcement of a foreign judgment); over distraint levied on immovable or movable property, and over proceedings concerned with the validity of measures for enforcement.

This jurisdiction is also the subject of international conventions, namely the Hague Convention of 15 April 1958 on the jurisdiction of the contractual forum in matters relating to the international sale of goods, and the Hague Convention of 25 November 1965 on the choice of court.[85]

It is unnecessary to stress the importance of this jurisdiction, particularly in commercial relations.

However, although agreement was readily reached on the basic principle of including such a jurisdiction in the Convention the Committee spent much time in drafting Article 17.

Like the draftsmen of the Convention between Germany and Belgium, the report of which may usefully be quoted, the Committee's first concern was "not to impede commercial practice, yet at the same time to cancel out the effects of clauses in contracts which might go unread. Such clauses will therefore be taken into consideration only if they are the subject of an agreement, and this implies the consent of all the parties. Thus, clauses in printed forms for business correspondence or in invoices will have no legal force if they are not agreed to by the party against whom they operate."

The Committee was further of the opinion that, in order to ensure legal certainty, the formal requirements applicable to agreements conferring jurisdiction should be expressly prescribed, but that "excessive formality which is incompatible with commercial practice"[86] should be avoided.

In this respect, the version adopted is similar to that of the Convention between Germany and Belgium, which was itself based on the rules of the Hague Convention of 15 April 1958 , in that a clause conferring jurisdiction is valid only if it is in writing, or if at least one of the parties has confirmed in writing an oral agreement.[87]

Since there must be true agreement between the parties to confer jurisdiction, the court cannot necessarily deduce from a document in writing adduced by the party seeking to rely on it that there was an oral agreement. The special position of the Grandy Duchy of Luxembourg in this matter necessitated an additional restriction which is contained in the second paragraph of Article I of the Protocol.

The question of how much weight is to be attached to the written document was left open by the Committee. In certain countries, a document in writing will be required only as evidence of the existence of the agreement; in others, however, it will go to the validity of the agreement.

Like the Conventions between Belgium and the Netherlands and between France and Belgium, and also the Benelux Treaty and the Hague Convention, the first paragraph of Article 17 provides that the court agreed on by the parties shall have exclusive jurisdiction. This solution is essential to avoid different courts from being properly seised of the matter and giving conflicting or at least differing judgments. In order to meet practical realities, the first paragraph of Article 17 also covers specifically cases of agreement that a particular court in a Contracting State or the courts of a Contracting State are to have jurisdiction, and is similar in this to the 1958 Hague Convention. As Professor Batiffol pointed out in his report on that Convention, an agreement conferring jurisdiction generally on the courts of a Contracting State "may have no legal effect if, in the absence of any connecting factor between the contractual situation and the State whose courts have been agreed on as having jurisdiction, the law of that State provides no way of determining which court can or should be seised of the matter".[88] But as Batiffol remarks, this is a matter which the parties should consider at the appropriate time.

The first paragraph of Article 17 applies only if at least one of the parties is domiciled in a Contracting State. It does not apply where two parties who are domiciled in the same Contracting State have agreed that a court that State shall have jurisdiction, since the Convention, **[38]** under the general principle laid down in the preamble determines only the international jurisdiction of courts (see Commentary, Chapter III, Section 1, International legal relationships).

Article 17 applies where the agreement conferring jurisdiction was made either between a person domiciled in one Contracting State and a person domiciled in another Contracting State, or between a person domiciled in a Contracting State and a person domiciled outside the Community, if the agreement confers jurisdiction on the courts of a Contracting State; it also applies where two persons domiciled in one Contracting State agree that a particular court of another Contracting State shall have jurisdiction.

The second paragraph of Article 17 provides that agreements conferring jurisdiction shall have no legal force if they are contrary to the provisions of Article 12 (insurance) or Article 15 (instalment sales),

85. By 1 September 1966 neither of these Conventions had entered into force.

86. Hague Conference on private international law, documents of the eighth session. Fréderica, Report on the work of the Second Committee, p. 303.

87. Hague Conference on private international law, Final Act of the tenth session. Convention on the choice of court Article 4.

88. Hague Conference on private international law, documents of the eighth session, p. 305.

or if the courts whose jurisdiction they purport to exclude have exclusive jurisdiction by virtue of Article 16.

The intention behind the Convention is to obviate cases of refusal of recognition and enforcement on the basis of Articles 28 and 34, and so, as already stated, to promote the free movement of judgments.

The third paragraph of Article 17 provides that if the agreement conferring jurisdiction was concluded for the benefit of only one of the contracting parties, that party shall retain the right to bring proceedings in any other court which has jurisdiction.[89] Agreements conferring jurisdiction cannot of course affect the substantive jurisdiction of the courts.

Article 18

Article 18 governs jurisdiction implied from submission. If a defendant domiciled in a Contracting State is sued in a court of another Contracting State which does not have jurisdiction under the Convention, two situations may arise: the defendant may either, as he is entitled to, plead that the court has no jurisdiction under the Convention, in which case the court must declare that it does not have jurisdiction; or he may elect not to raise this plea, and enter an appearance. In the latter case, the court will have jurisdiction.

Unlike the case of conventions based on indirect jurisdiction, the defendant may, by virtue of the Convention, rely on its provisions in the court seised of the proceedings and plead lack of jurisdiction. It will be necessary to refer to the rules of procedure in force in the State of the court seised of the proceedings in order to determine the point in time up to which the defendant will be allowed to raise this plea, and to determine the legal meaning of the term "appearance".

Moreover, by conferring jurisdiction on a court in circumstances where the defendant does not contest that court's jurisdiction, the Convention extends the scope of Title II and avoids any uncertainty. The main consequence of this rule is that if a defendant domiciled in a Contracting State is, notwithstanding the provisions of the second paragraph of Article 3 , sued in another Contracting State on the basis of a rule of exorbitant jurisdiction, for example in France on the basis of Article 14 of the Civil Code, the court will have jurisdiction if this is not contested. The only cases in which a court must declare that it has no jurisdiction and where jurisdiction by submission will not be allowed are those in which the courts of another State have exclusive jurisdiction by virtue of Article 16.

Section 7

Examination as to jurisdiction and admissibility

Article 19

As has already been stated (see pages 316–317), a court must of its own motion examine whether it has jurisdiction. Article 19 emphasizes that the court must of its own motion declare that it has no jurisdiction if it is seised of a matter in which the courts of another Contracting State have exclusive jurisdiction by virtue of Article 16.

This rule is essential since the exclusive jurisdictions are conceived to be matters of public policy which cannot be departed from by the free choice of the parties. Moreover, it corresponds to Article 171 of the French Code of Civil Procedure, by virtue of which territorial jurisdiction is automatically examined where the parties are not permitted to reach a settlement.[90]

If this Article deserves particular attention, it is mainly because, in order that the general rules of jurisdiction **[39]** are observed, it grants wide powers to the court seised of the proceedings, since that court will of its own motion have to examine whether it has jurisdiction.

The words "principally concerned" have the effect that the court is not obliged to declare of its own motion that it has no jurisdiction if an issue which comes within the exclusive jurisdiction of another court is raised only as a preliminary or incidental matter.

Article 20

Article 20 is one of the most important Articles in the Convention: it applies where the defendant does not enter an appearance; here the court must of its own motion examine whether it has jurisdiction under the Convention. If it finds no basis for jurisdiction, the court must declare that it has no jurisdiction. It is obvious that the court is under the same obligation even where there is no basis for exclusive juris-

89. See also the Conventions between France and Belgium Article 3 , between France and Italy, Article 2, and between Belgium and the Netherlands, Article 5 and the Benelux Treaty, Article 5.

90. The same is true in the Federal Republic of Germany: see Rosenberg, *op. cit.*, paragraph 38 (I)(3).

diction. Failure on the part of the defendant to enter an appearance is not equivalent to a submission to the jurisdiction. It is not sufficient for the court to accept the submissions of the plaintiff as regards jurisdiction; the court must itself ensure that tp.e plaintiff proves that it has international jurisdiction.[91]

The object of this provision is to ensure that in cases of failure to enter an appearance the court giving judgment does so only if it has jurisdiction, and so to safeguard the defendant as fully as possible in the original proceedings. The rule adopted is derived from Article 37 (2) of the Italian Code of Civil Procedure, by virtue of which the court must of its own motion examine whether it has jurisdiction where the defendant is a foreigner and does not enter an appearance.

The second paragraph of Article 20 is also designed to safeguard the rights of the defendant, by recognizing the international importance of the service of judicial documents. The service of judicial documents abroad although governed differently in each of the Member States, can broadly be separated into two main systems. The German system is based on the cooperation of the public authorities of the place of residence of the addressee which have jurisdiction to deliver to him a copy of the instrument. A German court cannot in general give judgment in default of appearance unless it receives conclusive evidence that the instrument has been delivered to the addressee.[92,93] The system contrasts with those in force in Belgium, France, Italy, Luxembourg and the Netherlands,[94] all of which are characterized by the "desire to localize in the territory of the State of the forum all the formalities connected with the judicial document whose addressee resides abroad".[95]

Under the laws of these countries, service is properly effected, and causes time to begin to run, without there being any need to establish that the document instituting the proceedings has actually been served on its addressee. It is not impossible in these circumstances that, in some cases, a defendant may have judgment entered against him in default of appearance without having any knowledge of the action.

The Hague Convention of 1 March 1954 on civil procedure, to which the six Member States are party, does not solve the difficulties which arise under such legislation.

The Committee also tried to solve the problems arising when service is effected late, bearing in mind that the aim of the Convention is to promote, so far as possible the free movement of judgments.

The search for a solution was obviously helped by the drafting at the tenth session of the Hague Conference on private international law of the Convention on the service abroad of judicial and extrajudicial documents in civil or commercial matters, which was opened for signature on 15 November 1965. This is the reason why the solution adopted in the second paragraph of Article 20 is only transitional.

This provision summarizes Article 15 of the Hague Convention, which is in fact derived from Article 20 of this present Convention since the work of the Committee served as a basis for discussion at the meetings of the Special Commission which was established by the Hague Conference and which drew up the preliminary draft which was submitted for discussion at the tenth session.

[40] Under the second paragraph of Article 20, where a defendant domiciled in one Contracting State is sued in the courts of another State and does not enter an appearance, the court must stay the proceedings so long as it is not shown that the defendant has been able to receive the document instituting the proceedings in sufficient time to enable him to arrange for his defence or that all necessary steps have been taken to this end.

This provision is based on the old Article 8 of the Netherlands Law of 12 June 1909, Stb No 141.[96]

The second paragraph of Article 20 requires first that notification of the proceedings has been given to the party who has not entered an appearance, that is either to him in person or at his domicile, and

91. Bülow, *op. cit.*

92. Rigaux, La signification des actes judiciaires à l'étranger. Revue critique de droit international privé, p. 448 *et seq.*

93. See German Code of Civil Procedure, Article 335 (1) (2) and Article 202.

94. Belgium: Code of Civil Procedure, Article 69*bis*, and Judgment of the Cour de cassation of 4 March 1954. Revue des huissiers de Belgique, May–June 1954, p. 15.

France: Code of Civil Procedure, Article 69 (10), as interpreted by the French Cour de cassation. See Revue critique de droit international privé, No. 1, January-March 1961, p. 174, *et seq.*

Italy: Code of Civil Procedure, Articles 142 and 143. Luxembourg: Arrêté-loi of 1 April 1814.

Netherlands: Code of Civil Procedure, Article 4 (8).

95. Rigaux, *id.*, p. 454.

96. This Article reads as follows: "Where the defendant does not enter an appearance, the court may not give judgment in default if the plaintiff does not show that the defendant received the writ of summons. The plaintiff may ask for a new date to be fixed for the hearing."

secondly that it has been delivered in sufficient time to enable the defendant to arrange for his defence. It does not require that the defendant should actually have been notified in sufficient time. The defendant must be responsible for any delay caused by his own negligence or by that of his relations or servants. The critical time is thus the time at which service was properly effected, and not the time at which the defendant received actual knowledge of the institution of proceedings.

The question of "sufficient time" is obviously a question of fact for the discretion of the court seised of the matter.

The court may give judgment in default against a defendant if it is shown that "all necessary steps have been taken" for him actually to have received in sufficient time the document instituting the proceedings.

This means that a court will be able to give judgment in default against a defendant even if no affidavit can be produced to confirm service on the defendant of the document instituting the proceedings, provided it is shown that all the necessary approaches have been made to the competent authorities of the State in which the defendant is domiciled in order to reach him in sufficient time. Where necessary, it must also be shown that "all the investigations required by good conscience and good faith have been undertaken to discover the defendant".[97]

As already stated, the second paragraph of Article 20 is only a transitional provision. Under the third paragraph of that Article, where the State of the forum and the State in which the document had to be transmitted have both ratified the new Hague Convention, the court seised of the matter will no longer apply the second paragraph of Article 20 but will be exclusively bound by Article 15 of the Hague Convention. Thus any possibility of conflict between Article 15 of the Hague Convention and the second paragraph of Article 20 of the EEC Judgments Convention is resolved in favour of the Hague Convention.

The Committee also considered it important to ensure certainty and speed in the transmission of judicial documents. In order to achieve this, it considered as a possible solution the transmission of such documents by registered post. However, it did not adopt this system for, although it meets the requirement of speed, it does not offer all the necessary safeguards from the point of view of certainty. In the end the Committee adopted the system which is set out in Article IV of the Protocol.

This Article simply adds a new method of transmission to those already provided for by the Hague Convention of 1 March 1954 on civil procedure, or by the agreements concluded between the Contracting States in application of that Convention. It corresponds moreover, to the facility provided for by Article 10 (b) of the new Hague Convention.

Under the system adopted in the Protocol, documents can be transmitted by public officers in one Contracting State directly to their colleagues in another Contracting State, who will deliver them to the addressee in person or to his domicile.

According to the assurances which were given to the Committee by representative of the "Union internationale des huissiers de justice et d'officiers judiciaires", it will be easy for a public officer in one country to correspond with the appropriate public officer in another country. In case of difficulty it would moreover be possible for the officer in the State in which judgment was given to invoke the assistance of the national associations of public officers, or on the central office of the "Union" which has its headquarters in Paris.

[41] In the opinion of the Committee these arrangements meet the requirements of speed and certainty. Direct communication between public officers allows a considerable gain in time by avoiding any recourse to intermediary bodies such as Ministries for Foreign Affairs, Ministries of Justice or prosecutors' offices.

Certainty is further guaranteed since if, for example, the address is incomplete or inaccurate, the officer in the State in which service is to be effected may well be able to undertake investigations in order to find the addressee.

As for the linguistic difficulties which could arise in the context of a grouping of the six countries, these could be overcome by attaching to the instrument a summary in the language of the addressee.

Like Article 10 (b) of the Hague Convention, Article IV of the Protocol allows a Contracting State to object to this method of transmission.

97. Cour d' appel de Poitiers, 9.7.1959 (Gazette du Palais, 1959.II.183); *cf.* GAVALDA, Revue critique de droit international privé, 1960, No. 1 , p. 174.

Section 8

Lis pendens – related actions

Article 21

As there may be several concurrent international jurisdictions, and the courts of different States may properly be seised of a matter (see in particular Articles 2 and 5), it appeared to be necessary to regulate the question of *lis pendens*. By virtue of Article 21, the courts of a Contracting State must decline jurisdiction if necessary of their own motion, where proceedings involving the same cause of action and between the same parties are already pending in a court of another State. In cases of *lis pendens* the court is therefore obliged to decline jurisdiction, either on the application of one of the parties, or of its own motion, since this will facilitate the proper administration of justice within the Community. A court will not always have to examine of. its own motion whether the same proceedings are pending in the courts of another country, but only when the circumstances are such as to lead the court to believe that this may be the case.

Instead of declining jurisdiction, the court which subsequently seised of a matter may, however, stay its proceedings if the jurisdiction of the court first seised is contested. This rule was introduced so that the parties would not have to institute new proceedings if, for example, the court first seised of the matter were to decline jurisdiction. The risk of unnecessary disclaimers of jurisdiction is thereby avoided.

Jurisdiction is declined in favour of the court first seised of the matter. The Committee decided that there was no need to specify in the text the point in time from which the proceedings should be considered to be pending, and left this question to be settled by the internal law of each Contracting State.

Article 22

The solution offered by this Article to the problem of related actions differs in several respects from that adopted to regulate the question of *lis pendens*, although it also serves to avoid the risk of conflicting judgments and thus to facilitate the proper administration of justice in the Community.

Where actions are related, the first duty of the court is to stay its proceedings. The proceedings must, however be pending at the same level of adjudication, for otherwise the object of the proceedings would be different and one of the parties might be deprived of a step in the heirarchy of the courts.

Furthermore, to avoid disclaimers of jurisdiction, the court may decline jurisdiction only if it appears that the court first seised has jurisdiction over both actions, that is to say, in addition, only if that court has not jurisdiction over the second action. The court may decline jurisdiction only on the application of one of the parties, and only if the law of the court first seised permits the consolidation of related actions which are pending in different courts. This last condition takes into account the specific problems of German and Italian law. In German law, consolidation is in general permitted only if both actions are pending in the same court. In Italian law, the constitution does not permit a court to decide whether it will hear an action itself or refer it to another court. It will, however, always be possible for a German or Italian court which is subsequently seised of a matter to stay its proceedings.

[42] Finally, since the expression "related actions" does not have the same meaning in all the Member States, the third paragraph of Article 22 provides a definition. This is based on the new Belgian Judicial Code (Article 30).

The Convention does not regulate the procedure for the consolidation of related actions. This is a question which is left to the internal laws of the individual States.

Article 23

This Article deals with a situation which will occur only very rarely, namely where an action comes within the exclusive jurisdiction of several courts. To avoid conflicts of jurisdiction, any court other than the court first seised of the action is required under Article 21 or Article 22 to decline jurisdiction in favour of that court.

Section 9

Provisional and protective measures

Article 24

Article 24 provides that application may be made to the courts of a Contracting State for such provisional measures, including protective measures, as may available under the internal law of that State irrespective of which court has jurisdiction as to the substance of the case. A corresponding provision will be found in nearly all the enforcement conventions.[98]

In each State, application may therefore be made to the competent courts for provisional or protective measures to be imposed or suspended, or for rulings on the validity of such measures, without regard to the rules of jurisdiction laid down in the Convention.

As regards the measures which may be taken, reference should be made to the internal law of the country concerned.

CHAPTER V: RECOGNITION AND ENFORCEMENT

A. GENERAL CONSIDERATIONS

As a result of the safeguards granted to the defendant in the original proceedings, Title III of the Convention is very liberal on the question of recognition and enforcement. As already stated, it seeks to facilitate as far as possible the free movement of judgments, and should be interpreted in this spirit. This liberal approach is evidenced in Title III first by a reduction in the number of grounds which can operate to prevent the recognition and enforcement of judgments and secondly, by the simplification of the enforcement procedure which will be common to the six countries.

It will be recalled that Article 1, which governs the whole of the Convention, provides that the Convention shall apply in civil and commercial matters whatever the nature of the court or tribunal. It follows that judgments given in a Contracting State in civil commercial matters by criminal courts or administrative tribunals must be recognized and enforced in the other Contracting States. Under Article 25, the Convention applies to any judgment, whatever the judgment may be called. It also applies to writs of execution (Vollstreckungsbefehl, Article 699 of the German Code of Civil Procedure)[99] and to the determination of costs (Kostenfestsetzungsbeschlug des Urkundsbeamten, Article 104 of the German Code of Civil Procedure) which, in the Federal Republic, are decisions of the registrar acting as an officer of the court. In decisions based on Article 104 of the German Code of Civil Procedure, the Costs are determined in accordance with a schedule laid down by law and on the basis of the judgment of the court deciding on the substance of the matter.[100] In the event of a dispute as to the registrar's decision, a fully constituted court decides the issue.

[43] It follows from Article 1 that Title III cannot be invoked for the recognition and enforcement of judgments given on matters excluded from the scope of the Convention (status and legal capacity of persons, rules governing rights in property arising out of matrimonial relationship, wills and succession, bankruptcy and other similar proceedings, social security, and arbitration including arbitral awards).

On the other hand, Title III applies to any judgment given by a court or tribunal of a Contracting State in those civil and commercial matters which fall within the scope of the Convention, whether or not the parties are domiciled within the Community and whatever their nationality.

B. COMMENTARY ON THE SECTIONS

Section 1

Recognition

Article 26

Recognition must have the result of conferring judgments the authority and effectiveness accorded to them in the State in which they were given.

The words "*res judicata*" which appear in a number of conventions have expressly been omitted since judgments given in interlocutory proceedings and *ex parte* may be recognized, and these do not always have the force of *res judicata*. Under the rules laid down in Article 26:

1. judgments are to be recognized automatically;
2. in the event of a dispute, if recognition is itself the principal issue, the procedure for enforcement provided for in the Convention may be applied;

98. Benelux Treaty and Convention between Belgium and the Netherlands (Article 8); Convention between Germany and Belgium (Article 15 (2)); between France and Belgium (Article 9); between Italy and Belgium (Article 14); between Italy and the Netherlands (Article 10); between France and Italy (Article 32); and between Germany and the Netherlands (Article 18 (2)).

99. The Vollstreckungsbefehl is issued hy the court registrar.

100. See also Article 18 (2) of the Hague Convention of 1 March 1954 on Civil Procedure.

3. if the outcome of proceedings depends on the determination of an incidental question of recognition the court entertaining those proceedings has jurisdiction on the question of recognition.

The first of these rules lays down the principle that judgments are to be recognized; recognition is to be accorded without the need for recourse to any prior special procedure. It is thus automatic, and does not require a judicial decision in the State in which recognition is sought to enable the party in whose favour judgment has been given to invoke that judgment against any party concerned, for example an administrative authority, in the same way as a judgment given in that State. This provision means that certain legal provisions which in some countries, such as Italy, make the recognition of a foreign judgment subject to a special procedure (dichiarazione di efficacia) will be abolished. The Italian delegation stated that it was able to concur in this solution since the scope of the Convention was limited to matters relating to property rights.

Furthermore, this system is the opposite of that adopted in numerous conventions, according to which foreign judgments are recognized only if they fulfil a certain number of conditions. Under Article 26 there is presumption in favour of recognition, which can be rebutted only if one of the grounds for refusal listed in Article 27 is present.

The second rule concerns the case where the recognition of a judgment is itself the point at issue, there being no other proceedings involved and no question of enforcement. For example, a negotiable instrument is declared invalid in Italy by reason of fraud. The negotiable instrument is presented to a bank in Belgium. Reliance is placed on the Italian judgment. The bank is faced with two contradictory instruments. The Italian judgment would normally have to be recognized, but it may be that one of the grounds for refusal set out in Article 27 applies. In the event of a dispute it is hardly the task of the bank to decide on the grounds for refusal, and in particular on the scope of Belgian international public policy. The second rule of Article 26 offers a solution in cases of this kind. It allows the party seeking recognition to make use of the simplified procedure provided by the Convention for enforcement of the judgment. There is thus unification at the stage of recognition not only of the legal or administrative procedures which govern this matter in a number of States, but also in those countries which, like Belgium do not allow actions for a declaration that a judgment is not to be recognized. Only the party seeking recognition may make use of this simplified procedure, which was evolved solely to promote the enforcement of judgments, and hence their recognition. It would moreover be difficult to apply the procedure laid down if the party opposing recognition could also avail himself of it; the latter will have to submit his claims in accordance with the ordinary rules of the internal law of the State in which recognition is sought.

[44] The third rule concerns the case where recognition of a judgment is raised as an incidental question in the course of other proceedings. To simplify matters, the Committee provided that the court entertaining the principal proceedings shall also have jurisdiction on the question of recognition.

It will immediately be noticed that two conditions which are frequently inserted in enforcement treaties are not referred to in the Convention: it is not necessary that the foreign judgment should have become *res judicata*,[101] and the jurisdiction of the court which gave the original judgment does not have to be verified by the court of the State in which the recognition is sought unless the matter in question falls within the scope of Sections 3, 4 or 5 of Title II.

Article 27

Public policy

Recognition may be refused if it is contrary to public policy in the State in which the recognition is sought. In the opinion of the Committee this clause ought to operate only in exceptional cases. As has already been shown in the commentary on Article 4, public policy is not to be invoked as a ground for refusing to recognize a judgment given by a court of a Contracting State which has based its jurisdiction over a defendant domiciled outside the Community on a provision of its internal law, such as the provisions listed in the second paragraph of Article 3 (Article 14 of the French Civil Code, etc.).

Furthermore, it follows from the last paragraph of Article 27 that public policy is not to be used as a means of justifying refusal of recognition on the grounds that the foreign court applied a law other than that laid down by the rules of private international law of the court in which the recognition is sought.

101. The condition of *res judicata* is required by the Conventions between Germany and Italy, France and Italy, and Italy and the Netherlands. It is not required in the Conventions between Belgium and the Netherlands, Belgium and Italy, Germany and Belgium and Germany and the Netherlands, in the Benelux Treaty, or in the application of the Convention between France and Belgium, in spite of the wording of this last Convention (Article 11 (2)).

The wording of the public policy provision is similar to that adopted in the most recent conventions,[102] in that it is made clear that there are grounds for refusal, not of the foreign judgment itself, but if recognition of it is contrary to public policy in the State in which the recognition is sought. It is no part of the duty of the court seised of the matter to give an opinion as to whether the foreign judgment is, or is not, compatible with the public policy of its country. Indeed, this might be taken as criticism of the judgment. Its duty is rather to verify whether recognition of the judgment would be contrary to public policy.

Safeguarding the rights of the defendant

Where judgment is given in default of appearance, recognition must be refused if the defendant was not duly served with the document which instituted the proceedings in sufficient time to enable him to arrange for his defence. Where judgment is given abroad in default of appearance, the Convention affords the defendant double protection.

First, the document must have been duly served. In this connection reference must be made to the internal law of the State in which the judgment was given, and to the international conventions on the service abroad of judicial instruments. Thus, for example, a German court in which recognition of a Belgian judgment given in default of appearance against a person who is Germany is sought could, on the basis of the Agreement between Belgium and Germany of 25 April 1959, which was entered into to simplify application of the Hague Convention of 1 March 1954 on civil procedure, refuse recognition if the document instituting the proceedings was sent from Belgium to Germany by registered post since the Federal Republic of Germany does not permit this method of transmitting documents.

Secondly, even where service has been duly effected, recognition can be refused if the court in which recognition is sought considers that the document was not served in sufficient time to enable the defendant to arrange for his defence.

Looking at the second paragraph of Article 20, which lays down that the court of the State in which judgment is given must stay the proceedings if the document instituting the proceedings was not served on the defendant in sufficient time, it might be assumed that Article 27 (2) would apply only in exceptional cases. It must not be forgotten, however, that the second **[45]** paragraph of Article 20 requires the court of the State in which judgment is given to stay proceedings only where the defendant is domiciled in another Contracting State.

Incompatibility with a judgment already given in the State in which recognition is sought

There can be no doubt that the rule of law in a State would be disturbed if it were possible to take advantage of two conflicting judgments.[103]

The case where a foreign judgment is irreconcilable with a judgment given by a national court is, in the existing conventions, either treated as a matter of public policy,[104] as in the Convention between France and Belgium, the Benelux Treaty and the Convention between Belgium, and Germany, or is regulated by a special provision.

In the opinion of the Committee, to treat this as a matter of public policy would involve the danger that the concept of public policy would be interpreted too widely. Furthermore, the Italian courts have consistently held that foreign judgments whose recognition is sought in Italy and which conflict with an Italian judgment do not fall within the scope of public policy. This is why the enforcement conventions concluded by Italy always contain two provisions, one referring to public policy, which serves the purpose of providing a safeguard in exceptional cases, and the other whereby the judgment must not conflict with an Italian judgment already given, or be prejudicial to proceedings pending in an Italian court.[105]

There are also several other conventions which contain clause providing for refusal of recognition of a judgment which conflicts with another judgment already given by the courts of the State in which recognition is sought.

102. Conventions between Germany and Belgium, Italy and Belgium; Hague Convention on the recognition and enforcement of foreign judgments in civil and commercial matters.

103. Niboyet, Traite de droit international privé français, Paris 1949, Vol. VI, No. 2028.

104. Batiffol, Traité élémentaire de droit international privé, Paris 1959, No. 761: "... any judgment which irreconcilable with a French judgment previously given is contrary to public policy. This rule holds good even if the judgment is not final" (Civ. 23 March 1936, Sirey 1936.1.175 , R.1937–198); Riezler, *op. cit.*, pp. 521 and 547.

105. Conventions between Germany and Italy, Article 4; between France and Italy, Article 1 (5); between Belgium and Italy, Article 1 (4); and between the Netherlands and Italy, Article 1 (3).

In certain conventions, the judgment given in the State in which recognition is sought has to have become *res judicata*,[106] in others it is sufficient for the judgment to be final and conclusive at that stage of procedure,[107] and finally there are some which do not regulate the point.[108]

The Committee preferred a form of wording which does not decide whether the judgment should have become *res judicata* or should merely be final and conclusive and left this question to the discretion of the court in which recognition is sought.

The Committee also considered that, for refusal of recognition, it would be sufficient if the judgment whose recognition was sought were irreconcilable with a judgment given between the same parties in the State in which recognition was sought. It is therefore not necessary for the same cause of action to be involved. Thus, for example, a French court in which recognition of a Belgian judgment awarding damages for failure to perform a contract is sought will be able to refuse recognition if a French court has already given judgment in a dispute between the same parties declaring that the contract was invalid.

The form of words used also covers the situation referred to in Article 5 (3)(c) of the Hague Convention on the recognition and enforcement of foreign judgments, under which recognition may be refused if the proceedings which gave rise to the judgment whose recognition is sought have already resulted in a judgment which was given in a third State and which would be entitled to recognition and enforcement under the law of the State in which recognition is sought. It is to be anticipated that the application of the provisions of Title II regarding *lis pendens* and related actions will greatly reduce the number of irreconcilable judgments.

[46] *PRELIMINARY QUESTIONS*

Recognition is not to be refused on the sole ground that the court which gave the original judgment applied a law other than that which would have been applicable under the rules of private international law of the State in which recognition is sought. However the Convention makes an exception for preliminary questions regarding the status or legal capacity of natural persons, rules governing rights in property arising out of a matrimonial relationship, wills and succession, unless the same result would have been reached by the application of the rules of private international law of the State in which recognition is sought.

The Convention between Belgium and Germany contains a rule which is similar, but confined to cases where the judgment concerns a national of the State in which it is sought to give effect to that judgment. It is pointed out in the report of the negotiators of that Convention that this exception is justified by the fact that States reserve to themselves the right to regulate the status of their nationals. The wording used is similar to that of Article 7 of the Hague Convention on the recognition and enforcement of foreign judgments in civil and commercial matters.

Article 28

The very strict rules of jurisdiction laid down in Title II and the safeguards granted in Article 20 to defendants who do not enter an appearance, make it possible to dispense with any review, by the court in which recognition or enforcement is sought, of the jurisdiction of the court in which the original judgment was given.

The absence of any review of the substance of the case implies complete confidence in the court of the State in which judgment was given; it is similarly to be assumed that that court correctly applied the rules of jurisdiction of the Convention. The absence of any review as whether the court in which the judgment was given had jurisdiction avoids the possibility that an alleged failure to comply with those rules might again be raised as an issue at the enforcement stage. The only exceptions concern, first, the matters for which Title II lays down special rules of jurisdiction (insurance, instalment sales and loans) or exclusive rules, and which, as has been shown, are in the six countries either of a binding character or matters of public policy, and, secondly, the case provided for in Article 59; reference should be made to the commentary on that Article.

106. Hague Convention on the jurisdiction of the contractual forum in matters relating to the international sales of goods, Article 5 (3).

107. Conventions between France and the United Kingdom Article 3 (1) (a); between the United Kingdom and Belgium, Article 3 (1) (a); between France and Germany on the Saar, Article 30 (1)(d); between Austria and Belgium on maintenance, Article 2 (2)(b); between Austria and Belgium (general), Article 2 (2)(b).

108. Hague Convention of 15 April 1958 concerning the recognition and enforcement of decisions relating to maintenance obligations towards children, Article 2 (4), and the Conventions concluded by Italy. Hague Convention on the recognition and enforcement of foreign judgments in civil and commercial matters (Article 5).

The second paragraph contains a provision which is already included in a number of conventions (Convention between Germany and Belgium; Hague Convention Article 9) and avoids recourse to timewasting duplication in the exceptional cases where re-examination of the jurisdiction of the court of origin is permitted.

The last paragraph of Article 28 specifies that the rules of jurisdiction are not matters of public policy within the meaning of Article 27; in other words, public policy is not to be used as a means of justifying a review of the jurisdiction of the court of origin.[109] This again reflects the Committee's desire to limit so far as possible the concept of public policy.

REVIEW AS TO SUBSTANCE

Article 29

It is obviously an essential provision of enforcement conventions that foreign judgments must not reviewed.

The court of a State in which recognition of a foreign judgment is sought is not to examine the correctness of that judgment; "it may not substitute its own discretion for that of the foreign court[110] nor refuse recognition" if it considers that a point of fact or of law has been wrongly decided.[111]

STAY OF PROCEEDINGS

Article 30

Article 30 postulates the following situation: a party may, in the course of litigation, wish to plead a judgment which has been given in another Contracting State but has not yet become *res judicata.* In order to remedy the inconvenience which would result if such judgment were reversed, Article 30 allows the court to stay the proceedings upon the principal issue of which it **[47]** is seised, until the foreign judgment whose recognition is sought has become *res judicata* in the State in which it was given. This power does not prevent the court from examining, before staying the proceedings, whether the foreign judgment fulfils the conditions for recognition laid down in Article 27.

Section 2

Enforcement

(a) **Preliminary remarks**

As has already been shown the Committee endeavoured to give the Convention a progressive and pragmatic character by means of rules of jurisdiction which break new ground as compared with the enforcement conventions concluded hitherto.

This means, of course, that at the enforcement stage solutions must be found which follow from the rules of jurisdiction.

The progress achieved by Title II of the Convention would be rendered nugatory if a party seeking enforcement in a Contracting State of a judgment given in his favour were impeded by procedural obstacles.

The aim of Title II of the Convention is to strengthen the role of the court of the State in which the judgment was given. It must not be forgotten that that court must declare that it does not have jurisdiction if there are rules of exclusive jurisdiction which give jurisdiction to the courts of another State (Article 19); the court must also declare that it does not have jurisdiction, in cases where the defendant does not enter an appearance, if its jurisdiction is not derived from the Convention (first paragraph of Article 20).

Moreover, the court must stay the proceedings in the absence of proof that the defendant has been able to arrange for his defence (second paragraph of Article 20).

This role, as set out in Title II, is thus of prime importance.

It follows that the intervention of the court in which enforcement is sought is more limited than is usual under enforcement conventions. That court has in practice only two points to examine: public policy and whether the defendant has had the opportunity of defending himself. The other reasons for refusal – conflicting judgments, preliminary questions, review of jurisdiction in relation to certain specific

109. For a similar provision, see Article 13 (2) of the Benelux Treaty.

110. P. Graulich, Principes de droit international privé. Conflits de lois. Conflits de juridictions. No. 254.

111. Batiffol, Traité élémentaire de droit international privé, No. 763.

topics – can in fact, be regarded as akin to public policy. Since moreover, the Convention is confined to matters relating to property rights, public policy will only very seldom have any part to perform.

This limitation on the powers of the court in which enforcement is sought led to a simplification of the enforcement procedure. Furthermore, as the position of the defendant in the original proceedings is well protected it is proper that the applicant for enforcement be enabled to proceed rapidly with all the necessary formalities in the State in which enforcement is sought, that he be free to act without prior warning and that enforcement be obtained without unnecessary complications.

The Committee discussed the enforcement procedure at length before adopting it. There were several possibilities open to it: reference back to national laws but subject to certain rules of the Convention, ordinary contentious procedure, summary contentious procedure or *ex parte* application.

Each of these solutions had its advantages and disadvantages. The Committee finally adopted a system for the whole Community based on *ex parte* application. This rapid and simple procedure will apply in all six States.

This uniform solution has the advantage of creating a proper balance as between the various provisions of the Convention: uniform rules of jurisdiction in the six countries and identical procedures for enforcement.

(b) **Conditions for enforcement**

As has been shown, the Convention is based on the principle that a foreign judgment is presumed to be in order. It must, in principle, be possible to enforce it in the State in which enforcement is sought. Enforcement can be refused only if there is a ground for refusing recognition.[112] The foreign judgment must, however, be enforceable in the State in which it was given in order to be enforceable in the State in which enforcement is sought.

[48] If a judgment from which an appeal still lies or against which an appeal has been lodged in the State in which it was given cannot be provisionally enforced in that State, it cannot be enforced in the State in which enforcement is sought. It is an essential requirement of the instrument whose enforcement is sought that it should be enforceable in the State in which it originates. As Niboyet points out, there is no reason for granting to a foreign judgment rights which it does not have in the country in which it was given.[113]

Under no circumstances may a foreign judgment be reviewed as to its substance (Article 34).

(c) **Enforcement procedure**

Before examining the Articles of the section on enforcement it seems appropriate to give on outline of the procedure which will be applicable in the six States.

1. The application, accompanied by the documents required under Articles 46 and 47, must be submitted to the authority specified in Article 32. The procedure for making the application governed by the law of the State in which enforcement is sought.

   The applicant must give an address for service of process or appoint a representative ad litem in the jurisdiction of the court applied to.

2. The court applied to must give its decision without delay, and is not able to summon the other party. At this stage no contentious proceedings are allowed.

The application may be refused only for one of the reasons specified in Articles 27 and 28.

3. If enforcement is authorized:
   (a) the party against whom enforcement is sought may appeal against the decision within one month of service of the decision (Article 36);
   (b) the appeal must be lodged, in accordance with the rules governing procedure in contentious matters, with the court specified in Article 37;
   (c) if an appeal has been lodged against the foreign judgment in the State in which it was given, or if the time for such an appeal has not yet expired the court seised of the appeal against the decision authorizing enforcement may stay the proceedings or make enforcement conditional on the provision of security (Article 38);

112. On the disadvantages resulting from a difference between the conditions for recognition and for enforcement, see Rigaux, *op. cit.*, p. 207, No. 39.

113. Niboyet, Droit international privé français. Vol. VI, No. 1974.

(d) the judgment given on the appeal against the decision authorizing enforcement may not contested by an ordinary appeal. It may be contested only by an appeal in cassation[114] (Article 37);
(e) during the time specified for an appeal against the decision authorizing enforcement the applicant may take only protective measures; the decision authorizing enforcement carries with it the power to proceed to such measures (Article 39).

4. If enforcement is refused:
(a) the applicant may appeal to the court specified in Article 40;
(b) the procedure before that court is contentious, the other party being summoned to appear (Article 40);
(c) the judgment given on this appeal may be contested only by an appeal in cassation[114] (Article 41).

Article 31

Under this Article "a judgment given in a Contracting State and enforceable in that State shall be enforced in another Contracting State when, on the application of any interested party, the order for its enforcement has been issued there".

As can be seen, this provision is almost identical with that contained in the European Convention providing a uniform law on arbitration.[115] The Committee did, in fact, take the view that judgments given in one **[49]** Contracting State should be enforceable in any other Contracting State as easily as arbitral awards.

The legal systems of the Member States are already familiar with authorization of enforcement by means of an enforcement order. This is so, for example, in the case of judgments and decisions given by the European Community institutions (Article 92 of the ECSC Treaty, Article 192 of the EEC Treaty, Article 164 of the Euratom Treaty). It is also true of judgments and decisions falling within the scope of the Mannheim Convention.[116]

The Convention of 30 August 1962 between Germany and the Netherlands also provides that judgments given in one of the two States are to be enforced in the other if enforcement is authorized by means of enforcement order.

A rule similar to that in Article 31, that is to say an *ex parte* procedure, was contained in the Franco-German Treaty on the Saar of 27 October 1956. Business circles in the Saar have said that the rule has proved entirely satisfactory.

About 80% of enforcement proceedings have been successfully completed by means of the first *ex parte* written phase of the procedure. In the majority of cases judgment debtors have refrained from contesting the proceedings by means of an appeal. This is easily explained by the fact that cases of refusal of enforcement are exceptional, and the risk of having to bear the costs of the proceedings restrains the judgment debtor, unless he feels certain of winning his case.

Article 31 does not purport to determine whether it is the judgment given in the State of origin, or the decision authorizing the issue of the enforcement order, which is enforceable in the State in which enforcement is sought.

The expression "on the application of any interested party" implies that any person who is entitled to the benefit of the judgment in the State in which it was given has the right to apply for an order for its enforcement.

Article 32

Article 32 specifies the authority in each of the Contracting States to which the application must be submitted and which will have jurisdiction. It was considered to be in the interests of the parties that each relevant authority be indicated in the Convention itself.

The court to which local jurisdiction is given is that for the place of domicile of the party against whom enforcement is sought, or, if that party is not domiciled in the State in which enforcement is sought, the court for the place of enforcement, that is, where the judgment debtor has assets. The jurisdiction of the court for the place of enforcement is thus of minor importance.

114. In the Federal Republic of Germany by a "Rechtsbeschwerde".

115. European Convention providing a uniform law on arbitration, Strasbourg, 20 January 1966. Article 29 of Annex I: "An arbitral award may be enforced only when it can no longer be contested before arbitrators and when an enforcement formula has been apposed to it by the competent authority on the application of the interested party."

116. Revised Convention for the Navigation of the Rhine signed at Mannheim on 17 October 1868.

The provision requiring applications to be submitted to the court for the place where the judgment debtor is domiciled was included for the following reason. It is quite possible that in the State in which enforcement is sought the judgment debtor may possess property situated in the jurisdiction of different courts. If jurisdiction had been given only to the court for the place of enforcement, a choice between several courts would have been open to the applicant. Thus, an applicant who was unsuccessful in one court could, instead of availing himself of the methods of appeal provided for in the Convention, have applied to another court which would not necessarily have come to the same decision as the first court, and this without the knowledge of the other party, since the procedure is *ex parte*.

Article 33

Under Article 33, the procedure and formalities for making the application are to be governed by the law of the State in which enforcement is sought.

Reference must therefore be made to the national laws for the particulars which the application must contain the number of copies which must be submitted to the court, the authority to which the application must be submitted, also, where necessary, the language in which it must be drawn up, and whether a lawyer should be instructed to appear.

The provisions to which reference must be made are the following:

Belgium:
The matter will be governed by the Judicial Code (see Articles 1025 and 1027);

Federal Republic of Germany, Netherlands and Italy:
The question will be governed by the law implementing the Convention;

France:
Code of Civil Procedure, Article 1040;

[50] Luxembourg:
A lawyer must be instructed in accordance with the general law under which no one can officially address the court except through an *avoué*. Article 856 or Article 512 of the Code of Civil Procedure is generally invoked in support of this proposition.

The application must be accompanied by the documents required to be produced under Articles 46 and 47.

In the view of the Committee, if the applicant does not produce the required documents, enforcement should not be refused, but the court may stay the proceedings and allow the applicant time to produce the documents. If the documents produced are not sufficient and the court cannot obtain sufficient information, it may refuse to entertain the application.

Finally, the applicant must, in accordance with the law of the State in which enforcement is sought, either give an address for service of process or appoint a representative ad litem within the area of jurisdiction of the court applied to. This provision is important in two respects: first for communicating to the applicant the decision given on the application (Article 35), and secondly in case the party against whom enforcement is sought wishes to appeal, since such an appeal must be lodged "in accordance with the rules governing procedure in contentious matters" (Article 37).

The respondent must therefore summon the applicant to appear; the furnishing of an address for service or the appointment of a representative enables the summons to be served rapidly, in accordance with the law of the country in which enforcement is sought, without risk of error and without all the hazards connected with the service of legal documents abroad. It will in fact usually happen that the applicant is domiciled outside the State in which enforcement is sought.

The appointment of a representative *ad litem* has been provided for because the furnishing of an address for service is unknown in German law.

The two methods will, of course, produce the same result.

Article 34

Article 34 provides that the court applied to shall give its decision without delay; "the party against whom enforcement is sought shall not at this stage of the proceedings be entitled to make any submissions on the application".

The Committee considered but rejected the idea of imposing on the court to which application is made a fixed period for giving its decision. Such a time limit is unknown in judicial practice, and there would in any case be no way of enforcing it.

The Convention does not allow the court to which application is made to ask the respondent to make submissions, even in exceptional cases. Such a possibility would have meant that the proceedings were not fully *ex parte*. Certain courts might be inclined to hear the respondent, which would in fact result in the *ex parte* procedure systematically becoming inter partes. Moreover, there would be a reduction in the element of surprise which is necessary in an enforcement procedure if the respondent is not to have the opportunity withdrawing his assets from any measure of enforcement.

The rights of the respondent are safeguarded, since he can institute contentious proceedings by appealing against the decision authorizing enforcement.

As has been shown above, the application may be refused only for one of the reasons specified in Articles 27 and 28, and the foreign judgment may not reviewed as to its substance. Consequently, fresh claims which have not been submitted to the foreign court are inadmissible; the court seised of the application may authorize or refuse enforcement, but it cannot alter the foreign judgment.

The court may, however, refuse the application if it does not satisfy the requirements of Articles 32 and 33.

Article 35

Article 35 provides that the appropriate officer of the court shall without delay bring the decision given on the application to the notice of the applicant in accordance with the procedure laid down by the law of the State in which enforcement is sought. It is important that the applicant be informed of the decision taken. This demonstrates the value of an address for service or of the appointment of a representative *ad litem* particularly where the applicant is domiciled abroad.

[51] The manner in which the decision is communicated to the applicant will be a matter for the national law of the State in which enforcement is sought, irrespective of whether enforcement is authorized or refused.

Article 36

If enforcement is authorized, the decision must be notified to the party against whom enforcement has been granted. That party may appeal against the decision from the time it is served on him. As regards the period within which an appeal may be lodged and the moment from which it begins to run, Article 36 makes a distinction between the following situations:

(a) if the party is domiciled in the State in which the decision was given, the period is one month; the moment from which time begins to run determined by the law of that State, from which there is no reason to derogate;

(b) if the party is domiciled in another Contracting State, the period is two months, and runs from the date when the decision was served, either on him in person or at his residence.[117]

In France and the Netherlands, the day of delivery to the prosecutor office is not counted for purposes of computation of time. In Belgium, the day of delivery to the postal authorities is not counted (Article 40 of the Judicial Code), nor is the day on which an instrument is dispatched by a Belgian Consul to a foreign authority.[118]

The purpose of this rule, which derogates from some national laws, is to protect the respondent and to prevent his being deprived of a remedy because he had not been informed of the decision in sufficient time to contest it.

No extension of time may be granted on account of distance, as the time allowed is sufficient to enable the party concerned to contest the decision, if he is so minded;

(c) if the party is domiciled outside the Community, the period within which an appeal may be lodged runs from the date when the decision is served or is deemed to have been served according to the law of the State in which the decision was given. In this case the period of one month may be extended on account of distance in accordance with the law of that State.

Computation of time is governed by the internal law of the State in which the decision was given.

Article 37

Article 37 specifies for each country the court with which an appeal can be lodged.

117. Service on a party at his residence means delivering the instrument to a person who is present and empowered by law to receive a copy of the instrument or, if there is no such person, to a competent authority.

118. Belgian Court of Cassation, 4 March 1954; Revue des huissiers de Belgique, May to June 1954, p. 15.

In that court the proceedings are contentious. Accordingly it is incumbent upon the person against whom enforcement has been authorized to summon the other party to appear.

The court seised of the appeal will have to examine whether it was properly lodged and will have to decide upon the merits of the appeal, taking account of the additional information supplied by the appellant. It will therefore be open to the appellant to establish, in the case of a judgment originally given in default of appearance, that the rights of the defendant were disregarded, or that a judgment has already been given in a dispute between the same parties in the State in which enforcement is sought which is irreconcilable with the foreign judgment. The appellant may also plead Article 38 if he has lodged an appeal against the judgment whose enforcement is sought in the State in which it was given.

It is no part of the duty of the court with which the appeal against the decision authorizing enforcement is lodged to review the foreign judgment as to its substance. This would be contrary to the spirit of the Convention. The appellant could, however, effectively adduce grounds which arose after the foreign judgment was given. For example, he may establish that he has since discharged the debt. As Batiffol points out such grounds are admissible In enforcement proceedings.[119, 120]

The second paragraph of Article 37 provides that the judgment given on the appeal may be contested only by an appeal in cassation and not by any other form of appeal or review.

This rule was requisite for the following reasons. First, the grounds for refusing enforcement are very limited and involve public policy. in the State in which enforcement is sought. No useful purpose is served by further argument on this concept. Next, the situation is different from that in which purely national proceedings are involved. The proceedings on the merits of the case itself have already taken place in the State in which the judgment was given, and the Convention in no way **[52]** interferes with the rights of appeal. It is true that the Convention applies to judgments which are enforceable only provisionally, but in this case the court with which the appeal is lodged may, as provided in Article 38, stay the proceedings. An excessive number of avenues of appeal might be used by the losing party purely as delaying tactics, and this would constitute an obstacle to the free movement of judgments which is the object of the Convention.

Since appeals in cassation are unknown in the Federal Republic of Germany, it has been provided, in order to establish a certain parity amongst the Contracting States that an appeal on point of law (Rechtsbeschwerde) shall lie against a judgment of the Court of Appeal (Oberlandesgericht).

Article 38

Article 38 covers cases where an ordinary appeal has been lodged against the judgment in the State in which that judgment was given, and also cases where the period within which such an appeal may be lodged has not yet expired. The court with which the appeal against enforcement under the first paragraph of Article 37 is lodged may either stay the proceedings, authorize enforcement, make enforcement conditional on the provision of such security as it thinks fit, or specify the time within which the defendant must lodge his appeal.

This provision originates in the Convention between Germany and Belgium (Article 10), and its "object is to protect the judgment debtor against any loss which could result from the enforcement of a judgment which has not yet become *res judicata* and may amended".[121]

Article 38 deals only with judgments which notwithstanding that they may be appealed against, are enforceable in the State in which they were given.

Only the court seised of the appeal has the power to stay the proceedings, and such a stay can be granted only on the application of the party against whom enforcement is sought. This is because that party does not appear at the first stage of the proceedings and cannot be required to do so.

Article 39

Article 39 contains two very important rules. First it provides that during the time specified for the lodging of an appeal the applicant for enforcement may take no enforcement measures other than protective measures namely those available under the law of the State in which enforcement is sought. Similarly, if an appeal has actually been lodged, this rule applies until the appeal has been determined. Secondly it provides that the decision authorizing enforcement carries with it the power to proceed to any such protective measures. Article 39 also allows the judgment creditor in certain States, for example in the

119. Batiffol, *op. cit.*, p. 863 , note 57.

120. For the Federal Republic of Germany, see Article 767 of the Code of Civil Procedure; see also Baumbach-Lauterbach, Zivilprozeßordnung, paragraph 723, note 1.

121. Convention between Germany and Belgium. See Report of the negotiators.

Federal Republic of Germany, to initiate the first phase of the enforcement of the foreign instrument. The object of this provision is to ensure at the enforcement stage a balance between the rights and interests of the parties concerned, in order to avoid either of them suffering any loss as a result of the operation of the rules of procedure.

On the one hand, an applicant who, in consequence of a foreign judgment, is in possession of an enforceable instrument, must be able to take quickly all measures necessary to prevent the judgment debtor from removing the assets on which execution is to be levied. This is made possible by the *ex parte* procedure and by the provision in Article 39 that the decision authorizing enforcement carries with it the power to proceed such protective measures. The power arises automatically. Even in those States whose law requires proof that the case calls for prompt action or that there is any risk in delay the applicant will not have to establish that either of those elements is present; power to proceed to protective measures is not a matter for the discretion of the court.

On the other hand, the fact that the enforcement procedure is ex parte makes it essential that no irreversible measures of execution can be taken against the defendant. The latter may be in a position to establish that there are grounds for refusal of enforcement; he may, for example, be able to show that the question of public policy was not examined in sufficient detail. To safeguard his rights it accordingly appeared to be necessary to delay enforcement, which is usually carried out by sequestration of the movable and immovable property of the defendant, until the end of the time specified for appeal (see Article 36) or, if an appeal is actually lodged, until it has been determined. In other words, this is a counter-balance to the *ex parte* procedure; the effect of the decision authorizing enforcement given pursuant to Article 31 is limited in that during the time specified for an appeal, or if an appeal has been lodged, no enforcement measures can be taken on the basis of that decision against the assets of the judgment debtor.

[53] *Articles 40 and 41*

These Articles relate to the case where an application for enforcement is refused.

Article 40 provides that the applicant may appeal to the appeal court which has jurisdiction in the State in which enforcement is sought.

The Committee did not think it necessary that the Convention should fix the period within which appeals would have to be lodged. If the applicant has had his application refused, it is for him to give notice of appeal within such time as he considers suitable. He will have regard, no doubt, to the length of time it will take him to assemble all the relevant documents.

Upon appeal the proceedings are contentious, since the party against whom enforcement is sought is summoned to appear. The inter partes procedure is necessary in order to avoid numerous appeals. If the procedure on appeal had remained *ex parte* it would have been essential to provide for additional proceedings to enable the defendant to make his submissions if the appellate court were to reverse the decision at first instance and authorize enforcement. The Committee wished to avoid a plethora of appeals. Moreover, the dismissal of the application reverses the presumption of validity of the foreign judgment.

The summoning of the party against whom enforcement is sought is to be effected in manner prescribed by the national laws.

The appellate court can give judgment only if the judgment debtor has in fact been given an opportunity to make his submissions. The object of this provision is to protect the rights of the defendant and to mitigate the disadvantages which result from certain systems of serving instruments abroad. These disadvantages are all the more serious in that a party against whom enforcement is sought and who is not notified in time to arrange for his defence no longer has any judicial remedy against the judgment given on the appeal other than by way of an appeal in cassation, and then only to the extent that this is allowed by the law of the State in which enforcement is sought (Article 41).

Because of the safeguards contained in Article 40, Article 41 provides that the judgment given on the appeal may not be contested by an ordinary appeal, but only by an appeal in cassation. The reason why a special form of appeal (Rechtsbeschwerde) is provided for in the Federal Republic of Germany has already been explained (Article 37).

The procedure for the forms of appeal provided for in Articles 40 and 41 is to be determined by the national laws which may, where necessary, prescribe time limits.

Article 42

Article 42 covers two different situations.

The first paragraph of Article 42 empowers the court of the State in which enforcement is sought to authorize enforcement in respect of certain matters dealt with in a judgment and to refuse it in respect of others.[121] As explained in the report annexed to the Benelux Treaty, which contains a similar provision, "this discretion exists in all cases where a judgment deals with separate and independent heads of claim, and the decision on some of these is contrary to the public policy of the country in which enforcement is sought, while the decision on others is not".

The second paragraph of Article 42 allows an applicant to request the partial enforcement of a judgment, and *ex hypothesi* allows the court addressed to grant such a request. As mentioned in the report on the Benelux Treaty, "it is possible that the applicant for enforcement himself wants only partial enforcement, e.g. where the judgment whose enforcement is sought orders the payment of a sum of money, part of which has been paid since the judgment was given".[122]

As is made clear in the Conventions between Germany and Belgium, and between Belgium and Italy, which contain similar provisions, the applicant may exercise this option whether the judgment covers one or several heads of claim.

Article 43

Article 43 relates to judgments which order a periodic payment by way of penalty. Some enforcement conventions contain a clause on this subject (see Benelux Treaty, Article 14; Convention between Germany and the Netherlands, Article 7).

[54] It follows from the wording adopted that judgments given in a Contracting State which order the payment of a sum of money for each day of delay, with the intention of getting the judgment debtor to fulfil his obligations, will be enforced in another Contracting State only if the amount of the payment has been finally determined by the courts of the State in which judgment was given.

Article 44

Article 44 deals with legal aid.

A number of enforcement conventions deal with this matter.[123]

The provisions adopted by the Committee supplements the Hague Convention of 1 March 1954 on civil procedure, which has been ratified by the six States, so that a party who has been granted legal aid in the State in which judgment was given also qualifies automatically for legal aid in the State in which enforcement is sought, but only as regards the issuing of the order for enforcement. Thus the automatic extension of legal aid achieved by the Convention does not apply in relation to enforcement measures or to proceedings arising from the exercise of rights of appeal.

The reasoning underlying Article 44 is as follows.

First, as maintenance obligations fall within the scope of the Convention consideration was given to the humanitarian issues which were the basis for a similar provision in the 1958 Hague Convention.

Above all it must not be forgotten that if a needy applicant were obliged, before making his application for enforcement, to institute in the State in which enforcement is sought proceedings for recognition of the decision granting him legal aid in the State in which the judgment was given, he would be in a less favourable position than other applicants. He would in particular not have the advantage of the rapidity of the procedure and the element of surprise which Title III is designed to afford to any party seeking the enforcement of a foreign judgment.

It is moreover because of this consideration that the automatic extension of legal aid has been limited to the procedure for issuing the order for enforcement, and has not been extended to the proceedings on appeal. Once these proceedings have been set in motion, the applicant for enforcement, or, in case of appeal, the respondent, may, in accordance with the 1954 Hague Convention, take the necessary steps, in the State in which enforcement is sought, to obtain legal aid, in the same way as nationals of that State.

Under Article 47 (2) an applicant must, on making his application, produce documents showing that he is receipt of legal aid in the State in which judgment was given.

121. See Benelux Treaty (Articles 14 (4)); the Conventions between France and Italy (Article 3); between Italy and the Netherlands (Article 3); between Germany and Belgium (Article 11); between Belgium and Italy (Article 10) and between Germany and the Netherlands (Article 12).

122. See also the Conventions between Germany and Belgium (Article 11) and between Belgium and Italy (Article 10).

123. Hague Convention of 15 April 1958 concerning the recognition and enforcement of decisions relating to maintenance obligations towards children (Article 9); Conventions between Italy and the Netherlands (Article 6) and between Germany and the Netherlands (Article 15).

Article 45

This Article deals with security for costs. A similar rule is included in the Hague Convention of 1 March 1954 but as regards the obligation to provide security it exempts only nationals of the Contracting States who are also domiciled in one of those States (Article 17). Under Article 45, any party, irrespective of nationality or domicile, who seeks enforcement in one Contracting State of a judgment given in another Contracting State may do so without providing security. The two conditions nationality and domicile prescribed by the 1954 Convention do not apply.

The Committee considered that the provision of security in relation to proceedings for the issuing of an order for enforcement was unnecessary.

As regards the proceedings which take place in the State in which judgment was given, the Committee did not consider it necessary to depart from the rules of the 1954 Convention.

Section 3

Common provisions

This Section deals with the documents which must be produced when application is made for the recognition or enforcement of a judgment.

[55] Article 46 applies to both recognition and enforcement. Article 47 applies only to applications for enforcement. It should be noted that at the recognition stage there is no reason to require production of the documents referred to in Article 47.

Article 47 (1) provides for the production of documents which establish that the judgment is enforceable in the State in which it was given. The requirement that the judgment be, in law, enforceable in that State applies only in relation to its enforcement (not to its recognition) abroad. (Article 31).

Article 47 (2), which relates to documents showing that the applicant is receiving legal aid in the State in which judgment was given is also relevant only enforcement proceedings. The documents are in fact intended to enable a party receiving legal aid in the State in which judgment was given to qualify for it automatically in the proceedings relating to the issue of the order for enforcement (Article 44). However, recognition requires no special procedure (Article 26). If recognition were itself the principal issue in an action Article 44 and, consequently, Article 47 (2) would apply, since Article 26 refers to Sections 2 and 3 of Title III.

Under Article 46 (1), a copy of the judgment which satisfies the conditions necessary to establish its authenticity must be produced, whether it is recognition or enforcement which is sought.

This provision is found in all enforcement treaties and does not require any special comment. The authenticity of a judgment will be established in accordance with the maxim *locus regit actum*; it is therefore the law of the place where the judgment was given which prescribes the conditions which the copy of the judgment must satisfy in order to be valid.[124]

Under Article 46 (2), if the judgment was given in default, a document which establishes that the party in default was served with the document instituting the proceedings must also be produced.

The court in which recognition or enforcement is sought must, if the foreign judgment was given in default, be in a position to verify that the defendant s right to defend himself was safeguarded.

Article 47 provides that the following documents must be produced:

(a) documents which establish that the judgment is enforceable according to the law of the State in which it was given. This does not mean that a separate document certifying that the judgment has become enforceable in that State is necessarily required. Thus in France, "provisional enforceability" would be deduced from an express reference to it in judgments given pursuant to Article 135a of the Code of Civil Procedure. Decisions given in summary proceedings will be provisionally enforceable (Article 809 of the Code of Civil Procedure); and so will decisions in ex parte proceedings (Article 54 of the Decree of 30 March 1808). But whether other judgments are enforceable can be determined only when the date on which they were given has been considered in relation to the date on which they were served and the time allowed for lodging an appeal.[125]

124. Weser: Traité franco-belge du 8 juillet 1899. Étude critique No. 247.

125. *Belgium*: Judicial Code: see Article 1029 for decisions in parte proceedings, Article 1039 for decisions in summary proceedings, and Articles 1398 and 1496 for judgments.

Federal Republic of Germany: "Vollstreckungsklausel" – Under Article 725 of the Code of Civil Procedure, the order for enforcement is worded as follows:

"This copy of the judgment shall be given to … (name of the party) for the purpose of enforcement." This order must be added at the end of the copy of the judgment and must be signed by the appropriate officer of the court

Documents which establish that the judgment has been served will also have to be produced, since some judgments may be enforceable and consequently fall within the scope of the Convention even if they have not been served on the other party. However, before enforcement can be applied for, that party must at least have been informed of the judgment given against him and also have had the opportunity to satisfy the judgment voluntarily;

(b) where appropriate, a document showing, in accordance with the law of the State in which the judgment was given, that the applicant is in receipt of legal aid in that State.

Article 48

In order to avoid unnecessary formalities, this Article authorizes the court to allow time for the applicant to produce the documentary evidence proving service of the document instituting the proceedings, required under Article 46 (2), and the documentary evidence showing that the applicant was in receipt of legal aid in the State in which judgment was given (Article 47 (2)).

[56] The court may dispense with the production of these documents by the applicant (the Committee had in mind the case where the documents had been destroyed) if it considers that it has sufficient information before it from other evidence.

The second paragraph relates to the translation of the documents to be produced. Again with the object of simplifying the procedure, it is here provided that the translation may be certified by a person qualified to do so in anyone of the Contracting States.

Article 49

This Article provides that legalization or other like formality is not necessary as regards the documents to be produced and, in particular, that the certificate provided for in the Hague Convention of 5 October 1961 abolishing the requirement of legalization for foreign public documents is not required. The same applies to the document whereby an applicant appoints a representative, perhaps a lawyer, to act for him in proceedings for the issue of an order for enforcement.

CHAPTER VI: AUTHENTIC INSTRUMENTS AND COURT SETTLEMENTS

Article 50

In drawing up rules for the enforcement of authentic instruments, the Committee has broken no new ground. Similar provisions are, in fact, contained in the Conventions already concluded by the six States,[126] with the sole exception of the Convention between Germany and Italy.

Since Article 1 governs the whole Convention, Article 50 applies only to authentic instruments which have been drawn up or registered in matters falling within the scope of the Convention.

In order that an authentic instrument which has been drawn up or registered in one Contracting State may be the subject of an order for enforcement issued in another Contracting State, three conditions must be satisfied:

(a) the instrument must be enforceable in the State in which it was drawn up or registered;
(b) it must satisfy the conditions necessary to establish its authenticity in that State;
(c) its enforcement must not be contrary to public policy in the State in which enforcement is sought.

The provisions of Section 3 of Title III are applicable as appropriate. It follows in particular that no legalization or similar formality is required.

---

and sealed with the seal of the court.

Luxembourg: see Articles 135, 136 and 137 of the Code of Civil Procedure, Article 164 for judgments in default, Article 439 for Commercial Courts (tribunaux de commerce) and Article 5 of the Law of 23 March 1893 summary jurisdiction.

Netherlands: see Articles 339, 350, 430 and 433 of the Code of Civil Procedure, also Articles 82 and 85 of that Code.

126. Conventions between France and Belgium (Article 16); between Belgium and the Netherlands (Article 16); Benelux Treaty (Article 18); Conventions between Germany and Belgium (Article 14); between Italy and Belgium (Article 13); between Germany and the Netherlands (Article 16); between Italy and the Netherlands (Article 8); and between France and Italy (Article 6).

Article 51

A provision covering court settlements was considered necessary on account of the German and Netherlands legal systems,[127] under German and Netherlands law settlements approved by a court in the course of proceedings are enforceable without further formality (Article 794 (1) of the German Code of Civil Procedure and Article 19 of the Netherlands Code of Civil Procedure).

The Convention, like the Convention between Germany and Belgium, makes court settlements subject to the same rules as authentic instruments, since both are contractual in nature. Enforcement can therefore be refused only if it is contrary to public policy in the State in which it is sought.

[57] CHAPTER VII: GENERAL PROVISIONS

Article 52

As regards the determination of domicile (Article 52), reference should be made to Chapter IV (A) (3) which deals with the matter.

Article 53

Article 53 provides that, for the purposes of this Convention, the seat of a company or other legal person or association of natural or legal persons shall be treated as its domicile.

The Convention does not define what is meant by the seat of a legal person or of a company or association of natural or legal persons any more than it defines domicile.

In determining the location of the seat, the court will apply its rules of private international law. The Committee did not think it possible to particularize the concept of seat in any other way, and considered that it could not be achieved by making a reference to Article , in view of the different approaches which the various Member States of the Community adopt in this matter. Moreover, the Committee did not wish to encroach upon the work on company law which is now being carried out within the Community.

It did not escape the attention of the Committee that the application of Article 16 (2) of the Convention could raise certain difficulties. This would be the case for example, where a court in one State ordered the dissolution of a company whose seat was in that State and application was then made for recognition of that order in another State under whose law the location of the company's seat was determined by its statutes, if when so determined, it was in that other State. In the opinion of the Committee, the court of the State in which recognition were sought would be entitled, under the first paragraph of Article 28, to refuse recognition on the ground that the courts of that State had exclusive jurisdiction.

Article 53 does not deal with the preliminary question of the recognition of companies or other legal persons or associations of natural or legal persons; this must be resolved either by national law or by the Hague Convention of 1 June 1956 on the recognition of the legal personality of companies, firms, associations and foundations,[128] pending the entry into force of the Convention which is at present being prepared within the EEC on the basis of Article 220 of the Treaty of Rome.

Article 53 refers to companies or other legal persons and to associations of natural or legal persons; to speak only of legal persons would have been insufficient, since this expression would not have covered certain types of company, such as the "offene Handelsgesellschaft" under German law, which are not legal persons. Similarly, it would not have been sufficient to speak only of companies, since certain bodies, such as associations and foundations, would then not have been covered by this Convention.

CHAPTER VIII: TRANSITIONAL PROVISIONS

Article 54

As a general rule, enforcement treaties have no retroactive effect,[129] in order "not to alter a state of affairs which has been reached on the basis of legal relations other than those created between the two States as a result of the introduction of the Convention".[130]

127. See the Conventions between Germany and Belgium (Article 14 (1)); between Germany and the Netherlands (Article 16); between Germany and Italy (Article 9); and the Hague Convention on the choice of court (Article 10).

128. Ratified on 20 April 1966 by Belgium, France and the Netherlands.

129. Conventions between France and Belgium (Article 19); between Belgium and the Netherlands (Article 27); between Germany and Belgium (Article 17); between Germany and Italy (Article 18); between Germany and the Netherlands (Article 20); between Italy and Belgium (Article 17); and between Italy and the Netherlands (Article 16).

130. See Report of the negotiators of the Convention between Germany and Belgium.

So far as the author is aware only the Benelux Treaty applies to judgments given before its entry into force.

[58] A solution as radical as that of the Benelux Treaty did not seem acceptable. In the first place, the conditions which a judgment must fulfil in order to be recognized and enforced are much stricter under the Benelux Treaty (Article 13) than under the EEC Convention. Secondly, the ease with which recognition and enforcement can be granted under the EEC Convention is balanced by the provisions of Title II which safeguard the interests of the defendant. In particular, those provisions have made it possible, at the stage of recognition or enforcement, to dispense with any review of the jurisdiction of the court of origin (Article 28). But, of course, a defendant in the State in which judgment was originally given will be able to rely on these protective provisions only when the Convention has entered into force. Only then will he be able to invoke the Convention to plead lack of jurisdiction.

Although Article 54 was not modelled on the Benelux Treaty, its effect is not very different.

The rules adopted are as follows:

1. The Convention applies to proceedings which are instituted and in which, therefore, judgment is given after the entry into force of the Convention.
2. The Convention does not apply if the proceedings were instituted and judgment given before the entry into force of the Convention.
3. The Convention does apply, but subject to certain reservations, to judgments given after its entry into force in proceedings instituted before its entry into force.

In this case, the court of the State addressed may review the jurisdiction of the court of origin, since the defendant originally had no opportunity to contest that jurisdiction in that court on the basis of the Convention.

Enforcement will be authorized if the jurisdiction of the court of origin:

(i) either was based on a rule which accords with one of the rules of jurisdiction in the Convention; for example, if the defendant was domiciled in the State in which the judgment was given;

(ii) or was based on a multilateral or bilateral convention in force between the State of origin and the State addressed. Thus if, for example, an action relating to a contract were brought in a German court, the judgment given could be recognized and enforced in Belgium if the obligation had been was to be performed in the Federal Republic since the jurisdiction of the German court would founded on Article 3 (1) (5) of the Convention between Germany and Belgium.

If the jurisdiction of the court of origin is founded on one of those bases, the judgment must be recognized and enforced, provided of course that there is no ground for refusal under Article 27 or 28. Recognition will be accorded without any special procedure being required (Article 26); enforcement will be authorized in accordance with the rules of Section 2 of Title III, that is to say, on *ex parte* application.

It follows from Article 54, which provides that the Convention applies only to legal proceedings instituted after its entry into force, that the Convention will have no effect on proceedings in progress at the time of its entry into force. If, for example, before the entry into force of the Convention, proceedings were instituted in France in accordance with Article 14 of the Civil Code against a person domiciled in another Contracting State that person could not plead the Convention for the purpose of contesting the jurisdiction of the French court.

CHAPTER IX: RELATIONSHIP TO OTHER INTERNATIONAL CONVENTIONS

Title VII deals with the relationship between the Convention and other international instruments governing jurisdiction, recognition and the enforcement of judgments. It covers the following matters:

[59] 1. the relationship between the Convention and the bilateral agreements already in force between certain Member States of the Community (Article 55 and 56)[131]:

2. the relationship between the Convention and those international agreements which, in relation to particlar matters, govern or will govern jurisdiction and the recognition or enforcement of judgments (Article 57);

3. the relationship between the Convention and the Convention of 15 June 1869 between France and Switzerland which is the only enforcement convention concluded between a Member State of the EEC and a non-member State to contain rules of direct jurisdiction (Article 58);

131. Mention has been made of the Benelux Treaty although, as it has not been ratified by Luxembourg, it has not yet entered into force; this is to avoid any conflict between the Convention and that Treaty should it enter into force.

4. the relationship between the Convention and any other instruments, whether bilateral or multilateral which may in the future govern the recognition and enforcement of judgments (Article 59).

It was not thought necessary to regulate the relationship between the Convention and the bilateral conventions already concluded between Member States of the EEC and non-member States since, with the exception of the Convention between France and Switzerland, such conventions all contain rules of indirect jurisdiction. There is, therefore, no conflict between those conventions and the rules of jurisdiction laid down in Title II of the Convention. Recognition and enforcement would seem to raise no problem, since judgments given in those non-member States must be recognized in accordance' with the provisions of the bilateral conventions.

Articles 55 and 56

Article 55 contains a list of the Conventions which will be superseded on the entry into force of the EEC Convention. This will, however, be subject to:

1. the provisions of the second paragraph of Article 54, as explained in the commentary on that Article;
2. the provisions of the first paragraph of Article 56 the consequence of which is that these conventions will continue to have effect in relation to matters to which the EEC Convention does not apply (status, legal capacity, etc.);
3. the provisions of the second paragraph of Article 56 concerning the recognition and enforcement of judgments given before the EEC Convention enters into force. Thus a judgment given in France before the EEC Convention enters into force and to which by virtue of Article 54 this Convention would therefore not apply, could be recognized and enforced in Italy after the entry into force of the EEC Convention under the terms of the Convention of 3 June 1930 between France and Italy. Without such a rule, judgments given before the Convention enters into force could be recognized and enforced only in accordance with the general law, and this would in several Contracting States involve the possibility of a review of the substance of the judgment, which would unquestionably be retrograde step.

Article 57

The Member States of the Community, or some of them, are already parties to numerous international agreements which, in relation to particular matters govern jurisdiction or the recognition or enforcement of judgments. Those agreements include the following:

1. The revised Convention for the navigation of the Rhine signed at Mannheim on 17 October 1868[132];
2. The International Convention for the unification of certain rules relating to international carriage by air, and Additional Protocol, signed at Warsaw on 12 October 1929[133];
3. The International Convention on certain rules concerning civil jurisdiction in matters of collision signed at Brussels on 10 May 1952[134];
4. The International Convention relating to the arrest of sea-going ships, signed at Brussels on 10 May 1952[135];
5. The Convention on damage caused by foreign aircraft to third parties on the surface, signed at Rome on 7 October 1952[136];

[60] 6. The International Convention concerning the carriage of goods by rail (CIM), and Annexes, signed at Berne on 25 October 1952[137];

7. The International Convention concerning the carriage of passengers and luggage by rail (CIV) and Annexes, signed at Berne on 25 October 1952[138];
8. The Agreement on German external debts, signed at London on 27 February 1953[138];

132. These Conventions have been ratified by the following Member States of the European Economic Community (list drawn up on 15 September 1966): Belgium, the Federal Republic of Germany, France and the Netherlands.

133. Belgium, the Federal Republic of Germany, France, Italy, Luxembourg and the Netherlands.

134. Belgium and France.

135. Belgium and France.

136. Belgium and Luxembourg.

137. Belgium, the Federal Republic of Germany, France, Luxembourg and the Netherlands.

138. Belgium, the Federal Republic of Germany, France, Luxembourg and the Netherlands.

9. The Convention on civil procedure concluded at The Hague on 1 March 1954[139];
10. The Convention on the contract for the International carriage of goods by road (CMR) and Protocol of Signature, signed at Geneva on 19 May 1956[139];
11. The Convention concerning the recognition and enforcement of decisions relating to maintenance obligations in respect of children, concluded at The Hague on 15 April 1958[140]
12. The Convention on the jurisdiction of the contractual forum in matters relating international sale of goods, concluded at The Hague on 15 April 1958[141];
13. The Convention on third party liability in the field of nuclear energy, signed at Paris on 29 July 1960,[142a] and the Additional Protocol, signed at Paris on 28 January 1964,[142b] the Supplementary Convention to the Paris Convention of 29 July 1960, and Annex, signed at Brussels on 31 January 1963,[142c] and Additional Protocol to the Supplementary Convention signed at Paris on 28 January 1964.[142d]
14. The Convention on the liability of operators of nuclear ships, and Additional Protocol, signed at Brussels on 25 May 1962[143];
15. The Convention of 27 October 1956 between the Grand Duchy of Luxembourg, the Federal Republic of Germany and the French Republic on the canalization of the Moselle.[144]

The structure of these agreements varies considerably. Some of them govern only jurisdiction, like the Warsaw Convention of 12 October 1929 for the unification certain rules relating to international carriage by air, or are based on indirect jurisdiction, like the Hague Convention of 15 April 1958 concerning the recognition and enforcement of decisions relating to maintenance obligations in respect of children, or contain rules of direct or even exclusive jurisdiction such as the International Convention of 25 October 1952 concerning the carriage of goods by rail (CIM), which lays down in Article 43 (5) that actions arising from the contract of carriage may be brought only in the courts of the State to which the defendant railway belongs.

The approach adopted by the Committee means that agreements relating to particular matters prevail over the Convention. It follows that, where those agreements lay down rules of direct or exclusive jurisdiction, the court of the State of origin will have to apply those rules to the exclusion of any others; where they contain provisions concerning the conditions governing the recognition and enforcement of judgments given in matters to which the agreements apply, only those conditions need be satisfied, so that the enforcement procedure set up by the EEC Convention will not apply to those judgments.

The Committee adopted this approach in view of the fact that the Member States of the Community, when they entered into these agreements, had for the most part contracted obligations towards non- Member States which should not be modified without the consent of those States. Moreover, the following points must be borne in mind:

1. The rules of jurisdiction laid down in these agreements have been dictated by particular considerations relating to the matters of which they treat, e. g. the flag or port of registration of a vessel in the maritime conventions; the criterion of domicile is not often used to establish jurisdiction in such agreements.
2. The EEC Convention lays down that judgments are in principle to be recognized, whereas agreements relating to particular matters usually subject the recognition and enforcement of judgments to a certain number of conditions. These conditions may well differ from the grounds for refusal set out in Articles 27 and 28; moreover they usually include a **[61]** requirement, which the Convention has dropped that the court of origin had jurisdiction.
3. The simplified enforcement procedure laid down by the Convention is the counterpart of Title II, the provisions of which will not necessarily have to be observed where the court of the State of origin has to apply another convention. Consequently, where agreements relating to particular matters refer for the enforcement procedure back to the ordinary law of the State in which enforcement is sought, it is that law which must be applied. There is, however, nothing to prevent

139. The six States.
140. Belgium, the Federal Republic of Germany, France, Italy and the Netherlands.
141. Italy.
142. (a) and (b) France and Belgium; (c) and (d) France.
143. Not ratified.
144. Ratified by the three States concerned.

a national legislature from substituting the Convention procedure for its ordinary civil procedure for the enforcement of judgments given in application of agreements governing particular matters.

Article 58

This Article deals only with certain problems of jurisdiction raised by the Convention of 15 June 1869 between France and Switzerland.

Under Article 1 of that Convention, a Swiss national domiciled in France may sue in the French courts a French national domiciled in a third State.

This option, granted by that Convention to Swiss nationals domiciled in France, might, in the absence of Article 58, conflict with the EEC Convention, according to which a defendant domiciled in a Contracting State may be sued in the courts of another Contracting State only in certain defined situations, and in any case not on the basis of rules of exorbitant jurisdiction such as those of Article 14 of the French Civil Code.

Under Article 58, a Swiss national domiciled in France can exercise the option which the Convention between France and Switzerland grants him to sue in France a Frenchman domiciled in another Contracting State without there being any conflict with the EEC Convention, since the jurisdiction of the French Court will be recognized under the terms of Article 58. As a result of this provision, the rights secured by Swiss nationals domiciled in France are safeguarded, and France can continue to honour the obligations which it has entered into with respect to Switzerland. This is, of course, only an option which is granted to Swiss nationals, and there is nothing to prevent them from making use of the other provisions of the EEC Convention.

Article 59

It will be recalled that under Article 3 of the Convention, what are known as the rules of "exorbitant" jurisdiction are no longer to be applied in cases where the defendant is domiciled in the Community, but that under Article 4 they are still fully applicable where the defendant is domiciled outside the Community, and that, in such cases, judgments given by a court whose jurisdiction derives from those rules are to recognized and enforced in the other Contracting States.

It must first be stressed that Article 59 does not reduce the effect of Article 4 of the Convention, for the latter Article does not prevent a State, in an agreement with a third State, from renouncing its rules of exorbitant jurisdiction either in whole or only in certain cases, for example, if the defendant is a national of that third State or if he is domiciled in that State. Each State party to the EEC Convention remains quite free to conclude agreements of this type with third States, just as it is free to amend the provisions of its legislation which contain rules of exorbitant jurisdiction; Article 4 of the Convention imposes no common rule, but merely refers back to the internal law of each State.

The only objective of Article 59 is to lessen the effects within the Community, of judgments given on the basis of rules of exorbitant jurisdiction. Under the combined effect of Articles 59 and 28, recognition or enforcement of a judgment given in a State party to the Convention can be refused in any other Contracting State:

1. where the jurisdiction of the court of origin could only be based on one of the rules of exorbitant jurisdiction specified in the second paragraph of Article 3. It would therefore be no ground for refusal that the court of origin founded its jurisdiction on one of those rules, if it could equally well have founded its jurisdiction on other provisions of its law. For example, a judgment given in France on the basis of Article 14 of the Civil Code could be recognized and enforced if the litigation related to a contract which was to be performed in France;

[62] 2. where a convention on the recognition and enforcement of judgments exists between the State addressed and a third State, under the terms of which judgments given in any other State on the basis of a rule of exorbitant jurisdiction will be neither recognized nor enforced where the defendant was domiciled or habitually resident in the third State. Belgium would thus not be obliged to recognize or enforce a judgment given in France against a person domiciled or habitually resident in Norway where the jurisdiction of the French courts over that person could be based only on Article 14 of the Civil Code since a convention between Belgium and Norway exists under which those two countries undertook not to recognize or enforce such judgments. Article 59 includes a reference not only to the defendant's domicile but also to his habitual residence, since in many non-member States this criterion is in practice equivalent to the concept of domicile as this is understood in the Member States of the Community (see also Article 10 (1)) of the Hague Convention on the recognition, and enforcement of foreign judgments in civil and commercial matters).

As regards the recognition and enforcement of judgments. Article 59 thus opens the way towards regulating the relations between the Member States of the EEC and other States, in particular the increasing number which are members of the Hague Conference. This seemed to justify a slight encroachment on the principle of free movement of judgments.

CHAPTER X: FINAL PROVISIONS

Articles 60 to 62 and 64 to 68

These Articles give rise to no particular comment.

Article 63

Article 63 deals with the accession of new Member States to the European Economic Community.

It is desirable, in the opinion of the Committee, that, in order to be able to fulfil the obligations laid down in Article 220 of the Treaty establishing the European Economic Community, such States should accede to the Convention. The legal systems of such States might however, prevent the acceptance of the Convention as it stands, and negotiations might be necessary. If such were the case, any agreement concluded between the Six and a new Member State should not depart from the basic principles of the Convention. That is why Article 63 provides that the Convention must be taken as a basis for the negotiations, which should be concerned only with such adjustments as are essential for the new Member State to be able to accede to the Convention.

The negotiations with that State would not necessarily have to precede its admission to the Community.

Since the adjustments would be the subject of a special agreement between the Six and the new Member State, it follows from the second paragraph of Article 63 that these negotiations could not be used as an opportunity for the Six to reopen debate on the Convention.

CHAPTER XI: PROTOCOL

Article I

Article I of the Protocol takes account of the special position of the Grand Duchy of Luxembourg. It provides that any person domiciled in Luxembourg who is sued in a court of another Contracting State pursuant to Article 5 (1) (which provides, in matters relating to a contract, that the courts for the place of performance **[63]** of the obligation shall have jurisdiction), may refuse the jurisdiction of those courts. A similar reservation is included in the Benelux Treaty (Protocol, Article I), and it is justified by the particular nature of the economic relations between Belgium and Luxembourg, in consequence of which the greater part of the contractual obligations between persons resident in the two countries are performed or are to be performed Belgium. It follows from Article 5 (1) that a plaintiff domiciled in Belgium could in most cases bring an action in the Belgian courts.

Another characteristic of Luxembourg economic relations is that a large number of the contracts concluded by persons resident in Luxembourg are international contracts. In view of this, it was clearly necessary that agreements conferring jurisdiction which could be invoked against persons domiciled in Luxembourg should be subject to stricter conditions than those of Article 17. The text adopted is based on that of the Benelux Treaty (Article 5 (3)).

Article II

Article II of the Protocol also has its origin in the Benelux Treaty. The latter applies inter alia judgments given in civil matters by criminal courts, and thus puts an end to a controversy between Belgium and the Netherlands on the interpretation of the 1925 Convention between Belgium and the Netherlands. As the report annexed to the Treaty explains,[145] the reluctance of the Netherlands authorities to enforce judgments given by foreign criminal courts in civil claims is due to the fact that a Netherlander charged with a punishable offence committed in foreign country may be obliged to appear in person before the foreign criminal court in order to defend himself even in relation to the civil claim, although the Netherlands does not extradite its nationals. This objection is less pertinent than would appear at first sight under certain systems of law, and in particular in France, Belgium and Luxembourg, the judgment in a criminal case has the force of res judicata in any subsequent civil action.

145. Benelux Treaty: see the commentary on Article 13 and Article II of the Protocol.

In view of this, the subsequent civil action brought against a Netherlander convicted of a criminal offence will inevitably go against him. It is therefore essential that he should be able to conduct his defence during the criminal stage of the proceedings.

For this reason the Convention, like the Benelux Treaty, provides (see the Protocol) that a person domiciled in a Contracting State may arrange for his defence in the criminal courts of any other Contracting State.

Under Article II of the Protocol, that person will enjoy this right even if he does not appear in person and even if the code of criminal procedure of the State in question does not allow him to be represented. However, if the court seised of the matter should specifically order appearance in person, the judgment given without the person concerned having had the opportunity to arrange for his defence, because he did not appear in person, need not be recognized or enforced in the other Contracting States.

This right is, however, accorded by Article II of the Protocol only to persons who are prosecuted for an offence which was not intentionally committed; this includes road accidents.

Article III

This Article is also based on the Benelux Treaty (Article III of the Protocol). It abolishes the levying, in the State in which enforcement is sought, of any charge, duty or fee which is calculated by reference to the value of the matter in issue, and seeks to remedy the distortion resulting from the fact that enforcement gives rise to the levying of fixed fees in certain countries and proportional fees in others. This Article is not concerned with lawyers' fees. In the opinion of the Committee, while it was desirable to abolish proportional fees on enforcement, there was no reason to suppress the fixed charges, duties and fees which are payable, even under the internal laws of the Contracting States, whenever certain procedural acts are performed, and which in some respects can be regarded as fees charged for services rendered to the parties.

Article IV

(See the commentary on Article 20 (2), page 66 *et seq.*)

[64] *Article V*

(See the commentary on Article 6 (2), page 27 *et seq.*

Article VI

This Article relates to the case where legislative amendments to national laws affect either the provisions of the laws mentioned in the Convention as might happen in the case of the provisions specified in the second paragraph of Article 3 or affect the courts listed in Section 2 of Title III. Information on these matters must be passed to the Secretary General of the Council of the European Communities to enable him, in accordance with Article 64 (e), to flotify the other Contracting States.

ANNEX

Committee of experts who drafted the Convention on jurisdiction and the enforcement of judgments civil and commercial matters

CHAIRMAN

Professor A. Bulow	Staatssekretär a.D. im Bundesministerium der Justiz der Bundesrepublik Deutschland
Belgium	
Mr P. Jenard	
Chairman of the Working Party	Directeur au ministere des affaires étrangères et du commerce exterieur
Mr H. Meuleman	Directeur général au ministère de la justice
Mr M. Rouserez	Magistrat délégué au ministère de la justice
Mr Ch. van Reepinghen	Commissaire royal à la réforme judiciaire
Mr E. Krings	Commissaire royal à la réforme judiciaire
Professor R. van der Elst	Avocat, professeur à l'universite libre de Bruxelles
Germany	
Mr H. Arnold	Ministerialrat im Bundesministerium der Justiz

France

Mr J. Baudoin	Sous-directeur des affaires civiles et du sceau – Ministère de la justice
Mr P. Bellet	Premier vice-président du tribunal de grande instance de la Seine
Mr Y. Cotte	Chef de bureau "Droit europeen et international" – Ministere de la justice

Italy

Professor L. Marmo	Consigliere di Corte di cassazione Ministero di grazia e giustizia
Mr Caldarera	Consigliere di Corte di cassazione addetto al servizio del contenzioso diplomatico del ministero degli affari esteri
Mr G. di Blasi	Magistrato, ministero degli affari esteri
Professor R. Miccio	Consigliere di Corte d'appello, ministero di grazia e giustizia

Luxembourg

Mr A. Huss	Procureur général d'Etat
Mr F. Goerens	Avocat général

Netherlands

Mr Th. van Sasse van Ysselt	Directeur, Afdelingschef bij het ministerie van justitie
Mr C. W. Dubbink	Raadsheer in de Hoge raad der Nederlanden

Observers

Benelux Committee on the unification of law

Mrs M. Weser	Member of the Committee

Hague Conference on private international law

Mr M. H. van Hoogstraten	Secretary-General to the Conference
Mr G. Droz	First Secretary to the Permanent Bureau of the Conference

Commission of the European Economic Community – Directorate-General for Competition

Mr W. Hauschild	Head of Division
Miss M. Van Es	Member of Division

THE SCHLOSSER REPORT

Report on the Convention on the Association of the Kingdom of Denmark, Ireland and the United Kingdom of Great Britain and Northern Ireland to the Convention on jurisdiction and the enforcement of judgments in civil and commercial matters and to the Protocol on its interpretation by the Court of Justice

(Signed at Luxembourg, 9 October 1978)

BY PROFESSOR DR PETER SCHLOSSER

of the Chair of German, international and foreign civil procedure, of the general theory of procedure and of civil law at the University of Munich

Pursuant to Article 3 (2) of the Act of Accession of 22 January 1972 a Council working party, convened as a result of a decision taken by the Committee of Permanent Representatives of the Member States, prepared a draft Convention on the accession of the Kingdom of Denmark, Ireland and the United Kingdom of Great Britain and Northern Ireland to the Convention of 27 September 1968 on jurisdiction and the enforcement of judgments in civil and commercial matters and to the Protocol of 3 June 1971 on its interpretation by the Court of Justice. This working party was composed of government experts from the nine Member States and representatives from the Commission. The rapporteur, Mr P. Schlosser, Professor of Law at the University of Munich, drafted the explanatory report which was submitted to the governments at the same time as the draft prepared by the experts. The text of this report, which is a commentary on the Convention of Accession signed at Luxembourg on 9 October 1978, is now being published in this issue of the Official Journal.

INDEX

CHAPTER 1 – PRELIMINARY REMARKS

1. Under Article 3 (2) of the Act of Accession, the new Member States undertook "to accede to the Conventions provided for in Article 220 of the EEC Treaty, and to the Protocols on the interpretation of those Conventions by the Court of Justice, signed by the original Member States and to this end to enter into negotiations with the original Member States in order to make the necessary adjustments thereto". As a first step the Commission of the European Communities made preparations for the impending discussions on the contemplated adjustments. On 29 November 1971, it submitted to the Council an interim report on the additions considered necessary to the two Conventions signed in 1968, namely the Convention on jurisdiction and the enforcement of judgments in civil and commercial matters (hereinafter referred to as "the 1968 Convention') and the Convention on the mutual recognition of companies and legal persons. Following consultations with the new Member States, the Commission on 15 September 1972 drew up a comprehensive report to the Council on the main problems arising from adjusting both Conventions to the legal institutions and systems of the new Member States. On the basis of this report, the Committee of Permanent Representatives decided on 11 October 1972 to set up a Working Party which was to be composed of delegates of the original and the new Member States of the Community and of a representative of the Commission. The Working Party held its inaugural meeting on 16 November 1972 under the chairmanship of the Netherlands delegate in accordance with the rota. On this occasion, it decided to focus its attention initially on negotiations concerning adjustments to the 1968 Convention which had already been ratified by the original Member States of the EEC and to the Protocol of 3 June 1971 on its interpretation ("the Interpretation Protocol of 1971"), and to postpone the work entrusted to it regarding the Convention on the mutual recognition of companies and legal persons. At its second meeting, the Working Party elected the author of this report as its rapporteur. On the basis of a request made by the Working Party at its third meeting in June 1973, the Committee of Permanent Representatives appointed Mr Jenard, the "Directeur d'administration aupres du ministere beige des Affaires Etrangeres", as its permanent chairman.

2. The Working Party initially considered proposing the legal form of a Protocol for the accession of the new Member States to the 1968 Convention, and that the adjustments contemplated should be annexed thereto. However, this method would have introduced some confusion into the subject. A distinction would then have had to be made between three different Protocols, i.e. the Protocol referred to in Article 65 of the 1968 Convention, the Interpretation Protocol of 1971 and the new Protocol on accession. Furthermore, there were no grounds for dividing the new provisions required in consequence of the accession of the new Member States to the 1968 Convention by putting some into a protocol and others into an act of accession annexed to it. The Working Party therefore presented the outcome of its discussions in the form of a draft Convention between the original Member States and the new Member States of the EEC. This draft Convention makes provision for accession both to the 1968 Convention and to the Interpretation Protocol of 1971 (Title I) as well as for the necessary changes to them (Titles II and IV). The accession of Denmark, Ireland and the United Kingdom to the 1968 Convention extends also to the Protocol referred to in Article 65 which is an integral part of the 1968 Convention. The Working Party also proposed adjustments to this Protocol (Title III).

The decision of the Working Party to adopt the legal form of a Convention incorporating adjustments instead of replacing the 1968 Convention by a new Convention has the advantage that the unchanged provisions of the 1968 Convention do not require renewed ratification.

Accordingly three different "Conventions" will in future have to be distinguished:

The Convention on jurisdiction and the enforcement of judgments in civil and commercial matters in its original form will be referred to as "the 1968 Convention".[1]

The expression "Accession Convention" refers to the draft Convention proposed by the Working Party.

After ratification of the Accession Convention certain provisions of the 1968 Convention will exist in an amended form. References in this report to the amended form will be indicated by the addition of that word, e.g. "Article 5 (2) as amended".

CHAPTER 2 – REASONS FOR THE CONVENTION

3. The structure of this report does not closely follow the structure of the proposed new Accession Convention. In many places, this report can only be understood, or at any rate is easier to understand, if it is read in conjunction with the corresponding parts of the reports on the 1968 Convention and on the

Interpretation Protocol of 1971 which were drawn up by the present permanent chairman and erstwhile rapporteur of the Working Party (hereinafter referred to as "the Jenard report"). The structure of this report is based on that of these earlier reports.

4. The second chapter of the Jenard report sets out the reasons for concluding a Convention. They apply with at least as much force to the new Member States as they did to the relationships between the original Member States of the EEC, but they do not call for further close examination here. The obligation on the new Member States to accede to the 1968 Convention is laid down in Article 3 (2) of the Act of Accession to the EEC Treaty. However, in order to give a clear view of the legal position, it may be helpful to supplement the references in the Jenard report to the laws in force in the original Member States of the EEC and to the existing Conventions between these States with details concerning the new Member States.

A

THE LAW IN FORCE IN THE NEW MEMBER STATES

1. United Kingdom

5. The legal position in the United Kingdom is characterized by six significant features.

6. (a) In the first place, there is a distinction between recognition and enforcement at common law on the one hand and under the foreign judgments (reciprocal enforcement) Act 1933 on the other.

At common law, a judgment given in a foreign State may serve as a basis for proceedings before courts in the United Kingdom, if the adjudicating court was competent to assume jurisdiction. This legal consequence follows irrespective of whether or not there is reciprocity. In this connection, recognition and enforceability are not limited to the use of the foreign judgment as evidence. The United Kingdom court dealing with the case may not in general review the substance of the foreign judgment. There are, of course, a limited number of grounds for refusing recognition.

For recognition and enforcement under the Foreign judgments (reciprocal enforcement) Act 1933 on the other hand the successful party does not have to institute fresh proceedings before courts in the United Kingdom on the basis of the foreign judgment. The successful party merely has to have the judgment registered with the appropriate court. However, this simplified recognition and enforcement procedure is available only where the judgment to be recognized was given by a Superior Court, and, more important, where a convention on the reciprocal recognition and enforcement of judgments is in force between the State of origin and the United Kingdom. Once the foreign judgment is registered, it has the same legal force and effect as a judgment given by the court of registration.

7. (b) Both these methods are available in the United Kingdom only for the enforcement of judgments which order payment of a specific sum of money. Consequently maintenance orders made by foreign courts which stipulate periodic payments are not generally enforceable in the United Kingdom. However, the Maintenance orders (reciprocal enforcement) Act which came into force in 1972 makes it possible for international treaty obligations to be concluded in this field.

8. (c) Both at common law and under the 1933 Act, it is a requirement for recognition and enforcement that the judgment should be "final and conclusive between the parties". This requirement is clearly satisfied where the adjudicating court can no longer alter its judgment or can only do so in very exceptional circumstances. Similarly, neither the fact that the period during which an appeal may be made is still running nor even a pending appeal prevent this requirement from being satisfied. However, maintenance orders which stipulate periodic payments are excluded from recognition since they may be varied to take account of changed circumstances unless they are covered by the above mentioned Maintenance orders (reciprocal enforcement) Act 1972.

9. (d) It is possible to institute proceedings on the basis of a foreign judgment or to make an application for its registration under the 1933 Act during a period of six years from the date on which the judgment was given.

10. (e) United Kingdom law distinguishes between the recognition and enforcement of foreign judgments in the same way as the other States of the Community. If a foreign judgment fulfils the common law requirements for its recognition or if it is registered with a United Kingdom court, it becomes effective also in fields other than enforcement. A clear distinction is made between recognition and enforcement of foreign judgments in, for example, the bilateral Conventions with France and Germany.

The requirements mentioned in paragraphs 7 and 9 are not set out in those Conventions as requirements for recognition.

11. (f) Finally, it should be noted that the United Kingdom although not a federal State, is not a single legal and judicial area. It consists of three areas with different legal systems: England and Wales, Scotland and Northern Ireland. Whilst the common law rules described in paragraph 6 apply uniformly to the whole of the United Kingdom, the different judicial systems in each of the three legal areas of this State have to be taken into consideration when the 1933 Act is applied. Applications for registration have to be made in England and Wales to the High Court of Justice, in Scotland to the Court of Session, and in Northern Ireland to the High Court of Justice of Northern Ireland. If registration is granted, the judgment can be enforced only in the area in which the relevant courts have jurisdiction, which extends to the whole of England and Wales, of Scotland or of Northern Ireland respectively (see paragraph 209; for maintenance orders, see paragraphs 210 and 218). Recognition of a judgment is, nevertheless, independent of its registration.

2. Ireland

12. The common law provisions of Irish law are similar to those which apply in the United Kingdom. The only statutory provisions of Irish law on the recognition and enforcement of foreign judgments are contained in the Maintenance orders (reciprocal enforcement) Act 1974. This Act gives effect to an international agreement between Ireland and the United Kingdom for the reciprocal recognition of maintenance orders made by courts in those States. The agreement is expressed to terminate on the coming into force of the 1968 Convention for both States.

3. Denmark

13. Under paragraph 223a of the Law of 11 April 1916, foreign judgments can be recognized only if a treaty providing reciprocity has been concluded with the State of origin, or if binding effect has been given to judgments of a foreign State by Royal Decree. Denmark has concluded no bilateral conventions on recognition and enforcement. There is only one Royal Decree of the type referred to and it concerns judgments given by German courts.[2]

B

EXISTING CONVENTIONS

14. Apart from Conventions relating to particular matters (see paragraph 238 *et seq.*), the United Kingdom is the only new Member State to be bound to other Member States of the EEC by bilateral Conventions on the recognition and enforcement of judgments. These are the Conventions with France, Belgium, the Federal Republic of Germany, Italy and the Netherlands listed in the new version of Article 55 (see paragraph 237). These bilateral Conventions serve to implement the. Foreign judgments (reciprocal enforcement) Act for the United Kingdom (see paragraph 6) and therefore contain provisions which more or less follow the same pattern. The requirements for recognition and enforcement correspond to the criteria mentioned in paragraphs 6 to 11 above. Rules providing for "direct" jurisdiction[3] are not included.

C

GENERAL ARRANGEMENT OF THE PROPOSED ADJUSTMENTS

15. Neither Article 3 (2) of the Act of Accession nor the terms of reference given to the Working Party provide any clear guide of what is meant by "necessary adjustments".

The term could be given a very narrow interpretation. The emphasis would then have to be laid above all on the requirement of necessity, in the sense of indispensability. At the beginning of the Working Party's discussions it became clear, however, that such a narrow view of the contemplated adjustments was bound to make it more difficult for the 1968 Convention to take root in the legal systems of the new Member States. There are a variety of reasons for this.

1. *SPECIAL STRUCTURAL FEATURES OF THE LEGAL SYSTEMS OF THE NEW MEMBER STATES*

16. The 1968 Convention implicitly proceeded from a legal background common to the original Member States of the EEC. By contrast the legal systems of the new Member States unmistakably contain certain special structural features. It would hardly have been reasonable to expect these States to adjust their national law to the legal position on which the 1968 Convention is based.

On the contrary, adjustment of the Convention seemed the more obvious course on occasion. This applies, for example, to the distinction made in Articles 30 and 38 between ordinary and extraordinary appeals (see paragraph 195 *et seq.*), which does not exist in United Kingdom and Irish law, to the system of registering judgments in the United Kingdom instead of the system of granting enforcement orders (see paragraph 208) and to the concept of the trust which is a characteristic feature of the common law[4] (see paragraph 109 *et seq.*). The same also applies to the inter-relation existing in Denmark between judicial and administrative competence in maintenance cases (see paragraph 66 *et seq.*).

2. *AMBIGUITIES IN THE EXISTING TEXT*

17. In certain cases, enquiries about the precise meaning of some provisions of the 1968 Convention by the States obliged to accede to it clearly showed that their interpretation was often uncertain and controversial. The Working Party decided therefore to propose that certain provisions of the 1968 Convention should be given a more precise wording or an authoritative interpretation. This applies, for example, to the provisions about granting legal aid in enforcement proceedings (see paragraph 223). The Working Party also dealt in this way with the provisions of Article 57 on the relation between the 1968 Convention and other Conventions, (see paragraph 238 *et seq.*). In most cases, however, the information requested could be given in a sufficiently clear and uniform way, so that this report need do no more than refer to it.

3. *FURTHER DEVELOPMENTS IN THE LAW OF THE ORIGINAL MEMBER STATES OF THE EEC*

18. In yet other cases, enquiries by the new Member States about the content of some provisions of the 1968 Convention revealed that in the original Member States of the EEC too the law had in the meantime evolved in such a way that general adjustments rather than adjustments restricted to relations with the new Member States seemed advisable. This applies particularly to proceedings in matters of family law in which ancillary relief, and especially maintenance claims, are now often combined with the main proceedings concerning status. In family and matrimonial matters, such combined proceedings have replaced the traditional system of separating status proceedings from subsequent proceedings in many countries during the years following the signing of the 1968 Convention. This is the reason for the revised Article 5 (2) proposed by the Working Party (see paragraphs 32 and 90). The development of consumer protection law in the Member States led to a completely new version of Section 4 of Title II, and in one case the 1968 Convention was amended as a result of judgments of the Court of Justice of the European Communities (see paragraph 179).

4. *SPECIFIC ECONOMIC EFFECTS*

19. Finally, it became apparent that certain provisions of the 1968 Convention in their application to the new Member States would have economic repercussions unequalled in the original Member States. Thus, the worldwide significance of the British insurance market prompted the Working Party to recommend amendments concerning jurisdiction in insurance matters (see paragraph 136). The new paragraph (7) of Article 5 (see paragraph 122) is justified by the special position occupied by British maritime jurisdiction.

CHAPTER 3 – SCOPE OF THE CONVENTION

20. As already discussed in the Jenard report, the provisions governing the scope of the 1968 Convention contain four significant elements. These required some further explanation in the context of the relationship of the original Member States to each other. They are:

1. Limitation to proceedings and judgments on matters involving international legal relationships (I).
2. Duty of the national courts to observe the provisions governing the scope of the 1968 Convention of their own motion (II).
3. Limitation of the Convention to civil and commercial matters (III).
4. A list (Article 1, second paragraph) of matters excluded from the scope of the Convention (IV).

In the relationship of the original Member States to each other there was no problem about a fifth criterion which is much more clearly brought out in the tide of the 1968 Convention than in Article 1 which defines its scope. The 1968 Convention only applies where court proceedings and court decisions are involved. Proceedings and decisions of administrative authorities do not come within the scope of the 1968 Convention. This gave rise to a particular problem of adjustment in relation to Denmark (V).

I. MATTERS INVOLVING INTERNATIONAL LEGAL RELATIONSHIPS

21. The accession of the new Member States to the 1968 Convention in no way affects the application of the principle that only proceedings and judgments about matters involving international legal relationships are affected, so that reference need only be made to Section I of Chapter III of the Jenard report.

II. BINDING NATURE OF THE CONVENTION

22. Under Articles 19 and 20 of the 1968 Convention the provisions concerning "direct jurisdiction" are to be observed by the court of its own motion: in some cases, i.e. where exclusive jurisdiction exists, irrespective of whether the defendant takes any steps; in other cases only where the defendant challenges the jurisdiction. Similarly, a court must also of its own motion consider whether there exists an agreement on jurisdiction which excludes the court's jurisdiction and which is valid in accordance with Article 17.

An obligation to observe the rules of jurisdiction of its own motion is by no means an unusual duty for a court in the original Member States. However, the United Kingdom delegation pointed out that such a provision would mean a fundamental change for its courts. Hitherto United Kingdom courts had been able to reach a decision only on the basis of submissions of fact or law made by the parries. Without infringing this principle, no possibility existed of examining their jurisdiction of their own motion.

However, Article 3 (2) of the Act of Accession cannot be interpreted as requiring the amendment of any provisions of the Conventions referred to on the ground that introduction of those provisions into the legal system of a new Member State would necessitate certain changes in its long established legal practices and procedures.

It does not necessarily follow from Articles 19 and 20 of the 1968 Convention that the courts must, of their own motion, investigate the facts relevant to deciding the question of jurisdiction, that they must for example inquire where the defendant is domiciled. The only essential factor is that uncontested assertions by the parties should not bind the court. For this reason the following rule is reconcilable with the 1968 Convention: a court may assume jurisdiction only if it is completely satisfied of all the facts on which such jurisdiction is based; if it is not so satisfied it can and must request the parties to provide the necessary evidence, in default of which the action will be dismissed as inadmissible. In such circumstances the lack of jurisdiction would be declared by the court of its own motion, and not as a result of a challenge by one of the parties. Whether a court is itself obliged to investigate the facts relevant to jurisdiction, or whether it can, or must, place the burden of proof in this respect on the party interested in the jurisdiction of the court concerned, is determined solely by national law. Indeed some of the legal systems of the original Member States, for example Germany, do not require the court itself to undertake factual investigations in a case of exclusive jurisdiction, even though lack of such jurisdiction has to be considered by the court of its own motion.

III. CIVIL AND COMMERCIAL MATTERS

23. The scope of the 1968 Convention is limited to legal proceedings and judgments which relate to civil and commercial matters. All such proceedings not expressly excluded fall within its scope.

In particular, it is irrelevant whether an action is brought "against" a named defendant (see paragraphs 124 *et seq.*). It is true that in such a case Article 2 *et seq.* cannot operate; but otherwise the 1968 Convention remains applicable.

The distinction between civil and commercial matters on the one hand and matters of public law on the other is well recognized in the legal systems of the original Member States and is, in spite of some important differences, on the whole arrived at on the basis of similar criteria. Thus the term "civil law" also includes certain important special subjects which are not public law, especially, for example, parts of labour law.

For this reason the draftsmen of the original text of the 1968 Convention, and the Jenard report, did not include a definition of civil and commercial matters and merely stated that the 1968 Convention also applies to decisions of criminal and administrative courts, provided they are given in a civil or commercial matter, which occasionally happens. In this last respect, the accession of the three new Member States presents no additional problems. But as regards the main distinction referred to earlier considerable difficulties arise.

In the United Kingdom and Ireland the distinction commonly made in the original EEC States between private law and public law is hardly known. This meant that the problems of adjustment could not be solved simply by a reference to these classifications. In view of the Judgment of the Court of Justice of the European Communities of 14 October 1976,[5] which was delivered during the final stages of the discussions and which decided in favour of an interpretation which made no reference to the "applicable" national law, the Working Party restricted itself to declaring, in Article 1, paragraph 1, that revenue, customs or administrative matters are not civil or commercial matters within the meaning of the Convention. Moreover, the legal practice in the Member States of the Community, including the new Member States, must take account of the above judgment which states that, in interpreting the concept of civil and commercial matters, reference must be made "first, to the objectives and scheme of the Convention and, secondly, to the general principles which stem from the corpus of the national legal systems".

As a result of this all that this report can do is to throw light on the Court's instructions by setting out some details of comparative law.

A

ADMINISTRATIVE LAW IN IRELAND AND THE UNITED KINGDOM

24. In the United Kingdom and in Ireland the expression "civil law" is not a technical term and has more than one meaning. It is used mainly as the opposite of criminal law. Except in this limited sense, no distinction is made between "private" and "public" law which is in any way comparable to that made in the legal systems of the original Member States, where it is of fundamental importance. Constitutional law, administrative law and tax law are all included in "civil law". Admittedly the United Kingdom is already a party to several Conventions which expressly apply only to "civil and commercial matters". These include all the bilateral Conventions on the enforcement of foreign judgments concluded by the United Kingdom. None of these, however, contains any rules which decide the circumstances under which an original court before which an issue is brought may assume jurisdiction. They govern only the recognition and enforcement of judgments and deal with questions of jurisdiction only indirectly as a condition of recognition. Moreover, these Conventions generally only apply to judgments ordering the payment of a specific sum of money (see paragraph 7). In drafting them, a pragmatic approach dispensing with a definition of "civil and commercial matters" proved, therefore, quite adequate.

B

ADMINISTRATIVE LAW IN THE CONTINENTAL MEMBER STATES

25. In the legal systems of the original Member States, the State itself and corporations exercising public functions such as local authorities may become involved in legal transactions in two ways. Having regard to their special functions and the fact that they are formally part of public law they may act outside private law in a "sovereign" capacity. If they do this, their administrative act ("Verwaltungsakt", "décision exécutoire") is of a special nature. The State and some other public corporations may, however, also engage in legal transactions in the same way as private individuals. They can conclude contracts subject to private law, for example with transport undertakings for the carriage of goods or persons in accordance with tariffs generally in force or with a property owner for the lease of premises. The State and public corporations can also incur tortious liability in the same way as private individuals, for example as a result of a traffic accident in which an official car is involved. The real difficulty arises from distinguishing between instances in which the State and its independent organs act in a private law capacity and those in which they act in a public law capacity. A few guidelines on how this difficulty may be overcome are set out below.

The difficulties of finding a dividing line are of three kinds. The field of activities governed by public law differs in the various continental Member States (1). Public authorities frequently have a choice of the form in which they wish to act (2). The position is relatively clear only regarding the legal relations between the State and its independent organs (3).

1. *THE VARYING EXTENT OF PUBLIC LAW*

26. The most important difference between national administrative laws on the continent consists in the legal rules governing the duties of public authorities to provide supplies for themselves and for public tasks. For this purpose the French legal system has established the separate concept of administrative contracts which are governed independently of the "Code civil" by a special law, the "Code des marchés publics". The administrative contract is used both when public authorities wish to cover their own requirements and when public works, such as surface or underground construction, land development, etc., have to be undertaken. In such situations the French State and public corporations do not act in the capacity of private persons. The characteristic result of this is that, if the other parties to the contract do not perform their obligations, the State and public corporations do not have to bring an action before the courts, but may impose unilaterally enforceable sanctions by an administrative act ("decision executoire"). The legal situation in Germany is quite different. There the administrative contract plays a completely subordinate role. Supplies to the administrative agencies, and in particular the placing of contracts for public works, are carried out solely on the basis of private law. Even where the State undertakes large projects like the construction of a dam or the channelling of a river, it concludes its contracts with the firms concerned like a private individual.

2. *CHOICE OF TYPE OF LAW*

27. However, the borderline between the public law and the private law activities of public agencies is not rigidly prescribed in some of the legal systems. Public authorities have, within certain limits, a right to choose whether in carrying out their functions they wish to use the method of a "sovereign act", i.e. an administrative contract, or merely to conclude a private transaction.

In respect of those areas where public authorities may act either under private or public law, it is not always easy to decide whether or not they have acted as private individuals. In practice a clear indication is often lacking.

3. *RELATIONSHIP OF PUBLIC AUTHORITIES TO ONE ANOTHER*

28. Relations between public authorities may also be governed either by private or by public law. If governed by public law, such relations are not subject to the 1968 Convention, even if, as in Italy, they are not considered part of administrative law. However, relations of States and public corporations with each other would fall almost without exception within the sphere of private law, if they contain international aspects (and are not subject to public international law). It is hard to imagine how, for example, it would be possible for relations under public law to exist between two local authorities in different States. However, such relations could, of course, be established in future by treaties.

C

CIVIL AND CRIMINAL LAW

29. The Working Party considered it obvious that criminal proceedings and criminal judgments of all kinds are excluded from the scope of the 1968 Convention, and that this matter needed, therefore, no clarification in the revised text (see paragraph 17). This applies not only to criminal proceedings *stricto sensu*. Other proceedings imposing sanctions for breaches of orders or prohibitions intended to safeguard the public interest also fall outside the scope of civil law. Certain difficulties may arise in some cases in classifying private penalties known to some legal systems like contractual penalty clauses, penalties imposed by associations, etc. Since in many legal systems criminal proceedings may be brought by a private plaintiff, a distinction cannot be made by reference to the party which instituted the proceedings. The decisive factor is whether the penalty is for the benefit of the private plaintiff or some other private individual. Thus the decisions of the Danish industrial courts imposing fines, which are for the benefit of the plaintiff or some other aggrieved party, certainly fall within the scope of the 1968 Convention.

IV. MATTERS EXPRESSLY EXCLUDED

30. The second paragraph of Article 1 sets out under four points the civil matters excluded from the scope of the 1968 Convention. The accession of the new Member States raises problems in respect of all four points.

A

STATUS OR LEGAL CAPACITY OF NATURAL PERSONS, RIGHTS IN PROPERTY ARISING OUT OF A MATRIMONIAL RELATIONSHIP, WILLS AND SUCCESSION

31. The Working Party encountered considerable difficulties when dealing with two problems relating to point (1) of the second paragraph of Article 1. The first problem was that of maintenance proceedings ancillary to status proceedings (1) and the second problem was the meaning of the term "regimes matrimoniaux" (rights in property arising out of a matrimonial relationship) (2). Apart from these two problems, the enquiries directed to the Working Party by the new Member States in respect of point (1) of the second paragraph of Article 1 were relatively easy to answer (3).

1. *MAINTENANCE JUDGMENTS ANCILLARY TO STATUS PROCEEDINGS (ANCILLARY MAINTENANCE JUDGMENTS)*

32. When the 1968 Convention was drawn up, the principle still applied in the original Member States that disputes relating to property could not be combined with status proceedings, nor could maintenance proceedings be combined with proceedings for the dissolution of a marriage or paternity proceedings. It was therefore possible, without running the risk of creating disadvantages caused by artificially separating proceedings which in reality belonged together, to exclude status matters, but not maintenance proceedings, from the scope of the 1968 Convention. Once this rule comes up against national legislation which allows combined proceedings comprising maintenance claims and status matters, it will perforce give rise to great difficulties. These difficulties had already become serious in the original Member States, as soon as the widespread reform of family law had led to an increasing number of combined proceedings in those countries. Accordingly a mere adjustment of the 1968 Convention as between the original and new Member States would have provided only a piecemeal solution. Time and opportunity were ripe for an adjustment of the 1968 Convention, even as regards the relationships between the original Member States, to take account of the developments in the law which had taken place (see paragraph 18).

33. (a) The solution proposed by the Working Party is the outcome of a lengthy and intensive study of the possible alternatives. A distinctive feature of the 1968 Convention is the inter-relation of the application of its rules of jurisdiction at the adjudicating stage and the prohibition against reopening the question of jurisdiction at the recognition stage. Consequently, on the basis of the original text of the Convention only two completely clear-cut solutions present themselves as regards the treatment of ancillary maintenance judgments. The first is that the adjudicating court dealing with a status matter may give an ancillary maintenance judgment only when it has jurisdiction under the 1968 Convention; the maintenance judgment must then be recognized by the foreign court which may not re-examine whether the original adjudicating court had jurisdiction. The second possible solution is that ancillary maintenance judgments should also be excluded from the scope of the 1968 Convention under point (1) of the second paragraph of Article 1 as being ancillary to status judgments. However, both solutions have practical drawbacks. The second would result in ancillary maintenance judgments being generally excluded from recognition and enforcement under the 1968 Convention, even though the great majority of cases are decided by courts which would have had jurisdiction under its provisions. In an unacceptably high number of cases established maintenance claims would then no longer be able to move freely. The first solution would constitute a retrograde step from the progressive and widely acclaimed achievement of combined proceedings and judgments in status and maintenance matters.

34. In view of the above, the simplest solution would have been to include rules of jurisdiction covering status proceedings in the 1968 Convention. However, the reasons given earlier against taking that course are still valid. Therefore, the only way out is to opt for one of the two alternatives outlined above, whilst mitigating its drawbacks as far as possible. In the view of the Working Party, to deprive maintenance judgments ancillary to status proceedings of the guarantee of their enforceability abroad, or to recognize them only to a severely limited extent, would be the greater evil.

35. The Working Party therefore tried first of all to find a solution along the following lines. National courts dealing with status matters should have unrestricted power to decide also on maintenance claims, even when they cannot use their jurisdiction in respect of the maintenance claim on any provision of the 1968 Convention; ancillary maintenance judgments should in principle be recognized and enforced, but the court addressed may, contrary to the principles of the 1968 Convention which would otherwise apply, re-examine whether the court which gave judgment on the maintenance claims had jurisdiction under the provisions of Title II. However, the principle that the jurisdiction of the court of origin should not be re-examined during the recognition and enforcement stages was one of the really decisive

achievements of the 1968 Convention. Any further restriction of this principle, even if limited to one area, would be justifiable only if all other conceivable alternatives were even more unacceptable.

36. The proposed addition to Article 5 would on the whole have most advantages. It prevents maintenance judgments which are ancillary to status judgments being given on the basis of the rule of exorbitant jurisdiction which generally applies in family law matters, namely the rule which declares the nationality of only one of the two parties as sufficient. One can accept that maintenance proceedings may not be combined with status proceedings where the competence of the court concerned is based solely on such exorbitant jurisdiction. For status proceedings, jurisdiction will continue to depend on the nationality of one of the two parties. The maintenance proceedings will have to be brought before another court with jurisdiction under the 1968 Convention.

(b) The significance of the new approach is as follows:

37. It applies uniformly to the original and to the new Member States alike.

38. The jurisdiction of the court of origin may not be re-examined during the recognition and enforcement stages. This still follows from the third paragraph of Article 28 even after the addition made to Article 5. The court of origin has a duty to examine very carefully whether it has jurisdiction under the 1968 Convention, because a wrong decision on the question of jurisdiction cannot be corrected later on.

39. Similar rules apply in respect of *lis pendens*. It was not necessary to amend Articles 21 and 23. As long as the maintenance claim is pending before the court seised of the status proceedings it may not validly be brought before the courts of another State.

40. The question whether the court seised of the status proceedings has indeed jurisdiction also in respect of the maintenance proceedings, without having to rely solely on the nationality of one of the parties to the proceedings, is to be determined solely by the *lex fori*, including of course its private international law and procedural law. Even where the courts of a State may not as a rule combine a status matter with a maintenance claim, but can do so if a foreign legal system applicable under the provisions of their private international law so provides, they have jurisdiction in respect of the maintenance claim under the provisions of Article 5 (2) of the 1968 Convention as amended. This is subject to the proviso that the court concerned in fact had jurisdiction in respect of both the status proceedings and the maintenance claim under the current provisions of its own national law.

41. The 1968 Convention prohibits the assumption of a combined jurisdiction which may be provided for under the national law to cover both status and maintenance proceedings only where the court's jurisdiction would be based solely on the nationality of one of the two parties. This concerns principally the exorbitant jurisdictions which are referred to in the second paragraph of Article 3, and provided for in Article 15 of the Belgian Civil Code (Code civil), and Articles 14 and 15 of the French and Luxembourg Civil Code (Code civil), governing proceedings which do not relate only to status and are therefore not excluded pursuant to point (1) of the second paragraph of Article 1. Maintenance actions combined with status proceedings continue to be permitted, even if the jurisdiction of the court is based on grounds other than those which are normally excluded by the 1968 Convention as being exorbitant. Jurisdiction on the basis of both parties having the same nationality is excluded by the 1968 Convention in respect of ordinary civil and commercial matters (Article 3, second paragraph), but in respect of combined status and maintenance proceedings, it cannot be considered as exorbitant, and consequently should not be inadmissible. The plaintiff's domicile is recognized in any case as a basis for jurisdiction in maintenance actions.

Finally, the proposed addition to Article 5 (2) deprives courts of jurisdiction to entertain maintenance claims in combined family law proceedings only where their jurisdiction in respect of the status proceedings is based solely on the nationality of one of the two parties. Where the jurisdiction of a court depends on the fulfilment of several conditions, only one of which is that one of the parties should possess the nationality of the country concerned, jurisdiction does not depend solely on the nationality of the two parties.

Article 606 (3) of the German Code of Civil Procedure is intended to ensure, in conjunction with Article 606a, that in matrimonial matters a German court always has jurisdiction, even when only one of the spouses is German. The fact that this provision is only supplementary to other provisions governing jurisdiction does not change the fact that jurisdiction may be based solely on the nationality of one of the parties. Once Article 5 (2) of the 1968 Convention comes into force in its amended form maintenance claims can no longer be brought and decided under that particular jurisdiction.

42. Article 5 (2) does not apply where the defendant is not domiciled in a Contracting State, or where maintenance questions can be decided without the procedural requirement of a claim or petition by one spouse against the other (see paragraph 66).

2. *RIGHTS IN PROPERTY ARISING OUT OF A MATRIMONIAL RELATIONSHIP*

43. The exclusion of "rights in property arising out of a matrimonial relationship' from the scope of the Convention (Article 1 second paragraph, point (1)) raises a problem for the United Kingdom and Ireland.

Neither of these countries has an equivalent legal concept, although the expression "matrimonial property" is used in legal literature. In principle, property rights as between spouses are governed by general law. Agreements between spouses regulating their property rights arc no different in law from agreements with third parries. Occasionally, however, there are special statutory provisions affecting the rights of spouses. Under English law (Matrimonial Homes Act 1967) and Irish law (Family Home Protection Act 1976), a spouse is entitled to certain rights of occupation of the matrimonial home. Moreover, divorce courts in the United Kingdom have, under the Matrimonial Causes Act 1973, considerable powers, though varying in extent in the different parts of the country, to order the payment of capital sums by one former spouse to the other. In England even a general redistribution of property as between former spouses and their children is possible.

The concept of "rights in property arising out of a matrimonial relationship" can also give rise to problems in the legal systems of the original Member States. It does not cover the same legal relations in all the systems concerned.

For a better understanding of the problems involved, they arc set out more fully below (a), before the solution proposed by the Working Party is discussed (b).

44. (a) Three observations may give an indication of what is meant by "matrimonial regimes" (rights in property arising out of a matrimonial relationship) in the legal systems of the seven continental Member States. They will deal with the character of the concept which is confined exclusively to relationships between spouses (paragraph 45), with the relationship with the provisions which apply to all marriages irrespective of the particular "matrimonial regime" between the spouses (paragraph 46), and finally with the possibility of third parties becoming involved (paragraph 47).

45. For the purpose of governing the relations between spouses in respect of property, these legal systems do not, or at least not predominantly, employ the legal concepts and institutions otherwise used in their civil law. Instead, they have developed exclusive legal institutions the application of which is limited to relations between spouses, and whose most important feature is a comprehensive set of rules governing property. However, there is not merely one such set of rules in each legal system. Instead, spouses have a choice between several, ranging from general "community of property" to strict "separation of property". Even the latter, when chosen by the spouses, is a special form of 'property regime", although special features arising from marriage can then hardly be said to exist any longer. The choice of a "property regime" must take the form of a 'marriage contract' which is a special legal concept and should not be confused with the conclusion of the marriage itself. If the spouses do not make a choice, one of the sets of rules governing property rights applies to them by law (known as the "statutory matrimonial regime").

In some legal systems (France and Belgium) the "matrimonial regime" existing at the beginning of a marriage can subsequently be changed only in exceptional circumstances. In others (Germany) the spouses are free to alter their "matrimonial regime' at any time.

Disputes concerning "matrimonial regimes' can arise in various forms. There may be a dispute about the existence and interpretation of a marriage contract. In certain circumstances, a spouse may apply to the court for conversion of one "matrimonial regime" into a different one. Some "matrimonial regimes" provide for different rules in respect of different types of property. A dispute may then arise as to the type of property to which a particular object belongs. Where the "matrimonial regime" in question differentiates between the management of different types of property, there may be disagreement as to which spouse may manage which items of property. The most frequent type of dispute relating to "matrimonial regimes" concerns the winding up of the "matrimonial regime" after termination of the marriage, particularly after divorce. The "statutory matrimonial regime" under German law ("Zugewinngemeinschaft" or community of acquisitions) then results in an equalization claim by the spouse whose property has not increased in value to the same extent as that of his partner.

46. Some provisions apply to all marriages, irrespective of the particular "matrimonial regime" under which spouses live, especially in Germany and France. Significantly the German and French texts of the 1968 Convention use the term in the plural ("die Güterstände", "les regimes matrimoniaux").

This can be explained as follows: the Code civil, for instance, deals with property aspects of marriage in two different parts of the code. Title V of the third book (on the acquisition of property) refers in detail to the "contrat de mariage" and then "régimes matrimoniaux", while property aspects of the relations between spouses are also covered by Articles 212 to 226 in Title V of the first book. The new French divorce law of 11 July 1975[6] introduced into the new version of Article 270 et seq. of the Code civil equalization payments normally in the form of lump sum compensation (Article 274) which are independent of the particular "regime" applicable between the spouses. German law in the fourth book of the Bürgerliches Gesetzbuch makes a similar distinction between the legal consequences in respect of property rights which generally follow from marriage (Title V, Article 1353 *et seq.*) and those which follow from "matrimonial property law', which varies according to the various "matrimonial regimes". Under both systems (Article 1357 (2) of the Bürgerliches Gesetzbuch, Article 220 (2) of the French Code civil) it is possible, for example, to prevent a spouse from engaging in certain legal transactions which he is normally entitled to engage in his capacity as spouse. According to Article 285 of the Code civil[7] the court can, after divorce, make orders concerning the matrimonial home irrespective of the "matrimonial regime" previously applicable. Similar possibilities exist in other States.

French legal literature refers to provisions concerning property rights which apply to all marriages as "regime matrimonial primaire". Other legal systems have no such special expression. It is within the spirit of Article 1, second paragraph, point (1) of the 1968 Convention to exclude those provisions concerning property rights affecting all marriages from its scope of application, in so far as they are not covered by the term "maintenance claims" (see paragraph 91 *et seq.*)

In all legal systems of the Community it is possible to conceive of relations affecting rights between spouses which are governed by the general law of contract, law of tort or property law. Some laws contain provisions specifically intended to govern cases where such relations exist between spouses. For example, Article 1595 of the French Code civil contains restrictions on the admissibility of contracts of sale between spouses. Case law has sometimes developed special rules in this field which are designed to take account of the fact that such transactions commonly occur in relations between spouses. All this does not alter the position that legal relations governed by the general law of contract or tort remain subject to the provisions of the 1968 Convention, even if they are between spouses.

47. Finally, legal provisions comprised in the term "matrimonial regimes" are not limited to relations between the spouses themselves. For example, in Italian law, in connection with the liquidation of a "fondo patrimoniale" disputes may arise between parents and children (Article 171 (3) of the Codice civile), which under Italian law unequivocally concern relations arising out of "matrimonial property law" ("il regime patrimoniale delia famiglia"). German law contains the regime of "continued community of property" ("fortgesetzte Gütergemeinschaft"), which forms a link between a surviving spouse and the issue of the marriage.

48. (b) These findings raise problems similar to those with which the Working Party was faced in connection with the concept "civil and commercial matters". It was, however, possible to define the concept of "matrimonial regimes" not only in a negative manner (paragraph 49), but also positively, albeit rather broadly. This should enable implementing legislation in the United Kingdom and Ireland, in reliance on these statements, to indicate to the courts which legal relations form part of "matrimonial regimes" within the meaning of the 1968 Convention (paragraph 50). Consequently no formal adjustment of the 1968 Convention became necessary.

49. As a negative definition, it can be said with certainty that in no legal system do maintenance claims between spouses derive from rules governing "matrimonial regimes'; nor are maintenance claims confined to claims for periodic payments (see paragraph 93).

50. The mutual rights of spouses arising from "matrimonial regimes" correspond largely with what are best described in English as "rights in property arising out of a matrimonial relationship". Apart from maintenance matters property relations between spouses which are governed by the differing legal systems of the original Member States otherwise than as "matrimonial regimes" only seldom give rise to court proceedings with international aspects.

Thus the following can be said in respect of the scope of point (1) of the second paragraph of Article 1 as far as "matrimonial regimes" are concerned:

> The Convention does not apply to the assumption of jurisdiction by United Kingdom and Irish courts, nor to the recognition and enforcement of foreign judgments by those courts, if the subject matter of the proceedings concerns issues which have arisen between spouses, or exceptionally between a spouse and a third party, during or after dissolution of their marriage, and which affect rights in property arising out of the matrimonial relationship. The expression "rights in property" includes all rights of administration and disposal – whether by marriage contract or by statute – of property belonging to the spouses.

3. *THE REMAINING CONTENTS OF ARTICLE 1, SECOND PARAGRAPH, POINT (1) OF THE 1968 CONVENTION*

51. (a) The non-applicability of the 1968 Convention in respect of the statUs or legal capacity of natural persons concerns in particular proceedings and judgments relating to:

- the voidability and nullity of marriages, and judicial separation,
- the dissolution of marriages,
- the death of a person,
- the status and legal capacity of a minor and the legal representation of a person who is mentally ill; the status and legal capacity of a minor also includes judgments on the right to custody after the divorce or legal separation of the parents; this was the Working Party's unanimous reply to the express question put by the Irish delegation,
- the nationality or domicile (see paragraph 71 *et seq.*) of a person,
- the care, custody and control of children, irrespective of whether these are in issue in divorce, guardianship, or other proceedings,
- the adoption of children.

However, the 1968 Convention is only inapplicable when the proceedings are concerned directly with legal consequences arising from these matters. It is not sufficient if the issues raised are merely of a preliminary nature, even if their preliminary nature is, or has been, of some importance in the main proceedings.

52. (b) The expression "wills and succession" covers all claims to testate or intestate succession to an estate. It includes disputes as to the validity or interpretation of the terms of a will setting up a trust, even where the trust takes effect on a date subsequent to the death of the testator. The same applies to proceedings in respect of the application and interpretation of statutory provisions establishing trusts in favour of persons or institutions as a result of a person dying intestate. The 1968 Convention does not, therefore, apply to any disputes concerning the creation, interpretation and administration of trusts arising under the law of succession including wills. On the other hand, disputes concerning the relations of the trustee with persons other than beneficiaries, in other words the "external relations" of the trust, come within the scope of the 1968 Convention (see paragraph 109 *et seq.*)

B. BANKRUPTCY AND SIMILAR PROCEEDINGS

53. Article 1, second paragraph, point (2), occupies a special position among the provisions concerning the legal matters excluded from the 1968 Convention. It was drafted with reference to a special Convention on bankruptcy which was being discussed at the same time as the 1968 Convention.

Leaving aside special bankruptcy rules for very special types of business undertakings, the two Conventions were intended to dovetail almost completely with each other. Consequently, the preliminary draft Convention on bankruptcy, which was first drawn up in 1970, submitted in an amended form in 1975,[8] deliberately adopted the principal terms "bankruptcy", "compositions" and "analogous proceedings"[9] in the provisions concerning its scope in the same way[10] as they were used in the 1968 Convention. To avoid, as far as possible; leaving lacunae between the scope of the two Conventions, efforts are being made in the discussions on the proposed Convention on bankruptcy to enumerate in detail all the principal and secondary proceedings involved[11] and so to eliminate any problems of interpretation. As long as the proposed Convention on bankruptcy has not yet come into force, the application of Article 1, second paragraph, point (2) of the 1968 Convention remains difficult. The problems, including the matters arising from the accession of the new Member States, are of two kinds. First, it is necessary to define what proceedings are meant by bankruptcy, compositions or analogous proceedings as well as their constituent parts (1). Secondly, the legal position in the United Kingdom poses a special problem as the bankruptcy of "incorporated companies" is not a recognized concept in that country (2).

1. *GENERAL AND INDIVIDUAL TYPES OF PROCEEDINGS EXCLUDED FROM THE SCOPE OF THE 1968 CONVENTION*

54. It is relatively easy to define the basic types of proceedings that are subject to bankruptcy law and therefore fall outside the scope of the 1968 Convention. Such proceedings are defined in almost identical terms in both the Jenard and the Noel-Lemontey reports[12] as those

> "which, depending on the system of law involved, are based on the suspension of payments, the insolvency of the debtor or his inability to raise credit, and which involve the judicial authorities for the

purpose either of compulsory and collective liquidation of the assets or simply of supervision by those authorities."

In the legal systems of the original States of the EEC there are only a very few examples of proceedings of this kind, ranging from two (in Germany) to four (Italy and Luxembourg). In its 1975 version (8) the Protocol to the preliminary draft Convention on bankruptcy enumerates the proceedings according to types of proceedings and States concerned. A list is reproduced in Annex I to this report. Naturally, the 1968 Convention does not, a fortiori, cover global insolvency proceedings which do not take place before a court as, for example, can be the case in France when authorization can be withdrawn from an insurance undertaking for reasons of insolvency.

The enumeration in Article 17 of the preliminary draft Convention on bankruptcy cannot, before that Convention has come into force, be used for the interpretation of Article 1, second paragraph, point (2) of the 1968 Convention. Article 17 mentions the kind of proceedings especially closely connected with bankruptcy where the courts of the State where the bankruptcy, proceedings are opened are to have exclusive jurisdiction.

It is not desirable at this stage to prescribe this list, or even an amended list, as binding. Further amendments may well have to be made during the discussions on the Convention on bankruptcy. To prescribe a binding list would cause confusion, even though the list to be included in the Protocol to the Convention on bankruptcy will, after the latter's entry into force, prevail over the 1968 Convention pursuant to Article 57, since it is part of a special Convention. Moreover, the list, as already mentioned, does not include all bankruptcies, compositions and analogous proceedings. For instance, it has become clear during the discussions on the Convention on bankruptcy that the list will not cover insurance undertakings which only undertake direct insurance,[13] without thereby bringing the bankruptcy of such undertakings within the scope of the 1968 Convention. Finally the Working Party was not sure whether all the proceedings included in the list as it stood at the beginning of 1976 could properly be regarded as bankruptcies, compositions or analogous proceedings, before the list formally comes into force. This applied particularly to the proceedings mentioned in connection with the liquidation of companies (see paragraph 57).

2. *BANKRUPTCY LAW AND THE DISSOLUTION OF COMPANIES*

55. As far as dissolution, whether or not by decision of a court, and the capacity to be made bankrupt are concerned, the legal treatment of a partnership[14] established under United Kingdom or Irish law is comparable in every respect to the treatment of companies established under continental legal systems. Companies[15] within the meaning of United Kingdom or Irish law, however, are dealt with in a fundamentally different way. The Bankruptcy Acts do not apply to them,[16] but instead they are subject to the winding-up procedure of the Companies Acts[17]; even if they are not registered companies. Winding-up is not a special bankruptcy procedure, but a legal concept which can take different forms and serves different purposes. A common feature of all winding-up proceedings is a disposal of assets and the distribution of their proceeds amongst the persons entitled thereto with a view of bringing the company to an end. The start of winding-up proceedings corresponds, therefore, to what is understood by "dissolution" on the continent. The dissolution of a company on the other hand is identical with the final result of a liquidation under continental legal systems.

A distinction is made between winding-up by the court, voluntary winding-up and winding-up subject to the supervision of the court. The second kind of winding-up takes place basically without the intervention of the court, either at the instance of the members alone or of the members together with the creditors. Only as a subsidiary measure and exceptionally can the court appoint a liquidator. The third kind of winding-up is only a variation on the second. The court has certain supervisory powers. A winding-up of a company by the court requires an application either by the company or by a creditor which is possible in a number of circumstances of which insolvency is only one. Other grounds for a winding-up include: the number of members falling below the required minimum, failure to commence, or a lengthy suspension of, business and the general ground "that the court is of the opinion that it is just and equitable that the company should be wound up".

56. The legal position outlined has the following consequences for the application of Article 1, second paragraph, point (2), and Article 16 (2) of the 1968 Convention in the Continental (b) and other (a) Member States.:

57. (a) A voluntary winding-up under United Kingdom or Irish law cannot be equated with court proceedings. The same applies to the non-judicial proceedings under Danish law for the dissolution of a

company. Legal disputes incidental to or consequent upon such proceedings are therefore normal civil or commercial disputes and as such are not excluded from the scope of the 1968 Convention. This also applies in the case of a winding-up subject to the supervision of the court. The powers of the court in such a case are not sufficiently clearly defined for the proceedings to be classed as judicial.

A winding-up by the court cannot, of course, be automatically excluded from the scope of the 1968 Convention. For although most proceedings of this kind serve the purpose of the liquidation of an insolvent company, this is not always the case. The Working Party decided to exclude from the scope of the 1968 Convention only those proceedings which are or were based on Section 222 (e) of the British Companies Act[18] or the equivalent provisions in the legislation of Ireland and Northern Ireland. This would, however, involve too narrow a definition of the proceedings to be excluded, as the liquidation of an insolvent company is frequently based on one of the other grounds referred to in Section 222 of the British Companies Act, notably in (a), which states that a special resolution of the members is sufficient to set proceedings in motion. There is no alternative therefore to ascertaining the determining factor in the dissolution in each particular case. The English version of Article 1, second paragraph, point (2), of the 1968 Convention has been worded accordingly. It was not, however, necessary to alter the text of the Convention in the other languages. If a winding-up in the United Kingdom or Ireland is based on a ground other than the insolvency of the company, the court concerned with recognition and enforcement in another Contracting State will have to examine whether the company was not in fact insolvent. Only if it is of the opinion that the company was solvent will the 1968 Convention apply.

56. The legal position outlined has the following consequences for the application of Article 1, second paragraph, point (2), and Article 16 (2) of the 1968 Convention in the Continental (b) and other (a) Member States:

58. Only in that event does the problem arise of whether exclusive jurisdiction exists for the courts at the seat of the company pursuant to Article 16 (2) of the 1968 Convention. In the United Kingdom and Ireland this is the case for proceedings which involve or have involved a solvent company.

The term "dissolution" in Article 16 (2) of the 1968 Convention is not to be understood in the narrow technical sense in which it is used in legal systems on the Continent. It also covers proceedings concerning the liquidation of a company after "dissolution". These include disputes about the amount to be paid out to a member; such proceedings are nothing more than stages on the way towards terminating the legal existence of a company.

59. (b) If a company established under a Continental legal system is dissolved, i.e. enters the stage of liquidation, because it has become insolvent, court proceedings relating to the "dissolution of the company" are only conceivable as disputes concerning the admissibility of, or the mode and manner of conducting, winding-up proceedings. All this is outside the scope of the 1968 Convention. On the other hand, all other proceedings intended to declare or to bring about the dissolution of a company are not the concern of the law of winding-up. It is unnecessary to examine whether the company concerned is solvent or insolvent. It also makes no difference, if bankruptcy law questions arise as a preliminary issue. For instance, when litigation ensues as to whether a company should be dissolved, because a person who allegedly belongs to it has gone bankrupt, the dispute is not about a matter of bankruptcy law, but of a type which falls within the scope of the 1968 Convention. The Convention also applies if, in connection with the dissolution of a company not involving the courts, third parties contend in legal proceedings that they are creditors of the company and consequently entitled to satisfaction out of assets of the company.

C. *SOCIAL SECURITY*

60. Matters relating to social security were expressly excluded from the scope of the 1968 Convention. This was intended to avoid the difficulties which would arise from the fact that in some Member States this area of law comes under public law, whereas in others it is on the border-line between public and private law. Legal proceedings by social security authorities against third parties, for example against wrongdoers, in exercise of rights of action which they have acquired by subrogation or by operation of law, do come within the scope of the 1968 Convention.

D. *ARBITRATION*

61. The United Kingdom requested information on matters regarding the effect of the exclusion of "arbitration" from the scope of the 1968 Convention, which were not dealt with in the Jenard report. Two divergent basic positions which it was not possible to reconcile emerged from the discussion on the

interpretation of the relevant provisions of Article 1, second paragraph, point (4). The point of view expressed principally on behalf of the United Kingdom was that this provision covers all disputes which the parties had effectively agreed should be settled by arbitration, including any secondary disputes connected with the agreed arbitration. The other point of view, defended by the original Member States of the EEC, only regards proceedings before national courts as part of "arbitration" if they refer to arbitration proceedings, whether concluded, in progress or to be started. It was nevertheless agreed that no amendment should be made to the text. The new Member States can deal with this problem of interpretation in their implementing legislation. The Working Party was prepared to accept this conclusion, because all the Member States of the Community, with the exception of Luxembourg and Ireland, had in the meantime become parties to the United Nations Convention of 10 June 1958 on the recognition and enforcement of foreign arbitral awards, and Ireland is willing to give sympathetic consideration to the question of her acceding to it. In any event, the differing basic positions lead to a different result in practice only in one particular instance (see paragraph 62).

1. *DECISIONS OF NATIONAL COURTS ON THE SUBJECT MATTER OF A DISPUTE DESPITE THE EXISTENCE OF AN ARBITRATION AGREEMENT.*

62. If a national court adjudicates on the subject matter of a dispute, because it overlooked an arbitration agreement or considered it inapplicable, can recognition and enforcement of that judgment be refused in another State of the Community on the ground that the arbitration agreement was after all valid and that therefore, pursuant to Article 1, second paragraph, point (4), the judgment falls outside the scope of the 1968 Convention? Only if the first interpretation (see paragraph 61) is accepted can an affirmative answer be given to this question.

In support of the view that this would be the correct course, it is argued that since a court in the State addressed is free, contrary to the view of the court in the State of origin, to regard a dispute as affecting the status of an individual, or the law of succession, or as falling outside the scope of civil law, and therefore as being outside the scope of the 1968 Convention, it must in the same way be free to take the opposite view to that taken by the court of origin and to reject the applicability of the 1968 Convention because arbitration is involved.

Against this, it is contended that the literal meaning of the word "arbitration" itself implies that it cannot extend to every dispute affected by an arbitration agreement; that "arbitration" refers only to arbitration proceedings. Proceedings before national courts would therefore be affected by Article 1, second paragraph, point (4) of the 1968 Convention only if they dealt with arbitration as a main issue and did not have to consider the validity of an arbitration agreement merely as a matter incidental to an examination of the competence of the court of origin to assume jurisdiction. It has been contended that the court in the State addressed can no longer re-open the issue of classification; if the court of the State of origin, in assuming jurisdiction, has taken a certain view as to the applicability of the 1968 Convention, this becomes binding on the court in the State addressed.

2. *OTHER PROCEEDINGS CONNECTED WITH ARBITRATION BEFORE NATIONAL COURTS*

63. (a) The 1968 Convention as such in no way restricts the freedom of the parties to submit disputes to arbitration. This applies even to proceedings for which the 1968 Convention has established exclusive jurisdiction. Nor, of course, does the Convention prevent national legislation from invalidating arbitration agreements affecting disputes for which exclusive jurisdiction exists under national law or pursuant to the 1968 Convention.

64. (b) The 1968 Convention does not cover court proceedings which are ancillary to arbitration proceedings, for example the appointment or dismissal of arbitrators, the fixing of the place of arbitration, the extension of the time limit for making awards or the obtaining of a preliminary ruling on questions of substance as provided for under English law in the procedure known as "statement of a special case" (Section 21 of the Arbitration Act 1950). In the same way a judgment determining whether an arbitration agreement is valid or not, or because it is invalid, ordering the parties not to continue the arbitration proceedings, is not covered by the 1968 Convention.

65. (c) Nor does the 1968 Convention cover proceedings and decisions concerning applications for the revocation, amendment, recognition and enforcement of arbitration awards. This also applies to court decisions incorporating arbitration awards – a common method of recognition under United Kingdom law. If an arbitration award is revoked and the revoking court or another national court itself decides the subject matter in dispute, the 1968 Convention is applicable.

V. JUDICIAL NATURE OF PROCEEDINGS AND JUDGMENTS

66. As between the original Member States, and also as between those States and the United Kingdom and Ireland, the 1968 Convention could and can in one particular respect be based on a surprisingly uniform legal tradition. Almost everywhere the same tasks pertaining to the field of private law are assigned to the courts. The authorities which constitute "courts" can everywhere be recognized easily and with certainty. This is also true in cases where proceedings are being conducted in "court" which are not the result of an action by one party "against" another party (see paragraphs 23 and 124 *et seq.*). The accession of Denmark raised new problems.

Although the Working Party had no difficulty in confirming that the Industrial Court under the Danish Industrial Court Act of 21 April 1964 (Bulletin No 124) was, in spite of its unusual structure, clearly to be considered a court within the meaning of the 1968 Convention, it was more difficult to decide how to classify proceedings in maintenance matters, which, in Denmark, failing an amicable settlement, are almost always held before administrative authorities and terminate with a decision by the latter.

1. *THE LEGAL POSITION IN DENMARK*

This method appeared simpler than attempting to amend a large number of separate provisions of the 1968 Convention.

67. The legal position may be summed up as follows. Maintenance matters are determined as regards the obligation to pay either by agreement or by a court judgment. The amount of the payment and the scale of any necessary modifications arc, however, determined by an authority known as the "Amtmand', which under Danish law is clearly not a court but an administrative authority which in this case plays a judicial role. It is true that decisions given in such proceedings come under The Hague Convention on the recognition and enforcement of decisions relating to maintenance obligations, but this is only because under that Convention the matter does not specifically require a court judgment.

Wherever the 1968 Convention refers to "court" or "judge" it must in the future be taken to include Danish administrative authorities when dealing with maintenance matters (as in Article 2, first paragraph, Article 3, first paragraph, Article 4, first paragraph, Article 5 (2), Article 17, Article 18, Articles 20 to 22, Article 27 (4), Article 28, third paragraph and Article 52). This applies in particular to Article 4, first paragraph, even though in the French, Italian and Dutch texts, unlike the German version, the word "court" does not appear.

2. *ARTICLE Va OF THE PROTOCOL AND ITS EFFECT*

68. There would, however, be an imbalance in the scope of the 1968 Convention, if it excluded maintenance proceedings of the type found in Denmark on the sole ground that they do not take place before courts.

The amendment to the 1968 Convention thus made necessary is contained in the proposal for the adoption of a new Article Va in the Protocol.

This method appeared simpler than attempting to amend a large number of separate provisions of the 1968 Convention.

Wherever the 1968 Convention refers to "court" or "judge" it must in the future be taken to include Danish administrative authorities when dealing with maintenance matters (as in Article 2, first paragraph, Article 3, first paragraph, Article 4, first paragraph, Article 5 (2), Article 17, Article 18, Articles 20 to 22, Article 27 (4), Article 28, third paragraph and Article 52). This applies in particular to Article 4, first paragraph, even though in the French, Italian and Dutch texts unlike the German version, the word "court" does not appear.

Similarly, wherever the 1968 Convention refers to "judgments", the decisions arrived at by the Danish administrative authorities in maintenance matters will in future be included in the legal definition of the term "judgment" contained in Article 25. Its content is extended in this respect by the addition of Article Va to the Protocol, so that it is now to be understood as reading:

> "For the purposes of this Convention, "judgment" means any judgment given by a court or tribunal of a Contracting State including in matters relating to maintenance, the Danish administrative authorities whatever the judgment may be called ...".

CHAPTER 4 – JURISDICTION

A
GENERAL REMARKS

69. In section A of Chapter 4 of his report, Mr Jenard sets out the main ideas underlying the rules of jurisdiction of the 1968 Convention. None of this is affected by the accession of the new Member States. The extent to which three features of the law in the United Kingdom and in Ireland are consistent with the application of the 1968 Convention must, however, be clarified. These features are: the far-reaching jurisdiction of the Superior Courts (1), the concept of domicile (2) and, lastly, the discretionary powers enjoyed by the courts to determine territorial jurisdiction (3).

1. *FIRST INSTANCE JURISDICTION OF THE SUPERIOR COURTS*

70. The Continental Member States of the Community have geographically defined jurisdictions where courts of first instance are competent to give judgments even in the most important civil disputes. There arc many courts of equal status; approximately 50 "Landgerichte" in Germany, and an equal number of "tribunaux de grande instance" in France and "Tribunali" in Italy. Where the 1968 Convention itself lays down both the international and local jurisdiction of the courts, as for example in Articles 5 and 6, jurisdiction is given to only one of the many courts with equal status in a State. There is little room for such a distinction in the judicial systems of Ireland and the United Kingdom in so far as a Superior Court has jurisdiction as a court of first instance.

In Ireland, the High Court is the only court of first instance with unlimited jurisdiction. It can, exceptionally, sit outside Dublin. Nothing in the 1968 Convention precludes this. In addition to the High Court, there is a Circuit Court and a District Court. In respect of these courts too, the expression "the Court" is used in the singular and there is only one Court for the whole country, but each of its judges is permanently assigned to a specific circuit or district. The local jurisdiction laid down in the 1968 Convention means, in the case of Ireland, the judge assigned to a certain "circuit" or "district".

In the United Kingdom three Superior Courts have jurisdiction at first instance: the High Court of Justice for England and Wales, the Outer House of the Court of Session for Scotland and the High Court for Northern Ireland. Each of these courts has, however, exclusive jurisdiction for the entire territory of the relevant part of the United Kingdom (see paragraph 11). Thus the same comments as those made in connection with the territorial jurisdiction of the Irish High Court apply also to each judicial area. The possibility of transferring a case from London to a district registry of the High Court does not mean transfer to another court. Bearing in mind that foreign judgments have to be registered separately in respect of each of the judicial areas of the United Kingdom in order to become enforceable therein (see paragraph 208), the distinction between international and local jurisdiction becomes largely irrelevant in the United Kingdom. The rules in the 1968 Convention governing local jurisdiction are relevant to the Superior Courts of first instance in the United Kingdom only in so far as a distinction has to be made between the courts of England and Wales, Scotland and Northern Ireland. The competence of the other courts (County Courts, Magistrates' Courts, and, in Scotland, the Sheriff Courts) presents no particular problems.

2. *THE CONCEPT OF "DOMICILE" AND THE APPLICATION OF THE CONVENTION*

71. (a) The concept of domicile is of fundamental importance for the 1968 Convention in determining jurisdiction (e.g. Articles 2 to 6, 8, 11, 12 (3), 14, 17 and 32). In the legal systems of the original Member States of the EEC, its meaning differs to some extent. In the Federal Republic of Germany, it expresses a person's connection with a local community within the national territory. In France and Luxembourg, it denotes a person's exact address. In Belgium, for purposes of jurisdiction the term denotes the place where a person is entered in the register of population as having his principal residence (Article 36 of the Code judiciaire). These differences explain why,. in determining a person's domicile, e.g. German law places greater emphasis on the stability of the connection with a specific place than do some of the other legal systems.

Notwithstanding these differences the basic concept of "domicile" is the same in all the legal systems of the original Member States of the EEC, namely the connection of a person with a smaller local unit within the State. This made it possible in Article 52 of the 1968 Convention to leave a more precise definition of the term to the law of the State in which the "domicile" of a person had to be ascertained. It did not lead to an uneven application of the provisions of the 1968 Convention. Clearly, for the purposes of applying them in the original Member States of the Community it is irrelevant whether the concept of domicile refers to a specific address or to a local community.

72. (b) The concept of domicile under the law in Ireland and the United Kingdom differs considerably in several respects from the Continental concept.

First, this concept does not refer to a person's connection with a particular place and even less with a particular residence within a place, but to his having his roots within a territory covered by a particular legal system (see paragraph 11). A person's domicile only indicates whether he comes under the legal system of England and Wales, Scotland, Northern Ireland, or possibly under a foreign legal system. A person's legal connection with a particular place is denoted by the word "residence", not "domicile'. According to United Kingdom law, a person always has one "domicile" and can never have more than" one. At birth a legitimate child acquires the domicile of its father, an illegitimate child that of its mother. A child retains its domicile of its parents throughout its minority.

After it reaches its majority, it may acquire another domicile but for this there are very strict requirements: the usual place of residence must have been transferred to another country – with the intention of keeping it there permanently or at least for an unlimited period.

73. (c) Article 52 of the 1968 Convention does not expressly provide for the linking of the concept of domicile with a particular place or a particular residence, nor does it expressly prohibit it from being connected with a particular national territory. The United Kingdom and Ireland would, consequently, be free to retain their traditional concept of domicile when the jurisdiction of their courts is invoked. The Working Party came to the conclusion that this would lead to a certain imbalance in the application of the 1968 Convention. In certain cases, the courts of the United Kingdom or Ireland could assume jurisdiction on the basis of their rules on the retention of domicile, although by the law of all the other Member States of the Community, such a person would be domiciled at his actual place of residence within their territory.

The Working Party therefore requested the United Kingdom and Ireland to provide in their legislation implementing the 1968 Convention (see paragraph 256), at any rate for the purposes of that Convention, for a concept of domicile which would depart from their traditional rules and would tend to reflect more the concept of "domicile" as understood in the original States of the EEC.

In Article 69 (5) of the Convention for the European patent for the common market which was drawn up concurrently with the Working Party's discussions, the concept of "Wohnsitz" is translated as "residence" and for the meaning of the expression reference is made to Articles 52 and 53 of the 1968 Convention. To prevent confusion, the proposed new Article Vc of the Protocol makes it clear that the concept of "residence" within the meaning of the Community Patent Convention should be ascertained in the same way as the concept of "domicile" in the 1968 Convention.

74. (d) It should be noted that the application of the third paragraph of Article 52 raises the problem of different concepts of domicile, when considering which system of law determines whether a person's domicile depends on that of another person. The relevant factor, in such a case, may be where the dependent person is domiciled. Under United Kingdom private international law, the question whether a person has a dependent domicile is not determined by that person's nationality, but by his domicile in the traditional sense of that concept. The re-definition of "domicile" in connection with the first paragraph of Article 52 in no way affects this.

If a foreigner under age who has settled in England is sued in an English court, that court must take account of the different concepts of domicile. As a first step it must establish where the defendant had his "domicile" before settling in England. This is decided in accordance with the traditional meaning of that concept. The law thus found to be applicable will then determine whether the minor was in a position to acquire a "domicile" in England within the meaning of the 1968 Convention The English court must then ascertain whether the requirements for a "domicile" in the area covered by the English court concerned are satisfied.

75. (e) There is no equivalent in the law of the United Kingdom to the concept of the "seat" of a company in Continental law. In order to achieve the results which under private international law are linked on the continent with the "seat" of a company, the United Kingdom looks to the legal system where the company was incorporated ("law of incorporation", Section 406 of the Companies Act 1948). The "domicile" of a company in the traditional sense of the term (see paragraph 72) is taken to be the judicial area in which it was incorporated. The new Member States of the Community are not obliged to introduce a legal concept which corresponds to that of a company's "seat" within the meaning of the continental legal systems, just as in general they are not obliged to adapt their concept of domicile. However, should the United Kingdom and Ireland not change their law on this point, the result would

again be an imbalance in the application of the 1968 Convention. It would, therefore, be desirable for the United Kingdom to introduce for the purposes of the Convention an appropriate concept in its national legislation such as "domicile of a company", which would correspond more closely to the Continental concept of the "seat" of a company than the present United Kingdom concept of "law of incorporation".

Such a provision would not preclude a company from having a "domicile" in the United Kingdom in accordance with legislation in the United Kingdom and a "seat" in a Continental State in accordance with the legislation of that State. As a result of the second sentence of Article 53, a company is enabled under the laws of several of the original States of the EEC to have a "seat" in more than one State. The problems which might arise from such a sitUation can be overcome by the provisions in the 1968 Convention on lis pendens and related actions (see paragraph 162).

3. *DISCRETIONARY POWERS REGARDING JURISDICTION AND TRANSFER OF PROCEEDINGS*

76. The idea that a national court has discretion in the exercise of its jurisdiction either territorially or as regards the subject matter of a dispute does not generally exist in Continental legal systems. Even where, in the rules relating to jurisdiction, tests of an exceptionally flexible nature are laid down, no room is left for the exercise of any discretionary latitude. It is true that Continental legal systems recognize the power of a court to transfer proceedings from one court to another. Even then the court has no discretion in determining whether or not this power should be exercised. In contrast, the law in the United Kingdom and in Ireland has evolved judicial discretionary powers in certain fields. In some cases, these correspond in practice to legal provisions regarding jurisdiction which are more detailed in the Continental States, while in others they have no counterpart on the Continent. It is therefore difficult to evaluate such powers within the context of the 1968 Convention. A distinction has to be made between the international and national application of this legal concept.

77. (a) In relationships with the courts of other States and also, within the United Kingdom, as between the courts of different judicial areas (see paragraph 11) the doctrine of *forum conveniens* – in Scotland, *forum non conveniens* – is of relevance.

The courts are allowed, although only in very rare and exceptional cases, to disregard the fact that proceedings may already be pending before foreign courts, or courts of another judicial area.

Exceptionally, the courts may refuse to hear or decide a case, if they believe it would be better for the case to be heard before a court having equivalent jurisdiction in another State (or another judicial area) because this would increase the likelihood of an efficient and impartial hearing of the particular case.

There are several special reasons why in practice such discretionary powers are exercised: the strict requirements traditionally imposed by the laws of the United Kingdom and Ireland regarding changes of domicile (see paragraph 72); the rules allowing establishment of jurisdiction by merely serving a writ or originating summons in the territory of the State concerned (see paragraphs 85 and 86); the principles developed particularly strongly in the procedural law of these States requiring directness in the taking of evidence with the consequent restrictions on making use of evidence taken abroad or merely in another judicial area; and finally, the considerable difficulties arising in the application of foreign law by United Kingdom or Irish courts.

78. According to the views of the delegations from the Continental Member States of the Community such possibilities are not open to the courts of those States when, under the 1968 Convention, they have jurisdiction and are asked to adjudicate.

Article 21 expressly prohibits a court from disregarding the fact that proceedings are already pending abroad. For the rest the view was expressed that under the 1968 Convention the Contracting States are not only entitled to exercise jurisdiction in accordance with the provisions laid down in Title 2; they are also obliged to do so. A plaintiff must be sure which court has jurisdiction. He should not have to waste his time and money risking that the court concerned may consider itself less competent than another. In particular, in accordance with the general spirit of the 1968 Convention, the fact that foreign law has to be applied, either generally or in a particular case, should not constitute a sufficient reason for a court to decline jurisdiction. Where the courts of several States have jurisdiction, the plaintiff has deliberately been given a right of choice, which should not be weakened by application of the doctrine of *forum conveniens*. The plaintiff may have chosen another apparently "inappropriate" court from among the competent courts in order to obtain a judgment in the State in which he also wishes to enforce it. Furthermore, the risk of a negative conflict of jurisdiction should not be disregarded: despite the United Kingdom court's decision, the judge on the Continent could likewise decline jurisdiction. The practical reasons in favour of the doctrine of *forum conveniens* will lose considerably in significance, as soon as the 1968 Convention becomes applicable in the United Kingdom and Ireland. The implementing legislation will necessitate not inconsiderable changes in the laws of those States, both in respect of the definition of the concept of domicile (see paragraph 73) and on account of the abolition of jurisdictional competence based merely on service of a writ within the area of the court (see paragraph 86). To correct rules of jurisdiction in a particular case by means of the concept of *forum conveniens* will then be largely unnecessary. After considering these arguments the United Kingdom and Irish delegations did not press for a formal adjustment of the 1968 Convention on this point.

79. (b) A concept similar to the doctrine of *forum conveniens* is also applied within the territory of the State, though the term itself is not used in that context. This may be due to the fact that the same result can be achieved by the device of transferring the case to another court having alternative jurisdiction within the same State or the same legal area (see paragraph 11). The Working Party had to examine to what extent the 1968 Convention restricted such powers of transfer. In this connection certain comments made earlier may be repeated: the powers of the Superior Courts in Ireland or in a judicial area of the United Kingdom (see paragraph 70) to decide as a court of first instance remain unchanged. For the rest, the following applies:

80. (aa) The previous legal position in Ireland and the United Kingdom remains essentially the same. Each court can transfer proceedings to another court, if that court has equivalent jurisdiction and can better deal with the matter. For example, if an action is brought before the High Court, the value of which is unlikely to exceed the amount which limits the jurisdiction of the lower court, the High Court has power to transfer the proceedings to such a court, but it is not obliged to do so. A Circuit Court in Ireland, a County Court or Magistrates' Court in England and a Sheriff Court in Scotland – but not an Irish District Court (see paragraph 70) – may transfer proceedings to another court of the same category or exceptionally to a court of another category, if the location of the evidence or the circumstances for a fair hearing should make such a course desirable in the interest of the parties.

Some Continental legal systems also provide for the possibility, albeit on a much smaller scale, of a judge having discretion to confer jurisdiction on a court which would not otherwise have it. This is the case under, for instance, Article 36 of the German Code of Civil Procedure, if proper proceedings are not possible before the court which originally had jurisdiction. Under Section 356 of the new French Code of Civil Procedure[19] proceedings may be transferred to another court of the same type if a risk of lack of impartiality exists.

81. (bb) The 1968 Convention in no way affects the competence as regards subject matter of the courts of a State. The national legal systems are thus free to provide for the possibility of transfer of cases between courts of different categories.

For the most part, the 1968 Convention does not affect the territorial jurisdiction of the courts within a State, but only their international jurisdiction. This is clearly reflected by the basic rule on jurisdiction contained in Article 2. Unless the jurisdiction of a court where proceedings are instituted against a person domiciled in the United Kingdom or Ireland is derived from a provision of the 1968 Convention which at the same time determines local jurisdiction, as for example Article 5, the 1968 Convention does not prevent a transfer of the proceedings to another court in the same State. Even in respect of exclusive jurisdiction, Article 16 only lays down the international jurisdiction of the courts of a State, and does not prevent a transfer within that State.

Finally, the 1968 Convention does not of course prevent a transfer to the court which actually has local jurisdiction under the Convention. This would occur where both parties agree to the transfer and the requirements for jurisdiction by consent pursuant to Article 17 are satisfied.

The only type of case which remains problematic is where an action is brought before a court in circumstances where the 1968 Convention gives the plaintiff a choice of jurisdiction. An action in tort or a liability insurance claim is brought at the place where the harmful event occurred or a maintenance claim at the domicile of the maintenance creditor. It appears obvious that in special exceptional cases a transfer to another court of the same State must be permitted, when proper proceedings are not possible before the court which would otherwise have jurisdiction. However, the Working Party did not feel justified in incorporating these matters expressly in the 1968 Convention. They could be covered by a rule of interpretation to the effect that the court having local jurisdiction may, in exceptional cases, include the court which is designated as having local jurisdiction by the decision of another court. The courts for the place "where the harmful event occurred" could thus be a neighbouring court designated by another court, if the courts for the place of the harmful event, should be unable to hear the proceedings.

In so far as a court's discretionary powers to confer jurisdiction on other courts and in particular to transfer proceedings to another court are not defined in detail such discretionary powers should, of course, only be used in the spirit of the 1968 Convention, if the latter has determined, not only international but also local jurisdiction. A transfer merely on account of the cost of the proceedings or in order to facilitate the taking of evidence would be possible only with the consent of the plaintiff, who had the choice of jurisdiction.

B

COMMENTS ON THE SECTIONS OF TITLE II

Section 1

General provisions

82. The proposed adjustments to Articles 2[20] to 4 are confined to inserting certain exorbitant jurisdictions in the legal systems of the new Member States into the second paragraph of Article 3. The occasion has been taken to adjust the text of that Article to take account also of an amendment to the law which has been introduced in Belgium. Detailed comments on the proposed alterations (I) precede two more general remarks on the relevance of this provision to the whole structure of the 1968 Convention (II).

I. *Detailed comments*

83. 1. *Belgium*

In Belgium, Articles 52, 52 *bis* and 53 of the law of 25 March 1876 had already been superseded before the coming into force of the 1968 Convention by Articles 635, 637 and 638 of the Judicial Code. Nevertheless only Article 638 of the Judicial Code is mentioned in the second paragraph of Article 3 in its revised version. It corresponds to Article 53 of the law of 25 March 1876 and provides that where Belgian courts do not possess jurisdiction based on other provisions, a plaintiff resident in Belgium may sue any person before the court of his place of residence. The version of Article 3, valid hitherto, erroneously classed the jurisdiction based on Articles 52 and 52 *bis* of the abovementioned law as exorbitant.

84. 2. *Denmark*

The provisions of Danish law included in the second paragraph of Article 3 state that a foreigner may be sued before any Danish court in whose district he is resident or has property when the document instituting the proceedings is served. On this last point the provision corresponds to similar German provisions included in the list of exorbitant jurisdictions. On the first point reference may be made to what follows concerning Ireland (see paragraph 85). There is a separate Code of Civil Procedure for Greenland (see paragraph 253); special reference had therefore to be made to the corresponding provisions affecting that country.

85. 3. *Ireland*

According to the principles of common law which are unwritten and apply equally in the United Kingdom and Ireland, a court has jurisdiction in principle if the plaintiff has been properly served with the court process. The jurisdiction of Irish (and United Kingdom) courts is indirectly restricted to the extent of the limits imposed on the service of a writ of summons. Service is available without special leave only within the territory of Ireland (or the United Kingdom). However, every service validly effected there is sufficient to establish jurisdiction; even a short stay by the defendant in the territory concerned will suffice. Service abroad will be authorized only where certain specified conditions are satisfied. As regards legal relations within the. EEC – especially because of the possibility of free movement of judgments resulting from the 1968 Convention – there is no longer any justification for founding the jurisdiction of a court on the mere temporary presence of a person in the State of the court concerned. This common law jurisdiction, for which of course no statutory enactment can be cited, had therefore to be classed as exorbitant.

86. 4. *United Kingdom*

As regards the United Kingdom it will suffice for point (a) of Article 3, second paragraph, of the 1968 Convention as amended, to refer to what has been said above in the case of Ireland. Points (b) and (c) deal with some characteristic features of Scottish law. To establish jurisdiction merely by service of a writ of summons during the temporary presence of the defendant is a rare, though not totally unknown, practice in Scotland. Scottish courts usually base their jurisdiction in respect of a defendant not permanently resident there on other factors, namely that he has been in Scotland for at least 40 days, or that he owns immovable property in Scotland or that he owns movable property which has been impounded in Scotland. In such cases service on the defendant is also required, but this may be effected by post or, exceptionally, by posting it on the court notice board. In the case of Germany, the 1968 Convention has already classed jurisdiction based solely on the existence of property in Germany as exorbitant. Any jurisdiction based solely on the seizure of property within a country must be treated in the same way.

II. *The relevance of the second paragraph of Article 3 to the whole structure of the 1968 Convention*

87. 1. *The special significance of the second paragraph of Article 3*

The rejection as exorbitant of jurisdictional bases hitherto considered to be important in the new Member States should not, any more than the original version of the second paragraph of Article 3, mislead anyone into thinking that the scope of the first paragraph of Article 3 would thereby be more closely circumscribed. Only particularly extravagant claims to international jurisdiction by the courts of a Member State are expressly underlined. Other rules founding jurisdiction in the national laws of the new Member States are compatible with the 1968 Convention also only to the extent that they do not offend against Article 2 and Articles 4 to 18. Thus, for example, the jurisdiction of English courts in respect of persons domiciled in the Community can no longer be based on the ground that the claim concerns a contract which was concluded in England or is govern ed by English law. On the other hand, the rules on the jurisdiction of English courts in connection with breaches of contract in England or claims connected with the commission or omission of an act in England largely correspond to the provisions in Article 5 (1) to (3).

2. *Impossibility of founding jurisdiction on the location of property*

88. With regard to Germany, Denmark and the United Kingdom the list in the second paragraph of Article 3 contains provisions rejecting jurisdiction derived solely from the existence of property in the territory of the State in which the court is situated. Such jurisdiction cannot be asserted even if the proceedings concern a dispute over rights of ownership, or possession, or the capacity to dispose of the specific property in question. Persons domiciled on the Continent of Europe may not be sued in Scotland, even if the aim of the action is to recover movable property situated or seized there or to determine its ownership. Interpleader actions (England and Wales) and multiple poinding (Scotland) are no longer permissible in the United Kingdom in respect of persons domiciled in another Member State of the Community, in so far as the international jurisdiction of the English or Scottish courts does not result from other provisions of the 1968 Convention. This applies, for example, to actions brought by an auctioneer to establish whether ownership of an article sent to him for disposal belongs to his customer or a third party claiming the article.

There is, however, no reason why United Kingdom legislation should not introduce appropriate measures pursuant to Article 24, to provide protection to persons (such as auctioneers) faced with conflicting legal claims. This might, for instance, take the form of a court order authorizing an article to be temporarily withdrawn from auction.

As regards persons who are domiciled outside the Community, the provisions which hitherto governed the jurisdiction of courts in the new Member States remains unaffected. Even the rules of jurisdiction mentioned in the second paragraph of Article 3 may continue to apply to such persons. Judgments delivered by courts which thus have jurisdiction must also be recognized and enforced in other States of the Community unless one of the exceptions in the new paragraph 5 of Article 27 or in Article 59 as amended applies.

This latter provision is the only one concerning which the list in Article 3, second paragraph is not only of illustrative significance but has direct and restrictive importance. (see paragraph 249).

Section 2

Special jurisdictions[21]

89. In the sphere of special, non-exclusive jurisdictions the problems of adjustment were confined to judicial competence as regards maintenance claims (I), questions raised by trusts in United Kingdom and Irish law (II) and problems in connection with jurisdiction in maritime cases (III). In addition, the Working Party dealt with a few less important individual questions (IV).

Reference should be made here to the judgments of the Court of Justice of the European Communities of 6 October 1976 (12/76; 14/76) and of 30 November 1976 (21/76) which were delivered shortly before or after the end of the negotiations.[22]

I. *Maintenance claims*

90. The need for an adjustment of Article 5 (2) arose because the laws of the new Member States – as was also by then the case with the laws of many of the original States of the EEC – allow status proceedings to be combined with proceedings concerning maintenance claims (see paragraphs 32 to 42). As far as other problems were concerned no formal adjustment was required. However, certain special features of United Kingdom and Irish law give rise to questions of interpretation; the views of the Working Party as to their solutions should be recorded. They concern a more precise definition of the term "maintenance" (1) and how maintenance entitlements are to be adjusted to changed circumstances in accordance with the system of jurisdiction and recognition established by the 1968 Convention (2).

1. *The term "maintenance"*

91. (a) The 1968 Convention refers simply to "maintenance" in Article 5 (2), the only Article which uses the expression. Several legal concepts used within one and the same national legal system can be covered by this term. For example, Italian law speaks of "alimenti" (Article 433 *et seq.* of the codice civile) to indicate payments amongst relations and spouses, but payments after divorce are "assegni"[23]. The new French divorce law,[24] too, does not speak of "aliments", but 'devoir de secours". In addition French legal terminology uses the expressions "devoir d'entretien" and "contribution aux charges du menage". All those are "maintenance" within the meaning of Article 5 (2) of the 1968 Convention.

92. (b) The Article says nothing, however, about the legal basis from which maintenance claims can emanate. The wording differs markedly from that of the Hague Convention of 2 October 1973 on the recognition and enforcement of decisions relating to maintenance obligations. Article 1 of that Convention excludes from its scope maintenance claims arising from tort, contract and the law of succession. However, there is no significant difference regarding the concept of maintenance as used in the two Conventions. The 1968 Convention is in any case not applicable to maintenance claims under the law of succession (second paragraph, point (1) of Article 1). "Maintenance" claims as the legal consequence of a tortious act are, in legal theory, claims for damages, even if the amount of compensation depends on the needs of the injured party. Contracts creating a "maintenance" obligation which previously did not exist are, according to the form employed, gifts, contracts of sale or other contracts for a consideration. Obligations arising therefrom, even where they consist in the payment of "maintenance', are to be treated like other contractual obligations. In such cases Article 5 (1) rather than 5 (2) of the 1968 Convention applies as far as jurisdiction is concerned; the outcome hardly differs from an application of Article 5 (2). "Maintenance" obligations created by contract are generally to be fulfilled at the domicile or habitual residence of the maintenance creditor. Thus actions may also be brought there. Article 5 (2) is applicable, however, where a maintenance contract merely crystallizes an existing maintenance obligation which originated from a family relationship.

Judicial proceedings concerning "maintenance" claims are still civil and commercial matters even where Article 5 (2) is not applicable because the claim arises from a tortious act or a contract.

93. (c) The concept of maintenance does not stipulate that the claim must be for periodic payments. Under Article 1613 (2) of the German Civil Code, for example, the maintenance creditor may in addition to regular payments, claim payment of a lump sum on the ground of exceptional need. Under Article 1615 (e) of the Code a father may agree with his illegitimate child on the payment of a lump sum settlement. Article 5 (4), third sentence, of the Italian divorce law of 1 December 1970 allows divorced spouses to agree on the payment of maintenance in the form of a lump sum settlement. Finally, under Article 285 of the French Civil Code, as amended by the divorce law of 11 July 1975, the French courts can order maintenance in the form of a single capital payment even without the agreement of the spouses. The mere fact that the courts in the United Kingdom have power to order not only periodic payments by one spouse to the other after a divorce, but also the payment of a single lump sum of money, does not therefore prevent the proceedings or a judgment from being treated as a maintenance matter. Even the creation of charges on property and the transfer of property as provided on the Continent, for example in Article 8 of the Italian divorce law, can be in the nature of maintenance.

94. (d) It is difficult to distinguish between claims for maintenance on the one hand and claims for damages and the division of property on the other.

95. (aa) In Continental Europe a motivating factor in assessing the amount of maintenance due to a divorced spouse by his former partner is to compensate an innocent spouse for his loss of matrimonial status. A typical example is contained in Article 301 of the Civil Code in its original form, which still applies in Luxembourg. In its two paragraphs a sharp distinction is drawn in respect of post-matrimonial relations between a claim for maintenance and compensation for material and non-material damages.

Yet material damages generally consist in the loss of the provision of maintenance which the divorced party would have enjoyed as a spouse. Thus the claims deriving from the two paragraphs of Article 301 of the Civil Code overlap in practice, especially since they can both take the form of a pension or a single capital payment. It remains to be seen whether the new French divorce law of 1 July 1975, which makes a clearer distinction between "*prestatiops compensatoires*" and "*devoir de secours*', will change this situation.

Under Section 23 (1) (c) and (f) and Section 27 (6) (c) of the English Matrimonial Causes Act 1973, an English divorce court, too, may order a lump sum to be paid by one divorced spouse to the other or to a child. However, English law, which is characterized by judicial discretionary powers and which does not favour inflexible systematic rules, does not make a distinction as to whether the payments ordered by the Court are intended as damages or as maintenance.

96. (bb) The 1968 Convention is not applicable at all where the payments claimed or ordered are governed by matrimonial property law (see paragraph 45 *et seq.*). Where claims for damages arc involved, Article 5 (2) is not relevant. Whether or not that provision applies depends, in the case of a lump sum payment, solely on whether a payment under family law is in the nature of maintenance.

The maintenance nature of the payment is likely to predominate in relation to children. As between spouses, a division of property or damages may well be the underlying factor. Where both spouses are earning well, payment of a lump sum can only serve the purpose of a division of property or compensation for non-material damage. In that case the obligation to pay is not in the nature of maintenance. If payment is in pursuance of a division of property, the 1968 Convention does not apply at all. If it is to compensate for non-material damage, there is no scope for the application of Article 5 (2). A divorce court may not adjudicate in the matter in either case, unless it has jurisdiction under Article 2 or Article 5 (1).

97. (e) All legal systems have to deal with the problems of how the needs of a person requiring financial support are to be met when the maintenance debtor defaults. Others also liable to provide maintenance, if necessary a public authority, may have to step in temporarily. They, in turn, should be able to obtain a refund of their outlay from the (principal) maintenance debtor. Legal systems have therefore evolved various methods to overcome this problem. Some of them provide for the maintenance claim to be transferred to the payer, thereby giving it a new creditor, but not otherwise changing its nature. Others confer on the payer an independent right to compensation. United Kingdom law makes particular use of the latter method in cases where the Supplementary Benefits Commission has paid maintenance. As already mentioned in the Jenard report[25] claims of this type are covered by the 1968 Convention, even where claims for compensation are based on a payment made by a public authority in accordance with administrative law or under provisions of social security legislation. It is not, however, the purpose of the special rules of jurisdiction in Article 5 (2) to confer jurisdiction in respect of compensation claims on the courts of the domicile of the maintenance creditor or even those of the seat of the public authority whichever of the two abovementioned methods a legal system may have opted for.

2. *Adjustment of maintenance orders*

98. Economic circumstances in general and the particular economic position of those obliged to pay and those entitled to receive maintenance are constantly changing. The need for periodical adjustments of maintenance orders arises particularly in times of creeping inflation.

Jurisdiction to order adjustments depends on the general provisions of the 1968 Convention. Since this is a problem of great practical importance it may be appropriate to preface its discussion in detail with a brief comparative legal survey.

99. (a) Continental legal systems differ according to whether the emphasis of the relevant legal provisions is placed on the concept of an infringement of the principle of finality of a maintenance judgment or more on the concept of an adjustment of the question of the claim (aa). In this respect, as in many others, the provisions of United Kingdom (bb) and Irish (cc) law do not fit into this scheme.

100. (aa) The provisions of German law relating to adjustments of maintenance orders are based on the concept of a special procedural remedy in the nature of a review of the proceedings (Wiederaufnahmeklage).

Since there are no special provisions governing jurisdiction, the general provisions governing jurisdiction in maintenance claims are considered applicable. This means that the original court making the maintenance order may have lost its competence to adjust it. Enforcement authorities, even when they are courts, have no power, either in general or in maintenance cases, to adjust a judgment to changed circumstances. Provisions giving protection against enforcement of a judgment for social reasons apply irrespective of whether or not the amount ordered to be paid in, the judgment is subject to variation. This is also true regarding the subsidiary provision of Article 765 (a) of the Zivilprozeßordnung (Code of Civil Procedure),[26] which is of general application and states that enforcement measures may be rescinded or disallowed in very special circumstances, if they constitute an undue hardship for the debtor.

Accordingly legal theory and case law accept that a foreign maintenance order may be adjusted by a German court, if the latter has jurisdiction.[27]

In the legal systems in the other original Member States of the EEC the problem has always been regarded as one of substantive law and not as a remedy providing protection against enforcement of judicial decisions. Accordingly jurisdiction depends on the general principles applying to maintenance cases.[28] Indirect adjustments cannot be obtained by invoking, as a defence against measures of enforcement, a change in the circumstances which were taken into account in determining the amount of the maintenance.

In general, the 1968 Convention is based on a similar legal position obtaining in all the original Member States: in the case of proceedings for adjustment of a maintenance order the jurisdiction of the court concerned has to be examined afresh.

101. (bb) In the United Kingdom, the most important legal basis for amendment of maintenance orders is Section 53 of the Magistrates' Courts Act of 1952 in conjunction with Sections 8 to 10 of the Matrimonial proceedings (Magistrates' Courts) Act 1960 which will be suspended in 1979 by the Domestic proceedings and Magistrates' Courts Act 1978. According to these Acts, the Court may revoke or vary maintenance orders, or revive them after they have been revoked or varied. In addition, the court in whose district the applicant is now resident also has jurisdiction in such matters.[29] In principle, the court's discretion is unfettered in such cases, but an application for variation may not be based on facts or evidence which could have been relied on when the original order was made.[30] The same applies under Section 31 of the Matrimonial causes Act 1973. A divorce court can vary or discharge an order it has made with regard to maintenance, irrespective of whether the original basis for its jurisdiction still exists or not.

102. To these possibilities must be added another characteristic aspect of the British judicial system. Enforcement of judgments is linked much more closely than on the Continent to the jurisdiction of the particular court which gave the judgment (see paragraph 208). Before a judgment can be enforced by the executive organs of another court, it must be registered with that other court. After registration, it is regarded as a judgment of that court. A further consequence is that, after such registration, the court with which it is registered is empowered to amend it. Hitherto, the United Kingdom has also applied this system in cases where foreign maintenance judgments have been registered with a British court to be enforced in the United Kingdom.[31]

103. (cc) In Ireland the District Court has jurisdiction to make maintenance orders in respect of spouses and children of a marriage and also in respect of illegitimate children. The Court also has power to vary or revoke its maintenance orders. The jurisdiction of the Court is exercised by the judge for the district where either of the parties to the proceedings is ordinarily resident or carries on any profession or occupation or, in the case of illegitimate children, the judge for the district in which the mother of the child resides. A judge who makes a maintenance order loses jurisdiction to vary it if these requirements as to residence, etc., are no longer fulfilled. Apart from the possibility of having a maintenance order varied there is a right of appeal to the Circuit Court from such orders made by the District Court. The Circuit Court also has jurisdiction to make maintenance orders in proceedings relating to the guardianship of infants. It may also vary or revoke its maintenance orders. Its jurisdiction is exercised by the judge for the circuit in which the defendant is ordinarily resident at the date of application for maintenance or at the date of application for a variation of a maintenance order, as the case may be. An appeal lies to the High Court.

The High Court may order maintenance to be paid, including alimony pending suit and permanent alimony following the granting of divorce *a mensa et thoro*. It has jurisdiction to vary its own maintenance orders and appeals against its orders lie to the Supreme Court.

104. (b) Although it nowhere states this expressly, the 1968 Convention is based on the principle that all judgments given in a Member State can be contested in that State by all the legal remedies available under the law of that State, even when the basis on which the competence of the courts of that State was founded no longer exists. In France, a French judgment may be contested by an appeal, appeal in cassation and an application to set aside a conviction, even if the defendant has long since ceased to be domiciled in France. It follows from the obligation of recognition that no Contracting State can claim

jurisdiction with regard to appeals against judgments given in another Contracting State. This also covers proceedings similar to an appeal, such as an action of reduction in Scotland or a "Wiederaufnahmeklage" in Germany. Conversely, every claim to jurisdiction which is not based on proceedings to pursue a remedy by way of appeal must satisfy the provisions of the 1968 Convention. This has three important consequences (see paragraphs 105 to 107) for decisions concerning jurisdiction for the adjustment of maintenance orders. A fourth concerns recognition and enforcement and is mentioned now as a connected matter. (See paragraph 108).

105. On no account may the court of the State addressed examine whether the amount awarded is still appropriate, without having regard to the jurisdiction provisions of the 1968 Convention. If the proceedings are an appeal, the courts of the State of origin will remain competent. Alternatively the new action may be quite distinct from the original proceedings, in which case the jurisdiction provisions of the 1978 Convention must be observed.

106. (bb) Under the legal systems of all six original EEC States, the adjustment of maintenance orders, at any rate as far as jurisdiction is concerned, is not regarded as a remedy by way of appeal (see paragraph 100). Accordingly the courts of the State of origin lose their competence to adjust maintenance orders within the original scope of the 1968 Convention, if the conditions on which their jurisdiction was based no longer exist. The 1968 Convention could not, however, be applied consistently, if the courts in the United Kingdom were to claim jurisdiction to adjust decisions irrespective of the continued existence of the facts on which jurisdiction was originally based.

107. Applications for the adjustment of maintenance claims can only be made in courts with jurisdiction under Article 2 or Article 5 (2), as amended, of the 1968 Convention. For example, if the maintenance creditor claims adjustment due to increases in the cost of living, he may choose between the international jurisdiction of the domicile of the maintenance debtor and the local jurisdiction of the place where he himself is domiciled or habitually resident. However, if the maintenance debtor seeks adjustment because of a deterioration in his financial circumstances, he can only apply under the international jurisdiction referred to in Article 2, i.e. the jurisdiction of the domicile of the maintenance creditor, even where the original judgment (pursuant to Article 2 where it is applicable) was given in the State of his own domicile and the parties have retained their places of residence.

108. If a maintenance debtor wishes effect to be given in another State to an adjusted order, account must be taken of the reversed roles of the parties. Adjustment at the instance of the maintenance debtor can only be aimed at a remission or reduction of the amount of maintenance. Reliance on such a decision in another Contracting State does not therefore involve "enforcement" within the meaning of Sections 2 and 3 of Title III, but rather recognition as referred to in Section 1 of that Title. It is true that the second paragraph of Article 26 makes provision for a special application to obtain recognition of a judgment, and the provisions of Sections 2 and 3 of Title III concerning enforcement are applicable to such an application. If, in these circumstances, recognition is to be granted to a judgment which has been amended on the application of the maintenance debtor, the position is as follows: the applicant within the meaning of Articles 34 and 36 is not the creditor but the debtor, and therefore, according to Article 34, the creditor is the party who is not entitled to make any submissions. The right of appeal of the party against whom enforcement is sought, provided for in Article 36, lies with the creditor in this case. As applicant, the maintenance debtor has the right laid down in the second paragraph of Article 42, read together with the second paragraph of Article 26, to request recognition of part only of an adjusting order. For the application of Article 44 it has to be determined whether, as plaintiff, he was granted legal aid in the original proceedings.

II. *Trusts*

1. *Problems which the Convention in its present form would create regard to trusts*

109. A distinguishing feature of United Kingdom and Irish law is the trust. In these two States it provides the solution to many problems which Continental legal systems overcome in an altogether different way. The basic structure of a trust may be described as the relationship which arises when a person or persons (the trustees) hold rights of any kind for the benefit of one or more persons (the beneficiaries) or for some object permitted by law, in such a way that the real benefit of the property accrues, not to the trustees, but to the beneficiaries (who may, however, include one or more of the trustees) or other object of the trust. Basically two kinds of legal relationships can be distinguished in a trust; they may be defined as the internal relationships and the external relationships.

110. (a) In his external relationships, i.e. in legal dealings with persons who are not beneficiaries of the trust, the trustee acts like any other owner of property. He can dispose of and acquire rights, enter into commitments binding on the trust and acquire rights for its benefit. As far as these acts are concerned no adjustments to the 1968 Convention are necessary. Its provisions on jurisdiction are applicable, as in legal dealings between persons who are not acting as trustees. If a Belgian lessee of property situated in Belgium, but belonging to an English trust, sues to be allowed into occupation, Article 16 (1) is applicable, irrespective of the fact that the property belongs to a trust.

111. (b) Problems arise in connection with the internal relationships of a trust, i.e. as between the trustees themselves, between persons claiming the status of trustees and, above all, between trustees on the one hand and the beneficiaries of a trust on the other. Disputes may occur among a number of persons as to who has been properly appointed as a trustee; among a number of trustees doubts may arise as to the extent of their respective rights to one another; there may be disputes between the trustees and the beneficiaries as to the rights of the latter to or in connection with the trust property, as to whether, for example, the trustee is obliged to hand over assets to a child beneficiary of the trust after the child has attained a certain age. Disputes may also arise between the settlor and other parties involved in the trust.

112. The internal relationships of a trust are not necessarily covered by the 1968 Convention. They are excluded from its scope when the trust deals with one of the matters referred to in the second paragraph of Article 1. Thus as a legal institution the trust plays a significant role in connection with the law of succession. If a trust has been established by a will, disputes arising from the internal relationships arc outside the scope of the 1968 Convention (see paragraph 52). The same applies when a trustee is appointed in bankruptcy proceedings; he would correspond to a liquidator ("Konkursverwalter") in Continental legal systems.

113. Where the 1968 Convention is applicable to the internal relationships of a trust, its provisions on jurisdiction were in their original form not always well adapted to this legal institution. To base jurisdiction on the domicile of the defendant trustee would not be appropriate in trust matters. A trust has no legal personality as such. If, however, an action is brought against a defendant in his capacity as trustee, his domicile would not necessarily be a suitable basis for determining jurisdiction. If a person leaves the United Kingdom to go to Corsica, it is right and proper that, in the absence of any special jurisdiction, claims directed against him personally should be brought only before Corsican courts. If, however, he is a sole or joint trustee or co-trustee of trust property situated in the United Kingdom and hitherto administered there, the beneficiaries and the other trustees cannot be expected to seek redress in a Corsican court.

Moreover, the legal relationships between trustees *inter se*, and between the trustees and the beneficiaries, are not of a contractual nature; in most cases, the trustees are not even authorized to conclude agreements conferring jurisdiction by consent. Jurisdiction for actions arising from the internal relationships of a trust can be based, therefore, neither on Article 5 (1) nor – as a rule – on agreements conferring jurisdiction by consent pursuant to Article 17. To overcome this difficulty simply by amending the 1968 Convention so as to allow a settlor to stipulate which courts are to have jurisdiction would only partly solve the problem. Such an amendment would not include already existing trusts, and the most suitable jurisdiction for possible disputes cannot always be foreseen when creating a trust.

2. *The solution proposed*

114. (a)The solution proposed in the new paragraph(6) of Article 5 is based on the argument that trusts, even though they have no legal personality, may be said to have a geographical centre of operation. This would fulfil functions similar to those fulfilled by the "seat" of business associations without legal personality. It is true that United Kingdom and Irish law have so far provided only a tentative definition of such a central point of a trust. However, the concept of the domicile of a trust is not, at present, unknown in legal practice and theory.[32] In his manual on Private International Law the Scottish Professor Anton gives the following definition[33]:

> "The domicile of a trust is thought to be basically a matter depending upon the wishes of a truster and his expressed intentions will usually be conclusive. In their absence the truster's intentions will be inferred from such circumstances as the administrative centre of the trust, the place of residence of the trustees, the situs of the assets of the trust, the nature of the trust purposes and the place where these are to be fulfilled."

No doubt these notions about the domicile of a trust were developed mainly for the purpose of determining the legal system to be applied, usually either English or Scottish law. The principal characteristics of "domicile" so defined .and some of the factors on which it is based would also justify making it the basis for founding jurisdiction. The proposed new provision does not, strictly speaking, create a special jurisdiction. It covers only a very limited number of cases and is, therefore, added to Article 5 rather than to Article 2. For the non-exclusive character of the new provision see paragraph 118.

115. (b) The following are some detailed comments on the Working Party's proposal (see paragraph 181).

116. The concepts "trust", "trustee" and "domicile" have not been translated into the other Community languages, since they relate to a distinctive feature of United Kingdom and Irish law. However, the Member States can give a more detailed definition of the concept of a trust in their national language in their legislation implementing the Accession Convention.

117. The phrase "created by the operation of a statute, or by a written instrument, or created orally and evidenced in writing" is intended to indicate clearly that the new rules on jurisdiction apply only to cases in which under United Kingdom or Irish law a trust has been expressly constituted, or for which provision is made by Statute. This is important, because these legal systems solve many problems with which Continental systems have to deal in a completely different way, by means of so-called "constructive" or "implied" trusts. Where the latter are involved, the new Article 5 (6) is not applicable, as for instance where, after conclusion of a contract of sale, but prior to the transfer of title, the vendor is treated as holding the property on trust for the purchaser (see paragraph 172). Trusts resulting from the operation of a statutory provision are unlikely to fall within the scope of the 1968 Convention. Since in the United Kingdom, for example, children cannot own real property, a trust in their favour arises by operation of statute, if the circumstances are such that adult persons would have acquired ownership.

118. It should be noted that the new provision is not exclusive. It merely establishes an additional jurisdiction. The trustee who has gone to Corsica (see paragraph 113) can also be sued in the courts there. However, a settlor would be free to stipulate an exclusive jurisdiction (see paragraph 174).

119. If proceedings are brought in a Contracting State, relating to a trust which is subject to a foreign legal system, the question arises as to which law determines the domicile of that trust. The new version of Article 53 proposes the same criterion as that adopted in the 1968 Convention for ascertaining the "seat" of a company. As far as the legal systems of England and Wales, Scotland Northern Ireland and Ireland are concerned, application of this provision should present no serious difficulty. There are at present no rules of private international law in the legal systems of the Continental Member States of the Community for determining the domicile of a trust. The courts of those States will have to evolve such rules to enable them to apply the trust provisions of the 1968 Convention. Two possibilities exist. It could be contended that the domicile of a trust should be determined by the legal system to which the trust is subject. One could, however, also contend that the court concerned should decide the issue in accordance with its own *lex fori* which would have to evolve its own appropriate criteria.

120. In principle, the exclusive jurisdictions provided for by Article 16 take priority over the new Article 5 (6). However, it is not easy to establish the" precise extent of that priority.

In legal disputes arising from internal trust relationships, the legal relations referred to in the provisions in question usually play only an incidental role, if any. The trustee requires court approval for certain acts of management. Even where the management of immovable property is concerned, any such applications to the court do not affect the proprietary rights of the trustee, but only his fiduciary obligations under the trust. Article 16 (1) does not apply. One could, however, envisage a dispute arising between two people as to which of them was trustee of certain property. If one of them instituted proceedings against the other in a German court claiming the cancellation of the entry in the land register showing the defendant as the owner of the property and the substitution of an entry showing the plaintiff as the true owner, there can be no doubt that, under Article 16 (1) or (3), the German court would have exclusive jurisdiction. However, if a declaration is sought that a particular person is a trustee of a particular trust which includes certain property, Article 16 (1) does not become applicable merely because that property includes immovable property.

III. *Admiralty jurisdiction*

121. The exercise of jurisdiction in maritime matters has traditionally played a far greater role in the United Kingdom than in the Continental States of the Community. The scope of the international competence of the courts, as it has been developed in the United Kingdom, has become of worldwide significance for admiralty jurisdiction. This factor is reflected not least in the Brussels Conventions of 1952 and 1957 (see paragraph 238 *et seq.*). It would have been inappropriate to limit the exercise of

admiralty jurisdiction to the basis of jurisdiction included in the 1968 Convention in its original form. If a ship is arrested in a State because of an internationally recognized maritime claim, it would be unreasonable to expect the creditor to seek a decision on his claim before the courts of the shipowner's domicile. For this reason, the Working Party gave lengthy consideration to the possible inclusion of a special section on admiralty jurisdiction in Title II. Article 36 of the Accession Convention is derived from an earlier draft prepared for that purpose (see paragraph 131). Parallel negotiations on Article 57 of the 1968 Convention did, however, lead to a generally acceptable interpretation which will enable States party to a Convention on maritime law to assume jurisdiction on any particular matter dealt with in that Convention, even in respect of persons domiciled in a Community State which is not a party to that Convention (see paragraph 236 *et seq.*). Furthermore, all delegations are in support of a Joint Declaration urging the Community States to accede to the most important of all the Conventions on maritime law, namely the Brussels Convention of 10 May 1952 (see paragraph 238). The Working Party, confident that this Joint Declaration will be adopted and implemented, finally dropped its plans for a section dealing with admiralty jurisdiction. This would also avoid interfering with the general principles of the 1968 Convention, and maintain a clear dividing line between its scope and that of other Conventions.

Two issues remain outstanding, however, since they are not fully covered by the Brussels Conventions of 1952 and 1957: jurisdiction in the event of the arrest of salvaged cargo or freight (the new Article 5 (7)) (1) and actions for limitation of liability in maritime matters (the new Article 6a) (2). Moreover, until Denmark and Ireland accede to the Brussels Arrest Convention of 10 May 1952, transitional provisions had also to be introduced (3). Finally, a particularity affecting only Denmark and Ireland (4) still remained to be settled.

1. *Jurisdiction in connection with the arrest of salvaged cargo or freight*

122. (a) The Brussels Convention of 1952 allows a claimant, inter alia, to invoke the jurisdiction of a State in which a ship has been arrested on account of a salvage claim (Article 7 (1) (b)). Implicit in this provision is a rule of substantive law. A claim to remuneration for salvage entitles

the salvage firm to a maritime lien on the ship. A similar lien in favour of a salvage firm can also exist on the cargo; this can be of some economic importance, if it is the cargo rather than the ship which was salvaged, or if the salvaged ship is so badly damaged that its value is less than the cost of the salvage operation. The value of the cargo of a modern supertanker can amount to a considerable sum. Finally, prior rights can also arise in regard to freight. If freight is payable solely in the event of the safe arrival of the cargo at the place of destination, it is appropriate that the salvage firm should have a prior right to be satisfied out of the claim to freight which was preserved due to the salvage of the cargo.

Accordingly United Kingdom law provides that a salvage firm may apply for the arrest of the salvaged cargo or the freight claim preserved due to its intervention and may also apply to the court concerned for a final decision on its claims to remuneration for salvage. Jurisdiction of this kind is similar in scope to the provisions of Article 7 of the Brussels Convention of 1952. As there is no other Convention on the arrest of salvaged cargo and freight which would remain applicable under Article 57, the United Kingdom would, on acceding to the 1968 Convention, have suffered an unacceptable loss of jurisdiction if a special provision had not been introduced.

123. (b) The proposed solution applies the underlying principle of Article 7 of the Brussels Convention of 1952 to jurisdiction after the arrest of salvaged cargo or freight claims.

Under Article 24 of the 1968 Convention, there is no limitation on national laws with regard to the granting of provisional legal safeguards including arrest. However, they could not provide that arrest, whether authorized or effected, should suffice to found jurisdiction as to the substance of the matter. The exception introduced in Article 5 (7) (a) is confined to arrest to safeguard a salvage claim.

Article 5 (7) (b) introduces an extension of jurisdiction not expressly modelled on the Brussels Convention of 1952. It is a result of practical experience. After salvage operations whether involving a ship, cargo or freight arrest is sometimes ordered, but not actually carried into effect, because bailor other security has been provided. This must be sufficient to confer jurisdiction on the arresting court to decide also on the substance of the matter.

The object of the provision is to confer jurisdiction only with regard to those claims which arc secured by a maritime lien. If the owner of a ship in difficulties has concluded a contract for its salvage, as his contract with the cargo owner frequently obliges him to do, any disputes arising from the former contract will not be governed by this provision.

2. *Jurisdiction to order a limitation of liability*

124. It is not easy to say precisely how the application of Article 57 of the 1968 Convention links up with that of the International Convention of 10 October 1957 relating to the limitation of the liability of owners of seagoing ships[34] (see end of paragraph 128) and with relevant national laws. The latter Convention contains no express provisions directly affecting international jurisdiction or the enforcement of judgments. The Working Party did not consider that it was its task to deal systematically with the issues raised by that Convention and to devise proposals for solving them. It would, however, be particularly unfortunate in certain respects if the jurisdictional lacunae of the 1957 Convention on the limitation of liability were carried over into the 1968 Convention and were supplemented in accordance with the general provisions on jurisdiction of that Convention.

A distinction needs to be drawn between three differing aspects arising in connection with the limitation of liability in matters of maritime law. First, a procedure exists for setting up and allocating the liability fund. Secondly, the entitlement to damages against the shipowner must be judicially determined. Finally, and distinct from both, there is the assessment of limitation of liability regarding a given claim.

The procedural details giving effect to these three aspects vary in the different legal systems of the Community.

125. Under one system, which is followed in particular in the United Kingdom, limitation of liability necessitates an action against one of the claimants – either by way of originating proceedings or, if an action has already been brought against the shipowner, as a counterclaim. The liability fund is set up at the court dealing with the limitation of liability issue, and other claimants must also lodge their claims with the same court.

126. Under the system obtaining in Germany, for example, proceedings for the limitation of liability are started not by means of an action brought against a claimant, but by a simple application which is not directed "against" any person, and which leads to the setting up of the fund.

If the application is successful, all claimants must lodge their claims with that court. If any disputes arise about the validity of any of the claims lodged, they have to be dealt with by special proceedings taking the form of an action by the claimant against the fund administrator, creditor or shipowner contesting the claim. Under this system an independent action by the shipowner against the claimant in connection with limitation of liability is also possible. Such an action leads not to the setting up of a liability fund or to an immediately effective limitation of liability, but merely establishes whether liability is subject to potential limitation, in case of future proceedings to assess the extent of such liability.

127. The new Article 6a does not apply to an action by a claimant against the shipowner, fund administrator or other competing claimants, nor to the collective proceedings for creating and allocating the liability fund, but only to the independent action brought by a shipowner against a claimant (a). Otherwise the present provisions of the 1968 Convention which are relevant to limitation of maritime liability apply (b).

128. (a) The actual or potential limitation of the liability of a shipowner can, however, in all legal systems of the Community be used otherwise than as a defence. If a shipowner anticipates a liability claim, it may be in his interest to take the initiative by asking for a declaration that he has only limited or potentially limited liability for the claim. In that case he can choose from one of the jurisdictions which are competent by virtue of Articles 2 to 6. According to these provisions, he cannot bring an action in the courts of his domicile. Since, however, he could be sued in those courts, it would be desirable also to allow him to have recourse to this jurisdiction. It is the purpose of Article 6a to provide for this. Moreover, apart from the Brussels Convention of 1952, this is the only jurisdiction where the shipowner could reasonably concentrate all actions affecting limitation of his liability. The result for English law (see paragraph 125) is that the fund can be set up and allocated by that same court. In addition, Article 6a makes it clear that proceedings for limitation of liability can also be brought by the shipowner in any other court which has jurisdiction over the claim. It also enables national legislations to give jurisdiction to a court within their territory other than the court which would normally have jurisdiction.

129. (b) For proceedings concerning the validity as such of a claim against a shipowner, Articles 2 to 6 are exclusively applicable.

In addition, Article 22 is always applicable. If proceedings to limit liability have been brought in one State, a court in another State which has before it an application to establish or to limit liability may stay the proceedings or even decline jurisdiction.

130. (c) A clear distinction must be drawn between the question of jurisdiction and the question which substantive law on limitation of liability is to be applied. This need not be the law of the State whose courts have jurisdiction for assessing the limitation of liability. The law applicable for the limitation of liability also defines more precisely the type of case in which limitation of liability can be claimed at all.

131. 3. *Transitional provisions*

All the delegations hope that Denmark and Ireland will accede to the Brussels Convention of 10 May 1952 (see paragraph 121). This will, however, naturally take some time, and it is reasonable to allow a transitional period of three years after the entry into force of the Accession Convention. It would be harsh if, within that period, in the two States concerned jurisdiction in maritime matters were to be limited to what is authorized under the terms of Articles 2 to 6a. Article 36 of the Accession Convention therefore contains transitional provisions in favour of those States. These provisions correspond, apart from variations in the drafting, to the provisions which the Working Party originally proposed to recommend for the special section on maritime law as general rules of jurisdiction regarding the arrest of seagoing ships. In preparing these provisions the Working Party drew heavily, in fact almost exclusively, on the rules of the 1952 Brussels Convention relating to the arrest of seagoing ships (see paragraph 121).

Since they are temporary, the transitional provisions do not merit detailed comments on how they differ from the text of that Convention.

132. 4. *Disputes between a shipmaster and crew members*

The new Article Vb of the Protocol annexed to the 1968 Convention is based on a request by Denmark founded on Danish tradition. This has become part of the Danish Seamen's Law No 420 of 18 June 1973 which states that disputes between a crew member and a shipmaster of a Danish vessel may not be brought before foreign courts. The same principle is also embodied in some consular conventions between Denmark and other States. Following a specific request from the Irish delegation, the scope of this provision has also been extended to Irish ships.

IV. *Other special matters*

133. 1. *Jurisdiction based on the place of performance*

In the course of the negotiations it emerged that the French and Dutch texts of Article 5 (1) were less specific than the German and Italian texts on the question of the designation of the obligation. The former could be misinterpreted as including other contractual obligations than those which were the subject of the legal proceedings in question. The revised versions of the French and Dutch texts should clear up this misunderstanding.[35]

134. 2. *Jurisdiction in matters relating to tort*

Article 5 (3) deals with the special tort jurisdiction. It presupposes that the wrongful act has already been committed and refers to the place where the harmful event has occurred. The legal systems of some States provide for preventive injunctions in matters relating to tort. This applies, for example, in cases where it is desired to prevent the publication of a libel or the sale of goods which have been manufactured or put on the market in breach of the law on patents or industrial property rights. In particular the laws of the United Kingdom and Germany provide for measures of this nature. No doubt Article 24 is applicable when courts have an application for provisional protective measures before them, even if their decision has, in practice, final effect. There is much to be said for the proposition that the courts specified in Article 5 (3) should also have jurisdiction in proceedings whose main object is to prevent the imminent commission of a tort.

135. 3. *Third party proceedings and claims for redress*

In Article 6 (2), the term "third party proceedings" relates to a legal institution which is common to the legal systems of all the original Member States, with the exception of Germany. However, a jurisdictional basis which rests solely on the capacity of a third party to be joined as such in the proceedings cannot exist by itself. It must necessarily be supplemented by legal criteria which determine which parties may in which capacity and for what purpose be joined in legal proceedings. Thus the provisions already existing in, or which may in future be introduced into, the legal systems of the new Member

States with reference to the joining of third parties in legal proceedings, remain unaffected by the 1968 Convention.

Section 3
Jurisdiction in insurance matters

136. The accession of the United Kingdom introduced a totally new dimension to the insurance business as it had been practised hitherto within the European Community. Lloyd's of London has a substantial share of the market in the international insurance of large risks.[36]

In . view of this situation the United Kingdom requested a number of adjustments. Its main argument was that the protection afforded by Articles 7 to 12 was unnecessary for policy-holders domiciled outside the Community (I) or of great economic importance (II). The United Kingdom expressed concern that, without an adjustment of the 1968 Convention, insurers within the Community might be forced to demand higher premiums than their competitors in other States.

There were additional reasons for each particular request for an adjustment. As regards contracts of insurance with policy-holders domiciled outside the Community the United Kingdom sought the unrestricted admissibility of agreements conferring jurisdiction to be vouchsafed so that appropriate steps could be taken with regard to the binding provisions contained in the national laws of many policy-holders insuring with English insurers (I). Requests for adjustments also referred, in conjunction with the other requests for adjustments, to the scope of Articles 9 and 10 which seemed to require clarification (III). Finally there were requests for a few minor adjustments (IV).

The original request of the United Kingdom in respect of the first two problems, namely that the insurance matters in question should be excluded from the scope of Articles 7 to 12 was too far-reaching in view of the general objectives of the 1968 Convention. In particular a number of features of the mandatory rules of jurisdiction, which differ for the various types of insurance, had to be retained (see paragraphs 138, 139 and 143). However, the special structure of the British insurance market had to be taken into account not least so that it would not be driven to resort systematically to arbitration. Although the 1968 Convention does not restrict the possibility of settling disputes by arbitration (see paragraph 63), national law should be careful not to encourage arbitration simply by making proceedings before national courts too complicated and uncertain for the parties. The Working Party therefore endeavoured to extend the possibilities of conferring jurisdiction by consent. For the form of such agreements see paragraph 176.

I. *Insurance contracts taken out by policy-holders domiciled outside the Community*

13 7. As already indicated earlier (see note 36), insurance contracts with policy-holders domiciled outside the Community account for a very large part of the British insurance business. The 1968 Convention does not expressly stipulate to what extent such contracts may provide for jurisdiction by consent. Article 4 applies only to the comparatively rare case where the policy-holder is the defendant in subsequent proceedings. In so far as the jurisdiction of courts outside the Community can be determined by agreement, the general question arises as to what restrictions should be imposed on such agreements having regard to the exclusive jurisdictions provided for by the 1968 Convention (see paragraphs 148, 162 *et seq.*). The main problem in this connection was the jurisdiction under Articles 9 and 10 which, it was thought, could not be excluded. However, this difficulty did not affect insurance contracts only with policy-holders domiciled outside the Community. It also affects, more generally, agreements on jurisdiction which are authorized by Article 12.

In view of the great importance for the United Kingdom of the question of agreements on jurisdiction with policy-holders domiciled outside the Community, it was necessary to incorporate the admissibility in principle of such agreements on jurisdiction expressly in the 1968 Convention. If, therefore, a policy-holder domiciled outside the Community insures a risk in England, exclusive jurisdiction may be conferred by agreement on English courts as well as on the courts of the policy-holder's domicile or others.

This basic rule had however to be limited again in two ways in the new paragraph (4) of Article 12.

138. 1. *Compulsory insurance*

Where a statutory obligation exists to take out insurance no departure from the provisions of Articles 8 to 11 on compulsory insurance can be permitted, even if the policy-holder is domiciled outside the Community. If a person domiciled in Switzerland owns a motor car which is normally based in

Germany, then the car must, under German law, be insured against liability. Such an insurance contract may not contain provisions for jurisdiction by consent concerning accidents occurring in Germany.

The possibility of invoking the jurisdiction of German courts (Article 8) cannot be contractually excluded. This is so even although the relevant German law of 5 April 1965 on compulsory insurance (Bundesgesetzblatt I, page 213) does not expressly prohibit agreements on jurisdiction. However, in practice German law prevents the conclusion of agreements on jurisdiction in the area of compulsory insurance because approval of conditions of insurance containing such a provision would be withheld.

Compulsory insurance exists in the following Member States of the Community for the following articles, installations, activities and occupations, although this list does not claim to be complete:

FEDERAL REPUBLIC OF GERMANY[37]*:*

1. Federal

Liability insurance compulsory for owners of motor vehicles, airline companies, hunters, owners of nuclear installations and handling of nuclear combustible materials and other radioactive materials, road haulage, accountants and tax advisers, security firms, those responsible for schools for nursing, infant and child care and midwifery, automobile experts, notaries' professional organizations, those responsible for development aid, exhibitors, pharmaceutical firms;

Life insurance for master chimney sweeps;

Accident insurance for airline companies and usufructuaries;

Fire insurance for owners of buildings which are subject to a charge, usufructuaries, warehouse occupiers, pawnbrokers;

Goods insurance for pawnbrokers;

Pension funds for theatres, cultural orchestras, district master chimney sweeps, supplementary pension funds for the public service.

2. Länder

There is no uniformity as between the Länder of the Federal Republic of Germany, but there is in particular compulsory fire insurance for buildings, compulsory pension funds for agricultural workers, the liberal professions (doctors, chemists, architects notaries) and (in Bavaria, for example) members of the Honourable Company of Chimney Sweeps and for example, a supplementary pension fund for workers in the Free and Hanseatic City of Bremen. In Bavaria there is compulsory insurance for livestock intended for slaughter.

BELGIUM:
Motor vehicles, hunting, nuclear installations, accidents at work, transport accidents (for paying transport by motor vehicles).

DENMARK:
Motor vehicles, dogs, nuclear installations, accountants.

FRANCE:
Operators of ships and nuclear installations, sand motor vehicles, operators of cable-cars, chair-lifts and other such mechanical units, hunting, estate agents, managers of property, syndics of co-owners, business managers, operators of sports centres, accountants, agricultUral mutual assistance schemes, legal advisers, physical education establishments and pupils, operators of dance halls, managers of pharmacists' shops in the form of a private limited liability company (S.il.r.\.), blood transfusion centres, architects, motor vehicle experts, farmers.

LUXEMBOURG:
Motor vehicles, hunting and hunting organizations, hotel establishments, nuclear installations, fire and theft insurance for hotel establishments;

Insurance against the seizure of livestock in slaughterhouses.

NETHERLANDS:
Motor vehicles, nuclear installations, tankers.

UNITED KINGDOM:
Third party liability in respect of motor vehicles;
Employers' liability in respect of work;
Insurance of nuclear installations;
Insurance of British registered ships against oil pollution;
Compulsory insurance scheme for a number of professions, e.g. solicitors and insurance brokers.

139. 2. *Insurance of immovable property*

The second exception referred to at the end of paragraph 137 is particularly designed to ensure that Article 9 continues to apply even when the policy-holder is domiciled outside the Community. However, this exception has further implications. It prohibits jurisdiction agreements conferring exclusive jurisdiction on the courts mentioned in Article 9. This applies even where the national law of the State in which the immovable property is situated allows agreements conferring jurisdiction in such circumstances.

II. *Insurance of large risks, in particular marine and aviation insurance*

140. The United Kingdom's request for special rules for the insurance of large risks was probably the most difficult problem for the Working Party. The request was based on the realization that the concept of social protection underlying a restriction on the admissibility of provisions conferring jurisdiction in insurance matters is no longer justified where the policy-holders are powerful undertakings. The problem was one of finding a suitable demarcation line. Discussions on the second Directive on insurance had already revealed the impossibility of taking as criteria abstract, general factors like company capital or turnover. The only solution was to examine which types of insurance contracts were in general concluded only by policy-holders who did not require social protection. On this basis, special treatment could not be conceded to industrial insurance as a whole.

Accordingly, the Working Party directed its attention to the various classes of insurance connected with the transport industry. In this area there is an additional justification for special treatment for agreements on jurisdiction: the risks insured are highly mobile and insurance policies tend to change hands several times in quick succession. This leads to uncertainty as to which courts will have jurisdiction and the difficulties in calculating risks are thereby greatly increased. On the other hand, there are here, too, certain areas requiring social protection. Particular complications were caused by the fact that there is a well integrated insurance market for the transport industry. The various types of risk for different means of transport are usually covered under one single policy. The British insurance industry in particular has developed standard policies which only require for their completion a notification by the insured that the means of transport (which can be of many different types) have set off.

The result of a consideration of all these matters is the solution which figures in the new paragraph (5) of Article 12, as supplemented by Article 12a: agreements on jurisdiction are in principle to be given special treatment in marine insurance and in some sectors of aviation insurance. In the case of insurance of transport by land alone no exceptional rules of any kind appeared justified.

In order to avoid difficulties and differences of interpretation, a list had to be drawn up of the types of policy for which the admissibility of agreements on jurisdiction was to be extended. The idea of referring for this purpose to the list of classes of insurance appearing in the Annex to the First Council Directive of 24 July 1973 (73/239/EEC) proved inadequate. The classification used there took account of the requirements of State administration of insurance, and was not directed towards a fair balancing of private insurance interests. There was thus no alternative but to draw up a separate list for the purposes of the 1968 Convention. The following comments apply to the list and the classes of insurance not included in it.

141. 1. *Article 12 a (1) (a)*

This provision applies only to hull insurance and not to liability insurance. The term "seagoing ships" means all vessels intended to travel on the sea. This includes not only ships in the traditional sense of the word but also hovercraft, hydrofoils, barges and lighters used at sea. It also covers floating apparatus which cannot move under its own power, e.g. oil exploration and extraction installations which are moved about on water. Installations firmly moored or to be moored on the seabed are in any event expressly included in the text of the provision. The provision also covers ships in the course of construction, but only in so far as the damage is the result of a maritime risk. This is damage caused by the fact that the ship is on the water and not therefore, damage which occurs in dry-dock or in the workshops of shipyards.

142. 2. *Article 12a (1) (b)*

In the same way as (1) (a) covers the value of the hull of a ship or of an aeroplane, (1) (b) covers the value of goods destroyed or lost in transit, but not liability insurance for any loss or damage caused by those goods. The most important single decision taken on the provision was the addition of the words "consists of or includes". The reason for this is that goods in transit are frequently not conveyed by the same means of transport right to their final destination. There may be a sequence of journeys by land, sea and air. There would be unwarranted complications for the insurance industry in drafting policies and settling claims, if a fine distinction had always to be drawn as to the section of transit in which loss or damage had occurred. Moreover it is often impossible to ascertain this. One has only to think of container transport to realize how easily a loss may be dis.covered only at the destination. Practical considerations therefore required that agreements on jurisdiction be permitted, even where goods are carried by sea or by air for only part of their journey. Even if it can be proved that the loss occurred in the course of transport on land, agreements on jurisdiction permitted by the new paragraph (5) of Article 12 remain effective. The provision applies even if the shipment does not cross any national border.

143. The exception in respect of injury to passengers and loss of or damage to their baggage, which is repeated in Article 12a (2) (a) and (b), is justified by the fact that such persons as a group tend to have a weaker economic position and less bargaining power.

144. 3. *Article 12a (2) (a)*

Whether these provisions also cover all liability arising in connection with the construction, modification and repair. of a ship; whether therefore the provision includes all liability which the shipyard incurs towards third parties and which was caused by the ship; or whether the expression "use or operation" has to be construed more narrowly as applying only to liability arising in the course of a trial voyage – all these are questions of interpretation which still await an answer. The exception for compulsory aircraft insurance is intended to leave the Member States free to provide for such protection as they consider necessary for the policy-holder and for the victim.

145. 4. *Article 12a (2) (b)*

As there is no reason to treat combined transport any differently for liability insurance than for hull insurance, it is equally irrelevant during which section of the transport the circumstances causing the liability occurred (see paragraphs 142 and 143).

146. 5. *Article 12a (3)*

The most important application of this provision is stated in the text itself. In the absence of a provision to the contrary in the charter party, an air crash would cause the carrier to lose his entitlement to freight and the owner his charter-fee from the charterer. Another example might be loss caused by the late arrival of a ship. For the rest the notion is the same as that used in Directive 73/239/EEC.

147. 6. *Article 12a (4)*

Insurance against ancillary risks is a familiar practice, especially in United Kingdom insurance contracts. An example would be "shipowner's disbursements" consisting of exceptional operational costs, e.g. harbour dues accruing whilst a ship remains disabled. Another example is insurance against "increased value", providing protection against loss arising from the fact that a destroyed or damaged cargo had increased in value during transit.

The provision does not require an ancillary risk to be insured under the same policy as the main risk to which it relates. The Working Party therefore deliberately opted for a somewhat different wording from that in Directive 73/239/EEC for the "ancillary risks" referred to in that Directive. The definition in that Directive could not be used since it is concerned with a different subject, the authorization of insurance undertakings.

148. III. *The remaining scope of Articles 9 and 10*

The revised text of Article 12, like the original text, does not expressly deal with the effect of agreements on jurisdiction or the special jurisdictions for insurance matters set out in Section 3. Nevertheless, the legal position is clear from the systematic construction of Section 3 of the 1968 Convention, as amended. Agreements on jurisdiction cover all legal proceedings between insurer and policy-holder, even where the latter wishes, pursuant to the first paragraph of Article 10, to join the insurer in the court in which he himself is sued by the injured party. However, jurisdiction clauses in insurance contracts cannot be binding upon third parties. The provisions of the second paragraph of Article 10 concerning a direct action by the injured party are thus not affected by such jurisdiction clauses. The same is true of the third paragraph of Article 10.

IV. *Other problems of adjustment and clarification in insurance law*

149. 1. *Co-insurance*

The substantive amendment in the first paragraph of Article 8 covers jurisdiction where several co-insurers are parties to a contract of insurance. What usually happens is that one insurer acts as leader for the other co-insurers and each of them underwrites a part of the risk, possibly a very small part. In such cases, however, there is no justification for permitting all the insurers, including the leader, to be sued in the courts of each State in which anyone of the many co-insurers is domiciled. The only additional international jurisdiction which can be justified would be one which relates to the circumstances of the leading insurer. The Working Party considered at length whether to refer to the leading insurer's domicile, but the effect of this would have been that the remaining co-insurers could be sued there even if the leader was sued elsewhere. An additional jurisdiction based on the leading insurer's circumstances is justifiable only if it leads to a concentration of actions arising out of an insured event. The new version of the first paragraph of Article 8 therefore refers to the court where proceedings are brought against the leading insurer. Co-insurers can thus be sued for their share of the insurance in that court, at the same time as the leading insurer or subsequently. However, the provision does not impose an obligation for proceedings to be concentrated in one court; there is nothing to prevent a policy-holder from suing the various co-insurers in different courts. If the leading insurer has settled the claim out of court, the policy-holder must ,bring any action against the other co-insurers in one of the courts having jurisdiction under points (1) or (2) of the new version of the first paragraph of Article 8.

The remaining amendments to the first paragraph of Article 8 merely rephrase it for the sake of greater clarity.

150. 2. *Insurance agents, the setting up of branches*

There was discussion on the present text of the second paragraph of Article 8 of the 1968 Convention because its wording might give rise to the misunderstanding that jurisdiction could be founded not only on the intervention of an agent of the insurer, but also on that of an independent insurance broker of the type common in the United Kingdom. The discussion revealed that this provision was unnecessary in view of Article 5 (5). The Working Party therefore changed the present paragraph three into paragraph two. The addition of the words "or other establishment" is intended merely to ensure consistency between Article 5 (5) and the third paragraph of the new Article 13. The latter provision is necessary in addition to the former in order to prevent Article 4 being applicable.

151. 3. *Reinsurance*

Reinsurance contracts cannot be equated with insurance contracts. Accordingly, Articles 7 to 12 do not apply to reinsurance contracts.

152. 4. *The term "policy-holder"*

The previous authentic texts of the 1968 Convention use the term "preneur d'assurance" and the equivalent in German, Italian and Dutch; the nearest English equivalent of the term proved to be "the policy-holder". However, this should not give rise to the misunderstanding that the problems arising from a transfer of legal rights are now any different from those existing before the accession of the new Member States to the Convention. The rightful possessor of the policy document is not always the "preneur d'assurance". It is of course conceivable that the whole legal status of the other party to the contract with the insurer might pass to another person by inheritance or some other means, in which case the new party to the contract would become the "preneur d'assurance'. However, this case must be clearly distinguished from the transfer of individual rights arising out of the contract of insurance, especially in the form of assignment of the sum assured to a beneficiary. Such an assignment may be made in advance and may be contingent, for instance, upon the occurrence of a claim. In this event it is conceivable that the insurance policy might be passed on to the beneficiary at the same time as the assignment of the right to the sum assured so that he can claim his entitlement from the insurer, if the case arises. The beneficiary would not thereby become the "preneur d'assurance". Hence, where a court's jurisdiction is dependent on individual characteristics of the "preneur d'assurance", the situation remains unchanged as a result of prior assignment of any claim to the sum assured which might arise, even if the policy document is transferred at the same time.

152. (a) 5. Agreements on jurisdiction between parties to a contract from the same State

For the amendment to Article 12 (3) ("at the time of conclusion of the contract"), see paragraph 161 (a).

Section 4

Jurisdiction over consumer contracts

153. I. *Principles*

Leaving aside insurance matters, the 1968 Convention pays heed to consumer protection considerations only in one small section, that dealing with instalment sales and loans. This was consistent with the law as it then stood in the original Member States of the Community since it was in fact at first only in the field of instalment sales and loans that awareness of the need to protect the consumer against unfairly worded contracts became widespread. Since that time legislation in the Member States of the Community has become concerned with much broader-based consumer protection. In particular there has been a general move in consumer protection legislation to ensure appropriate jurisdictions for the consumer. Intolerable tensions would be bound to develop between national legislation and the 1968 Convention in the long run if the Convention did not afford the consumer much the same protection in the case of transfrontier contracts as he received under national legislation. The Working Party therefore decided to propose that the previous Section 4 of Title II be extended into a section on jurisdiction over consumer contracts, establishing at the same time for future purposes that only final consumers acting in a private capacity should be given special protection and not those contracting in the course of their business to pay by instalments for goods and services used. The Working Party was influenced on this last point by the proceedings in the Court of Justice of the European Communities in response to a reference from the French Cour de cassation concerning the interpretation of "instalment sales and loans", proceedings which centred on the question of whether the existing Section 4 of Title II covered instalment sales contracts concluded by businessmen (Case 150/77: *Société Bertrand* v. *Paul Ott KG*).

The basic principle underlying the provisions of the new section is to draw upon ideas emerging from European Community law as it has evolved and is currently evolving. Consequently, most of the existing provisions on instalment sales and loans have been incorporated in the new section, which also draws on Article 5 of the preliminary draft Convention on the law applicable to contractual and non-contractual obligations. On points of drafting detail, however, improvements were made on the wording of the preliminary draft Convention. One substantive change was necessary, since to accord with the general structUre of the 1968 Convention reference had to be made to the place where the parties are domiciled, rather than habitually resident. Details are as follows:

154. II. *The scope of the new Section*

Using the device of an introductory provision defining the scope of the Section, the proposal follows the practice previously adopted at the beginning of Sections 3 and 4 of Title II.

1. *Persons covered*

155. The only new point of principle is a provision governing the persons covered by the section, including in particular the legal definition of the section's central term, the "consumer'. The substances of the definition is taken from Article 5 of the preliminary draft Convention on the law applicable to contractUal and non-contractual obligations the most recent version of which was used by the Working Party. The amendments made were only drafting improvements.

2. *Subject matter covered*

156. As regards the subject matter covered by the new section, a clear distinction is drawn between instalment sales, including the financing of such sales, and other consumer contracts. The consequent effect on the precedence of the provisions of Sections 3 and 4 is as follows: Section 3 is a more specific provision than Section 4 and hence takes precedence over it. A contract of insurance is not a contract for the supply of services within the meaning of the 1968 Convention. Within Section 4, the provisions on instalment sales are more specific than the general reference to consumer sales in the first paragraph of Article 13.

157. (a) As in the past, instalment sales are subject to the special provisions without any further preconditions. The sole change lies in the stipulation that the special provisions apply only where the purchaser is a private consumer. The rules governing instalment sales also apply automatically to the legal institution of hire purchase, which has developed into the commonest legal form for transacting instalment sales in the United Kingdom and Ireland. For reasons which are not material for jurisdiction purposes, instalment sales in those countries usually take the form in law of a contract of hire with an option to purchase for the hirer. In form the instalments represent the hire fee, whereas in substance they form the purchase price. At the end of the prescribed "hire" period, once all the prescribed instalments of the "hire fee" have been paid, the "hirer" is entitled to purchase the article for a nominal price. As the term "instalment sale" under the continental legal systems by no means implies that ownership of the article must necessarily pass to the purchaser at the same time as physical possession, hire purchase is in practice tantamount to an instalment sale.

Contracts to finance instalment sales to private consumers are also subject to the special provisions without any further preconditions. Contrary to the legal position obtaining hitherto, the Working Party has made actions arising out of a loan contract to finance the purchase of movable property subject to the special provision, even if the loan itself is not repayable by instalments or if the article is purchased with a single payment (normally with the funds lent). Credit contracts are not, moreover, contracts for the supply of services, so that, apart from point (2) of the first paragraph of Article 13, the whole of Section 4 does not apply to such contracts. Contracts of sale not falling under point (1) of the first paragraph of Article 13 do not, for instance, come under point (2) of that paragraph, although Section 4 may be applicable to them subject to the further conditions contained in point (3) (see paragraph 158).

158. (b) On the other hand, consumer contracts other than those referred to in paragraph 157 are subject to the special provisions only if there is a sufficiently strong connection with the place where the consumer is domiciled. In this, the new provisions once again follow the preliminary draft Convention on the law applicable to contractual and non-contractual obligations. Both the conditions referred to in point (3) of the first paragraph of Article 13 – an offer or advertising in the State of the consumer's domicile, and steps necessary for the conclusion of the contract taken by the consumer in that State – must be satisfied. The introductory phrase should, moreover, ensure that Articles 4 and 5 (5) will apply to all consumer contracts, as has until now been the case only for instalment sales and for loans repayable by instalments. One particular consequence of this is that, subject to the second paragraph of Article 13, Section 4 does not apply where the defendant is not domiciled in the EEC.

For further details of what is meant by "a specific invitation" or "advertising" in the State of the consumer's domicile and by "the steps necessary for the conclusion of the contract", see the report currently being drawn up by Professor Giuliano on the Convention on the law applicable to contractual and non-contractual obligations.

3. *Only a branch, agency or other establishment within the Community*

159. The exclusion from the scope of Section 4 of contracts between consumers and firms domiciled outside the EEC would not be reasonable where such firms have a branch, agency or other establishment within the EEC Under the national laws upon which jurisdiction is to be founded in such cases pursuant to Article 4, it would often be impossible for the consumer to sue in the courts which would be guaranteed to have jurisdiction for his purposes in the case of contracts with parties domiciled within the EEC Insurers with branches, agencies or other establishments in the FEC are treated as regards jurisdiction in like manner to those domiciled within the Community (Article 8) and for the same reasons the other parties to contracts with consumers must also be deemed to be domiciled within the EEC if they have a branch, agency of other establishment in the Community. It is, however, only logical that it should not be possible to invoke exorbitant jurisdictions against such parties simply because their head office lies outside the EEC

4. *Contracts of transport*

160. The last paragraph of Article 13 is again taken from Article 5 of the preliminary draft Convention on the law applicable to contractual and non-contractual obligations. The reason for leaving contracts of transport out of the scope of the special consumer protection provisions in the 1968 Convention is that such contracts are subject under international agreements to special sets of rules with very considerable ramifications, and the inclusion of those contracts in the 1968 Convention purely for jurisdictional purposes would merely complicate the legal position. Moreover, the total exclusion of contracts of transport from the scope of Section 4 means that Sections 1 and 2 and hence in particular Article 5 (1) remain applicable.

161. III. *The substance of the provisions of Section 4*
There are only a few points requiring a brief explanation of the substance of the new provisions.

1. *Subsequent change of domicile by the consumer*
In substance, the new Article 14 closely follows the existing Article 14, while extending it to actions arising from all consumer contracts. The rearrangement of the text is merely a rewording due to the availability of a convenient description for one party to the contract, the "consumer", which was better placed at the beginning of the text so as to make it more easily comprehensible. The Working Party's decision means in substance that, as in the case with the existing Article 14, the consumer may sue in the courts of his new State of domicile if he moves to another Community State after concluding the contract out of which an action subsequently arises. This only becomes practical, however, in the case of the instalment sales and credit contracts referred to in points (1) and (2) of the first paragraph of Article 13. For actions arising out of other consumer contracts the new Section 4 will in virtually all cases cease to be applicable if the consumer transfers his domicile to another State after conclusion of the contract. This is because the steps necessary for the conclusion of the contract will almost always not have been taken in the new State of domicile. The cross-frontier advertising requirement also ensures that the special provisions will in practice not be applicable to contracts between two persons neither of whom is acting in a professional or trading capacity.

2. *Agreements on jurisdiction*
161 a. The new version of Article IS, too, is in substance based on the existing version relating to instalment sales and loans. The only addition is intended to make it clear that it is at the time of conclusion of the contract, and not when proceedings are subsequently instituted, that the parties must be domiciled in the same State. It was then necessary to align and clarify Article 12 (3) in the same way.

Although Article 13 is not expressed to be subject to Article 17, the Working Party was unanimously of the opinion that agreements on jurisdiction must, in so far as they are permitted at all, comply with the formal requirements of Article 17. Since the form of such agreements is not governed by Section 4, it must be governed by Article 17.

Section 5

Exclusive jurisdiction

162. The only amendment proposed by the Working Party to the cases of exclusive jurisdiction provided for in Article 16 is a technical amendment in Article Vd of the Protocol annexed to the 1968 Convention, to clarify Article 16 (4). The Working Party did, however, spend some time discussing paragraphs (1) and (2) of that Article. Details of the information supplied to the new Member States regarding exclusive jurisdiction in actions relating to the validity of the constitution of companies or to their dissolution have already been given elsewhere (see paragraph 56 et seq.). It is only necessary to add that a company may have more than one seat. Where under a legal system it is possible for a company to have two seats, and it is that system which, pursuant to Article 53 of the 1968 Convention, is to determine the seat of the company, the existence of two seats has to be accepted. It is then open to the plaintiff to choose which of the two seats he will use to base the jurisdiction of the court for his action. Finally, it should be pointed out that Article 16 (2) also applies to partnerships established under United Kingdom and Irish law (see paragraph 55).

Thus essentially the only exclusive jurisdiction left to be dealt with more fully here is that in respect of actions relating to rights in rem in, or tenancies of, immovable property. There were five problems with regard to which the new Member States had requested explanations.

163. There was no difficulty in clarifying that actions for damages based on infringement of rights in rem or in damage to property in which rights in rem exist do not fall within the scope of Article 16 (1). In that context the existence and content of such rights in rem, usually rights of ownership, are only of marginal significance.

164. The Working Party was unable to agree whether actions concerned only with rent, i.e. dealing simply with the recovery of a debt, are excluded from the scope of Article 16 (1) as, according to the Jenard report, was the opinion of the Committee which drafted the 1968 Convention.[38] However, the underlying principle of the provision quite clearly does not require its application to short-term agreements for use and occupation such as, for example, holiday accommodation.

165. Two of the three remaining problems which the Working Party examined relate to the differences between the law of immovable property on the continent and the corresponding law in the United

Kingdom and Ireland; they require therefore somewhat more detailed comments. There is, first, the question what are rights in rem (1) within the meaning of Article 16 (1), and, secondly, the problem of disputes arising in connection with the transfer of immovable property (2). Certain other problems emerged as a result of developments which have taken place in the meantime in international patent law (3).

1. *Rights "in rem" in immovable property in the Member States of the Community*

166. (a) The concept of a right *in rem* – as distinct from a right *in personam* – is common to the legal systems of the original Member States of the EEC, even though the distinction does not appear everywhere with the same clarity.

A right *in personam* can only be claimed against a particular person; thus only the purchaser is obliged to pay the purchase price and only the lessor of an article is obliged to permit its use.

A right *in rem*, on the other hand, is available against the whole world. The most important legal consequence flowing from the nature of a right *in rem* is that its owner is entitled to demand that the thing in which it exists be given up by anyone not enjoying a prior right.

In the legal systems of all the original Member States of the EEC without exception, there are only a restricted number of rights *in rem*, even though they do not rigidly apply the principle. Some rights *in rem* are defined only in outline, with freedom for the parties to agree the details. The typical rights *in rem* are listed under easily identifiable heads of the civil law, which in all six countries is codified.[39] In addition, a few rights *in rem* are included in some special laws, the most important of which are those on the co-ownership of real property. Apart from ownership as the most comprehensive right *in rem*, a distinction can be made between certain rights of enjoyment and certain priority rights to secure liabilities. All the legal systems know the concept of usufruct, which confers extensive rights to enjoyment of a property. More restricted rights of enjoyment can also exist in these legal systems in various ways.

167. (b) At first glance there appears to be in United Kingdom and Irish law too a small, strictly circumscribed group of statutory rights corresponding to the Continental rights in rem. However, the position is more complicated, because these legal systems distinguish between law and equity.

In this connection it has always to be borne in mind that equity also constitutes law and not something merely akin to fairness lying outside the concept of law. As a consequence of these special concepts of law and equity in the United Kingdom and in Ireland, equitable interests can exist in immovable property in addition to the legal rights.

In the United Kingdom the system of legal rights has its origin in the idea that all land belongs to the Crown and that the citizen can only have limited rights in immovable property. This is the reason why the term "ownership" does not appear in the law of immovable property. However, the estate in fee simple absolute in possession is equivalent to full ownership under the Continental legal systems. In addition the Law of property Act 1925 provides for full ownership for a limited period of time ("term of years absolute"). The same Act limits restricted rights in immovable property ("interests or charges in or over land") to five. All the others are equitable interests, whose number and content are not limited by the Act. Equitable interests are not, however, merely the equivalent of personal rights on the Continent. Some can be registered and then, like legal rights, have universal effect, even against purchasers in good faith. Even if not registered they operate in principle against all the world; only purchasers in good faith who had no knowledge of them are protected in such a case.[40] If the owner of an estate in fee simple absolute in possession grants another person a right of way over his property for the period of that person's life, this cannot amount to a legal right. It can only be an equitable interest, though capable of registration.[41] Equitable interests can thus fulfil the same functions as rights *in rem* under the Continental legal systems, in which case they must be treated as such under Article 16 (1). There is no limit to the number of such interests. The granting of equitable interests is on the contrary the method used for achieving any number of subdivisions of proprietary rights.[42]

168. (c) If an action relating to immovable property is brought in a particular State and the question whether the action is concerned with a right in rem within the meaning of Article 16 (1) arises, the answer can hardly be derived from any law other than that of the situs.

2. *Actions in connection with obligations to transfer immovable property*

169. The legal systems of the original and the new Member States of the Community also differ as regards the manner in which ownership of immovable property is transferred on sale. Admittedly the legal position even within the original Member States differs in this respect.

170. (a) German law distinguishes most clearly between the transfer itself and the contract of sale (or other contract designed to bring about a transfer). The legal position in the case of immovable property

is no different from that obtaining in the case of movable property. The transfer is a special type of legal transaction which in the case of immovable property is called "Auflassung" (conveyance) and which even between the parties becomes effective only on entry in the land register. Where a purchaser of German immovable property brings proceedings on the basis of a contract for sale of immovable property which is governed by German law, the subject matter of such proceedings is never a right *in rem* in the property. The only matter in issue is the defendant's personal obligation to carry out all acts necessary to transfer and hand over the property. If one of the parties fails to fulfil its obligations under a contract for sale of immovable property, the remedy in German law is not a court order for rescission, but a claim for damages and the right to rescind the contract.

Admittedly it is possible with the vendor's consent to protect the contractual claim for a transfer of ownership by means of a caution in the land register. In that case the claim has, as against third parties, effects which normally only attach to a right *in rem*. The consequence for German domestic law is that nowadays rights secured by such a caution may be claimed against third parties in the jurisdiction competent to deal with the property concerned.[43] However, any proceedings for a transfer of ownership against the vendor himself would remain an action based on a personal obligation.

171. (b) Under French, Belgian and Luxembourg law, which is largely followed by Italian law, the ownership, at any rate as between the parties, passes to the purchaser as soon as the contract of sale is concluded, just as it does in the case of movable property, unless the parties have agreed a later date (see, e.g., Article 711 and 1583 of the french Civil Code and Article 1376 of the Italian Civil Code). The purchaser need only enter the transfer of ownership in the land register ("transcription") to acquire a legal title which is also effective against third parties. For the purchaser to bring proceedings for performance of the contract is therefore normally equivalent to a claim that the property be handed over him. Admittedly this claim is based not only on the obligation which the vendor undertook by the contract of sale, but also on ownership which at that point has already passed to the purchaser. This means that the claim for handing over the property has as its basis both a personal obligation and a right *in rem*. The system of remedies which is available in the event of one party to a contract not complying with its obligations is fully in accordance with this. Accordingly, French domestic law has treated such actions as a "matière mixte" and given the plaintiff the right to choose between the jurisdiction applicable to the right *in rem* and the jurisdiction applicable to the personal obligation arising from the contract, i.e. the law of the defendant's domicile or of the place of performance of the contract.[44]

The 1968 Convention does not deal with this problem. It would seem that the personal aspect of such claims predominates and Article 16 (1) is inapplicable.

172. (c) In the United Kingdom ownership passes on the conclusion of a contract of sale only in the case of movable property. In the case of a sale of immovable property the transfer of ownership follows the conclusion of the contract of sale and is effected by means of a separate document, the conveyance. If necessary, the purchaser has to bring an action for all necessary acts to be performed by the vendor. However, except in Scotland, in contrast with German law, the purchaser's rights prior to the transfer of ownership are not limited to a personal claim against the vendor. In fact the purchaser has an equitable interest (see paragraph 167) in the property which, provided the contract is protected by a notice on the Land Register, is also effective against third parties. Admittedly the new paragraph (6) of Article 5 does not apply (see paragraph 114 *et seq.*), because a contract of sale does not create a trust within the meaning of Article 5 (6), even if it is in writing. It is only in one respect that a purchaser's equitable interest does not place him in" as strong a position as the French owner of immovable property prior to "transcription" (see paragraph 171): the vendor's cooperation is still required to make the new owner's legal title fully effective.

This legal position would justify application of the exclusive jurisdiction referred to in Article 16 (1) even less than the corresponding position under French law. The common law has developed the concept of equitable interests so as to confer on parties to an agreement which originally gave them nothing more than merely personal rights a certain protection as against third parties not acting in good faith. As against the other party to the contract the claim remains purely a personal one, as does a claim, under German law, to transfer of ownership (see paragraph 170) secured by a caution in the Land Register. In Scotland contracts in favour of a third party are enforceable by that party (*jus quaesitum tertii*).

Actions based on contracts for the transfer of ownership or other rights *in rem* affecting immovable property do not therefore have as their object rights *in rem*. Accordingly they may also be brought before courts outside the United Kingdom. Admittedly, care will have to be exercised in that case to ensure that the plaintiff clearly specifies the acts to be done by the defendant so that the transfer of ownership (governed by United Kingdom law) does indeed become effective.

173. 3. Jurisdiction in connection with patent disputes

Since the 1968 Convention entered into force, two Conventions on patents have been signed which are of the greatest international importance. The Munich Convention on the grant of European patents was signed on 5 October 1973 and the Luxembourg Convention for the European patent for the common market was signed on 15 December 1975. The purpose of the Munich Convention is to introduce a common patent application procedure for the Contracting States, though the patent subsequently granted is national in scale. It is valid for one or more States, its substance in each case being basically that of a corresponding patent granted nationally. The aim of the Luxembourg Convention is to institute in addition a patent granted ab initio for all States of the Community in a standard manner and with the same substance, based on Community law; such a patent necessarily remains valid or expires uniformly throughout the EEC.

Both instruments contain specific provisions on jurisdiction which take precedence over the 1968 Convention. However, the special jurisdiction provisions relate only to specific matters, such as applications for the revocation of patents pursuant to the Luxembourg Convention. Article 16 (4) of the 1968 Convention remains relevant for actions for which no specific provision is made. In the case of European patents under the Munich Convention it is conceivable that this provision might be construed as meaning that actions must be brought in the State in which the patent was applied for and not in the State for which it is valid and in which it is challenged. The new Article Vd of the Protocol annexed to the 1968 Convention is designed to prevent this interpretation and ensure that only the courts of the State in which the patent is valid have jurisdiction, unless the Munich Convention itself lays down special provisions.

Clearly, such a provision cannot cover a Community patent. under the Luxembourg Convention, since the governing principle is that the patent is granted, not for a given State, but for all the Member States of the EEC. Hence the exception at the end of the new provision. However, even in the area covered by the Luxembourg Convention patents valid for one or more, but not all, States of the Community are possible. Article 86 of that Convention allows this for a transitional period to which no term has yet been set. Where the applicant for a patent takes up the option available to him under this provision and applies for a patent for one or more, but not all, States of the EEC, the patent is not a Community patent even though it comes under some of the provisions of the Luxembourg Convention but merely a patent granted for one or more States. Accordingly, the courts of that State have exclusive jurisdiction under Article Vd of the Protocol annexed to the 1968 Convention. The same is true for any case in which a national patent is granted in response to an international application, e.g. under the Patent cooperation Treaty opened for signature at Washington on 19 June 1970.

It only remains to be made clear that Article 16 (4) of the 1968 Convention and the new Article Vd of the Protocol annexed to the Convention also cover actions which national legislation allows to be brought at the patent application stage, so as to reduce the risk of a patent being granted, and the correctness of the grant being subsequently challenged.

Section 6

Jurisdiction by consent[45]

174. Article 17, applying as it does only if the transaction in question is international in character (see paragraph 21), which the mere fact of choosing a court in a particular State is by no means sufficient to establish, presented the Working Party with four problems. First, account had to be taken of the practice of courts in the United Kingdom (excluding Scotland) and Ireland of deducing from the choice of law to govern the main issue an agreement as to the courts having jurisdiction. Secondly, there was the problem, previously ignored by the 1968 Convention, of agreements conferring jurisdiction upon a court outside the Community or agreements. conferring jurisdiction upon courts within the Community by two parties both domiciled outside the Community. Thirdly, special rules had to be made for provisions in trusts. And finally, the Working Party had to consider whether it was reasonable to let Article 17 stand in view of the interpretation which had been placed upon it by the Court of Justice of the European Communities. It should be repeated (see paragraph 22) that the existence of an agreement conferring jurisdiction on a court other than the court seised of the proceedings is one of the points to be taken into account by the court of its own motion.

1. *Choice-of-law clause and international jurisdiction*

175. Nowhere in the 1968 Convention is there recognition of a connection between the law applicable to a particular issue and the international jurisdiction of the courts over that issue. However, persons

who, relying on the practice of United Kingdom or Irish courts, have agreed on choice-of-law clauses before the entry into force of the Accession Convention, arc entitled to expect protection. This explains the transitional provision contained in Article 35 of the proposed Accession Convention. The term "entry into force" within the meaning of this provision refers to the date on which the Accession Convention comes into effect in the State in question. For the various systems of law applying in the United Kingdom, see paragraph 11.

2. *Agreements conferring jurisdiction on courts outside the Community*

176. (a) In cases where parties agree to bring their disputes before the courts of a State which is not a party to the 1968 Convention there is obviously nothing in the 1968 Convention to prevent such courts from declaring themselves competent, if their law recognizes the validity of such an agreement. The only question is whether and, if so, in what form such agreements are capable of depriving Community courts of jurisdiction which is stated by the 1968 Convention to be exclusive or concurrent. There is nothing in the 1968 Convention to support the conclusion that such agreements must be inadmissible in principle.[46] However, the 1968 Convention does not contain any rules as to their validity either. If a court within the Community is applied to despite such an agreement, its decision on the validity of the agreement depriving it of jurisdiction must be taken in accordance with its own *lex fori*. In so far as the local rules of conflict of laws support the authority of provisions of foreign law, the latter will apply. If, when these tests are applied, the agreement is found to be invalid, then the jurisdictional provisions of the 1968 Convention become applicable.

177. (b) On the other hand, proceedings can be brought before a court within the Community by parties who, although both domiciled outside the Community, have agreed that that court should have jurisdiction. There is no reason for the Convention to include rules on the conditions under which the court stipulated by such parties must accept jurisdiction. It is however important for the Community to ensure, by means of more detailed conditions, that the effect of such an agreement on jurisdiction is recognized throughout the EEC. The new third sentence of the first paragraph of Article 17 is designed to cater for this. It covers the situation where, despite the fact that both parties are domiciled outside the Community, a court in a Community State ("X") would, were it not for a jurisdiction agreement, have jurisdiction, e.g. on the ground that the place of performance lies within that State. If in such a case the parties agree that the courts of another Community State are to have exclusive jurisdiction, that agreement must be observed by the courts of State X, provided the agreement meets the formal requirements of Article 17. Strictly speaking, it is true, this is not a necessary adjustment. Such sitUations were possible before, in relations between the original Member States of the Community. However, owing to the frequency with which jurisdiction is conferred upon United Kingdom courts in international trade, the problem takes considerably greater importance with the United Kingdom's accession to the Convention than hitherto.

3. *Jurisdiction clauses in trusts*

178. A trust (see paragraph 111) need not be established by contract. A unilateral legal instrument is sufficient. As the previous version of Article 17 dealt only with "agreements" on jurisdiction, it needed to be expanded.

4. *The form of agreements on jurisdiction in international trade*

179. Some of the first judgments given by the Court of Justice of the European Communities since it was empowered to interpret the 1968 Convention were concerned with the form of jurisdiction clauses incorporated in standardized general conditions of trade.[47] The Court of Justice's interpretation of Article 17 of the 1968 Convention does protect the other party to a contract with anyone using such general conditions of trade from the danger of inadvertently finding himself bound by standard forms of agreement containing jurisdiction clauses without realizing it. However, the Court's interpretation of that Article,. which many national courts have also shown a tendency to follow,[45] does not cater adequately for the customs and requirements of international trade. In particular, the requirement that the other party to a contract with anyone employing general conditions of trade has to give written confirmation of their inclusion in the contract before any jurisdiction clause in those conditions can be effective is unacceptable in international trade. International trade is heavily dependent on standard conditions which incorporate jurisdiction clauses. Nor are those conditions in many cases unilaterally dictated by one set of interests in the market; they have frequently been negotiated by representatives of the various interests. Owing to the need for calculations based on constantly fluctuating market prices, it has to be possible to conclude contracts swiftly by means of a confirmation of order incorporating

sets of conditions. These are the factors behind the relaxation of the formal provisions for international trade in the amended version of Article 17. This is however, as should be clearly emphasized, only a relaxation of the formal requirements. It must be proved that a consensus existed on the inclusion in the contract of the general conditions of trade and the particular provisions, though this is not the place to pass comment on whether questions of consensus other than the matter of form should be decided according to the national laws applicable or to unified EEC principles. Dealing with the form of jurisdiction agreements in a separate second sentence in the first paragraph of Article 17, rather than in passing in the first sentence as hitherto, is designed merely to obviate rather cumbersome wording.

Section 7

Examination of own motion

Adjustments and further clarification were not necessary.

Section 8

"Lis pendens" and related actions[48]

180. As regards lis pendens, there are two structural differences between the laws of the United Kingdom and Ireland, on the one hand, and the Continental legal systems on the other. However, neither of them necessitated a technical amendment of the 1968 Convention.

1. *Discretion of the court*

181. The rules governing *lis pendens* in England and Wales, and to some extent in Scotland, are more flexible than those on the Continent. Basically, it is a question for the court's discretion whether a stay should be granted. The doctrine of *lis pendens* is therefore less fully developed there than in the Continental States. The practice is in a sense an application of the doctrine of forum conveniens (see paragraph 77 *et seq.*). Generally a court will in fact grant an application for a stay of proceedings, where the matter in dispute is already pending before another court. Where proceedings are pending abroad, the courts in England and Wales exercise great caution, and if they grant a stay of proceedings at all, they will do so only if the plaintiff in England or Wales is also the plaintiff in the proceedings abroad. Scottish courts take into account to a considerable extent any conflicting proceedings which a Scottish defendant may have instituted abroad, or which are pending against him abroad.

After the United Kingdom has acceded to the 1968 Convention, it will no longer be possible for this practice to be maintained in relation to the other Member States of the Community. United Kingdom courts will have to acknowledge the existence of proceedings instituted in the other Member States, and even to take notice of them of their own motion (see paragraph 22).

2. *Moment at which proceedings become pending*

182. The fact that the moment at which proceedings become pending is determined differently in the United Kingdom and Ireland from the way it is determined on the Continent is due to peculiarities of procedural law in those States. In the original Member States of the Community a claim becomes pending when the document instititUting the proceedings is served.[49] Filing with the court is sometimes sufficient. In the United Kingdom, except Scotland, and in Ireland, proceedings become pending as soon as the originating document has been issued. In Scotland, however, proceedings become pending only when service of the summons has been effected on the defender. The moment at which proceedings become pending under the national procedural law concerned is the deciding factor for the application of Article 21 of the 1968 Convention. The addition to the text of Article 20 does not concern this point. It is justified by the fact that in the United Kingdom and in Ireland foreigners who are abroad do not receive the original writ but only notification of the order of the court authorizing service.

Section 9

Provisional measures

183. .No particular adjustments had to be made to the provisions of the 1968 Convention concerning provisional measures. The change in emphasis which the accession of further Member States introduced into the 1968 Convention consists in this field entirely in the wide variety of provisional measures

available in the law of Ireland and of the United Kingdom. This will involve certain difficulties where provisional judgments given in these States have to be given effect by the enforcement procedures of the original Member States of the Community. However, this problem does not affect only provisional measures. The integration of judgments on the main issue into the respective national enforcement procedures also involves difficulties in the relationship between Ireland and the United Kingdom on the one hand and the original Member States of the Community on the other (see paragraph 221 *et seq.*).

CHAPTER 5 – RECOGNITION AND ENFORCEMENT

A

GENERAL REMARKS – INTERLOCUTORY COURT DECISIONS

184. Article 25 emphasizes in terms which could hardly be clearer that every type of judgment given by a court in a Contracting State must be recognized and enforced throughout the rest of the Community. The provision is not limited to a judgment terminating the proceedings before the court, but also applies to provisional court orders. Nor does the wording of the provision indicate that interlocutory court decisions should be excluded from its scope where they do not provisionally regulate the legal relationships between the parties, but. are for instance concerned only with the taking of evidence. What is more, the legal systems of the original Member States of the Community describe such interlocutory decisions in a way which corresponds to the terms given, by way of example, in Article 25. Thus, in France court decisions which order the taking of evidence are also called "jugements (d'avant dire droit)". In Germany they are termed "(Beweis) beschlüsse" of the court. Nevertheless, the provisions of the 1968 Convention governing recognition and enforcement are in general designed to cover only court judgments which either determine or regulate the legal relationships of the parties. An answer to the question whether, and if so which, interlocutory decisions intended to be of procedural assistance fall within the scope of the 1968 Convention cannot be given without further consideration.

1. *RELATIONSHIP OF THE CONTINENTAL STATES WITH EACH OTHER*

185. This matter is of no great significance as between the original Member States of the EEC, or as between the latter and Denmark. All seven States are parties to the 1954 Hague Convention relating to civil procedure. The latter governs the question of judicial assistance, particularly in the case of evidence to be taken abroad, and its provisions take precedence over the 1968 Convention by virtue of Article 57. In any case, it is always advisable in practice to make use of the machinery of the Hague Convention, which is particularly suited to the processes required for obtaining judicial assistance. See paragraph 238, and note 59 (7) on the Hague Convention of 15 November 1965 on the service abroad of judicial and extrajudicial documents in civil or commercial matters and on the Hague Convention of 18 March 1970 on the taking of evidence abroad in civil or commercial matters.

2. *RELATIONSHIP OF THE UNITED KINGDOM AND IRELAND WITH THE OTHER MEMBER STATES*

186. It is only with the accession of the United Kingdom and Ireland to the 1968 Convention that the problem assumes any degree of importance. Ireland has concluded no convention judicial assistance of any kind with the other States of the European Community. Agreements on judicial assistance do, however, exist between the United Kingdom and the following States: the Federal Republic of Germany (Agreement of 20 March 1928), the Netherlands (Agreement of 17 November 1967). The United Kingdom is also party to the Hague Conventions of 1965 and 1970 referred to in paragraph 185. It has concluded no other agreements with Member States of the Community.

3. *PRECISE SCOPE OF TITLE III OF THE 1968 CONVENTION*

187. If it were desired that interlocutory decisions by courts on the further conduct of the proceedings, and particularly on the taking of evidence, should be covered by Article 25 of the 1968 Convention, this would also affect decisions with which the parties would be totally unable to comply without the court~s cooperation, and the enforcement of which would concern third parties, particularly witnesses. It would therefore be impossible to "enforce" such decisions under the 1968 Convention. It can only be

concluded from the foregoing that interlocutory decisions which are not intended to govern the legal relationships of the parties, but to arrange the further conduct of the proceedings, should be excluded from the scope of Title III of the 1968 Convention.

B

COMMENTS ON THE INDIVIDUAL SECTIONS

Section 1

Recognition

188. With two exceptions (4), no formal amendments were required to Articles 26 to 30. The Working Party did, however, answer some questions raised by the new Member States regarding the interpretation of these provisions. Basically, these concerned problems arising in connection with the application of the public policy reservation in Article 27 (1) – (2), the right to a hearing Article 27 (2) – (3), and the nature of the obligation to confer recognition, as distinct from enforceability (1). The fact that Article 28 makes no reference to the provisions of Section 6 of Title II on jurisdiction agreements. is intentional and deserves mention. When considering such agreements it must be borne in mind that the court seised of the proceedings in the State of origin must of its own motion take note of any agreement to the contrary (see paragraphs 22 and 174).

1. *Article 26*

189. Article 26, second paragraph, introduces a special simplified procedure for seeking recognition, modelled on the provisions governing the issue of orders for enforcement. However, this is not the only way in which recognition may be sought. Every court and public authority must take account of judgments which qualify for recognition, and must decide whether the conditions for recognition exist in a particular case, unless this question has already been determined under Article 26, second paragraph. In particular, every court must itself decide whether there is an obligation to grant recognition, if the principal issue in a foreign judgment concerns a question which in the fresh proceedings emerges as a preliminary issue. Each of these two recognition procedures involves a problem which the Working Party discussed.

190. (a) If proceedings are conducted in accordance with Article 26, second paragraph, the court may of its own motion take into account grounds for refusing recognition if they appear from the judgment or are known to the court. It may not, however, make enquiries to establish whether such grounds exist, as this would not be compatible with the summary nature of the proceedings. Only if further proceedings are instituted by way of an appeal lodged pursuant to Article 36 can the court examine whether the requirements for recognition have been satisfied.

191. (b) The effects of a court decision are not altogether uniform under the legal systems obtaining in the Member States of the Community. A judgment delivered in one State as a decision on a procedural issue may, in another State, be treated as a decision on an issue of substance. The same type of judgment may be of varying scope and effect in different countries. In France, a judgment against the principal debtor is also effective against the surety, whereas in the Netherlands and Germany it is not.[50]

The Working Party did not consider it to be its task to find a general solution to the problems arising from these differences in the national legal systems. However, one fact seemed obvious.

Judgments dismissing an action as unfounded must be recognized. If a German court declares that it has no jurisdiction, an English court cannot" disclaim its own jurisdiction on the ground that the German court was in fact competent. Clearly, however, German decisions on procedural matters are not binding, as to the substance, in England. An English court may at any time allow (or, for substantive reasons, disallow) an action, if proceedings are started in England after such a decision has been given by a German court.

2. *Article 27 (1) – public policy*

192. (a) The 1968 Convention does not state in terms whether recognition may be refused pursuant to Article 27 (1) on the ground that the judgment has been obtained by fraud. Not even in the legal systems of the original Contracting States to the 1968 Convention is it expressly stated that fraud in obtaining a judgment constitUtes a ground for refusing recognition. Such conduct is, however, generally considered as an instance for applying the doctrine of public policy.[51] The legal situation in the United Kingdom and Ireland is different inasmuch as fraud constitutes a special ground for refusing recognition in addition to the principle of public policy. In the conventions on enforcement which the United Kingdom concluded with Community. States, a middle course was adopted by expressly referring to

fraudulent conduct, but treating it as a special case of public policy.[52]

As a result there is no doubt that to obtain a judgment by fraud can in principle constitute an offence against the public policy of the State addressed. However, the legal systems of all Member States provide special means of redress by which it can be contended, even after the expiry of the normal period for an appeal, that the judgment was the result of a fraud (see paragraph 197 *et seq*.). A court in the State addressed must always, therefore, ask itself, whether a breach of its public policy still exists in view of the fact that proceedings for redress can be, or could have been, lodged in the courts of the State of origin against the judgment allegedly obtained by fraud.

193. (b) Article 41 (3) of the Irish Constitution prohibits divorce and also provides, as regards marriages dissolved abroad:

> "No person whose marriage has been dissolved under the civil law of any other State but is a subsisting valid marriage under the law for the time being in force within the jurisdiction of the Government and Parliament established by this Constitution shall be capable of contracting a valid marriage within that jurisdiction during the lifetime of the other party to the marriage so dissolved."

In so far as the jurisdiction of the 1968 Convention is concerned, this Article of the Constitution is of importance for maintenance orders made upon a divorce. The Irish courts have not yet settled whether the recognition of such maintenance orders would, in view of the constitutional provisions cited, be contrary to Irish public policy.

3. *The right to a hearing (Article 27 (2))*

194. Article 27 (2) is amended for the same reason as Article 20 (see paragraph 182). The object of the addition to Article 20 was to specify the moment when proceedings became pending before the Irish or British courts; in Article 27 (2) it is intended to indicate which documents must have been served for the right to a hearing to be respected.

4. *Ordinary and extraordinary appeals*

195. The 1968 Convention makes a distinction in Articles 30 and 38 between ordinary and extraordinary appeals. No equivalent for this could be found in the Irish and United Kingdom legal systems. Before discussing the reason for this and explaining the implications of the solutions proposed by the Working Party (b), something should be said about the distinction between ordinary and extraordinary appeals in the Continental Member States of the EEC, since judges in the United Kingdom and Ireland will have to come to terms with these concepts which to them are unfamiliar (a).

196. (a) A clearly defined distinction between ordinary and extraordinary appeals is nowhere to be found.

Legal literature and case law[53] have pointed out two criteria. In the first place neither an appeal ("Berufung") nor an objection to a default judgment ("Einspruch") has to be based on specific grounds; a party may challenge a judgment by alleging any kind of defect. Secondly execution is postponed during the period allowed for an appeal or objection, or after an appeal or objection has been lodged, unless the court otherwise directs or unless, exceptionally, different legal provisions apply.

Some legal systems contain a list of ordinary appeal procedures.

197. Part 1, Book 4 of the French Code de procedure civile of 1806, which still applies in Luxembourg, referred to extraordinary forms of appeal by which a judgment could be contested. It did not say, however, what was meant by ordinary appeals. Book 3 referred merely to "courts of appeal". However, in legal literature and case law appeals ("appel") and objections to default judgments ("opposition") have consistently been classified as ordinary appeals. The new French Code de procedure civile of 1975 now expressly clarifies the position. In future only objections (Article 76) and appeals (Article 85) are to be classified as ordinary appeals.

198. The Belgian Code judiciaire of 1967 has retained the French system which previously applied in Belgium. Only appeals and objections are considered as ordinary appeals (Article 21).

199. There is. no distinction in Netherlands law between ordinary and extraordinary appeals. Academic writers classify the forms of appeal as follows: objections ("Verzet" – where a judgment is given in default), appeals ("Hoger beroep"), appeals in cassation ("Beroep in cassatie") and appeals on a point of law ("Revisie") are classed as ordinary appeals. "Revisie" is a special form of appeal which lies only against certain judgments of the Hoge Raad sitting as a court of first instance.

200. The Italian text of Articles 30 and 38 refers to "impugnazione" without distinguishing between ordinary and extraordinary appeals. However, Italian legal literature distinguishes very clearly between

ordinary and extraordinary appeals. Article 324 of the Codice di procedura civile states that a judgment does not become binding as between the parties until the periods within which the following forms of appeal may be lodged have expired: appeals on grounds of jurisdiction ("regolamento di competenza"), appeals ("appello"), appeals in cassation ("ricorso per cassazione"), or petitions for review ("revocazione"), where these are based on one of the grounds provided for in Article 395 (4) and (5). These forms of appeal are classified as ordinary.

201. In Denmark, too, the distinction between ordinary and extraordinary appeals is recognized only in legal literature. The deciding factor mentioned there is whether a form of appeal may be lodged within a given period without having to be based on particular grounds, or whether its admissibility depends on special. consent by a court or ministry. Accordingly, appeals ("Anke") and objections to default judgments ("Genoptagelse af sager, i hvilke der er afsagt udeblivelsesdom") are classified as ordinary appeals.

202. Book 3 of the German Code of Civil Procedure ("Zivilprozeßordnung") is headed "Rechtsmittel" ("means of redress") and it governs "Berufung" (appeals), "Beschwerde" (complaints) and "Revision" (appeals on a point of law). These are frequently said to have in common the fact that the decision appealed against does not become binding ("rechtskräftig") until the period within which these means of redress may be lodged has expired. However, Article 705 of the Code defines "Rechtskraft" as the stage when these means of redress are no longer available. The material difference between the means of redress and other forms of appeal is that the former need not be based on particular grounds of appeal, that they are addressed to a higher court and that, as long as the decision has not become binding, enforcement is also postponed pursuant to Article 704 unless the court, as is almost invariably the case, allows provisional enforcement. If the expression "ordinary appeal" is used at all, a reference to "Rechtsmittel" (means of redress) is intended.

German legal writers, in accordance with the phraseology used by the law, do not classify objections to default judgments as a means of redress ("Rechtsmittel").[54] It does not involve the competence of a higher court. However, it has the effect of suspending execution and is not tied to specific grounds of appeal, just like an objection in the other original Member States of the Community. It must, therefore, be included under "ordinary appeals" within the meaning of Articles 30 and 38 of the 1968 Convention.

203. In its judgment of 22 November 1977[55] the European Court held that the concept of an "ordinary appeal" was to be uniformly determined in the original Member States according to whether there was a specific period of time for appealing, which started to run "by virtue of" the judgment.

204. (b) In Ireland and the United Kingdom nothing which would enable a distinction to be drawn between ordinary and extraordinary appeals can be found in either statutes, cases or systematic treaties on procedural law. The basic method of redress is the appeal. Not only is this term used where review of a judgment can be sought within a certain period, without being subject to special grounds for appeal; it is also the name given to other means of redress. Some have special names such as; for default judgments, "reponing" (in Scotland) or "application to set the judgment aside" (in England, Wales and Ireland); or again "motion" (in Scotland) or "application" (in England, Wales and Ireland) "for a new trial", which correspond roughly to a petition for. review in Continental legal systems. They are the only forms of redress against a verdict by a jury. A further distinctive feature of the appeal system in these States is the fact that the enforceability of a judgment is not automatically affected by the appeal period or even by the lodging of an appeal. However, the appellate court will usually grant a temporary stay of execution, if security is given. Finally there do exist in the United Kingdom legal procedures whose function corresponds to the ordinary legal procedures of Continental legal systems, but which are not subject to time limits. The judge exercises his discretion in deciding on the admissibility of each particular case. This is the case, for example, with default judgments. The case law of the European Court could therefore not be applied to the new Member States.

The Working Party therefore made prolonged efforts to work out an equivalent for the United Kingdom and Ireland of the Continental distinction between ordinary and extraordinary appeals, but reached no satisfactory result. This failure was due in particular to the fact that the term "appeal" is so many-sided and cannot be regarded, like similar terms in Continental law, as a basis for "ordinary appeals'. The Working Party therefore noted that the legal consequences resulting from the distinction drawn in Articles 30 and 38 between ordinary and extraordinary appeals do not have to be applied rigidly, but merely confer a discretion on the court. Accordingly, in the interests of practicality and clarity, a broad definition of appeal seemed justified in connection with judgments of Irish and United Kingdom courts. Continental courts will have to use their discretion in such a way that an equal balance in the application of Articles 30 and 38 in all Contracting States will be preserved. To this effect they will have to make only cautious use of their discretionary power to stay proceedings, if the appeal is one which is available in Ireland or the United Kingdom only against special defects in a judgment or which may still be lodged after a long period. A further argument in favour of this pragmatic solution was that, in accordance with Article 38, a judgment is in any event no longer enforceable if it was subject to appeal in the State of origin and the appellate court suspended execution or granted a temporary stay of execution.

5. *Conflicts with judgments given in non-contracting States which qualify for recognition*

205. In one respect the provisions of the 1968 Convention governing recognition required formal amendment. A certain lack of clarity in some of these provisions can be accepted since the European Court of Justice has jurisdiction to interpret them. However, Member States cannot be expected to accept lack of clarity where this might give rise to diplomatic complications with non-contracting States. The new Article 27 (5) is designed to avoid such complications.

This may be explained by way of an example. A decision dismissing an action against a person domiciled in the Community is given in non-contracting State A. A Community State, B, is obliged to recognize the judgment under a bilateral convention. The plaintiff brings fresh proceedings in another Community State, C, which is not obliged to recognize the judgment given in the non-contracting State. If he is successful, the existing text of the 1968 Convention leaves it open to doubt whether the judgment has to be recognized in State B.

In future, it is certain that this is not the case. In order to avoid unnecessary discrepancies, the text of the new provision is based on Article 5 of the Hague Convention of 1 February 1971 on the recognition and enforcement of foreign judgments in civil and commercial matters. Its wording is slightly wider in scope than would have been required to avoid diplomatic complications. A judgment given in a non-contracting State takes priority even where it has to be recognized, not by virtue of an international convention but merely under national law. For obligations under conventions not to recognize certain judgments, see paragraph 249 *et seq*.

Section 2
Enforcement

1. *Preliminary remarks*

206. The Working Party's efforts were almost entirely confined to deciding which courts in the new Member States should have jurisdiction in enforcement proceedings, and what appeal procedures should be provided in this context. In this connection four peculiarities of United Kingdom and, to a certain extent, Irish law had to be considered.

The Working Party took no decision on amendments to deal with the costs of the enforcement procedure. On this point, however, reference should be made to the judgment of the Court of Justice of the European Communities of 30 November 1976 (Case 42/76). According to that decision, Article 31 prohibits a successful plaintiff from bringing fresh proceedings in the State in which enforcement is sought. But the Contracting States are obliged to adopt rules on costs which take into account the desire to simplify the enforcement procedure.

207. The Working Party also abandoned attempts to draft provisions in the Convention on seizure for international claims, although it was clear that problems would occur to a certain extent if debtors and third party debtors were domiciled in different States. If, in one State, the court of the debtor's domicile has jurisdiction over seizure for such claims, then the State of domicile of the third party debtor may regard the making of the order for seizure applicable to the latter as a violation of its sovereignty, and refuse to enforce it. In such a situation the creditor can seek assistance by obtaining a declaration that the judgment is enforceable in the State of domicile of the third party debtor, and enforcing the debtor's claim against the third party in that State, provided that this State assumes international jurisdiction over such a measure.

208. (a) United Kingdom and Irish law does not have the exequatur system for foreign judgments. In these countries an action on the basis of the foreign judgment is necessary unless, as in the United Kingdom, a system of registration applies to the judgments of certain States (including the six original Member States with the exception of Luxembourg) (see paragraph 6). In that case the foreign judgments, if they are to be enforced, must be registered with a court in the United Kingdom. They then have the same force as judgments of the registering court itself. The application has to be lodged by the creditor in person or by a solicitor on his behalf. Personal appearance is essential; lodging by post will not suffice. If the application is granted, an order to that effect will be entered in the register kept at the

court.

Except in Scotland, however, the United Kingdom has no independent enforcement officer like the French "huissier" or the German "Gerichtsvollzieher" (see paragraph 221). Only the court which gave the judgment or where the judgment was registered can direct enforcement measures. Since this system of registration affords the same protection to a foreign judgment creditor as does the exequatur system on the Continent, the United Kingdom registration system could also be accepted for applying the provisions of the 1968 Convention.

209. (b) A special feature of the constitution of the United Kingdom has already been mentioned in the introductory remarks (see paragraph 11): England and Wales, Scotland and Northern Ireland are independent judicial areas. A new paragraph had to be added to Article 31 to cover this. Similarly the appeal possibilities provided for in Articles 37 and 40 apply separately to each registration. If a judgment has been validly registered with the High Court in London, another appeal is again possible against a subsequent registration with the Court of Session in Edinburgh.

210. (c) As far as the enforcement of foreign judgments is concerned the United Kingdom traditionally concedes special treatment to maintenance orders (see paragraph 7). Until now they have been enforced only in respect of a few Commonwealth countries and Ireland, and their enforcement is entrusted to courts different from those responsible for enforcing other judgments. Since the 1968 Convention contains no provisions precluding different recognition procedures for different types of judgment, there is no reason why maintenance orders cannot be covered by a special arrangement within the scope of the 1968 Convention. This will permit the creation of a uniform system for the recognition of maintenance orders from the Community and the Commonwealth and, in view of the type of court having jurisdiction, the setting up of a central agency to receive applications for enforcement (see paragraph 218). For agreements concerning maintenance see paragraph 226.

211. (d) Finally there were still problems in connection with judgments ordering performance other than the payment of money. Judgments directing a person to do a particular act are not generally enforceable under United Kingdom and Irish law, but only in pursuance of special legal provisions. These provisions cover judgments ordering the delivery of movable property or the transfer of ownership or possession of immovable property, and injunctions by which the court may in its discretion order an individual to do or refrain from doing a certain act. Enforcement is possible either by the sheriff's officer using direct compulsion or indirectly by means of fines or imprisonment for contempt of court. In Scotland, in addition to judgments for the transfer of possession or ownership of immovable property and preventative injunctions, there are also "decrees *ad factum prestandum*" by means of which the defendant can be ordered to perform certain acts, particularly to hand back movable property.

212. (aa) If an application is made in the Federal Republic of Germany for the enforcement of such a judgment given in Ireland or the United Kingdom, the court must apply the same means of compulsion as would be applicable in the case of a corresponding German judgment, i.e. a fine or imprisonment. In the reverse situation, the United Kingdom and Irish courts may have to impose penalties for contempt of court in the same way as when their own orders are disregarded.

213. (bb) The system for enforcing orders requiring the performance of a specific act is fundamentally different in other States of the Community, e.g. Belgium, France and Luxembourg. The defendant is ordered to perform the act and at the same time to pay a sum of money to the plaintiff to cover a possible non-compliance with the order. In France he is initially only threatened with a fine ("astreinte"). In case of non-compliance, a separate judgment is required and is hardly ever as high as the fine originally threatened. In Belgium the amount of the fine is already fixed in the judgment ordering the act to be performed.[56] With a view to overcoming the difficulties which this could cause for the inter-State enforcement of judgments ordering specific acts. Article 43 provides that, if the sanction takes the form of a fine ("astreinte"), the original court should itself fix the amount. Enforcement abroad is then limited to the "astreinte". French," Belgian, Dutch and Luxembourg judgments can be enforced without difficulty in Germany, the United Kingdom and Italy if the original court has proceeded on that basis.

However, the 1968 Convention leaves open the question whether such a fine for disregarding a court order can also be enforced when it accrues not to the judgment creditor but to the State. Since this is not a new problem arising out of the accession of the new Member States, the Working Party did not express a view on the matter.

2. *Formal adjustments as regards courts having jurisdiction and authorized appeals*

214. Apart from the inclusion of a term equivalent in the Irish and United Kingdom legal systems to ordinary appeal (see paragraph 195), and apart from Article 44 which deals with legal aid (see paragraph

223), the formal adjustments to Articles 32 to 45 relate exclusively to the courts having jurisdiction and the possible types of appeal against their decisions. (See paragraph 108 for adjustments relating to maintenance.)

215. (a) For applications for a declaration of enforceability (see paragraph 208) of judgments other than maintenance orders only one court has been given jurisdiction in each of Ireland, England and Wales, Scotland and Northern Ireland. This is due to the peculiarities of the court systems in these countries (see paragraphs 11, 208 and 209).

216. If the judgment debtor wishes to argue against the authorization of enforcement, he must lodge his application to set the registration aside not with a higher court, as in Germany, France and Italy, but, as in Belgium and the Netherlands, with the court which registered the judgment. The proceedings will take the form of an ordinary contentious civil action.

A corresponding position applies regarding the appeal which the applicant may lodge if his application is refused, although in such a case it is a higher court which has jurisdiction in all seven Continental Member States of the Community.

217. The adjustment of the second paragraph of Article 37 and of Article 41 gave rise to difficulties with regard to the solution adopted for Articles 32 and 40.

In the original Member States of the Community an appeal against judgments of courts on which jurisdiction is conferred by Articles 37 and 40 could only be lodged on a point of law and with the highest court in the State. It was therefore sufficient to make the same provision apply to the appeals provided for in the 1968 Convention and, in the case of Belgium, simply to bypass the Cour d'appel. The purpose of this arrangement is to limit the number of appeals, in the interests of rapid enforcement, to a single appeal which may involve a full review of the facts and a second one limited to points of law. It would therefore not have been enough to stipulate for the new Member States that only one further appeal would be permitted against the judgment of the court which had ruled on an appeal made by either the debtor or the creditor. Instead, the second appeal had to be limited to points of law.

Ireland and the United Kingdom will have to adapt their appeal system to the requirements of the 1968 Convention. In the case of Ireland, which has only a two-tier superior court system, the Supreme Court is the only possibility. Implementing legislation in the United Kingdom will have to determine whether the further appeals should go direct to the House of Lords or, depending on the judicial area concerned (see paragraph 11), to the Court of Appeal in England and Wales, to the court of the same name in Northern Ireland or to the Inner House of the Court of Session in Scotland. The concept of "appeal on a point of law" is the nearest equivalent as far as United Kingdom law is concerned to the "Rechtsbeschwerde" of German law and the appeal in cassation in the legal systems of the other original Member States of the Community, the common feature of which is a restriction of the grounds of appeal to an incorrect application of the law (as opposed to an incorrect assessment of the facts). Even in relation to appeals in cassation and "Rechtsbeschwerde" the distinction between points of law and matters of fact is not identical; for the United Kingdom and Ireland, too, this will remain a matter for its own legislation and case law to clarify.

Traditionally the leave of the Minister for Justice is required for an appeal to the highest Danish court at third instance. The Working Party was initially doubtful whether it should accept this in the context of the 1968 Convention. It emerged, however, that the Convention does not guarantee a third instance in all circumstances. In. order to relieve the burden on their highest courts, Member States may limit the admissibility of the appeals provided for in Article 41. The Danish solution is only one manifestation of this idea. There was also no need in the case of Denmark to stipulate that the appeal to the highest court should be limited to a point of law. When granting leave the Ministry of Justice can ensure that the appeal concerns only questions of law requiring further elucidation. Denmark has given an assurance that leave will always be granted, if the court of second instance has not made use of its discretion to refer a matter to the European Court of Justice or if enforcement of a foreign judgment has been refused on legal grounds.

218. (b) In Ireland the proposed arrangement also applies to maintenance orders. In the United Kingdom, however, maintenance orders are subject to a special arrangement (see paragraph 210). In England and Wales and in Northern Ireland registration is a matter for the Magistrates' Courts, and in Scotland for the Sheriff Courts. These courts also have jurisdiction in respect of other maintenance matters including the enforcement of foreign maintenance orders. Foreign maintenance creditors cannot, however, have recourse to any of the above courts directly, but must apply to the Secretary of State,[57] who will transmit the order to the appropriate court. This arrangement was made in the interest of the foreign maintenance creditors, because Magistrates' Courts and Sheriff Courts have lay justices

and no administrative machinery.

As regards jurisdiction in respect of appeals which may be brought by either the creditor or the debtor under the 1968 Convention, the usual system will continue to apply, i.e. the appeal is decided by the court which registered the order or refused such registration. It is impossible for a maintenance order to be amended during registration proceedings, even if it is claimed that the circumstances have changed (see paragraph 104 *et seq.*).

The special situation regarding maintenance orders in the United Kingdom offers a series of advantages to the maintenance creditor. After forwarding the order to the Secretary of State, he has virtually no further need to concern himself with the progress of the proceedings or with their enforcement. The rest will be done free of charge. The Secretary of State transmits the order to the appropriate court and, unless the maintenance creditor otherwise requests, the clerk of that court will be regarded as the representative *ad litem* within the meaning of Article 33, second paragraph, second sentence. In England and Wales and in Northern Ireland the clerk in question will also be responsible for taking the necessary enforcement measures and for ensuring that the creditor receives the proceeds obtained. Only in Scotland need the creditor under the order seek the services of a solicitor when applying for enforcement following registration of an order. The Law Society of Scotland undertakes to provide solicitors whose fees are, if necessary, paid in accordance with the principles of legal aid. Should the maintenance debtor move to another judicial area in the United Kingdom (see paragraph 11), a maintenance order will, unlike other judgments, be automatically registered with the court which then has jurisdiction. For agreements concerning maintenance, see paragraph 226.

3. *Other adjustment problems*

219. (a) The United Kingdom asked whether Article 34 excludes the possibility of notifying the debtor that an application for registration of a foreign judgment has been lodged. One of the aims of Article 34 is to secure the element of surprise, which is essential if measures of enforcement are to be effective. Therefore, although this provision does not expressly forbid notifying the debtor in the proceedings of the application for the grant of an enforcement order, such notification should be confined to very exceptional cases. An example might be an application for registration made a long time after the original judgment was given. In any case, the court may not consider submissions from the debtor, whether or not he was notified in advance.

220. (b) The appeal provided for in Article 36 can be based, *inter alia*, on the grounds that the judgment does not come within the scope of the 1968 Convention, that it is not yet enforceable, or that the obligation imposed by the judgment has already been complied with. However, the substance of the judgment to be enforced or the procedure by which it came into existence can be reviewed only within the limits of Articles 27 and 28. For the adjustment of maintenance orders, see paragraph 108.

221. (c) The Working Party discussed Article 39 at length. The provision in question is modelled on the French legal system and legal systems related to it, to which the institution of "huissier" is familiar. Under these systems, measures of enforcement. in respect of movable property or contractual claims belonging to the debtor can be taken, without involving the court, by instructing a "huissier" to deal with their execution. It is for the creditor to choose between the available methods of enforcement. The enforcing agency has no discretion whatsoever in the matter. The legal position obtaining in the United Kingdom (especially in England and Wales and also in Scotland) and Ireland is quite different. In the United Kingdom it is the court which has given or registered the judgment which has jurisdiction over measures of enforcement. In Ireland it is the court which has given or enforced the judgment. The court also has some discretion as to which enforcement measures it will sanction. Protective measures confined to securing enforcement of a claim do not yet exist.

This position will have to be altered by the implementing legislation of these States, which will have to introduce protective measures, in so far as this consequence does not arise as an automatic result of the entry into force of the 1968 Convention for one of these States (see paragraph 256).

The 1968 Convention does not guarantee specific measures of enforcement to the creditor. Neither is it in any way incompatible with the 1968 Convention to leave the measures of enforcement entirely to the court. The 1968 Convention contains no express provision obliging the Member States to employ an institution similar to the French "huissier". Even within its original scope, creditors have to apply directly to the court in the case of certain measures of enforcement; in Germany, for example, they would be required to do so in the case of enforcement against immovable property. It is certain however that in the German text the phrase "in das Vermögen des Schuldners" ("against the property of the party against whom enforcement is sought") does not mean that measures of enforcement are permissible as against third parties. The words quoted above could be omitted without changing the meaning of the provision. The question under what conditions measures of enforcement are possible against persons other than the judgment debtor is to be answered solely on the basis of national law. But the qualifications contained in Article 39 must also be observed.

The court enforcing the judgment need not be the one which grants the order of enforcement or registers the foreign judgment. Therefore, for the purposes of enforcement under the 1968 Convention, Denmark can retain its present system, by which execution is entrusted to a special enforcement judge.

222. (d) For the problems presented by the system of "*astreintes*", which applies in some Member States, see paragraph 213.

223. (e) In its present form, Article 44 does not provide for the case of a party who had been granted only partial legal aid in the State in which the judgment was given. Although this did not involve an adjustment problem specifically due to the accession of the new Member States, the Working Party decided to propose an amendment. The Working Party's discussions revealed that if the text were to remain in force in its present form, it could result in some undesirable complications. The Working Party's proposal was largely based on the formulation of Article 15 of the Hague Convention of 2 October 1973 on the recognition and enforcement of decisions relating to maintenance obligations which has now come into force. This provision opts for a generous solution: even if only partial legal aid was granted in the State of origin, full aid is to be granted in the enforcement proceedings.

This has a number of further advantages:

As the main application of Article 44 as amended relates to maintenance claims, the amended version contributes to the harmonization of provisions in international conventions.

Moreover, it leads to a general simplification of applications.

Since the rules concerning the granting of partial legal aid are not the same in all the Contracting States, the amended version also ensures a uniform application of the legal aid provisions.

Lastly, it secures the surprise effect of enforcement measures abroad, by avoiding procedural delays caused by difficult calculations concerning the applicant's share in the costs.

The first paragraph of Article 44 does not, however, oblige States which do not at present have a system of legal aid in civil matters to introduce such a system.

224. (f) The reason for the new second paragraph of Article 44 relates to the jurisdiction of the Danish administrative authorities (see paragraph 67) whose services are free. No question of legal aid therefore arises. The new provision is designed to ensure that the enforcement of Danish maintenance orders is not, for this reason, at a disadvantage in the other EEC countries by comparison with maintenance orders from EEC countries other than Denmark.

Section 3

Common provisions

225. The discussion of Articles 46 to 49 centred on whether the new Member States, in accordance with their legal tradition, could require an affidavit, in particular to the effect that none of the grounds for refusing recognition, specified in Articles 27 and 28, obtain. Affidavit evidence is certainly admissible in appellate proceedings, where the debtor appeals against registration or against a declaration of enforceability, or the creditor against a refusal to register. However, all the other means of giving evidence which are normally admissible must also be available in those proceedings.

The addition to Article 46 (2) is proposed for the reasons given in paragraphs 182 and 194.

CHAPTER 6 – AUTHENTIC INSTRUMENTS AND COURT SETTLEMENTS

226. In England and Ireland there is no equivalent of enforceable instruments. In Scotland, instruments establishing a clearly defined obligation to perform a contract can be entered in a public register. An extract from the public register can then serve as a basis for enforcement in the same way as a court judgment. Such extracts are covered by Article 50.

In the United Kingdom, the courts having jurisdiction for recognition and enforcement of maintenance orders are different from those concerned with other kinds of judgment (see paragraphs 210 and 218). It is for the internal Jaw of the United Kingdom to determine whether foreign court settlements concerning maintenance should be treated as maintenance orders or as other judgments.

CHAPTER 7 – GENERAL PROVISIONS

227. The outcome of the discussion of Articles 52 and 53 has already been recorded elsewhere (see paragraphs 73 *et seq.*, and 119).

CHAPTER 8 – TRANSITIONAL PROVISIONS

228. Article 54 continues to apply to the relationships between the original Member States. For their relationships with the new Member States, and the relationships of the new Member States with each other, an appropriate transitional provision is included in Article 34 of the proposed Accession Convention. It is closely modelled on Article 54 of the 1968 Convention, but takes into account the fact that the latter has already been in force in its present form between the original Member States since 1 February 1973, and also the fact that some amendments are to be made to it. Finally, the Interpretation Protocol of 3 June 1971 also had to be taken into account in the transitional rules. The detailed provisions are as follows[58]:

I. JURISDICTION

229. 1. The provisions on jurisdiction in the 1968 Convention apply in the new Member States only in their amended version and only to proceedings instituted after the Accession Convention has come into force, and hence after the 1968 Convention has come into force, in the State in question (Article 34 (1)).

230. 2. The amended version also applies to proceedings instituted in the Original Member States after that date. Jurisdiction in respect of proceedings instituted in the original Member States before that date but after 1 February 1973 will continue to be determined in accordance with the original text of the 1968 Convention (Article 34 (1)). It is to be noted, as regards the relationships of the old Member States with each other, that under Article 39 of the Accession Convention the amended version can only come into force simultaneously for all six of them.

If we assume that the Accession Convention comes into force for the original Member States of the Community and Denmark on 1 January 1981 and an action is brought in Germany against a person domiciled in Denmark on 3 January 1981, then a judgment on 1 July 1981 finding in favour of the plaintiff would be enforceable irrespective of transitional provisions, even if, say, the United Kingdom did not become a party to the Convention until 1 December 1981. However, if in this example the action was brought and judgment given against a person domiciled in the United Kingdom, Article 34 (1) would not govern recognition and enforcement in the United Kingdom. That would be a true transitional case.

Paragraphs (2) and (3) of Article 34 deal with judgments during the transitional period, i.e. judgments given after the Accession Convention has come into force in the State addressed but in proceedings which were instituted at a time when, either in the State of origin or in the State addressed, the Accession Convention was not yet in force. In Article 34 (2) and (3) a distinction is drawn between cases involving only the original Member States of the Community and those involving new Member States as well.

II. RECOGNITION AND ENFORCEMENT

1. *END OF THE TRANSITIONAL PERIOD*

231. The recognition and enforcement of judgments are in all respects governed by the Convention as amended, provided the transitional period had already ended at the time of institution of the proceedings. For this purpose, the Accession Convention must have come into force by that time both in the State of origin and in the State subsequently addressed (Article 34 (1)). It is not sufficient for the Accession Convention to be in force in the former State only, since rules of exorbitant jurisdiction may still be invoked under Article 4 of the 1968 Convention against domiciliaries of the State subsequently addressed if that State was not also a party to the Accession Convention at the time of institution of the proceedings. This would render an obligation to recognize and enforce a judgment in that State without any preliminary review unacceptable.

If we assume that the Accession Convention comes into force for the original Member States of the Community and Denmark on 1 January 1981 and an action is brought in Germany against a person domiciled in Denmark on 3 January 1981, then a judgment on 1 July 1981 finding in favour of the plaintiff would be enforceable irrespective of transitional provisions even if, say, the United Kingdom did not become a party to the Convention until 1 December 1981. However, if in this example the action was brought and judgment given against a person domiciled in the United Kingdom, Article 34 (1) would not govern recognition and enforcement in the United Kingdom. That would be a true transitional case.

Paragraphs (2) and (3) of Article 34 deal with judgments during the transitional period, i.e. judgments given after the Accession Convention has come into force in the State addressed, but in proceedings which were instituted at a time when, either in the State of origin or in the State addressed, the Accession Convention was not yet in force. In Article 34 (2) and (3) a distinction is drawn between cases involving only the original Member States of the Community and those involving new Member States as well.

2. *AMONG THE ORIGINAL MEMBER STATES OF THE COMMUNITY*

232. Article 34 (2) makes the recognition and enforcement of judgments among the original Member States of the Community subject without any restriction to the 1968 Convention as amended, even if the actions were started before the entry into force of the Accession Convention, which will necessarily be simultaneous in those States (see the end of paragraph 230). This amounts indirectly to a statement that the situation as regards the recognition and enforcement of judgments among those States remains that in Article 54 of the 1968 Convention in the case of judgments given before the entry into force of the Accession Convention. The most important implication of Article 34 (2) is that in proceedings for the recognition of judgments among the original Member States of the Community there is to be no consideration of whether the court giving the judgment whose recognition is sought would have had jurisdiction after the entry into force of the Accession Convention. If the action was started after 1 February 1973 then the jurisdiction of the court giving the judgment whose recognition is sought may no longer be examined. The point is of note since that court's jurisdiction could still have been founded on exorbitant jurisdictional rules where domiciliaries of the new Member States are concerned.

To illustrate the point with an example, if a Frenchman were in 1978 to bring an action in the French courts pursuant to Article 14 of the Civil Code against a person domiciled in Ireland, which would be possible under Article 4 of the 1968 Convention, and judgment was given in favour of the plaintiff in 1982; then, assuming the Accession Convention came into force for the original Member States of the Community and Ireland in 1981, the judgment would have to be recognized and enforced in Germany, but not in Ireland.

3. *WHERE NEW MEMBER STATES ARE INVOLVED*

233. The arrangements obtaining under Article 34 (3) for the recognition and enforcement of judgments between the original Member States and the new Member States, or as between the new Member States, differ somewhat from those applying among the original Member States. Article 34 (3) is concerned with the possibility of recognition and enforcement being sought in one of the new Contracting States of a judgment from an original Contracting State or from another new Contracting State. Apart from the cases referred to in paragraph 231, this is possible after the end of the transitional period, subject to three requirements being met.

234. (a) The judgment must have been given after the Accession Convention came into force in both States.

235. (b) In addition, the proceedings must have been instituted, in the words of the Convention, before "the date of entry into force of this Convention, between the State of origin and the State addressed". The purport of this is that, at the time when the proceedings were instituted, the Accession Convention may have come into force either in the State of the court giving the judgment for which recognition is sought, or in the State in which recognition and enforcement are subsequently sought, but not in both of these States.

236. (c) Finally, the jurisdiction of the court giving the judgment for which recognition is sought must satisfy certain criteria which the court in the State addressed must check. These criteria exactly match what Article 54 of the 1968 Convention laid down regarding transitional cases which were pending when that Convention came into force between the six original Member States. In proceedings for recognition, the jurisdiction of the court which gave judgment is to be accepted as having been valid, provided one of two requirements is met:

(aa) The judgment must be recognized where the court in the State of origin would have had jurisdiction if the Accession Convention had already been in force as between the two States at the time when the proceedings were instituted.

(bb) The judgment must also be recognized where the court's jurisdiction was covered at the time when the proceedings were instituted by another International convention which was in force between the two States.

Reverting to the example in paragraph 232, the position would be as follows: the French judgment would indeed have been given after the Accession Convention had come into force in Ireland and France. The proceedings would have been instituted at a time when the Accession Convention was not yet in force in France (or in Ireland). Had this Convention already been in force as between France and Ireland at that time, the French courts would no longer have been able to found their jurisdiction on Article 14 of the Civil Code and hence, it must further be assumed, would have been unable to assume jurisdiction. Lastly, there is no bilateral convention between France and Ireland concerning the direct or indirect jurisdiction of the courts. Consequently, the judgment would not have had to be recognized in Ireland.

If one changes the example so that it now concerns France and the United Kingdom, one has to take into consideration the Convention between those two States of 18 January 1934 providing for the reciprocal enforcement of judgments. However, jurisdiction deriving from Article 14 of the Civil Code is not admitted under that Convention; thus the judgment would not have to be recognized in the United Kingdom either.

If the example concerned Germany and the United Kingdom, and the defendant resident in the United Kingdom had agreed orally before the commencement of the proceedings that the German courts should have jurisdiction, then under the 1968 Convention the judgment would have to be recognized and enforced in the United Kingdom. Under Article IV (1) (a) of the Convention between the United Kingdom and Germany of 14 July 1960, oral agreement is sufficient to give grounds for jurisdiction for the purposes of recognition ("indirect" jurisdiction). However, the German court would have had to be a "Landgericht", since "Amtsgericht" judgments are not required to be recognized under that Convention (Article I (2)). In the event of a written agreement on jurisdiction, even the judgment of an "Amtsgericht" would have to be recognized, under Article 34 (3) of the Accession Convention, as the "Amtsgericht" would in that case have assumed jurisdiction under circumstances in which jurisdiction would also have had to be assumed if the Accession Convention had been in force between Germany and the United Kingdom.

CHAPTER 9 – RELATIONSHIP TO OTHER CONVENTIONS

I. ARTICLES 55 AND 56

237. The Working Party included in Article 55 the bilateral conventions between the United Kingdom and other Member States of the Community. No such conventions have been concluded by Ireland and Denmark.

II. ARTICLE 57[59]

1. *THE BASIC STRUCTURE OF THE PROPOSED PROVISION*

238. Great difficulties arose when an attempt was made to explain to the new Member States the exact scope of Article 57, the main reason being the statement that the Convention "shall not affect" any conventions in relation to particular matters, without stating how the provisions in such conventions could be reconciled with those of the 1968 Convention where they covered only part of the matters governed by the latter, which is usually the case. Special conventions can be divided into three groups. Many of them contain only provisions on direct jurisdiction, as in the case with the Warsaw Convention of 12 October 1929 for the unification of certain rules relating to international carriage by air and the Additional Protocols thereto,* and the Brussels Convention relating to the arrest of seagoing ships which is of great importance for maritime law (Article 7) (see paragraph 121). Most conventions govern only the recognition and enforcement of judgments, and merely refer indirectly to jurisdiction in so far as it constitutes a precondition for recognition. This is the case with the Hague Convention of 15 April 1958 on the recognition and enforcement of decisions relating to maintenance obligations towards children. Finally, there are also Conventions which contain provisions directly regulating jurisdiction as well as recognition and enforcement, as for example the Berne Convention on carriage by rail and the Mannheim Convention for the navigation of the Rhine. It is irrelevant for present purposes whether the conventions contain additional provisions on the applicable law or rules of substantive law.

* Not to be confused with the Brussels Convention of the same date for the unification of certain rules relating to penal jurisdiction in matters of collision.

239. (a) It is clear beyond argument that where a special convention contains no provisions directly governing jurisdiction, the jurisdiction provisions of the 1968 Convention apply. It is equally clear that where all the Contracting States are parties to a special convention containing provisions on jurisdiction, those provisions prevail. But for situations between these two extremes the solution provided by Article 57 is a great deal less dear. This is particularly the case for a number of questions, which arise where only the State of origin .and the State addressed are parties to the special convention. The problems become acute where only one of these two States is a party. If both States are parties to a special convention which governs only direct jurisdiction, will the provisions of the 1968 Convention regarding examination of jurisdiction by the court of its own motion (Article 20), *lis pendens* (Article 21) and enforcement apply? Do the provisions of the 1968 Convention on the procedure for recognition and enforcement apply, if a special convention on the recognition and enforcement judgments does not deal with procedure? Can a person domiciled in a Contracting State which is not a party to a special convention be sued in the courts of another Contracting State on the basis of jurisdiction provisions in the special conventions, or can the State of domicile which is not a party to the special convention claim that the jurisdiction rules of the 1968 Convention must be observed? Must a judgment given in a court which has jurisdiction only under a special convention be recognized and enforced even in a Contracting State which is not a party to that particular special convention? And, finally, what is the position where the special convention does not claim to be exclusive?

240. Tentative and conflicting views were expressed within the Working Party as to how these problems were to be solved in interpreting Article 57 in its original form. It became clear that it would not be practicable to provide a precise solution to all of them, particularly since it is impossible to predict the form of future conventions. It was however appropriate, in the interests of clarifying the obligations about to be assumed by the new Member States, to include in the Accession Convention an authentic interpretation which concerns some problems which are of special importance. The opportunity was taken to make a drafting improvement to the present Article 57 of the 1968 Convention – the new paragraph 1 of this Article – which will speak of recognition or enforcement. By reason of the purely drafting nature of the amendment to the text, the provision laying down the authentic interpretation of the new Article 57 (1) also applies to the present version.

The solution arrived at is based on the following principles. The 1968 Convention contains the rules generally applicable in all Member States; provisions in special conventions are special rules which every State may make prevail over the 1968 Convention by becoming a party to such a convention. In so far as a special convention does not contain rules covering a particular matter the 1968 Convention applies. This is also the case where the special convention includes rules of jurisdiction which do not altogether fit the inter-connecting provisions of the various parts of the 1968 Convention, especially those governing the relationship between jurisdiction and enforcement. The overriding considerations are simplicity and clarity of the legal position.

The most important consequence of this is that provisions on jurisdiction contained in special conventions are to be regarded as if they were provisions of the 1968 Convention itself, even if only one Member State is a Contracting Party to such a special convention. Even Member States which are not Contracting Parties to the special convention must therefore recognize and enforce decisions given by courts which have jurisdiction only under the special convention. Furthermore, in the context of two States which are parties to a special convention, a person who wishes to obtain the recognition or enforcement of a judgment may rely upon the procedural provisions of the 1968 Convention on recognition and enforcement.

At the same time, the Working Party did not wish to reach a final conclusion on the question whether the general principle outlined above could be consistently applied in all its ramifications. To take a critical example, it was left open whether exclusive jurisdiction under the provisions of a special convention must invariably be applied. The same applies to the question whether a case of *lis pendens* arising from a special convention is covered by Article 21 of the 1968 Convention. The Working Party therefore preferred to provide expressly for the application or Article 20 and to leave the solution of the outstanding problems to legal literature and case law. For the implications of an authentic interpretation of Article 57 for maritime jurisdiction, see paragraph 121.

2. *EXAMPLES*

241. A river boatman domiciled in the Netherlands is liable for damages arising from an accident which occurred on the upper Rhine. It is however no longer possible to determine whether the harmful event occurred on German or French territory or from where the damage emanated.

242. It is not possible in such a case for either German or French courts to assume jurisdiction under Article 5 (3) or any other provision of the 1968 Convention. According to Article 34 (2) (c) and Article 35a of the revised Rhine navigation Convention of 17 October 1868 in the version of the Protocol of 25 October 1972,[60] jurisdiction in such cases belongs to the court of the State which was the first or only one seised of the matter. That court must, however, take into account Article 20 of the 1968 Convention, even though no equivalent of this Article exists in the Rhine navigation Convention. For example, if the defendant fails to enter an appearance, the court must of its own motion (see paragraph 22) ascertain whether all means have been exhausted of determining exactly where the accident occurred, for only if this cannot be determined does the court have jurisdiction under the abovementioned provisions of the Rhine navigation Convention.

243. If the court first seised of the matter was French, then any judgment of that court must be recognized in Germany. The Rhine navigation Convention is even stricter than the 1968 Convention in forbidding any re-examination of the original judgment in the State addressed. According to the correct interpretation of Article 57 of the 1968 Convention the judgment creditor has the choice of availing himself of the enforcement procedure provided by the Rhine navigation Convention or by the 1968 Convention. However, if he proceeds under the 1968 Convention the court may not refuse recognition on any of the grounds given in Article 27 or Article 28 of the 1968 Convention. Unlike the enforcement procedure itself, the conditions for recognition and enforcement are exclusively governed by the special conventions - in this example, the Rhine navigation Convention.

244. If, however, a judgment has been given in the court with jurisdiction at the place of destination pursuant to Article 28 (1) of the Warsaw Convention of 12 October 1929 for the unification of certain rules relating to international carriage by air, the 1968 Convention applies fully to both recognition and enforcement, because the Warsaw Convention contains no provisions at all on these matters. The same applies where in maritime law the jurisdiction of the court of origin was based on the provisions governing arrest contained in the 1952 Brussels Convention (see paragraph 121).

245. If the boatman in the above example on Rhine navigation had been domiciled in Luxembourg, which is not a party to the Rhine navigation Convention, the position would be as follows: any jurisdiction assumed in France or Germany pursuant to the Rhine navigation Convention can no longer be regarded in Luxembourg as an infringement of the 1968 Convention. Under the provisions and procedure of the 1968 Convention, Luxembourg is obliged to recognize and enforce a judgment given by the German or French Rhine navigation courts. If, conversely, the boatman is sued in the court of his Luxembourg domicile, which is also permissible, under the 1968 Convention, Germany and France would have to accept this, even though they are parties to the Rhine navigation Convention which does not recognize jurisdiction based on domicile.

3. *UNDERTAKINGS IN CONVENTIONS BETWEEN STATES NOT TO RECOGNIZE JUDGMENTS*

246. Whether Article 57 also covers conventions under which one Member State of the Community undertakes not to recognize judgments given in another Member State remains an open question. It could be argued that the admissible scope of such conventions was governed exclusively by Article 59.

International obligations of this sort can result from a special convention which provides for the exclusive jurisdiction of the courts of one of the Contracting Parties. Such an obligation can however also result indirectly from the fact that the exercise of jurisdiction under the special convention is linked to a special regime of liability. For example, the Paris Convention of 1960 on third party liability in the field of nuclear energy, apart from laying down rules of jurisdiction, recognition and enforcement:

1. places the sole liability for damage on the operator of a nuclear installation;
2. makes his liability an absolute one;
3. sets maximum limits to his liability;
4. requires him to insure against his liability;
5. allows a Contracting State to provide additional compensation from public funds.

The recognition and enforcement of a judgment which is given in a State not party to such a special convention and which is based on legal principles quite different from those outlined above could seriously undermine the operation of that special convention.

The 1968 Convention should always be interpreted in such a way that no limitations of liability contained in international conventions are infringed. The question however remains open whether this result is to be achieved by applying the public policy provision of Article 27 (1), by analogy with the new paragraph (5) of Article 27, or by a broad interpretation of Article 57.

For conventions limiting liability in maritime law, see paragraph 124 *et seq.*

4. *PRECEDENCE OF SECONDARY COMMUNITY LAW*

247. Within the Working Party opinion was divided as to whether secondary Community law, or national laws adopted pursuant to secondary Community law, prevail over international agreements concluded between the Member States, in particular in the case of a convention provided for in Article 220 of the Treaty of Rome. There was, however, agreement that national and Community law referred to above should prevail over the 1968 Convention. This decision is embodied in Article 57; the provision is based on Article 25 of the preliminary draft Convention on the law applicable to contractual and non-contractual obligations.

5. *CONSULTATIONS BEFORE THE FUTURE ACCESSION BY MEMBER STATES OF THE COMMUNITY TO FURTHER AGREEMENTS*

248. By their accession to the Convention, the new Member States are also bound by the Joint Declaration made by the Contracting States at the time of the signing of the 1968 Convention. In the Declaration the States declare that they will arrange for regular periodic contacts between their representatives. The Working Party was unanimously of the opinion that consultations should also take place when a Member State intended to accede to a convention which would prevail over the 1968 Convention by virtue of Article 57.

III. ARTICLE 59

249. This provision refers only to judgments given against persons domiciled or habitually resident outside the Community. Such persons may also be sued on the basis of jurisdictional provisions which could not be invoked in the case of persons domiciled within the Community, and which are classed as exorbitant and disallowed pursuant to the second paragraph of Article 3. Nevertheless, any judgment which may have been given is to be recognized and enforced in accordance with the 1968 Convention. As the Jenard report explains, it is intended that the Contracting States should remain free to conclude conventions with third States excluding the recognition and enforcement of judgments based on exorbitant jurisdictions even though the 1968 Convention permits this in exceptional cases. The aim of the proposed amendment to Article 59 is further to limit the possibility of recognition and enforcement.

250. The way this will work may be illustrated by an example. If a creditor has a claim to be satisfied in France against a debtor domiciled in that country, then Danish courts have no jurisdiction under any circumstances to decide this issue, even if the debtor has property in Denmark and even if the claim is secured on immovable property there. Supposing the debtor is domiciled in Norway, then if Danish national law so allows Danish courts may very well claim jurisdiction, e.g. on the basis of the presence in Denmark of property owned by the debtor. Normally, the judgment given in such a case would also be enforceable in the United Kingdom. The United Kingdom could however undertake in a convention with Norway an obligation to refuse recognition and enforcement of such a judgment. This kind of treaty obligation may not however extend to a. case where the jurisdiction of the Danish courts is based on the ground that immovable property in, Denmark constitutes security for the debt. In such circumstances, the judgment would be enforceable even in the United Kingdom.

CHAPTER 10 – FINAL PROVISIONS

1. IRELAND

251. Ireland has no territorial possessions outside the integral parts of its territory.

2. UNITED KINGDOM

252. The term "United Kingdom" does not include the Channel Islands, the Isle of Man, Gibraltar or the Sovereign Base Areas in Cyprus. There is no obligation on the United Kingdom to extend the scope of the 1968 Convention to include these territories, even though it is responsible for their external relations. It might, however, be useful if the United Kingdom were to extend the 1968 Convention and it should be authorized to do so. It would have to undertake the necessary "adjustments" itself, and there was no need to provide for them in the Accession Convention. The following adjustments would be required: indication of any "exorbitant jurisdictions in the second paragraph of Article 3; a declaration as to whether in the newly included territories every appeal should be regarded as an ordinary appeal for the purposes of Articles 30 and 38; a declaration as to whether registration in any such territory in

accordance with the second paragraph of Article 31 is effective only within its area; establishing which courts are competent under Articles 32, 37 and 40, the form in which the application should be made, and whether the adjustments in respect of the United Kingdom contained in the second paragraph of Article 37 as amended and in Article 41 as amended should also apply in the newly included territories. If any international conventions should apply to any one of the territories in question, appropriate adjustments would also have to be made to Article 55.

The penultimate paragraph of the proposed addition to Article 60 relates to the fact that judgments of courts in these territories which do not belong to the United Kingdom can be challenged in the last instance before the Judicial Committee of the Privy Council. It would be illogical to bring Privy Council decisions within the scope of the 1968 Convention if they related to disputes arising in territories to which the 1968 Convention does not apply.

3. DENMARK

253. For the purposes of EEC law, Greenland is included in the European territory of Denmark. The special constitutional positions of the Faroe Islands led to a solution corresponding closely to that proposed for the territories for whose foreign relations the United Kingdom is responsible. This had to allow for the fact that both appellate and first instance proceedings which relate to the Faroes and are therefore conducted under the Code of Civil Procedure specially enacted for these islands can be brought in Copenhagen.

4. CHANGES IN A STATE'S TERRITORY

254. The Working Party was unanimous that any territory which becomes independent of the mother country thereby ceases to be a member of the European Community and, consequently, can no longer be a party to the 1968 Convention. It was unnecessary to provide for this expressly and, in any case, to have drafted such a provision would have gone beyond the Working Party's terms of reference.

CHAPTER 11 – ADJUSTMENTS TO THE PROTOCOL OF 3 JUNE 1971 ON THE INTERPRETATION BY THE COURT OF JUSTICE OF THE EUROPEAN COMMUNITIES OF THE 1968 CONVENTION

1. FORMAL ADJUSTMENTS

255. Formal adjustments to the Interpretation Protocol were few and fairly obvious. It became necessary to make only one short addition to its provisions: the courts in the new Member States which, in accordance with Article 2 (1) and Article 3, are required to request the Court of Justice to give preliminary rulings on questions of interpretation, had to be designated.[61] In the United Kingdom, unlike the other Member States, not only the highest court within the country has been included, as it is more difficult to refer a matter to the House of Lords than it is to have recourse to the highest courts on the continent. Therefore, at least the appellate proceedings provided for in the second paragraph of Article 37 and in Article 41 of the 1968 Convention should in the United Kingdom also terminate in a court which is obliged to request a preliminary ruling from the Court of Justice. The expression "appellate capacity" in Article 2 (2) should not be construed in a narrow technical sense, but in the sense of any challenge before a higher jurisdiction, so that it might be taken also to include the French "contredit'.

The remaining formal adjustments concerned merely the scope (Article 1) and territorial application of the Protocol. Article 6, which deals with the latter point, is wholly based on Article 60 of the 1968 Convention (see paragraphs 251 to 254). Which authorities are to be designated as competent within the meaning of the third paragraph of Article 4 is a question to be decided entirely by the new Member States.

2. THE SPECIAL NATURE OF IMPLEMENTING LEGISLATION IN THE UNITED KINGDOM AND IRELAND

256. The extension of the Interpretation Protocol to the United Kingdom and Ireland will, however, in all probability also present a procedural problem. A long-standing legal tradition in these States does not allow provisions of international treaties to become directly applicable as national law. In the United Kingdom legislation has to be passed transforming such provisions into national law. In many cases the legislative enactment does not follow precisely the wording of the treaty. The usual form of legislation

in this State often calls for a more detailed phraseology than that used in a treaty. The treaty and the corresponding national law are, therefore, to be carefully distinguished.

If the implementing legislation in the United Kingdom follows the usual pattern, courts in that country would only rarely be concerned with the interpretation of the 1968 Convention, but mostly with interpretation of the national implementing legislation. Only when the latter is not clear would it be open to a court, under the existing rules of construction in that country, to refer to the treaty on which the legislation is based, and only when the court is then faced with a problem of interpretation of the treaty may it turn to the European Court of Justice. If the provisions of implementing legislation are clear in themselves, the courts in the United Kingdom may as a rule refer neither to the text of the treaty nor to any decision by an international court on its interpretation.

This would undoubtedly lead to a certain disparity in the application of the Interpretation Protocol of 3 June 1971. The Working Party was of the opinion that this disparity could best be redressed if the United Kingdom could in some way ensure in its implementing legislation that the 1968 Convention will there too be endowed with the status of a source of law, or may at any rate be referred to directly when applying the national implementing legislation.

In the event of a judgment of the European Court of Justice being inconsistent with a provision of the United Kingdom implementing legislation, the latter would have to be amended.

It is also the case in Ireland that international agreements to which that State is a party are not directly applicable as national law. Lately, however, a number of Acts putting international agreements into force in national law have taken the form of an incorporation of the text of the agreement into national law. If the Act putting into force the 1968 Convention as amended by the Accession Convention were to take this form, the problems described above in relation to the United Kingdom would not arise in the case of Ireland.

ANNEX I

Extract from the Protocol to the preliminary draft Bankruptcy Convention (1975) (see paragraph 54)

Certain details of this list have been amended by later documents which, however, are not themselves final.

(aa) *Bankruptcy proceedings:*

Belgium:
"faillite" – "faillissement";

Denmark:
"Konkurs';

Federal Republic of Germany:
"Konkurs";

France:
"liquidation des biens";

Ireland:
"bankruptcy", "winding-up in bankruptcy of partnerships", "winding-up by the court under Sections 213, 344 and 345 of the Companies Act 1963", "creditors' voluntary winding-up under Section 256 of the Companies Act 1963";

Italy:
"fallimento";

Luxembourg:
"faillite";

Netherlands:
"faillissement";

United Kingdom:
"bankruptcy" (England, Wales and Northern Ireland), "sequestration" (Scotland), "administration in bankruptcy of the estates of persons dying insolvent" (England, Wales and Northern Ireland), "compulsory winding-up of companies", "winding-up of companies under the supervision of the court".

(bb) *Other proceedings*:

Belgium:
"concordat judiciaire" – "gerechtelijk akkoord",
"sursis de paiement" – "uitstel van betaling";

Denmark:
"tvangsakkord",
"likvidation af insolvente aktieselskaber eller anpartsselskaber",
"likvidation af banker eller sparekasser, der har standset deres betalinger";

Federal Republic of Germany:
"gerichtliches Vergleichsverfahren";

France:
"reglement judiciaire",
"procédure de suspension provisoire des poursuites et d'apurement collectif du passif de certaines entreprises";

Ireland:
"arrangements under the control of the court", "arrangements, reconstructions and compositions of companies whether or not in the course of liquidation where sanction of the court is required and creditors' rights are affected";

Italy:
"concordato preventivo",
"amministrazione controllata",
"liquidazione coatta amministrativa" – in its judicial stage;

Luxembourg:
"concordat préventif de la faillite",
"sursis de paiement",
"régime special de liquidation applicable aux notaires";

Netherlands:
"surséance van betaling",
"regeling, vervat in de wet op de vergadering van houders van schuldbrieven aan toonder";

United Kingdom:
"compositions and schemes of arrangement" (England and Wales),
"compositions" (Northern Ireland),
"arrangements under the control of the court" (Northern Ireland),
"judicial compositions" (Scotland),
"arrangements, reconstructions and compositions of companies whether or not in the course of liquidation where sanction of the court is required and creditors' rights are involved",
"creditors' voluntary winding-up of companies",
"deeds of arrangement approved by the court" (Northern Ireland).

ANNEX II

1. When references are given to Articles without any further mention, reference is to the 1968 version of the Convention.

2. The Royal Decree of 13 April 1938, reproduced in "Bundesanzeiger" 1953, No 105, p. 1 and in Bülow-Arnold, "Internationaler Rechtsverkehr", 925.5.

3. For this concept, see the Jenard report, Chapter II, B and C, and Chapter IV, A and B.

4. Zweigert-Kotz, "Einführung in die Rechtsvergleichung auf dem Gebiet des Privatrechts" Vol. 1 (1971), p. 78 *et seq.*

5. Case No 29/76 [1976/ ECR 1541. The formal part of the judgment reads as follows:

1. In the interpretation of the concept "civil and commercial matters" for the purposes of the application of the Convention of 27 September 1968 on jurisdiction and the enforcement of judgments in civil and commercial matters, in particular Title III thereof, reference must not be made to the law of one of the States concerned but, first, to the objectives and scheme of the Convention and, secondly, to the general principles which stem from the corpus of the national legal systems;
2. A judgment given in an action between a public authority and a person governed by private law, in which the public authority has acted in the exercise of its powers, is excluded from the area of application of the Convention.

6. Law No 75–617, JO 1975, 7171.

7. In the text of Law No 75–617 (note 6).

8. Document of the Commission of the European Communities XI/449/75–F.

9. The word "analogous" does not appear in Article 1 (1) simply because the proceedings in question are listed in a Protocol.

10. See the Report on the Convention on bankruptcy, winding-up arrangements, compositions and similar proceedings by Noel-Lemontey (16.775/XIV/70) Chapter 3, section I.

11. See preliminary draft Bankruptcy Convention, Article 17 and Protocol thereto, Articles 1 and 2 (note 8).

12. *Op. cit.*

13. 1975 preliminary draft (see note (8)), Article 1 (1), subparagraph (3), and Article II of the Protocol. See Noel-Lemontey report (note 10) for reasons for exclusion.

14. Although it does not have its own legal personality it corresponds by and large to the "offene Handelsgesellschaft" in German law and the "societe en nom collectif" in French law.

15. In the form of a "private company" it corresponds to the continental "Gesellschaft mit beschrankter Hafnmg" (company with limited liability) and in the form of a "public company" to the continental "Aktiengesellschaft" (joint stock company).

16. UK: Bankruptcy Act 1914, ss.119 and 126. See Tridmann-Hicks-Johnson, "Bankruptcy Law and Practice" (1970), page 272.

17. In respect of Great Britain – Companies Act 1948; in respect of Northern Ireland – Companies Acts 1960 and Companies (Amendment) Act 1963; in respect of Ireland – Company Act 1963, s.213.

18. "if ... the company is unable to pay its debts".

19. Decree No 75–1123 of 5 December 1975, (JO) 1975, 1251.

20. The adjustment proposed for Article 57 admittedly has certain repercussions on the scope of Article 20 (see paragraph 240).

21. The following cases may be mentioned with regard to difficulties of interpretation which have arisen hitherto in judicial practice in "Connection with the application of Articles 5 and 6: Corte Cassazione Italiana of 4 June 1974, "Giur. it." 1974, 18 (with regard to the concept of place of performance); Corte Cassazione Italiana No. 3397 of 20 October 1975 (place of performance in the case of deliveries via a forwarding agent who has an obligation to install); Tribunal de Grande Instance Paris D 1975, 638 with commentary by Droz (place where the harmful event occurred in cases of illegal publication in the press); Court of Justice of the European Communities, 6 October 1976, Case No. 12/76 [1976/ ECR 1473.

22. In the judgments referred to the formal parts of the judgments read as follows:

The "place of performance of the obligation in question" within the meaning of Article 5 (1) of the Convention of 27 September 1968 on jurisdiction and the enforcement of judgments in civil and commercial matters is to be determined in accordance with the law which governs the obligation in question according to the rules of conflict of laws of the court before which the matter is brought (Case No. 12/76).

In disputes in which the grantee of an exclusive sales concession is charging the grantor with having infringed the exclusive concession, the word "obligation" contained in Article 5 (1) of the Convention of 27 September 1968 on jurisdiction and the enforcement of judgments in civil and commercial matters refers to the contractual obligation forming the basis of. the legal proceedings, namely the obligation of the grantor which corresponds to the contractual right relied upon by the grantee in support of the application (Case No. 14/76 [1976] ECR 1497).

In disputes concerning the consequences of the infringement by the grantor of a contract conferring an exclusive concession, such as the payment of damages or the dissolution of the contract, the obligation to which reference must be made for the purposes of applying Article 5 (1) of the Convention is that which the contract imposes on the grantor and the non-performance of which is relied upon by the grantee in support of the application for damages or for the dissolution of the contract (Case No. 14/76).

In the case of actions for payment of compensation by way of damages, it is for the national court to ascertain whether, under the law applicable to the contract, an independent contractual obligation or an obligation replacing the unperformed contractual obligation is involved (Case No. 14/76).

When the grantee of an exclusive sales concession is not subject either to the control or to the direction of the grantor, he cannot be regarded as being at the head of a branch, agency or other establishment of the grantor within the meaning of Article 5 (5) of the Convention of 27 September 1968 (Case No. 14/76).

Where the place of the happening of the event which may give rise to liability in tort, delict or quasi-delict and the place where that event results in damage are not identical, the expression "place where the harmful event occurred" in Article 5 (3) of the Convention of 27 September 1968 on jurisdiction and the enforcement of judgments in civil and commercial matters must be undersrood as being intended to cover both the place where rhe damage occurred and the place of the event giving rise to it (Case No. 21/76 [1976] ECR 1735).

The result is that the defendant may be sued, at the option of the plaintiff, either in the courrs for the place where the damage occurred or in the courts for the place of the event which gives rise to and is at the origin of that damage (Case No. 21/76).

23. Divorce law of 1 December 1970, No 898, Article 5.

24. Law of 11 July 1975, new Article 281 of the Code civil.

25. Chapter III, end of Section IV.

26. Stein-Jonas (Münzberg) (note 27), paragraph 765 a II 3 with reference to case law in note 28).

27. Stein-Jonas (Leipold), *Kommentar zur Zivilprozeßordnung*, 19th ed., paragraph 323 II 2 c and other references.

28. In the case of France: Cour de Cassation of 21 July 1954 D 1955, 185.

29. Magistrates" Court Rules 1952 r 34 (2), and Rayden's *Law and Practice in Divorce and Family Matters* (1971), p. 1181.

30. Bromley, *Family Law*, 4th ed. (1971), p. 451 containing references to case law.

31. Section 9 of the Maintenance Orders (Reciprocal Enforcement) Act 1972.

32. A. E. Anton, *Private International Law* (1967), p. 470; Graveson, *The Conflict of Laws* (1969), p. 565; Lord President Clyde in *Clarks Trustee Petitioners* (1966) SLT 249, 251.

33. *Op. cit.*

34. The new Convention on limitation of liability for maritime claims, signed in London on 19 November 1976, was not yet in force at the end of the Working Party's discussions.

35. The Court of Justice of the European Communities has already decided in this sense see judgment of 6 October 1976 (Case No. 14/76).

36. In 1974 the premium income from overseas business amounted to no less than £3,045 million, £520 million of which consisted of business with Member States of the EEC, and 10% of which was accounted for by re-insurance business. A sizeable proportion of this insurance market consisted of marine and aviation insurance. For these classes alone the overseas premium income amounted to £535 million including £50 million worth of business with other EEC countries.

37. Extract from *Pflichtversicherung in den Europäischen Gemeinschaften*, a study by Professor Ernst Steindorff, Munich.

38. The Landgericht of Aachen (NJW 76,487) refused to endorse this standpoint.

39. Germany: Burgerliches Gesetzbuch, Book 3, Sections 3–8; France: Code civil, Book 2, and Book 3, Title XVII, Title XVIII, Chapters II and III; Italy: Codice civile, Book 3, Titles 4–6, Book 6, Title 3, Chapter 2, Section III, and Chapter 4.

40. Megarry and Baker, *The Law of Real Property*, 5th ed. (1969), p. 71 *et seq.*, p. 79 *et seq*

41. Megarry and Baker, *op. cit.*, p. 546.

42. R. David, *Les grands systemes de droit contemporains*, 5th ed. (1973) No. 311.

43. Stein-Jonas (Pohle) (note 27), paragraph 24 III 2.

44. Code de procedure civile, Article 46, third indent; Vincent, *Procedure Civile*, 16th ed. (1973) No. 291.

45. From past case law: Brunswick Landgericht, Recht der internationalen Wirtschaft/Außenwirtschaftsdienst des Betriebsberaters (RIW 1 A WD) 74,346 (written confirmation must actually be preceded by oral agreement); Hamburg Oberlandesgericht (RIW/AWD) 1975, 498 (no effective jurisdiction agreement where general terms of business are exchanged which are mutually contradictory); Munich Oberlandesgericht (RIW/AWD) 75,694; Italian Corte di Cassazione No. 3397 of 20 October 1975 (written confirmation, containing a jurisdiction clause for the first time, is not of itself sufficient); Bundesgerichtshof, MDR 77, p. 1013 (confirmation of an order by the seller not sufficient when the buyer has previously refused the incorporation); Heidelberg Landgericht (RIWI A WD) 76, p. 532 (reference to general conditions of sale not sufficient); Frankfurt Oberlandesgericht (RIWI A WD) 76, p. 532 (reference to general conditions of sale for the first time in the confirmation of the order from the supplier; reminder from the seller does not conclusively incorporate the jurisdiction clause included in the conditions); Dusseldorf Oberlandesgericht (RIW/AWD) 76, p. 297 (jurisdiction clause contained in the condition of a bill of lading of no effect against persons who themselves have given no written declaration); Pretura of Brescia, Foro it. 1976 No. 1, Column I 250 (subsequent national law prevails over Article 17); Tribunal of Aix-en-Provence of 10 May 1974, Dalloz 74, p. 760 (jurisdiction agreements in favour of the courts of the employer's domicile may be entered into even in contracts of employment); Tribunal de commerce of Brussels, Journal des Tribunaux 1976, 210 (Article 17 has precedence over contrary national law).

46. As correctly stated by von Hoffmann (RIW/AWD) 1973,57 (63); Droz ("Compétence judiciaire et effets des jugements dans le marché commun") No. 216 *et seq.*, Weser ("Convention communautaire sur la compétence judiciaire et l'exécution des décisions") No. 265.

47. In the case of an orally concluded contract, the requirements of the first paragraph of Article 17 of the Convention of 27 September 1968 on jurisdiction and the enforcement of judgments in civil and commercial matters as to form are satisfied only if the vendor's confirmation in writing accompanied by notification of the general conditions of sale has been accepted in writing by the purchaser (Case No. 25/76, [1976] ECR 1851). The fact that the purchaser does not raise any objections against a confirmation issued unilaterally by the other parry does not amount to acceptance on his part of the clause conferring jurisdiction unless the oral agreement comes within the framework of a continuing trading relationship between the parties which is based on the general conditions of one of them, and those conditions contain a clause conferring jurisdiction (Case No. 25/76).

Where a clause conferring jurisdiction is included among the general conditions of sale of one of the parties, printed on the back of a contract, the requirement of a writing under the first paragraph of Article 17 of the Convention of 27 September 1968 on jurisdiction and the enforcement of judgments in civil and commercial matters is fulfilled only if the contract signed by both parties contains an express reference to those general conditions (Case No. 24/76, [1976] ECR 1831).

In the case of a contract concluded by reference to earlier offers, which were themselves made with reference to the general conditions of one of the parties including a clause conferring jurisdiction, the requirement of a writing under the first paragraph of Article 17 of the Convention is satisfied only if the reference is express and can therefore be checked by a party exercising reasonable care (Case No. 24/76).

48. For further questions in Section 8, see paragraphs 22 and 240.

49. Germany: Article 253 (1) of the Zivilprozeßordnung; France: Article 54 of the Code de procédure civile.

50. For details see Droz (note 46) No. 448.

51. Italy: Article 798 (1) together with Article 395 (1) of the Codice di procedura civile; France: Batiffol, *Droit international prive*, 5th ed. (1971), No. 727.

52. Article 3 (1) (c) (2) of the German-British Treaty of 14 July 1960; Article 3 (I) (c) (ii) of the Franco-British Treaty of 18 January 1934.

53. From a comparative law point of view: Walther J. Habscheid, *Introduction à la procédure judiciaire, les systèmes de procédures civiles*, published by the Association internationale de droit comparé, Barcelona 1968.

54. Stein-Jonas (Grunsky) (note 27), introduction to paragraph 511 I 1; Rosenberg-Schwab, *Zivilprozeßrecht*, 11th ed., paragraph 135 I 1 b.

55. Case No. 43177 (*Industrial Diamond Supplies* v. *Riva*).

56. Cour de Cassation, 25 February 1937 Pas. 1937 I 73.

57. Exact name and address: If the judgment is to be executed in Scotland – Secretary of State for Scotland, Scortish Office, New St Andrew's House, St James Centre, Edinburgh EHI 3 SX; Otherwise – Secretary of State for the Home Department, Home Office, 50 Queen Anne's Gate, London SWIH 9AT.

58. Typical case law examples for Article 54: Hamburg Landgericht (RIWI A WD) 74, 403 *et seq*.; Frankfurt Oberlandesgericht (RIW 1 A WD) 76, 107.

59. The original and new Member States of the Community, or some of them, are already parties to numerous international conventions governing jurisdiction and the recognition and enforcement of judgments in particular areas of law. The following should be mentioned, including those already listed in the Jenard report:

1. The revised Mannheim Convention for the navigation of the Rhine of 17 October 1868 together with the Revised Agreement of 20 November 1963 and the Additional Protocol of 25 October 1972 (Belgium, Germany, France, Netherlands, United Kingdom);
2. The Warsaw Convention of 12 October 1929 for the unification of certain rules relating to international carriage by air and the Amending Protocol of 28 September 1955 and Supplementary Convention of 18 September 1961 (all nine States) with the Additional Protocols of 8 March 1971 and 25 September 1975 (not yet in force);
3. The Brussels International Convention of 10 May 1952 on certain rules concerning civil jurisdiction in matters of collision (Belgium, Germany, France, United Kingdom);
4. The Brussels International Convention of 10 May 1952 relating to the arrest of seagoing ships (Belgium, Germany, France, United Kingdom);
5. The Rome Convention of 7 October 1952 relating to damage caused by foreign aircraft to third parties on the surface (Belgium, Luxembourg);
6. The London Agreement of 27 February 1953 on German external debts (all nine States);
7. (a) The Hague Convention of 1 March 1954 on civil procedure (Belgium, Denmark, Germany, France, Italy, Luxembourg, Netherlands),
   (b) The Hague Convention of 15 November 1965 on the service abroad of judicial and extrajudicial documents in civil and commercial matters (Belgium, Denmark, France, Italy, Luxembourg, Netherlands, United Kingdom),
   (c) The Hague Convention of 18 March 1970 on the taking of evidence abroad in civil or commercial matters (Denmark, France, Italy, Luxembourg, United Kingdom);
8. The Geneva Convention of 19 May 1956 together with its Protocol of Signature on the contract for the international carriage of goods by road (CMR) (Belgium, Denmark, Germany, France, Italy, Luxembourg, Netherlands, United Kingdom);
9. The Convention of 27 October 1956 between the Grand Duchy of Luxembourg, the Federal Republic of Germany and the French Republic on the canalization of the Moselle, with the Additional Protocol of 28 November 1976 (the three signatory States);
10. The Hague Convention of 15 April 1958 on the recognition and enforcement of decisions relating to maintenance obligations in respect of children (Belgium, Denmark, Germany, France, Italy, Netherlands);
11. The Hague Convention of 15 April 1958 on the jurisdiction of the contractual forum in matters relaring to the international sale of goods (not yet ratified);
12. The Paris Convention of 29 July 1960 on third parry liabiliry in the field of nuclear energy (Belgium, France, Germany), together with the Paris Additional Protocol of 28 January 1964 (Belgium, Denmark, France, Germany, Italy), and the Brussels Convention and Annex thereto of 31 January 1963 supplementary to the Paris Convention of 29 July 1960 and the Paris Additional Protocol to the Supplementary Convention of 28 January 1964 (Denmark, France, Germany, Italy, United Kingdom);
13. The Supplementary Convention of 26 February 1966 to the International Convention of 25 February 1961 concerning the carriage of passengers and luggage by rail (CIV) on the liability of railways for death or injury to passengers, amended by Protocol II of the Diplomatic Conference for the entry into force of the

CIM and CIV International Agreements of 7 February 1970 concerning the extension of the period of validity of the Supplementary Convention of 26 February 1966 (all nine States);

14. The Brussels Convention of 25 May 1962 on the liability of operators of nuclear ships and Additional Protocol (Germany)
15. The Brussels International Convention of 27 May 1967 for the unification of rules relating to the carriage of passengers' luggage by sea (not yet in force);
16. The Brussels International Convention of 27 May 1967 for the unification of certain rules relating to maritime liens and mortgages (not yet in force);
17. The Brussels International Convention of 29 November 1969 on civil liability for oil pollution damage (Belgium, Denmark, France, Germany, Netherlands, United Kingdom) and the International Convention to supplement that Convention of 18 December 1971 on the establishment of an international fund for compensation for oil pollution damage (Denmark, France, Germany, United Kingdom);
18. The Berne International Conventions of 7 February 1970 on the carriage of goods by rail (CIM) and the carriage of passengers and luggage by rail (CIV), together with the Additional Protocol and Protocol I of 9 November 1973 of the Diplomatic Conference for the implementation of the Conventions (all nine States with the exception of Ireland for Protocol I);
19. The Athens Convention of 13 December 1974 on the carriage by sea of passengers and their luggage (not yet in force);
20. The European Agreement of 30 September 1957 covering the international carriage of dangerous goods by road (ADR) (United Kingdom) and the Additional Protocol of 21 August 1975 (United Kingdom) (not yet in force);
21. The Geneva Convention of 1 March 1973 on the contract for the international carriage of passengers and baggage by road (CUR) (not yet in force);
22. The Hague Convention of 2 October 1973 on the recognition and enforcement of decisions relating to maintenance obligations (no Community Member State is a party to this Convention).

60. See note 59 (1).

61. The expression "court" should not be taken as meaning the opposite of other jurisdictions (such as tribunals) but means the legal body which is declared competent in each case.

APPENDIX 2

CHOICE OF LAW MATERIALS

APPENDIX 2.1

CHOICE OF LAW

Identifying which legal regime applies

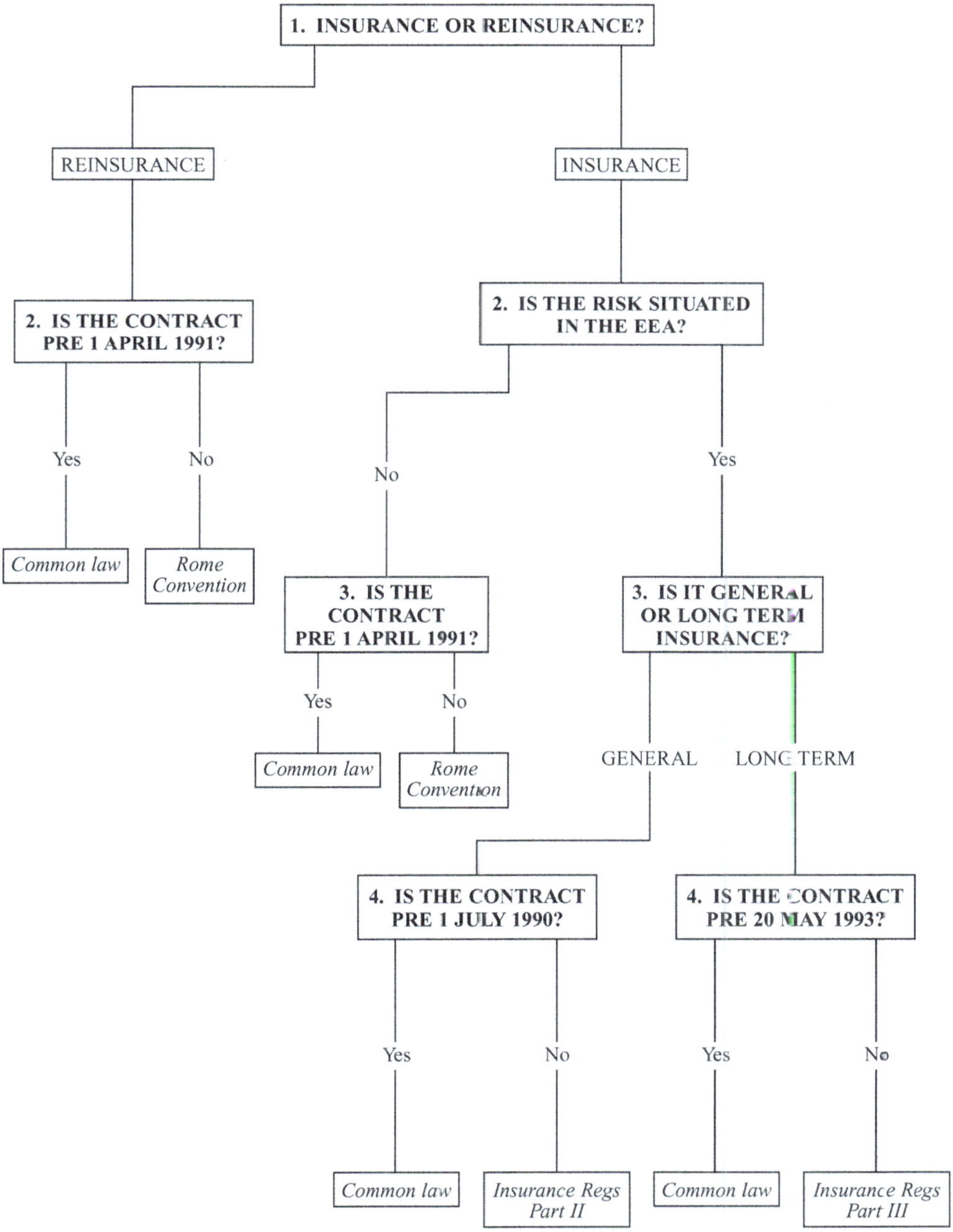

APPENDIX 2.2

CHOICE OF LAW

Applicable law under the Rome Convention

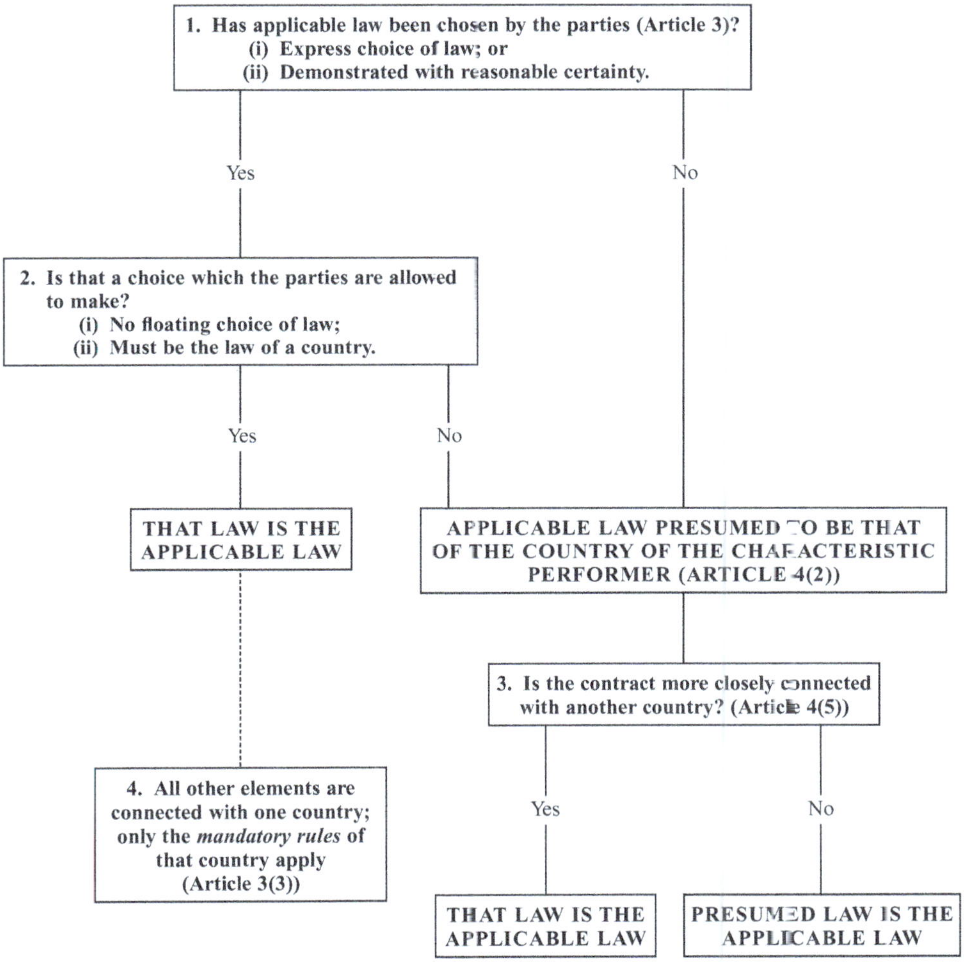

5. **Is it a *consumer contract*? If Yes, different rules apply (Article 5).**
6. **The court may apply English *overriding rules* which are mandatory irrespective of the law otherwise applicable to the contract (Article 7(2)).**
7. **The application of any rule of law so specified may be refused if it is manifestly incompatible with English *public policy* (Article 16).**

THE CONTRACTS (APPLICABLE LAW) ACT 1990

(appending the Rome Convention)

[1990, c. 36]

An Act to make provision as to the law applicable to contractual obligations in the case of conflict of laws.

[26th July 1990]

BE IT ENACTED by the Queen's most Excellent Majesty, by and with the advice and consent of the Lords Spiritual and Temporal, and Commons, in this present Parliament assembled, and by the authority of the same, as follows:

Meaning of "the Conventions"

1. In this Act—

(a) "the Rome Convention" means the Convention on the law applicable to contractual obligations opened for signature in Rome on 19th June 1980 and signed by the United Kingdom on 7th December 1981;

(b) "the Luxembourg Convention" means the Convention on the accession of the Hellenic Republic to the Rome Convention signed by the United Kingdom in Luxembourg on 10th April 1984; and

(c) "the Brussels Protocol" means the first Protocol on the interpretation of the Rome Convention by the European Court signed by the United Kingdom in Brussels on 19th December 1988;

and the Rome Convention, the Luxembourg Convention and the Brussels Protocol are together referred to as "the Conventions".

Conventions to have force of law

2.—(1) Subject to subsections (2) and (3) below, the Conventions shall have the force of law in the United Kingdom.

(2) Articles 7(1) and 10(1)(e) of the Rome Convention shall not have the force of law in the United Kingdom.

(3) Notwithstanding Article 19(2) of the Rome Convention, the Conventions shall apply in the case of conflicts between the laws of different parts of the United Kingdom.

(4) For ease of reference there are set out in Schedules 1, 2 and 3 to this Act respectively the English texts of—

(a) the Rome Convention;

(b) the Luxembourg Convention; and

(c) the Brussels Protocol.

Interpretation of Conventions

3.—(1) Any question as to the meaning or effect of any provision of the Conventions shall, if not referred to the European Court in accordance with the Brussels Protocol, be determined in accordance with the principles laid down by, and any relevant decision of, the European Court.

(2) Judicial notice shall be taken of any decision of, or expression of opinion by, the European Court on any such question.

(3) Without prejudice to any practice of the courts as to the matters which may be considered apart from this subsection—

(a) the report on the Rome Convention by Professor Mario Giuliano and Professor Paul Lagarde which is reproduced in the Official Journal of the Communities of 31st October 1980 may be considered in ascertaining the meaning or effect of any provision of that Convention; and

(b) any report on the Brussels Protocol which is reproduced in the Official Journal of the Communities may be considered in ascertaining the meaning or effect of any provision of that Protocol.

Revision of Conventions etc.

4.—(1) If at any time it appears to Her Majesty in Council that Her Majesty's Government in the United Kingdom—

(a) have agreed to a revision of any of the Conventions (including, in particular, any revision connected with the accession to the Rome Convention of any state); or

(b) have given notification in accordance with Article 22(3) of the Rome Convention that either or both of the provisions mentioned in section 2(2) above shall have the force of law in the United Kingdom,

Her Majesty may by Order in Council make such consequential modifications of this Act or any other statutory provision, whenever passed or made, as Her Majesty considers appropriate.

(2) An Order in Council under subsection (1) above shall not be made unless a draft of the Order has been laid before Parliament and approved by a resolution of each House.

(3) In subsection (1) above—

"modifications" includes additions, omissions and alterations;

"revision" means an omission from, addition to or alteration of any of the Conventions and includes replacement of any of the Conventions to any extent by another convention, protocol or other description of international agreement; and

"statutory provision" means any provision contained in an Act, or in any Northern Ireland legislation, or in—

(a) subordinate legislation (as defined in section 21(1) of the Interpretation Act 1978); or

(b) any instrument of a legislative character made under any Northern Ireland legislation.

Consequential amendments

5. The enactments specified in Schedule 4 to this Act shall have effect subject to the amendments specified in that Schedule.

Application to Crown

6. This Act binds the Crown.

Commencement

7. This Act shall come into force on such day as the Lord Chancellor and the Lord Advocate may by order made by statutory instrument appoint; and different days may be appointed for different provisions or different purposes.

Extent

8.—(1) This Act extends to Northern Ireland.

(2) Her Majesty may by Order in Council direct that all or any of the provisions of this Act shall extend to any of the following territories, namely—

(a) the Isle of Man;

(b) any of the Channel Islands;

(c) Gibraltar;

(d) the Sovereign Base Areas of Akrotiri and Dhekelia (that is to say, the areas mentioned in section 2(1) of the Cyprus Act 1960).

(3) An Order in Council under subsection (2) above may modify this Act in its application to any of the territories mentioned in that subsection and may contain such supplementary provisions as Her Majesty considers appropriate; and in this subsection "modify" shall be construed in accordance with section 4 above.

Short title

This Act may be cited as the Contracts (Applicable Law) Act 1990.

Section 2

SCHEDULE 1

THE ROME CONVENTION

The High Contracting Parties to the Treaty establishing the European Economic Community,

Anxious to continue in the field of private international law the work of unification of law which has already been done within the Community, in particular in the field of jurisdiction and enforcement of judgments,
Wishing to establish uniform rules concerning the law applicable to contractual obligations,

Have agreed as follows:

TITLE I: SCOPE OF THE CONVENTION

Article 1

Scope of the Convention

1. The rules of this Convention shall apply to contractual obligations in any situation involving a choice between the laws of different countries.
2. They shall not apply to:
   (a) questions involving the status or legal capacity of natural persons, without prejudice to Article 11;
   (b) contractual obligations relating to:
      – wills and succession,
      – rights in property arising out of a matrimonial relationship,
      – rights and duties arising out of a family relationship, parentage, marriage or affinity, including maintenance obligations in respect of children who are not legitimate;
   (c) obligations arising under bills of exchange, cheques and promissory notes and other negotiable instruments to the extent that the obligations under such other negotiable instruments arise out of their negotiable character;
   (d) arbitration agreements and agreements on the choice of court;
   (e) questions governed by the law of companies and other bodies corporate or unincorporate such as the creation, by registration or otherwise, legal capacity, internal organisation or winding up of companies and other bodies corporate or unincorporate and the personal liability of officers and members as such for the obligations of the company or body;
   (f) the question whether an agent is able to bind a principal, or an organ to bind a company or body corporate or unincorporate, to a third party;
   (g) the constitution of trusts and the relationship between settlors, trustees and beneficiaries;
   (h) evidence and procedure, without prejudice to Article 14.
3. The rules of this Convention do not apply to contracts of insurance which cover risks situated in the territories of the Member States of the European Economic Community. In order to determine whether a risk is situated in these territories the court shall apply its internal law.
4. The preceding paragraph does not apply to contracts of re-insurance.

Article 2

Application of law of non-contracting States

Any law specified by this Convention shall be applied whether or not it is the law of a Contracting State.

TITLE II: UNIFORM RULES

Article 3

Freedom of choice

1. A contract shall be governed by the law chosen by the parties. The choice must be express or demonstrated with reasonable certainty by the terms of the contract or the circumstances of the case. By their choice the parties can select the law applicable to the whole or a part only of the contract.
2. The parties may at any time agree to subject the contract to a law other than that which previously governed it, whether as a result of an earlier choice under this Article or of other provisions of this Convention. Any variation by the parties of the law to be applied made after the conclusion of the contract shall not prejudice its formal validity under Article 9 or adversely affect the rights of third parties.
3. The fact that the parties have chosen a foreign law, whether or not accompanied by the choice of a foreign tribunal, shall not, where all the other elements relevant to the situation at the time of the choice are connected with one country only, prejudice the application of rules of the law of that country which cannot be derogated from by contract, hereinafter called "mandatory rules".
4. The existence and validity of the consent of the parties as to the choice of the applicable law shall be determined in accordance with the provisions of Articles 8, 9 and 11.

Article 4

Applicable law in the absence of choice

1. To the extent that the law applicable to the contract has not been chosen in accordance with Article 3, the contract shall be governed by the law of the country with which it is most closely connected. Nevertheless, a severable part of the contract which has a closer connection with another country may by way of exception be governed by the law of that other country.
2. Subject to the provisions of paragraph 5 of this Article, it shall be presumed that the contract is most closely connected with the country where the party who is to effect the performance which is characteristic of the contract has, at the time of conclusion of the contract, his habitual residence, or, in the case of a body corporate or unincorporate, its central administration. However, if the contract is entered into in the course of that party's trade or profession, that country shall be the country in which the principal place of business is situated or, where under the terms of the contract the performance is to be effected through a place of business other than the principal place of business, the country in which that other place of business is situated.
3. Notwithstanding the provisions of paragraph 2 of this Article, to the extent that the subject matter of the contract is a right in immovable property or a right to use immovable property it shall be presumed that the contract is most closely connected with the country where the immovable property is situated.
4. A contract for the carriage of goods shall not be subject to the presumption in paragraph 2. In such a contract if the country in which, at the time the contract is concluded, the carrier has his principal place of business is also the country in which the place of loading or the place of discharge or the principal place of business of the consignor is situated, it shall be presumed that the contract is most closely connected with that country. In applying this paragraph single voyage charter-parties and other contracts the main purpose of which is the carriage of goods shall be treated as contracts for the carriage of goods.
5. Paragraph 2 shall not apply if the characteristic performance cannot be determined, and the presumptions in paragraphs 2, 3 and 4 shall be disregarded if it appears from the circumstances as a whole that the contract is more closely connected with another country.

Article 5

Certain consumer contracts

1. This Article applies to a contract the object of which is the supply of goods or services to a person ("the consumer") for a purpose which can be regarded as being outside his trade or profession, or a contract for the provision of credit for that object.
2. Notwithstanding the provisions of Article 3, a choice of law made by the parties shall not have the result of depriving the consumer of the protection afforded to him by the mandatory rules of the law of the country in which he has his habitual residence:
   - if in that country the conclusion of the contract was preceded by a specific invitation addressed to him or by advertising, and he had taken in that country all the steps necessary on his part for the conclusion of the contract, or
   - if the other party or his agent received the consumer's order in that country, or
   - if the contract is for the sale of goods and the consumer travelled from that country to another country and there gave his order, provided that the consumer's journey was arranged by the seller for the purpose of inducing the consumer to buy.
3. Notwithstanding the provisions of Article 4, a contract to which this Article applies shall, in the absence of choice in accordance with Article 3, be governed by the law of the country in which the consumer has his habitual residence if it is entered into in the circumstances described in paragraph 2 of this Article.
4. This Article shall not apply to:
   (a) a contract of carriage;
   (b) a contract for the supply of services where the services are to be supplied to the consumer exclusively in a country other than that in which he has his habitual residence.
5. Notwithstanding the provisions of paragraph 4, this Article shall apply to a contract which, for an inclusive price, provides for a combination of travel and accommodation.

Article 6

Individual employment contracts

1. Notwithstanding the provisions of Article 3, in a contract of employment a choice of law made by the parties shall not have the result of depriving the employee of the protection afforded to him by the mandatory rules of the law which would be applicable under paragraph 2 in the absence of choice.
2. Notwithstanding the provisions of Article 4, a contract of employment shall, in the absence of choice in accordance with Article 3, be governed:
   (a) by the law of the country in which the employee habitually carries out his work in performance of the contract, even if he is temporarily employed in another country; or
   (b) if the employee does not habitually carry out his work in any one country, by the law of the country in which the place of business through which he was engaged is situated;

unless it appears from the circumstances as a whole that the contract is more closely connected with another country, in which case the contract shall be governed by the law of that country.

Article 7

Mandatory rules

1. When applying under this Convention the law of a country, effect may be given to the mandatory rules of the law of another country with which the situation has a close connection, if and in so far as, under the law of the latter country, those rules must be applied whatever the law applicable to the contract. In considering whether to give effect to these mandatory rules, regard shall be had to their nature and purpose and to the consequences of their application or non-application.
2. Nothing in this Convention shall restrict the application of the rules of the law of the forum in a situation where they are mandatory irrespective of the law otherwise applicable to the contract.

Article 8

Material validity

1. The existence and validity of a contract, or of any term of a contract, shall be determined by the law which would govern it under this Convention if the contract or term were valid.
2. Nevertheless a party may rely upon the law of the country in which he has his habitual residence to establish that he did not consent if it appears from the circumstances that it would not be reasonable to determine the effect of his conduct in accordance with the law specified in the preceding paragraph.

Article 9

Formal validity

1. A contract concluded between persons who are in the same country is formally valid if it satisfies the formal requirements of the law which governs it under this Convention or of the law of the country where it is concluded.
2. A contract concluded between persons who are in different countries is formally valid if it satisfies the formal requirements of the law which governs it under this Convention or of the law of one of those countries.
3. Where a contract is concluded by an agent, the country in which the agent acts is the relevant country for the purposes of paragraphs 1 and 2.
4. An act intended to have legal effect relating to an existing or contemplated contract is formally valid if it satisfies the formal requirements of the law which under this Convention governs or would govern the contract or of the law of the country where the act was done.
5. The provisions of the preceding paragraphs shall not apply to a contract to which Article 5 applies, concluded in the circumstances described in paragraph 2 of Article 5. The formal validity of such a contract is governed by the law of the country in which the consumer has his habitual residence.
6. Notwithstanding paragraphs 1 to 4 of this Article, a contract the subject matter of which is a right in immovable property or a right to use immovable property shall be subject to the mandatory requirements of form of the law of the country where the property is situated if by that law those requirements are imposed irrespective of the country where the contract is concluded and irrespective of the law governing the contract.

Article 10

Scope of the applicable law

1. The law applicable to a contract by virtue of Articles 3 to 6 and 12 of this Convention shall govern in particular:
   (a) interpretation;
   (b) performance;
   (c) within the limits of the powers conferred on the court by its procedural law, the consequences of breach, including the assessment of damages in so far as it is governed by rules of law;
   (d) the various ways of extinguishing obligations, and prescription and limitation of actions;
   (e) the consequences of nullity of the contract.
2. In relation to the manner of performance and the steps to be taken in the event of defective performance regard shall be had to the law of the country in which performance takes place.

Article 11

Incapacity

In a contract concluded between persons who are in the same country, a natural person who would have capacity under the law of that country may invoke his incapacity resulting from another law only if the other party to the contract was aware of this incapacity at the time of the conclusion of the contract or was not aware thereof as a result of negligence.

Article 12

Voluntary assignment

1. The mutual obligations of assignor and assignee under a voluntary assignment of a right against another person ("the debtor") shall be governed by the law which under this Convention applies to the contract between the assignor and assignee.
2. The law governing the right to which the assignment relates shall determine its assignability, the relationship between the assignee and the debtor, the conditions under which the assignment can be invoked against the debtor and any question whether the debtor's obligations have been discharged.

Article 13

Subrogation

1. Where a person ("the creditor") has a contractual claim upon another ("the debtor"), and a third person has a duty to satisfy the creditor, or has in fact satisfied the creditor in discharge of that duty, the law which governs the third person's duty to satisfy the creditor shall determine whether the third person is entitled to exercise against the debtor the rights which the creditor had against the debtor under the law governing their relationship and, if so, whether he may do so in full or only to a limited extent.
2. The same rule applies where several persons are subject to the same contractual claim and one of them has satisfied the creditor.

Article 14

Burden of proof, etc.

1. The law governing the contract under this Convention applies to the extent that it contains, in the law of contract, rules which raise presumptions of law or determine the burden of proof.
2. A contract or an act intended to have legal effect may be proved by any mode of proof recognised by the law of the forum or by any of the laws referred to in Article 9 under which that contract or act is formally valid, provided that such mode of proof can be administered by the forum.

Article 15

Exclusion of renvoi

The application of the law of any country specified by this Convention means the application of the rules of law in force in that country other than its rules of private international law.

Article 16

Ordre public

The application of a rule of the law of any country specified by this Convention may be refused only if such application is manifestly incompatible with the public policy ("ordre public") of the forum.

Article 17

No retrospective effect

This Convention shall apply in a Contracting State to contracts made after the date on which this Convention has entered into force with respect to that State.

Article 18

Uniform interpretation

In the interpretation and application of the preceding uniform rules, regard shall be had to their international character and to the desirability of achieving uniformity in their interpretation and application.

Article 19

States with more than one legal system

1. Where a State comprises several territorial units each of which has its own rules of law in respect of contractual obligations, each territorial unit shall be considered as a country for the purposes of identifying the law applicable under this Convention.
2. A State within which different territorial units have their own rules of law in respect of contractual obligations shall not be bound to apply this Convention to conflicts solely between the laws of such units.

Article 20

Precedence of Community law

This Convention shall not affect the application of provisions which, in relation to particular matters, lay down choice of law rules relating to contractual obligations and which are or will be contained in acts of the institutions of the European Communities or in national laws harmonised in implementation of such acts.

Article 21

Relationship with other conventions

This Convention shall not prejudice the application of international conventions to which a Contracting State is, or becomes, a party.

Article 22

Reservations

1. Any Contracting State may, at the time of signature, ratification, acceptance or approval, reserve the right not to apply:
   (a) the provisions of Article 7(1);
   (b) the provisions of Article 10(1)(e).
2. Any Contracting State may also, when notifying an extension of the Convention in accordance with Article 27(2), make one or more of these reservations, with its effect limited to all or some of the territories mentioned in the extension.
3. Any Contracting State may at any time withdraw a reservation which it has made; the reservation shall cease to have effect on the first day of the third calendar month after notification of the withdrawal.

TITLE III: FINAL PROVISIONS

Article 23

1. If, after the date on which this Convention has entered into force for a Contracting State, that State wishes to adopt any new choice of law rule in regard to any particular category of contract within the scope of this Convention, it shall communicate its intention to the other signatory States through the Secretary-General of the Council of the European Communities.
2. Any signatory State may, within six months from the date of the communication made to the Secretary-General, request him to arrange consultations between signatory States in order to reach agreement.
3. If no signatory State has requested consultations within this period or if within two years following the communication made to the Secretary-General no agreement is reached in the course of consul-

tations, the Contracting State concerned may amend its law in the manner indicated. The measures taken by that State shall be brought to the knowledge of the other signatory States through the Secretary-General of the Council of the European Communities.

Article 24

1. If, after the date on which this Convention has entered into force with respect to a Contracting State, that State wishes to become a party to a multilateral convention whose principal aim or one of whose principal aims is to lay down rules of private international law concerning any of the matters governed by this Convention, the procedure set out in Article 23 shall apply. However, the period of two years, referred to in paragraph 3 of that Article, shall be reduced to one year.
2. The procedure referred to in the preceding paragraph need not be followed if a Contracting State or one of the European Communities is already a party to the multilateral convention, or if its object is to revise a convention to which the State concerned is already a party, or if it is a convention concluded within the framework of the Treaties establishing the European Communities.

Article 25

If a Contracting State considers that the unification achieved by this Convention is prejudiced by the conclusion of agreements not covered by Article 24(1), that State may request the Secretary-General of the Council of the European Communities to arrange consultations between the signatory States of this Convention.

Article 26

Any Contracting State may request the revision of this Convention. In this event a revision conference shall be convened by the President of the Council of the European Communities.

Article 27

1. This Convention shall apply to the European territories of the Contracting States, including Greenland, and to the entire territory of the French Republic.
2. Notwithstanding paragraph 1:
   (a) this Convention shall not apply to the Faroe Islands, unless the Kingdom of Denmark makes a declaration to the contrary;
   (b) this Convention shall not apply to any European territory situated outside the United Kingdom for the international relations of which the United Kingdom is responsible, unless the United Kingdom makes a declaration to the contrary in respect of any such territory;
   (c) this Convention shall apply to the Netherlands Antilles, if the Kingdom of the Netherlands makes a declaration to that effect.
3. Such declarations may be made at any time by notifying the Secretary-General of the Council of the European Communities.
4. Proceedings brought in the United Kingdom on appeal from courts in one of the territories referred to in paragraph 2(b) shall be deemed to be proceedings taking place in those courts.

Article 28

1. This Convention shall be open from 19 June 1980 for signature by the States party to the Treaty establishing the European Economic Community.
2. This Convention shall be subject to ratification, acceptance or approval by the signatory States. The instruments of ratification, acceptance or approval shall be deposited with the Secretary-General of the Council of the European Communities.

Article 29

1. This Convention shall enter into force on the first day of the third month following the deposit of the seventh instrument of ratification, acceptance or approval.
2. This Convention shall enter into force for each signatory State ratifying, accepting or approving at a later date on the first day of the third month following the deposit of its instrument of ratification, acceptance or approval.

Article 30

1. This Convention shall remain in force for 10 years from the date of its entry into force in accordance with Article 29(1), even for States for which it enters into force at a later date.

2. If there has been no denunciation it shall be renewed tacitly every five years.
3. A Contracting State which wishes to denounce shall, not less than six months before the expiration of the period of 10 or five years, as the case may be, give notice to the Secretary-General of the Council of the European Communities. Denunciation may be limited to any territory to which the Convention has been extended by a declaration under Article 27(2).
4. The denunciation shall have effect only in relation to the State which has notified it. The Convention will remain in force as between all other Contracting States.

Article 31

The Secretary-General of the Council of the European Communities shall notify the States party to the Treaty establishing the European Economic Community of:

(a) the signatures;
(b) the deposit of each instrument of ratification, acceptance or approval;
(c) the date of entry into force of this Convention;
(d) communications made in pursuance of Articles 23, 24, 25, 26, 27 and 30;
(e) the reservations and withdrawals of reservations referred to in Article 22.

Article 32

The Protocol annexed to this Convention shall form an integral part thereof.

Article 33

This Convention, drawn up in a single original in the Danish, Dutch, English, French, German, Irish and Italian languages, these texts being equally authentic, shall be deposited in the archives of the Secretariat of the Council of the European Communities. The Secretary-General shall transmit a certified copy thereof to the Government of each signatory State.

PROTOCOL

The High Contracting Parties have agreed upon the following provision which shall be annexed to the Convention:

Notwithstanding the provisions of the Convention, Denmark may retain the rules contained in Sloven (Statute on Maritime Law) paragraph 169 concerning the applicable law in matters relating to carriage of goods by sea and may revise these rules without following the procedure prescribed in Article 23 of the Convention.

Section 2

SCHEDULE 2

THE LUXEMBOURG CONVENTION

The High Contracting Parties to the Treaty establishing the European Economic Community,

Considering that the Hellenic Republic, in becoming a Member of the Community, undertook to accede to the Convention on the law applicable to contractual obligations, opened for signature in Rome on 19 June 1980,

Have decided to conclude this Convention, and to this end have designated as their plenipotentiaries:

(Designation of plenipotentiaries)

Who, meeting within the Council, having exchanged their full powers, found in good and due form,

Have agreed as follows:

Article 1

The Hellenic Republic hereby accedes to the Convention on the law applicable to contractual obligations, opened for signature in Rome on 19 June 1980.

Article 2

The Secretary-General of the Council of the European Communities shall transmit a certified copy of the Convention on the law applicable to contractual obligations in the Danish, Dutch, English, French, German, Irish and Italian languages to the Government of the Hellenic Republic.

The text of the Convention on the law applicable to contractual obligations in the Greek language is annexed hereto. The text in the Greek language shall be authentic under the same conditions as the other texts of the Convention on the law applicable to contractual obligations.

Article 3

This Convention shall be ratified by the Signatory States. The instruments of ratification shall be deposited with the Secretary-General of the Council of the European Communities.

Article 4

This Convention shall enter into force, as between the States which have ratified it, on the first day of the third month following the deposit of the last instrument of ratification by the Hellenic Republic and seven States which have ratified the Convention on the law applicable to contractual obligations.

This Convention shall enter into force for each Contracting State which subsequently ratifies it on the first day of the third month following the deposit of its instrument of ratification.

Article 5

The Secretary-General of the Council of the European Communities shall notify the Signatory States of:

(a) the deposit of each instrument of ratification;
(b) the dates of entry into force of this Convention for the Contracting States.

Article 6

This Convention, drawn up in a single original in the Danish, Dutch, English, French, German, Greek, Irish and Italian languages, all eight texts being equally authentic, shall be deposited in the archives of the General Secretariat of the Council of the European Communities. The Secretary-General shall transmit a certified copy to the Government of each Signatory State.

SCHEDULE 3
THE BRUSSELS PROTOCOL

The High Contracting Parties to the Treaty establishing the European Economic Community,

Having regard to the Joint Declaration annexed to the Convention on the law applicable to contractual obligations, opened for signature in Rome on 19 June 1980,

Have decided to conclude a Protocol conferring jurisdiction on the Court of Justice of the European Communities to interpret that Convention, and to this end have designated as their Plenipotentiaries:

(Designation of plenipotentiaries)

Who, meeting within the Council of the European Communities, having exchanged their full powers, found in good and due form,

Have agreed as follows:

Article 1

The Court of Justice of the European Communities shall have jurisdiction to give rulings on the interpretation of—

(a) the Convention on the law applicable to contractual obligations, opened for signature in Rome on 19 June 1980, hereinafter referred to as "the Rome Convention" ;
(b) the Convention on accession to the Rome Convention by the States which have become Members of the European Communities since the date on which it was opened for signature;
(c) this Protocol.

Article 2

Any of the courts referred to below may request the Court of Justice to give a preliminary ruling on a question raised in a case pending before it and concerning interpretation of the provisions contained in the instruments referred to in Article 1 if that court considers that a decision on the question is necessary to enable it to give judgment:

(a) – in Belgium:
la Cour de cassation (het Hof van Cassatie) and le Conseil d'Etat (de Raad van State),

- in Denmark:
  Hjesteret,
- in the Federal Republic of Germany:
  die obersten Gerichtschoife des Bundes,
- in Greece:
  taanwgtataAikasthgria,
- in Spain:
  el Tribunal Supremo,
- in France:
  la Cour de cassation and le Conseil d'Etat,
- in Ireland:
  the Supreme Court,
- in Italy:
  la Corte suprema di cassazione and il Consiglio di Stato,
- in Luxembourg:
  la Cour supérieure de Justice, when sitting as Cour de cassation,
- in the Netherlands:
  de Hoge Raad,
- in Portugal:
  o Supremo Tribunal de Justiôa and o Supremo Tribunal Administrativo,
- in the United Kingdom:
  the House of Lords and other courts from which no further appeal is possible;

(b) the courts of the Contracting States when acting as appeal courts.

Article 3

1. The competent authority of a Contracting State may request the Court of Justice to give a ruling on a question of interpretation of the provisions contained in the instruments referred to in Article 1 if judgments given by courts of that State conflict with the interpretation given either by the Court of Justice or in a judgment of one of the courts of another Contracting State referred to in Article 2. The provisions of this paragraph shall apply only to Judgments which have become *res judicata*.
2. The interpretation given by the Court of Justice in response to such a request shall not affect the Judgments which gave rise to the request for interpretation.
3. The Procurators-General of the Supreme Courts of Appeal of the Contracting States, or any other authority designated by a Contracting State, shall be entitled to request the Court of Justice for a ruling on interpretation in accordance with paragraph 1.
4. The Registrar of the Court of Justice shall give notice of the request to the Contracting States, to the Commission and to the Council of the European Communities; they shall then be entitled within two months of the notification to submit statements of case or written observations to the Court.
5. No fees shall be levied or any costs or expenses awarded in respect of the proceedings provided for in this Article.

Article 4

1. Except where this Protocol otherwise provides, the provisions of the Treaty establishing the European Economic Community and those of the Protocol on the Statute of the Court of Justice annexed thereto, which are applicable when the Court is requested to give a preliminary ruling, shall also apply to any proceedings for the interpretation of the instruments referred to in Article 1.
2. The Rules of Procedure of the Court of Justice shall, if necessary, be adJusted and supplemented in accordance with Article 188 of the Treaty establishing the European Economic Community.

Article 5

This Protocol shall be subJect to ratification by the Signatory States. The instruments of ratification shall be deposited with the Secretary-General of the Council of the European Communities.

Article 6

1. To enter into force, this Protocol must be ratified by seven States in respect of which the Rome Convention is in force. This Protocol shall enter into force on the first day of the third month following the deposit of the instrument of ratification by the last such State to take this step. If, however, the Second Protocol conferring on the Court of Justice of the European Communities certain powers to interpret the Convention on the law applicable to contractual obligations, opened for signature in Rome on 19 June 1980, concluded in Brussels on 19 December 1988, enters into force on a later date, this Protocol shall enter into force on the date of entry into force of the Second Protocol.
2. Any ratification subsequent to the entry into force of this Protocol shall take effect on the first day of the third month following the deposit of the instrument of ratification provided that the ratification, acceptance or approval of the Rome Convention by the State in question has become effective.

Article 7

The Secretary-General of the Council of the European Communities shall notify the Signatory States of:

(a) the deposit of each instrument of ratification;
(b) the date of entry into force of this Protocol;
(c) any designation communicated pursuant to Article 3(3);
(d) any communication made pursuant to Article 8.

Article 8

The Contracting States shall communicate to the Secretary-General of the Council of the European Communities the texts of any provisions of their laws which necessitate an amendment to the list of courts in Article 2(a).

Article 9

This Protocol shall have effect for as long as the Rome Convention remains in force under the conditions laid down in Article 30 of that Convention.

Article 10

Any Contracting State may request the revision of this Protocol. In this event, a revision conference shall be convened by the President of the Council of the European Communities.

Article 11

This Protocol, drawn up in a single original in the Danish, Dutch, English, French, German, Greek, Irish, Italian, Portuguese and Spanish languages, all 10 texts being equally authentic, shall be deposited in the archives of the General Secretariat of the Council of the European Communities. The Secretary-General shall transmit a certified copy to the Government of each Signatory State.

Section 5

SCHEDULE 4
CONSEQUENTIAL AMENDMENTS

The Equal Pay Act 1970 (c. 41)
The Equal Pay Act (Northern Ireland) 1970 (c. 32 (N.I.))

1. In Section 1(11) of the Equal Pay Act 1970 and section 1(12) of the Equal Pay Act (Northern Ireland) 1970, for the words "proper law of" there shall be substituted the words "law applicable to".

The Consumer Credit Act 1974 (c. 39)

2. In sections 43(2)(c) and 145(3)(c) and (4)(b) of the Consumer Credit Act 1974, for the words "proper law of", in each place where they occur, there shall be substituted the words "law applicable to".

The Patents Act 1977 (c. 37)

3. In section 82(5) and (6) of the Patents Act 1977, for the words "proper law of" there shall be substituted the words "law applicable to".

The Unfair Contract Terms Act 1977 (c. 50)

4. In section 27(1) of the Unfair Contract Terms Act 1977, for the words "proper law of" there shall be substituted the words "law applicable to" and for the words "of the proper law" there shall be substituted the words "of the law applicable to the contract".

The Aviation Security Act 1982 (c. 36)

5. In section 19(5) of the aviation security act 1982, for the words "of which the proper law" there shall be substituted the words "the law applicable to which".

The Income and Corporation Taxes Act 1988 (c. 1)

In section 347b(1)(a) of the Income and Corporation Taxes Act 1988, for the words "proper law of" there shall be substituted the words "law applicable to".

THE GIULIANO–LAGARDE REPORT

REPORT on the Convention on the law applicable to contractual obligations*
by Mario Giuliano, Professor, University of Milan (who contributed the introduction and the comments on Articles 1, 3 to 8, 10, 12, and 13) and Paul Lagarde, Professor, University of Paris I (who contributed the comments on Articles 2, 9, 11, and 14 to 33)
Official Journal C 282, 31/10/1980, pp. 1–50

INTRODUCTION

1. Proposal by the Governments of the Benelux countries to the Commission of the European Communities.

On 8 September 1967 the Permanent Representative of Belgium extended to the Commission, in the name of his own Government and those of the Kingdom of the Netherlands and the Grand Duchy of Luxembourg, an invitation to collaborate with the experts of the Member States, on the basis of the draft Benelux convention, in the unification of private international law and codification of the rules of conflict of laws within the Community.

The object of this proposal was to eliminate the inconveniences arising from the diversity of the rules of conflict, notably in the field of contract law. Added to this was "an element of urgency", having regard to the reforms likely to be introduced in some Member States and the consequent "danger that the existing divergences would become more marked".

In the words of Mr T. Vogelaar, Director-General for the Internal Market and Approximation of Legislation at the Commission, in his opening address as chairman of the meeting of government experts on 26 to 28 February 1969:

> "This proposal should bring about a complete unification of the rules of conflict. Thus in each of our six countries, instead of the existing rules of conflict and apart from cases of application of international Agreements binding any Member State, identical rules of conflict would enter into force both in Member States' relations inter se and in relations with non-Community States. Such a development would give rise to a common corpus of unified legal rules covering the territory of the Community's Member States. The great advantage of this proposal is undoubtedly that the level of legal certainty would be raised, confidence in the stability of legal relationships fortified, agreements on jurisdiction according to the applicable law facilitated, and the protection of rights acquired over the whole field of private law augmented. Compared with the unification of substantive law, unification of the rules of conflict of laws is more practicable, especially in the field of property law, because the rules of conflict apply solely to legal relations involving an international element."[1]

2. Examination of the proposal by the Commission and its consequences.

In examining the proposal by the Benelux countries the Commission arrived at the conclusion that at least in some special fields of private international law the harmonization of rules of conflict would be likely to facilitate the workings of the common market.

Mr Vogelaar's opening address reviews the grounds on which the Commission's conclusion was founded and is worth repeating here:

> "According to both the letter and spirit of the Treaty establishing the EEC, harmonization is recognized as fulfilling the function of permitting or facilitating the creation in the economic field of legal conditions similar to those governing an internal market. I appreciate that opinions may differ as to the precise delimitation of the inequalities which directly affect the functioning of the common market and those having only an indirect effect. Yet there are still legal fields in which the differences between national legal systems and the lack of unified rules of conflict definitely impede the free movement of persons, goods, services and capital among the Member States.

* The text of the Convention on the law applicable to contractual obligations was published in Official Journal No. L 266 of 9 October 1980. The Convention, open for signature in Rome on 19 June 1980, was signed on that day by the Plenipotentiaries of the following seven Member States: Belgium, Germany, France, Ireland, Italy, Luxembourg and the Netherlands.

Some will give preference to the harmonization or unification of substantive law rather than the harmonization of rules of conflict. As we know, the former has already been achieved in various fields. However, harmonization of substantive law does not always contrive to keep pace with the dismantling of economic frontiers. The problem of the law to be applied will therefore continue to arise as long as substantive law is not unified. The number of cases in which the question of applicable law must be resolved increases with the growth of private law relationships across frontiers.

At the same time there will be a growing number of cases in which the courts have to apply a foreign law. The Convention signed on 27 September 1968 on jurisdiction and the enforcement of judgments in civil and commercial matters uniformly governs the international jurisdiction of the courts within the Community. It should help to facilitate and expedite many civil actions and enforcement proceedings. It also enables the parties. in many matters, to teach agreements assigning jurisdiction and to choose among several courts. The outcome may be that preference is given to the court of a State whose law seems to offer a better solution to the proceedings. To prevent this 'forum shopping', increase legal certainty, and anticipate more easily the law which will be applied, it would be advisable for the rules of conflict to be unified in fields of particular economic importance so that the same law is applied irrespective of the State in which the decision is given.

To sum up, there are three main considerations guiding our proposal for harmonizing the rules of conflict for a few well-defined types of legal relations. The first is dictated by the history of private international law: to try to unify everything is to attempt too much and would take too long. The second is the urgent necessity for greater legal certainty in some sectors of major economic importance. the third is the wish to forestall any aggravation of the differences between the rules of private international law of the various Member States."[2]

These were in fact the motives which prompted the Commission to convene a meeting of experts from the Member States in order to obtain a complete picture of the present state of the law and to decide whether and to what extent a harmonization or unification of private international law within the Community should be undertaken. The invitation was accompanied by a questionnaire designed to facilitate the discussion.[3]

3. Favourable attitude of Member States to the search for uniform rules of conflict, the setting of priorities and establishment of the working group to study and work out these rules.

The meeting in question took place on 26 to 28 February 1969. It produced a first survey of the situation with regard to prospects for and possible advantage of work in the field of unification of rules of conflict among Member States of the European Communities.[4]

However, it was not until the next meeting on 20 to 22 October 1969 that the government experts were able to give a precise opinion both on the advisability and scope of harmonization and on the working procedure and organization of work.

As regards advisability of harmonization the Member States' delegations (with the sole exception of the German delegation) declared themselves to be fundamentally in agreement on the value of the work in making the law more certain in the Community. The German delegation, while mentioning some hesitation on this point in professional and business circles, said that this difference of opinion was not such as to affect the course of the work at the present time.

As regards the scope of harmonization, it was recognized (without prejudice to future developments) that a start should be made on matters most closely involved in the proper functioning of the common market, more specifically:

1. the law applicable to corporeal and incorporeal property;
2. the law applicable to contractual and non-contractual obligations;
3. the law applicable to the form of legal transactions and evidence;
4. general matters under the foregoing heads (renvoi, classification, application of foreign law, acquired rights, public policy, capacity, representation).

As for the legal basis of the work, it was the unanimous view that the proposed harmonization, without being specifically connected with the provisions of Article 220 of the EEC Treaty, would be a natural sequel to the Convention on jurisdiction and enforcement of judgments.

Lastly, on the procedure to be followed, all the delegations were in favour of that adopted for work on the Conventions already signed or in process of drafting under Article 220 and of seeking the most suitable ways of expediting the work.[5]

The results of the meeting were submitted through the Directorate-General for the Internal Market an Approximation of Legislation to the Commission with a proposal to seek the agreement of Member States for continuance of the work and preparation of a preliminary draft Convention establishing uniformity of law in certain relevant areas of private international law.

The Commission acceded to the proposal. At its meeting on 15 January 1970 the Committee of Permanent Representatives expressly authorized the Group to continue its work on harmonization of the rules of private international law, on the understanding that the preliminary draft or drafts would give priority to the four areas previously indicated.

Following the abovementioned decision of the Permanent Representatives Committee, the Group met on 2 and 3 February 1970 and elected its chairman, Mr P. Jenard, Director of Administration in the Belgian Ministry of Foreign Affairs and External Trade, and its vice-chairman, Prof. Miccio, Counsellor to the Italian Court of Cassation.

Having regard to the decision of the previous meeting that the matters to be given priority should be divided into four sectors, the Group adopted the principle that each of the four sectors should have its own rapporteur appointed as follows, to speed up the work:

1. in the case of the law applicable to corporeal and incorporeal property, by the German delegation;
2. in the case of the law applicable to contractual and extracontractual obligations, by the Italian delegation;
3. in the case of the law applicable to the form of legal transactions and evidence, by the French delegation;
4. in general matters, by the Netherlands delegation, in agreement with the Belgian and Luxembourg delegations.

As a result the following were appointed: Prof. K. Arndt, Oberlandsgerichtspräsident a.d.: Prof. M. Giuliano, University of Milan; Prof. P. Lagarde, University of Paris I; Mr T. van Sasse van Ysselt, Director in the Netherlands Ministry of Justice.

Other matters were dealt with at the same meeting, notably the kind of convention to be prepared, as to which the great majority of delegates favoured a universal convention not based upon reciprocity ; the method of work ; participation of observers from the Hague Conference on Private International Law and the Benelux Commission on Unification of Law.[6]

4. Organization, progress and initial results of the Group's work at the end of 1972.

The Group took as its starting point the examination and discussion of the questionnaires prepared by the rapporteurs, Messrs Giuliano, Lagarde and van Sasse van Ysselt in their respective fields. They were discussed at a meeting of the rapporteurs chaired by Mr Jenard on 1 to 4 June 1970. The three questionnaires were subjected to a thorough analysis, extending both to the rules of conflict (national or established by convention) in force in the Community Member States and to the evolutionary trends already apparent in case law and legal theory in certain countries or worthy of consideration in relation to certain present-day requirements in international life. This oral analysis was further supplemented by the written replies given by each rapporteur on the basis of the statutes, case law and legal theory of his own country (of the three Benelux countries in the case of Mr van Sasse) to the questionnaires drawn up by his colleagues and himself.[7]

This preliminary work and material enabled each of the rapporteurs to present an interim report, with draft articles on the matter considered, as a working basis for the Group meetings. It was agreed that these meetings would be devoted to an examination of Mr Giuliano's report on the law applicable to contractual and non-contractual obligations and to the subject matter of Mr Lagarde's and Mr van Sasse van Ysselt's report to the extent that this was relevant to Mr Giuliano's subject.

It was agreed that Mr Arndt's report on the law applicable to corporeal and incorporeal property would be discussed later, Mr Arndt having explained that a comparative study of the principal laws on security rights and interests should precede his report and that the need for such a study had been generally recognized.

Apart from the meeting of rapporteurs in June 1970, the work fully occupied 11 Group plenary sessions, each with an average duration of five days.[8]

At its meeting in June 1972 the Group completed the preliminary draft convention on the law applicable to contractual and non-contractual obligations and decided that it should be submitted, together with the reports finalised at a meeting of rapporteurs on 27 and 28 September 1972, to the Permanent Representatives Commitee for transmission to the Governments of the Community Member States.[9]

5. Re-examination of Group work in the light of observations by the Governments of original and new Member States of the EEC and results achieved in February 1979.

It follows from the foregoing observations that the 1972 draft dealt both with the law applicable to contractual obligations and with that applicable to non-contractual obligations. At the same time it provided solutions relating to the law governing the form of legal transactions and evidence, questions of interpretation of uniform rules and their relationship with other rules of conflict of international origin, to the extent to which these were connected with the subject of the preliminary draft.

Following the accession of the United Kingdom, Denmark and Ireland to the EEC in 1973 the Commission extended the Group to include government experts from the new Member States and the Permanent Representatives Commitee authorized the enlarged Group to re-examine in the light of observations from the Governments of the original and of the new Member States of the EEC, the preliminary draft convention which the Commission had submitted to it at the end of 1972. The Group elected Prof. Philip as vice-chairman.

Nevertheless the preliminary draft was not re-examined immediately. The need to allow the experts from the new Member States time to consult their respective Governments and interested parties on the one hand and the political uncertainties in the United Kingdom concerning membership of the European Communities (which were not settled until the 1975 referendum) on the other, resulted in a significant reduction (if not suspension) of the Group's activities for about three years. It was not until the end of 1975 that the Group was able properly to resume its work and proceed with the preparation of the Convention on the law applicable to contractual obligations. In fact the Group decided at its meeting in March 1978 to limit the present convention to contracts alone and to begin negotiations for a second Convention, on non-contractual obligations, after the first had been worked out. Most delegations thought it better for reasons of time to finish the part relating to contractual obligations first.

The original preliminary draft, with the limitation referred to, was re-examined in the course of 14 plenary sessions of the Group and three special meetings on transport and insurance contracts ; each of the plenary sessions lasted two to five days.[10] At the meeting in February 1979 the Group finished the draft convention, decided upon the procedure for transmitting the draft to the Council before the end of April and instructed Professors Giuliano and Lagarde to draw up the report ; this was then finalised at a meeting of rapporteurs on 18 to 20 June 1979 in which one expert per delegation participated, and transmitted in turn to the Council and to the Governments by the chairman, Mr Jenard.

6. Finalization of the Convention within the Council of the European Communitees.

On 18 May 1979 the Group's chairman, Mr Jenard, sent the draft Convention to the President of the Council of the European Communities with a request that the Governments make their comments on the draft by the end of the year so that the Convention could then be concluded during 1980.

On 20 July 1979 Mr Jenard sent the President of the Council a draft report on the Convention, which was the predecessor of this report.

The General Secretariat of the Council received written comments from the Belgian, Netherlands, Danish, Irish, German, Luxembourg and United Kingdom Governments. In addition, on 17 March 1980, the Commission adopted an opinion on the draft Convention, which was published in Official Journal of the European Communities No. L 94 of 11 April 1980.

On 16 January 1980 the Permanent Representatives Commitee set up an ad hoc working party on private international law, whose terms of reference were twofold:

- to finalize the Convention text in the light of the comments made by Member States' Governments,
- to consider whether, and if so within what limits, the Court of Justice of the European Communities should be given jurisdiction to interpret the Convention.

The ad hoc working party met twice, from 24 to 28 March and 21 to 25 April 1980, with Mr Brancaccio from the Italian Ministry of Justice in the chair.[11] Working from the Governments' written comments and others made orally during discussions, the working party reached general agreement on the substantive provisions of the Convention and on the accompanying report.

The only problems unresolved by the working party concerned the problem of where the Convention stood in relation to the Community legal order. They arose in particular in determining the number of ratifications required for the Convention to come into force and in drafting a statement by the Governments of the Member States on the conferral of jurisdiction on the Court of Justice.

Following a number of discussions in the Permanent Representatives Committee, which gradually brought agreement within sight, the Council Presidency deemed circumstances to be ripe politically for the points of disagreement to be discussed by the Ministers of Justice with a good chance of success at a special Council meeting on 19 June 1980 in Rome.

At that meeting, a final round of negotiations produced agreement on a number of seven Member States required to ratify in order for the Convention to come into force. Agreement was also reached on the wording of a joint statement on the interpretation of the Convention by the Court of Justice, which followed word for word the matching statement made by the Governments of the original six Member States of the Community when the Convention on jurisdiction and enforcement was concluded on 27 September 1968 in Brussels. In adopting the statement, the Representatives of Governments of the Member States, meeting within the Council, also instructed the ad hoc Council working party on private international law to consider by what means point 1 of the statement could be implemented and report back by 30 June 1981.

With these points settled, the President-in-Office of the Council, Tommaso Morlino, Italian Minister of Justice, recorded the agreement of the Representatives of the Governments of the Member States, meeting within the Council, on the following:

- adoption of the text of the Convention and of the two joint statements annexed to it;
- the Convention would be open for signing from 19 June 1980;
- the Convention and accompanying report would be published in the Official Journal of the European Communities for information.

The Convention was signed on 19 June 1980 by the plenipotentiaries of Belgium, the Federal Republic of Germany, France, Ireland, Italy, Luxembourg and the Netherlands.

7. Review of the internal sources and nature of the rules in force in the EEC Member States relating to the law applicable to contractual obligations.

The chief aim of the Convention is to introduce into the national laws of the EEC Member States a set of uniform rules on the law applicable to contractual obligations and on certain general points of private international law to the extent that these are linked with those obligations.

Without going here into details of positive law, though it may be necessary to return to it in the comments on the uniform rules, a short survey can now be given of the internal sources and the nature of the rules of conflict at present in force in the Community countries in the field covered by the Convention. This survey will bring out both the value and the difficulties of the unification undertaken by the Group and of which the convention is only the first fruit.

Of the nine Member States of the Community, Italy is the only one to have a set of rules of conflict enacted by the legislature covering almost all the matters with which the Convention is concerned. These rules are to be found for the most part in the second paragraph of Article 17 and in Articles 25, 26, 30 and 31 of the general provisions constituting the introduction to the 1942 Civil Code, and in Articles 9 and 10 of the 1942 Navigation Code.

In the other Member States of the Community, however, the body of rules of conflict on the law applicable to contractual obligations is founded only on customary rules or on rules originating in case law. Academic studies and writings have helped considerably to develop and harmonize these rules.

The position as just stated has not been altered substantially either by the French draft law supplementing the Civil Code in respect of private international law (1967) or by the Benelux Treaty establishing uniform rules of private international law signed in Brussels on 3 July 1969. These two texts are certainly an interesting attempt to codify the rules of conflict and also, in the case of the Benelux countries, to make these rules uniform on an inter-State level. The Group did not fail to take account of their results in its own work. However, the entry into force of the Benelux Treaty has not been pursued, and the French draft law seems unlikely to be adopted in the near future.

8. Universal application of the uniform rules.

From the very beginning of its work the Group has professed itself to be in favour of uniform rules which would apply not only to the nationals of Member States and to persons domiciled or resident within the Community but also to the nationals of third States and to persons domiciled or resident therein. The provisions of Article 2 specify the universal application of the convention.

The Group took the view that its main purpose was to frame general rules such as those existing in legislative provisions currently in force in Italy and in the Benelux Treaty and the French draft law. In such a context these general rules, which would become the "common law" of each Member State for settling conflicts of laws, would not prejudice the detailed regulation of clearly delimited matters arising from other work, especially that of the Hague Conference on private international law. The application of these particular conventions is safeguarded by the provisions of Article 21.

9. On the normally general nature of the uniform rules in the Convention and their significance in the unification of laws already undertaken in the field of private international law.

At the outset of its work the Group had also to determine the nature and scope of the uniform rules of conflict to be formulated. Should they be general rules, to be applied indiscriminately to all contracts, or would it be better to regulate contractual obligations by means of a series of specific rules applicable to the various categories of contract, or again should an intermediate solution be envisaged, namely by adopting general rules and supplementing them by specific rules for certain categories of contract?

Initially the rapporteur advocated the latter method. This provided that, in default of an express of implied choice by the parties, the contract would be governed (subject to specific provisions for certain categories) by one system of law.

When the Group tackled the question of whether to supplement the general rules for determining the law applicable to the contract by some specific rules for certain categories of contract it became clear that the point was no longer as significant as it had been in the context of the rapporteur's initial proposals. The Group's final version of the text of Article 4 provided satisfactory solutions for most of the contracts whose applicable law was the subject of specific rules of conflict in the rapporteur's proposals, notably because of its flexibility. The Group therefore merely provided for some exceptions to the rule contained in Article 4, notably those in Articles 5 and 6 concerning the law applicable respectively to certain consumer contracts and to contracts of employment in default of an express or implied choice by the parties.

The normally general nature of the uniform rules made it necessary to provide for a few exceptions and to allow the judge a certain discretion as to their application in each particular case. This aspect will be dealt with in the comments on a number of Articles in Chapter III of this report.

As declared in the Preamble, in concluding this Convention the nine States which are parties to the Treaty establishing the European Economic Community show their desire to continue in the field of private international law the work of unification already undertaken in the Community, particularly in matters of jurisdiction and enforcement of judgments. The question of accession by third States is not dealt with in the Convention (see page 41, penultimate paragraph).

TITLE I: SCOPE OF THE CONVENTION

Article 1

Scope of the Convention

1. As provided in Article 1 (1) the uniform rules in this Convention apply generally to contractual obligations in situations involving a conflict of laws.

It must be stressed that the uniform rules apply to the abovementioned obligations only "in situations involving a choice between the laws of different countries". The purpose of this provision is to define the true aims of the uniform rules. We know that the law applicable to contracts and to the obligations arising from them is not always that of the country where the problems of interpretation or enforcement are in issue. There are situations in which this law is not regarded by the legislature or by the case law as that best suited to govern the contract and the obligations resulting from it. These are situations which involve one or more elements foreign to the internal social system of a country (for example, the fact that one or all of the parties to the contract are foreign nationals or persons habitually resident abroad, the fact that the contract was made abroad, the fact that one or more of the obligations of the parties are to be performed in a foreign country, etc.), thereby giving the legal systems of several countries claims to apply. These are precisely the situations in which the uniform rules are intended to apply.

Moreover the present wording of paragraph 1 means that the uniform rules are to apply in all cases where the dispute would give rise to a conflict between two or more legal systems. The uniform rules also apply if those systems coexist within one State (*cf.* Article 19 (1)). Therefore the question whether a contract is governed by English or Scots law is within the scope of the Convention, subject to Article 19 (2).

2. The principle embodied in paragraph 1 is however subject to a number of restrictions.

First, since the Convention is concerned only with the law applicable to contractual obligations, property rights and intellectual property are not covered by these provisions. An Article in the original preliminary draft had expressly so provided. However, the Group considered that such a provision would be superfluous in the present text, especially as this would have involved the need to recapitulate the differences existing as between the various legal system of the Member States of the Community.

3. There are also the restrictions set out in paragraph 2 of Article 1.

The first of these, at (a), is the status or legal capacity of natural persons, subject to Article 11 ; then, at (b), contractual obligations relating to wills and succession, to property rights arising out of matrimonial relationships, to rights and duties arising out of family relationships, parentage, marriage or affinity, including maintenance obligations in respect of illegitimate children. The Group intended this enumeration to exclude from the scope of the Convention all matters of family law

As regards maintenance obligations, within the meaning of Article 1 of the Hague Convention on the law applicable to maintenance obligations, the Group considered that this exclusion should also extend to contracts which parties unter a legal maintenance obligation make in performance of that obligation. All other contractual obligations, even if they provide for the maintenance of a member of the family towards whom there are no legal maintenance obligations, would fall within the scope of the Convention.

Contrary to the provisions of the second paragraph of Article 1 in the original preliminary draft, the current wording of subparagraph (b) does not in general exclude gifts. Most of the delegations favoured the inclusion of gifts where they arise from a contract within the scope of the Convention, even when made within the family, provided they are not covered by family law. Therefore the only contractual gifts left outside the scope of the uniform rules are those to which family law, the law relating to matrimonial property rights or the law of succession apply.

The Group unanimously affirmed that matters relating to the custody of children are outside the scope of the Convention, since they fall within the sphere of personal status and capacity. However, the Group thought it inappropriate to specify this exclusion in the text of the Convention itself, thereby intending to avoid an a contrario interpretation of the Convention of 27 September 1968.

To obviate any possibility of misconstruction, the present wording of subparagraphs (a) and (b) uses the same terminology as the 1968 Convention on jurisdiction and enforcement of judgments.

4. Subparagraph (c) excludes from the scope of the uniform rules in the first instance obligations arising from bills of exchange, cheques, promissary notes.

In retaining this exclusion, for which provision had already been made in the original preliminary draft, the Group took the view that the provisions of the Convention were not suited to the regulation of obligations of this kind. Their inclusion would have involved rather complicated special rules. Moreover the Geneva Conventions to which several Member States of the Community are parties govern most of these areas. Also, certain Member States of the Community regard these obligations as non-contractual.

Subparagraph (c) also excludes other negotiable instruments to the extent that the obligations under such other negotiable instruments arise out of their negotiable character. If a document, though the obligation under it is transferable, is not regarded as a negotiable instrument, it falls outside the exclusion. This has the effect that such documents as bills of lading, similar documents issued in connection with transport contracts, and bonds, debentures, guarantees, letters of indemnity, certificates of deposit, warrants and warehouse receipts are only excluded by subparagraph (c) if, they can be regarded as negotiable instruments; and even then the exclusion only applies with regard to obligations arising out of their negotiable character. Furthermore, neither the contracts pursuant to which such instruments are issued nor contracts for the purchase and sale of such instruments are excluded. Whether a document is characterized as a negotiable instrument is not governed by this Convention and is a matter for the law of the forum (including its rules of private international law).

5. Arbitration agreements and agreements on the choice of court are likewise excluded from the scope of the Convention (subparagraph (d)).

There was a lively debate in the Group on whether or not to exclude agreements on the choice of court. The majority in the end favoured exclusion for the following reasons: the matter lies within the sphere of procedure and forms part of the administration of justice (exercise of State authority); rules on this matter might have endangered the ratification of the Convention. It was also noted that rules on jurisdiction are a matter of public policy and there is only marginal scope for freedom of contract. Each court is obliged to determine the validity of the agreement on the choice of court in relation to its own law, not in relation to the law chosen. Given the nature of these provisions and their fundamental diversity, no rule of conflict can lead to a uniform solution. Moreover, these rules would in any case be frustated if the disputes were brought before a court in a third country. It was also pointed out that so far as concerns relationships within the Community, the most important matters (valitidity of the clause and form) are governed by Article 17 of the Convention of 27 September 1968. The outstanding points, notably those relating to consent, do not arise in practice, having regard to the fact that Article 17 provides that these agreements shall be in writing. Those delegations who thought that agreements on choice of court should be included within the Convention pointed out that the validity of such an agreement would often be dealt with by the application of the same law that governed the rest of the contract in which the agreement was included and should therefore be governed by the same law as the contract. In some systems of law, agreement as to choice of court is itself regarded as a contract and the ordinary choice of law rules are applied to discover the law applicable to such a contract.

As regards arbitration agreements, certain delegations, notably the United Kingdom delegation, had proposed that these should not be excluded from the Convention. It was emphasized that an arbitration agreement does not differ from other agreements as regards the contractual aspects, and that certain international Conventions do not regulate the law applicable to arbitration agreements, while others are inadequate in this respect. Moreover the international Conventions have not been ratified by all the Member States of the Community and, even if they had been, the problem would not be solved because these Conventions are not of universal applications. It was added that there would not be unification within the Community on this important matter in international commerce.

Other delegations, notably the German and French delegations, opposed the United Kingdom proposal, emphasizing particularly that any increase in the number of conventions in this area should be avoided, that severability is accepted in principle in the draft and the arbitration clause is independent, that the concept of "closest ties" difficult to apply to arbitration agreements, that procedural and contractual aspects are difficult to separate, that the matter is complex and the experts' proposals show great divergences; that since procedural matters and those relating to the question whether a dispute was arbitrable would in any case be excluded, the only matter to be regulated would be consent; that the International Chamber of Commerce – which, as everyone knows, has great experience in this matter – has not felt the need for further regulation.

Having regard to the fact that the solutions which can and have been considered generally for arbitration are very complex and show great disparity, a delegate proposed that this matter should be studied separately and any results embodied in a Protocol. The Group adopted this proposal and consequently excluded arbitration agreements from the scope of the uniform rules, subject to returning to an examination of these problems and of agreements on the choice of court once the Convention has been finally drawn up.

The exclusion of arbitration agreements does not relate solely to the procedural aspects, but also to the formation, validity and effects of such agreements. Where the arbitration clause forms an integral part of a contract, the exclusion relates only to the clause itself and not to the contract as a whole. This exclusion does not prevent such clauses being taken into consideration for the purposes of Article 3 (1).

6. Subparagraph (e) provides that the uniform rules shall not apply to questions governed by the law of companies, and other bodies corporate or unincorporate such as the creation, by registration or otherwise, legal capacity, internal organization or winding-up of companies, and other bodies corporate or unincorporate and the personal legal liability of officers and members as such for the obligations of the company or body.

This exclusion in no way implies that this aspect was considered unimportant in the economic life of the Member States of the Community. Indeed, this is an area which, by virtue of its economic importance and the place which it occupies in many provisions of the Treaty establishing the EEC, appears to have the strongest possible reasons for not being separated from Community work in the filed of unification of private international law, notably in conflicts of laws pertaining to economic relations.

Notwithstanding the foregoing considerations, the Group had thought it inadvisable, even in the original preliminary draft, to include companies, firms and legal persons within the scope of the Convention, especially in view of the work being done on this subject within the European Communities.[12]

Confirming this exclusion, the Group stated that it affects all the complex acts (contractual, administrative, registration) which are necessary to the creation of a company or firm and to the regulation of its internal organization and winding-up, i.e. acts which fall within the scope of company law.

On the other hand, acts or preliminary contracts whose sole purpose is to create obligations between interested parties (promoters) with a view to forming a company or firm are not covered by the exclusion.

The subject may be a body with or without legal personality, profit-making or non-profit-making. Having regard to the differences which exist, it may be that certain relationships will be regarded as within the scope of company law or might be treated as being governed by that law (for example, société de droit civil, nicht-rechtsfähiger Verein, partnership, Vennootschap onder firma, etc.) in some countries but not in others. The rule has been made flexible in order to take account of the diversity of national laws.

Examples of "internal organization" are: the calling of meetings, the right to vote, the necessary quorum, the appointment of officers of the company or firm, etc. "Winding-up" would cover either the termination of the company or firm as provided by its constitution or by operation of law, or its disappearance by merger or other similar process.

At the request of the German delegation the Group extended the subparagraph (e) exclusion to the personal liability of members and organs, and also to the legal capacity of companies or firms. On the other hand the Group did not adopt the proposal that mergers and groupings should also be expressly mentioned, most of the delegations being of the opinion that mergers and groupings were already covered by the present wording.

As regards legal capacity, it should be made clear that the reference is to limitations, which may be imposed by law on companies and firms, for example in respect of acquisition of immovable property, not to *ultra vires* acts by organs of the company or firm, which fall under subparagraph (f).

7. The solution adopted in subparagraph (f) involves the exclusion from the scope of the uniform rules of the question whether an agent is able to bind a principal, or an organ to bind a company or body corporate or unincorporate, to a third party.

The exclusion affects only the relationships between the principal and third parties, more particularly the question whether the principal is bound vis-à-vis third parties by the acts of the agent in specific cases. It does not affect other aspects of the complex field of agency, which also extends to relationships between the principal and the agent and to agent-third party relationships. The exclusion is justified by the fact that it is difficult to accept the principle of freedom of contract on this point. On the other hand, principal-agent and agent-third party relationships in no way differ from other obligations and are therefore included within the scope of the Convention in so far as they are of a contractual nature

8. The exception in subparagraph (g) concerns "trusts" in the sense in which they are understood in the common law countries. The English word "trust" is properly used to define the scope of the exclusion. On the other hand similar institutions under continental laws falls within the provisions of the Convention because they are normally contractual in origin. Nevertheless it will be open to the judge to treat them in the same way as the institutions of the common law countries when they exhibit the same characteristics.

9. Under subparagraph (h) the uniform rules do not apply to evidence and procedure, subject to Article 14.

This exclusion seems to require no comment. The scope and extent to which the exclusion is subject to limitation will be noted in the commentary on Article 14.

10. The question whether contracts of insurance should or should not be included in the sope of the uniform rules was discussed at length by the Group. The solution finally adopted was that which appears in paragraph 3.

Under this paragraph the provisions of the Convention do not apply to contracts of insurance covering risks situated in the territories of Member States of the European Economic Community. This exclusion takes account of work being done within the Community in the field of insurance. Thus the uniform rules apply to contracts of insurance covering risks situate outside those territories. The States are nevertheless free to apply rules based on those in the Convention even to risks situate in the Community, subject to the Community rules which are to be established.

Insurance contracts, where they cover risks situate outside the Community, may also, in appropriate cases, fall under Article 5 of the Convention.

To determine whether a risk is situate in the territories of the Member States of the Community the last phrase of paragraph 3 states that the judge is required to apply his own national law. This expression means the rules in force in the judge's country, to the exclusion of the rules of private international law as stated by Article 15 of the Convention.

11. By virtue of paragraph 4 of Article 1 the exclusion provided for in paragraph 3 does not affect reinsurance contracts. In fact these contracts do not raise the same problems as contracts of insurance, where the need to protect the persons insured must necessarily be taken into account. Thus the uniform rules apply to reinsurance contracts.

Article 2

Application of law of non-Contracting States

This Article underlines the universal character of the uniform rules laid down in this Convention. The Convention does not apply only in situations involving some form of connection with one or other of the Contracting States. It is of universal application in the sense that the choice of law which it lays down may result in the law of a State not party to the Convention being applied. By way of example, under Article 3, parties to a contract may opt for the law of a third State, and in the absence of any choice, that same law may be applied to the contract under Articles 4 and 5 if it is with that State that the contract has the closest links. In other words, the Convention is a uniform measure of private international law which will replace the rules of private international law in force in each of the Contracting States, with regard to the subject matter which it covers and subject to any other convention to which the Contracting States are party (see Article 21).

The solution is consistent with that adopted in most of the Hague Conventions on private international law that deal with choice of laws (*stricto sensu*). The text follows that of the Hague Convention drafted during the XIIIth session (Conventions of 14 March 1978 on the law applicable to matrimonial property regimes, Article 2, and on the law applicable to agency, Article 4).

TITLE II: UNIFORM RULES

Article 3

Freedom of choice

1. The rule stated in Article 3 (1) under which the contract is governed by the law chosen by the parties simply reaffirms a rule currently embodied in the private international law of all the Member States of the Community and of most other countries.

In French law the rule conferring this power (or "autonomie de la volonté" as it is called) upon the parties is founded on case law dating back to the judgment delivered on 5 December 1910 by the Court of Cassation in *American Trading Company* v. *Quebec Steamship Company Limited.* The French draft law of 1967 to supplement the Civil Code in matters of private international law merely confirms the state of French law in this matter by providing in the first paragraph of Article 2312: "Contracts of an international character and the obligations arising from them shall be subject to the law under which the parties intended to place themselves."

The firm establishment of the rule in French case law was accompanied by corresponding developments in legal theory. The most eminent contemporary writers declare themselves fundamentally in favour of the principle of the parties' freedom of contract in determining the law applicable to the contract, or, according to the opinion of some legal writers, the "localization" of the contract in a specific legal system.[13]

The same applies to the law of the German Federal Republic, where the subject of contractual obligations was not dealt with by the legislature in the final version of the "introductory law" of 1896. The rule conferring upon the parties the power to specify the law applicable to their contract is nevertheless founded on case law which has been developed and strengthened in recent decades despite the opposition of the great majority of earlier German legal theorists. At all events present-day theory is in entire agreement with the position taken by the case law.[14]

Unlike the situation in France and Germany, in Italy the principle of freedom of contract of the contracting parties was expressly enacted as early as 1865 in the preliminary provisions of the Civil Code. It is currently based upon the first paragraph of Article 25 of the preliminary provisions of the 1942 Civil Code, in which the freedom of the parties to choose the law applicable to their contract is formally accepted, as in Articles 9 and 10 of the Navigation Code, where it is provided that the power of the parties to designate the applicable law may also be exercised in seamen's contracts and in contracts fot the use of ships, boats and aircraft. According to the preponderant view of theorists and consistent decisions by the Court of Cassation, the law applicable to the contract must be determined primarily on the basis of the express will of the parties; only in default of such a nomination will the law of the contract be determined by the connecting factors stipulated in the abovementioned provisions.[15]

As regards Belgium, Luxembourg and the Netherlands, the rule that the contracting parties enjoy freedom of contract in choosing the applicable law has also been sanctioned by judicial practice and by contemporary legal writers.

In its judgment of 24 February 1938 in *SA Antwerpia* v. *Ville d'Anvers* the Belgian Court of Cassation stated for the first time, in terms clearly suggested by the French judgment of 5 December 1910, that: "the law applicable to contracts, both to their formation and their conditions and effects, (is) that adopted by the parties".[16] Several Belgian writers have contributed to the firm establishment of the rule in theory and in practice.[17]

In the Netherlands the Hoge Raad put the finishing touches to the developments in case law in this field in its judgment of 13 May 1966 in the *Alnati* case. The previous decisions of the Supreme Court and the differing views of writers on the precise scope of the freedom of contract rule would not have permitted definition of the state of Netherlands law in this matter with sufficient certainty.[18]

At all events the 1969 Benelux Treaty on uniform rules for private international law, even though the signatory States have not pursued its entry into force, is clear evidence of their present views on this subject. Article 13 (1) of the uniform law states: "Contracts shall be governed by the law chosen by the parties as regards both essential and ancillary provisions."

English law recognizes that the parties to a contract are free to choose the law which is to govern it ("the proper law of the contract"). This principle of freedom of choice is founded on judicial decisions.[19] In *Vita Food Products Inc.* v. *Unus Shipping Co. Ltd* [20] Lord Wright indicated that the parties' choice must be bona fide and legal and could be avoided on the ground of public policy. In certain areas the parties' freedom of choice is subject to limitations imposed by statute,[20a] the most important of these being in the field of exemption clauses.[20b]

The law of Scotland is to similar effect[20c] and Irish law draws its inspiration from the same principles as the English and Scottish legal systems.

Under English law (and the situation is similar in Scots law and Irish law), in the case where the parties have not expressly chosen the law to govern their contract,[20d] the court will consider whether the parties' choice of law to be applied can be inferred from the terms of the contract. The most common case in which the court may infer a choice of the proper law is where the contract contains an arbitration or choice of jurisdiction clause naming a particular country as the seat of arbitration or litigation. Such a clause gives rise to an argument that the law of the country chosen should be applied as the proper law of the contract. This inference however is not conclusive and can be rebutted by any contrary inferences which may be drawn from the other provisions of the contract and the relevant surrounding circumstances.[20e]

Finally, as regards Denmark, the principle of the freedom of contracting parties to choose the law applicable to their contract already seems to have inspired several opinions by Supreme Court judges during this century. Today at all events this principle forms the basis of Danish case law, as can be seen from the judgment in 1957 in *Baltica* v. *M.J. Vermaas Scheepvaart bedrijf*, with full support from legal writers.[21]

2. The principle of the parties' freedom to choose the law applicable is also supported both by arbitration decisions and by international treaties designed to unify certain rules of conflict in relation to contracts.

The rule, which had already been cited in 1929 by the Permanent Court of International Justice in its judgment in the case of the Brazilian Loans,[22] very clearly underlay the award made by the arbitration tribunal on 29 August 1958 in *Saudi Arabia* v. *Arabian American Oil Company (Aramco)* in which it was stated that the "principles of private international law to be consulted in order to find the law applicable are those relating to freedom of choice, by virtue of which, in an agreement which is international in character, the law expressly chosen by the parties must be applied first ...".[23] Similarly in the arbitration findings given on 15 March 1963 in *Sapphire International Petroleums Ltd* v. *National Iranian Oil Company*, the sole arbitrator, Mr Cavin, affirmed that it is the will of the parties that determines the law applicable in matters of contract.[24] The rule was reaffirmed even more recently by the sole arbitrator,

Mr Dupuy, in the award which he made on 19 January 1977 in *Libyan Arab Republic* v. *California Asiatic Oil Company and Texaco Overseas Petroleum Company*.[25]

As regards international treaties, the rule of freedom of choice has been adopted in the Convention on the law applicable to international sales of goods concluded at the Hague on 15 June 1955 which entered into force on 1 September 1964. Article 2 of this Convention, which is in force among several European countries, provides that: "The sale shall be governed by the internal law of the country nominated by the contracting parties."

Article VIII of the European Convention on international commercial arbitration concluded at Geneva on 21 April 1961, which entered into force on 7 January 1964, provides that the parties are free to determine the law which the arbitrators must apply in a dispute.

The same principle forms the basis of the 1965 Convention for the settlement of disputes relating to investments between States and nationals of other States, which entered into force on 14 October 1966, when it provides in Article 42 that "the Tribunal shall rule on the dispute in accordance with the rules of law adopted by the parties".

The Hague Convention of 14 March 1978 on the law applicable to agency provides in Article 5 that "the internal law chosen by the principal and the agent is to govern the agency relationship between them".[26]

3. The parties' choice must be express or be demonstrated with reasonable certainty by the terms of the contract or the circumstances of the case. This interpretation, which emerges from the second sentence of Article 3 (1), has an important consequence.

The choice of law by the parties will often be express but the Convention recognizes the possibility that the Court may, in the light of all the facts, find that the parties have made a real choice of law although this is not expressly stated in the contract. For example, the contract may be in a standard form which is known to be governed by a particular system of law even though there is no express statement to this effect, such as a Lloyd's policy of marine insurance. In other cases a previous course of dealing between the parties under contracts containing an express choice of law may leave the court in no doubt that the contract in question is to be governed by the law previously chosen where the choice of law clause has been omitted in circumstances which do not indicate a deliberate change of policy by the parties. In some cases the choice of a particular forum may show in no uncertain manner that the parties intend the contract to be governed by the law of that forum, but this must always be subject to the other terms of the cntract and all the circumstances of the case. Similarly references in a contract to specific Articles of the French Civil Code may leave the court in no doubt that the parties have deliberately chosen French law, although there is no expressly stated choice of law. Other matters that may impel the court to the conclusion that a real choice of law has been made might include an express choice of law in related transactions between the same parties, or the choice of a place where disputes are to be settled by arbitration in circumstances indicating that the arbitrator should apply the law of that place.

This Article does not permit the court to infer a choice of law that the parties might have made where they had no clear intention of making a choice. Such a situation is governed by Article 4.

4. The last sentence of Article 3 (1) acknowledges that the parties' choice of the law applicable may relate to the whole of the contract or to only part thereof. On the question whether severability (dépeçage) was to be allowed, some experts observed that the contract should in principle be governed by one law, unless that contract, although apparently a single contract, consists in reality of several contracts or parts which are separable and independent of each other from the legal and economic points of view. In the opinion of these experts, no reference to severability should have been made in the text of the Convention itself. In the view of others, on the contrary, severability is directly linked with the principle of freedom of contract and so would be difficult to prohibit. Nevertheless when the contract is severable the choice must be logically consistent, i.e. it must relate to elements in the contract which can be governed by different laws without giving rise to contradictions. For example, an "index-linking clause" may be made subject to a different law; on the other hand it is unlikely that repudiation of the contract for non-performance would be subjected to two different laws, one for the vendor and the other for the purchaser. Recourse must be had to Article 4 of the Convention if the chosen laws cannot be logically reconciled.

In the opinion of these experts the danger that the argument of severability might be used to avoid certain mandatory provisions is eliminated by the operation of Article 7. The experts concerned also emphasized that severability should not be limited to cases of express choice of law.

The solution adopted in the last sentence of Article 3 (1) is prompted by exactly this kind of idea. The Group did not adopt the idea that the judge can use a partial choice of law as the basis for a presumption in favour of one law invoked to govern the contract in its entirety. Such an idea might be conducive to error in situations in which the parties had reached agreement on the choice of law solely on a specific point. Recourse must be had to Article 4 in the case of partial choice.

5. The first sentence of Article 3 (2) leaves the parties maximum freedom as to the time at which the choice of applicable law can be made.

It may be made either at the time the contract is concluded or at an earlier or later date. The second sentence of paragraph 2 also leaves the parties maximum freedom as to amendment of the choice of applicable law previously made.

The solution adopted by the Group in paragraph 2 corresponds only in part to what seems to be the current state of the law on this point in the Member States of the Community.

In the Federal Republic of Germany and in France the choice of applicable law by the parties can apparently be made even after the contract has been concluded, and the courts sometimes deduce the applicable law from the parties' attitude during the proceedings when they refer with clear agreement to a specific law. The power of the parties to vary the choice of law applicable to their contract also seems to be very widely accepted.[27]

Case law in the Netherlands seems to follow the same line of interpretation.[28]

In Italy, however, the Court of Cassation (sitting as a full court) stated in its judgment of 28 June 1966 No. 1680 in *Assael Nissim* v. *Crespi* that: "the parties" choice of applicable law is not admissible if made after the contract has been drawn up."[29]

According to this dictum, which Italian commentators do not wholly support[30] the choice can be made only at the time the contract is concluded. Once the choice is made, the parties no longer have the option of agreeing to nominate a law other than that nominated at the time of concluding the contract.

In the laws of England and Wales, Scotland, Northern Ireland and Ireland, there is no clear authority as to the law which governs the possibility of a change in the proper law.

6. The liberal solution adopted by the Group seems to be in accordance with the requirement of logical consistency. Once the principle of freedom of contract has been accepted, and having regard to the fact that the requirement of a choice of law by the parties may arise both at the time of conclusion of the contract and after that time, it seems quite logical that the power of the parties should not be limited solely to the time of conclusion of the contract. The same applies to a change (by a new agreement between the parties) in the applicable law previously chosen.

As to the way in which the choice of law can be changed, it is quite natural that this change should be subject to the same rules as the initial choice.

If the choice of law is made or changed in the course of proceedings the question arises as to the limits within which the choice or change can be effective. However, the question falls within the ambit of the national law of procedure, and can be settled only in accordance with that law.

7. The second sentence of Article 3 (2) states that a change in the applicable law after the contract has been concluded shall not prejudice its formal validity under Article 9 or adversely affect the rights of third parties. The purpose of the reservation concerning the formal validity of the contract is to avoid a situation whereby the agreement between the parties to subject the contract to a law other than that which previously governed it could create doubts as to the validity of the contract during the period preceding the agreement between the parties. The preservation of third-party rights appears to be entirely justified. In certain legal systems, a third party may have acquired rights in consequence of a contract concluded betwen two other persons. These rights cannot be affected by a subsequent change in the choice of the applicable law.

8. Article 3 (3) provides that the choice of a foreign law by the parties, whether or not accompanied by the choice of a foreign tribunal, shall not, where all other elements relevant to the situation at the time of the choice are connected with one country only, prejudice the application of the law of that country which cannot be derogated from by contract, hereinafter called "mandatory rules"

This solution is the result of a compromise between two lines of argument which have been diligently pursued within the Group: the wish on the one hand of certain experts to limit the parties' freedom of choice embodied in this Article by means of a correcting factor specifying that the choice of a foreign law would be insufficient per se to permit the application of that law if the situation at the moment of choice did not involve another foreign element, and on the other the concern of other experts, notably the United Kingdom experts, that such a correcting factor would be too great an obstacle to the freedom of the parties in situations in which their choice appeared justified, made in good faith, and capable of serving interests worthy of protection. In particular these experts emphasized that departures from the principle of the parties' freedom of choice should be authorized only in exceptional circumstances, such as the application of the mandatory rules of a law other than that chosen by the parties; they also gave several examples of cases in which the choice of a foreign law by the parties was fully justified, although there was apparently no other foreign element in the situation.

The Group recognized that this concern was well founded, while maintaining the principle that the choice by the parties of a foreign law where all the other elements relevant to the situation at the time of the choice are connected with one country only shall not prejudice the application of the mandatory rules of the law of that country.

9. Article 3 (4) merely refers questions relating to the existence and validity of the parties' consent as to the choice of the law applicable to the provisions of Articles 8, 9 and 11. We will return to these matters in the comments on those Articles.

Article 4

Applicable law in the absence of choice

1. In default of an express or implied choice by the parties, there is at present no uniform way of determining the law applicable to contracts in the legal systems of the Member States of the Community.[31]

In French and Belgian law no distinction is to be drawn between the express and hypothetical (or presumed) will of the parties. Failing an express choice of applicable law, the courts look for various "pointers" capable of showing that the contract is located in a particular country. This localization is sometimes regarded subjectively as equivalent to the probable wish of the parties had such a wish been expressed, sometimes objectively as equivalent to the country with which the transaction is most closely connected.[32]

The objective concept seems to be receiving more and more support from legal writers and from case law. Following this concept, the Paris Court stated in its judgment of 27 January 1955 (*Soc. Jansen* v. *Soc. Heurtey*) that, in default of an indication of the will of the parties, the applicable law "is determined objectively by the fact that the contract is located by its context and economic aspects in a particular country, the place with which the transaction is most closely connected being that in which the contract is to be performed in fulfilment of the obligation characteristic of its nature".[33]

It is this concept of the location of the contracts that is referred to, in terms clearly modelled on the above judgment, in the second paragraph of Article 2313 of the French draft, which states that in default of the expressed will of the parties "the contract is governed by the law with which it is most closely connected by its economic aspects, and notably by the main place of performance".

Similarly, in German law the solution adopted by the courts in determining the law of the contract in the absence of choice by the parties is based largely upon the search for "pointers" capable of showing the "hypothetischer Parteiwille", the presumed will of the parties, having regard to the general interests at stake in each particular case. If this gives no result, the law applicable to the contract according to German case law is determined by the place of performance: more precisely, by the place of performance of each of the obligations arising from the contract, because the German courts take the view that if the various contractual obligations are to be performed in different countries, each shall be governed by the law of the country in which it is performed.[34]

In English law where the parties have not expressly chosen the proper law and no choice can be inferred, the law applicable to the contract is the system of law with which the transaction has its "closest and most real connection".[35] In such a case the judge does not seek to ascertain the actual intentions of the contracting parties, because that is non-existent, but seeks "to determine for the parties what is the proper law which, as just and reasonable persons, they ought to have intended if they had thought about the question when they made the contract".[36] In this inquiry, the court has to consider all the circumstances of the case. No one factor is decisive; instead a wide range of factors must be taken into account, such as for instance, the place of residence or business of the parties, the place of performance, the place of contracting and the nature and subject-matter of the contract.

Scots law adopts a similar approach,[36a] as does the law of Ireland.

In Italian law, where the presumed will of the parties plays no part, the matter is settled expressly and directly by the legislature. Failing a choice of law by the parties, the obligations arising from the contract are governed by the following:

(a) contracts for employment on board foreign ships or aircraft, by the national law of the ship or aircraft (Naval Code Article 9);
(b) marine, domestic and air hiring contracts, charters and transport contracts, by the national law of the ship or aircraft (Naval Code Article 10);
(c) all other contracts, by the national law of the contracting parties, if common to both; otherwise by the law of the place where the contract was concluded (preliminary provisions of the Civil Code, Article 25, first subparagraph).

The abovementioned laws are of subsidiary effect only; they apply only in default of an expression of the parties' will as to the law applicable. Italian case law so holds and legal writers concur with this view.[37]

To conclude this short survey, only the provisions of the third and fourth paragraphs of Article 13 of the 1969 Benelux Treaty which has not entered into force remain to be mentioned. According to the third paragraph, in default of a choice by the parties "the contract shall be governed by the law of the country with which it is most closely connected", an according to the fourth paragraph "when it is impossible to determine that country, the contract shall be governed by the law of the country in which it was concluded". One may note a tendency in Netherlands case law to formulate special rules of reference for certain types of contract (see *Journal du Droit Int. 1978*, pp. 336–344 and *Neth. Int. Law Rev. 1974*, pp. 315–316), i.e. contracts of employment, agency contracts and contracts of carriage.

The foregoing survey has shown that, with the sole exception of Italy, where the subsidiary law applicable to the contract is determined once and for all by hard-and-fast connecting factors, all the other Community countries have preferred and continue to prefer a more flexible approach, leaving the judge to select the preponderant and decisive connecting factor for determining the law applicable to the contract in each specific case among the various elements of the contract and the circumstances of the case.

2. Having considered the advantages and disadvantages of the solutions adopted by the legislatures and the case law of the Member States of the Community and after analysing a range of ideas and alternatives advanced both by the rapporteur and by several delegates, the Group agreed upon the uniform rule embodied in Article 4.

The first paragraph of this Article provides that, in default of a choice by the parties, the contract shall be governed by the law of the country with which it has the closest connection.

In order to determine the country with which the contract is most closely connected, it is also possible to take account of factors which supervened after the conclusion of the contract.

In fact the beginning of the first paragraph does not mention default of choice by the parties; the expression used is "to the extent that the law applicable to the contract has not been chosen in accordance with Article 3". The use of these words is justified by reference to what has been said in paragraph 4 of the commentary on Article 3.

However, the flexibility of the general principle established by paragraph 1 is substantially modified by the presumptions in paragraphs 2, 3 and 4, and by a strictly limited exception in favour of severability at the end of paragraph 1.

3. According to Article 4 (2), it is presumed that the contract has the closest connection with the country in which the party who is to effect the performance which is characteristic of the contract has his habitual residence at the time when the contract is concluded, or, in the case of a body corporate or unincorporate, its central administration. If the contract is concluded by that party in the course of his trade or profession, the country concerned is that in which his principal place of business is situated or, if the contract is to be performed through a place of business other than the principal place of business, the country in which that other place of business is situated. Article 4 (2) establishes a presumption which may be rebutted in accordance with Article 4 (5).

The kind of idea upon which paragraph 2 is based is certainly not entirely unknown to some specialists. It gives effect to a tendency which has been gaining ground both in legal writings and in case law in many countries in recent decades.[38] The submission of the contract, in the absence of a choice by the parties, to the law appropriate to the characteristic performance defines the connecting factor of the contract from the inside, and not from the outside by elements unrelated to the essence of the obligation such as the nationality of the contracting parties or the place where the contract was concluded.

In addition it is possible to relate the concept of characteristic performance to an even more general idea, namely the idea that his performance refers to the function which the legal relationship involved fulfils in the economic and social life of any country. The concept of characteristic performance essentially links the contract to the social and economic environment of which it will form a part.

Identifying the characteristic performance of a contract obviously presents no difficulty in the case of unilateral contracts. By contrast, in bilateral (reciprocal) contracts whereby the parties undertake mutual reciprocal performance, the counter-performance by one of the parties in a modern economy usually takes the form of money. This is not, of course, the characteristic performance of the contract. It is the performance for which the payment is due, i.e. depending on the type of contract, the delivery of goods, the granting of the right to make use of an item of property, the provision of a service, transport, insurance, banking operations, security, etc, which usually constitutes the centre of gravity and the socio-economic function of the contractual transaction.

As for the geographical location of the characteristic performance, it is quite natural that the country in which the party liable for the performance is habitually resident or has his central administration (if a body corporate or unincorporate) or his place of business, according to whether the performance in question is in the course of his trade or profession or not, should prevail over the country of performance where, of course, the latter is a country other than that of habitual residence, central administration or the place of business. In the solution adopted by the Group the position is that only the place of habitual residence or of the central administration or of the place of business of the party providing the essential performance is decisive in locating the contract.

Thus, for example, in a banking contract the law of the country of the banking establishment with which the transaction is made will normally govern the contract. It is usually the case in a commercial contract of sale that the law of the vendor's place of business will govern the contract. To take another example, in an agency contract concluded in France between a Belgian commercial agent and a French company, the characteristic performance being that of the agent, the contract will be governed by Belgian law if the agent has his place of business in Belgium.[39]

In conclusion, Article 4 (2) gives specific form and objectivity to the, in itself, too vague concept of "closest connection". At the same time it greatly simplifies the problem of determining the law applicable to the contract in default of choice by the parties. The place where the act was done becomes unimportant. There is no longer any need to determine where the contract was concluded, with all the difficulties and the problems of classification that arise in practice. Seeking the place of performance or the different places of performance and classifying them becomes superfluous.

For each category of contract it is the characteristic performance that is in principle the relevant factor in applying the presumption for determining the applicable law, even in situations peculiar to certain contracts, as for example in the contract of guarantee where the characteristic performance is always that of the guarantor, whether in relation to the principal debtor or the creditor.

To counter the possibility of changes in the connecting factor ("conflits mobiles") in the application of paragraph 2, it has been made clear that the country of habitual residence or of the principal place of business of the party providing the characteristic performance is the country in which he is habitually resident or has his central administration or place of business, as appropriate, "at the time of conclusion of the contract".

According to the last part of paragraph 2, if the contract prescribes performance by an establishment other than the principal place of business, it is presumed that the contract has the closest connection with the country of that other establishment.

4. Article 4 (3) establishes that the presumption in paragraph 2 does not operate to the extent that the subject of the contract is a right in immovable property or a right to use immovable property. It is presumed in this case that the contract is most closely connected with the country in which the immovable property is situated.

It is advisable to state that the provision in question merely establishes a presumption in favour of the law of the country in which the immovable property is situate. In other words this is a presumption which, like that in paragraph 2, could also be rebutted if circumstances so required.

For example, this presumption could be rebutted if two persons resident in Belgium were to make a contract for renting a holiday home on the island of Elba (Italy). It might be thought in such a case that the contract was most closely connected with the country of the contracting parties' residence, not with Italy.

Finally it should be stressed that paragraph 3 does not extend to contracts for the construction or repair of immovable property. This is because the main subject-matter of these contracts is the construction or repair rather than the immovable property itself.

5. After a long and animated discussion the Group decided to include transport contracts within the scope of the convention. However, the Group deemed it inappropriate to submit contracts for the carriage of goods to the presumption contained in paragraph 2, having regard to the peculiarities of this type of transport. The contract for carriage of goods is therefore made subject to a presumption of its own, namely that embodied in paragraph 4. This presumption may be rebutted in accordance with Article 4 (5).

According to this fourth paragraph it is presumed in the case of contracts for the carriage of goods that if the country in which the carrier has his principal place of business at the time the contract is concluded is also the country of the place of loading or unloading or of the principal place of business of the consignor, the contract is most closely connected with that country. The term "consignor" refers in general to any person who consigns goods to the carrier (Afzender, Aflader, Verzender, Mittente, Caricatore, etc).

Thus the paragraph 4 presumption rests upon a combination of connecting factors. To counter the possibility of changes in the connecting factor in applying the paragraph, it has been made clear here also that the reference to the country in which the carrier has his principal place of business must be taken to refer to the carrier's place of business "at the time the contract is concluded".

It appears that for purposes of the application of this paragraph the places of loading and unloading which enter into consideration are those agreed at the time when the contract is concluded.

It often happens in contracts for carriage that a person who contracts to carry goods for another does not carry them himself but arranges for a third party to do so. In Article 4 (4) the term "the carrier" means the party to the contract who undertakes to carry the goods, whether or not he performs the carriage himself.

In addition, the third sentence of paragraph 4 provides that in applying that paragraph single-voyage charterparties and other contracts whose main purpose is the carriage of goods shall be treated as contracts for the carriage of goods. The wording of paragraph 4 is intended to make it clear that charterparties may be considered to be contracts for the carriage of goods in so far as that is their substance.

6. Contracts for the carriage of passengers remain subject to the general presumption, i.e. that provided for in Article 4 (2).

This solution was adopted by majority vote within the Group. Certain delegations favoured the special presumption emodied in paragraph 4, arguing that, as with other types of transport, the need was for a combination of connecting factors, in view of the fact that reference solely to the place where the carrier, who provides the characteristic performance, has his principal place of business may not be a significant connecting factor: by way of example they cited the case of transportation of French or English passengers between London and Paris by an American airline. It was also emphasized that in a mixed contract (passengers and goods) the difficulty of applying two different laws would arise.

Nevertheless the other delegations were against the special presumption, their principal arguments being: the application of several laws to passengers on the same journey would involve serious difficulties; the formulation of paragraph 4 is such that it would hardly ever apply to carriage of passengers, so recourse would usually be had to the first paragraph of Article 4, which does not give the judge sufficiently precise criteria for decision; contracts of carriage normally contain a clause conferring jurisdiction on the court of the carrier's principal place of business, and paragraph 2 would operate so that the law of the court of competent jurisdiction would coincide with the applicable law.

In any event it should be stated that the judge will not be able to exclude consideration of the country in which the carrier has his principal place of business in seeking the places with which the contract is most closely connected.

Finally it is useful to note that the Group repeatedly stressed in the course of the discussions on transport problems that the international conventions took precedence in this matter.

7. Article 4 (2) does not apply when the characteristic performance connot be determined. The case then falls under paragraph 1, i.e. the contract will be governed by the law of the country with which it is most closely connected.

The first part of Article 4 (5) contains precisely that provision.

However, that paragraph also provides for the possibility of disregarding the presumptions in paragraphs 2, 3, and 4 when all the circumstances show the contract to have closer connections with another country. In this case the law of that other country is applied.

The grounds for the latter provision are as follows. Given the entirely general nature of the conflict rule contained in Article 4, the only exemptions to which are certain contracts made by consumers and contracts of employment, it seemed essential to provide for the possibility of applying a law other than those referred to in the presumptions in paragraphs 2, 3 and 4 whenever all the circumstances show the contract to be more closely connected with another country.

Article 4 (5) obviously leaves the judge a margin of discretion as to whether a set of circumstances exists in each specific case justifying the non-application of the presumptions in paragraphs 2, 3 and 4. But this is the inevitable counterpart of a general conflict rule intended to apply to almost all types of contract.

8. Article 4 (1) allows parts of the contract to be severed under certain conditions. The last sentence of this paragraph provides that if one part of the contract can be separated from the rest and is more closely connected with another country, then by way of exception the law of that other country can be applied to that part of the contract.

Discussion of the matter within the Group revealed that no delegation wished to encourage the idea of severability (*dépeçage*). However, most of the experts were in favour of allowing the court to effect a severance, by way of exception, for a part of the contract which is independent and separable, in terms of the contract and not of the dispute, where that part has a closer connection with another country (for example, contracts for joint venture, complex contracts).

As to whether or not the possibility of severance should be mentioned in the text of the convention itself most delegations were in favour of its being mentioned. It was emphasized in particular that mere reference to the matter in the report would be insufficient by itself, because in some Member States of the Community it is not usual to take account of the report. It was also emphasized that to include it in the text would reduce the risk of variation in the application of the convention on this point, because the text would specify the conditions under which severance was allowed.

The wording of the last sentence in paragraph 1 embodies precisely this idea. The words "by way of exception" are therefore to be interpreted in the sense that the court must have recourse to severance as seldom as possible.

9. It should be noted that the presumptions mentioned in paragraphs 2, 3 and 4 of Article 4 are only rebuttable presumptions.

Article 5

Certain consumer contracts

1. Article 5 of the convention establishes a specific conflict rule for certain contracts made by consumers. Most of the experts who have participated in the Group's work since 1973 have taken the view that consumer protection, the present aim of several national legislatures, would entail a reversal of the connecting factor provided for in Article 4 or a modification of the principle of freedom of choice provided for in Article 3. On the one hand the choice of the parties should not adversely affect the mandatory provisions of the State in which the consumer is habitually resident; on the other, in this type of contract it is the law of the buyer (the weaker party) which should normally prevail over that of the seller.

2. The definition of consumer contracts corresponds to that contained in Article 13 of the Convention on jurisdiction and enforcement of judgments. It should be interpreted in the light of its purpose which is to protect the weaker party and in accordance with other international instruments with the same purpose such as the Judgments Convention. Thus, in the opinion of the majority of the delegations it will, normally, only apply where the person who supplies goods or services or provides credit acts in the course of his trade or profession. Similarly, the rule does not apply to contracts made by traders, manufacturers or persons in the exercise of a profession (doctors, for example) who buy equipment or obtain services for that trade or profession. If such a person acts partly within, partly outside his trade or profession the situation only falls within the scope of Article 5 if he acts primarily outside his trade or profession. Where the receiver of goods or services or credit in fact acted primarily outside his trade or profession but the other party did not know this and, taking all the circumstances into account should not reasonably have known it, the situation falls outside the scope of Article 5. Thus if the receiver of goods or services holds himself out as a professional, e.g. by ordering goods which might well be used in his trade or profession on his professional paper the good faith of the other party is protected and the case will not be governed by Article 5.

The rule extends to credit sales as well as to cash sales, but sales of securities are excluded. The Group has specifically avoided a more precise definition of "consumer contract" in order to avoid conflict with the various definitions already given by national legislation. The rule also applies to the supply of services, such as insurance, as well as supply of goods.

3. Paragraph 2 embodies the principle that a choice of law in a consumer contract cannot deprive the consumer of the protection afforded to him by the law of the country in which he has his habitual residence. This principle shall, however, only apply under certain conditions set out in the three indents of paragraph 2.

The first indent reales to situations where the trader has taken steps to market his goods or services in the country where the consumer resides. It is intended to cover inter alia mail order and door-step selling. Thus the trader must have done certain acts such as advertising in the press, or on radio or television, or in the cinema or by catalogues aimed specifically at that country, or he must have made business proposals individually through a middleman or by canvassing. If, for example, a German makes a contract in response to an advertisement published by a French company in a German publication, the contract is covered by the special rule. If, on the other hand, the German replies to an advertisement in American publications, even if they are sold in Germany, the rule does not apply unless the advertisement appeared in special editions of the publication intended for European countries. In the latter case the seller will have made a special advertisement intended for the country of the purchaser.

The Group expressly adopted the words "steps necessary on his part" in order to avoid the classic problem of determining the place where the contract was concluded. This is a particularly delicate matter in the situations referred to, because it involves international contracts normally concluded by correspondence. The word "steps" includes inter alia writing or any action taken in consequence of an offer or advertisement.

According to the second indent Article 5 shall apply in all situations where the trader or his agent has received the order of the consumer in the country in which the consumer has his habitual residence. This provision is a parallel to Article 3 (2) of the 1955 Hague Convention on international sales.

There is a considerable overlap between the first and the second indents. This overlap is, however, not complete. For example, the second indent applies in situations where the consumer has addressed himself to the stand of a foreign firm at a fair or exhibition taking place in the consumers country or to a permanent branch or agency of a foreign firm established in the consumer's country even though the foreign firm has not advertised in the consumer's country in a way covered by the first indent. The word "agent" is intended to cover all persons acting on behalf of the trader.

The third indent deals with a situation which is rather special but where, on the other hand, a majority of delegations found a clear need for protecting the consumer under the provisions of Article 5. It covers what one might describe as "border-crossing excursion-selling", i.e. for example, a situation where a store-owner in country A arranges one-day bus trips for consumers in a neighbouring country B with the main purpose of inducing the consumers to buy in his store. This is a practice well-known in some areas. The situation is not covered by the first indent because there it is required that the consumer has taken in his own country all the steps necessary on his part for the conclusion of the contract. The third indent is, unlike the rest of paragraph 2, limited to contracts for the sale of goods. The condition that the journey was arranged by the seller shall not be understood in the narrow way that the seller must himself have taken care of the transportation. It is sufficient that the seller has arranged the journey by way of an agreement with the transportation company.

In describing the situation in which Article 5 applies to consumer contracts, the Group has not followed the text of Article 13 (1) of the Judgments Convention as amended by the Accession Convention. On the one hand Article 5 contains no special provision for hire purchase contracts and loans on deferred terms. On the other hand, Article 13 of the Judgments Convention has no provisions parallel to the second and third indents of Article 5 (2).

4. Article 5 (3) introduces an exception to Article 4 of the Convention. According to this paragraph, notwithstanding the provisions of Article 4 and in the absence of choice in accordance with Article 3, a contract made by a consumer shall "be governed by the law of the country in which the consumer has his habitual residence if it is entered into in the circumstances described in the second paragraph of Article 5".

The wording of paragraph 3 is sufficiently clear, and calls for no additional examination

5. Under the terms of paragraph 4 thereof, Article 5 applies neither to contracts of carriage (a) nor to contracts relating to the supply of services provided exclusively in a country other than that in which the consumer is resident (b). The exclusion of contracts of carriage is justified by the fact that the special protective measures for which provision is made in Article 5 are not appropriate for governing contracts of this type. Similarly, in the case of contracts relating to the supply of services (for example, accommodation in a hotel, or a language course) which are supplied exclusively outside the State in which the consumer is resident, the latter cannot reasonably expect the law of his State of origin to be applied in derogation from the general rules of Articles 3 and 4. In the cases referred to under (b) the contract is more closely connected with the State in which the other contracting party is resident, even if the latter has performed one of the acts described in paragraph 2 (advertising, for example) in the State in which the consumer is resident.

6. The intention of paragraph 5 is to ensure that Article 5, notwithstanding the exclusions made in paragraph 4, shall apply to contracts providing for what is in English normally called a "package tour", i.e. an ordinary tourist arrangement consisting of a combination of travel and accommodation for an inclusive price. If a package tour starts with transportation from the country in which the consumer has his habitual residence the contract would not be excluded according to paragraph 4. The importance of paragraph 5 is, therefore, that it ensures application of Article 5 also in situations where the services provided for under a package tour start with transportation from another country. However, Article 5 of course only applies to package tours where the general conditions of paragraphs 1 and 2 are fulfilled, i.e. that the contract can be regarded as a consumer contract and that it is entered into in one of the situations mentioned in paragraph 2.

When formulating paragraph 5, the Group met with difficulty in defining a "package tour". The Group confined itself to a definition which underlines the main elements of this type of contract well known in practice, leaving it to the courts to solve any possible doubt as to the exact delimitation. The accommodation which is a part of a package tour must normally be separate from the transportation, and so paragraph 5 would not apply to the provision of a sleeper on a train.

Article 6

Individual employment contracts

1. Re-examination of the specific conflict rule in the matter of contracts of employment led the Group to make fundamental changes to this Article, which already appeared (as Article 5) in the original preliminary draft, and to harmonize its approach with that of the present Article 5 on consumer contracts.

In both cases the question was one of finding a more appropriate arrangement for matters in which the interests of one of the contracting parties are not the same as those of the other, and at the same time to secure thereby more adequate protection for the party who from the socio-economic point of view is regarded as the weaker in the contractual relationship.

2. On this basis, Article 6 (1) sets a limit on the parties' freedom to choose the applicable law, as permitted by Article 3 of the convention, affirming that this choice in contracts of employment "shall not have the result of depriving the employee of the protection afforded to him by the mandatory rules of the law which would be applicable under paragraph 2 in the absence of choice".

The purpose of this text is as follows:

> if the law applicable pursuant to paragraph 2 grants employees protection which is greater than that resulting from the law chosen by the parties, the result is not that the choice of this law becomes completely without effect. On the contrary, in this case the law which was chosen continues in principle to be applicable. In so far as the provisions of the law applicable pursuant to paragraph 2 give employees better protection than the chosen law, for example by giving a longer period of notice, these provisions set the provisions of the chosen law aside and are applicable in their place.

The mandatory rules from which the parties may not derogate consist not only of the provisions relating to the contract of employment itself, but also provisions such as those concerning industrial safety and hygiene which are regarded in certain Member States as being provisions of public law.

It follows from this text that if the law of the country designated by Article 6 (2) makes the collective employment agreements binding for the employer, the employee will not be deprived of the protection afforded to him by these collective employment agreements by the choice of law of another State in the individual employment contract.

Article 6 applies to individual employment contracts and not to collective agreements. Consequently, the fact that an employment contract is governed by a foreign law cannot affect the powers which an employee's trade union might derive from collective agreements in its own country.

The present wording of Article 6 speaks of "contract of employment" instead of "employment relationship" as in the original preliminary draft. It should be stated, however, that the rule in Article 6 also covers the case of void contracts and also de facto employment relationships in particular those characterized by failure to respect the contract imposed by law for the protection of employees.

3. According to Article 6 (2), in the absence of choice by the parties and notwithstanding the provisions of Article 4, the contract of employment is governed as follows:

(a) by the law of the country in which the employee habitually carries out his work in performance of his contract, even if he is temporarily employed in another country; or
(b) if the employee does not habitually carry out his work in any one country, by the law of the country in which the place of business through which he was engaged is situated,

unless it appears from the circumstances as a whole that the contract of employment is more closely connected with another country, in which case the law of that other country applies.

After a thorough examination of the various problems raised by contracts of employment in private international law, in the course of which particular consideration was given both to the draft Regulation prepared in this connection by the EEC Commission and to the latest trends in the legal literature and case law of the Member States of the Community, the Group finally adopted the following solution. If the employee habitually works in one and the same country the contract of employment is governed by the law of that country even if the employee is temporarily employed in another country. This is the rule which appears in subparagraph 2 (a). On the other hand, if the employee does not habitually work in one and the same country the contract of employment is governed by the law of the country in which the place of business through which he was engaged is situated. This is the rule which appears in subparagraph 2 (b).

These solutions obviously differ substantially from those which would have resulted from the Article 4 presumption.

However, the last sentence of Article 6 (2) provides that if it appears from the circumstances as a whole that the contract is more closely connected with another country, the law of the latter country is applied.

4. As regards work done outside the jurisdiction of any State, the Group considered that the rule adopted in Article 6 could in principle be applied. In the case of work on an oil-rig platform on the high seas, the law of the country of the undertaking which engaged the employee should be applied.

The Group did not seek a special rule for the work of members of the crew on board a ship.

Article 7

Mandatory rules

1. The wording of Article 7 of the original preliminary draft has been considerably improved in the course of the Group's re-examination of the text of the convention since 1973, in order to permit a better interpretation in the various situations in which it will have to be applied.

The Group reiterated at its last meeting that Article 7 merely embodies principles which already exist in the laws of the Member States of the Community.

The principle that national courts can give effect under certain conditions to mandatory provisions other than those applicable to the contract by virtue of the choice of the parties or by virtue of a subsidiary connecting factor, has been recognized for several years both in legal writings and in practice in certain of our countries and elsewhere.

For example, the principle was recognized in the abovementioned 1966 judgment of the Netherlands Supreme Court in the *Alnati* case (cited *supra*, commentary on Article 3 (1)) in which the Court said that, although the law applicable to contracts of an international character can, as a matter of principle, only be that which the parties themselves have chosen, "it may be that, for a foreign State, the observance of certain of its rules, even outside its own territory, is of such importance that the courts must take account of them, and hence apply them in preference to the law of another State which may have been chosen by the parties to govern their contract".

This judgment formed the basis for the second paragraph of Article 13 of the non-entered-into-force Benelux Treaty of 1969 on uniform rules of private international law, which provides that "where the contract is manifestly connected with a particular country, the intention of the parties shall not have the effect of excluding the provisions of the law of that country which, by reason of their special nature and subject-matter, exclude the application of any other law".

The same attitude, at any event, underlies Article 16 of the Hague Convention of 14 March 1978 on the law applicable to agency, whereby, in the application of that convention, effect may be given to the mandatory rules of any State with which the situation has a significant connection, if and to the extent that, by the law of that State, those rules are applicable irrespective of the law indicated by its conflict rules.

On the other hand, despite the opinion of some jurists, it must be frankly recognized that no clear indication in favour of the principle in question seems discernible in the English cases (*Ralli Bros* v. *Sota y Aznar*; *Regazzoni* v. *Sethia*; *Rossano* v. *Manufacturers Life Insurance Co.*).[40]

2. The wording of Article 7 (1) specifically provides that in the application of the convention "effect may be given to the mandatory rules of the law of another country with which the situation has a close connection if and in so far as, under the law of the latter country, those rules must be applied whatever the law applicable to the contract".

The former text did not specify the nature of the "connection" which must exist between the contract and a country other than that whose law is applicable. Several experts have observed that this omission might oblige the court in certain cases to take a large number of different and even contradictory laws into account. This lack of precision could make the court's task difficult, prolong the proceedings, and lend itself to delaying tactics. Accepting the force of these observations, the Group decided that it is essential that there be a genuine connection with the other country, and that a merely vague connection is not adequate. For example, there would be a genuine connection when the contract is to be performed in that other country or when one party is resident or has his main place of business in that other country. Among the suggested versions, the Group finally adopted the word "close" which seemed the most suitable to define the situation which it wished to cover.

The connection in question must exist between the contract as a whole and the law of a country other than that to which the contract is submitted. The Group rejected the proposal by one delegation designed to establish a connection between the point in dispute and a specific law. In fact this proposal would have given rise to a regrettable dismemberment of the contract and would have led to the application of mandatory laws not foreseeable by the parties. Nevertheless the Group preferred to replace the word "the contracts" by "the situation".

Since the former text seemed to some delegations to be lacking in clarity, the Group decided to improve the wording. In the new text it has therefore stated that the legal system of the country of which these mandatory provisions are an integral part must be examined to find out whether these provisions apply in the particular case whatever the law applicable to the contract. Furthermore, in the French text the word "loi" has been replaced by the word "droit" in order to avoid any doubts as to the scope of the rule, which is to cover both "legislative" provisions of any other country and also common law rules. Finally, after a long discussion, the majority of the Group, in view of the concern expressed by certain delegations in relation to constitutional difficulties, decided that it was preferable to allow the courts a discretion in the application of this Article.

3. Article 7 (1) adds in relation to the mandatory rules that their nature and purpose, and the consequences of their application or non-application, must be taken into account in order to decide whether effect should be given to them.

Thus the application of the mandatory provisions of any other country must be justified by their nature and by their purpose. One delegation had suggested that this should be defined by saying that the nature and purpose of the provisions in question should be established according to internationally recognized criteria (for example, similar laws existing in other countries or which serve a generally recognized interest). However, other experts pointed out that these international criteria did not exist and that consequently difficulties would be created for the court. Moreover this formula would touch upon the delicate matter of the credit to be given to foreign legal systems. For these reasons the Group, while not disapproving this idea, did not adopt this drafting proposal.

Additionally, in considering whether to give effect to these mandatory rules, regard must be had to "the consequences of their application or non-application".

Far from weakening the rule this subsequent element – which did not appear in the original preliminary draft - defines, clarifies and strengthens it. In fact, the judge must be given a power of discretion, in particular in the case where contradictory mandatory rules of two different countries both purport simultaneously to be applicable to one and the same situation, and where a choice must necessarily be made between them.

To complete the comments on Article 7 (1) it only remains to emphasize that the words "effect may be given" impose on the court the extremely delicate task of combining the mandatory provisions with the law normally applicable to the contract in the particular situation in question. The novelty of this provision, and the fear of the uncertainty to which it could give rise, have led some delegations to ask that a reservation may be entered on Article 7 (1) (see Article 22 (1) (a)).

4. Article 7 (2) states that "nothing in this Convention shall restrict the application of the rules of the law of the forum in a situation where they are mandatory irrespective of the law otherwise applicable to the contract".

The origin of this paragraph is found in the concern of certain delegations to safeguard the rules of the law of the forum (notably rules on cartels, competition and restrictive practices, consumer protection and certain rules concerning carriage) which are mandatory in the situation whatever the law applicable to the contract may be.

Thus the paragraph merely deals with the application of mandatory rules (lois d'application immédiate; leggi di applicazione necessaria; etc) in a different way from paragraph 1.[40a]

Article 8

Material validity

1. Article 8 (1) provides that the existence and validity of a contract, or of any term of a contract, shall be determined by the law which would govern it under this Convention if the contract or term were valid.

The paragraph is intended to cover all aspects of formation of the contract other than general validity. As we have emphasized previously in paragraph 9 of the comments on Article 3, this provision is also applicable with regard to the existence and validity of the parties' consent as to choice of the law applicable.

The word "term" has been adopted to cover cases in which there is a dispute as to the validity of a term of the contract, such as a choice of law clause.

2. Notwithstanding the general rule in paragraph 1, paragraph 2 provides a special rule which relates only to the existence and not to the validity of consent.

According to this special rule a party may rely upon the law of the country in which he has his habitual residence to establish that he did not consent if it appears from the circumstances that it would not be reasonable to determine the effect of his conduct in accordance with the law specified in paragraph 1.

The solution adopted by the Group in this respect is designed inter alia to solve the problem of the implications of silence by one party as to the formation of the contract.

The word "conduct" must be taken to cover both action and failure to act by the party in question; it does not, therefore, relate solely to silence.

The words "if it appears from the circumstances" mean that the court must have regard to all the circumstances of the case, not solely to those in which the party claiming that he has not consented to the contract has acted. The Court will give particular consideration to the practices followed by the parties inter se as well as their previous business relationships.

According to the circumstances, the words "a party" can relate either to the offeror or to the offeree.

The application of paragraph 2 can result in a decision releasing a party who would have been bound under the terms of paragraph 1, but it can never produce the opposite effect of holding that a contract exists which is non-existent by its proper law.

Article 9 (4) contains a special rule relating to acts intended to have legal effect, such as, in accordance with the law of many countries, an offer. Such acts have not been mentioned in Article 8. Nonetheless, the rules in Article 8 apply to such acts by way of analogy.

Article 9

Formal validity

Article 9 deals with the formal validity of contracts and acts intended to have legal effect. The first four paragraphs lay down rules governing all contracts and acts intended to have legal effect. The last two paragraphs lay down special rules peculiar to certain types of contract. I. General rules (paragraphs 1 to 4 inclusive)

The scope of these general rules needs to be specified before indicating the various laws which they declare to be applicable.

A. The scope of the general rules – 1. Acts to which they apply

Article 9 applies to contracts and unilateral acts intended to have legal effect. The preliminary draft of 1972 used only the term "act intended to have legal effect" (*acte juridique*) which, in the terminology originating from Roman law, includes both categories. The inclusion in Article 9 of both contracts and acts intended to have legal effect, mentioned successively, is due merely to a wish to ensure clarity, since the rules to be applied are based on the same principles in both cases.

Unilateral acts intended to have legal effect which fall within the scope of the Article are those which are related to an existing or contemplated contract. Acts relating to a concluded contract can be extremely varied: notice of termination, remission of a debt, declaration of rescission or repudiation, etc.

But the act must be connected with a contract. A unilateral undertaking, unconnected with a contract, as for example, in some legal systems, a recognition of a debt not arising under a contract, or a unilateral act creating, transferring or extinguishing a right in rem, would not fall within the scope of Article 9 or of any other provision in the Convention since the latter is concerned only with contractual obligations.

Such an act must also, quite clearly, relate to a contract falling within the scope of the convention. Article 9 does not apply to the formal validity of acts relating to contracts excluded from the convention under Article 1 (2) and (3).

There is no provision expressly referring to "public acts". This omission is intentional. First, the concept of a public act is not recognized in all the legal systems and could raise awkward problems of definition. Moreover, it seems wrong for there to be special provisions governing the formal validity of private law acts concluded before public officials. Indeed, as has recently been pointed out,[41] it is because a public official can draw up an instrument only in accordance with the law from which he derives his authority that the formal validity for the act concluded before him is necessarily subject to that law. If, for example, a notary has not observed the law from which he derives his authority, the contract he has drawn up will not of course be a valid notarial act. But it will not be entirely void if the law which governs its substance (and which may also determine its formal validity by virtue of Article 9) does not require a special form for that type of contract.

The general rules accordingly apply to "public acts". This has the advantage of validating acts drawn up by a public official who has thought it appropriate, as happens in the Netherlands, to follow the forms laid down by the foreign law which governs the substance of the contract.

2. Article 9 does not define what is to be understood by the "formal validity" of acts. It seemed realistic to leave open this difficult problem of definition, especially as its importance has been slightly reduced in consequence of the solutions found for the problem of the connecting factor which to some extent equate formal and material validity.

It is nevertheless permissible to consider "form", for the purposes of Article 9, as including every external manifestation required on the part of a person expressing the will to be legally bound, and in the absence of which such expression of will would not be regarded as fully effective.[42] This definition does not include the special requirements which have to be fulfilled where there are persons under a disability to be protected, such as the need in French law for the consent of a family council to an act for the benefit of a minor, or where an act is to be valid against third parties, for example the need in English law for a notice of a statutory assignment of a chose in action.

B. Laws to be applied – 1. The principle of applying in the alternative the lex causae or the lex loci actus.

The system contained in Article 9 is a compromise between *favor negotii*, which tends to take a liberal attitude regarding the formalities required for acts, and the due observance of formalities which, most often, is merely giving effect to requirements of substance.

In supporting the former attitude, it did not seem possible to follow the example of the Hague Convention of 5 October 1961 concerning conflict of laws with regard to testamentary dispositions. Favor testamenti is justified by the fact that a will is an act of final disposition which by definition cannot be reenacted if its validity is challenged after the testator's death. This consideration does not affect other acts intended to have legal effect in the case of which excessive freedom with regard to formalities would result in robbing of all effect the requirements in this field which are specified by the various legal systems, very often with a legitimate aim in view. Moreover, the connection between questions of form and questions of evidence (Article 14) makes it desirable to limit the number of laws applicable to formal validity.

On the other hand, in order to avoid parties being caught unawares by the annulment of their act on the ground of an unexpected formal defect, Article 9 has, nonetheless, laid down a fairly flexible system based on applying in the alternative either the law of the place where the contract was entered into (or in the case of a unilateral act the law of the country where the act was done) or else the law which governs its substance.

This choice of applicable laws appears to be sufficient and this is why the possibility of applying the law of the common nationality or habitual residence of the parties was rejected.[43] On the other hand no priority has been accorded either to the *lex causae* or to the *lex loci actus*. If the act is valid to one of these two laws, that is enough to prevent defects of form under the other from affording grounds for nullity.[44]

The Group did not examine the question of which of the two laws would apply to an action brought to annul the contract for formal defect in a case where the contract would be null and void according to both these laws. If, for example, the limitation period for bringing an action for annulment on the ground of a formal defect is not the same in the two legal systems, it may seem to be in keeping with the spirit of this Article to apply the law which provides for the shorter period and, in this respect, is more favourable than the other to the validity of the act.

Renvoi must be rejected as regards formal validity as in all other matters governed by the Convention (*cf.* Article 15).

2. Problems raised by applying the law governing the substance of the contract to the question of formal validity

The *lex causae* is already recognized as applicable, either as the principal law or as a subsidiary option, to the question of formal validity by the law of the Contracting States and its application is fully justified by the logical connection between substance and form.[45]

The law governing the substance of the contract must be determined by reference to Articles 3, 4 and 6 of the Convention (for contracts provided for under Article 5, see II below, Special rules peculiar to certain contracts). Article 3 (2) specifically governs the formal consequences of a voluntary change by the parties in the law governing the substance of the contract. This text means that, on this assumption of changes in the connecting facts, it is enough for the contract to be formally valid in accordance with one or other of the laws successively called upon to govern the substance of the contract.

A difficulty will arise when a contract is subject to several laws, either because the parties have selected the law applicable to a part only of their contract (Article 3 (1)), or because the court itself, by way of exception, has proceeded to sever the contract (Article 4 (1)). Which of the laws governing the substance of the contract is to determine its formal validity? In such a case it would seem reasonable to apply the law applicable to the part of the contract most closely connected with the disputed condition on which its formal validity depends.

Article 8 (1), dealing with material validity, says that the existence and validity of a contract or of any term of a contract shall be determined by the law which would govern it under the Convention if the contract or term were valid. This is to avoid the circular argument that where there is a choice of the applicable law no law can be said to be applicable until the contract is found to be valid. A similar point arises in relation to formal validity under Article 9, and although the text does not expressly say so it is intended that "the law which governs it under this Convention" should be the law which would govern the contract if it were formally valid.

3. Problems raised by applying the *locus regit actum* rule to the question of formal validity

The application of the law of the country in which a contract was entered into or in which a unilateral act was done, in order to determine the formal validity of the contract or act, results from the age-old maxim locus regit actum, recognized alike, usually as a principal rule, by the law of the Contracting States.[46]

However a classic difficulty arises in determining the country in which the contract was entered into when the contract has been made between persons in different countries.

To resolve this difficulty it is first necessary to describe exactly what is meant by persons being or not being in the same country. Where the contract is concluded through the offices of one or more agents, Article 9 (3) indicates clearly that the place to be taken into consideration is where the agents are acting at the time when the contract is concluded. If the parties' agents (or one party and the agent of the other) meet in a given country and conclude the contract there, this contract is considered, within the meaning of paragraph 1, to be concluded between persons in that country, even if the party or parties represented were in another country at the time. Similarly, if the parties' agents (or one party and the agent of the other) are in different countries at the time when they conclude the contract, this contract is considered, within the meaning of paragraph 2, to be concluded between persons in different countries even if both the parties represented were in fact in the same country at the time.

The question of finding which law is the law of the place where the contract was entered into and therefore determines the formal validity of a contract made between persons in different countries, in the sense just indicated, has been very widely debated. Solutions consisting in fixing the conclusion of the contract either in the place where the offer was made or in the place where the acceptance was made have been rejected as rather artificial.[47] The solution consisting in applying to offer and acceptance separately the law of the country in which each was made, directly based on the Frankenstein draft for a European code of private international law and retained in the preliminary draft of 1972, and by the 1978 Swiss draft of Federal law on private international law, Article 125 (2), was also rejected. It is clear that there are numerous requirements as to formal validity which are laid down with regard to the contract itself, taken as a whole and not stage by stage. This is the case where, for example, two signatures are required or where the contract has to be made in duplicate. Accordingly, rather than split the law determining the formal validity of a contract, it seemed preferable to look for a law which would be applicable to the formal validity of the contract as a whole.

The choice was therefore between a liberal solution, retaining the application in the alternative of the law of one or other of the countries which the persons concluding the contract were at the time it was entered into, and a strict solution, requiring the cumulative application of these various laws. The liberal solution was adopted by Article 9 (2). When a contract is concluded between persons in different countries, it is formally valid if it satisfies the requirements as to form laid down by the law of one of those countries or of the law governing the substance of the contract.

4. Reservation regarding mandatory rules

Article 7 of the Convention, which contains a reservation in favour of the application of mandatory rules, may lead to the rejection of the liberal system based on the application in the alternative of either the law governing the substance of the contract or the law of the place where it was entered into. It may happen that certain formal requirements laid down by the law of the country with which a contract or act has a close connection have a mandatory character so marked that they could be applied even though the law of that country is not one of those which would normally determine formal validity under Article 9.

In this connection mention was made of the rules regarding form laid down by the law of the country where an employment contract is to be carried out, especially the requirement that a non-competition clause should be in writing, even though the oral form is permitted by the law of the place where the contract was entered into or under the law chosen by the parties.

Of course, under the system established by Article 7, it will be for the court hearing the case to decide whether it is appropriate to give effect to these mandatory provisions and consequently to disregard the rules laid down in Article 9.

II. Special rules peculiar to certain contracts (paragraphs 5 and 6)

Paragraphs 5 and 6 provide special rules for the formal validity of certain contracts made by consumers and of contracts the subject matter of which is a right in immovable property or a right to use immovable property. It would have been conceivable with regard to such contracts merely to apply Article 7 quite simply and, as an exception to Article 9, to allow, for example, the application of certain formal provisions for consumer protection laid down by the law of the consumer's habitual place of residence, or of certain mandatory requirements as to form imposed by the law of the country where the immovable property is situated.

This solution, however, was not thought adequate to ensure the effective application of these laws because of the discretionary power which Article 7 gives to the court hearing the case. It was accordingly decided to exclude the first four paragraphs of Article 9 completely in the case of contracts of these kinds.

The fifth paragraph of Article 9 deals with the contracts mentioned in Article 5 (1), entered into in the circumstances described in Article 5 (2), taking into account Article 5 (4) and (5).

Just as Article 5 protects the consumer, despite any choice of law specified in the contract, by imposing, as regards substance, the mandatory rules of the law of the country in which he has his habitual residence (Article 5 (3)), Article 9 (5) imposes the rules of that same country with regard to formal validity. This is justified by the very close connection, in the context of consumer protection, between mandatory rules of form and rules of substance.

For the same reasons, it might have been expected that the formal validity of employment contracts would also have been made subject to mandatory attachment to the rules of a particular national law.

This idea, though at first contemplated, was finally rejected. Indeed, contrary to Article 5 which provides explicitly that consumer contracts, in the absence of any choice by the parties, shall be subject as regards formal validity to the law of the country where the consumer has his habitual residence, for the purpose of determining the connecting factors applying to employment contracts Article 6 of the Convention only introduces rebuttable presumptions which must be disregarded in cases where it appears from the circumstances that the employment contract is more closely connected with a country other than that indicated by these presumptions. Consequently, if it had been decided that the law governing the substance of the contract should be mandatory for determining the formal validity of employment contracts, it would have been impossible, at the time a contract was entered into, to determine the law governing its formal validity because of the uncertainty caused by Article 6. Therefore no special rule was laid down regarding the formal validity of employment contracts, but thanks to Article 7, it is to be expected that the mandatory rules regarding formal validity laid down by the law of the country where the work is to be carried out will frequently be found to apply.

The sixth paragraph of Article 9 deals with contracts the subject matter of which is a right in immovable property or a right to use immovable property. Such contracts are not subject to a mandatory connecting factor as regards substance, Article 4 (3) merely raising a presumption in favour of the law of the country where the immovable property is situated. It is clear, however, that if the law of the country where the immovable property is situated lays down mandatory rules determining formal validity, these must be applied to the contract, but only in the probably rather rare cases where, according to that law, these formal rules must be applied even when the contract has been entered into abroad and is governed by a foreign law.

The scope of this provision is the same as that of Article 4 (3).

Article 10

Scope of the applicable law

1. Article 10 defines the scope of the law applicable to the contract under the terms of this Convention.[48]

The original preliminary draft contained no specific rule on this point. It confined itself to the provision in Article 15 that the law which governs an obligation also governs the conditions for its performance, the various ways in which it can be discharged, and the consequences of non-performance. However, since Article 11 of the preliminary draft defined in detail the scope of the law applicable to non-contractual obligations, the principal subject of Article 15 was the scope of the law of the contract.

2. Article 10 (1) lists the matters which fall within the scope of the law applicable to the contract. However, this list is not exhaustive, as is indicated by the words "in particular".

The law applicable to the contract under the terms of his Convention governs firstly its interpretation (subparagraph (a)).

Secondly the law applicable to the contract governs the performance of the obligations arising from the contract (subparagraph (b)).

This appears to embrace the totality of the conditions, resulting from the law or from the contract, in accordance with which the act is essential for the fulfilment of an obligation must be performed, but not the manner of its performance (in so far as this is referred to in the second paragraph of Article 10 or the conditions relating to the capacity of the persons who are to perform it (capacity being a matter excluded from the scope of the uniform rules, subject to the provisions of Article 11) or the conditions relating to the form of the act which is to be done in performance of the obligation.

The following therefore fall within the provisions of the first paragraph of Article 10: the diligence with which the obligation must be performed; conditions relating to the place and time of performance; the extent to which the obligation can be performed by a person other than the party liable; the conditions as to performance of the obligation both in general and in relation to certain categories of obligation (joint and several obligations, alternative obligations, divisible and indivisible obligations, pecuniary obligations); where performance consists of the payment of a sum of money, the conditions relating to the discharge of the debtor who has made the payment, the appropriation of the payment, the receipt, etc.

Within the limits of the powers conferred upon the court by its procedural law, the law applicable to the contract also governs the consequences of total or partial failure to perform these obligations, including the assessment of damages insofar as this is governed by rules of law.

The assessment of damages has given rise to some difficulties. According to some delegations the assessment of the amount of damages is a question of fact and should not be covered by the Convention. To determine the amount of damages the court is obliged to take account of economic and social conditions in its country; there are some cases in which the amount of damages is fixed by a jury; some countries use methods of calculation which might not be accepted in others.

Other delegations countered these arguments, however, by pointing out that in several legal systems there are rules for determining the amount of damages; some international conventions fix limits as to the amount of compensation (for example, conventions relating to carriage); the amount of damages in case of non-performance is often prescribed in the contract and grave difficulties would be created for the parties if these amounts had to be determined later by the court hearing the action.

By way of compromise the Group finally decided to refer in subparagraph (c) solely to rules of law in matters of assessment of damages, given that questions of fact will always be a matter for the court hearing the action.

The expression "consequences of breach" refers to the consequences which the law or the contract attaches to the breach of a contractual obligation, whether it is a matter of the liability of the party to whom the breach is attributable or of a claim to terminate the contract for breach. Any requirement of service of notice on the party to assume his liability also comes within this context.

According to subparagraph 1 (d), the law applicable to the contract governs the various ways of extinguishing obligations, and prescription and limitation of actions. This Article must be applied with due regard to the limited admission of severability (dépeçage) in Articles 3 and 4.

Subparagraph (e) also makes the consequences of nullity subject to the applicable law. The working party's principal objective in introducing this provision was to make the refunds which the parties have to pay each other subsequent to a finding of nullity of the contract subject to the applicable law.

Some delegations have indicated their opposition to this approach on the grounds that, under their legal systems, the consequences of nullity of the contract are non-contractual in nature. The majority of delegations have nevertheless said they are in favour of including such consequences within the scope of the law of contracts, but in order to take account of the opposition expressed provision had been made for any Contracting State to enter a reservation on this matter (Article 22 (1) (b)).

3. Article 10 (2) states that in relation to the manner of performance and the steps to be taken in the event of defective performance regard shall be had to the law of the country in which performance takes place.

This is a restriction which is often imposed in the national law of many countries as well as in several international conventions. Many jurists have supported and continue to support this restriction on the scope of the law applicable to the contract even when the contractual obligation is performed in a country other than that whose law is applicable.

What is meant, however, by "manner of performance" of an obligation? It does not seem that any precise and uniform meaning is given to this concept in the various laws and in the differing views of learned writers. The Group did not for its part wish to give a strict definition of this concept. It will consequently be for the *lex fori* to determine what is meant by "manner of performance". Among the matters normally falling within the description of "manner of performance", it would seem that one might in any event mention the rules governing public holidays, the manner in which goods are to be examined, and the steps to be taken if they are refused.[49]

Article 10 (2) says that a court may have regard to the law of the place of performance. This means that the court may consider whether such law has any relevance to the manner in which the contract should be performed and has a discretion whether to apply it in whole or in part so as to do justice between the parties.

Article 11

Incapacity

The legal capacity of natural persons or of bodies corporate or unincorporate is in principle excluded from the scope of the Convention (Article 1 (2) (a) and (e)). This exclusion means that each Contracting State will continue to apply its own system of private international law to contractual capacity.

However, in the case of natural persons, the question of capacity is not entirely excluded. Article 11 is intended to protect a party who in good faith believed himself to be contracting with a person of full capacity and who, after the contract has been entered into, is confronted by the incapacity of the other contracting party. This anxiety to protect a party in good faith against the risk of a contract being held voidable or void on the ground of the other party's incapacity on account of the application of a law other than that of the place where the contract was concluded is clearly present in the countries which subject capacity to the law of the nationality.[50]

A rule of the same kind is also thought necessary in the countries which make capacity subject to the law of the country of domicile. The only countries which could dispense with it are those which subject capacity to the law of the place where the contract was entered into or to the law governing the substance of the contract.

Article 11 subjects the protection of the other party to the contract to very stringent conditions. First, the contract must be concluded between persons who are in the same country. The Convention does not wish to prejudice the protection of a party under a disability where the contract is concluded at a distance, between persons who are in different countries, even if, under the law governing the contract, the latter is deemed to have been concluded in the country where the party with full capacity is.

Secondly, Article 11 is only to be applied where there is a conflict of laws. The law which, according to the private international law of the court hearing the case, governs the capacity of the person claiming to be under a disability must be different from the law of the country where the contract was concluded.

Thirdly, the person claiming to be under a disability must be deemed to have full capacity by the law of the country where the contract was concluded. This is because it is only in this case that the other party may rely on apparent capacity.

In principle these three conditions are sufficient to prevent the incapacitated person from pleading his incapacity against the other contracting party. This will not however be so "if the other party to the contract was aware of his incapacity at the time of the conclusion of the contract or was not aware thereof as a result of negligence". This wording implies that the burden of proof lies on the incapacitated party. It is he who must establish that the other party knew of his incapacity or should have known of it.

Article 12

Voluntary assignment

1. The subject of Article 12 is the voluntary assignment of rights.

Article 12 (1) provides that the mutual obligations of assignor and assignee under a voluntary assignment of a right against another person (the debtor) shall be governed by the law which under this Convention applies to the contract between the assignor and assignee.

Interpretation of this provision gives rise to no difficulty. It is obvious that according to this paragraph the relationship between the assignor and assignee of a right is governed by the law applicable to the agreement to assign.

Although the purpose and meaning of the provision leave hardly any room for doubt, one wonders why the Group did not draft it more simply and probably more elegantly. For example, why not say that the assignment of a right by agreement shall be governed in relations between assignor and assignee by the law applicable to that agreement.

Such a form of words had in fact been approved initially by most of the delegations, but it was subsquently abandoned because of the difficulties of interpretation which might have arisen in German law where the expression "assignment" of a right by agreement includes the effects of it upon the debtor this was expressly excluded by Article 12 (2).

The present wording was in fact finally adopted precisely to avoid a form which might lead to the idea that the law applicable to the agreement for assignment in a legal system in which it is understood as "Kausalgeschäft" also determines the conditions of validity of the assignment with respect to the debtor.

2. On the contrary, under the terms of Article 12 (2) it is the law governing the right to which the assignment relates which determines its assignability, the relationship between the assignee and the debtor, the conditions under which the assignment can be invoked against the debtor and any question whether the debtor's obligations have been discharged.

The words "conditions under which the assignment can be invoked" cover the conditions of transferability of the assignment as well as the procedures required to give effect to the assignment in relation to the debtor.

Notwithstanding the provisions of paragraph 2, the matters which it covers, with the sole exception of assignability, are governed, as regards relations between assignor and debtor if a contract exists between them, by the law which governs their contract in so far as the said matters are dealt with in that contract.

Subrogation

1. The substitution of one creditor for another may result both from the voluntary assignment of a right (or assignment properly so called) referred to in Article 12 and from the assignment of a right by operation of law following a payment made by a person other than the debtor.

According to the legislation in various Member States of the Community, "subrogration" involves the vesting of the creditor's rights in the person who, being obliged to pay the debt with or on behalf of others, had an interest in satisfying it: this is so under Article 1251-3 of the French Civil Code and Article 1203-3 of the Italian Civil Code. For example, in a contract of guarantee the guarantor who pays instead of the debtor succeeds to the rights of the creditor. The same occurs when a payment is made by one of a number of debtors who are jointly and severally liable or when an indivisible obligation is discharged.

Article 13 of the Convention embodies the conflict rule in matters of subrogation of a third party to the rights of a creditor. Having regard to the fact that the Convention applies only to contractual obligations, the Group thought it proper to limit the application of the rule adopted in Article 13 to assignments of rights which are contractual in nature. Therefore this rule does not apply to subrogation by operation of law when the debt to be paid has its origin in tort (for example, where the insurer succeeds to the rights of the insured against the person causing damage).

2. According to the wording of Article 13 (1), where a person (the creditor) has a contractual claim upon another (the debtor), and a third person has a duty to satisfy the creditor, or has in fact satisfied the creditor in discharge of that duty, the law which governs the third person's duty to satisfy the creditor shall determine whether the third person is entitled to exercise against the debtor the rights which the creditor had against the debtor under the law governing their relationship and, if so, whether he may do so in full or only to a limited extent.

The law which governs the third person's duty to satisfy the creditor (for example, the law applicable to the contract of guarantee, where the guarantor has paid instead of the debtor) will therefore determine whether and to what extent the third person is entitled to exercise the rights of the creditor against the debtor according to the law governing their contractual relations.

In formulating the rule under analysis the Group made a point of considering situations in which a person has paid without being obliged so to do by contract or by law but having an economic interest recognized by law as anticipated by Article 1251-3 of the French Civil Code and Article 1203-3 of the Italian Civil Code. In principle the same rule applies to these situations, but the court has a discretion in this respect.

As regards the possibility of a partial subrogation such as that provided for by Article 1252 of the French Civil Code and by Article 1205 of the Italian Civil Code, it seems right that this should be subject to the law applicable to the subrogation.

In addition, when formulating Article 13 the Group envisaged the possibility that the legal relationship between the third party and the debtor was governed by a contract. This contract will obviously be governed by the law which is applicable to it by the terms of this Convention. Article 13 in no way affects this aspect of the relationship between the third party and the debtor.

3. Article 13 (2) extends the same rule in paragraph 1 to cases in which several person are liable for the same contractual obligation (co-debtors) and the creditor's interest has been discharged by one of them.

4. As well as the problem of voluntary assignment of rights and the problem of assignment of rights by operation of law (Articles 12 and 13), there exists the problem of assignment of duties. However, the Group did not wish to resolve this problem, because it is new and because there are still many uncertainties as to the solution to be given.

Article 14

Burden of proof, etc.

Article 14 deals with the law to be applied to certain questions of evidence.

There is no rule of principle dealing with evidence in general. In the legal systems of the Contracting States, except as regards the burden of proof, questions of evidence (both as regards facts and acts intended to have legal effect and as regards foreign law) are in principle subject to the law of the forum. This principle is, however, subject to a certain number of exceptions which are not the same in all these legal systems. Since it was decided that only certain questions of evidence should be covered in Article 14, it was thought better not to bind the interpretation thereof by a general provision making the rules of evidence subject to the law of the forum on questions not decided by the Convention, such as, for example, the taking of evidence abroad or the evidential value of legal acts. In order that there should be no doubt as to the freedom retained by the States regarding questions of evidence not decided by the Convention, Article 1 (2) (h) excludes evidence and procedure from the scope of the Convention, expressly without prejudice to Article 14.

Two major questions have been covered and are each the subject of a separate paragraph. These are the burden of proof on the one hand and the recognition of modes of proving acts intended to have legal effect on the other. After considerable hesitation the Group decided not to deal with the problem of evidential value.

A. Burden of proof

The first paragraph of Article 14 provides for the application of the law of the contract "to the extent that it contains, in the law of contract, rules which raise presumptions of law or determine the burden of proof". Presumptions of law, relieving the party in whose favour they operate from the necessity of producing any evidence, are really rules of substance which in the law of contract contribute to making clear the obligations of the parties and therefore cannot be separated from the law which governs the contract. By way of example, where Article 1731 of the French Civil Code provides that "where no inventory of the state of the premises has been taken, the lessee shall be deemed to have received them in good tenantable repair and must, in the absence of proof to the contrary, restore them in such condition", the Article is in reality determining the obligation of the lessee to restore the let premises. It is therefore logical that the law of the contract should apply here.

The same observation applies to rules determining the burden of proof. By way of example, Article 1147 of the French Civil Code provides that a debtor who has failed to fulfil his obligation shall be liable for damages "unless he shows that this failure is due to an extraneous cause outside his control". This text determines the burden of proof between the parties. The creditor must prove that the obligation has not been fulfilled, the debtor must prove that the failure is due to an extraneous cause. But in dividing the burden, the text establishes the debtor's obligations on a vital point, since the debtor is liable for damages even if the failure to fulfil is not due to a proven fault on his part. The rule is accordingly a rule of substance which can only be subject to the law of the contract.

Nevertheless the text of the first paragraph of Article 14 does contain a restriction. The burden of proof is not totally subject to the law of the contract. It is only subject to it to the extent that the law of the contract determines it with regard to contractual obligations ("in the law of contract"), that is to say only to the extent to which the rules relating to the burden of proof are in effect rules of substance.

This is not always the case. Some legal systems recognize rules relating to the burden of proof, sometimes even classed as presumptions of law, which clearly are part of procedural law and which it would be wrong to subject to the law of the contract. This is the case, for example, with the rule whereby the claim of a party who appears is deemed to be substantiated if the other party fails to appear, or the rule making silence on the part of a party to an action with regard to facts alleged by the other party equivalent to an admission of those facts.

Such rules do not form part of "the law of contract" and accordingly do not fall within the choice of law rule established by Article 14 (1).

B. Admissibility of modes of proving acts intended to have legal effect

Paragraph 2 of Article 14 deals with the admissibility of modes of proving acts intended to have legal effect (in the sense of *voluntas negotium*).

The text provides for the application in the alternative of the law of the forum or of the law which determines the formal validity of the act. This liberal solution favouring proof of the act is already recognized in France and in the Benelux countries.[51] It seems to be the only solution capable of reconciling the requirements of the law of the forum with the desire to respect the legitimate expectations of the parties at the time of concluding their act.

The law of the forum is normally employed to determine the means which may be used for proving an act intended to have legal effect, which in this context includes a contract. If, for example, that law allows a contract to be proved by witnesses, it should be followed, irrespective of any more stringent provisions on the point contained in the law governing the substance or formal validity of the act.

On the other hand, in the opposite case, if the law governing the formal validity of the act only requires oral agreement and allows such an agreement to be proved by witnesses, the expectations of parties who had relied on that law would be disappointed if such proof were to be held inadmissible solely on the ground that the law of the trial court required written evidence of all acts intended to have legal effect. The parties must therefore be allowed to employ the modes of proof recognized by the law governing formal validity.

Nevertheless this liberalism should not lead to imposing on the trial court modes of proof which its procedural law does not enable it to administer. Article 14 does not deal with the administration of modes of proof, which the legal system of each Contracting State makes subject to the law of the trial court. Admitting the application of a law other than that of the forum to modes of proof ought not to lead to the rules of the law of the forum, as regards the administration of the modes of proof, being rendered nugatory.

This is the explanation of the proviso which in substance enables a court, without reference to public policy, to disregard modes of proof which the law of procedure cannot generally allow, such as an affidavit, the testimony of a party or common knowledge. Consideration was also given to the case of rights subject to registration in a public register, holding that the authority charged with keeping that register could, owing to that provision, only recognize the modes of proof provided for by its own law.

Such being the general system adopted, a proviso had to be added regarding the law determining formal validity applicable as an alternative to the law of the forum.

The text refers to "any of the laws referred to in Article 9 under which that contract or act is formally valid". This expression means that if, for example, the act is formally valid under the law governing the substance of the contract but is not formally valid under the law of the place where it was done, the parties may employ only the modes of proof provided for by the first of these two laws, even if the latter is more liberal as regards proof. The reference in Article 14 (2) to the law governing formal validity is clearly based on the assumption that the law governing formal validity has been observed. On the other hand, if the act is formally valid according to both laws (lex causae and lex loci actus) mentioned in Article 9, the parties will be able to employ the modes of proof provided for by either of those laws.

C. There is no provision dealing with the evidential value of acts intended to have legal effect. The preliminary draft of 1972 contained a provision covering two questions derived, in Roman law countries, from the concept of evidential value; the question how far a written document affords sufficient evidence of the obligations contained in it and the question of the modes of proof to add to or contradict the contents of the document - "outside and against the content" of such a document, according to the old phraseology of the Code Napoléon (Article 1341). Despite long discussion, no agreement could be reached between the delegations and it was therefore decided to leave the question of evidential value outside the scope of the Convention.

Article 15

Exclusion of renvoi

This Article excludes renvoi.

It is clear that there is no place for renvoi in the law of contract if the parties have chosen the law to be applied to their contract. If they have made such a choice, it is clearly with the intention that the provisions of substance in the chosen law shall be applicable; their choice accordingly excludes any possibility of renvoi to another law.[52]

Renvoi is also excluded where the parties have not chosen the law to be applied. In this case the contract is governed, in accordance with Article 4 (1), by the law of the country with which it is most closely connected. Paragraph 2 introduces a presumption that that country is the country where the party who is to effect the performance which is characteristic of the contract has his habitual residence. It would not be reasonable for a court, despite this express localization, to subject the contract to the law of another country by introducing renvoi, solely because the rule of conflict of laws in the country where the contract was localized contained other connecting factors. This is equally so where the last paragraph of Article 4 applies and the court has decided the place of the contract with the aid of indications which seem to it decisive.

More generally, the exclusion of renvoi is justified in international conventions regarding conflict of laws. If the Convention attempts as far as possible to localize the legal situation and to determine the country with which it is most closely connected, the law specified by the conflicts rule in the Convention should not be allowed to question this determination of place. Such, moreover, has been the solution adopted since 1951 in the conventions concluded at The Hague.

Article 16

"Ordre public"

Article 16 contains a precise and restrictively worded reservation in favour of public policy ("*ordre public*").

First it is expressly stated that, in the abstract and taken as a whole, public policy is not to affect the law specified by the Convention. Public policy is only to be taken into account where a certain provision of the specified law, if applied in an actual case, would lead to consequences contrary to the public policy ("*ordre public*") of the forum. It may therefore happen that a foreign law, which might in the abstract be held to be contrary to the public policy of the forum, could nevertheless be applied, if the actual result of its being applied does not in itself offend the public policy of the forum.

Secondly, the result must be "manifestly" incompatible with the public policy of the forum. This condition, which is to be found in all the Hague Conventions since 1956, requires the court to find special grounds for upholding an objection.[53]

Article 16 provides that it is the public policy of the forum which must be offended by the application of the specified law. It goes without saying that this expression includes Community public policy, which has become an integral part of the public policy ("*ordre public*") of the Member States of the European Community.

Article 17

No retrospective effect

Article 17 means that the Convention has no retrospective effect on contracts already in existence. It applies only to contracts concluded after it enters into force, but the entry into force must be considered separately for each State since the Convention will not enter into force simultaneously in all the contracting States (see Article 29). Of course, there is no provision preventing a court of a contracting State with respect to which the Convention has not yet entered into force from applying it in advance unter the concept of *ratio scripta*.

Article 18

Uniform interpretation

This Article is based on a formula developed by the United Nations Commission on International Trade Law.

The draft revision of the uniform law on international sales and the preliminary draft of the Convention on prescription and limitation of actions in international sales contained the following provision: "In the interpretation and application of this Convention, regard shall be had to its international character and to the necessity of promoting uniformity". This provision, whose wording was slightly amended, has been incorporated in the United Nations Convention on contracts for the international sale of goods (Article 7) signed in Vienna on 11 April 1980.

Article 18 operates as a reminder that in interpreting an international convention regard must be had to its international character and that, consequently, a court will not be free to assimilate the provisions of the Convention, in so far as concerns their interpretation, to provisions of law which are purely domestic. It seemed that one of the advantages of this Article might be to enable parties to rely in their actions on decisions given in other countries.

It is within the spirit of this Article that a solution must be found to the problem of classification, for which, following the example of the Benelux uniform law, the French draft and numerous conventions of The Hague, the Convention has refrained from formulating a special rule.

Article 18 will retain its importance even if a protocol subjecting the interpretation of the Convention to the Court of Justice of the European Communities is drawn up pursuant to the Joint Declaration of the Representatives of the Governments made when the Convention was opened for signature on 19 June 1980.

Article 19

States with more than one legal system

This Article is based on similar provisions contained in some of the Hague Conventions (see, for example, the Convention on the law applicable to matrimonial property regimes, Articles 17 and 18 and the

Convention on the law applicable to agency, Articles 19 and 20).

According to the first paragraph, where a State has several territorial units each with its own rules of law in respect of contractual obligations, each of those units will be considered as a country for the purposes of the Convention. If, for example, in the case of Article 4, the party who is to effect the performance which is characteristic of the contract has his habitual residence in Scotland, it is with Scottish law that the contract will be deemed to be most closely connected.

Paragraph 2, which is of special concern to the United Kingdom, covers the case where the situation is connected with several territorial units in a single country but not with another State. In such a case there is a conflict of laws, but it is a purely domestic matter for the State concerned which consequently is under no obligation to resolve it by applying the rules of the Convention.

Article 20

Precedence of Community law

This Article is intended to avoid the possibility of conflict between this Convention and acts of the Community institutions, by according precedence to the latter. The text is based on that of Article 52 (2) of the Convention of 27 September 1968 as revised by the Accession Convention of 9 October 1978.

The Community provisions which will have precedence over the Convention are, as regards their object, those which, in relation to particular matters, lay down rules of private international law with regard to contractual obligations. For example, the Regulation on conflict of laws with respect to employment contracts will, when it has been finally adopted, take precedence over the Convention.

The Governments of the Member States have, nevertheless, in a joint declaration, expressed the wish that these Community instruments will be consistent with the provisions of the Convention.

As regards the form which these instruments are to take, the Community provisions contemplated by Article 20 are not only acts of the institutions of the European Communities, that is to say principally the Regulations and the Directives as well as the Conventions concluded by those Communities, but also national laws harmonized in implementation of such acts. A law or regulation adopted by a State in order to make its legislation comply with a Directive borrows, as it were, from the Directive its Community force, thus justifying the precedence accorded to it over this Convention.

Finally, the precedence which Article 20 accords to Community law applies not only to Community law in force at the date when this Convention enters into force, but also to that adopted after the Convention has entered into force.

Article 21

Relationship with other Conventions

This Article, which has its equivalent in the Hague Conventions on the law applicable to matrimonial property regimes (Article 20) and on the law applicable to agency (Article 22) means that this Convention will not prejudice the application of any other international agreement, present or future, to which a Contracting State is or becomes party, for example, to Conventions relating to carriage. This leaves open the possibility of a more far-reaching international unificatin with regard to all or part of the ground covered by this Convention.

This provision does not of course eliminate all possibility of difficulty arising from the combined application of this Convention and another concurrent Convention, especially if the latter contains a provision similar to that in Article 21. But the States which are parties to several Conventions must seek a solution to these difficulties of application without jeopardizing the observance of their international obligations.

Moreover, Article 21 must be read in conjunction with Articles 24 and 25. The former specifies the conditions under which a contracting State may become a party to a multilateral Convention after the date on which this Convention enters into force with respect thereto. The latter deals with the case where the conclusion of other Conventions would prejudice the unification achieved by this Convention.

Article 22

Reservations

This Article indicates the reservations which may be made to the Convention, the reasons for which have been set out in this report as regards Articles 7 (1) and 10 (1) (e). Following the practice generally applied, in particular in the Hague Conventions, it lays down the procedure by means of which these reservations can be made or withdrawn.

TITLE III: FINAL PROVISIONS

Article 23

Unilateral adoption by a contracting State of a new choice of law rule

Article 23 is an unusual text since it allows the contracting States to make unilateral derogations from the rules of the Convention. This weakening of its mandatory force was thought desirable because of the very wide scope of the Convention and the very general character of most of its rules. The case was envisaged where a State found it necessary for political, economic or social reasons to amend a choice of law rule and it was thought desirable to find a solution sufficiently flexible to enable States to ratify the Convention without having to denounce it as soon as they were forced to disregard its rules on a particular point.

The possibility of making unilateral derogations from the Convention is, however, subject to certain conditions and restrictions.

First, derogation is only possible if it consists in adopting a new choice of law rule in regard to a particular category of contract. For example, Article 23 would not authorize a State to abandon the general principle of the Convention. But it would enable it to adopt, under the conditions specified, a particular choice of law rule different from that of the Convention with respect, for example, to contracts made by travel agencies or to contracts for correspondence courses where the specialist nature of the contract could justify this derogation from the common rule. It is of course understood that the derogation procedure shall only be imposed on States if the contract for which they wish to adopt a new choice of law rule falls within the scope of the Convention.

Secondly, such a derogation is subject to procedural conditions. The State which wishes to derogate from the Convention must inform the other signatory States through the Secretary-General of the Council of the European Communities. The latter shall, if a State so requests, arrange for consultation between the signatory States in order to reach unanimous agreement. If, within a period of two years, no State has requested consultation or no agreement has been able to be reached, the State may then amend its law in the manner indicated.

The Group considered whether this procedure should apply to situations where the contracting States would wish to adopt a rule of the kind referred to in Article 7 of the Convention, i.e. a mandatory rule which must be applied whatever the law applicable to the contract. It was considered that the States should not be bound to submit themselves to the Article 23 procedure before adopting such a rule. But to escape the application of Article 23 the rule in question must meet the criteria of Article 7 and be explicable by the strong mandatory character of the rule of substantive law which it lays down. It is not the intention that the contracting States should be able to avoid the conditions of Article 23 by disguising under the form of a mandatory rule of the Article 7 kind a rule of conflict dealing with matters whose absolute mandatory nature is not established.

Articles 24 and 25

New Conventions

The procedure for consultation imposed under Article 23 on a State intending to derogate from the Convention by amending its national law is also imposed on a State which wishes to derogate from the Convention on becoming a party to another Convention.

This system of "freedom under supervision" imposed on contracting States applies only to conventions whose main object or whose principal aim or one of whose principal aims is to lay down rules of private international law concerning any of the matters governed by this Convention. Consequently the States are free to accede to a Convention which consolidates the material law of such and such a contract, with regard, for example, to transport and which contains, as an ancillary provision, a rule of private international law. But, within the area thus defined, the consultation procedure applies even to Conventions which were open for signature before the entry into force of the present Convention.

Article 24 (2) further restricts the scope of the obligation imposed on the States by specifying that the procedure in the first paragraph need not apply:

1. if the object of the new Convention is to revise a former Convention. The opposite solution would have had the unfortunate effect of obstructing the modernization of existing Conventions;
2. if one or more contracting States or the European Communities are already parties to the new Convention;
3. if the new Convention is concluded within the framework of the European Treaties particularly in the case of a multilateral Convention to which one of the Communities is already party. These rules are in harmony with the precedence of Community law provided for under Article 20.

Article 24 therefore establishes a clear distinction between Conventions to which contracting States may freely become parties and those to which they may become parties only upon condition that they submit to consultation procedure.

For Conventions of the former class, Article 25 provides for the case where the conclusion of such agreements prejudiced the unification achieved by this Convention. If a contracting State considers that such is the case, it may request the Secretary-General of the Council of the European Communities to open consultation procedure. The text of the Article implies that the Secretary-General of the Council possesses a certain discretionary power. The Joint Declaration annexed to this Convention in fact provides that, even before the entry into force of this Convention, the States will confer together if one of them wishes to become a party to such a Convention.

For Conventions of the latter class, the consultation procedure is the same as that of Article 23 except that the period of two years is here reduced to one year.

Article 26

Revision

This Article provides for a possible revision of the Convention. It is identical with Article 67 of the Convention of 27 September 1968.

Articles 27 to 33

Usual protocol clauses

Article 27 defines the territories of the Member States to which the Convention is to apply (cf. Article 60 of the revised Convention of 27 September 1968). Articles 28 and 29 deal with the opening for signature of the Convention and its ratification. Article 28 does not make any statement on the methods by which each contracting State will incorporate the provisions of the Convention into its national law. This is a matter which by international custom is left to the sovereign discretion of States. Each contracting State may therefore give effect to the Convention either by giving it force of law directly or by including its provisions into its own national legislation in a form appropriate to that legislation. The most noteworthy provision is that of Article 29 (1) which provides for entry into force after seven ratifications. It appeared that to require ratification by all nine contracting States might result in delaying entry into force for too long a period.

Article 30 lays down a duration of 10 years, automatically renewable for five-year periods. For States which ratify the Convention after its entry into force, the period of 10 years or five years to be taken into consideration is that which is running for the first States in respect of which the Convention entered into force (Article 29 (1)). Article 30 (3) makes provision for denunciation in manner similar to the Hague Conventions (see for example Article 28 Agency Convention). Such a denunciation will take effect on expiry of the period of 10 years or five years as the case may be (cf. Article 30 (3)). This Article has no equivalent in the Convention of 27 September 1968. The difference is explained by the fact that this Convention, unlike that of 1968, is not directly based on Article 220 of the Treaty of Rome. It is a Convention freely concluded between the States of the Community and not imposed by the Treaty.

Articles 31 and 33 entrust the management of the Convention (deposit of the Convention and notification to the signatory States) to the Secretary-General of the Council of the European Communities.

No provision is made for third States to accede to the Convention. The question was discussed by the Group but it was unable to reach agreement. In these circumstances, if a third State asked to accede to the Convention, there would have to be consultation among the Member States.

On the other hand a solution was found to the position, vis-à-vis the Convention, of States which might subsequently become members of the European Community.

The Group considered that the Convention itself could not deal with this question as it is a matter which falls within the scope of the Accession Convention with new members. Accordingly it simply drew up a joint declaration by the contracting States expressing the view that new Member States should be under an obligation also to accede to this Convention.

Protocol relating to the Danish Statute on Maritime Law – Article 169

The Danish Statute on Maritime Law is a uniform law common to the Scandinavian countries. Due to the method applied in Scandinavian legal cooperation it is not based upon a Convention but a result of the simultaneous introduction in the Parliaments of identical bills.

Article 169 of the Statute embodies a number of choice of law rules. These rules are partly based upon the bills of lading Convention 1924 as amended by the 1968 Protocol (The Hague-Visby rules). To the extent that that is the case, they are upheld as a result of Article 21 of the present Convention, even after its ratification by Denmark.

The rule in Article 169, however, provides certain additional choice of law rules with respect to the applicable law in matters of contracts of carriage by sea. These could have been retained by Denmark under Article 21 if the Scandinavian countries had cooperated by means of Conventions. It has been accepted that the fact that another method of cooperation has been followed should not prevent Denmark from retaining this result of Scandinavian cooperation in the field of uniform legislation. The rule in the Protocol permitting revision of Article 169 without following the procedure prescribed in Article 23 corresponds to the rule in Article 24 (2) of the Convention with respect to revision of other Conventions to which the States party to this Convention are also party.

NOTES relating to the report on the Convention on the law applicable to contractual obligations

1. Minutes of the meeting of 26 to 28 February 1969.
2. Minutes of the meeting of 26 to 28 February 1969, pages 3, 4 and 9.
3. Commission document 12.665/XIV/68.
4. Minutes of the meeting of 26 to 28 February 1969.
5. Minutes of the meeting of 20 to 22 October 1969.
6. Minutes of the meeting of 2 and 3 February 1970.
7. See the following Commission documents: 12.153/XIV/70 (questionnaire prepared by Professor Giuliano and replies of the rapporteurs); 6.975/XIV/70 (questionnaire prepared by Mr Van Sasse van Ysselt and replies of the rapporteurs); 15.393/XIV/70 (questionnaire prepared by Professor Lagarde and replies of the rapporteurs).
8. The meetings were held on the following dates: 28 September to 2 October 1970; 16 to 20 November 1970; 15 to 19 February 1971; 15 to 19 March 1971; 28 June to 2 July 1971; 4 to 8 October 1971; 29 November to 3 December 1971; 31 January to 3 February 1972; 20 to 24 March 1972; 29 to 31 May 1972; 21 to 23 June 1972.
9. Minutes of the meeting of 21 to 23 June 1972, page 29 *et seq.*
10. The meetings were held on the following dates: 22 to 23 September 1975; 17 to 19 December 1975; 1 to 5 March 1976; 23 to 30 June 1976; 16 to 17 December 1976; 21 to 23 February 1977; 3 to 6 May 1977; 27 to 28 June 1977; 19 to 23 September 1977; 12 to 15 December 1977; 6 to 10 March 1978; 5 to 9 June 1978; 25 to 28 September 1978; 6 to 10 November 1978; 15 to 16 January 1979; 19 to 23 February 1979.
11. The list of government experts who took part in the work of this ad hoc working party or in the work of the working party chaired by Mr Jenard is attached to this report.
12. The work done on company law by the European Communities falls into three categories. The first category consists of the Directives provided for by Article 54 (3) (g) of the EEC Treaty. Four of these Directives are already in force. The first, issued on 9 March 1968 (OJ No. L 65, 14.3.1968), concerns disclosure, the extent to which the company is bound by acts done on its behalf, and nullity, in relation to public limited companies. The second, issued on 13 December 1976 (OJ No. L 26, 31.1.1977), concerns the formation of public limited companies and the maintenance and alteration of their capital. The third, issued on 9 October 1978 (OJ No. L 295, 20.10.1978), deals with company mergers, and the fourth, issued on 25 July 1978 (OJ No. L 222, 14.8.1978), relates to annual accounts. Four other proposals for Directives made by the Commission are currently before the Council. They concern the structure of "sociétés anonymes" (OJ No. C 131, 13.12. 1972), the admission of securities to quotation (OJ No. C 131, 13.12.1972), consolidated accounts (OJ No. C 121, 2.6.1976) and the minimum qualifications of persons who carry out legal audits of company accounts (OJ No. C 112, 13.5. 1978). The second category comprises the Conventions provided for by Article 220 of the EEC Treaty. One of these concerns the mutual recognition of companies and legal persons. It was signed at Brussels on 29 February 1968 (the text was published in Supplement No. 2 of 1969 to the Bulletin of the European Communities). The draft of a second Convention will shortly be submitted to the Council; it concerns international mergers. Finally, work has progressed with a view to creating a Statute for European companies. This culminated in the proposal for a Regulation on the Statute for European companies, dated 30 June 1970 (OJ No. C 124, 10.10.1970).
13. For the text of the judgment, see: Rev. crit., 1911, p. 395; Journal dr. int. privé, 1912, p. 1156. For comments, *cf.* Batiffol and Lagarde, *Droit international privé* (2 vol.), sixth edition, Paris, 1974–1976, II, No. 567–573, pp. 229–241.
14. Kegel, *Internationales Privatrecht: Ein Studienbuch*, third edition, München-Berlin, 1971, §18, pp. 253–257; Kegel, "Das IPR im Einführungsgesetz zum BGB", in Soergel/Siebert, *Kommentar zum BGB* (Band 7), 10th edition, 1970, Margin Notes 220–225; Reithmann, *Internationales Vertragsrecht. Das internationale Privatrecht der Schuldverträge*, third edition, Köln, 1980, margin notes 5 and 6; Drobnig, *American-German Private International Law*, second edition, New York, 1972, pp. 225–232.
15. Morelli, *Elementi di diritto internazionale privato italiano*, 10th edition, Napoli, 1971, Nos 97–98, pp. 154–157; Vitta, *op. cit.*, III, pp. 229–290.
16. Rev. crit., 1938, p. 661.
17. Frederic, "La vente en droit international privé", in *Recueil des Cours de l'Ac. de La Haye*, Tome 93 (1958-I), pp. 30–48; Rigaux, Droit international privé, Bruxelles, 1968, Nos 348–349; Vander Elst, Droit international privé.

Règles générales des conflits de lois dans les différentes matières de droit privé, Bruxelles, 1977, No. 56, p. 100 *et seq*.

18. The text of the judgment in the *Alnati* case (Nederlandse Jurisprudentie 1967, p. 3) is published in the French in Rev. crit., 1967, p. 522. (Struycken note on the *Alnati* decision). For the views of legal writers: *cf.* J.E.J. Th. Deelen, *Rechtskeuze in het Nederlands internationaal contractenrecht*, Amsterdam, 1965; W.L.G. Lemaire, *Nederlands internationaal privaatrecht*, 1968, p. 242 *et seq*.; Jessurun d'Oliveira, Kotting, Bervoets en De Boer, Partij-invloed in het Internationaal Privaatrecht, Amsterdam 1974.

19. The principle of freedom of choice has been recognized in England since at least 1796: *Gienar* v. *Mieyer* (1796), 2 Hy. Bl. 603.

20. [1939] A.C. 277, p. 290.

20a. See, e.g., the Employment Protection (Consolidation Act 1978, s. 153(5) and the Trade Union and Labour Relations Act 1974, s. 30(6)).

20b. Unfair Contract Terms Act 1977, s. 27(2).

20c. Anton, *Private International Law*, pp. 187–192.

20d. This includes cases where the parties have attempted to make an express choice but have not done so with sufficient clarity.

20e. *Compagnie d'Armement Maritime SA* v. *Compagnie Tunisienne de Navigation SA* [1971] A.C. 572, at pp. 584, 587 to 591, 596–600, 604–607.

21. Lando, "Contracts", in *International Encyclopedia of Comparative Law*, vol. III, Private International Law (Lipstein, Chief editor), sections 51 and 54, pp. 28–29; Philip, *Dansk International Privat-og Procesret*, second edition, Copenhagen, 1972, p. 291.

22. C.P.J.I., Publications, Série A, Nos 20 to 21, p. 122.

23. *International Law Reports*, vol. 27, pp. 117–233, p. 165; Riv. dir. int., 1963, pp. 230–249, p. 244.

24. For a summary of this award, including extensive quotations, see: Lalive, "Un récent arbitrage suisse entre un organisme d'Etat et une société privée étrangère", in Annuaire suisse de dr. int., 1963, pp. 273–302, especially pp. 284–288.

25. Int. Legal Mat., 1979, pp. 3–37, at p. 11; Riv. dir. int., 1978, pp. 514–517, at p. 518.

26. The first Convention, dated 1 October 1976, was in force between the following eight European countries: Belgium, Denmark, Finland, France, Italy, Norway, Sweden, Switzerland. The Republic of Niger also acceded to the convention. For the text of the second and third conventions, see: Associazione Italiana per l'Arbitrato, *Conventions multilaterales et autres instruments en matière d'arbitrage*, Roma, 1974, pp. 86–114. For the text of the fourth convention see: Conf. de La Haye de droit international privé, Recueil des conventions (1951–1977), p. 252. For the state of ratifications and accessions to these Conventions at 1 February 1976, see: Giuliano, Pocar and Treves, *Codice delle convenzioni di diritto internazionale privato e processuale*, Milano, 1977, pp. 1404, 1466 *et seq*., 1497 *et seq*.

27. Kegel, Das IPR cit., margin notes 269–273 and notes 1 and 3; Batiffol and Lagarde, Droit international privé cit. II, No 592, p. 243; judgment of the French Cour de Cassation of 18 November 1959 in *Soc. Deckardt c. Etabl. Moatti*, in Rev. crit., 1960, p. 83.

28. *Cf.* Trib. Rotterdam, 2 April 1963, S § S 1963, 53; Kollewijn, "De rechtskeuse achteraf", Neth. Int. Law Rev. 1964 225; Lemaire Nederlands Internationaal Privaatrecht, 1968, 265.

29. Riv. dir. int. priv. proc., 1967, pp. 126 *et seq*.

30. V. Treves T., "Sulla volontà delle parti di cui all'art. 25 delle preleggi e sul momento del suo sorgere", in Riv. dir. int. priv. proc., 1967, pp. 315 *et seq*.

31. For a comparative survey *cf.* Rabel, *The Conflict of Laws. A comparative study*, II, second edition, Ann Arbor, 1960, Chapter 30, pp. 432–486.

32. Batiffol and Lagarde. Droit international privé, cit., II, Nos 572 *et seq*., pp. 236 *et seq*., and the essay of Batiffol, Subjectivisme et objectivisme dans le droit international privé des contrats, reproduit dans choix d'articles rassemblés par ses amis, Paris 1976, pp. 249–263.

33. Rev. crit., 1955, p. 330.

34. According to German case law, "hypothetischer-Parteiwille" does not involve seeking the supposed intentions of the parties, but evaluating the interests involved reasonably and equitably, on an objective basis, with a view to determing the law applicable (BGH, 14 April 1953, in IPRspr., 1952–53, No. 40, pp. 151 *et seq*.). According to another case, "in making this evaluation of the interests involved, the essential question is where the centre of gravity of the contractual relationship is situated" (BGH, 14 July 1955, in IPRspr., 1954–1955, No. 67, pp. 206 *et seq*.). The following may be consulted on this concept: Kegel, *Internationales Privatrecht* ct. § 18, pp. 257 et seq.; Kegel, Das IPR cit., Nos 240–268, and the numerous references to judicial decisions given in the notes; Reithmann, Internationales Vertragsrecht, cit., pp. 42 *et seq*.

35. See *Bonython* v. *Commonwealth of Australia* [1951] A.C. 201 at p. 219; *Tomkinson* v. *First Pennsylvania Banking and Trust Co.* [1961] A.C. 1007 at pp. 1068, 1081 and 1082; *James Miller and Partners Ltd* v. *Whitworth Street Estates (Manchester) Ltd* [1970] A.C. 583 at pp. 603, 605 and 606, 601 to 611; *Compagnie d'Armement Maritime SA* v. *Compagnie Tunisienne de Navigation SA* [1971] A.C. 572 at pp. 583, 587, 603; *Coast Lines Ltd* v. *Hudig and Veder Chartering NV* [1972] 2 Q.B. 34 at pp. 44, 46, 50.

36. *Mount Albert Borough Council* v. *Australian Temperance and General Mutual Life Assurance Society* [1938] A.C. 224 at p. 240, *per* Lord Wright; *The Assunzione* [1974] P. 150 at pp. 175 and 179, *per* Singleton L.J.

36a. Anton, *Private International Law*, pp. 192–197.

37. See to this effect: Cour de Cassation, judgment of 28 March 1953 (n. 827), *supra*; Cour de Cassation (full court), judgment of 28 June 1966 (n. 1680), *supra*; Cour de Cassation, judgment of 30 April 1969 (n. 1403), in Officina Musso c. Société Sevplant (Riv. dir. int. priv. proc., 1970, pp. 332 *et seq*. For comments: Morelli, Elementi di diritto internazionale privato, *cit.* n. 97, p. 155; Vitta. Dir intern. privato (3 V) Torino 1972–1975 III, pp. 229–290.

38. See especially Vischer, *Internationales Vertragsrecht*, Bern, 1962, especially pp. 89–144. This work also contains a table of the decisions in which this connection has been upheld. See also the judgment of 1 April 1970 of the Court of Appeal of Amsterdam, in *NAP NV* v. *Christophery*.

39. This is the solution adopted by the Court of Limoges in its judgment of 10 November 1970, and by the Tribunal de commerce of Paris in its judgment of 4 December 1970 (Rev. crit., 1971, pp. 703 *et seq.*). The same principle underlies the judgment of the Supreme Court of the Netherlands of 6 April 1973 (N.I. 1973 N. 371). See also Article 6 of the Hague Convention of 14 March 1978 on the law applicable to agency.

40. For the judgments mentioned in the text see: Rev. crit. 1967 pp. 521–523; [1920] 2 K.B. 287; [1958] A.C. 301; [1963] 2 Q.B. 352 and more recently: R. Van Rooij, *De positie van publiekrechtelijke regels op het terrein van het internationaal privaatrecht*, 1976, 236 et seq.; L. Strikwerda, Semipubliekrecht in het conflictenrecht, 1978, 76 *et seq.*

40a. On this Article, see the reflections of Vischer, "The antagonism between legal security and search of justice in the field of contract", in Recueil de l'Académie de La Haye, Tome 142 (1974 II) pp. 21–30; Lando, *op. cit.*, nn. 200–203, pp. 106–110; T. Segre , "Il diritto comunitario della concorrenza come legge d'applicazione necessaria", in Riv. dir. int. priv. et proc. 1979, pp. 75–79; Drobnig, comments on Article 7 of the draft convention in European Private International Law of obligations edited by Lando–Von Hoffman-Siehr, Tübingen 1975, pp. 88 *et seq.*

41. V. Delaporte, Recherches sur la forme des actes juridiques en droit international privé. Thesis Paris I, 1974, duplicated, No. 123 *et seq.*

42. V. Delaporte, *op. cit.*, No. III.

43. The possibility of applying a common national law is expressly provided for by Article 26 of the preliminary provisions to the Italian Civil Code. See also Article 2315 of the French draft of 1967.

44. The solution adopted has been influenced by that approved, though in a wider setting, by the Corte di Cassazione italiana, 30 April 1969, Riv. dir. int. priv. e pro. 1970, 332 et seq. It is contrary to that given by the Cour de Cassation of France, 10 December 1974, Rev. crit. dr. inter. pr. 1975, 474, note A.P. The alternative solution also prevails in the United Kingdom, *Van Grutten* v. *Digby* (1862), 31 Beav. 561; *cf.* Cheshire and North, *Private International Law*, 10th edition, p. 220.

45. Solution adopted in German (principal law), Article 11 E.G.B.G.B.; in Italy (subsidiary) Article 26 prel. pro. and in France (Cour de Cassation, 26 May 1963, Rev. crit. dr. int. pr. 1964, 513, note Loussouarn; 10 December 1974, see note 44 above), and implicitly allowed by the Benelux Treaty (Article 19).

46. See references cited in the previous note.

47. See, for example, Article 13 (4) of the Benelux Treaty 1969, which has not entered into force.

48. For a comparative outline on this subject, see: Toubiana: Le domaine de la loi du contrat en droit international privé (contrats internationaux et dirigisme économique) Paris, 1972, especially. pp. 1–146; Lando, *Contracts in International Encyclopedia of Comparative Law*, vol. III, Private international law (Lipstein, chief editor) sections 199–231, pp. 106–125.

49. See, on this subject, Article 4 of the Hague Convention of 1955 on the law applicable to international sales of corporeal movables.

50. See the Benelux Treaty 1969 (Article 2) not entered into force, the preliminary provisions of the Italian Civil Code (Article 1), the law introducing the German Civil Code (Article 7) and French judicial decisions. Rec. 16 January 1861, Lizardi, D.P. 1861.1.193, S. 1861.1.305.

51. See Article 20 (3) of the Benelux Treaty 1969 not entered into force and, in France, Cass. 24 February 1959 (Isaac), D. 1959 J. 485; 12 February 1963 (*Ruffini* v. *Sylvestre*), Rev. crit. d.i.p., 1964, p. 121.

52. *Cf.* Kegel, IPR, fourth edition, p. 173; Batiffol and Lagarde, sixth edition, p. 394; Article 2 of the Convention of 15 June 1955 on the law applicable to international sales of corporeal movables; Article 5 of the Convention of 14 March 1978 on the law applicable to agency. Dicey and Morris, 9th edition, pp. 723–724.

53. See Acts and Documents of the Hague Conference, IXth Session, vol. III, Wills (1961) explanatory report, p. 170.

THE INSURANCE DIRECTIVES

Second Council Directive 88/357/EEC of 22 June 1988 on the coordination of laws, regulations and administrative provisions relating to direct insurance other than life assurance and laying down provisions to facilitate the effective exercise of freedom to provide services and amending Directive 73/239/EEC

Official Journal L 172, 04/07/1988, pp. 1–14

THE COUNCIL OF THE EUROPEAN COMMUNITIES,

Having regard to the Treaty establishing the European Economic Community, and in particular Articles 57 (2) and 66 thereof,

Having regard to the proposal from the Commission,[1]

In cooperation with the European Parliament,[2]

Having regard to the opinion of the Economic and Social Committee,[3]

Whereas it is necessary to develop the internal insurance market and, to achieve this objective, it is desirable to make it easier for insurance undertakings having their head office in the Community to provide services in the Member States, thus making it possible for policy-holders to have recourse not only to insurers established in their own country, but also to insurers which have their head office in the Community and are established in other Member States;

Whereas, pursuant to the Treaty, any discrimination with regard to freedom to provide services based on the fact that an undertaking is not established in the Member State in which the services are provided has been prohibited since the end of the transitional period; whereas this prohibition applies to services provided from any establishment in the Community, whether it is the head office of an undertaking or an agency or branch;

Whereas, for practical reasons, it is desirable to define the provision of services taking into account both the insurer's establishment and the place where the risk is situated; whereas therefore a definition of the situation of the risk should also be adopted; whereas, moreover, it is desirable to distinguish between the activity pursued by way of establishment and the activity pursued by way of freedom to provide services;

Whereas it is desirable to supplement the First Council Directive 73/239/EEC of 24 July 1973 on the coordination of laws, regulations and administrative provisions relating to the taking-up and pursuit of the business of direct insurance other than life assurance,[4] hereinafter referred to as the "first Directive", as last amended by Directive 87/343/EEC,[5] in order particularly to clarify the powers and means of supervision vested in the supervisory authorities; whereas it is also desirable to lay down specific provisions regarding the taking-up, pursuit and supervision of activity by way of freedom to provide services;

Whereas policy-holders who, by virtue of their status, their size or the nature of the risk to be insured do not require special protection in the State in which the risk is situated should be granted complete freedom to avail themselves of the widest possible insurance market; whereas, moreover, it is desirable to guarantee other policy-holders adequate protection;

Whereas the concern to protect policy-holders and to avoid any disturbance of competition justifies coordinating the relaxation of the matching assets rules, provided for by the first Directive;

Whereas the provisions in force in the Member States regarding insurance contract law continue to differ; whereas the freedom to choose, as the law applicable to the contract, a law other than that of the State in which the risk is situated may be granted in certain cases, in accordance with rules taking into account specific circumstances;

Whereas the scope of this Directive should include compulsory insurance but should require the contract covering such insurance to be in conformity with the specific provisions relating to such insurance, as provided by the Member State imposing the insurance obligation;

Whereas the provisions of the first Directive on the transfer of portfolio should be reinforced and supplemented by provisions specifically covering the transfer of the portfolio of contracts concluded for the provision of services to another undertaking;

Whereas the scope of the provisions specifically concerning freedom to provide services should exclude certain risks, the application to which of the said provisions is rendered inappropriate at this stage by the specific rules adopted by the Member States' authorities, owing to the nature and social implications of such provisions; whereas, therefore, these exclusions should be re-examined after this Directive has been in force for a certain period;

Whereas, in the interests of protecting policy-holders, Member States should, at the present stage in coordination, be allowed the option of limiting the simultaneous pursuit of activity by way of freedom to provide services and activity by way of establishment; whereas no such limitation can be provided for where policy-holders do not require this protection;

Whereas the taking-up and pursuit of freedom to provide services should be subject to procedures guaranteeing the insurance undertaking's compliance with the provisions regarding both financial guarantees and conditions of insurance; whereas these procedures may be relaxed in cases where the activity by way of provision of services covers policy-holders who, by virtue of their status, their size or the nature of the risk to be insured, do not require special protection in the State in which the risk is situated;

Whereas it is necessary to initiate special cooperation with regard to freedom to provide services between the competent supervisory authorities of the Member States and between these authorities and the Commission; whereas provision should also be made for a system of penalties to apply where the undertaking providing the service fails to comply with the provisions of the Member State of provision of service;

Whereas, pending future coordination, the technical reserves should be subject to the rules and supervision of the Member State of provision of services where such provision of services involves risks in respect of which the State receiving the service wishes to provide special protection for policy-holders; whereas, however, if such concern to protect the policy-holders is unjustified, the technical reserves continue to be subject to the rules and supervision of the Member State in which the insurer is established;

Whereas some Member States do not subject insurance transactions to any form of indirect taxation, while the majority apply special taxes and other forms of contribution, including surcharges intended for compensation bodies; whereas the structure and rate of these taxes and contributions vary considerably between the Member States in which they are applied; whereas it is desirable to avoid a situation where existing differences lead to disturbances of competition in insurance services between Member States; whereas, pending future harmonization, the application of the tax system and of other forms of contributions provided for by the Member State in which the risk is situated is likely to remedy such mischief and whereas it is for the Member States to establish a method of ensuring that such taxes and contributions are collected;

Whereas it is desirable to prevent the uncoordinated application of this Directive and of Council Directive 78/473/EEC of 30 May 1978 on the coordination of laws, regulations and administrative provisions relating to Community co-insurance[6] from leading to the existence of three different systems in every Member State; whereas, therefore, the criteria defining "large risks" in this Directive should also define risks likely to be covered under Community co-insurance arrangements;

Whereas it is desirable to take into account, within the meaning of Article 8C of the Treaty, the extent of the effort which needs to be made by certain economies showing differences in development; whereas, therefore, it is desirable to grant certain Member States transitional arrangements for the gradual application of the specific provisions of this Directive relating to freedom to provide services,

HAS ADOPTED THIS DIRECTIVE:

TITLE I: GENERAL PROVISIONS

Article 1

The object of this Directive is:
(a) to supplement the first Directive 73/239/EEC;
(b) to lay down special provisions relating to freedom to provide services for the undertakings and in respect of the classes of insurance covered by that first Directive.

Article 2

For the purposes of this Directive:
(a) "first Directive" means:
Directive 73/239/EEC;
(b) "undertaking":
- for the purposes of applying Titles I and II, means:
any undertaking which has received official authorization under Article 6 or 23 of the first Directive,
- for the purposes of applying Title III and Title V, means:
any undertaking which has received official authorization under Article 6 of the first Directive;
(c) "establishment":
means the head office, agency or branch of an undertaking, account being taken of Article 3;
(d) "Member State where the risk is situated" means:
- the Member State in which the property is situated, where the insurance relates either to buildings or to buildings and their contents, in so far as the contents are covered by the same insurance policy,
- the Member State of registration, where the insurance relates to vehicles of any type,
- the Member State where the policy-holder took out the policy in the case of policies of a duration of four months or less covering travel or holiday risks, whatever the class concerned,
- the Member State where the policy-holder has his habitual residence or if the policy-holder is a legal person, the Member State where the latter's establishment, to which the contract relates, is situated, in all cases not explicitly covered by the foregoing indents;
(e) "Member State of establishment" means:
the Member State in which the establishment covering the risk is situated;
(f) "Member State of provision of services" means:
the Member State in which the risk is situated when it is covered by an establishment situated in another Member State.

Article 3

For the purposes of the first Directive and of this Directive, any permanent presence of an undertaking in the territory of a Member State shall be treated in the same way as an agency or branch, even if that presence does not take the form of a branch or agency, but consists merely of an office managed by the undertaking's own staff or by a person who is independent but has permanent authority to act for the undertaking as an agency would.

Article 4

For the purposes of this Directive and the first Directive, general and special policy conditions shall not include specific conditions intended to meet, in an individual case, the particular circumstances of the risk to be covered.

TITLE II: PROVISIONS SUPPLEMENTARY TO THE FIRST DIRECTIVE

Article 5

The following is added to Article 5 of the first Directive:
"(d) 'large risks" means:
(i) risks classified under classes 4, 5, 6, 7, 11 and 12 of point A of the Annex;
(ii) risks classified under classes 14 and 15 of point A of the Annex, where the policy-holder is engaged professionally in an industrial or commercial activity or in one of the liberal professions, and the risks relate to such activity;
(iii) risks classified under classes 8, 9, 13 and 16 of point A of the Annex in so far as the policy-holder exceeds the limits of at least two of the following three criteria:

first stage: until 31 December 1992:
- balance-sheet total: 12,4 million ECU,
- net turnover: 24 million ECU,
- average number of employees during the financial year: 500.

second stage: from 1 January 1993:
- balance-sheet total: 6,2 million ECU,
- net turnover: 12,8 million ECU,
- average number of employees during the financial year: 250.

If the policy-holder belongs to a group of undertakings for which consolidated accounts within the meaning of Directive 83/349/EEC[7] are drawn up, the criteria mentioned above shall be applied on the basis of the consolidated accounts.

Each Member State may add to the category mentioned under (iii) risks insured by professional associations, joint ventures or temporary groupings."

Article 6

For the purposes of applying the first subparagraph of Article 15 (2) and Article 24 of the first Directive, the Member States shall comply with Annex 1 to this Directive as regards the matching rules.

Article 7

1. The law applicable to contracts of insurance referred to by this Directive and covering risks situated within the Member States is determined in accordance with the following provisions:

(a) Where a policy-holder has his habitual residence or central administration within the territory of the Member State in which the risk is situated, the law applicable to the insurance contract shall be the law of that Member State. However, where the law of that Member State so allows, the parties may choose the law of another country.

(b) Where a policy-holder does not have his habitual residence or central administration in the Member State in which the risk is situated, the parties to the contract of insurance may choose to apply either the law of the Member State in which the risk is situated or the law of the country in which the policy-holder has his habitual residence or central administration.

(c) Where a policy-holder pursues a commercial or industrial activity or a liberal profession and where the contract covers two or more risks relating to these activities and situated in different Member States, the freedom of choice of the law applicable to the contract shall extend to the laws of those Member States and of the country in which the policy-holder has his habitual residence or central administration.

(d) Notwithstanding subparagraphs (b) and (c), where the Member States referred to in those subparagraphs grant greater freedom of choice of the law applicable to the contract, the parties may take advantage of this freedom.

(e) Notwithstanding subparagraphs (a), (b) and (c), when the risks covered by the contract are limited to events occurring in one Member State other than the Member State where the risk is situated, as defined in Article 2 (d), the parties may always choose the law of the former State.

(f) For the risks referred to in Article 5 (d) (i) of the first Directive, the parties to the contract may choose any law.

(g) The fact that, in the cases referred to in subparagraph (a) or (f), the parties have chosen a law shall not, where all the other elements relevant to the situation at the time of the choice are connected with one Member State only, prejudice the application of the mandatory rules of the law of that Member State, which means the rules from which the law of that Member State allows no derogation by means of a contract.

(h) The choice referred to in the preceding subparagraphs must be expressed or demonstrated with reasonable certainty by the terms of the contract or the circumstances of the case. If this is not so, or if no choice has been made, the contract shall be governed by the law of the country, from amongst those considered in the relevant subparagraphs above, with which it is most closely connected. Nevertheless, a severable part of the contract which has a closer connection with another country, from amongst those considered in the relevant subparagraphs, may by way of exception be governed by the law of that other country. The contract shall be rebuttably presumed to be most closely connected with the Member State in which the risk is situated.

(i) Where a State includes several territorial units, each of which has its own rules of law concerning contractual obligations, each unit shall be considered as a country for the purposes of identifying the law applicable under this Directive.

A Member State in which various territorial units have their own rules of law concerning contractual obligations shall not be bound to apply the provisions of this Directive to conflicts which arise between the laws of those units.

2. Nothing in this Article shall restrict the application of the rules of the law of the forum in a situation where they are mandatory, irrespective of the law otherwise applicable to the contract.

If the law of a Member State so stipulates, the mandatory rules of the law of the Member State in which the risk is situated or of the Member State imposing the obligation to take out insurance may be applied if and in so far as, under the law of those States, those rules must be applied whatever the law applicable to the contract.

Where the contract covers risks situated in more than one Member State, the contract is considered for the purposes of applying this paragraph as constituting several contracts each relating to only one Member State.

3. Subject to the preceding paragraphs, the Member States shall apply to the insurance contracts referred to by this Directive their general rules of private international law concerning contractual obligations.

Article 8

1. Under the conditions set out in this Article, insurance undertakings may offer and conclude compulsory insurance contracts in accordance with the rules of this Directive and of the first Directive.

2. When a Member State imposes an obligation to take out insurance, the contract shall not satisfy that obligation unless it is in accordance with the specific provisions relating to that insurance laid down by that Member State.

3. When, in the case of compulsory insurance, the law of the Member State in which the risk is situated and the law of the Member State imposing the obligation to take out insurance contradict each other, the latter shall prevail.

4. (a) Subject to subparagraphs (b) and (c) of this paragraph, the third subparagraph of Article 7 (2) shall apply where the insurance contract provides cover in several Member States of which at least one imposes an obligation to take out insurance.

(b) A Member State which, on the date of notification of this Directive, requires that any undertaking established within its territory must obtain approval for the general and special conditions of its compulsory insurance, may also, by way of derogation from Articles 9 and 18, require such conditions to be approved in the case of any insurance undertaking offering such cover, within its territory, under the conditions provided for in Article 12 (1).

(c) A Member State may, by way of derogation from Article 7, lay down that the law applicable to a compulsory insurance contract is the law of the State which imposes the obligation to take out insurance.

(d) Where a Member State imposes compulsory insurance and the insurer must notify the competent authorities of any cessation of cover, such cessation may be invoked against injured third parties only in the circumstances laid down in the legislation of that State.

5. (a) Each Member State shall communicate to the Commission the risks against which insurance is compulsory under its legislation, stating:

- the specific legal provisions relating to that insurance,
- the particulars which must be given in the certificate which an insurer must issue to an insured person where that State requires proof that the obligation to take out insurance has been complied with. A Member State may require that those particulars include a declaration by the insurer to the effect that the contract complies with the specific provisions relating to that insurance.

(b) The Commission shall publish the particulars referred to in subparagraph (a) in the Official Journal of the European Communities.

(c) A Member State shall accept, as proof that the insurance obligation has been fulfilled, a certificate, the content of which is in conformity with the second indent of subparagraph (a).

Article 9

1. The last subparagraph of Article 9 and the last subparagraph of Article 11 (1) of the first Directive are replaced by the following:

"However, the information referred to in (a) and (b) concerning the general and special conditions and the scales of premiums shall not be required in the case of risks referred to in Article 5 (d)."

2. Article 8 (3) and Article 10 (3) of the first Directive are replaced by the following:

"3. This coordination shall not prevent the Member States from maintaining or introducing laws, regulations or administrative provisions concerning, in particular, the necessity for managers and directors to be technically qualified and the approval of articles of association, the general and special conditions of insurance policies, the scales of premiums and any other document necessary for the normal exercise of supervision.

However, with regard to the risks referrred to in Article 5 (d), Member States shall not lay down provisions requiring the approval or systematic notification of general and special policy conditions, scales of premiums, or forms and other printed documents which the undertaking intends to use in its dealings with policy-holders. They may require only non-systematic notification of these conditions and other documents, for the purpose of verifying compliance with laws, regulations and administrative provisions in respect of such risks, and this requirement may not constitute a prior condition for an undertaking to be able to carry on its activities.

With regard to the risks referred to in Article 5 (d), Member States may not retain or introduce prior notification or approval of proposed increases in premium rates except as part of a general price control system.

This coordination shall also not prevent Member States from subjecting undertakings requesting or having obtained authorization for class 18 in point A of the Annex to checks on their direct or indirect resources in staff and equipment, including the qualification of their medical teams and the quality of the equipment, available to the undertakings to meet their commitments arising from this class of insurance."

Article 10

The following paragraph is added to Article 19 of the first Directive:

"3. Each Member State shall take all steps necessary to ensure that the authorities responsible for supervising insurance undertakings have the powers and means necessary for supervision of the activities of insurance undertakings established within their territory, including activities engaged in outside that territory, in accordance with the Council Directives governing those activities and for the purpose of seeing that they are implemented.

Those powers and means must, in particular, enable the supervisory authorities to:

- make detailed inquiries about the undertaking's situation and the whole of its business, *inter alia* by:
- gathering information or requiring the submission of documents concerning insurance business,
- carrying out on-the-spot investigations at the undertaking's premises,
- take any measures with regard to the undertaking which are appropriate and necessary to ensure that the activities of the undertaking remain in conformity with the laws, regulations and administrative provisions with which the undertaking has to comply in each Member State and in particular with the scheme of operations in so far as it remains mandatory, and to prevent, or remove any irregularities prejudicial to the interests of policy-holders,
- ensure that measures required by the supervisory authorities are carried out, if need be by enforcement, where appropriate through judicial channels.

Member States may also make provision for the supervisory authorities to obtain any information regarding contracts which are held by intermediaries."

Article 11

1. Article 21 of the first Directive is hereby deleted.

2. Each Member State shall, on the conditions laid down by national law, authorize undertakings which are established within its territory to transfer all or part of their portfolios of contracts for which that State is the State where the risk is situated to an accepting office established in that same Member State, if the supervisory authorities of the Member State in which the head office of the accepting office is located certify that the latter possesses the necessary margin of solvency after taking the transfer into account.

3. Each Member State shall, on the conditions laid down by national law, authorize undertakings established within its territory to transfer all or part of their portfolios of contracts concluded in the circumstances referred to in Article 12 (1) to an accepting office established in the Member State of provision of services if the supervisory authorities of the Member State in which the head office of the accepting office is located certify that the latter possesses the necessary margin of solvency after taking the transfer into account.

4. Each Member State shall, on the conditions laid down by national law, authorize undertakings established within its territory to transfer all or part of their portfolios of contracts concluded in the circumstances referred to in Article 12 (1) to an accepting office established in the same Member State if the supervisory authorities of the Member State in which the head office of the accepting office is located certify that the accepting office possesses the necessary margin of solvency after taking the transfer into account and if it fulfils the conditions in Articles 13 to 16 in the Member State of provision of services.

5. In the cases referred to in paragraphs 3 and 4, the supervisory authorities of the Member State in which the transferring undertaking is established shall authorize the transfer after obtaining the agreement of the supervisory authorities of the Member State of provision of services.

6. If a Member State, on the conditions laid down by national law, authorizes undertakings established within its territory to transfer all or part of their portfolios of contracts to an accepting office established in another Member State which is not the Member State of provision of services, it shall ensure that the following conditions are fulfilled:

- the supervisory authorities of the Member State in which the head office of the accepting office is located shall certify that the latter possesses the necessary margin of solvency after taking the transfer into account,
- the Member State in which the accepting office is established agrees,
- the accepting office fulfils the conditions in Articles 13 to 16 in the Member State of provision of services, the law of that Member State provides for the possibility of such a transfer and that Member State agrees to the transfer.

7. A transfer authorized in accordance with this Article shall be published, under the conditions laid down by national law, in the Member State in which the risk is situated. Such transfer shall be automatically valid against the policy-holders, the insured persons and any other person having rights and obligations arising out of the contracts transferred.

This provision shall not affect the right of Member States to provide policy-holders with the option of cancelling the contract within a given period after the transfer.

TITLE III: PROVISIONS PECULIAR TO THE FREEDOM TO PROVIDE SERVICES

Article 12

1. This Title shall apply where an undertaking, through an establishment situated in a Member State, covers a risk situated, within the meaning of Article 2 (d), in another Member State; the latter shall be the Member State of provision of services for the purposes of this Title.

2. This Title shall not apply to the transactions, undertakings and institutions to which the first Directive does not apply, nor to the risks to be covered by the institutions under public law referred to in Article 4 of that Directive.

This Title shall not apply to insurance contracts covering risks classified under the following numbers of point A of the Annex to the first Directive:

- No 1:
  as regards accidents at work,
- No 10:
  not including carrier's liability,
- No 12:
  as regards motorboats and boats which the Member State concerned makes subject to the same arrangements as land motor vehicles at the time of notification of this Directive,
- No 13:
  as regards nuclear civil liability and pharmaceutical products liability,
- Nos 9 and 13:
  as regards compulsory insurance of building works.

These exclusions will be examined by the Council not later than 1 July 1998.

3. Pending the coordination referred to in Article 7 (2) (c) of the first Directive, the Federal Republic of Germany may retain the prohibition on the simultaneous undertaking in its territory, under the arrangements for the provision of services, of health insurance with other classes.

Article 13

Member States' legislation shall provide that an undertaking established in a Member State may cover within that State, by way of provision of services, at least:

- large risks as defined in Article 5 (d) of the first Directive,
- risks other than those defined in Article 5 (d) of the first Directive coming within classes for which its establishment there has no authorization.

Article 14

Any undertaking which intends to provide services shall first inform the competent authorities of the head office Member State, and, where appropriate, of the Member State of the establishment concerned, indicating the Member State or Member States within the territory of which it contemplates providing services and the nature of the risks which it proposes to cover.

Those authorities may require provision of the information or proof referred to in Article 9 or 11 of the first Directive.

Article 15

1. Subject to the provisions of Article 16, each Member State within the territory of which an undertaking intends to provide services may make access to such activity subject to administrative authorization; to that end, it may require that the undertaking:

(a) produce a certificate issued by the competent authorities of the head office Member State attesting that it possesses for its activities as a whole the minimum solvency margin calculated in accordance with Articles 16 and 17 of the first Directive and that the authorization, in accordance with Article 7 (1) of the said Directive, enables the undertaking to operate outside the Member State of establishment;

(b) produce a certificate issued by the competent authorities of the Member State of establishment indicating the classes which the undertaking has been authorized to practise and attesting that those authorities do not object to the undertaking providing services;

(c) submit a scheme of operations containing the following particulars - the nature of the risks which the undertaking proposes to cover in the Member States of provision of services,

- the general and special conditions of the insurance policies which it proposes to use there,
- the premium rates which the undertaking envisages applying for each class of business,
- the forms and other printed documents which it intends to use in its dealings with policy-holders, in so far as these are also required of established undertakings.

2. The competent authorities of the Member State of provision of services may require that the particulars referred to in paragraph 1 (c) be supplied to them in the official language of that State.

3. The competent authorities of the Member State of provision of services shall have a period of six months from receipt of the documents referred to in paragraph 1 in which to grant or refuse authorization on the basis of the compliance or non-compliance of the particulars in the scheme of operations submitted by the undertaking with the laws, regulations and administrative provisions applicable in that State.

4. If the competent authorities of the Member State of provision of services have not given a decision by the end of the period referred to in paragraph 3, authorization shall be deemed to be refused.

5. Any decision to refuse authorization or to refuse a certificate as referred to in paragraph 1 (a) or (b) must be accompanied by the precise grounds and communicated to the undertaking in question.

6. Each Member State shall institute the right to take legal action in the courts against a refusal of authorization or refusal to issue the certificate referred to in paragraph 1 (a) or (b).

Article 16

1. Each Member State within the territory of which an undertaking intends to provide services covering the risks referred to in Article 5 (d) of the first Directive shall require that the undertaking:

(a) produce a certificate issued by the competent authorities of the head office Member State attesting that it possesses for its activites as a whole the minimum solvency margin calculated in accordance with Articles 16 and 17 of the first Directive and that the authorization, in accordance with Article 7 (1) of the said Directive, enables the undertaking to operate outside the Member State of establishment;

(b) produce a certificate issued by the competent authorities of the Member State of establishment indicating the classes which the undertaking has been authorized to practice and attesting that those authorities do not object to the undertaking providing services;

(c) state the nature of the risks which it proposes to cover in the Member State of provision of services.

2. Each Member State shall institute the right to apply to the courts in the event of a refusal to issue the certificate referred to in paragraph 1 (a) or 1 (b).

3. The undertaking may commence activities as from the certified date on which the authorities of the Member State of provision of services are in possession of the documents referred to in paragraph 1.

4. This Article shall also apply where the Member State, in the territory of which an undertaking intends to provide services covering risks other than those referred to in Article 5 (d) of the first Directive, does not make access to such activity conditional on administrative authorization.

Article 17

1. Where an undertaking referred to in Article 14 intends to amend the information referred to in Article 15 (1) (c) or Article 16 (1) (c), it shall submit the amendments to the competent authorities of the Member State of provision of services. These amendments shall enter info force in accordance with the rules in Articles 15 (3) and 16 (3) respectively.

2. Where an undertaking referred to in Article 14 intends to extend its activities to risks other than those referred to in Article 5 (d) of the first Directive, it shall follow the procedure described in Articles 14 and 15.

3. Where an undertaking referred to in Article 14 intends to extend its activities to risks referred to in Article 5 (d) of the first Directive or Article 16 (4) of this Directive, it shall follow the procedure described in Articles 14 and 16.

Article 18

1. This coordination shall not prevent the Member States from maintaining or introducing laws, regulations or administrative provisions concerning, in particular, approval of general and special policy conditions, of forms and other printed documents for use in dealing with policy-holders, of scales of premiums and of any other document necessary for the normal exercise of supervision provided that the rules of the Member State of establishment are not sufficient to achieve the necessary level of protection and the requirements of the Member State of provision of services do not go beyond what is necessary in that respect.

2. However, with regard to the risks referred to in Article 5 (d) of the first Directive, Member States shall not lay down provisions requiring approval or systematic notification of general and special policy conditions, scales of premiums, forms and other printed documents which the undertaking intends to use in its dealings with policy-holders. They may require only non-systematic notification of these conditions and other documents, for the purpose of verifying compliance with laws, regulations and administrative provisions in respect of such risks, although this requirement may not constitute a prior condition in order for an undertaking to carry on its activities.

3. With regard to the risks referred to in Article 5 (d) of the first Directive, Member States may not retain or introduce prior notification or approval of proposed increases in premium rates except as part of a general price control system.

Article 19

1. Any undertaking providing services shall submit to the competent authorities of the Member State of provision of services all documents requested of it for the purposes of implementing this Article, in so far as undertakings established there are also obliged to do so.

2. If the competent authorities of a Member State ascertain that an undertaking providing services within its territory does not comply with the legal rules in force in that State which are applicable to it, such authorities shall request the undertaking concerned to put an end to the irregular situation.

3. If the undertaking in question fails to comply with the request referred to in paragraph 2, the competent authorities of the Member State of provision of services shall inform the competent authorities of the Member State of establishment accordingly. The authorities of the Member State of establishment

shall take all appropriate measures to ensure that the undertaking concerned puts an end to the irregular situation. The nature of those measures shall be communicated to the authorities of the Member State of provision of services.

The competent authorities of the Member State of provision of services may also apply to the competent authorities for the head office of the insurance undertaking if the services are being provided by agencies or branches.

4. If, despite the measures thus taken by the Member State of establishment, or because such measures prove inadequate or are lacking in the Member State in question, the undertaking persists in violating the legal rules in force in the Member State of provision of services, the latter Member State may, after informing the supervisory authorities of the Member State of establishment, take appropriate measures to prevent further irregularities, including, in so far as it is strictly necessary, the prevention of the further conclusion of insurance contracts by that undertaking by way of provision of services within its territory. In the case of risks other than those referred to in Article 5 (d) of the first Directive, such measures shall include withdrawal of the authorization referred to in Article 15. The Member States shall ensure that within their territory it is possible to make the notifications necessary for these measures.

5. These provisions shall not affect the right of Member States to punish irregularities committed within their territory.

6. If the undertaking which has committed the offence has an establishment or possesses property in the Member State of provision of services, the supervisory authorities of the latter may, in accordance with national legislation, apply the administrative penalties prescribed for that offence by way of enforcement against that establishment or property.

7. Any measure adopted pursuant to paragraphs 2 to 6 involving penalties or restrictions on the provision of services must be properly justified and communicated to the undertaking concerned. Every such measure shall be subject to the right to apply to the courts in the Member State in which the authorities adopted it.

8. Where measures have been taken pursuant to Article 20 of the first Directive, the competent authorities of the Member State of provision of services shall be informed of them by the authority which has taken them and shall, where the measures have been taken under the terms of paragraphs 1 and 3 of the said Article, take any steps necessary to safeguard the interests of insured persons.

In the event of withdrawal of authorization on the basis of Article 22 of the first Directive, the competent authorities of the Member State of provision of services shall be informed of such action and shall take appropriate measures to prevent the establishment concerned from continuing to conclude insurance contracts by way of provision of services within the territory of that State.

9. Every two years the Commission shall submit to the Council a report summarizing the number and type of cases in which, in each Member State, decisions refusing authorizations have been communicated under Article 15 or measures have been taken in accordance with paragraph 4. Member States shall cooperate with the Commission by providing it with the information required for this report.

Article 20

In the event of an insurance undertaking being wound up, commitments arising from contracts underwritten in the course of the provision of services shall be met in the same way as those arising under that undertaking's other insurance contracts, without distinction of nationality as far as the insured and the beneficiaries are concerned.

Article 21

1. Where insurance is offered by way of provision of services, the policy-holder shall, before any commitment is entered into, be informed of the Member State in which the head office, agency or branch with which the contract is to be concluded is established.

Any document issued to the policy-holder must contain the information referred to in the preceding subparagraph.

The requirements in the first two subparagraphs shall not apply to the risks referred to in Article 5 (d) of the first Directive.

2. The contract or any other document granting cover, together with the insurance proposal where it is binding upon the proposer, must specify the address of the insurance establishment which is granting the cover and also that of the head office.

Article 22

1. Every establishment must inform its supervisory authority in respect of operations effected by way of provision of services of the amount of the premiums, without deduction of reinsurance, receivable by Member State and by group of classes. The groups of classes shall be defined as follows:

- accident and sickness (1 and 2),
- fire and other damage to property (8 and 9),
- aviation, marine and transport (3, 4, 5, 6, 7, 11 and 12),
- general liability (13),
- credit and suretyship (14 and 15),
- other classes (16, 17 and 18).

The supervisory authority of each Member State shall forward this information to the supervisory authorities of each of the Member States of provision of services.

2. Where an establishment earns in a Member State, in respect of the operations referred to in the first subparagraph of paragraph 1, a volume of premiums, without deduction of reinsurance, higher than 2,500,000 ECU, it must keep an underwriting account, comprising the items listed in Annex 2A or 2B, broken down by group of classes for that Member State.

However, where an undertaking, with all its establishments taken together, earns in a Member State, in respect of the operations referred to in the first subparagraph of paragraph 1, a volume of premiums, without deduction of reinsurance, higher than 2,500,000 ECU, the supervisory authority of the Member State of provision of services may ask the supervisory authority of the Member State of the head office that an underwriting account be kept, in future, for the operations effected in its country by each of the establishments of that undertaking.

The underwriting account referred to in the first or second subparagraph of this paragraph shall be forwarded by the supervisory authority of the Member State of establishment to the supervisory authority of the Member State of provision of services on the latter's request.

Article 23

1. Where the provision of services is subject to authorization by the Member State of provision of services, the amount of the technical reserves relating to the contracts concerned shall be determined, pending further harmonization, under the supervision of that Member State in accordance with the rules it has laid down or, failing such rules, in accordance with established practice in that Member State. The covering of these reserves by equivalent and matching assets and the localization of those assets shall be under the supervision of that Member State in accordance with its rules or practice.

2. In all other cases, determination of the amount of the technical reserves, and their covering by equivalent and matching assets and the localization of those assets shall be under the supervision of the Member State of establishment, in accordance with its rules or practice.

3. The Member State of establishment shall ensure that the technical reserves relating to all the contracts which the undertaking concludes through the establishment concerned are sufficient, and that they are covered by equivalent and matching assets.

4. In the case referred to in paragraph 1, the Member State of establishment and the Member State of provision of services shall exchange any information necessary for carrying out their respective duties under paragraphs 1 and 3.

Article 24

Notwithstanding this Directive, the Member States shall be entitled to require undertakings operating by way of provision of services in their territories to join and participate in any scheme designed to guarantee the payment of insurance claims to policy-holders and injured third parties, on the same terms as established undertakings.

Article 25

Without prejudice to any subsequent harmonization, every insurance contract concluded by way of provision of services shall be subject exclusively to the indirect taxes and parafiscal charges on insurance premiums in the Member State in which the risk is situated within the meaning of Article 2 (d), and also, with regard to Spain, to the surcharges legally established in favour of the Spanish "Consorcio de compensación de Seguros" for the fulfilment of its functions relating to the compensation of losses arising from extraordinary events occurring in that Member State.

By way of derogation from the first indent of Article 2 (d), and for application of this Article, the moveable property contained in a building situated in the territory of a Member State, except for goods in commercial transit, shall be a risk situated in that Member State, even though the building and its contents are not covered by the same insurance policy.

The law applicable to the contract pursuant to Article 7 shall not affect the fiscal arrangements applicable.

Each Member State shall, subject to future harmonization, apply to those undertakings which provide services in its territory, its own national provisions for measures to ensure the collection of indirect taxes and parafiscal charges due under the first subparagraph.

Article 26

1. The risks which may be covered by way of Community co-insurance within the meaning of Directive 78/473/EEC shall be those defined in Article 5 (d) of the first Directive.

2. The provisions of this Directive regarding the risks defined in Article 5 (d) of the first Directive shall apply to the leading insurer.

TITLE IV: TRANSITIONAL ARRANGEMENTS

Article 27

1. Greece, Ireland, Spain and Portugal may apply the following transitional arrangements:

(i) until 31 December 1992, they may apply, to all risks, the regime other than that for risks referred to in Article 5 (d) of the first Directive,

(ii) from 1 January 1993 to 31 December 1994, the regime for large risks shall apply to risks referred to under (i) and (ii) of Article 5 (d) of the first Directive; for risks referred to under (iii) of the abovementioned Article 5 (d), these Member States shall fix the thresholds to apply therefor;

(iii) Spain

- from 1 January 1995 to 31 December 1996, the thresholds of the first stage described in Article 5 (d) (iii) of the first Directive shall apply,
- from 1 January 1997, the thresholds of the second stage shall apply.

Portugal, Ireland and Greece

- from 1 January 1995 to 31 December 1998 the thresholds of the first stage described in Article 5 (d) (iii) of the first Directive shall apply,
- from 1 January 1999 the thresholds of the second stage shall apply.

The derogation allowed from 1 January 1995 shall only apply to contracts covering risks classified under classes 8, 9, 13 and 16 situated exclusively in one of the four Member States benefiting from the transitional arrangements.

2. Until 31 December 1994, Article 26 (1) of this Directive shall not apply to risks situated in the four Member States listed in this Article. For the transitional period from 1 January 1995, the risks defined under Article 5 (d) (iii) of the first Directive situated in these Member States and capable of being covered by Community co-insurance within the meaning of Directive 78/473/EEC shall be those which exceed the thresholds referred to in paragraph 1 (iii) of this Article.

TITLE V: FINAL PROVISIONS

Article 28

The Commission and the competent authorities of the Member States shall collaborate closely for the purpose of facilitating the supervision of direct insurance within the Community.

Every Member State shall inform the Commission of any major difficulties to which application of this Directive gives rise, *inter alia* any arising if a Member State becomes aware of an abnormal transfer of insurance business to the detriment of undertakings established in its territory and to the advantage of branches and agencies located just beyond its borders.

The Commission and the competent authorities of the Member States concerned shall examine these difficulties as quickly as possible in order to find an appropriate solution.

Where necessary, the Commission shall submit appropriate proposals to the Council.

Article 29

The Commission shall forward to the Council regular reports, the first on 1 July 1993, on the development of the market in insurance transacted under conditions of freedom to provide services.

Article 30

Where this Directive makes reference to the ECU, the exchange value in national currencies to be used with effect from 31 December of each year shall be the value which applies on the last day of the preceding October for which exchange values for the ECU are available in all Community currencies.

Article 2 of Directive 76/580/EEC[8] shall apply only to Articles 3, 16 and 17 of the first Directive.

Article 31

Every five years, the Council, acting on a proposal from the Commission, shall review and if necessary amend any amounts expressed in ECU in this Directive, taking into account changes in the economic and monetary situation of the Community.

Article 32

Member States shall amend their national provisions to comply with this Directive within 18 months of the date of its notification[9] and shall forthwith inform the Commission thereof.

The provisions amended in accordance with this Article shall be applied within 24 months of the date of the notification of the Directive.

Article 33

Upon notification of this Directive, Member States shall ensure that the texts of the main laws, regulations or administrative provisions which they adopt in the field covered by this Directive are communicated to the Commission.

Article 34

The Annexes shall form an integral part of this Directive.

Article 35

This Directive is addressed to the Member States.

Done at Luxembourg, 22 June 1988.

For the Council: The President – M. Bangemann

ANNEX 1: MATCHING RULES

The currency in which the insurer's commitments are payable shall be determined in accordance with the following rules:

1. Where the cover provided by a contract is expressed in terms of a particular currency, the insurer's commitments are considered to be payable in that currency.

2. Where the cover provided by a contract is not expressed in terms of any currency, the insurer's commitments are considered to be payable in the currency of the country in which the risk is situated. However, the insurer may choose the currency in which the premium is expressed if there are justifiable grounds for exercising such a choice.

This could be the case if, from the time the contract is entered into, it appears likely that a claim will be paid in the currency of the premium and not in the currency of the country in which the risk is situated.

3. The Member States may authorize the insurer to consider that the currency in which he must provide cover will be either that which he will use in accordance with experience acquired or, in the absence of such experience, the currency of the country in which he is established:

- for contracts covering risks classified under classes 4, 5, 6, 7, 11, 12 and 13 (producers' liability only), and
- for contracts covering the risks classified under other classes where, in accordance with the nature of the risks, the cover is to be provided in a currency other than that which would result from the application of the above procedures.

4. Where a claim has been reported to an insurer and is payable in a specified currency other than the currency resulting from application of the above procedures, the insurer's commitments shall be considered to be payable in that currency, and in particular the currency in which the compensation to be paid by the insurer has been determined by a court judgment or by agreement between the insurer and the insured.

5. Where a claim is assessed in a currency which is known to the insurer in advance but which is different from the currency resulting from application of the above procedures, the insurers may consider their commitments to be payable in that currency.

6. The Member States may authorize undertakings not to cover their technical reserves by matching assets if application of the above procedures would result in the undertaking – whether head office or branch – being obliged, in order to comply with the matching principle, to hold assets in a currency amounting to not more than 7 % of the assets existing in other currencies.

However:

(a) in the case of technical reserve assets to be matched in Greek drachmas, Irish pounds and Portuguese escudos, this amount shall not exceed:
- 1 million ECU during a transitional period ending 31 December 1992,
- 2 million ECU from 1 January 1993 to 31 December 1998;

(b) in the case of technical reserve assets to be matched in Belgian francs, Luxembourg francs and Spanish pesetas, this amount shall not exceed 2 million ECU during a transitional period ending 31 December 1996.

From the end of the transitional periods defined under (a) and (b), the general regime shall apply for these currencies, unless the Council decides otherwise.

7. The Member States may choose not to require undertakings - whether head offices or branches - to apply the matching principle where commitments are payable in a currency other than the currency of one of the Community Member States, if investments in that currency are regulated, if the currency is subject to transfer restrictions or if, for similar reasons, it is not suitable for covering technical reserves.

8. The Member States may authorize undertakings – whether head offices or branches – not to hold matching assets to cover an amount not exceeding 20 % of their commitments in a particular currency.

However, total assets in all currencies combined must be at least equal to total commitments in all currencies combined.

9. Each Member State may provide that, whenever under the preceding procedures a commitment has to be covered by assets expressed in the currency of a Member State, this requirement shall also be considered to be satisfied when up to 50 % of the assets in expressed in ECU.

ANNEX 2A: UNDERWRITING ACCOUNT

1. Total gross premiums earned.
2. Total cost of claims.
3. Commission costs.
4. Gross underwriting result.

ANNEX 2B: UNDERWRITING ACCOUNT

1. Gross premiums for the last underwriting year.
2. Gross claims in the last underwriting year (including reserve at the end of underwriting year).
3. Commission costs.
4. Gross underwriting result.

Notes:

1. OJ No. C 32, 12.2.1976, p. 2.
2. OJ No. C 36, 13.2.1978, p. 14, OJ No. C 167, 27.6.1988 and Decision of 15 June 1988 (not yet published in the Official Journal).
3. OJ No. C 204, 30.8.1976, p. 13.
4. OJ No. L 228, 16.8.1973, p. 3.
5. OJ No. L 185, 4.7.1987, p. 72.
6. OJ No. L 151, 7.6.1978, p. 25.
7. OJ No. L 193, 18.7.1983, p. 1.
8. OJ No. L 189, 13.9.1976, p. 13.
9. This Directive was notified to Member States on 30 June 1988.

Council Directive 90/619/EEC of 8 November 1990 on the coordination of laws, regulations and administrative provisions relating to direct life assurance, laying down provisions to facilitate the effective exercise of freedom to provide services and amending Directive 79/267/EEC

Official Journal L 330, 29/11/1990, pp. 50–61

THE COUNCIL OF THE EUROPEAN COMMUNITIES,

Having regard to the Treaty establishing the European Economic Community, and in particular Articles 57 (2) and 66 thereof,

Having regard to the proposal from the Commission,[1]

In cooperation with the European Parliament,[2]

Having regard to the opinion of the Economic and Social Committee,[3]

Whereas it is necessary to develop the internal market in life assurance and in the operations referred to in First Council Directive 79/267/EEC of 5 March 1979 on the coordination of laws, regulations and administrative provisions relating to the taking-up and pursuit of the business of direct life assurance,[4] hereinafter called the "First Directive" as last amended by the Act of Accession of Spain and Portugal; whereas, in order to achieve that objective, it is desirable to make it easier for assurance undertakings having their head office in the Community to provide services in the Member States, thus making it possible for policy-holders to have recourse not only to assurers established in their own country, but also to assurers which have their head office in the Community and are established in other Member States;

Whereas, under the Treaty, any discrimination with regard to freedom to provide services based on the fact that an undertaking is not established in the Member State in which the services are provided has been prohibited since the end of the transitional period; whereas that prohibition applies to services provided from any establishment in the Community, whether it be the head office of an undertaking or an agency or branch;

Whereas, for practical reasons, it is desirable to define provision of services taking into account both the assurer's establishment and the place where the commitment is to be covered; whereas, therefore, commitment should also be defined; whereas, moreover, it is desirable to distinguish between activities pursued by way of establishment and activities pursued by way of freedom to provide services;

Whereas it is desirable to supplement the First Council Directive in order in particular to clarify the powers and means of supervision vested in the supervisory authorities; whereas it is also desirable to lay down specific provisions regarding the taking-up, pursuit and supervision of activity by way of freedom to provide services;

Whereas policy-holders who, by virtue of the fact that they take the initiative in entering into a commitment in another State and thus place themselves under the protection of the legal system of that other State, do not require special protection in the State of the commitment, should be granted complete freedom to avail themselves of the widest possible market in life assurance and in the operations referred to in the First Directive; whereas other policy-holders should also be afforded adequate protection;

Whereas in the management of some group pension funds, the multiplicity and complexity of the various schemes and their close connection with social security schemes call for careful study; whereas they should therefore be excluded from the scope of the provisions specific to freedom to provide services contained in this Directive; whereas they will form the subject matter of another Directive;

Whereas the provisions in force in the Member States regarding contract law applicable to the activities referred to in the First Directive continue to differ; whereas the freedom to choose, as the law applicable to the contract, a law other than that of the State of the commitment may be granted in certain cases, in accordance with rules which take into account specific circumstances;

Whereas the First Directive's provisions on transfer of portfolio should be reinforced and supplemented by provisions specifically concerning the transfer to another undertaking of the portfolio of contracts concluded by way of freedom to provide services;

Whereas, in the interests of protecting policy-holders, Member States should, at the present stage of the coordination process, be given the option of limiting the simultaneous pursuit of activity by way of freedom to provide services and activity by way of establishment; whereas no such limitation can be provided for where policy-holders do not require such protection;

Whereas the taking-up and pursuit of activity by way of freedom to provide services should be subject to procedures guaranteeing the assurance undertaking's compliance with provisions regarding financial guarantees, conditions of assurance and premium rates; whereas those procedures may be relaxed where the activity pursued by way of freedom to provide services covers policy-holders who, by virtue of the characteristics of the commitment they propose to enter into, do not require special protection in the State of the commitment;

Whereas for life assurance contracts entered into by way of the free provision of services the policy-holder should be given the opportunity of cancelling the contract within a period of between 14 and 30 days;

Whereas the First Directive adopted the principle of prohibiting the simultaneous pursuit of the activities covered by Directive 73/239/EEC[5] (called the First Directive on the coordination of non-life insurance) as last amended by Directive 88/357/EEC[6] and those covered by the First Directive; whereas, while it authorized the continued existence of existing composite undertakings, it stated that they may not set up agencies or branches for life assurance; whereas the specific nature of the commitments entered into in the insurance field under the freedom of services regime nevertheless justifies, at least on a transitional basis as from notification of this Directive to Member States, the introduction of a degree of flexibility in the application of the above principle;

Whereas nothing in this Directive would prevent a composite undertaking from dividing itself into two undertakings, one active in the field of life assurance, the other in non-life insurance; whereas in order to allow such division to take place under the best possible conditions, it is desirable to permit Member States, in accordance with Community rules of competition law, to provide for appropriate tax arrangements, in particular with regard to the capital gains such division could entail;

Whereas it is necessary to make provision for special cooperation in the sphere of freedom to provide services between the competent supervisory authorities of the Member States and between those authorities and the Commission; whereas provision should also be made for a system of penalties to apply where the undertaking providing the service fails to comply with the provisions of the Member State in which the service is provided;

Whereas the technical reserves, including mathematical reserves, should be subject to the rules of and supervision by the Member State in which the service is provided where the provision of services involves commitments in respect of which the State in which the service is received wishes to provide special protection for policy-holders; whereas, however, if such concern to protect policy-holders is unjustified, the technical reserves, including mathematical reserves, should remain subject to the rules of and supervision by the Member State in which the undertaking is established;

Whereas some Member States do not subject life assurance contracts and the other operations covered by the First Directive to any form of indirect taxation, while others apply special taxes; whereas the structure and rate of those taxes vary considerably between the Member States in which they are applied; whereas it is desirable to avoid a situation where those differences lead to distortions of competition between undertakings in the various Member States; whereas, pending further harmonization, the application of the tax arrangements provided for by the Member State in which the commitment is entered into is a means of remedying such mischief; whereas it is for the Member States to establish a method of ensuring that such taxes are collected;

Whereas the First Directive makes express provision for specific rules concerning the authorization of agencies and branches of undertakings whose head offices are outside the Community;

Whereas provision should be made for a flexible procedure to make it possible to assess reciprocity with third countries on a Community basis; whereas the aim of this procedure is not to close the Community's financial markets but rather, as the Community intends to keep its financial markets open to the rest of the world, to improve the liberalization of the global financial markets in other third countries; whereas, to that end, this Directive provides for procedures for negotiating with third countries and, as a last resort, for the possibility of taking measures involving the suspension of new applications for authorization or the restriction of new authorizations;

Whereas it is desirable to take into account, within the meaning of Article 8c of the Treaty, the extent of the effort which needs to be made by certain economies showing differences in development; whereas, therefore, it is desirable to grant certain Member States transitional arrangements for the gradual application of the specific provisions of this Directive relating to freedom to provide services;

Whereas, in view of the differences in the national legislations, it is also appropriate to grant to those Member States which so wish transitional arrangements enabling them to adapt their legislation before applying in their entirety, as regards group insurance contracts linked to a contract of employment or the intervention of a broker, the provisions of this Directive relating to the case where the policy-holder takes the initiative to conclude a contract by way of provision of services;

Whereas it will be particularly important to allow those Member States who so wish a sufficiently long period to be able to adopt the appropriate provisions in order to ensure the professional qualification and independence of insurance brokers; whereas taking into account the growing role such brokers play in advising those buying insurance and facing an increasing range of products as a result of the freedom to provide services, their professional qualification and independence will become essential elements for protection of the consumer,

HAS ADOPTED THIS DIRECTIVE:

TITLE I: GENERAL PROVISIONS

Article 1

The object of this Directive is to:

(a) supplement Directive 79/267/EEC;

(b) lay down specific provisions relating to freedom to provide services in respect of the activities referred to in the said Directive, such provisions being set forth in Title III of this Directive .

Article 2

For the purposes of this Directive:

(a) "First Directive":
means Directive 79/267/EEC;

(b) "undertaking":
- for the purposes of Titles I and II, means any undertaking which has received official authorization under Article 6 or Article 27 of the First Directive,
- for the purposes of Titles III and IV, means any undertaking which has received official authorization under Article 6 of the First Directive;

(c) "establishment":
means the head office, an agency or a branch of an undertaking, having regard to Article 3;

(d) "commitment":
means a commitment represented by one of the kinds of insurance or operation referred to in Article 1 of the First Directive;

(e) "Member State of the commitment":
means the Member State where the policy-holder has his habitual residence or, if the policy-holder is a legal person, the Member State where the latter's establishment, to which the contract relates is situated;

(f) "Member State of establishment":
means the Member State in which the establishment covering the commitment is situated;

(g) "Member State of provision of services":
means the Member State of the commitment where the commitment is covered by an establishment situated in another Member State;

(h) "parent undertaking":
means a parent undertaking within the meaning of Articles 1 and 2 of Directive 83/349/EEC[7];

(i) "subsidiary":
means a subsidiary undertaking within the meaning of Articles 1 and 2 of Directive 83/349/EEC, any subsidiary undertaking of a subsidiary undertaking shall also be regarded as a subsidiary of the parent undertaking which is at the head of those undertakings.

Article 3

For the purposes of the First Directive and of this Directive, any permanent presence of an undertaking in the territory of a Member State shall be treated in the same way as an agency or branch, even if that presence does not take the form of a branch or agency, but consists merely of an office managed by the undertaking's own staff or by a person who is independent but has permanent authority to act for the undertaking as an agency would.

TITLE II: PROVISIONS SUPPLEMENTARY TO THE FIRST DIRECTIVE

Article 4

1. The law applicable to contracts relating to the activities referred to in the First Directive shall be the law of the Member State of the commitment . However, where the law of that State so allows, the parties may choose the law of another country.

2. Where the policy-holder is a natural person and has his habitual residence in a Member State other than that of which he is a national, the parties may choose the law of the Member State of which he is a national.

3. Where a State includes several territorial units, each of which has its own rules of law concerning contractual obligations, each unit shall be considered a country for the purposes of identifying the law applicable under this Directive.

A Member State in which various territorial units have their own rules of law concerning contractual obligations shall not be bound to apply the provisions of this Directive to conflicts which arise between the laws of those units.

4 . Nothing in this Article shall restrict the application of the rules of the law of the forum in a situation where they are mandatory, irrespective of the law otherwise applicable to the contract.

If the law of a Member State so stipulates, the mandatory rules of the law of the Member State of the commitment may be applied if and in so far as, under the law of that Member State, those rules must be applied whatever the law applicable to the contract.

5. Subject to the preceding paragraphs, the Member States shall apply to the assurance contracts referred to in this Directive their general rules of private international law concerning contractual obligations.

Article 5

The following paragraph is added to Article 23 of the First Directive:

"3. Each Member State shall take all steps necessary to ensure that the authorities responsible for supervising assurance undertakings have the powers and means necessary for supervision of the activities of assurance undertakings established within their territory, including activities engaged in outside that territory, in accordance with the Council Directives governing those activities and for the purpose of ensuring that they are implemented.

Those powers and means must, in particular, enable the supervisory authorities to:

- make detailed inquires about the undertaking's situation and the whole of its business, *inter alia,* by:
- gathering information or requiring the submission of documents concerning assurance business,
- carrying out on-the-spot investigations at the undertaking's premises,
- take any measures, with regard to the undertaking, which are appropriate and necessary to ensure that the activities of the undertaking remain in conformity with the laws, regulations and administrative provisions with which the undertaking has to comply in each Member State and in particular with the scheme of operations insofar as it remains mandatory, and to prevent or remove any irregularities prejudicial to the interests of policy-holders,
- ensure that measures required by the supervisory authorities are carried out, if need be by enforcement, where appropriate through judicial channels.

Member States may also make provision for the supervisory authorities to obtain any information regarding contracts which is held by intermediaries."

Article 6

1. Article 25 of the First Directive is hereby deleted.

2. Each Member State shall, under the conditions laid down by national law, authorize undertakings which are established within its territory to transfer all or part of their portfolios of contracts for which that State is the State of the commitment, to an accepting office establishing in that same Member State if the supervisory authorities of the Member State in which the head office of the accepting office is situated certify that the latter possesses the necessary margin of solvency after taking the transfer into account.

3. Each Member State shall, under the conditions laid down by national law, authorize undertakings established within its territory to transfer all or part of their portfolios of contracts concluded in the

circumstances referred to in Article 10 (1) to an accepting office established in the Member State of provision of services if the supervisory authorities of the Member State in which the head office of the accepting office is situated certify that the latter possesses the necessary margin of solvency after taking the transfer into account.

4. Each Member State shall, under the conditions laid down by national law, authorize undertakings established within its territory to transfer all or part of their portfolios of contracts conluded in the circumstances referred to in Article 10 (1) to an accepting office established in the same Member State if the supervisory authorities of the Member State in which the head office of the accepting office is situated certify that the accepting office possesses the necessary margin of solvency after taking the transfer into account and if it fulfils the conditions set out in Articles 11, 12, 14 and 16 in the Member State of provision of services.

5. In the cases referred to in paragraphs 3 and 4, the supervisory authorities of the Member State in which the transferring undertaking is established shall authorize the transfer after obtaining the agreement of the supervisory authorities of the Member State of provision of services.

6. If a Member State, under the conditions laid down by national law, authorizes undertakings established within its territory to transfer all or part of their portfolios of contracts to an accepting office established in another Member State which is not the Member State of provision of services, it shall ensure that the following conditions are fulfilled:

- the supervisory authorities of the Member State in which the head office of the accepting office is situated certify that the latter possesses the necessary margin of solvency after taking the transfer into account,
- the Member State in which the accepting office is established agrees,
- the accepting office fulfils the conditions set out in Articles 11, 12, 14 and 16 in the Member State of provision of services, the law of that Member State provides for the possibility of such a transfer and that Member State agrees to the transfer.

7. A transfer authorized in accordance with this Article shall be published, under the conditions laid down by national law, in the Member State of the commitment. Such transfer shall be automatically valid against policy-holders, assured persons and any other person having rights or obligations arising out of the contracts transferred.

This provision shall not affect the right of Member States to provide that policy-holders may cancel the contract within a given period after the transfer.

Article 7

Article 22 (2) of the First Directive is replaced by the following :

"2. The Italian Republic shall take all steps to ensure that the requirement that undertakings established in its territory cede part of their underwriting to the 'Istituto Nazionale di Assicurazioni' is abolished no later than 20 November 1994."

Article 8

1. The heading of Title III of the First Directive is replaced by the following:

"TITLE III A

Rules applicable to agencies or branches established within the Community and belonging to undertakings whose head offices are outside the Community."

2. The following heading is placed after Article 32 of the First Directive:

"TITLE III B

Rules applicable to subsidiaries of parent undertakings governed by the laws of a third country and to acquisitions of holdings by such parent undertakings."

Article 9

The following Articles are added to Title III B of the First Directive:

"Article 32a

The competent authorities of the Member States shall inform the Commission:

(a) of any authorization of a direct of indirect subsidiary one or more parent undertakings of which are governed by the laws of a third country. The Commission shall inform the Committee referred to in Article 32b (6) accordingly;

(b) whenever such a parent undertaking acquires a holding in a Community insurance undertaking which would turn the latter into its subsidiary. The Commission shall inform the Committee referred to in Article 32b (6) accordingly.

When authorization is granted to the direct or indirect subsidiary of one or more parent undertakings governed by the law of third countries, the structure of the groupe shall be specified in the notification which the competent authorities shall address to the Commission.

Article 32b

1. The Member States shall inform the Commission of any general difficulties encountered by their insurance undertakings in establishing themselves or carrying on their activities in a third country.

2. Initially no later than six months before the date referred to in the second paragraph of Article 30 of Directive 90/619/EEC,* and thereafter periodically, the Commission shall draw up a report examining the treatment accorded to Community insurance undertakings in third countries, in the terms referred to in paragraphs 3 and 4, as regards establishment and the carrying on of insurance activities, and the acquisition of holdings in third-country insurance undertakings. The Commission shall submit those reports to the Council, together with any appropriate proposals.

3. Whenever it appears to the Commission, either on the basis of the reports referred to in paragraph 2 or on the basis of other information, that a third country is not granting Community insurance undertakings effective market access comparable to that granting Community to insurance undertakings effective market access comparable to that granted by the Community to insurance undertakings from that third country, the Commission may submit proposals to the Council for the appropriate mandate for negotiation with a view to obtaining comparable competitive opportunities for Community insurance undertakings. The Council shall decide by a qualified majority.

4. Whenever it appears to the Commission, either on the basis of the reports referred to in paragraph 2 or on the basis of other information, that Community insurance undertakings in a third country are not receiving national treatment offering the same competitive opportunities as are available to domestic insurance undertakings and that the conditions of effective market access are not being fulfilled, the Commission may initiate negotiations in order to remedy the situation.

In the circumstances described in the first subparagraph, it may also be decided at any time, and in addition to initiating negociations, in accordance with the procedure laid down in Article 32b (6), that the competent authorities of the Member States must limit or suspend their decisions:

- regarding requests pending at the moment of the decision or future requests for authorizations, and
- regarding the acquisition of holdings by direct or indirect parent undertakings governed by the laws of the third country in question.

The duration of the measures referred to may not exceed three months.

Before the end of that three-month period, and in the light of the results of the negotiations, the Council may, acting on a proposal from the Commission, decide by a qualified majority whether the measures shall be continued.

Such limitations or suspension may not apply to the setting up of subsidiaries by insurance undertakings or their subsidiaries duly authorized in the Community, or to the acquisition of holdings in Community insurance undertakings by such undertakings or subsidiaries.

5. Whenever it appears to the Commission that one of the situations described in paragraphs 3 and 4 has arisen, the Member States shall inform it at its request:

(a) of any request for the authorization of a direct or indirect subsidiary one or more parent undertakings of which are governed by the laws of the third country in question;

(b) of any plans for such an undertaking to acquire a holding in a Community insurance undertaking such that the latter would become the subsidiary of the former.

This obligation to provide information shall lapse whenever an agreement is reached with the third country referred to in paragraph 3 or 4 when the measures referred to in the second and third subparagraphs of paragraph 4 cease to apply.

6. The Commission shall be assisted by a committee composed of the representatives of the Member States and chaired by the representative of the Commission.

The representative of the Commission shall submit to the committee a draft of the measures to be taken. The committee shall deliver its opinion on the draft within a time limit which the chairman may lay down according to the urgency of the matter. The opinion shall be delivered by the majority laid down in Article 148 (2) of the Treaty in the case of decisions which the Council is required to adopt on a proposal from the Commission. The votes of the representatives of the Member States within the committee shall be weighted in the manner set out in that Article. The chairman shall not vote.

The Commission shall adopt the measures envisaged if they are in accordance with the opinion of the committee.

If the measures envisaged are not in accordance with the opinion of the committee, or if no opinion is delivered, the Commission shall, without delay, submit to the Council a proposal relating to the measures to be taken. The Council shall act by a qualified majority.

If, on the expiry of a period to be laid down in each act to be adopted by the Council under this paragraph but which may in no case exceed three months from the date of referral to the Council, the Council has not acted, the proposed measures shall be adopted by the Commission, save where the Council has decided against the said measures by a simple majority.

7. Measures taken under this Article shall comply with the Community's obligations under any international agreements, bilateral or multilateral, governing the taking-up and pursuit of the busin of insurance undertakings.

* OJ No. L 330, 29.11.1990, p. 50."

TITLE III: PROVISIONS RELATING SPECIFICALLY TO THE FREEDOM TO PROVIDE SERVICES

Article 10

1. This Title shall apply where an undertaking, through an establishment situated in a Member State, covers a commitment in another Member State.

2. This Title shall apply to :
   - the types of insurance referred to in Article 1 (1) of the First Directive.
   - the operations referred to in Article 1 (2) (a) and (b) of the First Directive.

3. This Title shall not apply to the operations and bodies referred to in Article 1 (2) (c), (d) and (e), Article 1 (3) and Articles 2, 3 and 4 of the First Directive.

4. An undertaking shall not cover a commitment in another Member State unless it is authorized under Article 6 of the First Directive to cover such a commitment in its Member State of establishment.

Article 11

Any undertaking which intends to provide services shall first inform the competent authorities of the head office Member State, and, where appropriate, of the Member State of the establishment concerned, indicating the Member State or Member States within whose territory it intends to provide services and the nature of the commitments it proposes to cover.

Article 12

1. Subject to Article 13, each Member State within whose territory an undertaking intends, by way of freedom to provide services, to cover commitments within the meaning of Article 10 may make the taking-up of such activity conditional on official authorization insofar as the commitments are not entered into in accordance with the arrangements referred to in Article 13; to that end, it may require that the undertaking:

(a) produce a certificate issued by the competent authorities of the head office Member State certifying that it possesses for its activities as a whole the minimum solvency margin calculated in accordance with Article 19 of the First Directive and that, in accordance with Article 6 (1) of the said Directive, the authorization enables the undertaking to operate outside the Member State of establishment;

(b) produce a certificate issued by the competent authorities of the Member State of establishment indicating the classes in respect of which the undertaking is authorized to transact business and certifying that those authorities do not object to the undertaking's transacting business by way of freedom to provide services;

(c) submit a scheme of operations concerning the following particulars:
   - the nature of the commitments which the undertaking proposes to cover in the Member State of provision of services,
   - the general and special conditions of the assurance policies which it proposes to use there,
   - the premium rates which the undertaking envisages applying and the technical bases which it proposes to use for each class of business,

- the forms and other printed documents which it intends to use in its dealings with policy-holders, insofar as these are also required of established undertakings.

2. The competent authorities of the Member State of provision of services may require that the particulars referred to in paragraph 1 (c) be supplied to them in the official language of that State.

3. The competent authorities of the Member State of provision of services shall have a period of six months from receipt of the documents referred to in paragraph 1 in which to grant or refuse authorization on the basis of the compliance or non-compliance of the particulars in the scheme of operations submitted by the undertaking with the laws, regulations and administrative provisions applicable in that State.

Such authorization may not be refused on the grounds that some operations in the scheme of operations, which are subject in the Member State of establishment of the undertaking to supervision by the authorities responsible for the supervision of insurance undertakings, are not subject to such supervision in the Member State of provision of services.

4. If the competent authorities of the Member State of provision of services have not taken a decision by the end of the period referred to in paragraph 3, authorization shall be deemed to be refused.

5. Any decision to refuse authorization or to refuse a certificate as refer
to in paragraph 1 (a) or (b) shall be accompanied by the precise grounds therefor and communicated to the undertaking in question.

6. Each Member State shall make provision for the right to apply to the courts in respect of a refusal of authorization or refusal to issue the certificate referred to in paragraph 1 (a) or (b).

Article 13

1. Commitments covered by way of freedom to provide services shall be subject to Article 14 where the policy-holder takes the initiative in seeking a commitment from the undertaking.

The policy-holder shall be deemed to have taken the initiative:

- where, on the one hand, the contract is entered into by both parties in the Member State in which the undertaking is established or by each of the parties in that party's own State of establishment or of habitual residence, and where, on the other hand, the policy-holder has not been contacted in his State of habitual residence by the undertaking or through an insurance intermediary or any person authorized to act for it or by means of any solicitation of business addressed to him personally,
- where the policy-holder approaches an intermediary established in the Member State in which the policy-holder has his habitual residence and carrying on the professional activities defined in Article 2 (1) (a) of Directive 77/92/EEC,[8] in order to obtain information on assurance contracts offered by undertakings established in Member States other than his State of habitual residence or with a view to entering into a commitment through the intermediary with such an undertaking. In that event the policy-holder shall sign a statement, the text of which is set out, under item A in the Annex, expressly so requesting.

2. Before entering into a commitment in the cases referred to in the first and second indents of paragraph 1, the policy-holder shall sign a statement, the text of which is set out under item B in the Annex, to the effect that he notes that the commitment is subject to the rules of supervision of the Member State of establishment which is to cover the commitment.

Article 14

1. Each Member State within whose territory an undertaking intends, by way of freedom to provide services, to cover commitments in accordance with Article 13 shall require that the undertaking abide by the following procedure:

(a) production of a certificate issued by the competent authorities of the head office Member State certifying that it possesses for its activities as a whole the minimum solvency margin calculated in accordance with Article 19 of the First Directive and that, in accordance with Article 6 (1) of the said Directive, the authorization enables the undertaking to operate outside the Member State of establishment;

(b) production of a certificate issued by the competent authorities of the Member State of establishment indicating the classes in respect of which the undertaking is authorized to transact business and certifying that those authorities do not object to the undertaking's transacting business by way of freedom to provide services;

(c) statement of the nature of the commitments which it proposes to cover in the Member State of provision of services.

The above procedure shall not apply where an activity falling within this Directive is not subject, in the Member State of the commitment, to supervision by the administrative authorities responsible for supervising private insurance.

2. Each Member State shall make provision for the right to apply to the courts in respect of a refusal to issue the certificate referred to in paragraph 1 (a) or (b).

3. The undertaking may commence activities as from the certified date on which the authorities of the Member State of provision of services are in possession of the documents referred to in paragraph 1.

4. This Article shall also apply where the Member State in whose territory an undertaking intends, by way of freedom to provide services, to cover commitments in accordance with arrangements other than those referred to in Article 13 of this Directive does not make the taking-up of such activity conditional on official authorization.

5. Member States may not prevent the policy-holder from entering into any commitment which may be lawfully undertaken in the Member State of establishment unless it is contrary to public policy in the Member State of the commitment.

Article 15

1. Each Member State shall prescribe that a policy-holder who concludes an individual life-assurance contract in one of the cases referred to in Title III shall have a period of between 14 and 30 days from the time when he was informed that the contract had been concluded within which to cancel the contract.

The giving of notice of cancellation by the policy-holder shall have the effect of releasing him from any future obligation arising from the contract.

The other legal effects and the conditions of cancellation shall be determined by the law applicable to the contract as defined in Article 4, notably as regards the arrangements for informing the policy-holder that the contract has been concluded.

2. The Member States need not apply paragraph 1 to contracts of six months' duration or less.

Article 16

Member States' legislation shall provide that an undertaking established in a Member State may cover within that State by way of freedom to provide services from an establishment in another Member State at least:

- the commitments within the meaning of Article 10, where they are entered into in accordance with the arrangements in Article 13,
- the commitments within the meaning of Article 10 entered into in accordance with arrangements other than those laid down in Article 13, where they fall within classes in respect of which the undertaking established in the first Member State lacks authorization there in accordance with Article 6 of the First Directive.

If, however, in the latter case that undertaking has such authorization, the first Member State may prevent such provision of services.

Article 17

1. Where an undertaking referred to in Article 11 intends to amend the information referred to in Article 12 (1) (c) or 14 (1) (c), it shall submit the amendments to the competent authorities of the Member State of provision of services. Those amendments shall be subject to the provisions of Article 12 (3) and 14 (3), as the case may be.

2. Where the undertaking intends to extend its activities to commitments within the meaning of Article 10 in accordance with arrangements other than those laid down in Article 13 or 14 (4), it shall follow the procedure laid down in Articles 11 and 12.

3. Where the undertaking intends to extend its activities to commitments in accordance with the arrangements laid down in Article 13 or 14 (4), it shall follow the procedure laid down in Articles 11 and 14.

Article 18

1. Undertakings which, by virtue of Article 13 (3) of the First Directive, carry on simultaneously the activities referred to in the Annex to Directive 73/239/EEC and those listed in Article 1 of the First

Directive may accept commitments in any of the classes referred to in the First Directive by way of provision of services as referred to in Article 13 of this Directive. They may also accept commitments by way of provision of services as referred to in Article 12 if the law of the Member State of provision of services so allows at the time of notification of this Directive, or thereafter and until 31 December 1995 in the other Member States.

2. This Article will be reviewed in the light of the report to be prepared by the Commission in accordance with Article 39 (2) of the First Directive.

Article 19

1. Member States of provision of services may maintain or introduce laws, regulations or administrative provisions justified on policy-holder protection grounds, concerning, in particular, approval of general and special policy conditions, of forms and other printed documents for use in dealings with policy-holders, of scales of premiums and of any other document necessary for the normal exercise of supervision on condition that the rules of the Member State of establishment are insufficient to achieve the necessary level of protection and the requirements of the Member State of provision of services do not go beyond what is necessary in that respect.

2. However, with regard to commitments entered into in accordance with the arrangements described in Article 13, Member States of provision of services shall not lay down provisions requiring approval or notification of general and special policy conditions, scales of premiums, forms and other printed documents which the undertaking intends to use in its dealings with policy-holders.

3. They may require only non-systematic notification of these conditions and other documents, for the purpose of verifying compliance with laws, regulations and administrative provisions in respect of such commitments, although this requirement may not constitute a prior condition in order for an undertaking to carry on its activities.

Article 20

1. Any undertaking providing services shall submit to the competent authorities of the Member State of provision of services all documents requested of it for the purposes of implementing this Article, insofar as undertakings established there are also obliged to do so.

2. If the competent authorities of a Member State establish that an undertaking providing services within its territory does not comply with the legal provisions applicable to it in that State, such authorities shall request the undertaking concerned to put an end to the irregular situation.

3. If the undertaking in question fails to comply with the request referred to in paragraph 2, the competent authorities of the Member State of provision of services shall inform the competent authorities of the Member State of establishment accordingly. The latter authorities shall take all appropriate steps to ensure that the undertaking concerned puts an end to that irregular situation. The nature of those measures shall be communicated to the authorities of the Member State of provision of services.

The competent authorities of the Member State of provision of services may also apply to the competent authorities responsible for the head office of the assurance undertaking if the services are being provided by agencies or branches.

4. If, despite the steps thus taken by the Member State of establishment, or because such steps prove inadequate or are lacking in the Member State in question, the undertaking persists in violating the legal provisions in force in the Member State of provision of services, the latter Member State may, after informing the supervisory authorities of the Member State of establishment, take appropriate steps to prevent further irregularities, including, insofar as it is strictly necessary, the prevention of the further covering of commitments by the undertaking by way of freedom to provide services within its territory. In the case of commitments covered by way of freedom to provide services in accordance with arrangements other than those referred to in Article 13 of this Directive, such steps shall include withdrawal of the authorization referred to in Article 12. Member States shall ensure that within their territory it is possible to effect the notifications necessary for such steps.

5. These provisions shall not affect the right of Member States to punish irregularities committed within their territory.

6. If the undertaking which has committed the irregularity has an establishment or owns property in the Member State of provision of services, the supervisory authorities of the latter may, in accordance with national law, apply the administrative penalties prescribed for such irregularity by way of enforcement against such establishment or property.

7. Any step taken under paragraphs 2 to 6 involving penalties or restrictions on the provision of services must be properly justified and communicated to the undertaking concerned. Every such measure shall be subject to the right to apply to the courts in the Member State in which the authorities adopted it.

8. Where steps are taken under Article 24 of the First Directive, the competent authorities of the Member State of provision of services shall be informed accordingly by the authority which takes them and, where the steps are taken under paragraphs 1 and 3 of the said Article, take whatever action is necessary to safeguard the interests of assured persons.

In the event of withdrawal of authorization under Article 26 of the First Directive, the competent authorities of the Member State of provision of services shall be informed accordingly and shall take appropriate steps to prevent the establishment concerned from continuing to conclude assurance contracts by way of freedom to provide services within the territory of that Member State.

9. Every two years the Commission shall submit to the Council a report summarizing the number and type of cases in which, in each Member State, decisions refusing authorization have been communicated under Article 12 or measures have been taken under paragraph 4. Member States shall cooperate with the Commission by providing it with the information required for the report.

Article 21

In the event of an assurance undertaking being wound up, commitments arising from contracts underwritten by way of freedom to provide services shall be met in the same way as those arising from that undertaking's other assurance contracts, no distinction being made on grounds of the nationality of assured persons or beneficiaries.

Article 22

1. Where an operation is offered by way of freedom to provide services, the policy-holder shall, before any commitment is entered into, be informed of the Member State in which the head office, agency or branch with which the contract is to be concluded is established.

Any document issued to the policy-holder or to the insured shall contain the information referred to in the preceding subparagraph.

2. The contract or other document granting cover, together with the assurance proposal where it is binding upon the proposer, shall specify the address of the establishment which grants the cover and that of the head office.

Article 23

Every establishment must inform its supervisory authority in respect of operations effected by way of provision of services of the amount of the premiums, without deduction of reinsurance, receivable by Member State and by each of classes I to VI, as defined in the Annex to the First Directive.

This information shall be provided separately for commitments covered in accordance with the arrangements in Article 12 and for those covered in accordance with the arrangements in Article 14.

The supervisory authority of each Member State shall forward this information to the supervisory authorities of each of the Member States of provision of services which so requests.

Article 24

1. Where the provision of services is conditional upon authorization by the Member State of provision of services, the amount of the technical reserves, including mathematical reserves, and the rules on profit sharing and on the surrender and paid-up values of the contracts concerned shall be determined under the supervision of that Member State in accordance with the rules it has laid down or, failing such rules, in accordance with established practice in that Member State. The covering of those reserves by equivalent and matching assets, the location of those assets and the application of the rules on profit sharing and on surrender and paid-up values shall be under the supervision of that Member State in accordance with its rules or practice.

2. In all other cases, those various operations shall be under the supervision of the Member State of establishment, in accordance with its rules or practice.

3. The Member State of establishment shall ensure that the reserves relating to all the contracts which the undertaking concludes through the establishment concerned are sufficient and covered by equivalent and matching assets.

4. In the circumstances referred to in paragraph 1, the Member State of establishment and the Member State of provision of services shall exchange any information necessary for carrying out their respective duties under paragraphs 1 and 3.

Article 25

Without prejudice to any subsequent harmonization, every assurance contract concluded by way of freedom to provide services shall be subject only to the indirect taxes and parafiscal charges on assurance premiums of the Member State of the commitment within the meaning of Article 2 (e) and, in the case of Spain, to the surcharges legally fixed to assist the Spanish body "Consorcio de Compensacion de Seguros" in its function of compensating for losses resulting form the occurrence of exceptional events in that Member State.

The law applicable to the contract pursuant to Article 4 shall not affect the tax arrangements applicable.

Subject to future harmonization, each Member State shall apply to undertakings which provide services in the territory its own national provisions concerning measures to ensure the collection of indirect taxes and parafiscal charges due under the first paragraph.

TITLE IV: TRANSITIONAL PROVISIONS

Article 26

The following transitional arrangements shall apply for the benefit of Spain until 31 December 1995 and of Greece and Portugal until 31 December 1998 :

- they may limit the commitments for which they are the Member State of provision of services to those entered into in accordance with the arrangements referred to in Article 13,
- they may require that the technical reserves, including mathematical reserves, relating to those commitments, should be calculated, covered and located in accordance with their national legislation in force.

Article 27

1. In the case of group assurance contracts entered into by virtue of the insured person's contract of employment or professional activity, any Member State may, until 31 December 1994, limit the commitments for which it is the Member State of provision of services to those entered into in accordance with the arrangements referred to in Article 12.

2. Member States may, up to three years at the latest after the date of application laid down in the second paragraph of Article 30, consider that the policy-holder shall be deemed to have taken the initiative only in the case provided for in the first indent of Article 13 (1).

TITLE V: FINAL PROVISIONS

Article 28

The Commission and the competent authorities of the Member States shall collaborate closely with a view to facilitating the supervision of the kinds of insurance and the operations referred to in the First Directive within the Community.

Each Member State shall inform the Commission of any major difficulties to which application of this Directive gives rise, inter alia any arising if a Member State becomes aware of an abnormal transfer of business referred to in the first Directive to the detriment of undertakings established in its territory and to the advantage of agencies and branches located just beyond its borders.

The Commission and the competent authorities of the Member States concerned shall examine such difficulties as quickly as possible in order to find an appropriate solution.

Where necessary, the Commission shall submit appropriate proposals to the Council.

Article 29

The Commission shall forward to the European Parliament and the Council regular reports, the first on 20 November 1995, on the development of the market in assurance and operations transacted under conditions of freedom to provide services.

Article 30

Member States shall amend their national provisions to comply with this Directive within 24 months of the date of its notification[9] and shall forthwith inform the Commission thereof.

The provisions amended in accordance with the first paragraph shall be applied within 30 months of the date of notification of this Directive.

Article 31

Upon notification of this Directive, Member States shall ensure that the texts of the main laws, regulations or administrative provisions which they adopt in the field covered by this Directive are communicated to the Commission.

Article 32

This Directive is addressed to the Member States.

Done at Brussels, 8 November 1990.

For the Council: The President – P. Romita

ANNEX

A. Statement to be signed by the policy-holder under Article 13 (1), second indent:

> "I hereby state that I wish (name of intermediary) to provide me with information on assurance contracts offered by undertakings established in Member States other than (Member State of habitual residence of policy-holder). I understand that such undertakings are subject to the supervisory arrangements of the State in which they are established and not to the supervisory arrangements of (Member State of habitual residence of policy-holder)."

B. Statement to be signed by the policy-holder under Article 13 (2):

> "I hereby take note that (name of assurer) is established in Member State of establishment of assurer) and I realize that supervision of that assurer is the responsibility of the supervisory authorities in (Member State of establishment of assurer) and not the responsibility of the authorities in (Member State of habitual residence of policy-holder)."

Notes:

1. OJ No. C38 of 15.2.1989, p. 7 and OJ No. C72 of 22.3.1990, p. 5.
2. OJ No. C175, 16.7.1990, p. 107, and Decision of 24 October 1990 (not yet published in the Official Journal).
3. OJ No. C298, 27.11.1989, p. 2.
4. OJ No. L 63, 13.3.1979, p. 1.
5. OJ No. L 228, 16.8.1973, p. 3.
6. OJ No. L 172, 4.7.1988, p. 1.
7. OJ No. L 193, 18.7.1983, p. 1.
8. OJ No L 26, 31.1.1977, p. 14.
9. This Directive was notified to the Member States on 20 November 1990.

APPENDIX 2.6

STATUTORY INSTRUMENTS MADE UNDER THE FINANCIAL SERVICES AND MARKETS ACT 2000

THE FINANCIAL SERVICES AND MARKETS ACT 2000 (LAW APPLICABLE TO CONTRACTS OF INSURANCE) REGULATIONS 2001

(SI 2001, No. 2635)

The Treasury, in exercise of the powers conferred on them by sections 424(3), 417(1)[1] and 428(3) of the Financial Services and Markets Act 2000,[2] hereby make the following Regulations:

PART I: GENERAL

Citation and commencement

1. These Regulations may be cited as the Financial Services and Markets Act 2000 (Law Applicable to Contracts of Insurance) Regulations 2001 and come into force on the day on which section 19 of the Act comes into force.

Interpretation

2.—(1) In these Regulations—

"the Act" means the Financial Services and Markets Act 2000;

"the 1990 Act" means the Contracts (Applicable Law) Act 1990[3];

"applicable law", in relation to a contract of insurance, means the law that is applicable to that contract;

"contract of general insurance" and "contract of long-term insurance" have the meanings given by the Regulated Activities Order;

"EEA State of the commitment" means, in relation to a contract of long-term insurance entered into on a date—

(a) if the policyholder is an individual, the EEA State in which he resides on that date; or

(b) otherwise, the EEA State in which the establishment of the policyholder to which the contract relates is situated on that date;

"establishment", in relation to a person ("A"), means—

(a) A's head office;

(b) any of A's agencies;

(c) any of A's branches; or

(d) any permanent presence of A in an EEA State, which need not take the form of a branch or agency and which may consist of an office managed by A's staff or by a person who is independent of A but has permanent authority to act for A as if he were an agency;

"large risk" has the meaning given by Article 5(d) of the first non-life insurance directive and includes risks specified by paragraph (iii) of that definition insured by professional associations, joint ventures or temporary groups;

"mandatory rules" means the rules from which the law allows no derogation by way of contract;

"the Regulated Activities Order" means the Financial Services and Markets Act 2000 (Regulated Activities) Order 2001.[4]

(2) References to the EEA State where the risk covered by a contract of insurance is situated are to—

(a) if the contract relates to buildings or to buildings and their contents (in so far as the contents are covered by the same contract of insurance), the EEA State in which the property is situated;

(b) if the contract relates to vehicles of any type, the EEA State of registration;

(c) if the contract covers travel or holidays risks and has a duration of four months or less, the EEA State in which the policyholder entered into the contract;

(d) in any other case—

(i) if the policyholder is an individual, the EEA State in which he resides on the date the contract is entered into;

(ii) otherwise, the EEA State in which the establishment of the policyholder to which the contract relates is situated on that date.

(3) References to the country in which a person resides are to—

(a) if he is an individual, the country in which he has his habitual residence;

(b) in any other case, the country in which he has his central administration.

(4) Where an EEA State (including the United Kingdom) includes several territorial units, each of which has its own laws concerning contractual obligations, each unit is to be considered as a separate state for the purposes of identifying the applicable law under these Regulations.

Scope of these Regulations

3.—(1) These Regulations do not apply to contracts of reinsurance.

(2) These Regulations apply to contracts of insurance which are entered into by friendly societies as follows—

(a) Part II applies to a contract of insurance entered into by a friendly society to which section 37(3) of the Friendly Societies Act 1992[5] applies;

(b) Part III applies to a contract of insurance entered into by a friendly society to which section 37(2) of that Act applies; and

(c) Part II applies to any other contract of insurance entered into by a friendly society which covers a risk situated in an EEA State with the following modifications—

(i) paragraph (1) of regulation 4 does not apply;

(ii) regulation 4 applies only where the policyholder is an individual; and

(iii) regulation 7 applies as if for the words "the 1990 Act is deemed to apply" in each case there were substituted the words "the general rules of private international law of that part of the United Kingdom concerning contractual obligations apply".

PART II: CONTRACTS OF GENERAL INSURANCE

Applicable law

4.—(1) This Part applies to a contract of general insurance which covers risks situated in an EEA State.

(2) If the policyholder resides in the EEA State in which the risk is situated, the applicable law is the law of that EEA State unless, if such a choice is permitted under the law of that EEA State, the parties to the contract choose the law of another country.

(3) If the policyholder does not reside in the EEA State in which the risk is situated, the parties to the contract may choose as the applicable law either—

(a) the law of the EEA State in which the risk is situated; or

(b) the law of the country in which the policyholder resides.

(4) If the policyholder carries on a business (including a trade or profession) and the contract covers two or more risks relating to that business which are situated in different EEA States, the freedom of the parties to choose the applicable law conferred by this regulation extends to the law of any of those EEA States and of the country in which the policyholder resides.

(5) If any of the EEA States referred to in paragraph (3) or (4) grant greater freedom of choice of the applicable law, the parties to the contract may take advantage of that freedom.

(6) Notwithstanding paragraphs (2) to (4), if the risks covered by the contract are limited to events occurring in one EEA State other than the EEA State in which the risk is situated, the parties may choose the law of the former EEA State as the applicable law.

(7) Notwithstanding paragraphs (2) to (4), if the risk covered by the contract is a large risk the parties may choose any law as the applicable law.

(8) Where the foregoing provisions of this regulation allow the parties to the contract to choose the applicable law and if no choice has been made, or no choice has been made which satisfies the requirement set out in regulation 6(1), the applicable law is the law of the country, from amongst those considered in the relevant paragraph ("the relevant countries"), which is most closely connected with the contract; however, where a severable part of the contract has a closer connection with another relevant country, the law applicable to that part is, by way of exception, the law of that relevant country.

(9) For the purposes of paragraph (8), the contract is rebuttably presumed to be most closely connected with the EEA State in which the risk is situated.

Mandatory rules

5.—(1) Nothing in regulation 4 restricts the application of the mandatory rules of any part of the United Kingdom, irrespective of the applicable law of the contract.

(2) If the parties to the contract choose the applicable law under regulation 4 and if all the other elements relevant to the situation at the time when the parties make their choice are connected with one EEA State only, the application of the mandatory rules of that EEA State is not prejudiced.

Choice of law

6.—(1) Any choice made by the parties under regulation 4 must be expressed or demonstrated with reasonable certainty by the terms of the contract or the circumstances of the case.

(2) Where the parties to the contract may choose the applicable law under regulation 4, and where the risk to which the contract relates is covered by Community co-insurance (within the meaning of Council Directive 78/473/EEC on the coordination of laws, regulations and administrative provisions relating to Community co-insurance[6]), co-insurers other than the leading insurer (within the meaning of that Directive) are not to be treated as parties to the contract.

The 1990 Act

7.—(1) Subject to the preceding provisions of this Part, the 1990 Act is to be treated as applying to the contract for the purposes of determining the applicable law.

(2) In determining whether the mandatory rules of another EEA State should be applied in accordance with regulation 5(2) where the parties have chosen the law of a part of the United Kingdom as the applicable law, the 1990 Act is to be treated as applying to the contract.

(3) In determining what freedom of choice the parties have under the law of a part of the United Kingdom, the 1990 Act is to be treated as applying to the contract.

PART III: CONTRACTS OF LONG-TERM INSURANCE

Applicable law

8.—(1) This Part applies to a contract of long-term insurance if—

(a) where the policyholder is an individual, he resides in an EEA State;

(b) otherwise, the establishment of the policyholder to which the contract relates is situated in an EEA State.

(2) The applicable law is the law of the EEA State of the commitment unless, if such a choice is permitted under the law of that EEA State, the parties choose the law of another country.

(3) If the policyholder is an individual and resides in one EEA State but is a national or citizen of another, the parties to the contract may choose the law of the EEA State of which he is a national or citizen as the applicable law.

Mandatory rules

9. Nothing in regulation 8 affects the application of the mandatory rules of any part of the United Kingdom, irrespective of the applicable law of the contract.

The 1990 Act

10.—(1) Subject to the preceding provisions of this Part, the 1990 Act is to be treated as applying to the contract for the purposes of determining the applicable law.

(2) In determining what freedom of choice the parties have under the law of a part of the United Kingdom, the 1990 Act is to be treated as applying to the contract.

Explanatory note

(This note if not part of the Regulations.)

These Regulations specify the law that applies to contracts of insurance, the effecting or carrying out of which constitutes a regulated activity within the meaning of the Financial Services and Markets Act 2000 ("the Act").

Regulation 3 specifies the scope of the Regulations and makes certain modifications to the application of the Regulations to friendly societies which are not covered by the insurance directives (within the meaning of Schedule 3 to the Act).

Regulation 4 specifies the applicable law for contracts of general insurance (as defined by the Financial Services and Markets Act 2000 (Regulated Activities) Order 2001 ("the Regulated Activities

Order") (SI 2001/544)) which cover risks in an EEA State.

Regulation 6 makes provision as to how the parties' choice of law must be expressed and specifies that where the risk is covered by Community co-insurance, as defined by Council Directive 78/473/EEC on the coordination of laws, regulations and administrative provisions relating to Community co-insurance (OJ L 151, 7.6.78, p. 25) the leading insurer is to be treated as the only insurer.

Regulation 8 specifies the applicable law for contracts of long-term insurance (as defined by the Regulated Activities Order) where the policyholder has his habitual residence in an EEA State or the establishment of the policyholder to which the contract relates is in an EEA State. The applicable law is the law of that EEA State unless the law of that State or these Regulations permits the parties to choose a different law.

In circumstances specified by regulations 5 and 8, mandatory rules apply to a contract of insurance regardless of the applicable law.

Where these Regulations apply and regulation 4 or 8 does not specify the applicable law, the Contracts (Applicable Law) Act 1990 is to be treated as applying for the purpose of determining the applicable law. That Act is also to be treated as applying for the purpose of determining what freedom of choice the parties have under the law of a part of the United Kingdom and, in the case of contracts of general insurance, what mandatory rules of other EEA States apply.

Notes:

1. See the definition of "prescribed".
2. 2000 c. 8.
3. 1990 c. 36.
4. SI 2001/544.
5. 1992 c. 40.
6. OJ L 151, 7.6.78, p. 25.

THE FINANCIAL SERVICES AND MARKETS ACT 2000 (LAW APPLICABLE TO CONTRACTS OF INSURANCE) (AMENDMENT) REGULATIONS 2001

(SI 2001, No. 3542)

The Treasury, in exercise of the powers conferred on them by sections 424(3), 417(1)[1] and 428(3) of the Financial Services and Markets Act 2000,[2] hereby make the following Regulations:

Citation and commencement

1. These Regulations may be cited as the Financial Services and Markets Act 2000 (Law Applicable to Contracts of Insurance) (Amendment) Regulations 2001 and come into force on 1st December 2001.

Amendment of the Financial Services and Markets Act 2000 (Law Applicable to Contracts of Insurance) Regulations 2001

2. In regulation 3 of the Financial Services and Markets Act 2000 (Law Applicable to Contracts of Insurance) Regulations 2001,[3] omit the word "and" at the end of paragraph (2)(c)(ii) and, for paragraph (2)(c)(iii), substitute—

"(iii) regulation 7(1) applies as if for the words 'the 1990 Act is to be treated as applying', there were substituted 'a court in any part of the United Kingdom must apply the general rules of private international law of that part of the United Kingdom concerning contractual obligations'; and

(iv) regulation 7(2) and (3) apply as if for the words 'the 1990 Act is to be treated as applying' in each case, there were substituted the words 'the general rules of private international law of that part of the United Kingdom concerning contractual obligations apply'."

Explanatory note

(This note is not part of the Regulations.)

These Regulations make certain drafting amendments to the Financial Services and Market Act 2000 (Law Applicable to Contracts of Insurance) Regulations 2001 (SI 2001/2635).

Notes:

1. See the definition of "prescribed".
2. 2000 c. 8.
3. SI 2001/2635.

INDEX